Cold Wars

What was the Cold War that shook world politics for the second half of the twentieth century? Standard narratives focus on the Soviet–American rivalry as if the superpowers were the exclusive driving forces of the international system. Lorenz M. Lüthi offers a radically different account, restoring agency to regional powers in Asia, the Middle East, and Europe, and revealing how regional and national developments shaped the course of the global Cold War. Despite their elevated position in 1945, the United States, Soviet Union, and United Kingdom quickly realized that their political, economic, and military power had surprisingly tight limits given the challenges of decolonization, Asian–African Internationalism, pan-Arabism, pan-Islamism, Arab–Israeli antagonism, and European economic developments. A series of Cold Wars ebbed and flowed as the three world regions underwent structural changes which weakened or even severed their links to the global ideological clash, leaving the superpower Cold War as the only major conflict that remained by the 1980s.

Lorenz M. Lüthi is Associate Professor at McGill University and a leading historian of the Cold War. His first book, *The Sino-Soviet Split: Cold War in the Communist World*, won the 2008 Furniss Award and the 2010 Marshall Shulman Book Prize. His publications on the Vietnam War, Asian–African Internationalism, and Non-Alignment have broken new ground in Cold War history.

Cold Wars

Asia, the Middle East, Europe

Lorenz M. Lüthi

McGill University, Montréal

CAMBRIDGE
UNIVERSITY PRESS

CAMBRIDGE
UNIVERSITY PRESS

University Printing House, Cambridge CB2 8BS, United Kingdom

One Liberty Plaza, 20th Floor, New York, NY 10006, USA

477 Williamstown Road, Port Melbourne, VIC 3207, Australia

314–321, 3rd Floor, Plot 3, Splendor Forum, Jasola District Centre,
New Delhi – 110025, India

103 Penang Road, #05–06/07, Visioncrest Commercial, Singapore 238467

Cambridge University Press is part of the University of Cambridge.

It furthers the University's mission by disseminating knowledge in the pursuit of
education, learning, and research at the highest international levels of excellence.

www.cambridge.org
Information on this title: www.cambridge.org/9781108418331
DOI: 10.1017/9781108289825

First published 2020
Reprinted 2022

Printed in the United Kingdom by TJ Books Limited, Padstow, Cornwall

A catalogue record for this publication is available from the British Library.

Library of Congress Cataloging-in-Publication Data
Names: Luthi, Lorenz M., 1970– author.
Title: Cold Wars : Asia, the Middle East, Europe / Lorenz Lüthi, McGill
University, Montreal.
Description: New York : Cambridge University Press, 2020. | Includes
bibliographical references and index.
Identifiers: LCCN 2019031573 (print) | LCCN 2019031574 (ebook) | ISBN
9781108418331 (hardback) | ISBN 9781108289825 (epub)
Subjects: LCSH: Cold War – Diplomatic history. | World politics – 1945–1989.
| Decolonization. | International relations – History – 20th century.
Classification: LCC D843 .L866 2020 (print) | LCC D843 (ebook) | DDC
909.82/5–dc23
LC record available at https://lccn.loc.gov/2019031573
LC ebook record available at https://lccn.loc.gov/2019031574

ISBN 978-1-108-41833-1 Hardback
ISBN 978-1-108-40706-9 Paperback

For Catherine

Contents

Maps

Acknowledgments

Fifteen years of teaching, research, and writing have gone into this book, and many more years of thinking beforehand. Along the way, I explored topics and countries about which I had known little previously. I often found myself like a little boy standing in a giant candy store with hungry eyes wide open. In the process of producing this book, I have received much support, encouragement, and constructive criticism from numerous people and institutions.

This project would not have been possible without the generous funding of four research grants and two conference grants from the Social Science and Humanities Research Council (SSHRC) of Canada, a research grant from the Fonds de Recherche du Québec – Société et culture (FRQSC), a fellowship from the John Simon Guggenheim Memorial Foundation, a New Directions Fellowship from the Andrew W. Mellon Foundation, and a fellowship from the Deutscher Akademischer Austausch Dienst (DAAD). All these funding institutions – including McGill's support to apply (thank you to Kathleen Holden!) – enabled me to conduct wide-ranging research in almost two dozen archives on four continents, to take leave from teaching and service for longer periods of time, and to acquire new skills.

I have benefited greatly from the knowledge and support of the staff of the National Archives of Australia, the Foreign Ministry Archive of the People's Republic of China, the Jiangsu Provincial Archive, the Nehru Memorial Museum and Library, the National Archives of India, the Archive of Foreign Policy of the Russian Federation, the Russian State Archive of Contemporary History, the Archive of Yugoslavia, the Archive of the Ministry of Foreign Relations in Bulgaria, the Political Archive of the Office for Foreign Affairs of Germany, the Federal Archives of Germany, the Federal Commissioner for the Documents of the State Security Service of the former German Democratic Republic (Stasi-Archive), the Archive of the German Caritas Association, the Federal Archive of Switzerland, the Archive of the International Olympic Committee, the Austrian State Archive, the Archives of the Ministry of

Foreign Affairs of France, the National Library of Sweden, the British Library, the National Archives of the United Kingdom, the Labour History Archive and Study Centre, Library and Archives Canada, the United Nations Archive, the John F. Kennedy Presidential Library, the Lyndon Baines Johnson Presidential Library, the Richard Nixon Presidential Library, the Jimmy Carter Presidential Library, and the Special Collections Department of UCLA Library. During my stays at various places during my travels, Reinhard Wolf, Karin Schiebold, Martin Kaufmehl, and Sarah and Christian Miescher have provided me with a comfortable bed, great food, and even better company.

Over the course of fifteen years, many research assistants have contributed to this project. My gratitude goes to Sarah Balakrishnan, Petia Draguieva, Sarah Ghabrial, Hussein Hassan, Stephanie Hu, Ira Hubert, Disha Jani, Garima Karia, Jean-Robert Lalancette, Robert Larson, Liu Jing, Mao Xiaosong, Laila Matar, Simeon Mitropolitski, Jonathan Newburgh, Joyce Ng, Dafe Oputu, Jonah Ross-Marrs, Maya Shopova, Philip Stachnik, Erik Underwood, Eliza Wood, Brian Wright, Boyao Zhang, Zhang Qian, and Yuan Yi Zhu.

Numerous colleagues have provided me with historiographical references, raised ideas and objections, assisted in archival research, or read chapters. I want to express my thanks to Malek Abisaab, Hussam Ahmed, Anastassios Anastassiadis, Pierre Asselin, Megan Bradley, Mark A. Brawley, Gregg Brazinsky, Subho Basu, Cai Jiahe, Giancarlo Casale, Jovan Čavoški, Roland Cerny-Werner, Paul Chamberlin, Chen Hao, Dai Chaowu, Ruud van Dijk, Lyubodrag Dimič, Sean Fear, Yakov Feygin, F. Gregory Gause, Christopher Goscha, Maximilian Graf, Bernd Greiner, Pierre Grosser, Eric Helleiner, Daniel Heller, David Holloway, Talbot Imlay, Kristy Ironside, Jabin Jacob, Wanda Jarząbek, Juliet Johnson, Matthew Jones, Pierre Journod, Andy B. Kennedy, James C. Kennedy, Piotr Kosicki, Lynn Kozak, James Krapfl, Erik Kuhonta, Guy Laron, Brian Lewis, Li Danhui, Catherine Lu, Laura Madokoro, Setrag Manoukian, Leonard Moore, Michael C. Morgan, Wolfgang Mueller, Farid Abdel-Nour, Lien-Hang Nguyen, Phi-Van Nguyen, Maria Popova, Laila Parsons, T. V. Paul, Krzysztof Pelc, Jeronim Perović, Lou Pingeot, Jacques Portes, Vincent Pouliot, Srinath Raghavan, János Rainer, J. Simon Rofe, Douglas Selvage, Mahesh Shankar, Shen Zhihua, Balazs Szalontai, Eric Tagliacozzo, Jeremy Tai, Christopher Tang, Joshua Teitelbaum, Martin Thomas, Oldřich Tůma, Peter Vámos, Hamish van der Ven, Adrian Vickers, Robert Vitalis, Steven Wagner, Wang Dong, Juan Wang, Manfred Wilke, Robert Wisnovsky, and John Zucchi. I fear that I have forgotten somebody – thank you, too!

I am also grateful to my colleagues, who participated in the book manuscript workshop at McGill in September 2018, for their innumerable (and mostly accepted) criticisms and suggestions for improvement. Thank you to Subho Basu, Gregg Brazinsky, Jeffrey Byrne, Cindy Ewing, Kristy Ironside, Juliet Johnson, Piotr Kosicki, Laila Parsons, Vincent Pouliot, Judith Szapor, and David Welch. O. Arne Westad has read and commented on the whole manuscript even if he could not attend – thank you, too!

Of course, I take full responsibility for all mistakes remaining in the text.

Several chapters have been partially published in previous publications. I want to thank the President and Fellows of Harvard College and the Massachusetts Institute of Technology for granting permission to reprint parts of "The Non-Aligned Movement and the Cold War, 1961–1973," originally published in the *Journal of Cold War Studies* (18/4, pp. 98–147); the University of Pennsylvania Press for granting permission to reprint parts of "Non-Alignment, 1946–65: Its Formation and Struggle against Afro–Asianism," originally published in *Humanity* (7/2, pp. 201–23); the Taylor & Francis Group for granting permission to reprint parts of "Non-Alignment, 1961–1974," originally published in *Neutrality and Neutralism in the Global Cold War: Between or Within the Blocs?* (edited by Sandra Bott, Jussi M. Hanhimaki, Janick Schaufelbuehl, and Marco Wyss, pp. 90–107); and the Woodrow Wilson Center Press / Stanford University Press for granting permission to reprint parts of "Strategic Shifts in East Asia," originally published in *The Regional Cold Wars in Europe, East Asia, and the Middle East: Connections and Turning Points* (edited by myself, pp. 223–44).

I am very grateful to my editor, Michael Watson at Cambridge University Press, for his support of this project from the moment of our first meeting, two anonymous reviewers who came to opposite conclusions about the manuscript, Ian McIver for shepherding the manuscript through production, Rachel Harrison for pre-copy editing, Kay McKechnie for copy-editing, and Caroline Diepeveen for indexing. Thank you also to Marc Desrochers and Valentin Rakov for repeatedly fixing my irritable laptop.

Last but not least, this book would not have been possible without the love, support, and patience of Catherine, who had heard about this project virtually since the first months of our relationship, let me go to many archives around the world to conduct research on people long dead, and listened to my excited, detailed, and entirely boring reports about my many archival finds. Without you, this book would not have been written!

Note on Names, Transliterations, and References

For reasons of space, the full bibliography appears online at www .cambridge.org/luthi and the author's institutional website, but full references are also given when a reference is first cited in each chapter.

Names appear according to historical custom. Usually, for Korean, Chinese, and Vietnamese individuals, they occur in the sequence of last name – first name, and for the rest in the reverse order. I tried to keep exceptions to a minimum. Any name with a widespread English spelling that diverges from the correct transliteration is exempt from the below-mentioned transcription rules, as for example: Warsaw (Warszawa), Khrushchev (Khrushchyev), Gamal Abdel Nasser (Gamal abd al-Nasir), Chiang Kai-shek (Jiang Jieshi), etc. For Vietnamese names, I follow the inconsistent but customary usage, which can be confusing: For example, Ho Chi Minh appears as Ho (last name) in the short version, but Vo Nguyen Giap appears as Giap (first name) in the short version, etc. Some country names have changed since 1945, but they will appear in their historical form as well, such as Burma (Myanmar) and Ceylon (Sri Lanka). I applied the following transcription conventions for the multitude of languages used in this book:

> All European languages using the Latin alphabet (English, German, Polish, Czech, Hungarian, Romanian, Italian, and French) keep their diacritical marks.

> For Cyrillic languages, I followed the transliteration tables generally used by the Library of Congress (ALA-LC Romanization table; see www.loc.gov/catdir/cpso/roman.html), with the following exceptions: 1. Soft vowels such as ю, я, and ё are transliterated as *yu* (not *iu*), *ya* (not *ia*), and *ye* (not *ë*). 2. The following signs and diacritical marks are dropped: ′ for the soft sign ь, ″ for the Russian hard sign ъ, ŭ for the Bulgarian unstressed vowel ъ, ˘ on ῐ (й), ˙ on ė (э), and ˉ above a cluster of Latin letters (*ts*, *yu*, *ya*),

indicating that they jointly stand for one transliterated Cyrillic letter (ц, ю, я).

Vietnamese and Korean names lose their diacritical marks, due to publishing constraints and because they often appear without any in numerous documents.

For Chinese, the Pinyin system applies.

For Arabic and Persian, common spellings of names in English-language sources are used.

Abbreviations

AAPSO	Afro–Asian People's Solidarity Organization
ABM	Anti-Ballistic Missile (Treaty, 1972)
ASEAN	Association of Southeast Asian Nations
CCP	Chinese Communist Party
CENTO	Central Treaty Organization (Baghdad Pact)
CIA	Central Intelligence Agency
CMEA	Council for Mutual Economic Assistance
CoCom	Coordinating Committee for Multilateral Export Controls
Cominform	Communist Information Bureau
Comintern	Communist International (Third International)
CPSU	Communist Party of the Soviet Union
CSCE	Conference on Security and Cooperation in Europe
DRV	Democratic Republic of Vietnam (1945–76; North Vietnam)
EC	European Communities (1967–93; ECSC, EEC, and EURATOM)
ECHR	European Court of Human Rights (since 1959)
ECSC	European Coal and Steel Community (1951–93)
EDC	European Defense Community
EEC	European Economic Community (1957–67)
EFTA	European Free Trade Association (since 1960)
EPC	European Political Cooperation
EU	European Union (since 1993)
EURATOM	European Atomic Energy Community (since 1957)
Fatah	Palestinian National Liberation Movement (reverse acronym)
FLN	Front de libération nationale (National Liberation Front of Algeria)
FRG	Federal Republic of Germany (West Germany)
G-77	Group of 77
GDR	German Democratic Republic (East Germany)

GMD	*Guomindang* (Nationalist Party of China)
IBEC	International Bank of Economic Cooperation (CMEA)
ICP	Indochinese Communist Party
ICSC	International Commission for Supervision and Control (Vietnam)
ICWA	Indian Council of World Affairs
IDF	Israel Defense Forces
IIB	International Investment Bank (CMEA)
IMF	International Monetary Fund
INF	Intermediate Nuclear Forces
KGB	Komitet Gosudarstvennoy Bezopasnosti (Committee for State Security)
KOR	Komitet Obrony Robotników (Workers' Defense Committee)
LTBT	Limited Test Ban Treaty (1963)
MAD	Mutual Assured Destruction
MLF	Multi-Lateral Force
MNF	Multinational Force (Lebanon)
NATO	North Atlantic Treaty Organization
NEFA	North-East Frontier Agency (after 1954)
NEFT	North-East Frontier Tracts (until 1954)
NEP	New Economic Policy
NLF	National Liberation Front (South Vietnam)
NPT	Nuclear Non-Proliferation Treaty (1968)
OAPEC	Organization of Arab Petroleum Exporting Countries
OECD	Organization for Economic Cooperation and Development
OEEC	Organization for European Economic Cooperation
OSCE	Organization for Security and Cooperation in Europe
Panchsheel	Five Principles of Peaceful Coexistence (1954)
PCF	Parti Communiste Français (French Communist Party)
PCI	Partito Comunista Italiano (Italian Communist Party)
PFLP	Popular Front for the Liberation of Palestine
PLA	People's Liberation Army (China)
PLA	Palestinian Liberation Army
PLO	Palestine Liberation Organization
PRC	People's Republic of China
PRG	Provisional Revolutionary Government (South Vietnam)
ROC	Republic of China

ROPCiO	Ruch Obrony Praw Człowieka i Obywatela (Movement for Defense of Human and Civic Rights)
RVN	Republic of Vietnam (1955–76; South Vietnam)
SALT	Strategic Arms Limitation Treaty (1972)
SALT II	Strategic Arms Limitation Treaty (1979)
SDI	Strategic Defense Initiative
SEATO	Southeast Asia Treaty Organization
SED	Sozialistische Einheitspartei Deutschlands (Socialist Unity Party of Germany)
sihua	*si xiandaihua* (Four Modernizations; PRC)
SRV	Socialist Republic of Vietnam (since 1976)
START	Strategic Arms Reduction Treaty (1991)
START II	Strategic Arms Reduction Treaty (1993)
START III	Strategic Arms Reduction Treaty (2010)
SVN	State of Vietnam (until 1955)
UAR	United Arab Republic
UK	United Kingdom
UN	United Nations
UNCTAD	United Nations Conference on Trade and Development
UNEF	United Nations Emergency Force (Sinai)
UNESCO	United Nations Educational, Scientific and Cultural Organization
UNIFIL	United Nations Interim Force in Lebanon
US	United States (of America)
USSR	Union of Soviet Socialist Republics
VCP	Vietnamese Communist Party
VWP	Vietnamese Workers Party (since 1951)
WAPA	Warsaw Pact

Introduction

Almost a decade ago, when I attended a performance of Richard Wagner's opera *Die Walküre* in Berlin, the narrative structure of this book emerged before my eyes. Wagner's idea of a network of stories that intersect and influence each other has fascinated me since the early 1990s when I first saw the complete performance of his four-part operatic cycle *Der Ring des Nibelungen*. Its second part, *Die Walküre*, sparked my vision of writing a reinterpretation of the Cold War as an interconnected set of narratives that focuses on how middle and smaller actors at the regional level shaped that global conflict.

What was the Cold War that shook world politics for the second half of the twentieth century? When did it start? How did it transform over time? And when did it end? The standard answers focus on the start of the Cold War in Europe in the period between 1917 and 1947, and its development as a Soviet–American rivalry. In this version, narratives in the rest of the world are generally secondary to the main story of Soviet–American conflict over the continent of Europe. The predominant focus on the bilateral global conflict has led historians to write interpretations of each side's policies and of vertical relations between one of them and a middle power or smaller actor. Only a few books on the global Cold War focus on multiple continents. *Cold Wars: Asia, the Middle East, Europe* sprang from my growing unease about the sporadic attention that Cold War scholarship has paid to structural change at the regional and national levels, and to horizontal interconnections among different world regions, as if only the superpowers were the exclusive driving forces of change in the international system.[1] The regional focus, which I advocate, reveals that events in several world regions significantly affected structural change, and thus critically shaped the course of the global Cold War itself.

Cold Wars: Asia, the Middle East, Europe pursues four interrelated goals. *First*, it aims to redirect the interpretative focus from the global, or systemic, Cold War to the regional, sub-systemic, Cold Wars. Returning agency to middle powers such as China and smaller actors such as the Vatican enables us to appreciate better two obscured facets in the global Cold War. One is that the global Cold War did not cause *all* regional conflicts of the period. Often, the great powers co-opted pre-existing regional or national developments and tried to nudge them in their favor. The other, even more important, facet is that the *reverse* often happened! The great powers might have believed that they were puppet masters pulling strings across the world, but the puppets had their own agendas and frequently pulled at their end of the strings to make the self-declared puppeteers dance. Concentrating on regional and national developments illuminates their impact on structural change in the international system over the course of the whole global Cold War. Ultimately, without the structural changes at the sub-systemic level, the end of the systemic Cold War would not have been possible in the late 1980s.

Second, focusing on regional conflicts forces us to reintegrate decolonization into the Cold War narrative. Nation-state formation in Vietnam, India, Pakistan, Iraq, Syria, Lebanon, and Palestine/Israel all had roots in the pre-1945 period. A historical account that takes the drivers of regional conflicts seriously allows us to acknowledge different starting points of the ideological rivalry, which dominated the global Cold War after 1945, in different regions of the world. Consequently, the chapters on Asia and the Middle East occur before those on Europe, because conflicts in Asia, as for example the Chinese Civil War that started in 1927, generally preceded those in Europe.

Third, the dynamic nature of the global Cold War enabled regional and national developments to exert a substantial impact on structural change. In 1945, the world was run by the Big Three. The United Kingdom, the Soviet Union, and the United States were great powers in a *league of their own* even if their respective strengths were not equal to each other. Each of them had acquired a sphere of influence in the mid and late 1940s – the Arab League, the Socialist Camp, and the Free World – that was hard to control and riven with internal conflict. In parallel to the transformation of the triangular relationship of the Big Three into a *nuclear superpower duopoly* without the United Kingdom by the 1960s, the internal weaknesses of the three spheres precipitated the *diffusion of power at the regional and national levels*. This double development entailed the simultaneous concentration of the superpower rivalry at the top and the decentering of power at the lower levels of the international system.

Fourth, the book also focuses on interconnections and spillover effects within and among the three world regions of Asia, the Middle East, and Europe. Events within each of them often were interconnected, which is why Parts II to VII (Chapters 5–22) are organized along geographical lines. Furthermore, events in one world region often influenced developments in the other two. In general, such influence flowed from Asia toward the Middle East and Europe, and from the Middle East toward Europe. This is yet another good reason to position the chapters on Asia ahead of those on the Middle East and Europe. A fitting example is the outbreak of the Korean War in 1950, which affected China, Vietnam, India, the Arab League, Europe, and Germany. Although less frequently, spillover effects also went the other way. For example, the triple crisis in Poland, Hungary, and Egypt in the fall of 1956 had an impact on China, and the Afghanistan War and the Iranian Revolution in 1979 influenced Asia.

Although I am proposing that historians of international relations collectively step outside the well-established paradigm of Cold War superpower bipolarity, I do not argue that the Soviet Union and the United States did not matter at all. Still, we need to change the focus – or better adopt multiple foci – in order to decenter the Cold War in a systematic fashion, to move structural developments into the foreground, to restore middle powers and smaller actors to visibility, and to link events horizontally to each other (and not only vertically to the great powers). Only then can we reintegrate the United Kingdom, the Soviet Union, and the United States at their proper places in the overall Cold War narrative again. As mentioned above, this requires the incorporation of conflicts and developments that pre-dated and interacted with the global Cold War – such as decolonization, nation-state formation, the Arab–Israeli conflict, and even Western European integration. Ultimately, this approach substantially revises the Eurocentric standard interpretation of the Cold War.

For almost fifty years after World War I, the world experienced a three-way ideological conflict between imperialism, communism, and liberal democracy/capitalism. Throughout the interwar period, it was dominated by European imperial powers and a rising Imperial Japan. London, Paris, Rome, and Tokyo all continued to increase territorial control in the Middle East, Africa, and East Asia after World War I. By the end of World War II, the United Kingdom was about to lose its colonial possessions in South Asia, but it was still the world's foremost imperial power, dominating East Africa, the Persian Gulf, and Southeast Asia while having just established preponderance in the Middle East through the Arab League. In 1945, Italy and Japan ceased being colonial powers as the result of defeat in World War II. France tried to re-establish control in Indochina and cling to its possessions in Africa. In comparison, since the Bolshevik Revolution in 1917, Soviet Russia / the Union of Soviet Socialist Republics (USSR) had aimed at the revolutionary overthrow of the imperialist–capitalist world system and the establishment of a stateless and classless society across the globe. For that purpose, it established a network of communist parties throughout the world in the wake of the Bolshevik Revolution and, during most of its existence, used military force to create and maintain the Socialist Camp. Finally, the United States sought both decolonization and the containment of communism. During both world wars, it had developed reformist ideas aimed at the overhaul of the international system. The United States thereby attempted to make the world less prone to radical challenges from the extreme right and the extreme left, establishing the self-described Free World after 1945 in the process. In the two decades after World War II, worldwide decolonization ended most colonial empires, including the British Empire. The United Kingdom ceased being one of the Big Three in the Cold War, though it continued to participate as an ally of the United States. In the 1960s, the USSR and the United States maintained the ideological conflict in the form of the newly established nuclear superpower duopoly.

Thus, the Cold War occurred in multiple incarnations at different levels in the international system and in different geographical areas of the world. It raged at the global level between the Big Three until the 1960s and between the Soviet–American superpowers afterward. Yet, at the regional level, the Cold War spawned only a few conflicts exclusively by itself – most notably in Korea, Germany, and Afghanistan. In most cases, the Cold War interacted with pre-existing developments – be they domestic conflicts like in China since 1927 and Vietnam since 1945, or in regional confrontations such as the Arab–Israeli conflict, or in spin-off conflicts as for instance Sino–Indian hostility. Regional actors – middle and small alike – were not just lifeless punching bags that only responded to the strikes of the Big Three or the two superpowers. On the contrary, they possessed agency – i.e. the ability to shape their own future through their own actions.[2] Of course, the degree of agency spanned a wide range of capabilities – from a rising communist China, at one extreme, to the dispersed Palestinians, at the other. Still, these different assertions of agency cumulatively caused structural change to the global system over the course of the Cold War. Hence, just as the Soviet Union and the United States reached a nuclear superpower duopoly in the 1960s, the *diffusion of military, political, and economic power* was under way at the regional and national levels of the Cold War.

Furthermore, the regional Cold Wars emerged at different times, depending on specific preconditions. In Asia (defined as East, Southeast, and South Asia), the Chinese Civil War that started in 1927 was the first major regional Cold War even before the global conflict had started. In Europe, ideologically motivated tensions briefly emerged after the Bolshevik Revolution in 1917, but major conflict arose only by the mid 1940s. In the Middle East (defined as the area stretching from Morocco to Pakistan and from the Arabian peninsula to Turkey), the Cold War entered tentatively by the mid 1950s and then definitely by the mid 1960s. Regional actors not only had agency to respond to particular context-specific developments, but they also formulated alternatives to the ideological conflict. India spawned Asian–African Internationalism and Non-Alignment in the 1940s. Communist China tried to promote anti-Western and anti-Soviet agendas in the 1960s. Muslim nations produced competing pan-Islamist conceptions between the 1930s and the 1970s. Christian democrats in Europe, together with the Vatican, pursued policies situated in between the revolutionary left and unfettered capitalism. Western European communists formulated a Eurocommunist alternative to Soviet-style communism in the 1970s. Not all these alternatives survived into the post-Cold War period, but most exerted major influence on structural change during the Cold War. In short, the regional Cold Wars emerged in different world regions at different times, and the various regional actors shaped them in parallel and sometimes interrelated fashion.

Since the Cold War was a dynamically developing global system with distinctive regional incarnations, it ended in different ways in various parts of the world. In order to determine the end of a specific regional Cold War, it is necessary to define its principal characteristics. In Asia, the Cold War primarily was a combination of decolonization and ideological conflict. On the one side were the communist-dominated national liberation movements in China and Vietnam that had emerged in close cooperation with each other since the 1920s. On the other side stood the US allied non-communist states from South Korea to South Asia. The regional Cold War ended structurally in Asia in the late 1970s with the Sino–Vietnamese conflict and the rapprochement between the People's Republic of China, the United States, and anti-communist Southeast Asian states. In the Middle East, none of the regional Cold War conflicts – bar the Afghanistan War in 1979–89 – stemmed from the global conflict, but all had local roots dating back to the collapse of the Ottoman Empire at the end of World War I and the Arab–Zionist/Israeli conflict that arose afterward. The global Cold War was drawn into the Middle East by the 1950s and then imposed itself on the region by the mid 1960s. It mostly ended with structural changes in the late 1970s, i.e. when the region transcended the global Cold War with the Israeli–Egyptian peace treaty and the rise to power of pan-Islamist movements that rejected the East–West conflict. In comparison, conflict in Europe was mainly a result of the global Cold War. Still, the regional Cold War faltered in the late 1970s, too, with the advent of major structural transformations, such as the economic decline and ideological exhaustion of the Socialist Camp, the increasing economic integration of socialist Eastern Europe into the world economy, the rise of a civil society in Poland challenging the status quo, and the economic rebound of Western Europe after the crises of the 1970s. As the three world regions underwent structural changes and, in the process, weakened or even severed their links to the global ideological clash, the superpower Cold War was the only major conflict that remained. It took Moscow and Washington until the late 1980s to understand this.

The literature on the Cold War is so vast that it deserves its own book-length treatment. Dominated by American-based authors during the Cold War, the first four decades of scholarly production mainly focused on the United States and its conflict with the Soviet Union.[3] The collapse of the Socialist Camp in the late 1980s offered access to hitherto closed archives, opening up new avenues of historical inquiry. As more and more primary evidence became available, historians found new answers to old questions. Who started the Korean War in 1950? Was Stalin serious when he offered a peace treaty to a unified Germany in 1952? Were the Vietnamese communists essentially nationalists or genuine communists? Furthermore, much of the historiography produced during the Cold War focused on Europe and, though to a much lesser degree, on East Asia, Indochina, and the Arab–Israeli conflict. The unlocking of archives after the end of the Cold War inspired research in previously neglected areas, such as Southeast Asia beyond Indochina, South Asia, Africa, and Latin America.[4]

After the end of the Soviet–American conflict in 1989, Cold War historians, who often were based outside the United States, insisted on decentering the Cold War and even on replacing the superpower lens. Area specialists further pointed to the phenomenon of "the tail wagging the dog," i.e. the phenomenon of a smaller ally forcing the hand of a superpower.[5] In short, they all called for the equitable inclusion of middle powers and smaller actors in the historical inquiry. A quarter of a century later, the state of historiographical affairs in this regard is mixed at best. On the basis of newly available sources, area specialists have written remarkable pieces on China, Vietnam, India, the Palestinians, Yemen, Algeria, and Germany, for example.[6] Even historians of the global Cold War have increasingly included the Global South in their interpretations.[7] But, in general, decentering the Cold War was more successful in fields other than diplomatic and political history, such as cultural studies or political science.[8]

The strange bifurcation between international history and regional studies continues to this day. Most historians writing general interpretations of the global Cold War still use the Soviet–American conflict as the primary interpretative lens without systematically integrating the findings of area specialists, or even re-examining their own choice of approach.[9] This kind of interpretative schism is replicated in several, though not all, subfields. The Vietnam War attracts a vast number of historians who write exclusively on the American side, but they rarely incorporate – though with a few notable exceptions – what area specialists have written on the basis of Vietnamese-language sources.[10] Since the publication of Edward Said's famous book on Orientalism in the late 1970s, the historiography on the Middle East is, broadly speaking, actually split into three interpretative clusters that barely converse with each other: intellectual, cultural and social historians working with Arab language sources, diplomatic historians mainly tied to an American-centric or bipolar Cold War frame of interpretation, and Israeli scholars working on Israeli–Arab relations.[11] In the same vein, books on the Cold War in Europe are focusing on individual events or are national case studies, often in relation to one or both superpowers.[12] With a few exceptions, historians of Germany have failed to produce integrated interpretations of the divided past between 1945 and 1990.[13] Instead, they either continue to treat the two Germanys as separate entities, or consider the East German experience an outright aberration.[14] In many subfields of Cold War studies, the often-heard calls for decentering or for adopting new approaches have gone mostly unheard.

Cold Wars: Asia, the Middle East, Europe resurrects these calls by integrating different experiences and multiple viewpoints. Based on the synthesis of publications from numerous fields of area and Cold War studies and on primary research in archives on four continents, the book restores middle powers and smaller actors to their actual role in the structural evolution of the Cold War. But it does not follow a rigid pattern of applying identical approaches in each chapter. On the contrary, the interpretative lens chosen in each case varies from the global to the regional and the national. Ultimately, the choice of lens depended on my personal judgment as to what approach would be the most fruitful in understanding the topic under investigation. Despite this eclectic method, the book pursues a larger, integrated question: how did regional and national actors – collectively and individually – influence and transform the structure of the global Cold War, and thereby produce the necessary conditions for its end?

No book is a comprehensive treatment of the historical past. I decided to focus on Asia, the Middle East, and Europe for two basic reasons. First, these three regions stood at the geographic frontline of the Cold War, where the largest number of conflicts and the most lethal ones occurred between the 1940s and the 1980s.[15] Second, it was primarily these three regions that generated the structural changes which enabled the superpowers to end the global Cold War in the late 1980s. Developments in Africa and Latin America appear in several chapters when they connect to the larger themes of the book.[16] But even with this reduced focus on three world regions, I needed to take decisions on what to include and what to leave out. Various notable countries in Asia, the Middle East, and Europe thus do not appear prominently in the book, mainly because they did not contribute to structural change over time. And while China, Vietnam, India, the Palestinians, Germany, and the Vatican all receive chapter-length treatments, Indonesia, Pakistan, Algeria, France, and Poland do not, though their stories appear in several sections of various chapters.

Cold Wars: Asia, the Middle East, Europe employs the literary technique of the frame story – i.e. the device of using a general story to set the stage for detailed narrative strings within it. This book in effect is a *double frame story* with fifteen narrative strings in between. The *outer* frame (Chapters 1 and 23) provides the structural support for the book's overall argument. It consists of the emergence of the systemic Cold War from 1917 to 1957 and its end with the termination of the superpower clash in the late 1980s. The *inner* frame comprises the beginning of the regional Cold Wars after World War II (Part I) and their end at the turn of the 1970s/1980s (Part VII). This *inner* frame supports fifteen narrative threads (Parts II to VI). These fifteen chapters describe how middle powers and smaller actors shaped their own fate. Collectively, the developments in Parts II to VI caused structural change to the global system over the period from the 1950s to the 1970s, which led to the end of the regional (sub-systemic) Cold Wars, as covered in Part VII. As these fifteen narratives (Chapters 5 to 19) unfold in the center section of the book, they produce a colorful tapestry – a *network of narratives interconnected at multiple knots*.

Chapter 1 "From High Imperialism to Cold War Division" sets the stage for the remaining chapters. The period from 1917 to 1957 witnessed the transformation of the world from one dominated by European imperial states into one divided between the two ideological blocs – the USSR and the Anglo–American powers. The 1950 outbreak of the Korean War, which was merely a local conflict, triggered the spread of Cold War division from Europe and East Asia to Southeast Asia, South Asia, and the Middle East. With the Suez Crisis of 1956, the United Kingdom lost its international influence outside Europe.

Part I on *Elusive Unities* explores the international system after World War II. The Big Three monopolized most of the influence in the world. Although not a Cold War creation, the "Arab League" (Chapter 2) was a British attempt to fortify its imperial influence in the Middle East, Africa, and the Asian world beyond World War II. But the internal unity of the Arab League was weak, and British leadership collapsed during the Suez Crisis in late 1956. Stalin's Soviet Union ran the "Socialist Camp" (Chapter 3), which emerged over the period from 1944 to 1949 and included Eastern Europe and parts of mainland East Asia. Yet the inner strength of the Socialist Camp was brittle, particularly after Stalin's death. The self-described "Free World" (Chapter 4) consisted of two American spheres of influence, one in democratic Western Europe and the other among mostly authoritarian allies in Asia and the Middle East. Its internal unity faced serious tests during Charles de Gaulle's decade-long rule in France and the parallel domestic conflicts in multiple countries during the 1960s.

Part II on *Asia* focuses on three countries emerging from the colonial period. Chapter 5 on China explores the civil war from 1927 to 1949 as an early Cold War conflict, and communist China as a revolutionary pariah from 1949 to 1971. Once the People's Republic of China (PRC) joined the United Nations in 1971, however, it became a status quo power. Chapter 6 on Vietnam sketches the long path of the Vietnamese Communist Party from a peripheral group in the 1930s to the hegemon of Indochina in the 1970s. Its anti-colonial struggle against France after World War II turned into a 25-year-long Cold War conflict by early 1950. Chapter 7 covers India's unsuccessful struggle to prevent the Cold War from entering South Asia. Because of a series of military conflicts with its neighbors Pakistan and China, India declined from a position of widespread international admiration to pariah status. The developments of these three states were closely interconnected – in the form of the faltering Sino–Vietnamese relationship, the collapse of Sino–Indian friendship, and the emerging Indo–Vietnamese partnership.

Part III on the *Middle East* stands at the intersection of the successive collapses of Ottoman, French, and British imperialism in the region and the rise of the Zionist project in Palestine. The resulting clashes – the Arab–Israeli War in 1948 and the Suez Crisis in 1956 – were not Cold War conflicts (Chapter 8). On the contrary, both the USSR and the United States supported Israel in the first conflict and Egypt in the second. Still, their antagonism made its first tentative entry into the Middle East in the wake of the Korean War. Only in the period from 1964 to 1974 (Chapter 9), however, did the global Cold War fully enter the Middle East when the superpowers lined up behind the opposite sides in the June War of 1967. Yet, by the early 1970s, Egypt and Saudi Arabia tried to push the global Cold War out of the region, with the October War of 1973 being an important watershed. The conflict of the Arab states with Israel affected the fate of Palestinians in their quest to establish their own state (Chapter 10). The Chinese and Vietnamese revolutionary experiences, as described in Part II, had a major impact on developments in the Middle East, particularly before the Suez Crisis and between the June and the October Wars.

Part IV on *Alternative World Visions* addresses three transnational phenomena that weave together developments from Parts II and III. Asian–African Internationalism (Chapter 11) originally emerged as India's response to decolonization immediately after World War II. In 1955, the Cold War imposed itself on the movement at the famous Bandung Conference, which was simultaneously the movement's endpoint. The concept of Non-Alignment (Chapter 12) was an Indian invention as well, although Yugoslavia and Egypt forged it into a movement by 1961 with the intent of providing a global voice to unaligned middle powers and smaller countries. Yet it soon fell victim to the June War of 1967 and the Indochina conflict. Finally, various forms of competing pan-Islamisms (Chapter 13) emerged during the Cold War – in Pakistan, Egypt, Saudi Arabia, and Iran.

Part V on *Europe between the Superpowers* turns from Asia and the Middle East to Europe. Chapter 14 on nuclear weapons links a multitude of developments from all three world regions and thus serves as a transition from Parts II–IV to Parts V–VI. It brings together the transformation of Soviet–American–British post-World War II dominance into the nuclear superpower duopoly since the 1960s, and nuclear proliferation to China, France, Israel, India, and Pakistan. Chapters 15 and 16 describe the competitive economic integration in Western and Eastern Europe from the late 1940s to the 1970s, disclosing, in the process, the different degree of American and Soviet influence in the continent. Part VI on *European Détente* explores divided Germany (Chapter 17), the Conference on Security and Cooperation in Europe (CSCE; Chapter 18), and the Vatican's relations with the Socialist Camp (Chapter 19). The uniting theme among these three chapters is how the two Germanys and Poland managed to come to terms with each other by the early 1970s.

Part VII on the *End of the Regional Cold Wars* weaves together the structural transformations described in Parts II–VI, and the manner by which this development produced the termination of the regional Cold Wars in the Middle East, Asia, and Europe at the turn of the 1970s/1980s. Chapter 20 focuses on how the Middle East transcended the global Cold War with the Israeli–Egyptian peace treaty and the rise of Islamic movements to influence and even state power. Chapter 21 starts with the final collapse of long-standing communist unity among the national liberation movements of China, Vietnam, and Cambodia, and continues with India's brief but aborted attempts to escape its isolation in the region through improving relations with Pakistan, China, and Southeast Asia. Chapter 22 on the end of the Cold War in Europe brings together the economic collapse of the Socialist Camp, the Polish Crisis, the economic turnaround of Western Europe, and the structural changes of East–West relations on the continent.

Chapter 23 on "The End of the Superpower Conflict" returns to the stage of the international system – a stage that had radically changed in shape and size over the course of the previous thirty years. Contrary to widespread popular and scholarly convictions, the United States did not win the Cold War with a knockout punch. Quite the opposite, the Soviet Union simply lost by running out of steam. Initially, Mikhail S. Gorbachev's reforms aimed at making the Soviet Union competitive again for the continuation of the Cold War, but by 1988, it was clear that the USSR was losing ground in almost every field of domestic and foreign policy. The collapse of the Soviet empire in Eastern Europe in 1989 preceded the collapse of the USSR two years later. The final chapter (24) sketches the long-term legacies of the Cold War in Asia, the Middle East, and Europe.

The internal organization of *Cold Wars: Asia, the Middle East, Europe* allows readers to consume it in one go, to read it with a geographical focus, or to pick just one or two chapters. Each of the seven parts (Chapters 2–22) of the book starts with a brief introduction, summarizing the main points of its three chapters and how they relate to each other. The Soviet Union and the United States figure prominently in Chapters 1, 3–4, 14–16, and 23, Asia in Chapters 1, 3–7, 11–12, and 21, the Middle East in Chapters 1–2, 8–10, 13, and 20, and Europe in Chapters 1, 3–4, 14–19, and 22. To make the book more accessible to a larger audience, I decided to keep the coverage of historiographical debates at a minimum in all chapters. Specialists will anyway understand what intervention each chapter makes.

Terms appear in this book as Cold War participants used them at the time. George Orwell was the first to use the term "Cold War" in an essay published in mid October 1945. Hence, this book uses "Cold War" only for the period after World War II.[17] "Socialist Camp" frequently occurs in Soviet and Eastern European documents. The "Free World" is a self-description of the Western side in the Cold War. "US imperialism" commonly occurs in the vocabulary of American antagonists. Since I make the argument that the United States and the Soviet Union reached an enhanced status in the international system on the basis of large numbers of nuclear weapons only by the 1960s, I will use the term "superpower" merely for the second half of the Cold War. I avoid using "bipolarity" and even "tripoliarity" but instead use the contemporaneous term "the Big Three" – the United Kingdom, the Soviet Union, and the

United States – for the two decades after World War II. In any case, the frequently used terms "bipolarity" and "tripoliarity" not only are misleading for the first half of the Cold War but also imply that medium and smaller powers were orienting themselves to one of the poles under the inescapable influence of some mysterious form of political or ideological magnetism. On the contrary, as this book shows over and again, many countries attempted to avoid turning toward any of the assumed poles, but engaged with the Cold War to exploit new opportunities for the promotion of their own, unrelated agendas. All of these and other frequently used historical and scholarly terms appear in the text of the book *without* quotation marks. Equally, the book uses "Eastern Europe" to denote what many area specialists now call "East Central Europe." Again, "Eastern Europe" is a historical term that pre-dated the Cold War and acquired additional prominence in the context of the continent's division along the Iron Curtain running from north to south. Yet, inasmuch as "Eastern Europe" nowadays is a highly politicized term, so is the younger term "East Central Europe."[18] Socialism and communism are used interchangeably. I am aware that there is a theoretical difference between the two, but even communist parties at the time employed them inconsistently in daily usage.

1   From High Imperialism to Cold War Division

The political and ideological roots of the world's Cold War division after World War II date back to the final years of the previous world war, when Soviet Russia and the United States emerged as promoters of competing visions for reordering a world that was still dominated by imperial powers, particularly the United Kingdom. But the parallel Soviet–American retreat from international relations during the 1920s allowed the imperialist world order to flourish one last time. During the interwar period, London, Paris, and Rome increased their influence in the larger Middle Eastern region and Africa, and Tokyo did the same in East Asia. In 1945, the joint British–Soviet–American defeat of German, Italian, and Japanese aggression in World War II provided the United Kingdom, the Soviet Union, and the United States with unparalleled but shared political, military, and moral clout. No other country could rival them in terms of political and military power. Germany, Italy, and Japan all were defeated, China was weak, and France re-emerged humiliated by occupation. Yet the Big Three could not have been more different from each other. The United Kingdom emerged bankrupt from the war and under pressure to withdraw from its colonies in South Asia but not yet from the rest of its empire. The Soviet Union had survived a brutal and devastating attack by Germany. World War II caused massive destruction in its western territories, and hence forced Moscow to pursue a cautious imperial-revolutionary policy first at its European periphery and then in East Asia. And the United States emerged as an internationalist economic and military power that stood ready to decolonize the world and restore peace, stability, and prosperity on a global scale.

The world's Cold War division between the Soviet Union and the two Western great powers unfolded over roughly a dozen years after 1945. It was not predetermined, but was the collective result of ideological clashes, unilateral decisions, political disagreements, and misperceptions. It did not evolve along a steady path, but in fits and starts – with 1945 and 1950 as key years. In the years after World War II, the three great powers particularly clashed over their former enemies Germany and Japan. Soviet behavior in Eastern Europe and the resumption of the Chinese

Civil War by the official government of China – a US associate in the emerging Cold War – further complicated the situation. Without the outbreak of the Korean War – a local clash at the world's periphery – in 1950, the Soviet–Western conflict probably would have remained confined to Europe and East Asia. Convinced that the Soviet Union was intrinsically expansionist, the United States used the Korean War to implement a new containment strategy of linked defensive alliances surrounding the communist world. And in 1956, another local conflict – the Suez Crisis, which the imperialist United Kingdom helped to spark – tentatively invited the Cold War into the Middle East.

By early 1957, the structural foundations of the global Cold War had been put in place. The Soviet Union and its partners – the Eastern European satellites and a few voluntary allies like Albania, China, and North Vietnam – formed an almost contiguous bloc of revolutionary regimes on the Eurasian landmass. In the wake of the Korean War, the United States had established a network of alliances that spanned from Europe across the Middle East to Asia and was designed to contain the so-called Soviet bloc. During the same time, however, the British Empire declined as a global power. By the end of World War II, only South Asia had been on the course to independence, while London still commanded a global empire that reached from Africa across the Middle East to Southeast Asia and beyond. Yet, within a dozen years, it had lost most of its influence in the Arab world, the region crucial to holding together the empire, and thereby much of its sway over its former and remaining colonies around the Indian Ocean. Moreover, the emergence of the Cold War in the period after World War II sowed the seeds for structural changes in the following quarter of a century, as numerous later chapters reveal. For example, India and Egypt refused to take sides in the Cold War; Germany's division eventually convinced West Germany to pursue policies of engagement with the eastern half of the country; and the United Kingdom transformed itself from an imperial power into a European player.

Conflicting Visions for a Post-Imperial World, 1917–45

At the eve of World War I, the international system of states looked markedly different from today. Although historical maps show recognizable outlines for the mostly independent countries of the American double continent, the borders and names of many territories in Europe, Asia, the Middle East, and Africa appear unfamiliar. Germany extended beyond today's southwestern and northeastern borders, the Austro–Hungarian Empire included territories from twelve present-day countries, Poland did not exist, and much of the Russian borderlands were part of the

Tsarist Empire. Many parts of the Middle East belonged to the Ottoman Empire, though Egypt was under British suzerainty, Libya under Italian control, and Tunisia, Algeria, and Morocco under French and Spanish rule. Apart from Siam (Thailand) and the Empire of Japan, almost all Asian countries were either colonies or protectorates of imperial powers. China was disintegrating into an ever-changing system of feuding warlords after the anti-Qing revolution in 1911/12, and South Asia was divided into multiple, mainly British, colonial possessions and hundreds of princely states. With the exception of Ethiopia, all of sub-Saharan Africa was under British, French, Belgian, German, or Portuguese imperial rule.

Map 1. Europe and the Ottoman Empire, 1914

Even if World War I undermined the political strength of imperialism, it did not trigger outright decolonization in Asia, the Middle East, or Africa. The United Kingdom remained the dominant power in international relations, controlling large parts in three world regions. After World War I, Germany's colonies in China, the Western Pacific, and Africa were simply transferred to the United Kingdom, Portugal, Japan, or the mandate system of the newly established League of Nations. The Arab parts of the Ottoman Empire – Iraq, Transjordan (today's Jordan), Palestine, Syria, and Lebanon – fell under British and French mandate rule. To make matters worse, imperialism seemed to gather renewed momentum in the 1930s when Japan increased its colonial holdings on the Asian mainland, and Italy took Ethiopia.

In 1918, a quarter of the world's population of 1.7 billion lived under British rule. World War I had not undercut the economic and military domination of the world by the United Kingdom, even if it had helped to undermine the country's ability to maintain this exalted position in the long term. The war had devastated world trade, which hit the free-trading and credit-granting imperial power particularly hard. International trade did not return to pre-World War I levels during the 1920s, while the United Kingdom spent vast resources on restoring the pound to the prestigious rank of the world's lead currency. But even if the financial and economic resources were less plentiful than before World War I, they were still sufficient for the United Kingdom to outrank all other aspiring great powers – with the exception of the United States. But the Great Depression, which started with the stock market crash in New York in 1929, removed that potential rival from the international scene, and then let world trade collapse once more.[1]

During the interwar years, the United Kingdom followed divergent policies toward two of its imperial domains that are of interest to this book: South Asia and the Middle East. The period between the world wars witnessed a general weakening of economic integration between the United Kingdom and the British Raj because competitors – European countries, the United States, and Japan – managed to enter the South Asian market. In parallel, the British grip on political control subsided as well. As promised during World War I, London devolved power toward self-rule twice – in 1919 and 1935 – even if conservative politicians in the United Kingdom, like the Westminster backbencher Winston Churchill, opposed this development. In any case, South Asians increasingly manned the Indian Civil Service, Mahatma Gandhi's and Jawaharlal Nehru's non-sectarian Indian Congress and Muhammad Ali Jinnah's Muslim League worked for independence, and British forces lost *de facto* control outside the Raj's urban and economic centers over the course of the 1930s. By World War II, Indian independence was in the offing, though before 1945 even the anti-imperialist Labour Party saw this only as a long-term possibility.[2]

In the Middle East, London's imperial interests focused on the British–French-built Suez Canal in Egypt and the formerly Ottoman territories to the east. The canal was the crucial link to the Raj, imperial possessions in East Asia and eastern Africa, and the dominions of Australia and New Zealand. With Italian imperial designs growing in Ethiopia and Japanese pretensions arising in the Western Pacific by the mid 1930s, the Suez Canal acquired additional strategic importance. Thus, British troops in Egypt did not shy away from suppressing political unrest after World War I with military force, but ultimately the United Kingdom gave in to popular Egyptian pressure by making a deal with King Faruq in 1936 that included troop withdrawals from Egypt proper in exchange for occupation rights of the canal zone for another twenty years. In the rest of the Middle East, British imperialists dreamed of the development of a new empire on the basis of the mandate territories in Palestine, Transjordan, and Iraq, which the United Kingdom had acquired from the collapsing Ottoman Empire after World War I. The goal was to create a secure land corridor in the east of the Suez Canal to the Persian Gulf, where the United Kingdom had imperial and oil interests. Although fears about Soviet expansion played a role in this new imperial project, the greatest threat to its success was Arab nationalism, which the new British presence and the increasing Zionist immigration was sparking. Though the United Kingdom agreed with collaborationist King Faisal to provide Iraq with formal independence in 1932, the British-administered mandate thereby simply turned into a close ally under British patronage. But in 1936–39, the United Kingdom resorted to outright military force in Palestine to suppress the Arab rebellion.[3]

Against the background of this seemingly robust imperialist world system in the interwar period, two challengers of colonialism – Soviet Russia and the United States – emerged. Vladimir I. Lenin's government had pursued *revolutionary change* in the world since the Bolshevik Revolution in November 1917. By February 1919, the future Soviet dictator Iosif V. Stalin described the world as being divided into "two camps" – the American–British–French–Japanese imperialist–capitalist camp and the socialist camp headed by revolutionary Russia. A month later, the Soviet government established the Comintern (the Third International), which one historian considered a response to the creation of the League of Nations during the concurrent Paris Peace Conference. Centrally run from Moscow by the Russian Communist (Bolshevik) Party, this "league of parties" was designed to establish and then guide fraternal outfits in other countries toward global revolution. When revolution in the advanced industrial countries of Europe failed to occur, Lenin called on the Comintern to use national liberation movements in the colonized world as vehicles to overthrow governments in imperialist–capitalist countries. Unsurprisingly, the victorious powers of World War I did not invite the new Russian government to the Paris Peace Conference. In any case, Lenin would have rejected a summons to a gathering that he considered a desperate attempt by the doomed global order to extend its life. From the beginning, Lenin's Soviet Russia was an outcast in international relations, not only of its own volition but also due to the outside reaction to its revolutionary pretensions.[4]

Yet the revolutionary zeal of the new Soviet government soon abated. A long civil war left the country's economy in tatters, and the attempt to export the revolution by military means into Europe failed due to the resistance of the newly recreated Polish state. In 1921, Lenin himself introduced the *New Economic Policy* (NEP), which marked the abandonment of communist ideas. After his death in 1924, his successor Stalin also retreated from the emphasis on promoting world revolution in exchange for building a strong socialist state in the Union of Soviet Socialist Republics (USSR) first. Given the rise of right-wing and militarist regimes in Germany and Japan in the 1930s, his Soviet Union even engaged with the hitherto despised bourgeois international order by acceding to the League of Nations and establishing relations with the United States. In that vein, the last Comintern congress in 1935 called for the establishment of anti-fascist popular fronts, which included non-leftist parties, as the organization's primary goal. But Stalin still did not completely abandon support for world revolution. He tried to influence domestic politics through Comintern-created communist parties in Germany in 1932–33 and in Spain in the second half of the decade. But the results turned out to be the opposite of his original expectations, as his policies had helped the rightists Adolf Hitler and Francisco Franco to gain power instead. In the Middle East and Asia, Soviet influence on local communist parties decreased as well, both as the result of changes in Comintern strategy and local reversals of fortune.[5]

Stalin's foreign policy immediately before and during World War II followed a mix of pragmatism and ideology. Weakened by its self-inflicted internal convulsions, the Soviet Union faced the possibility of a two-front war. In the east, Japan was building an empire on the Asian mainland that was supposed to include parts of Siberia. In the west, Hitler's Germany announced its designs to expand into Eastern Europe and the USSR.

Stalin thus wanted to prevent, or at least delay, a two-front war on the Eurasian continent through diplomatic means. In 1939, he concluded a deal with Hitler, who for his own reasons temporarily wanted to avoid a two-front war in Europe. The agreement divided the northern part of Eastern Europe into Soviet and German buffer zones. And in April of 1941, Stalin signed a five-year non-aggression treaty with Japan. Whether or not any other Soviet policy could have prevented Germany's attack two months later is still debated among historians. But the German invasion and the resulting massive destruction of the western USSR, where most of the Soviet population lived, pressed home the country's vulnerability at its exposed western borders. That Moscow, after the end of World War II, would follow a pragmatic policy of searching for some form of a security arrangement through a buffer zone at its periphery thus was plausible. However, during the war, Stalin had already prepared small groups of exiled communists from Eastern Europe and Germany for the task of seizing power and imposing revolutionary regimes in Soviet occupied territories in the immediate post-war period.[6]

The United States, too, emerged as a great power during the final two years of World War I. Unlike the Soviet Union, it saw itself not as a revolutionary force that aimed at overthrowing the existing international order, but as a *reformer*. Some historians have suggested that Woodrow Wilson's Fourteen Points of early 1918 were a direct response to Lenin's Bolshevik Revolution in late 1917. Like Lenin, Wilson envisioned a reordering of the world's imperialist core in Europe. Eight of his Fourteen Points addressed the redrawing of the continent's borders, five the need to prevent renewed war, and one the creation of an international organization that would transform the world's anarchic state system into one governed by rules. His visions were about remaking the world in the image of the United States – a successful and self-determined nation state that had emerged from nothing in just one and a half centuries.[7]

Yet the predominantly European focus of Wilson's proposals, particularly with regard to national self-determination, reflected the shortcomings of his own thinking. Wilson spent as little thought on the decolonization of Asia, the Middle East, and Africa as he did on embracing the end of racial discrimination in the United States. Even if he had instrumental reasons not to alienate the allied British and French empires at the Paris Peace Conference, his agreement to the transfer of German and Ottoman possessions to other imperial powers and the establishment of the League's mandate system conformed with the American policy of putting non-white people – like the Filipinos since 1898 – under long-term paternalist tutelage. But the universal applicability of his rhetoric on national self-determination attracted the attention of many anti-imperialist leaders from Asia, the

Middle East, and Africa. Wilson's refusal even to give their appeals a hearing at the Paris Peace Conference left them disappointed. It convinced some, like the Vietnamese Nguyen Ai Quoc (Ho Chi Minh), that Leninism provided the answers which Wilsonianism refused to give.[8]

Wilson's ultimate failure in reordering Europe and the world had both substantial short-term and political long-term consequences. After World War I, the US government did not believe that it should make a formal economic or even military commitment to international stability, particularly to European countries that suffered from economic and political crises in the post-war period. Wilson's United States even withdrew from the world entirely of its own volition, unlike Lenin's Russia. Still, the White House did not completely retreat even if the US Congress tried to bind the hands of the president in foreign affairs as much as possible. Under Wilson's successor, Warren G. Harding, the country took the lead in establishing the Washington treaty system (1921–22), which aimed at keeping the Japanese Empire contained and the internally fragmented Republic of China safe from an imperial race for colonies. The next president, Calvin Coolidge, collaborated with Wall Street banks in 1924 in reordering the financial system in Europe. The resulting Dawes Plan helped to end the economic crisis in Germany and to bring Europe a semi-decade of prosperity. But the stock market crash in New York in 1929, particularly the subsequent American shifting of its economic burden onto foreign debtors on all continents, heralded the global Great Depression. By the mid 1930s, nationalist legislation and politicized congressional investigations into the reasons for the US entry into World War I had pushed the country into a stridently isolationist position.[9]

By the late 1930s, President Franklin D. Roosevelt understood that his country could not stay perpetually aloof from the world in the face of German, Italian, and Japanese militarism. In August 1941, while the United States was still a non-belligerent in World War II, the president and British Prime Minister Churchill drafted the Atlantic Charter, which later became the seminal statement of war aims for all Allied powers, including Stalin's Soviet Union. The document contained many of Wilson's Fourteen Points – national self-determination, free trade, global cooperation for the sake of peace and prosperity, disarmament of aggressors, and a renunciation of the use of force in international relations – but it also included a non-transfer principle for territories, and the right of every nation to free and democratic choice of government. The charter thereby re-emphasized, expanded, and universalized the *reformist* ideas of Wilson's Fourteen Points, even if the conservative Churchill, and later France's equally conservative Charles de Gaulle, hoped to limit its applicability in order to protect their countries' imperial possessions in Asia, the Middle

East, and Africa. But unlike Wilson, Roosevelt abhorred imperialism – out of principle and pragmatism. Colonialism was not only a moral wrong, but the failure to decolonize, he feared, would also develop into a renewed threat to world peace. Still, in negotiations with Stalin during World War II, he was willing to make territorial compromises in Eastern Europe and Northeast Asia, which contradicted his own non-transfer principle but which he felt were necessary to keep the war alliance together. And his principled rejection of colonialism also did not mean that he had shed all of Wilson's racialist and paternalist ideas toward colonized people either. While he believed that the United States should bring independence to "1,100,000,000 brown people ... [who] are ruled by a handful of whites," he still advocated the idea of temporary tutelage for some countries – Korea and Indochina, for example – because they supposedly needed time and assistance to prepare for self-rule.[10]

From the Atlantic Charter emerged the United Nations (UN) system and the Bretton Woods agreements on the International Monetary Fund (IMF) and the World Bank. Originally, the United Nations included just the allies fighting Germany, Italy, and Japan, but by 1945 it had turned into Roosevelt's reformed and pragmatic reincarnation of the League of Nations. The United Nations Organization was supposed to ensure international peace through cooperation among the great powers while providing the appearance of collaboration among all nations. Of course, Roosevelt counted the United States, the Soviet Union, and the United Kingdom among the great powers by default. Yet, as a pragmatic politician, he also included the weak Republic of China (ROC) and humiliated France as permanent members of the Security Council to flank Stalin's revolutionary Soviet Union. For its part, the Bretton Woods system incorporated the lessons learned from the American oversights from the immediate post-World War I world – the failure of the economically most powerful country to make a commitment to international stability after the war, the quick fix of Europe's financial problems in the mid 1920s, and the collapse of the world economy during the Great Depression. Toward the end of World War II, Roosevelt spent much personal capital convincing Congress and the American people of the need for the United States to make a political and economic commitment to the world in order to avoid another global collapse and possibly World War III.[11]

The Dawn of a New World Order, 1945–50

World War II ended in 1945 with the unparalleled Soviet–American–British military control of vast parts of the world. Tsar Alexander I, whose armies had marched to Paris in 1814 to defeat French Emperor Napoleon and restore the pre-revolutionary Bourbon monarchy, would have been stunned by the degree of territorial control which Stalin exercised in Eastern Europe by mid 1945. And Queen Victoria would have gasped at how quickly the United States had equaled British naval control in the Pacific and the Atlantic, thereby gaining domination of the Western Pacific islands, Japan, Korea, North Africa, and Western Europe. Even if the United Kingdom with its global empire appeared to be a diminished great power, it still controlled much of eastern Africa, the Middle East, South Asia, and Malaya (today's Malaysia). Nevertheless, London continued to believe that the United Kingdom was still a great power at the helm of a worldwide colonial empire. Giving up all of the colonial possessions was not on the agenda at all. Discussions in London during World War II revolved primarily around preserving and reforming the global empire, including the possibility of trimming it in some places while extending it elsewhere.[12]

The victorious Big Three had experienced the war in fundamentally different ways. As mentioned above, the German attack on the USSR had caused large-scale destruction and death while it reinforced Stalin's will to seek security through territorial control beyond his country's borders. In comparison, the United States did not experience foreign occupation, physical destruction, or a high rate of war-related deaths. On the contrary, its geographical isolation from Europe and Asia had kept it secure, while the war had helped finally overcome the Great Depression, put the country back on track toward prosperity, and extend American power far beyond the country's shores. Like the United States, the United Kingdom benefited from its island position away from the continental battlegrounds in Europe, but it experienced destruction due to German aerial bombardment. Its loss was mostly in global financial health, but the United Kingdom still was in a much better economic state than the semi-destroyed Soviet Union.[13] In 1945, the USSR could claim the moral high ground because it had defeated the bulk of German troops in a long and brutal war. But the United States could equally do so because it had defeated Japan almost single-handedly, had fought together with the United Kingdom to defeat Hitler's Germany and Benito Mussolini's Italy, and had provided unparalleled and massive material aid to its fighting Allies in the process.

Unilateral decisions, ideological preconceptions, and misperceptions undermined the possibility of the Soviet–American–British war alliance transforming itself into a lasting arrangement for global peace. Stalin's imposition of communist-dominated regimes in Poland, Romania, Bulgaria, and the Soviet occupation zone of Germany in 1944–45 not only went beyond justified security needs but also contradicted the principle of democratic choice of national governments, as promulgated in the Atlantic

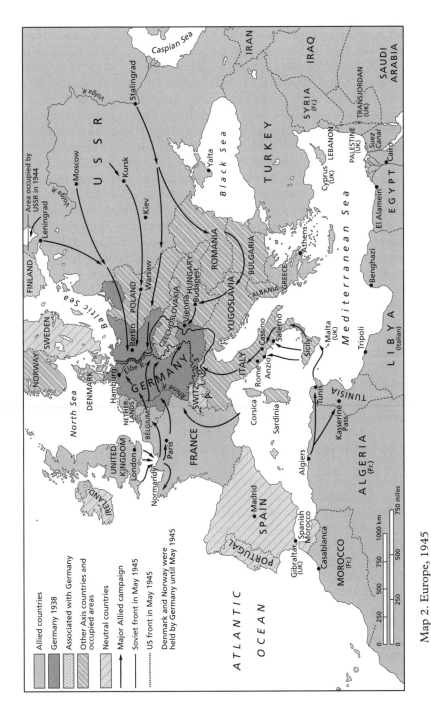

Map 2. Europe, 1945

Charter. Soviet attempts to extract territorial and oil concessions from Turkey and Iran in 1945–46 and the island-grabbing in Northeast Asia even after formal Japanese surrender on September 2, 1945, all irritated the United States. Harry S. Truman's ascent to the presidency after Roosevelt's death in April 1945 may have changed the style of American policy toward the Soviet Union, though it initially did not alter the US proclivity for multilateral cooperation. But Stalin's long-held ideological belief in the inevitability of war in international relations induced him to reject multilateral solutions once World War II was over. The self-perception of weakness in relation to the capitalist United States caused him to forego economic cooperation, and instead to erect a facade of strength in order to disguise his country's fragility and thereby delay the outbreak of a World War III, which Leninist–Stalinist ideology foresaw as inevitable. At the same time, however, he also believed that Anglo–American cooperation, which emerged in response to his actions at the Soviet periphery, would not last because, as Marxism–Leninism promulgated, capitalist–imperialist powers were incapable of cooperating with each other in the long term. Instead, he hoped that US–British disagreements would lead to cooperation between Moscow and London against Washington. Thus, relations among the Big Three, or so Stalin hoped, would change to the benefit of his Soviet Union. Finally, the American use of nuclear weapons to defeat Japan in August 1945 convinced both the United States and the USSR – erroneously – of the war-terminating capabilities of such arms. As a result, the great dictator quickly ordered the Soviet A-bomb program into high gear at the expense of the country's reconstruction. The temporary US application of veiled nuclear threats in negotiations with the USSR in the fall of 1945, i.e. after the defeat of Japan, further undermined much of the remaining good will among the Big Three.[14]

The collapse of wartime trust hence created a tit-for-tat retaliatory system that dominated the relations among the Big Three as early as at the turn of 1945/46. Soviet demands for territorial aggrandizement in Iran, Turkey, and Japan, as well as the American refusal to grant the USSR occupation rights in Italy and Japan, marked only the beginning. By early 1946, the Big Three were also at loggerheads over how to deal with Germany, which had been divided into several occupation zones among the three and France. Still, at the Paris Conference from July to October 1946, they were able to come to agreement with regard to the smaller enemy states Italy, Hungary, Bulgaria, Romania, and Finland.[15]

If the Soviet Union had contributed much to the deterioration of relations before early 1946, it was the United States that took the lead in dividing Europe, and eventually the world, afterward. Based on George Frost Kennan's famous Long Telegram from the US embassy in Moscow,

Washington had come to believe that Stalin's Soviet Union was historically, ideologically, and pathologically expansionist. But Kennan did not endorse a comprehensive American military reaction to the perceived Soviet threat, because he was convinced that the USSR was internally weak and thus acting cautiously. Instead, he advocated a calculated policy of actively denying crucial West German and Japanese human and industrial resources to the Soviet Union while harnessing them for the restoration of economic stability in both world regions. Kennan's idea of creating strong points of economic self-defense at either end of the Soviet Union generated the so-called Marshall Plan for Europe in mid 1947 and a similar economic recovery scheme for Japan a year later.[16]

By early 1947, the intersection of decolonization with the emerging Cold War forced Truman to go beyond Kennan's targeted policy of encountering Soviet pressure exclusively at crucial points. British Prime Minister Clement Attlee had decided to start the process of imperial withdrawal from South Asia two months after his ascent to power in July 1945. His decision did not amount to a fundamental renunciation of imperialism, but was related to long-time political developments in that particular world region. Faced with severe financial problems in the wake of World War II, London also reviewed other commitments. By February 1947, Attlee announced the reduction of the British economic and military commitment to the Greek government, which struggled with a communist insurgency sponsored by Yugoslavia and the Soviet Union. In view of past Soviet pressure on Turkey, President Truman called on Congress to grant funds to provide military and economic aid to either country in order to strengthen resistance to communist subversion and outside threats. The Truman Doctrine was born.[17]

By mid 1947, American economic and military commitments to non-communist Europe had *de facto* divided the continent, forcing Stalin to respond. Faced with sole responsibility for the reconstruction of Soviet-occupied Eastern Europe in competition with Marshall Plan aid to the continent's western half, Stalin increased political, military, and economic control over his dominion there. This included the Stalinization of Poland, Romania, Bulgaria, Hungary, and the Soviet zone of occupation in East Germany, but also the successful pro-Soviet coup in relatively independent Czechoslovakia in February 1948. Yet he concurrently failed at bringing the Yugoslav, Italian, and French communist parties to heel, and he also launched the politically self-defeating blockade of West Berlin in June 1948. Stalin's attempt to starve half of Germany's capital into submission over the duration of almost one year convinced the three Western Allies – the United States, the United Kingdom, and France – to create a West German state and a European defensive alliance, the North Atlantic Treaty (later North Atlantic Treaty Organization; NATO). The prospect of a deepening division of Europe eventually persuaded Stalin to end the blockade in May 1949, but his sudden change of mind failed to undo the damage.[18]

At least, in 1949, Stalin could record two successes, even if one was not of his own making. By August, Moscow tested its first nuclear device, which allowed the Soviet Union to catch up with American atomic preponderance in the long term. However, the communist victory in the Chinese civil war only two months later fell into his lap unexpectedly. This internal conflict pre-dated the Cold War, though the Comintern had established the victorious Chinese Communist Party (CCP) in 1921. But unlike in Eastern Europe, where Stalin imposed communist regimes in 1945, his support for the Chinese communists had been insignificant since the early 1930s. And it was the governing *Guomindang* (Nationalist Party) – not the CCP – that provoked the resumption of the civil war in 1946, in the hope of receiving increased US military and economic aid in the context of the unfolding Cold War in Europe. Yet the United States chose to withdraw support from the internationally recognized Chinese government in 1948/49, in the expectation that the USSR would be drawn into the quagmire, overextend its limited resources, and thereby weaken itself in Europe. Just as the United States decided to retreat, Stalin re-established closer contacts with the CCP. After the foundation of the People's Republic of China (PRC) on October 1, the Chinese communist leader Mao Zedong traveled to Moscow with the desire to establish a friendship and alliance treaty.[19]

The Korean War as Watershed, 1950–55

Few events in the Cold War had such a far-reaching impact on the division of the world as the Korean War. The North Korean attack on the southern half of the peninsular country in mid 1950 occurred at a time of great fluidity in East–West relations. The Soviet A-bomb test and Chinese communist victory had created an inflated sense of vulnerability in the United States. Due to increasing policy disagreements with the Truman administration, Kennan decided to leave his position as the main strategic adviser by the end of 1949. His successor, Paul H. Nitze, advocated in the national security paper NSC-68 of April 1950 the military containment of an inherently expansionist communist world system at *all* points of its periphery, no matter how important to US or international security. President Truman shared this bleak threat assessment but did not act on the recommendations for massive rearmament because he disliked the associated enormous budget and tax increases.[20]

Concurrent with the change in Washington's threat perception in early 1950, the Cold War formally arrived in East Asia. During Mao's stay in Moscow, the PRC and the Soviet Union recognized the government of the Vietnamese communists who were fighting against colonial France, and then signed a bilateral friendship and military assistance treaty, aimed at the supposedly imperialist United States. The start of the Korean War on June 25, 1950, hence occurred in the context of raised American strategic anxieties and increased communist activity in East Asia. However, the Korean War was *primarily* a local conflict. The northern leader, Kim Il-sung, certainly did not expect the domestic conflict to grow into a crisis that would reshape the global Cold War.[21]

Korea's division into two mutually hostile and ideologically antagonistic regimes had been an unintended byproduct of the emerging Cold War. During World War II, Roosevelt had believed that the Japanese colony was not ready for self-rule, and hence he persuaded Stalin of the need for a joint military occupation and temporary UN tutelage to prepare the country for independence. In the end, two competing regimes emerged in the two Korean zones of Soviet–American occupation after August 1945. Since both claimed exclusive representation of the whole country, they increasingly engaged in propaganda and sabre rattling to that end. At the turn of 1949/50, Kim Il-sung concluded that time for unification under his leadership was running out. Through diplomatic maneuvers between Stalin and Mao, including the provision of embellished reports about the revolutionary situation in South Korea, he managed to convince the new Sino–Soviet allies to provide political backing and military aid. Stalin and Mao had their own, mutually incompatible reasons to endorse Kim's plans, though both also entertained reservations about the planned military operation. Without a doubt, the massive military attack in late June was well prepared and rapidly executed. Within weeks, North Korean troops had occupied much of the south except for the harbor city of Busan, where American and South Korean troops offered determined resistance.[22]

The Truman administration placed the local Korean conflict within the context of the exaggerated threat assessments of NSC-68. It believed not only that the aggression was merely a diversionary attack designed to mask Soviet preparations for creating trouble in Europe, but also that a lack of American reaction would undermine US credibility on a global scale. The president faced little resistance in Congress in obtaining approval for a massive increase of the defense budget as envisioned by NSC-68. The United States also easily received international support for military action against North Korea, exploiting the Soviet boycott of the United Nations over the continued exclusion of the PRC. By mid

September, American and UN troops had expelled North Korean troops from the south. Using the momentum of their counterattack, US forces soon crossed the former line of division and pushed toward the Chinese border, particularly after the UN General Assembly approved the move with 47 to 5 votes in a legally non-binding poll that endorsed the reunification of Korea. The PRC intervened of its own volition in late October – out of both fear of an attack on Manchuria and an ideological commitment to a fellow communist regime. By early 1951, the frontline had stabilized around the former line of division where it stayed until armistice in mid 1953 and where it marks the *de facto* border of the two Koreas today.[23]

Apart from destroying a country that had escaped World War II virtually unscathed, the Korean War had a long-term impact on the global Cold War. Parallel to its military intervention, the United States implemented the exaggerated defense recommendations of NSC-68 in the following five years. Truman and his successor Dwight D. Eisenhower broadened the policy of containing the communist world. Since mid 1950, it included the militarization of the North Atlantic Treaty (NATO) with an integrated command system and the alliance's geographical inclusion of two previous Cold War hot spots – Turkey and Greece. Equally important was the decision to rearm West Germany because of its frontline status in Europe. In order to avoid popular resistance in Europe to such a development so soon after the end of World War II, France proposed the establishment of an integrated army, the European Defense Community (EDC), within which West Germany would be allowed to get access to weapons.[24]

Washington followed similar containment strategies in East Asia. Immediately after the start of the Korean War, the United States made unilateral defense commitments to both embattled South Korea and the Republic of China, which was still ruled by the *Guomindang* after its flight from the mainland to Taiwan in 1949. The originally hesitant American policy toward Japan, the former World War II enemy, changed as well; in September 1951, the United States and its Cold War allies signed a peace treaty, followed by a bilateral defensive alliance. However, Washington ultimately decided to establish an East Asian "hub and spokes" network of alliances with Australia and New Zealand, the Philippines, South Korea, and the ROC. On the one hand, the pro-Western countries in the region were unwilling to enter into a NATO-style multilateral alliance with their past war enemy Japan. On the other hand, the United States also did not trust the authoritarian impulses of some of these countries, and thus opted mostly for bilateral alliances that maximized US influence in each case. In the context of US containment in Asia, however, strategic imperatives trumped Roosevelt's vocal commitment to decolonization. Although Washington in the late 1940s had grown dissatisfied with French foot dragging toward decolonization of Indochina, the Sino–Soviet treaty and, particularly, the outbreak of the Korean War in 1950 triggered an American military commitment to colonial France in its fight against Vietnamese communism. However, the United States continued to be displeased with France's stubborn unwillingness to decolonize, which it considered one of the causes of conflict in Indochina.[25]

Exaggerated assessments of the Soviet threat to the Middle East fed American alliance policies there, too, but the United States could rely on pre-existing regional anti-communism. In view of Soviet meddling in Kurdish territories in 1945, Turkey and Iraq had signed a bilateral treaty of friendship in March the following year. In the fall, Turkey announced its intention to conclude alliances with all Arab states, but only Transjordan (today's Jordan), which was just emerging from British mandate rule, agreed to join. By the spring of 1947, these three countries had established a rudimentary anti-Soviet bloc – despite resistance from Syria, Egypt, and Saudi Arabia. However, the multilateral defensive pact, which the Arab League eventually signed just a week before the outbreak of the Korean War, was directed against Israel, not the Soviet Union. In the context of Turkey's accession to NATO in 1952, the Truman administration proposed the creation of the Middle Eastern Defense Organization (MEDO), which was supposed to link NATO's southeastern member with Iran and Pakistan in the defense of the Middle East and the Suez Canal. MEDO never saw the light of day due to a lack of interest among Arab states. But Eisenhower proposed to the imperially minded Churchill, who had been re-elected as UK prime minister in 1951, to use British influence in the Middle East to implement MEDO in the form of the UK-led Baghdad Pact that included Pakistan, Iran, Turkey, and one Arab state – Iraq.[26]

The pact's creation paralleled, and was partially influenced by, events in Indochina in 1954. Despite Washington's substantial commitment to Paris – made in the wake of the outbreak of the Korean War – for the fight against Vietnamese communism, the United States grew dissatisfied with France's lack of military success and continued unwillingness to transfer power. Given the increasingly dire French military situation in Vietnam in the spring of 1954, the Eisenhower administration decided not to intervene unilaterally but to call for multilateral military action to stop communist aggression in Indochina. However, neither France nor the United Kingdom was willing to act multilaterally until other means of ending the war, including negotiations, had been exhausted. While the Geneva Conference in mid 1954 failed to solve the parallel Korean problem, it at least produced a compromise agreement on the temporary division of

Vietnam and the neutralization of Laos and Cambodia. As a non-belligerent, the United States stayed aloof from the Indochina negotiations in order to keep all options open for future action. Appalled by the supposed concessions which France and the United Kingdom had made at Geneva to the communist world – the Soviet Union, the PRC, and the Vietnamese communists – the United States established the Southeast Asia Treaty Organization (SEATO) on September 8, 1954. This new alliance brought together the Philippines, Thailand, Pakistan, Australia, New Zealand, France, the United Kingdom, and the United States in defense of Indochina against communist expansion.[27]

The analogous foundation of the British-led Baghdad Pact and American-led SEATO in 1954–55 closed the semi-ring of Western anti-communist alliances, which reached from Norway across Europe, the Middle East, South Asia, and Southeast Asia to the East Asian rim. Its completion, however, occurred shortly after Stalin's death in March 1953, just as the new Soviet leadership tried to reduce Cold War tensions. Nikita S. Khrushchev and his fellow leaders in the Kremlin understood that Stalin's confrontational policies were co-responsible for the economic problems at home and the military encirclement abroad. Moscow thus sought negotiations with Washington to resolve some of the accumulated problems. While the German issue eluded any solution for unrelated reasons, as described further below, the Soviet Union and the PRC cooperated closely at Geneva to eliminate the Indochina conflict by means of a compromise agreement. Even if they pressured a recalcitrant communist Vietnam to agree to the division of the country and the neutralization of Laos and Cambodia, the resulting Geneva Accords still did not satisfy American security needs. Similarly ephemeral was Khrushchev's attempt in 1955 to repair relations with Yugoslavia, which Stalin had expelled from the socialist world in 1948 for its refusal to submit to his dictates. At least, the new Kremlin leaders succeeded in abandoning Stalin's disinterest in the Afro–Asian world, particularly in one of its most important emerging representatives – India.[28]

At the time of Soviet attempts to relax international tensions, two crucial non-communist countries rejected the dark American perception of the threat supposedly emanating from the USSR, as expressed in NSC-68. To India, US alliance building brought the Cold War unnecessarily to South Asia. American containment policies turned its Muslim neighbor Pakistan into the most allied American ally in the Cold War – once through a bilateral agreement and twice through multilateral alliances – and, in the process, into a military threat to India. Indeed, SEATO's creation in September 1954 convinced Prime Minister Jawaharlal Nehru to rescind his vociferous opposition to an Indonesian proposal to convene an Asian–African Conference. Later that year, Nehru took the lead in preparing what would become the Bandung Conference in April 1955, insisted on inviting the PRC, and convinced Yugoslav President Josip Broz Tito to join his non-aligned stance in international affairs. Concurrently, Nehru also accepted an invitation to visit Moscow in mid 1955 in an exercise of even-handedness between the Cold War blocs. By the same token, Egypt's Gamal Abdel Nasser had opposed the creation of MEDO and the Baghdad Pact. He was convinced that the United States and the United Kingdom were using the pretext of an exaggerated Soviet threat to fortify Britain's imperialist position in the region while simultaneously provoking the projection of Soviet influence into it. In the run-up to the Bandung Conference, Nasser committed his country to the Asian–African Movement and afterward even to Nehru's non-alignment.[29]

Furthermore, the Geneva Conference in mid 1954 had an impact on Europe. The traumatic loss of its colonial possessions in Indochina shook France's identity to the core. As a reaction to the self-perceived decrease in its international standing, the National Assembly was loath to integrate France into the supranational structure of the European Defense Community (EDC). Its refusal in late August 1954 to ratify the EDC treaty, which it had proposed four years earlier, reopened the debate about West German armament. But even if France's parliament demolished the outcome of four years of international negotiations, the country's government was unwilling to compromise its other anti-Soviet commitments. Paris not only agreed to join SEATO the following month, but, in October, also approved West Germany's direct membership in NATO and rearmament within it.[30]

The prospect of West Germany joining the American-led alliance system in Western Europe predictably triggered Soviet misgivings. The USSR proposed a pan-European security conference, which two decades later would become the Conference on Security and Cooperation (CSCE). A conference of the European socialist states in Moscow decided in December of 1954 to create a counter-NATO – the Warsaw Pact – and approved the right of communist East Germany to arm itself against the supposed resurgence of (West) German militarism. The creation of the Warsaw Pact formally occurred in mid May 1955, a week after West Germany's accession to NATO. On the surface a reaction to these developments, the pact was in reality a Soviet ploy designed to gain leverage in negotiations with the United States on the parallel dissolution of both alliances. However, the Geneva Summit of the World War II Allies in the summer of 1955, the first major conference of that sort in

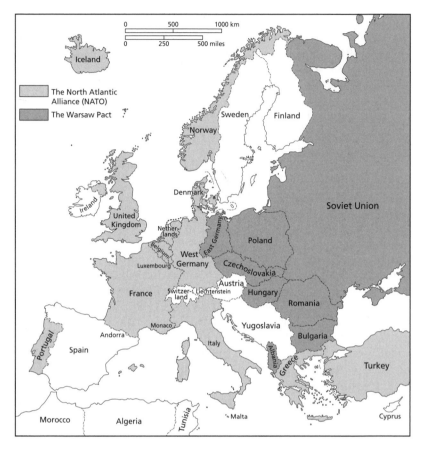

Map 3. American and Soviet alliance systems in Europe, 1955

a decade, did not reverse Europe's division into two hostile alliances, even if Moscow had hoped it would at least reduce Cold War tensions.[31]

The clarifications of Cold War fault lines in Europe by mid 1945 allowed Western and Eastern European countries to test the limits of independence within their respective blocs. Pro-American West Germany sought rapprochement with the Soviet Union in the fall of 1955, and Poland and Hungary sought political autonomy in the wake of Nikita Khrushchev's Secret Speech the following February. However, the parallel political crises in Warsaw and Budapest in October 1956 revealed that Moscow was only willing to allow some limited form of domestic autonomy but definitely not neutrality in the Cold War. Similarly, Washington's castigation of Paris and London in the concurrent Suez Crisis, to which we turn now, reminded the declining great power United Kingdom and the resurgent France that they had become dependent on American economic good will and military protection. Hence, in the wake of the Korean War, the events in late 1956 further cemented the division of Europe into antagonistic spheres of Soviet and Western influence.[32]

The Suez Crisis, 1956

The Suez Crisis in 1956 marked simultaneously the endpoint of British global pretensions *and* an important step in the Cold War's subsequent, though slow and hesitant, entry into the Middle East. Stalin's attempts to get territorial concessions from Iran and Turkey had undermined the Soviet–American–British World War II alliance in 1945–46, but afterward the great powers did not engage for some time in any competition in this world region. On the contrary, Washington and Moscow both supported the creation of the state of Israel at the expense of Palestinians in 1947–48. Truman aimed at ensuring that the new state would not fall under Soviet influence, and Stalin hoped to diminish the British hold in the Middle East. Subsequently, Washington and London tried to sponsor a peace process between the Jewish state and its Arab neighbors, but this happened largely outside the Cold War context. The two Western powers and France also imposed on themselves a ban of weapons deliveries to the Middle East in order to prevent an arms race and the expansion of the Cold War into the region. Stalin's USSR respected the ban, mostly because it had no specific interests in the Middle East at that time.[33] Yet American–British alliance building in the wake of the Korean War, as described above, brought the Cold War for the first time to the Middle East, even if Egypt refused to participate in the alliance building, joined the Asian–African Movement, and subscribed to Nehru's non-alignment. After an Israeli incursion into Egyptian-held Gaza in late February 1955, Nasser used his meeting with Nehru and Chinese Prime Minister Zhou Enlai on his way to the Bandung Conference of Asian–African nations to ask for weapons deliveries. Ultimately, Khrushchev supported Egypt with weapons in the Soviet–Czechoslovak arms deal that broke the Western arms embargo in September 1955. In mid May 1956, Nasser's Egypt even recognized the PRC – the only major power excluded from the United Nations – in an attempt both to emphasize his commitment to Asian–African Internationalism and to undermine a complete arms embargo against the Middle East that was under discussion in the UN General Assembly.[34]

The Suez Crisis itself started two months later, on July 26, 1956, with the Egyptian nationalization of the Canal Company. This surprise step was triggered by American demands for Egypt to commit itself to the West in the global Cold War in exchange for loans to build the Aswan Dam at the upper Nile. Incensed by this disrespect for Egypt's sovereignty and non-aligned stance, Nasser decided to forego US aid dollars and, instead, nationalize the foreign-owned company. While he portrayed the event as the final act of his country's decolonization, he also had a sober reason to nationalize – it allowed him to tap into the company's annual income and massive financial assets to bankroll the construction of the dam. Cairo's daring maneuver enraged London and Paris, because British and French citizens were the main shareholders in the canal company. But the Eisenhower administration calmly indicated to the British government that it would not endorse the use of force, or threats thereof, as long as Nasser did not infringe on the right of passage through the canal. London and Paris, however, were convinced that Nasser's decision to nationalize the company meant "that NATO and Western Europe were at the mercy of one irresponsible and faithless individual." In the end, Israel, France, and the United Kingdom clandestinely prepared a joint military intervention in Egypt with the goal of seizing the canal and possibly overthrowing the supposedly dangerous Nasser.[35]

The Israeli–French–British intervention on October 29–30 forced the USSR and the United States once more onto the same side, even if they did not agree on anything else with regard to the Middle East. Unlike in 1947/48, however, Washington and Moscow in 1956 supported the Arab side. The United States was exasperated that its NATO allies had acted covertly behind its back. Through economic and diplomatic means, it strong-armed the three aggressors out of Egypt. Washington not only feared that the intervention would alienate Cairo even more, but it was also irritated that this unnecessary crisis had redirected the world's attention from the ongoing anti-Soviet revolution in Budapest. Ultimately, the crisis cost the United States much standing in the Middle East due to the implicit American association with the aggressors – despite its forceful actions against them. The Soviet Union, in comparison, used the unexpected opportunity to suppress the Hungarian Revolution with military force while drawing close to Nasser's Egypt by portraying itself as the true anti-imperialist defender of Arab interests.[36] Poignantly, American containment policy that was supposed to keep the Soviet Union out of the Middle East had created a situation that allowed the USSR to enter it.

In the wake of the Suez Crisis, the United States faced a heap of shards in the Middle East. Its own heavy-handed Cold War policy toward Nasser had triggered a chain of events that led to the American association, at least in Arab minds, with Israeli and European imperialism. Furthermore, British participation in the intervention discredited the United Kingdom as an American partner to contain Soviet influence in the Middle East. In its tendency to see the Cold War mainly as a zero-sum game, Washington concluded that it had lost Cairo to Moscow, and thus tried to establish close cooperation with conservative Arab monarchies to contain the spread of Nasser's supposedly pro-Soviet nationalism throughout the region. While the establishment of formal alliances did not materialize, the United States could still enlist Saudi Arabia and Jordan as informal, and eventually long-term, Cold War partners. In turn, such American policies once more drove Nasser closer to the Soviet side. By the spring of 1958, the charismatic Egyptian president went on his first visit to Moscow. And some months later, by mid 1958, the anti-monarchical revolution in Iraq led to an existential crisis in the British-led Baghdad Pact. By 1959, Iraq withdrew, and the alliance moved its headquarters to Turkey, renamed itself the Central Treaty Organization (CENTO), and made the United States an associate member.[37]

Conclusion

In the dozen years after the end of World War II, the international system witnessed the ascent of the two great powers to global pre-eminence, at the expense of the imperialist United Kingdom. The Soviet Union was an ideologically committed world revolutionary and anti-imperialist agent that established communist hegemony in Eastern Europe while showing little interest in the colonized Afro–Asian world. The United States was a reformist but pragmatic internationalist power that, as soon as the Cold War unfolded, struggled with its own anti-colonial commitments. Ideological clashes, political disagreements, unilateral decisions, and misperceptions triggered the bilateral confrontation. In the late 1940s, the Cold War division of the world was still confined to Europe and, to a lesser degree, East Asia. The rupture of the war alliance among the Big Three had started with disagreements over Europe and the Middle East in 1945–46, helped to harden the Korean division, influenced the Chinese Civil War, and eventually was completed during Stalin's Berlin Blockade in 1948–49.

Following the outbreak of the Korean War in mid 1950, American containment policies extended the Cold War division to regions at the whole periphery of the communist world. The Soviet Union itself had contributed to East Asia's division both by signing the friendship and alliance treaty with the PRC and by providing support for North Korean war plans in early 1950. The exaggerated US reaction to the local conflict on the Korean peninsula put the Soviet Union on the defensive while it alienated countries in the Afro–Asian world – particularly India and

Egypt. The communist world hoped to decrease Cold War tensions through negotiating a compromise deal on Indochina in 1954, but France's loss of its colonies caused Washington to extend its alliance building into Southeast Asia while it caused Paris to complicate the Cold War in Europe. The Soviet Union reacted to West German membership in NATO by creating the Warsaw Pact in 1955, followed by the establishment of friendly relations with India, and entered the Middle East on the coattails of the Suez Crisis.

Yet the seemingly deep division of the Eurasian world by the mid 1950s into two antagonistic blocs turned out to be more brittle than expected, as the next three chapters reveal. The rash and improvised bloc formation had produced shoddy and unsound construction on all sides. In 1958, the pro-Western Iraqi monarchy fell in a coup that undermined the Baghdad Pact, while the supposedly pro-Soviet Nasser turned against the Soviet Union by persecuting Arab communists in Egypt and Syria. Under de Gaulle's leadership, France implemented, starting in the same year, a policy of independence from the United States that would lead to his country's withdrawal from the military organization of NATO. And starting in the early 1960s, the socialist world suffered from the consecutive defection of Albania, the PRC, and Romania.

Part I

Elusive Unities

Introduction to Chapters 2 to 4

The Big Three – the United Kingdom, the Soviet Union, and the United States – were the only global powers in 1945. They had led the worldwide alliance against National Socialist Germany, militarist Japan, and Fascist Italy to victory in World War II. At the end of the war, 10 Downing Street ruled a global empire but faced financial troubles; the Kremlin ran the militarily strong but economically destroyed Soviet Union; and the White House led the economically and militarily dominant United States. Into the 1960s, these three countries continued to shape international relations, but also experienced significant changes in their relations with each other. During this period, the Cold War spread geographically from Europe and East Asia to Southeast Asia, South Asia, and the Middle East (Chapter 1). As the Soviet Union and the United States ascended to superpower status in the late 1950s and over the course of the 1960s, the United Kingdom tried to keep up by establishing its own nuclear weapons program (see also Chapter 14). As late as 1963, when the three negotiated the Limited Test Ban Treaty, Moscow and Washington still considered London an equal. But, in reality, British global power had been declining slowly since 1945 and then greatly after the Suez Crisis in 1956. And the United Kingdom ended up cooperating with the United States against the USSR in the divided Cold War world.

In the second half of the mid 1940s, each of the Big Three held a sphere of influence in the European–Middle Eastern–Asian world. Apart from the Arab League, the Socialist Camp, and the Free World, *no* other structural mechanism had emerged in the larger Eurasian world in the 1940s. The United Kingdom tried to steer the Arab League, which had been established even before the end of World War II, as its main vehicle to maintain imperial power across the world (Chapter 2). The Soviet Union led the Socialist Camp in Eastern Europe since 1944/45 and in East Asia starting in the late 1940s (Chapter 3). And the United States headed the Free World in Western Europe and Japan after 1945 and a string of authoritarian allies in East Asia and the Middle East following the outbreak of the Korean War in 1950 (Chapter 4).

Chapters 2 to 4 reveal that these three spheres of influence greatly diverged in nature, internal cohesion, and political structure. The Arab League was loosely led by the United Kingdom and subsisted as a group of Middle Eastern states still in the process of post-colonial nation state formation. The Socialist Camp was authoritarian in character and run centrally from Moscow. And the Free World consisted of a mixture of liberal democracies and anti-communist authoritarian states. All three passed through comparable arcs of development over the first two decades of the Cold War. After an initial period of relative coherence, each experienced a phase of intense internal dissent.

As Chapter 2 shows, the United Kingdom gradually lost its influence over the Arab League, largely because of its support for the creation of Israel by 1947/48, its Cold War alliance building in the Middle East in the first half of the 1950s, and particularly its imperialist behavior during the Suez Crisis in 1956. Afterward, the Arab League transformed itself from a vehicle of British imperial influence into an independent regional actor, despite concurrent Soviet and American attempts to get a foothold in the Middle East (see also Chapter 9). Unlike the USSR and the United States, Great Britain was unable to maintain influence in its sphere past the 1950s.

Chapter 3 reveals that the Soviet Union faced unrest as early as 1947/48 when it tried to tighten its control over Eastern Europe. In the 1950s and 1960s, it dealt with successive crises in its three European frontline states – in East Germany in 1953, in Hungary in 1956, and in Czechoslovakia in 1968. The ideological conflicts, which underpinned all three crises, also caused major disagreements with socialist states in Eastern Europe's strategic hinterland – Yugoslavia, Poland, Romania, and Albania – and with the People's Republic of China in East Asia. Ultimately, however, the USSR was able to restore a semblance of unity in a diminished Socialist Camp by the late 1960s.

Finally, as Chapter 4 shows, the United States faced challenges from the bickering Western European democracies, particularly France, and the authoritarian states in Asia and the Middle East, which had joined the anti-Soviet alliance system of the United States after the outbreak of the Korean War. In the 1960s, members of the Free World were also confronted with increased domestic conflict. Still, by the 1970s and 1980s (see Chapter 22), the American-led Free World managed to restore unity of action.

Why does this all matter to this book? The geographical extension of the Cold War in the first post-World War II decade, the decline of the United Kingdom among the Big Three after 1956, and the elusive internal cohesion of all three spheres of influence – the Arab League, the Socialist Camp, and the Free World – all contributed to the emergence of *a new world system by the 1960s*. The resulting rise of a nuclear superpower duopoly (see Chapter 14) made the Soviet Union and the United States superpowers, while, at the same time, political, conventional military, and economic power *dispersed* in Asia, the Middle East, and Europe. These parallel developments over the course of the two post-World War II decades essentially created opportunities for middle powers and smaller actors to affect long-term structural change to the global Cold War, as Parts II to VI (see Chapters 5–19) reveal. Their experiences and pathways were often interconnected and mutually influential. Collectively, they heralded the end of the Cold War in the 1980s (see Chapters 20–23). Without the elusiveness of internal unity of the Arab League, the Socialist Camp, and the Free World, as described in Part I, it is likely that the Cold War would have taken another road.

2   The United Kingdom and the Arab League

The *Arab League* arose from the interplay of British imperial strategy, nation state formation in the Middle East, regional anti-imperialism, and Arab anti-Zionism. The league was *not* a creation of the early Cold War. Before the end of World War II, a century of European imperialism had stimulated the construction of Arab identity. Recently established borders in the Arab world did not extinguish the idea of a unitary Arab nation, primarily because they were creations imposed by outside imperial powers. Still, they generated competing forms of nationalism based on territoriality. The main lines of intra-Arab conflict from the late 1920s to the 1960s ran between Saudi Arabia, the Hashemite kingdoms of Jordan (Palestine and Transjordan) and Iraq, and Egypt. The Holy sites – Mecca, Medina, and Jerusalem – were important markers of political legitimacy, which is why Arab states so strenuously contested control over them.

Unlike the Soviet Union in the Socialist Camp or the United States in the Free World, the great power hegemon of the Middle East was not a formal player in the Arab League. Although, by 1931, the United Kingdom had established the British Commonwealth in order to tie former colonies to London, Arab countries would not be able to join because they had never been formal British colonies. Hence, London needed to think about how to integrate the Levant into its global strategy, given the area's geographical centrality to Britain's long-term imperial interests across the globe. London signaled its interest in creating the Arab League in the second half of World War II. Once seven Arab states had established the organization in early 1945, London was able to maintain its authority in the region for roughly a decade. Yet British influence faced constraints from the very beginning. Saudi Arabia wanted to keep all foreign influence at bay. And Egypt, the largest of all Arab countries, challenged British strategic supremacy in the Suez Canal Zone after World War II.

Ultimately, the British delusion of being able to reinforce its imperial influence in the region during the Suez Crisis in 1956 undermined the country's great power status among the Big Three. The crisis thus marked a change from British to future American and Soviet influence. But neither

Washington nor Moscow were able to establish preponderance immediately. The Arab world turned out to be remarkably resistant to the imposition of Cold War division until the mid 1960s. Anti-imperialist and non-aligned commitments ran deep, though some of the Arab states – Egypt above all – tried to play the United States and the USSR against each other. The only firm relationship that emerged in the wake of 1956 was the US–Israeli partnership that lasts to this day.

Britain's influence in the Middle East in 1945 and its decline over the course of the following twelve years had major structural effects on the global Cold War that were entirely different from concurrent developments in Asia and Europe. The Cold War did not divide the Middle East into antagonistic communist and non-communist spheres. Britain's loss of influence after 1956 also meant that the only existing regional structure – the Arab League – took on a life of its own during the remainder of the Cold War. Even if the Arab League was internally weak, it still provided an important centripetal force to the fractured Middle East after World War II. Thus, it helped to delay the entry of the Cold War into the region until the 1950s and 1960s, as Chapters 8 and 9 reveal. The remarkably high degree of Arab unity in 1973 even enabled Egypt to push the Cold War out of the core of the Middle East. Unlike Moscow and Washington, London had lost its sphere of influence long before the end of the Cold War. Its imperial collapse in late 1956 forced Great Britain to rethink its role in global affairs. This was particularly important because the Suez Crisis happened a few months before the signing of the Rome Treaties, which marked a greater step toward integration of continental Western Europe, as Chapter 15 shows. Similar to the Arab League, this process originated in the interwar yearning for greater unity, joint strength, and regional peace, although it turned out to be much more successful than the Arab League. As Britain's imperial project and, by extension, its global aspirations crumbled, it needed to transform itself into a regional power able to engage in the multilateral integration process of the European continent, which it had tried to quash since the late 1940s for the purpose of preserving its empire.

British Imperial Strategy and the Middle East

Looking back from the vantage point of the present, the British Empire at the end of World War II appeared to be on the road to oblivion. But in 1945, neither the United Kingdom nor its main war allies, the Soviet Union and the United States, would have agreed. British leaders retained a global outlook despite their country's lingering "financial Dunkirk" and India's imminent independence. In that respect, they were not much different from Iosif V. Stalin, who headed an economically destroyed Soviet Union but nevertheless entertained long-term plans for world revolution. Until the mid 1950s, British leaders firmly believed that the United Kingdom would continue in its role as a global power. Their strategic plans comprised dispatching significant parts of the British land, sea, and air forces to the Mediterranean to check presumed Soviet influence in the Middle East, and posting the British Navy on all of the world's seas, even on the Pacific, to rival the US Navy.[1]

While British strategic planning displayed remarkable continuities from the pre-World War I to the post-World War II period, it remained as flexible in adjusting to ever changing conditions as it had been since the American Revolution, when Great Britain lost a major colonial possession for the first time. In the wake of World War I, London had agreed to long-term devolution of power in South Asia. But in the interwar period, the British Empire also acquired a new sphere of influence in the strategically important region of the formerly Ottoman Levant – first through a shared arrangement with France, but after May 1945 alone. The core of the Middle East formed a crucial link between Great Britain, the Mediterranean, eastern Africa, the Persian Gulf, South Asia, Malaya (today's Malaysia), Australia, and New Zealand. It retained the strategic potential of replacing the Suez Canal Zone, from where London knew it would have to withdraw within a decade or so after World War II. In effect, Great Britain had begun to adjust its imperial strategy as early as the 1920s. By 1931, it established the Commonwealth, which initially encompassed only the former settlement colonies of New Zealand, Australia, and Canada. After World War II, the association agreed to allow former British colonies without European majority populations to accede as well. The Commonwealth was supposed to serve London to maintain influence in its former domains in Africa and Asia in the long term.[2]

But the Arab world did not fit in with this project. British dominance of the Middle East in 1945 had arisen on the basis of the mandate system of the League of Nations. The former Ottoman territories were supposed to become independent in due course, regardless of British imperial visions. While London and Paris had dragged their feet in granting self-rule throughout the 1930s, World War II eventually forced Great Britain to rethink its role in the Middle East, as we will see further below. France's collapse in 1940 at least allowed the United Kingdom to extend *de facto* influence to all of the Arab mandate territories in the Levant. Thus, by 1943, London started to look at the Middle East as the all-important brace that would hold the British imperial positions in the eastern hemisphere together. Fortuitously, it seized on the long-standing but ambiguous attempts by Egypt and Levantine countries to form some sort of regional association under British strategic leadership.

Great Britain's plan to create a formal sphere of influence in the Middle East was based on the time-honored policy of seizing opportunities while reducing liabilities. Thus, when London eventually faced its financial Dunkirk in February 1947, it cut its losses where it had no other choice. Over the course of four short days, it formally announced its withdrawal from civil war-torn Greece with immediate effect, from South Asia within half a year, and from Palestine after fifteen months. While the United Kingdom happily passed responsibility for Greece – which had little strategic signifi-cance to its imperial strategy – to the United States, it still intended to maintain long-term informal influence in independent South Asia and the decolonizing Levant. But London had no intention to give up its formal imperial influence in Africa, other parts of the Middle East, the Persian Gulf region, Southeast Asia, and the Commonwealth. On the contrary, it planned to revitalize its empire in parallel with restoring its own economic health to a point where it was capable of maintaining and even increasing influence globally. Eventually, the Suez Crisis in the fall of 1956, when British imperial ambitions clashed with Arab anti-imperialism, signified the turning point toward the formal decolonization of the global empire within a dozen years.[3]

Ottomans, Turks, and Arabs

The creation of the Arab League in 1945 marked an important waypoint in the region's long-term political development. In the early sixteenth century, Ottoman Sultan Selim I had claimed the title of caliph, the religious successor of Prophet Muhammad, in the wake of his conquest of the Hijaz, the region of the holy Muslim cities Mecca and Medina. By the late seventeenth century, his successors had fashioned the multiethnic and multireligious Ottoman Empire, which encompassed lands stretching from Ukraine to Egypt and from Kuwait to Morocco. They ruled from Istanbul by relying on local elites to run the empire. In the Hijaz, the clan of the Hashemites remained in power as the guardians of the holy cities, for example. But by the nineteenth and early twentieth century, the empire witnessed the parallel phenomena of internal weakness and external pressure. Russia, Austria, the United Kingdom, Italy, France, and Spain gradually pushed the Ottoman Empire out of the Black Sea region and the Balkans, or assumed political and even territorial control in Arab North Africa from Egypt to Morocco. Under the influence of European nationalist political thought, the core of the weakened Ottoman state redefined itself as Turkish, while its Arab parts started to ponder a separate identity for themselves.[4]

World War I doomed the Ottoman Empire, which by 1914 had been reduced to its Turkish core, the Levant in the eastern Mediterranean, and the Hijaz further south. The Ottoman Empire had decided to join the war on the side of Germany and Austria in order to settle accounts with the United

Kingdom, France, and Russia. In turn, the United Kingdom supported the brewing Arab nationalist revolt in the Hijaz, particularly in the wake of its double defeat by Ottoman troops at Gallipoli and Baghdad. In May 1916, the British diplomat Mark Sykes and his French counterpart François Georges-Picot agreed to divide the Levant into future spheres of influence. In accordance with its global imperial interests, the British wartime government saw the Arab Middle East mainly as a strategic asset and a source of oil that would help the United Kingdom to wean itself from American energy supplies. By November 1917, the British foreign minister, Arthur Balfour, also promised Zionist representatives support for the establishment of a homeland for Jews in Palestine. The Ottoman government eventually capitulated in October 1918, after enemy troops had occupied all of its territory except parts of the Turkish core. A year later, at the Paris Peace Conference, the United Kingdom and France reconfirmed the Sykes–Picot agreement, with London taking over Palestine, Transjordan (today's Jordan), and Iraq, and Paris acquiring Syria and Lebanon. In the spring of 1920, the two European imperial powers agreed to turn the former Ottoman provinces into mandates under the auspices of the recently established League of Nations, though the Levant remained *de facto* under their divided administration. However, as British and French troops occupied their respective spheres of influence, they stepped into political quagmires. Based on British wartime promises and their own dreams of creating a unified state in the Levant and the Arabian peninsula, the Hashemites had founded kingdoms in the Hijaz under the Grand Sharif of Mecca Hussein bin Ali, and in Syria–Lebanon and Transjordan under his sons Faisal and Abdullah, respectively. When France arrived in Damascus, however, it abolished the pro-British monarchy in favor of a presidential system.[5]

In effect, the Ottoman collapse in 1918 destroyed long-held political certainties throughout its former Arab domains. But it simultaneously provided a jolt to various strands of nationalism. Egypt, the largest Arab country demographically, managed to acquire a limited degree of independence by 1922, though it had to accept British control of the Suez Canal Zone, the country's defense, and Sudan. Egyptian nationalism was well developed, but some of the country's elites did not yet see the country as Arab. Iraqi scholars had focused on the construction of a unifying national identity in view of their country's artificial borderlines, ethnic diversity, and religious schisms. The anti-British rebellion in Iraq in 1920 brought together Arabs and non-Arabs as well as Sunni and Shia, but the following year London nonetheless installed King Faisal, the Hashemite monarch recently sacked by the French in Syria, in Baghdad to defend its strategic and resource interests. Under pressure from nationalists and Islamic scholars, Faisal eventually negotiated the Anglo–Iraqi Treaty of 1922, which opened the way to a degree of self-rule under British patronage ten years later. In comparison, French troops encountered a significant tradition of elite and populist nationalist thinking in Syria and Lebanon. Both countries remained a hotbed of political activity throughout a quarter century. In Palestine, where the mandate was yet another artificial creation, Muslim and Christian Arabs living at the core of the territory – in the former Ottoman province of Jerusalem – had fostered a sense of integrated local community for centuries. The development of an Arab Palestinian nationalism, however, occurred mainly in response to Zionist immigration since 1881 and particularly as a result of increased

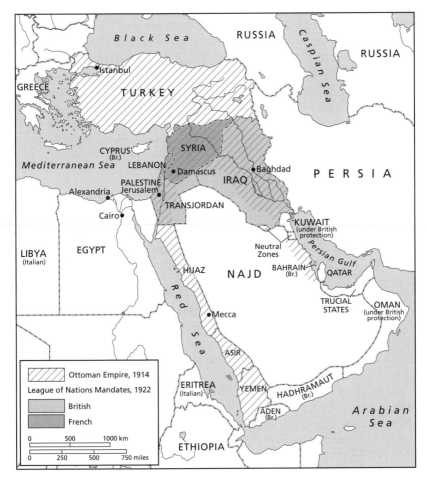

Map 4. The Middle East before and after the collapse of the Ottoman Empire

Jewish settlement in the interwar period. In short, after 1918, many different forms of Arab nationalism emerged. Pan-Arabism as a political force arose only a decade later.[6]

The transformation of the Ottoman Empire into a secular Turkish state in 1923 gave the Arab world final political impetus. The Allied dismemberment of the Turkish core after capitulation sparked a four-year war of independence. In early 1919, Turkish nationalists and communists appealed to Soviet Russia for military aid. Even if Moscow was just establishing the Comintern as a world revolutionary organization, its policy toward Turkey mainly focused on embarrassing the imperialist powers there instead of promoting fundamental change. Eventually, by July 1923, the Allied powers recognized the new Turkish state within today's borders. On March 3, 1924, the secular Turkish Republic unilaterally abolished the Caliphate. Within four days, King Hussein of the Hijaz, the guardian of Medina and Mecca, appointed himself caliph, but did not garner much recognition in the wider Muslim world. Anyway, his dream lasted only until October 13, when Saudi Sultan Ibn Saud occupied Mecca, with Medina and Jeddah to follow within fourteen months. King Hussein's defeat not only cost him his royal status but also meant surrendering almost a thousand years of family rule over the Hijaz to an upstart dynasty from the Najd in today's central Saudi Arabia.[7]

Creating the Arab League, 1932–45

In early September 1932, a month before receiving greater self-rule from the United Kingdom, Iraqi King Faisal proposed the creation of a Hashemite-led Arab federation that would include his country, Syria, Transjordan, Palestine, and the Hijaz. Although he thereby claimed leadership of the Arab world, he was convinced that his proposal would help resolve tensions between Zionist immigrants and Arabs in Palestine. Jews would end up living in a small "corner" of a large, unified Levant. After Ibn Saud had established the Kingdom of Saudi Arabia within a fortnight by merging the Najd and the Hijaz, Faisal's proposal implicitly developed an anti-Saudi tilt. But since it received little resonance, he shelved his idea the following summer, shortly before he died unexpectedly.[8]

Three years later, Italian colonialism and Arab anti-imperialism sparked interest in unity once more. In October 1935, Fascist Italy marched into Ethiopia to occupy Africa's last independent country. Sandwiched between Italy's new colony and its older possession in today's Libya, British-dominated Egypt was in a dire situation. To make matters worse, the royal government faced mass protests demanding complete UK withdrawal. Taking into account this difficult situation, London offered military retreat from the country as long as it was permitted to keep troops in the Suez Canal

Zone. In August 1936, Egypt signed an agreement in line with this proposal, though with the provision of revision within twenty years.[9] Soon thereafter, Cairo showed interest in military cooperation with other Arab capitals, including an alliance with Baghdad. But for some time Iraq had been negotiating the Saadabad Pact with Turkey, Iran, and Afghanistan – all non-Arab states. Signed in July 1937, the pact envisioned the peaceful resolution of territorial disputes and the increase of economic cooperation at the expense of dependency on the Soviet Union.[10]

At the same time, to make matters even more complicated, the core of the Levant experienced increasing political instability. Early in 1936, a massive strike in Syria called for the end of French mandate rule. By September, Paris agreed to an independence treaty, followed by a similar agreement with Lebanon two months later. And in April 1936, a three-year long Arab nationalist uprising against British mandate rule and Zionist immigration erupted in Palestine. In the aftermath of all these events, Arab states prepared for the first National Arab Congress in the Syrian spa town of Bloudan in September 1937. The congress met in the wake of the recently published report of the British Peel Commission, which proposed to resolve the ongoing unrest in Palestine through partition into Arab and Jewish parts. Unsurprisingly, the congress decided to reject the proposal, to call for the creation of an Arab Palestine, to demand an end of Zionist immigration, and to establish an economic boycott of Jewish and British goods.[11]

The outbreak of World War II in Europe in 1939 forced London and Paris yet again to reconsider their respective positions in the Middle East. National Socialist Germany's anti-Semitic propaganda targeted Arab resentment of Zionist immigration. German actions thereby mirrored the policies which the two war allies had pursued during World War I against Germany's ally, the Ottoman Empire. In the end, however, London decided to stay away from Arab unity plans, because it considered them a "hornet's nest." Paris, in comparison, simply refused to ratify the 1936 treaties with Syria and Lebanon. After France's defeat by Germany in June 1940, the United Kingdom occupied the two Middle Eastern countries with the goal of removing them from control of German-allied Vichy France. Many of the French civilian and military officials, who had switched sides to Charles de Gaulle's Free France in good time, stayed in office. Furthermore, Britain decided to rely on the strongly anti-communist Saudi Arabia for the maintenance of its interests in the region. For its part, Riyadh feared potential Soviet expansion into neutral Turkey and beyond, at a time when Stalin was still in alliance with Adolf Hitler. Yet the Arab states remained split about unity. Expecting British defeat by Germany in the summer of 1940, royal Iraq once more tried to work for an Arab federation under its leadership, but met opposition from Riyadh and Cairo.[12]

The German attack on the Soviet Union in June 1941 increased British fears about Hitler's territorial designs on the wider Middle East. Within two months, London and Moscow agreed to occupy neutral Iran in order to remove German influence and establish an Allied supply route to the USSR. With regard to Turkey, however, the United Kingdom hoped that the country's own armed forces would be sufficient to block a German advance. At long last, London reconsidered its negative attitude toward Arab unity given the German military successes in the Balkans and in North Africa. Prompted by Saudi Arabia, the United Kingdom started to contemplate how to use the Arab yearning for unity to counteract German influence. Would a smaller union in the Levant be sufficient, or should the Arabian peninsula be included? What seemed to be certain, however, was that Egypt, while interested in leading the Arabs, would not join any union at the expense of its sovereignty. In the end, the prospect of continued Arab discord convinced London to go slow for the time being.[13]

The simultaneous British victory at Al-Alamin and Soviet triumph in Stalingrad at the turn of 1942/43 tipped the scales of World War II in Europe in favor of the Allies. In its wake, British standing in the Middle East improved. Despite continued disputes among Arab governments, London publicly offered political assistance toward a unity scheme under the condition that "the initiative ... would ... come from the Arabs themselves." But why the sudden change of mind? Prime Minister Winston Churchill and military post-war planners saw continued British influence in the Suez Canal Zone as the most crucial asset in projecting power into the Indian Ocean and beyond. But in view of Arab expectations of complete post-war sovereignty, the United Kingdom needed a political tool to extend its imperial influence in a less noticeable fashion throughout all of the Levant. This also included the policy of preventing de Gaulle's Free France from returning to the Middle East after the war.[14]

In 1943, Egypt eventually seized the moment to shape the Arab Middle East. Working closely with London, Cairo pursued pan-Arab policies against the idea of a small Levantine union under Hashemite leadership. Since the emerging Egyptian-led Arab League was no more than an association of sovereign states, it did not fulfill the Hashemite hopes for a loose federation or even a close union. Moreover, the Egyptian emphasis on existing territories as membership units effectively bolstered the mandate borders from the post-World War I period. Supported by the Levant's Shia and Kurdish minorities, which feared marginalization in a Sunni-Arab dominated union, Egypt managed to impose a league that rendered the Levant divided into smaller territorial units and hence too feeble to challenge Egyptian leadership and, by extension, British strategic interests. As Cairo was establishing its own sphere of influence in the

Middle East in close cooperation with the United Kingdom, it still pursued a policy of decolonization in the wider Arab world. From the Churchill government it demanded – unsuccessfully – the release of imprisoned Palestinian leaders so that they could attend a preparatory conference for the league. And from de Gaulle, it sought – also in vain – the inclusion of delegates from French North Africa.[15]

The preparatory conference for the foundation of the Arab League met in Alexandria, Egypt, from September 25 to October 7, 1944. Of the seven Arab governments attending, only five signed the protocol – Egypt, Lebanon, Transjordan, Iraq, and Syria – though Yemen followed soon thereafter. Saudi Arabia refused to sign for two months since it believed that the other participants had not taken its interests seriously. At the gathering itself, the issue of a unified Levant resurfaced briefly, but the four governments involved could not reach an agreement. Syria pushed its own republican system while the two Hashemite kingdoms preferred a monarchical order. Rebuffing Levantine unification altogether, Lebanon managed to extract a statement of respect for its multireligious setup and independence. Also, the unexpected arrival of the exiled Palestinian leader Musa al-Alami raised the problem of how to include a non-governmental representative of an Arab nation, the destiny of which was dear to all. He was allowed to sit alongside all the other delegations, spoke only – though passionately – about the Palestinian issue, and did not sign the protocol. Ultimately, the seven Arab countries announced the establishment of a league of sovereign states, the creation of a council, the principle of non-violence in intra-Arab disputes, and the formation of a commission that would write the league covenant. A special declaration voiced "deep grief for the horrors" that European Jews were suffering in the Holocaust, but warned that this injustice could not validate the Zionist dream of a homeland for Jews at the expense of Arabs in Palestine. Saudi Arabia decided to join the league by November, mainly because it was concerned about the possibility of Levantine domination and the need to create unity in the face of American policies supporting a Jewish homeland. Immediately after the conference, Cairo reported to London that the emerging Arab League would accept British leadership in the military defense of the Middle East. The United Kingdom happily accepted the proposal which fit well with its imperial visions.[16]

On March 22, 1945, the seven Arab countries signed the covenant that established the league, the council, and a secretariat. Although technically not all founding members were fully independent yet, the covenant stipulated that any other Arab state could join only if it was. Consequently, while a Palestinian representative was invited to participate in the league's work, the territory itself had to wait for membership until future independence. While Arab diplomats had been working on

the text of the covenant from February 14 to March 3, the region underwent major readjustments in international affairs. On their return from
the Yalta Conference with Stalin in mid February, Churchill and US
President Franklin D. Roosevelt met with the Saudi and Egyptian kings
in Cairo and at the Suez Canal, respectively. The British prime minister
signaled that the Arab world would have greater weight in world politics
by becoming founding members of the soon-to-be-established United
Nations, though this would require declaring war on Hitler's Germany
first. In a meeting among themselves, the Saudi king, his Egyptian counterpart, and the Syrian president decided to comply. While Iraq had
joined the allies two years before, Saudi Arabia, Egypt, Syria, and
Lebanon did so within a fortnight at Churchill's encouragement.
Transjordan and Yemen, however, decided to stay neutral, and thus did
not receive an American invitation to attend the San Francisco conference that established the United Nations in the summer. King Abdullah
was displeased that the Saudi king and the Syrian "upstart president" but
not he – the "Hashemite ruler" – had been invited to Egypt when
Churchill and Roosevelt were passing through.[17]

The Arab League's outward unity of purpose papered over its internal
conflicts. In early March, Cairo and Riyadh had worked for an Arab
defense treaty in parallel to the negotiations on the league covenant, but
backed off the plan since Baghdad, the original proponent of an Arab
federation in the 1930s, feared Saudi–Egyptian domination. Paired with
its apprehension of Soviet political expansionism that might divide the
Arab world, Iraq instead pushed for close military cooperation with the
United Kingdom. The Palestinian delegate al-Alami complained that his
nation had not received a seat in the council. And Lebanon accused most
of the other members of pursuing their regional interests under the disguise of Arab unity. Unsurprisingly, neighboring Turkey called the league
a "three-headed monster" that was tearing itself apart at its birth.[18]

Opposing Imperialism, 1945–62

Despite its internal conflicts, most of the league's members agreed on one
issue: the decolonization of all Arab lands. Since the 1930s, Arab unity had
revolved around the goal of ending both mandate rule in the Levant and
French colonialism in North Africa. A Saudi–Egyptian–Syrian meeting in
Cairo in February 1945 had reached agreement on strong trilateral unity,
close relations with the United Kingdom, the renunciation of plans for
a Greater Syria, opposition to French colonialism, and hostility toward
communism in the Middle East. Over the following period of more than
one and a half decades, the decolonization of the Arab world occurred in

fits and reversals. Given the league's close association with United Kingdom, much of the anti-imperialist activities focused on France. A British military intervention in May of 1945 had foiled de Gaulle's attempt to reassert control, which forced France to leave Syria and Lebanon for good in 1946. Thus, since the end of World War II, the United Kingdom had wielded predominant political and military influence in the Middle East. The same year, it signed a treaty with Transjordan that turned the Hashemite emirate into the formally independent Jordanian kingdom, though it remained under British political influence and military control. Further afield, the Arab League did not threaten British interests. In line with the Saudi–Egyptian–Syrian agreement to focus on French colonialism, it delayed action on the decolonization of the British protectorates in the Trucial States (today's United Arab Emirates), Qatar, Bahrain, Kuwait, and Aden (part of today's Yemen).[19]

These general agreements notwithstanding, Egypt pursued policies that primarily served its own interests. In December 1945, Cairo prematurely demanded from London the revision of the 1936 treaty. Negotiations lasted for more than eight years, mainly due to disagreements over Sudan. There, Egypt was as much a decolonizer as it was seeking influence for itself. At the same time, Egypt began its slow decline into a domestic political crisis – due to party politics, popular dissatisfaction with the monarchy, and the royal government's failure to renegotiate speedily the 1936 treaty, which ultimately led to the military coup in 1952. In its wake, the nationalist colonel Gamal Abdel Nasser ascended to power in Cairo. The regime's quick decoupling of the Sudan issue from the revision of the 1936 treaty cut the deadlock in the negotiations with the United Kingdom by October 1954. Sudan obtained independence by January 1, 1956, while London withdrew its last troops from the Suez Canal Zone half a year later. The two Anglo–Egyptian agreements thus made the Levant even more important to British imperial strategy.[20]

Further west, the Egyptian-led Arab League raised the decolonization of the French colonies of Tunisia, Algeria, and Morocco at the United Nations. From the end of World War II in 1945 to Algerian independence in 1962, however, France insisted that the international organization was not competent to discuss matters of colonial policy of individual member states. Its rigidity on this issue even increased after the Arab League, with support from sympathetic Asian states like India, put French colonialism in all of Africa and Southeast Asia on the UN agenda in 1952. Yet, while French threats of a boycott of the United Nations and the country's humiliation in Indochina delayed the decolonization of the Maghreb for some time, Paris at least agreed by 1955 to grant independence to Tunisia and Morocco. But Algeria was a different case. Constitutionally bound to

France and with a significant population of French settlers, Paris claimed deeper political and emotional bonds. By late November 1954, just after the eight-year-long Vietnamese communist struggle against French colonialism had ended, the European colonial power faced a similar rebellion in Algeria. De Gaulle's return to power in mid 1958, which occurred against the background of the worsening crisis in Algeria, eventually set developments into motion that led to independence in 1962. Nasser's Egypt was a central hub for weapons supplies to Algeria's National Liberation Front, while newly independent Tunisia and Morocco exploited UN procedures to increase international pressure on France.[21]

Dealing with Israel, 1945–50

Resistance to the emerging Jewish state, however, provided the strongest glue to the internally weak Arab League. Given the increasing levels of violence between Arab and Jewish armed militias, the league's council in September of 1945 demanded from London a complete stop of Jewish immigration. In the wake of the subsequent Anglo–American establishment of a commission tasked with reviewing both the fate of European Jews and the Palestine Mandate, the Arab League feared that London would lift the 1939 restrictions on Jewish immigration. In early December, the league decided on a boycott of Jewish businesses with the goal of depriving the Zionist project of financial assets. It was not the first Arab boycott, but the one adopted at Bloudan in 1937 had never been implemented consistently. Although the new boycott failed to prevent the establishment of Israel in 1948, its fast execution by league members was a heavy burden on the economies of Lebanon, Syria, and Jordan, which were closely intertwined with economy of Palestine.[22]

Ultimately, the Anglo–American commitment to the creation of a Jewish homeland posed a severe test for Britain's influence on the Arab League. Support for the Zionist cause since 1917 had linked the United Kingdom to what Arabs perceived as an imperialist project. In Arab eyes, the European colonial venture unfolded in their midst just after British policy had expelled French imperialism from the Levant. Late in 1945, the United States emphasized its support for unrestricted Jewish immigration. The report of the Anglo–American commission from April 1946 called for facilitated immigration and the creation of a UN mandate to prevent a Jewish–Arab war. In response, the Arab League convened its first summit at Inshas, near Cairo, where its members agreed to oppose further Jewish immigration and to regard any Anglo–American policy contrary to this goal as a hostile act to all Arab states. The extraordinary league council meeting at Bloudan a fortnight later even discussed the adoption of concrete steps. While Iraq advocated a hard line, Saudi Arabia, Syria, and Egypt only proposed adopting realistic measures that did not generate inflated Palestinian expectations. This included the denial of future Arab economic (oil) concessions to Anglo–American companies, a suspension of support for Anglo–American interests at the United Nations, and a moral boycott. The Bloudan decisions, however, did not affect a crucial oil pipeline project – the Saudi pipeline from the Persian Gulf to the Lebanese harbor of Sidon.[23]

Just as the United Kingdom and the United States proposed the partition of Palestine in the summer of 1946, the resurging internal conflicts of the Arab League stymied its ability to react. Jordan once more proposed the formation of a Greater Syria. Running a landlocked, demographically small, and economically weak country, King Abdullah sought to undo the developments of the past decade by seeking unification with Syria, Lebanon, Iraq, and – through clandestine contacts with the Jewish Agency – with the non-Jewish parts of Palestine. His design aimed at replacing what he considered an Egyptian and Saudi-dominated Arab League with a state that ultimately would incorporate the three most Holy cities of Islam – Jerusalem, Mecca, and Medina – under his leadership.[24]

Because in early 1947 London had declared its unwillingness to govern Mandatory Palestine beyond 1948, the crisis over that contested territory rapidly escalated. In September 1947, a UN proposal endorsed partition. It enjoyed support from both the United States and the USSR, and was approved by the General Assembly in late November against all Arab votes. The proposal envisioned a chessboard-like division of Palestine into three Jewish and three Arab parts, with Jerusalem internationalized in order to guarantee unrestricted access to a city that was holy to Muslims, Jews, and Christians alike. Zionists welcomed the proposed division, because it allotted more than 50 percent of the Palestinian territory to a future Jewish state. Arab reactions included warnings of World War III and calls for an economic boycott against the Anglo–American powers. In October, the Arab League even pondered military action, although it understood that its members collectively had few resources available. Following the report's adoption by the General Assembly, the league established a Liberation Army with the goal of creating a unitary Arab state in Palestine. Apart from lacking enough trained officers, funding, and weapons, the army was also a victim of intra-Arab conflicts. Militarily weak, Syria saw the Liberation Army as an insurance against Jordan's plans for a Greater Syria. In turn, Jordan's Abdullah prohibited – though without effect – the use of his kingdom as a staging ground for the Liberation Army. The volunteer army primarily focused on taking Jerusalem. Within months, the military situation turned against the Palestinian Arabs.[25]

With the withdrawal of British forces on May 14, 1948, the Jewish Agency declared the foundation of Israel, which in turn triggered military interventions by Egypt, Syria, Iraq, Lebanon, and Jordan. By early 1949, the Israel Defense Forces (IDF) had defeated all invading Arab armies, seized all of Palestine except Gaza, East Jerusalem, and the West Bank, and driven half of the Palestinian Arabs out of their homes and towns. Palestinians blamed the *Nakba* – the national disaster – on Arab failures to coordinate military action. Indeed, the Egyptian royal government intervened mainly to prevent Jordan from occupying Arab Palestine alone, and to redirect the political energy of nationalist, pan-Arabist, and pan-Islamist members of its armed forces and of the Muslim Brotherhood outward. Jordan's Abdullah resumed his pre-war contacts with Jewish leaders as early as the second half of July 1948, just after his troops had occupied the West Bank and East Jerusalem. As a reaction to Jordan's unilateralism, the Arab League decided in early September to establish an All-Palestine Government in Egyptian-occupied Gaza. Once the Arab League had appointed one of Abdullah's long-time enemies, Grand Mufti of Jerusalem Mohammed Amin al-Husseini, to head that government, the Jordanian king barred him from returning to Jerusalem.[26]

Defeat by Israel simultaneously united and divided the Arab League. On the one hand, an American arms embargo that had been designed to prevent Arab intervention in Palestine convinced the Arab League by February 1948 to reconfirm the two-year-old Bloudan decisions by denying further oil concessions, though the boycott never materialized. Following the foundation of Israel, Iraq shut down the Kirkuk oil pipeline to the refineries in Haifa. Shortly thereafter, Egypt denied passage through the Suez Canal to any ship with cargo bound for Israel. This combined embargo-boycott made the importation of oil to Israel exorbitantly expensive. The boycott continued after the Lausanne Conference from April to September 1949, at which Israel refused to commit to the return of Palestinian refugees in exchange for peace.[27] Furthermore, in the wake of defeat, Cairo demanded weapon supplies from London to deter Israel. The request led to a new round of international diplomacy to stabilize the Middle East. The United States feared an uncontrolled arms race, while the United Kingdom hoped in vain that a bilateral arms deal would lead to a solidification of its influence in Egypt. Ultimately, Washington and London agreed on a common strategy and convinced Paris to declare jointly, by late May 1950, a voluntary self-limitation of arms deliveries in order to guarantee the territorial status quo of the region. The prospect of such a declaration persuaded the Arab League to discuss the formation of a NATO-style defensive alliance among themselves. Bar the two pro-British Hashemite monarchies, its members signed a collective security treaty with a thinly veiled anti-Israeli objective on June 18, 1950.[28]

On the other hand, the Hashemite refusal to join the collective security treaty pointed toward continued conflict along old lines. Baghdad had opposed the idea of a defense treaty as an anti-Hashemite ploy since 1945. Instead, it had pursued, together with fraternal Jordan, an anti-Soviet military alliance with Turkey. For a while, the two Hashemite monarchies even toyed with the idea of leaving the Arab League altogether.[29] By fall of 1948, in the final months of the Arab–Israeli war, Palestinian leaders with pro-Jordanian sympathies denounced the Grand Mufti's All-Palestine government in Gaza while starting to agitate for annexation of the West Bank and East Jerusalem by the Hashemite kingdom. Yet Abdullah's plan to use annexation as a first step toward building a Greater Syria quickly ran into trouble. A series of three coups in Syria from April to December caused the country's successive governments to vacillate. When Damascus eventually reaffirmed its relationship with Cairo and Riyadh, the aging King Abdullah replaced his dream for a Greater Syria with one for a Greater Jordan. In secret negotiations in late 1949, he tried to work out with the Israeli government the division of Jerusalem and their mutual borders in Palestine, though without success.[30]

During a visit to Iraq in the waning days of 1949, Abdullah announced that he would offer Arabs in the West Bank and East Jerusalem citizenship and a vote in the parliamentary elections on April 11. But on April 1, the Arab League prohibited its members from entertaining contacts with Israel (as Abdullah had in early 1950), threatened Jordan's expulsion from the organization in case of annexation, and reconfirmed the ongoing boycotts against Israel. Three and a half weeks later, the newly elected parliament in Amman approved annexation of the West Bank. In response, Egypt demanded Jordan's expulsion, but Iraq asked for the recognition of the fact of annexation. Since the league covenant required unanimity with regard to expulsion, Jordan did not lose its membership, but disagreements remained. It was in this context in mid June that five of the seven league members signed the anti-Israeli collective security treaty, but also warned that the Anglo–American–French declaration on limiting arms supplies could not be used to freeze the territorial status quo in Palestine. Yet the events in the first half of 1950 had achieved exactly that – at least until the June War in 1967. Ultimately, Abdullah could not enjoy his enlarged kingdom for long. On July 20, 1951, an assassin with links to the Grand Mufti and the governments in Cairo and Riyadh shot him dead just as he entered Al-Aqsa Mosque in Jerusalem.[31] In the end, all the troubles within the Arab League since 1945 merely revealed to London that its dominant influence in the Middle East remained fragile.

From Korea to Suez, 1950–56

The Korean War helped bury the intra-Arab conflicts temporarily and reconfirm the league's pro-Western stance. On July 7, Egypt abstained in the UN Security Council vote that sanctioned military intervention against North Korea. Implicitly drawing on the Bloudan decisions from 1946, the only Arab member in the council accused the international organization of using double standards in assessing Jewish aggression in the Middle East in 1947 and communist aggression in Korea three years later. Already before the vote, Cairo had announced its neutrality in the Korean conflict, publicly toying with the idea of closing the Suez Canal to any ships carrying UN troops and war material to East Asia. But Egypt quickly faced resistance from Jordan, Lebanon, and Iraq, which all demanded league support for the United Nations. Abdullah even called for the reactivation of the dormant anti-Soviet Saadabad Pact of 1937.[32]

In mid August, however, the Arab League managed to close ranks again. The seven members dropped the issue of Jordan's annexation of the West Bank, reaffirmed the double boycott against Israel, demanded the internationalization of Jerusalem and the return or compensation of Palestinian refugees, agreed to put French North Africa on the agenda at the United Nations, and asked the international organization to admit the league as a regional organization. In an effort to put pressure on the United States, which they considered primarily responsible for Israel's creation, league members declared their neutrality only with regard to the Korean War but not the global Cold War. Consequently, the league decided to maintain recognition of the Republic of China on Taiwan at the expense of the newly established People's Republic of China on the mainland. Interested in global unity against communist aggression, the United States responded by reversing its five-year-old opposition to the league's association with the United Nations, and successfully sponsored – despite Israeli disapproval – accreditation of the league as a regional organization with permanent observer status in October. It was only the second regional organization to obtain such a status, following the Organization of American States in 1948. The subsequent emergence of a strengthened and unified Arab voice at the United Nations initiated the establishment of the informal Arab caucus there. Within weeks, it evolved into the Asian–Arab caucus, and eventually served as an organizational basis for the emerging Asian–African Movement.[33]

The failure of the Asian–Arab caucus to mediate in the Korean conflict at the turn of 1950/51, however, led the Arab League to abandon its position of neutrality in that war in favor of a pro-Western stance. In February, Iraq joined the Arab collective security treaty, in the hope of refocusing the alliance's geographically limited anti-Israeli proclivity toward a more general anti-communist position. Yet, in the context of Western alliance building against the Soviet Union after the outbreak of the Korean War, in late October Egypt publicly opposed an Anglo–American–French–Turkish proposal to fold the Arab collective security treaty into a larger Cold War alliance. By February 1952, Washington, too, decided to turn away from that idea because it feared that Cairo's discontent about the unresolved Anglo–Egyptian questions on Suez and Sudan would become a major obstacle to its anti-Soviet alliance building in the region. In parallel to these developments, post-Abdullah Jordan signed the Arab collective security treaty as the final league member in January 1952, and Iraq's ratification in August allowed the pact to come into force. But by then, the July revolution in Egypt threatened to throw everything into disarray again. The new military government in Cairo initially signaled its wish to work more closely with the Arab League, while giving up its proclivity for making unilateral decisions. In the same vein, it removed the league's first General Secretary, Abdul Rahman Hassan Azzam, because of his closeness to the deposed royal regime, though it still managed to install another Egyptian, Abdel Khalek Hassouna, as successor. Egyptian institutional dominance thus continued, as did the country's unilateralism despite initial promises to the contrary.[34]

In early 1953, London and Washington hoped that they could strike a deal with Cairo by linking British withdrawal from Suez to Egyptian membership in an anti-Soviet alliance. Hatched by the incoming Eisenhower administration, the plan was for the United Kingdom to take the lead in establishing the alliance without formal US membership. Pakistan, which had shown interest in joining an anti-Soviet alliance for anti-Indian reasons, tried to convince Egypt to join. But when the new military regime in Egypt attempted to manipulate the Arab League to support its positions in the negotiations with the United Kingdom, it merely alienated Iraq, Jordan, Syria, and Lebanon. All four even refused to attend a foreign ministers meeting of the league in April as a sign of protest. By May, Cairo's emerging leader Nasser publicly stated that his country refused to link British withdrawal from Suez to Egyptian membership in any Cold War alliance. In mid August, Nasser chaired the first chief of military staff meeting of the Arab collective security treaty, demanding that all present should learn lessons from the *Nakba* and to prepare collectively for the defense against all "aggression and evil designs." By late 1953, Cairo even announced publicly its "neutralist" stance in the Cold War.[35]

Even though by 1954 London signed treaties with Cairo that stipulated Sudanese independence and complete British withdrawal from Suez, it still pursued its own regional defense project, though without recalcitrant Egypt. But Nasser, together with recently crowned King Saud, continued to oppose the emerging British-led Baghdad Pact between Turkey, Iraq,

Pakistan, and Iran. Cairo and Riyadh saw this military arrangement mostly as a British attempt to prolong its colonial influence, but also as an "evil design" meant to destroy the Arab collective security treaty. Still, Egypt and Saudi Arabia were unable to prevent the multilateral anti-Soviet alliance under British patronage from forming. Even a joint last-minute threat to leave the Arab League did not change Iraq's decision to sign a bilateral agreement with Turkey on February 24, 1955, that would lead to the five-member Baghdad Pact within eight months.[36]

The Iraqi decision set off a vicious cycle of escalatory international developments that ended in the Suez Crisis – and the concomitant British collapse in the Middle East – in 1956. It occurred just four days before an Israeli military incursion into Gaza that left around three dozen Egyptian and ten Israeli soldiers dead, thereby ending a long period of relative calm at Israeli–Arab borders. Military hardliners in Israel had decided on a show of military force to deter Egypt, after they had concluded – wrongly – that the emerging Baghdad Pact would include all of Israel's neighbors, including Egypt. In response to Iraq's decision and Israel's incursion, however, Nasser sought a closer military alliance with Saudi Arabia and Syria, with the dual purpose of blocking the further expansion of the Baghdad Pact and of containing Israel. In the wake of the Gaza clash, the Egyptian leader also took the emerging Asian–African Movement – which was scheduled to meet in Bandung in April – more seriously by deciding to attend in person. On his way to Indonesia, Nasser asked India's Prime Minister Jawaharlal Nehru and China's counterpart Zhou Enlai for arms so that Egypt could break the five-year Anglo-American–French embargo. But in May, after his return from Bandung, Nasser directly turned to the Soviet Union with a request for arms that would turn into the Soviet–Czechoslovak arms deal of September 1955.[37]

Anti-communist Saudi Arabia did not mind Egypt's cooperation with the USSR, as long as it was directed against Israel. By late October of 1955, Cairo, Riyadh, and Damascus even signed military agreements to counterbalance the Baghdad Pact. The following May, Egypt recognized the PRC, almost a year after Nasser had met Chinese Premier Zhou in Burma and Indonesia. Because communist China was not a UN member, Egypt hoped to secure access to military supplies outside a total arms embargo in the Middle East that was under consideration at the United Nations. With Egypt gradually undermining Western containment policy in the Middle East, the United States in turn reconsidered its offer to help finance the hydro-electrical and flood-regulating Aswan Dam project at the Upper Nile. When Washington announced its decision to withdraw funding, Nasser reacted by nationalizing the Suez Canal Company on July 26, 1956, so that his country could tap into the passage fees and the company's assets to fund the dam. His surprise move occurred just six weeks after the last British soldier had left, as stipulated by the Anglo–Egyptian agreement of 1954. Nasser publicly emphasized that "restoring the Canal to Egypt" was a crucial step in the "holy march" from colonial exploitation "toward industrialization, development and reconstruction."[38]

Nasser's nationalization of the Suez Canal Company triggered the well-known Israeli–Franco–British military intervention on October 29, but it also split the Arab League yet again. On the one hand, each of the three aggressors had its own reasons for military action. Jerusalem wanted to occupy the Sinai in order to obtain strategic depth while breaking the canal blockade. Paris yearned to punish Nasser for his support of the Algerian insurgency. And London had wanted, even before July, to dispose of the supposedly pro-Soviet Egyptian leader in order to reorganize the Middle East once more under its own leadership.[39] In the face of instant Anglo–French bellicosity after nationalization, however, Washington had notified London and Paris that it considered Cairo's decision entirely within Egypt's rights, and that military action was only warranted if Nasser failed to run the canal properly. By late October, the British government had to acknowledge that Egypt was entirely capable of doing so. By then, however, the Israeli–Franco–British conspiracy for joint intervention was already under way.[40]

On the other hand, Nasser's Egypt did not receive full support from fellow Arab states either. Unsympathetic to the provocative nature of the canal's nationalization, Iraq presciently emphasized to the United Kingdom that "it was essential to keep Israel out of this dispute," and "vital" for the Anglo–American–French powers to "work together." King Saud decried Nasser's "irresponsible" action, which had unilaterally created a "fait accompli" that affected all Arab states. As international mediation and negotiations failed due to British, French, and Egyptian intransigence in the late summer, Riyadh tried to buy Cairo's agreement to a compromise settlement with economic aid. But Nasser called for joint Arab preparations, including an oil embargo, in "the event of Anglo–French aggression, made with American support."[41]

The failure of the triple intervention of October 29 completely changed the nature of international relations in the Middle East. The United States was furious about being hoodwinked by its two NATO allies and Israel, particularly at a time when the anti-Soviet revolution in Hungary seemed to succeed. Through diplomatic and economic means, Washington forced the three aggressors into accepting a UN armistice on November 6 and then into consenting to military withdrawal. Since the collaboration with Israel had painted the United Kingdom and France "in true Zionist colours," London's long-held influence in the Middle East collapsed, while Paris failed to gain any advantage in Algeria.[42] The main beneficiary of the British collapse was the Soviet Union. Before the nationalization of the Suez Canal Company, it had been skeptical about replacing the United States in financing the Aswan Dam but it had been willing to support anti-imperialist tendencies in the Arab world in general. As London readied itself for armed action by August, Moscow warned that "military preparations ... would inevitably spread" hostilities beyond the Middle East, while its communist ally in Beijing publicly accused the United Kingdom, France, and the United States of using old-style "gunboat" diplomacy. Two days into the war at the Suez Canal, on October 31, the Soviet leadership concluded that the concurrent anti-Soviet unrest in Hungary and the triple intervention against Egypt were an Anglo–American–French imperialist attempt to change the balance of global power – a challenge which it could not let go unanswered.[43] In the shadow of war at Suez, Moscow suppressed the Hungarian Revolution while threatening nuclear missile strikes against the United Kingdom and France. These empty nuclear bluffs did not cause London or Paris to agree to an armistice – Washington's arm twisting did – but they earned the USSR much undeserved credit in Egypt.[44]

The triple intervention greatly affected inter-Arab relations, too. At the beginning of the crisis, fellow Arab states showed solidarity with Egypt. On November 6, for example, Saudi Arabia cut its diplomatic relations with the two European powers and even established an oil embargo against them. Five days later, the heads of state of the Arab League met in Beirut to discuss the organization's strategic reorientation, though the Egyptian delegation attended without Nasser. Damascus and Cairo advocated accepting military and economic aid from Moscow – "the one true friend of the Arab world" – while Iraq, Lebanon, and Saudi Arabia opposed "Soviet penetration." Taking charge in leading the opposition to Egypt, King Saud blamed Nasser for inviting Soviet influence, for causing the war-related debris blocking the Suez Canal, and for provoking the wanton destruction of oil pipelines by free-lancing hotheads. Simultaneously, however, he continued to oppose the Baghdad Pact because of the intra-Arab controversies it had caused. Even if the crisis had increased Nasser's pan-Arabist appeal among many ordinary people in the Middle East, he himself was "worried about the future," as he told the Sudanese prime minister: "He admitted that the Egyptians had not fought and that Egypt was saved 'by United Nations and world opinion' ... He denied that he was a Communist."[45]

At least, after three decades of mutual hostility since the mid 1920s, the Suez Crisis brought reconciliation between Hashemite Jordan and Saudi Arabia, which enabled Amman to abrogate the 1946 treaty with London and get rid of British military personnel and political influence within a year. The United States tried to exploit these developments by proposing an alliance with the two reconciled kingdoms, designed to contain the supposedly pro-Soviet Egypt. Yet US plans did not work out, because Saudi Arabia opposed the formal involvement of foreign powers in the Middle East in principle. By the early 1960s, it would be one of the founding members of the Non-Aligned Movement – under the leadership of Josip Broz Tito's Yugoslavia and, paradoxically, Nasser's Egypt. Western containment strategy suffered yet another setback with the revolution in Iraq in mid 1958 that replaced the British-installed monarchy with an increasingly pro-Soviet regime. Baghdad's withdrawal in 1959 from the pact that bore its name convinced the United States to encourage the creation of the Central Treaty Organization (CENTO), which brought together the non-Arab members of the defunct pact in an anti-Soviet alliance.[46] By the late 1950s, British influence had collapsed everywhere in the Middle East. The brace that was supposed to keep UK imperial interest in the eastern hemisphere together was broken beyond repair.

Hiatus and Resurrection, 1957–64

The seven years following the Suez Crisis marked the period of what the political scientist Malcolm Kerr once called the Arab Cold War. What he meant, of course, was not the Soviet–American clash after the British collapse in the Middle East, but the extraordinarily high level of political animosity within the Arab League. Much of the intra-Arab conflict was caused by Nasser, who tried to exploit his newly acquired popularity for the establishment of a pan-Arab state. Given Saudi Arabia's strident anti-communism and rivalry with Egypt, King Saud was convinced that Nasser acted in both his exalted self-interest and that of the USSR. The Saudi–Egyptian enmity was so deep that each of the two countries tried to have the other's head of government assassinated. The rivalry also paralyzed the Arab League to such a degree that even the membership applications of newly independent Arab states – like Morocco, Tunisia, and Kuwait – became bones of contention.[47]

Egypt's attempt to unite the core of the Arab world under its own leadership was equally based on pan-Arabist and anti-communist visions. Given their ideologically skewed Cold War perceptions, Saudi Arabia and the United States overlooked the fact that Egypt shared their anti-communist stance. Nasser's cooperation with the Soviet Union was strategic, not ideological. Although by late 1958 Cairo extracted financial and technical aid from Moscow for the construction of the Aswan Dam, Egypt's relations with the USSR worsened quickly thereafter due to Nasser's persecution of Arab communists.[48] Also, by late summer of 1957, Syria had become a battleground in the global Cold War when its long brewing domestic crisis entered into a critical phase. In mid August, its government exposed

American participation in the preparations for an overthrow of what many perceived to be an increasingly pro-Soviet regime in Damascus. Pro-American King Saud tried mediation to defuse the crisis and to build up his own sphere of influence. He thereby provoked Nasser into dispatching Egyptian troops in mid October to prevent Syria from falling under either Soviet or Saudi control. By February 22, 1958, Egypt and Syria merged to form the United Arab Republic (UAR) under Cairo's leadership. The following day, Nasser announced that the merger was only the start of complete Arab liberation from imperialist, including Zionist, influence and that future steps would overcome the artificial borders imposed on the Arab Nation at the end of World War I. On March 7, the Egyptian-controlled Palestinian government in Gaza joined the UAR. Within twenty-four hours, Yemen acceded to the United Arab States, which the UAR had formed to allow other Arab states that did not want to give up sovereignty immediately to join. For half a year, the two Hashemite monarchies and the Saudi kingdom discussed the possibility of forming a counter-federation, but the anti-royal Iraqi revolution in mid July quickly put a stop to this idea.[49]

The prospect of the formation of a unitary Arab state encouraged pan-Arabist activities throughout the Levant. In Lebanon, pan-Arab supporters agitated for the country to join the UAR. The staunchly pro-Western government suspected Egyptian machinations, and appealed to the Arab League to call on Cairo to stop interfering in its internal affairs. The Egyptian-dominated league, however, failed to reassure the Lebanese government, which then brought the dispute to the United Nations. The Security Council was divided along Cold War lines, but at least dispatched a fact-finding mission. In the wake of the Iraqi revolution in mid July, the United States and the United Kingdom heeded requests by Lebanon and Jordan, respectively, to send troops to stabilize either country in view of pan-Arabist unrest. By August, Saudi Arabia and Egypt agreed on a political armistice that helped end rumors about Cairo's plans to turn the Arab League into an Egyptian-led Arab Federation. In an unexpected twist – auspicious for Saudi Arabia – Iraq announced the same month that it had no intention to join the UAR, largely because Nasser had given the Iraqi revolutionaries the cold shoulder. In effect, the Egyptian leader had liked neither their seemingly pro-Soviet policies nor the prospect of additional conflict with the United States. He even supported an insurgency against the new regime in Baghdad – though with little success.[50]

Nasser's pan-Arab dreams suffered major setbacks in 1961–62. Cairo's Arab unity policies had alienated both Washington and Moscow. The United States had agreed to a slow rapprochement with Israel – a development which formed the basis of the close bilateral relationship that remains to this day. At the same time, Nasser's suppression of communists in the UAR had soured relations with both the USSR and the PRC. Ultimately, however, Syrian dissatisfaction with Egyptian dominance led to the collapse of the UAR on September 28, 1961, followed by Yemen's defection from the now meaningless United Arab States. Within a year, the Egyptian president even threw his country into a ruinous five-year war against Saudi Arabia to defend Republican Yemen and, ultimately, increase his influence in the Arabian peninsula. Thus, by 1962, Cairo was almost completely isolated in the Arab world. During an Arab League meeting in August, Egypt threatened to withdraw from the organization altogether. Nasser's only major success in international affairs at that time was sponsoring the establishment of the Non-Aligned Movement, together with Yugoslavia's Tito and India's Nehru, in 1961. While this enabled him to showcase Egypt during the preparatory conference in Cairo in early June of 1961, his participation in the first Non-Aligned Conference in Belgrade in early September of 1961 was overshadowed by the mounting crisis within the UAR that would lead to Syrian secession three weeks later.[51]

But in 1963, Nasser's Egypt benefited from unexpected developments in the Arab world. In the first ten weeks of the year, military coups in Baghdad and Damascus removed two of Cairo's three greatest Arab rivals from power. The new regimes quickly approached Egypt with requests to talk about a federation, which Nasser, however, regarded with suspicion. But the episode seemed to have encouraged Nasser to mend fences all around. In June 1963, he sent a high-ranking delegation to Moscow for reconciliation talks. In response, Nikita S. Khrushchev traveled to Egypt in May 1964 to inspect the Soviet-financed Aswan Dam.[52] Trying to pursue a middle-of-the-road policy with regard to all powers, the Egyptian president also received, by mid December 1963, Chinese Prime Minister Zhou, who himself tried to counterbalance Soviet and Indian influence in the Middle East.[53] After Zhou's departure, Nasser suddenly called for an Arab League summit meeting in Cairo in mid January, largely with the intention of preventing Syria, which again had become more radical, from taking the initiative on policy toward the Israel/Palestine question. Years of disputes over the diversion of the Jordan waters for agricultural purposes had strained the difficult Arab–Israeli relationship. At the summit, Nasser hoped to defang the water issue while simultaneously addressing the Palestinian issue in a constructive manner. The ultimate goal was to restore Arab unity against the possibility of Israel arming itself with nuclear weapons. The summit's two achievements consisted of the very fact that it happened at all and the decision to allow Palestinians to create their own organization. But Nasser's attempt to improve relations with other Arab states took a heavy toll on his patience; all delegations publicly reprimanded him for past mistakes at the summit. At least, the most important remaining rival in the Arab world, Saudi Arabia, was willing to talk about ending the Yemen conflict.[54]

A second summit in Cairo in early September 1964 deepened Arab attempts at coordinating policies toward Israel. In its wake, Nasser traveled to Saudi Arabia to sign an agreement aimed at ending the Yemen conflict, which nevertheless would continue for three years. Nonetheless, in September, Nasser also could welcome the Non-Aligned states, including Saudi Arabia, to the movement's second conference in an Egypt, which he had restored to some level of international standing. But reconciliation with the Arab states remained a fragile plant. Half a year before, Saudi Crown Prince Faisal had launched a pan-Islamist program that, by the 1970s, would become an important competitor to the Arab League and the Non-Aligned Movement. At least, Arab solidarity held with regard to Israel. When, in late 1964, Egypt discovered that the Federal Republic of Germany (West Germany) clandestinely delivered weapons to Israel, Arab relations with that European country entered into an accelerating downward spiral. By May 1965, Bonn had exchanged ambassadors with Tel Aviv, to which all Arab League members responded by breaking relations with West Germany.[55]

Conclusion

By the early 1960s, the Arab League had almost doubled in size with the entrance of Libya in 1951, Sudan in 1956, Morocco and Tunisia in 1958, Kuwait in 1961, and Algeria in 1962. The Arab League had emerged from two mutually exclusive impulses that had kept its inner conflicts running for almost three decades since the early 1930s. The organization was established on the basis of both the *collective* Arab yearning for unity and *individual* attempts to prevent other Arab states from dominating the Middle East. The initial fault lines ran between Saudi Arabia, the Hashemite monarchies, and Egypt. Until the Suez Crisis in 1956, Riyadh and Cairo cooperated to undermine Hashemite interests. Afterward Saudi Arabia reconciled with Jordan in order to oppose Egyptian dominance. The Cold War played an ambiguous role in the first twenty years of the Arab League. One the one hand, it was a source of intra-Arab conflict, but on the other, the league was also the main obstacle to its entrance into the region. Iraq and Saudi Arabia both were anti-communist countries in the period from 1945 to 1958, though they were unable to cooperate with each other. Baghdad was not averse to working with non-Arabs – Turkey, Iran, Pakistan, the United Kingdom, and the United States – to contain Soviet influence. Riyadh, however, was a non-aligned player, which eschewed formal alliances with non-Arab countries despite its own pro-American stand. In that respect, Saudi Arabia was close to both Egypt's royal government and its revolutionary successor from 1952 onwards. Yet Nasser's Egypt was also willing to pursue an active policy of playing the great powers off against each other – only to end up antagonizing all of them by the early 1960s. In 1963–64, Egypt was able to restore a semblance of Arab unity to escape from its international isolation. By then, however, the Arab League had long severed its links with the United Kingdom; instead, it would become an important regional actor on its own during the wars with Israel in 1967 and 1973.

The United Kingdom had sought imperial preponderance in the Middle East since World War I. The goal was to dominate a strategic territory that would reinforce British control of imperial possessions on the rim lands of the Indian Ocean – from East Africa to the Persian Gulf, South Asia, Malaya, and the Commonwealth members Australia and New Zealand. To that end, the United Kingdom used the mandate system of the League of Nations during the interwar period, military force against France in 1940 and 1945, and patronage over the Arab League. Until World War II, London had feared the Arab unity project, but eventually decided to support Cairo in its quest to unite the Arab Middle East because this offered the best option to prolong British dominance in the Suez Canal Zone and the Levant. But the organization quickly turned against the imperialist interests of the United Kingdom. Long-term British support for the Zionist cause, the establishment of Israel, and the creation of a British-led, anti-Soviet Cold War alliance – the Baghdad Pact – undermined British influence. Still, the pre-eminent though waning position in the region from 1945 to 1956 allowed the United Kingdom to prop up its global empire and thereby claim standing among the world's other great powers – the Soviet Union and the United States – in the early global Cold War. Poignantly, it more or less also helped to keep the Cold War out of the region for a decade. But London's imperialist reflexes in 1956 destroyed much of its remaining influence in the Arab world, while it undercut its status among the Big Three and allowed the Soviet–American race for influence in the region to start. The mere possession of nuclear weapons allowed the United Kingdom to play the continued role of a great power in the global Cold War until 1963, when Moscow and Washington still accepted London as an equal in the trilateral negotiations on the Limited Test Ban Treaty, as Chapter 14 reveals. Afterward, with British global standing greatly diminished, a system consisting of an American–Soviet nuclear superpower duopoly coupled with the simultaneous diffusion of non-nuclear power throughout the world emerged, as Parts II to VI collectively show.

3   The Soviet Union and the Socialist Camp

The *Socialist Camp* was a Soviet creation. In the wake of its military advance in the later stages of World War II, the USSR established an *empire of imposition* in much of Eastern Europe. The Yugoslav communist Milovan Djilas remembered Iosif V. Stalin asserting in April 1945: "Everyone imposes his own system as far as his army can reach." The other socialist states that joined the Socialist Camp soon after World War II – Yugoslavia, mainland China, North Vietnam, and Albania – were run by communist parties that had been established with Soviet political inspiration and organizational assistance between 1918 and 1941. The Middle East was hardly in Stalin's crosshairs, nor was the region attracted to his ideological visions of decolonization. The Socialist Camp's unquestioned center was Moscow, from where Stalin ruled the USSR and many of its member states – through the help of either subservient puppets or willing collaborators.[1]

But the seemingly monolithic nature of the Socialist Camp was deceptive. In reality, it resembled a block of cast iron – hard in appearance but brittle under stress. It derived its ostensible sturdiness from the militarized and centralized nature of the state, society, and economy that had emerged from the long struggles which the various communist parties took part in to obtain power in their respective countries. These struggles continued afterward on the basis of the ideological belief that socialist states were engaged in a near-perpetual conflict with the so-called imperialist–capitalist world. Yet, at the same time, the camp suffered from internal weakness because of the intrinsic shortcomings of its ideology. Marxism, the allegedly scientific ideological belief system that underpinned the Socialist Camp, was silent about the exact path to the future. Karl Marx and his devotees had offered a seemingly logical explanation of human development as a linear evolution from slave society to the paradisiacal communist end of history. At the beginning of each historical phase, one socio-economic class liberated itself in a revolution; by Marx's time, history had reached the capitalist stage, in which the bourgeoisie yielded political and economic power while it exploited the proletariat. But Marxist ideology failed to sketch the precise revolutionary steps necessary for mankind to move further into the penultimate socialist stage of history, and eventually into the final communist stage.[2]

Leninism tried to fill that void by inserting the idea of the communist vanguard party that would push history down its scientifically predetermined path under the leadership of supposedly wise party leaders who claimed to have grasped the Truth. Yet Leninism and all the other elaborations of Marxism – Stalinism and Maoism, for example – were just bastard descendants from the original theory.[3] In reality, all communist parties struggled with themselves, and often also against each other, to identify the proper pathway toward socialism and communism. The ideologically undetermined nature of the final two steps toward the end of history was one of the principal sources of the many disagreements that arose among countries run by communist party dictatorships, particularly after Stalin's death.

The Socialist Camp, which Stalin created during and after World War II, exhibited congenital structural defects that allowed its members to challenge Soviet leadership and thereby transform the so-called Soviet bloc over several decades, as Chapters 5, 6, and 16 to 19 collectively show in greater detail. The camp's overall ideological rigidity created much conflict between the Soviet core and, predominantly, those parts that had joined voluntarily in the late 1940s. Despite the camp's ideological claim to international solidarity, socialist states fostered and even exploited nationalist inclinations, which in turn led to multiple conflicts in the realm of ideology, politics, and economics. Insecure about its own sphere of influence in the global Cold War, the Soviet Union repeatedly used military interventions or the threat thereof to bring other socialist states in line. This heavy-handed approach to solving problems, however, had two negative effects in the long term. First, it alienated those socialist states – like China – and communist parties – mostly in Western Europe – that never had been under complete Soviet control. Second, it deterred the Eastern European socialist states under Soviet control from undertaking necessary reforms. Thus, by the late 1960s, the Soviet Union was able to enforce cohesion in a rump-Socialist Camp in Eastern Europe, though at the price of continued low-level conflicts and the essential unreformability of the Soviet system.

Exporting Communism, 1917–47

Similar to revolutionary France after 1789, Soviet Russia after 1917 (the Union of Soviet Socialist Republics/USSR since 1922) aimed at overthrowing the existing system of states. At home, it claimed to create a socialist and eventually communist society that would terminate the exploitation of the masses by the capitalist bourgeoisie and the state itself. On a global scale, it hoped to replace the imperialist–capitalist system led by the United Kingdom and the United States with a stateless international system that would liberate the colonized and the proletariat. With the Comintern (the Third International), Soviet Russia had established numerous communist parties in the world since 1919 in the hope of exporting revolution. While this endeavor failed in the short term, some of these parties played an important role in the rise of communist regimes in the non-European world, particularly in China and Vietnam.[4]

The actual spread of Soviet-style revolution occurred in the wake of the Soviet advance into Eastern Europe in 1944 and 1945. The creation of like-minded socialist states at the western border of the USSR served immediate security needs following a brutal war, but was also the first step in the historical mission to advance revolution on a global scale. Stalin could thereby rely on national groups of communists, which had escaped from right-wing regimes in Europe in the 1930s or fled after the outbreak of World War II. Many of the communist leaders of post-war Europe not only knew each other from their exile in Moscow, but had also survived numerous Stalinist purges by maneuvering politically or even betraying compatriots. Though they were not a cohesive group, they shared the experience of exile, physical survival, and political training, on the one hand, and the mission to establish communist regimes in their home countries, on the other. The number of members in each national exile group generally was small. Once they had returned to their respective home countries at the end of the war, they usually could not rely on networks of cadres because right-wing governments and the war had wiped out most party organizations. They also had to compete with non-communist politicians and parties that had survived the war and German occupation in the local resistance, prison, or the underground. Soviet military commanders quickly established real and purported coalition governments in Hungary, Poland, and Romania. In Bulgaria, however, they simply co-opted a national unity government that had fought German occupation and emerged as the *de facto* regime even before the arrival of Soviet troops. In all cases, the occupiers tried to control governments either through local communist parties or through the outright intimidation and arrest of non-communist politicians.[5]

However, the Soviet establishment of communist rule was not uniform in Eastern Europe. For example, the dispatch of a group of exiled communists to Germany's capital, Berlin, in April 1945 resembled, on the surface at least, Soviet standard practice. But the group around Walter Ulbricht was tiny, had to compete with the rapidly re-emerging and popular Social Democratic Party, and needed to take into account political developments in the other 70 percent of Germany occupied by the United States, the United Kingdom, and France. In order to overcome its organizational shortcomings and lacking political appeal, in April 1946 Stalin ordered Ulbricht's small communist party to merge with the much larger Social Democratic Party in the Soviet-occupied zone of Germany. In Czechoslovakia, Soviet military commanders did not exercise control in the period immediately after World War II because Soviet troops had not arrived when Germany surrendered in May of 1945. Still, with Moscow's support, centrists and leftists, including the communists, formed a national unity government that was sympathetic to political cooperation with the USSR. In Yugoslavia, the communists came to power with little Soviet military help but on the basis of their military struggle against the German occupation. Stalin's armed forces quickly withdrew from the northeastern part of the country, which they had temporarily occupied on the march to Hungary. In parallel, after German withdrawal in October 1944, the Albanian resistance transformed itself into a government headed by the communist party, which had been founded in Moscow as late as 1941 and was closely run by Yugoslav communists.[6]

Thus, the Socialist Camp that emerged in Eastern Europe at the end of World War II was by no means a unitary bloc with analogous regimes. In some countries, Soviet-installed and subservient communist parties controlled coalition governments. In others, communist parties had come to power independently and were not necessarily deferential to the center of world revolution in Moscow. In any case, Stalin's war-torn USSR lacked the human and political capabilities to establish monolithic and central control from Bulgaria to East Germany and from Albania to Poland – an area that had suffered much war-related damage and dislocation. Although the great dictator originally believed that the communists could win elections, the meager results of Soviet-installed communist parties in the relatively free elections in Hungary (November 1945) and East Germany (October 1946) clearly revealed that communist rule was neither firmly established nor popular. In other cases, like in Poland (June 1946) and Romania (November 1946), communist parties simply resorted to outright vote rigging to get their way.[7]

Tightening the Screws, 1947–53

An external Cold War event in mid 1947, however, forced the Soviet Union to assert greater control in Eastern Europe. After the United States had concluded that Soviet–American disagreements made the emergence of a stable, prosperous, self-reliant, and united Europe unattainable, it introduced the Marshall Plan (the European Recovery Program) to rebuild Western Europe. Stalin understood the inherent threat of an important feature of the plan – the offer of economic aid to all of Europe. Thus, accepting Marshall Plan aid would have threatened to undercut his grip in his sphere of influence, but rejecting it would have forced the war-torn USSR to shoulder the exclusive responsibility for reconstruction of the eastern half of the continent. The dictator decided after some hesitation to allow the dispatch of Soviet and Eastern European delegations to the conference in Paris in July 1947, but then suddenly ordered their withdrawal in the hope of throwing the gathering into disarray. He failed in this endeavor, while simultaneously exposing the extent of his inability to control all of Eastern Europe. Czechoslovakia refused to withdraw its delegation until an ultimatum and promises of economic aid from Stalin left it without much choice. Subsequently, the remaining Western European participants successfully negotiated an American recovery program for the western half of the continent.[8]

Faced with the need to assume economic reconstruction in Eastern Europe in competition with the United States, the USSR tried to impose greater political and ideological uniformity in its sphere of influence. At the first conference of the Cominform (Communist Information Bureau) in Poland's Szklarska Poręba on September 22–28, 1947, Soviet representative Andrei Zhdanov revived Stalin's Two-Camp Theory from 1919. He postulated that the world was divided into the "anti-imperialist and democratic camp" led by the "superior social system, the Soviet Union" and the "imperialist and anti-democratic camp" headed by the United States. In the face of the "aggressive" and "expansionist course" of American foreign policy, Zhdanov regretted the dissolution of the Comintern in 1943 which, or so he claimed, some communist parties had misunderstood as "the liquidation of all links, all contact between fraternal Communist Parties." As an alternative, he called for "consultation and voluntary co-ordination of action."[9]

The exact meaning of Zhdanov's surprise speech only became evident in subsequent months. As in East Germany in 1946, Moscow ordered the ruling communist parties in Romania, Poland, and Hungary to swallow social democratic parties with which they had formed a coalition. With regard to Czechoslovakia, Zhdanov's calls for greater coordination accelerated ongoing attempts by the Czech and Slovak twin communist parties to purge non-communist coalition members from the government – a policy that eventually led to a pro-Soviet coup d'état on February 25, 1948. Similarly, under Stalin's orders, other Eastern European communist parties expunged members who had proposed a national path toward socialism, in order to conform to the Soviet vision of a unitary bloc.[10]

Stalin's heavy hand, however, did not succeed everywhere. At the first Cominform conference, the communist parties of Italy (PCI) and France (PCF) received much criticism for their recent participation in elections and for advocating peaceful transition toward socialism. Even if they had just been dismissed from coalition governments in the so-called May Crisis in 1947, when the United States demanded that Italy and France expel communist ministers as a precondition for Marshall Plan aid, neither had abandoned its commitment to democratic politics because both feared that revolutionary action would damage their appeal. The sudden implementation by the PCI of policies conforming to Zhdanov's Two-Camp Theory in late 1947, however, broke the party's popular front alliance with the Italian Socialists, and probably was co-responsible for its clear defeat in the national elections in mid April 1948. The bitterly fought vote brought the country to the brink of civil war; a right-wing fanatic even made an attempt on the life of PCI leader Palmiro Togliatti. Similarly, the PCF organized massive labor strikes against the pro-American policies of the government in late 1947 and engaged in political violence against the elected, non-communist officials. The Stalinist character, which it would retain into the 1960s, was responsible for the rapid loss of members and the party's political isolation until 1981.[11]

Further afield, in the Balkans and Asia, Moscow's new assertive policy both repelled and attracted communist parties at the same time. On the one hand, Soviet–Yugoslav disagreements in the spring of 1948 revealed the congenital fragility of socialist unity. Although the ideological and political tensions between Josip Broz Tito and Stalin dated to the war years, they burst into full-fledged conflict after the first conference of the Cominform over Yugoslavia's long-standing plans to form a union with Bulgaria and Albania, and over disagreements about communist involvement in the ongoing Greek Civil War. The second Cominform conference on June 19–23, 1948, formally criticized the Yugoslav communists as revisionists who "have left the Marxist–Leninist road." The Soviet Union thereby elevated political disagreements between two communist states to the level of ideological disputes, triggering the *de facto* expulsion of Yugoslavia from the Socialist Camp. In the aftermath, Stalin ordered the cutting of all military and economic links; the great dictator even tried to have Tito assassinated. Stalin's heavy hand and the outbreak of the Korean War a year later convinced Yugoslavia to turn to the United States for economic and military assistance to deter the Soviet threat.[12]

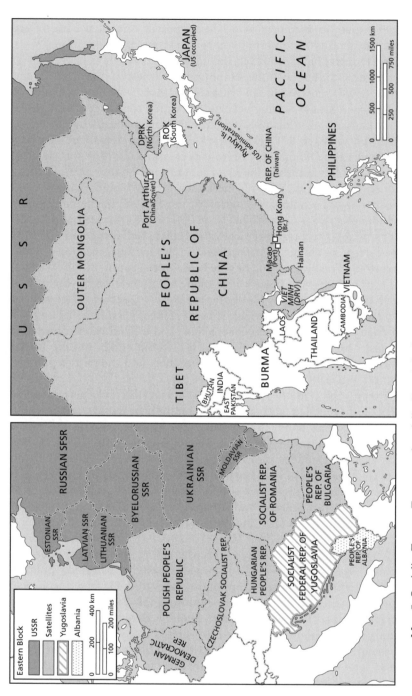

Map 5. Socialist Eastern Europe and socialist East Asia, late 1940s

On the other hand, the anti-Yugoslav resolutions of the second Cominform conference in June 1948 convinced communist parties outside Stalin's firm control to acquiesce. Both the Chinese and Albanian parties had been Soviet creations – in 1921 and 1941, respectively – but had suffered from Stalin's neglect. In dire need of economic aid after the impending victory in the civil war, the leader of the Chinese Communist Party (CCP), Mao Zedong, decided in mid 1948 "to lean" toward the USSR lest he risked being branded a "second Tito." On Mao's request in mid 1950, Stalin also sent Pavel Yudin, a decorated Marxist–Leninist theoretician, as ambassador to the newly established People's Republic of China (PRC) to help edit the chairman's writings according to the Stalinist canon. For similar reasons, the Albanian Communist Party used the Cominform resolutions of June 1948 to break free from Yugoslav tutelage and to position itself as a loyal Stalinist party within the Socialist Camp. With their parallel and deliberate entry into the camp, the Chinese and Albanian communists started a journey of bilateral friendship that lasted until Sino–Yugoslav rapprochement in the late 1970s. Last but not least, with the establishment of the PRC in October 1949, the Vietnamese communists rekindled their old contacts with the Chinese comrades. Stalin, who had never been interested in Southeast Asia, reacted by entrusting the Indochinese revolution to Mao in early 1950.[13]

Apart from deepening the world's division as described in Chapter 1, the Korean War had numerous direct and indirect influences on the Stalinization of the socialist world in East Asia and Eastern Europe. The advance of American troops through the Korean peninsula toward the People's Republic of China (PRC) in the last quarter of 1950 provided the Chinese communists with a welcome pretext for socializing society and economy in the atmosphere of an existential threat emanating from an ideological enemy. The new regime had originally planned to permit the continuation of capitalist methods of economic organization in order to allow the country to recover from decades of civil war. The Korean War provided the opportunity to establish a socialist order in the PRC itself and to weed out opposition at an earlier date than projected. The new Chinese leadership thereby used Stalinist methods from the 1930s, including show trials and the instigation of systematic lethal violence against supposed class enemies. In addition, the CCP made the reading of Stalin's bible of communism, the so-called *Short Course* of 1938, mandatory for cadres above a certain rank. Similarly, after the Chinese intervention in the Korean War and the reoccupation of the northern half of the country by early 1951, North Korea's strongman Kim Il-sung introduced his own form of Stalinist dictatorship through purges of supposedly unreliable cadres, the socialization of society and economy, and the introduction of a personality cult.[14]

The military conflict in Northeast Asia had consequences even in Eastern Europe. The *de facto* formation of two hostile military blocs in the wake of the Korean War was yet another impetus for the Socialist Camp to focus on economic and political consolidation in Eastern Europe. The experience was not uniform but was still analogous for much of the period until 1953. Usually with Stalin's approval but sometimes against his explicit counsel for caution, Poland, Czechoslovakia, Hungary, Romania, Bulgaria, Albania, and the German Democratic Republic (GDR, East Germany; established in 1949) implemented policies similar to those which the great dictator had pushed through in the Soviet Union in the 1930s. They included the nationalization of businesses and factories, heavy industrial development projects, radical rural reform, the use of indoctrination and mass terror, and show trials of alleged traitors, saboteurs, and supposed Titoists. However, these policies also expressed a widely shared belief among Eastern European communist leaders, which an East German slogan from the time perfectly captured: "To learn from the Soviet brother means to learn how to be victorious."[15]

De-Stalinization, 1953–56

In 1954, the famous Soviet author Ilya Ehrenburg compared de-Stalinization to a *Thaw* that melted the shield of Stalinist ice, which had been heavily weighing on the Socialist Camp. The dictator's death on March 5, 1953, had shattered the emotional and intellectual certainty of millions of communist cadres throughout the world. Stalin had symbolized the center of world revolution for a quarter of a century. But his successors understood that he had created a dysfunctional socio-economic and political system, and that his foreign policy had helped to create an international environment in which the Soviet Union was isolated and under threat. The question was how to crack the shield of ideological ice, reform the Soviet system, and undo the damage in international politics. In effect, de-Stalinization started in the USSR within a fortnight of Stalin's passing with the rehabilitation of individual victims.[16]

The post-Stalinist leadership quickly reviewed the political excesses in socialist Eastern Europe. Since it feared that the survival of the communist regimes in some countries was under threat, the new leadership invited delegations from the GDR, Hungary, and Albania to Moscow in June 1953 for discussions about past mistakes and future reforms. The Soviet bid to impose a *New Course* produced three entirely different outcomes. East German attempts to undo some of the recently intro-duced Stalinist economic policies publicly revealed the regime's illegiti-macy and brittleness. The party's inability to deal with the rising popular dissatisfaction triggered the workers' uprising in East Berlin on June 16, 1953. Spreading through the whole country within twenty-four hours, it forced Walter Ulbricht and his fellow party leaders to flee to the Soviet military headquarters for safety. The uprising came as a surprise to the Soviets, who quickly came to the dubious conclusion that hostile forces in the West had instigated a counter-revolution. If Soviet occupation forces had not put down the revolt quickly, it possibly would have overthrown the communist regime in East Germany and maybe even spread to neighboring Poland. The unrelated arrest on June 26 of Lavrentii Beria, who was accused by his fellow post-Stalinist Soviet leaders of seizing power in Moscow, allowed Ulbricht to brand his reform-minded internal critics as Beria's allies, and thereby enabled him to abrogate the New Course altogether. With regard to Hungary, Moscow insisted on the prime ministerial appointment of the moderate Imre Nagy, who subse-quently introduced sensible socio-economic reforms. But Stalin's self-styled best disciple Mátyás Rákosi was allowed to stay on as party leader – a function which he subsequently used to orchestrate Nagy's sacking in April 1955 on trumped-up charges. Albania's long-time dictator Enver Hoxha, by comparison, stymied any Soviet attempt to impose reform from the very beginning by quickly purging possible rivals and moderates. In Romania, Bulgaria, and Poland, however, communist parties acted on their own initiative to relax repression or undo some of the excessive socio-economic policies of the late Stalinist era. Only Czechoslovakia continued with the same repressive policies – even in the face of protests, which it quickly suppressed with military force.[17]

With de-Stalinization continuing at an irregular pace in the USSR itself, the emerging Soviet strongman Nikita S. Khrushchev tried to relax foreign relations beyond the Socialist Camp. In view of the West German entry into NATO in May 1955, he proposed to US President Dwight D. Eisenhower negotiations on disarmament. Even if the Soviet leader himself did not believe that the proposal would lead to any success, he still hoped that it would help ease international tensions during the Soviet–American–British–French summit in Geneva in July. As it turned out, his assessment was spot on. The legendary *Geneva Spirit* celebrated the willingness of the great powers to negotiate at the highest level, but also served to disguise the lack of real agreement. Khrushchev's attempt to mend fences with Tito two months earlier had been similarly ephem-eral. The Russian leader's visit to Belgrade was full of contrition about Stalin's erroneous decisions seven years earlier, but the Yugoslav host was not willing to give up his non-aligned position in international affairs and submit to Soviet leadership again.[18]

Eventually, the year 1956 revealed the limits of de-Stalinization throughout the whole socialist world. The need to deal systematically with Stalin's crimes against party and country convinced the Soviet leadership to commission a report that formed the basis of Khrushchev's famous Secret Speech on February 25. Read to a closed nocturnal meeting, which occurred after the official end of the twentieth congress of the Communist Party of the Soviet Union (CPSU), it documented Stalin's crimes against the party and his mistakes in foreign policy. While this critical assessment finally opened the door to cultural liberalization and socio-economic reform in the USSR itself, it encountered mostly rejection within the Socialist Camp. Once the communist regimes in Eastern Europe and East Asia had the chance to escape Stalin's long shadow, many decided to cling to the dictator's legacy. De-Stalinization threatened to open a Pandora's box that could undermine regime stability and survival.[19]

Only Poland and Hungary provided a brief exception. The death of Poland's own Stalin – Bolesław Bierut – shortly after Khrushchev's Secret Speech raised the possibility of the return of Władysław Gomułka, who had been removed from power for his criticism of the Yugoslav expulsion from the Cominform in 1948. The brutal suppression of protesters in Poznań in mid 1956 further discredited the interim Polish party leadership to such a degree that it proposed of its own accord that Gomułka should return to power at the eighth plenum on October 19–21. The Soviet leadership tried to prevent this through military intimidation and the dispatch of a high-ranking delegation under Khrushchev's leadership. Yet the two sides managed to resolve the conflict with an agreement that allowed increased Polish autonomy in domestic affairs as long as the country did not question the socialist form of its government and its membership in the Warsaw Pact.[20]

However, on October 23, just as the Polish crisis subsided, the Hungarian Revolution erupted. In the summer, the Soviet leadership had forced Rákosi into retirement, but decided not to reinstall the recently sacked Nagy. But Gomułka's return to power in neighboring Poland triggered mass demonstrations in Budapest, to which the regime's security forces first replied with lethal force before crumbling within twenty-four hours. Events in Budapest unfolded faster than Moscow could react. Day after day, the Soviet leadership had to endorse one compromise after another, which the Hungarian comrades were making under popular pressure. When the Soviet leaders started to entertain the idea of using Nagy in some form to placate the unrest, the Hungarian party had already reappointed him as prime minister. By October 30,

Moscow believed that the situation in Budapest was beyond political and military control, and decided to withdraw its occupation forces. In response, Nagy endorsed popular demands for Hungary to depart from the Warsaw Pact and become a Western-style, multi-party democracy. With that, however, he had crossed the line, which the Polish and Soviet comrades had drawn to defuse the crisis in Warsaw. After a night of discussions, the CPSU Presidium decided in the morning of November 1 to intervene. Leaving the Socialist Camp was beyond question for Hungary, particularly given its geographical frontline status in Europe's Cold War. The Suez Crisis, as described in the previous chapter, provided the perfect cover for the military intervention.[21]

The Sino–Soviet Rift, 1956–60

In the years between 1956 and 1968, socialist fraternal parties criticized de-Stalinization not because Soviet reforms did not go far enough but because the Soviet comrades had supposedly allowed them to run out of control. A case in point was communist China, but so were East Germany and Albania. Mao Zedong quickly realized that the Secret Speech was a threat to him personally – primarily because of the criticism of policy mistakes, the personality cult, and single-handed decision-making. He decided to endorse criticisms of Stalin in principle, but only if they concerned mistakes which the great dictator supposedly had committed in relation to the Chinese Revolution. This allowed Mao to avoid discussions of the essence of Khrushchev's assessment, which could also be used against him, while it simultaneously enabled him to appear as the true victim of Stalin's errors. Still, he was unable to suppress all of his party's attempts to limit his power. The first session of the eighth congress of the Chinese Communist Party (CCP) in September of 1956 curtailed his prerogatives, removed his writings (in the versions revised with Soviet assistance earlier in the decade) from the list of mandatory readings for party members, and called for collective leadership by the Politburo.[22]

It did not take long for Mao to seize an opportunity to return to his pre-eminent status in decision making. Despite the minor and inconsistent role which a CCP delegation played in the resolution of the Polish October and the Hungarian Revolution, the Chinese leaders convinced themselves that their resolve and ideologically correct advice to the CPSU had saved the unity of the Socialist Camp. Mao himself concluded that, while Stalinism had erroneous aspects, it still was Marxism, and that the "so-called de-Stalinization thus is simply de-Marxification, it is *revisionism*." Still, the chairman feared the possibility of a Hungarian-style revolution in the PRC itself. In an effort to learn from Stalin's mistakes, he proposed the controlled liberalization of domestic politics in order to incite potential counter-revolutionaries to come forward and to catch them in the process. However, the criticism which Chinese cadres and specialists raised in the spring of 1957 during supervised and controlled meetings revealed the great depth of political disaffection. The party leadership thus decided to react with a major purge of alleged counter-revolutionaries, using methods akin to those employed by Stalin in the Soviet Union of the 1930s.[23]

The launch of the Great Leap Forward in 1958 had its roots in these Stalinist purges and Khrushchev's concurrent but unrelated announcement that the USSR would surpass the United States in heavy industrial production within ten years. In order not to be outdone by the supposedly revisionist Khrushchev, Mao instigated the Great Leap Forward – a major socio-economic initiative designed to compel the PRC into the communist stage of history ahead of the USSR. The rapid communization of industry, agriculture, and societal life served as a deliberate ideological challenge to Soviet leadership of the Socialist Camp. The chairman even claimed that his country would improve Stalin's methods and find the pathway toward communism, which the late dictator supposedly had failed to do. But Mao's reckless ideas only led to rapid chaos in China's economy and massive, lethal spring famines over several years.[24]

Mao's manifest move in April 1960 to disclose publicly the ideological disagreements between his PRC and the allegedly revisionist USSR poured more oil onto the fire, particularly as that year's spring famine cost tens of millions of Chinese lives. The Soviet downing of an American U-2 spy plane on May 1, 1960, served as additional ammunition for Mao's attack on the supposedly revisionist Khrushchev. Under double pressure from Mao and from conservative generals at home, the Soviet leader thus decided to ruin the French–American–British–Soviet summit in Paris later that month. Yet this solved neither Khrushchev's disputes with the Chinese comrades nor his disagreements with the American imperialists. The fallout between the largest communist countries eventually occurred at the eighth Romanian Party Congress in June 1960 where Khrushchev attacked Mao, whom he by now considered "an exact copy" of Stalin. Shortly thereafter, Moscow announced the withdrawal of all Soviet military and economic advisers and specialists from the PRC. However, this provided Beijing with the opportunity to blame the Soviet Union for the unrelated collapse of China's economy. Through Vietnamese communist mediation, the CPSU and the CCP eventually agreed on a temporary ideological truce at the Moscow meeting of the world's communist parties in November 1960.[25]

The Berlin Crisis, 1958–61

Ulbricht's criticism of de-Stalinization was less crude than Mao's and anyway aimed more at Khrushchev's policy of peaceful coexistence with the West than at Soviet reforms. Liberated from the need to follow the *New Course* after Beria's arrest in June 1953, he continued to establish a socialist East Germany that was supposed to outcompete the larger, capitalist part of the divided country – the Federal Republic of Germany (FRG). While he had given up hope for a rapid reunification, he still believed that the construction of a successful and prosperous socialist East Germany would persuade capitalist West Germany to seek reunification on his terms. His policies after June 1953 continued along the same Stalinist lines as in the years before, i.e. he tried to introduce a heavily centralized, planned, and militarized socio-economic system. But there was one major blemish in his calculations: the FRG still developed much faster. Taking note, East German citizens voted with their feet, first across the long line of the country's division, and then, after its closure in 1957, across the lightly guarded border in divided Berlin. But Ulbricht did not blame his own policies for the refugee stream. Instead, he held Khrushchev's lack of economic and political support responsible for the malaise. Given that his policy of convincing the FRG to join the GDR had not succeeded, his revised goal became the eradication of the Western presence in Berlin, which was enormously appealing to disaffected East German citizens.[26]

Ulbricht's self-inflicted destabilization of the GDR – a front state in the European Cold War – increasingly worried the Soviet leaders. In September 1958, Khrushchev issued his famous Berlin ultimatum, demanding negotiations on West Berlin while threatening unilateral action. He pointed out – with some justification – that the original agreements of the victorious World War II Allies with regard to the occupation of Germany and Berlin had become meaningless given the realities of the Cold War. But the Soviet leader was probably not completely serious about removing the Western presence from Berlin because he would thereby have lost an important political lever for extracting concessions from the imperialist–capitalist world on a whole range of related and unrelated issues. Indeed, the ultimatum netted Khrushchev an invitation to the United States for September 1959 for talks with US President Dwight D. Eisenhower. Having reached American recognition of Soviet equality in the Cold War, the Soviet leader withdrew his Berlin ultimatum while in the United States. During his subsequent visit to Beijing at the occasion of the tenth anniversary of the PRC, Khrushchev wasted no time rubbing in his newly achieved rank in international relations.[27]

Having been denied the prize he had coveted so much, Ulbricht decided to escalate the crisis around Berlin in the following two years gradually through propaganda and provocations on the ground. The resulting increase of the refugee stream to West Berlin allowed him to push Khrushchev to accept his plan to close the borders in Berlin completely.[28] The collapse of the Soviet rapprochement policies in the wake of the U-2 affair in May 1960 reduced the potential damage which radical action in Berlin would cause to Soviet–American relations.[29] In early August 1961, Khrushchev warned the members of the Warsaw Pact of a collapse of the GDR if the Socialist Camp refused to provide political, military, and economic support. Otherwise revanchist West Germany, in a repetition of the aggression of 1939 and 1941, "will move forward to the Polish border ... [and] to our Soviet border." By collectively strengthening the East German position, he concluded, "we strengthen our own position." In the night from August 12 to 13, East German forces occupied the perimeter of West Berlin, severing the last physical connections between both sides of the city and, by extension, the country. Ulbricht had not gotten West Berlin, but at least he had obtained a second chance to construct socialism in the GDR under stable demographic conditions, while saving the stability of the Socialist Camp in the process. Ironically, with the refugee stream stopped, he opted for relatively liberal economic policies to try to surpass the FRG. Ultimately, he failed in this endeavor too, while the permanent imprisonment of the East German population served as an enduring public declaration of defeat in the global competition between socialism and capitalism.[30]

Albania, China, Romania, and Vietnam, 1960–65

The Berlin Wall did not stop the centrifugal forces that de-Stalinization had unleashed elsewhere in the Socialist Camp. On the contrary, the Warsaw Pact meeting shortly before the closure of the borders in Berlin triggered the Soviet–Albanian split. Ulbricht had called the gathering to receive political backing for his plans in Berlin, but Albania provoked its own exclusion from the meeting by dispatching a low-ranking delegation in a show of contempt. The incident was the last straw in the mounting Soviet–Albanian dispute. The small Balkan country had rejected de-Stalinization and Soviet attempts of rapprochement with Yugoslavia from the very beginning. The Sino–Soviet clash at the 8th Romanian Party congress in June 1960 had irritated the Albanian party, although it had refused to take sides yet. The refusal to back Moscow during the temporary Sino–Soviet ideological reconciliation in late 1960 cost Tirana all of its Soviet economic aid. Over the course of the first eight months of 1961, military relations with the USSR that were crucial to Albania's

security also deteriorated to such a degree that Moscow decided to withdraw its entire Mediterranean fleet from Albania's sole naval base.[31]

The Soviet–Albanian fallout in August 1961 fueled the Sino–Soviet split.
After the collapse of the Great Leap Forward in late 1960, the Politburo had
sidelined Mao in daily decision-making. His fellow leaders Zhou Enlai, Liu
Shaoqi, and Deng Xiaoping also abolished many of his outlandish policies
for the sake of market mechanisms to jumpstart China's economy. The
chairman, however, feared that this would reintroduce capitalism into
China through the back door. Following the riotous eighth Romanian
Party Congress, he had not only embraced the Albanian party as the only
communist party supposedly standing up to Khrushchev but also granted
economic assistance to replace what the revisionist Soviet leader just had
cut. Mao exploited both the Soviet–Albanian fallout in August of 1961 and
the subsequent decision of the twenty-second CPSU Congress to remove
Stalin's body from the Lenin Mausoleum in Moscow to push his anti-
revisionist and anti-Soviet positions at home. The use of ideologically supercharged rhetoric allowed him to tie the sensible economic recovery policies,
which Zhou, Liu, and Deng implemented in the PRC, to the economic
reform policies of the supposedly revisionist Khrushchev. Mao's political use
of the Soviet–Albanian split and his attacks on Soviet revisionism for domestic purposes ultimately helped him to regain pre-eminence in decision-
making in the summer of 1962. But while he had thereby won an important
battle against his fellow leaders, he had not won the war against Soviet and
domestic revisionism. Over the following four years, he continued to exploit
Sino–Soviet disagreements for domestic political gain. The USSR delivered
timely ammunition for this enterprise when it negotiated the Limited Test
Ban Treaty (LTBT) with the United States and the United Kingdom in the
summer of 1963. Mao's campaign against Soviet ideological revisionism
and supposed surrender to US imperialism included the public claim that
the center of world revolution had moved from Moscow to Beijing. In mid
1966, he launched the Cultural Revolution with the purpose of purging
allegedly revisionist and capitalist internal enemies and establishing an
ideologically pure communist society.[32]

In comparison, the Romanian–Soviet estrangement was less about
ideology than about the reassertion of national autonomy against Soviet
hegemony. Despite some policy corrections following Stalin's death,
Romania never underwent de-Stalinization until the collapse of communism in late 1989. Instead, its communist leaders played the nationalist
card to gain legitimacy. After proving its loyalty to the USSR during the
Hungarian Revolution, Bucharest managed to convince Moscow by 1958
to withdraw Soviet occupation troops. Romania used the argument that
the country was surrounded by socialist states (even if Yugoslavia was not

a member of the Socialist Camp) and thus not in need of Soviet military protection. During the Sino–Soviet clashes at its party congress in June 1960, the Romanian party sided with the CPSU. In the spring of 1963, Bucharest tried to mediate between Beijing and Moscow. But the subsequent talks between the CCP and the CPSU party delegations in the Soviet capital in mid-year – which occurred in parallel and close proximity to the successful Soviet–American–British negotiations on the Limited Test Ban Treaty – were nothing more than shouting matches. In the wake of the failed Sino–Soviet reconciliation, the USSR proposed Outer Mongolian membership in the Warsaw Pact, with the implicit intention of turning the European military alliance into an anti-Chinese accord. Romania was the only member to balk at assuming alliance obligations outside Europe, forcing Khrushchev to drop the idea. Irritated, Romania moved toward a middle position between the quarreling communist brothers. Moreover, Bucharest clandestinely indicated to Washington late in 1963 that it would not honor its military alliance obligations toward Moscow in the case of global war.[33]

By the mid 1960s, the ideological divisions ran so deep in the Socialist Camp that it was unable to cooperate in the face of the second military attack by US imperialism against one of its members. The American military advance through the Korean peninsula toward northeastern China in late 1950 had led to greater, though uneasy, coordination between the USSR and the PRC. The American escalation of the Vietnam War after August 1964, however, did not help to bridge the deep divisions between the two communist powers. Beijing and Moscow engaged in bickering over ideology and military strategy, and each accused the other of encouraging American aggression. While the Democratic Republic of Vietnam (DRV; North Vietnam) could benefit from the military and economic aid competition between its two main allies, their squabbles, and the Cultural Revolution after mid 1966, still gravely complicated its efforts on the battlefield.[34]

The Intervention in Czechoslovakia and its Repercussions, 1968–75

The Socialist Camp entered the second half of the 1960s without Yugoslavia, China, and Albania. Hence Moscow grew concerned about the camp's continued fragmentation and the multitude of problems which it faced at many places along its periphery, particularly in Indochina and the Middle East. Following Khrushchev's fall in October 1964, the new Soviet leadership under the duumvirate of Leonid I. Brezhnev and Aleksei N. Kosygin signaled to Ulbricht its displeasure over his economic reform program, particularly since the East German leader insinuated that his GDR was moving toward the communist end of history ahead of the USSR. Luckily for the Soviet leaders, Ulbricht's comrades did not share his enthusiasm for reform either, but set about gradually curtailing his program.[35]

The political liberalization that started in Czechoslovakia in early 1968 was another matter. As one of the three important socialist frontline states in the European Cold War, Czechoslovakia had resisted de-Stalinization and survived the existential crises of the other two frontline states – the GDR in 1953 and 1961, and Hungary in 1956. Oddly out of step with developments in the rest of the Socialist Camp since the end of World War II, the Czechoslovak Communist Party under the leadership of its new first secretary, Alexander Dubček, embarked on political reforms in 1968 at a time when this proved inopportune. In the wake of the Sino–Soviet clashes at the Romanian Party Congress in June 1960 and Khrushchev's renewed denunciations of Stalin at the twenty-second CPSU Congress in October 1961, Czechoslovakia had started its own economic reforms, which continued even after the rise of the conservative Brezhnev. The ensuing political reforms in the spring of 1968 aimed at creating a "socialism with a human face" that included the abolition of censorship, the free circulation of Western media products, the opening of the borders to West Germany and Austria for tourists, and reforms in the field of nationality and economic policies. For the first time since February 1948, the Czechoslovak Communist Party enjoyed some degree of genuine popularity. At no point did the reform program question the leading role of the party, the socialist nature of the Czechoslovak state, or the country's membership in the Warsaw Pact. In that respect, the Prague Spring, with its exclusive focus on internal socialist reforms, was closer to the Polish October than the Hungarian Revolution a dozen years earlier.[36]

Yet the USSR and Czechoslovakia's socialist neighbors saw another Hungarian Revolution unfolding. Over the spring and summer of 1968, they convinced themselves that Czechoslovakia was on the verge of leaving the Socialist Camp and that this threatened to undermine their security. Gomułka, who had benefited from the compromise with Khrushchev on internal autonomy in late 1956, feared that Czechoslovakia might turn into a "bourgeois democracy." And the Hungarian leader János Kádár compared the situation in Prague with the one in Budapest in October 1956. By late July 1968, Moscow was convinced that a Hungarian-style "counter-revolutionary coup" via a "peaceful, evolutionary path" was on the way. The combined intervention of Soviet and allied Warsaw Pact troops on August 20–21 aimed at restoring the correct kind of socialism. In mid

November, Brezhnev announced what would become his Cold War doctrine: socialist states had only limited sovereignty, and the USSR had the right to intervene wherever it believed the socialist order was under threat.[37]

The Soviet policy of shoring up a *rump*-Socialist Camp in Eastern Europe in the face of increasing disunity within the larger socialist world managed to enforce a semblance of unity – but at enormous costs. The intervention rendered the rump-camp essentially unreformable. As we shall see in Chapter 16 on the Council for Mutual Economic Assistance (CMEA), the economies of the European socialist countries were suffering from a range of economic problems by the late 1960s, including energy shortages, the inability to innovate, and the emergence of the rival market in the European Economic Community (today's European Union) in the western half of the continent. Even though Soviet leaders understood the need for economic reforms, the intervention in Czechoslovakia in August 1968 dampened the rump-camp's enthusiasm to undertake them. Within some socialist states, like East Germany, the regime further tightened the screws to stamp out alleged counter-revolutionary activities – a move that additionally limited the party's ability to harness potentially useful but unorthodox ideas. And conservative forces in the German Democratic Republic (GDR) went into action in 1970–71 to replace Ulbricht, whose ideas on economic restructuring and attempts at rapprochement with the FRG were highly suspect to them. In comparison, the Soviet-installed regime in Czechoslovakia followed an ostensible policy of official non-acknowledgment of the Prague Spring, which drove – and in some respects was designed to do so – its citizens into acquiescence, resignation, and even withdrawal from the public sphere.[38]

Thus, the dozen or so years after 1968 – the so-called Brezhnev years – signified a period of economic stagnation and political ossification in most of the *rump*-Socialist Camp. At the beginning of the 1970s, Soviet and East European leaders fully realized that their countries were lagging behind the capitalist world in economic development. The solution pursued, however, once more did not entail a conceptual rethink of the Soviet economic system, but simply the importation of Western technology on the basis of Western loans in order to modernize production. Unsuccessful, this policy ultimately caused a lowering of living standards and a massive increase in foreign debt – a double phenomenon that raised the specter of state bankruptcies in Bulgaria, Poland, and East Germany within a little more than a decade. Hedged in by languid party bureaucracies, massive foreign debt, disillusioned populations, and Soviet energy supply problems, communist regimes in the rump-camp were still unable to embark on economic reform in the 1980s. Instead, the lack of economic power threatened Soviet hegemony over Eastern Europe in the final decade of the Cold War, as this book's concluding chapters reveal.[39]

Equally dramatic was the damage that the intervention in Czechoslovakia caused in the wider socialist world. Among the European socialist states, Romania and Yugoslavia sharply criticized the alleged Soviet restoration of socialism. Both had warned beforehand that such a move would undermine the cause of socialism at a global level, and both had supported Czechoslovakia's reformers through high-level visits, political advice, and public declarations. After August 20–21, both feared a similar Soviet military intervention because of their ideologically heterodox stances. Romania's leader, Nicolae Ceaușescu, publicly criticized the Soviet intervention, despite the fact that his support for the Czechoslovak cause had primarily domestic reasons and was not at all based on his own love of reform. He subsequently used the middle position, into which he maneuvered his country, to offer himself as an intermediary in international relations, such as during Sino–American rapprochement in 1969 and in the Middle East in the early 1970s. In turn, Western leaders courted him, and Romania entered the International Monetary Fund (IMF) in late 1972 as the first socialist country. But Ceaușescu's Stalinist domestic policies turned Romania into Europe's poor house by the 1980s, and him into one of the most loathed communist leaders. In comparison, in the fall of 1968, Tito's Yugoslavia turned away from its recent pro-Soviet stance, which it had assumed following the Middle East crisis the previous year, back toward non-alignment.[40]

Among East Asian socialist states, the reaction to the events in Czechoslovakia was mixed. The Chinese communists had been completely unsympathetic to the Czechoslovak revisionists on ideological grounds. But the intervention raised fears of a similar Soviet action against the PRC designed to restore Soviet-style communism there. Mao thus invented the term "socialist imperialism" to criticize the Soviet-led intervention in Czechoslovakia. The further deterioration of bilateral relations, including several military clashes at the border in 1969, helped trigger Sino–American rapprochement in 1971–72. The DRV, however, sided with the USSR. Although Beijing's ally since the early 1950s, Hanoi grew concerned by April 1968 that Prague's revisionism would undermine the remaining fraternal unity, which it considered crucial for its war effort. It vociferously supported military intervention in Czechoslovakia. The year 1968 thus became an important marker in the country's decade-long march from pro-Chinese positions toward a pro-Soviet stance.[41]

And finally, the heavy-handed Soviet policies toward Czechoslovakia drove Western European communist parties away, although the intervention in August 1968 was only a waypoint in a long process of alienation from the USSR. Shortly before his death in a Soviet hospital in August 1964, Stalin's man in Italy, PCI leader Togliatti, penned a manifesto that called on his party to find its own path toward socialism. By early 1966, his successor, Luigi Longo, convinced the party to return to positions from before the first Cominform conference in 1947. Like Ceaușescu and Tito, Longo warned the Soviet leaders not to meddle in Czechoslovakia in July 1968. On holiday in Moscow at the time of the actual intervention, he hurriedly flew to Paris to find a common position of dissent with the PCF, but failed. The French party itself was still undergoing a political transformation after its long-time Stalinist leader, Maurice Thorez, had died on the way to a Soviet hospital, just a month before Togliatti's demise. Shortly before Khrushchev's overthrow on October 14, 1964, the PCF declared its autonomy from the Socialist Camp. Yet the subsequent political opening toward the non-communist left did not bring any success in the elections in December 1965, March 1966, and June 1968. The PCF remained torn over the Soviet intervention in Czechoslovakia. At least, at the Moscow conference of the world's communist parties in June of 1969, the PCI and the PCF sternly criticized Soviet policies toward both Prague and Beijing. But internal debates about the correct political path continued to paralyze both parties for some time.[42]

Thus, the emergence of Eurocommunism took another six years. Under the reform leadership of Enrico Berlinguer, the PCI was the first of all Western European communist parties to try to transform European communism into a modern democratic force. In January 1974, it organized a conference of Western European communist parties with the goal of defining a third way between Western liberalism and Soviet communism, but failed due to the strident anti-Americanism of other parties. In November 1975, eventually, the PCI and the PCF agreed on a joint Eurocommunist platform that discarded violent revolution in favor of the democratic path toward socialism. On that occasion, the two parties rejected Soviet leadership because of Moscow's unwillingness to accept dissent. Indeed, the Soviet refusal to allow the dissident Andrei D. Sakharov to travel to Stockholm to accept the Nobel Peace Prize had brought the two parties together. Half a year later, twenty-nine European communist parties met in East Berlin to discuss a common program but the anti-Soviet criticism of the Italian, French, and recently legalized Spanish parties spoiled any chance of a consensus.[43] Within thirty years, Stalin's revolutionary empire had crumbled.

Conclusion

The Socialist Camp in Europe was brittle from the very beginning. In order to construct a stable sphere of influence that could provide security to the USSR, Stalin chose to install communist regimes against the popular will of the majority. Geography dictated some of the solutions which he imposed. Without a communist East Germany occupied by Soviet troops, Moscow would have lost its claim to hegemony over Czechoslovakia, another state on the Cold War frontline, and Poland in the hinterland. Furthermore, the frontline state Hungary geographically connected the northern and southern parts of the Soviet sphere of influence in Eastern Europe. Ironically, the greatest challenges to Soviet hegemony occurred exactly in these three frontline states: in 1953, 1956, 1958–61, and 1968. Several other states in the Socialist Camp – Yugoslavia, Albania, the PRC, and communist Vietnam – joined Stalin's empire on their own accord. But all of them – bar one – chose to leave again, as did some of the communist parties outside the socialist world.

While Soviet security needs were crucial for the establishment of Stalin's hegemony over Eastern Europe, they cannot exclusively explain his need to implant communist regimes there. In reality, ideology mattered to him as much as it did to so many of the member states of the Socialist Camp. Although cautious, Stalin had always been a communist believer willing to export revolution whenever possible. Similarly, Mao was a hard-core believer, too, otherwise he would not have embarked on the radical and misguided Great Leap Forward. Ceaușescu might have used nationalism to position his country in between the Cold War powers, but he also remained a committed Stalinist to his last breath. Security interests cannot explain why Hoxha found it necessary to decry Tito's Yugoslavia or Khrushchev's Soviet Union as revisionist. Ultimately, the camp needed Stalin and his brand of rule to survive. His death in 1953 questioned the *raison d'être* of his entire empire. De-Stalinization, while politically necessary, shattered the ideological unity of the Socialist Camp. No amount of good will or force could bring it back together. The attempt in 1968 to shore up a rump-camp only prolonged its agony.

4   The United States and the Free World

The term *Free World* emerged in American political discourse in May 1940 in the wake of Germany's attack on Belgium, the Netherlands, and France. It denoted all those democracies that resisted the aggression of authoritarian and "world revolutionary" states, such as Adolf Hitler's National Socialist Germany, its Italian fascist brother, its militarist ally Japan, and its most recent collaborator – Iosif V. Stalin's Soviet Union. In January 1941, US President Franklin D. Roosevelt explicitly called on Congress to grant military aid to the "free world." But in the wake of the American entry into the war on the side of the Soviet Union eleven months later, Roosevelt used the term primarily to mean the "United Nations" which struggled against Germany, Italy, and Japan. In US public discourse, it more generally referred to the post-war period of peace. By June 1945, however, Western newspapers again depicted the Free World as a group of liberal democracies, which, this time, were primarily in conflict with Stalin's USSR.[1]

Stalin's quip that each great power would establish its political system in whatever territory its army occupied generally did not apply to the US sphere of influence that emerged after the end of World War II. At its core, the American-led Free World included democracies that joined voluntarily (the United Kingdom, Australia, New Zealand, and Turkey), democracies that re-emerged after liberation (Norway, Denmark, the Netherlands, Luxembourg, Belgium, France, Italy, and Greece), and democracies that were established by the United States after the war (Germany and Japan). In spite of Washington's commitment to promoting decolonization, its support for democracy and self-determination lapsed in several cases during the Cold War. Hence, as the Soviet–American conflict unfolded, the Free World included states, particularly in Asia, that were anti-communist but authoritarian (the Republic of China on Taiwan, the Republic of Vietnam, Pakistan, Indonesia, Cambodia, and the Philippines). In the Arab world, anti-communist partners (Iraq until 1958, and Jordan and Saudi Arabia after 1956) were cooperating with the United States, but were not formally allied. In one case only – the Republic of Korea (South Korea) – the United States itself installed, though without a premeditated plan, an authoritarian regime. And in another case – Iran in 1953 – it was involved in overthrowing a government suspected of pro-Soviet sympathies. Still, the American spheres of influence were fundamentally different from Soviet hegemony. Washington led a Free World that included a substantial number of democracies; Moscow ruled a Socialist Camp that consisted only of authoritarian regimes.

The shared commitment to anti-communism created a surprisingly flexible structure that helped to hold the politically heterogeneous and geographically fragmented Free World together. This structure allowed members to pursue their own internal and external policies to a much larger degree than most of the members of the Socialist Camp. Unlike the Soviet Union, the United States never used military force to suppress political change in an allied European country, as, for example, in Charles de Gaulle's recalcitrant France in the 1960s, though it made its displeasure known through diplomatic channels. In general, the American hegemon left its allies in Europe almost completely free to run their own affairs, and even awarded them with far-reaching participation in deciding questions of collective interest. The mostly authoritarian partners in Asia and the Middle East, too, enjoyed a greater amount of agency, even if some of them were heavily dependent on American economic and military aid. While the loose structure of the Free World occasionally threatened to undermine cohesion, it ultimately allowed American Cold War partners to launch extraordinary initiatives. As some of the later chapters reveal, Western European countries greatly shaped their own integration process – though with gentle American support. West Germany and the Vatican pioneered détente in Europe in the 1960s – despite US reluctance. And the European Community successfully struggled to include human rights in the Conference on Security and Cooperation in Europe (CSCE) in the early 1970s – against the long-time opposition of the United States. All of this not only testified to the continued flexibility of the Free World during the Cold War but also allowed structural change that helped to end the global Cold War during the late 1980s.

The Realm of Democracies in Western Europe

If the Soviet World War II advance across East Europe was akin to a winter storm blanketing a ruined landscape under Stalinist ice, the analogous American advance across Western Europe resembled a spring-like rain front prompting democratic rebirth. Unlike the USSR, the United States did not impose its political and socio-economic system on the formerly German-occupied countries. To be sure, Washington welcomed the rapid re-emergence of democracies, but every single European country which American and British troops liberated had a pre-World War II democratic tradition. In each case, governments either proceeded to remove collaborators (Denmark), returned from exile in London (Norway, the Netherlands, Luxembourg, and Belgium), or rebuilt themselves on the basis of pre-war traditions (France). Only Greece was an exception to this phenomenon, as Great Britain helped the self-appointed, royal exile government to return from Cairo to Athens where it enjoyed little authority.[2]

The post-war governments in Western Europe exhibited a wide range of pluralistic and democratically legitimized configurations. As one of the few Western European countries not occupied by Germany during the war, the United Kingdom held general elections on July 5, 1945, which the Conservative wartime Prime Minister Winston Churchill lost to the Labour candidate Clement Attlee. Later that year, Norway voted a Labor majority government into power, while neighboring Denmark elected a Liberal minority government. The Dutch reconfirmed in 1946 the continuation of pre-war politics with an electoral victory of a Catholic–Labor coalition. Democratically chosen national unity governments that included communists arose in Luxembourg in late 1945 and Belgium early the following year. In France, the self-appointed leader of wartime Free France, Charles de Gaulle, arrived in Paris in mid 1944 in the wake of American troops to head a three-party republican–socialist–communist provisional government. This coalition obtained democratic legitimacy in the first post-war election in June 1946. By then, however, the general had retired because he had been unable to obtain the presidential system to which he aspired. Instead, France returned for a dozen years to a pre-war parliamentary system headed by a weak president of the Council of Ministers (prime minister) – until de Gaulle's return to power in 1958. Greece, after two years of a provisional government following liberation in 1944, voted for a coalition of center-right parties. The new government, however, could not avoid the *only* civil war in democratic post-war Europe. But the communist-led insurrection eventually collapsed in the wake of the Stalin–Tito split in mid 1948.[3]

Unlike Moscow, Washington did not feel threatened by the political heterogeneity that emerged in its European sphere of influence. It never sent tanks or troops to suppress a popular uprising or overthrow a government with which it disagreed, as the Soviet Union did in 1953, 1956, and 1968. And no coup or uprising occurred in any of the European democracies, with the exception of the takeover of Greece by a right-wing military junta in 1967, about which Washington was embarrassed, at least initially. However, the United States included one existing authoritarian state in Europe's defense against Soviet communism – Portugal – though it refused to ally with Francisco Franco's Spain. In general, democratic rule in American-led Western Europe was firmly entrenched, even if some governments might have been weak in terms of political staying power – most notably in France, where twenty-two different presidents of the Council of Ministers headed twenty-seven different governments between 1944 and 1958.[4]

The United States recognized and worked with European leaders, even if this occasionally turned out to be difficult. Roosevelt accepted the provisional French government under de Gaulle's leadership, although Washington had wished for a more cooperative partner in Paris. Only during the so-called May Crisis in 1947 did the administration of President Harry S. Truman exercise diplomatic pressure on the French coalition government to expel all communist ministers, using the veiled threat of denying future economic aid. By 1947, unrelated developments in domestic politics anyway had removed communist participation in Luxembourg and Belgium, the other national unity governments in democratic Europe.[5]

As one historian once argued, the western half of Europe *asked* for US military protection and economic aid in 1946–47, and thereby heralded an American *empire by invitation*. During the war, Roosevelt certainly had envisioned the rise of a global, liberal democratic post-war order, and he probably had expected the world to be peaceful and united, particularly in Europe. The Stalinist imposition of communist regimes in Eastern Europe against the will of the majority there, the increasing division of the continent, and Soviet military and ideological threats convinced many of the war-torn post-war democracies in Western Europe that joining the American sphere of influence voluntarily was preferential to being forcibly incorporated into the Soviet empire. In response to Western European entreaties, Washington offered military and economic aid, though under the condition that the European democracies would resolve historical animosities among themselves first. While the Brussels Pact – the Western European defense organization of 1948 – never amounted to much, the Marshall Plan fostered economic integration on the continent, as described in a later chapter.[6]

Turning Enemies into Allies

In the immediate post-World War II year, the political and economic reconstruction of the former enemies quickly turned into a major, strategically necessary task. Roosevelt and Churchill had announced at the Casablanca Conference in early 1943 that the Allies "were determined to accept nothing less than unconditional surrender of Germany, Japan, and Italy." But when the Roosevelt administration started to ponder policies for post-war Italy in May 1943, the Mediterranean country was on the verge of switching sides in the war. In the wake of Benito Mussolini's fall from power in July and Italy's declaration of war on Germany soon thereafter, the Big Three agreed on the post-war establishment of a democratic order that included all politicians that had "always opposed fascism." With regard to Germany and Japan, Washington wanted to drive defeat home to prevent the re-emergence of political myths that would allow revanchist movements, similar to Hitler's National Socialist Party after 1918, to regain power. Yet, before the end of the war, the Roosevelt administration did not settle on concrete plans for Germany. Its officials actually disagreed on whether or not to dismember and de-industrialize that country. For Japan, in comparison, Washington formulated a vague plan of demilitarization, political liberalization, and institutional and economic reform.[7]

Anyway, developments on the ground quickly rendered most wartime plans moot. In Italy in 1943, the American–British–Canadian occupation forces entered a constitutional monarchy with more or less functioning political institutions, despite two decades of fascist government. But the country was also caught in an intense political competition between the socialist- and communist-led partisan movement, on the one hand, and non-leftist parties close to the Catholic Church, on the other. Following the allied landing in Sicily in July 1943, King Vittorio Emmanuelle III had replaced Mussolini with another card-carrying fascist, Marshall Pietro Badoglio. When the new government switched sides to the Allies soon thereafter, Hitler's Germany intervened to restore Mussolini as a puppet in the northern and central parts of Italy. Following the liberation of the capital Rome in June 1944, the Committee of National Liberation convinced the king to replace Badoglio with its chairman, the independent Ivanoe Bonomi, who would lead an anti-fascist provisional government for almost a year until after German surrender in May 1945.[8]

Independently from Stalin, who was preparing compliant communist exile groups in the Soviet capital to assume power on his behalf in Eastern Europe, Washington and London had decided by August 1943 to keep Moscow out of the formal administration of post-war Italy. The Soviet Union anyway did not participate in the liberation of Italy, while Roosevelt and Churchill also distrusted Stalin's designs on the Mediterranean country. But in 1945, Soviet–Western disagreements over unrelated issues still influenced developments in Italy. The post-liberation, anti-fascist coalition government of Christian Democrats, Socialists, and Communists, which had swept into power in June 1945 on a wave of popular excitement, did not survive even half a year. In the first post-war poll on June 2, 1946, voters approved the abolition of the discredited monarchy, endorsed the establishment of a republic, and elected the second and final coalition government between Christian Democrats, Socialists, and Communists. Despite the unfolding of the Cold War, the four World War II Allies were still able to agree on a peace treaty with Italy (and Romania, Hungary, Bulgaria, and Finland) that was signed on February 10, 1947. But three months later, as in France, the United States made the dismissal of communists from the coalition government a pre-condition for future economic aid.[9]

With regard to Germany, the Big Three had agreed at the Potsdam Conference in July 1945 to keep the country as a political and economic unit, but to rebuild its institutions from scratch. Unlike in Italy, however, the United States and its British and French allies only occupied around 70 percent of the country, with Stalin's USSR controlling the remainder. The overall worsening of relations among the Allies in the year after German surrender paralyzed any joint decision-making. The post-war economic crisis in the three Western zones, which was mainly caused by a lack of American–British–French coordination, convinced the United States to push for their step-wise economic merger. Because the extended post-World War I misery had created economic chaos in Germany, which in turn had facilitated the emergence of radical right-wing movements, the United States feared a recurrence of a similar development after World War II, though this time with a pro-Soviet bent. The decision to merge the Western zones, however, turned out to be an important fork in the road toward West German statehood by 1949. Consequently, it rendered the conclusion of a peace treaty with all of Germany unfeasible until after the end of the Cold War.[10]

Japan's post-war experience was, once again, different from Italy's and Germany's. After unconditional surrender in August 1945, Japan retained its Meiji institutions but was put under the military governorship of the strongminded American General Douglas MacArthur. Even if the Soviet Union had contributed to the country's defeat by attacking the Japanese colony of Manchuria on August 8, 1945, President Truman was determined to avoid the kind of conflict that had just emerged over Germany. Washington decided not to allow Moscow a share in the occupation, administration, and reconstruction of Japan, particularly after the USSR continued with territorial seizures even after Japan had formally surrendered on September 2. Yet, unwilling to reject Stalin's request for an occupation zone directly, President Truman passed the buck to MacArthur, who offered a completely destroyed part in central Honshu that was flanked by American occupation forces. Moscow did what the general had expected: it thanked him for the offer but dropped its original request.[11]

Because Washington had originally expected the war against Japan to continue for more than a year, it was not fully prepared for the occupation task. MacArthur and his staff consisted of seasoned military personnel and idealistic civilian administrators, who shared the conviction that Japan needed radical reform. While MacArthur and his closest military advisers wrote a new Japanese constitution in the image of the American model, the sundry group of mostly young administrators tried to impose progressive reforms across Japan – without much oversight from Washington. By late April 1947, Japanese citizens went to the first universal and free polls. The new prime minister would be appointed under the articles of MacArthur's constitution, i.e. by the Diet (the Japanese bicameral parliament) and no longer by the emperor. The Socialists unexpectedly won the plurality in the upper and lower house, while the pro-Soviet communists fared poorly.[12]

The Socialist election victory in late April and the eventual confirmation by the Diet of what turned out to be a short-lived and faction-ridden minority government happened just at the time when Washington pressured Paris and Rome to expel communist coalition partners from their respective governments. Yet simultaneity does not mean causality. Developments in Europe itself, not the surprise election results in Japan, led to American strong-arm tactics in France and Italy because the Truman administration assumed – correctly – that the PCF and PCI were under Stalin's influence. In comparison, the US occupation regime of Japan under MacArthur supported the institutional and socio-economic reform agenda of the Socialist minority government. The problem, which the Truman administration faced in Tokyo at the end of 1947, was not the new government but the unmanageable MacArthur – at a moment when the United States was rethinking its global strategy.[13]

In this context, the United States reviewed its policies toward Italy. After the first Cominform conference in September 1947, the Mediterranean country was heading toward a crisis, including the possibility of a communist coup or a communist-inspired civil war. In mid November, Washington decided to implement policies that fostered closer Italian ties to other Western European democracies, to formulate policies to "combat communist propaganda," and to prepare for the period after a possible political cataclysm in the country. Also against the background of the ongoing Greek Civil War and the pro-Soviet coup

in Czechoslovakia in early 1948, the United States used the newly established Central Intelligence Agency to finance the campaign of the Italian
Christian Democrats before the national elections in April. To this day, it
is not completely clear whether this indirect intervention or the concurrent self-destructive policies, which the Italian communists adopted after
the first Cominform conference, were responsible for the decisive victory
of the Christian Democrats. But the unexpected electoral triumph
secured non-communist rule in Italy for the rest of the Cold War.[14]

At the same time, the greater American emphasis on the political and
economic stability of West Germany and Japan as potential bulwarks
against the USSR and as regional workshops for the Free World triggered
the overhaul of policies toward all three former war enemies. This policy
adjustment paralleled the arrival of Marshall Plan aid to Germany and
Italy, and of analogous US economic assistance to Japan. Yet much of the
subsequent economic miracles in the two European countries was due to
sensible domestic policies that created two analogous social market economies capable of distributing newly created wealth across all strata. A similar
phenomenon occurred in Japan following the massive inflow of American
capital in the wake of the outbreak of the Korean War. In 1951, the United
States also decided to end its occupation regime there with a unilateral
peace treaty, signed only by the Western World War II Allies.[15] Thus, by
the early 1950s, the Cold War had witnessed Italy's re-emergence as
a sovereign and universally recognized republic, West Germany's rise
as an occupied and semi-sovereign democracy, and Japan's reappearance
as a sovereign but only partially recognized state. All three former World
War II enemies had joined American spheres of influence within less than
a decade after the war, not by invitation, but by incorporation.

Authoritarian Allies

With the creation of a ring of anti-communist alliances around the Socialist
Camp in the wake of the Korean War, the United States started to integrate
undemocratic and authoritarian regimes in Asia and the Middle East into
the defense of the Free World. Yet direct US involvement in the creation of
these allies varied from country to country. With regard to the Republic of
China on Taiwan, authoritarianism pre-dated the Cold War, or, as in the
case of the Republic of Vietnam, at least anteceded the American alliance.
In the Middle East, the integration into anti-Soviet alignments provided
legitimacy to the existing undemocratic regimes. In the Republic of Korea
and Iran, however, the United States created an authoritarian regime or
was involved in the overthrow of a leftist government that threatened
American-led alliance building, respectively.

In the East Asia of the early 1950s, three authoritarian allies joined the self-proclaimed Free World: the Republic of Korea, the Republic of China, and the Republic of Vietnam. Their individual genesis varied greatly, though their accession to the Free World occurred in the wake of the outbreak of the Korean War in mid 1950. During the Cold War, however, successive White House administrations remained uneasy about the authoritarian nature of all three regimes, even if they served an important purpose in the overall American Cold War strategy at the Asian periphery of the Socialist Camp. In general, Washington faced the same kind of problem. Whenever the United States called for reform, each regime cynically raised the specter of domestic collapse or even threatened defection to the other side of the Cold War.[16]

South Korea as an American ally emerged almost accidentally. During World War II, Roosevelt and Stalin had agreed to put the Japanese colony under international tutelage, because its people supposedly were not yet ready for self-rule. The sudden Japanese surrender in August 1945 forced Washington to shift personnel trained for occupation duty in Japan to an occupation zone in southern Korea. Trained only in the Japanese language, the ill-equipped US military and civilian officials quickly alienated the local population when they employed the former Japanese colonial administration as a conduit to run the unfamiliar occupation zone. To make matters worse, American officials in Korea allied with the small exile government that had returned in time and consisted mainly of the 70-year-old Syngman Rhee, the long-time exiled anti-Japanese nationalist. As early as spring 1947, however, planners in Washington considered South Korea unimportant in terms of US national security.[17]

Still, as a result of the Soviet–American deadlock in the talks about Korea, Washington decided in 1948 to apply its West German policy of building up a state in the southern half of Korea, albeit as an anti-communist state with little democratic legitimacy. It remained under the rule of the authoritarian Syngman Rhee until 1960. Before the outbreak of the Korean War, he at least introduced urgently needed land reforms but otherwise failed at economic development until his downfall. The Korean War and the new, post-NSC-68 policy of stopping communist expansion everywhere in the world eventually opened the path for the Republic of Korea to join the American alliance system. Throughout the 1950s, Washington funded much of the South Korean state budget. Aware of the government's ineptitude, it tried to push for domestic reforms – though without any success. By the late 1950s, the United States gave up on the aging Rhee, hoping that a more reform-minded successor would soon emerge in his place. With the exception of thirteen months of democratic rule in the early 1960s, however, Washington ended up with a military dictatorship in Seoul until 1987.[18]

In comparison, the US ally in Taiwan was the anti-communist shadow of the former wartime partner on mainland China. During World War II, Roosevelt had hoped in vain that Chiang Kai-shek's Republic of China (ROC) would become a great power capable of stabilizing post-war Asia. Washington also was aware that Chiang was responsible for restarting the civil war with the Chinese communists in 1946. The Generalissimo had hoped to use the emerging Cold War to extract more economic and military aid from Truman. As Chiang's ROC developed into an unreformable drain on US resources, Washington decided at the turn of 1948/49 to allow China to slip into the Soviet orbit. The hope was that a communist-led China would turn to the USSR and become a similarly huge liability to America's principal Cold War enemy. By mid 1949, Chiang moved his government from the mainland to Taiwan in order to escape communist seizure. But Washington continued its policy of indifference until the outbreak of the Korean War once more changed the equation. Truman sent the Seventh Fleet to the Taiwan Strait to deter a communist Chinese attempt to expand the conflict in Northeast Asia. Even if Washington subsequently provided economic and military aid to Taipei in the context of its new strategy of containment, it continued, as in South Korea, to face an ally that resisted calls for domestic reform.[19]

South Vietnam, too, turned out to be an unreformable ally against communist expansion in Southeast Asia. In the second half of the 1940s, the Truman administration had been uneasy about the French reassertion of colonial control in all of Indochina. France fought a wide range of Indochinese nationalists after 1945, but particularly the well-organized communists. Ho Chi Minh and his comrades had proclaimed the Democratic Republic of Vietnam (DRV) on September 2, 1945, but failed to garner recognition by any state. While France was an important US ally in the unfolding European Cold War, Washington wanted Paris to devolve power in Indochina with the ultimate goal of complete decolonization. Much to American frustration, the European ally created empty shells of states in Vietnam, Laos, and Cambodia in 1948 and 1949. The situation changed dramatically with the foundation of the People's Republic of China (PRC) on October 1, 1949. In January 1950, during his visit to Moscow, Mao Zedong decided to recognize the DRV, and even managed to convince Stalin to follow suit. When the United States and other Western allies responded by recognizing France's three Indochinese creations, the Cold War had formally arrived in Southeast Asia. The Sino–Soviet Friendship Treaty of February 14, 1950, and the outbreak of the Korean War four months later convinced the United States to support France in a struggle that was no longer about French reassertion of colonial control but about containment of communist expansion.[20]

In the following four years, Washington nonetheless became aware that Paris was losing the war on the battlefield and the struggle for hearts and minds. In the spring of 1954, the United States refused to back France's military effort and, in the summer, stayed aloof from the Geneva Accords that formally, though temporarily, divided Vietnam into a communist North and a non-communist South. For a year after mid 1954, Washington hesitated to support the southern State of Vietnam given the inconclusive internal power struggle there. Only when Prime Minister Ngo Dinh Diem emerged as a strongman by mid 1955 did Washington choose to support him as the sole South Vietnamese leader capable of resisting communist expansion. Despite the North Vietnamese propaganda vilification of Diem as an American puppet, he was a politician with a long record of nationalism since the 1920s. While deeply flawed as president, Diem had his own, strongly anti-communist vision of Vietnam's future. Keenly aware of the danger of being seen as an American puppet, he remained resistant to US calls for political, economic, and rural reform.[21]

The rise of these three authoritarian allies in East Asia set precedents for US policies in other parts of Asia and in the Middle East. In the name of the defense of the Free World, Washington allied with authoritarian countries that switched sides in the Cold War, like Indonesia in 1965 and Cambodia in 1970. As anti-Soviet containment entered the Middle East, the United States also fostered close relationships with autocratic monarchies there, like Jordan or Saudi Arabia. In Iran in 1953, Washington cooperated with London to support internal political forces that overthrew the leftist and increasingly authoritarian Prime Minster Mohammad Mosaddeq. Yet this "involvement by invitation," as one historian called it, led to the reinstatement of the monarch, Shah Mohammad Reza Pahlavi, who turned out to be no democrat either. In other cases, Washington chose to maintain existing Cold War partnerships when dictatorships replaced democratic forms of government, as in Pakistan in 1958, in Turkey on three occasions (1960, 1971, and 1980), or in the Philippines in 1972. Thus, from the mid 1940s, the United States was willing to include, in the name of the defense of the Free World, the democracies in Europe and Japan, and numerous non-democratic countries in Asia and the Middle East as long as they were sufficiently anti-communist.[22]

The French Challenge, 1958–66

The Korean War clarified and hardened the lines of Cold War division not only in East Asia but also in Europe. With Turkey's and Greece's accession to NATO in early 1952 and the creation of the British-led

Baghdad Pact in the Middle East soon thereafter, Western containment of the Soviet Union ran along an unbroken chain of countries from Norway to Pakistan and beyond. Yet, just as American alliance making succeeded, conflicts within the Free World erupted. US President Dwight D. Eisenhower's refusal to provide continued support to the French struggle in Vietnam in the spring of 1954 had a deep impact on the bilateral relationship. The American denial of support for what France considered vital to its national interest led members of the French National Assembly from right to left to question the value of the American-inspired military integration of Western Europe. Fearing that France's entanglement in a supranational European alliance would limit the country's global room to maneuver, the National Assembly rejected ratification of the anti-Soviet European Defense Community (EDC) on August 30, 1954.[23]

More important, however, was the American refusal to back the British and French imperialist reflexes during the Suez Crisis in late October 1956. To make matters worse, Washington used economic and financial measures to force its two NATO allies out of the Middle East. This humiliation compelled both to rethink their role in world affairs and their relationship to the American hegemon. London ultimately decided to mend fences with Washington as a partner in the Cold War and to try to extend its great power status with the further development of its nuclear forces. Paris, however, drew different conclusions. By mid 1956, France had concluded – wrongly – that the Soviet Union was catching up in nuclear armament, and therefore questioned the US ability to guarantee security in Western Europe. More importantly, the United States had failed twice to provide support – once in the spring of 1954 and again in the fall of 1956 – when France's supposed national interests were at stake. President of the Council of Ministers Guy Mollet, a long-time Socialist nuclear weapons skeptic, thus ordered the start of France's own nuclear weapons project – the *force de frappe* (nuclear strike force) – on November 30, 1956.[24]

De Gaulle's appointment on June 1, 1958, as what turned out to be the last president of the Council of Ministers of the Fourth Republic further increased tensions within the Free World. He quickly started to reshape France, both in constitutional terms and at the international level. Within half a year, de Gaulle had replaced the parliamentary republic, which he had disparaged for a dozen years, with a presidential system of his own liking.[25] In foreign affairs, he aimed at establishing his Fifth Republic as the leader of continental Europe and a champion of the decolonizing world. This required the reduction of Anglo–American influence on the continent, rapprochement with the USSR, reconciliation with (West)

Germany, the withdrawal from Algeria, the establishment of good relations with the PRC, and criticism of the American intervention in Vietnam after August 1964.

De Gaulle quickly set out to try to restore his country to great power status. After only four months in power, he demanded from US President Eisenhower and British Prime Minister Harold Macmillan the reorganization of NATO under trilateral leadership. His scheme aimed both at elevating France to equality with the Anglo–American powers and at regaining national control over the country's armed forces outside the integrated command structures of the Western alliance. Despite his triumphant trip to Washington in April 1960, de Gaulle's proposal created a serious dilemma for the United States. Agreeing to it would have meant a complete overhaul, and possibly even the *de facto* dissolution, of NATO. But rejecting it would provoke France to withdraw from the alliance altogether. With neither being palatable options, Washington delayed as much as possible. By early 1963, however, the bilateral relationship had faltered over France's double rejection of American plans to share nuclear knowhow within NATO only with the United Kingdom and of the British request for membership in the European Economic Community (EEC). Yet the United States responded in kind when it negotiated the Limited Test Ban Treaty in mid 1963 with the Soviet Union and the United Kingdom, denying great power status to the ascendant nuclear power France. De Gaulle's disagreements with the newly sworn-in President Lyndon B. Johnson over Vietnam in late 1963 further harmed the strained relationship with the United States. By spring 1966, the French president announced the withdrawal of his country's forces from the integrated military structures of NATO, and demanded the removal of the alliance's headquarters from the French capital within one year.[26]

This double challenge to NATO rested on the stepwise success of the French nuclear weapons project. Although France had approached West Germany and Italy with the purpose of building a joint European A-bomb after Mollet's basic decision to go nuclear, de Gaulle quickly ended these plans once he had returned to power. On his first day as first president of the newly established Fifth Republic, on January 9, 1959, he ordered the first test series in the desert of southern Algeria to proceed within little more than a year. By 1964, France had managed to produce warheads small enough to be mounted on the country's own *Mirage* warplanes. Even if the French parliamentary opposition relentlessly mocked the relatively small *force de frappe* as de Gaulle's "bombinette," the nuclear program was still politically powerful enough for the French president to withdraw from NATO in 1966.[27]

De Gaulle's visions of a Europe outside American hegemony specifically included some form of rapprochement with Nikita S. Khrushchev's USSR. Since his return to power, he had pursued the project of a *Europe of Fatherlands* that reached from the Azores to the Urals. But the general's timing was off on several counts. In November 1958, two months after de Gaulle had demanded equality with the Anglo–American powers in NATO, the Soviet leader threw down the gauntlet with the Berlin Ultimatum. As Moscow and Washington were edging toward Eisenhower's invitation for Khrushchev to visit the United States in September of 1959, France and the USSR improved their bilateral relationship. Before his departure for the United States, Khrushchev received, for the first time, one of de Gaulle's ministers, who had come with the purpose of inviting the Soviet leader to France for March 1960. Khrushchev's visit to Paris just before de Gaulle's trip to Washington in April was closely linked to Franco–American relations in more than just proximity of time. The general wanted to claim a role equal to Khrushchev's and Eisenhower's in international affairs. But the Franco–Soviet rapprochement was overshadowed by disagreements over France's colonial struggle in Algeria since 1954, and was eventually cut short by Khrushchev's sabotage of the Paris Summit following the U-2 incident in May 1960. The closure of the Berlin borders in August 1961 and the Soviet–American–British Nuclear Test Ban Treaty of mid 1963 suspended de Gaulle's hoped-for resumption of Franco–Soviet rapprochement until 1966.[28]

Just as de Gaulle was challenging the United States and the United Kingdom over NATO in September 1958, he also received the German federal chancellor, Konrad Adenauer, for talks at his country house at Colombey-les-Deux-Églises. The German leader had initially been skeptical about the invitation, but the meeting turned out to be an unexpected success. The two politicians quickly established a warm personal relationship, which rested on de Gaulle's general commitment to German unity and European integration. Indeed, Paris took a hard line in response to Khrushchev's ultimatum on Berlin only two months later, but irritated Bonn through its rapprochement with Moscow in 1959–60. De Gaulle's policy toward NATO – the alliance which guaranteed West Germany's political and military survival in the Cold War, at least in Adenauer's eyes – and his rejection of British membership in the EEC were both sources of Franco–German tensions in the early 1960s. In order to undermine attempts by President John F. Kennedy to shape European economic and military integration policies, de Gaulle again courted Adenauer with the idea of closer Franco–West German cooperation in mid 1962. The German chancellor was willing to settle on a friendship treaty – eventually signed on January 22, 1963 – not because he shared de Gaulle's anti-Americanism but because it helped to bury the historical Franco–German rivalry. His single-handed decision to negotiate and sign the treaty, however, irritated many of his pro-American friends in his party, the Christian Democratic Union, and ultimately was responsible for his resignation in the fall of 1963. While the Franco–German treaty provided France with a partner in Europe, it simultaneously deprived de Gaulle of his personal German friend.[29]

As important as all of these developments in France's foreign policy were, none of them had really been the cause for de Gaulle's return to power in May 1958. Algeria was. Less than four months after the Geneva Accords that had ended France's eight-year war in Indochina by July 1954, France was sliding into what would become another eight-year war against an anti-colonial independence movement – the National Liberation Front of Algeria (FLN). Unlike Indochina, Algeria was a settlement colony, and thus many in France had deeper political and emotional attachments to it than to the distant colonial possessions in Indochina. Moreover, one of the reasons for France to intervene in Egypt in October 1956 had been the hope of ending Nasser's support of the FLN. The rebellion of right-wing French officials in Algeria in May 1958 eventually smoothed de Gaulle's path back to power after twelve years of self-exile at Colombey-les-Deux-Églises. Historians still debate whether or not popular expectations for victory in Algeria under de Gaulle's leadership misaligned with his previous but undisclosed decision to extricate France from its colonial legacy. Ultimately, international pressure, the independence of French sub-Saharan colonies in the late 1950s, and the increasing military support of the FLN by Czechoslovakia, the PRC, and the USSR changed the context in which France looked at its North African colony. De Gaulle entered into negotiations with the FLN-led Algerian provisional government in early 1961 – just after the end of the first series of A-bomb tests in the Algerian desert – which opened the path to the Evian Accords a year later. Despite the overall French public support for Algerian independence in the early 1960s, de Gaulle was the target of several assassination attempts by right-wing opponents of decolonization.[30]

In many respects, Sino–French recognition in late January 1964 was the consequence of de Gaulle's checkered record of achievements in international affairs since 1958. On the one hand, there were major disappointments, like France's failed transformation to equality in its relationship with the United States, the abortive rapprochement with the USSR, and Soviet–American–British cooperation on the limitation of nuclear testing at the expense of France and the PRC in mid 1963. On the other hand, de

Gaulle had achieved some successes, such as France's withdrawal from Algeria, which helped to restore the country to respectability in the decolonized world. But communist China was a different game. In 1950, the need for American support in the war against the Vietnamese communists had forced France to withhold recognition of the newly established PRC. Even if Paris retained diplomatic links with Taipei, neither side invested much in the relationship. France's withdrawal from Algeria in 1962 removed a major political obstacle to mutual recognition for the PRC. But it was de Gaulle himself who sought the establishment of diplomatic relations with Mao's China in the wake of the Soviet–American–British agreement on the Nuclear Test Ban Treaty in mid 1963. The Chinese leaders were flattered by the French initiative – particularly since they hoped that recognition would provide an opening for further recognition in Western Europe and francophone Africa. But they responded by proposing a procedure, which would make de Gaulle look like a petitioner begging Mao for a favor. The proud French president would not accept that; in the end, he imposed a method through which France would not even abide by the PRC demand to break official relations with the ROC on Taiwan. Here, too, de Gaulle snatched defeat from the jaws of victory. The unilateral and surprise step unnecessarily irritated the United States, violated the mutual consultation clause in the Franco–German treaty from the previous year, let post-Adenauer West Germany doubt France's commitment to German unity, and, above all, did not bring any increase in French influence on mainland China.[31]

Ultimately, Franco–Chinese rapprochement was linked to US policies in Indochina. After President John F. Kennedy's assassination on November 22, 1963, de Gaulle had been briefly willing to forego recognition of the PRC, but the talks with the new president, Lyndon B. Johnson, on Indochina went nowhere, as mentioned above. The French president thus hoped that a closer relationship with China would help France to influence events in Southeast Asia. The US escalation of the Vietnam War in August 1964 met with much criticism from virtually all American allies and from many countries in the Afro–Asian world, but de Gaulle, unsurprisingly, turned out to be one of the most vocal detractors. With France having fought two consecutive, eight-year-long wars against national liberation movements, de Gaulle was convinced that the United States was heading for disaster. His subsequent attempts to defang the unfolding crisis were based on two additional motivations: his fear that a greater American commitment to Vietnam would reduce US security obligations to Western Europe (despite his own anti-American policies with regard to NATO), and his pursuit of elevating France's standing as peacemaker in the Third World. After the American escalation in late 1964, the French president briefly tried to mediate in Indochina: he soon decided to improve relations with Cambodia and North Vietnam, particularly during a personal trip to Phnom Penh in September 1966, in the hope of moving all sides in the conflict to make concessions. Here, too, he failed.[32]

Popular Unrest

The disunity of the Free World ran deeper than just disagreements among its Atlantic partners, because it affected the societies of the Western democracies themselves. Much of the widespread popular criticism leveled at governmental policies carried some justification, because it pointed to shortcomings and problems within the liberal–capitalist system. However, this should not come as a surprise; public political debates are an inherent and functional aspect of democratic systems. In comparison, member states of the Socialist Camp tried to suppress anything that was closely reminiscent of public debate; public dissatisfaction thus had no other channel than outright rebellion. After a post-war decade of relative domestic quiet in the Free World, unrest started to erupt in the late 1950s. The US ally Japan experienced public criticism over the country's close relationship to the American Cold War hegemon at the expense of its supposedly traditional links to mainland China. Dissatisfaction reached a peak during the renewal of the security alliance with the United States in 1960, which occurred in the context of massive and violent demonstrations in Tokyo, including the storming of the parliament building.[33]

In the United States itself, the experience of the Great Depression, World War II, and the advent of the Cold War had forged a conservative consensus within much of American mainstream society. But this consensus started to crumble over the course of the 1950s. It broke apart not only within the white, male-dominated society because of the advent of the sexual revolution, but also across ethnic, gender, and generational lines within American society at large. In any case, the seeming conformity of the early Cold War consensus had covered up long-standing fissures – such as the systematic discrimination of people of color, particularly African Americans, and of women of all ethnic backgrounds. With the ubiquitous external propaganda about the struggle between the Free World and the evils of communism as a backdrop, civil rights leaders, the women's movement, and student protesters all challenged the status quo at home. Added to this volatile mix of dissatisfaction was the rising criticism of US Cold War policy, particularly with regard to the nuclear arms race and the Vietnam War. What President Richard M. Nixon cynically called the Silent Majority emerged over the course of the 1960s in response to civil unrest. This majority, in reality, included not-so-silent racists in the south as well as outspoken conservatives, agitated parents, and strident Cold Warriors. Ultimately, the American intervention in the Vietnam War after August 1964 fused the various protest movements together, particularly as the old generation – even in the form of the civil rights-championing President Lyndon B. Johnson – sent young, underprivileged, and often ethnic minority conscripts on a mission to assault the body of the Third-World country Vietnam.[34]

In West Germany, political conflict emerged just as the Adenauer era, with its paternalist approach to democracy, ended in 1963. With the post-war generation coming of age, questions about parental involvement in Hitler's Germany triggered conflict between the younger and the older generation – between those who challenged the supposedly petty-bourgeois status quo and those who were happy with the peace and material wellbeing which the post-war economic miracle had created. Starting in 1965, students in the walled-in capitalist enclave of West Berlin criticized what they saw as the government's acquiescence to American war crimes in Vietnam. For their political campaign, they received logistical and political support from the East German regime on the other side of the wall. But the West German student movement mainly took cues from similar protests in the United States, particularly during the visit of the pro-American Shah of Iran to West Berlin in early June 1967. During demonstrations in front of the opera house – where the autocratic monarch was enjoying Mozart's Enlightenment opera *The Magic Flute* – the West Berlin policeman Karl-Heinz Kurras shot the student-demonstrator Benno Ohnesorg execution-style. To make matters even more confusing, Kurras had been working for the East German security organs since 1955 and had passed on state secrets to his handlers in the GDR. Ohnesorg's killing and Kurras's subsequent acquittal triggered massive student protests in West Berlin and other cities in West Germany. Ultimately, it also prompted the rise of left-wing terrorism, which plagued the FRG for more than two decades and was supported logistically by East German state security services. In early February 1968, a student conference on the Vietnam War in West Berlin garnered international attention as it occurred just weeks after the start of the Tet Offensive, during which Vietnamese communist forces sought a decisive victory against the South Vietnamese Republic and the United States. The violence of subsequent demonstrations in several West German cities, including a right-wing assassination attempt on one of the student leaders, convinced the federal parliament to pass state-of-emergency legislation by May 30 to suppress internal unrest. In turn, this development seemed to confirm the supposedly fascist nature of the West German state to the protesting students and their sympathizers.[35]

De Gaulle's France experienced a similarly intense, though shorter, period of student protest. The long-term cause for student activism was the general crisis of the university system that had led to initial but localized protest on campuses in Paris in the fall of 1967. Student protest erupted in late March in the context of the Tet Offensive and in the wake of conflict between university administrations, on the one hand, and anarchist, Maoist, and Trotskyite students, on the other. Increasingly, the goal of the demonstrators was no longer just the reform of the university system but the overhaul of de Gaulle's Fifth Republic. This extension of demands increasingly attracted working-class protest. The swelling of street demonstrations threatened to thwart the opening of the North Vietnamese–American peace talks, which de Gaulle was hosting in the French capital. On May 10–11, student–worker demonstrators occupied central Paris, erecting symbolic barricades memorializing the Paris Commune and its resistance to Imperial Germany in the spring of 1871. Afraid of losing his hold on power, on May 29 de Gaulle secretly fled the chaos in a military helicopter bound for former enemy territory – Germany. Rumors about his disappearance led to demands from the street for his resignation on the 30th. On that day, however, the president announced parliamentary snap elections for June 23. The shift of the conflict from the street to the ballot box, as well as de Gaulle's mobilization of massive counter-demonstrations in June, convinced the student–worker demonstrators to back off. The election turned into a referendum on the protesting students and workers; the massive victory for the Gaullist party halted their momentum.[36]

Protest in 1968 was not only confined to the United States, Germany, or France, but was an international phenomenon that occurred even behind the Iron Curtain. In general, activist students in the United States and Western Europe criticized from the left what they believed were conservative governments and conformist societies, while their counterparts in the socialist world pushed for some form of cultural pluralism or even multiparty democracy, as for example during the Prague Spring. Given their fundamentally incompatible life experiences, they often admired from afar what their counterparts on the other side of the Iron Curtain criticized. Thus, in the few instances where they met, as for example in Prague or East Berlin in the spring and summer of 1968, they spoke past each other and parted in mutual disappointment. Western European utopianism had clashed with Eastern European realism.[37]

Ultimately, the Soviet-led intervention in Czechoslovakia in mid August 1968 reminded many what was at stake in the European Cold

War. The brutal military action to suppress a socialist alternative to Soviet-style communism particularly damaged de Gaulle's recently repaired reputation. Just two years before, after the French rupture with NATO, he had resumed his project of building a *Europe of Fatherlands* by visiting the USSR. During the Israeli–Arab War of June 1967, the French president had split from the Free World and joined the Soviet-led Socialist Camp in support of the Arab side, though France had provided assistance to Israel's nuclear weapons project and delivered Israel's entire air force beforehand. But Soviet actions in August 1968 undercut de Gaulle's quest to reposition France among the superpowers. Even if his criticism of Washington's war in Vietnam against a communist-inspired nationalist liberation movement was astute (though not entirely unselfish), Moscow's imperial aggression in Eastern Europe readjusted Western European public opinion about the nature of the global Cold War. At the end of the day, it also discredited protest movements in many European countries, particularly the radicalized students in walled-in West Berlin. Yet de Gaulle did not fall immediately. He received a final gesture of respect when newly elected US president, Richard M. Nixon, went on his first trip abroad to Paris to obtain advice from de Gaulle on world politics, including on China and Vietnam. By turning the referendum on institutional reform in late April 1969 into a *de facto* plebiscite of his leadership, however, the French president provided his domestic opponents with the opportunity to end the Gaullist decade of mixed success once and for all. After one and a half years living quietly in Colombey-les-Deux-Églises, the first president passed away in early November 1970, shortly before his eightieth birthday.[38]

While protest in Europe had reached its peak in 1968 and then quickly declined, civil unrest continued in the United States for several years. Despite Nixon's promise to end the war in Vietnam during his election campaign, he escalated the bombing of the communist North and even carried the war into Cambodia by the spring of 1970. In the belief that the Silent Majority was backing him, the law-and-order president alienated protesters even more, whether they were ethnic minorities, women, or students. The shootings of two anti-Vietnam War demonstrators and two student bystanders at Kent State University on May 4, 1970, marked the depressing low point in the polarization of American politics under Nixon. The economic downturn induced by the long war in Indochina, the American withdrawal from Vietnam in 1973, and Nixon's resignation in the wake of the Watergate Scandal the following year moved much of the conflict from the street back into the political arena. The presidential election of 1976 provided two competing visions for a new beginning – one from the Democratic left with the election of President Jimmy Carter, and the other from the narrowly defeated Republican candidate for nomination Ronald Reagan, who would run again four years later. Both strongly criticized Nixon's amoral policies abroad and his unethical actions at home, though from opposite political positions.[39]

Unity despite Disagreements, 1969–73

De Gaulle's departure from power and the decline of protest in Europe did not resolve all disagreements among the governments of the Free World. The European NATO partners continued to criticize American involvement in Indochina, which they found unnecessary and detrimental to global stability and peace. At least, France continued to host the US–Vietnamese talks, which ended with the Paris Accords in January 1973.[40] Generally, however, this period saw the democracies of the Free World reviewing their respective positions. In some cases, this led to greater cooperation among them, but, in others, to additional conflict. France understood that it could not play the leading role in international relations which de Gaulle had envisioned. Nixon's United States realized it could no longer afford to stabilize the Free World economically on the basis of the Bretton Woods agreements. Exogenous shocks, like the Arab oil embargo, further tested the cohesion of the Free World.

Georges Pompidou's succession of de Gaulle as president in June 1969 changed French foreign policy, even if the new leader had been a staunch Gaullist since the end of World War II. Pompidou recognized that France was only a middle power. Still, the new president hoped to preserve much of the country's independence in international affairs, particularly by staying out of the military structures of NATO. But his greater realism still led to a rapprochement with the Anglo–American powers. Paris swiftly ended de Gaulle's blockade of London's membership in the renamed European Communities (EC). Pompidou's decision was not based on a rediscovered love for the United Kingdom but on the realistic assessment that France needed a functioning and enlarged EC for its own modernization project. Likewise, the United Kingdom entered the community mostly for economic reasons. Pompidou also abandoned his predecessor's public anti-Americanism during a visit to Washington in early 1970. While disagreements on many issues, like Vietnam and the Middle East, remained, the United States and France supported the policy of the new West German chancellor, Willy Brandt, of establishing better relations with the USSR, socialist Eastern Europe, and the GDR, largely because they hoped it would help détente on the old continent. Ultimately, West Germany's *Ostpolitik* opened the door to the Conference on Security and Cooperation in Europe, during which the NATO allies ended up working together closely despite substantial disagreements.[41]

But economic developments in the late 1960s and early 1970s erected new barriers to greater collaboration. The American involvement in the Vietnam War had caused an increase in US governmental spending and a slow rise in inflation and unemployment by the late 1960s. Simultaneously, France kept its positive bilateral trading balance, which enabled Paris to exchange surplus US dollars for American gold. This all put pressure on the fixed exchange rates and the gold pegging, which the Bretton Woods system had introduced in 1944, and which had helped to stabilize the global economy since. To make matters worse, Great Britain devalued the pound in November 1967 to recapture economic competi-tiveness in the otherwise rigid Bretton Woods system. Subsequent public debates in the United States about the need to devalue the US dollar merely helped to accelerate the outflow of gold, currency, and invest-ments, which in turn exacerbated the financial and economic situation in the United States even more. After months of internal discussions, President Nixon abruptly announced in mid August 1971 a ninety-day freeze on wages and prices, the introduction of a 10 percent import tariff on manufactured goods, and the temporary suspension of dollar–gold convertibility. One of the main goals of the new policy was to force the revaluation of Western European and Japanese currencies unilaterally. He had thereby *de facto* abolished the Bretton Woods system of perma-nently fixed exchange rates and the gold pegging. Within only two years, the exchange rates of most important Western currencies were floating freely. But Nixon's unilateral step caused inflationary pressures in Western Europe and Japan, which were additionally exacerbated by the Arab oil production cutbacks to counterbalance price decreases following the *de facto* devaluation of the US dollar after 1971.[42]

In late 1973, members of the Organization of Arab Petroleum Exporting Countries (OAPEC) decided to implement an oil embargo against the United States, Canada, the United Kingdom, the Netherlands, and Japan as punishment for their pro-Israeli involvement in the October War. In the wake of the oil production cutbacks since 1971, the embargo created severe energy supply shortages and price shocks in the Free World, but it also paradoxically caused both greater cohesion and greater division there. With Washington taking leadership, the Organization for Economic Cooperation and Development (OECD) – which brought together all NATO partners, several Western European neutrals, and Japan – decided on greater coordination of energy policies in order to manage the current crisis and avoid future shocks. Yet the embargo was also the first stress test for cohesion of the European Communities (EC) after the admission of the United Kingdom at the beginning of 1973. Deplorably, community members affected by the

Arab oil embargo did not resort to coordination within the framework of the much heralded common foreign policy. Particularly the United Kingdom tried to appease Arab demands while refusing to help other community members, like the Netherlands, with oil supplies from non-Arab production sources. British behavior during the oil embargo in 1973–74 and the country's referendum on EC membership in mid 1975 both revealed that the United Kingdom was still not fully committed to the European project.[43]

Conclusion

The American Cold War spheres of influence in Europe, Asia, and the Middle East varied in genesis, nature, and cohesion. At the core of the Free World was a capitalist and largely democratic Western Europe and Japan. The United States had to deal with much dissent from both during the Cold War. Disagreements had accumulated by the 1960s for a variety of reasons. But the multiple crises of 1968 – on the battlefield in Vietnam, in the streets of Western cities, and in Soviet-occupied Czechoslovakia – undermined the credibility of some of the extreme criticism. Unlike the socialist states, however, democracies never elevated their disagreements to fundamental debates on ideological correctness. They derived their legitimacy from the consent of the ruled – obtained by periodic free and nearly universal elections – but not from their ability to interpret the hallowed texts of Adam Smith or John Maynard Keynes correctly. Even if interests in the core of the Free World continued to diverge by the early 1970s, the United States, the Western European democracies, and Japan were at least able to restore a minimal Cold War consensus.

The American spheres of influence in the other parts of Asia and in the Middle East looked less promising as *bona fide* parts of the Free World. To be sure, Washington did not install the regimes there – South Korea being the only exception – but it still sought alliances with authoritarian regimes, or continued partnerships with countries that became authoritarian, in the name of defending the Free World. In several cases, Washington was troubled by the authoritarian nature of some of its allies, but its attempts to change them lacked long-term conviction and political commitment. This diffident attitude paralleled the waning of US commitments to decolonization, as described earlier. Ultimately, a number of authoritarian allies in Europe – Portugal and Greece – and in East Asia – Taiwan, South Korea, the Philippines – underwent democratization in the 1970s and 1980s, respectively, which at least testified to the continued, strong allure of the idea of the Free World during the Cold War.

Part II

Asia

Introduction to Chapters 5 to 7

Over several decades, three countries played major roles in Asia's Cold War. China, Vietnam, and India all were dynamic agents in the shaping of their own fates, and definitely not just passive battlegrounds in the global competition between the United States and the Soviet Union. Their decolonization occurred in parallel to that of the Middle Eastern countries (Chapter 2), but was intertwined with the Cold War in more profound ways. As early as 1927, China became a major regional theater of the ideological conflict that would be typical for the Cold War, when Chiang Kai-shek's *Guomindang* (Nationalist Party) turned on the Soviet-sponsored Chinese Communist Party and started an intermittent civil war that lasted for over two decades.[1] During a pause in this conflict in the period of 1937–45, China fortuitously got rid of formal colonial interference as Japanese occupation terminated the Western presence, and Washington's defeat of Tokyo in 1945 ended Japanese imperialism. In early 1946, the civil war resumed in the form of a local Cold War, ending with Chinese communist victory three years later. In Indochina, the Japanese occupation in 1941–45 ended the French colonial presence, though after Japan's surrender on September 2, 1945, France tried to reassert control in a war that by early 1950 turned into a local Cold War conflict for twenty-five years – until 1975, when the Vietnamese communists won. South Asia emerged from the British Empire in 1947 concurrently with London's shift of its imperial focus to the Middle East, as we saw in Chapter 2. Still, the subcontinent was drawn into the Cold War in the wake of the Korean War in the early 1950s, as American-led alliance building arose along the periphery of the Socialist Camp.

The developments of China, Vietnam, and India during the Cold War displayed remarkable similarities. They all were countries torn apart by internal conflict. Although China's civil war ended with communist victory on the mainland in 1949, the country remains divided into the People's Republic of China and the Republic of China on Taiwan to this day. Anti-imperialists in Vietnam split into communists and non-communists in the interwar period, ultimately leading to the thirty-year division of the country after World War II. In comparison, the partition of South Asia in 1947, when India and Pakistan emerged independent from the British Empire, ran along sectarian, not Cold War, lines. This, however, did not prevent the entry of the global Soviet–American competition into the region, which did not help to reduce the bitterness of partition either.

Moreover, each of the three countries shared a set of particular characteristics with one of the other two. China and Vietnam experienced communist victory and authoritarian governments, while India turned into a republic with a shaky democracy. China and India rivalled each other in their pretensions to global leadership, while communist Vietnam saw itself at best as one of several world revolutionary agents. And Vietnam and India faced contested post-colonial borders and undefined territoriality, which led to extended armed conflict in their respective world regions.

The trilateral relationship between China, Vietnam, and India underwent significant structural changes in the three decades following the end of World War II. In the late 1940s, the PRC established close relations with communist Vietnam, while Jawaharlal Nehru's India remained unaligned. In the mid 1950s, or so it seemed, Delhi and Beijing were finding a common understanding, while Vietnamese–Indian relations remained distant. In the decade from 1962, however, Beijing drove Delhi and Hanoi into each other's arms. With the start of Sino–American rapprochement and China's entry into the United Nations in 1971, the revolutionary PRC turned into a global status quo power while the DRV assumed China's former role as a radical world revolutionary force. In comparison, India emerged as an isolated country that desperately sought status, particularly with regard to its Chinese rival.

The developments in Asia's Cold War had a lasting impact on the regional Cold Wars in the Middle East and Europe, as Parts III to VII reveal. China and Vietnam injected their revolutionary agendas into the Arab world. All three Asian states played major roles in the Asian–African Movement and Non-Alignment – sometimes constructive and at other times destructive. The Sino–Indian rivalry after 1962 had an impact on nuclear proliferation. In the 1970s, the PRC exerted influence on German–German relations and the Conference on Security and Cooperation in Europe. Eventually, the three Asian countries clashed in the Third Indochina War in 1978–79 (see Chapter 21), which divided them anew.

5   China

In 1949, the Chinese Communist Party (CCP) provided the country with a stable central government for the first time in more than a century. The foundation of the People's Republic of China (PRC) on October 1 concluded a long period of inner turmoil that had witnessed the gradual collapse of the Qing dynasty, internal rebellions, imperialist interventions, and a failed republic. The CCP won as the result of good leadership, sheer luck, the mutual elimination of its internal and external enemies, and the ineptitude, stubbornness, and recklessness of its main internal rival – the *Guomindang* (GMD; Nationalist Party). In its self-perception, the party had defeated domestic and foreign enemies singlehandedly, and thereby helped the Chinese people to stand up after a century of humiliation. Since its foundation in 1921, the CCP had presented itself as the country's redeemer, with the goal of restoring China to past glory and greatness while modernizing it in the process.[1] Along the path from small party to victory and beyond, CCP leaders were torn between nationalism and ideology. Although the party was established with Comintern assistance in the wake of World War I, it had left the shadow of Soviet guidance by the 1930s, and even toyed with the idea of aligning with the United States in the mid 1940s. Yet, as the Cold War emerged, the United States continued to support the internationally recognized government of China – the GMD-led Republic of China (ROC).

Communist leaders disagreed among themselves over how exactly to restore China to independence, prosperity, and global power. For almost a quarter of a century after 1949, their debates were marked by the opposite ambitions of revolutionizing the existing world order and of accepting it. This fundamental paradox caused two conflicting impulses. First, the PRC struggled against the United Nations as the supposedly highest form of imperialism – US Cold War imperialism – while it concurrently pursued policies to obtain membership in lieu of the GMD-led ROC on Taiwan. Second, the Chinese communist leaders imposed policies at home that aimed at revolutionizing Chinese society into a socialist utopia, while simultaneously trying to focus on the sound development of the country's underdeveloped economy. Once the PRC had obtained status in international relations with its admission to the United Nations in 1971, however, it abandoned ideological radicalism for pragmatic foreign and economic policies.

The Sino–Soviet split in the 1960s and the Sino–American rapprochement in the early 1970s not only marked two of the most important developments in the middle period of the global Cold War, but also generated the conditions by which the PRC could join the United Nations. Yet China's revolutionary and then pragmatic outlook caused ripple effects throughout Asia, the Middle East, and Europe. As subsequent chapters reveal, PRC policies influenced the course of the Indochina conflict and developments in South Asia significantly. Communist China attracted Egyptian interest as early as the mid 1950s, and Syrian and Palestinian admiration in the 1960s. The People's Republic engaged with – and then destroyed – the Asian–African Movement, while it simultaneously struggled against Non-Alignment throughout the 1950s and 1960s. Furthermore, China recurrently intruded in European affairs, particularly in the German–German relationship and European negotiations on continent-wide security.

Toward 1949

Qing China was one of the biggest prizes in the Western race for imperial influence in Asia. The country's socio-economic, cultural, and governmental achievements had fascinated Europeans for centuries. In the early 1800s, however, the Celestial Empire started to decline internally, just before Western imperialist aggression reached its peak. Foreign interventions since 1839 imposed outside control and set off domestic rebellions, but also introduced the country to Western ideas of society, economics, government, science, philosophy, and religion. The steady collapse of central authority continued after the revolution of 1911/12, which ended monarchical rule while establishing the internally fragmented Republic of China.[2]

Chinese nationalism drew equally on the perception of past national glory and Western ideas on the modern nation state. The country's seminal nationalist leader, Sun Yat-sen, established the *Guomindang*, which, by the early 1920s, ruled its own statelet in the southern province of Guangdong. To this day, the GMD on Taiwan and the CCP on the mainland revere him as the founder of Chinese nationalism. Comintern agents helped to establish the CCP in 1921, and then convinced the young outfit and the GMD to enter into an anti-imperialist united front. Sun's successor in 1925, Chiang Kai-shek, was less sympathetic to the USSR and communism. During the so-called Northern Expedition, which unified much of China in 1926–28, he turned against the CCP, thereby making China the first theater of a regional ideological conflict two decades before the global Cold War even started. Japanese imperialist aggression and Soviet mediation in the Chinese civil war led to the establishment of the second united front in 1937. Even if this united front collapsed *de facto* in 1940, it at least suspended the civil war for the duration of World War II. Still, China's territory remained divided three ways: collaborationist regimes set up by the Japanese occupiers on the seaboard existed alongside the internationally recognized ROC in the southwest, and a communist controlled zone in the northwest.[3]

Despite its domestic fragmentation and external weakness, the gradual elimination of imperialist influence occurred on republican China's watch, and not as a result of communist policies. Defeat in World War I had removed Germany as a colonial power, although imperial Japan obtained the German colony in Shandong. Japanese designs pushed Soviet influence – inherited from imperial Russia – out of Manchuria by the 1930s. During the Japanese occupation of China proper from 1937 to 1945, Tokyo undermined the European and American presence when it captured many of those places where foreign powers had enjoyed privileges since the nineteenth century. Given the rising nationalist sentiments among the Chinese people, the Western powers decided to relinquish most of their legal claims in Japanese-occupied China by 1943. This left Japan as virtually the last power with colonial possessions in China, but its defeat by the United States in World War II in the Pacific removed the last imperialist player too. With the exception of British and Portuguese rights in Hong Kong and Macao, respectively, Western colonial control did not return to China in 1945.[4]

Notwithstanding its limited contribution to defeating Japan, the ROC emerged as a global power during World War II. The alliance with the United States provided Chiang Kai-shek's government with enhanced prestige in domestic politics and with increasing international legitimacy. Moreover, US President Franklin D. Roosevelt elevated the ROC in early 1942 to one of the permanent members in the Security Council of the yet-to-be-established United Nations. But in 1946, Chiang's GMD restarted the civil war against the CCP in the hope of exploiting the unfolding Cold War in Europe for economic and military aid from the United States. Despite massive American assistance, the GMD lost the civil war and evacuated from the mainland to Taiwan in 1949.[5]

In comparison to the GMD, the CCP offered a different vision of restoring China to its former greatness and glory. Throughout the 1920s, the Comintern had sponsored the foundation of communist parties across the globe. Lenin's idea of anti-imperialist revolutions in the colonized world that would foment socialist revolutions in the imperialist–capitalist world appealed to those Chinese leftists who gathered in Shanghai in 1921 to establish the CCP under Comintern guidance. Lenin's vision promised the elevation of the humiliated country to an influential role in world affairs. Yet, with the end of the first united front in 1927 and the concurrent Soviet inward turn, the CCP progressively slipped away from Comintern influence. During the following decade, it also experienced the difficult struggle for survival against the GMD. By the late 1930s, the party's emerging leader, Mao Zedong, started to rethink the larger meaning of the Chinese Revolution to the world. In mid 1941, with World War II raging concurrently in Asia and Europe, he came to believe that the CCP was a participant in a global united front of progressive forces – consisting of "Kuomintang–Communist co-operation" in China, the USSR, the United States, and the United Kingdom – against imperialism, militarism, and fascism. The collapse of this imagined alliance and the GMD resumption of civil strife in 1946, in Mao's political imagination, turned Chiang Kai-shek into a "counter-revolutionary" and China's domestic conflict into "a counter-revolutionary war directed by US imperialism." The CCP did not win the civil war on the basis of Maoist ideas of people's war from the 1930s, as often claimed. It succeeded because it could exploit the military and political weakness of the GMD, benefit from Chiang Kai-shek's stubbornness and recklessness, convince whole armies of the enemy to defect, and pursue a conventional war based on captured heavy weaponry.[6]

For some years before victory in the fall of 1949, the CCP had been ambiguous about China's position in the world. During the last years of World War II, the party had hoped to work closely with the United States, the world's most powerful country. As the Cold War started and the United States continued to support the internationally recognized GMD-led ROC, the party decided to "lean to one side" – to the "anti-imperialist front headed by the Soviet Union," from which it hoped to obtain "genuine and friendly help." The expulsion of Yugoslavia from the Socialist Camp in 1948 convinced Chairman Mao of the political necessity to align closely with the USSR, lest he appear as another Tito in Stalin's eyes. This all required, however, the acceptance of Soviet ideas about the fundamental nature of the world system, even if the CCP would adapt them to its own needs. Borrowing from Stalin's Two-Camp Theory from 1919, Mao had anyway developed his own Two-Camp Theory as early as 1946. In his version, the United States and the Soviet Union were struggling over influence in the world's vast intermediate zone (Europe, Asia, and Africa), with China being the ultimate prize.[7] This view not only seemed to provide a cogent explanation for the reasons behind US support for the CCP's last enemy – the GMD – in the revolutionary liberation war, but it also elevated China once more to a pre-eminent position in world affairs.

Setting out as a Pariah, 1949–53

As early as mid August 1945, the Chinese communists had requested participation in the United Nations in a form separate from the GMD-led ROC, marshalling their supposed contribution to the defeat of Japan as justification. Four years later, on November 15, 1949, Prime Minister Zhou Enlai demanded – again without result – from UN General Secretary Trygve Lie membership for the PRC in lieu of the defeated ROC. Implicitly, this included the claim to one of the five veto-yielding permanent seats in the Security Council, which would have afforded the young state immediate global status. Within one year, all socialist states recognized New China, as did some Western European and several newly decolonized countries – all in all eighteen governments. Protesting against the exclusion of the PRC, the USSR decided to abstain from meetings of the Security Council starting on January 14, 1950.[8]

Parallel to its attempts at achieving far-reaching international recognition, the young PRC continued to be concerned with its physical survival. Mao was convinced that the United States had not accepted the defeat of the ROC. Hence he believed that New China needed to defend itself assertively on three fronts from which a possible US intervention could come: South Korea, the ROC on Taiwan, and French Indochina. Given the earlier decision to lean toward one side, Mao traveled to Moscow in December 1949 to seek military and economic aid. The resulting Sino–Soviet Friendship and Alliance Treaty of February 1950 and the outbreak of the Korean War four months later rattled the United States to such a degree that it committed itself economically and militarily to South Korea, the ROC in Taiwan, and the French struggle against Vietnamese communism in Indochina. The American reaction to communist China's assertive policies turned Mao's erstwhile fears into self-fulfilling prophecies.[9]

As a result of the Soviet UN boycott, the Security Council passed several resolutions in late June and early July 1950 that authorized collective military action to expel North Korea's troops from South Korea, despite the fact that neither was a member state. Also, on June 27, US President Harry S. Truman decided to send the Seventh Fleet into the Taiwan Strait to deter a possible Chinese attack on the ROC-held island. A US-led coalition of sixteen UN members intervened in South Korea in mid September and expelled North Korean troops within two weeks.

Although the PRC had not participated in the original attack in late June, the Chinese leaders had not only endorsed it beforehand but had also started to plan, together with the Vietnamese communists, a similar campaign against French colonial troops in Indochina. But following the UN decision to send troops to Korea and the US decision to dispatch the Seventh Fleet to the Taiwan Strait, the PRC refocused its attention on its northeastern border.[10]

New China's concerns over Korea went beyond mere security anxieties, even in the face of US troops advancing through North Korea to the Chinese border in early October. Since the end of the civil war, the Chinese leaders were committed to the internationalist duty of defending and promoting revolution in all of East Asia. Yet, as China's supposed "volunteer troops" swooped through North Korea in late October into the southern half of the country, the PRC found itself at war not only with US imperialism but also with the United Nations. Despite a recent vote rejecting the seating of New China, however, the international organization still invited a PRC delegation to attend a Security Council meeting in New York on the presence of Chinese troops in Korea. But six weeks of discussions in late 1950 did not lead to a diplomatic solution to the conflict in Northeast Asia. Instead, Washington accused Beijing of aggression in Korea, and the PRC charged the United States with bellicosity toward China over the Taiwan issue. By early 1951, the Korean conflict had turned into a stalemate around the original line of division, the 38th parallel. Even if the ongoing war allowed the PRC to mobilize the Chinese people for the country's revolutionary transformation, the extended duration of the conflict turned out to be costly in both financial and reputational terms. In July 27, 1953, four months after Stalin's death, all warring parties agreed to an armistice in Korea.[11]

Between Moderation and Assertiveness, 1953–55

The ceasefire in Korea allowed the Chinese leaders to recalibrate their revolutionary commitments abroad. Toward the end of 1953, Zhou promoted foreign policy ideas that would eventually be enshrined as the five principles of peaceful coexistence – *Panchsheel* – in the preamble of the Sino–Indian agreement on Tibet of April 29, 1954. The PRC thereby committed itself to a peaceful foreign policy and non-interference in the domestic affairs of other countries – just at the time of the opening of the international Geneva Conference on the restoration of peace in Korea and Indochina.[12] During the next three months, Zhou worked closely with North Korean, North Vietnamese, Soviet, British, and French delegations in Geneva to achieve a compromise peace on two of the three fronts on which Mao had feared an American attack on the PRC. In May, the Chinese delegation to Geneva confirmed that *Panchsheel* would be its guiding principle for any agreement on Korea and Indochina. Communist China's ultimate goal was to create a peaceful international environment conducive to internal socio-economic development. This included not only ending conflicts at the country's periphery but finding robust international agreements to thwart them from restarting. Yet the two Koreas failed to come to a settlement. With regard to Indochina, the Chinese leaders put pressure on the Vietnamese communists to make concessions in the hope of preventing the United States from finding a pretext for military intervention in the future. The conference eventually reached a compromise agreement by neutralizing Laos and Cambodia, and by temporarily dividing Vietnam into a communist government in the north and a non-communist counterpart in the south. Still, the United States used the fact that it had "not been a belligerent" in the Indochina War to avoid signing what it called a "capitulation" of the Free World to the Socialist Camp.[13]

On the basis of the Geneva Accords, the PRC focused on internal development. In early fall, Zhou for the first time introduced ideas similar to the famous Four Modernizations (*sige xiandaihua*; or *sihua*) that would trigger China's rise to prosperity and power after 1978. In his public discussions of the first Five-Year Plan (1953–57) on September 23, 1954, he called for the modernization of industry, agriculture, communications and transport, and defense. But external peace did not necessarily mean that the Chinese leaders agreed among themselves about internal development. Frustrated both by the country's slow economic development and by the supposed lack of revolutionary spirit, Mao soon started to promote economic development ideas antithetical to Zhou's visions. His Socialist High Tide (1955–56) abandoned the coordinated development of agriculture, China's largest economic sector.[14]

At the same time, Beijing tried to implement *Panchsheel* in its relations with Asian countries. Toward the end of the Geneva Conference, Zhou proposed a pan-Asian collective security pact that was supposed to enshrine the five principles. The scheme was designed to thwart American plans to create the anti-communist Southeast Asia Treaty Organization (SEATO). The Chinese prime minister also responded positively to an earlier Indonesian idea about an East Asia anti-aggression pact that explicitly referred to *Panchsheel*. The foundation of SEATO on September 8, 1954, however, triggered Indian–Indonesian planning for the Asian–African Conference in Bandung in April 1955, which made Zhou's ideas obsolete.[15]

Yet, despite a more peaceful international environment after the Geneva Conference, the Chinese leaders were still willing to embark on assertive policies toward the United States – particularly with regard to Taiwan, the one of the three fronts at risk of a potential American attack that had not been a topic at the Geneva Conference. After the end of the negotiations in Switzerland, Zhou blamed the United States for the lack of agreement on Korea, the problems during negotiations on Indochina, the continued division of China, and even Cold War conflicts outside Asia. Given this assessment, Beijing decided to take action in the Taiwan Strait. On September 3, the People's Liberation Army (PLA) started to shell ROC-held positions on small islands off the coast of mainland China. The long-planned establishment of SEATO five days later increased the Chinese feeling of hostile encirclement. The PRC leaders now decided to use the Taiwan Strait Crisis to deter US support for the ROC, in the hope that this would lead to the collapse of the GMD regime there, quick reunification, and eventually PRC membership in the United Nations. In order to put additional pressure on Washington, Beijing sentenced thirteen US Air Force personnel, whose airplane had been shot down during the Korean War, to long prison or even life terms for spying in late November.[16]

The sudden worsening of the international situation in the Taiwan Strait had unexpected effects on China's relationship with *both* the Asian–African countries and the United Nations. Angered by the foundation of SEATO, Indian Prime Minister Jawaharlal Nehru turned his initially negative stance toward an Indonesian proposal to convene an Asian–African Conference into enthusiastic support. During his seminal visit to Beijing in October 1954, Nehru and Zhou discussed the participation of the PRC in the conference. Despite much resistance by fellow co-organizers Ceylon (today's Sri Lanka) and Pakistan, India and Burma (today's Myanmar) managed to invite the PRC to the conference in April 1955 in Bandung, Indonesia. In comparison, China's relationship with the United Nations developed in the opposite direction. The United States used the sentencing of the thirteen US airmen, who had fought in the Korean War as UN personnel, to convince the General Assembly in early December to condemn the non-member PRC. Zhou complained to Indian diplomats about the "unfairness" of the US policy toward the PRC. Yet the international condemnation led to a Chinese invitation for UN General Secretary Dag Hammarskjöld to visit Beijing in early 1955. While Zhou committed the PRC to the ideals of the United Nations, Hammarskjöld, in return, explained that the trial of the US airmen amounted to a tribunal of UN personnel authorized to fight in Korea.[17]

After Hammarskjöld's departure, the PRC reassessed the overall direction of its foreign policy. The analysis of the discussions with the general secretary persuaded the Chinese leaders that UN membership was unlikely to occur soon. Not only had Beijing concluded that Hammarskjöld had visited Beijing "as a representative of the interests of the United States," but it also believed that Washington manipulated the international organization to China's detriment. Thus, the Chinese leaders decided to be in "no hurry" to pursue UN membership but to wait for the international organization to invite the PRC in the future. This change of mind occurred just at the time when the PRC received the official invitation to attend the Asian–African Conference. In this context, Mao even started to toy with the idea of establishing an alternative "People's United Nations."[18]

Simultaneously, Beijing decided to start up its nuclear weapons project. Mao had understood a decade earlier that nuclear weapons did not have military but primarily psychological and political value. As early as 1946, he had mocked the American A-bomb as a "paper tiger," but in early 1955 he still hoped that the successful development of Chinese nuclear weapons would break the US atomic preponderance in international relations and thereby elevate the PRC to equal status. The decision to go nuclear followed from both the realization that the PRC would not join the United Nations soon and another reassessment of the ongoing Taiwan Strait Crisis. The conflict had revealed overall Chinese communist weakness, since Beijing's assertiveness vis-à-vis Taipei had failed to deter Washington from supporting the ROC, or to bring about the fall of the GMD regime. On the contrary, the United States had made firm commitments to the defense of Taiwan, and with that to the continued ROC membership in the United Nations.[19]

This overall readjustment of China's foreign policy had an impact on seemingly unrelated issues, like Sino–Middle Eastern relations, within only a few months. Israel and the PRC had negotiated the establishment of trade relations since the turn of 1953/54. Yet, by spring of 1955, the PRC abrogated this nascent relationship by swinging support behind the Palestinians, in the hope of obtaining recognition from Arab states, none of which had yet recognized the PRC. In view of the approaching Asian–African Conference in Bandung, Zhou also decided to travel to Burma's capital, Rangoon, to meet with Prime Minister U Nu, the Egyptian leader Gamal Abdel Nasser, and Nehru. Luckily for him, in doing so he missed a direct flight to Jakarta that the secret service of the ROC bombed out of the sky.[20]

At the Asian–African Conference in Bandung on April 18–24, 1955, Zhou presented himself as a man of peace and reason, regardless of the ongoing Taiwan Strait Crisis and the swirling accusations of US involvement in the airplane bombing. In response to anti-communist attacks by pro-American conference participants, the prime minister publicly stated that he had come to seek "common ground." In closed meetings, several delegations raised their concerns about the ongoing Taiwan Strait Crisis and the imprisonment of US airmen. In a surprise announcement on April 23, Zhou offered to end the ongoing crisis and start direct talks with the United States. But within twenty-four hours Washington reacted negatively to the proposal. Still, the PRC terminated the shelling of the ROC-held islands a week after the Bandung Conference, in the hope that this would lead to negotiations with the United States. Through Indian mediation, the PRC and the United States eventually agreed to meet in informal ambassadorial talks in Geneva, although Washington continued to refuse to recognize Beijing. Hours before the start of the talks on August 1, the PRC released the last of the thirteen US airmen.[21]

Zhou's conciliatory attitude at Bandung improved communist China's international image. His support for the Palestinian cause also bought the sympathy of Arab countries. As a result, the PRC achieved formal recognition from Egypt, Syria, and Yemen within a few years. In his report to the State Council in mid May 1955, Zhou himself called the Bandung Conference a great success for the Asian–African world, global peace, and China's foreign policy. He stressed once more that the PRC was committed to the principles of the United Nations, even if the United States had "robbed" New China of its rightful place in it.[22]

Radicalization, 1955–60

The PRC gambled away much of its improved image during the following half-decade. While Zhou was at Bandung polishing the country's reputation, Mao launched the radical Socialist High Tide in agriculture at home. Its failure came into focus by the spring of 1956, just when the Soviet leader Nikita S. Khrushchev criticized his predecessor Stalin for policy mistakes and disregard for collective leadership. These kinds of accusations could have applied to Mao as well. Over the subsequent summer, the chairman attempted to prevent de-Stalinization at home while his fellow CCP leaders tried to curb his decision-making prerogatives and reverse his rural policies. At the first session of the eighth party congress in September, Mao saw his policies overturned and his writings – "Mao Zedong Thought" (*Mao Zedong Sixiang*) – removed from the party constitution as mandatory political reading for party members. Remarkably, however, he was able to regain his pre-eminent position by promoting radical policies quickly – first in domestic affairs in the wake of the Polish October and Hungarian Revolution, and then in external relations in the first half of 1958. This included sharp ideological attacks on the Yugoslav communists, which contradicted the principles of non-interference in domestic affairs promulgated in *Panchsheel* in 1954.[23]

In August 1958, Mao conceived the simultaneous start of the second Taiwan Strait Crisis and the launch of the radical phase of the Great Leap Forward as his double challenge to the USSR. On the one hand, he hoped to punish Khrushchev for his supposed appeasement of the United States over the concurrent Middle East crisis in Lebanon and Jordan. As a secondary goal, he intended to chasten the United States for the lack of progress in the ambassadorial talks over the three previous years. On the other hand, Mao claimed that the Great Leap Forward would enable the PRC to assume leadership in the Socialist Camp. He planned to use the artificially created external crisis in the Taiwan Strait to produce a domestic atmosphere conducive to the launching of his utopian socio-economic development project for China. Given the rapidly developing problems of the Great Leap Forward, however, as early as the beginning of 1959 Beijing retracted the claim that China was heading the Socialist Camp in lieu of the Soviet Union.[24]

But Mao's political radicalism undermined China's recently improved standing in various parts of the world. The PRC had vocally backed Egypt against Great Britain and France during the Suez Crisis in the fall of 1956. Afterward, it also supported, alongside the USSR, the communist movement in Syria. Nasser's persecution of communists in the wake of the creation of the bi-national United Arab Republic in February of 1958 soured China's relationship with many of the Middle Eastern countries. Shortly thereafter, the Chinese suppression of the Tibetan Uprising brought not only international condemnation – including a UN resolution – but also the collapse of China's relations with India. By August of 1959, border guards from the two countries shot at each other along the undemarcated border in the Himalayas. And finally, the PRC considered Khrushchev's visit to the United States in September 1959 ideological treason against world revolution and a betrayal of Soviet support for China's claim on Taiwan. The Soviet leader's third and last trip to the PRC shortly thereafter revealed the depth of ideological and political differences. The conversations between Mao and Khrushchev on October 2 ended in a shouting match.[25]

Notwithstanding the tens of millions of Chinese deaths that the Great Leap Forward caused during the spring famine in 1960, Mao was unwilling to give up on his political radicalism. In April, he made the brewing ideological disagreements with the USSR public when he approved of the release of the so-called Lenin polemics. Incensed by the Chinese rhetorical attacks, Khrushchev responded in July 1960 by recalling all Soviet advisers from China and terminating most development projects in the PRC. This sudden reversal did not cause the collapse of the Great Leap Forward, but it conveniently served as a pretext for the Chinese leaders to claim publicly Soviet responsibility for the country's economic problems. Yet the ultimate failure of Mao's economic brainchild later in the year opened up the opportunity for Zhou to reintroduce centrally planned and coordinated economic policies. While a CCP delegation went to Moscow in the fall of 1960 to praise Mao's radical ideas, the prime minister quietly reassumed his leading role in restoring China's economic health, two years after Mao's pretensions to lead the Socialist Camp.[26]

Moderation vs. Renewed Radicalization, 1960–65

In early 1961, Mao conceded that the Great Leap Forward had failed and officially endorsed the return to central economic planning. As Prime Minister Zhou and the party leaders Liu Shaoqi and Deng Xiaoping instituted moderate economic policies, including the reintroduction of small private plots and small-scale markets in the countryside, Mao withdrew from daily decision-making into philosophical and theoretical work. Although the PRC was willing to relax the ideologically charged relationship with the USSR, it did not restore the previously close economic relationship. In the first half of the 1960s, communist China shifted its economic foreign policy toward the capitalist world, except the United States. Beijing was even willing to establish commercial relations with countries – like Japan – that had recognized the ROC, its rival across the Taiwan Strait. This pragmatic policy was driven by the desire to reduce the overreliance on one economic partner – the USSR – but also by the double need to import large quantities of foodstuff and advanced technology. By late 1964, China had achieved a certain level of economic recovery that allowed Zhou to call once again for the Four Modernizations – this time in agriculture, industry, defense, and science and technology.[27]

In parallel, the PRC focused on diplomacy to reduce its international isolation. The Sino–Indian border clashes in 1959 and Sino–Soviet border conflicts the following year had revealed the need to negotiate on the non-demarcated borders with virtually all neighbors. Over the early 1960s, the PRC managed to come to compromise agreements with most – except Vietnam, India, and the USSR. In the hope of enhancing its own standing in Western Europe, and maybe even in the former French colonies in Africa, communist China also reacted positively to France's inquiries about mutual diplomatic recognition in the fall of 1963. Although

Beijing tried to impose a procedure of diplomatic recognition that would have made Paris look like a petitioner, at the turn of the year, France's President Charles de Gaulle dictated a solution, which denied the PRC much of the desired boost in status. Official relations were established in late January 1964, but France did not take the initiative to break relations with the ROC even though the PRC demanded such a step.[28]

Yet domestic and external pragmatism was stymied once again by renewed ideological radicalism. Fearing what he considered the reintroduction of capitalism through the back door, Mao started to use anti-Soviet and anti-American rhetoric to elevate the PRC to "the center of world revolution" in mid 1962. One of the first consequences of this new radicalism was the military attack on supposedly bourgeois India across the Himalayas in October in order to punish the southern neighbor for supposed border violations. In the wake of the conflict, Beijing tried to revive the Asian–African Movement as an alternative to the United Nations. Still, in the annual votes at the United Nations, the PRC continued to fail year after year to receive the necessary majority. Thus, by the end of 1963, Mao refined his Two-Camp Theory from the late 1940s, arguing that the United States and the Soviet Union struggled over two intermediate zones – over the developed zone encompassing Europe and Japan, and over the underdeveloped zone, including Asia, Africa, and Latin America. He emphasized the need for the PRC to focus on the second of the two zones.[29]

Chinese leaders hoped that the country's first nuclear test on October 16, 1964, would help the country gain greater international influence, particularly among the Asian–African countries. For that purpose, the PRC had accelerated the preparations for its first test as early as August of 1963, in the wake of the Soviet–American–British Limited Test Ban Treaty (LTBT). As the country's nuclear program stood ready for the first test in early fall of 1964, the Chinese leaders briefly discussed postponing or even cancelling it for political and reputational reasons. Just a year before, the PRC had called for the worldwide elimination of nuclear weapons, despite the fact that it had ordered its own program into high gear at the same time. In view of their fears about a joint Soviet–American surgical air strike against the program, the Chinese leaders decided to go ahead with the test. After the successful explosion on October 16, PRC embassies monitored the reaction of Asian–African countries carefully. While the vast majority of these countries praised the "Afro–Asian bomb" and the obliteration of the white, imperialist nuclear monopoly, China briefly hoped – but again, in vain – that the test would lead to PRC membership in the United Nations.[30]

Instead, the PRC actively promoted the Asian–African Movement as an alternative to the United Nations – preferably under its own leadership. China therefore seized on Indonesia's withdrawal from the United Nations, which occurred on January 1, 1965, in protest against Malaysia's elevation to a two-year term on the UN Security Council. Zhou publicly asserted that the PRC would not join the United Nations at all, even in the event of a positive vote in the General Assembly. At the same time, he demanded a revolutionary shakeup of the organization to cleanse it of US imperialist influence. During the tenth anniversary celebration of the Bandung Conference in mid April, Zhou met with Indonesia's President Sukarno to discuss world affairs, including the possibility of an alternative United Nations based on political and economic collaboration among underdeveloped Asian–African nations.[31]

But China's stridently revolutionary agenda – particularly its anti-Indian, anti-American, and anti-Soviet rhetoric – did not find many supporters in the Asian–African world. During a visit to Tanzania in early June 1965, Zhou went so far as to demand socialist revolutions against the post-colonial governments of recently independent countries in Africa. In this manner, he by and large undermined much of that continent's good will toward the PRC. The coup against Algerian Prime Minister Ahmed Ben Bella on June 19 removed not only the host of the second Asian–African Conference, scheduled to open only a few days later, but also one of China's allies in the region. The military overthrow of President Sukarno's government later in the fall further reduced the number of China's collaborators in the Asian–African Movement. A year later, Indonesia's pro-American government even led the country back into the United Nations. Finally, the Egyptian invitation of the Soviet Union to the postponed Asian–African Conference convinced the PRC to boycott the gathering, which triggered the movement's complete collapse in November 1965.[32]

Chinese radicalism toward the Asian–African world went hand in hand with greater support for national liberation movements there. For example, China was the first country to recognize the recently created Palestine Liberation Organization (PLO) in May 1965 (and ahead of the Arab League); it also supported the national unification struggle of the Vietnamese communists. Even before the American military intervention in Vietnam in early August 1964, the Chinese leaders had prepared for the possible escalation of the conflict. Their decision to support the North Vietnamese comrades was influenced by a mix of security concerns, commitments to national liberation, ideological considerations, and domestic needs. Yet Chinese aid to the communist Vietnamese struggle did not prevent Beijing from seeking, via several intermediaries, a secret understanding with Washington to keep the war in Indochina geographically limited.[33]

Finally, China's external radicalization was accompanied by a similar internal development. Deeply distrustful of Liu and Deng, who together with Zhou had restored China's economy to a low level of health, Mao decided to move against them at the turn of 1964/65. The emerging Cultural Revolution was primarily a purge of what Mao considered ideologically unreliable or even capitalist cadres. As an unintended effect, however, the Cultural Revolution suspended economic development, including Zhou's Four Modernizations, once more. Mao's rhetorical linking of his alleged internal enemies to the Soviet traitors of world revolution required the destruction of the alliance with the socialist ally prior to the launch of the Cultural Revolution in mid 1966. The collapse of party and state authority in China during the first months of the Cultural Revolution included the massive reduction of the country's diplomatic corps abroad. By late 1966, even socialist countries that had taken pro-Chinese positions in the Sino–Soviet Split, like communist Korea and communist Vietnam, dissociated themselves from the developments in China's domestic policies.[34]

Opening Up to the Outside World, 1968–72

Within two years, Mao's Cultural Revolution had run into deep trouble. Although he had achieved the removal of thousands of supposedly unreliable cadres, including Liu and Deng, students whom he had mobilized as Red Guards to implement revolution paralyzed the country internally and damaged the country's reputation externally. By the spring of 1968, Mao ordered the reduction of Chinese propaganda abroad. He even called his own slogan that "Beijing is the center of world revolution" inappropriate because it erroneously declared communist China to be the world's "core" in international affairs.[35]

However, it was the Soviet-led Warsaw Pact intervention in Czechoslovakia in August 1968 that triggered a major overhaul of China's domestic and foreign policies. In the wake of the intervention, the PRC denounced the Soviet Union as a socialist–imperialist power – an enemy to China as dangerous as the reactionary–imperialist United States. Far worse, however, was the possibility of an analogous Soviet intervention in the PRC, designed, as the Chinese leaders feared, to restore Soviet-style socialism there as well. During the second half of October, Mao ordered the end of the Cultural Revolution and the restoration of party and state organs by the spring of 1969.[36]

Even if Zhou equated the Soviet aggression against Czechoslovakia with the concurrent American intervention in Vietnam, the PRC still treated its two main enemies differently. Following the November 1968 election victory of US presidential candidate Richard M. Nixon – a man who had promoted the need for Sino–American reconciliation just a year before – Chinese leaders abandoned their strict insistence on uncompromising military struggle in Vietnam. Previously, Beijing had rejected Hanoi's negotiations with Washington, which had begun in Paris in May, as an ideological mistake. In late January 1969, however, Chinese media carried a translation of Nixon's inaugural speech as a sign of good will. Shortly thereafter, Beijing's relations with Moscow worsened. As a result of a decision from early 1968 to assume an assertive defense of Chinese territorial claims at the Ussuri River, Beijing found itself in lethal military border clashes with Moscow by March 1969, which triggered veiled Soviet counter-threats of a nuclear strike.[37]

The concurrent lack of progress in Sino–American rapprochement in the early weeks of the incoming Nixon administration left China completely without "friends" in international affairs, as Mao bemoaned in mid March. This development reconfirmed the pressing double need to restore the country's internal institutions and diplomatic capabilities. Following the ninth CCP congress in April, during which the party apparatus was re-established, the PRC re-dispatched twenty ambassadors to positions that had been orphaned since 1966–67. The choice of mainly Western countries was a sign that the PRC was looking forward to an opening toward the non-socialist world.[38]

Yet the grave state of Sino–Soviet relations over the summer of 1969 worked on the psyche of the Chinese leaders. By late August they fell into a war psychosis, expecting an imminent Soviet military intervention similar to the one in Czechoslovakia the year before. A hastily arranged meeting between the chairman of the Soviet Council of Ministers Aleksei Kosygin and Zhou Enlai in the wake of Ho Chi Minh's funeral in early September did not lead to rapprochement, particularly since Moscow was unwilling to stop its veiled nuclear threats. Soviet psychological warfare and the continued lack of positive signals from a hesitant Nixon administration merely exacerbated the war scare in Beijing. On the advice of the Pakistani government, the United States eventually decided to withdraw the Seventh Fleet from the Taiwan Strait – one of China's three fronts – in mid October as a sign of good will. But only after the US ambassador to Poland was able to corner the Chinese chargé d'affaires during a reception at the Yugoslav embassy in early December did Sino–American rapprochement start. As a sign of good will before the resumption of the informal ambassadorial talks, Mao ordered the release of several American citizens, who had been arrested earlier in the year when their yacht had strayed into Chinese waters.[39]

The year 1970 turned out to be a period of slow consolidation for the PRC. The decline of political radicalism in China itself allowed the economy to recover. The following year, the Chinese leaders even discussed resuming the construction of large and integrated factories with the help of capitalist countries, after a hiatus of half a decade due to the Cultural Revolution. But the pro-Western coup in Cambodia in March 1970 temporarily suspended Sino–American rapprochement. Yet China's diplomatic reappearance on the world stage still produced results in relations with non-socialist states. The Canadian recognition of the PRC in October 1970 opened the floodgates of recognition by a large number of countries, mostly from Western Europe, in the first half of the decade. China's concurrent decision to abandon its revolutionary support of national liberation movements throughout the world – though with a few exceptions, such as Vietnam – also helped the country to regain international respect and credibility. Consequently, the votes supporting PRC membership in the United Nations increased drastically in 1969 and 1970, even if the necessary two-thirds majority still remained out of reach.[40]

Few observers expected the far-reaching changes that would occur in 1971. With the help of the Pakistani government, Nixon's national security advisor Henry Kissinger secretly visited the PRC in July to discuss the improvement of relations and even a presidential visit early the following year. The subsequent public revelation of Kissinger's trip and the announcement of Nixon's future journey to Beijing broke the last dams preventing PRC admission to the United Nations. Although Washington desperately tried to prevent Taipei's replacement, a substantial number of pro-American UN members renounced their Cold War loyalty to the rapidly fading hardline US stance on China. On October 25, 1971, the necessary votes came together to replace the ROC in the United Nations with the PRC. Even if the Chinese leaders had denounced the international organization as "an instrument of great power politics" less than three years before, they happily accepted the unexpected membership, including the coveted permanent seat on the Security Council. As Zhou told UN General Secretary Kurt Waldheim, Beijing had expected membership in 1972 at the earliest. Despite their own surprise and complete lack of preparation, the Chinese leaders marveled at the "great victory" they had scored after twenty-two years of exclusion. With that, all of the world's declared nuclear powers had become permanent members in the council, and, simultaneously, all permanent members were nuclear powers.[41]

According to the testimony of numerous observers, Nixon's visit to China on February 21–28, 1972, shook the world or even changed history's course. Official Chinese accounts often stress that Nixon's handshake with Zhou at the airport was a belated attempt to make amends for the refusal by US Secretary of State John Foster Dulles to do so at the Geneva Conference in 1954. Since the American president visited of his own volition, Chinese propaganda portrayed his journey to Beijing as the pilgrimage of a repentant sinner to the magnanimous philosopher-king Mao. In any case, the Chinese leader had already reaped some benefits of Sino–American rapprochement prior to Nixon's arrival. Kissinger's secret visit on July 9–11, 1971, had brought conflicts among the Chinese leaders to the fore that led, within one month, to the removal of the hardline anti-American Lin Biao, whom, poignantly, Mao had originally chosen as his successor. Thus, the supreme Chinese leader not only got rid of a potential rival, but could also portray Nixon's visit as a success of his long-term confrontational policy toward the United States. Yet, substantially, the visit was much less prolific. The two sides agreed to disagree on Taiwan, did not find a common agreement on the ongoing war in Indochina, and did not establish formal relations for another seven years.[42]

Quo Vadis, 1972–76?

As the PRC settled into its new role as a permanent member of the Security Council in late 1971, it started its transformation from a revolutionary challenger of the world system into a status-quo power. Against initial US apprehensions about PRC ideological aggressiveness in the international organization, New China's voting record was mostly pragmatic. Zhou himself admitted that the PRC owed reasonable policies to all of those countries that had supported its membership in 1971. Indeed, in the long-term, communist China subscribed to the basic ideas of international law, which it had rejected for such a long time.[43]

Yet the period until Mao's death in September 1976 was still marked by a remarkable degree of Chinese ambivalence about the country's place in international affairs. In August 1972, Zhou told visiting UN General Secretary Kurt Waldheim that PRC admission to the United Nations had moved the world to the "crossroads" between the end of the Cold War and the collapse of the world system as in the late 1930s. Even if no global crisis developed in subsequent years, Sino–American rapprochement was heading toward a dead end by 1973. The Chinese leaders quickly realized that Nixon had used his visit to Beijing in February of 1972 to increase his leverage over Moscow during his journey there only three months later. Indeed, in May 1972, the two superpowers signed deals on nuclear arms limitation, mutual trade, collaboration in outer space, and cooperation in solving regional crises across the world. Thus, by early 1973, Mao emphasized to the visiting Kissinger that the United

States was pursuing an anti-Chinese policy by making peace with the USSR. Ultimately, as Nixon's secretary of state concluded, the PRC wanted the United States to take up stronger positions to prevent the spread of Soviet influence in Asia, the Middle East, and Europe. But Leonid I. Brezhnev's return visit to the United States in mid 1973 further undercut Mao's strategic calculations, and even questioned his decision to seek rapprochement in the first place, particularly since the PRC had little leverage left over the United States in the wake of the recent American withdrawal from Vietnam. His disappointment with the stuttering relationship was apparent during US President Gerald Ford's visit in early December 1975: "It seems to me at present there is nothing very much between our two countries, your country and mine. Probably this year, next year, and the year after there will not be anything great happening between our two countries. Perhaps afterward the situation might become a bit better."[44]

This disappointment led Mao to rethink his Two-Camp Theory from the post-World War II period. In 1974, Beijing started to propagate the Three-World Theory as an alternative. The new paradigm divided the international system into a bloc of two superpowers, the advanced industrialized countries of Europe and Japan, and the underdeveloped rest. China claimed a continued leadership role in the developing world, but indicated that it was willing to replace revolution with economic collaboration. Primarily, however, the theory served to guide China's policy toward the First and Second Worlds. Given the continued Sino–Soviet split, the lack of progress in Sino–American rapprochement, and the ongoing US–Soviet détente, the PRC focused its diplomatic efforts on Western Europe in a mixture of political pragmatism and strategic thinking. First of all, a substantial number of Western European countries had shifted recognition from the ROC to the PRC in the early 1970s. More importantly, or so the Chinese leaders believed, the Western European integration process not only appeared to produce a rising economic powerhouse – and thus a source of technology – but also looked like a budding military bloc in between the superpowers.[45] In that vein, as we will see in Chapter 18, communist China also demanded participation in the Conference on Security and Cooperation in Europe in 1972–75. As a belligerent in World War II and member of the UN Security Council, it claimed a stake in what it considered a pan-European peace conference, which, if concluded with Chinese input, would allow the USSR to redirect military capabilities toward East Asia.

Even if the long-term success of Sino–American rapprochement was in doubt by 1973, the events of the previous two years still had a major impact on PRC relations with its two communist neighbors. Mao Zedong understood that his invitation of Nixon to Beijing bore the potential of alienating

North Vietnam and North Korea, which both entertained antagonistic relations with the United States. Indeed, as the next chapter shows, the Democratic Republic of Vietnam (North Vietnam) resented China's collaboration with American imperialism; the Nixon visit even helped to trigger a North Vietnamese decision to launch a military offensive in the spring of 1972. With regard to the Korean peninsula, the American president agreed with Zhou during his visit to Beijing to restrain their respective allies, which had coexisted in an uneasy truce since the end of the Korean War in 1953. In any case, North Korea's relations with China had deteriorated since the start of the Cultural Revolution, followed by tensions with South Korea and the United States. In early 1968, Pyongyang sent a team to Seoul to assassinate South Korean President Park Chung-hee (which failed), and then seized the US Navy vessel *Pueblo* cruising in international waters off the North Korean coast. Surprisingly, Nixon's visit in 1972 led to a short-lived Thaw between the two Koreas in mid year Given the delicate balance on the Korean peninsula, however, Mao did not dare to make the kind of political gesture toward South Korea that had led to the opening with the United States.[46]

China's awkward dance between the two Koreas encapsulated the larger ideological problem which the PRC faced in the wake of the rise of capitalist Asia. In 1949, the PRC had been established with the goal of exploiting the supposedly superior socialist economic model to restore the country to economic prosperity and former global status. But the comparative record of development between New China and capitalist Asia in the two decades after 1949 spoke volumes. While the PRC suffered a major self-induced economic setback during the disastrous and lethal Great Leap Forward and then experienced stuttering growth during the Cultural Revolution, Japan re-emerged from its near-destruction in 1945 as the major economic force in Asia. Its transformation from a defeated militarist state to a successful capitalist one had induced the Chinese leaders in the early 1960s to seek closer economic relations with their ideological antagonist in Asia. Indeed, over several years in the early 1970s, Japan had captured a quarter of PRC foreign trade. Economic developments on the Korean peninsula in the early 1970s even more clearly revealed to the Chinese leadership that the socialist economic model did not fare well in comparative terms. Although the PRC disliked the military dictatorship in Seoul, it understood that capitalist South Korea was economically outperforming the communist northern half of the country. But the delicate balance on the peninsula, as mentioned above, did not yet allow the PRC to reap the economic benefits from a strategic relationship with South Korea. At least, on January 13, 1975, during one of his last public appearances before his death from cancer within a year, Zhou announced for the third time in two decades the launch of *sihua*. However, the brief but final political resurgence of the radical faction in the Cultural Revolution – the Gang of Four around Mao's wife Jiang Qing – in the following year delayed its implementation once more.[47]

Mao's death in September 1976 symbolically ended the revolutionary period in the history of the PRC. His immediate successor, Hua Guofeng, was a transitional figure until Deng's advent to supreme power. His outstanding achievement was the arrest of the Gang of Four around Jiang Qing in October 1976. But at Mao's death, the seeds for the long-term changes in China's internal policies, which are so apparent today, had already been planted. As the rehabilitated Deng struggled with Hua for supreme leadership of the PRC, he emphasized in May 1978 the urgent need to implement Zhou's *sihua*. In the last four months of the year, he managed to supersede his internal rival and convince the party to adopt the Four Modernizations.[48]

Conclusion

In retrospect, the 200-year development from giant empire to failed state and back to great power must be startling to all observers. Yet the teleological history of China's rise, as promoted by the country's Communist Party, is less straightforward than assumed. Chinese leaders disagreed among themselves as to what method was best to achieve the country's return to greatness. Was China to challenge the international system or ascend to power within it? Was it supposed to be a revolutionary force or a conventional great power? As the Great Leap Forward and the Cultural Revolution failed to propel China into the communist future, the Chinese leaders rejected their utopian goals for less ideological but more pragmatic aims. Sino–American rapprochement and the entry into the United Nations in 1971 helped to undermine the basis for the revolutionary impulse in China's domestic and foreign policies. Once accepted into the midst of the nations, the PRC was willing to engage with the world on the latter's terms and in peaceful competition, not in antagonistic rivalry. The remarkable economic success after 1978 seems, retrospectively, to justify this decision. But with the hindsight of history, it is anyway hard to imagine a revolutionary China beyond the 1970s. As future chapters reveal, the turn to a less ideological internal and external development reduced domestic and international conflict in many aspects. Paradoxically, however, it increased conflict with Vietnam, China's southern neighbor. But ultimately, it also helped to prevent the spread of revolution by the Vietnamese communists in the late 1970s and early 1980s.

6   Vietnam

Without doubt, the Indochina conflict was one of the most divisive events in the Cold War. For almost three decades, the Vietnamese communists fought internal adversaries, colonial France, and the United States to achieve ultimate victory. Any interpretation of the conflict hence needs to focus on their motivations and policies. For many decades, scholars have speculated whether the Vietnamese communists were just nationalists or genuine communists. The query's binary thrust, however, obscures historical reality. The Vietnamese communists pursued a set of five interrelated goals according to a flexible order of priorities: struggle for sheer survival, national reunification under their leadership, socialist construction, hegemony over all of Indochina, and world revolution.

Still, the Vietnamese communist leaders did not completely agree among themselves on this agenda. The high degree of continuity in the party leadership was responsible for why their disputes lasted so long. Ho Chi Minh, Truong Chinh, Vo Nguyen Giap, Pham Van Dong, and Le Duan were the most powerful Vietnamese communist leaders for three decades or more each. Some, such as Ho, were internationalists and patriots, and others, such as Le Duan, were Stalinists, Indochinese nationalists, and world revolutionaries. Their varied biographical backgrounds often influenced their political outlook. "Ho, the enlightened" had long-standing links to the Comintern and to the Chinese Communist Party (CCP). Truong Chinh – "Long March" – was a great admirer of the Chinese revolutionary Mao Zedong. But the other leaders were essentially homegrown revolutionaries who had little knowledge of the outside world. Their differences over the ultimate goals of their revolution also had roots in the country's past. Vietnamese monarchs had claimed, with little success, hegemony over Laos and Cambodia; some communists in effect chased the old royal dreams. With the exception of the early nineteenth century, Vietnam also did not carry its present name, did not exercise power across all of its current area, and was not unified under one government. Unsurprisingly, during the interwar period, intellectuals from all political backgrounds engaged in a lively debate about national identity and post-colonial borders. To a large degree, Vietnam is a creation of decolonization and nation building in the twentieth century.[1]

The Vietnamese Revolution occurred, of course, in the context of its Chinese communist counterpart, as we saw in the previous chapter. It drew on this successful model in the late 1940s, but rejected some of its extreme characteristics two decades later. Structurally, the Vietnamese Revolution had far-reaching consequences on a range of Cold War issues, as future chapters will show. Sino–Vietnamese conflict led to Vietnamese–Indian rapprochement in the 1970s. The anti-imperialist claims of Vietnamese communists exerted a great influence on the Non-Aligned Movement, but ultimately were co-responsible for its collapse by the early 1980s. The Vietnamese revolutionary agenda also appealed to young protesters in the Free World, who came to see the US military intervention in Indochina in the mid 1960s as a symbol of all the ills of the Western socio-economic model. It similarly provided a model to Palestinian officials and fighters, who claimed to pursue a revolutionary war against the Zionist occupation in the Middle East. In the end, however, this long-term commitment to revolution by the Vietnamese communists helped China to seek an opening to the United States after Mao's death in 1976. By the late 1970s and early 1980s, the Vietnamese revolutionary agenda was increasingly out-of-place in a rapidly changing world.

From Early Beginnings to Revolution, 1930–45

In the 1920s, imperial France tried to install ideas of ethnic hierarchy in Indochina to fortify its colonial rule – a practice that other European imperial powers had pioneered elsewhere. By declaring people from Annam superior to those from Tonkin, Cochinchina, Cambodia, and Laos, the French colonial administration tried to elevate and bind them into the imperial system. But, in doing so, it unwittingly triggered a heated debate among Indochinese intellectuals about national identity. Hailing mostly from Annam, these intellectuals tried to imagine how their country's borders would look in the post-colonial future. Should it contain only the part in which they lived, combine some of the five, or encompass all of them? It was in this particular context that the term "Vietnam" ("Southern Viet") re-emerged in the 1920s, symbolizing a new beginning grounded in a short period of early nineteenth-century history.[2]

Although the communists were not central contributors to this debate, the discussion about the name of their party reveals that they certainly were part of it. In late 1920s, the Comintern instructed the Annamite Ho Chi Minh to create an "Indochinese Communist Party" (ICP) and

Map 6. Indochina

similar parties in Thailand, Malaya (Malaysia), Indonesia, and the Philippines. Although the most successful among Ho's creations, the ICP still emerged only in fits and starts. At the foundational meeting in Hong Kong in February 1930, he proposed to call the new political outfit the Vietnamese Communist Party (VCP) because almost no member hailed from Laos and Cambodia. Taking into account Comintern criticism, the plenum of the new party renamed the outfit the Indochinese Communist Party (ICP) within less than a year. The party thereby followed Comintern practice of working for anti-imperialist revolutions within territorial boundaries imposed by European imperialism. Due to persecution by the British and French colonial security services, the party did not grow significantly over the course of the 1930s. For much of the decade, Ho himself went to Moscow and, by 1938, to China in an attempt to reactivate his old contacts.[3]

In June 1940, just when National Socialist Germany was overrunning France, Ho met with Vo Nguyen Giap and Pham Van Dong, two fellow Annamites, in southern China, where they revived a dormant united front organization – the Viet Nam Independence League (Viet Minh) – that had been established in 1936. The goal was to attract non-Communist nationalists to the cause of national liberation. The eighth ICP plenum in spring of 1941 decided to call the future post-colonial state the "Democratic Republic of Vietnam." The name reflected the recently promulgated Maoist concept of a two-stage revolution in the colonial world – envisioning, first, an anti-imperialist national revolution through a united front with non-communists, and then a socialist revolution against them. While the focus of the reinstated Viet Minh was primarily on Vietnam, the eighth plenum still did not abandon Laos and Cambodia. On the contrary, the ICP intended to build up separate national independence leagues that were supposed to join a planned Indochinese Independence League in the future. Despite French colonial harassment, the party managed to establish roots in northern Vietnamese border areas by late 1941. But the expansion of imperial Japanese dominance into Indochina early in the following year greatly hindered party building throughout all of Vietnam. Under Truong's party management and Giap's military leadership, the ICP nevertheless managed to maintain a small base area in northern Vietnam during World War II.[4]

The seeds for the revolution in August 1945 were planted a full year before. In liberated Paris, Charles de Gaulle annulled the orders, which the defunct Vichy government had issued in 1940, for the French colonial administration in Indochina to collaborate with imperial Japan. Because World War II was turning against Japan, Tokyo began to toy with the idea of granting "independence" to the Asian nations under its control in order to prevent the return of European colonialism. On March 9, 1945, imperial Japan announced the abolition of the French colonial administration, through which it had ruled Indochina. At the same time, it declared Cambodia, Laos, and "Annam" – encompassing Tonkin, Annam, and Cochinchina – independent. Tokyo enlisted representatives from three royal houses to head the former French colonies – Norodom Sihanouk, Sisavang Vong, and Bao Dai. When Japan transferred power to the new Annamese government in June and July, Bao Dai adopted "Vietnam" as the official name of his country.[5]

The March coup opened up unexpected opportunities for the ICP. It replaced the French colonial system with a weak, Japanese-sponsored monarchy, just at a time when imperial Japan was about to lose the war. An emergency party meeting chaired by Truong, however, decided to wait until conditions for revolution matured *in the wake* of the anticipated landing of Allied troops in Indochina. But by late spring, the ICP realized its misjudgment. The Allies were attacking Japan directly across the western Pacific while the three royal governments started to collaborate with each other. In June, Ho implemented a new set of policies toward the outside world, which included good relations with the prospective American victor of the Pacific War, a reduction of tensions with the *Guomindang*-led Republic of China (ROC), and the demand for France's recognition of Vietnam's independence. Collaboration with a small number of low-ranking American intelligence officers in Hanoi intensified for a short time after.[6]

In the words of a contemporaneous party document, the "hour of General Insurrection ... struck" in mid August when Japan offered to surrender to the United States. In an unrelated development, Bao Dai's government had just entered into a week-long internal impasse over postwar policy. All the while, the country suffered from a famine that years of forced Japanese food exports had caused. At the ninth plenum of the ICP on August 13–15, Ho revised the party position from the spring on the benefits of the Allied landing, and instead claimed that the arrival of foreign troops after Japanese surrender would *complicate* the situation. Thus, he urged the party to exploit concurrent French–British–American–Chinese disagreements and to "build up a ... Democratic Republic of Vietnam" immediately.[7]

In the absence of functioning French and Japanese administrative institutions, the August revolution primarily targeted Bao Dai's paralyzed and weak government. Riding on popular discontent over the raging famine, an ICP-led insurrection started on August 16 in Hanoi, from where it spread south within ten days. On August 25, Bao Dai abdicated and handed over the government to the Viet Minh. On September 2, the day of Japan's official surrender, Ho publicly proclaimed the establishment of the Democratic Republic of Vietnam (DRV) in Hanoi. The official declaration invoked the revolutionary history of the United States and France, and ended with an appeal to the Allied nations to "acknowledge the independence of Viet Nam." But since the World War II Allies had decided at the Potsdam Conference to divide Indochina at the 16th parallel into a British and Chinese occupation zone, no country recognized the DRV.[8]

With the arrival of ROC troops in Hanoi, also on September 2, it became obvious that the new state's grasp on power was tenuous. The ICP itself had only around 5,000 members. Non-communist nationalists and the Chinese army sympathetic to them contested the party's claim to rule. By September 8, the first British advance troops arrived in Saigon, soon followed by their French counterparts. Originally, the late President Franklin D. Roosevelt had envisioned a shared Sino–British occupation to prevent the return of French colonialism. But Churchill's successful prevention of the French re-establishment of colonial control in Syria and Lebanon in May had "deeply insulted" de Gaulle, who considered British behavior an unforgivable betrayal. In late summer, the French president explicitly prohibited his representatives in Indochina from cooperating with any of the war allies, otherwise "we will see the dastardly game which the English played in Syria repeat itself in Indochina." Fortuitously, the British commander in Indochina shared de Gaulle's conviction that France had a case to reclaim colonial authority. Unenthusiastic about the unwanted occupation duties in Indochina, the new Labour government in London retroactively acquiesced to the re-establishment of French rule south of the 16th parallel.[9]

From Anti-Colonial War to Cold War Struggle, 1945–50

Within less than one year, France managed to reoccupy much of Indochina, particularly after early 1946 when the ROC withdrew its troops for the final phase of the civil war at home. The return of French colonial rule posed a serious challenge to the DRV. The young state quickly decided to focus on self-defense in the north in order to create a base capable of sponsoring guerilla warfare below the 16th parallel. Simultaneously, the ICP-run Viet Minh tried to acquire democratic legitimacy through the manipulation of the elections in January 1946. Yet the Vietnamese communists had also realized that the ICP was a political liability, and thus officially dissolved it before the polls. Still, it continued to exist in clandestine form until it re-emerged in 1951 under a different name. Furthermore, the Vietnamese communist attempt at gaining democratic legitimacy went hand in hand with a campaign of persecuting and even assassinating non-communist nationalists – among them the brother of future South Vietnamese President Ngo Dinh Diem.[10]

The arrival of French troops in northern Indochina in 1946 threatened the survival of the DRV itself. The communist leadership decided to avoid war by negotiating with colonial France, but the talks in Paris ended in failure by the autumn. At the start of war soon thereafter, the Vietnamese communists moved their military activities from the cities to the countryside. Initially, their armed forces proved no match for the superior French troops. But Truong eventually imposed Maoist ideas of conventional warfare concurrently used by the CCP in the civil war in Manchuria: withdrawal, consolidation, and general offensive. At the beginning, he also saw Laos, Cambodia, and even Thailand merely as battlefield extensions, or at least logistical bases, for the war in Vietnam. But as the war continued, the clandestine ICP built up resistance organizations in the two neighboring Indochinese kingdoms, in the hope of bringing them into an Indochinese Federation after French withdrawal. Looking beyond Indochina, DRV leaders even toyed with the idea of building up a Southeast Asian federation.[11]

As Giap's troops began to contest French military supremacy, both the DRV and France modified their political approaches to the war. The Vietnamese communists also benefited from the successes of their Chinese comrades in 1949, even though the two fraternal parties kept their unfolding military cooperation at a clandestine level. Paris, in comparison, embarked on the double policy of lessening the popular appeal of the DRV and increasing the chances of support from a strongly anticolonial United States. In March 1949, France created the State of Vietnam (SVN) – headed by Bao Dai – as a counter-model to the DRV. In a similarly underhanded manner, France granted formal independence to Laos and Cambodia later that year.[12]

The Cold War formally arrived in Indochina by January 1950. On the 18th, as the first country in the world to do so, the newly established People's Republic of China (PRC) recognized the four-year-old DRV. Mao convinced Stalin to follow suit by January 30, one day after the French Assembly had ratified the treaties that created the supposedly independent Associated States of Vietnam, Laos, and Cambodia. On February 8, Washington and London recognized the three French-sponsored countries. Following the conclusion of the Sino–Soviet Friendship and Alliance Treaty six days later, the United States also approved financial and military support for France in the struggle against communism in Indochina. With Thailand's decision to recognize the French creations in Indochina and then to suppress communist activities at home, the Vietnamese communist dream of a Southeast Asian federation evaporated.[13]

From War to a Negotiated Solution, 1950–54

In the spring of 1950, just as Mao's China endorsed North Korean plans to attack the southern part of the country, the PRC and the DRV jointly planned a military offensive in Tonkin. A month after the start of the Korean War, Ho rhetorically linked the national liberation of Indochina to Chinese communist victory in 1949: "Close solidarity between the peoples of Viet Nam, Cambodia and Laos constitutes a force capable of defeating the French colonialists and the US interventionists. The US imperialists have failed in China, they will fail in Indochina." In the fall, while US-led UN troops intervened in the Korean War and soon thereafter the supposed Chinese volunteers counter-intervened, Vietnamese communist troops cleared the northern border area of French control, facilitating future PRC–DRV military cooperation.[14]

These rapid political changes pointed toward the pressing need for institutional reforms in the DRV. In mid February 1951, the clandestine ICP publicly reappeared, holding its second congress under a new name – the Vietnamese Workers Party (VWP). Alienated by this sudden development, many non-communist members of the Viet Minh defected to Bao Dai's SVN. In order to emphasize the importance of the southern revolution, the newly elected Central Committee elevated the party committee in charge of Cochinchina, run by Le Duan since 1946/47, to the Central Office for South Vietnam. While the geographical redefinition of the party's name reflected the continued failure of the ICP to attract Laotian and Cambodian members, it did not mean that the renamed VWP abandoned revolution in neighboring Indochinese countries. As early as November 1950, the DRV had organized a meeting of Vietnamese, Laotian, and Cambodian "peoples" to discuss collaboration. A month after its second congress, the VWP created the "Joint National United Front of Vietnam, Laos, and Cambodia." While its manifesto suggested that the new organization worked toward "genuine independence for the three peoples," the VWP had no intention of relinquishing its hegemony in a future "Party of the *Vietnam–Khmer–Laotian Federation*." For that purpose, the ICP had already created communist parties in Laos and Cambodia earlier in 1950. The newly founded Pathet Lao functioned like the defunct Viet Minh – as a communist front organization. In Cambodia, the VWP first revived Khmer Issarak, an older non-communist national liberation movement, and then sponsored the foundation of a communist party, the Khmer People's Revolutionary Party, which later would become the Khmer Rouge.[15]

As the war intensified in Vietnam in 1951, northern communist troops and southern guerillas were able to win some battles against the French army. Given the organizational extension of Vietnamese communist influence into the neighboring Indochinese countries, Giap also expanded military action into Laos with the goal of overstretching the French enemy forces. These parallel political and military developments brought profound changes to the nature of the DRV. Stalinist and Maoist ideas of mass mobilization increasingly influenced political organization. In the end, the emergence of a highly militaristic and regimented but economically, socially, and culturally underdeveloped communist state was primarily a response to the necessities of war.[16]

Once the Korean armistice was signed in mid 1953, Paris faced the question of why it should continue fighting communism in Indochina after Washington had cut a deal in Northeast Asia. As early as June, French President of the Council of Ministers (Prime Minister) Joseph Laniel had floated the idea of negotiations for an "honorable peace." In October, Ho accepted Laniel's offer to negotiate. As a diplomatic solution appeared on the horizon, both sides tried to secure territory in order to increase leverage at the negotiation table. In a combined attempt to support the royal government of Laos and to disrupt Vietnamese communist offensives, the French army decided to seize the strategically important town of Dien Bien Phu in mountainous northwestern Tonkin in November 1953. The DRV seemingly did not react but continued its military offensive deep into Laos. By early February, its troops had almost reached the royal capital Luang Prabang. Yet, in reality, Giap planned a major attack on Dien Bien Phu, designed to achieve a spectacular victory before the start of the not-yet-scheduled negotiations.[17]

As a sign of the relaxation of international tensions following Stalin's death in March 1953, the foreign ministers of the four major World War II Allies – the Soviet Union, the United States, the United Kingdom, and France – met in Berlin in early 1954 to discuss Germany primarily. On the last day, they issued a joint communiqué proposing a conference on Korea and Indochina to start in late April in Geneva. The announcement intensified French and DRV preparations for the battle at Dien Bien Phu, which eventually began on March 13. France had hoped that the airfield near the township would facilitate the supply of reinforcements. Within less than two weeks, Vietnamese communist artillery positioned in caves which had been dug into surrounding hillsides had obliterated it completely. On May 7, the encircled French troops surrendered. Even if the battle had not decided the war, it undermined France's will to fight.[18]

Buoyed by the victory, the DRV joined the talks on Indochina, which began in Geneva the following day. In view of the long history of claims on all of Indochina, a confident Vietnamese communist delegation had arrived in the Swiss city with maximalist demands in its luggage: complete

French withdrawal, a united independent Vietnam, free elections in all three Indochinese countries, and the inclusion of Pathet Lao and the Khmer Issarak in the conference. But over the course of more than two months, the delegation itself proposed the military and administrative disentanglement of the DRV and the SVN, agreed to the 17th parallel as a temporary line of division, withdrew its demands for Pathet Lao and Khmer Issarak participation, and pledged to respect the sovereignty and territorial integrity of the kingdoms of Laos and Cambodia. Pragmatism and fear about a possible intervention by US imperialism convinced the DRV to sign a compromise agreement, which was supposed to buy time for the national revolution. The reduction of demands was also rooted in the realization that victory at Dien Bien Phu had only been a single battlefield success, which had exhausted Vietnamese communist capabilities. Sober-minded advice from the Chinese and Soviet comrades helped as well. The PRC bluntly told the DRV that the continued denial of its political involvement in Laos and Cambodia was disingenuous and counterproductive. In the end, Moscow and Beijing both practiced *communist self-containment*. They were concerned that the geographical enlargement of the DRV would trigger American military intervention and also alienate non-aligned India, an important anti-imperialist country and potential friend.[19]

The Geneva Accords of July 20–21 granted all three Indochinese countries independence, guaranteed the neutralization of Laos and Cambodia, temporarily divided Vietnam, and foresaw nationwide elections in that country within two years. However, the United States did not sign the accords – technically because it had "not been a belligerent." While the conference had been going on, the United States continued to plan the establishment of a regional, anti-communist military alliance, which eventually was founded in Manila on September 8, 1954. Bringing together the United States, the Philippines, Thailand, Australia, New Zealand, Pakistan, France, and the United Kingdom, the Southeast Asia Treaty Organization (SEATO) claimed to guarantee the security of "the general area of the Southwest Pacific not including the area north of 21 degrees 30 minutes North latitude." The twisted wording thinly disguised the fact that it covered virtually all the territories of the non-members Vietnam, Cambodia, and Laos.[20]

By the end of the summer of 1954, the conditions that would shape developments in Indochina for the next two decades had been put in place. The DRV received, for the first time, undisputed rule over territory – north of the 17th parallel. However, the transfer of comrades from the southern guerilla bases to the north left it with much less leverage in the SVN. In addition, the DRV had lost much of its influence in

Cambodia and Laos. In the nine months after the withdrawal of 132,000 French and SVN personnel from the north, approximately 900,000 civilians left as well – non-communist nationalists, educated and professional elites, and Catholics. While they would form a large part of the future elite in the southern SVN, this exodus created *de facto* a political monoculture in the northern DRV. The greatest losers of the Geneva Accords, however, were the southern guerilla fighters who had gone to war on a battlefield of secondary importance. About 260,000 persons left the southern base areas for the north. Around 10,000 fighters were ordered to stay behind covertly, in a flagrant violation of the Geneva Accords.[21]

Toward Renewed War, 1954–63

India's Prime Minister Jawaharlal Nehru, who was the first foreign guest to visit the territorially reconstituted DRV on October 17, noted that Hanoi had a "rather fearful look." Indeed, North Vietnam, as it would be called informally for the next two decades, had suffered over 300,000 casualties. The country's industry and agriculture lay in ruins. Many of the best people to run the economy had left for the south. In early 1955, on Truong's proposal, the VWP decided to radicalize the land reform, which had begun two years earlier. The new policy was both an ideologically motivated copy of the concurrent Socialist High Tide in the PRC and a reaction to the famines that had been caused by bad weather, Catholic farmers fleeing south, and the SVN refusal to resume the customary rice shipments from south to north. Against this background, the VWP decided in March 1955 to focus on the socialist construction in the north and to use diplomatic means to overcome the country's temporary division.[22]

The DRV took American interference in the south for granted long before the United States had actually decided to support the SVN. Relying on Mao's Two-Camp Theory of 1946, its leadership considered the world divided into "two blocs." As the American-led bloc was rife with internal strife, it was supposedly forced to provoke conflict around the globe. North Vietnamese propaganda particularly attacked the southern government headed by Ngo Dinh Diem, who was one of the leading non-communist nationalists and whom Bao Dai had appointed prime minister during the Geneva Conference. From the very beginning, Hanoi's rhetoric tried to portray Diem as an American puppet. The DRV leaders had fully understood that he was a genuine nationalist and thus constituted a major threat to their long-term plans of reuniting the country under their own leadership. When Diem survived internal challenges in his first year in office and then refused to participate in preparations for nationwide elections, North Vietnam grew disillusioned. By the fall of 1955, the southern strongman had even overthrown Bao Dai, renamed the SVN the Republic of Vietnam (RVN), and used a rigged election to appoint himself president. Diem's emergence as a stable, yet authoritarian, leader eventually convinced the United States to support him as the only man capable in the south of resisting communist expansion.[23]

Diem's refusal to hold elections confirmed long-held southern communist skepticism about the Geneva Accords. Le Duan himself had been disappointed by the results of the 1954 conference, but had loyally explained to the southern comrades why they should regroup to the north. After Diem's rejection of elections, Le Duan urged the party leadership in the north to resume armed struggle in the south. In August 1955, the eighth plenum of the VWP Central Committee decided in principle on preparations for a future insurgency. But even if Saigon had taken unilateral steps to prevent reunification, Hanoi was careful not to violate the 1954 agreements openly in order to maintain the moral high ground. Hence, the DRV sent its prime minister, Pham Van Dong, to India in early April 1955, where he confirmed his country's commitment to *Panchsheel*. At the Asian–African Conference in Bandung some weeks later, Nehru convinced the DRV delegation to promise publicly that it would not intervene in the internal affairs of its Indochinese neighbors. While DRV influence in Cambodia was negligent anyway, the VWP in reality was working closely with Pathet Lao.[24]

The period from mid 1956 to early 1957 witnessed fundamental changes in the leadership in Hanoi that would eventually reverberate throughout the next quarter of a century. Because of the disastrous results of his Chinese-inspired rural reforms, Truong was forced to resign as general secretary at the tenth plenum in late summer of 1956. The sudden dismissal of the long-standing party leader, who since 1954 had been firmly committed to the idea of focusing on socialist construction in North Vietnam, opened up new possibilities for those who advocated armed struggle in the south for national reunification. Le Duan's election as general secretary in January 1957 – albeit ad interim – elevated a hardline leader to power for the next quarter of a century. He advocated the development of North Vietnam primarily as a "stable and powerful base" for supporting the national revolution in the south, urged the quick resumption of the military struggle against the "US–Diem imperialists and feudalists," and placed Vietnam's revolution within the framework of the "progressive people's movement throughout the world."[25]

In late 1957, Le Duan grew concerned by the apparent strengthening of Diem's government. A year later, he even visited South Vietnam covertly to get a better picture of the situation. At the fifteenth plenum in May 1959, Le Duan warned of the dire situation in the south: the Diem regime was on the cusp of annihilating the remnants of communist presence. The subsequent decision by the VWP Central Committee, Resolution 15, committed the party to a southern strategy once more, although details remained ambiguous. The third party congress in September 1960 eventually ratified many of Le Duan's visions. He was also formally elected first secretary, as the position was now called, while a substantial number of southerners joined him in the Politburo. Three months later, the VWP officially established the National Liberation Front of South Vietnam (NLF). Bringing together communist and non-communist nationalists, it resembled the defunct Viet Minh.[26]

At that same time, the ongoing crisis in royal Laos rapidly worsened. Formally led by the king's half-brother Souphanouvong but guided by the VWP, Pathet Lao had started civil war in May 1959. On January 1, 1961, Cambodia's head of state, former King Sihanouk, called for an international conference to restore peace in the neutral country. The Laos Conference in Geneva from May 1961 to July 1962 reconfirmed the Geneva Accords of 1954, but neither the DRV nor the United States subsequently honored the new agreement. Yet the American willingness to participate in the conference and sign an accord suggested to the DRV that the United States might be willing to come to a similar agreement on Vietnam.[27]

While the world focused on the Laos Conference the crisis in Vietnam matured. In the wake of the third party congress, Le Duan embarked on a long-term campaign of monopolizing power in his hands through the use of the secret police. But just as the DRV started to organize the southern insurgency, incoming US president, John F. Kennedy, decided to support Diem's counterinsurgency warfare. In the face of a militarily more effective South Vietnamese regime, the Politburo of the VWP officially decided in late 1962 to resume armed struggle. The concurrent Chinese emphasis on national liberation in the struggle against the supposedly revisionist USSR opened up the additional possibility of receiving much needed military aid.[28]

However, a coincidental event eventually set the DRV on its ten-year maximalist course to seek reunification by military means. A member of the Catholic minority in the largely non-Christian state, Diem had grown increasingly dictatorial. On November 1, 1963, his own generals removed him, though with implicit American endorsement. His sudden fall and violent death reopened the debate about strategy in Hanoi. The moderate faction in the central leadership saw the recent developments in Saigon as a chance to negotiate reunification, but the radicals proposed military escalation to overthrow the supposedly weak generals. At the ninth plenum in December, Le Duan asserted that the international situation was beneficial and that the party should wage war against the US imperialists and their southern puppets. Resolution 9 asserted that "complete victory" in South Vietnam would come as the result of a military offensive combined with a popular uprising. This radicalization of policies went hand in hand with a purge of moderate party leaders, many close to Ho, while it simultaneously produced a more uncompromising and insular leadership around Le Duan.[29]

Battling US Imperialism, 1964–68

As the DRV prepared for the anticipated final step toward national unification, the United States decided to enter fully into the fray. Three weeks after Diem's fall and death, US President John F. Kennedy was assassinated as well. His successor, Lyndon B. Johnson, believed that a hardline stance on Vietnam would bolster his credentials as a reliable Cold Warrior. The news of an attack by North Vietnamese torpedo boats on an American reconnaissance ship in the Gulf of Tonkin on August 2, 1964 – including the canard of a similar attack two days later – served as a pretext for the new president to escalate the war. In March 1965, the first ground troops arrived in South Vietnam, destined to defend the RVN against internal insurgents and northern infiltrators.[30]

The US participation in counter-insurgency warfare in the RVN and the concurrent American escalation of the strategic bombing of the DRV forced Hanoi to rethink its southern strategy once again. Le Duan's radical faction still advocated sticking to the chosen course of action while keeping any revolutionary activity in Laos and Cambodia as a low priority. Thus, the Vietnamese leaders showed little interest when Sihanouk, who had just terminated Cambodia's relations with the United States and the RVN because of grave political differences, asked for strategic collaboration. Simultaneously, the DRV benefited from increased Chinese and Soviet commitments. Nikita S. Khrushchev's overthrow in mid October 1964 elicited Soviet economic and military support for a socialist fraternal country under imperialist attack. Yet the rapidly evolving split between Beijing and Moscow forced Hanoi to tread carefully between the self-declared "center of world revolution" and Soviet revisionism. From 1965 to 1968, the PRC provided anti-aircraft artillery troops to defend northern cities, and supplied small arms, food, and clothing to the southern insurgents, while the Soviet Union delivered sophisticated weaponry, including fighter planes and anti-aircraft missiles. Although Beijing insisted on uncompromising military struggle until final victory, Moscow repeatedly advocated a negotiated solution to the war.[31]

The American military escalation opened up old splits among the DRV leaders. By early 1966, Le Duan's radical faction called for a "victory of the type of the battle of Dien Bien Phu" with the goal of achieving a position of strength from which Hanoi could dictate the terms for peace to Saigon and Washington. Ultimately, it believed, the "liberation of the South Vietnamese population ... was the precondition for national unity." Le Duan's sidekick, Le Duc Tho, informed the NLF that South Vietnam had become "the center of the world revolutionary storm," which would trigger similar developments in Southeast Asia, South Asia, Africa, and Latin America. Yet the uncompromising dedication to national revolution in the RVN had dire consequences for the DRV. American strategic bombing, supposed to destroy North Vietnam's will to fight, drastically reduced living standards.[32]

The internal battle about overall strategy reached its peak with a purge of the moderate faction in the second half of 1967. By then, the Vietnamese communist cause had fallen into a dire state in both halves of the country. The war-related destruction in the DRV had undermined the economy. In the south, according to Soviet and Polish reports, US armed forces were routing NLF forces. Le Duan's reputation started to lose its polish at home. The first secretary and his allies in the party used the secret police to remove proponents of a negotiated solution, many of whom were close to Ho and Giap. Until his death a little more than two years later, the aging Ho retained no real power, while Giap was sidelined. The political monoculture that had dominated the DRV since 1954 had reached the highest levels of the VWP.[33]

Secure in power, Le Duan proceeded in the fall of 1967 to implement plans for a combined offensive and uprising in South Vietnam during Tet (Chinese lunar New Year) in late January 1968. The radicals in Hanoi hoped for a victory similar to "Dien Bien Phu" during a US presidential election year. According to a later Soviet assessment, the Tet Offensive was the final bid to win complete military victory; in case of failure, Hanoi was willing to negotiate. Socialist ambassadors picked up signs of a mass mobilization in December, concluding that a major offensive in South Vietnam would occur early the following year. Vietnamese comrades confirmed that 1968 would be a decisive year. The radicals in Hanoi were so confident about the future victory that they even discussed post-war reconstruction of North Vietnam, the reunification with the south, and infrastructure projects for all of Indochina.[34]

The Tet Offensive unfolded over three periods. Starting in the night of January 30–31, regular North Vietnamese troops and southern insurgents attacked over one hundred cities in South Vietnam, but were unable to hold on to any except, for a month, the old imperial capital Hué. There, the occupiers systematically executed an estimated two thousand officials and supporters of the southern regime. From May 7 to August 17, regular troops and insurgents resumed attacks but gained no victories. The final six-week phase started immediately thereafter and included futile attacks on American bases. A general popular uprising did not occur, as Hanoi had anticipated, nor was the offensive a military success. On the contrary, the Vietnamese communists lost 75,000 regular and insurgent troops, and a South Vietnamese and American counteroffensive in the second half of 1968 succeeded at clearing out NLF strongholds in the southern country-side. US bombing runs on North Vietnam more than before threatened to "undermine ... the national independence" of the DRV. As early as March of 1968, it had dawned on the North Vietnamese leaders that the United States was not defeated on the battlefield. The DRV had to "fight 5, 10, 20 years or longer" for victory and reunification.[35]

In political terms, the Tet Offensive achieved somewhat better results. Even if the communist onslaught had generated short-lived popular support for the RVN, the southern regime quickly gambled away its newly enhanced legitimacy through its own incompetence and misrule. In the United States, President Johnson was under enormous domestic pressure to end the war. On March 31, 1968, he announced his decision not to run for office again and even proposed peace talks. Four days later, the DRV agreed to negotiations. In Hanoi's eyes, Washington had blinked in the spring of 1968 as much as Paris had done following its defeat at Dien Bien Phu fourteen years earlier. Prime Minister Pham was convinced that the DRV would be able to negotiate from a "position of strength." In the long run, Hanoi hoped that negotiations would lead to a Geneva-style agreement that was signed by Washington.[36]

Fighting while Negotiating, 1968–73

Despite the ongoing negotiations with the United States in Paris, the DRV continued fighting. According to Le Duc Tho, who led the delegation in the French capital, North Vietnam hoped to exploit the concurrent internal problems of the United States – the racial tensions as well as Martin Luther King's and Robert Kennedy's assassinations – for a combined diplomatic–military offensive. Yet, at the same time, the DRV believed that the Republican presidential candidate, Richard M. Nixon, would be a more generous negotiating partner than Johnson's vice president, Hubert Humphrey, who ran as the Democratic candidate.[37]

Concurrently, 1968 witnessed major changes in the Sino–North Vietnamese relationship. In the spring, Beijing had sharply criticized Hanoi for giving up the long-standing policy of uncompromising military struggle. Probably as a result of this dispute, the two sides agreed in the summer on the withdrawal of Chinese troops stationed in North Vietnam since 1965. The bilateral relationship cooled down even further after the Soviet-led Warsaw Pact intervention in Czechoslovakia in August. Beijing denounced Moscow as a socialist–imperialist power, while the DRV closed ranks with the USSR. By November 17, 1968 – two weeks after Nixon's election victory – Mao eventually supported the North Vietnamese decision to negotiate, largely because he wanted to give the new president a chance. But Premier Pham believed that the Chinese leader acted solely out of cynical motivations, in the hope of preserving some influence in the DRV.[38]

The following year turned out to be difficult for Hanoi. The DRV requested much foreign aid from the Socialist Camp to reconstruct the country. The need to rebuild the decimated southern insurgent forces also meant reduced military activities there. Vindicated by the failures of 1968, the remnants of the moderate faction in Hanoi resurfaced with demands for less fighting and more negotiations. Le Duan's hard-line policies faced criticism even outside the party. Anti-war organizations sprang up in several cities, though the security apparatus quickly stamped them out.[39]

The major obstacle to progress, however, was the lack of success in Paris, where Washington and Hanoi pursued mutually exclusive goals. The United States wanted the DRV to promise not to subvert or even attack the RVN, which it considered a non-communist version of Vietnamese nationalism. The Nixon administration ultimately hoped to withdraw its armed forces in an "honorable solution," a goal that the Laniel government had formulated one and a half decades earlier. To that end, the White House invested much in "Vietnamization," i.e. shifting the burden of fighting the insurgency to RVN troops. In comparison, the DRV arrived in Paris with maximalist demands. Hanoi wanted Washington to withdraw and, in the process, "take down the puppet regime" in Saigon. In its place, a "coalition government" of NLF cadres, representatives from communist front organizations, and politically palatable members of the defunct regime should emerge. The DRV particularly feared the possibility that the United States would succeed in stabilizing the regime in Saigon before withdrawal.[40] Thus, in order to counterbalance the despised "puppet regime" in Saigon, Hanoi created the Provisional Revolutionary Government of South Vietnam (PRG) in June 1969. During the negotiations that year, Hanoi remained stubbornly inflexible. According to a Soviet assessment, the North Vietnamese delegation suffered from a Geneva complex: it feared that the DRV would again be cheated after concluding a compromise agreement.[41]

By the spring of 1970, the DRV focused again on Laos and Cambodia. The escalating war since 1964/5 had triggered North Vietnamese and American military incursions into neighboring Indochinese lands, which had destabilized Cambodia and even restarted civil war in Laos. On March 18, Sihanouk's own prime minister, the pro-American Lon Nol, overthrew the Cambodian head of state. After the coup, the DRV, Pathet Lao, and the Khmer Rouge supported the creation of an exiled Cambodian government in Beijing, led by the felled Sihanouk. According to Canadian diplomats visiting Hanoi, the coup in Phnom Penh "seemed to mark a watershed." In its wake, North Vietnam decided to reactivate its dormant Indochina policies; it was finally receptive to Sihanouk's proposal for quadrilateral collaboration with Pathet Lao, the PRG, and his exile government. During a two-day meeting in southern China in late April 1970, the four sides agreed to coordinate policies in the struggle against "American imperialism." At a follow-up meeting near Hanoi a month later, the North Vietnamese leaders reconfirmed close Indochinese coordination and promised to honor Cambodia's neutrality following Sihanouk's future return to liberated Phnom Penh.[42]

Throughout 1971, both Hanoi and Washington continued to face difficulties in the ongoing war. The DRV was unable to solve its military problems in the south, suffered from mounting economic problems despite reduced US bombing, and experienced increasing popular dissatisfaction. The United States, in comparison, was approaching a "fork in the road." By spring, the withdrawal of US ground forces from the RVN had reached a critical point after which South Vietnamese forces needed to take over most of the fighting. Yet the southern armed forces had failed in a major offensive operation – Lam Son 719 – in February. On May 31, the United States submitted in Paris what it considered a final compromise offer that included, for the first time, a set date for complete withdrawal while it allowed northern troops that had infiltrated the RVN to remain there. It simultaneously insisted that the South Vietnamese solve their political problems by themselves, i.e. without American action, as demanded by the DRV. The proposal thus separated the termination of military conflict in South Vietnam from the question of the political future of the RVN.[43]

Despite this compromise offer, the DRV felt it was pushed against the wall by the Sino–American surprise announcement in mid July 1971 that Nixon would visit the PRC the following February. The American president hoped that the opening to China would help end the war in Indochina. Deeply aware of the political sensitivity of Sino–American rapprochement, however, Premier Zhou Enlai quickly traveled to Hanoi to "calm the tempers." Since the North Vietnamese leaders were furious that the PRC was abetting the imperialist enemy, Beijing felt compelled to boost its military aid to Hanoi after a decrease since 1968. Even if Nixon realized by early 1972 that he could not manipulate the Chinese leaders, the DRV was deeply offended by the welcome the PRC gave the president and Zhou's simultaneous advice to seek a negotiated end to the war.[44]

In the wake of the Nixon visit in February 1972, Hanoi decided on a major military offensive that had been in preparation for some months. North Vietnamese leaders saw the planned campaign as a repetition of "February 1968," designed to achieve "changes in ... the RVN" and break another sitting US president in an election year. Ultimately, the Spring Offensive of late March was supposed to have a "positive influence over the world revolutionary movement," while simultaneously punishing the world's "counter-revolutionary forces, led by the United States and China." As in 1968, the military effort was the final bid in the gamble for victory, which, however, failed militarily and politically. After almost eight years of war, the DRV was economically ruined, its population exhausted, the country unable to continue the war, and – as the DRV leaders clearly understood by late summer of 1972 – Nixon certain to win the elections in November.[45]

Given the possibility of renewed escalation after Nixon's re-election, the North Vietnamese leaders gave up their maximalist demands for the simultaneous US withdrawal and removal of the presumed "puppet regime" in Saigon. Pham publicly emphasized that "North Vietnam had no desire to humiliate the United States." To foreign diplomats, he even admitted that Hanoi had misjudged the situation. In comparison, the United States saw its chances of obtaining more concessions from the DRV increase. After cynically delaying a final agreement in the Paris negotiations, the Nixon administration escalated the bombing of North Vietnam in the aftermath of the presidential election. Eventually, by January 27, 1973, the DRV signed the Paris Accords, which had been modeled on the US compromise offer of May 31, 1971. The North Vietnamese leaders ultimately heeded the Chinese advice to "let the Americans leave," because the situation in the RVN would "change in six months or a year" for the better anyway. Almost five years of negotiations-while-fighting had only brought an American signature, but no glorious victory over US imperialism on the battlefield or even on a global scale. The peace agreement ended an eight-year war that cost millions of Vietnamese and 58,000 American lives.[46]

Unifying Vietnam, Dominating Indochina, and Pursuing World Revolution

The Paris Accords allowed the DRV to rebuild "in order to bring the national-democratic revolution to an end," as Pham stressed in February.

Yet the North Vietnamese leaders also wanted to grant their own population some respite, though small-scale military conflict continued. Hanoi focused on economic reconstruction of the DRV with foreign – mostly socialist – help while it continued to keep a close eye on the developments in the RVN. In December 1973, North Vietnam decided on a military reunification campaign because it had concluded that "a solution of the South Vietnam problem is not possible through democratic means." Initially, DRV leaders did not plan a repeat of 1968 or 1972 but a war of attrition. However, the eventual military operation from early January to April 30, 1975, was a conventional campaign planned by Giap, the hero of 1954. The timing was motivated by the mistaken perception of the increasing consolidation of the regime in Saigon, but also by internal unrest and widespread dissatisfaction in the DRV itself, which the North Vietnamese leaders conveniently attributed to supposed southern subversion. Ultimately, however, Hanoi moved against Saigon after it had judged – correctly – that Washington would not counter-intervene. Its assessment of southern strength turned out to be incorrect. Despite its massive military might, the regime in Saigon had failed to produce much popular support or even legitimacy by the early 1970s. Originally, the DRV planned for a two-year war of attrition to start in early 1975, but won a lightning victory against a quickly disintegrating RVN within only a few months.[47]

With the collapse of the RVN, the PRG became the new government of South Vietnam. Having violated the Paris Accords with its military offensive, the DRV did not even bother to put into place the long-talked-about three-way coalition government. On July 2, 1976, the two countries were simply amalgamated into the Socialist Republic of Vietnam (SRV). The change of name was supposed to symbolize the end of the national phase of the Vietnamese Revolution, which purportedly had included non-communist participation, and the beginning of the socialist revolution under exclusive communist rule. In reality, this rhetorical transition from the united front to a single-party state was a sham. DRV leaders admitted to East German diplomats that the VWP and the NLF had been all along a "unitary party despite carrying different names." After victory in April 1975, the new government started to persecute members of the old regime and non-communist nationalists. By then, the vibrant political debates of the 1930s about the nature and scope of the future nation had become nothing but a faint memory.[48]

In the wake of the national triumph, foreign diplomats wondered about the future direction of Vietnamese foreign policy. The chief editor of the central party newspaper *Nhan Dan* provided a succinct answer as early as mid May 1975. After the impending communist victories in Laos and Cambodia, Vietnam would pursue the "expulsion of US imperialism from all of Southeast Asia," particularly from "Thailand and the Philippines," which the Vietnamese communists had eyed as early as the 1930s. At first, it seemed that the North Vietnamese commitments to Laos and Cambodia since spring 1970 brought immediate success. Thereby, the three parallel conflicts in Indochina had become one single war, at least in North Vietnamese eyes. Parallel to Beijing's hosting of Nixon in mid February 1972, the North Vietnamese leaders received Sihanouk and representatives of Pathet Lao in Hanoi to coordinate anti-imperialist strategy. Within a month of the Paris Accords in early 1973, the civil war participants in Laos concluded a similar ceasefire agreement that comprised the withdrawal of all foreign troops. However, the DRV did not withdraw its troops from Laos, as it had promised in writing. Pathet Lao itself resumed fighting, with military backing from the DRV, by late March 1975. Before the end of the year, it had overthrown the 600-year-old monarchy and announced the establishment of the Lao People's Democratic Republic.[49]

In comparison, the 1975 changeover from Lon Nol to the Khmer Rouge, Sihanouk's ally, was not to Hanoi's liking. In May 1973, the DRV had hoped to get a quick negotiated solution for Cambodia similar to the Paris Accords. But the war continued over the next one and a half years. Parallel to the military reunification campaign in Vietnam in early 1975, the Khmer Rouge started its own large-scale attack on the Lon Nol regime. Phnom Penh fell on April 17. Subsequently, Hanoi tried to increase its influence on the Khmer Rouge, which had developed autonomously over one and a half decades. Le Duan was the first foreign guest to arrive in the new Democratic Kampuchea in August 1975, but proved unable to iron out bilateral disagreements in talks with Pol Pot, Phnom Penh's new leader. By late 1975, Hanoi had grave misgivings about the radical Maoist policies that the Khmer Rouge implemented. And by mid 1976, the two communist countries were engaged in bickering over territory.[50]

Furthermore, DRV relations with the long-time ally to the north, the PRC, had worsened even beforehand. In the spring of 1972, the Chinese leaders did not want to see a "new Dien Bien Phu" in Vietnam, the Swiss embassy reported, because victory would provide the DRV with "preponderance in all of Indochina." North Vietnam, however, saw the Spring Offensive in March 1972 as a political tool to foil the "attempt of the United States and the PRC to seek a solution to the Indochina Question behind the back of the Indochinese people." After the failure of the offensive, Zhou advised the North Vietnamese leaders to focus on negotiating a speedy US withdrawal. Yet, as soon as American troops withdrew from

Indochina, armed clashes at the Sino–Vietnamese border occurred. Their continuation in the following two years further cooled the bilateral relationship. In late 1975, Hanoi concluded that Beijing was pursuing hegemonic goals in Indochina, particularly in Democratic Kampuchea. Eventually, by the late 1970s the SRV attacked the PRC rhetorically as a revisionist and counter-revolutionary power, employing language similar to that used by Beijing in the 1960s in its propaganda war against Moscow.[51]

The deterioration of its relations with Cambodia and the PRC in the year of national triumph did not prevent communist Vietnam from trying to pursue world revolution once more. For two decades, the radical leadership in Hanoi had placed the Vietnamese national struggle within the context of a larger world revolutionary movement fighting the imperialist United States and, since 1972, the reactionary PRC. Before the start of the final military offensive to unify Vietnam in late 1974, Le Duan confirmed his country's "internationalist duty" toward Southeast Asia: "Who would have thought that Laos and Cambodia will come over to the side of socialism? Once this will have happened, Thailand cannot stand aside. . . . I believe that socialism will achieve hegemony." Three years later, he even saw Vietnam as the leading standard bearer of world revolution in Asia. Vietnam had the "duty" to support the "revolutions in Southeast Asia," especially in the member states of the counter-revolutionary Association of Southeast Asian Nations (ASEAN), which cooperated with "the imperialist countries, particularly the USA, Japan, and the West European countries." Indeed, this regional organization, founded in 1967, had adopted the anti-communist mission of SEATO, which was dissolved in 1977 following the end of the Vietnam War.[52]

Conclusion

In their three-decade-long struggle, the Vietnamese communists won the country's independence, national unity, and exclusive power on the basis of tenacity, cunning, international socialist solidarity, and diplomatic and military victories over their internal rivals and external enemies. From the very beginning, they had pursued the ultimate goal of ruling all of Vietnam. They had briefly achieved that goal in 1945, demanded it at the Geneva Conference in 1954, and single-mindedly pursued it from 1960 to 1975. Yet the length of the struggle also brought to power a radical faction in Hanoi. The leadership around Le Duan not only monopolized state and party authority, but also pursued maximalist goals on the battlefield and at the negotiation table. Le Duan's imprudent radicalism, designed to achieve national unification quickly and, in the process, humiliate US imperialism on a global scale, was co-responsible for the unnecessary suffering and death of many Vietnamese, Laotian, and Cambodian people. As a result of his radicalism, the DRV faced major economic problems in 1968 and in 1972.

The expansive Vietnamese communist vision of revolution seems, in retrospect, to confirm the validity of the so-called Domino Theory, which US President Dwight D. Eisenhower had promulgated in April 1954.[53] Yet Washington proceeded from the assumption of an international revolutionary movement that was centrally guided by Moscow or Beijing. In reality, the Vietnamese communists had been their own masters since the early 1940s. The American fear of the spread of communism might explain the reasons for intervention in Indochina, but this justified neither the brutal counter-insurgency warfare nor the massive strategic bombing of all three Indochinese countries. Thus, the United States was co-responsible for the suffering and death in all three countries, too. Still, it was the DRV that almost *consistently* entertained designs on the southern half of the nation, while the RVN and the United States *never* seriously considered the roll back of communism in North Vietnam.

The economic problems of the DRV in 1968 and 1972 seem to suggest that a more intensive bombing campaign of the North, as proposed by some US officials at the time, might have thrown North Vietnam into oblivion and thereby ended the war. Yet an occupied DRV – with remnants of the VWP and the NLF holed up in rural areas once more – would have continued to pose a serious security problem to the RVN. Following the precedent of 1945/46, a collapse of the DRV in 1968 or 1972 very likely would not have terminated Vietnamese communism. Anyway, neither Saigon nor Washington ever had the intention, nor the stomach, to occupy North Vietnam in order to stamp out the communist threat. From the very beginning, the United States did not want this war to be more than a localized Cold War conflict designed to preserve a non-communist Vietnamese nationalist project and simultaneously contain communist expansion. In any case, the occupation of the DRV would certainly have led to a Chinese counterintervention – similar to the one in the Korean War in 1950, as Beijing had warned Washington secretly in the spring of 1965 – with the possibility of this localized war spreading to all of East Asia.[54]

What, then, could have prevented Vietnamese communist expansion? Something similar to Sino–US rapprochement in 1971–72, as mentioned in the previous chapter? For Beijing, the opening to the world was an end in itself because it ushered in diplomatic recognition and entry into the United Nations. But Hanoi did not seek global status in that international organization. Communist Vietnam pursued regional hegemony and world revolution. Moreover, once the PRC had achieved its ultimate goal in the early 1970s it slowly transformed itself into a less ideological power. In comparison, once the DRV had accomplished national reunification in 1975, it became even more radical. In the end, as we will see in Part VII, it was the establishment of full Sino–American diplomatic relations in early 1979 that helped to contain Vietnamese communist expansionism once and for all.

7   India

India's journey in the initial three decades of independence must startle any observer. By the mid twentieth century, the country had emerged from the British Empire as a model for many newly independent states. Despite initial doubts, India's first prime minister, Jawaharlal Nehru, had quickly become a dedicated supporter of the United Nations. With the parliamentary elections in 1951, the South Asian country turned into the world's largest democracy. In the context of the world's Cold War division, India chose to follow a policy of promoting non-aligned peace. Nehru rejected India's acquisition of atomic weapons, and even called for universal nuclear disarmament. In the first half of the 1950s, the emerging decolonized world, the Socialist Camp, and the Free World all looked to India for moral and political guidance. But two decades later, India was internationally isolated.

The plunge in India's global reputation stemmed from the country's difficult relationship with two of its neighbors: bi-territorial Pakistan in the northwest and northeast, and China to the north. India's conflict with its Muslim sibling caused three wars within a quarter of a century. And the country's only equivalent in the Global South, the People's Republic of China (PRC), fought a border war with the South Asian giant. Even worse, by the mid 1960s, Pakistan and the PRC allied against India, which led India to abandon many of its Nehruvian ideals. Following the defeat by China in late 1962, it imposed its first State of Emergency and then embarked on an armament campaign against both neighbors. After the second war with Pakistan in 1965, India found itself increasingly isolated in the world. The rapprochement between the United States and the PRC, which had occurred through Pakistani mediation in 1971, compelled India to turn toward the Soviet Union and communist Vietnam. This all happened just at the time when India faced a refugee crisis emanating from East Pakistan, caused by the brutal West Pakistani suppression of the emerging nationalist movement in the future Bangladesh. Six weeks after the PRC had replaced the Republic of China (ROC) on Taiwan in the United Nations in October 1971, the new permanent Security Council member cast its very first veto – against India, over the Pakistan issue. The UN General Assembly censured India for its behavior toward its Muslim neighbor. Facing both a loss in international status and a wide range of internal problems, India, under the leadership of Nehru's daughter Indira Gandhi, decided to restore its status by testing a nuclear device.

India's policies from the 1940s to the 1970s exerted major structural effects on the regional Cold Wars in Asia and the Middle East, as future chapters also show in greater detail. The South Asian giant opened the Asian–African Movement to Chinese communist participation in the mid 1950s, with the indirect result that the PRC destroyed the movement when it tried to seize its leadership a decade later. In the aftermath of the Sino–Indian border war in 1962, Nehru's India for the first time made a firm commitment to the emerging Non-Aligned Movement, which quickly superseded the Asian–African Movement. The Sino–Indian conflict, however, fueled the nuclear arms race in South Asia. India's breakup of its bi-territorial Muslim neighbor in 1971 threw West Pakistan into an identity crisis. In its wake, West Pakistani elites tried to redefine their lacerated state as a Middle Eastern country, and eventually embraced political Islam. India's heavy-handed policies in 1971 thus were indirectly responsible for the events that ultimately led to the Afghanistan War toward the end of the decade.

Establishing India, 1945–54

India's independence in mid August 1947 was foreordained and unplanned at the same time. For a quarter of a century, London had gradually devolved power from its colonial administration to local bodies of self-rule. The interwar period thus witnessed not only the decline of British power but also a drop in economic influence, as India opened up to the world market. But until the end of World War II, most British politicians could not imagine letting the Empire in South Asia go. In the face of the dire state of finances, the newly elected post-war government under Clement Attlee decided in September of 1945 to start a process that would lead to formal South Asian independence within two years. The hastily implemented handover of power bestowed massive political and economic problems on the newly independent subcontinent, and also was co-responsible for the bitter and bloody partition into a conjunct, multi-religious India and a bi-territorial, Muslim-majority Pakistan.[1]

In constitutional, administrative, and political terms, India was barely ready for independence in 1947. That it survived the initial years and emerged as a functioning state and even moral world leader is, to a large extent, the achievement of its first prime minister, Jawaharlal Nehru. Until his death in 1964, he ran external relations as his "monopoly." He served not only as his own foreign minister for the entire length of his seventeen-year premiership, but also as his own defense minister for more than half of it.[2]

From 1947 to 1964, Nehru struggled to come to terms with Pakistan and China. This pointed to a fundamental question, which he himself never really managed to answer: What actually was India? Like Indochina, India was the product of Western imperialism, but it lacked a unitary pre-colonial state that could serve as a focal point for nation building.[3] On the ground, India resembled an irregular patchwork of religion, language, culture, ethnicity, class, and caste, with innumerable communal conflicts arising along its feeble seams. Seen from afar, however, it looked like a giant wedge of Swiss cheese sticking out into the Indian Ocean. The straight sides stood for the coastlines, and the holes for the 500 or so princely states. But where the curved and polished peel was supposed to be in the northwest, north, and northeast, there were only rugged and ill-defined border areas.

In August 1945, shortly after release from a British colonial prison, Nehru was convinced that territorial unity was the only means by which to secure independence: "Small states in the world of tomorrow have no future as the present [world] war shows." But how did he imagine the territorial extent of a united, post-colonial India? In his book *The Discovery of India*, which he had written in prison, Nehru promoted the idea that the ancient Indus Valley civilization could serve as a basis. This would have included territories as far as Afghanistan, but neither the southern tip nor much of the Himalayas. Probably because he was unable to define India as something other than just a geographical space, he envisioned an even larger political "unit" – "a south Asia federation of India, Iraq, Iran, Afghanistan and Burma."[4]

With the British decision in 1947 to partition South Asia into Pakistan and India, the dream of a united subcontinent abruptly ended. The subsequent population exchanges not only led to a traumatic bloodbath but also forced Nehru to rethink his conception of the country. Moreover, when the Hindu Maharaja of Muslim-majority Kashmir hesitated to accede to Pakistan in August 1947, the spurned bi-territorial country launched tribal guerilla warfare to seize the kingdom. In turn, the monarch sought union with India, only to see his realm ending up divided between the hostile twins of decolonization. Twice, in 1947–48 and in 1965, Pakistan and India went to war over Kashmir, but the former kingdom remains divided to this day.[5]

Map 7. South Asia

In the absence of internal cohesion, well-defined borders served to delineate national unity. With regard to the land borders in the north-west and northeast, the double trauma of South Asian and Kashmiri dismemberment had clarified the territorial question there. Nehru hence started to look to "the sentinel at the northern gates of India," as he called the Himalayas. Here, he faced three border sectors in rugged mountain terrain – one between Pakistani-occupied Kashmir and Nepal in the west, one at the tiny kingdom of Sikkim sandwiched between Nepal and Bhutan in the middle, and one along the extended border running from Bhutan to Burma in the east. The eastern sector turned out to pose the thorniest problem. A generation before, India's Foreign Secretary – the British colonial agent Sir Henry McMahon – had tried to secure the territories located to the south of the Himalayan crest line – today's Arunachal Pradesh in northeastern India and parts of northern Myanmar (Burma) – for the British Empire. Negotiated with the Tibetan theocratic authorities and the weak Chinese central government, the Simla Agreement of 1914 consisted of a *thick pencil line* drawn on a small two-part map, approximately *six miles wide* on the ground, and frequently crisscrossing the Himalayan crest line. Successive Chinese governments refused to recognize it. The year 1914 thus bore not only World War I but also a disaster-in-waiting in the Himalayas.[6]

The British Empire had never really controlled the Indian North-East Frontier Tracts (NEFT) located between the Himalayan crest line and the northern edges of India's Assam in the Brahmaputra River plain. Tribal societies had dodged any outside political authority for centuries. Two years after independence, Nehru emphasized the "new importance" of that territory to India against the background of civil war in China and the possibility of "separatist tendencies" in the NEFT. The PRC invasion of Tibet in October 1950 exacerbated the situation even more. Becoming "more frontier-conscious," the prime minister stated as early as November 1949 that "we are not going to tolerate any breach" of the McMahon Line. A general statement by China's Prime Minister Zhou Enlai in August 1951 that there was no territorial conflict between the PRC and India seemed to satisfy Nehru. Contrary to the recommendations from his closest advisers, he decided not to raise the McMahon line in negotiations with China. When the PRC republished old maps in the early 1950s that showed the NEFT and even parts of Assam as Chinese territory, Nehru was forced to placate an agitated public with references to past Chinese assurances. By 1954, Delhi created the North-East Frontier Agency (NEFA) under central administration to shore up central authority.[7]

With the borders in the Himalayas unresolved by the early 1950s, Nehru contemplated the meaning of the ongoing Chinese occupation of Tibet. The Indian prime minister considered "Chinese suzerainty" an established fact, but was unhappy about the harsh treatment of the Tibetans. Still, he was not really bothered by the appearance of battle-hardened Chinese troops north of the Himalayan crest line. Due to "the inhospitable terrain and climate of Tibet," they did not constitute a military threat to India. Attacking India from this "icy wilderness" would be "foolish," a confident Nehru wrote by mid 1952.[8]

India and the World, 1945–54

While Nehru tried to define India's post-colonial borders, he simultaneously attempted to find a place for his country in the world. As early as

August 1945 – two years before independence and despite his initial skepticism about the viability of the United Nations – he believed that India would soon belong to the circle of four great powers, together with three of the five permanent UN Security Council members: the United States, the Soviet Union, and the Republic of China. Thus, he did not hesitate to demand at least a non-permanent seat on the UN Security Council as early as 1946 from where his soon-to-be-independent country would lead "poorly represented" Asia. However, by 1948, he concluded that the United Kingdom and France deserved to be in the circle of permanent members, while he believed that civil-war-torn "China is rather out of the picture."[9]

Though he was not a rigid pacifist himself, Nehru in general abhorred brute force. At independence, he did not want India to acquire a large conventional army, or even "evil" nuclear weapons. On the contrary, he believed that a "relatively small but a highly efficient army" was sufficient. But the First Kashmir War with Pakistan in 1947–48 convinced him of the need for a "strong" army. Defeat at the hands of China fifteen years later eventually persuaded him to pursue a conventional armament campaign, although he remained a dedicated anti-nuclear crusader until his death in 1964. Like Mao Zedong, however, he had recognized that the essence of nuclear weapons did not lie in their military capabilities but in their symbolic power that provided enhanced status in international politics.[10]

By the early 1950s, Nehru had grown concerned about the triple crisis in Korea, the Taiwan Strait, and Indochina. After the North Korean attack in late June of 1950, he accused the United States of exaggerating the communist threat, and even of "mixing up … the Korean issue" with Taiwan and Indochina. Yet, at the same time, he decided to remain neutral in the French colonial war in Southeast Asia; he did not recognize the Indochinese governments when they emerged in 1949/50. During the battle of Dien Bien Phu four years later, Nehru lamented "the grave international situation that has arisen." He was convinced that "the question of war and peace – *world war* and peace – hangs in the balance" at the imminent Geneva Conference. This was why he wanted the Sino–Indian negotiations on Tibet to come to a successful conclusion *before* the start of the Geneva Conference on April 26, 1954. He hoped that the preamble with the five Chinese-proposed principles of peaceful coexistence (*Panchsheel*) would serve as a model for the multinational negotiations in Switzerland. But since the Tibet agreement was not ready for signature in time, Nehru announced his own proposals for a ceasefire in Indochina along the lines of *Panchsheel* before the start of the Geneva Conference. While he rejected US plans for the anti-communist Southeast Asia Treaty

Organization (SEATO), he also warned the USSR and China to contain the spread of Vietnamese communism throughout Indochina. By late May, Nehru even sent his confidante and India's UN ambassador V. K. Krishna Menon to Geneva as a roving diplomat to mediate during negotiation deadlocks.[11]

Even if Nehru entertained sympathies for the nationalist nature of the Vietnamese communist struggle, he was still troubled by the danger of communist expansion. Thus, in May 1954, his government guaranteed Burma (Myanmar) military support in case of communist aggression – Delhi even informed Beijing about the pledge – and considered similar promises to Thailand, Cambodia, and Laos. In early June, India publicly warned that the Soviet support for Vietnamese communist positions on Laos and Cambodia would antagonize many Asian nations. Chinese Prime Minister Zhou eventually convinced the Vietnamese communist delegation to back down on the issue. Furthermore, India's unofficial involvement at the Geneva Conference led to its formal inclusion as the neutral member in the trilateral International Commission for Supervision and Control (ICSC) of the Geneva agreements for Vietnam, together with communist Poland and the US ally Canada. Little did Nehru know that the original two-year commitment would last for two painful decades.[12]

While he hoped that the Geneva Accords would help bring about "final peace" in Indochina, he likened the US creation of the anti-communist SEATO in early September to a bully "hitting a man into the face." The arrival of Cold War alliances in South Asia had worried Nehru, who for some time had been a strong proponent of India's non-alignment in the Cold War. He had rejected earlier British and American plans for the establishment of an anti-Soviet alliance system in the Middle East, which Pakistan wanted to join. Because with such an alliance the "Cold War ... [would] come right to our north-western frontiers," he warned, it could drag India into a "shooting war" with Pakistan. In that vein, he considered SEATO, which also included Pakistan, "an angry [American] reaction" to the negotiated solution to the Indochina problem, which the United States was unwilling to accept. After the establishment of the Baghdad Pact – comprising Turkey, Iraq, the United Kingdom, Iran, and *once more* Pakistan – a year later, Nehru again condemned the United States for creating "tension" and increasing India's defense "burden."[13]

Dealing with China, 1952–60

Despite his criticisms about overblown Western fears of world communism, Nehru himself grew alarmed about the Chinese threat. When, in mid

1952, the PRC requested negotiations on India's privileges in Tibet, which dated back to the British colonial period, Nehru read into the absence of any reference to the Himalayan border lines an implicit Chinese attempt to revise what he himself had come to consider a settled issue. In the long run, however, he feared that India had "only two alternatives": to match Chinese military power with a massive Indian armament program, or to "seek a modus vivendi for co-existence with China." Since he had just concluded that the PRC would not attack from the icy Himalayas, and because he believed that India lacked the economic capabilities to fund a large army, Nehru discarded the first option.[14]

Still, Nehru did not mix his fears of communist China with his principles about the representative character of the United Nations. After the *Guomindang*-led ROC had lost the civil war and moved to Taiwan in 1949, he considered its continued presence in the United Nations "farcical." Even if Nehru wished for India to become a permanent Security Council member, he refused an American and a Soviet offer on that matter in 1950 and 1955, respectively. The prime minister was unwilling to take up the seat of the ROC on Taiwan or even accept a newly created sixth seat, as long as the PRC, representing hundreds of millions of people, continued to be excluded.[15]

By 1952, Nehru also started to reconsider India's positions in the Himalayas. He recognized that Indian rights and privileges in Tibet were "an inheritance from British days" and thus untenable for an anti-imperialist country like India. Once the Korean War had ended with an armistice in late July 1953, Nehru believed that the time was ripe for proposing negotiations on Tibet to the Chinese leaders. Signed on April 29, 1954, the Sino–Indian agreement contained – apart from the high-sounding *Panchsheel* in the preamble – detailed technical agreements codifying trade and pilgrimages, including the Indian renunciation of the inherited British privileges in Tibet. The combination of these two disparate issues – one in the preamble and the other in the actual text – suggests that Nehru saw them as a single unit, by which India gave up its rights in Tibet while, in turn, the PRC implicitly respected India's northern borders as they existed. While Nehru continued to fear that "our relations with China might worsen," he simultaneously hoped "that China and the Soviet Union may not continue to be as friendly as they are now." In frequent communications with the Indonesian prime minister, Ali Sastroamidjojo, during the course of the Geneva Conference, Nehru alluded to his desire to use Sino–Indian rapprochement to draw the PRC away from its alliance with the USSR.[16]

Nehru implicitly equated Zhou's seminal visit to Delhi during a break in the Geneva Conference in late June 1954 to a pilgrimage to his temple of world peace. Nehru did not miss the opportunity to advise his guest against exporting revolution to the rest of Asia. During his reciprocal visit to China in October, he discussed with his host the participation of the PRC in the impending Asian–African Conference. The foundation of SEATO in early September had convinced Nehru to swing his support behind the Indonesian idea of convening a gathering of decolonized Asian–African countries in Indonesia. Following Zhou's impressive performance at the Bandung Conference in April 1955, Nehru was satisfied that the Asian–African meeting had removed some of the mutual "misapprehensions and fears." In the unkind words of a Pakistani observer, however, Zhou simply had evolved from Nehru's "god-son" to "everyone's godfather." During a series of two visits to India at the turn of 1956/57, Zhou conducted wide-ranging talks with Nehru that marked the high point of Sino–Indian relations. His first call comprised a lavish friendship tour through the country, designed to establish *Hindi-Chini bhai-bhai* – Indo-Chinese brotherhood. During his second visit at the turn of the year, the two leaders finally discussed the borders. The Chinese guest promised "to convince the Tibetan Government to recognise the McMahon Line as an accomplished fact."[17]

Zhou's contorted pledge quickly turned out to be like an ephemeral snowflake in a Himalayan blizzard. Sino–Indian relations entered a hiatus in 1957 and then descended quickly into conflict. The radicalization of Chinese domestic politics in the run-up to the Great Leap Forward led to uncompromising positions in foreign policy. The relentless ideological attacks on the Yugoslav communists in 1958 rattled Nehru to such a degree that he started to fear that the PRC had renounced the spirit of *Panchsheel*. Even worse, in the spring, Beijing had published brand-new maps – not mere re-editions of pre-revolutionary versions – that claimed both the NEFA territory in the northeast and Aksai Chin in the barren high plateau at the northwestern sector. In a letter to Zhou in December 1958, Nehru pointed out that the two had agreed two years earlier to respect the McMahon line. In a harshly worded reply on January 23, 1959, Zhou bluntly denied any border agreement.[18]

The military conflict, which started at the McMahon line in August 1959, was a consequence of the Chinese military suppression of the unrelated Tibetan Uprising that had started in March. With both sides sending troops to the non-demarcated and ill-defined border in the aftermath of the revolt, the possibilities for violent clashes multiplied. On August 7 and 25, Chinese troops fired on Indian soldiers. Clashes lasted on and off until October. "India and China have fallen out," a frustrated Nehru noted, "and the future appears to be one of continuing tension." Regardless of his disregard for the Himalayas only fifteen years earlier when he wrote about India in a British colonial prison, the prime minister now redefined that region as an area of "basic security" to the country.[19]

Eventually, Zhou accepted an invitation by Nehru to come to Delhi from April 20 to 25, 1960, to discuss the border issues. The Chinese prime minister had decided in advance to table a compromise agreement for the sake of preserving Sino–Indian friendship. Zhou proposed for the NEFA territory to go to India and for the smaller Aksai Chin, which was strategically crucial to China, to go to the PRC. But Nehru was unwilling to bargain and insisted on legal claims stemming from the British colonial period. Even after Zhou had recognized the impasse, he strenuously continued to propose mutually acceptable principles through which the border disputes could be resolved in the future. At the concluding press conference, Zhou deplored the failure of his visit. Even some Indian observers recognized that he was trying to impress the Indian public with his wish to find a settlement. Despite his own intransigence, however, Nehru publicly called Zhou a "hard rock."[20]

Nehru was unwilling to agree to the proposed Chinese compromise deal because he had fallen victim to his past public statements on the PRC. Despite his own fears about China, Nehru for years had remained publicly upbeat about the northern neighbor. The recent Sino–Indian propaganda war, with its exaggerated claims on both sides, also had cornered him to a much greater degree than his Chinese counterpart. Unlike Zhou, Nehru headed a country with a vibrant public discourse and a rigid constitutional framework that left him with little wiggle room. By the spring of 1960, *Hindi-Chini bhai-bhai* had become "Hindi-Chini bye-bye."[21]

The Sino–Indian Rupture, 1960–63

Throughout 1960, India and China failed to find a solution to the disputed borders in low-level negotiations. Both sides fortified the border – or where they claimed it was – at various sectors in the Himalayas. By 1961, each side had established positions behind those of the other, resulting in a zigzag pattern of military posts. Unsurprisingly, armed clashes occurred in the Aksai Chin region in May 1962. Instead of pulling back, both sides continued to fortify their positions over the summer. But Nehru remained certain that, beyond "shouting at each other, not much would happen" in the Himalayas.[22]

If domestic pressure to defend the borders drove India's assertive policies, internal developments in the PRC triggered China's decision to go to war. By late July 1962, Mao had staged a comeback in daily decision-making, calling for ideologically radical policies. This included the *sanni yitie* agenda – the three *ni* and one *ti* – which targeted the quartet of his supposed international enemies: US President John F. Kennedy (Ke-*ni*-di), Soviet party Chairman Nikita S. Khrushchev (*Ni*-ji-ta He-lu-xiao-fu), Indian Prime Minister Jawaharlal Nehru (*Ni*-he-lu), and Yugoslav President Josip Broz Tito (*Tie*-tuo). On October 17, the Chinese leader approved the final preparations for a self-defense operation. The battle plan included a pre-emptive strike against what the PRC perceived – wrongly – to be an impending Indian assault across the McMahon line, followed by a punitive attack designed to destroy India's military infrastructure south of the disputed border.[23]

On October 20, China's one-month-long "self-defense–counterattack" campaign started. At the western sector, Chinese troops occupied Aksai Chin and then moved beyond. In the NEFA territory, Chinese troops traveled down the southern Himalayan slope on military roads that India had built to supply its defense uphill. Within weeks, Chinese troops arrived at the northern edge of Assam in the Brahmaputra River plain. The massive invasion was accompanied first by an offer of a ceasefire and negotiations, and then by anti-Indian, anti-American, and eventually even anti-Soviet propaganda. On November 21, Beijing announced its withdrawal 20 kilometers behind the "illegal McMahon line" at the eastern sector and the same distance behind the "line of actual control" in the west, which left the PRC in *de facto* possession of Aksai Chin. Despite China's political assertiveness and military superiority, the PRC and its few allies continued to uphold the view that India had harbored aggressive designs all along. Indonesian foreign minister Subandrio concluded during a visit to Beijing that the Chinese leaders were "sincere in believing [the] Indians [had] begun aggression." The Democratic Republic of Vietnam (DRV) also sided with its communist friend to the north. Foreign minister Xuan Thuy told a visiting Indian diplomat in August 1963 that China, because it was "a socialist country[,] would not ... and had not ... committed aggression."[24]

The force and swiftness of the Chinese operation surprised Nehru. He quickly called the war the "greatest menace ... to India since the attainment of independence." The situation worsened so fast that President Sarvepalli Radhakrishnan declared the country's first State of Emergency on October 26. Thousands of Communist Party members and Indian citizens of Chinese descent were imprisoned for years without due process. The State of Emergency stayed in effect until early January 1968. Nehru himself had difficulties understanding Beijing's motivations for the war, while Indian diplomats speculated that China was trying to undermine their country's stand in the Afro–Asian world and, as a greater objective, to punish the USSR for its policy of coexistence with the imperialist United States and "bourgeois India." Hence Nehru's government called the Chinese announcement of partial withdrawal an unacceptable propaganda ploy. The prime minister was willing to negotiate on the border, but only after the status quo ante had been "restored." More worryingly, the war had revealed India's precarious military capabilities. Within days of the Chinese attack, India turned to the Western world for emergency military aid. Even the USSR, which was in a politically tight spot given its still valid alliance with the PRC, provided military aid, but largely to counterbalance increased Western influence. In an unprecedented show of solidarity, forty nations "answered Mr. Nehru's message requesting support and aid for India" before the partial Chinese withdrawal.[25]

Military defeat was as a wake-up call for Nehru's government. Delhi massively increased its military procurement, even if it had already decided to raise it in 1959. For a moment, new defense minister T. T. Krishnamachari was willing to cooperate with SEATO in containing the expansion of communism in South Asia and Indochina. But ultimately, the turn to the West did not mean that India gave up its Non-Aligned status. Befriended Non-Aligned countries like Yugoslavia and Egypt sponsored a mediation attempt by non-aligned Asian–African countries during the war because they were keen on preventing India's exit from the Non-Aligned Movement. Even the Western powers did not favor such a development, because they believed that a friendly India in the movement was more useful to their Cold War interests than an allied one outside it.[26]

Equally worrying was Pakistan's attempt to exploit India's humiliation. Following the Sino–Indian border clashes in 1959, the staunchly anti-communist Pakistan had been willing to improve relations with India for the double purpose of solving the Kashmir conflict and coordinating policies against the Chinese communist threat. But while Delhi was exploiting the Sino–Soviet split for a rapprochement with Moscow in mid 1960, the USSR threatened Pakistan with war after it had shot down an American U-2 spy plane on May 1 that had started its mission at a military airport in Peshawar. Once the Pakistani military dictator, Muhammad Ayub Khan, had concluded that the "crypto-Communist" Nehru would never come to any agreement on Kashmir, Islamabad decided to seek rapprochement with Beijing. By May 1962, Pakistan and the PRC had agreed to negotiate on their un-demarcated borders, including those of Kashmir to the west of Aksai Chin. Nehru quickly grew concerned about this development: "[The] cold war is already very much in evidence in our relations with China and Pakistan."[27]

Immediately after the outbreak of the border war, Ayub Khan was more concerned with the Chinese threat than with the danger of India's imminent rearmament through international military aid. The Chinese victory was "sobering" and the PRC military preponderance a "jeopardy to Pak[istan's] security." Soon, however, Western arms deliveries to India changed Pakistani perceptions. By late November, Ayub Khan stressed that "Indian imperialism is a greater threat to Pakistan than international communism." Suspecting that Pakistan would exploit Indian weakness for rapprochement with the PRC, Nehru in turn compared Pakistan to a "jackal going to clean up after the tiger's kill." Initially, he had been open to talks with Ayub Khan, even on Kashmir, but after Pakistan's shift of stance, India announced that the settlement of disputes with the PRC would take precedence over coming to terms with its Muslim neighbor.[28]

In this context, Pakistan made good on its desire to find an arrangement with the PRC. The bilateral border accords of March 2, 1963, which included Pakistani-occupied Kashmir, marked the start of the rapidly improving friendship between the two unequal neighbors. Nehru concluded that his country was engaged in a double struggle against two hostile but allied neighbors. Even worse, Pakistan simultaneously sought rapprochement with fellow Muslim Indonesia, with the aim of isolating India within the Asian–African world. Indian diplomats suspected that the pro-Chinese Indonesian President Sukarno, who they believed had "developed a personal dislike for Nehru," was maneuvering to take over as Asia's principal leader after the aging Indian prime minister's passing. Similarly, Ayub Khan believed that a Kashmir settlement "would have to await Nehru's departure."[29]

Quo Vadis, 1964–66?

In the spring of 1964, the 75-year-old Nehru faced a multitude of unresolved problems in domestic and foreign affairs. Defeat at the hands of China had dented his reputation, but he nonetheless soldiered on. Independently from each other, foreign dignitaries noticed the great degree of exhaustion that was etched into his striking face. On May 27, at 6:30 a.m., Nehru suffered a heart attack. By two o'clock, an era had ended. His successor, Lal Bahadur Shastri, shared many of Nehru's basic conceptions about India's foreign policy – above all the renunciation of nuclear weapons and the aspiration to work for world peace. Shortly after his formal election as prime minister, Shastri confirmed to the visiting Soviet leader Anastas I. Mikoyan that "there would be no deviations from Nehru's policies."[30] But India's new leader still had inherited a tangled legacy of problems – foremost with regard to China and Pakistan – that would plague his short time in office.

Worried about the Chinese nuclear weapons program, Shastri called on the Non-Aligned on October 7 to send a delegation to Beijing "to persuade China to desist from developing nuclear weapons." Once the PRC had exploded its first nuclear device on the 16th, India's government feared that Chinese nuclear capabilities would open the door to UN membership for its communist neighbor. Under public pressure, Shastri's government started to ponder the acquisition of nuclear weapons, simply because "the problem was now that China had them." Despite an implicit American offer of a nuclear umbrella, his government decided to give up the strict Nehruvian position against nuclear weapons by allowing preliminary research to go forward.[31]

Moreover, Delhi was concerned about Beijing's radicalism in the Afro–Asian world, which it believed would make 1965 a "decisive year for India." In June, the Asian–African Movement was supposed to meet in Algiers for its second conference in June, a decade after Bandung. India was not enthusiastic about the conference because it believed a hostile Sino–Indonesian–Pakistani front was seizing the movement. But Beijing's strident positions alienated other participants too – particularly Algeria, China's close Arab ally and the conference's designated host. Thus, Shastri decided to confront the three hostile lions in the Algerian den in person. The unexpected overthrow of Algeria's President Ben Bella on June 19, shortly before the conference's scheduled opening, allowed the Indian prime minister to join other Asian–African countries in calling for a postponement. After Egypt invited the USSR in August, China decided to boycott the deferred gathering. By November, the Asian–African Movement cancelled the conference – and thereby finished itself off.[32]

At the same time, Islamabad and Delhi went twice to war over their disputed borders. In late January of 1965, Pakistan had crossed into Indian-claimed territory at the Rann of Kutch, an area of marshland at the southern sector of India's western border. Subsequently, Ayub Khan tried to link the solution of that problem to the settlement of the Kashmir issue, but Shastri refused. A ceasefire on June 30 restored the status quo ante. On September 1, Pakistan attacked Indian Kashmir but ran into massive resistance and even counterattacks. Delhi had judged – correctly – that Beijing's threat of armed conflict in the Himalayas was only for the psychological support of its new South Asian friend. Under military pressure from India, Pakistan agreed to a UN-proposed ceasefire on September 22.[33]

Despite China's demise in the Afro–Asian world and Pakistan's recent defeat, Shastri's India suffered from the blues in late 1965. The war had worsened the budgetary and food situation, because Western countries had suspended economic assistance. Moreover, the Pakistani government had successfully appealed to fellow Muslims in the Islamic world for political support. India's post-war refusal to withdraw from occupied Pakistani territory additionally damaged its image. Both the conflict itself and Chinese threats once more increased public pressure on Shastri to jumpstart the Indian nuclear weapons project, which was supposed to counterbalance the two hostile neighbors and to reduce dependence on the American nuclear umbrella. Acknowledging Delhi's international isolation in late 1965, Indian diplomats warned that time was running out to match the rival to the north of the Himalayas. Despite China's recent sabotage of the Asian–African Movement, they asserted, the PRC would seek an improvement of relations with the USSR following Khrushchev's overthrow a year earlier, continue to benefit politically from its nuclear test in the Afro–Asian world, and take advantage of its improving trade relations with Western Europe. All would lead to PRC membership in the United Nations in lieu of the ROC on Taiwan.[34]

Fortuitously, Moscow helped Delhi to re-emerge from its reputational cul-de-sac with an offer of mediation. From January 3 to 10, 1966, Soviet Prime Minister Aleksei N. Kosygin coaxed Lal Bahadur Shastri and Muhammad Ayub Khan to agree on the restoration of the status quo before August 5. The so-called Tashkent Agreement was a short-lived triumph for Soviet diplomacy. Only hours after its signing, however, Shastri suffered a fatal heart attack. His untimely death silenced Indian skeptics of the accord, but not Pakistani critics. Anyway, the tragedy did not prevent the Tashkent Agreement from crumbling soon thereafter. The Kashmir conflict remains as unsolved as the Himalayan border problems to this day.[35]

Indira's India, 1966–71

On January 24, 1966, Nehru's daughter, Indira Gandhi, was confirmed as India's third prime minister. Although she promised the nation that she would continue her father's policies, the subsequent years witnessed distinct departures from Nehruvian positions. Domestically, Gandhi moved to the left, given popular and political pressures as well as economic and rural problems. In foreign policy, she deviated from her father's internationalism because it had not brought the country many dividends. Also, relations with the United States deteriorated over disagreements with regard to the concurrent Vietnam War and political strings that were attached to American wheat supplies. And the late Shastri had bequeathed her with an already tempered version of Nehru's absolute rejection of nuclear weapons. The third Chinese nuclear test on May 9, 1966, once again led to public demands to produce an Indian bomb for the "defence of territorial integrity." Over the following three years, Gandhi, however, refused to commit the massive resources needed to build up, at best, a "modest system" of nuclear weapons. In the spring of 1967, India once more sought a guarantee of nuclear deterrence against China from both the United States and the USSR.[36]

In May 1967, Delhi decided "not to sign any treaty on [nuclear] non-Proliferation unless it was in conformity with our national interests." Gandhi's reasons were obvious: "One of the non-signatories is our neighbor, namely, China, who is full of hostile intentions toward our country ... and not subject to the discipline which arises from membership in the United Nations." After Moscow and Washington had signed the Nuclear Non-Proliferation Treaty on July 1, 1968, Delhi reduced its participation in international nuclear negotiations. In August, an Indian representative told Australian officials that his government "had no intention at the present time to manufacture nuclear weapons, but that it was unwilling to commit itself to the same attitude in the unknown international circumstances of, say, ten to fifteen years ahead."[37]

Gandhi similarly inherited Shastri's shifting policy toward communist North Vietnam. Despite Indian membership as the neutral representative in the ICSC since 1954, Gandhi's government welcomed the US military intervention in the Vietnam War ten years later because it "helped to set a limit" to China's power in Asia. Soon, however, India became troubled by the massive US bombing campaign against North Vietnam. Ultimately, both Shastri and Gandhi were convinced that a solution to the Vietnam conflict "could not be found by force of arms." In 1968, the prime minister herself demanded at the United Nations that the United States respect the right of the Vietnamese people "to shape their destiny by themselves." She had come to believe – incorrectly – that the southern National Liberation Front (NLF) was "essentially a nationalist organization," but anticipated – accurately – that the "anti-Chinese" North Vietnam would develop into an "Asian Yugoslavia" after the end of the war. Like her father, who tried to wean the PRC away from the Soviet Union in the mid 1950s, Gandhi tried to draw the DRV away from communist China. By late 1969, Delhi openly worked for an improvement of relations with Hanoi. But its membership in the ICSC forced India to preserve its impartial stance in the ongoing political developments in Indochina.[38]

Gandhi's subsequent tilt toward the USSR was driven by her increasing frustration over US policies toward both Southeast and South Asia. In early 1968, she received Kosygin in Delhi for Republic Day – as it turned out just a few days before the start of the Tet Offensive in Vietnam on

January 30–31. Moscow's subsequent arms sales to Islamabad, however, harmed the new relationship, and the Soviet-led WAPA intervention in Czechoslovakia the following August rocked it even more. India publicly condemned Soviet actions in Eastern Europe as a "clear violation of the U.N. Charter." Nonetheless, following the outbreak of the Sino–Soviet border clashes in March 1969, Delhi and Moscow exchanged military intelligence on Beijing, and India even rushed to support publicly Soviet territorial claims against China at the Ussuri River. Two months later, the USSR proposed a collective security system to several South Asian countries to fill the anticipated power vacuum in all of Asia following the expected American withdrawal from Vietnam. While Pakistan rejected the idea as blatantly anti-Chinese, India hoped to use the collective agreement for an improvement of relations with its Muslim neighbor.[39] Yet, as Sino–Soviet tensions decreased in 1970 and the East Pakistan Crisis developed, the Soviet idea lost its appeal.

The Pakistani Watershed, 1971–72

The East Pakistan Crisis, which gave birth to Bangladesh, had been in the making for almost a quarter of a century. A plethora of East Pakistani grievances led to the rise of the Awami League (People's League): the institutionally sanctioned underrepresentation in the national parliament, disagreements over language policies, and a military coup in 1958 against a new constitution that was designed to distribute power more equally. Trumped-up charges against the league's leader, Sheikh Mujibur Rahman, triggered mass demonstrations and civil unrest in 1968. Under public pressure, Ayub Khan resigned in March 1969. His successor Agha Muhammad Yahya Khan announced elections for December 1970 on the basis of equal representation. The Awami League won virtually all seats in the country's eastern half, and thereby the majority in the national parliament. Pakistan suddenly faced the real possibility of a breakup. After three months of futile negotiations, Yahya Khan decided, on March 25, 1971, to solve the national crisis by suppressing the Awami League with armed force.[40]

In the following eight months, India witnessed the unfolding of a civil war and of a humanitarian crisis of unimaginable proportions at its eastern border. As early as June 1963, Defense Minister T. T. Krishnamachari had been concerned about a possible breakup of Pakistan, particularly about the ensuing chaos in its eastern half that would invite Chinese influence, result in "refugees … streaming into India," and compel his country to "bring in the United Nations." While the PRC underwent a de-radicalization in its domestic and foreign policies in 1971, the other two predictions remained spot on. Millions of East Pakistanis fled across the border to India, while Delhi tried – unsuccessfully – to mobilize international pressure on Islamabad and to organize relief for the humanitarian crisis in West Bengal. Early on, Gandhi's government toyed with the idea of recognizing Bangladesh, providing support for the insurgents, and staging a military intervention.[41]

The East Pakistan Crisis even caused Delhi to move further away from Washington toward Moscow. In 1971, Richard M. Nixon's United States relied on Pakistani diplomatic services for its opening to the PRC. The revelation of Henry Kissinger's secret visit to Beijing in July, which occurred thanks to Islamabad's logistical support, not only alienated the DRV from the PRC, but also created a rift between India and the United States. While Delhi publicly welcomed the overdue Sino–American rapprochement and even expressed its hope that this development would finally lead to "China's entry into the U.N.," it privately feared a hostile Sino–American–Pakistani "encirclement." On September 9, 1971, India and the Soviet Union signed a friendship treaty that had been under negotiation since 1969. India's Foreign Secretary S. K. Banerjee frankly admitted to Australian diplomats that the situation in East Pakistan had spurred the treaty's rapid conclusion and that Delhi hoped it would help deter Beijing from delivering arms to Islamabad. Unsurprisingly, Pakistan denounced the Soviet–Indian arrangement as a "pact of aggression" against itself and China.[42]

With the situation in East Pakistan worsening, Gandhi was convinced that "war was coming," though "not on Indian initiative." In essence, the prime minister was facing a serious dilemma. On the one hand, Delhi itself did not expect that Beijing would intervene in support of Islamabad. Indeed, Sino–Pakistani talks in early November 1971 ended without any results. On the other hand, India risked gravely damaging its international reputation in a war against Pakistan, which foreign diplomats, however, reckoned it would win within "six to eight weeks." In any case, Indian military support for the East Pakistani insurgents dramatically increased in mid November. On December 3, Islamabad reacted with air strikes against northwestern India. The following day, India recognized Bangladeshi independence, the world's first nation to do so. Pakistan's troops surrendered to the Indian army after a two-week-long war in East Pakistan. The Indian military intervention destroyed the strategic threat, which the bi-territorial Muslim neighbor had posed to India for almost two decades. Australian diplomats observed that the loss of the eastern half had turned Pakistan from a South Asian country into a Middle Eastern one. But victory came at a steep political price for Delhi. India had alienated anti-communist countries in Southeast Asia with its "patronising attitudes," and Arab countries with its war against a fellow Muslim country.[43]

The war over East Pakistan occurred against the background of communist China's entry into the United Nations. Despite the Himalayan border conflict, Delhi had always supported Beijing's membership in lieu of Taipei's. Still, the PRC cast its first ever veto as permanent Security Council member against India in the discussions on the East Pakistan Crisis. Facing an internal deadlock, however, the Security Council eventually decided to refer the issue to the General Assembly. The assembly approved a non-binding resolution close to an American and Chinese-supported Security Council draft resolution, demanding the immediate withdrawal of all Indian and Pakistani troops to their respective national territories. Delhi flouted the resolution, primarily because it failed to address "the root cause of the present crisis, viz., the brutal attempt of the Pakistan military machine to repress by force the national aspirations of the people of Bangla Desh."[44]

India entered the New Year with a feeling of international isolation but also in a state of defiance. Facing a shared hostile Sino–American front, Delhi decided to seek rapprochement with Hanoi. On January 7, 1972, India and the DRV established full diplomatic relations – eighteen years after Nehru had warned the PRC and the USSR of Vietnamese communist expansionism. The decision contradicted the country's neutral membership in the ICSC. But similar to Hanoi, Delhi saw Nixon's impending visit to Beijing as a Sino–American attempt to contain India's "independent policies." A fortnight later, Delhi announced that the territory of the North-East Frontier Agency south of the McMahon line would be renamed Arunachal Pradesh – "Land of the Dawn-Lit Mountains" – and become a Union Territory, under direct rule by the central government. The intention was to incorporate tribal people into the Indian political process after secessionist feelings had bubbled up in the wake of the creation of Bangladesh. Yet the decision was also a delayed response to the temporary Chinese occupation of the NEFA territory in late 1962.[45] Delhi thereby created facts on the ground in a disputed border territory just at a time when the PRC was distracted by the ongoing changes in its international standing.

Nuclear Triumph and Political Defeat, 1972–77

In the months after Nixon's pilgrimage to Mao in February 1972, Indira Gandhi decided to test a nuclear device. On May 18, 1974, *Smiling Buddha* exploded in Rajasthan's Thar Desert. The single underground test with an unwieldy device was officially designated a peaceful nuclear explosion. India subsequently stressed it would "not use nuclear power for military purposes." Still, Gandhi had overturned her father's strict anti-nuclear stance. US–Pakistani collaboration and the simultaneous

Sino–American rapprochement had undercut the implicit American nuclear umbrella.[46]

But most importantly, *Smiling Buddha* was about status in international relations. Gandhi portrayed the test as a means to allow India to "stand in line" with the other great powers. An unspoken but obvious historical link between India, China, great power status, and nuclear capabilities existed. Nehru's India had refused to become a permanent UN Security Council member in the 1950s because the PRC had been kept out. His successor, Shastri, had concluded that the first Chinese nuclear test in October 1964 would open the door to UN membership. With the PRC admission to the international organization in October 1971, all declared nuclear powers were Security Council members. But if Delhi had believed that nuclear capabilities would elevate India to global status, it had badly misjudged. Yugoslav President Tito, who had fought together with Nehru against the nuclear arms race, was deeply disappointed, fearing that the test might encourage other countries in the region to follow suit. Western non-nuclear powers like Japan, Australia and Canada were concerned about the test's negative impact on concurrent non-proliferation efforts. A month after the test, Pakistan used the fear of a supposed Hindu bomb to prod thirty-seven Muslim countries at the fifth Islamic Conference to demand guarantees from the United Nations "against nuclear powers threating non-nuclear countries."[47]

The nuclear test temporarily helped to increase Gandhi's flagging fortunes at home. Just as the East Pakistan Crisis arose in March of 1971, she had won the mid-term elections with a campaign promise for a tough stance toward the Muslim neighbor. But accusations of vote rigging dogged her for years as public dissatisfaction with the economic malaise grew. With the help of the pliant President Fakhruddin Ali Ahmed, the prime minister imposed the third State of Emergency on June 25, 1975. In force for twenty-one months, it allowed her to imprison political opponents without trial and to censor the press. In March 1977, however, Gandhi lost the majority in parliament and even her own seat during national elections. Morarji Desai, once her deputy, became India's fourth prime minister, heading the two-month-old Janata Party. The Congress Party, which had been ruling India since independence, was out of power. Insult followed injury. On October 3, Gandhi was arrested on charges of corruption dating back to her eleven-year tenure as prime minister.[48]

Conclusion

Indira Gandhi's arrest completed the journey that had started with Jawaharlal Nehru's release from a colonial prison thirty-two years before. In between, India went through a remarkable development from a newly independent country to a globally respected and internally tranquil democracy, and finally to an internationally disaffected and politically fractured nation. The territorial conflicts with its two main neighbors – Pakistan and the PRC – triggered not only four wars within a quarter of a century but also redirected the country's political development. As Islamabad and Beijing manipulated the global Cold War to their own advantage, the non-aligned Delhi was drawn into Soviet–American conflict against its will. Consequently, Nehru's successors felt obliged to forsake one after another of his ideals. And as India faced external conflict, it emasculated its own democracy with several states of emergency.

Nehru's principles on foreign relations received much praise and admiration in the 1950s. But the geographical context and the narcissistic policies of India's neighbors turned them into long-term liabilities. As a result, his country missed the chance of achieving international status within the United Nations – an outcome which his successors tried to mend by jettisoning his refusal to develop nuclear capabilities. In other cases, Nehru's own policy choices created unnecessary problems. His soft line toward China in the early 1950s and then his hard-line stance in the early 1960s both did not serve India's long-term interests well.

In March of 1977, when Morarji Desai became prime minister, India was heading into an uncertain future. In the previous decade or so, Indira Gandhi had discarded her father's commitment to non-aligned internationalism and instead followed a policy of safeguarding unilaterally what she defined as India's national interest. In the process, her style of government had become autocratic. She lost the election in 1977 not because of the Chinese or Pakistani threat, but due to a surge of democratic opposition to her rule. As Chapter 21 shows, her successor Desai did not inherit a good hand of cards. His tumultuous and internally divided government turned off voters within a short period of time. At least in foreign policy, he tried to revise some of Gandhi's commitments to communist Vietnam and the USSR while seeking a relaxation of relations with post-Maoist China. But factors beyond his control doomed his attempts to failure – Vietnam's intervention in Cambodia in 1978, China's punitive military campaign against Vietnam in early 1979, the Soviet intervention in Afghanistan later that year, the subsequent collapse of superpower détente, and the near collapse of the Non-Aligned Movement over the Iraq–Iran War in the fall of 1980. All foreshadowed Indira Gandhi's return to power in early 1980 and the restoration of previous policies.

Part III

The Middle East

Introduction to Chapters 8 to 10

As in Asia, decolonization in the Middle East intersected with the long-term effects of European imperialism and the influence of the global Cold War. Resembling Vietnam and India, many Arab states did not emerge from pre-colonial antecedents, but were mainly French and British creations (Chapter 2). Like China in Asia (Chapter 5), Egypt was the rare exception in the Middle East. Nation state formation in the region occurred relatively late as a result of previous European interventions. And similar to South Asia (Chapter 7), the Middle East experienced partition imposed from the outside. In 1947, when Muslim Pakistan and multi-religious India emerged from the British Empire, the United Nations approved the partition of British Mandatory Palestine into a Jewish majority and a Muslim–Christian Arab state. In the subsequent quarter of a century, these two parallel partitions caused war between Pakistan and India on three occasions and between Israel and the Arabs on as many as four. Mutual hostility, unresolved territorial issues, and questions of political standing all were closely connected to each other in either case. Neither conflict was rooted in the global Cold War but each became intertwined with the Soviet–American conflict in due course.

The Zionist nation state building project, which led to the establishment of Israel in 1948, emerged in response to intensifying anti-Semitism in the European nation states of the late nineteenth century. It was a colonial project by its very nature and use of methods. It aimed to create a European-style Jewish majority settler state outside Europe, and it instrumentally exploited British imperialism to that end. The death of 6 million Jews in the Holocaust during World War II added moral urgency to the project. Together, however, these developments triggered another national tragedy – the displacement of Palestinians. The Arab inability to protect Palestinian interests merely exposed the fact that nation state building processes – for example in Jordan – were still ongoing, as were post-colonial struggles between Arab states for political leadership of the region – for instance between Egypt and Saudi Arabia.

The global Cold War in the wake of the Korean conflict added yet again more complexity.

The four Middle Eastern wars between 1947 and 1973 revolved, at their heart, around Israel's place in the Arab-majority region. In the first war over the creation of Israel in 1947–48, the USSR and the United States sided with the new state against the Arabs. But the conflict generated the Palestinian refugee crisis, which remains unresolved to this day. During the Suez Crisis in 1956, the two great powers again found themselves on the same side, but this time in support of Egypt fighting an Israeli invasion. Only the June War in 1967 and the October War in 1973 split the superpowers in the Middle East, with the USSR supporting the Arab side and the United States backing Israel. The global Cold War thus had a significant impact on the Middle East for only *one decade* – from the mid 1960s to the mid 1970s. Previously, Arab states such as Egypt and Saudi Arabia had proven remarkably resistant to taking sides in the Soviet–American conflict, just at a time when the Arab League was severing relations with its British imperial sponsor (Chapter 2). By 1972-73, both Egypt and Saudi Arabia tried to push the USSR, and thereby the global Cold War, out of the region again. Yet the June and the October Wars once more increased the suffering of the Palestinian people. The first led to the Israeli occupation of all of Palestine and to yet another refugee crisis, and the second signified the abandonment of the Palestinians by their long-term patron Egypt. In the late 1970s, the structural changes that the Middle East had experienced since 1945 triggered the bilateral Egyptian–Israeli peace treaty that would become an important marker of the end of the Cold War in the Middle East (Part VII, Chapter 20).

The links between the Middle Eastern regional Cold War and its Asian counterpart reach far beyond the parallel partitions of imperial South Asia and Mandatory Palestine in the late 1940s. The PRC provided crucial political and material aid to the Palestinian cause starting in 1964, and Vietnamese communism, particularly its insurgency in the southern half of the country, served as a model for the Palestinian struggle (Chapters 5 and 6). But the Vietnamese–Palestinian relationship also reveals that anti-imperialist movements cooperated mostly at the rhetorical or propaganda level. They failed to create close institutional links or to form coordinated strategies in shaking off what they considered the regional variations of the global American imperialist system. While both focused all of their respective resources on their own national project, they mostly saw themselves as separate actors working independently toward the common goal of universal liberation from oppression. In Vietnam, the independent path turned out to be successful, but not so in the Palestinian case. Structural constraints, internal conflicts, a determined enemy that saw itself as having no other place to go, and the lack of a stable strategic hinterland like North Vietnam all sentenced the Palestinian project to failure almost from the beginning.

The regional Cold Wars in Asia (Part II) and the Middle East (Part III) are central to topics covered in Part IV (Chapters 11–13) – Asian–African Internationalism, Non-Alignment, and pan-Islamism. Egypt and Saudi Arabia were players in all three, and the Palestinians in two. The Asian–African Movement was an important pillar of support for the Palestinian cause. Non-Alignment underwent a serious test during the June War in 1967, since one of the founding members – Egypt – was a combatant, while the Cold War blocs lined up on opposite sides of the war. Saudi-inspired pan-Islamism, which emerged in reaction to Nasser's Egypt in the second half of the 1960s, became heir to the defunct Asian–African Movement and its embattled Non-Aligned sibling. Unlike the internal structure of the other six parts, which contain three chapters each on thematically related but chronologically parallel developments, Part III consists of two sequential chapters on the complex and multilateral Arab–Israeli conflict – Chapter 8 on the 1948–64 period and Chapter 9 on the 1964–74 period – and a third chapter (10), spanning both periods, on the Palestinians.

8   Arab–Israeli Relations, 1948–64

The Zionist nation state building project in Palestine, which culminated in the creation of Israel in 1948, was a settler-colonial venture from the very beginning. Zionist leaders designed it as such, they worked together with a European imperial power to obtain it, and Ottomans, Arabs, and Palestinians all came to see it in this manner. What made this project distinctive, however, was its tragic historical dimension outside of the Middle East. The persecution of Jews in Europe, which increased during nation state formation in the nineteenth century and culminated in the Holocaust in World War II, provided the project with moral urgency. The rise of the Arab League as the self-appointed guardian of the Palestinians in 1937, US President Harry S. Truman's call for Jewish mass emigration to Palestine in 1945, and the subsequent involvement of the United Nations made the Palestine Question into an issue of global diplomacy – just as the Cold War began.

Unlike Chapter 2, which mainly deals with conflicts among Arab states between 1932 and 1964, this chapter focuses on the Zionist–Arab conflict over Palestine before 1948 and its transformation into the Israeli–Egyptian conflict afterward. Since its foundation, Israel disagreed with Egypt on the issue of the return of Palestinian refugees to their homes, which Chapter 10 will cover in greater detail. In addition, the two countries also pursued conflicting strategic interests in the region. David Ben-Gurion's Israel wanted to break Egypt's naval blockade of the Suez Canal and the Strait of Tiran, which had cut off his country's access to the Red Sea – and in extension to the Indian Ocean – since the late 1940s. In comparison, Gamal Abdel Nasser's Egypt wanted a land bridge across Israel's Negev Desert to reunite geographically the Arab world, which the foundation of the Jewish state in the area between the Mediterranean Sea and the Gulf of Aqaba had cut into two. The eventual escalation of the Israeli–Egyptian conflict in early 1955 was one of the key factors that triggered the Suez Crisis, during which Israel tried to break Egypt's dual naval blockade. US mediation eventually forced Israel out of Egypt's Sinai by March 1957 and froze the Israeli–Egyptian conflict for a decade without any solution. Ultimately, the dozen years after World War II first established and then fortified the regional structures that would produce the June War of 1967 (Chapter 9).

Despite the unfolding Cold War in Europe and East Asia, the United States and the USSR often saw eye to eye on the issue of Palestine/Israel. In 1947, both supported the UN partition proposal and recognized Israel within a year. But in the aftermath, each kept its distance. In the Suez Crisis of 1956, both considered Israel the aggressor and cooperated at the United Nations to restore the status quo ante. Still, Anglo–American Cold War fears about Soviet expansionism in the Middle East triggered a joint attempt in 1955 to find a comprehensive solution to the Arab–Israeli conflict – in the so-called Alpha plan – lest the Soviet Union benefit from continued conflict in the Middle East. Not only did the endeavor fail, but it also allowed the Soviet Union to enter the region in 1955. Even if communist influence in the Middle East remained marginal in the wake of the Suez Crisis, the United States still formed a strategic – anti-communist and anti-Egyptian – partnership with Israel that would have long-term effects in the region. Thus, by 1964, three years before the frozen Israeli–Egyptian conflict would heat up again, the foundations for the global Cold War to enter the Middle East had been fully put in place.

Toward Jewish Statehood, 1948

In essence, Zionism is a secular rebellion against the long-time Jewish destiny of living in diaspora in expectation of the Messiah's future return. It emerged in response to the formation of nation states in Europe in the nineteenth century. While Zionism reacted to the exclusionary ideas of various strands of European ethno-nationalism, it simultaneously adopted the idea of the nation itself. Yet not all Jews subscribed to the notion of a secular return to Palestine. The overwhelming majority of those who decided to escape discrimination, particularly from Russia and Eastern Europe where 75 percent of the world's Jews lived in the late nineteenth century, chose emigration to the Americas, South Africa, or Australasia. Those who decided to go to Palestine were a relatively small and self-selected group. They experienced the physical passage to the Holy Land as a rebirth.[1]

Leading Zionists understood that emigration to Palestine alone was not sufficient to establish a homeland. After experiencing anti-Semitism during the Dreyfus Affair in France in 1894, the Viennese journalist Theodor Herzl feared that even assimilated Jews in Western Europe were not safe. Hence, in 1896, he publicly called for the creation of a *Judenstaat* (state of the Jews). At the founding congress of the World Zionist Organization in Basel the following year, he called for "Jewish sovereignty over Palestine – our never-to-be-forgotten, historical home." A resolution adopted at the congress called for the Jewish "settlement" of Ottoman Palestine with support of the European colonial powers. As early as 1895, Herzl himself had admitted in his diary that a future *Judenstaat* could only be built on the basis of a Jewish majority population. This, however, necessitated the "removal" and "benevolent expropriation" of non-Jewish people already living there.[2]

In the wake of Franco–British plans in 1916 to divide the Ottoman Levant, the pro-Zionist prime minister, David Lloyd George, agreed in late 1917 to issue the so-called Balfour Declaration promising the creation of a national Jewish home in Palestine. A year later, Britain's Hashemite ally Faisal promised support for the idea, though he quickly rescinded his assurances after popular protests. With the creation of the British-administered mandate by the League of Nations in 1922, Palestine emerged for the first time in the borders of what is today Israel, the West Bank, and Gaza. In the period after World War I, the Zionist project benefited from British imperial interests in the region, from exploiting the belief in the empire's civilizing mission, and from the prevalent but questionable assumption that the population living in Palestine did not form a nation and thus had no claim to the territory.[3]

Local resistance to the Zionist project dated back to the late Ottoman period. Widespread European and Zionist views to the contrary, Palestine was neither abandoned nor empty. Its overall population had grown over the period of the nineteenth century and developed a sense of local identity before Zionist immigration even started. In the late nineteenth century, the Ottoman Empire forbade the sale of land to Jewish immigrants. But neither this nor subsequent prohibitions achieved the aim of preventing Jewish immigrants from acquiring property and thereby gaining a stake in Palestine. Ultimately, the Zionist goal of creating a Jewish majority state was not conducive to frictionless cohabitation. Beyond necessary economic interactions, Jewish relations with other communities were often shaped by mutual mistrust, hostility, and even violence. Although Palestinians opposed Zionism, Arab leaders still could not agree on a common position in the 1920s and early 1930s. Seeking to unify large parts of the Levant under his family's leadership, for example, Iraq's King Faisal believed in 1932 that a greater Hashemite Kingdom, in which Jews would live in a "corner" in Palestine, would diminish communal tensions.[4]

The Arab revolt in Palestine that started in 1936 occurred in the context of comparable nationalist stirrings in Egypt and Syria, but also revealed clear anti-Zionist objectives. Increasing communal tensions had created a situation in which a local incident – the murder of two Jews and the retaliatory killing of two Arabs – escalated into a major conflict that encompassed political demonstrations against British mandate rule, economic boycotts of Jewish businesses, and the militarization of the conflict on both sides. This escalation occurred against the background of increased immigration from Hitler's anti-Semitic National Socialist Germany, which had led to a doubling of the Jewish population in Palestine from 1932 to 1935 alone. The revolt itself turned Palestinian nationalism into a mass phenomenon as it spread through cities and the countryside. The Peel Commission, which the British government sent to the mandate territory in late 1936 to investigate the causes of the revolt, proposed partition the following year. Its recommendations envisioned the award of today's northwestern third of Israel to a Jewish state, a corridor from Jaffa to Jerusalem under British control, and the merger of the rest of Palestine with Transjordan (today's Jordan) into an Arab state. The publication of the Peel Commission report triggered even greater unrest. At the Arab National Congress in Bloudan in September 1937, Arab states claimed political leadership in the Palestine Question, demanded the repeal of the Peel recommendations, called for the creation of an Arab Palestine, pleaded for an end to Zionist immigration, and established an economic boycott of Jewish and British goods. After military suppression and a failed mediation attempt, London issued a White Paper in May 1939 that dropped the idea of a Jewish state altogether. Instead, it called for restrictions of land sales to the Jewish population while limiting new immigration to 75,000 over the course of the following five years, after which point the Arab side would assume the right to decide on immigration. But the Arab victory in 1939 was Pyrrhic. The Peel report of 1937 had firmly implanted in Zionist minds the certainty that a Jewish state was attainable in principle. In comparison, the revolt's brutal suppression by the British crippled the Palestinian leadership and civil society for decades to come.[5]

The five-year limitation of Jewish immigration corresponded almost exactly to World War II in Europe. The period of 1939–45, however, witnessed fundamental adjustments to the international framework in which the Zionist project unfolded. The systematic killing of 6 million Jews in the Holocaust provided moral urgency to the project of establishing a safe homeland for Jews. By May 1942, a Zionist conference in New York called for the immediate mass emigration of European Jews to Palestine, envisioned a Jewish majority state in all of Palestine, and pressed for American support. But only a year later, the Arab unity project gathered momentum under Egypt's leadership, culminating in the

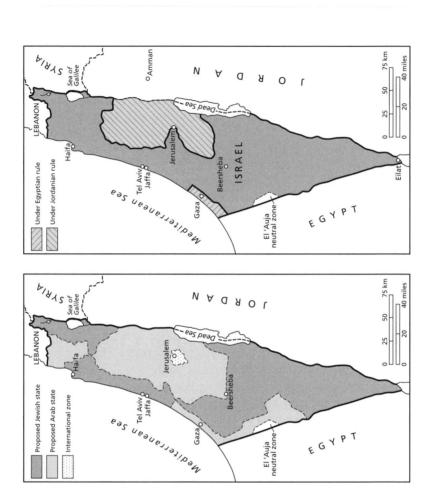

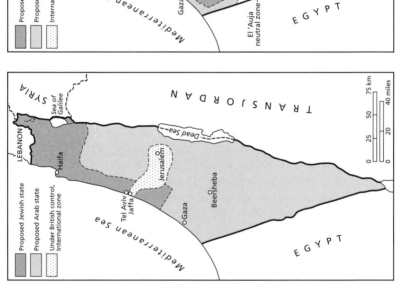

Map 8. The partition of Palestine according to (1) the Peel Commission in 1937, (2) the UN partition proposal in 1947, and (3) after the end of the war in 1949

foundation of the Arab League on March 22, 1945. Saudi Arabia warned the United States about the "Zionist wish to expel this noble [Palestinian] people and allow Jews from every quarter of the globe to occupy this holy Islamic and Arab homeland." During their preparatory conference in October 1944, the future Arab League members at least recognized the "horrors" of the Holocaust, but still rejected the creation of a Jewish homeland in Palestine. In a meeting at the Suez Canal in mid February 1945, King Ibn Saud emphasized that it was a European, not an Arab, responsibility to find a solution to the settlement of "Jewish refugees," while US President Franklin D. Roosevelt promised that "he would do nothing to assist the Jews against the Arabs." Both the Arab League Covenant and its Annex on Palestine claimed the mandate territory exclusively for Arabs. Only two months later, however, the Jewish Agency, the umbrella organization of all Jewish organizations in Palestine, demanded that the British government "establish Palestine as a Jewish State."[6]

As Jewish survivors of the Holocaust emerged from concentration camps, hiding, or exile at the end of World War II, they faced an uncertain future. Many who had lived in Eastern Europe before the war did not want to return, or fled from post-war anti-Semitism there. Given the existence of strict immigration laws in most of the world's countries, over 250,000 Jews from numerous European countries ended up in the western occupation zones of Germany in 1945–47. There, they competed for scarce resources with the non-Jewish population, or were housed in Allied camps for displaced persons, often behind barbed wire and in abysmal sanitary conditions. Trauma, linguistic and cultural differences, and disagreements over rigid rules in the camps quickly led to conflict between Jewish Holocaust survivors, on the one hand, and Allied officials, on the other. If they had not yet considered emigrating to a Zionist Palestine, many started to see it not only as a possible future but also as the only one left. Hence, the British government found itself caught between its promises from 1939 to limit Jewish emigration to Palestine and a rising number of illegal Jewish immigrants arriving in Palestine after World War II.[7]

As violence between Arabs, Zionists, and the British in Palestine increased over the second half of 1945, the international context changed once more. Truman had become president after Roosevelt's death in April, and Clement Attlee replaced Winston Churchill as prime minister three months later. Attlee in the next two years came to see the British Mandate in Palestine through the lens of the Empire in South Asia, where a sizeable Muslim minority had taken interest in developments in the Levant. But London continued to consider the mandate territory a crucial link in holding its global Empire together. Contrary to both the White Paper of 1939 and Roosevelt's six-month-old promise to Ibn Saud, Truman called on Attlee on August 16, 1945, to allow almost unlimited Jewish immigration to Palestine. He had been deeply shaken by the fate which Jews had suffered in the Holocaust, but simultaneously seemed to be unaware of the complex realities on the ground in Palestine. The British government rejected the American proposal on the grounds of infeasibility, while Arab countries rebuffed it on principle. In November, the recently founded Arab League formally objected to any further Jewish immigration, and a month later decided on an economic boycott of Jewish businesses in Palestine. It particularly criticized the idea of "relieving persecution of one people by the persecution of another," and warned that, with the realization of the Zionist project in Palestine, "Arabs would definitely lose their national rights in their own country."[8]

The Peel Commission, the emergence of the Arab League, and Truman's plea had *de facto* internationalized the Palestine Question. But an Anglo–American Commission of Inquiry, established in late 1945, failed to come up with a viable solution within the following half year. The Jewish Agency at least welcomed the commission's proposal of annulling the immigration restrictions of the White Paper in view of massive illegal immigration. In comparison, the Arab League toyed with a moral and economic boycott of the Anglo–American powers. By the spring of 1947, just as London was negotiating partition of and withdrawal from South Asia in Delhi, it decided to submit the Palestine Question to the United Nations. In early September, the UN Special Committee on Palestine issued a majority report, which the General Assembly adopted in a slightly altered form on November 29 as Resolution 181. It envisioned the political partition of Palestine in a chessboard-like manner, even though the mandate territory was supposed to remain one economic unit. The northeast, a strip along the Mediterranean from Haifa to Tel Aviv, and the largely unpopulated Negev Desert would go to a Jewish state, while the northwest, an enlarged West Bank, and an extended Gaza strip would form an Arab state – with Jerusalem internationalized within the West Bank. Fifty-five percent of Palestine would be part of a Jewish state, although the Jewish population in the territory was less than half of its Arab counterpart of 1.3 million. A population of 500,000 Jews and 400,000 Arabs lived in the territory allotted to a future Jewish state. The United Kingdom agreed to the UN proposal because Attlee saw the partition of Palestine in terms similar to South Asia's recent – and, in his view, successful – partition into India and Pakistan. Despite the unfolding Cold War, both the United States and the USSR supported it as well, largely because they saw no feasible alternative.[9]

While the Jewish Agency considered the geographical and economic entanglement of the planned partition to be impractical, it nevertheless supported the proposal. The UN endorsement of the idea of a Jewish state, no matter how flawed the details of the plan were, constituted a victory for Zionism. Unsurprisingly, Arab leaders rejected partition on principle, warning that its implementation would be the source of "a third World War." Even before the report's official adoption by the UN General Assembly, the Arab League reviewed its military options, though it realized that it lacked sufficient capabilities. In early December, the league publicly announced its decision to take military steps, while Egypt imposed a Suez Canal embargo on ships owned by Jewish businesses in Palestine. The Arab League was aware that outright intervention by its members would violate the UN resolution, but was still convinced that "volunteers" would circumvent international criticism. It was in this context that the Arab League established the Arab Liberation Army of volunteers, which was supposed to fight for the establishment of a unitary Arab state in Palestine. The league decided in late February 1948 to coordinate military and civilian strategies, and to refuse oil pipeline concessions to companies from any country that supported partition. On May 14, the British Mandate in Palestine expired. That same day, the chairman of the Jewish Agency, David Ben-Gurion, proclaimed the state of Israel.[10]

The Arab–Israeli War, 1948–49

Palestinians and Israelis alike have claimed in retrospect that British mandate rule was anti-Arab and anti-Zionist, respectively, and thus had created the conditions that made the war of 1948 inevitable. Technically, the Arab–Israeli war started with the invasion by the armies of Arab neighbor states one day after Israel's foundation. But by then, Resolution 181 had already been obsolete for months. Palestinian forces and the Zionist paramilitary organization Haganah had clashed since December of 1947. The following month, several thousand members of the Arab Liberation Army started to infiltrate Palestine. At the same time, the Jewish Agency under Ben-Gurion pursued a campaign of psychological pressure and then physical force to compel Palestinian civilians to leave their homes. In December 1947 alone, over 20,000 Palestinians fled from the Haifa region. In February 1948, Jewish military units started to destroy Arab villages so that their inhabitants had no place to return. Starting in April, the expulsion of Palestinians became more systematic. After July, the Israel Defense Forces (IDF) reoccupied territories which had been temporarily lost since December, and then seized areas that had not even been assigned to the Jewish state in the UN partition proposal. By October, the IDF controlled 77 percent of Mandatory Palestine – including all the territories allotted by Resolution 181, the northeast, parts of Jerusalem, and a land bridge linking the city to other Jewish-held territory in the west. Some 782,000 Jews and 69,000 Arabs lived in Israel's enlarged territory in November 1948. Over 750,000 Palestinians had fled or were expelled from their homes in what Arabs call the *Nakba* – the catastrophe. As early as June 1948, Prime Minister Ben-Gurion had prohibited the return of Palestinian refugees to territories under Israeli control. On December 11, 1948, the UN General Assembly adopted Resolution 194 that called for the voluntary return of "refugees" to their homes, and demanded that the Holy City of Jerusalem be transferred to UN control.[11]

Both sides had been unwilling to make concessions even before the fighting started in late 1947. In continuation of their ten-year rejection of a Jewish state, Palestinians and Arab states had rebuffed Resolution 181 and prepared for military escalation. However, Palestinian local militias and irregulars, the Arab Liberation Army, Egyptian Muslim Brotherhood volunteers, and Arab armies did not fight under central command, or in a well-coordinated fashion. Shortly after Israel's foundation, Iraq cut oil deliveries with the intent of crippling the new state's economy, and Egypt tightened its Suez Canal blockade to include ships with cargo bound for Israel. But Jordan broke Arab political unity when it re-established its pre-war contacts with the Jewish Agency-turned-Israel in July to work out the division of Jerusalem and surrounding territories. As Israeli forces retook ground temporarily lost to the invading Arab armies, the head of the Arab League rejected peace talks, which Israel had offered in early August, on principle. Humiliated by the losses in Palestine, however, the league in late 1948 fell into open dispute about how to proceed.[12]

In comparison, the Jewish Agency was relatively well prepared – particularly in political and organizational terms – for war. Ben-Gurion had understood as early as the 1920s that the national aspirations of Palestinians and Jews were mutually exclusive. By the late 1930s, he had even accepted the notion that the Palestinians formed a nation. But he had also convinced himself that diplomacy could not solve the conflict, that the establishment of a Jewish majority state was more important than any agreement with the Palestinians, and that only military superiority would force Arabs to accept a Jewish state in their midst. Inspired by the population exchange proposals in the Peel report of 1937, Zionist leaders in the following decade regularly returned to pondering the relocation – preferably voluntary, but compulsory if necessary – of Palestinians, but not of Jews. Since the Jewish Agency did not believe that the UN partition plan of 1947 was a viable solution – even though the agency formally agreed to it and the Jewish population would have disproportionally benefited from it – Ben-Gurion was ready to ignore it as soon as Palestinian and Arab leaders had rejected it. Despite later claims that the Jewish population was on the brink of extermination in the first half of 1948 by a demographically larger enemy, Zionist armed forces were bigger, better organized, and increasingly better equipped. Of the 150,000 combatants that participated in the war, almost two-thirds were conscripted Jews/Israelis or Jewish volunteers from abroad. On the Arab side, only Jordan's Arab Legion with 4,500 soldiers was an effective fighting force. It was in this context that the Jewish Agency, and later the Israeli government, pursued the policy of expelling Palestinians from their homes in those territories that ended up in Israeli hands by early 1949. At the end of the war, Palestinians in particular and Arabs in general concluded that Israel was a colonial, aggressive, and unjust state, and that it was backed by the majority of the UN members, including the American and Soviet Cold War antagonists.[13]

The principled Arab refusal to negotiate peace with Israel compelled the United Nations to mediate in reaching armistice agreements. UN diplomat Ralph Bunche started to arbitrate between Israel and Egypt shortly after the assassination of his predecessor Folke Bernadotte by Jewish right-wing extremists in mid October 1947. He managed to get representatives of both countries to the negotiation table in Rhodes by early 1949 and even to sign an armistice. Until July, similar agreements with Lebanon, Jordan, and Syria followed. Based on Resolution 194, the American-led UN Palestine Conciliation Commission also convened the Lausanne Conference from April to September with representatives from Israel and Arab states – but without a Palestinian delegation. The hope was to turn the armistices into a peace agreement. Given that Arab states still refused to participate in peace talks or negotiate directly with Israel, the conference ran along parallel tracks. Nevertheless, secret informal Arab–Israeli meetings occurred outside the official framework. But irreconcilable positions doomed the conference to failure. The Arab side insisted on Israeli acceptance of Resolution 181, which it had originally rejected in 1947, and the return of refugees to their homes according to Resolution 194. The Israeli side dug in its heels in the hope that time would allow the young state to consolidate its territorial gains and make the return of refugees less likely. In principle, Israel was willing to pay compensation to Palestinians for abandoned properties, but only in the wake of a comprehensive peace settlement. Midway through the conference, the United Kingdom also proposed territorial exchanges, according to which Israel would agree to an Arab land bridge through the

Negev – which had enormous symbolic importance as it tied the Arab world together again – and other territorial adjustments in exchange for the incorporation of Gaza and territories taken by Israel in the 1948 war. But Israel refused any territorial reduction on principle. An Israeli offer to allow the return of 100,000 refugees both came too late in the negotiations and was too little for the Arabs to break the deadlock. Eventually, in the 1950s, Israel allowed the return of 40,000 under a family reunification scheme.[14]

Arab–Israeli hostility also evolved far from Lausanne. When the UN General Assembly in New York admitted Israel on May 11, 1949, the representatives of the six Arab members staged a walk-out in protest. Despite the armistice of February, Egypt tightened the Suez Canal ban once more, while the Arab League's economic boycott and the Iraqi oil embargo continued. In late October, the league's council decided to create an anti-Israeli collective security pact that was formally established in June of 1950, though initially without the Hashemite twins Iraq and Jordan. The same league meeting also adopted a resolution prohibiting each member state from pursuing separate negotiations with Israel, while demanding from Israel adherence to the UN resolutions from 1947 and 1948. Still, Jordan negotiated with Israel on the formal division of Jerusalem and the West Bank in the spring of 1950. Hence, the league council decided on April 1 to prohibit all members from pursuing a "separate peace" or any other agreement with Israel. Lastly, on January 28, 1950, Egypt occupied the Saudi-held islands of Tiran and Sanafir at the mouth of the Gulf of Aqaba, followed by a unilaterally announced extension of territorial waters a year later. Egypt thereby controlled access to the harbor of Eilat, Israel's only maritime outlet to the Red Sea and the Indian Ocean. Yet, until 1955, Egypt's enforcement of its own passage regulations remained light.[15]

Ambiguous Truce, 1949–55

The six-year period after early 1949 witnessed a relative calm in Arab–Israeli relations despite the lack of a peace agreement, continued low-intensity border conflicts, and the combined Arab blockades. Israel focused on the construction of its state, society, and economy while receiving Jewish immigrants and refugees from Europe and the Arab world. Although both the United States and the USSR had voted for partition and quickly recognized Israel, they decided to stay aloof. Truman grew concerned that the socialist Ben-Gurion would turn Israel toward the Soviet Union in the unfolding global Cold War. But Iosif V. Stalin had little interest in the Arab world, though he had supported, via allied Czechoslovakia, the Israeli war effort with arms in 1948. When Israel failed to turn toward the USSR in 1949, Stalin even engaged in anti-Zionist propaganda abroad and pursued Jews at home until his death in March 1953. With the goal of preventing an arms race and maintaining the territorial status quo, London, Washington, and Paris implemented a self-imposed ban on weapons supplies to the region in May of 1950. Responding to the reluctant attitude of the United States and the Soviet Union, Israel pursued a policy of *non-identification* with the global Cold War in order to preserve decent relations with both. It was only after the start of the Korean War in June 1950 that Ben-Gurion followed his pro-Western inclinations by supporting the US/UN condemnation of the North Korean attack. In its wake, he came to see the United States as a possible protector, similar to how Herzl had looked to the British Empire for support of the early Zionist project. Still, Israel objected to the US policy of giving the Arab League associated status as a *regional* organization at the United Nations in October 1950. It considered the league primarily an outfit based on ethnicity rather than geography. And because the United Kingdom took the lead in coordinating the Free World's anti-Soviet policies in the Middle East in the early 1950s, Ben-Gurion's hope for a security guarantee from the United States did not come to fruition for another decade.[16]

The irreconcilable positions of Israel and its Arab neighbors also did not lessen during negotiations under the umbrella of the UN Palestine Conciliation Commission in Geneva in 1950 and in Paris in 1951. As in Lausanne, entrenched positions precluded any chance for rapprochement or even agreement. Israel demanded direct negotiations and a non-aggression treaty before even considering the release of frozen financial assets to Palestinian refugees or compensation. Arab states, though ready to give a unilateral non-aggression promise, were unwilling to sign any formal agreement because this would implicitly recognize Israel. Various UN attempts to restart talks in 1952–54 failed as well. At least, informal talks had taken place.[17]

Still, Ben-Gurion was convinced that the Arab side neither wanted peace nor accepted Israel in the borders of 1949. The implication of his views was that Israel would live in perpetual conflict, and thus needed to guarantee its own security unilaterally through superior military deterrence. Hence, continuing negotiations, even under the UN umbrella, would only send a sign of weakness to the Arab side, he concluded. The Egyptian Revolution in July 1952 briefly lifted Ben-Gurion's spirits, because it seemed that Cairo might become the "key" to a change in the deadlock: "If there is peace with Egypt, other Arabs states will follow." Indeed, in February 1953, the Egyptian foreign minister, Mahmoud

Fawzi, told Bunche that "Egypt can accept one partition but not two" – i.e. his country was ready to acknowledge the existence of Israel in a partitioned Palestine but unwilling to accept that a Jewish state cut the Arab world into two. Yet, in November, Egypt once more tightened the Suez Canal blockade to include ships under foreign flags that were sailing to and from Israel.[18]

Foreign Minister Moshe Sharett replaced Ben-Gurion as prime minister in February 1954. His tenure of less than two years was marked by his constant struggle with hardliners in the military and with his predecessor (and eventual successor) in office. The hardliners were willing to risk war with Egypt through military provocation in the Strait of Tiran and the Suez Canal designed to break the naval blockades. Without Sharett's knowledge, army intelligence launched an incendiary bombing campaign against American institutions in Cairo in the summer of 1954. The operation aimed at preventing an Egyptian–American alliance from emerging in the wake of the conclusion of the Anglo–Egyptian agreement on British military withdrawal from the Suez Canal Zone. The amateurish campaign not only failed, but its ringleaders were also arrested and quickly put on trial in Cairo.[19]

More importantly, Arab hostility denied Israel access to oil in a region that enjoyed it in abundance. Iraq's supply embargo and Egypt's naval blockade confronted Israel with the choice of importing crude oil from the Persian Gulf around Africa or from Venezuela across the Atlantic to the dormant refinery in Haifa. When the British owners decided to close down the processing plant in March 1950, Ben-Gurion threatened to nationalize it. In mid July, the Israeli government, its UK counterpart, and the British owners agreed on a steady and affordable oil supply from British-held Qatar to Haifa. In any case, Israel managed to acquire two additional oil suppliers – the Soviet Union and Iran – in subsequent years. Hence, starting in 1951, the Arab League tried to use diplomacy to convince Persian Gulf sheikhdoms, Iran, and foreign oil and shipping companies to end deliveries to Israel.[20]

In view of the increasingly rigid Arab boycotts, Israel tried to establish diplomatic relations with non-Arab countries in the Middle East and beyond. Iran and Turkey had recognized Israel in March 1950. However, the Palestine issue repeatedly interfered in the endeavor of obtaining diplomatic recognition from other countries in the region. In February 1955, Israel grew concerned when, during the signing of the Baghdad Pact, Turkey and Iraq exchanged letters promising to work for the implementation of "United Nations resolutions concerning Palestine." Similarly, Jawaharlal Nehru's India had been concerned about Arab and domestic Muslim opposition to recognition of Israel after May 1948. Eventually it followed Turkey and Iran in recognizing Israel on September 17, 1950, though full diplomatic relations did not develop for several decades. But India's eastern neighbor Burma (today's Myanmar) was one of the few success stories of Israel's early foreign policy, largely because both governments shared socialist points of view. Israel even sent one of the largest delegations to the first Asian Socialist Conference in Burma in early 1953. For this reason, at the Asian–African preparatory conference in Bogor, Indonesia, in late 1954, Burma proposed, together with India and Ceylon (today's Sri Lanka), to invite Israel to the impending Asian–African Conference in Bandung. But the two Muslim countries Pakistan and Indonesia warned that the ensuing Arab boycott would "jeopardize" the success of the conference even before its start. Further east, Israel was the first Middle Eastern country to recognize the People's Republic of China (PRC) on January 6, 1950, but its pro-American stance after the start of the Korean War prevented reciprocal recognition. Israel tried again via Burma in December of 1953, and a year later a trade mission traveled to China. But due to the instrumental reason of increasing its own recognition throughout the world, the PRC decided to abandon the nascent relationship with Israel at Bandung, and to support the Palestinians instead.[21]

For obvious historical reasons, Germany was one of the thorniest issues in Israel's foreign relations. After 1949, the western part of defeated Germany experienced an *economic miracle* within a comparatively secure Western Europe, while Israel built up its state and society within a hostile Arab environment. By 1951, the Israeli government decided to seek reparations for Jewish property lost during the Hitler period, including financial support for the integration of Jewish refugees in Israel. West Germany agreed in 1952 to pay 3.5 billion German marks, mostly in goods and services. But East Germany refused even to negotiate – for economic reasons but also with the goal of increasing its political appeal in the Arab world. Several Arab states understood that Germany carried a moral obligation toward Jewish victims. But there was much anger about the West German support for Israel at a time when Palestinian refugees were still waiting to receive any compensation from Israel for their financial and property losses, or adequate support for their life in exile.[22]

The Cold War and the Arab–Israeli Conflict, 1954–56

In 1953, incoming US President Dwight D. Eisenhower was committed to an even-handed approach to Arab–Israeli relations, even if he supported the idea of a British-led alliance against the USSR that included Turkey,

Iraq, Iran, and Pakistan. In his first year in office, he primarily focused on advancing Anglo–Egyptian negotiations on the Suez Canal. He hoped that an early return of the waterway to full Egyptian control would prevent Cairo from declaring neutrality or even switching sides in the Cold War. As the bilateral agreement crystalized in the spring of 1954, London proposed to Washington a joint Anglo–American–French peace effort in the region. When both Arabs and Israelis alike demanded arms supplies in late summer, the need to promote a peace deal grew pressing. Nasser emphasized that "the other Arab States were likely to follow an Egyptian lead" if there was a chance of peace. His country was even willing to cede territory if an Arab land bridge replaced the "Negev as a wedge in Jewish hands." And the Egyptian leader was ready to agree to a "compensation scheme" for Palestinians instead of insisting on their return to their homes. In early 1955, he doubled down by calling for an end of the "cold war" with Israel. However, he had not forgotten the assassination of Jordan's King Abdullah in 1951 in the wake of negotiations with Israel. Nasser was aware that he risked having "his throat cut," too. Indeed, he had survived an attempt on his life in late October by members of the Muslim Brotherhood, which had already been responsible for the assassination of two Egyptian prime ministers in 1945 and 1948. Given all these signals from Nasser's Egypt, British and American regional specialists in early 1955 surreptitiously worked out the so-called Alpha proposals that called for compromises on the Negev, borders, refugees, the economic blockades, Jerusalem, and water usage in the Jordan Valley.[23]

But in an instance of unfortunate timing, the Western anti-communist alliance in the Middle East received a huge boost on February 24, 1955, when Iraq and Turkey signed the Baghdad Pact, followed by the consecutive accessions of the United Kingdom, Pakistan, and Iran within eight months. The event infuriated *both* Israel and Egypt. With hardliner David Ben-Gurion having just rejoined the government as defense minister, Israel reacted four days later with a strike against an Egyptian army base in Gaza that left around three dozen Egyptian soldiers and ten Israeli soldiers dead. The raid was the most severe military confrontation since 1949, and probably designed to deter Egypt from joining the Baghdad Pact. But Cairo itself was one of the pact's staunchest critics on the Arab side. On March 1, a doubly exasperated Nasser told the British foreign secretary Selwyn Lloyd that his government was willing to live with the Baghdad Pact, but Arab leaders would not negotiate with the Israeli government until Ben-Gurion "ceased to point the pistol at their heads." Still, the Anglo–Americans believed that their recently worked-out Alpha proposals had a chance. In exploratory conversations in early April, foreign minister Fawzi welcomed the general idea but insisted on the transfer of all of the Negev to Egypt or Jordan. Scheduled to leave for the Asian–African Conference in Bandung, Nasser himself was less optimistic, though.[24]

Nasser's three-week trip to Asia turned out to be a transformative experience for him. He not only returned with his international stature grown, but he had also explored the possibility of arms deals with Pakistan, India, and China. And the Arab League members had managed to set aside their disputes to convince the conference of twenty-nine countries to adopt a resolution in support of the Palestinian people. Israel protested against both its exclusion and the "anti-Israel resolution." After another Israeli attack on Egyptian positions in Gaza on May 18, Nasser considered any Alpha talks "useless." Three days later, he asked the Soviet ambassador in Cairo for weapons to break the five-year-old Anglo–American–French arms supply ban. To an American diplomat, a "despondent" Nasser confessed that he wished for a reduction of tensions, but "if the Israelis want war they will have it." To add insult to injury, on June 1, the Israeli government revealed its intention of seeking a mutual defense treaty with the United States. The rise of tensions with Arab countries since February had shaken Israeli domestic politics to such a degree that the elections on July 20 had become an open race. Long coalition negotiations afterward prevented Ben-Gurion from forming his second government until early November.[25]

Given the worsening conditions in the Middle East, Washington felt the pressure to issue a public statement on the Middle East. In the summer of 1955, however, the Eisenhower administration was unwilling to sign a security pact with Israel. But Nasser's acceptance on August 9 of a Soviet invitation for a visit to Moscow deepened US fears that the American failure to deliver weapons in the quantities requested by Egypt would drive that country into the arms of Washington's Cold War antagonist. Then, on August 22, Israeli–Egyptian military clashes erupted again at the Gaza frontier; forty soldiers and civilians lost their lives, mostly on the Arab side. Finally, four days later, US Secretary of State John F. Dulles announced support for a peace plan along the lines of the still undisclosed Anglo–American Alpha proposals. Arab governments cautiously welcomed Dulles's statement, but Israel rejected territorial concessions, particularly in the Negev, in exchange for peace.[26]

The American proposal soon faced setback after setback. The border clashes with Israel had convinced Egypt to accelerate negotiations on arms supplies with the USSR and to tighten the naval blockade at the Strait of Tiran. On September 12, Soviet and Egyptian diplomats signed a commercial arms deal in Prague. It freed the Arab country from constraints imposed by the Western arms ban from 1950, but also threatened to cause an arms race in the Middle East and bring Soviet influence into the region. Nasser understood that the deal might trigger another Korean War-style conflict if the United States overreacted. While Washington and London feared that Cairo was slipping into Moscow's orbit, they finally managed to convince Tehran to join the Baghdad Pact to complete the British-led anti-Soviet alliance. But even now, the United States rejected Israeli bids for arms supplies or even a security guarantee.[27]

On November 2, after more than three months of coalition negotiations, Ben-Gurion became prime minister once more. His government simultaneously included advocates of preventive war against Egypt – like Chief of General Staff Moshe Dayan – and opponents thereof – like Foreign Minister Moshe Sharett, who would soon resign, however. Ben-Gurion himself emphasized that he was ready for a peace settlement but also prepared for war. At any rate, he ordered a strike for the night of November 2–3 against an Egyptian base near the joint border, which left fifty Egyptian soldiers dead. For Nasser, the clash was one more proof that Ben-Gurion's Israel was not serious about peace. In its wake, the Oil Committee of the Arab League decided to renew pressure on Arab and non-Arab oil suppliers to cease oil deliveries to Israel.[28]

On November 9, after consultations between the American and British governments on the situation in the Middle East, Prime Minister Anthony Eden offered British good offices for a compromise solution on the borders based on the 1947 UN partition plan. He did not refrain from accusing the USSR of fomenting conflict through arms supplies, as if the British-led Baghdad Pact had not contributed to the tensions in the region at all. Arab reactions were again more positive than the Israeli response. Despite the latest clashes, Nasser was still convinced that the Arab states would eventually recognize Israel, but blamed Ben-Gurion for the deadlock. The new Israeli prime minister, however, saw a combination of sinister Arab and Western forces at work. He even suspected a British imperial plot designed to secure Israeli territory in the Negev to station UK troops in the Middle East. A final American attempt to save the Alpha proposals in January and February 1956 failed.[29]

The continued deterioration of the situation triggered a mediation attempt by UN General Secretary Dag Hammarskjöld in the spring of 1956. At that time, Nasser had convinced himself that war was almost inevitable, that the United States would deliver arms to Israel, and that the United Kingdom would fight alongside Israel. Still, he continued to emphasize his willingness to recognize Israel if the peace settlement included "a land link between Egypt and Jordan." With the arrival of Soviet arms in Egypt in March, however, the Anglo–American powers lost patience. Prime Minister Eden started to speculate how the Middle

East would look like without Nasser, and Dulles began to reconsider the American offer to help finance the Aswan Dam. At this juncture, Hammarskjöld stepped in for a month of shuttle diplomacy between April 6 and May 6 which resulted in an armistice agreement. Blaming mostly Ben-Gurion's hardline stance for the intractability of the problems in the Middle East, Hammarskjöld gave the armistice agreement, which he had mediated, only two or three months to live. Dulles was similarly gloomy about the future of the region, but largely because he believed that "the Russians were doing all they could" to destabilize it in their favor.[30]

Freezing the Arab–Israeli Conflict, 1956–57

Nasser's mistaken belief that the United States was delivering substantial quantities of weapons to Israel just at a time when the United Nations was deliberating a global arms embargo for the Middle East led him to recognize the PRC in mid May. His goal was to secure a military supplier outside future UN restrictions. In return, he received a Chinese pledge never to recognize Israel. While Nasser sent a military delegation to China and even accepted an invitation to visit Beijing (although he would never go), Fawzi confirmed to foreign governments that his country remained staunchly "anti-Communist." Yet Cairo's diplomatic recognition of Washington's main Cold War antagonist in East Asia alarmed the Eisenhower administration. On July 19, Dulles announced the cancellation of funding for the Aswan Dam, despite the danger of Soviet money replacing it. Concurrently, the United States also decided to agree to the concealed delivery of twelve jet fighters to Israel from Canadian stocks. In response to the announcement by Dulles, Nasser nationalized the Suez Canal Company on the 26th in order to use its assets and earnings to finance the dam.[31]

Nationalizing the company was not about Israel, even though it was the indirect result of the recent worsening of Arab–Israeli relations. Still, Ben-Gurion recognized that Nasser's assertive step potentially provided Israel with the pretext to use military force to break the Egyptian naval blockades. Until early October, however, he adopted a wait-and-see attitude. Once the London conference – which debated the internationalization of the canal in August and September – had failed because of Egypt's refusal to attend, Ben-Gurion announced on October 1 that Israel would challenge the blockades in the Suez Canal and the Strait of Tiran militarily.[32] In the following two weeks, France secretly agreed to Israel's request to deliver 75 fighter jets, which replaced the US offer of 12 planes. Concurrently, the two countries also worked out a war plan "to the effect that Israel would attack over Sinai and go up to the East bank [of the canal]; France and, presumably, Great Britain would then intervene 'in order to separate the two parties' with the real purpose to re-occupy the Canal Zone." In clandestine talks, the three states hashed out the details for the intervention between October 22 and 24 at Sèvres, near Paris.[33] Israeli troops attacked Egypt on the 29th with a pair of moves toward the Suez Canal and the southern tip of the Sinai peninsula, both of which aimed at breaking the two Egyptian naval blockades. Paris and London responded within one day with a concocted ultimatum to both warring parties to withdraw from the Canal Zone. Since Israeli troops would not arrive at the canal's east bank until November 2, the ultimatum in reality demanded unilateral Egyptian evacuation of the west bank. Unsurprisingly, Nasser's Egypt refused to withdraw from its own territory, which triggered the British–French military intervention on November 5.[34]

Washington resented the triple intervention at the Suez Canal. It not only felt deceived by London and Paris, but the unnecessary crisis also drew attention away from the concurrent anti-Soviet revolution in Hungary. The United States applied economic and financial pressure to force its two straying NATO allies into accepting a ceasefire on November 6 and even into withdrawal the following month. Two days before, on November 4, Israeli troops had, however, occupied the two islands at the Strait of Tiran, from where Egypt had executed its naval blockade. Under American diplomatic pressure and Soviet threats of intervention, Israel agreed four days later to withdraw in principle but without agreeing to a specific date. It thereby gave up its one-week-old demand to withdraw only after concluding a peace agreement and obtaining the right of passage through the Suez Canal. While British and French troops departed from Egypt on December 22–23, Israel until early January tried to link its withdrawal to Egyptian concessions on Suez and the Strait of Tiran.[35]

Four days before the ceasefire on November 6, Soviet–American collaboration in the United Nations General Assembly had helped to establish the United Nations Emergency Force (UNEF), tasked with re-establishing calm at the Suez Canal, in the Sinai, at the Strait of Tiran, and in Gaza. At this point, Ben-Gurion realized that the Israeli–Franco–British intervention "had not succeeded in upsetting Nasser" and that, consequently, the three countries needed to seek "unity" with the United States to safeguard their own interests. Because Franco–British control over the canal had become an illusion, his government endorsed the idea of stationing UN troops at the Canal Zone instead while it still demanded territorial concessions along the western coast of the Gulf of Aqaba and in the Strait of Tiran. These claims were related to Israel's resolve to focus on the use of the gulf for imports of Iranian oil. To increase its stake in future negotiations, Ben-Gurion's cabinet decided in late November to build an oil pipeline that would run from Eilat through the Negev, first to Beersheba, and later even to Haifa.[36]

With the goal of preventing Israel from delaying withdrawal from the Sinai to obtain concessions, Hammarskjöld informed Ben-Gurion on January 5 that negotiations on the Strait of Tiran would occur only after full withdrawal. Two days later, Israeli foreign minister Golda Meir announced that her country would comply within two months by withdrawing unconditionally to the lines of control before October 29. In response, Nasser hinted about his willingness to make a deal with Israel on the Suez Canal in the wake of complete withdrawal. After a review of American policies toward the Middle East, Eisenhower demanded freedom of navigation through the Suez Canal six weeks later, and promised the Israeli government that American warships would ensure free passage through the Strait of Tiran. In view of the impending Israeli withdrawal from the islands, Meir announced on March 1 that future Egyptian interference with Israeli shipping there "will be regarded by Israel as an attack entitling her to exercise her inherent right of self-defence."[37]

As Israel completed its internationally enforced withdrawal by mid March, the Egyptian army, advancing across the Sinai, pushed UNEF troops to the border with Israel. The Jewish state refused to allow the stationing of UN troops on its side of the boundary, which meant that Egypt alone hosted UN troops on a small strip running along its border. During a five-day visit to Cairo in late March, Hammarskjöld managed to work out an implicit agreement to allow Israeli shipping through the Strait of Tiran, but no formal deal on the Suez Canal was reached. Yet, through trial and error, Egypt and Israel soon established a tacit understanding for the canal – as long as Israeli ships did not carry oil or arms. The arrangement held until early 1959.[38]

In a speech to the Knesset on April 2, Ben-Gurion tried to sound upbeat: Israel had supposedly destroyed Egyptian bases of aggression and lowered Nasser's prestige at home and abroad. But he warned that the lack of a real agreement on the Strait of Tiran might force Israel to go to war in the future. Without a doubt, the Suez Crisis had deeply shaken Nasser, who confessed to Hammarskjöld in the spring of 1957 that "the last eight months had been very difficult ones for Egypt and that he had . . . lost confidence in everyone." Anyway, the situation at the Strait of Tiran had not calmed down because Saudi Arabia resented the continued Egyptian occupation of the two islands, and hence disagreed with Egypt's practice of allowing Israeli ships to pass. And on April 24, the same day as Egypt announced the opening of the Suez Canal after the clearing of war-related debris, Israel started to pump oil from Eilat through its new pipeline to Beersheba.[39]

In the end, UN and US diplomacy had defused the crisis on the water-ways on either side of the Sinai, but had failed to resolve it. Still, Nasser remained certain into 1957 that a comprehensive "Arab-Israel settle-ment" would be possible, as long as it was "without piecemeal solutions which would give Israel what it wanted, for example on Suez or Aqaba."[40] He would be proven wrong. The conflict remained frozen for a decade – until the spring of 1967.

Quo Vadis, 1957–64?

The cooling of the conflict occurred just as the conflict among the Arab states started to heat up, as described in Chapter 2. The fear of a Soviet-dominated Egypt brought the United States and Saudi Arabia into a strategic partnership, though not a formal alliance. But by the summer of 1957, Syria threatened to slide into internal chaos, which provoked Egypt to intervene militarily to keep Saudi *and* Soviet influence out. In early 1958, it even merged with Syria to form the United Arab Republic (UAR), with Yemen joining on the basis of a complementary federal structure, the United Arab States. By the summer, pan-Arabism rocked Lebanon and Iraq. Yet, by the turn of 1958/59, Nasser had overplayed his hand. Neither Lebanon nor Iraq had joined the UAR, and his persecution of communists in the new double state had alienated the USSR and the PRC. In September 1961, Syrian elites had enough of Egyptian domina-tion, and the country regained independence by seceding from the UAR. After Yemen exited from the obsolete United Arab States, Nasser's Egypt went to war with Saudi Arabia in 1962 over it.

Israel benefited from the relative calm that the intra-Arab turmoil provided through implementing a range of focused policies. On October 24, the last day of the Franco–Israeli–British conspiracy at Sèvres, Paris had formally agreed to deliver a research reactor that would form the basis of Israel's nuclear weapons project. The outcome of the subsequent Suez Crisis convinced Ben-Gurion once more that Israeli security needed to be based primarily on military – including nuclear – deterrence, particularly since the conquest of territory – like the Sinai – for defensive purposes was no longer an internationally accepted option, at least for the time being. Although the mid 1958 return to power of Charles de Gaulle, who wanted to improve France's relations with the Arab world, threatened the nuclear project, Israel nevertheless received sufficient French help to complete the reactor, located near the small desert town Dimona, by 1963–64.[41] Despite American dissatisfaction with Israel's behavior during the Suez Crisis and concerns over its secretive nuclear project, an Israeli–American partnership started to emerge at virtually the same time. Since the outbreak of the Korean War, Ben-Gurion had wanted the United States to act as a great power protector. What changed for the United States after the Suez Crisis was the perceived threat of a Soviet-dominated Egypt at the heart of the Middle East. Thus, Israel gradually transformed itself from an American liability in the region's conflict into a US asset in the global Cold War. American–Israeli rapprochement even survived President Kennedy's attempt to improve relations with Nasser, which, however, floundered in the wake of the Egyptian intervention in Yemen in 1962. Still, the United States refused to enter into major arms deals with Israel until early 1966 when it reluctantly sold warplanes to counterbalance rising Arab air power. Two years prior, however, Washington had permitted the Israeli purchase of used American-made tanks from West Germany, which eventually led to the collapse of Arab relations with the Western European country by mid 1965.[42] Finally, after the Suez debacle, Israel itself pursued the strategic policy of allying itself with the enemies of its enemies, i.e. with states immediately beyond the Arab world. This included, above all, close relations with Turkey, Iran, and Ethiopia. As decolonization in sub-Saharan Africa gathered momentum in 1957, Israel used development aid to overcome strong criticism of Israeli imperialism in Palestine. In Ghana's case, it could exploit that country's arduous competition with Egypt for leadership in Africa. In 1963, however, Israel's focus shifted from West to East Africa in order to curtail Arab influence that would impede the free approach to and passage through the Red Sea.[43]

These parallel developments in intra-Arab affairs and Israeli foreign relations started to concern Nasser by late 1963. He recognized that he had maneuvered his country into a difficult spot. The relationship with Syria had turned back to a state of tension after a series of coups over the course of the year. Egypt had entered into a military stalemate with Saudi Arabia in Yemen, which undermined morale at home. The ten-year-old water dispute between Israel and its eastern neighbors over the Jordan Valley had escalated once more. And Israel seemed to be on the verge of going nuclear, which, as Nasser feared, might force Egypt into a preventive war.[44] His country's relations with the United States and the USSR remained difficult, despite his attempts to relax relations with the Soviet Union since mid 1963. Only the PRC seemed to be interested in Egypt when Zhou Enlai invited himself to visit Cairo in December 1963. But Nasser understood that Beijing's charm offensive was instrumental – i.e. it was about mobilizing anti-Soviet support and isolating Egypt's Non-Aligned friend India in the Asian–African world in the wake of the Sino–Indian border war a year before.[45]

On December 23, 1963, just a week after his talks with Zhou, Nasser called the first Arab League Summit for January in Cairo. He wanted to restore a semblance of Arab unity, but he was mainly motivated by the need to prevent a radical Syria from seizing the initiative against Israel. At the summit, Nasser listened to much pent-up criticism about Egypt's over-bearing policies since the Suez Crisis, but he was at least able to get an agreement on the need for Palestinians to take the initiative in creating their own organization while blurring other lines of intra-Arab conflict. In comparison, the Israeli government under new prime minister Levi Eshkol saw the summit mostly as a show. But he at least appreciated that Nasser – while trying to re-establish his leadership in the Arab world – was attempting to contain the militancy of other league members.[46] Similarly, Nikita S. Khrushchev's two-week visit to Egypt in May 1964 served Nasser's goal of repairing a strained relationship. But disagreements about the nature of Arab socialism arose in tense political talks that included Algeria's President Ben Bella and Iraq's President Abdul Salam Aref. Still, the Soviet leader promised additional economic aid while publicly supporting Arab anti-imperialist – i.e. anti-Israeli – positions, though neither he nor Nasser engaged in anti-American polemics.[47] Nasser's restorative policies continued at the second Arab League Summit in September and even included, in its wake, another attempt to improve relations with Saudi Arabia with regard to Yemen. At the summit itself, intra-Arab conflicts about how to deal with Israel broke out again, but Egypt was able to check Syrian demands for the "liquidation" of Israel by imposing a generally defensive posture. This time, however, the Israeli government was alarmed about the seemingly aggressive Arab propaganda claims, particularly about the call for "the liberation of Palestine from Zionist imperialism," which it considered an "attempt to destroy" Israel.[48] Intra-Arab competition thus threatened the region with a new conflict, which would come in 1967, as the next chapter shows.

Conclusion

The Cold War did not cause Arab–Israeli tensions but complicated them still further. The Zionist nation state building project had emerged against the background of the dual rise of European ethno-nationalism and high imperialism in the late nineteenth century. It adopted – and subsequently never questioned – both the European concept of ethno-nationalism and the idea of colonial settlement in non-European lands. The Holocaust provided moral urgency to establishing a Jewish homeland, though at a time when the Zionist project in Palestine was already well advanced. With a clear goal before their eyes and mostly indifferent to Palestinian national aspirations, Zionists under Ben-Gurion's leadership established an enlarged Israel by 1948. At that time, however, the post-Ottoman Arab states were at odds with one another, incapable of confronting the crisis in Palestine in an effective manner. The United States and the USSR agreed to support Israel's creation, but both distrusted the new country; one because it feared that it would turn communist, and the other because it did not do so.

American fears of Soviet penetration of the Middle East in the wake of the Korean War generated the idea of a British-led Turkish–Iraqi–Pakistani–Iranian pact of containment that fit into the global American network of anti-Soviet alliances. The Baghdad Pact not only split the Arab world, but sowed distrust between Egypt and Israel and drove both to search for allies – one in the USSR, the other in France. Anglo–American Cold War policies thus helped to accelerate pre-existing developments that led to the Suez Crisis in 1956. Here, the United States and the Soviet Union ended up on the same side again – though they entertained hostile images of each other. Washington feared that the Israeli–Franco–British intervention, if unchecked, would open the floodgates to Soviet influence, and Moscow believed that the intervention needed kerbing because otherwise the imperialists would take over all of the Middle East. Ultimately, American and UN diplomacy froze the Egyptian–Israeli conflict just before the intra-Arab Cold War, another consequence of the Suez Crisis, heated up.

While the global Cold War did not shape events in the late 1950s and early 1960s, it still lingered in the background. The United States tried to contain what it considered Soviet influence in Egypt and Syria, which stimulated its rapprochement with Israel. Moscow attempted to increase influence in both Arab states, but misjudged Cairo's motives. With the emergence of the United Arab Republic in 1958, the USSR lost influence in Syria. Its regional political allies, the Arab communists, moved into the crosshairs of Nasser's United Arab Republic. The intense intra-Arab competition for leadership created a situation by 1964, in which Egypt, Saudi Arabia, and Syria struggled in a three-way contest. Israel and the Palestinians were just the political battlegrounds of this contest, which would shape the decade starting in 1964, as Chapters 9 and 10 reveal.

9   Arab–Israeli Relations, 1964–75

The decade after 1964 witnessed two major cataclysmic conflicts – the June War in 1967 and the October War in 1973. Three larger develop-ments from two decades after World War II converged in this period: the rise of the Arab League as a regional player, the Israeli–Egyptian conflict at the center of the Middle East, and the global Cold War. In the eight years after the Suez Crisis in late 1956, the Arab League had shed its imperialist patron Great Britain and overcome its internal disunity. American mediation and UNEF forces had frozen, but not resolved, the Israeli–Egyptian conflict by early 1957. The 1950s had witnessed the first, brief incursions of the global Cold War into the Arab world – in the form of the Baghdad Pact in 1955, the Soviet–Czechoslovak–Egyptian arms deal in the same year, and the American–Soviet competi-tion for Egypt's allegiance in 1956. Yet, after the Suez Crisis, the Middle East was surprisingly resistant to American and Soviet influence, with the brief exception of the parallel crises in Lebanon, Jordan, and Iraq in mid 1958.

After 1964, superpower influence in the Middle East grew for two reasons. On the one hand, the conflict between Israel and its Arab neigh-bors deepened, which triggered the June War in 1967. On the other hand, the June War committed both superpower blocs to the Middle East. As the Socialist Camp and Free World almost uniformly lined up behind the Arab side and Israel, respectively, the global Cold War superimposed itself on a pre-existing regional conflict. Until the fall of 1970, superpower antagon-ism supported local actors in buttressing the Israeli–Arab stalemate. Egypt's decision in late 1970 to seek a unilateral arrangement with Israel, however, required the prior weakening of Soviet influence in the region. Thus, while Middle Eastern countries had enticed the superpowers to permeate the region in the second half of the 1960s, one of the regional actors – Egypt, supported by Saudi Arabia – took active steps to push one of the hegemons and, in the process, the global Cold War out of the region again. Following the trajectory of the preceding chapter, this one focuses on the Israeli–Egyptian conflict from 1964 to 1974, with the subsequent

212

chapter addressing the Palestinian Question during the period from 1945 to 1975.

Structurally, the ten-year period after 1964 put the conditions in place which enabled Israel and Egypt to sign the peace treaty of March 1979, as Chapter 20 shows. The Egyptian expulsion of the Soviet military advisers in mid 1972 started the transition of the region from an arena of Cold War competition into a field of unilateral American influence, even if the United States ultimately failed to take full advantage. Gripped by Cold War thinking, Washington did not seize the opportunity but left it up to Cairo and Tel Aviv to seek peace by themselves in 1977, though it eventually helped as midwife. The period from 1964 to 1974 also connected all regional Cold Wars in Asia, the Middle East, and Europe to each other, as previous and future chapters reveal. Chinese communist radicalism inspired Syria, which then was responsible for creating the crisis that led to the June War in 1967. The Sino–Soviet border clash in March 1969 convinced Moscow to adopt more constructive policies toward the Middle East. The Sino–American rapprochement in July 1971 triggered a similar Egyptian–Chinese rapprochement that would develop into a deeper relationship in the second half of the 1970s. Similarly, North Vietnamese communism in the late 1960s radicalized Syrians and Palestinians. At the same time, Israeli–Arab conflict influenced German–German relations, since it helped East Germany to gain international recognition. And the Arab oil embargo in the wake of the October War in 1973 provided a major test for West European cohesion.

Toward June 1967

In the four years after early 1963, a progressively radical Syria emerged as one of the causes for the June War. A coup in March brought the *Baath* (Rebirth) Party to power. The new regime quickly revamped government, economy, and society in a manner reminiscent of states in the Socialist Camp. A Baath congress in February 1964 declared Syria – in lieu of Egypt – the "true" representative of Arab unity and the "true" champion of the Palestinians, while calling for an improvement of relations with the People's Republic of China (PRC). Subsequently, the country demanded the "liquidation" of Israel. Syrian relations with the PRC, however, only matured after the successful Chinese nuclear test in mid October 1964, which the Asian country used to increase its influence across the world. In that vein, Chinese officials did not hesitate to equate Israel with Taiwan, and Israeli policy toward the Arab states with US imperialism in Asia.[1]

A coup in February 1966 brought to power the Baath Party's anti-Nasserite wing, which proclaimed North Vietnam's struggle against American imperialism the model for Palestinian resistance against Israeli imperialism. Because the Baath regime understood that it was too weak for a showdown with Israel, it sought rapprochement with Egypt for unified action. Gamal Abdel Nasser agreed to sign a defense treaty on November 4, 1966, convinced that this would help restrain Syrian provocations against Israel. But Egypt thereby relinquished its ability to take the initiative. An Israeli military incursion into the West Bank on November 13 in retaliation for the killing of three Israeli soldiers by a Palestinian-laid mine within Israel left a Palestinian village completely destroyed and fifteen Jordanian soldiers dead. Humiliated and under pressure to make a stand on the Palestinian issue, Jordan's King Hussein accused Nasser of failing to support other Arabs while UNEF troops, stationed on Egypt's side of the border with Israel, conveniently protected Egypt.[2]

Syria's radicalization since 1963 repeatedly forced Egypt to try to regain the initiative. The two Arab summits in the first nine months of 1964 had looked like a success, but little went according to plan. Egypt had suffered from an economic crisis for several years, which convinced Nasser to nationalize parts of the economy in 1961 and 1964. Moreover, Nikita S. Khrushchev's overthrow on October 14, 1964, came as a "considerable shock" after the prior improvement of relations with the USSR. The successful Chinese nuclear test two days later, which radicalized PRC foreign policy toward the Afro–Asian world, induced Egypt to seek nuclear assistance from China to catch up with Israel. The discovery of West German deliveries of US arms to Israel later the same month set off an escalatory diplomatic row between Cairo and Bonn.[3]

Thus, Nasser "proclaimed 1965 as a year of decision," but his difficulties continued. Apart from the fallout with West Germany, they included the resumption of the war with Saudi Arabia in Yemen and the US refusal to extend food assistance. Cairo also had to parry Beijing's revolutionary foreign policy, particularly with respect to the radical regimes in Damascus and Algiers, though Algeria's Ben Bella fell in a coup on June 19. Soon thereafter, Nasser rethought his country's foreign policy. During a visit to Moscow in late August, he not only invited the USSR to the postponed second Asian–African Conference – a provocation of the PRC in the wake of the Sino–Soviet split – but also canceled his own trip to China, scheduled to occur immediately afterward. Beijing's subsequent termination of nuclear talks with Cairo elicited Moscow's promise to extend the Soviet nuclear umbrella over Egypt to deter Israel.[4] In order to implement a tougher policy against Israel – which now included propaganda claims for its "destruction" – Nasser tried to resolve two vexing issues in his country's affairs. First, he once more attempted to end the conflict in Yemen. A trip to Jeddah before his visit to Moscow in August and a return visit by Saudi King Faisal soon afterward merely resulted in yet another short-lived agreement. Second, Nasser also decided to crack down on his most vociferous and violent critics at home – the Muslim Brothers.[5]

The year 1966, too, did not bring any of the dividends Nasser had hoped for. The economy continued to tank while relations with Saudi Arabia soured once more. Cairo concluded that Washington backed both Israel *and* Saudi Arabia against Egypt. It was in this context that Syria offered the rapprochement that led to the defense treaty of November 1966, as mentioned above. In the wake of the deadly Israeli attack in the West Bank, the Defence Council of the Arab League decided on December 10 to station Iraqi and Saudi troops in the frontline state of Jordan – against Amman's explicit wishes – to demonstrate solidarity with the Palestinian cause. At the same time, the council discussed calling for the withdrawal of UNEF troops, which had been stationed for a decade at the Egyptian–Israeli border at Cairo's exclusive discretion. It thereby envisioned removing *one of the two devices* that had kept the Arab–Israeli conflict frozen for a decade, the other being unhindered passage for Israeli ships through the Strait of Tiran.[6]

Nasserite Egypt matched Syria's military provocations of Israel in early 1967 with anti-imperialist, anti-American, and anti-Israeli rhetoric, and with public pronouncements of Arab revolutionary unity. Alarmed, the USSR requested that Syria and Egypt avoid war. At least, Cairo tried to improve its relationship with London, which had been in hiatus for a decade, in order to signal an interest in international diplomacy. But when Syria began to provoke military clashes with Israel again on April 7, Egypt once more followed by increasing its belligerent rhetoric. Blaming US imperialism for all the ills in the Middle East since 1945, Nasser accused the United States of "permanent war" against the Arab world: "In reality, our struggle is not directed against Faisal, Hussein, [or Tunisia's] crazy Bourgiba ..., because they are all American tools. ... We are standing on the side of the revolutionary forces, which struggle against colonialism in the Arab countries." Contrary to Nasser's insinuations, however, Faisal generally supported Nasser's anti-Israeli and pro-Palestinian positions, despite the war in Yemen and his dislike of Egypt's leanings to the USSR.[7]

The Syrian–Egyptian competition of brinkmanship continued in May. Faulty Soviet warnings and fabricated Syrian intelligence convinced Nasser that an Israeli attack on Syria was imminent. On May 14, he responded by sending troops to the Sinai, although his best troops were still bogged down with the five-year war in Yemen. Two days later, Egypt asked the United Nations to withdraw its forces from the border with Israel. Cairo's formal request for withdrawal on the 18th officially ended the UNEF deployment. On May 20, UN General Secretary U Thant announced that he would leave New York for Cairo within forty-eight hours for discussions on the unfolding crisis. On the 22nd, however, Nasser declared the closure of the Strait of Tiran to ships bound for Eilat – a move that aimed at hitting Israel "at a very sensitive spot." Thereby, the Egyptian leader removed the *second of the two mechanisms* that had kept the Arab–Israeli conflict frozen since 1957, just before U Thant arrived in Cairo. The general secretary instantaneously warned that the closure of the Strait of Tiran would provoke Israel into war. Nasser dismissed the advice, stating that Egypt had merely returned to the situation before the Israeli attack on October 29, 1956. Foreign Minister Mahmoud Riad added that Israel fortunately had no military allies, unlike eleven years before, and thus would not dare to attack the combined armies of seven Arab countries stationed in the Sinai, Syria, and Jordan. In any case, he reassured U Thant, "we have no plans to attack Israel. We realize that any attack by us would create an international crisis." A year later, Cairo admitted that "something . . . had gone wrong" with planning in May 1967, most likely because of "miscalculations on the basis of misinformation."[8]

The Egyptian depiction of Arab cohesion and strength was a fantasy. King Hussein considered Nasser's provocative steps "extremely dangerous." Unaware of Egyptian intentions, Saudi Arabia assumed a Soviet plot behind Nasser's actions, designed to pressure the United States "in relation to Vietnam," but was convinced that Egypt would not go as far as engaging "with superior Israeli troops." In reality, the Soviet leaders did not conspire at all, but found themselves with egg all over their faces. By May 22, Moscow had realized that its ten-day-old warning about the imminent Israeli attack on Syria had no basis in fact, but instead had triggered what it considered Cairo's dangerous closure of the Strait of Tiran. On the 19th, Israel had already criticized Egypt's demand for UNEF withdrawal as a dangerous provocation. However, its own refusal to allow the stationing of UN troops on its side of the border ten years earlier had eliminated any possibility of preventing such a withdrawal in the first place. Moreover, it did not permit UNEF troops to cross into Israel but let the withdrawal from Egypt proceed. Still, on the 23rd, Israeli Prime Minister Levi Eshkol showed restraint in a speech to the Knesset when he called on the world to restore free passage through the recently closed Strait of Tiran. Ultimately, however, Nasser's decision to close the waterway amounted to "an act of war" against Israel, as former foreign minister, Golda Meir, had declared a decade earlier and Israeli officials had warned for several days before May 22.[9]

Yet Israel was neither unprepared nor blameless for the crisis. With Eshkol, a less hawkish prime minister had replaced Ben-Gurion in mid 1963, but he faced generals who argued that Israel needed to expand its borders for security reasons, as the country had done in 1948. Ben-Gurion himself had abandoned this strategic idea in late 1956 in favor of military and nuclear deterrence. The outcome of the Suez Crisis had convinced him that territorial changes in the Middle East were no longer internationally acceptable. Still, in 1957, Israeli generals had updated contingency plans to annex Egypt's Sinai, Jordan's West Bank, and Syria's Golan Heights. Until early 1966, Eshkol remained convinced that radical Syria was the only "source of active trouble," with Jordan and Egypt mainly focusing on their domestic problems. Foreign Minister Abba Eban even believed that Arab disunity offered the opportunity for a American–Soviet–British–French joint peace effort in the Middle East, similar to the recent Soviet-brokered Tashkent agreement between Pakistan and India. The increase of Syrian-sponsored attacks by the Palestine Liberation Organization (PLO) on Israel after the February 1966 coup in Damascus, however, augmented Israeli interests in counterinsurgency tactics, which South Vietnam employed against communist insurgents. It was these kinds of search-and-destroy tactics which Israel used against Palestinian civilians and Jordanian troops in the West Bank in mid November, and thereby sparked the stiff Arab response mentioned above.[10]

Israeli generals were adamant in using the Syrian provocations in early 1967 to implement parts of their ten-year-old contingency plans. They were convinced that Cairo would not come to the aid of Damascus if Israel militarily engaged with Syria only. Nasser's decision to send troops to the Sinai on May 14 shattered this misconception. To reduce tensions in the Middle East, Eshkol deliberately adopted a restrained tone in his speech to the Knesset on the Strait of Tiran on May 23, and then sent Eban to the United States to discuss possible US steps to defuse the crisis. In Washington, the foreign minister described a gravely increased sense of Israeli insecurity, but the administration of President Lyndon B. Johnson was convinced that no Arab attack was imminent. Referring to Dwight D. Eisenhower's promise of February 1957, Eban tried to obtain an unequivocal US promise to guarantee free passage through the Strait of Tiran, but the American side stalled. Still, after his return to Israel, Eban claimed in the cabinet that he had received such a commitment.[11]

But generals on both sides were itching for a showdown. In Cairo, the Egyptian high command planned an air strike against Israel, which Nasser managed to stop on May 26 before it could be carried out. The seeming disconnect between Eban's reports from the Washington talks and intelligence about Egypt's planned air strike allowed Israeli generals to put pressure on Eshkol. The announcement of an Egyptian–Jordanian defense treaty on May 30 opened the way for the June War. The rhetorical belligerency on all sides had convinced King Hussein to enter into a pact with the man whom he had just recently criticized as dangerous to help Jordan defend the West Bank. But the Egyptian–Jordanian pact merely played into the hands of the Israeli generals. On June 1, Eshkol formed a national unity government, and appointed the uncompromising Moshe Dayan, formerly chief of general staff in 1956, as defense minister. Israeli intelligence indicated that the United States had not made any naval preparations to open the Strait of Tiran nor did it seem to be opposed to an Israeli attack. On the 2nd, Eshkol, Dayan, and a small number of cabinet members decided to go to war within three days. Rejecting a limited military operation, the generals proposed an ambitious campaign similar to that of 1956, designed to occupy the Sinai, open the Strait of Tiran, and destroy the Egyptian army. At that moment, East Jerusalem, the West Bank, Gaza, and the Golan Heights were secondary targets, at best.[12]

The June War of 1967

Israel's French-made warplanes destroyed the Egyptian, Jordanian, and Syrian air forces on the ground on June 5. "It took 80 minutes to execute a plan which had been in the making for ten years," Dayan's adviser Shimon Peres later claimed. Without air cover, the Arab armies were routed within days. By June 7, Israeli troops had reached the Suez Canal; two days later, they took Sharm al-Sheikh at the Strait of Tiran. With unexpected daily successes, Israel's war aims grew. On the 7th, Israeli forces occupied East Jerusalem and then the West Bank. The following day, when Egypt agreed to a UN ceasefire proposal, Dayan ordered an attack on Syria's Golan Heights, which fell to Israeli forces on June 10. Unlike Israel, none of the Arab states had developed any offensive military plans before the war, and the defensive posture of Egypt, the most powerful Arab state, turned out to be flawed. The five-year-old commitment to Yemen against Saudi Arabia had weakened the numerical strength of the country's army on the Sinai. Apart from misjudging the situation, Egyptian generals had also misinformed Nasser about combat readiness. As one Arab observer concluded, the main reason for the defeat in 1967 lay in the triple lack of diplomatic flexibility before the war, a "unified strategy" among all Arab countries, and a workable military plan.[13]

Map 9. Israel and the Occupied Territories after the June War in 1967

Defeat was costly to Egypt in terms of lives, war material, and reputation. Moreover, the war closed the Suez Canal for eight years, depriving the country of an important source of revenue. Nasser quickly admitted that the Arabs "had over-estimated their own strength." But he also claimed that defeat was due to the lack of Soviet support, while Israel supposedly had enjoyed American co-belligerency: "There are no longer two superpowers, but only one, that imposes its will on the world: in Vietnam, ... Africa, Indonesia, and now in Arab lands." The misguided *idée fixe* of Anglo–American co-belligerency on Israel's side provoked Cairo into breaking relations with both powers on June 6. Given the magnitude of the *Naksa* – the setback – Nasser announced his resignation three days later. Moscow tried to dissuade him with the promise of sending a high-ranking delegation to Cairo. But only the outpouring of popular support on the 10th swept him back into office, from where he ordered the arrest of the military top brass. Convinced that Egypt could reverse the *Naksa* in the impending resumption of the war, Nasser ordered military resupplies from the Socialist Camp on June 12. By then, Egyptian leaders had come to believe that there was no alternative to a "natural alliance" with the USSR, despite their earlier criticism of the Soviet Union. By the month's end, a more realistic outlook settled in. Contrite, Foreign Minister Riad admitted to East German diplomats that his country had made no real military plans against Israel before June 5, apart from spouting "big slogans." In international affairs, he claimed, Cairo had assumed too many obligations since 1952 – the struggle against the Baghdad Pact, support for Algeria against France, and the war against Saudi Arabia in Yemen – all of which had led to conflict with "the only world power" – the United States. In early July, Egyptian leaders asked themselves whether to align their country with the Soviet Union or to seek a "compromise with the United States" that would produce Israeli withdrawal and US economic aid. However, as the situation had developed by then, they still had no choice but to turn to the USSR.[14]

Jordan's defeat was even more dramatic. The loss of control over Al-Aqsa Mosque and East Jerusalem, the third holiest Muslim city, went hand in hand with the annihilation of its armed forces, the arrival of over one hundred thousand Palestinians from the West Bank, and the forfeiture of a territory that generated 40 percent of the country's economic gross product. King Hussein freely admitted that his country paid a "brutal price for our stupidity." By late June, he understood that resuming the war was not an option. Instead, he fell back on his grandfather Abdullah's policies: Jordan "must very discreetly seek separate settlement with Israel."[15]

Syria lost the Golan Heights only at the end of war. Despite its pre-war goading of Nasser and its military provocations of Israel, it had been wholly unprepared. Barely involved in the war until the Israeli assault on the Golan Heights, the Baath regime quickly adopted Nasser's viewpoint about American involvement and Soviet lack thereof. But it took much longer for Syria to acknowledge the magnitude of Egypt's and Jordan's defeat. And the loss of the Golan Heights turned public opinion against the regime. In response, the internally split Baath leadership called on the Socialist Camp to break relations with Israel, shifted the blame for the Arab defeat on Nasser, and demanded Egypt's resumption of fighting.[16]

In the larger Arab world, the sense of pre-war unity had diminished, too. The supposedly crazy Habib Bourgiba complained as early as June 8 "that, for a second time, Nasser had recklessly and without previous consultation led the Arab States into a hopeless war with Israel." King Faisal, who had originally supported Egyptian escalation, made "his inveterate enemy" the main culprit of the *Naksa*. If Nasser had really wanted to defeat Israel, the Saudi monarch surmised, he would have ended the five-year war in Yemen beforehand. But, instead, he "had embarked on a gigantic bluff. Unfortunately for Nasser … the Jews had called his bluff … if he [Faisal] had been in Israel's place he would have done exactly the same." Only Algeria came out in full support during the war by sending troops. After Egypt had accepted the UN ceasefire, Algeria's leader Houari Boumédiène met Leonid I. Brezhnev and Aleksei N. Kosygin in Moscow on June 12 to demand military aid and Soviet troops for the resumption of the war on *all* fronts. But the Soviet leaders were not keen on "starting World War III." Disappointed by the "cowards," Boumédiène returned home to call for the continuation of the conflict against Israel through military, economic, and political means. Even the oil embargo, which Nasser had called for in late May, became a source of conflict. Officially adopted at a conference of oil-producing Arab countries in Baghdad on the first day of the war, it aimed at all countries that supported Israel. But by mid June, disagreements arose. Boumédiène called for a one-year-long oil embargo, but Faisal did not want to endanger his country's economic well-being and good relationship with the Anglo–American powers.[17]

Unlike eleven years earlier, the superpowers and their Cold War allies lined up behind the warring parties – except for each side's dissenters Romania and France. After inadvertently contributing to the crisis, Moscow had signaled to Cairo on May 25 that it would prefer Egypt "to prevent breaches of the peace." In the first days of the war, the Soviet Union worked for a ceasefire at the United Nations. Only after the Israeli attack on the Golan Heights – which happened despite the UN call for a ceasefire – did the USSR cut relations with Israel, followed by most of the other Warsaw Pact states and Yugoslavia. An emergency meeting of the pact on June 9 discussed steps to avoid a "global war" and military assistance to the Arabs to undo the war's outcomes. Romania nevertheless blamed the USSR for inciting Arab states with arms supplies before June 5 while "leaving them high and dry" during the actual war. On June 22, the long-promised Soviet delegation finally arrived in Egypt. Politburo member Nikolai V. Podgorny discussed with Nasser a close Cold War alignment, a defense agreement, support for Arab demands for an unconditional Israeli withdrawal, and economic assistance to replace the financial losses resulting from the closure of the Suez Canal. The talks also revealed a mutually shared displeasure with communist China. With the PRC at the peak of the Cultural Revolution, Mao had advised Nasser to disperse the Egyptian army in the mountains and among the people in order to wage guerrilla warfare against Israel. The defeated president drily replied that the Sinai was mainly flat, a desert, and mostly uninhabited. Disillusioned Arab diplomats in Beijing bitterly complained how the ideologically supercharged PRC had failed their countries "in the hour of distress."[18]

On June 5, Washington claimed to London that it had been "caught completely unaware" by the recent Israeli attack. In reality, the Johnson administration had expected the war, but it had neither dissuaded nor encouraged Israel beforehand because it did not believe that it had any leverage in the Middle East. US policy during the war was caught in the four-way dilemma between the official June 5 statement of neutrality, support for the war by the American Jewish Community, the accidental but lethal Israeli attack on a US Navy ship on the 8th, and the distraction of the ongoing Vietnam War. Washington quickly joined Moscow at the United Nations to seek a ceasefire. Already before the end of the war, however, the United States embraced Israel's proposal to use the war for a comprehensive solution of the Arab–Israeli conflict. The Johnson administration thereby agreed to the implicit supposition of making Israeli withdrawal dependent on a prior peace agreement. This stance became official US policy with the president's public address on June 19, in which he called on all Middle Eastern nations to "accept the right of others to life," and to pursue "justice for refugees," "free maritime passage," limits to the arms race in the region, and "respect for political independence and territorial integrity." The United States could thereby rely on the support of most of its NATO allies for a policy that supported Israel but still demanded compromises from it. Only France raised criticism. President Charles de Gaulle understood that Israel had won the war because his own country had delivered all the warplanes which Israel had successfully deployed against the Arab states. But he firmly believed that Israel was in the "wrong" and that it had made the solution of the Arab–Israeli conflict "more difficult ... for perhaps another quarter of a century." Ultimately, however, he faulted the United States. The American escalation of the Vietnam War since 1964 had created an international situation, which had made great power cooperation impossible and, hence, had increased the likelihood of regional bouts of violence like the June War. Still, the French president was clear-eyed enough to see that Israel was unlikely to give up all occupied territories, although he too demanded complete withdrawal.[19]

When Eshkol celebrated "victory ringing in our ears" in the Knesset on June 12, he defined his expectations: "Be under no illusion that the State of Israel is prepared to return to the situation that reigned up to a week ago. ... We look, not backward, but forward – to peace." But what would this peace look like? Military triumph had not removed the political pre-war disagreements within the government. And the unexpected territorial gains at the eastern front only revealed that the Israeli government had no ready-made plans for the future. Eshkol's cabinet officially decided to propose a peace-for-land deal to Egypt and Syria on June 19. But despite subsequent Israeli claims that the two Arab states rebuffed the offer after it was sent to the United States for onward delivery, it was never intended to reach the addressees: it was just meant to serve as a show of good will to the Americans. Washington was by no means the right messenger, because Cairo and Damascus had broken relations with it a fortnight earlier. In a speech in Sharm al-Sheikh on the 20th, Eshkol offered to meet Arab leaders to negotiate peace, but he did not mention withdrawal. The only issue on which Israeli leaders completely agreed was East Jerusalem's speedy annexation. With regard to the West Bank and Gaza, internal discussions produced ideas ranging from outright annexation to the establishment of a bi-territorial Palestinian state with transit rights across Israeli territory. The reality, however, was that Israel had become an occupying power in the West Bank, Gaza, and the Sinai in June 1967.[20]

As the dust of war settled, superpower diplomacy sprang into action. While Podgorny negotiated with Nasser in Cairo, Kosygin and Johnson met in Glassboro, New Jersey, on June 23–25. Yet their talks merely disclosed how much each superpower had already made one-sided commitments, creating thereby an impasse that would paralyze the Middle East for several years to come. In view of the likely resumption of war in the Middle East, the Soviet leader demanded unconditional Israeli withdrawal before peace talks. But the president saw no alternative to a peace agreement before withdrawal, since Israel had gotten nothing except another war after unconditional retreat ten years earlier. In July, the United States tried to push Israel and Jordan to make peace, particularly after King Hussein had indicated interest. But since dismembered Jordan no longer posed any real military threat, Israel was ambivalent. When Hussein insisted on negotiating on the return of East Jerusalem, Eshkol's interest quickly waned. As Ben-Gurion had argued fifteen years before, the real key to peace in the Middle East was Egypt. Thus, by early August, both the United States and Israel tried to establish unofficial contacts – but without success.[21]

Ultimately, anti-Israeli unity resolidified the Arab states over the course of July and August. On June 14, Sudan had raised the idea of an Arab League summit, but met with opposition from Algeria, which feared such a meeting would only deepen disunity. By mid July, the leaders of the five revolutionary states – Algeria, Egypt, Sudan, Syria, and Iraq – met in Cairo where they decided to go for renewed military action. A visit by Boumédiène and Iraq's Abdul Rahman Arif to Moscow on July 17–18, however, did not elicit support for what Brezhnev and Kosygin considered an "unrealistic" and "ill-timed" idea. Instead, the Soviet leaders counseled coordination of policies and patience in rebuilding defensive capabilities with Soviet help. After Boumédiène's and Arif's return to Cairo, the five Arab leaders still stuck to the military solution, in the hope that it would force the USSR to become more deeply involved in the Middle East. At the same time, Nasser also argued that "armed struggle" did not preclude "political action," including temporarily setting aside disagreements with the "reactionary Arab countries." An Arab League meeting of foreign ministers in Khartoum on August 1–5 still did not reduce the depth of disagreements, though it at least managed to call for a summit later in the month. Because conservative Saudi Arabia shared the rigid anti-Israeli positions of the revolutionary Arab states, it agreed to Egypt's request to discuss an end to the distracting war in Yemen. Yet, at the oil conference in Baghdad in mid August, Saudi Arabia once more blocked the idea of an oil embargo against countries siding with Israel.[22]

Contrary to all expectations, the Khartoum Summit on August 29 – September 1 reached a compromise agreement. King Hussein's personal diplomacy since August 15 had mobilized the moderate Arab states to build up a united front in favor of a pragmatic approach. The Sudanese host deemed the absence of obstinate Syria "no great loss." Instead of an oil embargo, the summit decided, oil-producing Arab countries were supposed to finance the rearmament and reconstruction of the two front states of Jordan and Egypt, including the provision of funds for revenue lost due to the closure of the Suez Canal. On a higher plane, the summit's participants concurred that both superpowers had forsaken the

Arab world. Unlike in 1956, when the Soviet Union and the United States had supported the Arab side, they now seemed to seek a compromise solution at the United Nations – to the detriment of Arab states. Thus, the league decided that its members should use diplomatic means on a global scale – at the superpower level and the United Nations – to recover the occupied territories. Still, their officially adopted policy of the *three no's* – no peace agreement, no recognition, and no direct negotiations with Israel before withdrawal – was a political compromise between radicals and moderates. The Arab League did not plan to reject Israel in perpetuity.[23] As Riad later confirmed, most Arab states wanted a "political solution" in the Middle East. He even claimed that the summit had dispatched the pre-war rhetoric about the "destruction of Israel ... to the realm of myths." At Khartoum, Nasser also encouraged Hussein to seek some form of accommodation with Israel in order to regain the West Bank and East Jerusalem. Finally, in the context of this newly found, pragmatic unity, Cairo agreed to Riyadh's demand for unilateral and unconditional withdrawal from Yemen.[24]

From Khartoum to Amman, 1967–70

Unsurprisingly, Israel saw the *three no's* as a complete rejection. The supposedly rigid Arab stance played well into its campaign of appealing to the world's sympathy. Government propaganda disseminated the spurious claim that in May Israel had received "funeral let[ter]s" from both superpowers, and that the June War had been a victory "by a narrow margin." A spate of events in the fall seemed to bolster Israel's case. In late September, the Khartoum Summit boycotter Syria once more called for Israel's destruction. Within another month, Egypt sank an Israeli destroyer with Soviet-delivered missiles, triggering a retaliatory air strike against Egyptian oil refineries. Cairo's contacts with Moscow also appeared worrying, even if Nasser publicly declared that the "key" to the solution of the Arab–Israeli conflict was the United States, because it was the only power able to convince Israel to make concessions. But Cairo tried to work on Moscow to elicit a more dynamic Soviet anti-imperialist policy toward Indochina, Indonesia, and Africa with the goal of forcing Washington's hand in the Middle East.[25] Yet the Johnson administration was not as powerful as Egypt hoped; it too grew exasperated with Israel's increasingly inflexible positions. But this did not prevent the United States from arming Israel with modern warplanes to deter Egypt's re-emerging Soviet-delivered air force – given that de Gaulle's critical stance had turned France into a less willing arms supplier.[26]

On November 22, after months of deliberations, the UN Security Council adopted Resolution 242. It mostly reiterated Johnson's five-month-old bid: withdrawal from territories occupied in June, respect for each other's "right to live in peace," freedom of navigation, settlement of the Palestinian refugee issue, and mutual guarantees of territorial integrity and political independence. The language of the British-drafted resolution was deliberately vague in order to prevent a veto by one of the council's permanent members and to attract broad support beyond. The sequence of peace and withdrawal was left undefined, as was the question of how much occupied land Israel would have to vacate – all or only some. Egypt and Jordan supported the resolution. Israel dithered for three years. Syria, Iraq, Algeria, Sudan, and the PLO rejected it. Finally, in December, Nasser sent a privately delivered message to Johnson, expressing his wish for "good relations," though full diplomatic links did not resume until late 1973.[27]

In accordance with Resolution 242, U Thant appointed Swedish diplomat Gunnar Jarring his special representative to the Middle East. After twenty-two months of shuttle diplomacy, however, the UN envoy decided "to terminate his efforts" when he concluded that his mission had reached an "impasse." Jarring repeatedly ran into Israeli–Arab disagreements on the procedural and substantial implementation of the vaguely worded UN resolution. Sporadic outbreaks of fighting also regularly wrecked minor concessions just made. Israel submitted frequent proposals – a tactic primarily designed to show good will, keep Jarring busy, prevent the Arabs from reverting to military action, and curb renewed discussions in the Security Council. Encouraged by Nasser and Johnson, Hussein tried to find a solution in private negotiations with Israeli officials, during which he offered territorial concessions – but to no avail. In the second year of Jarring's mission, the Arab side became more rigid. Since the deadlock favored Israel's settlement activities in the West Bank, Nasser by late 1968 concluded that Jarring's mission was "useless."[28]

The year 1969 witnessed major changes that would lead to more conflict the following year. On February 26, Eshkol died of cancer. Golda Meir, sick herself, agreed to serve as interim prime minister – for five years. Rigid and personally burned by the internationally enforced withdrawal in 1957, she surrounded herself with military hawks, shared Ben-Gurion's perception of unforgiving Arab hostility, and pursued Eshkol's policy of seeking full peace for some land. From the beginning, her government hoped that Nasser's departure from the political stage would change Egyptian positions.[29]

A month before Eshkol's death, Richard M. Nixon had succeeded Johnson as US president. Faced with a range of major international problems, the new president decided to seek advice from de Gaulle, the old detractor of American foreign policy. The French leader counseled withdrawal from Vietnam, recognition of the PRC, and active great power cooperation at the United Nations with regard to the Arab–Israeli conflict. Otherwise, no agreement would ever emerge in the Middle East, allowing Israel to "become more and more imperialistic." By late March, the United States proposed to U Thant a "package" deal on the Middle East designed to reach an overall negotiated agreement on all issues raised in Resolution 242 but "before implementation of any part" of it. Unnerved by the recent border clashes with the PRC, the USSR reacted positively to the renewed American commitment to the Middle East.[30]

But violence in the Middle East escalated rapidly. On March 8, 1969, Egypt shelled Israeli positions across the Suez Canal. The resulting eighteen-month-long War of Attrition consisted of monthly, ever intensifying military confrontations. Both Jordan and Egypt had concluded that Israel did not want to accept Resolution 242. King Hussein believed that Israel had "gambled away [the] victory" of 1967. For Cairo, there were only three courses of action left to break the impasse: "another war," a solution imposed by Israel, or the implementation of Resolution 242. The first two would not resolve Israel's quest for peace because they would only generate more Arab resistance, only the third could do so. Thus, the overall goal of the Egyptian escalation on March 8 was to force the great powers at the United Nations to come up with a path toward implementation of Resolution 242. The timing of the Egyptian raid on March 8 was related to substantial Soviet arms deliveries, which Nasser believed would "let us intensify the commando operations until we are militarily capable of crossing the canal." But getting a bridgehead on the eastern side of the canal would ultimately require increased coordination with "the four [Arab] states at the eastern front."[31]

The American–Soviet–British–French talks at the United Nations on the Middle East that started in April 1969 met with immediate Israeli rejection. Fearful that Israel would never withdraw from any territory occupied in 1967, Egypt, however, was ready to accept the US "package" deal. But Nasser insisted that Israel needed to withdraw from all occupied territories – otherwise, there would be war. Anxious about a deterioration of Egypt's military strength, Moscow decided to provide Cairo with missiles and Soviet-piloted warplanes, which arrived in the Canal Zone between December and March.[32]

A chance event on August 21, 1969 – the arson attempt on Al-Aqsa Mosque by a deranged Australian evangelical tourist – additionally fanned the flames. Nasser quickly accused Israel of failing to protect the Holy Sites in Jerusalem. An emergency Arab League meeting on the 26th decided to establish a joint army against Israel. At a conference in early September, Egypt, Syria, Iraq, and Jordan reviewed the political situation, military preparedness, and the steps necessary to increase Arab unity. But a heart attack shortly thereafter forced Nasser to take a six-week break. The concurrent arrival of the first batch of powerful American F-4 Phantom fighter planes, which the outgoing Johnson administration had agreed to deliver to Israel in late 1968, aroused Arab anger once more. It was against this background that Jarring terminated his mediation mission on September 10, as mentioned above. By late October, a convalesced Nasser decided that Egypt would only negotiate from a position of strength acquired by renewed war. At virtually the same time, Dayan reformulated Israel's security needs. Israel would not give up control over the West Bank, the Golan Heights, Gaza, and a strip of land on the Sinai from Eilat to Sharm al-Sheikh.[33]

The hardening of Arab and Israeli positions convinced the United States in early December to advance a peace plan that had been developed in bilateral talks with the USSR since the spring. The plan committed the United States for the first time to seek complete Israeli withdrawal from all occupied territories except East Jerusalem, to request Egypt to allow free maritime passage for Israeli ships through the Suez Canal and the Strait of Tiran, and to persuade Israel to allow the return of some Palestinian refugees. Jordan was pleased, Egypt did not respond, and Israel called it a danger to its existence.[34]

By late 1969, all signs pointed toward renewed war. Angered by the continued American arms deliveries, Cairo eventually called Washington's peace plan a sham. Instead, Nasser sought to increase Arab unity in a personal meeting with Saudi Arabia's Faisal in Cairo on December 18–19 and at the Arab League Summit in Rabbat, Morocco, soon thereafter. But the oil-producing members were not willing to finance the war policy of a man whom they considered a Soviet "instrument." The radical secular Arab states could not even agree on anything among themselves. A fortnight later, Israel escalated the War of Attrition with deep penetration bombings of the Egyptian hinterland. Convinced that the United States was preoccupied with the war in Vietnam, the USSR responded by sending additional air and naval forces to Egypt. By mid April of 1970, Soviet-piloted fighter planes engaged with Israeli aircraft in the skies over the Suez Canal.[35]

Given Moscow's increased military involvement, Washington approached Cairo with the request to take the diplomatic initiative. "In a last appeal for peace," Nasser publicly responded by calling on Nixon

either to continue enabling Israeli aggression and risk global consequences, or to help resolve the crisis. After consultations with Israeli
and Soviet officials, US Secretary of State William P. Rogers publicly
outlined a plan on June 19, 1970, that envisioned a ninety-day ceasefire
and the resumption of Jarring's mission. Although Nasser welcomed the
plan, Israel immediately rejected it while continuing to attack Soviet
missile positions and shoot down Soviet-piloted airplanes. During his
medical stay in Moscow from June 29 to July 17, Nasser charted out
possible compromises with Brezhnev and Kosygin; in exchange for Israeli
withdrawal, he agreed to grant passage rights to Israel in the Suez Canal
and the Strait of Tiran. On his return to Cairo, Nasser finally decided to
agree to the Rogers Plan but remained pessimistic about its chances of
success. At least, it brought ninety days for Egypt's armed forces to rest,
regroup, and absorb more Soviet-supplied weapons. The reactions of the
other Arab states reflected the long-standing splits between radical and
conservative/moderate regimes. The official Egyptian acceptance on the
22nd, however, allowed the United States to put pressure on Israel. On
July 31, the Meir government, unnerved by a coalition crisis over the
issue, agreed. The ceasefire went into effect on August 7, even if it
remained shaky for some time.[36]

While the Rogers Plan allowed the guns to fall silent at the Suez Canal,
it exacerbated the crisis in Jordan once King Hussein had accepted it on
July 26. Following the June War three years earlier, the PLO and other
Palestinian resistance organizations had left the West Bank for Amman.
Since the late 1960s, they had created their own quasi-statelets within the
kingdom, threatening Hussein's authority. Naturally, they opposed the
Rogers Plan and decried Nasser's and Hussein's successive endorse-
ments. The descent into civil war in Jordan started with the hijacking of
several Western civilian airliners on September 6 by a Jordan-based
Palestinian splinter group. On the 15th, the king decided to form
a military government to counter the Palestinian challenge. As civil war
ensued within a day, the superpowers threw their support behind the
imperiled monarchy. Washington provided military, diplomatic, and
political aid; Moscow leaned on Damascus and Baghdad to call off their
military interventions. On the 20th, Nasser called the heads of Arab
League member states to Cairo for an emergency summit. Seven days
later, the Egyptian leader successfully mediated a ceasefire between King
Hussein and PLO leader Yasser Arafat. After having succeeded in avert-
ing further bloodshed, Nasser suffered another heart attack on
September 28 when he was seeing off Arab delegations at the airport.
He passed away at his home in the early evening hours. As the news
percolated through the world, the Arab Middle East fell into deep

mourning. When Israel celebrated Jewish New Year the following day, even "crocodile tears" were in short supply.[37]

No War, No Peace, 1970–72

Many observers considered Nasser's successor, Anwar Sadat, a transitional figure. A junior member of the officers' revolt in 1952, he rose through the ranks under Nasser. Even before he became president in October 1970, he had realized that Egypt above all needed economic reform. Sadat also questioned Nasser's foreign policy, and he was dissatisfied with both superpowers, particularly, however, with the USSR. To an American diplomat, the new president declared that "Egypt wanted nothing to do with the rivalry" between the superpowers, but instead aimed at ending Israel's second occupation of the Sinai and reopening the Suez Canal. But there was one important continuity with Nasser. Sadat too believed that no Egyptian leader could afford to recognize Israel: "Our people will crush anyone who would decide this!" Still, 1971, his "year of decision," witnessed marked changes in Egypt's foreign policy. Sadat tried to bridge old, intra-Arab cleavages by seeking improved relations with conservative Saudi Arabia as well as closer links with radical Syria and Libya. Echoing Riad's words from mid 1967 that Egypt had assumed too many obligations, however, Sadat's foreign policy was supposed to serve primarily Egyptian interests.[38]

With regard to Israel, Sadat in early November was willing to extend the ninety-day ceasefire one more time for a similar period. But he was frustrated by Israel's continued refusal to implement Resolution 242, because it allowed the country to cement the status quo. When the second ninety-day period was up in early February, Sadat proposed signing a foreign-mediated interim agreement, which would lead to Israeli withdrawal from the eastern bank of the Suez Canal as a first step of implementing Resolution 242. But on February 9, Meir rejected Sadat's offer as insufficient. The United States grew equally frustrated by Israel's continued insistence on maximalist goals. In the spring, Egyptian officials warned American diplomats that "there were only three doves left" in the Egyptian government – luckily, Sadat was still among them. But Israel believed time was working in its favor; according to Eban, Israel would not "pluck the fruit before it is ripe." On April 1, Sadat repeated the proposal of an interim agreement, with Israel budging a little three weeks later with an offer to open the Suez Canal without withdrawing from the eastern bank.[39]

As early as October 2, 1970, Sadat had told an American official that he had not seen eye to eye on everything with the recently deceased Nasser, and that he believed there were no disagreements between the United States and Egypt – apart from Israel. In a personal letter to US President Nixon ten weeks later, the new Egyptian leader expressed his hope for an improvement of relations, but also asked for "understanding of the realities of our positions." Like Nasser, Sadat believed that only the United States could push Israel into concessions. His dovish approach to Israel in early 1971 quickly earned him the visit from Rogers in early May. Ahead of the first visit of a US secretary of state in eighteen years, Sadat had fired his pro-Soviet vice president, Ali Sabri. In his talks with Rogers, he minced no words: the USSR was not interested in helping Egypt to recover Arab lands, but in increasing its military presence in the Middle East. Should his proposed interim agreement materialize with the help of American mediation, Egypt would send Soviet troops home and re-establish full diplomatic relations with the United States.[40]

Still, on May 27, Moscow and Cairo signed a friendship treaty. Podgorny's visit to Egypt in early January, which had occurred to celebrate the completion of the Aswan Dam project after over fifteen years of construction, had revealed major tensions in the bilateral relationship. The Soviet guest tried to convince his Egyptian host of Nasser's anti-imperialist position and of a solid alliance with the USSR. Shortly after Rogers' visit to Cairo, Egyptian diplomats in Moscow observed a "tense and nervous" atmosphere among the Soviet leaders. On May 25, a high-ranking Soviet delegation traveled to Cairo, obviously concerned about Sadat's political drift. It hoped to commit Nasser's successor to the old anti-imperialist policies by proposing a friendship treaty. Sadat initially did "not intend" at all to sign, but eventually changed his mind in order to extract as much economic and military aid as possible, and to use the treaty to put pressure on the United States. Israel drew the opposite conclusions – Sadat's Egypt had descended into even greater Soviet dependency.[41]

The treaty stood at the start of a period during which the momentum, which Sadat had created since October, seemed to peter out. In June and early July, the Nixon administration focused on the secret trip of security adviser Henry Kissinger to China on July 9–11. The subsequent Sino-American announcement of Nixon's scheduled visit to Beijing in February 1972 put enormous pressure on the Soviet Union and North Vietnam, and convinced Cairo's friend Delhi to close ranks with Moscow against Beijing, Washington, and Islamabad in the run-up to the Indian intervention in East Pakistan later in the year. In comparison, Egypt hoped that Sino-American rapprochement would convince the PRC to pursue a more constructive policy in the Middle East. In September, Sadat once more tried to signal flexibility to Nixon with regard to Egypt's desire for "permanent peace with Israel." A month later, during a visit to Moscow, a disheartened Sadat tilted back to the USSR with a request to overcome the recent "chill" in the bilateral relationship. He returned to Cairo with promises of additional warplanes and missiles. In November, he publicly vented his frustrations about American inaction: "There is no longer any hope for [a] peaceful solution ... to fight is our decision." But, then, the East Pakistan War occurred, and the USSR shifted urgently needed military goods from Egypt to its new ally India.[42]

In the first half of 1972, Sadat remained torn about the direction of his policy toward Israel. Three weeks before Nixon went to Beijing, Sadat traveled to Moscow where he failed to receive additional weapons. On his way home, he stopped over in Yugoslavia for talks with Josif Broz Tito, who advised him to engage with Nixon in the context of the emerging Sino–American rapprochement. Mahmoud Riad's semi-official trip to Beijing a month after Nixon's visit there helped to re-establish relations with China, but he received advice from Mao contrary to Tito's: Since peace was not possible in the Middle East, Egypt should be ready for a long war. In view of the upcoming Nixon visit to Moscow in late May, Egypt increasingly feared that the Arab–Israeli conflict would become frozen in a superpower deal, in a repetition of the situation between 1957 and 1967. In late April, Sadat was again in Moscow, this time because the Soviet leaders wanted to reassure him that they would not sell Egypt out in the talks with the American president. It was in this context that a Romanian mediation attempt occurred. Hoping to receive the Nobel Peace Prize for solving the Arab–Israeli conflict, the megalomaniac Nicolae Ceauşescu met Sadat in Cairo in early April and invited Meir to Bucharest a month later, but his timing was off given the concurrent vacillations of the Egyptian leader. Nixon's visit to Moscow in late May resulted in the conclusion of nuclear arms limitation agreements as symbols of a US–Soviet détente, but his talks with Brezhnev and Kosygin focused primarily on the crisis in Indochina and hardly touched on the Middle East.[43]

By mid 1972, decision time had come for Sadat. With Saudi advice and help, he once more signaled to Nixon that he wanted closer ties. Via the Saudi channel, the United States replied that it would not pressure Israel for concessions as long as there was a Soviet military presence in Egypt. On July 8, Sadat informed the Soviet ambassador about his dissatisfaction with Moscow's policy of slowing down arms deliveries, and even hinted at the expulsion of the Soviet personnel. But before taking that step, he sent Prime Minister Aziz Sedky on a final mission to Moscow on July 13–14 to demand additional weapons deliveries and the transfer of Soviet troops and advisers under Egyptian command. When the Kremlin refused to budge, Sadat changed strategy by gambling on reaching a negotiated solution to the Middle Eastern deadlock through US mediation. On July 17, he informed Nixon, using Soviet–American détente as a pretext, about his decision to send 10,000 Soviet troops and advisers home. It should not have come as a surprise to the United States because Egyptian politicians had talked about this step as early as mid 1967, and Sadat had hinted at it during Rogers' visit in May 1971. But when the news arrived in Washington, the Nixon administration discovered that it had no policy ready for this event.[44]

Sadat had chosen an inopportune moment. Occupied by the final round of fighting and diplomacy in Indochina, Nixon's attention to the Middle East was minimal. After his successful trips to Beijing and Moscow earlier in the year, the American president did not want to engage with a potentially explosive issue during an election year. Unsurprisingly, Cairo once more grew frustrated with Washington's policy of inaction. Sadat refused to heed Israeli, British, and American calls for direct negotiations since he was convinced that this would merely allow Israel to use the Sinai as a bargaining chip to obtain secure borders that "might even start at the canal." He was particularly dismayed that the United States continued to deliver arms to Israel. By mid October, Sadat sent Sedky back to the USSR for talks on the delivery of arms without Soviet advisers attached – with little result. Moscow was again not willing to budge even under the open threat of Cairo switching sides in the global Cold War. Disappointed, Sadat took his idea of a mediated interim agreement with Israel off the table. On October 24, he decided to go to war at the Suez Canal.[45]

Toward the October War and Beyond, 1972–74

As the dice were cast, Sadat embarked on meticulous military and diplomatic preparations. He obviously did not want to rush into war without battle plans or clear political goals, as Egypt had done in 1956 and in 1967. In a series of meetings between mid November and late January, Sadat committed the Arab League to a joint battle "for the liquidation of Israeli aggression" and the complete implementation of all aspects of Resolution 242. Unlike six years earlier, Jordan welcomed fraternal troops, because it had grown fed up with Israeli stalling in negotiations over East Jerusalem and the West Bank. But old disagreements did not disappear over night. It took Sadat until the fall of 1973 to bind in Syria. On September 21, 1973, the Egyptian president took the decision to go to war by October 6.[46]

Sadat did not plan a big battle for complete liberation. Nor was he willing to honor the recent agreements with other Arab states. "Given

Israel's overwhelming air of superiority," he had recognized, Egypt "would not be so foolish as to launch an all out attack." The impending conflict was about launching a political process at the international level about the Egyptian – not the Arab – struggle with Israel. Early in 1973, in one of his attempts to engage Washington, Sadat informed the Nixon administration that he considered the solution of the Egyptian–Israeli conflict an issue separate from the solution of the Palestinian Question. The West Bank was "an internal Jordanian matter," and "Gaza's self-determination should be worked out under UN auspices." It was a major break with long-term Arab positions, but Sadat shrewdly let the other Arab states, particularly Syria, believe that the looming war was about the liberation of all Arab land. Cairo thereby compelled Damascus into action in a manner similar to how Syria had forced Egypt to act before the June War in 1967 – under a false pretext. As Arab military unity re-emerged, skirmishes on all Israeli fronts multiplied. Just at the time when the Vietnam War was winding down with the Paris Accords of January 1973, a new Arab–Israeli war was in the offing.[47]

Learning lessons from the previous three wars with Israel, Sadat took time to plan for the looming clash. To support the Egyptian need for weapons, Kuwait, Qatar, and the United Arab Emirates provided 1.25 billion dollars of funds, of which 700 million dollars alone were used in March to purchase, in cash, weapons from the USSR to be delivered by the fall. Saudi Arabia and Libya helped to finance the acquisition of arms from the United Kingdom. By mid April, Saudi Arabia demanded that the United States should lean on Israel, otherwise it would not increase oil production to ease recent shortages and price increases in North America. Half a month later, Sadat raised the possibility of an Arab oil embargo. Within another fortnight, Algeria, Iraq, Kuwait, and Libya symbolically stopped pumping oil for a short period in a show of support. In late August, Faisal and Sadat agreed to use oil as a political tool in the coming war. In early September, the ten members of the Organization of Arab Petroleum Exporting Countries (OAPEC) discussed production cuts as "a political weapon."[48]

Beyond the Arab world, Sadat exploited the involvement of the Non-Aligned Movement in the Arab–Israeli conflict since 1967. After the conclusion of the Vietnam War in Paris earlier in the year, Tito tried to mobilize the movement for mediation in the Arab–Israeli conflict. Yet, at the fourth Non-Aligned Conference in Algiers in early September 1973, Arab member states forwarded a draft calling on the other members – all hailing from Africa and Asia – to sever relations with Israel. In line with the six-year-old Resolution 242, the final declaration of the conference demanded unconditional Israeli withdrawal and support for the Arab front states, and included a call on all states in the world to impose economic and political boycotts against Israel. Beginning in early October, just as the war was about to start, all twenty sub-Saharan African states successively severed relations with Israel. This Arab diplomatic achievement was particularly bitter for Israel, after it had invested many economic and military resources there since 1957 to counterbalance Arab hostility.[49]

Even though the period before the October War was a chronicle of a military clash foretold, the United States and Israel did not pay close attention. Egypt's war plans and its related political goals had been circulating among foreign diplomats in Cairo for almost half a year. From February to May, Sadat also had been willing to give diplomacy another chance – but re-elected President Nixon did not react to any of the Egyptian proposals to replicate the Paris Accords on Vietnam in the Middle East. In May, the US government even believed that Egypt would never dare to start a war against a militarily superior Israel. After the United States had vetoed a resolution, sponsored by Afro–Asian states, in support of Resolution 242 at the UN Security Council in late July, Cairo demanded from Washington the withdrawal of the acting head of the US interest section in Spain's embassy in Egypt within one month.[50]

Like the United States, Israel did not believe that war was probable – even on its eve, October 5. Israel's lack of war preparedness stemmed from intelligence failures and attitudinal shortcomings. In terms of assessing the danger of war in early October, Israeli intelligence services failed to provide a well-timed warning because of a successful Egyptian military deception campaign. But Israeli inertia after years of war readiness, fears of causing a false alarm, and bureaucratic infighting were culpable too. On a more general level, the government's default position was that the Arab neighbors would not go to war after the decisive defeat in 1967, and that Israeli military superiority and the presumed Arab incompetence served as adequate deterrents. It was precisely this dismissive attitude which had not only caused Israeli diplomacy to become maximalist in its goals and inflexible in its tactics since 1967, but also convinced Sadat of the necessity to go to war once more. Moreover, few of those responsible for intelligence gathering and policy making in Jerusalem could have imagined that Sadat would launch a war with limited goals – one which he was ready to lose on the battlefield but win in the political arena.[51]

On October 6, over one hundred thousand Egyptian troops crossed the Suez Canal. Within two days, they breached Israel's Bar Lev line encompassing a series of fortified defensive posts and succeeded in establishing several bridgeheads on the eastern bank. At the same time, Syrian tanks attacked the Golan Heights, but with less success. Unprepared, Israeli troops suffered heavy losses at both fronts. On October 9, Israel appealed to the United States for military resupplies, just as the first Soviet military supply flights arrived in Egypt and Syria after Brezhnev had decided, unilaterally, to support the Arabs in their anti-imperialist struggle. On the 12th, Meir accepted a US call for a ceasefire. But Sadat rejected it twenty-four hours later because it did not address the basic political issues underlying the conflict. The Egyptian rebuff persuaded the United States to start its own supply airlift to Israel on October 14/15. On the 16th, Israel managed to cross the Suez Canal at the middle section, which allowed the occupation of the southern half of the western bank within a week. With the war turning against Egypt, Sadat now appealed to the United States to work at the United Nations for a ceasefire. Betting on Arab solidarity, he simultaneously called on OAPEC to impose an oil embargo. Yet, at that time, Damascus realized that Cairo had tricked it into believing that the war was about the military liberation of all occupied Arab lands. Syria thus demanded – unsuccessfully – the resumption of Egyptian offensive operations in the Sinai to relieve pressure at the Golan Heights. On the 17th, OAPEC decided on an oil embargo against all countries supporting Israel, which included immediate price increases and monthly production cuts by 5 percent until Israel withdrew from the occupied territories. At the Soviet Union's invitation, Kissinger traveled to Moscow on October 19/20 to negotiate UN Security Council Resolution 338 (adopted on the 22nd), which called for a ceasefire and the implementation of Resolution 242. The war ended soon thereafter, with Egypt and Israel controlling roughly a similar amount of ground on the other side of the canal, and Israel gaining some Syrian territory east of the Golan Heights. The limited success in October 1973 made Sadat, whom many had considered a transitional figure after Nasser's death, into a hero who had led Egypt out of the six-year humiliation.[52]

As early as October 7, Sadat had contacted Nixon via Iranian diplomatic channels about his war aims. Resuming the old Egyptian practice of speaking for all Arabs, Sadat demanded Israel accept complete withdrawal from all occupied territories. In return, Egypt was willing to agree to the introduction of UN or international troops in all of these territories, to grant free passage to Israeli shipping through the Strait of Tiran and the Suez Canal, to end the state of belligerency since 1948, and to participate in an international peace conference that would involve all parties, including the Palestinians. Since he did not want the Arab–Israeli conflict to go back to the UN Security Council again, he clearly sought US leadership. He rejected the American call for a ceasefire on October 13 mainly on the grounds that it was not linked to a final settlement. During Kosygin's visit to Cairo some days later, he empha-sized the same points once more. On the 16th, the United States informed Egypt that it had grasped the political nature of Cairo's war aims, and that the current bloodletting in the Middle East had revealed "the necessity of a political settlement."[53]

In early November, Kissinger negotiated with Sadat the resumption of full US–Egyptian diplomatic relations. In January, he helped Israel and Egypt agree on military disengagement that provided for the withdrawal of all Israeli troops behind a line 20 miles to the east of the Suez Canal. In recognition of American diplomatic efforts, oil-producing Arab states – with the exception Syria and Libya – lifted the embargo against the United States on March 19. Israeli withdrawal also allowed Egypt to reopen the Suez Canal. Two wars and almost seven years of neglect, however, required thirteen months of repair until the canal could open on June 5, 1975 – exactly eight years after its war-related closure. But in the absence of a peace agreement, Israeli ships were not allowed passage, though Egypt permitted Israeli goods to sail on third-party ships. Anyway, Israeli ships continued to reach Eilat through the Israeli-occupied Strait of Tiran.[54]

Other participants in the events of the October War were less lucky. Disappointed by Egypt's national war goals and its fast acceptance of Resolution 338, Syria refused to subscribe to Sadat's visions or accept Kissinger's mediation. By May, it merely achieved an Israeli withdrawal from the territories lost in October 1973, but not from the Golan Heights. On the Israeli side, the major political fatality was Golda Meir. Under her leadership, the country had lost the lives of 2,656 soldiers in nineteen days – an enormous amount for the small country – and thereby the sense of invincibility which it had gained in 1967. A governmental report held the armed forces exclusively responsible for the lack of war preparedness. Its one-sided conclusions, however, caused a public uproar that forced Meir to resign on April 10, 1974.[55] Moscow equally suffered from the war's outcome, despite plans for an international peace conference in Geneva in late 1973. The USSR continued to refuse the resumption of full diplomatic relations with Israel until 1991. This snub deprived Moscow of the kind of influence that Washington enjoyed on both sides of the Egyptian–Israeli conflict for the next two decades.

The United States, with Sadat's endorsement, happily capitalized on its new, privileged role in Middle Eastern affairs. However, the continued lack of an overarching American peace plan, the further downward slide of the Nixon administration into the Watergate Scandal in 1974, and the overall American Cold War goal of keeping Soviet influence out of the region pushed the primary task of solving the root causes of the conflict into the background.[56] As the events of 1977 showed, the actual initiative for peace came from within the region itself.

Conclusion

The ten-year period after 1964 was characterized by the intra-Arab conflict between the two former parts of the United Arab Republic – Syria and Egypt. At the same time, the Egyptian–Saudi war over Yemen turned into peace in 1967 and then into close collaboration six years later. Sadat managed to forge a level of Arab unity by the fall of 1973 that had not existed since 1945. Yet he planned to exploit this newly found unity mostly for Egyptian goals. Sadat had learned the lessons from 1956 and 1967 – war against Israel required unity, meticulous preparations, and realistic goals. In 1967, the Arab states had not wanted to go to war, but their competitive brinkmanship had provoked Israel to inflict a stinging defeat. Six years later, they were determined to go to war by catching Israel off guard. Even if they obtained a military draw on the battlefield, Egypt still won a political victory. The transition from Nasser to Sadat had clearly led to a change of strategy, most notably in the form of a switch of association from the Soviet Union to the United States, but there were still some continuities. Cairo had toyed with the idea of seeking rapprochement with Washington as early as mid 1967, although by then it had no choice but to ally with the weaker of the two superpowers. Similarly, the idea of a limited war to establish a bridgehead on the eastern bank of the Suez Canal had emerged at the beginning of the War of Attrition in March 1969.

The period from 1967 to 1973 witnessed the high point of Israeli expansionism. The Zionist dream of a *Judenstaat* had been a settler colonial project from the beginning. For a short period in 1956–57 and then again in 1967 it had gone beyond that project's goal by seeking territorial expansion beyond the borders of Mandatory Palestine. Israeli behavior in the six years between the June War and the October War was remarkably similar to that of the European powers in the nineteenth century. It displayed excessive self-confidence based on military superiority, pursued policies seeking to dictate peace from a position of strength, and implemented manifest expansionism (Jerusalem) and territorial acquisition for security needs. But as in the nineteenth century, this kind of expansionism created new security dilemmas that required the geographical extension of its defense – such as bombing the Egyptian hinterland in the spring of 1970. In 1973, Israel was forced to recognize the limits of its power. Egyptian diplomacy had forged Arab unity, come up with a battle plan that put the politics of the weak ahead of self-deceptions of military grandeur, and managed to isolate

Israel in the Global South. The war aimed at forcing the Middle Eastern conflict onto the American agenda and compelling Israel to accept its strategic vulnerabilities.

At the international level, the Middle East in the decade after 1964 drew the two superpowers into the region. The June War revealed how much each had made commitments to one or the other side. For the following five years, the superpower Cold War helped to keep the Arab–Israeli conflict firmly in place. Movement in this deadlock came only when Egypt decided to cut military relations with the USSR in July 1972, though it took war against Israel fifteen months later to make the United States understand this point. In comparison, the United Nations had played various roles in the region for a quarter of a century – destructive in 1947, constraining in 1957–67, and doomed in 1967–69. UNEF did not return to the Middle East after the June War, though Sadat briefly suggested stationing foreign troops in the Sinai. By the early 1970s, the United Nations played no diplomatic role in the Arab–Israeli conflict, apart from issuing Security Council resolutions. Ultimately, it shared responsibility since 1947 for the plight of the Palestinian people. How they fared in the quarter of a century after the *Nakba* is the focus of the next chapter.

10 The Palestinians

Over 750,000 Palestinians fled or were expelled from their homes during the *Nakba* in 1947–49. The *Naksa* in 1967 displaced more than 280,000 Palestinians from the West Bank, East Jerusalem, and Gaza. Among them, 145,000 fled for a second time to other Arab states. To this day, Israel has neither allowed the return of refugees – bar 40,000 under a family reunification scheme in the 1950s and 14,000 in the summer of 1967 – nor participated in a compensation mechanism for Palestinian properties lost.[1]

In early 1949, the Palestinian nation ended up scattered across multiple locations – Israel, East Jerusalem, the West Bank, Gaza, and neighboring Arab states. As a long-term result of the British suppression of the Arab revolt in 1936–39, Palestinians lacked a central leadership to represent their cause. While Arab states disagreed on a joint standpoint, the Arab League paternalistically claimed decision-making supremacy in all Palestinian affairs from the very beginning. Independent Palestinian organizations eventually emerged in exile by the late 1950s, but the league ignored them when it called for what would become the Palestine Liberation Organization (PLO) in 1964. In 1967, the PLO leadership expected that the June War would topple Israel and establish a Palestinian state in its place. The rapid defeat dashed Palestinian hopes, but simultaneously liberated the PLO from Arab tutelage. By early 1969, one of the exiled organizations – Yasser Arafat's Fatah – assumed PLO leadership and soon thereafter pursued revolutionary policies. Under Fatah, the PLO almost took over Jordan in 1970, but the monarchy's military response forced the PLO to relocate to Lebanon by 1971. At the same time, however, Egypt was starting to withdraw from directing Palestinian affairs, which convinced the PLO leadership to alter its heavy reliance on revolution and to consider a negotiated solution with Israel. Even if the PLO was able to obtain observer status at the United Nations in late 1974, the prospect of establishing a state in all of former Mandatory Palestine had become all but an illusion, despite the emergence of a vibrant Palestinian civil society in Lebanon. The best that Palestinians could hope for by the mid 1970s was a state in the West Bank and Gaza.

The political fate of the Palestinians thus underwent major structural changes during the middle period of the Cold War. Until 1964, Palestinians were under Arab League tutelage but lacked a political organization of their own. After 1973, they ran their own affairs but lacked Egyptian support. The period in between witnessed the rise of Palestinian mass activism on the ground and agency at the international level. Fatah and the PLO were greatly inspired by Chinese and North Vietnamese communism. Both Asian states even provided political, organizational, and military support for the Palestinian revolutionary project. Yet Sino–American rapprochement in 1971–72 and the Paris Accords on Vietnam of early 1973 removed the political bonds between the Asian and the Palestinian revolutions.

The Palestinian Diaspora

No Palestinian organization or individual received membership status when the Arab League was established in March 1945. Internally divided, the league was incapable of protecting or even supporting Palestinians. A plan to purchase Arab land in Mandatory Palestine so that it could be denied to Jewish buyers quickly collapsed.[2] After August 1945 when US President Harry S. Truman called for increased Jewish immigration to Palestine, the Arab League rejected any change to the immigration restrictions outlined in the 1939 White Paper. Afterward it also fought international proposals for partition of the territory. At the start of the first Arab–Israeli war in late 1947, the league eventually grasped that it lacked real military capabilities to defend Palestinian interests.

The military weakness and political division of Arab states mirrored similar fault lines among Palestinians. While the revolt of 1936–39 had achieved a political victory when the United Kingdom issued the White Paper of 1939 that limited Jewish immigration, the three-year-long brutal suppression by the British forces had imprisoned, sent into exile, and even killed many of the Palestinian leaders. British officials prevented Palestinians from establishing an organized military force, contrary to the Zionists, who had built up the Haganah. Furthermore, a few Palestinian leaders with anti-British and anti-Zionist views – like the Grand Mufti of Jerusalem Mohammed Amin al-Husseini, for example – chose to collaborate with Adolf Hitler's National Socialist Germany during World War II. In comparison, Jews were victims of the Holocaust, and Zionists in general supported Allied war goals.[3] Thus, when military conflict between Jews and Arabs began in late 1947, Palestinians suffered long-term organizational, military, and political disadvantages.

Over 750,000 Palestinians fled or were expelled from the territory of what became Israel during the *Nakba*. Despite a decade of internal Zionist discussions about the removal of Palestinians, no concrete blueprint existed when war broke out in late 1947. Displacement occurred for a variety of reasons. In the first months, Palestinians from mostly urban regions fled their homes, as they had done in disturbances during the previous quarter of a century, as a temporary escape from violence. Zionist removal of Palestinians became more systematic in early 1948, focusing mainly on the countryside. In July, the Israeli government prohibited the return of all Palestinian refugees, though 40,000 were eventually allowed to come back under a family reunion scheme in the 1950s. In the five years after 1948, Israel razed 418 of over 500 Arab villages and established 370 new Jewish settlements with Hebrew names on or near their Arab predecessors – all with the goal of erasing legal Palestinian claims on plots of land. Vacant Palestinian neighborhoods in cities were either similarly destroyed, or cleared for redistribution to Jewish immigrants. Ten thousand businesses and 60 percent of Israel's cultivated land changed from Arab to Jewish hands during the war without compensation.[4]

More than 360,000 Palestinians alone fled to the West Bank and East Jerusalem, another 200,000 to Gaza, over 100,000 to Lebanon, at least 85,000 to Syria, and around 7,000 to Egypt. In neighboring Arab states, they often remained politically and economically disenfranchised, largely because the host governments, particularly in Lebanon, feared that the arrival of large numbers of refugees would upset domestic politics. Jordan was the only exception. With the annexation of the West Bank and East Jerusalem in the spring of 1950, it added 800,000 citizens to its population of 340,000 living in the East Bank (the former Transjordan).[5]

Scattered throughout several different political entities around Israel, Palestinians continued to suffer from a lack of political leadership. Although the incorporation of the West Bank and East Jerusalem into Jordan had provided some Palestinians with citizenship status in an Arab country, it simultaneously undermined the idea of a separate Palestinian state in the former mandate territory. To counter Jordanian designs, the Arab League had pre-emptively established an All-Palestine Government under the leadership of the Grand Mufti of Jerusalem, a political rival to Jordan's King Abdullah, in Egyptian-occupied Gaza in September 1948. Lacking legitimacy, resources, and organization, it moved to Cairo within a month where it lingered until Gaza was merged with Egypt and Syria into the United Arab Republic in 1958. In any case, following the Arab League appeasement of Jordan's annexation of the West Bank and East Jerusalem in 1950, the Grand Mufti closed ranks with Egypt's outlawed

Muslim Brotherhood, and participated in Pakistan's pan-Islamist activities. He eventually moved to Lebanon in 1959 after the new Iraqi regime, with which he entertained close contacts, had fallen out with Nasserite Egypt.[6]

The Anglo–American Alpha project of 1955, which collapsed within a year, aimed not only at ending the Arab–Israeli conflict but also at addressing the Palestine refugee problem. It emerged against the background of continued skirmishes at Israel's border that comprised a wide range of incidents – from individual attempts by Palestinians to cross into Israel for personal reasons to armed clashes that included both irregular and regular military units. Thus, in the first half of 1955, Washington and London discussed a possible compromise agreement between Israel and Arab states on the Palestinian refugees. Israel was to allow the return of 75,000 refugees, but all other refugees were to be resettled in the Arab world and receive collectively 100 million pounds as compensation. This sum had been previously determined by the UN Palestine Conciliation Commission, and took into account property abandoned by Jews departing from their homes in Arab states after 1948. Thirty percent of the funds were supposed to come from Israel, and 70 percent from the rest of the world. American and British representatives agreed that all Palestinian refugees, even those without claims, should receive a basic sum (100 pounds per family) to facilitate resettlement and integration into Arab host societies. For its part, the Israeli government had signaled in early 1949, before the start of the Lausanne Conference, that the country had obligations to pay for abandoned property, but made any compensation conditional upon the prior conclusion of a comprehensive Arab–Israeli peace. In late 1954, Gamal Abdel Nasser's Egypt indicated that it would agree to compensation instead of return – to be paid with funds from the world community to avoid driving Israel into bankruptcy.[7]

But the Alpha plans arose just at a time when the situation in the Middle East was deteriorating. The disproportionate Israeli incursions into Gaza in February and May 1955, Nasser's subsequent appeal to the Soviet Union to supply weapons, Israeli–Egyptian border clashes in August, the Soviet–Czechoslovak arms deal a month later, and David Ben-Gurion's return to power in November all undermined Alpha's chances of succeeding. In Gaza itself, Israeli incursions led to the reorganization and augmentation of the Egyptian-managed Palestinian border guards, causing an increase in border incidents starting in late 1955.[8] Palestinian refugees, however, continued to await return or compensation.

Given its inability to protect Palestinians in the war of 1947–49, the Arab League and some of its member states included one Palestinian representative in their diplomatic corps on a rotating basis. Ahmad al-Shuqayri, a Lebanese-born Palestinian and minister in the Grand Mufti's short-lived All-Palestine Government in Gaza, worked for the Syrian delegation at the United Nations in 1949–50, was assistant general secretary in the Arab League in 1950–56, and served as Saudi representative to the United Nations in 1957–63. The Grand Mufti had reportedly selected him to represent the Palestinians in the league. During the early 1950s, al-Shuqayri aimed for the return of refugees to all of Palestine while dismissing the creation of a Palestinian state in the West Bank only.[9]

In April 1955, the Grand Mufti and al-Shuqayri attended the Asian–African Conference in Bandung, where they discussed Palestinian affairs with China's Prime Minister Zhou Enlai. But with no help forthcoming from the People's Republic of China (PRC) and relations with the West souring after the Suez Crisis, al-Shuqayri turned to the USSR for support. Sitting behind Nikita S. Khrushchev at the fifteenth anniversary meeting of the United Nations in September 1960, al-Shuqayri, in his role as official Saudi representative, hastened to congratulate the Soviet leader after his notorious shoe-banging speech. The following year, he visited Moscow and Sochi in 1961 to plead – without result – for Soviet support of the Palestinian cause. Eventually, in 1963, Saudi Arabia fired al-Shuqayri as the head its UN mission; in the Saudi–Egyptian conflict over Yemen, he had disobeyed Prince Faisal's order to lodge a complaint against Egypt.[10]

Despite the devastation that the *Nakba* had brought to the Palestinian people, the 1950s witnessed the emergence of a younger generation of leaders in exile, particularly in Egypt. Palestinian students, workers, and women established organizations to represent Palestinian interests in Cairo, after the military coup in 1952 had allowed them to work, study, and become politically active. Egypt's involvement in the anti-colonial war in Algeria since 1954 and the Suez Crisis two years later provided a fertile context in which young Palestinians developed ideas about revolution, anti-imperialism, and liberation struggle. From the ranks of the Palestinian alumni of Egyptian universities sprang the *Palestinian National Liberation Movement* (a.k.a. Fatah, a reverse acronym meaning "conquest" in Arabic). It was formally established in October 1959 in Kuwait, a major center for anti-colonial agitation in the Arab world at the time. The organization's goal was to liberate Palestine from Zionism through war and revolution, and to restore the territory as an Arab-majority state in which Jews would live as resident aliens. After the collapse of the UAR in 1961, Fatah's founder Arafat and other leaders started to work closely with the ever-changing but leftist, anti-Nasserite, and anti-Israeli regimes in Damascus. There, he and al-Shuqayri repeatedly had contact with the reopened embassy of communist China.[11]

The Palestine Liberation Organization and Fatah

The sudden death of Ahmad Hilmi, the Palestinian representative of the Arab League, forced the league's members to review their stand on the Palestinian issue in mid 1963. Nasser had raised the issue of creating a new Palestinian "entity" as early as 1959 for a variety of reasons. He feared that Israel was working for the elimination of Palestinian claims. Besides, UN General Secretary Dag Hammarskjöld had proposed the integration of Palestinian refugees into the Arab host societies. And Nasser himself wanted to weaken the conservative rival Jordan that had annexed the West Bank. At several Arab League conferences in 1960, Amman was able to prevent what it considered Cairo's attempt to break up the kingdom. Subsequently, Nasser used Gaza as a laboratory for the construction of a Palestinian state, but the collapse of the UAR in September 1961 nixed his plans. Hilmi's death renewed the debate about the future of Palestine. At the Arab League Foreign Ministers Conference in September 1963, Iraq advocated the foundation of a Palestinian organization that would create a national assembly and then a government, but met with Jordanian opposition. Prompted by Egypt, the conference appointed al-Shuqayri, whom Saudi Arabia had recently sacked as UN ambassador, as Palestinian representative of the Arab League. For Cairo, neither the Grand Mufti nor Arafat were viable candidates because of their affiliation to various anti-Nasserite governments in Damascus.[12]

The first Arab League Summit in January 1964 not only helped to clear "the Arab atmosphere" but also decided on a new start in Palestinian affairs. Even though the gathering could not agree on the details of a future Palestinian organization, it still adopted a resolution that made "the people of Palestine the first factor in the pursuit of their cause." In concrete terms, al-Shuqayri was charged to discuss future policies with Arab states and other Palestinians. Yet the reality was that the league's members were still split on the issue. Egypt fully supported its own initiative. Jordan opposed the creation of a Palestinian state in the West Bank, but since it was happy to have reconciled with Egypt, it did not reject Nasser's ideas. Syria opposed what it considered a compromise decision that failed to create a Palestinian state on Jordanian territory. Saudi Arabia opposed al-Shuqayri in favor of the Grand Mufti. The Israeli government ridiculed the league's initiative because it believed that Jordan's rejection of Palestinian statehood in the West Bank would merely help cement the status quo. Al-Shuqayri himself received a mixed reception in the West Bank, largely because he had been chosen by the league. In the years before, he had gained some popularity for his passionate speeches at the United Nations, but he also faced accusations of opportunism for his service in the Saudi diplomatic corps and his lack of patriotism. Still, al-Shuqayri quickly set out to draft ambitious plans for a Palestinian state and army, which Nasser approved by February 1964. Soon thereafter, he traveled to Jordan, Iraq, and the Gulf sheikhdoms to raise political, financial, and military support – but with little success.[13]

The Palestine Liberation Organization (PLO) was formally established at the first Palestinian National Congress (PNC), which al-Shuqayri convened on May 28 – June 2 in East Jerusalem. Al-Shuqayri had hand-picked delegates from the old Palestinian elites. By convening the congress and publishing the PLO charter on its first day, al-Shuqayri tried to erase his image of being a stooge for the Arab League. The charter unambiguously called for the liberation of the "sacred homeland Palestine" through revolutionary force. For that purpose, the congress established the Palestinian Liberation Army (PLA), to be stationed in Gaza, Syria, and Iraq. Before the congress, however, Egypt and Jordan had both warned al-Shuqayri not to propose military force, nor advocate war against Israel, largely because they wanted to avoid armed military conflict. But the second Arab League Summit in September 1964 still recognized the PLO and approved all decisions taken by the first PNC – including the one on the military struggle against Israel, even if some league members were reluctant. Israel continued to consider the PLO a stillborn entity that weakened Palestinian claims to compensation, and anyway would disappear, as it hoped, as quickly as the All-Palestine Government had beforehand. The only worry was a possible diplomatic effort by al-Shuqayri to obtain international recognition for the PLO, including from the United Nations.[14]

The creation of the PLO posed a political challenge to Fatah. Already in late January 1964, Arafat's outfit had approached al-Shuqayri with a proposal for collaboration, but received a rejection. Fatah propaganda subsequently painted al-Shuqayri's PLO as a pawn of the Arab League. It formally boycotted the national congress, although its representatives participated as observers with the purpose of promoting their own rival outfit. Except for Algeria, which allowed Fatah to open an office, no Arab country supported Arafat's organization. But soon thereafter, Arafat managed to obtain financial support from Saudi Arabia, which sought to undermine al-Shuqayri. After a period of internal discussions on future strategy in the summer and fall of 1964, Fatah started to launch raids against Israel, mostly from the West Bank, at the turn of the year. Ultimately, Fatah was responsible for laying the mine in the West Bank that killed three Israeli soldiers in mid November 1966, triggering both the disproportionate and lethal Israeli military reaction and the Arab counter-response of greater military unity that led to the June War in 1967.[15]

The PLO emerged as an actor in international affairs just at a time when the PRC was descending into political radicalism prior to the start of the Cultural Revolution in 1966. In late 1963, Prime Minister Zhou Enlai had promised Nasser Chinese support against "Israeli imperialism" on his tour through the Middle East and Africa, which he wanted to use for the mobilization of the Afro–Asian world against the Soviet Union, the United States, and India. In March 1964, the PRC received Arafat and other Fatah representatives months before the formal foundation of the PLO. Al-Shuqayri himself traveled to Beijing a year later, just when the Chinese leaders were confronted with the American escalation of the Vietnam War. His comparison of Israeli imperialism with US imperialism – including the claim that Israel had no right to exist – fell on open ears with Chairman Mao Zedong, but not with Prime Minister Zhou Enlai. In any case, since the PRC had promised Egypt in 1956 never to recognize Israel, it allowed the PLO to open an office in Beijing in May 1965. Through Beijing's diplomatic and military representation in Damascus, China delivered small arms to Syria, but Egypt seized the tanks that the PRC tried to ship clandestinely to Gaza through the Suez Canal. Al-Shuqayri had turned to the PRC primarily because Soviet interest in the PLO after Khrushchev's fall in October 1964 remained minimal. In turn, Moscow believed that Beijing was unnecessarily adding fuel to the Arab–Israeli fire by aligning with the PLO. The Soviet leaders were particularly concerned with Mao's alleged statement that 100 million Arabs should have no problem with the "extermination of two million Jews."[16]

As the crisis in Arab–Israeli relations sharpened in the spring of 1967, Palestinians waited in anticipation. Some PLO leaders were convinced that the impending war, whatever the result, would lead to a revolutionary chain reaction in the Middle East. In late 1966, al-Shuqayri had boasted that 10,000 fighters – some of whom had supposedly received training in the PRC – were standing ready in Gaza. On May 25, three days after Nasser had announced the closure of the Strait of Tiran, Egypt mobilized the PLA in Gaza. Unlike the USSR, which hoped to prevent war in the Middle East, the PRC publicly pushed its support for the Palestinian struggle against Israel. Its ambassador to Egypt, Huang Hua, met with al-Shuqayri in Gaza on May 16, and attended a political rally there in early June. On this occasion, the PLO leader announced that the time for decision had come: "Either us or Israel." After victory in the impending war, or so he predicted, Jewish immigrants would return to "their countries of origin," and Palestine would emerge in federation with Jordan or as an independent Arab state. Once the June War had started, the PRC called on the PLO to emulate the anti-imperialist struggle of the Vietnamese communists.[17]

Responding to the *Naksa*

The *Naksa* in June 1967 meant that at least 280,000 Palestinians fled from East Jerusalem and the West Bank to Syria and the East Bank. Some 145,000 were fleeing yet again within twenty years. For the first time in history, more Palestinians lived outside Palestine than inside. Although East Jerusalem and the West Bank had not been among Israel's original war aims, the country's leaders ordered their swift occupation on June 7. The expulsion of Arab inhabitants from central parts of East Jerusalem and from several strategically located Palestinian villages – including the destruction of their homes – started immediately.[18]

Apart from the unanimous decision to annex East Jerusalem, the Israeli government faced the question of what to do with the West Bank. Foreign Minister Abba Eban admitted that his government "had certainly done no real thinking" about the territory. On June 5, Prime Minister Levi Eshkol had expected that the international community would force Israel out of any of the occupied territories as it had done in 1956–57. But just two days later, Defense Minister Moshe Dayan speculated about the possibility of removing all Palestinians from the occupied West Bank. Immediately after the war, foreign ministry representatives voiced criticism that some Israeli government officials "were losing their heads" in the hour of triumph. They instead urged the government to proceed "wisely" in solving "relations with Palestine Arabs." Initially, internal proposals raised the idea of returning the West Bank to Jordan, or of creating a Palestinian entity, but none advocated continued occupation. The Israeli government also welcomed interest among Palestinian leaders in collaborating to establish a Palestinian state in the West Bank and Gaza – but, oddly, it did not react officially to their inquiries. Given the new realities in the Middle East after June 10, some members of the US government pleaded in vain for Israel to withdraw from the West Bank, adhere to the UN resolutions of 1948, and compensate Palestinian refugees. These measures, or so the hope went, would enable Arab states to recognize Israel and make peace.[19]

The Israeli failure to work with Palestinian elites, popular Israeli enthusiasm for the occupation, and the refusal of Arab states to negotiate directly with Israel all rendered alternatives to direct control of the West Bank increasingly unfeasible. By early August, Israel introduced its currency in the occupied territories, an important step toward economic integration. Under international pressure, it agreed to allow refugees to return, but only 14,000 did so before the deadline on August 31. In any case, the Israel Defense Force (IDF) used lethal force at the Jordan River

to prevent any Palestinians, including women and children, from returning even before the deadline. In September, Eshkol decided to allow
settlers to move to the occupied West Bank, although he knew that
Israel thereby broke international law.[20]

The occupation of East Jerusalem and the West Bank on June 7 came as
a shock to Palestinians. In Gaza, the PLA had fought on June 5–6, losing
122 men. The IDF captured 6,000 PLA members, imprisoning 1,000
and deporting the rest to Egypt. Ultimately, the June War was a personal
naksa for the grandiloquent al-Shuqayri, who was forced to step down as
PLO chairman after internal discontent rose. Although his supporters in
Beijing suffered defeat in the Middle East in June 1967 as well, they at
least voluntarily removed the PRC from the scene by turning down an
invitation to attend an Asian–African solidarity conference in Egypt in
early July. Instead, Chinese propaganda attacked Leonid I. Brezhnev for
being a traitor of the Palestinian and the Vietnamese peoples, while Soviet
propaganda called al-Shuqayri a Chinese stooge. In late November, the
PRC denounced UN Resolution 242 as a Soviet–American superpower
deal concluded at the expense of the Palestinian people. But while Zhou
reassured PLO visitors in 1968 about China's continued support for the
liberation of Palestine, the PRC entered into unofficial low-level contact
with Israel the same year.[21]

Arab defeat in the June War was an opportunity for Fatah. Arafat's
outfit was one of the few Palestinian organizations that emerged almost
unscathed from the conflict, largely because it had barely participated in
the fighting. The weakening of the PLO and the preoccupation of Arab
states with themselves after June 10 removed many of the previous
political constraints. Still, some despairing Fatah members were ready
to relinquish the goal of liberating all of Palestine by advocating instead
the idea of a Palestinian state in the West Bank and Gaza. They met with
Arafat's fierce opposition. Within a fortnight of the war, he slipped into
the West Bank to raise *fedayeen* (literally: "somebody who is sacrificing
himself") and to organize a Chinese-inspired people's war of liberation.
But the West Bank was not suitable to Maoist ideas of warfare, and Fatah
lacked a hinterland of the type that the South Vietnamese insurgents had
in North Vietnam. In September, Palestinian commandos thus started
a bombing campaign against civilian targets in Israel, Jerusalem, and the
West Bank that shook Israeli society. In response, Israeli security forces
managed to arrest over 1,000 Palestinian *fedayeen* fighters before the end
of the year.[22]

On March 21, 1968, Fatah eventually vaulted itself into the world's
attention with the battle of al-Karama. Thousands of IDF soldiers
fought 300 *fedayeen* fighters, supported by Jordanian artillery and

warplanes, for a day in a Jordanian border town that carried the name "dignity" in Arabic. Israeli forces suffered many casualties, failed in the stated aim to crush Fatah, and retreated after destroying three-quarters of the city. Palestinians and sympathetic international observers quickly claimed similarities between the battle of al-Karama and the Tet Offensive in Vietnam less than two months earlier, although, in reality, there were significant differences in scale, characteristics, and objectives. Still, despite Fatah's own heavy casualties, the battle was a political triumph. Having destroyed the twenty-year-old image of Israeli military invincibility, Fatah subsequently attracted thousands of volunteers and the attention of Third World revolutionaries. Saudi King Faisal promised finances, and Nasser invited Arafat to Cairo for talks while transferring former PLA soldiers from Egypt to Fatah in Jordan. In the wake of the triumph on the battlefield, Fatah also increased its bombing campaign against civilian targets in Israel and the West Bank.[23]

In early July 1968, Arafat visited the USSR as a disguised member of Nasser's delegation. Given his frustration with the political standstill one year after the June War, the Egyptian president promoted the Fatah leader in Moscow in order to help a new ally while buying time to rebuild his army. However, the visit was not as successful as the two men had hoped. The Soviet Union did not approve of Fatah's *fedayeen* raids and bombing attacks against Israel. On the contrary, it feared that they opened the door to Chinese influence among Palestinians and increased US weapons deliveries to Israel. But the subsequent Soviet intervention in Czechoslovakia on August 20–21 undermined Moscow's image as a staunch anti-imperialist. In comparison, China's condemnation of Soviet socialist-imperialism confirmed to Fatah that Beijing was an ideologically more compatible partner. In any case, Arafat's organization had already sent thirty officers to the PRC for a five-month leadership course and 400 volunteers to Algeria for guerilla training. In early 1969, Arafat's Fatah thus rejected a Franco–Soviet peace proposal at the United Nations that promoted the creation of a Palestinian state in the West Bank and Gaza only. Subsequently, Moscow informed Fatah that it would not deliver any of the requested weapons as long as the organization persisted in "adding fuel to the fires of the Middle East conflict."[24]

The battle of al-Karama and Arafat's command over thousands of, partially Chinese-armed, *fedayeen* fighters in Jordan enabled him to claim leadership of the PLO in early February of 1969. The Chinese ambassador to Egypt, Huang Hua, reportedly played an important advisory role in Fatah's takeover. Under Arafat's leadership, the PLO adopted a hardline policy against Israel. Propaganda portrayed Zionism as a racist and expansionist ideology, and as a participant in global US imperialism. The PLO now aimed for the creation of a unitary state for Muslims, Christians, and Jews in all of former Mandatory Palestine. But Arafat's ascent to PLO leadership coincidentally happened a month before the outbreak of Sino–Soviet border clashes, which revealed the depth of conflict between Moscow and Beijing. In their aftermath, Beijing did not lose time in accusing Moscow of selling the Palestinians out, while it publicly sided with Arafat's hardline policy on the liberation of all of Palestine from Zionist occupation.[25]

Fatah's takeover of the PLO did not mean that Arafat was in control of all Palestinian organizations. The long-time activist Georges Habash had established one of Fatah's main rivals, the socialist Popular Front for the Liberation of Palestine (PFLP), shortly after the June War. An alternative to Fatah, it quickly gained notoriety through attacks on international air travel. On July 23, 1968, PFLP members commandeered an Israeli plane taking off from Rome. In late December and mid February, commando missions opened gunfire on Israeli airliners on airport runways in Athens and Zürich, respectively. But these attacks alienated even the otherwise sympathetic leftist regimes in Algeria and Syria. Arafat replied to the challenge by marginalizing the PFLP within the highest levels of the PLO.[26]

Changes in the global Cold War forced the PLO to adjust its international alignments. The Sino–Soviet border clashes in March 1969 had triggered a rethinking of foreign policy strategy in China. In the summer, the PRC re-established full diplomatic relations with twenty mostly Western states – relations that had been broken off at the beginning of the Cultural Revolution – and recalled Huang Hua from Egypt. By late 1969, informal Sino–American talks resumed. Within a little more than two years, they would lead to Richard M. Nixon's famous visit to Mao in February 1972. Consequently, Fatah and the PFLP started to focus their propaganda on the Vietnamese communist struggle against the United States, though early in 1969 Ho Chi Minh had been critical of Fatah's military activities against Israeli civilians because they alienated international sympathizers. The sixth PNC, which brought together many of the different Palestinian groups in early September 1969, for this reason censured the PFLP's attacks on Israeli airliners and bombing attacks on Israeli embassies in Europe. But the conference also called upon Fatah to limit its attacks to economic targets in Israel only. In its published statements, the PLO for the first time emphasized Soviet contributions to its cause ahead of Chinese assistance. During Arafat's visit to Moscow in mid February 1970, the PLO finally reached an agreement over the delivery of Soviet weapons, but in turn had to agree to respect UN

Resolution 242. Still, Arafat traveled to China a month later to prove his independent status in the Sino–Soviet conflict. Before his return to the Middle East, he also visited North Vietnam for talks and inspections of guerilla training camps where *fedayeen* fighters received military instruction.[27]

Numerous Defeats and One Victory

By the spring of 1970, the PLO and other Palestinian organizations commanded several *de facto* statelets in Jordan. Abdullah's annexation of the West Bank and East Jerusalem in 1950 and two refugee waves – in 1947–49 and 1967 – had made Palestinians the majority population in the kingdom. Living in refugee camps or in separate neighborhoods in Jordan's East Bank, Palestinians generally were poorly integrated. Instead, they formed their own, *fedayeen*-controlled entities outside the formal structures of the Jordanian society and state, similar to the communist-controlled insurgent strongholds in South Vietnam before the Tet Offensive. Starting in 1969, King Hussein tried to re-establish royal authority through an array of increasingly oppressive policies that aimed to enhance the cohesion of Jordanian society while weakening *fedayeen* domination of Palestinian communities. Using Arafat's absence during his visit to Moscow in February 1970, the monarch declared martial law to undermine the authority of Palestinian organizations. However, this move only triggered skirmishes between *fedayeen* units and Jordanian security forces. A quick ceasefire did not dissolve the parallel government structures but merely froze the conflict for a time. By mid June, almost a thousand lives had been lost in weeks of renewed fighting. Under an Iraqi threat of intervention in support of the Palestinians, King Hussein cunningly offered Arafat the prime minister's post. For a brief moment, the PLO even toyed with the idea of overthrowing royal rule by force. But internal conflict among Palestinian organizations and the inability to reach out to non-Palestinians in Jordan scuttled the chance for Palestinians to run a state, even if it was not a Palestinian one.[28]

To add to the Palestinian crisis in Jordan, the American bombshell of the Rogers Plan landed on June 19. The US proposal included a ninety-day ceasefire in the Arab–Israeli War of Attrition and the resumption of the Jarring mission. Before the end of July, Egypt, Jordan, and Israel had successively accepted the plan, with the ceasefire coming into effect on August 7. All Palestinian organizations as well as Syria and Iraq rejected the plan because they feared that it would permanently undermine Palestinian claims to all of Palestine. During a visit to Baghdad in mid

August, Arafat threatened to turn Amman into "another Hanoi" and thwart the Rogers Plan "by our gun barrels." DRV propaganda in turn supported the "comrades-in-arms and brothers" in Jordan in their "struggle against U.S. imperialism." Palestinian organizations in Jordan saw their chances of establishing a state in all of Palestine further diminished once the USSR threatened to terminate all arms deliveries because of the Palestinian rejection of the Rogers Plan. A PNC meeting in Amman in late August discussed Arafat's idea of seizing the moment by staging a coup d'état against King Hussein, but then flinched from implementing it.[29]

Instead, the PFLP took action on September 6. During the previous months, Georges Habash had posed for interviews in his Amman office below pictures of Mao Zedong and Vo Nguyen Giap. In late August, he had left for North Korea and China to collect weapons and funds. His military deputy Wadi Haddad organized the September 6 hijackings of three American and one Swiss airliner, which were forced to fly to an abandoned military airfield in Jordan and blown up six days later in the presence of the world's media. The PFLP hoped that this spectacular action would bring the plight of the Palestinians into the international limelight, torpedo the Rogers Plan, enable it to use passengers with Israeli citizenship as hostages to free Palestinian prisoners in Israel and Europe, and generally enhance the image of the PFLP among Palestinians. Stuck in North Korea on a two-week visit, Habash returned home via Beijing, where the Chinese leaders expressed their displeasure at the hijackings. Under the threat of being pushed to the sidelines, Arafat on September 14 called for a general strike in support of the Palestinian revolution. The following day, *fedayeen* units seized the Jordanian city of Irbid, declaring it to be a Vietnamese-style liberated area with a people's government.[30]

The hijackings and destruction of the airliners forced King Hussein to act, launching two weeks of fighting that Palestinians still remember as the *Black September*. On the 16th, the Jordanian crackdown of Palestinian organizations began with the goal of arresting Palestinian leaders and of establishing complete royal control over Amman and other cities. In many respects, the campaign was similar to the South Vietnamese and American operations after the Tet Offensive, which had cleared out communist-controlled areas in the spring and summer of 1968. As early as the 18th, Egypt, Sudan, and Libya called for an end to fighting in Jordan. But Syria and Iraq intervened in support of the Palestinian revolution – and with the goal of overthrowing the royal house – although Soviet pressure and fierce Jordanian military resistance soon forced both to retreat. Urged on by Egypt and Sudan, Jordan agreed to a draft cease-fire on September 26. Over 3,000 people, most of them Palestinian civilians, had lost their lives in ten days of fighting. Nasser personally mediated between King Hussein and Arafat on the 27th in a stormy meeting in Cairo to which the two antagonists had shown up with loaded guns. Instead of real shots, however, they contented themselves with firing off verbal accusations of being a revolutionary or a counter-revolutionary, respectively. In the end, both signed a compromise agreement that the Arab League had tabled and that essentially restored the status quo ante. The day after, Nasser passed away after suffering a massive heart attack.[31]

In the year after September 1970, the global context in which the PLO and other Palestinian organizations were operating changed once more. Nasser's successor, Anwar Sadat, quickly separated the pursuit of Egyptian national interests from the intractable Palestinian issue. A long-time supporter of the Palestinian cause, the PRC was dissatisfied with the performance of the *fedayeen* fighters in September of 1970. China had also suffered embarrassment when the Jordanian army had caught numerous unregistered Chinese military experts in the kingdom. At the global level, the PRC continued to seek rapprochement with the United States. The US intervention in Cambodia in the spring of 1970 only briefly interrupted China's new policy – though it caused Mao to link the Indochinese and the Palestinian revolutions to a worldwide struggle against American imperialism in public statements. But after mid 1970, Beijing resumed its wooing of Washington. Early in the following year, PRC diplomats hinted at a reduction of Cultural Revolution radicalism in China's foreign policy and a decrease in support for national liberation movements throughout the world, except in Indochina. Henry Kissinger's secret visit to Beijing in July 1971 eventually opened the doors to communist China's entry into the United Nations by October. Despite much continued rhetorical condemnation of Resolution 242 and the Rogers Plan, the PRC subsequently did not offer consistent support of the Palestinians at the United Nations Security Council or the General Assembly.[32]

But most problematic for the PLO was the resumption of civil war in Jordan, which King Hussein used to expel all Palestinian organizations from his country. By late 1970, Arafat admitted that the events in September had greatly damaged the Palestinian cause. Early in the New Year, he and moderate Palestinian leaders started to think about a political solution in lieu of revolutionary action, including the creation of a Palestinian state in the West Bank and Gaza alongside Israel. Yet, by late October 1970, King Hussein had started to prepare another campaign to dislodge Palestinian organizations from Jordan. In a gradually escalating military offensive, his army had managed by July 1971 to kill hundreds of leaders and *fedayeen* fighters, arrest thousands, and force the rest to flee to Lebanon, Syria, and even the West Bank into Israeli imprisonment. After gaining control over Jordan's East Bank, King Hussein followed the footsteps of his grandfather Abdullah by trying to integrate the Israeli-occupied West Bank into his kingdom through negotiations. In March 1972, he proposed the creation of a United Arab Kingdom that would unify Jordan and the West Bank as two autonomous regions. While he clearly hoped that this plan would undermine the popular appeal of the feuding Palestinian organizations and enhance his own in the eyes of many ordinary Palestinians, his proposal drew mostly rejection and derision from outside the royal palace.[33]

The expulsion from Jordan turned Lebanon into the host of the vast majority of Palestinian organizations. In the late 1940s, over 100,000 Palestinians had fled to Lebanon where they lived in refugee camps in coastal cities. The Lebanese government had been hesitant to allow the integration of the refugees since it feared that their arrival would threaten the fragile political balance between Sunni and Shia Muslims, Druze, and members of various Christian denominations. Still, after the June War, the country was directly drawn into the Palestine conflict when Palestinian organizations assumed control of the refugee camps, as they did in Jordan at the same time. In early 1969, Israel attacked Beirut's airport and blew up the airliners of Lebanon's flag carrier in a disproportionate retaliation to a PFLP attack on an Israeli airliner at Athens airport. The arrival of cadres and *fedayeen* fighters in mid 1971 further exacerbated the situation. Despite internal quarrels, PLO leaders established a military presence in southern Lebanon from where their commandos infiltrated and attacked northern Israel. An Israeli incursion to root out the Palestinian presence in September 1972 triggered clashes between Palestinian organizations and Lebanese security forces. Ultimately, Lebanon faced problems similar to those that Jordan had confronted in 1970, though Lebanese political parties, divided by religion and pro-Western vs. pro-Arab predispositions, sharply disagreed on how to deal with the increasing Palestinian presence in their country. Anyway, Arafat believed that Lebanon would only be a temporary base until after clandestine Palestinian organizations had been rebuilt in Jordan, i.e. in the country that hosted the largest number of Palestinians and offered direct access to the Israeli-occupied West Bank.[34]

In the wake of the expulsion from Jordan, both Fatah and the PFLP decided to resort to terrorism. The PLO set up a clandestine organization to overthrow the Jordanian monarchy, but Fatah and the PFLP could not agree on control over it. Thus, the two factions engaged in an international competition of terror, killing Jordanian politicians and foreign diplomats in the Middle East, bombing economic infrastructure in Europe, consecutively attacking the airport of Tel Aviv, and even assassinating each other's members. The best-known attack, however, was the PFLP kidnapping of members of the Israeli team at the Olympic Games in Munich in September 1972. The botched German rescue attempt led to the murder of eleven Israeli athletes and one German police officer, and the killing of five attackers by German security forces. Fatah refused to condemn the operation, because the International Olympic Committee had rejected a PLO request to allow Palestinians to participate in Munich. Arafat himself blamed West German, Israeli, and American disregard for the fate of the Palestinian people for the deaths in Germany.[35]

But the PFLP action in Munich damaged the Palestinian cause for a second time within only two years. International disapproval of the attack was widespread, even among friends. As early as 1971, the PRC had twice informed the PLO that it disapproved of terrorist activities. A week after the Munich attack, Huang Hua stated at the UN Security Council that the PRC did not support such "adventurist actions," though he did not shy away from blaming Israel's past policies for the problems in the Middle East. However, soon thereafter, Chinese diplomats indicated that the PRC did not see a good reason to stay involved in the Middle East as long as the superpowers were unwilling to resolve the Arab–Israeli conflict.[36]

After Fatah had restored supremacy in the PLO by the spring of 1973, it mothballed its terror campaign, largely because it wanted to join the ranks of the Non-Aligned Movement, where it hoped to mobilize worldwide support. Arafat was also motivated by his growing fears of American policy in the Middle East, particularly after Egypt's expulsion of the Soviet military presence in 1972. Moreover, he had convinced himself that the end of the American involvement in Indochina in April 1973 would allow the United States to focus on the "destruction" of Palestinian organizations. Still, PLO propaganda claimed that the organization had accepted the torch of anti-imperialist struggle from the Vietnamese communists after the Paris Accords of early 1973.[37]

The PLO did not know about the Egyptian plans for the October War until early September 1973. The modest *fedayeen* participation at the Egyptian and Syrian fronts at least brought the PLO the formal recognition from the Arab League as the sole representative of the Palestinian people during the 6th Summit in Algiers in late November. But this recognition, more than nine years after its foundation, did not amount to a triumph. In reality, Sadat had decided to exclude the PLO from any international effort in solving problems in the Middle East. The PLO had been cut loose. Thus, in recognition of the larger transformations in the region following the October War, the 12th PNC in early June 1974 decided to employ diplomacy to obtain a Palestinian state in the West Bank and Gaza. But Habash's PFLP called for continued armed struggle, the overthrow of Jordan's monarchy, and the establishment of a Palestinian state in all of former Mandatory Palestine. By then, it had restarted its raids against northern Israel, which provoked massive retaliatory air strikes against Palestinian refugee camps in Lebanon. Dissatisfied with the new moderate course of the PLO, the PFLP eventually withdrew from the organization in September. Yet even Fatah doubted that the Palestinian state in the West Bank, which it now advocated, would be "viable" at all.[38]

Arafat's new moderate policy aimed at appealing to both superpowers. Already before the October War, he had tried to establish contact with the United States, but without success. After the war, Arafat hoped to get a US-backed peace agreement for Palestine, but the Nixon administration refused to deal with the PLO beyond informal low-level talks in Morocco. The PLO had better luck with the Soviet Union. As Cairo's relations with Washington grew closer after the October War, the USSR faced the prospect of being frozen out of Middle East diplomacy. On November 15, Brezhnev publicly committed his country to the creation of a Palestinian state. Five days later, he promised Arafat to work for full Palestinian sovereignty in the West Bank, East Jerusalem, and Gaza within the framework of an international conference that would address all aspects of the Middle East conflict "as a package." However, American intransigence and the downfall of President Nixon over the Watergate Scandal ensured that the conference did not convene at all after the initial meetings in Geneva at the turn of 1973/74. At least, Arafat gained some success in early August 1974 during another visit to Moscow when Brezhnev agreed to allow the opening of a PLO office in the Soviet capital. Thus, in the three years to 1974, the USSR had replaced the PRC as the PLO's great power patron in international affairs.[39]

Political moderation ultimately earned the PLO one major victory in international affairs – its inclusion in the United Nations. In response to a PLO request, twenty Arab and twenty-three Afro–Asian states formally demanded that the United Nations invite the PLO to discuss the Palestine issue on September 13, 1974. But as Arafat stood in front of the General Assembly two months later, he threw away all the moderation that had enabled him to be there in the first place. Although he ended on a seemingly conciliatory note – "I have come bearing an olive branch and a freedom fighter's gun. Do not let the olive branch fall from my hands" – his long speech contained a detailed condemnation of the "racist" and "imperialist" nature of Zionism, praised the global networks of anti-imperialist revolutions from Indochina across the Middle East to Africa, and called for the establishment of a unitary state for Muslims, Christians, and Jews in all of former Mandatory Palestine. The subsequent rebuttal of the Israeli ambassador was no less strident. Still, a little over a week later, the General Assembly decided to provide the PLO with observer status as a non-state entity – against the opposition of the United States and Israel.[40]

In the end, Arafat's rhetoric reflected the revolutionary spirit that had spread among Palestinians, particularly in Lebanon, in previous years. The *Nakba*, the *Naksa*, and Black September had all served to mobilize mostly younger Palestinians to join popular civil organizations – and in some cases underground military units – with the goal of keeping the national struggle and the hope for a future Palestinian state alive. Thus, Lebanon in the early 1970s witnessed a flowering of Palestinian civil society and political activism, which quickly established links to socialist and non-aligned countries across the world. It used literature, film, music, poster art, newspapers, and radio to reach sympathizers in the Free World, the Socialist Camp, and the Global South. Yet this groundswell of popular activism still failed to translate into success in international politics.[41]

Arafat's diplomatic triumph at the United Nations did not last long. Egypt's pursuit of its national interests and the lack of Arab unity in support of the Palestinian issue led him to toy with the idea of dropping the olive branch in April 1975. In September, the PLO and a range of Arab states reacted with dismay to the Israeli–Egyptian conclusion of the US brokered second disengagement agreement on the Sinai, in which both signatories renounced the use of military force against each other. For the PLO, this amounted to an Egyptian "defection" from long-held Arab positions of support for both the Palestinians and the military liberation of any territory occupied by Israel. As Arab unity crumbled over the course of 1975, so did peace in Lebanon where most Palestinian organizations had established their bases since at least mid 1971. The fragile balance among the various religious groups had briefly led to civil strife in Lebanon as early as 1958. The increasing cross-border violence between Palestinian organizations in southern Lebanon and the IDF deepened pre-existing communal divisions in Lebanon. On April 13, 1975, the drive-by shooting by unknown gunmen at a church in Beirut incited a spiral of retaliatory attacks between Christians, Muslims and Palestinians. The fifteen-year-long civil war had started.[42]

Conclusion

In 1975, the outlook for the Palestinian cause was bleak in international politics despite the rise of Palestinian civil society, particularly in

Lebanon. The chances of establishing a state in all of former Mandatory Palestine had become all but an illusion. Disagreements among Palestinian organizations had damaged the cause for years. At the same time, the historical backer among the Arab states – Egypt – sought a bilateral arrangement with Israel. And once the PRC opened up to the West, the PLO also lost this long-time external patron. The United States was unwilling to engage with the PLO beyond some informal contacts. The PLO's new outside sponsor, the USSR, had to stomach the break with Egypt while it excluded itself from diplomacy with its continued refusal to re-establish diplomatic relations with Israel. All of this benefited Israel, which had followed an uncompromising policy toward the Palestinians from the very beginning. Due to the double failure by the international community and its own representatives, the Palestinian people in the West Bank and Gaza suffered deprivation and occupation. Palestinians in refugee camps in Jordan and Lebanon died by the thousands as a result of the Palestinian–Arab conflict and Israeli retaliatory attacks. The hope of many Palestinians to regain their homes lost in 1947–49 or in 1967, or to receive compensation through Israeli hands, continued to dwindle, even if Palestinian civilians themselves started to foster a sense of civil society in Lebanon in the early 1970s. As Chapter 20 reveals, the Israeli–Egyptian peace of 1979 brought yet another political shock.

Part IV

Alternative World Visions

Introduction to Chapters 11 to 13

As previous chapters have revealed, the imposition of the global Cold War on Asia and the Middle East faced resistance – particularly in India, Egypt, and Saudi Arabia. Even more, it provoked the creation of alternative visions for a world able to manage, contain, and possibly overcome the Cold War. Asian–African Internationalism emerged in the late 1940s as an early reaction to the unfolding post-war world, although it focused primarily on overcoming imperialism and colonialism. In comparison, Non-Alignment engaged with the Cold War while attempting to stay formally out of it as a third force. Various strands of pan-Islamism sought alternatives to the Cold War, and even worked to transcend it. Though the three offered different alternative visions to the contemporaneous Cold War world, they overlapped in terms of ideas and membership.

Asian–African Internationalism (Chapter 11) emerged in the spring of 1947 with a conference organized by soon-to-be independent India. Prime Minister of the Interim Government Jawaharlal Nehru had spawned the idea of collaboration among states from Asia to the Middle East and eastern Africa. The conference gathered mostly non-governmental delegations from sovereign and non-sovereign territories in Asia and the Middle East to discuss shared problems related to the post-colonial future. By 1949, Asian–African Internationalism turned into an informal association of governments dedicated to Indonesian independence. Using the regional status of the Arab League (Chapter 2) in the United Nations, Arab and Asian states formed the Arab–Asian bloc in late 1950. While Arab and Asian countries at the United Nations thereafter continued to press for decolonization in the Afro–Asian world, they also started to engage with the Cold War in an attempt to mediate in the Korean War. The extension of the Cold War into Southeast Asia, South Asia, and the Middle East in the wake of this North Asian conflict worried Nehru greatly (Chapter 7). At the famous Bandung Conference in April 1955, which brought together mostly Asian and Arab states, the Indian premier tried to reverse the globalization of the Cold War, which had taken place since the outbreak of the Korean War. He had not only insisted on the invitation of the People's Republic of China in the hope of detaching it from the Soviet Union, but he also tried to mute the conflicts between a large number of anti-communist participants, on the one hand, and neutralist and communist participants, on the other. Ultimately, Bandung was the high point of Asian–African Internationalism, but simultaneously also the start of its decline, since the unfolding of the Cold War had undermined its viability. Communist China's attempt to revive Asian–African Internationalism once more, while imposing its own anti-Indian, anti-American, and anti-Soviet agenda, slew it by late 1965.

Non-Alignment (Chapter 12) in the Cold War was also a creation of Nehru, at least intellectually. But Yugoslavia's Josip Broz Tito and Egypt's Gamal Abdel Nasser established the movement, which was based on bloc-free status in the Cold War, in 1961. Originally, the Indian prime minister had developed the idea of non-alignment in the late 1940s as a policy of active but neutralist engagement with the world to ensure global peace. In the period of 1954–56, he managed to convince Tito and Nasser of his ideas, but resisted their subsequent attempts to turn it into a formal movement. By 1961, the two pre-sidents had their way, with the Indian prime minister giving his grudging assent. Of all three movements discussed in this part, Non-Alignment was the only one that attracted a large number of sub-Saharan African countries. From 1961 to 1965, Non-Alignment also developed into the antagonist of Asian–African Internationalism, particularly in the context of China's radicalized policies toward the Afro–Asian world (Chapter 11). But victory in this struggle still left Non-Alignment deeply shaken. The June War in 1967 (Chapter 8) further taxed the movement's internal unity and political *raison d'être*, since the founding member Egypt was one of the belligerents in a conflict in which the superpower blocs lined up behind the two warring sides. The Soviet-led intervention in Czechoslovakia the following year (Chapter 3) forced Tito to pull back from instituting Non-Aligned collaboration with the Socialist Camp. Yet, against the background of the ongoing Indochina conflict (Chapter 6), Non-Alignment in the first half of the 1970s still sided increasingly with the Socialist Camp, undermining its own purpose in the long term.

In comparison, pan-Islamism (Chapter 13) was not even a single move-ment. Different actors promoted pan-Islamist ideas at different times. Pakistan launched the first pan-Islamist initiative in the 1930s, i.e. even before its formal creation in 1947. Its motivation was related to the South Asian Muslim desire to establish a separate state as a counterpoint to a supposedly Hindu-dominated India. By the 1940s, Egypt's Muslim

Brotherhood promoted pan-Islamist, anti-imperialist, and anti-governmental ideas in the British-occupied Suez Canal Zone (Chapter 2). The military regime, which came to power in 1952 and was soon under Nasser's sole leadership, tried to contain Pakistani pan-Islamism – with success – and suppress the Brotherhood – without long-term success – by promoting its own pan-Islamist ideas in collaboration with Saudi Arabia. But the tentative entry of the Cold War into the Middle East in the mid 1950s undermined such plans (Chapter 2). The Muslim Brotherhood experienced a second birth after the humiliating Egyptian defeat in the June War in 1967 and a political comeback during the Sadat years in the 1970s (Chapter 9). In 1965, Saudi Arabia launched its own pan-Islamist initiative, which was anti-communist, anti-Egyptian, and anti-secular at the same time. Experiencing initial difficulties, it rose to success in the wake of the arson attack on Al-Aqsa Mosque in Israeli-occupied East Jerusalem in 1969. By the 1970s, Saudi pan-Islamism expanded its influence throughout much of the Muslim world by exploiting its growing oil income. Finally, during the 1970s as well, Iranian pan-Islamism emerged in opposition to and exile from the Shah's regime. This form of a mainly anti-Western but simultaneously universalist pan-Islamism would become the great antagonist of Saudi pan-Islamism in 1979, and to this day, as Chapter 20 shows.

11   Asian–African Internationalism

To most observers, Asian–African Internationalism was closely linked to the Bandung Conference in April 1955. Memoirs and scholarly publications praise the so-called *Bandung Spirit* while depicting the meeting of the twenty-nine nations as the beginning of the cooperation among countries from the Global South. Yet one historian wrote as early as 1966 that "[t]wo conferences were held at Bandung in April 1955. One was the real conference, about which not very much is known, about which people care even less, and which has faded away like a bad dream. The other was a quite different conference, a crystallization of what people wanted to believe had happened." Equally confusing is how later generations remembered the name of the conference – usually as the Afro–Asian Conference. But on Jawaharlal Nehru's insistence, it bore the name the *Asian–African Conference*, because the Indian leader did not want it to be confused with an aphrodisiac.[1] Hence, in this book, *Asian–African* denotes the Bandung Conference and the associated movement, and *Afro–Asian* the geographic space of the two continents. Even then, the term *Asian–African* is still misleading. The gathering was essentially an Asian–Arab conference; only three countries from sub-Saharan Africa participated.

The conference at Bandung marked the highpoint of a particular brand of Asian–Africanism, but not its beginning. Its roots lie in the Asian internationalism that arose in the interwar years and at the foundational conference of the United Nations in 1945. Within a few years, it transformed itself into the Arab–Asian bloc in the UN General Assembly, and eventually became Asian–African Internationalism at the Bandung Conference. The famous conference influenced many subsequent international movements in the Global South, but the movement, which it allegedly spawned, faded as a political force within a decade.

Asian–African Internationalism was only one in an array of internationalist movements in the non-Western world during the twentieth century – including Socialist Internationalism, Non-Alignment, and various forms of pan-Islamism – that tried to promote formal decolonization, economic development of the Global South, international justice, and peace. While these movements stood in mutual competition, they were by no means rigidly separate from each other. Ideas and participants freely flowed back and forth. The leading figure in Asian–African Internationalism, Nehru, was a participant in the founding conference of the Comintern-sponsored League against Imperialism in Brussels in 1927, and inspired the foundation of the Non-Aligned Movement in the 1950s and early 1960s.[2] Similarly, the Egyptian Gamal Abdel Nasser saw his international star rising at the Bandung Conference, promoted pan-Islamism at the same time, and ended up hosting the second Non-Aligned Conference in 1964. Pakistan and Saudi Arabia both sent high-level delegations to Indonesia in 1955, even if the former had tried to launch a pan-Islamist movement in the late 1940s and the latter would join Non-Alignment and then succeed in launching its own pan-Islamist initiative in the 1960s.

In many respects, Asian–African Internationalism was an attempt by the emerging Global South to define an alternative to the post-World War II international system. Before the formation of Cold War blocs in the late 1940s, the decolonizing world regarded Asian–African Internationalism as a potential regional substitute to the global United Nations system. The fear was that countries from Europe and the Americas dominated the international organization to such a degree that concerns dear to the Global South seemed not to matter at all. Yet, as one after another newly decolonized state entered the United Nations, Asian–African Internationalism quickly came to consider itself the standard bearer of the United Nations system. But its attempts to use the international organization to raise issues of decolonization, or to mediate in the Cold War, generally failed. Its many internal conflicts and its inability to form a functioning regional organization, even under the umbrella of the United Nations, let Asian–African Internationalism fall prey to the dominant system of the Cold War and to other internationalist movements by the first half of the 1960s.

Beginnings, 1945–47

Although post-World War II Asian–African Internationalism had its roots in Nehru's ideas on Asian solidarity and cooperation, it simultaneously endorsed and struggled against older forms of anti-imperialist and pan-Asianist efforts. Nehru himself considered the conference of the Comintern-sponsored League against Imperialism in Brussels in 1927 an important antecedent. Even if he left the league in 1930 for ideological reasons, he still continued to see 1927 as an important marker in bringing together Asian countries that had been torn apart by Western colonialism. But at the same time, he also rejected the kind of pan-Asianism which militarist Japan started to promote in 1932, after it had launched its imperialist campaign on the Asian mainland. Tokyo used pan-Asianism as a fig leaf to disguise its own imperialist ambitions; Japan did not see the other Asian countries as equals but merely as objects in its search for regional dominance. As its fortunes in World War II turned in 1942, Japan cynically reframed pan-Asianism as a supposed instrument of Asian liberation from Western imperialism. The Greater East Asian Conference, to which the Japanese Empire invited pliable representatives from occupied Manchukuo (Manchuria), China, Burma (today's Myanmar), Thailand, and the Philippines in 1943, principally aimed at countering the universalist and anti-imperialist Atlantic Charter, which served as the political basis for establishment of the United Nations at the end of World War II.[3]

The founding conference of the United Nations that met in San Francisco from April to June 1945 actually witnessed the rise of Asian–African Internationalism. Among the fifty founding members were several countries that were not yet fully independent. Moreover, only six participants came from the Middle East and a meager three – the Republic of China (ROC), India, and the Philippines – from the rest of Asia. It was in this context that Middle Eastern and Asian diplomats approached the leader of the Indian UN delegation, Nehru's sister Vijaya Lakshmi Pandit, with the idea for an Asian conference. By then, Pandit and some members of her delegation had already grown frustrated by the West's political and intellectual indifference to Asian interests. Because Nehru was still skeptical about the success of the new global organization, he was receptive to the idea of an "Asian alternative." He even came to see India as the natural leader of Asian national liberation. Accordingly, by late 1945, Nehru professed solidarity with the Indonesian people and their new Republican government in the struggle against the reassertion of Dutch colonialism, and elevated UN support for the Indonesian "revolt against imperialist domination" to the "acid test . . . of the San Francisco Charter."[4]

Throughout the preparations of what would become the Asian Relations Conference in Delhi in the spring of 1947, Nehru remained ambivalent about the capacity of the United Nations to work for "the elimination of imperialism and colonialism." In early 1946, he envisioned an Asian alternative of "self-defence and mutual help," possibly a "close union of the countries bordering on the Indian Ocean," along the lines of the South Asian federation which he had imagined in 1945. Since Nehru was concerned with the ongoing conflicts in Indonesia and Palestine, he ultimately wanted to bring together all Asian countries – including those "of the Indian Ocean, from Australia to Egypt" – to discuss "their common problems." Nehru soon charged the Indian Council of World Affairs (ICWA) with organizing and hosting a conference of Asian countries.[5]

The use of a non-governmental institution not only reflected India's lack of full sovereignty but also facilitated the invitation of delegations from other Asian countries in a similar situation.

When Nehru was appointed prime minister of the Interim Government of India on September 2, 1946, he clarified his thinking about Asian–African Internationalism and India's apparently inevitable role in it. He not only placed the impending conference within the tradition of the anti-imperialist conference in Brussels in 1927, but also proudly recalled how he had stayed in contact with many of its participants "from Syria to Indo-China." The countries which he intended to invite not only reflected his expansive notion of Asia – "I would include Australia and New Zealand ... [as well as] East Africa" – but also included politically divided entities – "Jewish and ... Arab" delegates from Palestine, and Chinese representatives from "the Kuomintang and the Communists" – as well as observers from "the Asian Republics of the Soviet Union."[6] While the ICWA organizers took their cues from Nehru, they faced two interrelated problems: which countries should attend, and who should represent them? Obviously, it did not make sense to invite the European imperial governments, which legally represented colonized Asian countries. The ICWA eventually decided to include all countries and territories from the Asian continent plus Egypt, given its geographical and cultural links to other invited Arab states.[7]

A few days after Nehru had become the head of the Indian interim government, he sent out letters of invitation to prospective participants. Due to the fragmentation of communication lines within imperial domains, invitations took months to arrive at their destinations and replies took equally long to return. Eventually, 231 delegates and observers from twenty-eight countries and territories attended. They included Afghanistan, Bhutan, Burma, Cochin–Cambodia–Laos (French Indochina), the Democratic Republic of Vietnam, Ceylon (today's Sri Lanka), the Republic of China, Egypt, India, the Republic of Indonesia, Iran, Korea (South), Malaya (today's Malaysia and Singapore), Mongolia, Nepal, Hebrew University-Palestine (Palestine Jewish delegation), the Philippines, Thailand, Tibet, Turkey, and eight Soviet republics (Armenia, Azerbaijan, Georgia, Kazakhstan, Kirghizstan, Tajikistan, Turkmenistan, and Uzbekistan). Despite receiving an invitation, Japan was not able to attend because the Allied occupation authorities did not allow the delegation to leave the country.[8]

Lasting from March 23 to April 2, 1947, the conference took place at a crucial time in India's path toward independence. On February 20, British Prime Minister Clement Attlee had announced that the United Kingdom would grant India *full* self-government. His representative in charge of negotiating the transition, Lord Louis Mountbatten, held talks with Jawaharlal

Nehru, the leader of the All-India Muslim League Ali Jinnah, and the spiritual head of the Indian independence movement Mahatma Gandhi in parallel to the Asian Relations Conference. These negotiations occurred in a climate of communal strife in Delhi and other parts of India, which would only increase by late spring when the partition of India and the creation of Pakistan became a political reality long before independence on August 15. Against the background of the emerging partition, the All-India Muslim League, which later formed the first government of independent Pakistan, called for a boycott by Muslim states of the Asian Relations Conference – but without any success.[9]

The conference opened in the late morning of March 23 with Nehru emphasizing his conviction that "we stand at an end of an era and on the threshold of a new period of history ... Asia, after a long period of quiescence, has suddenly become important again in world affairs." From March 24 to April 1, the conference split into five subgroups to discuss issues of economic development, cultural collaboration, migration and citizenship issues, women's rights, and decolonization. On the final day, April 2, the head of the republican Chinese delegation proposed the creation of an Asian Relations Organization with the task of promoting peace, mutual understanding, and progress in Asia. All delegations accepted the proposal and agreed to meet in China for the next conference, tentatively scheduled for 1949.[10]

But Nehru's celebration of unanimity at the closing session covered up fundamental disagreements among some of the Asian countries. While the Chinese delegation consisted only of *Guomindang* representatives and thus did not force the world's emerging Cold War division onto the agenda, the participation of a Zionist delegation representing all of Palestine caused conflict with Arab participants. Just before the start of the conference, from March 17–22, the Arab League had met in Cairo to coordinate its positions with regard to discussion of the Palestine issue at the United Nations. Although this meeting was not related to the impending Asian Relations Conference, it still had an immediate impact on events in Delhi. On the conference's second day, the Zionist and the Egyptian delegations sparred over Palestine. When Nehru tried to end the discussion, the Jewish delegation walked out because it felt that he had cut off its turn to speak. The Indian organizers eventually managed to bring the delegation back to the conference hall; the two quarreling sides ended their exchange with a handshake while Nehru took the blame for the incident.[11]

Through the future foundation of the Asian Relations Organization, the participants of the Delhi conference hoped to create an institutional platform designed to defuse problems and promote exchange. To their own dismay, over the course of the conference participants had discovered that they knew little about each other. The idea of creating an organization also received a positive welcome from groups outside the Asian world. African American newspapers in the United States proudly announced that "darker peoples" finally had their own international organization dedicated to the struggle against white dominance. Yet much of the optimism about the new organization turned out to be just that. The conference only established a council supposed to discuss the creation of the organization before the next meeting. Nothing ever came of the idea.[12]

Indonesia, 1947–49

After the conference, many Asian countries shifted their focus away from mutual collaboration toward the plight of the Republic of Indonesia. In parallel to the foundation of the DRV in Hanoi on September 2, 1945, Indonesian nationalists had established a republic on the day of Japanese surrender in order to prevent the re-establishment of Dutch colonial rule. In view of India's own formal decolonization on August 15, 1947, Nehru took great interest in the anti-colonial struggle of the Southeast Asian nation. In the subsequent one and a half years, Nehru's government frequently raised Dutch imperialism at the United Nations and in diplomatic talks with other countries. By the end of 1948, however, the situation in Indonesia had deteriorated to such a degree that the Indian prime minister felt compelled to take action. While Nehru had initially been hesitant about a Burmese proposal to hold an Asian conference on the issue, he changed his position once Pakistan publicly pondered the dispatch of an Asian "police force" in support of the Republic of Indonesia. On December 31, Nehru's government invited Egypt, Turkey, Iran, Afghanistan, the ROC, Burma, Thailand, Ceylon, Pakistan, and Australia to attend a governmental conference in Delhi the following month. Nehru no longer deemed China a "suitable" location for the conference due to its "state of acute disintegration," despite the 1947 decision to meet there next.[13]

The exclusive invitation of *governmental* delegations from *sovereign* states reflected two major changes in Nehru's approach to Asian–African Internationalism since the Delhi conference in 1947. A number of Asian states had entered the United Nations – Afghanistan, Burma, Thailand, and Pakistan – with fewer Asian countries remaining outright colonies. With the emerging Cold War division of the world, Nehru considered "Soviet Asia ... [a] part of the larger world problem" that should "not be treated as an Asian problem." Moreover, despite the continued failure of the United Nations to pass the Indonesian acid test, which he had formulated in late 1945, Nehru had come to embrace the global organization in the face of no other available alternative: "[T]he

United Nations, in spite of its failings and weaknesses, ... should be encouraged and supported in every way." With regard to Indonesia, Nehru was adamant about placing the impending conference in Delhi within the United Nations system, and about using it to help the Security Council find a solution.[14]

The delegations to the conference met on January 19, 1949, to discuss agenda and procedure. A much larger number of countries than originally invited attended the conference: Afghanistan, Australia, Burma, Ceylon, Egypt, Ethiopia, India, Iran, Iraq, Lebanon, Pakistan, the Philippines, Saudi Arabia, Syria, and Yemen all sent delegates, while the ROC, Nepal, New Zealand, and Thailand dispatched observers. During the initial meeting, Arab countries insisted on putting the Palestinian issue on the agenda, given their defeat by Israel in the recent war. Nehru, however, demanded the exclusive focus on the original topic because he was convinced that the Arab flouting of UN Resolution 181 had damaged the Palestinian case.[15]

The actual conference started on the 20th with a speech by Nehru that set a moderate tone. Subsequently, the conference elected the host country, Pakistan, Ceylon, and Australia onto the committee tasked with drafting the resolutions. The four had already formed a core group of committed participants despite some initial disagreements. The Pakistani–Indian war over Kashmir, which had rattled the bilateral relationship since the fall of 1947 and which had ended just three weeks before the conference, did not preclude close cooperation between Muhammad Zafarullah Khan and Jawaharlal Nehru. In the end, the conference adopted three resolutions: recommendations to the Security Council for outright Indonesian independence, mechanisms of collaboration among the conference participants in support of these recommendations, and the start of preparations for the creation of an Asian organization within the framework of the United Nations, as planned in 1947. Nehru sent the first resolution in a personal letter to the Security Council. On January 28, the council adopted a similar resolution calling for the end of Dutch military activities, the release of all arrested Republican leaders, a negotiated settlement on independence, elections for an Indonesian constituent assembly by October 1, 1949, and the transfer of sovereignty not later than July 1, 1950.[16]

Despite the quick departure of some delegations, Nehru called another meeting on January 24 to discuss the creation of the proposed Asian organization. In the following months, however, few warmed to the idea. Many Arab countries rejected it since they feared that a future communist China might join. And Pakistan suddenly changed its mind, calling the idea premature while arguing that the participants in the January conference were too heterogeneous to form a regional organization working for a common objective beyond the Indonesian issue.[17] In reality, India's neighbor and rival was building up its own international outfit at the very same time – in the form of the Muslim World Congress.

The Arab–Asian Bloc in the United Nations, 1950–53

Buttressed by the massive Asian and Arab support for its independence, Indonesia joined the United Nations as its sixtieth member on September 29, 1950, in the aftermath of the Arab League obtaining permanent observer status as an accredited regional organization. The new member Indonesia quickly proposed to enlarge the group of collaborating Arab states into an Arab–Asian bloc along the lines of the two Delhi conferences in 1947 and 1949. Arab and Asian states had supported each other's concerns in the General Assembly for at least three years. Arab members had championed the Indonesian struggle in the fall of 1947, while Asian members – except the Philippines – had opposed the partition of Palestine shortly thereafter. In late 1950, after Indonesia's accession to UN membership, the "Arab–Asian bloc" arose not only as a term but also in action during the UN discussions. It brought together the seven Arab League members (Egypt, Iran, Iraq, Lebanon, Saudi Arabia, Syria, and Yemen) and six Asian nations (Afghanistan, Burma, India, Indonesia, Pakistan, and the Philippines).[18]

The first test case for the thirteen-nation bloc was mediation in the Korean War. On November 8, a month after the communist Chinese intervention in Korea against the US-led United Nations troops, the Security Council invited the non-member People's Republic of China (PRC) to send representatives to New York for a hearing. While a Chinese delegation traveled from Beijing to New York via Moscow, Prague, and London over the period of November 15–24, Security Council member India blocked further decisions on Korea so that the Chinese delegation could receive an unprejudiced hearing. On November 28, the United States and the PRC sparred at the UN Security Council, with each accusing the other of aggression in Korea and over Taiwan, respectively.[19]

In the context of this rhetorical Sino–American battle and the adoption of a resolution condemning Chinese aggression in Korea on December 7, the informal Arab-Asian bloc at the United Nations sprang into action in an attempt at bridging the divide. Headed by India, the bloc had appealed to the PRC on the previous day to stop the military advance southward on the Korean peninsula, but representatives from the Soviet Union and communist Eastern Europe mocked the idea as an open attempt to prevent certain communist victory in Korea. After the resolution condemning China was adopted on December 7, Vijaya Lakshmi Pandit visited the PRC delegation at its temporary home, the Waldorf Astoria hotel, to discuss calling a halt to the military advance at the 38th parallel. Yet, even if the Indian delegation spearheaded the Arab–Asian initiative, Nehru's government in Delhi remained skeptical about its success.[20]

On December 10–11, the Arab–Asian bloc met to discuss a ceasefire appeal supposed to prevent even harsher UN actions against non-member PRC. Its proposal of creating an Iranian–Indian–Canadian team to seek a negotiated end to the fighting in Korea was adopted by the General Assembly on the 13th by a margin of 52 to 5, against the opposition of the so-called "Soviet bloc" in the United Nations – the USSR, Ukraine, Belarus, Poland, and Czechoslovakia. Calling the proposal a "trap," the PRC delegation left New York on December 19 in protest. In anticipation of crossing the 38th parallel before the end of the year, Prime Minister Zhou Enlai rejected any ceasefire as "illegal," reiterated earlier Chinese demands for the United States to evacuate from Korea and Taiwan, and requested membership in the United Nations in lieu of the ROC.[21]

The diplomatic failure did not discourage the Arab–Asian bloc. An emergency meeting at Cairo airport on January 19, 1951, held by Nehru with Egyptian, Pakistani, and Arab League representatives tried to coordinate positions on Korea. As the fortunes of war in Korea were turning against China, Beijing showed interest in the "Arab–Asian proposal" of a ceasefire. However, the United States now rejected it, demanding a UN resolution against the PRC aggression while publicly offering a guarantee to respect China's borders in an attempt to defuse Chinese anxieties over its security. Anyway, the Arab–Asian ceasefire proposal suffered a stunning defeat of 44 to 7 at the Political Committee of the General Assembly, which gathered one representative each from all UN member states. Not even all the members of the Arab–Asian bloc voted for it.[22]

As the Korean armistice negotiations dragged on from 1951 to 1953, the Arab–Asian bloc shifted its focus toward French colonialism in North Africa. In early 1952, fifteen Asian, Arab, and African nations complained to the UN General Assembly and the Security Council about France's repressive policies in Tunisia. The bloc eventually managed to get both the Tunisian question and the related Moroccan issue on the agenda of the Political Committee by December, despite French threats to quit the global organization. Yet the Arab–Asian draft resolutions, which called for the start of negotiations on independence, did not garner majorities. Less far-reaching resolutions, introduced by Latin American countries on behalf of the United States, managed to get overwhelming majorities because they merely appealed to France to begin talks.[23]

The inability to achieve anything raised questions about the future of the Arab–Asian bloc. On December 23–24, 1952, shortly after the end of the annual General Assembly session, diplomats representing the bloc met in Cairo. The meeting's location – far away from the United Nations head-quarters in New York – was symbolic. Obviously, the bloc tried to look at its achievements of the past two years from afar. The Egyptian hosts also considered the fact that the Arab–Asian bloc met away from the UN headquarters proof that it "was becoming an independent organization." The new military government in Egypt, which had overthrown the unpopular monarchy in July, also tried to use the gathering to shore up internal and external support by focusing on the thorny issue of Arab–Israeli relations. The bloc meeting paralleled a week-long conference of the Arab League, which also met in Cairo to discuss the Tunisian and Moroccan issues as well as relations with Israel. Arab–Asian representatives eventually issued a warning to Paris that failure to find a solution in North Africa "in accordance with the provision of the United Nations charter" would make "it impossible [for them] to cooperate with France in the future."[24]

In spite of all the optimism about the Arab–Asian bloc coming into its own, 1953 turned out to be yet an even greater disappointment. The bloc members continued to push France on Tunisia and Morocco, but without any success. In frustration, Indonesia called for an emergency meeting of Arab–Asian diplomats at its Cairo embassy on August 26 to discuss the Moroccan issue, but subsequent cooperation failed once more to break the antagonistic American–British–French position on the issue.[25]

Toward Bandung, 1953–55

This lack of success led some bloc members to rethink their form of international cooperation. In October 1953, Jakarta approached Delhi with a proposal to "consolidate" the informal grouping in the United Nations "a little more." Nehru, however, was skeptical about the success of such an idea; his recent experiences with establishing "some machinery" among Asian nations had been "not particularly encouraging." The following January, Egypt joined in by proposing "a conference of Arab–Asian Prime Ministers." In March 1954, eventually, Indonesia's Prime Minister Ali Sastroamidjojo announced that he would suggest convening an "Afro–Asian" conference during the impending Colombo meeting of the prime ministers of Ceylon, India, Pakistan, Burma, and Indonesia.[26]

Nehru still remained skeptical. At that very time, he was observing how the United Kingdom and the United States tried to establish anti-Soviet defense agreements in the Middle East that included Pakistan and thus threatened to turn the Kashmir conflict into a Cold War clash in South Asia. The prime minister's attention also focused on India's negotiations with the PRC about Tibet, which ultimately led to the famous agreement on April 29, 1954, that included the five principles of coexistence. He was convinced that *Panchsheel* could serve as a global model "in the relations of various countries with each other." Finally, the Indian leader believed that the Arab–Asian world should await the outcome of the impending Geneva Conference on Korea and Indochina, scheduled to start in late April, before convening a conference by itself.[27]

The Colombo Conference met on April 28, just two days after the Geneva Conference had started and one day before Sino–Indian negotiations on *Panchsheel* and Tibet ended in agreement. The Indian agenda called for a declaration of non-aggression among the five, a non-transfer principle of colonies in Asia, opposition to Cold War bloc policies in South Asia, and an end to the Indochina conflict. Yet the five participants arrived in Colombo with different expectations. Nehru himself went to Ceylon with the Indochina conflict and Chinese membership in the United Nations in mind. Pakistan expected help to hammer out a deal with India on Kashmir. Ceylon was mostly concerned with the communist threat to Asia. Burma wanted to raise the issue of economic collaboration. And Indonesia, of course, intended to call for an Asian–African conference.[28]

The final communiqué of May 2 merged many of these ideas while adding some more. It called for the independence of the three Indochinese countries as well as of Tunisia and Morocco, Chinese membership in the United Nations for the sake of "stability in Asia," an end to colonialism on a global scale, attention to the suffering of Palestinian refugees, and preliminary preparations for a conference of African–Asian nations. However, this façade of unity papered over differences, most importantly on the Kashmir issue, the Indian desire for complete Indochinese decolonization, and relations with communist states such as the PRC. The acrimonious nature of the talks had required the addition of two more conference days at a different conference location – but to no avail. Western observers called the discussions in Ceylon "tense," and the results an obvious sign that Nehru could not get his agenda "rubber-stamped." Indeed, India lost the battle to get a more assertive resolution on Indochina, while it was unable to prevent its three smaller neighbors from expressing anti-communist sentiments.[29]

Two weeks after the end of the Geneva Conference on July 21, Indonesia again approached India with an unspecified proposal for a gathering of Asian and African nations, preferably before the impending opening of the annual session of the UN General Assembly. Over the summer, Jakarta had considered inviting members of the Arab–Asian bloc and other countries. Nehru welcomed the Indonesian initiative in principle, but pleaded for more time because such a conference needed "careful preparations." He also proposed that Indonesia act as host of the summit. A month later, eventually, Nehru changed his hesitant stance, primarily because the creation of the American-led Southeast Asia Treaty Organization (SEATO) brought Cold War bloc thinking to Asia once more. During the meetings with Sastroamidjojo in Delhi on September 21–29, the two agreed on a preparatory meeting by the Colombo Powers later in the year. Unenthusiastic about the whole enterprise, Ceylon announced that it did not want to get involved with any bloc formation in Asia, and was certain that other Colombo Powers shared its opinion.[30]

Because the preparatory conference on December 28–29 in the Indonesian town of Bogor addressed the limited range of two topics – the choice of participants and the agenda of the planned conference in Indonesia – it was far less contentious than the meeting in Colombo seven months earlier. Anyway, Nehru was the only one who had arrived prepared. The five countries quickly agreed to exclude South Africa on the basis of apartheid, not to invite either Korea since the Geneva Conference had failed to settle that issue, but, applying the same standard in reverse, to include both Vietnams. When Ceylon wanted to invite the ROC on Taiwan and prevent the inclusion of the PRC, Burma threatened not to attend. Pakistan was indifferent to the issue, but India and Indonesia sided with Burma. Thus, the PRC received an invitation while the ROC was left out. India and Burma both proposed inviting Israel, which Muslim Pakistan and Indonesia opposed because they feared a possible Arab boycott. As for Africa, Nehru proposed issuing invitations to Ethiopia, the Gold Coast (Ghana), Liberia, and the semi-independent Central African Federation (today's Zambia, Malawi, and Zimbabwe). The discussion on inviting Nigeria ended without decision because "nobody knew much about it." Two Asian countries – Bhutan and Outer Mongolia – did not even cross the minds of the assembled leaders in Bogor. Australia, a participant of the 1949 conference, was omitted because it was now considered not to be a part of Asia. Pakistan and Ceylon refused the inclusion of *Panchsheel*, largely because they opposed what they considered making concessions to communist countries. The final communiqué comprised thirteen of the seventeen points that Nehru had drafted beforehand. In the end, the five Colombo Powers invited another twenty-five nations, and collectively formed the joint secretariat in charge of organizing the conference at Bandung under Indonesian leadership.[31]

The Bogor participants assessed the outcome of the gathering in varying ways. Naturally, Indonesia was elated about the fact that the gathering had happened at all and that it had produced positive results. In Delhi, Nehru expressed to the visiting Yugoslav President Josip Broz Tito his "satisfaction over the outcome of a conference." Yet the other three participants were less enthusiastic. The Pakistani delegation prided itself on having been "negatively successful," particularly with regard to "prevent[ing] Pandit Nehru [from] having things all his own way." Ceylon was "lukewarm" about the impending gathering because it feared that India and the PRC would be "the dominating countries." The members of the Burmese delegation "returned from Bogor in a somewhat chastened mood." The meeting had revealed that theirs was "a small country which cannot match . . . her larger neighbors."[32]

Bandung, 1955

The twenty-nine countries attending the Bandung Conference on April 18–24 represented 61 percent of the world's population. Only the Central African Federation refused to accept the invitation, thus reducing the meager sub-Saharan African participation to three – Ethiopia, Liberia, and the Gold Coast. Widespread apprehension about the Indonesian ability to organize such an event notwithstanding, the government in Jakarta succeeded in hosting a conference that had to accommodate a large number of delegations, journalists, and other guests. Apart from the official delegations, non-governmental observers from Australia and from the French colonies in Tunisia, Morocco, and Algeria attended. Informal guests and self-invited participants arrived in Bandung as well.[33]

Unofficial talks started even before the conference, largely because India and Burma were stopover locations for many en route to Indonesia. North Vietnamese Prime Minister Pham Van Dong visited Delhi on April 9 to discuss the implementation of the Geneva Accords. In mid April, Burmese Prime Minister U Nu entertained Zhou, Nasser, and Nehru in Rangoon. The host and his Indian counterpart tried to dissuade their Chinese colleague "from violent action and talk" with regard to Taiwan at Bandung. Nasser, who was on his first official visit outside the Middle East, was mostly interested in discussing Arab apprehensions over Israel and obtaining arms.[34]

The conference at Bandung consisted of open sessions on April 18–19 and 24, and of supposedly closed sessions of committees on political, economic, and cultural issues in the intermittent days. Because "secrecy was non-existent," the contents of even confidential talks or the occasional heated quarrel instantly became common knowledge. While official record keeping was rudimentary, the accounts of participants, observers, and newspapers still provide ample evidence for historians to digest.[35]

Participants, observers, and historians have all lauded the *Bandung Spirit* that supposedly permeated the whole conference. The frequent walks of pairs or even groups of world leaders from their lodgings to the conference hall, which took on the air of processions, suggested such an atmosphere. Bandung's streets thereby turned into pedestrian zones that were reserved for official delegations and lined by thousands of cheering local residents. Equally important were the many informal talks among delegations outside the official meetings, which enabled representatives from different countries to meet each other. Although Indonesia was the official host, Nehru was "the centre" of such activities, playing "tactfully ... a quiet role" to make sure that countries "which previously had no contact were brought together." The lack of knowledge about each other was striking; Nasser later admitted that "it took him five days to achieve any bearings at all." Many delegations left the conference with the firm intention to visit other participants in the near future.[36]

From the very beginning, however, the conference was rife with discord. Even before the opening, when the five Colombo Powers met to discuss the final details of agenda and procedures, tempers flared. In view of limited time, Nehru proposed to cancel all opening speeches because written versions had anyway been submitted beforehand, but his Pakistani counterpart Mohammad Ali Bogra refused to go along with this suggestion. Hence, the first two days passed with "speechifying," which the US Cold War allies Iraq, Pakistan, the Philippines, Thailand, and Turkey exploited to denounce *Panchsheel* and communist imperialism. Zhou parried well by openly discarding his previously submitted speaking notes and giving instead an impromptu speech that "was conciliatory in the extreme." But the criticism of communism spilled over into the procedures of the Political Committee on April 21 when Ceylon's Premier Sir John Kotelawala equated Soviet control of the Baltics and Eastern Europe with old-style colonialism. Although the PRC was not mentioned in the rhetorical attack, Zhou objected and accused him, in broken English, of trying to "wreck the Conference." Nehru, too, reproached the Ceylonese premier, who himself curtly retorted: "And who the hell asked you?"[37]

The fracas over communist colonialism was related to disagreements over the Taiwan issue, which Zhou had not intended to raise at all. Against the background of the ongoing Taiwan Strait Crisis, started by the PRC in September of 1954, several delegations questioned China's commitment to *Panchsheel*. Ceylon raised the Taiwan issue on April 19, proposing that the five Colombo Powers, the Philippines, and Thailand meet informally with the PRC. Zhou welcomed the opportunity of quietly finding a peaceful solution to the Taiwan issue while stressing his concern over US unwillingness to do so. The eight eventually met for lunch on April 23, but the discussions quickly shifted from Taiwanese self-determination toward direct Sino–American contacts. On Mohammad Ali Bogra's and Jawaharlal Nehru's suggestion, Zhou Enlai released a surprise statement, announcing that China was "willing to ... enter into negotiations with the United States." Many conference participants considered this a breakthrough in resolving the Sino–American antagonism. The Chinese premier doubled his offer with a guarantee to respect the territorial and political integrity of neighboring countries. When the negative American reply arrived within twenty-four hours, Zhou was "genuinely upset."[38]

While this informal gathering mainly dealt with Taiwan, the official meetings addressed the lingering crises in North Africa and the Middle East. On the basis of an Arab proposal and with Zhou's support, the conference decided to honor the Tunisian, Moroccan, and Algerian observer delegations by seating them in all sessions. On April 23, the conference adopted an Egyptian resolution in support of independence for all three and calling on France "to bring about a peaceful settlement of the problem without delay." But it was the fate of Palestine that was particularly on the minds of Arab delegations. Even if no official Arab Palestinian delegate attended the conference, Ahmad al-Shuqayri arrived as part of the official Syrian delegation and Grand Mufti of Jerusalem Mohammed Amin al-Husseini participated informally.[39] The eight Arab delegations had managed on April 18, before the official start of the Bandung Conference, to agree on a common position on Palestine despite their concurrent disagreements on the Baghdad Pact. During the heated discussions in the Political Committee on April 20–21, Zhou emerged strongly in support of the Arab cause. The Syrian delegates, including al-Shuqayri, firmly believed that they had managed to convince the Chinese premier during discussions on previous nights. In any case, Zhou had arrived in Bandung determined to put the Arab Palestinian issue on the agenda, because it served mainland Chinese goals in the struggle against the ROC on Taiwan. On the 22nd, the conference adopted a non-binding declaration in support of the rights of the Palestinian people.[40]

On the whole, numerous principled disagreements lurked behind the scenes. Nehru's strong condemnation of NATO, SEATO, and the Baghdad Pact on April 22 triggered a fierce response from Turkey, Pakistan, and Iraq on their right to collective self-defense. The Indian prime minister backtracked the following day with an apology, but still believed that their insistence on collective self-defense was merely a pretext for Cold War pact systems. Conversely, his advocacy of *Panchsheel* did not convince delegations from pro-Western countries, which considered the five principles of peaceful coexistence simply too "vague." With a mass of proposals for new principles raised, Nasser was appointed to head a drafting committee that was supposed to reduce the number to the "lowest common denominator."[41]

The Ten Principles listed in the communiqué from the 23rd included four of five points of *Panchsheel* but *omitted* peaceful coexistence itself. They also enshrined respect for human rights, the equality of races and nations, the right to individual and collective self-defense, the abstention from "arrangements of collective defence to serve the particular interests of any of the big powers," a call for peaceful settlement of disagreements, and a commitment to international justice. Most importantly, however, was the explicit commitment in the final communiqué to the ideas and principles of the United Nations, which all participants, including the PRC, formally endorsed. The final communiqué also included a series of additional desires, which had not been controversial in any of the committee meetings, such as the appeal for economic cooperation and international development aid, the call for cultural collaboration, the demand for decolonization particularly in sub-Saharan Africa, and the plea for international disarmament.[42]

Regardless of the conflicts at the conference, the twenty-nine participants decided to meet at an unspecified time in the future, possibly in Egypt. Yet Nehru was able to prevent the creation of a permanent organization, which Indonesia, Ceylon, and Egypt had raised once more. To Zhou's applause, Nasser instead announced the creation of the Afro–Asian People's Solidarity Organization (AAPSO) with headquarters in Cairo.[43]

The Collapse of the Bandung Legacy, 1955–65

Despite the often-cited *Bandung Spirit* that supposedly sprang from the conference, Asian–African Internationalism had passed its peak as soon as the curtain fell on the conference. While the gathering's successes had many mothers, the subsequent failures had equally plentiful fathers. Geography was not sufficient to maintain a movement that represented states with 61 percent of the world's population. The twenty-nine participants fell into fifteen pro-Western, twelve non-aligned or neutralist, and two communist countries. From the very beginning, the pro-Western group seized the conference to make its case for anti-communist policies and Cold War alliances with the United States. As a jubilant Pakistani delegation claimed afterward, this approach seemed to have succeeded. Despite Zhou's great diplomatic performance, the Chinese prime minister had been forced to make one concession after another to "the majority of the delegations." Yet this success against communism also created a problem, as Pakistan realized with some dismay. A new "political vacuum" in the Cold War struggle had arisen after Bandung that required an updating of rhetoric: "We have to learn a new political A.B.C.; our old one has been destroyed at the Conference."[44]

Apart from the fundamental disagreements among the Bandung participants, the core group behind the conference – the Colombo Powers – lacked the necessary internal glue to carry on with Asian–African Internationalism. Public conflict had raged among them already at the Colombo meeting in 1954. Indonesia had been deeply troubled by the "unconcealed animosity which Bogra and Nehru had for each other." Despite Nehru's and U Nu's attempts to keep controversial issues, such as communism or the Taiwan issue, off the agenda at Bandung, Ceylon's Kotelawala did not hesitate to put them back on. The display of disunity among the five Bandung hosts continued after the conference. In the wake of the Suez Crisis in late October 1956, Kotelawala bypassed Nehru by directly approaching Nasser with the idea of convening another Asian–African summit. Soon thereafter, Indonesia called for a meeting of the Colombo Powers in Delhi to discuss the issue, but Pakistan decided not to attend because it wanted to exploit the "opportunity to extend its influence in the Middle Eastern Affairs at the expense of India." By the early 1960s, even the once close Indo-Indonesian relationship had degenerated into open hostility.[45]

Some of the Colombo Powers were generally skeptical about Asian–African Internationalism. Nehru himself confessed that, despite the unexpected successes at Bandung, there was no real future ahead for the movement. A Burmese participant suggested "that the importance of the Conference should not be exaggerated ... 'We are little people – even India ... [D]ecisions are still being made in Washington and London.'" While Ceylon was "inclined to favour further meetings if proposed," Kotelawala doubted that the next Asian–African Conference would meet in Cairo. Although he would propose such a meeting to Nasser in the wake of the Suez Crisis, by May 1955 he was still openly "contemptuous of Nasser," wondering how the fatuous colonel "had obtained and kept his position in Egypt" at all.[46]

In subsequent years, Nehru was unwilling to use his pre-eminent stature within the Afro–Asian world to counterbalance the conflicts among the Colombo Powers. The Indian leader had acted twice as conference host in the late 1940s and had been a central figure in 1955, but afterward, he was not ready to continue in this role. The lack of concord within the Afro–Asian world, Nehru warned by early 1957, precluded any success of a future conference. The emerging Sino–Indian conflict made him additionally reluctant to endorse a successor meeting. After shots were fired across the undemarcated Himalayan border in 1959 and war broke out in 1962, Delhi was convinced that any conference attended by both India and the PRC would damage the dormant Asian–African Movement beyond repair.[47]

Besides, Asian–African Internationalism suffered from having remarkably little *African* content. The non-Arab part of that continent was not represented at the 1947 and 1949 conferences at all. With Ethiopia, Liberia, and the Gold Coast attending Bandung in 1955, sub-Saharan Africa still provided only a token involvement. In any case, in the early 1950s, the Arab–Asian bloc in the United Nations had mostly directed its fire at French colonialism in Arab North Africa and apartheid in South Africa while disregarding the rest of the continent. In the second half of the decade, the bloc grew numerically as the result of sub-Saharan decolonization, which in turn rendered it large and unwieldy. While the Bandung Spirit took on its own mythological life in some parts of Africa after 1955, the continent in reality dissociated itself from Asian–African Internationalism rather quickly. Its emerging leader, the Ghanaian Kwame Nkrumah, who had not even attended the Bandung Conference, perceived himself as the non-Arab alternative to Nasser in Africa. Ghana's close relations with Israel at that time further precluded a warm relationship with Egypt. Suspicious that Nasser was inviting the Soviets to join the Asian–African Movement, including the AAPSO, Nkrumah hosted his own All-African People's Conference in Accra in December 1958.[48]

While pan-Africanism competed with Asian–African Internationalism for membership among the newly decolonized sub-Saharan nations, the Socialist Camp actively competed for the heart and soul of the Afro–Asian world. In the two weeks before the Bandung Conference, 188 delegates from thirteen countries, including the Soviet Union and North Korea, had flocked to an Asian Solidarity and Peace Conference in Delhi that was co-organized by the Communist Party of India. Nehru's government was embarrassed by the explicit leftist competition to the Bandung Conference. In December of 1957, Egypt hosted the first conference of AAPSO, which turned out to be heavily influenced by Soviet and socialist ideas and participants. Once this had become obvious before its opening, Nasser even refused to attend. In an attempt to undermine Nkrumah's All-African People's Conference in Accra a year later, however, Nasser organized a simultaneous Afro–Asian Economic Conference, which attracted a small number of non-Arab participants and a large Soviet "jet-borne delegation."[49]

By the 1960s, internal conflicts and external alternatives eventually tore apart what remained of Asian–African Internationalism. At the beginning of the decade, Indonesia emerged as the most vocal proponent of a second

Bandung Conference. In the wake of the Sino–Indian border clashes in 1959, Jakarta proposed the gathering as a means to contain the PRC, only to switch sides after the Sino–Indian border clashes in late 1962 and work with Beijing against Delhi. By April 1963, the PRC itself started to push for a second Asian–African summit. While Ceylon and Egypt were happy in cooperating "to bury . . . prospects of a Bandung Conference," Zhou Enlai undertook a two-part tour through Africa and Asia at the turn of 1963/64 to raise support for it. Quickly it became clear that the PRC – given the Sino–American Cold War antagonism, the Sino–Soviet Split, and the Sino–Indian border clashes – wanted to impose its anti-American, anti-Soviet, and anti-Indian agenda. Beijing was less interested in seeking formal decolonization of the remaining European colonies, which had been the initial focus of the Asian–African Movement in the late 1940s, than in forming a communist-inspired Afro–Asian alliance against the supposedly imperialist world system at large. The overthrow of Algeria's Ben Bella, one of China's closest allies in the Arab world, on June 19, 1965, postponed the convocation of the planned second Bandung Conference, originally scheduled to take place later that month in Algiers. In August, Nasserite Egypt decided to invite China's arch nemesis, the Soviet Union, to the deferred gathering. Given Zhou's call for communist revolutions in Africa in early June, Nasser speculated – correctly, as it turned out – that the majority of the Asian–African member states agreed with his own unilateral decision. Once Beijing realized that Moscow would attend, it decided to boycott and then to sabotage the second Bandung Conference. On October 9, Premier Zhou forecast that Soviet participation would turn the meeting into a "battlefront of the Sino–Soviet Split." But by then, the PRC had lost yet another friend in the coup in Indonesia on September 30. To Chinese cries of triumph, the Asian–African membership countries decided in early November to cancel the conference for good. Asian–African Internationalism was dead.[50]

As communist China was laying waste to Asian–African Internationalism, several alternatives emerged. Despite initial irritations about the United Nations in 1945, the Asian–African Movement had embraced the international organization by 1949. Thus, when the movement collapsed in late 1965, many of its activities, particularly in the realm of economics, moved into the United Nations Conference on Trade and Development (UNCTAD), which had been established in June 1964, and the Group of 77 (G-77), a coalition of developing nations within it.[51] Outside of the formal structures of the United Nations, Yugoslavia and Egypt established the Non-Aligned Movement by 1961, as described in the next chapter, even if Nehru, as the original proponent of non-alignment in the Cold War, had initially been hesitant at the prospect of establishing yet another association. Only against the background of the Sino–Indian border conflict in 1962 did Nehru decide to commit India to the emerging Non-Aligned Movement. The initial strength of the new association rested on its shared political convictions – not the shared geographical space – of its member states. Finally, the various forms of pan-Islamism, as covered in Chapter 13, presented yet another set of alternatives to Asian–African Internationalism. Indeed, the Bandung Conference was an important marker in the rise of Muslim internationalism; it was the hitherto largest meeting of countries from the Islamic world. Fourteen out of the twenty-nine participating countries were Muslim or Muslim majority, eight more had sizeable Muslim minorities, and three Muslim countries were observers. After the conference, Pakistan lauded Bandung for its supposed role in the renaissance of international Islam, although this was wishful thinking given that its own pan-Islamist initiative had lost steam two years earlier. It was once more Indonesia which tried to seize the memory of Bandung by organizing an Asian–African Islamic Conference in the same city in March 1965, a month before the tenth anniversary of the original meeting. In April, Saudi Arabia itself began to promote pan-Islamism, largely as a conservative alternative to Nasser's secular and leftist Arab nationalism and as a platform to rally the Islamic world against Israel. By 1969, Jeddah's efforts had borne fruit with the first Islamic Summit in Rabat, Morocco.[52]

Conclusion

Despite its eventual collapse in 1965, Asian–African Internationalism could celebrate several successes. Its focus on decolonization since 1947 put political pressure on the European colonial powers to grant independence to their overseas possessions. In early 1949, it moved the UN Security Council to call on the Netherlands to withdraw from Indonesia. In the early 1950s, it stridently rendered pressure on France to withdraw from North Africa. By the mid 1950s, Tunisia and Morocco had gained their sovereignty, while France started a brutal but ultimately unsuccessful war against Algerian independence. Thus, formal decolonization across the Afro–Asian world was among the greatest triumphs of the Bandung Movement. However, this was not the exclusive result of Asian–African pressure, but the combined effect of Asian–African Internationalism and anti-colonial pressures jointly emanating from the Socialist Camp and from within the Free World. But the successes of formal decolonization by the early 1960s also removed the sense of unity and purpose that had underpinned the three conferences between 1947 and 1955. Asian–African Internationalism eventually spawned a series of successor movements. One of them – the AAPSO – fell prey to the Cold War in the late

1950s, and another one – G-77 in UNCTAD – emerged within the United Nations. But two more flourished outside the Cold War division, as described in the following two chapters.

Yet Asian–African Internationalism also suffered from basic weaknesses and the ensuing failures. Geography was not a guarantee of unity – on the contrary. The Cold War was present at Bandung in terms of pro-American participants, ideological questions, and controversially fought debates. Fears of boycotts by the People's Republic of China (PRC) and the Arab states led to the exclusion of the Republic of China (ROC) in 1955, despite its participation in 1947 and 1949, and of Israel, in spite of the attendance of a Zionist delegation eight years earlier. Communist China and the Arab states even started to collaborate on the Palestinian issue – aimed directly at Israel and indirectly at Taiwan. The exclusion of most of non-Arab Africa raised doubts about Asian–African commitment to that world region, which might explain why sub-Saharan nations did not emerge as strong supporters of the Asian–African Movement once it fell on hard times after 1955. In the end, the lack of Institutionalization enabled a radicalized China to try to seize Asian–African Internationalism for its own anti-imperialist agenda in the early 1960s, and to destroy it in the process.

12 Non-Alignment

According to conventional wisdom, the Non-Aligned Movement was created at the famous meeting of Yugoslavia's Josip Broz Tito, Egypt's Gamal Abdel Nasser, and India's Jawaharlal Nehru on the Adriatic Island of Brioni in mid July 1956. Yet much of the event remains shrouded in mystery, largely because primary documentation is either inaccessible or lost. The Brioni myth mainly rests on the charisma of the three leaders and the stunning beauty of the location. Nehru later complained about the publicity given to the trilateral meeting, which he himself considered just a "friendly call." In the absence of a clear purpose for the talks, the Indian prime minister proposed to issue a communiqué that endorsed the Ten Principles of the Bandung Conference of April 1955.[1] Nehru left Brioni without the impression that the meeting had spawned a new movement. In the following four years, he also consistently opposed repeated calls for a non-aligned conference of a larger number of like-minded states.

Numerous misconceptions about the Non-Aligned Movement circulate to this day, most notably its conflation with Asian–African Internationalism. The confusion primarily stems from the overlapping programs and memberships, but also from Nehru's attempt to impose his rigid definition of non-alignment on the Asian–African Conference in Bandung in 1955. Moreover, the early Non-Aligned Movement endorsed Bandung's Ten Principles at its first conference in Belgrade in 1961. But Asian–African Internationalism was mainly based on geography and anti-imperialism, while Non-Alignment advocated bloc-free status in the Cold War. Numerous participants from the Bandung Conference – communist China and pro-American Pakistan, for example – were excluded from the sibling movement because they were formally aligned in the Cold War. By the early 1960s, the two often conflated movements became vicious rivals for allegiance in the emerging Global South, despite having joint roots in Nehruvian thinking.[2] Still, after the demise of Asian–African Internationalism in 1965, the Non-Aligned Movement remained internally split, and then tended to tilt toward the Socialist Camp during the June War in 1967, the East Pakistan crisis in 1971, and the Indochina conflict in the first half of the 1970s. Eventually, the pursuit of national interests by India and Egypt, which had both lost their Non-Aligned founding fathers Nehru and Nasser, undermined the movement even more.

Non-Alignment arose from three parallel developments in the early Cold War. Nehru had abhorred the Cold War division and concomitant militarization of the world since the late 1940s because he saw it as a danger to global peace. Tito pursued Non-Alignment with the purpose of fortifying Yugoslavia's independent position in world politics in the wake of Stalin's expulsion of his country from the Socialist Camp in 1948. Nasser had tried to impose anti-imperialism on the Arab League against Anglo–American attempts to include the Middle East in anti-Soviet containment policies since the 1952 coup. By the first half of the 1960s, Nasser and Tito managed to launch the Non-Aligned Movement on the basis of their charismatic appeal, but also by exploiting Nehru's moral leadership in the world. Despite internal conflicts, Non-Alignment helped to put nuclear disarmament on the international agenda very quickly. Yet, after the mid 1960s, the movement declined in international appeal because of a series of international crises that questioned its non-aligned commitments. By the late 1970s, revolutionary and pro-Soviet members tried to seize the movement as China had done with regard to the Asian–African movement in the early 1960s. As Chapters 20 and 21 show, Non-Alignment barely survived, but emerged weakened and without much influence in the 1980s. In its stead, Saudi and Iranian pan-Islamism rose to lead the Muslim world in the Middle East and beyond.

Origins, 1946–56

Non-Alignment emerged in response to the increasing Cold War division of the world and the ensuing possibility of global, and possibly nuclear, conflict. Nehru, Tito, and Nasser all independently from each other developed alternative ideas to the East–West bloc system, although they eventually agreed on Nehruvian positions by the mid 1950s, including the refusal to join formal Cold War alliances and the promotion of active policies to avoid war and foster world peace. Yet, at different times in the 1950s and 1960s, the three did not believe that non-alignment ruled out receiving foreign military aid from either side of the Cold War or even concluding defensive military alliances with the Soviet Union or the United States.

Nehru used the term "non-alignment" for the first time in May 1949. As early as March 1946, however, he had stressed that his country "would not like to entangle itself with other people's feuds." Alignments with power blocs were "essentially wrong" because they inevitably led to war, or so he believed. But for him, non-alignment did not amount to neutrality in the sense of abstention from world politics. Nehru insisted that India's non-alignment consisted of "positive" and "active" policies, designed to "preserve and ... establish peace on firm foundations." Still, over the course of the first two decades of India's independence, Nehru's non-alignment clashed with the country's security needs. In early 1953, Nehru was convinced that India's non-alignment precluded his country from receiving any foreign military aid, even after Pakistan's interest in joining the Western-sponsored, anti-Soviet alliance system in the Middle East had put Indian national security at risk. Yet, during the Sino–Indian war almost a decade later, the Indian prime minister welcomed Western arms supplies as long as they had no political strings attached: "It is one thing to get help from friendly countries ... ; it is quite another to hand over the defence of our country and all that this implies to powerful military blocs."[3]

Yugoslavia's non-alignment policy emerged as the result of the country's expulsion from the Cominform and the Socialist Camp in 1948. The following year, Tito terminated support for the communist guerillas in Greece with the purpose of improving relations with the non-socialist world. In late 1951, fearing a Soviet intervention in the context of the ongoing Korean War, Tito announced that his country would side with the US-sponsored North Atlantic Treaty Organization (NATO) in the event of World War III. Yugoslavia even signed an arms agreement with the United States that initiated greater military cooperation against the Soviet Union. In early 1953, Tito reassured US ambassador George V. Allen that Yugoslavia "would not ... return to [the] Cominform fold" and that "any form of neutralism or isolation was a practical and moral impossibility." Following Iosif V. Stalin's death in March 1953, however, Moscow took the initiative to normalize relations with Belgrade, but Yugoslavia remained unwilling to return to the Socialist Camp. Instead, Tito decided to pursue policies that would ensure the highest possible degree of independence between the blocs by establishing relations with the decolonizing Afro–Asian world. As his first extended trip to India, Burma (today's Myanmar), and Egypt at the turn of 1954/55 approached, he still publicly reconfirmed his commitment to the West in the event of World War III, and portrayed his impending visit to the non-aligned Nehru as a meeting of like-minded promoters of world peace.[4]

Tito's visit to India occurred at a crucial time. After the creation of the US-sponsored Southeast Asia Treaty Organization (SEATO) in September 1954, Nehru had swung his support behind the Indonesian idea of what would become the Asian–African Conference in Bandung in April 1955. The two-day preparatory meeting in the Indonesian city of Bogor in the last days of 1954 coincided with Tito's extended visit to India. In Delhi, the Yugoslav guest and the Indian host discussed equidistance from both Cold War blocs. The joint communiqué announced that they saw "non-alignment" as a "positive, active and constructive policy seeking to lead to a collective peace." In Nehru's eyes, Tito's Yugoslavia was the first European country to sign up to the Indian concept of non-alignment.[5]

Egypt's path to non-alignment following the military coup in mid 1952 was more direct than Yugoslavia's after 1948. In February 1953, Pakistan sent its foreign minister to Egypt to discuss preliminary ideas of a Western-sponsored, anti-Soviet alliance system in the Middle East. But Nasser rejected the idea "as another form of occupation" following "70 years" of British imperialism. Nehru's first talks with the military government in Cairo in June 1953 thus touched on the ongoing Egyptian–British negotiations with regard to the British military presence in the Suez Canal Zone. The prime minister returned home convinced that "in Egypt, as well as in the entire Middle East, India is looked upon ... as a guide and friend." Soon thereafter, the Egyptian military regime pondered the possibility of "neutralism" in the Cold War. The signing of a Turkish–Pakistani cooperation agreement in February 1954 – which would lead to the Baghdad Pact within a year – swayed Nasser to announce that his government's "policy was not one of neutrality but one of co-operation and non-co-operation ... with those who occupied its country and restricted its sovereignty." At a meeting in the Suez Canal Zone on February 5, 1955, Tito encouraged Nasser to adopt Nehru's non-aligned positions, which he himself had publicly endorsed in Delhi six weeks earlier. When the Indian prime minister passed through Cairo ten days later, both sides agreed to work for world peace and condemned the formation of military blocs. Nehru parted from Nasser convinced that they shared a "similarity of outlook in many matters."[6]

Nasser eventually embraced Nehru's non-aligned position over the course of 1955. At the Asian–African Conference in Bandung, he espoused positions close to, but still distinct from, Nehru's rigid non-alignment. Coincidentally, Nasser chaired the panel that found the compromise solution of the Ten Principles, which did not include non-alignment, however. The joint communiqué on Nehru's talks with Nasser in Cairo in July 1955 stressed their shared "conviction that involvement in military pacts or alignments with great powers does not serve the cause of peace." Yet Nasser obviously did not agree with Nehru's strict view that foreign military aid from either side in the Cold War was akin to membership in a military alliance. In May, a short time after his return from Bandung to Cairo, he had asked the Soviet ambassador for military aid. In late September 1955, Egypt announced, to the surprise of the Western world, an arms agreement with the USSR and Czechoslovakia. Tito himself had helped to convince Soviet leader Nikita S. Khrushchev in May to satisfy Nasser's requests. Paradoxically, the man who had been receiving weapons from the United States since 1951 assisted his new Egyptian friend in obtaining arms from the Soviet Union four years later. Ultimately, in a meeting in Cairo in early January of 1956, Tito managed to commit Nasser to the Nehruvian idea of "non-alignment" endorsed by himself a little over a year before.[7]

The Rise of the Non-Alignment, 1956–61

Tito and Nasser hoped that the seminal meeting on Brioni Island on July 18–19, 1956, would turn into an international event. But Nehru quickly poured cold water on their expectations. The Yugoslav president had originally invited only the Indian prime minister for a brief meeting toward the end of his guest's multi-week tour of Europe. Once they had reached agreement on a date, the two urged the Egyptian leader to reschedule a trip to Yugoslavia originally planned for August. Nehru was particularly keen on restraining Nasser's increasing political radicalism in foreign relations – such as the recent recognition of the PRC – by keeping him "in the neutralist camp." In the absence of clear ideas about what the meeting was supposed to achieve, Nehru simply proposed the endorsement of the Ten Principles of Bandung, issued fourteen months earlier. The Brioni communiqué furthermore called for an end to the world's division, for nuclear and conventional disarmament, and for the "development of under-developed areas in the world." Yet, as Nehru later confessed, the statement was a compromise, which "I doubt … anyone of us quite liked."[8]

The new triangular relationship underwent a serious test during the Suez Crisis. Nasser had not revealed to Nehru his intention to nationalize the Suez Canal Company during their joint flight from Yugoslavia to Egypt following the Brioni talks, or during their short talks in Cairo on July 20. The Indian prime minister only heard about it a week later, after he had returned to India. While Nehru and Tito did not dispute Egypt's right to nationalize, they both criticized the abrupt nature of Nasser's action. Subsequently, India tried to mediate between its non-aligned friend and its former colonial master. After the Israeli–Franco–British intervention in late October, it was the Arab–Asian bloc at the United Nations – not the supposedly nascent Non-Aligned Movement – that took the initiative in finding a diplomatic solution.[9]

The continued internal discord of the Arab–Asian bloc persuaded Nehru that convening an international conference would be politically damaging to the Asian–African Movement or any non-aligned initiative. Nevertheless, Yugoslavia's and Egypt's interest in a non-aligned conference increased over the following years. Tito tried to use his contacts with the emerging Global South to counterbalance the Cold War blocs, particularly after the relationship with the USSR, improved in May 1955, had faltered again. Meanwhile, Nasser tried to exploit his stardom, which he had so suddenly obtained at Bandung and during the Suez Crisis, to increase his international influence. Consequently, both Tito and Nasser repeatedly proposed a conference of non-aligned countries from the Afro–Asian world in the period from 1958 to 1960.[10]

Tito's first opportunity to call for a conference arose against the background of the ideological battle between Yugoslavia and the rest of the communist world, which started in late 1957. Nehru considered the Chinese propaganda attacks on Yugoslavia a breach of *Panchsheel* and the spirit of the Ten Principles of Bandung, which the PRC had signed in 1954 and 1955, respectively. Nasser too was irritated by the parallel Soviet ideological attacks on Yugoslavia. Thus, during his first visit to Moscow in the spring of 1958, he made a point of publicly thanking "the Soviet Union, China, *and* Yugoslavia" for their support during the Suez Crisis. But Nehru still remained dead set against any conference, even after Yugoslavia and Indonesia had proposed one in mid July for the purpose of discussing the ongoing, Egyptian-caused crisis in Lebanon. On his tour through the Middle East and South Asia at the turn of 1958/59, Tito once more beat the drum of non-alignment. After the Yugoslav leader had left Cairo for Jakarta in early December, Nasser asked Cambodia's Prince Norodom Sihanouk to raise the possibility of convening a conference during his impending visit to Delhi before Tito's arrival there in mid January. "Irritated" by Sihanouk's "unnecessary" visit, Nehru stuck to his guns.[11]

The collapse of Sino–Indian relations over the Tibetan revolt in March 1959 supplied yet another potential motive to bring the non-aligned together. In mid May, Nasser and Tito proposed a quadrilateral, neutralist summit meeting with Nehru and Indonesia's Sukarno, but the Indian prime minister still hesitated. Even if the proposal was about countering Soviet and American influence in the Middle East – and thus supposedly unrelated to India's ongoing conflict with China – Nehru doubted that the gathering would have any influence on world politics. When in the fall of 1959 the United States, the USSR, the United Kingdom, and France had agreed to meet in Paris in May 1960 for a summit, Tito grew anxious that the window for the non-aligned to gain influence in world affairs was closing quickly. But Nasser's ensuing proposal to convene a second Brioni meeting concurrently with the Paris Summit once more fared poorly with Nehru.[12]

Because Nasser had given up on the idea of a non-aligned conference by early 1960, he turned to Indonesia's Sukarno with a proposal to convene a second Bandung Conference instead. With India in mind, he proposed to use the gathering to convince the PRC of "a less aggressive Chinese policy" in the Himalayas. During a visit to Delhi in late March and early April, Nasser pushed Nehru to accept the idea because the conference would "publicly give Zhou Enlai the advice to reduce the Sino–Indian conflict in the spirit of the Bandung conference." But since Nehru was scheduled to negotiate with the Chinese prime minister on Sino–Indian territorial disputes three weeks later, he did not believe that such "dictatorial" measures would work.[13]

Eventually, the U-2 incident on May 1, 1960, influenced the fate of both Soviet–American relations and non-alignment. Khrushchev's sabotage of the impending Paris Summit allowed Tito to revive the idea of non-aligned diplomacy at the global level. During a visit to Yugoslavia in mid June 1960, Nasser and Tito discussed Nehru's negative attitude toward an Asian–African conference, and India's parallel enmities with China over the Himalayas and with Pakistan over Kashmir. The final communiqué of Nasser's weeklong visit declared that "the uncommitted nations should have a bigger say in world affairs," particularly after the "collapse of the Paris Summit."[14]

The fifteenth anniversary meeting of the UN General Assembly, which started on September 20, 1960, in New York, marked the actual birth of the Non-Aligned Movement. As the gathering unfolded, observers quickly realized that it would be different from previous years. The overlapping Asian–African bloc and non-aligned group made up seventy of the roughly one hundred UN member states, though the number of members increased during the gathering as mostly African nations were accepted into the United Nations. Yet the smaller, informal non-aligned group was politically more active than the larger Asian–African caucus.[15]

The central non-aligned figure in New York was Tito, even if Nehru appeared in public as the group's spokesman. The Yugoslav president actively sought out the representatives of newly independent African countries, particularly the leader of pan-Africanism, Ghana's Kwame Nkrumah. He hosted two non-aligned "summits" at the Yugoslav mission in New York on September 29 and October 4, which the non-aligned big five attended: Nehru, Nasser, Sukarno, Nkrumah, and Tito himself. At the second meeting, they pledged close cooperation. Yet the non-aligned group failed to achieve its envisioned objectives in New York. Tito and Nasser had hoped to mediate between the USSR and the United States, given the rise of tensions in the wake of the abortive Paris Summit. Several times, non-aligned and African states called on the two nuclear powers to disarm for the sake of world peace. Yet US President Dwight D. Eisenhower refused to meet the ranting and shoe-banging Khrushchev. Tito left New York "in a less optimistic mood than he had when he arrived." Nehru noted "that the General Assembly presented a rather frightening aspect, for it was a picture of the cold war almost at its worst."[16]

Tito took the initiative to forge the little momentum gained in New York into a concrete plan. A two-month trip to western and northern Africa in the spring of 1961 included many of the nations that had recently become independent – Ghana, Togo, Liberia, Guinea, Mali, Morocco, and Tunisia – and ended in talks with Nasser in Egypt. While the trip's official purpose was economic cooperation, Tito had probably intended for it to result in the call for a non-aligned conference all along. His talks with Nasser in mid April lasted for several days and included telegraphic discussions with Sukarno, who approved the idea of a non-aligned conference from afar. The three sent an invitation to a preparatory conference in Cairo in their name to twenty countries which they considered "non-aligned."[17]

The reaction to the invitation was mostly positive. However, in May, Sukarno announced that he would only attend the Cairo preparatory conference in the summer but not the actual conference in Belgrade later in the fall. He believed that a second Bandung Conference should have priority over a non-aligned gathering, since Afro–Asian problems were pressing. Nehru was also "not very keen" on the project, though for different reasons. After receiving the invitation letter, the father of non-alignment was primarily eager to guard the gates. He decried the lack of a definition of what non-alignment was supposed to be, and he was not happy with the list of invitees. Yugoslavia and Egypt eventually agreed for the preparatory conference to define both the term "non-alignment" and the conditions for participation. The conference on June 5–12 in Cairo delineated non-alignment as "an independent policy based on the coexistence of states," support for national liberation, and non-membership in a "multilateral military alliance concluded in the context of Great Power conflicts."[18] Thus, despite Nehru's consistent resistance, Tito and Nasser had managed to establish the Non-Aligned Movement within five years after the trilateral meeting in Brioni.

Nuclear Weapons, 1961–63

The first Non-Aligned Conference in Belgrade on September 1–5, 1961, brought together twenty-three countries from Asia and Africa, plus

Yugoslavia and Cuba. Despite its strenuous attempt to address problems of decolonization and economic development, the nuclear arms race dominated the Belgrade Conference from the very beginning. On August 31, Khrushchev announced the resumption of testing, thereby abandoning a three-year-old Soviet–American–British nuclear test moratorium. And on the opening day of the Belgrade Conference, the USSR conducted the first in a nine-week series of thirty-one tests.[19]

Khrushchev's announcement followed soon after the closure of the borders in Berlin. Combined, both pointed to a further worsening of the international atmosphere. In the first two days of the Belgrade Conference, one speaker after another demanded the USSR and the United States start nuclear disarmament negotiations for the sake of world peace, or at least expressed dismay over Khrushchev's announcement. Nehru, who had left Delhi convinced that the arms race would soon end with "an explosion," tried to steer the outrage toward a discussion about concrete action. But on September 3, Tito added fuel to the fire by expressing sympathy for Khrushchev's announcement while still calling for a worldwide test moratorium. As the conference threatened to break apart over the Soviet nuclear tests, Nasser proposed a "collective message" to Khrushchev and US President John F. Kennedy. The final declaration urged the "total prohibition of the production, possession and utilization of nuclear and thermo-nuclear arms," and called for *Non-Aligned participation* in both nuclear disarmament negotiations and an *inspection regime.*[20]

In the non-aligned spirit of working for world peace, Nehru and Nkrumah traveled to Moscow on September 6 with a collectively signed letter to Khrushchev. In the Soviet capital, the two Non-Aligned guests told the Soviet host that the August 31 announcement was the major reason for "the sudden worsening of the international situation." Khrushchev tried to bypass the issue by blaming the closure of the borders in Berlin, as if he had not been involved in the making of that crisis either. Nehru and Nkrumah left Moscow unconvinced by his explanations. Sukarno and Mali's Modibo Keïta carried a similar letter to Kennedy on September 12, reminding the US president of his earlier statements about the "terrible nature of modern war." The American leader reassured his guests of his willingness to talk with his Soviet counterpart about nuclear disarmament, but only under conditions that would guarantee a beneficial outcome. The recent developments in Berlin, however, undermined the viability of negotiations with Khrushchev, Kennedy feared.[21]

In early November, an overwhelming majority of the UN General Assembly requested that the USSR, the United States, and the United Kingdom resume negotiations on the prohibition of nuclear testing.

Moscow responded by proposing a test ban *without* a control regime – a proposition that also passed the vote in the UN Political Committee with the support of many Non-Aligned countries. Thereby, they disowned their own two-month-old demand for an inspection regime. Dissatisfied with such inconsistent behavior, Nehru publicly criticized his fellow Non-Aligned leaders during a concurrent visit to the United States for failing to condemn Soviet nuclear tests sufficiently. His stance became a source of conflict when he met Nasser and Tito in Cairo on November 18–19 on his way home. Originally planned as a short airport meeting with Nasser only, the meeting turned into a small Non-Aligned summit when Tito decided, on short notice, to fly to Egypt. He hoped to gather support against US threats of food aid withdrawal following Tito's September 3 speech at the Belgrade Conference. In the trilateral talks, Nehru reported Kennedy's displeasure with the pro-Soviet stances of the Non-Aligned. He also criticized the other two; they could not hope "to receive vast quantities of American aid" while ignoring the "American point of view."[22]

On November 21, half a month after the end of its series of thirty-one tests, the USSR accepted an American–British proposal to resume trilateral test ban talks. On January 29, 1962, however, negotiations broke down, largely because the Soviet Union refused to agree to any control regime. Yet, a fortnight later, Khrushchev proposed a summit in Geneva that would bring together all heads of governments of the Eighteen-Nation Committee on Disarmament at the United Nations, which included five NATO members, five socialist countries, and eight countries that were not formally allied with either side in the Cold War to discuss nuclear disarmament. Khrushchev's sudden proposition aimed at pre-empting an American decision to resume testing, but also at re-establishing good relations with the Non-Aligned. Yet, among the eight unallied members of the committee, only four were Non-Aligned – India, Egypt, Burma, and Ethiopia – while the other four "neutralists" – Nigeria, Sweden, Mexico, and Brazil – were members of neither formal military alliances nor the Non-Aligned Movement. In early March, the Kennedy administration announced the resumption of testing for late April unless Khrushchev was willing to agree to a "cheat-proof" test ban treaty. The USSR rejected the proposal because it still considered any inspection regime "a system of espionage."[23]

France's decision to stay away cast an ominous spell on the Eighteen-Nation Committee that started talks in Geneva on March 14. Unsurprisingly, the problem of inspections quickly emerged as the principal stumbling block. With Indian leadership, the eight unallied committee members tried to prevent both the resumption of American testing and the threatened Soviet countertesting. India proposed to replace the inspection regime demanded by the United States with a monitoring scheme run by the Non-Aligned. While Washington and London were willing to accept this idea on the condition that the Non-Aligned were technologically proficient to do so, Moscow considered even "neutral" inspectors spies. In a last ditch effort, Brazil proposed a test ban with a weak inspection regime run by scientists from unallied countries – but again to no avail. On April 25, the United States resumed testing. The Non-Aligned and neutralist committee members were understandably disappointed. Washington publicly stated that the tests were necessary in order to prevent Moscow from pulling ahead in nuclear weapons development, but urged the eight unallied committee members to continue pushing for a test ban with a control regime.[24]

As the Geneva talks entered into limbo for most of the summer of 1962, several unrelated developments came together to trigger the Soviet–American–British test ban talks in Moscow a year later. In May, the USSR had decided, unbeknownst to all, to send medium-range nuclear missiles to Cuba. In August, the United States proposed new measures to restart trilateral talks. Even if unallied pressure had helped to spur the US decision to ask the USSR for negotiations, Washington had actually grown more concerned with Beijing's nuclear bomb project, while it had not yet discovered Moscow's ongoing Cuban venture. Khrushchev rejected the American request but agreed to talk, obviously with the intent of using negotiations as a smokescreen for his Caribbean operation. But the generally negative Soviet attitude dismayed the unallied countries, which had hoped for the prohibition of at least atmospheric testing in order to prevent nuclear fallout on a global scale.[25]

The Limited Test Ban Treaty (LTBT), which the United States, the United Kingdom, and the USSR initialed in Moscow in late July 1963, was not the result of Non-Aligned influence at Geneva. The Cuban Missile Crisis in October 1962 had been a cathartic episode for Khrushchev, who had realized how his brinkmanship had almost brought the world to nuclear war. The subsequent US recognition that a global network of seismographic stations would replace the need for on-site inspections to supervise nuclear test explosions – provided they were conducted underground – also helped to minimize Soviet–American differences. Of course, the Non-Aligned welcomed the test ban treaty, even if it was only limited, as a big step forward to world peace.[26]

The Struggle against Asian–African Internationalism, 1963–65

The two years bracing the second Non-Aligned Conference in Cairo on October 5–10, 1964, witnessed the detrimental struggle against the PRC, a non-member but great rival in the Global South. Relations between Yugoslavia, Egypt, and India, on the one hand, and communist China, on the other, had been developing well by the mid 1950s. But by 1957–59, they deteriorated in parallel though for unrelated reasons, reaching a low point during the Sino–Indian border war in 1962. On the first day of the war, October 20, Nasser offered arbitration by "non-aligned African Asian nations," but failed to get a positive response from the Chinese leaders. It was in this context that Ceylon (today's Sri Lanka) proposed a summit of neutral Afro–Asian countries – including Burma, Ghana, Indonesia, Cambodia, and Egypt – to work out a mediation plan. Yugoslavia tried to coordinate its position with Egypt during bilateral negotiations in Cairo beforehand.[27]

The Colombo Conference on December 10–12, 1962, reflected the shifted power realities in Asia. Most participants were caught between a militarily rising China and a vulnerable India. The Egyptian representative Ali Sabri took the initiative to propose a pro-Indian approach for the mediation, but Cambodia's Sihanouk, Indonesia's Subandrio, and Burma's delegation took up positions sympathetic to the PRC. The compromise solution, which the Ceylonese Prime Minister Sirimavo Bandaranaike presented to Beijing and Delhi in early 1963, envisioned a Chinese withdrawal from all occupied Indian territories and an Indian abstention from reoccupying *some* of them. But Zhou demanded Indian abstention from reoccupying *all* territories, while Nehru was ready to accept all proposals without any preconditions.[28]

The failed Colombo mediation marked the *key moment* in the bifurcation of the Non-Aligned Movement from its Asian–African sibling. In its wake, the PRC decided to focus on the Bandung group, while India, disappointed by the lack of Afro–Asian support, seemed to give up the very movement, which Nehru had fathered in the late 1940s. Instead, Delhi sought rapprochement with the only other association with which it had close political affinity – Non-Alignment.[29]

In the fall of 1963, China redoubled its efforts to engage with the Afro–Asian world. The PRC was particularly interested in enticing away one of India's closest collaborators – Egypt. Probably aware of Nehru's apprehension in this regard, Nasser and Bandaranaike proposed in mid October a Non-Aligned conference for 1964 in order to prevent another Asian–African gathering. But during his two-part trip to Pakistan, Egypt, Albania, Algeria, Morocco, Tunisia, Ghana, Mali, Guinea, Sudan, Ethiopia, Somalia, Burma, and Ceylon at the turn of 1963/64, the Chinese prime minister consistently pushed for a second Bandung Conference. Sparked by Zhou's ongoing travel diplomacy, Nasser, Tito, and Bandaranaike took the initiative in late 1963 to invite the ambassadors of twenty other Non-Aligned countries to a preparatory meeting in Colombo for late March. But just before the Non-Aligned preparatory conference started, pro-Chinese Indonesia issued invitations to a similar meeting in April to prepare a rival Asian–African conference. In a shift from his skeptical position from the preceding decade, Nehru in the last weeks of his life enthusiastically welcomed the invitation for the second Non-Aligned Conference in Cairo in October, stating in parliament that "India will play an active role." For Egypt, the conference marked an increase of prestige, particularly since it followed the second Arab League Summit scheduled to take place in Cairo the previous month as well. China, with its 650 million inhabitants, protested its exclusion from a conference of countries from the Global South.[30]

The Cairo Conference on October 5–10 gathered delegations from forty-seven countries. The doubling in participation over the Belgrade gathering three years earlier was mainly due to decolonization in sub-Saharan Africa. As before, only Cuba among the invited Latin American countries attended. The final communiqué reconfirmed many of the points enshrined at the Belgrade Conference, such as anti-imperialism, national self-determination, peaceful coexistence, peaceful conflict resolution, and the rejection of military blocs. An additional declaration called for the non-proliferation of nuclear weapons, and committed all participants "not to produce, acquire, or test any nuclear weapons."[31]

Even if China was not invited, its rivalry with India was present in Cairo. In his speech on October 7, Nehru's successor, Lal Bahadur Shastri, demanded that the Non-Aligned "persuade China to desist from developing nuclear weapons." Coincidentally, on October 11, on the day after the Cairo Conference closed, Zhou ordered the planned test of his country's first nuclear device to go ahead. The nuclear explosion five days later was a success. The Chinese government was particularly pleased with the positive echo from the Afro–Asian countries. Even Egypt seemed to move away from India – and from recently adopted Non-Aligned positions on nuclear non-proliferation – toward China when it requested nuclear assistance. Furthermore, as early as October 12, the day after his order to go ahead with the bomb test, Zhou had discussed with Pakistani diplomats the agenda of a second Asian–African Conference. As one of the very few Afro–Asian countries worried about China's nuclear test, India bemoaned its rival's propaganda campaign targeted at the Afro–Asian–Latin American world.[32]

However, China's triumph in October 1964 evaporated within just one year. Overconfident, Beijing tried to impose its anti-Indian, anti-American, and anti-Soviet agenda on the scheduled conference, thereby laying waste to the Asian–African Movement in the process, as described in the previous chapter. With the death of Asian–African Internationalism in late 1965, Non-Alignment had finally escaped its sibling's long shadow. But the wounds that China's ideological frenzy had caused to Non-Alignment needed healing. Nasser had met Tito in early September 1965 to discuss the possible revival of Non-Aligned activities, but the two parted without a decision. Despite China's annihilation of the Bandung movement, India by late 1965 felt a deep isolation from the world at large.[33]

The Middle East, the USSR, and Czechoslovakia, 1966–69

Few of the Non-Aligned favored the convocation of a third conference in this situation – and neither Belgrade nor Cairo pressed for it. But Delhi pushed in May of 1966 for a meeting of its new prime minister, Indira Gandhi, with Tito and Nasser, mostly with the intention to "polish" the country's international standing, as foreign diplomats noted. Gandhi's vision was one of close Indian–Egyptian–Yugoslav trilateral cooperation, but definitely not one based on consensus by the whole movement. Many Non-Aligned members explicitly warned that the impending trilateral meeting could not speak in their name. Still, the summit in Delhi in October 1966 helped along the reconstruction of Non-Alignment. Tito assisted Gandhi and Nasser in repairing the Indian–Egyptian relationship, which had become strained in the wake of the successful Chinese nuclear test. In the end, Egypt and India also needed each other's support as bastions of secularism. As Nasser was in the process of cracking down on the Muslim Brothers, Gandhi needed to counterbalance Pakistan, which had recently made religion once more the center of its identity politics. But the talks in Delhi still exuded an atmosphere of uncertainty, with the communiqué resembling a laundry list of wishes and aspirations. Despite the fact that the meeting officially was not much more than an exchange of ideas, the three essentially agreed to run the Non-Aligned Movement jointly, without calling any further conference.[34]

Their intended collaboration underwent a serious test during the June War in 1967. Tito supported Nasser's pre-war decision to terminate the stationing of UN troops on the Egyptian side of the border with Israel and to close the Strait of Tiran to Jewish shipping. Shortly after Israel had started the war on June 5, Tito denounced it as the aggressor while defending all prior Arab provocations as purely defensive. During and after the war, Yugoslavia participated in, and even hosted, several Warsaw Pact (WAPA) meetings to discuss support for Egypt, despite its lack of membership in the Soviet-led military alliance.[35] Thereby, Belgrade had taken sides in the Middle East conflict, removing itself from the position of a future Non-Aligned mediator.

India's reaction to the June War was not as one-sided as Yugoslavia's. When the United States and Egypt officially broke off relations on June 8 in the midst of the short war, they agreed to stay in touch via third parties. Washington tasked Francisco Franco's neutral Spain with representing its interests in Egypt, and Cairo requested Gandhi's Non-Aligned India do the same in the United States. Unlike Tito, Indira Gandhi thereby implemented her father's long-time conviction that the Non-Aligned should mediate between warring parties. But India was also dependent on American deliveries of grain, which had been regularly shipped through the Suez Canal until early June 1967. Indian diplomats in Cairo were aghast at Egyptian political and military incompetence in June. Ambassador Apa B. Pant lamented that "non-alignment has obviously been the first casualty" when Egypt turned to the USSR for political and military support immediately after the war. Indeed, Delhi's support for Cairo never reached the extent of Belgrade's. Once Egyptian aid requests arrived, India expressed its willingness to help but announced that its capabilities to send food or civilian products were limited at best; it did not even offer any military aid. Prime Minister Gandhi stayed away from Nasser for four months after the war. While Tito toured the Arab Middle East in mid August on a diplomatic mission to start negotiations with Israel, she visited Cairo only on October 19–20 after a twelve-day tour of the socialist world. During the preparations for her visit to Egypt, it was clear to Pant that Nasser primarily saw her visit in terms of receiving a political boost.[36]

Tito continued to push for closer collaboration with the Socialist Camp in January 1968. After a trip through Afghanistan, Pakistan, and Cambodia, he discussed the Middle East with Gandhi and Aleksei N. Kosygin, chairman of the Soviet Council of Ministers, during India's Republic Day celebrations in Delhi. The trilateral talks raised the idea of inviting socialist states to a new Non-Aligned conference. To Gandhi, however, the sudden interest in such a collaboration merely displayed the deep programmatic crisis in the Non-Aligned Movement.[37]

But the USSR itself undermined any chance of future cooperation when it led the Warsaw Pact intervention in Czechoslovakia on August 20–21, 1968. Moreover, the event laid bare once more the cleavages within the Non-Aligned Movement. Since Tito's Yugoslavia feared it would be next on the list of Soviet-led interventions to restore socialism abroad, it harshly denounced Soviet imperialism. India's Gandhi expressed "her profound concern" about the violation of "the principle of non-interference" which "constitutes the very basis of peaceful coexistence." But Nasser found himself between a rock and a hard place after he had visited Moscow as recently as July. Immediately after the intervention in Czechoslovakia, the Egyptian government expressed support for Soviet policies, but when public opinion in Cairo quickly turned against Moscow, Nasser fell silent.[38]

Tito almost instantly reversed his recent Non-Aligned policies in favor of the Socialist Camp by pushing member states of the movement to agree to a conference focusing on non-interference. Delhi and Cairo tried to slow down Belgrade's new initiative by advocating thorough preparations. By January, however, Yugoslavia had managed to convince a sufficient number of Non-Aligned countries of the need for a consultative conference in Belgrade in July. Fifty-one of the fifty-seven countries which had attended the 1964 conference as participants or observers welcomed the invitation. But as a British diplomat observed, the Belgrade meeting was a "gathering of lesser men speaking with an uncertain voice." Nehru had been gone for five years, his daughter Indira Gandhi chose to stay at home in India, and a "chastened" Nasser decided not to attend either. The conference did not achieve renewed unity; some participants even publicly criticized the final communiqué on the day of its release.[39]

Radicalization and Disunity, 1969–76

The seven years after 1969 witnessed major developments in the Cold War that did not leave the Non-Aligned unaffected. The Vietnam War entered into its hottest phase during the presidency of Richard M. Nixon from 1969 to 1974. The PRC replaced the ROC in the United Nations in October 1971. China sought rapprochement with the United States in 1971–72. Moscow and Washington signed nuclear arms limitation agreements in May 1972. And the Middle East moved toward yet another clash in October 1973. Headlines about these epochal developments dominated the front pages of newspapers, but the Non-Aligned were unable to benefit. Particularly, Soviet–American détente deprived the movement of an important topic: the nuclear arms race. At the same time, the movement entered into a period of contradictory internal developments. While the jointly approved institutionalization in 1970 suggested that the member states wanted to collaborate more closely with each other, the movement simultaneously betrayed its foundational principle of non-participation in Cold War conflicts.[40]

The shift of Non-Aligned positions with regard to the long-lasting Indochina conflict signified a major departure from Nehru's original positions. For most of the 1960s, the founding member Cambodia had been able to navigate skillfully the problems which the war in neighboring Vietnam caused. Prince Sihanouk's overthrow by his own, pro-American prime minister, Lon Nol, in March 1970, however, led him into exile in

Beijing, where he established an exile government in coalition with the radical Khmer Rouge. The new situation forced the consultative conference of the Non-Aligned Movement in Dar es Salaam in mid April of 1970 to find a solution to deal with the contested right of Cambodia's representation. To make things even more complicated, the pseudo-government of the communist National Liberation Front (NLF) of South Vietnam – the Provisional Revolutionary Government (PRG) – requested full membership. While Lon Nol unsurprisingly did not receive much support, Sihanouk, a founding father of the movement, also gathered merely one-third of the vote. The third Non-Aligned Conference in Lusaka on September 7–12, 1970, eventually agreed to observer status for the PRG, but still could not decide on the Cambodian issue. Seven member states supported Lon Nol, and just seventeen Sihanouk – both far short of the majority.[41]

The Cambodian contest reached its apex at the Foreign Ministers Conference of the Non-Aligned Movement in Georgetown, Guyana, in early August 1972 in the wake of the scuffle about full membership of the PRG. A majority agreed to PRG membership, but five countries from Southeast Asia – Indonesia, Malaysia, Laos, Singapore, and Burma – and another three African countries were opposed. When the chairman of the conference, Guyana's Foreign Minister Sonny Ramphal, simply announced that the conference had reached consensus, the delegations of Indonesia, Malaysia, and Laos protested violation of procedure and walked out of the conference. With some of the staunchest supporters of Lon Nol's regime gone, the conference quickly decided to award Cambodia's representation to Sihanouk's exile government. In the end, Non-Aligned support for the PRG and Sihanouk meant that the Non-Aligned allied themselves with one side in the global Cold War. Backing the fallen Cambodian head of state also implied support for the Khmer Rouge. Little did the Non-Aligned Movement know in 1972 that, by doing so, it lent credibility to a radical movement that would establish a mass-murderous regime in the name of Maoism, racist nationalism, and rigid anti-imperialism within a few years.[42]

Apart from internal disunity, the particular national interests of two founding members, Egypt and India, further undermined the legitimacy of the movement. Despite the ongoing internal crisis in Jordan between the Palestine Liberation Organization (PLO) and the royal government, the Middle East did not play a role at the Lusaka Conference on September 7–12, 1970. In any case, Nasser decided to stay away from Zambia once a Palestinian splinter group had hijacked four Western airplanes on September 6. Instead, he led Arab League efforts to mediate between the PLO and Jordanian monarchy, after which he unexpectedly passed away. Nasser's successor, Anwar Sadat, understood that his country's closeness to the USSR was not conducive to the ultimate settlement of the Arab–Israeli conflict. In July 1972, just as Belgrade was reconciling with Moscow once more, Egypt expelled the Soviet military presence. At the fourth Non-Aligned Conference in Algiers on September 5–9, 1973, Sadat implicitly, but not openly, rallied support for his country's impending war against Israel. Tito, who emphasized both renewed cooperation with the Socialist Camp and international negotiations in the Middle East, seemed not to have understood Sadat's game.[43] Egypt wanted to exploit the Non-Aligned Movement – as it did the Arab League – for national goals, while Yugoslavia pursued an internationalist and pro-Soviet agenda.

At the same time, India's Indira Gandhi too disregarded the Non-Aligned Movement for her own agenda. Her country's decisive victory in the war against Pakistan in December 1971 not only led to Bangladesh's independence, but also tarnished the international reputation of the South Asian giant. The UN General Assembly called on Pakistan and India to negotiate a ceasefire, implying that both sides shared responsibility for the conflict. Only the USSR, its Eastern European allies (without Romania), Bhutan, and India itself voted against the call. *All* Non-Aligned countries, even India's long-time friend Yugoslavia, chose to vote for a statement that placed blame at the doorstep of Non-Aligned India. Delhi's subsequent continuation of the military conflict against Islamabad, despite the resolution of the UN General Assembly, alienated Muslim Non-Aligned countries even more, particularly since they believed that the *Hindu* Non-Aligned country wanted to humiliate a *Muslim*, though aligned, nation.[44]

India's subsequent dance around nuclear weapons became yet another issue of discord within the Non-Aligned Movement. In the wake of the Indian–Pakistani War and Nixon's visit to China in February 1972, Indira Gandhi took the formal decision to go nuclear. Yet India's quest for great power status met with a mixed reception in the Afro–Asian world and among the Non-Aligned. Following the successful nuclear test explosion in the spring of 1974, Yugoslavia was deeply concerned about India's actions, particularly after it had so strenuously mobilized the Non-Aligned world to support the Nuclear Non-Proliferation Treaty of 1968. Egypt showed interest in nuclear technology by approaching India, as it had approached China after the seminal Chinese test in 1964.[45]

Non-Aligned disunity was on full display in the year before the fifth conference on August 16–19, 1976, in Colombo. Maybe because the number of member states had trebled to eighty-five within fifteen years, the movement was unable to prevent Cold War conflicts from entering its ranks in full force. At the Foreign Ministers Conference in Lima in August 1975, the PLO, recently united Vietnam, and North Korea gained admission, but South Korea's bid for membership was rejected. During the preparations for the Colombo Conference, Cuba and the three new members, in close cooperation with the Soviet Union, tried to transform the Non-Aligned Movement into a global force against US imperialism. In comparison, Gandhi's India kept a low profile in the wake of its nuclear test in May 1974 while focusing on promoting economic cooperation within the Global South. Yugoslavia tried to pursue a policy of developing a "partnership between the Western countries and the non-aligned" because it disagreed with the unconstructive nature of concurrent Soviet policies toward the PRC, the Middle East, and the West. Unsurprisingly, Sadat's Egypt shared this pro-Western position, mainly because it was working closely with the United States to try to solve its conflict with Israel after October 1973. But Egypt's unilateralism in the Middle East and the ongoing civil war in Lebanon caused much public discord among Arab member states at the conference in Colombo.[46]

The diplomatic skills of Tito, Gandhi, and conference host Bandaranaike managed to keep the movement from falling apart at the Colombo meeting in August 1976. Only the declarations on Israel's continued occupation of Arab lands since 1967, on its denial of statehood to the Palestinians, on the apartheid regime in South Africa, and on the supposed US imperialist occupation of South Korea were hard-hitting, while those on most other issues were relatively moderate. The main problem, however, was that the four-day conference dealt with too many issues in too little time. Most of the countries were hardly prepared to discuss – or often not interested in discussing – issues that did not directly concern themselves. The conference's major achievement consisted of focusing on economic cooperation among member states while calling for changes to the global economic order. Due to their declaratory nature, the ensuing statements were mostly uncontroversial. The radicals thus left Colombo with mixed feelings. North Korea had only obtained a resolution against its rival (and non-member) South Korea, but had alienated the host country by moving an electronic spy ship to Colombo harbor during the conference. Cuba departed from the conference disappointed with the moderate results but happy that it was selected to host the sixth conference in September 1979. Vietnam considered the anti-imperialist wording of the resolutions an improvement over those of the Algiers Conference in 1973, but no more than that. Still, the recently united country was optimistic that the movement would become more anti-American in the future. When the Non-Aligned met again in Havana in September 1979, however, the compromises of Colombo faced a harsh test in a radically changed world, as Chapter 21 reveals.[47]

Conclusion

The Non-Aligned Movement was a Yugoslav–Egyptian co-production. The two countries collaborated closely in establishing and running the movement in the twenty years after 1956. Only once, in the fall of 1973, did they not see eye to eye. India was the odd member in this *ménage à trois*. Nehru was skeptical about the viability of Non-Alignment until he was forced to accept its inception in 1961. Only after the Sino–Indian War the following year did he make a commitment to the movement – largely for the instrumental reasons of counterbalancing Beijing's attempt to seize the Asian–African Movement. Under Indira Gandhi, India pursued its own national interests, with regard to Pakistan – by midwifing Bangladesh's birth – and China – by trying to catch up in terms of nuclear status.

In view of the larger membership, the Non-Aligned were numerically too weak throughout the 1960s, and politically too disparate in general to develop the influence that they had hoped for in 1961. The charismatic personalities of Tito, Nasser, and Nehru had managed to compensate for programmatic shortcomings in the early years. But by the early 1970s only one of the big three – the Yugoslav leader – remained. The successors of the other two lacked the political convictions to step into the large shoes left by their predecessors. The fundamental problem of the Non-Aligned Movement was that, beyond the claim that the non-aligned were just that, it had "no real common ethos except a feeling of having been badly done by," as a British report noted in 1973.[48]

Finally, the movement's fast growing membership included some countries that were clearly aligned with the Socialist Camp. How non-aligned could the Non-Aligned Movement remain if members like Cuba and Vietnam openly worked for it to take sides in the global Cold War? Yugoslavia might have breached the taboo by proposing to align with one of the blocs in the wake of the June War in 1967. But Tito had at least perfected the art of swinging back and forth between the Cold War blocs since the mid 1950s. Finally, even if criticism of the heavy-handed American intervention in Indochina was justified, the Non-Aligned took the anti-imperialism of various radical movements and countries in Southeast Asia at face value, without reflecting on their brutal nature and ideological orientation. By the mid 1970s, the movement had entered into an identity crisis, which the Colombo compromises of 1976 helped to disguise for a few more years only.

13 Pan-Islamism

On his way home from the negotiations about Pakistan's independence in London in late 1946, Muhammad Ali Jinnah spent three days in Cairo. The head of the All-India Muslim League proposed the creation of a global Islamic League in talks with Egypt's Prime Minister Mahmoud al-Nokrashy Pasha, the head of the Muslim Brotherhood Hassan al-Banna, two royal Saudi advisers, and Grand Mufti of Jerusalem Mohammed Amin al-Husseini.[1] His consultations were doubly symbolic for pan-Islamism during the Cold War. On the one hand, they brought together representatives from three of the four countries that spawned pan-Islamist initiatives during the Cold War. The future leaders of Pakistan had launched their bid for Islamic unity leadership in the 1930s, the Egyptian Brotherhood did so in the 1940s, Cairo's secular regime under Gamal Abdel Nasser followed in the wake of the 1952 coup, the Saudi monarchy tried in 1965, and Iranian clerics made an effort in the 1970s. On the other hand, the participation of the Grand Mufti in the Cairo meeting in 1946 emphasized the relevance of the Palestinian issue to visions of Islamic unity.

The political violence that extremists have committed in the name of Islam in recent decades has skewed the Western understanding of the politics of religion in the Middle East. Political Islam is complex, has multiple intellectual roots, and displays various political and sectarian differences. To this day it comprises numerous internal cleavages along the lines of denomination (Sunni versus Shia), ethnicity (Arab vs. non-Arab), levels of secularism or religiosity, and commitments to political moderation or violence. During the Cold War, it engaged with or rejected the USSR and the United States to varying degrees.

The multiple initiatives of pan-Islamism – be they governmental or non-governmental – during the Cold War competed with each other in attaining unity of the *ummah*, the global Muslim community. Generally, the different pan-Islamist initiatives embraced a set of analogous political premises in their struggle for transnational unity, such as the idea of a center or leading authority, the definition of a common cause (or enemy) to rally Muslims from all over the world, and sometimes even the willingness to launch *jihad* (Holy War). The various strands of pan-Islamism did not have their roots in the Cold War itself, even if the intellectual concept of a global Muslim community was relatively young. Only by the nineteenth century – in a reaction to Western imperialism, Christian ideas of empire, and European racialism – did Muslim leaders and thinkers fashion the idea of a single Islamic world that was defined by shared civilizational, religious, and even ethnic characteristics. Early pan-Islamists looked to the Ottoman caliph as the natural leader, just at the time when his empire was collapsing. The abrogation of the Caliphate by the Turkish Republic in 1924 ended the first phase of pan-Islamist thinking, but at the same time prepared the intellectual ground that allowed for the emergence of multiple forms of pan-Islamism – from South Asia to Egypt, Saudi Arabia, and Iran.[2] Particularly after 1945, Muslim leaders and thinkers promoted ideas that reflected long-standing debates on the future of the Muslim world, but also reacted to, tried to pre-empt, hoped to shape, or even rejected the Cold War as an ordering mechanism of international relations.

Like the Arab League, most of the pan-Islamist initiatives emerged in response to the identity crisis of the *ummah* following the abrogation of the Caliphate. In South Asia, this quickly sparked Muslim political activities that led to the establishment of Pakistan. In Egypt, it triggered the foundation of the Muslim Brotherhood by the late 1920s. However, Arab governments in the end showed greater interest in pan-Arabism than in pan-Islamism, which is why they eventually agreed to the creation of the secular Arab League by 1945. Still, pan-Islamist feelings did not subside. Since Muslim majority countries amounted to half of the participants in the Asian–African Conference in April 1955, some concluded that the Bandung meeting was the start of an Islamic renaissance at the international level. Yet the collapse of the Asian–African Movement in mid 1965 occurred at the very time when Saudi Arabia decided to seize the leadership of the *ummah*, even if the rising kingdom had rejected the idea of resurrecting the Caliphate under its leadership four decades before. As it succeeded in doing so by the 1970s, a competitor, however, emerged from the ranks of Iranian religious scholars and jurists in opposition and exile. In the wake of the Iranian Revolution in 1979, Sunni Saudi Arabia and Shia Iran engaged in a struggle over hearts and minds among the world's Muslims that continues to this day.

Pakistan

The collapse of the Ottoman Empire in October 1918 aroused existential fears among many Muslims across the world. The prospect of the end of the Ottoman Caliphate – the recently constructed symbol of a unified, global Islamic community – had haunted South Asian Muslims in particular for some time. Forming a significant religious minority in a Hindu majority society, they feared they would suffer the Jewish fate of being a people without a dominion. Hence, by late 1918, the All-India Muslim League launched a political campaign – the *Khilafat* Movement – that called for the lenient treatment of the Ottoman Empire by the victorious allies, including the restoration of Egypt and the Levant to the Caliphate. South Asian Muslims supported the military struggle of the Turkish secularists against the Western powers in 1919–23 because they had convinced themselves that only the Turkish Republic offered the hope of preserving the Caliphate. Hence its abolition by the secular republic in March 1924 came as a rude shock. Most South Asian Muslims rejected the subsequent Hashemite attempt to restore the Caliphate in the Hijaz, as well as a similar Egyptian royal bid in the two following years. Ultimately, they sided with Ibn Saud, the new ruler of the Hijaz, even though he rejected the idea of the restoration of the Caliphate. The demise of the *Khilafat* Movement by the mid 1920s and the concurrent worsening of relations between the Hindu-majority Congress and the All-India Muslim League set South Asian Muslim leaders on the path toward seeking special status for Muslims in a future post-colonial India. As early as 1930, the league argued that Muslims in South Asia formed a distinct nation. A decade later, the league's leader, Ali Jinnah, demanded the partition of India into a Muslim nation and a Hindu-majority state.[3]

Although Ali Jinnah had not been personally involved in the *Khilafat* Movement, the All-India Muslim League under his leadership still faced the problem of defining the relationship of a future Muslim state in South Asia to the larger Muslim world. One of the league's leaders, Choudhry Khaliquzzaman, attended a conference in Egypt in 1938 in support of an undivided Arab Palestine. There, he made the case for the creation of a South Asian Muslim nation. However, Arab politicians rejected the idea of a partitioned India, largely because they feared it would set a precedent for the creation of a Jewish homeland in Palestine. Given this background, Ali Jinnah's meeting with other Arab leaders in Cairo in late 1946 was a success for the simple reason that it occurred at all. After his return to India, he called for a Muslim boycott of the Asian Relations Conference scheduled in Delhi for the spring of 1947, at which half of the participating delegations came from Muslim lands. During his visit to Cairo in late 1946, Ali Jinnah had also alleged that the future India would be a Hindu imperialist power that posed an even greater threat to the Arab Middle East than Great Britain had in the past.[4] He obviously tried to prevent what he considered an Indian-led Asian–Arab rapprochement, but he failed.

With bloody partition and independence in August 1947, Pakistan emerged as the demographically largest Muslim country in the world – but only until Indonesian independence two years later. The bi-territorial country suffered from sectarian, linguistic, cultural, ethnic, and economic divisions. Apart from Islam and anti-Indian feelings, it had little to offer as a basis for creating a sense of national identity. Pakistan was as much an artificial nation founded for the members of one religious group as was Israel, which would emerge within the space of a year. One historian hence called it the "Muslim Zion." As in Israel, the mostly secular founders of the country tried to exclude religious leaders from politics. Predictably, the *ulama* – the religious scholars and jurists – rejected the idea of Pakistan in general. Their most prominent thinker, Abul Ala Maududi, considered the secular idea of the nation state antithetical to Islam. In his view, it was not sufficient to create a state solely in the name of Islam or on the basis of a Muslim majority population. On the contrary, the state needed to be Islamic in nature. As a former supporter of the *Khilafat* Movement, Maududi instead advocated the creation of a theo-democratic caliphate ruled by the community of all Muslims.[5]

Moreover, Pakistan's territorial extent remained uncertain at independence in 1947. For the next two decades, the country fought as many wars with India over Kashmir. The bi-territorial nature of the new state posed yet another problem. West Pakistan brought together Muslims from the area itself and those originally coming from northeastern India, while East Pakistan comprised mainly Bengalis. On the national level, elites from the western part ran the new state, while the eastern half was underrepresented at virtually all levels of government, despite its larger population. An attempt to make Urdu, which was spoken only in some parts of West Pakistan, the national language failed in 1948 due to determined resistance by the Bengali-speaking majority. To make matters worse, the new Muslim state had historical economic links to its larger Hindu sibling – connections that broke in 1947 and thereby threw the new state's economy into the doldrums.[6]

The secular Ali Jinnah still believed that Pakistan, as the largest Muslim country, would be the natural leader of the Islamic world, and that pan-Islamism could serve as a tool for nation building in the bi-territorial country. Hence, he supported Indonesian independence as early as July 1947 – one month before his country would achieve its own. But his backing for fellow Muslims across the world led to policies that were not always logically consistent. While Pakistan split from India in the summer of 1947, triggering a massive and bloody population exchange of Muslims and non-Muslims, it opposed the partition of Palestine into an Arab and a Jewish homeland just a few months later at the United

Nations. In any case, support of fellow Muslims did not help Pakistan to get the desired membership in the Arab League, the only major international organization of Muslim countries, because Pakistan was not an Arab country.[7]

Against the background of the rising Arab–Zionist crisis over Palestine and the concurrent Pakistani–Indian war over Kashmir, Ali Jinnah sent his trusted aide Feroz Khan Noon to Saudi Arabia, Jordan, Lebanon, Turkey, and Iraq in October 1947 with the goal of establishing formal relations. In August 1948, a month before his death, he publicly elevated the struggle with India over Kashmir to a level similar to the Indonesian war of independence and the raging Arab–Israeli conflict. Yet, by late 1948, the new government under Prime Minister Liaquat Ali Khan realized that, apart from Islam, Pakistan had little in common with the Arab countries.[8]

Starting in 1949, a pair of competing Pakistani initiatives – one unofficial and the other governmental – aimed at closing the gap between the country and the Arab Middle East. In February, the first conference of the new non-governmental but state-supported World Muslim Congress (Mutamar al-Alam al-Islami) convened in Karachi. It took its inspiration from interwar Islamic conferences in the Arab world, was chaired by the exiled Grand Mufti of Jerusalem, and aimed at promoting Islamic solidarity against India and Israel. In July 1949, the head of the Pakistan Muslim League, Choudhry Khaliquzzaman, called for the creation of a united "Islamistan." Yet the Egyptian government rejected his idea even before his arrival in Cairo during his unofficial trip to the Middle East in the last quarter of the year. After his return home, Khaliquzzaman complained about the discourteous reception he had received in the Middle East, particularly in Egypt and Saudi Arabia. Ultimately, Pakistan faced the problem that some Middle Eastern countries were more interested in regional collective security arrangements than in global religious unity. Khaliquzzaman thereafter called once more for the opening of the Arab League to non-Arab Muslim countries like Pakistan – but to no avail. As a member of the Pakistani delegation to the Asian–African Conference in Bandung in April 1955, he saw his pan-Islamist hopes revived for one last time; the conference, or so he believed, was a "Mecca of many hearts."[9]

In comparison, the Pakistani government followed a more pragmatic policy of cooperation with the Middle East. Its focus was mostly on economic development, particularly of the western half of the bi-territorial country. For reasons of geography and the political domination by West Pakistani elites, East Pakistan did not appear high on the pan-Islamist agenda of the national government. In general, Prime Minister Liaquat Ali Khan was more interested in promoting the "non-religious" aspects of Islam, such as social justice and fair economic development. Heeding the call of the late Ali Jinnah, Liaquat initiated a series of three economic conferences that promoted integration with the Middle East to help develop (West) Pakistan and reduce its economic dependency on India.[10] The semi-official first International Islamic Economic Conference brought together eighteen Muslim countries in Karachi from November 29 to December 5, 1949. In his opening speech, Pakistani finance minister, Ghulam Mohammad, called on the gathering to aim at "interlinking ... our economies" on the basis of principles prescribed by Islam, i.e. on a "middle path between democracy and communism." The location of the second conference in early October 1950 – Tehran – suggested that the idea of international cooperation among Muslims had taken hold outside Pakistan. But the conference suffered from a boycott by several Arab states after Iran had recognized Israel earlier in the year. The third conference four months later convened Muslim representatives from forty nations in Karachi again. In his speech to the conference on the opening day, Aga Khan III, a founding member of the All-India Muslim League, proposed for his country to adopt Arabic, which was not spoken in Pakistan at all, as the national language in order to integrate his country into the Arab world. While his proposal went nowhere, the Pakistani government still advocated the creation of an integrated railroad system to link the economies of Saudi Arabia, Jordan, Syria, Turkey, Iraq, Iran, and Pakistan. The relative success of two of the three conferences led the Pakistani government to forge ahead with initiatives seeking leadership of a united Muslim world. Shortly before his assassination in mid October 1951, Liaquat also approached the Egyptian and Iranian governments with the proposal of coordinating foreign policies.[11]

Liaquat's successor, Khawaja Nazimuddin, one of the few Bengalis in the national government, quickly sent foreign minister Muhammad Zafarullah Khan to Turkey, Syria, Lebanon, and Egypt in February 1952. Obviously on a mission to sound out his hosts, Zafarullah Khan proposed to turn the Arab–Asian bloc at the United Nations – which included non-Muslim countries – into a formal pan-Islamist "regional organization" that would remain neutral in the Cold War. However, a Pakistani invitation to discuss this idea, which was sent to twelve Muslim countries in mid March, only ended in repeated postponements and, finally, the cancellation of the conference.[12]

It was in this context that Pakistan faced the opportunity of entering the Western-led, anti-Soviet collective security arrangements in the Middle East. The prospect of finding alternative forms of integration with the Middle East triggered a major change in Pakistan's orientation in the Cold War, given that the country had repeatedly stressed its non-aligned status beforehand. Even after the start of the Korean War, Pakistan had tried to stay out of the Cold War, largely because it did not want to endanger Muslim minorities in the USSR or provoke the People's Republic of China (PRC). In mid February 1954, however, Pakistan signed a US-supported military agreement with Turkey, to which it even tried to invite post-revolutionary Egypt during the early stages in the year-long negotiations. The agreement provided Pakistan with arms, which it hoped to use against India to break the deadlock in the Kashmir conflict. Furthermore, it also hoped to implement surreptitiously its pan-Islamist "third way" visions within the confines of the Anglo–American policy of containing the USSR.[13]

In the wake of the pact's signing, Pakistan emphasized its continued interest in cooperation with Arab countries, possibly even in the form of an "Islamic Front" against Israel, India, and the emerging Asian–African Movement. But Egypt rejected the proposal because it feared that the emphasis on religion in the struggle against Israel would lead to world-wide Jewish support for that state. Nevertheless, the developing Cold War alignment with the West started to change Pakistan's perception of its role in international affairs. Starting in 1954, the government promoted the idea of Pakistan as a South Asian bridge between Europe, the Middle East, and Southeast Asia, destined to connect the Christian and the Muslim worlds in opposition to atheistic communism. This rhetorical adjustment helped to pave the way for the country to join the British-led Baghdad Pact in February 1955, and thereby made the United States the most important source of military and economic aid until the 1970s.[14]

In September 1956, the new Pakistani government under Prime Minister Huseyn Shaheed Suhrawardy openly called for the end of pan-Islamist policies. Deriding past attempts to collaborate with the Middle East as the futile policy by one "zero" in international relations to ally with a bunch of other "zeros," he proposed to engage instead with the world's big numbers directly – the United States, the USSR, and the PRC. Given the Pakistani government's dislike of Nasser, such talk did not endear the country to the Middle East in the concurrent Suez Crisis. Suhrawardy hoped to repair the damage by refusing to take part in a meeting in Delhi in mid November, which was convened by several Asian–African nations to discuss the Israeli–Franco–British intervention at Suez. Through personal diplomacy, he hoped to increase Pakistan's influence in Egypt at the expense of India's. But Nasser accepted Indian UNEF troops instead of the promised Pakistani detachments, and even refused to receive Suhrawardy in Cairo. Subsequently, Suhrawardy accused Nasser of being both pro-Soviet and anti-Pakistani. In mid November, his government tried to convince Saudi Arabia and Lebanon of the need to establish an anti-Nasser and anti-communist alliance in the Middle East – to no avail.[15]

Egypt

In Sunni Egypt, the royal government and the opposition Muslim Brotherhood had been competing for political influence since the second half of the 1920s. With the General Islamic Congress in 1926, Egypt's monarchy had briefly tried to claim pre-eminent status in the Islamic World through the restoration of the Caliphate under its leadership. Almost two decades later, Cairo eventually succeeded in obtaining regional supremacy by seizing leadership of the emerging Arab League. Still, the largely secular Egyptian monarchy continued to face religious competition at home. Co-founded by the schoolteacher Hassan al-Banna in 1928 in the wake of the Turkish abolition of the Caliphate, the Muslim Brotherhood aimed to restore Islam to its central role in society and government. Like other Islamic thinkers of the time, he was concerned that Western influence had undermined Islam. Unsurprisingly, the Brotherhood emerged first in Ismailia, a city in the Suez Canal Zone that hosted British troops and Canal Company officials. Through social programs, the Muslim Brotherhood expanded its ranks by the end of World War II, and in the late 1940s even managed to establish branches in Palestine and other Arab states. According to contemporaneous sources, the organization had several hundreds of thousand members in Egypt alone by late 1946 – out of 17 million inhabitants.[16]

After World War II, the opposition Muslim Brotherhood was powerful enough to influence the agenda of Egyptian politics. In August 1946, al-Banna threatened a revolt if the government would not take action to remove all British influence, including troops in the Suez Canal Zone, within one year. In November, members of the Brotherhood were arrested for creating disturbances during the ongoing negotiations with the United Kingdom on the revision of the 1936 treaty. In December 1947, Muslim Brothers organized massive demonstrations against the partition of Palestine. Soon thereafter, the organization sent its own paramilitary forces to the Sinai in anticipation of the Arab intervention in Palestine. As the fortunes of the Arab–Israeli war turned in 1948, al-Banna reportedly called on Arab people to "drive the Jews who live in their midst into the sea."[17]

When the Egyptian police found weapon caches in houses linked to the Muslim Brotherhood in October 1948, the government reacted by outlawing the organization on December 8, after years of gathering evidence of its secret organization and plans. Three weeks later, a student member of the Brotherhood assassinated Prime Minister Mahmoud al-Nokrashy Pasha. Despite claiming that his organization was not involved in the murder, al-Banna himself fell victim to a political assassination by the government two months later. Even after its prohibition, the Muslim Brotherhood remained a political reality, which led to its relegalization in 1951.[18]

With the Brotherhood seemingly silenced as a political threat at the turn of 1948/49, the Egyptian government was able to deal with Pakistani pan-Islamist proposals and competing ideas about collective security arrangements in the Middle East. Royal Egypt was largely unsympathetic to Pakistani ideas because they threatened its own predominance in the Middle East. In April 1951, at the time of the relegalization of the Muslim Brotherhood, Cairo publicly reconfirmed its policy of neutralism in the Cold War. Pakistan reacted to this development by trying to convince Egypt of its own "third way" during negotiations in February 1952.[19]

By then, however, the Free Officers were conspiring against King Farouk, who fell in a coup on July 22/23. Like the Muslim Brotherhood, the officers pursued anti-imperialist goals. Before the coup, both groups had collaborated in agitation and attacks on British authorities in the capital and the Suez Canal Zone. Afterward, the Brotherhood publicly declared its support for military rule. Since the Islamist organization had sympathizers in the army, it even managed to obtain two positions in the cabinet of the revolutionary government. Yet programmatic differences emerged quickly. As early as August, the head of the Brotherhood, Hassan al-Hudaybi, demanded the prohibition of all parties, the abolition of the constitution, and the introduction of Sharia law. Soon thereafter, the military regime outlawed all parties, but its subsequent policy of relegalization, though under strict conditions, caused relations with the Brotherhood to deteriorate rapidly.[20]

The political struggle between the secular regime and its Islamist opposition continued throughout the following two years. The Muslim Brotherhood successfully organized the General Islamic Congress in Jerusalem (al-Mutamar al-Islami al-Amm li al-Quds) in late December 1952, bringing together Islamic scholars to discuss the Palestinian Question. One of the conference's main purposes, however, was to launch the struggle against the formal control of Islamic unity by secular governments. By September 1953, Egypt's President Muhammad Naguib faced renewed demands by the Brotherhood to follow a harder line in the negotiations with the British on military withdrawal. The subsequent lack of success in the negotiations only increased Islamist pressure on the regime.[21]

At the turn of 1953/54, the military government publicly announced its neutral stance in the Cold War. At the same time, it decided to outlaw the

Muslim Brotherhood and arrest hundreds of its leaders. According to British government sources, the regime suppressed the Islamist opponents in response to their armed activities against UK military installations in the Suez Canal Zone, which threatened to undermine its position in the negotiations on withdrawal. Regime propaganda accused the outlawed Brotherhood of working with imperialism and the reactionary forces in Egypt to gain political power. Although the military government managed to weaken its last serious domestic rival, it still faced the problem of what to do with hundreds of arrested Islamists. Bringing them to court could possibly trigger political violence, but freeing them without charge would demonstrate its own weakness. In mid March, Muslim Brotherhood organizations from all Arab countries met in Damascus to discuss the situation, express support for their arrested Egyptian Brothers, and call for greater efforts to rid the Middle East of imperialism. After his sudden release from prison later that month, al-Hudaybi condemned all negotiations with the British and called for *jihad* in the Suez Canal Zone.[22]

The row with the Muslim Brotherhood happened just at the time when Turkey and Pakistan signed the US-sponsored bilateral military agreement in February of 1954. The prospect of including Iraq in the military arrangement divided the Arab Middle East. It not only threatened Egypt's neutralist leadership in the Arab world, but possibly made negotiations on Suez more difficult. In late April, King Saud visited Pakistan to discuss what he considered the negative implications of the Turkish–Pakistani pact for unity in the Arab Middle East. On his advice, Zafarullah Khan visited Cairo in mid May to allay Egyptian fears.[23]

The Turkish–Pakistani pact ultimately triggered closer Egyptian–Saudi cooperation. On June 11, 1954, the two countries announced the creation of an Arab collective security arrangement, which included the merger of their army commands. The new pact was supposed to provide Arab states with an alternative to joining the Turkish–Pakistani pact and thereby guarantee Arab unity against British imperialism at Suez. Yet the Turkish–Pakistani pact and the Pakistani proposal of an Islamic Front, mentioned above, divided the Arab League Council at its meeting in late June. In August 1954, during a pilgrimage to Mecca, Nasser met King Saud and Pakistani Prime Minister Mohammad Ali Bogra. The first meeting of the Islamic Congress (al-Mutamar al-Islami), as it later became known, ostensibly focused on Muslim unity, but essentially was designed by Egypt and Saudi Arabia to contain Pakistani pan-Islamist initiatives. The three leaders decided to meet yearly in Mecca during the annual pilgrimage season and to facilitate the pilgrimage to the holy city for ordinary Muslims. Nasser also agreed with Bogra to collaborate in arms procurements; in return, Pakistan promised to abstain from further military alliances with powers outside the Middle East. A month later, the Egyptian leader used the momentum to create an Islamic Center, in Cairo, as a think tank for Islamic policy in the Middle East and Africa.[24]

While the Islamic Congress to a certain degree was a reaction to the Turkish–Pakistani pact, it also helped the Egyptian regime to compete with the political appeal of the Muslim Brotherhood. The illegal but still powerful Islamist organization was unwilling to accept the Egyptian–British agreement on Suez that was initialed on July 27, 1954, and which envisioned complete UK military withdrawal within two years. It continued to engage in violence against British military installations in the Suez Canal Zone. In August, after his return from Mecca, Nasser labeled the Muslim Brothers enemies of the government. Not shy to counter-escalate, the Islamist organization called Nasser a traitor.[25]

The conflict between the secular regime and the Islamist organization reached its peak on October 26, 1954 – a week after the formal signing of the Suez agreement – when a working-class member of the Brotherhood attempted to assassinate Nasser. In the wake of the incident, a pro-regime mob rioted against the Islamist organization, and thousands of Muslim Brothers were arrested. In mid November, Nasser ordered the removal of Naguib from the presidency on the pretext of his alleged involvement in the assassination attempt. The execution of six Brothers on December 7 triggered protests by several delegations participating in the concurrent meeting of the Arab League Council in Cairo. Yet Nasser was convinced that the Muslim Brotherhood should be crushed once and for all. In a *Foreign Affairs* article in early 1955, he denounced the Islamist Organization as backward and "contrary to the spirit of Islam."[26]

If Nasser had thought that he had solved both his internal and external problems by the turn of 1954/55, he was mistaken. While the Muslim Brotherhood would remain weakened for a decade, the Saudi–Egyptian–Pakistani Islamic Congress failed to keep fellow Arab states from concluding agreements with outside powers. On February 28, 1955, Iraq and Turkey signed the anti-Soviet Baghdad Pact, which the United Kingdom, Pakistan, and Iran would join before the end of the year. In the context of the impending Asian–African Conference in Bandung in April, Nasser responded by sending the general secretary of the Islamic Congress, Anwar Sadat, on a six-week trip to Saudi Arabia, Yemen, Kuwait, Qatar, Malaya, Indonesia, India, Afghanistan, and Pakistan to discuss closer Islamic collaboration.[27]

Pakistan forced the issue of future pan-Islamist collaboration onto the agenda in late summer. Despite Egyptian efforts, the Islamic Congress had not grown in members beyond the original three when it convened for its second meeting in Mecca in August 1955. Quite the opposite: in the previous month, Pakistan had announced its intention to join the Baghdad Pact, breaking its promises made at the meeting a year before. But Egypt's disappointment with Pakistan's betrayal was insincere. In September, the month in which Pakistan formally joined the Baghdad Pact, Nasser himself concluded the famous arms deal with the USSR and Czechoslovakia. At the third meeting of the Islamic Congress in Mecca in early April 1956 and in meetings later that month, only Egypt and Saudi Arabia participated; Pakistan was not even asked to attend. The two countries, however, invited Yemen to join in their military arrangements. The resulting trilateral alliance was directed not only against the Baghdad Pact but also, in anti-imperialist fashion, against the British positions in the so-called Protectorate of Aden at the mouth of the Red Sea.[28]

The Suez Crisis eventually undermined this pan-Islamist alliance as well. Not only was Pakistan's Suhrawardy offended by Nasser's supposedly pro-Soviet foreign policy, but several Arab leaders had grown skeptical about Egypt's recent flirtation with the USSR. While Nasser's anti-imperialist rhetoric in 1956 had produced widespread popular support in the Middle East, Arab governments generally were critical about his policies during and after the Suez Crisis. The following year, Riyadh ended its support for the Islamic Congress, leaving Cairo to run it alone – without any success. While Saudi Arabia subsequently moved closer to the United States, and, as we will see below, developed its own, conservative variant of pan-Islamism, Egypt moved politically toward the left. Still, Nasser continued to invoke Islam with the purpose of denouncing communists at home. Starting in 1961, he also reorganized Egypt's premier university – al-Azhar – as an anti-imperialist and revolutionary tool to promote state-sponsored Islamic education throughout the Muslim world.[29]

In the decade after its second ban in 1954, some members of the Muslim Brotherhood underwent ideological radicalization. One of their most influential thinkers was the poet and literary critic Sayyid Qutb, who had grown disenchanted with the United Kingdom in World War II and with the United States during an extended stay in 1948–50. He joined the Brotherhood during the period of 1951–54 when it was briefly legal. Initially, in 1952, he supported the Free Officers' coup, but withdrew from work in the military government the following year. Immediately before and during his imprisonment from 1954 to 1964, Qutb produced several of his most influential writings. Some took cues from Maududi's criticism of Pakistan as a non-Islamic state. In general, he promoted revivalist Islamic ideas, adopted strongly anti-imperialist, anti-Western, and anti-communist positions, and called for the establishment of an

Islamic society even by means of *jihad*. A year after Qutb's release in mid 1965, Nasser's regime started once more to crack down on the activities of the still illegal Brotherhood and arrest many of its leading members, accusing them of masterminding a coup d'état. Simultaneously, the Saudi government uncovered a plot to kill King Faisal that was run by the Saudi branch of the Muslim Brotherhood and headed by a Saudi prince. The mass trials against the arrested Brothers in Egypt in the spring and summer of 1966 occurred against the background of popular dissatisfaction with the regime's economic and political performance. On August 20–21, seven members received death sentences and over a hundred long prison terms. On the 29th, three were hanged – Qutb among them.[30]

Within a year, the June War brought the *Naksa* to both the wider Arab world and Nasser's secularism. The experience of defeat amounted to a second birth of the Muslim Brotherhood. To some of Nasser's disappointed followers, the still outlawed Islamist organization appeared to be the only way out of the humiliation; others turned away from secularism by converting to other reformist versions of Islam. The Egyptian Islamist writer Muhammad Jalal Kishk even saw defeat in divine terms. According to him, the Jews had won in 1967 because they had been devout to their God; Muslims had lost because the false doctrines of nationalism and socialism had led them astray from Islam. Against the background of political unrest and economic problems in Nasser's Egypt in the late 1960s, the ideas of the Islamist martyr Qutb began to appear prophetic to many disillusioned citizens. For some Islamists, the *Naksa* turned into the transformative event of their lives.[31]

Nasser's successor, Sadat, faced a major political dilemma in late 1970. On the one hand, he understood that Egypt needed to find accommodation with Israel after two decades of bloodshed. On the other hand, he was a devout Muslim who had collaborated with al-Banna's Muslim Brotherhood in anti-British activities in World War II and had kept in contact with Islamist leaders as a member of the Free Officer's group and the Nasserite regime. He also recognized the danger to the life of any Egyptian politician who dared to recognize Israel. The Muslim Brotherhood had always been staunchly anti-Israeli, and Islamist radicals, inspired by Qutb's writings on *jihad*, using violence in the first half of the 1970s against all those Egyptian Muslims – officials and non-officials – whom they considered apostates. Still, Sadat sought rapprochement with the Islamists in the context of his anti-Soviet foreign and anti-leftist domestic policies. Hoping that he could pacify their passions and bind them into the body politic, the Egyptian president released Muslim Brothers, some of whom had been imprisoned for many years, in the period of 1971–75. Though radical Islamists started to commit violence, Sadat's collaboration with the Brotherhood was relatively successful – until 1977, when he went on a surprise visit to Jerusalem, as described in Chapter 20.[32]

Saudi Arabia

In control of Mecca and Medina since the mid 1920s, Saudi Arabia was in the pre-eminent position to establish its own brand of pan-Islamism. Unlike the governments of Pakistan or Egypt, which used religion mostly for instrumental purposes, the Saudi emirate (monarchy after 1932) promoted Islam for a mix of political and religious reasons. In the eighteenth century, the emirate had made conservative Wahhabism the state-sponsored form of Islam in exchange for political support from the religious establishment. The reformist-purist Wahhabi movement aimed at liberating Islam from foreign, particularly Ottoman, and other sectarian, mainly Sufi and Shia, influences. Still, when the Turkish Republic abolished the Caliphate in 1924, Saudi Arabia opposed the recreation of the Islamic institution, even under its own leadership.[33]

Although the Saudi emirate/kingdom remained small in terms of population during most of the twentieth century, its wealth in oil translated into increasing influence throughout the Islamic world, particularly in the second half of the Cold War. Since 1933, Saudi Arabia and the United States had jointly developed the kingdom's oil fields, which led not only to rising elite prosperity in the Arab country but also to a *quasi*-alliance between the conservative monarchy and the liberal democracy. Riyadh was drawn to Washington in and after World War II because the Americans, unlike the British, were both anti-imperialist *and* anti-communist.[34]

By the mid 1950s, Saudi Arabia had become critical of the Egyptian-sponsored Arab League, which it considered ineffectual in the struggle against Israel. At the same time, however, it agreed with Egypt on opposing formal alliances in the Cold War. Saudi Arabia even became a founding member of the Non-Aligned Movement in 1961, although it continued to receive military support from the United States. The agreement on the creation of the Egyptian–Saudi military command and the establishment of the Islamic Congress in Mecca, both in 1954, were logical consequences of its policy of creating Arab security structures that excluded all formal external influence from the Middle East. Yet, after Nasser's announcement of the Soviet and Czechoslovak arms deal in September 1955, Saudi doubts about Egypt started to grow. The pro-Soviet leanings of the Egyptian leader during and after the Suez Crisis further disturbed the conservative Saudi monarchy. By early 1957, the kingdom was willing to cooperate even more closely with the United States, although it still did not enter into a formal alliance beyond the military cooperation agreement of 1957.[35]

The power-sharing agreement between King Saud and his brother, Prince Faisal, of March 22, 1958, marked a turning point for Saudi pan-Islamism in the long term. Faisal, who had been involved in Saudi external relations since the 1930s, had articulated foreign policy positions that strongly opposed non-Islamic influence in the region while being anti-communist and anti-Zionist at the same time. Even if he supported the anti-communist arrangement with the United States, he believed that Muslims worldwide should not engage with Cold War blocs but find their identity and unity within Islamic civilization. After March of 1958, Saudi foreign policy seemed to align briefly with Egypt, which had just formed the United Arab Republic with Syria. This tentative rapprochement happened in the wake of the Egyptian revelation of a Saudi plot to kill Nasser in March 1958 – a scandal which had helped the Saudi royal family to force the overspending and erratic Saud into a power-sharing agreement with Faisal. Yet, once the Egyptian leader started to use Islam as a political tool against conservative Arab regimes, relations deteriorated once more. Starting in the late 1950s, Saudi Arabia offered refuge to persecuted Muslim Brothers. In May 1961, it invited Islamists from countries as far as sub-Saharan Africa and South Asia – including exiled Muslim Brothers and the Pakistani Islamist Maududi – to a non-governmental Islamic Conference in Mecca. During the annual pilgrimage season in May 1962, the kingdom established the non-governmental Muslim World League (Rabitat al-Alam al-Islami), which provided financial support to older organizations – like the Pakistani World Muslim Congress and the Muslim Brotherhood's General Islamic Congress – and coordinated their activities. In September 1962, the Yemeni revolution and civil war further deepened Egyptian–Saudi antagonism for half a decade.[36]

Before Saudi Arabia was able to challenge Egypt, however, it had to resolve the conflicts within the power-sharing agreement between the ailing and politically unpredictable Saud and Faisal. By November 1963, Saud had resigned himself to a ceremonial role. Five months later, he was sent into exile, and within another year, Faisal officially replaced him as king. By late 1966, in an ironic twist, the deposed monarch accepted Nasser's offer of exile in Egypt, despite past conflicts and assassination plots, and in return provided support to the former rival in the Yemeni conflict against his own brother. Shortly after the *de facto* assumption of power in late 1963, Faisal announced a social reform and economic modernization program, to be implemented with

American help. At the same time, he called on Arab countries to force Israel into suing for peace within five years. It was in this context that the new king started to promote his religious Wahhabi version of pan-Islamism throughout the Muslim world. The trigger was Indonesia's proposal in March 1964 to organize an Asian–African Islamic Conference in Bandung within twelve months, just before the tenth anniversary of the original Asian–African Conference in April of 1965. Saudi Arabia seized the opportunity to fund it, but withdrew from the actual conference shortly before its opening, because it had realized that Sukarno's pro-Chinese government was trying to use the gathering for its secular and anti-Indian policies. A month later, at the second congress of the Muslim World League in April 1965, Faisal finally unveiled his plan for an Islamic Pact. Its objectives were manifold: anti-communist, anti-Israeli, pro-Palestinian, anti-Nasserite, and supposed to supersede the Arab League.[37]

Subsequently, he tried to attract like-minded Muslim countries, such as Iran, Jordan, Pakistan, Turkey, Morocco, Tunisia, and several sub-Saharan African countries. His visit to Iran on December 8–14, 1965, aimed at removing bilateral territorial disputes in the Gulf and at laying the ground for the establishment of an Islamic alliance that would replace the American-led CENTO and fill the vacuum once the United Kingdom had decolonized the Trucial States (today's United Arab Emirates), Qatar, Bahrain, and Kuwait. When the Saudi king visited Jordan in late January 1966, his counterpart, Hussein, was not enthusiastic about the idea of a trilateral alliance with Shia Iran and Sunni Saudi Arabia, since it would divide the Arab world further. However, Faisal compared his vision of Islamic Unity with the recent second Vatican Council in Rome, in which Christians from various denominations had seemingly come together in unity. Nasser's Egypt reacted by portraying the Saudi initiative as an attempt to undermine the Arab League and keep the Western imperialists in the Middle East – a claim that Faisal publicly rejected.[38]

In April 1966, Faisal visited yet another anti-communist country in the region – Pakistan. Military dictator Ayub Khan supported the idea of an Islamic Pact in return for economic assistance. Faisal's visit to Pakistan's long-standing ally Turkey in late August was, however, not successful at all, but Morocco, Guinea, Mali, and Tunisia were receptive to Saudi ideas a few weeks later. Against the background of these Saudi initiatives, Nasser revived the Islamic Congress, which he and King Saud had co-founded in 1954 out of anti-Pakistani motives, by inviting representatives of selected Muslim countries to Cairo in October. At the same time, the Saudi plan for an Islamic Pact seemed to fade because of the rising Arab–Israeli military tensions that started in November 1966.[39]

The *Naksa* in June 1967 undermined Nasser's claim to lead the Arab world. Accordingly, by mid August, Saudi Arabia proposed Muslim unity outside the Arab League. The kingdom and the three non-Arab countries Pakistan, Turkey, and Iran envisioned an Islamic Summit in lieu of the Arab League meeting in Khartoum in August. Yet Nasser's subsequent rapprochement with King Faisal over Yemen and the temporary cooling of Saudi–Iranian relations undercut any such designs for some time. Only in October 1968 did Saudi Arabia successfully host a conference on Islamic theology and the Palestinian Question in Mecca. It brought together four pan-Islamist organizations – the Saudi Muslim World League, Pakistan's World Muslim Congress, the Muslim Brotherhood's General Islamic Congress, and the Indonesian Afro–Asian Islamic Organization. Its resolutions called for *jihad* to liberate the holy sites in Jerusalem, requested all Muslim countries cut relations with Israel, demanded minority rights for the Muslims living in non-Islamic majority states, and announced the creation of an Islamic development fund.[40]

The fire at the Al-Aqsa Mosque in Jerusalem on August 21, 1969, eventually caused the Saudi breakthrough in pan-Islamist leadership. In its wake, Nasser called for military action against Israel, and King Faisal even for *jihad*. An emergency Arab League meeting in Cairo on August 25 did not lead to a joint policy, but at least prompted an agreement to convene an Islamic Summit that included Muslim countries beyond the Arab world. Even Nasser supported a decision that essentially amounted to a victory for Faisal.[41]

The first Islamic Summit in Morocco on September 22–24, 1969, gathered delegates from 24 of the 40 invited predominantly Muslim countries. All participants – including those who had established diplomatic relations with Israel, like Iran and Turkey – condemned the Jewish state, called for international pressure to force its withdrawal from territories occupied in 1967, and demanded respect for the rights of the Palestinians. Yet the deep divisions within the Muslim world were clearly visible even before the summit, as Nasser and King Faisal fought over the agenda. While the Egyptian leader himself could not attend due to illness, the radical regimes in Iraq and Syria boycotted the meeting. Pakistan prevented the participation of the hastily invited Indian ambassador to Morocco because he was Sikh. In the end, conflict among participants led to the adoption of a mere declaration, not a binding resolution.[42]

Despite these disagreements, the summit was a big boost for Saudi pan-Islamism. It convinced Nasser to restore relations with Faisal in December, although the Saudi king continued to consider Egypt's president a Soviet stooge in the Middle East. The first Islamic Foreign Ministers Conference in Jedda in late March 1970, which met to discuss Jerusalem and Palestine, decided to establish the Organization of the Islamic Conference (Munazzamat al-Mutamar al-Islami). Yet Iraq and Syria once more boycotted the Saudi-inspired outfit, and Egypt, Sudan, and Libya were against establishing a secretariat for the organization because they feared that it could be used to spread Islamic conservatism.[43]

Following Nasser's death in late September 1970, his successor, the more devout Sadat, cooperated closely with Saudi Arabia. Faisal had worked with Sadat in the 1950s when Riyadh and Cairo had established the short-lived Islamic Congress. In late 1970, the Saudi king hoped to resume this personal relationship in order to convince Egypt that cutting relations with the USSR might entice the United States to help obtain Israeli withdrawal from territories occupied in 1967. Throughout 1971, Riyadh acted as mediator between Cairo and Washington. The Egyptian–Soviet Treaty of Friendship and Cooperation in May did not slow down the rapprochement between the two Arab countries. The Indian intervention in the Pakistani civil war, which lead to the breakup of the Muslim bi-territorial country at the turn of 1971/72, reinforced Saudi interests in improving bilateral affairs with Egypt to strengthen Islamic unity. The third Islamic Foreign Ministers Conference in Jedda, in early March 1972, condemned the creation of Bangladesh as anti-Islamic, despite the fact that it was a Muslim nation. The conference also decided on a *jihad* fund against Israel. With Saudi financial assistance and political backing, Sadat eventually expelled Soviet military advisers in mid July 1972, in the hope of improving relations with the United States. Although Saudi Arabia in 1973 was initially skeptical about Egyptian plans to attack Israel in the coming October War, it joined other oil-producing Arab countries in increasing prices, cutting production, and imposing an oil embargo.[44]

The rapprochement with Egypt paralleled a similar development in Saudi Arabia's relationship with Pakistan. As mentioned above, the bilateral relationship had suffered in 1955, once Karachi had decided to engage with American Cold War alliance building, but improved with Faisal's visit to Islamabad in 1966. In the wake of the June War in 1967, the two countries concluded a military agreement that included weapon deliveries by Islamabad to Riyadh. On Saudi Arabia's urging, the second Islamic Foreign Ministers Conference in December 1970 was convened in Karachi, in recognition of Pakistan's earlier pan-Islamist policies. Zulfikar Ali Bhutto, the first president after the end of the military dictatorship in December 1971, accentuated Islam in domestic and foreign policies. For opportunistic reasons, he allied with Pakistani Islamists, like Maududi, who had rejected the creation of the secular nation state in 1947. Bhutto's Pakistan also revived the focus on the Middle East from the immediate post-independence period. Anyway, the loss of East Pakistan had turned the rump-state from a South Asian country into part of the extended Middle East. The crowning victory of this new policy was the decision of the Muslim world, urged by Saudi Arabia, to award Pakistan with hosting the second Islamic Summit in Lahore in early 1974. The congress not only marked Pakistan's final integration into the wider Middle East, but was also a general success for Muslim unity and purpose. Furthermore, the conference accepted Bangladesh into its midst while accrediting the PLO as the sole representative of the Palestinians. Finally, the oil-producing countries, particularly Saudi Arabia and Iran, committed 1 percent of their oil revenues to the funding of the recently established Organization of the Islamic Conference.[45]

By the time of King Faisal's assassination at the hands of a disgruntled royal prince in March 1975, Saudi Arabia had developed into the pan-Islamist leader even beyond the Arab world. Large oil revenues had turned the kingdom into the richest Arab economy, enabling it to expand its political and religious influence abroad. By the first half of the 1970s, Saudi Arabia had re-established close relations with the governments of two important Muslim countries – Egypt and Pakistan – after it had supported Islamists in both in the previous decade. In parallel, Egypt and Pakistan sought rapprochement with their former domestic opponents and Saudi Arabia's Islamist associates in the wake of Sadat's and Bhutto's rise to power in 1970 and 1971, respectively. Thus, this emerging transnational partnership included an anti-communist Saudi Arabia, a pro-Western Egypt, a Pakistan drifting toward neutralism in the Cold War, and Islamists who were simultaneously anti-Soviet and anti-American. The Saudi-led network of various Islamist movements in the world would become critical in the wake of the Egyptian–Israeli peace agreement and the Soviet intervention in Afghanistan in 1979, as Chapter 20 reveals.[46]

Iran

By and large, Iranian pan-Islamism developed independently from its Pakistani and Arab counterparts. It emerged as a reaction to the growing authoritarianism of the Shah's regime, but only became a major international force after the success of the revolution in 1979, which is also the topic of Chapter 20. A quarter of a century earlier, the overthrow of Prime Minster Mohammad Mosaddeq and the return of Shah Mohammad Reza Pahlavi in August 1953 had insured that Iran would adopt a pro-Western stance – at least for some time. Yet the first decade of the Shah's rule was a period of political autocracy and economic standstill. Given increasing popular dissatisfaction and his own fears about a coup, Mohammad Reza took forward action in 1963 by launching the *White*

Revolution. The initiative included land reform, nationalization of forests and pastures, increased franchise (including for women), the strengthening of labor rights, and literacy campaigns to appeal to rural areas and the working class, while it also comprised privatization of state-owned businesses to provide an investment opportunity for compensated former landlords. The agenda included radical and reformist measures designed to address the economic malaise, but it did not include political reforms. Furthermore, by the mid 1960s, the Shah normalized relations with the USSR, indicating his intent to follow a policy of equidistance between the superpowers. Finally, Iran worked closely with Saudi Arabia in taking steps to control and eventually nationalize foreign oil companies operating in their respective countries, which, in the Iranian case, helped to finance the programs of the White Revolution.[47]

By the 1970s, the Shah's absolutism, the oil-revenue-fueled corruption, and the Westernization of society had generated opposition from communists, liberals, and particularly the *ulama*. In Shia Iran, religious scholars had traditionally played an important role in religious and political life. The end of the Ottoman Empire in 1918 and the Turkish abolition of the Caliphate in 1924 did not generate as deep a crisis for Shia Muslims as it did for Sunni Muslims. The creation of a modern central state under Reza Shah Pahlavi, the father of Shah Mohammad Reza, in the 1920s and 1930s was a much greater threat as it aimed at limiting the political power of the *ulama*. Still, many Islamic clerics and scholars supported the coup against the leftist Mosaddeq in 1953 in an alignment of political interests with the military and monarchist coup leaders, the United Kingdom, and the United States. The relationship between Shah and the *ulama* remained solid for the remainder of the decade, largely because they saw each other as bulwarks against communism and liberalism. But after the launch of the White Revolution in January 1963, political cooperation deteriorated over disagreements on land reform, local election laws, and the granting of extraterritorial rights to American civilian and military personnel. Quickly, the former partners found themselves in an open and even violent struggle over the right to make the kind of fundamental changes, which the White Revolution envisioned, to Iranian society. Members of the *ulama*, like the high-ranking Ayatollah (Islamic scholar) Ruhollah Khomeini, accused the Shah of being an apostate, while the regime responded by accusing the conservative *ulama* of working with its secularist enemy, Nasserite Egypt. Khomeini's six-week-long arrest in 1963 made him into a popular figure in the religious opposition and eventually into a first-rank Islamist leader. His continued hostility toward the regime, particularly his criticism of the Shah's granting of extraterritorial rights, led to his banishment to Turkey in November 1964 and exile in Najaf, one of the holiest Shia sites in neighboring Iraq, soon thereafter.[48]

In Najaf, Khomeini publicly rejected the Westernization of Iranian society and criticized the policies of the monarchy for being un-Islamic. But only by 1970, in his scholarly reflections on Islamic government, did he start to reject the monarchy itself as un-Islamic, infidel, and despotic. For that reason, believers had the duty not only to overthrow the un-Islamic monarch but also to replace the institution of the monarchy with absolute clerical rule. The intellectual sources of these changes in his thinking are not completely clear, but they might have come from older Shia writings on the state, from the reports about the situation in Iran by lower-class students who came to Najaf for study, and from the Islamist writer Jalal Ale-Ahmad. Even before officially breaking with the Tudeh (Communist) Party in 1948, Ale-Ahmad had turned to Islam. An early supporter of Khomeini, in 1962 he had published his famous book *Westoxication*, which in turn had a major intellectual impact on the charismatic cleric because of its criticism of Iran's Westernization under the Shah. In his revolutionary rhetoric, Khomeini called on all Muslims, regardless of the sectarian divide, to confront the West. But his anti-Westernism did not mean that he himself had turned communist or even pro-Soviet. Despite his borrowings from Marxism and his calls for an anti-Western revolution in Iran, he abhorred all foreign influence, and thus, by extension, rejected both superpowers.[49]

Although Khomeini's writings both addressed the whole *ummah* and were translated into Arabic, his focus in the 1970s was not yet on pan-Islamism but rather on the overthrow of the Shah's government in Iran. In exile in Najaf, he focused on working out the juristic foundations for clerical rule in Iran. But much of his criticism paralleled concepts developed by the Pakistani Islamist Maududi and the Egyptian Muslim Brother Qutb. One of Khomeini's associates, the cleric S. Ali Khamenei, even translated some of Qutb's work on Islamic ideology into Persian in 1975. Nevertheless, with substantial Shia minorities living in Pakistan, Afghanistan, Iraq, Syria, Bahrain, Saudi Arabia, and Lebanon, Iranian Islamist thinking had the potential to become pan-Islamist in due course. In the end, much of its intellectual appeal to Shias worldwide only unfolded *after* the revolution in Iran in 1979, which is a topic of Chapter 20. Once in power in Tehran, Khomeini had acquired the kind of influence that would allow him to call for similar revolutions in other Muslim states – and even the whole world.[50] Yet, as long as Khomeini was exiled in Najaf during the 1970s, there were only a few indications that the Islamist challenge to the Middle East, or the world, would come from anybody other than Arab Islamists.

Conclusion

By the mid 1970s, Saudi Arabia had emerged as an anti-communist partner of the United States that was allied with Pakistan and Egypt, and supported Islamic movements throughout the Sunni world. From the mid 1960s to the mid 1970s, the Sunni kingdom was even willing to cooperate with the Shia monarchy in Iran. Sadat's Egypt was a pro-American and anti-Soviet republic that used the Muslim Brotherhood to persecute communists at home, while it simultaneously sought rapprochement with Israel. Although the Muslim Brothers benefited from the reduction of repression in the short term, Sadat's policy toward Israel carried the danger of alienating them in the long term. Finally, Iran was sliding into an internal crisis under a Westernized and absolutist regime that oppressed the opposition, including the *ulama*. While some Islamists, such as those in Saudi Arabia and Egypt, were pro-Western in the Cold War, most rejected both superpowers as foreign meddlers.

Islamist – and by extension pan-Islamist – movements in the Muslim world were heterodox. Pakistan's version was non-Arab, Sunni, and complementarily governmental and non-governmental. Egypt's was Arab, Sunni, and competitively governmental and oppositional. Saudi Arabia's was Arab, Sunni, and royal. And Iran's was non-Arab, Shia, and oppositional. Even if some variants influenced each other intellectually, they mainly emerged from particular political circumstances and from different intellectual milieus. Maududi and Khomeini were Islamic scholars. Al-Banna and Qutb had studied education and philology, respectively, in secular institutions. The Saudi kings posed as self-proclaimed guardians of the Holy Sites. Pakistani and Egyptian leaders were promoters of Islam for the pragmatic advancement of national interest.

In terms of audience, pan-Islamists also differed from each other. Pakistani and Saudi pan-Islamism aimed at bringing together governments of the Muslim world, including from Sunni and Shia majority countries. However, Egyptian governmental and oppositional pan-Islamism mostly focused on the Arab (Sunni) world. The Iranian version concentrated at the beginning on Iran itself, but after the revolution in 1979 also on the Shia in the Arab world and eventually even the non-Muslim world. Successful pan-Islamists during the Cold War were only the Saudi monarchy and, after 1979, the Iranian *ulama*, even if they emerged in competition with each other. In comparison, the Pakistani and Nasserite versions of pan-Islamism had failed, mainly because they were secular and ostentatiously instrumental.

Part V

Europe between the Superpowers

Introduction to Chapters 14 to 16

As we shift our focus from Asia and the Middle East toward Europe, we encounter a world region where the Soviet challenge to the West had caused virtually all regional conflicts. This included the ideological competition between two economic blocs of Western and Eastern Europe, Germany's division, and the struggle over borders, human rights, and religion. Although Part VI (Chapters 17–19) reveals how the regional Cold Wars of Asia, the Middle East, and Europe were connected to each other in a myriad of ways, they were most clearly linked in the field of nuclear weapons (Chapter 14).

Chapter 14 begins with the nuclear projects of the victorious Big Three of World War II – the United States, the Soviet Union, and the United Kingdom – and how they motivated China, Israel, and France to embark on their own nuclear weapons projects by the mid 1950s. Although each of them reacted to unrelated global and regional developments, nuclear weapons still bound them together across geographical divides. In the second half of the 1950s, France provided aid to the Israeli project, while in 1963 the triangular negotiations of the Soviet–American–British Limited Test Ban Treaty estranged China and France from the Big Three to such a degree that it triggered Sino–French diplomatic recognition within half a year. Ultimately, the extraordinary quantity of nuclear weapons and delivery systems, which the United States and the USSR amassed by the late 1960s, set them apart from the United Kingdom and other nuclear powers in the elevated position of a *nuclear superpower duopoly*. However, the proliferation of nuclear weapons that had started in the 1960s was simultaneously co-responsible for the *regional diffusion of power* that tallied well with other global developments – China's reintegration into the world (Chapter 2), the rise of Gaullist France (Chapters 4, 14, and 15), and the emergence of Western European integration (Chapter 15).

Chapter 14 on nuclear weapons and Chapter 15 on Western European integration tell the parallel stories of the United Kingdom as a declining great power and of France's relative rise in the two decades after World War II. The United Kingdom ended the war militarily victorious but economically exhausted. Despite its hasty decolonization of South Asia and Palestine, it remained one of three ordering powers of the world by focusing on the Middle East as a brace to keep the remaining Empire together (Chapter 2), by embarking on its own nuclear weapons project (Chapter 14), and by briefly supporting Western European integration (Chapter 15). Still, the UK intervention at Suez in late 1956 damaged its standing in the Middle East. The subsequent decolonization of the Empire in Africa and the Middle East reduced British presence on the world stage. London's decision to rely on Washington's nuclear missile technology in the 1960s further undermined its status as a world power. The turn to the continent, most notably to France, during that time revealed that the United Kingdom needed Europe if it wanted to maintain global influence. In comparison, France experienced the reverse development in the two decades after World War II. Greatly diminished in its global stature by the German occupation during the war, Allied-liberated France was an unlikely candidate to become the leader of continental Europe. Yet Paris was a dedicated promoter of European integration from the beginning, and thus shaped the emerging European community with gentle support from the United States. In late 1956, in the wake of the Suez Crisis, it embarked on its own nuclear project to fortify its leading role in Europe, just as British power in the Middle East collapsed. With success achieved within one and a half decades, it surpassed the United Kingdom not only as a European but also as a nuclear power.

Chapters 15 and 16 contrast the economic organization of divided Europe on either side of the Iron Curtain. In a narrow sense, the European Community for Steel and Coal (ECSC) / European Economic Community (EEC) and the Council for Mutual Economic Assistance (CMEA) were reactions to the American announcement of the European Recovery Program (Marshall Plan) in June 1947 (Chapter 1). But the comparison between the ECSC/EEC and the CMEA reveals the fundamental difference between American hegemony and Soviet imperialism in Europe. The United States encouraged the ongoing integration, but usually did not impose its solutions. It was able to tap into long-standing Western European ideas and encouraged Western European leadership in the formation of the supranational community, but it refused to become a member. The Western European insight that integration would prevent another catastrophic war provided the internal glue that allowed the ECSC/EEC to succeed. In comparison, the USSR imposed contradictory economic ideas on Eastern Europe in the immediate post-war period, which turned out to be fatal birth defects for the CMEA. This organization was always dominated by its preponderant member, the Soviet Union, and never able to overcome the tensions between the economic nationalisms of its other members and the need for deeper integration in an increasingly complex world economy. The lack of a common economic experience prior to World War II and the imposition of communism on Eastern Europe deprived the CMEA of the glue to bind it together.

Chapters 14 to 16 thus combine several seemingly contradictory developments. They cover the trend toward a nuclear superpower duopoly in the global Cold War, the military and economic decline of the United Kingdom, the *regional diffusion* of military and economic power away from the Anglo–American powers toward the western half of the European continent, and the economic failure of the Soviet-led CMEA. These structural shifts jointly had a major effect on developments covered in Part VI (Chapters 17 to 19) and Part VII (Chapter 22).

14   Nuclear Weapons

Throughout the Cold War, the possession of nuclear weapons secured elevated status in international affairs.[1] Unlike the United States in World War II, the Soviet Union and the United Kingdom built, tested, and stockpiled nuclear weapons after the war in an attempt to extend their pre-eminent global status into the post-war period. But only the United States and the USSR succeeded in acquiring an enhanced status by the 1960s, thereby turning the equal relationship among the Big Three into a *nuclear superpower duopoly* during the second half of the Cold War. Due to technical and financial constraints, the United Kingdom lost great power status by the second half of the 1960s.

Other countries followed the same logic of securing status when they decided to build nuclear weapons. The People's Republic of China (PRC), Israel, and France all embarked on nuclear projects in the mid 1950s because they aimed at acquiring respect from the Soviet Union, the United States, regional neighbors, or any combination thereof. All three benefited from technical aid from one of the nuclear powers or other allies. Yet proliferation to this second generation of nuclear powers did not always lead to further proliferation to a third one. By the late 1950s, Washington and Moscow grew concerned about the numerical increase in nuclear powers, and thus took action, initially together with London, to impose an international non-proliferation regime in the 1960s. Not all second generation nuclear powers shared the goal of preventing further proliferation. Only Israel's strategy of *nuclear opacity* aimed at depriving its Arab neighbors of the pretext to seek nuclear weapons. France did not care much about proliferation, whereas China advocated it in order to break the nuclear monopoly by white people. Its first successful test in October 1964, however, triggered India's decision to go nuclear in an attempt to restore equal status, which in turn convinced Pakistan to seek nuclear weapons.

In structural terms, the Soviet–American nuclear competition made the two countries into *superpowers* by setting them *apart* from all other states, including the United Kingdom, by the second half of the 1960s.

For the rest of the Cold War, the two superpowers were committed to maintaining their elevated status while trying to deny other states equality. The USSR had always denied transferring nuclear knowhow to any of its Eastern European allies but not the PRC. In comparison, the United States had been willing to share military nuclear technology in a controlled fashion to maintain the deterrent capabilities of one ally – the United Kingdom – or to keep national nuclear ambitions of other allies – France and West Germany – at a low level. In the end, the Soviet–American policy of nuclear exclusivity since the 1960s achieved only a mixed record of success. It did not prevent the diffusion of power at the regional level; nuclear power did not translate necessarily into political or economic power, as previous chapters have shown and future ones will do. Even in the realm of nuclear power, exclusivity was no guarantee for absolute primacy. Paris refused to play along with Washington's nuclear stratagems. By the early 1970s, France even surpassed the United Kingdom in developing its own independent nuclear deterrent. West Germany turned into the most strident lobbyist for American nuclear commitments to Western European security in the 1970s. With the NATO double-track decision of late 1979, Bonn recommitted Washington to Western Europe's security through a regional nuclear deterrent, just half a year after the superpowers had reached an agreement on strategic weapons.

From Trilateral War Alliance to Nuclear Stand-Off

The United States launched its nuclear weapons program – codenamed "Manhattan" – at the end of 1941 in response to intelligence about National Socialist Germany's pursuit of a similar project. Neither President Franklin D. Roosevelt before his death in April 1945 nor his successor Harry S. Truman in the four months afterward envisioned the military use of the atomic bomb as a diplomatic tool to blackmail the USSR. They were determined to use the bomb, once it was ready, immediately, in the hope of ending the war quickly. Before the dropping of two American A-bombs on Hiroshima and Nagasaki on August 6 and 9, 1945, Truman was convinced of the instantaneous war-terminating capabilities of nuclear weapons: "Believe Japs will fold up before Russia comes in[to the war]," i.e. before August 15 as agreed at the Potsdam Conference a month before. "I am sure they will when Manhattan appears over their homeland." However, in the wake of the A-bombing of Japan, Washington decided to use its military power for diplomatic pressure against Moscow.[2] Hence, Hiroshima and Nagasaki tied World War II and the Cold War together.

The Soviet Union decided to pursue its own nuclear weapons program by March of 1943, in response to intelligence about the American program. The project suffered from war-related impediments but benefited from American technological knowledge obtained through espionage. Iosif V. Stalin drew three key lessons about nuclear weapons in the weeks after July 24, when Truman informed him about the imminent American use of the bomb against Japan during a break at the Potsdam Conference. Two of the three suggest that he had thought through the strategic implications of nuclear weapons much faster than the US president. First, he too believed that the A-bomb had war-terminating capabilities, i.e. that its use might end the war in the Pacific before the USSR had a chance to intervene and thereby make political claims in Asia. He thus moved the planned Soviet entry into the war against Japan ahead of its scheduled date in mid August. The actual Soviet attack on Japanese-held Manchuria fell in the three-day period between the American A-bombings – on August 8. After the Japanese offer of surrender on the 15th, both Truman and Stalin concluded that the A-bomb had forced Japan to capitulate, although Japanese archival evidence suggests that the Soviet military intervention closed the last avenue for Japan to seek a negotiated end to the war. Second, Stalin ordered the Soviet A-bomb project into high gear to catch up with the United States, regardless of the economic hardship that his war-torn country was experiencing after the war. He had deduced that the nuclear asymmetry possibly awarded the United States with political and diplomatic leverage over the Soviet Union. In effect, he did so even before the White House started to employ atomic diplomacy – the veiled threat of nuclear war for the purpose of extracting political concessions in bilateral negotiations – by September of 1945. Thus, the speedy Soviet acquisition of A-bombs was supposed to restore international status to the USSR. Third, with some delay, Stalin realized that nuclear weapons were primarily psychological weapons, despite their seminal use against Japan. Possible US nuclear blackmail in diplomatic talks, as would happen soon, would only work if the Soviet Union permitted itself to be intimidated. Consequently, when the United States actually used atomic diplomacy in the fall of 1945 in unrelated negotiations on European issues, it only led to uncompromising Soviet standpoints.[3] The interplay of US atomic diplomacy and the stiff Soviet response in the late summer and fall of 1945 contributed significantly to the unfolding of the global Cold War.

Attempts to place nuclear weapons under international control started in late 1945 after the United States had realized that its atomic diplomacy did not work. During the war, officials and nuclear scientists involved in the Manhattan project had already proposed some form of international control, but neither Roosevelt nor UK Prime Minister Winston Churchill were willing to share nuclear secrets with Stalin, whose commitment to the trilateral alliance they mistrusted. The American idea of sharing nuclear materials under UN supervision from late 1945 was primarily an attempt to break the diplomatic deadlock in Soviet–American relations. Within half a year, the US representative to the UN Atomic Energy Commission, Bernard Baruch, proposed the creation of a supranational body to control fissile material. But the Soviet–American mistrust, which was growing over the course of 1946, formed an insurmountable obstacle. At heart, Washington was not willing to disclose its nuclear secrets to Moscow or surrender its atomic monopoly as long as it lasted, and the Soviet Union did not expect this to happen. Hence, both sides played up their ideological disagreements in the public debate about the Baruch Plan at the United Nations, instead of trying to overcome them.[4]

After the plan's collapse in late 1946, the Cold War antagonism worsened for unrelated reasons. The Truman Doctrine of the following spring, the subsequent creation of the US National Security State, and the announcement of the Marshall Plan in mid 1947 collectively contributed to the Cold War division of Europe. The first Soviet test explosion of a nuclear device, a copy of the Nagasaki bomb built on the basis of espionage, on August 29, 1949, set off the Soviet–American nuclear arms race – a four-decade-long competition primarily for numerical dominance. When the Baruch Plan had been announced in 1946, the US nuclear stockpile stood at nine bombs, but it increased to 170 by 1949, to 1,169 by 1953, and to 22,229 by 1961. After the first Soviet test, the Truman administration also concluded that it needed to respond to the future Soviet acquisition of equal nuclear status by extending the race to thermonuclear bombs. Although the president understood that the extraordinarily powerful H-bomb (hydrogen bomb) had little military use, he nevertheless decided to build it. The rationale was simple: if the United States would not test, it would lose status and credibility once the USSR had succeeded in doing so. The United States detonated its first H-bomb on November 1, 1952, with the Soviet Union restoring equality in status with its own hybrid A-/H-bomb design on August 12, 1953. Yet the numbers of American and Soviet nuclear weapons never closely matched during Stalin's final years. From 1949 to 1953, the Soviet stockpile increased from one to 120, or from less than 1 percent of the US stockpile to 10 percent. While the United States committed its military strategy of deterrence to the construction of the *nuclear triad* of strategic bombers, land-based missiles, and submarine- and ship-based missiles during the 1950s, the Soviet Union relied on an outdated and insufficient bomber fleet despite attempts to develop long-range missiles.[5]

As the United States and the USSR used testing and stockpiling to reinforce status and deterrence, the United Kingdom joined the race for the same reason. British scientists had worked on the joint Anglo–American Manhattan project during World War II. After the war, the governing Labour Party and opposition Conservative Party agreed on the pursuit of an independent nuclear weapons program to ensure equality with the United States and the Soviet Union *and* to elevate the United Kingdom above the other Europeans. "If we are unable to make the bomb ourselves," Churchill's science adviser Lord Cherwell stressed in the early 1950s with an undisguised reference to the Empire, "we shall sink to the level of a second-class nation, only permitted to supply auxiliary troops, like the native levies who have been allowed small arms but not artillery." Originally, in 1946, Prime Minister Clement Attlee had supported American ideas to establish UN control over fissile materials. But in January 1947, once the Baruch Plan had collapsed, his cabinet made the formal decision to go nuclear, although preliminary work on the project had been conducted for more than a year. Lack of fissile materials and bureaucratic rivalries hampered the project until after the Soviet A-bomb test in late August 1949 and the start of the Korean War in June 1950. Churchill's return to office in October 1951 helped to focus and accelerate the project. But his cabinet understood that UK economic capabilities would never permit a complete replacement of US nuclear deterrent capabilities against the Soviet threat; at least, London could aim at enhancing its influence in Washington.[6]

The first British A-bomb test occurred on October 3, 1952, off the Australian coast. When both the United States and the USSR tested H-bombs within another ten months, the United Kingdom decided in mid 1954 to catch up to reinforce its status, although it too doubted the military utility of thermonuclear weapons. The first H-bomb test occurred on May 15, 1957. It helped to re-establish some notion of global status for the United Kingdom half a year after the disastrous Suez Crisis, which had significantly undermined the country's influence abroad. However, Great Britain not only suffered from economic constraints in building nuclear weapons but its self-developed bombers also turned out to be highly vulnerable in the case of war. With the Nassau Agreement of late 1962, Washington promised to provide London with submarine-based missiles to maintain deterrence. The first specially built British submarines went into service, with the American Polaris missile on board, in 1968, replacing the vulnerable bomber fleet.[7]

Nuclear Hopefuls, 1955–64

Several other countries embraced the logic of obtaining status by joining the nuclear club. The PRC, Israel, France, and the Federal Republic of

Germany (FRG; West Germany) all hoped to use nuclear weapons to enhance their positions at the global, regional, or national level. Communist China decided to embark on a nuclear weapons program in early 1955, primarily after it had become obvious that making the moral claim to membership in the United Nations, including the permanent seat in the Security Council, was futile. Like Stalin, Mao had understood early on, in 1946, that nuclear weapons were above all psychological weapons: "The atom bomb is a paper tiger which the US reactionaries use to scare people. It looks terrible, but in fact it isn't." A decade later, he even denied that a nuclear world war would be that horrific, because it would end the Cold War: "The whole world has 2 billion 700 million people, possibly it will lose a third [in a nuclear war, ... but] the imperialists will be hit completely, [and] the whole world will become socialist." But his China did not primarily seek nuclear weapons to bring about the communist end of world history. On the contrary, the PRC hoped that possession of nuclear weapons would establish a deterrent capability against, respect from, and ultimately equality with the United States in the existing world system. Moscow provided a significant amount of technological aid for the primary purpose of defusing Sino–Soviet tensions dating back to the Stalin period, but stopped in 1959 when ideological differences emerged. After the PRC had exploded its first nuclear device in mid October 1964, China raised the topic of UN membership within diplomatic channels. But Beijing had to wait another seven years, well beyond even its first H-bomb test on June 17, 1967, to accede to the international organization.[8]

Israel's quest for nuclear weapons had mainly a regional motivation. In the absence of ironclad security guarantees from the USSR or the United States, it hoped to gain Arab acquiescence to its existence, if not outright recognition, through military predominance in the Middle East. After the end of World War II, the Zionist leaders had already laid the foundations for Israel's doctrine of armed superiority. The 1955 decision to go nuclear was just another logical step. On October 22–24, 1956, Israel received promises of technical support from France, at the very moment when the two secretly negotiated with the United Kingdom on the joint intervention at the Suez Canal. Although President Charles de Gaulle canceled French assistance in May 1960 when he tried to restore relations with the Arab world in view of the impending negotiations over Algerian independence, his country's aid had still been sufficient to kick start Israel's bomb project. Unlike the United Kingdom and the PRC, which used testing to display their nuclear prowess for claims to global status, Israel chose another strategy to obtain regional pre-eminence. By all accounts, it did not undertake nuclear tests at all, although it probably had at least two warheads by 1967. Its strategy of *nuclear opacity* – of letting the

Arab neighbors guess at its capabilities and intentions – was a sufficient deterrent for military purposes, while this simultaneously denied a formal pretext for the Arab neighbors to seek nuclear weapons and thereby annul its deterrent capability. Israel thus remained an *undeclared* nuclear power.[9]

Defeat in the Suez Crisis in late 1956 convinced France to go nuclear, although it had made basic decisions about its nuclear program already two years earlier. Since World War II, the Fourth Republic had struggled to gain status equal to the United States and the United Kingdom. At least, de Gaulle had managed to obtain a permanent seat on the UN Security Council and a small occupation zone in Germany before he resigned in early 1946 over unrelated issues. A decade later, Paris was disappointed by Washington's lack of support for its policies during the final year of the First Indochina War in 1953–54 and the Suez Crisis in 1956. Soviet nuclear threats in the wake of the crisis in the Middle East convinced President of the Council of Ministers (prime minister) Guy Mollet, a socialist and long-time opponent of nuclear weapons, to launch a national A-bomb project to provide France with its own deterrent. Initially, Paris was willing to share nuclear secrets – both civilian and military – with West Germany and Italy. But once de Gaulle had returned to power in mid 1958, he rejected the idea of a European A-bomb. *La Grande Nation* was supposed to seize, not share, leadership of Europe, and thereby elevate itself to equality with the United States and the United Kingdom in NATO. The first French A-bomb test occurred on February 13, 1960, in the desert of Algeria, which at the time was still France's colony. Domestic detractors scoffed at de Gaulle's "bombinette," but, unlike the United Kingdom, France managed to build its own nuclear triad through its self-designed bombers, missiles, and submarines within a little more than one decade.[10]

In the process, France rejected cooperation with the Anglo–American partners in NATO. Since London was fearful that the Nassau Agreement of late 1962 would undermine the ongoing British application to join the European Economic Community (EEC), it convinced Washington to offer the same agreement to Paris. But de Gaulle did not want to risk the technical independence of the French deterrent force. On January 14, 1963, the president rejected not only the US missile offer but also the British application for EEC membership. Within eight days, he signed a treaty of friendship with Germany, and within three years, he expelled NATO from its headquarters in Paris. Considerations regarding international status eventually convinced de Gaulle to test an H-bomb, mainly because he wanted to beat Mao in that race. He did not succeed at that, nor did the French H-bomb test fulfill expectations of a publicity stunt when it occurred on August 24, 1968 – three days after the Soviet-led intervention in Czechoslovakia.[11]

West Germany's long-time first chancellor, Konrad Adenauer, never intended to embark on a national nuclear weapons program. The country's National Socialist past, NATO restrictions, and the domestic struggle over conventional rearmament before entry into the Western alliance in 1955 had erected prohibitively high political barriers. However, France's willingness to embark on a European bomb project between 1956 and 1958 seemed to bring the German co-possession of nuclear weapons into the realm of the possible. Ultimately, Adenauer's Germany sought limited access to decision-making and shared responsibility for American nuclear weapons within NATO. As Europe's main battlefield in a nuclear war, it wanted to have some say in the matter of nuclear planning. The country wanted to play the nuclear card to extract concessions from the USSR, possibly in the form of renouncing nuclear weapons in exchange for German reunification.[12] Yet the prospect of West German access to the nuclear button scared friend and foe, as we will see further below.

From the Thaw to Trilateral Nuclear Talks, 1953–61

The problem of nuclear proliferation occupied the United States and the Soviet Union for most of the Cold War. Originally, when Dwight D. Eisenhower entered the White House as the new president in January 1953, he was a proponent of worldwide proliferation. He had concluded that nuclear weapons were so powerful that they would make war meaningless. Thus, universal proliferation would establish a shared self-deterrence that would make the world safe for lasting peace. In retrospect, his idea might look reckless, but the reality was that the United States itself had released so much technical information about building A-bombs after August 1945 that it had helped to accelerate the Soviet program. Hence, in 1953, President Eisenhower did not face the question of whether or not proliferation would occur, but how he could shape it. He changed his mind when he received news about the global nuclear fallout from a large American atmospheric test in the Pacific in 1954. Radioactive poisoning as a result of continuous testing and, in the worst case, of nuclear war would make the world uninhabitable. By 1959, Eisenhower also started to doubt if all future nuclear powers would be sufficiently rational to see these weapons primarily as a self-deterrent: "The President ... could conceive of nothing worse than permitting Israel and Egypt to have a nuclear capability, as they might easily set out to destroy one another." Yet, despite such fears, Eisenhower had no problem with using veiled nuclear threats against China during the first and second Taiwan Straits crises in 1954/55 and 1958, respectively.[13]

Stalin's death in March 1953, less than two months after Eisenhower's inauguration, opened the possibility for the Soviet leadership to rethink nuclear strategy as well, though much time was lost to infighting over succession. Anyway, into the 1960s, the USSR suffered from a numerical disadvantage – its stockpile would remain at roughly 10 percent of the American counterpart – while it also lacked a delivery system beyond its inadequate bomber fleet. In an attempt to close the gap in the minds of the imperialists and to enhance Soviet standing in the world, Nikita S. Khrushchev started nuclear bluffing in November 1956, in the wake of the Suez Crisis, when he threatened the French and British imperialists with nuclear punishment by Soviet long-range nuclear missiles. No such missiles existed at that time, however. His country only achieved such a rocket capability in the period from October 4, 1957, to May 15, 1958, when it launched three progressively larger Sputnik satellites into orbit. But the spectacular triumph turned out to be a boomerang. Since the missile was excessively expensive, difficult to maintain, and unwieldy to operate, it could hardly be used in nuclear war. Only a few were deployed before Khrushchev axed the missile program in favor of developing two new, competing projects. Much worse, the Sputnik satellite launches convinced the United States to send medium-range nuclear missiles to the United Kingdom, Italy, and Turkey as a makeshift solution to restore deterrence. Moreover, the Eisenhower administration accelerated the long-range rocket program to close the supposed missile gap, and launched spy missions with high-flying U-2 airplanes to verify, or possibly invalidate, supposed Soviet nuclear capabilities.[14]

From the very beginning, the pursuit of nuclear weapons and the resulting arms race had met with internal criticism and popular opposition. As early as World War II, scientists in the Manhattan project had questioned the morality of nuclear weapons, as did Soviet nuclear scientists after Stalin's death. Appalled by the destructive power and the long-term health and environmental effects of the A-bombs that had been dropped on Hiroshima and Nagasaki, an informal coalition of peace activists, political and religious leaders, pacifists, and scientists from Japan, North America, Western Europe, and the Afro–Asian world demanded international control of fissile materials and even an end to the military use of nuclear power. Faced with such public demands, President Eisenhower responded with *Atoms for Peace* – a propaganda campaign to promote the civilian use of nuclear energy – in a speech at the United Nations in late 1953. The idea primarily aimed at mollifying critics at home and abroad. Given the global debate about nuclear fallout since 1954, Eisenhower later also added calls for a test ban in his push for *Atoms for Peace*. Yet this did not satisfy the expectations of the world's public opinion, which called for an outright ban of all nuclear weapons.[15]

Soviet–American–British talks on banning nuclear tests started in the fall of 1958 in the wake of global public pressure and due to three developments in their trilateral relations over the previous year: the renewed proposal for a test ban from re-elected President Eisenhower, the British H-bomb test, and the first Soviet Sputnik launch. But Khrushchev had withdrawn from the nuclear disarmament talks in Geneva in late 1957 to underline his newly found position of strength. In March 1958, he proposed a test moratorium, mainly for the purpose of splitting the unity of NATO in the context of the French offer of nuclear sharing with West Germany and Italy. Yet over the summer, Khrushchev grew troubled by the ideological radicalization of Mao, who was about to launch the radical phase of the Great Leap Forward. He worried about the extreme views of the Chinese leader about nuclear war – particularly the idea that it would end the Cold War with a communist victory – and about Mao's attempts to coerce the USSR into a nuclear exchange with the United States during the concurrent second Taiwan Strait Crisis. In the end, both convinced him to cancel nuclear assistance to China within a year.[16]

Before the end of 1958, the three nuclear powers agreed on the long-term goal of a test ban, but continued to bicker about how to control mutual compliance in the age before satellite reconnaissance. Khrushchev's concurrent ultimatum over the Berlin issue did not help to build trilateral trust, either. On the contrary, since both Moscow and Washington had turned the struggle over that divided city into a high-stakes game, any military conflict there could possibly escalate into nuclear war. At least, or so Khrushchev believed, he had obtained recognition as an equal in the global Cold War when he was invited to visit the United States in September 1959 – the first of the Soviet leaders ever to do so. In the talks with Eisenhower, Khrushchev ended the Berlin Crisis by withdrawing his ultimatum. The two leaders instead called for a French–American–British–Soviet summit in Paris for May 1960. But the Soviet leader himself ruined the four-power meeting after the USSR had managed to shoot down one of the American U-2 spy planes on May 1. The Soviet Union had tracked these flights for some time, and thus understood that the United States was trying to verify, or worse invalidate, Khrushchev's bluffs with nuclear missiles.[17]

Khrushchev decided to wait until early 1961, when a new American president would enter office, to reset relations with the United States. But John F. Kennedy started into his tenure poorly with a failed mission to liberate Cuba from Fidel Castro's revolution. Planned by the outgoing Eisenhower administration, the amphibious landing by Cuban exiles at the Bay of Pigs in mid April 1961 was a disaster. In early June, at the Vienna Summit, Khrushchev tried to browbeat Kennedy in revenge for the humiliation of the U-2 flights. Shortly thereafter, following the closure of the borders in Berlin, he decided to end the 1958 moratorium and to undertake a long series of nuclear tests, including the superbomb *Tsar Bomba*. The Soviet leader understood perfectly that the planned test with such a big thermonuclear device was a political stunt, since it was so large – even after Soviet nuclear scientists had negotiated its yield down by half – that it had neither military nor scientific use. *Tsar Bomba* was simply about size and intimidation. "Let this device hang over the heads of the capitalists, like a sword of Damocles," Khrushchev gloated before the October 30 test. He had announced the test publicly on August 31, using the false claim that the French tests earlier that year were in fact covert Anglo–American tests designed to circumvent the three-year moratorium. It was yet another one of Khrushchev's boomerangs. The announcement occurred one day before the opening of the first Non-Aligned Conference in Belgrade, alienating almost all of its anti-nuclear members immediately. Two weeks later, Khrushchev tried to hoodwink – albeit unsuccessfully – the Non-Aligned leaders Jawaharlal Nehru from India and Kwame Nkrumah from Ghana by claiming that the Soviet decision to test was a response to Western provocations in Germany that had caused the closure of the borders in Berlin. However, nine days before the political *Tsar Bomba* test on October 30, the Kennedy administration let the cat out of the bag: U-2 flights and early Corona satellites had confirmed that the USSR lacked the claimed missile capability. With neither a credible long-range missile capability nor the possibility of continuing his bluffs, Khrushchev was back to square one in the race for nuclear delivery vehicles.[18] No *Tsar Bomba* could change that.

The Cuban Missile Crisis and the Nuclear Test Ban Treaty, 1962–63

In August 1962, Washington offered Moscow renewed negotiations on a test ban – either comprehensive or limited. It seemed that the Kennedy administration had bowed to international and Non-Aligned pressure, but, in reality, the resurrection of Eisenhower's test ban idea had a hidden motive. Washington had grown concerned that Beijing would not be a rational nuclear player once it had tested a nuclear device. The White House hoped to include a mechanism in the test ban treaty that would terminate what it assumed was continued Soviet nuclear aid to China.

Khrushchev responded positively to Kennedy's idea of talking about nuclear arms limitation – but largely with the intent of covering up his own hidden agenda. By early 1962, the two competing nuclear long-range missile programs, which he had initiated after axing the missile that had launched the three Sputnik satellites, had suffered repeated setbacks and were nowhere near deployment. The USSR still lacked a reliable vehicle to deliver nuclear warheads to the American enemy in the case of a global war. Faced with US medium-range missiles, which Eisenhower had sent to the Turkish south shore of the Black Sea in 1958, a frustrated Khrushchev decided in April 1962 to give the Americans a taste of their own bitter medicine: "Why not throw a hedgehog at Uncle Sam's pants?" Because Cuba had turned to the USSR after the Bay of Pigs disaster, the Caribbean island became Khrushchev's Turkey from which he could threaten the United States with medium-range nuclear missiles in an attempt to restore strategic parity. While the Soviet Navy covertly moved rockets, warheads, related equipment, specialists, and troops across the Atlantic and along the US east coast to Cuba over the summer and fall of 1962, the Soviet government pretended to the Kennedy administration that it was ready to negotiate on the test ban.[19]

On October 22, 1962, the Cuban Missile Crisis burst onto the world stage, transfixing humankind for a long week. The United States had followed the Soviet military build-up on Cuba for months. Once Washington had evidence that Moscow – in contradiction to public and confidential reassurances – was stationing nuclear missiles on the island, President Kennedy publicly announced on the 22nd the imposition of a naval quarantine while demanding verifiable removal of missiles and nuclear warheads. As the world stood at the edge of nuclear war, Khrushchev blinked. His public agreement to withdraw the nuclear missiles damaged the global credibility of the USSR. However, he at least received Kennedy's secret assurance that the United States would withdraw the missiles from Turkey and abstain from overthrowing the Cuban regime. The crisis had several important consequences for international relations. First, the continued lack of a dependable nuclear delivery vehicle forced Moscow to focus on accelerating the development of its long-range missiles. Second, the Soviet Union thereby joined the United States in the symbolic race for numbers; within a decade, it had increased its stockpile of nuclear warheads to more than 50 percent of the American counterpart. Third, the Cuban Missile Crisis convinced Khrushchev to engage in serious test ban talks. The crisis actually had been a cathartic experience for him, as he told a visiting American journalist two months later: "If we don't have peace and the nuclear bombs start to fall, what difference will it make whether we are Communists or Catholics or

Capitalists or Chinese or Russians or Americans? Who could tell us apart? *Who will be left to tell us apart?* ... I was scared. ... I was frightened about what could happen to my country – your country and all the other countries that would be devastated by a nuclear war."[20]

Soviet–American–British test ban negotiations started at the turn of 1962/63. The three thus bypassed the Eighteen-Nation Committee on Disarmament at the United Nations, which encompassed five NATO members (including the United States, the United Kingdom, and France, which however boycotted the body), five Warsaw Pact members (including the USSR), four Non-Aligned, and four neutralist countries. The sticking point in the trilateral talks was Khrushchev's refusal to allow regular on-site inspections to verify the ban. He feared that permanently stationed foreign teams, even teams from Non-Aligned countries, would abuse their presence in the Soviet Union for espionage. But the radical Chinese propaganda during and after the Cuban Missile Crisis deeply worried the Kennedy administration. Washington wanted to sign any test ban treaty as long as it contained some form of a non-proliferation clause. In order to break the deadlock in the trilateral talks, the United States completed a series of underground tests to determine if global networks of seismographic stations could pinpoint the location of a test and help establish its precise yield. The successful tests made on-site inspections, which Khrushchev had blocked, unnecessary, as long as a test ban treaty limited testing to the underground. In the second half of July, diplomats of the Big Three negotiated the Limited Test Ban Treaty (LTBT) in Moscow. The minimum, on which they could agree, was the prohibition of testing in the atmosphere, the sea, and outer space, plus a weak non-proliferation regime – both of which fulfilled basic American wishes. Still, the treaty received a rousing welcome throughout the world, with the vast majority of countries acceding within five months.[21]

But the Soviet–American–British test ban treaty drove the PRC and France into each other's arms. It was negotiated and initialed at the time when the Soviet Communist Party and its Chinese counterpart were talking about ideological reconciliation, in parallel and in the Soviet capital as well. But the exchanges between the two hostile communist powers were not much more than shouting matches, until the initialing of the test ban treaty put an end to the undignified spectacle. Beijing understood that the LTBT was directed against its own nuclear ambitions. It quickly reacted by launching a global propaganda campaign for universal nuclear disarmament, while it secretly accelerated its own A-bomb program. The PRC succeeded in detonating its first nuclear device within less than fifteen months, on October 16, 1964. France, too, felt shunned. Despite the series of successful tests in the Algerian desert more than three years before, it was the only declared nuclear power that had not been invited to the test ban talks in Moscow. De Gaulle was primarily irritated at being denied recognition of his country's enhanced status. As the master of atomic France, he reached out to nuclear apprentice Mao in August 1963 with a feeler about establishing diplomatic relations. The clandestine negotiations quickly descended into a struggle about which of the two countries could enhance its international status at the expense of the other. Paris rejected Beijing's proposal for France to request recognition from the PRC publicly because this would have demoted de Gaulle to a mere petitioner before Mao. At the turn of 1963/64, the French president micro-managed the secret negotiations in Switzerland to dictate the terms of recognition to the PRC. After official recognition in late January 1964, de Gaulle considered it beneath France's dignity to heed the request of communist China to cut official links with its fraternal archrival, the Republic of China on Taiwan.[22] Although de Gaulle might have won the battle for status against Mao in early 1964, the French president still lost the race for the H-bomb against the Chinese nuclear newcomer, as mentioned above.

Toward the Nuclear Non-Proliferation Treaty, 1963–68

The weak non-proliferation clause of the LTBT was not sufficient to stop the spread of nuclear weapons. Bombing the Chinese nuclear project, as the Kennedy administration pondered in the summer of 1963, would have been at best a desperate attempt to delay the inevitable for a while.[23] Both the United States and the USSR were equally concerned that smaller powers, such as West Germany or Israel, would continue to aspire to nuclear weapons and thereby complicate international relations. The explosion of a Chinese atomic device in 1964 even threatened to set off a nuclear arms race in Asia. Hence, the Soviet Union and the United States focused on preventing further proliferation in the five years after the LTBT.

The USSR, other Eastern European countries, and even NATO members were concerned about West German access to nuclear weapons, particularly since the country hesitated ratifying the LTBT for almost a year. The West German vacillation had less to do with an outright rejection of non-proliferation than with denying East Germany the opportunity to gain status and diplomatic recognition in international relations by signing the treaty as well. Anyway, British–Soviet–East European concerns over West German access to nuclear weapons primarily aimed at Kennedy's proposal of establishing a Multi-Lateral Force (MLF). In April 1962, the American president resurrected a proposal of shared access to nuclear weapons. His goal was to counter the possibility of NATO's disintegration in the context of de Gaulle's quest for France's national *grandeur*. The MLF was about symbolic sharing in the form of twenty-five surface ships manned by multilateral NATO crews and armed with eight American nuclear missiles each. France opposed the project since it would enhance US influence in NATO at its own expense and possibly limit its control over its own independent nuclear forces. London rejected the idea since this kind of nuclear egalitarianism would have watered down its own elevated status in NATO while possibly allowing West Germany access to military nuclear technology. Not only were West Germany's friends dismayed, but also its enemies. Given that the USSR did not share military nuclear technology with the socialist countries in Eastern Europe, Warsaw and East Berlin tried to convince Moscow to push Washington to drop the MLF. Ultimately, Soviet and British pressure helped to erode American espousal within only a few years.[24]

When Lyndon B. Johnson succeeded the assassinated Kennedy as president in November 1963, the first proliferation issue which he faced was the potential nuclear arms race between Israel and Egypt. Concerned about proliferation, the Kennedy administration had managed, by mid August 1963, to extract a vague – though, as it turned out, insincere – Israeli pledge to use nuclear energy exclusively for peaceful purposes. The promise included permission for an unspecified number of American visits to the French-delivered reactor in the Negev town of Dimona. As the reactor neared completion at that very time, Egypt's Gamal Abdel Nasser put the rumored Israeli A-bomb project and other Israeli–Arab disputes on the agenda of the first Arab League Summit in January 1964. He had already warned the Kennedy administration in April 1963 that Egypt would launch a preventive war if Israel went nuclear. Faced with the possibility of renewed conflict, a nuclear arms race, or even both in the Middle East, the Johnson administration proposed the delivery of American-built nuclear-powered desalinization plants to Israel and Egypt, ostensibly to defuse the unrelated fresh water crisis, but in reality to obtain in return pledges from both countries to sign up for international control of their nuclear reactors. While Egypt had no significant nuclear power industry and thus agreed to the delivery of the plants, Israel understood the hidden agenda behind the proposal. Unsurprisingly, it did not sign up – and then even dragged its feet on the promised visits to Dimona – since it did not want to give up its opaque deterrence capabilities. The overall political changes, which the June War of 1967 brought to the Middle East, terminated the desalination project once and for all.[25]

Likewise, the Chinese nuclear test on October 16, 1964, raised the issue of non-proliferation once more. PRC embassies closely monitored the overwhelmingly positive reaction in the Afro–Asian world to the first non-white or "Afro–Asian bomb." However, communist China hoped in vain that the test would bring membership in the United Nations. Thus, during the first nine months of 1965, it supported Indonesia's quixotic attacks on the allegedly reactionary international organization, while it tried to exploit its nuclear success to seize and radicalize the Asian–African Movement as an alternative United Nations. Under the accurate assumption that Israel was clandestinely seeking nuclear weapons, Egypt turned to the PRC in November 1964 with a request for nuclear assistance. However, Cairo was one of Beijing's main adversaries in the struggle for control over the Asian–African Movement, and thus the possibility of a nuclear partnership vanished within less than a year. One of the few Afro–Asian countries that did not welcome the Chinese bomb test in October 1964 was India. It recognized that the Chinese nuclear test was an attempt to gain admission to the United Nations and to seize leadership in the Afro–Asian world. India's first prime minister, Jawaharlal Nehru, had understood the link between nuclear weapons and great power status as early as 1954, but remained an avid opponent of an Indian A-bomb project until his death a decade later. Still, since 1961, Indian nuclear scientists had advocated pursuing a nuclear weapons project in response to reports about China's program. Also, Delhi's diplomats had seen the Chinese attack on India across the Himalayas in October 1962 as an attempt to undermine their country's status in the Afro–Asian world and the Non-Aligned Movement. Unsurprisingly, after the Chinese bomb test two years later, Nehru's successor Shastri Lal Bahadur faced intense public pressure to catch up in the race for nuclear weapons, mainly because "the problem was now that China had them." Toward the end of the year, he took decisions that would ultimately lead to the explosion of an Indian nuclear device on May 18, 1974.[26]

The Johnson administration reviewed US non-proliferation policy at the end of 1964 in view of West German interests in nuclear weapons, the autonomy of the French nuclear project, the Chinese bomb test, the ensuing danger of Japan, India, and even Pakistan going nuclear, and continued concerns about a nuclear arms race in the Middle East. Although the American president initially rejected an internal proposal to seek an explicit non-proliferation treaty with the USSR, the White House soon revived the idea in light of intelligence suggesting that Israel and India were working toward the acquisition of nuclear weapons. At least, his administration finally gave up on the MLF by early 1966. But even if the United States wanted to negotiate with the Soviet Union on non-proliferation, the problem was how to get the other superpower to the negotiation table. Before 1966, Moscow refused to negotiate in earnest as long as Washington pursued the MLF. Afterward, the American intervention in Vietnam introduced "serious complications into Soviet relations with the United States," chairman of the Soviet Minister Council Aleksei N. Kosygin told UK Prime Minister Wilson in early 1966, adding: "The Americans talk of peace while pursuing aggression."[27]

Still, 1966 and 1967 brought limited rapprochement on non-proliferation among the two nuclear great powers. The complete break-down of Sino–Soviet relations in mid 1966, just before the launch of the Cultural Revolution in the PRC, induced Moscow to drop Vietnam as an obstacle to negotiations on non-proliferation with Washington, although the USSR continued to insist on barring the FRG from any access to nuclear weapons. West Germany's federal elections in late 1966 produced a coalition government between the Christian Democrats, who still pursued nuclear sharing, and the Social Democrats, who had rejected that idea a long time before. Although it took the FRG until late 1969 to commit formally to abstaining from nuclear weapons, the election result put the Soviet Union at sufficient ease to agree with the United States on the two non-transfer principles (articles 1 and 2 on active and passive proliferation) in what would become the Nuclear Non-Proliferation Treaty (NPT) of 1968. But despite the renewed possibility of a regional nuclear arms race in the wake of the Arab–Israeli war in early June of 1967, Kosygin and Johnson remained at loggerheads over both the Middle East and Vietnam during the Glassboro Summit later that month. As negotiations moved into the Eighteen-Nation Committee on Disarmament at the United Nations, the proposed Soviet–American frame-work of seeking a non-proliferation treaty without a commitment to nuclear disarmament faced worldwide opposition. The committee's members from both socialist Eastern Europe and NATO rejected the draft treaty's inherent division of the world into a small number of nuclear *haves* and a large number of *have-nots*, because it would cement global power and status in the hands of only a few. The Non-Aligned and neutralist members complained that the draft treaty did not even commit the *haves* to any form of nuclear disarmament. India, a Non-Aligned committee member, opposed signing any treaty as long as "China, who is full of hostile intentions toward our country," refused to join.[28]

In an example of hitherto unseen bilateral cooperation, Washington and Moscow shepherded the draft treaty through the United Nations in the first half of 1968. The two used diplomatic pressure on their allies – NATO and the Warsaw Pact – and befriended states – Latin America and

Africa – to have the treaty ready for signature by July 1, before the non-nuclear powers were scheduled to meet at a conference focusing on nuclear disarmament. The rush left a number of dissenting UN members – France, India, and Israel, but also Argentina and Brazil – deeply disappointed. The widespread dissatisfaction with the absent Soviet–American commitment to nuclear disarmament was an important, though not the only, impetus for the Soviet–American strategic arms limitation talks that would start soon. With ratification by the necessary number of states, the treaty finally went into force in 1970. American interests in getting the treaty there allowed the USSR to pressure the United States to react only mildly to its military intervention in Czechoslovakia in August 1968. Non-proliferation thus not only cemented the division of the world along nuclear capabilities but also reinforced once more the division of Europe.[29]

The Nuclear Superpower Duopoly: Soviet–American Negotiations on SALT and ABM, 1968–72

The late 1960s thus marked the final transition from the World War II cooperation among the Big Three toward a Soviet–American nuclear superpower duopoly, which would characterize global politics throughout the second half of the Cold War. Over the course of the 1960s, the USSR had caught up with the United States in number of nuclear warheads and managed to establish its own nuclear triad of bombers, long-range missiles, and submarine-based missiles. Late in the decade, the two powers thus passed the threshold where each side had sufficient nuclear capabilities to endure a full-scale nuclear attack by the other while still being capable of retaliating with a full-scale counter-strike. *Mutual Assured Destruction* (MAD) made nuclear war between the two less likely, but also set them as *superpowers* apart from all the other nuclear powers.[30] For the United Kingdom, this meant a major *loss* of status. In the 1950s, London had tried to catch up with Washington and Moscow in full knowledge that its economic and technological capabilities would not suffice to establish a nuclear force capable of defending the country independently. The Nassau agreement of late 1962, which provided American missiles, had saved the small UK nuclear deterrent force but made it dependent on US delivery vehicles. While the United Kingdom had been a party to the trilateral LTBT negotiations in Moscow in mid 1963, it was, however, only one of the eighteen members of the Committee on Disarmament at the United Nations in the negotiations leading to the NPT five years later.

Still, London believed it had one final arrow in its quiver – France. After the Nassau deal had killed its first application to join the European

Economic Community in early 1963, the United Kingdom reapplied in 1967. Even before becoming prime minister in mid 1970, the conservative Edward Heath had understood that his country needed to overcome the liability of the special American–British nuclear relationship. London was willing to offer Paris a special nuclear relationship in the hope of overcoming French mistrust and simultaneously lessen its own nuclear dependence on the United States. Although the incoming administration of US President Richard M. Nixon was skeptical about the EEC, it needed UK support in the impending nuclear negotiations with the USSR. Thus, Washington was willing to support Anglo–French nuclear cooperation – and even provide Paris with some nuclear assistance – in order to bring post-Gaullist France back into the military structures of NATO. Ultimately, France's preference for the advantageous status quo – the country could retain its independent nuclear triad while it enjoyed NATO's *de facto* protection given its central geographical location in Europe – prevented the rearrangement of nuclear dependencies among the three Western powers. At least, Paris did not veto London's bid for EEC membership any longer, while the United Kingdom continued to depend on American nuclear technology as a hanger-on.[31]

Consequently, the international negotiations on nuclear arms limitations in 1969–72 were a bilateral superpower affair. The United States and the USSR both had their own reasons to seek bilateral détente. The Nixon administration sought an exit from the Vietnam War, possibly through the improvement of relations with either Moscow or Beijing, or preferably both. Only a few months after the first Chinese H-bomb test in June 1967 did the future Republican presidential candidate Nixon write: "During the next decade the West faces two prospects which, together, could create a crisis of the first order: (1) that the Soviets may reach nuclear parity with the United States; and (2) that China, within three to five years, will have a significant deliverable nuclear capability." This required both negotiations with the Soviet Union and a "dialogue with mainland China" in order to pull that country "back into the world community – but as a great and progressing nation, not as the epicenter of world revolution." China at the same time also played on the minds of the Soviet leadership. After the Sino–Soviet border clashes in the first half of March 1969, Soviet General Secretary Leonid I. Brezhnev painted a gloomy picture of the future, particularly how a lengthy armed conflict with the PRC would tax Soviet military and economic capabilities. In August of 1969, the USSR publicly toyed with the idea of an airstrike on the Chinese nuclear weapons program in Xinjiang. Given the economic problems it was facing at home and in Eastern Europe, Moscow also sought a relaxation of global tensions to reduce Cold War pressures and to increase trade with the non-socialist world for its own modernization drive. Yet, while 1969 was a relatively favorable year for a possible superpower détente, the American expansion of the Vietnam War into neutral Laos and the Jordan Crisis in the following year delayed the improvement of relations.[32]

Several developments in 1971 pushed the two superpowers to come to an agreement on strategic nuclear weapons. The chance interactions of the Chinese and the American table tennis teams at the world championship in Nagoya, Japan, in the spring had triggered Sino–American rapprochement. After a secret visit to Beijing by Nixon's security adviser, Henry Kissinger, the two countries announced in mid July that the US president would visit the People's Republic of China in February 1972. Afraid of being left out of the triangular relationship, Brezhnev agreed to Nixon's appeal to find solutions to the world's major problems, and invited the American leader to come to Moscow in May of 1972. Sino–American rapprochement not only accelerated Soviet–American détente but also undermined the long-standing US policy of denying mainland Chinese entry into the United Nations. On October 25, the UN General Assembly voted to admit the PRC in lieu of the ROC. The news arrived in Beijing just as Kissinger was wrapping up discussions with Zhou Enlai on the brewing East Pakistan Crisis.[33]

With Nixon's visit to Moscow scheduled for May 1972, the two superpowers were under pressure to come to an agreement on nuclear weapons. Their negotiators managed to settle on three interlocking agreements that would underpin superpower détente in the 1970s. In the *Basic Principles*, Washington and Moscow concurred to continue the Cold War primarily in the realm of peaceful coexistence and in mutually beneficial cooperation, given that MAD left them no other choice. The Strategic Arms Limitation Treaty (SALT) aimed at limiting the nuclear arms race by capping the number of warheads and delivery vehicles on both sides. The Anti-Ballistic Missile (ABM) Treaty restricted the number of defensive missile systems, so that neither side could annul MAD unilaterally. The two superpowers obtained different benefits from the agreements. Before May 1972, Washington had used Beijing to play on Moscow's fears and extract concessions. Afterward, the United States pursued superpower détente at the expense of rapprochement with the PRC. In the end, Nixon did not get much aid from Brezhnev in resolving the ongoing Vietnam War, but his administration hoped that the grand deal of May 1972 would help to manage the transition of the USSR from strategic inferiority to equality. For its part, Moscow believed that it had reached the status of strategic equality in the early 1970s, but it did not plan to stop there. The ensuing superpower agreements initially helped the Soviet Union to outmaneuver the PRC, to create a basis for economic and cultural exchanges with the United States, and to influence the stage for détente in Europe, which will be covered in Chapter 18. In the long term, the Soviet Union strove for nuclear superiority.[34]

South Asia's Nuclear Competition, 1972–79

Just as Soviet–American détente occurred, the East Pakistan Crisis and the Sino–American rapprochement triggered a nuclear arms race in South Asia. Humiliated and broken apart by its Indian neighbor, rump-Pakistan decided on January 20, 1972, to embark on a nuclear weapons project. Although by then Zulfikar Ali Bhutto had been Pakistan's president for just a month, he had supported a national A-bomb program at least since March 1965, i.e. since before the national humiliation suffered in the Second Kashmir War. Serving as Pakistan's foreign minister in the mid 1960s, he had publicly stated that his country needed to proceed from the assumption that India was working toward acquiring an A-bomb, and hence had to catch up, no matter what the cost: " . . . we should have to eat grass and get one, or buy one, of our own." After suffering another humiliation within less than seven years, Bhutto's Pakistan was determined to prevent another defeat on the basis of a national nuclear project. Chinese specialists assisted in making a Canadian-delivered nuclear reactor functional, and provided important knowhow to Pakistan's bomb project despite international sanctions.[35]

India's decision to test a nuclear device was not related to Pakistan, but to China. Since October 1964, Delhi had gradually taken steps that put the country on the path toward a nuclear test. With communist China's ascent to the UN Security Council in October 1971, all *declared* nuclear powers had become permanent members, and all permanent members were nuclear powers. In early 1972, just when Pakistan decided to start its nuclear weapons project, Indian Prime Minister Indira Gandhi still rejected a proposal of India's atomic energy commission to go forward with a nuclear test because of its staggering economic costs. But with Nixon's visit to Beijing in February, India concluded that the United States had given up its policy of "containment" of China for a policy of "accommodation."[36] Within two months, Gandhi formally decided to test a nuclear device. The decision was so sensitive that she made sure not to leave anything on paper. After the surprise test of *Smiling Buddha* on May 18, 1974, India's minister of state for external affairs publicly linked the allegedly peaceful explosion to China: "We thought we had good relations [with the PRC] when it encroached [on us in 1962]. We were stabbed in the back. We cannot afford to make another mistake." The prime minister herself also saw the test as a rite of passage into the club of the world's great powers: "India, which was until sometime back a slave country, had the audacity to stand in line with them." Whether or not she hoped to use the test to get a permanent seat on the UN Security Council for India is unclear given the lack of access to Indian archival evidence. Unsurprisingly, however, Pakistan used the Indian surprise test to mobilize the Muslim world, demanding UN nuclear guarantees against its hostile neighbor.[37]

The prospect of a nuclear arms race in South Asia worried the world. Initially, neither of the two hostile countries pushed their nuclear programs with resolve. India did not test again until May 1998, when it exploded a thermonuclear device and a nuclear warhead. It also did not seriously proceed in developing a reliable missile-based delivery vehicle until the 1980s. Pakistan reached the capability to produce a nuclear bomb by the late 1980s, but only tested a series of nuclear devices in response to the Indian tests in 1998. During his term in office in 1977–81, US President Jimmy Carter considered nuclear disarmament, nonproliferation, the peaceful use of nuclear energy, and environmentalism closely interlinked problems, particularly in the wake of the Indian test in 1974. His administration tried to reverse the fatalistic laissez-faire approach to non-proliferation of the preceding administrations through actively preventing the diffusion of nuclear knowhow and technology to Egypt and, especially, India and Pakistan. The new American policy included attempts to impose international inspections of nuclear power plants in South Asia, and diplomatic intercessions to thwart the purchase of technology from third countries, like France, Canada, or the USSR. However, Carter thereby entered into the minefield of Indo-Pakistani enmity. In the end, his policy remained an inconsistent patchwork of non-proliferation attempts in the regional South Asian conflict and strategic decision-making in the global Cold War.[38]

SALT II vs. NATO Double-Track Decision, 1972–79

Because SALT was formally a five-year interim agreement, the two superpowers continued to negotiate on nuclear arms limitation soon after May 1972. Both the end of the Vietnam War and Brezhnev's visit to the United States in 1973 seemed to reconfirm the bilateral willingness to come to a comprehensive and long-term agreement. Yet a series of conflicts threw a monkey wrench into Soviet–American détente: the October War in late 1973, Nixon's increasing absorption with the Watergate Scandal and his eventual resignation in August 1974, and the unfolding crises at the Horn of Africa, in Afghanistan, and in Indochina over the

1975–78 period. Still, at the Vladivostok Summit in November 1974, Brezhnev and Ford were able to agree on important elements of a future agreement, particularly the capping of bombers, long-range nuclear missiles, sea-launched nuclear missiles, and the inclusion of newer missiles with multiple warheads.[39]

President Carter was not only committed to non-proliferation but also dedicated to nuclear arms limitation. Yet he dedicated his first year in office to seeking a solution to the Arab–Israeli conflict, though he eventually benefited from the initiative by new Israeli Prime Minister Menachem Begin and Egypt's President Anwar Sadat that would lead to the Camp David Accord in September 1978. In the end, Soviet activities at the Horn of Africa motivated him in the spring of 1978 to adopt Nixon's playbook by using the China card to force the USSR onto the defensive at a global level. The Soviet Union understood that developments in the Middle East, East Africa, and China came together to threaten the signing of SALT II. By June 1978, Moscow was convinced that the "international situation is very complicated," and, despite that the "policy of détente will doubtlessly continue," rapprochement with Washington was going to suffer "certain defeats" in the process. When the Soviet ally Vietnam marched into Cambodia half a year later, the USSR celebrated it as a surprise victory over the superpower rival. But Moscow grew deeply concerned over the visit of China's supreme leader Deng Xiaoping to Washington in late January 1979 – four weeks after the establishment of full diplomatic relations between the two countries. The strident Sino–American collaboration against the Soviet Union, as Moscow believed, made the conclusion of SALT II even more pressing for the sake of world peace. All in all, the USSR saw US actions at the turn of 1978/79 in the darkest colors possible. At the same time, the developing crises in Afghanistan and Iran convinced American President Carter in early 1979 to call for a superpower summit to sign SALT II, despite Vietnam's intervention in Cambodia and Beijing's subsequent punitive war against Hanoi. Brezhnev and Carter signed the second strategic arms limitation treaty at the Vienna Summit in June 1979, though they remained at odds on virtually all of the other issues that divided them – from Asia to the Middle East to Europe.[40]

After experiencing a difficult birth, SALT II met with resistance in the United States and among the American partners in NATO. Within months, the US Senate announced that it opposed ratification without major revisions in the realm of verification. Western European alliance partners, particularly West Germany's Chancellor Helmut Schmidt, feared that SALT II would decouple European NATO members from the American strategic nuclear deterrence, particularly after Bonn had committed in 1969 to abstaining from nuclear weapons in exchange for

American nuclear commitments to Western European security. Frustrated by Carter's refusal to consider European security concerns, Schmidt had gone public in October 1977, demanding the inclusion of Soviet intermediate-range nuclear missiles in nuclear arms limitation talks. The USSR had deployed SS-20 missiles in the western Soviet Union and in Eastern European Warsaw Pact member states since the mid 1970s for a mixture of defensive and offensive reasons. Only after the United States and the USSR had signed SALT II in June 1979 did Carter finally revise his hitherto hesitant position on the SS-20 threat to Western Europe. The NATO double-track decision of December 12, 1979, envisioned negotiations with the Soviet Union, designed to reduce if not eliminate the missiles, in the coming four years. While NATO announced the withdrawal of one thousand American nuclear warheads from Europe as a sweetener, it also wielded a big stick – the threat of deploying US Pershing II missiles and Tomahawk cruise missiles at the end of 1983 to counter the SS-20 threat – should negotiations fail.[41]

Conclusion

Within a fortnight, the USSR intervened in Afghanistan. In response, Carter withdrew SALT II from consideration in the Senate. Over the course of another four years, Moscow refused to negotiate on the SS-20 missiles, which caused Carter's successor, Ronald Reagan, to honor the NATO double-track decision by deploying Pershing II missiles and Tomahawk cruise missiles to Western Europe in late 1983.

While nuclear weapons played major political roles in the global and regional Cold Wars, their influence was not categorical. Without doubt, nuclear weapons nudged developments into one or the other direction. But the Soviet–American conflict would have started anyway without US atomic diplomacy in 1945. Or the PRC would have become a member of the United Nations at some point in the 1970s. Still, nuclear weapons were responsible for some of the most serious crises in the Cold War – above all, the Cuban Missile Crisis – before the advent of MAD. A major Cold War historian once claimed that Soviet–American possession of an abundant number of nuclear weapons stabilized the Cold War in its second half and thereby helped to guarantee peace in Europe.[42] It is certainly true that after the Berlin Crisis in 1961 and the Soviet intervention in Czechoslovakia in 1968, no major crisis rattled the European continent. But, as subsequent chapters suggest, this might have been related to structural changes in Europe. Also, despite MAD, the Afro–Asian world was torn by conflicts in the late 1960s and throughout the 1970s.

15 Western European Integration

"Victory has 100 fathers and defeat is an orphan," US President John F. Kennedy once quipped.[1] The post-World War II integration process in Europe certainly was the accomplishment of many parents – European and American alike. Two world wars and the emergence of right-wing authoritarianism in between all had reinforced the desire among post-war leaders to overcome past conflicts and create some form of an integrated Europe. Nationalist rivalries had twice brought physical destruction, socio-economic dislocation, and global decline. Breaking this cycle of self-destructive behavior required overcoming the central conflict in Europe – the Franco–German antagonism. Although French leaders took the initiative in working for economic integration in the 1920s and after 1945 in order to establish structural barriers to future military conflict, their German counterparts were by no means averse to their ideas.

The idea of Western European integration emerged in the 1920s when middle powers and smaller countries grew concerned about a pair of powerful states flanking the continent. From the 1920s to the post-World War II era, Western European leaders saw integration as the principal mechanism to contain Soviet expansionism, but they also struggled against the ambivalent position and even obstructionist policies of the United Kingdom. London insisted on its unfettered great power status well beyond World War II, as described in previous chapters. Similarly, from 1947 to 1961, it tried to impose its views on the integration project through pre-emptive and sometimes destructive policies. Afterward, given its waning global influence, it was forced to ask the Western European continentals to join the integration project on their terms.

Without any doubt, France was the most consistent proponent of integration since the 1920s. It shaped European integration after World War II with the double goal of restoring itself to great power status and of holding Germany down after three wars in less than a century. Yet, by the 1960s, President Charles de Gaulle made France into a domineering leader in Western Europe, sparking opposition and even pushback by the smaller partners. In the end, the Western European integration project survived the Gaullist challenge. After the president's resignation in the spring of 1969, France shelved its aspiration to be the project's principal leader and guardian of the gates to membership.

Finally, the United States played a judiciously self-restrained but still crucial role in the success of post-World War II integration. It made a commitment to Western European integration in 1947 for Cold War reasons, but generally abstained from providing ready-made solutions to European problems. On the condition that the Europeans work out their problems first, it strategically provided a long-term stable environment in which older European ideas of integration could evolve and succeed. Still, by the late 1960s, the United States withdrew its tacit political support, forcing the Western European integration project into greater self-reliance and self-determination.

Western European integration is one of the lasting structural legacies of the Cold War. It helped the semi-continent to overcome the devastating results of World War II relatively quickly by creating a vehicle for economic recovery and political cooperation. Despite external and internal challenges – from Great Britain in the 1950s and France in the 1960s – it was remarkably resilient. Although it had a strong congenital anti-Soviet bent, it survived the end of the Cold War despite the collapse of the USSR. In the 1990s, post-communist Eastern Europe was keen on being part of the continent's success story, particularly after the failure of its own integration project, as described in the next chapter.

The Global Economy from World War I to World War II

At the end of World War II, the global economy had experienced three decades of disintegration. In 1914, European imperial powers, with Great Britain paramount among them, had still occupied dominant positions within it. London, Paris, Brussels, The Hague, Berlin, Rome, Lisbon, and Madrid all were imperial commercial hubs connected in spoke-like fashion to their respective colonial possessions. In comparison, Washington, St. Petersburg, and Tokyo headed rising powers with their own hegemonic and even imperialist aspirations. Despite the parallel nature of European-dominated economic blocs before World War I, the imperial powers, their empires, and the smaller European states were linked to each other through international financial networks. In the decades before 1914, Great Britain and France were the world's leading lenders and investors.[2]

World War I and the interwar period significantly altered worldwide economic relations. The global conflict had exhausted all European participants economically while it allowed the United States to reverse its role from long-time debtor of the United Kingdom to creditor of Great Britain and France. After the Bolshevik Revolution in November 1917, Soviet Russia repudiated the international order on ideological grounds, and therewith rejected its own financial liabilities abroad, primarily toward France and Great Britain. The Paris Peace Conference in 1919 and subsequent negotiations erected a financial scheme in which Germany paid reparations to France and the United Kingdom, enabling both to repay war debt to the United States. Germany's refusal to honor its reparation obligations in 1922 led to the French occupation of the Ruhr Valley, a major German industrial region, for the purpose of extracting reparations. Only a restructuring of the financial scheme under the leadership of American banks – the so-called Dawes Plan of 1924 – ended the Ruhr Valley occupation and solved the payments crisis. The revised scheme functioned on the basis of short-term loans supplied to Germany by American banks, but was dependent on the continued stability of the US financial sector. The crash of the New York stock market in late October 1929 exacerbated the ongoing reduction of American lending to foreign countries, which had started in 1928 as a result of spiraling domestic stock market speculation. As liquidity in the United States collapsed, American banks exported the crisis abroad by recalling loans or refusing to grant new ones. In cascading fashion, the economies in Germany, France, Great Britain, and other parts of the world collapsed. Despite attempts in the early 1930s to recreate a stable international financial system, Western liberal democracies – led by the United States – and the rising right-wing authoritarian regimes – Italy, Germany, and Japan – chose to increase import tariffs and introduce protectionist policies to shield domestic industries, which in turn gave rise to self-contained trading blocs along existing or new imperial lines. The emergence of these economically closed parallel systems further lowered worldwide interdependence and, in its wake, structural barriers to military conflict.[3]

Paradoxically, just as the collapse of the world economy increased the importance of integrated trading blocs to the respective imperialist powers, colonial independence movements challenged the existing political and economic world order. While Japan and Italy were still building up their empires in the 1930s, political unrest – mainly in South Asia and the Middle East – forced the other European imperial powers – especially the United Kingdom – to reconsider their imperial strategies. It was also in this time that the worldwide depression reached colonial possessions, because imperial powers passed on the economic crisis or proved unable to alleviate the economic suffering on the ground. This all provided growing political legitimacy to anti-imperialist movements.[4]

World War II swept away the remnants of the old global economic order. The war destroyed industrial and other infrastructure on an unimaginable scale, particularly in two world regions. In East Asia, the devastation was mostly confined to Japan, but in Europe, it primarily affected a large triangular area between London, Leningrad, and Stalingrad, which encompassed parts of the United Kingdom and France, and all of the Netherlands, Germany, Austria, Poland, and the western Soviet Union. Unscathed by war, the United States emerged as the predominant power in the world; in 1945, its economy made up half of the world's economy. In comparison, the victorious European powers emerged exhausted and partially destroyed. The United Kingdom faced financial bankruptcy, France a long economic recovery, and the Soviet Union a monumental reconstruction task. By and large, the colonial holdings had shown economic and political loyalty to the imperialist powers in the worldwide struggle against right-wing authoritarianism and militarism, but expected national self-determination as a just reward after the end of the war.[5]

It was against this background that the United States set about reordering the world economy. Given both its spectacular rise in world politics within one and a half centuries and its worldwide economic predominance in 1945, Washington concluded that the new order should benefit from American savoir-faire and largesse. American policies were magnanimous and selfish at the same time, designed to get the world back on its feet while fortifying American preponderance in the process. An arrangement of interlocking international institutions – the United Nations and the Bretton Woods System (the International Monetary Fund and the World Bank) – aimed at creating political and economic stability on a global scale, facilitating reconstruction, and restoring an integrated world economy on the basis of trade liberalism. American-led global economic integration aspired to re-establish structural barriers to military conflict, but also tear down the residual imperial trading blocs, even of allies like the United Kingdom.[6] In the end, the destruction of parts of Europe in World War II, American global preponderance, and the unfolding of the early Cold War all provided incentives to the Western European democracies to revisit and refashion older ideas of economic and political integration in order to overcome the roots of past conflicts, rebuild their future, and generate cohesion against Soviet pressure.

Sources of European Integration, 1923–47

In 1923, the Bohemian Count Richard N. Coudenhove-Kalergi made the seminal, visionary case for a United States of Europe in his widely circulated and often-translated book *Pan-Europa*. Surveying the world, he saw the United States of America, the United Kingdom, the Empire of Japan, and Soviet Russia as leaders in their respective world regions. In comparison, continental Europe had fallen from international prominence after committing collective suicide in World War I. The only choice left to European countries, he stressed, was to unify voluntarily into a cohesive association. Otherwise, expansionist Soviet Russia would divide them against each other and ultimately absorb them by military force. Unsurprisingly, Coudenhove-Kalergi envisioned this United States of Europe without two of the European great powers – Soviet Russia, due to its lack of democracy, and the United Kingdom, because of its non-European empire. At its heart, he claimed, Europe needed to overcome the historical Franco–German antagonism that had prevented continent-wide unity and peace since the 1860s. Coudenhove-Kalergi's plan of unifying Europe's democracies consisted of four concrete steps: a series of conferences to resolve differences, the conclusion of non-aggression treaties, the establishment of a customs union, and finally the creation of a United States of Europe. As the founder and long-time head of the private Pan-European Union, he organized six international conferences between 1926 and 1943 to propagate his ideas.[7]

Through personal contacts, Coudenhove-Kalergi influenced several European leaders, particularly France's Presidents of the Council of Ministers (prime ministers) Édouard Herriot (in office: 1924–25) and Aristide Briand (1929). In 1924, France faced the humiliation of withdrawing – without economic compensation – from the Ruhr Valley as part of the Dawes Plan. Hence, in the fall, Herriot proposed an interdependent peace with Germany through the establishment of a supranational "trust" that would amalgamate French steel production in the Lorraine region and the German coal industry in the Ruhr Valley. He thereby returned to French ideas from World War I to seek structural economic integration to reduce the chance of renewed war between the two countries. Early the following year, he even promoted the idea of the "United States of Europe" to prevent Germany's rearmament and thwart its possible alignment with Soviet Russia. Before the end of 1925, the two old enemies concluded the Locarno Pact, a non-aggression treaty guaranteed by the deterrence commitments of other European powers. In the negotiations beforehand, German and French representatives had even discussed the idea of a bilateral customs union, but failed to come to an agreement.[8] On October 1, 1926, however, the two countries established, together with Belgium and Luxembourg, the International Steel Cartel, which aimed at coordinating production, pricing, and marketing. The organization did not survive Europe's economic and political upheavals of the early 1930s, but still it was the first genuine attempt at economic integration on the continent. By early September 1929, Briand returned to the more ambitious idea of creating a political, economic, and social federation of European states, which Herriot had raised in 1925. As the global economy slipped in the wake of the stock market crash in the United States, Briand invited twenty-seven countries to Paris on May 17, 1930, to discuss a "federal union in Europe" in order to avoid the "material and moral" collapse of the continent. Even though several rounds of talks occurred in the following two years, his death in March 1932 and the subsequent rise of Adolf Hitler's National Socialism in Germany put an end to the project.[9]

British reactions to the idea of a united Europe vacillated between hostility and support, foreshadowing the country's inconsistent policies in the following decades. The British government rejected Briand's proposal, largely because economic integration in Europe would have undermined the commercial "unity" of the United Kingdom with its Empire. But backbench Member of Parliament Winston Churchill hailed Briand's call for a United States of Europe as early as February 1930. When Germany and Austria decided to establish a customs union in 1931, he grew concerned about the rise of a unified German great power that threatened France, in particular, and peace in Europe, in general. Yet, as the chances of Franco–German reconciliation subsequently waned, his enthusiasm for a united Europe turned into disdain for French impotence. Shortly after Briand's death in March 1932, Churchill sarcastically compared the Frenchman's idea to Napoleon's failed dream of domination over Europe, calling instead for unity of the Anglo–American great powers.[10] Still, in May 1938, five years after Hitler's rise to power, he reversed his opinion once more by embracing Coudenhove-Kalergi's ideas. Two months after the German aggression against Poland in September 1939, opposition Labour Party leader Clement Attlee called for the creation in Europe of an "international authority superior to individual states and endowed … with rights over them." Echoing Coudenhove-Kalergi, Attlee also concluded that the continent faced a stark choice: "Europe must federate or perish." The statements of the two British politicians reflected widespread popular enthusiasm in the United Kingdom in the late 1930s for a European federation. After being elected prime minister in the wake of Germany's attack on France on May 10, 1940, Churchill even proposed to the beleaguered French government a supranational union. But the idea was mainly born out of desperation in the face of France's imminent capitulation. Bilateral relations subsequently worsened due to the different experiences of the United Kingdom at war and France under occupation, personality conflicts between Churchill and the leader of Free France, Charles de Gaulle, and the British move to push France out of the Levant in May 1945. Nevertheless, during the war, Churchill continued to favor a "United States of Europe" to guard against future Soviet domination, and a "Council of Europe" to overcome the European causes of both world wars.[11]

Out of power from July 1945 to October 1951, Churchill toured the world as elder statesmen and Westminster opposition member. Between November 1945 and September 1946, he gave speeches before the Belgian and Dutch parliaments and at the University of Zurich to make his case for the United States of Europe. Referring to Coudenhove-Kalergi and Briand by name, the former prime minister called on France and Germany to take the lead "in the re-creation of the European family." Yet he saw Great Britain merely as a co-sponsor, together with the United States and the Soviet Union, of an integrated Europe on the continent. Still, his renewed invocation of unity among the Big Three was insincere, because he himself had pierced this fiction with his "iron curtain" speech in the United States on March 5, 1946. Europe was to unite against the USSR, not to be co-sponsored by it. On a deeper level, however, his daydream of trilateral great power cooperation revealed his continued vacillation about whether the British claim to global status would be better served within a trilateral relationship with the Soviet Union and the United States, or within a united Europe. Attlee's Labour government, in comparison, prioritized a close bilateral relationship with the United States against the USSR. In May 1947, finally, Churchill demanded that the United Kingdom "play her full part as a member of the European family" when he called for the creation of a union of European democracies based on the collaboration of France with its former enemies Germany and Italy.[12]

In parallel to Churchill's World War II musings about Europe's future, continental governments in exile in London had pondered concrete ideas of greater post-war collaboration. In early September 1944, at the very time when American troops marched into Flanders, the exile governments from Belgium, the Netherlands, and Luxembourg agreed to establish a customs union after the war. Delayed by the need to stabilize their countries following liberation, the Benelux countries returned to the idea in the spring and summer of 1947. Ratified by all three in late October, the trilateral customs union started on January 1, 1948.[13]

Against the background of such debates, the United States rethought its hands-off policy toward the continent in 1946–47. The idea of a United States of Europe was not new to the American public. In August 1940, Coudenhove-Kalergi and his Jewish wife had fled Vienna to New York, where he established, together with Senator J. William Fulbright and other distinguished US politicians, the American Committee for a Free and United Europe. As wartime collaboration with the USSR collapsed after mid 1945, and the official, friendly US view of the Soviet ally changed into the perception of a hostile and expansionist enemy, Washington grew concerned about the economic malaise in Europe and the ensuing security problems. On March 12, 1947, President Harry S. Truman called on Congress to grant economic and military aid to support Greece and Turkey against communist interference in the wake of the British announcement to withdraw its troops from Greece. Coudenhove-Kalergi publicly lauded the Truman Doctrine in the belief that it broke Iosif V. Stalin's plans to "block and paralyze Europe's will to unite."[14]

In anticipation of its withdrawal from Greece, the United Kingdom had started to revise its security commitments to Europe as early as the beginning of 1947. On March 4, London and Paris signed the Dunkirk Treaty of mutual defense – a pact born not from mutual love but forged on the anvil of parallel strategic interests. Great Britain hoped to use France to deter the Soviet threat, while Paris tried to line up the United Kingdom to contain the German enemy. In May, London approached Brussels and The Hague with proposals for similar agreements. But by March 27, 1948, the United Kingdom and France concluded the five-member Brussels Pact with the three Benelux countries, which all preferred a multilateral agreement over a set of parallel bilateral treaties. The pact's military weakness during Stalin's Berlin blockade from June 1948 to May 1949 convinced the United States to take the lead in establishing a multilateral alliance against the USSR. Signed on April 4, 1949, the North Atlantic Treaty brought together the United States, Canada, the five members of the Brussels Pact, Italy, Portugal, Denmark, Norway, and Iceland in a mutual military assistance agreement. The alliance's first general secretary, Baron Hastings Lionel Ismay, once quipped that the treaty's purpose was "to keep the Russians out, the Americans in, and the Germans down."[15]

While the United States assumed leadership in establishing military security in Western Europe against the Soviet threat, it decided to act only in an advisory and financial role in the Western European reconstruction project. Thus, 1947 marked the year in which military and economic integration *parted ways* – one would be Atlantic, the other Western European. Since mid 1945, the United States had provided much aid to the continent but without any interest in integration or any success in rebuilding intra-European trade. On March 21, 1947, nine days after Truman had called for aid to Greece and Turkey, Fulbright introduced a resolution in the US Senate that called for American support for the creation of the United States of Europe. Churchill, as the foremost promoter of European unity, publicly hinted in mid May that this United States of Europe would only include the western half of the continent. During the spring, the United States recognized that the rise of an economically integrated and cohesive Western Europe was a precondition for that semi-continent's ability to resist the Soviet threat. When US Secretary of State George C. Marshall gave his famous commencement address at Harvard University on June 5, he emphasized the need for continued US economic aid, but also highlighted that the "initiative" for a transnational recovery program "must come from Europe." The Truman administration understood that imposing a solution on the Europeans would only lead to resentment and possibly renewed conflict. Marshall's proposal for an American-financed European Recovery Program was intentionally vague, because the United States wanted to force the Europeans to overcome historical antagonisms by running the program jointly. Still, Washington thereby turned from a bystander into a lobbyist for European integration. Officially, the recovery program aimed at all European countries, including the USSR, but few in the Truman administration expected Stalin to consent. Indeed, in the initial round of talks in Paris in late June and early July 1947, the Soviet Union tried to derail what Stalin considered an American attempt to interfere in Europe to the detriment of his country, but ultimately failed.[16]

Once all delegations from socialist Europe had left the French capital by July 12, negotiations among sixteen Western European countries (excluding Franco's Spain and the Western occupied zones of Germany) started. It was at this juncture that Paris returned to its interwar prominence in promoting European integration. In many respects, early Western European integration was a French-led project, in which Paris contested the interests of Washington and London. France's policy since mid 1944 had been driven by the fear of a renewed but unchecked German rise, while it concurrently aimed at restoring the country's status of equality with the Big Three – the United States, the United Kingdom, and the USSR. The French demand in 1944–45 for an occupation zone in Germany had reflected this strategic thinking, even if the ensuing French zone included only the smaller industrial region of the Saarland and not the larger Ruhr Valley. France welcomed the European Recovery Program, because it both needed continuous economic aid and shared American security concerns about Soviet expansionism. But the Marshall Plan raised anew the danger of Germany re-emerging as an unconstrained threat. In the end, the French government saw the American demand for a European initiative as an opportunity to shape integration, preferably along the lines proposed by its own interwar predecessors. Still, disagreements about the nature of integration quickly arose as the sixteen countries began to discuss the size and allocation of American financial aid among them, and between them and occupied Germany. The United

Kingdom refused a French proposal for a Europe-wide customs union similar to the one the Benelux countries had just ratified, largely because the scheme would have interfered with British rules governing trade with the Empire. France was also exasperated by unilateral Anglo–American plans to rehabilitate economic life in their combined occupation zones in Germany – including the Ruhr Valley – which threatened to undermine French influence and security. To make matters worse, as Truman's United States stepped up its economic commitment to Western Europe, Attlee's United Kingdom seemed to step away from the idea of creating a united continent. In the end, as subsequent pages suggest, France, however, achieved many of its goals over the following decade anyway.[17]

The United States focused on pushing for trade liberalization among the European countries. In November 1947, it convinced the Benelux countries, France, and Italy to agree on a central clearing mechanism for payments, a scheme that stimulated trade among the five. Ultimately, with the support of Paris, on April 16, 1948, Washington established the Organization of European Economic Cooperation (OEEC) to manage the distribution of 12.7 billion US dollars of recovery money to Western Europe – including the three Western occupation zones of Germany – and to oversee the lowering of trade barriers among all European participants in the recovery program. Through the OEEC, the non-member United States in 1949 also successfully lobbied for the transformation of the five-member clearing mechanism into a membership-wide payments union.[18]

Creating European Institutions, 1947–60

Marshall's announcement of the European Recovery Program in June of 1947 jolted integration proponents in many European countries into action. They shared a record of advocacy, which in some cases dated back to resistance against right-wing authoritarianism in the 1930s and World War II. A French committee – established in July 1947 and headed by President of the French National Assembly Édouard Herriot – supported Churchill's two-month-old call for a United States of Europe. In the fall, Coudenhove-Kalergi, who had returned from the United States, promoted the idea of a European Parliamentary Union. Together with the efforts of other like-minded, mostly non-governmental organizations, these visions eventually resulted in the convocation of the semi-official Congress of Europe in The Hague in May 1948. Churchill, in his role as the gathering's honorary chairman, called for the creation of a "Council of Europe" that was supposed to bring together all of the continent's democracies in unity against "Nazi domination" and Soviet despotism, and "in harmony with the great republic of the United States."[19]

The enthusiasm which the congress created inspired France and Belgium to lead the efforts in establishing a European parliamentary assembly. To Churchill's disappointment, the Attlee government once more rejected the idea of greater political union on the grounds of its incompatibility with the Empire, though London countered with a proposal of creating a European council to represent governments. After arduous negotiations, the representatives of ten European democracies – Belgium, Denmark, France, Ireland, Italy, Luxembourg, the Netherlands, Norway, Sweden, and the United Kingdom – agreed on May 5, 1949, to create the Council of Europe in accordance with British ideas. For symbolic reasons, they chose for its seat the city of Strasbourg in Alsace-Lorraine, the region that had been the long-time object of Franco–German nationalist competition. The new institution included a strong Council of Ministers and a weak Consultative Assembly that brought together selected members of parliaments from member states. A French proposal to call the dual structure the *European Union* did not find majority approval. As an ardent European *unionist*, Paris did not like the Council of Ministers because it represented sovereign governments and thus contradicted the idea of deeper political integration, while London, as a hesitant *federalist*, did not like the Consultative Assembly because it deemed that chamber dangerously uncontrollable.[20]

The preamble of the Council's Statute of May 5, 1949, was steeped in anti-Soviet rhetoric. It listed as the council's central goals "the pursuit of peace based upon justice and international co-operation," "the preservation of human society and civilization," and the guarantee of "individual freedom, political liberty and the rule of law, principles which form the basis of all *genuine democracy*." Greece, Turkey, Iceland, and the newly established Federal Republic of Germany (West Germany) joined the Council's ten original members within two years. Today, it includes almost all European countries – forty-seven in total – except Belarus and the Vatican. The very first meeting of the Consultative Assembly in August 1949 decided to draft a European Convention on Human Rights, which was ready for signature on November 4, 1950, and entered into force on September 3, 1953. It was adopted in response to the atrocities committed by National Socialist Germany between 1933 and 1945, and designed to enshrine and enforce human rights among the democracies that were members of the Council of Europe. On the basis of the convention's article 19, the Consultative Assembly established the European Court of Human Rights on January 21, 1959.[21]

However, neither the loose North Atlantic Alliance nor the British-imposed federalist Council of Europe satisfied France, the Benelux states,

Italy, and West Germany. When Paris proposed on May 9, 1950, the creation of the European Coal and Steel Community (ECSC) – Europe's first supranational institution and the foundation stone of the present European Union – the other five quickly joined in negotiations. The success of the idea benefited from the fortunate confluence of multiple developments. On the one hand, democratically elected governments led by Christian democrats had emerged in several European countries after World War II – in the Netherlands in 1946, in Italy in 1948, and in West Germany in 1949. In France, Christian democrats had been junior coalition members in all governments since 1946. As early as the nineteenth century, Europe's Christian democrats had pondered the problem of how to deal with the far-reaching political and socio-economic changes arising from the formation and industrialization of European nation states. They eventually positioned themselves between liberal capitalism and the revolutionary left by advocating the solution of the Social Question – i.e. the rise of a large and impoverished working class in the wake of industrialization – on the basis of Christian social teachings. Christian democrats reappeared as strong supporters of European integration after World War II on the basis of their international networks from the interwar period. Their shared commitment to integration partially stemmed from their long-standing internationalist traditions but also from the personal life experiences of some of the central Christian democratic protagonists after World War II, such as France's Foreign Minister Robert Schuman, Italy's Prime Minister Alcide de Gasperi, and Germany's Federal Chancellor Konrad Adenauer. Schuman and de Gasperi had family roots in regions – Lorraine and Trentino – that had been objects of intense nationalist competition since the nineteenth century – between Germany and France, and between Austria and Italy – though both remained at ease with having multiple national identities. Adenauer, in comparison, had understood, during his tenure as mayor of Cologne in the 1920s, that only bilateral economic cooperation could allay France's fears of a resurgent Germany. Finally, the three also shared similar experiences with right-wing nationalism in the interwar period and World War II. De Gasperi had been a political prisoner in Benito Mussolini's Italy, Adenauer put under house arrest and eventually into jail in Adolf Hitler's Germany, and Schuman incarcerated by German occupation troops before escaping to join the Resistance.[22]

On the other hand, American and French leaders in 1949 grew frustrated with British obstructionism regarding the European integration process. Given the perception of a growing Soviet threat, Washington encouraged Paris in October to come up with ideas to accelerate integration once more. At that time, France feared that it was in a race against time in the wake of West Germany's regained statehood in May 1949. German industrial war-making capabilities seemed on the verge of coming under exclusive national control once again. France's main economic planner Jean Monnet – a one-time diplomat after World War I, Anglophile businessman during the interwar period, and proponent of a European integration since World War II – came up with the idea of a supranational merger of Germany's and France's coal and steel industries, which Schuman officially proposed on May 9, 1950. The scheme relied on ideas that had circulated in the French foreign ministry since 1948, but also evoked the short-lived quadrilateral International Steel Cartel of 1926. Adenauer reacted with enthusiasm to Schuman's proposal, particularly since his new government had made reconciliation with France a top priority. In March 1950, he had even proposed a Franco–German union with joint citizenship and parliament. De Gasperi for his part understood that participation in the supranational ECSC would help Italy re-establish itself more firmly in European politics than was possible as a weak member of the US-led North Atlantic alliance. And the keenly integrationist Benelux states joined almost by default.[23]

Negotiations among the *Six* started on June 20, 1950 – five days before the unrelated outbreak of the Korean War – and continued until the signing of the Treaty of Paris on April 18 the following year. The ensuing European Coal and Steel Community (ECSC) was essentially a customs union for coal and steel, with joint external tariffs. Its supranational High Authority executed the treaty, the Council of Ministers brought together national governments to advise it, the Common Assembly gathered representatives from national parliaments to exercise oversight, and the Court of Justice ruled on legal disputes. All four institutions form the foundations of today's European Union – the Commission, the Council, the Parliament, and the Court – but they have always remained separate entities from those of the Council of Europe. The United Kingdom declined to join the ECSC. Attlee had been open to participating in negotiations but rejected the supranational elements of Schuman's proposal from the very beginning. In spite of his initial public endorsement of the French initiative, Churchill soon supported the prime minister from the opposition bench. Apart from an ideological dislike of supranational solutions, both Attlee's Labour government and Churchill's subsequent Conservative cabinet believed that joining this kind of European integration would undermine the remaining Empire and the Commonwealth. Even worse, it would transform their country from a great power equal to the USSR and the United States to a hanger-on of continental Western Europe, as Churchill professed in 1952: "I love France and Belgium, but we must not allow ourselves to be dragged down to that level." Still, the United Kingdom could not stay aloof from the new realities on the continent. In December 1954, it signed an association agreement with the ECSC in order to enjoy some of the economic benefits of the French-led integration project.[24]

Successful supranational integration in economics, however, still did not extend to the military sphere. North Korea's attack on the southern half of that country on June 25, 1950, convinced the United States of the need to rearm West Germany in order to deter the perceived threat of a similar attack emanating from communist East Germany. To prevent the rise of unchecked German militarism, French President of the Council of Ministers René Pleven proposed the creation of an integrated European army on October 26 – along lines similar to the ECSC. The United States was not enthusiastic about the French idea because it looked militarily unsound, but it was not willing to block further steps in the European integration process. After one and a half years of negotiations, on May 27, 1952, France, the Benelux countries, West Germany, and Italy signed the treaty of the European Defense Community (EDC), which merged all their national armies under NATO command but which also directly controlled the yet-to-be-built army of the Federal Republic of Germany. The treaty never went into force because France subsequently had doubts about losing national sovereignty over its armed forces and thereby its predominance in Western Europe. Eventually, on August 30, 1954, the National Assembly refused to ratify the EDC because of the Franco–American conflicts over the first Indochina War. Instead, prompted by Britain, the members of the Brussels Pact agreed to let West Germany and Italy join their non-operational alliance, which opened the path for their direct membership in NATO. Afraid of unchecked German rearmament, France ratified the pertinent Paris Agreement from October 23, 1954, only at Anglo–American prodding. The ensuing West German accession to NATO on May 6, 1955, both deepened Cold War bloc formation in Europe and cemented the bifurcation of Western Europe's military and economic integration.[25]

Ten years after World War II, Western European recovery looked impressive. Germany and Italy were undergoing economic miracles. After recuperating from war destruction caused by German occupation, the Dutch economy boomed during all of the 1950s. Belgium and Luxembourg, which both had a long-standing economic union, recovered quickly after liberation, mostly because of the low level of war-related damage. Open American markets after the war and US economic needs after the outbreak of the Korean War also allowed them to supply semi-finished products. But in France, post-war recovery was slower than in the neighboring countries. During the 1950s, the country's economy developed only at the OEEC average, though it exceeded that average in the following decade. As France faced structural problems in many sectors of its economy after World War II, the government imposed, under Jean Monnet's watch, reforms and economic modernization on a scale that postponed recovery by a decade. While the *Six* prospered economically, the United Kingdom lagged behind. This was partially due to the decline – caused, to a certain degree, by the American post-war policy of global liberalization – in its economic relationship with the Empire and the Commonwealth, which London had originally used to justify its refusal to enter the ECSC. That the recipient of the largest share of the Marshall Plan fared so poorly, however, raises the question of the degree to which the 12.7 billion US dollars had a direct economic effect on European recovery. In any case, the American aid program played primarily a psychological and political role because it inspired, encouraged, and even pushed the European partners to cooperate with each other in economics and create cohesion against the Soviet threat.[26]

By 1955, Western European integration had occurred in more or less concentric circles. Military integration had happened at the Atlantic level, the payments union among seventeen OEEC countries (the original sixteen plus West Germany), the Council of Europe among fourteen participants, the ECSC among six members, and the Benelux customs union among three neighbors. As ardent integrationists, the Benelux countries grew concerned that the collapse of the EDC might undermine cohesion or, worse, even reverse the process of integration. Just as West Germany entered NATO in May 1955, they demanded that the ECSC should turn into a general customs union among the *Six*. The other three welcomed the proposal, though with some hesitation. Eventually, the *Six* agreed at the Messina Conference on June 1–3, 1955, to "work for the establishment of a united Europe by the development of common institutions, the progressive fusion of national economies, [and] the creation of a common market." After almost two years of strenuous negotiations, the *Six* signed treaties for two new communities in Rome on March 25, 1957. The European Economic Community (EEC) created a general common market (customs union), and envisioned future agreements on a common agriculture policy, a common transport policy, and a common social fund. The European Atomic Energy Community (Euratom) coordinated research and civilian use of nuclear energy. The United States once more supported this new round of integration, since it replaced six individual countries with one supranational unit, with which Washington found it easier to negotiate and coordinate policies.[27]

From the very beginning, the United Kingdom was skeptical about the Benelux push for greater integration, though Conservative Prime

Minister Harold Macmillan initially allowed participation in the negotiations. Some members of his cabinet hoped to kill supranational integration in favor of a free trade area based on the OEEC. London continued to fear that participation in the Rome Treaties would undermine trade with the Empire and Commonwealth – at that time still three times larger than trade with the *Six* – and lead to a gradual loss of sovereignty in a process that would end in complete political union. But coupled with pragmatic thinking was the illusion that the country still belonged to the small circle of the world's great powers; the United Kingdom justified its rejection because it did not want to join what it considered a "club of defeated nations." Britain's dismissive attitude toward the Rome Treaties in March 1957 and its destructive attempts to derail ratification in the national parliaments of the *Six* afterward, however, could not mask the country's international loss of prestige following the Suez debacle in late 1956. The United Kingdom just about managed to hang on to great power status on the basis of its nuclear weapons, as described in the previous chapter. To London's chagrin, Washington supported the Rome Treaties as a guarantee to bind West Germany into a unified Europe that was able to stand up to the Soviet Union. As the common market of the *Six* came into effect on January 1, 1958, Britain realized that it needed some form of economic association to prevent being cut off. But since a free trade agreement with the *Six* was not in the cards, the United Kingdom managed to convince Sweden, Austria, Denmark, Norway, Portugal, and Switzerland to establish the European Free Trade Association (EFTA) – the *Seven* – by May 1960. This rival organization made little sense, since each of its members – except for Portugal – traded individually more with the *Six* than with the other members combined.[28]

Thus, fifteen years after World War II, the seventeen OEEC countries were divided into two parallel economic organizations and four unaffiliated countries (Turkey, Greece, Ireland, and Iceland). By then, the OEEC had become less important to the European integration process, particularly after the end of the Marshall Plan in the early 1950s. The Payments Union had fulfilled its purpose of restoring trade among OEEC members, and had even helped to establish payment parity between them and the United States. It faltered in 1956–60, largely because of the parallel establishment of the EEC and EFTA. In December 1960, the members of the OEEC decided to transform it into the Organization for Economic Cooperation and Development (OECD). As the new organization allowed non-European members like Canada, Japan, and the United States to join, it ceased being a tool for European integration.[29]

Crisis, Enlargement, and Reform, 1958–79

The crisis of European integration in 1958–69 did not stem from British obstructionism but from radical changes in France's political system. When de Gaulle returned to power on June 1, 1958, he shared some of the British reservations about the supranational character of the European integration process. Gaullist and communist members of the National Assembly had cooperated in bringing down the EDC in August 1954, although for different reasons. De Gaulle wanted to replace the American-backed supranational community of the *Six* with a federation of sovereign, continental European countries – misleadingly named the "European Political Union" – under French leadership, and without British participation and American backing. His anti-Anglo/American reflexes dated to the post-World War II period; he had not forgiven Churchill for the British move against French interests in the Levant in May of 1945. His ultimate goal was to establish France as an equal to the Big Three in international affairs. But in mid 1958, de Gaulle's anti-British impulses still prevailed over his anti-supranational convictions. Since he was primarily afraid that British free trade policies aimed at establishing London's dominance in Western Europe at the expense of Paris, de Gaulle quickly informed the United Kingdom that France resented British attempts to derail the ratification of the Rome Treaties, which in turn was the final straw for Macmillan to establish the EFTA. De Gaulle's anti-Anglo/American focus on continental Europe led him to invite West Germany's Chancellor Adenauer, an outspoken Atlanticist, to his country house in Colombey-les-Deux-Églises in September 1958 to promote European reconciliation under French leadership.[30]

De Gaulle's France First policy not only had an impact on the cohesion of the Free World, as described in Chapter 4, but also strained the operations of the three European communities in the realm of membership enlargement and internal politics. By the end of 1960, the British government realized that the anemic EFTA of the *Seven* had not solved the problem of being shut out of the vibrant common market of the *Six*. London had realized that it needed the EEC for its own modernization, given that the British economy was the slowest growing in Western Europe. Hence, the declining great power decided to join what it had mocked as a community of defeated nations only some years earlier. Macmillan's government received strong backing to apply for EEC membership from the incoming Kennedy administration. Washington had concluded that London's "peripheral" seven-member free trade association was an "anachronistic nonsense" embraced by a former imperial power that "had not yet adjusted to reality." Great Britain started formal negotiations on membership, including associated status for the Commonwealth countries, in the second half of 1961, with its close trading partners Ireland, Denmark, and Norway in tow. De Gaulle now faced the consequence of his own recent anti-British policies; the United Kingdom applied for membership in a supranational community which he had defended against earlier British attempts to destroy it. But London had chosen an inopportune moment, just when Paris was trying to rebuild the club as a French-led federated Europe. The unrelated Anglo–American Nassau Agreement on nuclear missiles in late 1962 provided de Gaulle with the perfect excuse to veto British membership on January 14, 1963, and thereby freeze the applications of the other three. A resurging France thus punished the declining United Kingdom for past and recent slights. As an alternative, de Gaulle sought a close Franco–German partnership with a bilateral treaty eight days later, designed to exclude Anglo–American influence from Europe.[31]

France's unilateral surprise decision to keep the United Kingdom out of the *Six* infuriated the other members, particularly since the hexagonal community was also concurrently at loggerheads over the Common Agricultural Policy (CAP). Because France was the only country among the *Six* to produce more food than needed, de Gaulle for years had pursued a joint agricultural policy that aimed at benefitting French farmers. This included guaranteed high prices for agricultural producers within the *Six* and high custom barriers for competitors from the outside. The row came to a head on June 30, 1965, during the so-called Empty Chair Crisis when de Gaulle withdrew his representative from the Council of Ministers of the EEC in protest against supranational decision-making procedures. The *Six* overcame the deadlock with the Luxembourg Compromise in early 1966. The joint defiance of the other five EEC members and his slim victory in the second round of the French presidential election late in 1965 had forced de Gaulle to seek de-escalation. Still, the compromise abolished the supranational procedure of qualified majority voting in favor of unanimity in decision-making, i.e. it *de facto* introduced national vetoes. However, the Empty Chair Crisis did not affect the ratification and implementation of the Merger Treaty, which the *Six* had signed on April 8, 1965. Coming into effect on January 1, 1967, it rationalized the parallel institutions of the ECSC, the EEC, and Euratom by amalgamating them into the European Communities (EC) with a joint European Commission (formerly High Authority), a joint European Council (formerly the Council of Ministers), and a joint Court of Justice. Only the Parliamentary Assembly remained unchanged since all three communities had shared it since 1958 anyway, though it had been renamed the European Parliament two years later.[32]

When the tenth anniversary of de Gaulle's return to power was approaching, the varnish of his policy of national *grandeur* was fading, as described in preceding chapters. His France had failed to achieve equality with the United States and the United Kingdom in NATO, while it had irritated the smaller partners in the EEC. West Germany continued to be committed to American-led Atlanticism in the global Cold War. His anti-Anglo/American policy of improving relations with the USSR had floundered during the Berlin Crisis in 1961 and at the Soviet–American–British Nuclear Test Ban Treaty two years later. An attempt to reach out to the People's Republic of China in 1963–64 also did not reap any of the expected benefits. Thus, when Labour Prime Minister Harold Wilson applied for British membership in the merged EC in early 1967 – again with Ireland, Denmark, and Norway in tow – de Gaulle initially announced that he would not to use the veto but then changed his mind within half a year out of fear that a larger community would erode French dominance. At least, the British application for membership included an unqualified UK commitment to integration, with neither demands for exemptions nor references to the Commonwealth. Since trade with the former colonies had significantly declined and the British economic growth rate still had been among the lowest in Western Europe for the entire decade, the United Kingdom's desire to stay aloof from the integration process had greatly weakened. By April 1969, de Gaulle, the main opponent of British membership in the EC, resigned as French president and went into self-imposed exile at his country house. His successor, Georges Pompidou, reversed the long-standing hostility toward the United Kingdom. For him, British membership was a strategic necessity for the shared economic modernization of all of Western Europe.[33]

The parallel phenomena of continued decline of British power and of crumbling French obstructionism occurred at a time of increased American skepticism about the European integration project. Washington had grown disappointed that, two decades after the Marshall Plan, it did not reap the strategic benefits it had expected. Originally, it had hoped that American-supported integration and economic growth in Western Europe would lead to greater military burden sharing among NATO members against the Soviet threat. Moreover, virtually all European leaders, not only de Gaulle, criticized the American involvement in Vietnam, where the White House believed it was defending the Free World against communist expansionism. Even worse, the American war effort in Southeast Asia heavily taxed the US economy, leading to increases in governmental debt, inflation, unemployment, and outflow of foreign capital. The negative US trading balance, particularly with Europe and Japan, also drained American gold reserves, given that the Bretton Woods system functioned on the basis of the gold standard and exchange rate stability (dollar pegging). In 1967, four non-EC members – the United Kingdom, Denmark, Finland, and Spain – devalued their currencies to regain international competitiveness in relation to both the United States and the European Communities. Given all these developments, US President Richard M. Nixon decided on August 13, 1971, to suspend the dollar–gold convertibility and to impose a 10-percent import tariff on manufactured goods, both of which called into question the Bretton Woods System and the underlying American commitment to global trade liberalism. Washington achieved its short-term goal in obtaining devaluation of the US dollar and the revaluation of the currencies of West Germany, the Benelux countries, Switzerland, and Japan, but he thereby set parts of the Bretton Woods System on the path to oblivion. With the start of freely floating exchange rates in March 1973, one of the system's foundation stones disappeared. In its wake, national currencies in Europe were devalued and revalued regardless of membership in the EC or EFTA. For example, the West German mark doubled in value compared to the US dollar and gained 50 percent on the French franc within a few years. These kinds of adjustments in exchange rates increased strains on both US–European trade relations and those within the European Communities, and temporarily created obstacles to further European integration. Yet they also created new opportunities for the EC to develop.[34]

In the second half of 1970, finally, negotiations on the three-year-old UK application for membership started in the wake of the Conservative election victory in June. Incoming Prime Minister Edward Heath had understood that the United Kingdom, given its global and economic decline, needed a strategic realignment with France. He had campaigned explicitly on joining the European Communities, which questioned the validity of Labour's subsequent claim that Wilson's EC application of 1967 had been responsible for the party's election defeat three years later. By the fall of 1971, the European Communities and the United Kingdom agreed on accession. London obtained minor concessions with regard to the Commonwealth, did not benefit from the CAP, and was to pay up to 20 percent of the EC budget within four years of membership. Between October 1971 and the following July, parliament approved the legislation to transfer existing EC legislation into UK law. Entry was set for January 1, 1973. On that date, two of the other three applicants joined as well. In a referendum in May 1972, 83 percent of Irish voters had approved membership, and in early October, 63.5 percent of Danish voters had done so, too. Norwegian voters, however, rejected membership in late September by 53.5 percent. Only the British people could not vote for or against joining the European Communities – but French voters did that for them. On April 23, 1972, France held a referendum on the accession treaty of the four applicants; 68 percent of those who went to the polls followed the call of de Gaulle's successor, President Pompidou, to vote in favor. Heath's decision to enter the EC without a popular vote was primarily a hurried defensive move in view of the deepening economic malaise in the country.[35]

When the United Kingdom joined the European Communities on January 1, 1973, the Conservative government continued to entertain the hope of reducing the community's supranational characteristics to a minimum, to reform the CAP, and to increase free trade with the outside world. In short, London still clung to its attempts to impose its decade-old positions, but this time from within. This position collided with the decision of the EC in October 1972 to create a European Union in the long term. After joining the European Communities, the United Kingdom also showed a remarkable lack of solidarity toward its new partners during the oil crisis in 1973–74. Interested in securing its own oil supplies, the United Kingdom buckled under Arab demands to disallow oil deliveries from third-party suppliers to the Netherlands, which suffered from a complete Arab oil embargo in the wake of the October War. Moreover, during the same year, British public opinion turned from being split about EC membership to rejecting it – an expression of the widespread dissatisfaction with the continued deterioration of the state of the economy. After a snap election in February 1974 that produced a hung parliament, Wilson returned as prime minister at the head of a minority government. On the promise of holding a referendum following renegotiations of the terms of EC membership, he handily won another snap election in October. In subsequent renegotiations, the United Kingdom demanded an increase of agricultural imports from the Commonwealth, the reduction of the country's contribution to the EC budget, and the re-establishment of parliamentary sovereignty in adopting EC law. After London had obtained minor concessions from the other eight only with regard to trade with the Commonwealth, the referendum on June 5, 1975, produced a 67.2 percent vote in favor of continued membership. Ironically, the Labour government was split about the issue, while the Conservative opposition campaigned in favor of membership – under the leadership of its new head, Margaret Thatcher.[36]

In the wake of British entry into the European Communities, the Franco–German engine, which had jumpstarted the integration process in 1950, sprang back to life. In May 1974, Helmut Schmidt and Valéry Giscard d'Estaing assumed the German chancellorship and French presidency, respectively, within less than a fortnight of each other. Not only were both deeply committed to a united Europe and influenced by Monnet's latest ideas on financial and democratic integration, but they also became close personal friends and partners in promoting that process. With the Franco–German engine running well once more after almost two decades of sputtering, the European Communities addressed two major issues that had become pressing in recent years. The first concerned the need to bring long-term stability into the exchange rates between all membership currencies. The devaluations of non-EC currencies and the resulting pressures on EC currencies in the late 1960s had led the community in 1969 to agree to the introduction of a joint reserve bank and a common currency. But these plans had floundered in 1971 over France's concerns about the weakness of the French franc and the turbulences following Nixon's unilateral measures to abrogate the Bretton Woods system. In the wake of the oil shock in 1973–74, Schmidt and Giscard d'Estaing proposed the European Monetary System, with the goal of institutionalizing and tightening an informal agreement from 1972 that kept exchange rates of membership currencies within a narrow band of permitted fluctuations. In many respects, the agreement that was reached in 1978 reintroduced a Bretton Woods-style monetary system of mutually pegged currencies in Europe but without a formal lead currency. Within a few years, however, most currencies ended up tied to the reliably stable West German mark. Ultimately, the European Monetary System was the beginning of Europe's currency emancipation from the United States after almost thirty years of beneficial dependence.[37]

The second issue that the EC addressed was internal democratization. European integration had been an elite-driven project since the late 1940s. Only the four recent applicants had held popular referenda about membership. The original *Six* had established the ECSC and the EC without direct democratic legitimization, and members of the European Parliament were not directly elected. Democratic legitimization in all EC institutions was only indirect, through democratically elected national governments and members of the European Parliament that were chosen by democratically elected national parliaments. Thus, the Commission and EC members pushed for the introduction of direct elections to the European Parliament for 1979. The goal was to increase citizen interest and input in the European project, though apathetic voter behavior in much of the following decade did not fulfill the ambition.[38]

Conclusion

By 1979, the European integration process had reached a form in which today's European Union is clearly discernible. The ECSC/EC helped to bring prosperity back to Western Europe within twenty-five years after World War II, created cohesive institutions that survived both British outside pressure and a French internal challenge, strengthened the liberal order in Western Europe against Soviet influence, persisted through the American withdrawal of political support in the early 1970s, and was open to new members. Thus, Greece, Spain, and Portugal joined in the 1980s in the hope of locking in their regained democratic forms of government and to access funds to modernize their economies. Until 1993, however, democracy and human rights were not official requirements for membership in the EC.[39] Yet the democratic nature of the participants in the European integration process had always been the implicit default position since Coudenhove-Kalergi's *Pan-Europa* in 1923.

There are some obvious reasons why the European integration process worked in the three decades after World War II. While the United States provided a stable and supportive framework within the context of the emerging global Cold War that allowed Europe to restore its place in the world, the ideas that shaped integration were homegrown. Many reached back to the interwar period. Economic interdependence between former antagonists, particularly between France and Germany, was crucial for the success of the project. Although the larger members of the original *Six*, particularly France, pushed the process of supranational integration, the smaller members had pioneered some of the basic building blocks in the 1940s, pressed for further integration by the mid 1950s, and served as a check on French dominance in the 1960s. Less obvious but equally important were a few other reasons. The collective life experience and similarity in political outlook of the founding fathers was an important lubricant in the initial years of integration. The fusion of the heavy industrial sector, explored in rudimentary form in the 1920s, was equally decisive. The integration of the central backbones of the economies of the original *Six* predetermined the further path of integration. At the same time, the seminal protectionist focus on the important heavy industrial sector ensured a high degree of economic independence from foreign, potentially destabilizing influence – be it from the USSR or the United States. Western European integration thus benefited from a combination of several, mutually reinforcing factors: the commitment to oppose the Soviet Union, the unwillingness to submit to British global interests, the resistance to internal French domination, the support of the United States, and the general agreement among the principal Western European continental actors about the overall direction of the project.

16   The Council for Mutual Economic Assistance

"The disintegration of the single, all-embracing world market must be regarded as the most important economic sequel of the Second World War," Iosif V. Stalin claimed in 1952, adding that "now we have two parallel world markets . . . confronting one another."[1] Since the Bolshevik Revolution in 1917, the Soviet Union had aimed at creating a socialist economic system that would supersede the imperialist–capitalist order on a global scale in due course. But until 1945, this system had existed only in one country. In the wake of the military advancements in World War II, the USSR created the conditions for its expansion into Eastern Europe. Contrary to his assertion of 1952, Stalin had only managed to create a shadow of the Western European integration process. But three years earlier, with the communist revolution in China, the opportunity to expand the socialist economic system into Asia had fallen into his lap.

The socialist economic system in Eastern Europe – the Council for Mutual Economic Assistance (CMEA) – was formally established in 1949. It was *not* a mirror image of Western European integration, even if the Marshall Plan of 1947 spurred its creation. The CMEA was primarily a defensive move to protect Soviet territorial gains in Eastern Europe. Most of the countries there did not join the CMEA because they genuinely believed in its purpose – that is, of rivaling the capitalist half of Europe after Stalin had forced them to cut relations with it on ideological grounds. Although the dictator clearly aimed at exporting the Soviet system to the world, he simultaneously seemed not to be convinced about the CMEA either. His successors understood that the organization was flawed. Within two decades, several socialist states opted out of the integrated socialist economic system – Yugoslavia due to political conflict, China and Albania for ideological reasons, and Romania for nationalist objectives. Because the USSR was the dominant member, it initiated reforms in every decade to provide the CMEA with greater purpose and direction. Competition with the capitalist economic system, particularly its increasingly dynamic Western European variant, was the primary motivation. But the structural and ideological foundations which Stalin had put in place before 1953 remained remarkably resistant to change. On the one hand, Eastern European socialist states were effective in carving out room to maneuver that allowed them to evade, stymie, or even sabotage Soviet initiatives. Thus, within two decades of the end of World War II, Soviet-controlled Eastern Europe turned from a source of assets looted and reparations collected into an economic liability for the USSR. On the other hand, proposals to introduce radical reforms – such as adopting Western European-style integration processes or even opening the CMEA up to the global economy – fell on deaf ears in Moscow, since the Soviet leaders were committed to socialist competition with capitalism until the 1980s. Anyway, the USSR arrogated the right to protect the integrity of the Socialist Camp by military force if any of the Eastern European CMEA members introduced reforms, as was the case in Hungary in 1956 and Czechoslovakia in 1968.

The CMEA was not a source of but a structural obstacle to effective economic development during its entire existence. Despite the Soviet understanding of its congenital flaws as early as the mid 1950s, neither the USSR nor the other member states ever managed to agree on a joint course of reform. Some Eastern European countries wished for fundamental transformations along the lines of the Western European integration model, others resisted any reform, and the Soviet Union stymied any proposals for change which threatened its domination in Eastern Europe. As a result, the CMEA remained trapped in a continuous state of necessary but unrealized reforms. The lack of structural adaptation to a rapidly changing world economy thus turned the CMEA into a failure by the 1970s. The vicious interaction between its unreformability and its deepening economic crisis forced CMEA members to open to, and in the process become dependent on, the global economy via international financial markets. Jointly, these structural developments were co-responsible for the collapse of Soviet domination in Eastern Europe in the 1980s and the desire of that semi-continent to join the European Community/European Union in the subsequent decade.

From Bolshevik Revolution to Eastern European Empire, 1917–45

For the first third of its 74-year existence, the Soviet state aimed at independence from the global economy. Foreign trade as a percentage of all economic activity fell from over 10 percent in pre-World War I Russia to 3–4 percent in 1930 and to 0.5 percent in 1937.[2] The Soviet Union accomplished this level of economic self-sufficiency because it declared ideological war on the imperialist–capitalist world system in

1917/18, risked far-reaching exclusion from global trade in response, and then made the conscious decision to seek economic independence. However, a certain level of trade always remained crucial to satisfy the need for technological imports, which were supposed to make the first proletarian state the most advanced country in the world.[3]

The Bolshevik Revolution of November 1917 aimed at smashing capitalism in Russia and destroying imperialism in the rest of the world. Within less than a year, the revolutionary government claimed overall management of the national economy, started to nationalize banks, industry and enterprises, and socialized all land. Over the course of 1918, its monetary system collapsed as a result of the war-related ruble depreciation and the ideological commitment to abolishing money. The assertion of control over foreign trade aimed at protecting the new state from foreign financial interventions and at using trade for the sole purpose of developing the national economy. On February 3, 1918, the Soviet government renounced all the foreign liabilities of its Tsarist predecessor, which destroyed its international creditworthiness and alienated European lenders. Revolutionary upheaval and civil war ensured that, throughout the first three years of Soviet power, the new state had a negative trading balance, with imports surpassing exports by a factor of ten or more.[4]

Revolutionary radicalism and the civil war completely ruined the economy within a few years. With victory in sight in the early 1920s, Soviet Russia managed to sign trade agreements with virtually all neighbors from Finland to Afghanistan. The first proletarian state imported machines, manufactured goods, medicine, and food, while it exported agricultural and raw materials. Gold and dwindling hard currency reserves were used to cover the continued post-1917 trade deficit. Still, the restoration of foreign trade preceded the New Economic Policy, which reintroduced a stable currency and internal market mechanisms in 1921–22. Yet the USSR continued to refuse to accept Tsarist liabilities with the counter-argument that foreign intervention in the civil war had caused much greater economic damage. Moscow managed to achieve a breakthrough in re-establishing foreign economic relations by reaching out to another pariah in Europe – Berlin. With the Rapallo Treaty of mid April 1922, the USSR and Germany canceled financial claims against each other and established formal trade relations. The treaty provided Germany with support to refuse paying reparations to Great Britain and France in 1922, which in turn triggered the French occupation of the Ruhr Valley and ultimately the reordering of reparations and war debt payments through the Dawes Plan in 1924. Within another two years, the Soviet Union established diplomatic and trade relations with France, the United Kingdom, Austria, and the Scandinavian countries.[5]

With Stalin's ascent to power in the late 1920s, the USSR chose to concentrate on "building socialism in one country." The new policy took until the early 1930s to come into focus, but had two major goals from the very beginning: to overcome the remnants of bourgeois society and capitalist economy at home, and to ready the country to withstand imperialist–capitalist interventions from abroad. Consequently, the focus on the domestic construction of a comprehensive socialist economy reduced the ideologically determined export of revolution. The Stalinist inward turn had a mix of pragmatic, ideological, and instrumental reasons. While the New Economic Policy – which itself was a retreat from building a communist society – had helped the Soviet economy to bounce back, the various dysfunctionalities it had created set off heated debates about the future of socio-economic development. Stalin's revolutionary economic transformation from above generated yet another dysfunctional system within a few years. Yet, at the same time, his government had come to believe that a "partial stabilization of capitalism" had occurred after the first years of the global Great Depression of the 1930s, which in turn led to the threat of a renewed "capitalist encirclement" of the Soviet Union.[6]

The Stalinist policy of "building socialism in one country" included various mutually reinforcing characteristics: central planning as a supposedly rational method of running a socialist economy, the development of heavy industry as the assumed overall engine of the economy, the nationalization of all remaining private businesses, and the complete socialization of the peasantry (collectivization). Foreign economic relations primarily had to serve the Stalinist modernization project, until the country was ready to produce everything on its own. Consequently, at the beginning of the 1930s, this policy triggered a short expansion in foreign trade, though never to the levels of the late Tsarist period. The first proletarian society exported agricultural products, raw materials, and oil as payment for the import of technology and scarce goods. In the end, Soviet economic independence was a self-chosen, long-term policy. In early 1941, Stalin summarized the main points of his economic model: "The main task of planning is to ensure the independence of the socialist economy from the capitalist encirclement ... It is a type of battle with world capitalism. The basis of planning is to reach the point where metal and machines are in our hands and we are not dependent on the capitalist economy."[7]

Three years of warfare in the wake of the invasion by National Socialist Germany and its Romanian and Hungarian allies in 1941 caused massive destruction to the western USSR. In 1941–45, 12 billion US dollars in Anglo–American aid reached the Soviet Union, equal to at least 4 percent of the national economic output. The first proletarian society emerged from World War II victorious, but greatly weakened. Its sheer survival in the brutal war seemed to confirm the viability of the Stalinist system. But the gap in economic power in comparison to the leading imperialist–capitalist power – the United States – had increased even more, largely because the war had caused no physical damage to American economic infrastructure. As Washington set about reordering the world economy in its own image, Moscow faced the question of entering the American-led Bretton Woods system. Stalin allowed the participation of a Soviet delegation in the negotiations of 1944. Soviet specialists internally argued for the ratification of the Bretton Woods agreements, since this would release billions of US dollars in reconstruction credits. In the last days of 1945, however, Stalin vetoed these plans. Upset by the collapse of the war alliance among the Big Three and steeped in his ideological convictions, he saw the new system primarily as an American attempt to dominate the world at the expense of the USSR. Hence, Soviet participation would have been a sign of weakness. In a misjudgment of American needs for Soviet membership in the Bretton Woods system, Stalin believed that Moscow could even extract more economic assistance from Washington in the future as a condition for participation.[8]

Opting out of the post-World War II international economic system increased the value of resources in occupied Eastern Europe. When Soviet troops arrived in 1943–45, they entered a region that had experienced fifteen years of turbulent economic development. The disintegration of the world economy after 1929 and the war ten years later had led to the partial integration of Poland, the Czech half of Czechoslovakia, and Yugoslavia into the economy of National Socialist Germany, or at least to alignment with it, as in the case of Slovakia, Hungary, Romania, and Bulgaria. At the war's end, Stalin ruled over a partially destroyed and socio-economically chaotic region that reached from the Baltic to the Black Sea. To complicate matters, the USSR had almost no interwar history of economic relations with the region. Before World War II, Eastern European countries traded to some degree with each other, but the bulk of Eastern European and Soviet trade occurred along parallel channels with countries in Western Europe.[9]

On the grounds of national security and revolutionary long-term goals, Stalin aimed at keeping control over Eastern Europe. However, at the end of the war, he had neither the necessary resources nor detailed plans to impose communist regimes. Initially, the Soviet dictator also acted cautiously. He ostensibly honored the percentage agreement, which UK Prime Minister Winston Churchill had concluded with him behind US President Franklin D. Roosevelt's back in October 1944 to fix post-war

Western and Soviet influence in Eastern Europe at various ratios. Still, Stalin was determined to ensure Soviet control from the very beginning. In a mirror image of the European governments which went into exile in London during World War II – including those from Poland, Czechoslovakia, and Yugoslavia – persecuted communists had fled European countries to seek refuge in Moscow since the 1930s. Those who survived the Stalinist purges underwent ideological training in the USSR to build up pro-Soviet regimes in their countries after the war. But when they returned home in the wake of the Soviet army, Stalin still allowed non-communists to enter provisional post-war governments. Yet Soviet authorities and the returned communists predetermined future economic development to a certain degree through the nationalization of industry, commerce, and banking as early as 1944.[10]

The lack of detailed Soviet plans for Eastern Europe resulted in incoherent economic developments. From 1944 to 1947, the struggle against war-induced inflation sparked Soviet-style monetary reforms, which *de facto* detached all Eastern European currencies from the Bretton Woods system. As early as October 1945, Soviet-style economic planning was introduced in Poland, to be followed soon in all other Eastern European countries and the Soviet occupation zone of Germany. By 1946, the USSR and the communist-dominated regimes in Eastern Europe started to discuss greater economic cooperation. Yet, at the same time, Eastern European countries also re-established interwar trade relations with Western Europe since the Soviet Union was unable to deliver goods and machines needed for reconstruction and recovery. In some cases, trade with Western countries grew faster than with the USSR.[11]

To complicate matters even further, the Soviet Union extracted economic assets from Eastern Europe. In the case of the former war enemies Hungary and Romania, the USSR calculated reparations on the basis of war damages to the USSR and costs of liberation. With regard to Germany, the Soviet government had pondered the idea of transferring economic assets and labor to the USSR as early as 1943. At the Yalta Conference of the Big Three in February 1945, Stalin thus had demanded that Churchill and Roosevelt approve a total of 20 billion US dollars of reparations to the Soviet Union. The two Western leaders did not reject the request outright because they did not want to endanger the war alliance, but they felt uncomfortable given the bad experiences with reparations following World War I. In the case of non-enemies, Soviet dismantling of assets started the following month in Silesia, the former German territory in post-war Poland. Eventually, the Paris Peace Treaties of early 1947 fixed reparation payments by Hungary and Romania at 200 and 300 million US dollars, respectively. In total, the

USSR dismantled economic assets in the eastern half of the continent – mostly from the Soviet zone of occupation of Germany – to the tune of 15 to 20 billion US dollars before the operation ceased in the mid 1950s.[12]

Reacting to the Marshall Plan, 1947–53

The Soviet Union responded with hesitation to the announcement of the European Recovery Plan by US Secretary of State George C. Marshall on June 5, 1947. On the one hand, Moscow placed the proposed program within the context of a more assertive American policy following the pronouncement of the Truman Doctrine three months earlier. On the other hand, the USSR was willing to participate in negotiations; it even instructed Eastern European socialist countries to prepare for the talks. Applying Marxist–Leninist ideology, Stalin believed that the US economy needed to increase access to foreign markets to ward off an imminent domestic economic crisis in the wake of World War II. For practical reasons, he believed, the Soviet Union should exploit the American offer to benefit its own reconstruction. Confronted with the details of an American-financed, integrated Europe at the Paris talks, however, Stalin decided to pull out – in a repetition of his withdrawal from the Bretton Woods agreements less than two years before. The dictator understood that American actions had put him on the defensive, which is what the Truman administration had hoped the Marshall Plan would do all along. He particularly feared the rise of an integrated Western Europe outside his political reach, the unchecked resurgence of Germany, and an increase of American influence in Eastern Europe. Since the 1920s, the USSR had called Richard N. Coudenhove-Kalergi's anti-Soviet *Pan-Europa* and similar ideas imperialist–capitalist attempts to prevent the supposedly certain emergence of an alternative United States of Europe led by the revolutionary proletariat. Thus, Soviet propaganda after mid 1947 portrayed the Marshall Plan as a second Dawes Plan, designed to turn the Soviet Union into an "agricultural colony" similar to what the original plan, or so it claimed, had done to Germany a quarter of a century before. However, Stalin's decision to force Eastern European countries not to participate in the Paris negotiations saddled the USSR with the need to provide alternative forms of support. He thereby provided his empire in Eastern Europe with the ability to "strike back" with economic demands.[13]

Faced with the possible rise of an integrated and American-financed bloc in the other half of the European continent, a defensive Stalin reorganized his Eastern European empire politically and economically to preserve Soviet control. At the first conference of the Cominform in

Szklarska Poręba in late September 1947, the Soviet representative Andrei Zhdanov postulated that the world was divided into two antagonistic camps, and, consequently, that it was time for the socialist countries to cooperate more closely. Stalin's pressure on Josip Broz Tito to submit to his dictates triggered the famous Soviet–Yugoslav break in mid 1948. Oddly enough, Tito had not wanted to participate in the Marshall Plan negotiations at all but bowed to Stalin's pressure just days before the Soviet delegation withdrew from the Paris talks. A year later, Moscow expelled Belgrade from the Socialist Camp into Washington's aid-laden arms.[14]

Stalin needed to address the economic problems which his rejection of the Marshall Plan had caused in Eastern Europe quickly. Poland and Hungary had planned for 13 to 20 percent of their reconstruction investments to come from foreign sources. After being forced to forego Marshall Plan aid, the two received emergency funding from the USSR to fill some of the gaps. In 1948, the Soviet Union reduced the amount of war reparations from the former war enemies Hungary and Romania, but not those to be paid by the emerging East Germany. In the Soviet occupation zone of Germany, the Soviet authorities started to prepare a currency reform at the turn of 1947/48 in response to a similar reform in the Anglo–American zone that, they feared, would increase Western economic influence in all of Germany. Poland and Czechoslovakia – the only Eastern European members of the International Monetary Fund (IMF) and the World Bank – were forced to cut their institutional ties with the Bretton Woods system by 1950 and 1954, respectively. Warsaw used the opportunity to accuse Washington of exploiting the two institutions to punish those countries that had balked at "acceding to the so-called Marshall Plan."[15]

Yet Soviet stopgap measures were neither part of a greater plan nor a match for the 12.7 billion US dollars of European Recovery Money that poured into Western Europe from 1948 to 1951. The double need to shore up external defense and internal control had overshadowed the thinking about the long-term implications which these steps had for Eastern Europe. Thus, 1948 was a year of renewed economic *disintegration* – a development both within and beyond Stalin's control. Under Soviet pressure, Czechoslovakia and Poland dropped a July 1947 agreement on closer economic and energy cooperation that focused on the joint exploitation of the former German territory of Silesia. A Bulgarian–Yugoslav project of political and economic integration similarly faltered, and then was used by Stalin to justify his break with Tito in mid 1948. Soviet trade with Czechoslovakia, Hungary, and Poland shrank in 1947–48 after a short peak in the immediate post-war period, largely because Soviet exports were unable to satisfy specific needs. Moreover, the Socialist Camp as a whole faced the prospect of future isolation from the rest of the world economy. In March 1948, a month after the pro-Soviet coup in Czechoslovakia, the United States adopted a licensing system for exports to the camp. The embargo list of the international Coordinating Committee (CoCom) – an organization that initially brought together North Atlantic Treaty member states as well as Iceland and Japan – greatly reduced East–West trade within a few years and terminated almost completely the Western delivery of machines and technology classified as strategically important. Partially in response to this development, in June 1948 the USSR imposed an economic embargo against the Western occupation zones of Germany and Berlin – the so-called Berlin Blockade – that lasted for eleven months and additionally deepened the continent's economic division.[16]

It was against this background that the Council for Mutual Economic Assistance (CMEA) was established on January 5–7, 1949. The apparent impetus was a Romanian proposal that called for the combined goal of coordinating economic policies and warding off damage caused by Anglo–American economic warfare. As at the foundation of the Cominform sixteen months earlier, the USSR invited representatives from Poland, Czechoslovakia, Hungary, Romania, and Bulgaria to Moscow, though without announcing the agenda. At the meeting itself, Stalin insisted that the new organization should be open not only to additional socialist states but also to "workers from Italy, France, and other countries that [had] entered the orbit of the Marshall Plan." The CMEA aimed at providing an alternative so that Europe "can help itself" without American financial aid, or so he claimed. No Western European country ever took up the offer, but Albania and the German Democratic Republic (GDR; East Germany) joined the council within one year. Until his death on March 5, 1953, however, Stalin seemed to remain ambivalent about the CMEA, probably because he feared the rise of a multilateral organization, which he could not control completely. The CMEA held only three meetings before the dictator's demise – in April and August of 1949, and in November of 1950. All together, its members discussed such diverse topics as the organizational set-up, technological and scientific cooperation, pricing, payments, standardization, and the construction of a small number of heavy industrial projects.[17]

The increase of trade among CMEA member states in the years after 1948 happened primarily because Soviet post-war policies to detach the Socialist Camp from the world economy left them with few alternatives. In that vein, the three meetings in 1949–50 severely criticized Czechoslovakia for its remaining trade with Yugoslavia and the capitalist world. Against the background of the unfolding global Cold War, the organization aimed at forming a parallel international economic system for the Socialist Camp. Indeed, by 1952, over two-thirds of each member's foreign trade was with each other or with the People's Republic of China (PRC), up from less than 20 percent before World War II. In comparison, during the 1948–52 period, trade with the non-socialist world declined by 19 percent for the USSR and on average by 24 percent for the other CMEA members.[18]

Paradoxically, all CMEA members pursued national development policies to create self-sustaining economies despite the growth of trade between them. The Stalinist economic model, as it had developed in the 1930s, served as a paradigm. In 1949/50, Poland, East Germany, and Hungary started to construct planned heavy industrial cities in the image of Magnitogorsk (Magnetic Mountain City) – named Nowa Huta (New Steel Mill), Stalinstadt/Eisenhüttenstadt (Stalin City/Steel Mill City), and Sztálinváros/Dunaújváros (Stalin City/Danube City). Czechoslovakia planned a modern urban extension of Ostrava, including the construction of two additional steel mills. Yet the necessary bituminous coal mines and iron ore deposits only existed in a few of the CMEA countries – primarily the USSR and, to a lesser degree, in Poland and Czechoslovakia. Thus, the parallel national attempts to obtain far-reaching economic independence only resulted in increased dependencies on a small number of raw material suppliers.[19]

Moreover, the introduction of the Soviet economic model in Eastern Europe envisioned the nationalization of industry, business, and commerce. To be sure, individual Eastern European governments had some leeway in deciding how exactly to proceed, taking into account different levels of economic development and national particularities. Highly developed Czechoslovakia faced problems different from those of mainly rural Romania or partially destroyed East Germany. Still, the introduction of the Soviet economic model, even if it happened differently in each country, reduced incentives for trade among CMEA members. Central planning created intrinsic incentives to prioritize domestic development, which was easier to forecast, over foreign trade, where price fluctuations and supply uncertainties evaded the predictive powers of the national plan.[20]

In this context, the parallel centrality of heavy industry to the Stalinist model and to the Western European Coal and Steel Community (ECSC) offers illuminating comparisons. The *Six* of the ECSC sought the integration of existing heavy industries in order to reduce sources of conflict and tap into each other's strengths without having to rely on American supplies. Their preferred method was trade liberalization among themselves – i.e. the reduction of governmental intervention – in the form of a customs union. In comparison, most of the CMEA members built up parallel national heavy industrial capabilities – each on its own, but all with Soviet support – while adopting massive state intervention in the form of Soviet-style central planning.

Even if trade among CMEA countries increased in the initial years of the organization, it was still mostly limited to the delivery of goods from a surplus producer to a recipient suffering from shortages. In order to simplify and standardize this form of goods exchange, early on the CMEA introduced the *clearing ruble* as an accounting tool for bilateral trade, only a few years after the Benelux states, France, and Italy had adopted a financial clearing mechanism among themselves proposed by the United States. Simultaneously, the CMEA froze prices at 1949/50 world market levels in the hope of preventing erratic swings. Yet, in the long run, this policy failed to take into account developments in actual production costs and supply-and-demand-induced fluctuations of world market prices. Unsurprisingly, the pricing of goods quickly became subject to negotiations within the CMEA that produced arbitrary and even chaotic results.[21]

Although Poland and Czechoslovakia exported coal to the USSR until the early 1960s, Eastern European countries benefited from the underpricing of both Soviet energy and raw material supplies in the long-term. To a certain degree, these price distortions compensated them for Stalin's decision to reorient Eastern Europe economically from the capitalist West to the socialist East, but within a few decades they developed into a huge drain on Soviet economic resources. The inclination of Eastern European countries to rely on annual increases of subsidized Soviet raw material and energy deliveries suffocated incentives to undertake painful but necessary reforms in the wasteful and energy-hungry Stalinist economic model, even once the USSR reached the limits of its supply capabilities in the 1970s, as we will see further below.[22]

In 1952, when Stalin announced the emergence of two antagonistic "parallel world markets," he emphasized that the United States, the United Kingdom, and France had gravely erred when they "imposed an economic blockade on the U.S.S.R., China and the European people's democracies, which did not join the 'Marshall plan' system." But his triumphant assessment had two major blemishes. The CMEA was not a world market at all; at best, it was a *regional platform for goods exchange* established for defensive purposes. Moreover, the Socialist Camp still needed trade with the rest of the world to import technology and goods otherwise unavailable, as much as the Soviet Union had before World War II. It used various methods to obtain Western technology despite the CoCom embargo – sometimes illicit, at other times fortuitous.

The USSR benefited from studying Western technology, which it found in occupied Eastern Europe and even in the PRC in the 1950s. One historian surmised that Stalin's empire was an "imperial scavenger" of Western technology, aiming to win the Cold War by simply outwitting the imperialist–capitalist embargo.[23]

As Western European integration deepened in the period from 1950 to 1954, the CMEA did not convene any meetings at all. Instead, the USSR and East Germany intensified their propaganda war against Western European integration. The campaign aimed at laying blame for Europe's and Germany's division exclusively at the doorstep of the Anglo–American imperialist powers, while trying to portray the Soviet-led Socialist Camp as a genuine promoter of continent-wide unity. This kind of propaganda echoed earlier Soviet criticisms, including the disparagement of Coudenhove-Kalergi's *Pan-Europa* and the Dawes Plan, but it failed to recognize the high degree of Western European agency in the integration process. Since Stalinist theory defined the USSR, and in extension the other socialist countries, as inherently "peaceful" and the imperialist–capitalist countries as essentially "belligerent," it was incapable of seeing that peacebuilding by supranational integration provided the strong glue that kept Western European countries together.[24] This kind of adhesive helped the Western European integration process through the crises of the 1960s and 1970s, but its complete lack within the CMEA doomed the organization to failure from the very beginning.

Toward Integration, 1953–61

Stalin's death provided his successors with the opportunity to rethink Soviet foreign and economic policies. Within a short time, they sought to relax relations with the capitalist world, reform the Stalinist economic system at home and in Eastern Europe, and transform the CMEA into a genuine multilateral organization. The Soviet effort to reduce Cold War tensions had primarily domestic goals, i.e. the reassignment of state expenses from the inflated military budget to the neglected civilian sector. It also included increasing trade with the non-socialist world *both* as a means to acquire technology and goods otherwise not available *and* as the main arena of competition between the socialist and capitalist systems. In this quest, however, the USSR encountered numerous obstacles. Stalin's co-responsibility for the outbreak of the Korean War had worsened the isolation of the Socialist Camp; in response, the United States established a network of anti-Soviet alliances around the Socialist Camp that reached from Scandinavia across Europe, the Middle East, and Southeast Asia to the Pacific Rim. Thus, President Dwight D. Eisenhower was not disposed to welcome Soviet endeavors to relax tensions. Even worse, in May 1955, West Germany acceded to NATO. As a countermeasure, the emerging Soviet leader Nikita S. Khrushchev established the Warsaw Pact (WAPA) with the same membership as the CMEA. The new alliance was primarily destined to serve as a bargaining chip in the hoped-for negotiations with the United States over the dissolution of the North Atlantic Alliance to end the Cold War, but failed to achieve that purpose. The Polish October and the Hungarian Revolution in late 1956 increased Cold War tensions anew, with Khrushchev adding more fuel to the fire through his Berlin Ultimatum two years later. Yet, despite all these complications, the USSR managed to increase its foreign trade with the non-socialist world, although it continued to struggle with hard currency shortages and quality problems. Attempts to earn Western money through oil exports met with initial resistance from NATO governments, which feared politically dangerous dependencies, and from American-owned oil companies trying to keep out a new competitor. Yet, by 1961, the Soviet leadership was still convinced that the economic system of the USSR was superior to that of its capitalist rival and would surpass it within a decade.[25]

Reforming the Stalinist economic system to make it competitive with Western capitalism turned out to be a major headache for post-Stalinist leadership in Moscow. Although the Soviet Politburo would eventually criticize Khrushchev in October 1964 for "hare-brained scheming" when it overthrew him, his economic policies in the preceding decade still represented genuine attempts at reform. Khrushchev's initial rival, Georgii M. Malenkov, originally started reforms shortly after Stalin's death by proposing to launch the New Course. The new line was supposed to prop up the Stalinist system by making concessions to popular consumption needs. Once Khrushchev had superseded Malenkov, he went even further by pushing economic decentralization, the reform of enterprise management, the increase of food production, and the adoption of lessons learned from studying capitalist economies. But by the early 1960s, his policies started to falter.[26] In comparison to domestic reform, reorganizing the Eastern European empire was an even more difficult, if not a fundamental problem. How could the hastily assembled CMEA be transformed from a defensive economic system into one that could prove the superiority of socialist economics? Stalin had imposed the Soviet model in Eastern Europe regardless of its national suitability. Czechoslovakia had been much more developed than even the USSR, and Romania much less. Within weeks of Stalin's death, the new Soviet leaders tried to impose Malenkov's New Course of minimal de-Stalinization in East Germany, Hungary, and Albania. But the Uprising in East Germany in June 1953 and the Hungarian Revolution in October 1956 merely exposed the fragility of the regimes there. Spooked, Eastern European CMEA members generally shunned domestic reform for the remainder of the 1950s.

Moscow's efforts to overcome the burdensome legacies of Stalinism went hand in hand with its attempts rebuild the CMEA. At the fourth council meeting in March 1954, Anastas I. Mikoyan called for "self-criticism" of past shortcomings, particularly with regard to the lack of coordination in heavy industrial construction, which had led to the creation of "uneconomical" national steel mill complexes far away from iron and bituminous coal mines. He particularly decried the fact that all member states "want to produce everything by themselves," even if they lacked national expertise and resources. Thus, Mikoyan demanded enhanced cooperation, increased standardization, and the application of economies of scale through the geographic concentration of production. At its fifth meeting three months later, the CMEA adopted policies to coordinate all national economic plans. The concurrent decision to increase trade with the capitalist world had both practical and ideological goals. It was designed to increase "the living standard of the people" by securing otherwise unavailable goods, but it also aimed at reducing international "tensions" and consolidating "peace." The sixth meeting in December 1955 adopted detailed plans to erase "parallelisms in production" by apportioning the standardized production of automobiles, trucks, tractors, railroad cars and engines, and a range of agricultural machines to individual countries. At the seventh meeting in May 1956, which occurred ten weeks after Khrushchev's famous Secret Speech criticizing Stalin's mistakes, the CMEA admitted Yugoslavia and the PRC as observers, though both allowed their status to lapse after political divergences arose soon thereafter.[27]

Turmoil in Poland and Hungary in the fall of 1956 and the establishment of the European Economic Community (EEC) in the following spring forced the USSR to rethink the economics of the Socialist Camp once more. Emergency aid to Warsaw and particularly Budapest put many CMEA projects on hold for a while. Ultimately, it also forced the USSR to replace the remainder of the sixth Five-Year Plan (1956–60) and the whole seventh Five-Year Plan (1961–65) with a special but less ambitious Seven-Year Plan (1959–65). A Soviet review of the country's relations with other socialist states at the turn of 1956/57 revealed that CMEA member states and the PRC wanted the USSR to treat them as partners, not as imperial subjects. At the same time, Western markets seemed to close to CMEA trade, though for unrelated reasons. The signing of the Rome Treaties in March 1957, which created the EEC with a common external tariff by January 1, 1958, threatened to remove access to the emerging market, which the USSR had envisioned as a natural trading partner for the CMEA. Although the eighth meeting in June 1957 publicly criticized the creation of the EEC as "an obstacle for the development of foreign trade and other forms of economic cooperation among all European countries," Poland and Czechoslovakia proposed to respond by adopting EEC-style supranational integration in the CMEA. The two countries thereby implicitly violated the ideological framework of socialist revolution by advocating copying the methods of the capitalist enemy, but failed to win the debate. At least, the eighth meeting decided to transform the bilateral ruble clearing of 1950 into a multilateral clearing mechanism. The Soviet State Bank would assume the miniscule supranational role of clearing payments automatically. However, voluntary participation meant that the mechanism cleared only 1.5 percent of intra-CMEA trade until 1963.[28]

Greater economic integration in the CMEA emerged in 1958, though it was uneven in terms of geography and economic sectors. Within four years, for example, three out of eight members generated 72.1 percent of all intra-CMEA trade: the USSR (38.7 percent), the GDR (18.5 percent), and Czechoslovakia (14.9 percent). The division of the CMEA into a more integrated northern group (including Poland) and a less cohesive southern group (Bulgaria and Romania) – with Hungary in between – would remain a fundamental feature of the organization until its demise three decades later. Given the general resistance to further specialization beyond the 1955 decision, integration occurred primarily in the energy sector where the geographical distribution of fossil fuel resources was particularly lopsided. After years of stopgap measures to alleviate energy bottlenecks, the organization's tenth meeting in December 1958 decided to construct the *Druzhba* (Friendship) pipeline connecting Soviet oil fields to Poland, East Germany, Czechoslovakia, and Hungary. At the time of its completion in 1963, however, it was already insufficient to satisfy the annually growing energy demands in Eastern Europe. In May 1959, after five years of discussions, the eleventh meeting also decided to link national electricity networks, but only at the local level across bilateral borders.[29]

And by 1960/61, the CMEA was drawn into the local Cold War between the two Germanys. At that time, East Germany was the only Eastern European country still headed by a party leader trained in Moscow during World War II and installed by Stalin afterward. An unreconstructed national Stalinist throughout the 1950s, Walter Ulbricht sought the economic separation of his country from the despised capitalist other half. Hence, at the fourteenth meeting in March 1961, he demanded greater CMEA integration to thwart a supposed West German imperialist-economic intervention that would exploit the open borders in divided Berlin. The timing of the speech was not coincidental. Ulbricht was preparing to close the borders in the city in order to stop the continued exodus of dissatisfied citizens – a predicament that had undermined the development of the country's economy for a long time. At the Warsaw Pact meeting on August 3, 1961, during which the other Eastern European member states were informed about the imminent changes in Berlin, Ulbricht demanded economic support and, in particular, his country's economic reintegration with the former German territories in Poland (Silesia and Pomerania). In the weeks after the closure of the borders in Berlin on August 12–13, the GDR used combined WAPA/ CMEA channels to negotiate increases of supplies from the other socialist states, but managed to get only limited support. For most CMEA members, the pursuit of national interests was more important than the promotion of international solidarity.[30]

The Dream of Supranational Integration, 1961–68

The growing dissatisfaction with Eastern European resistance to specialization and the hasty closure of the Berlin borders pushed Moscow to seek extensive reforms for the CMEA by late 1961. Remarkably, the USSR took cues from the economically successful integration of the *Six*, which, coincidentally, had attracted at that very time another four applicants. Despite ubiquitous propaganda to the contrary, Soviet leaders understood that the EEC had become an inescapable reality in international affairs, and potentially even a model to emulate. Khrushchev and his economic advisers envisioned turning the CMEA into a "unified economic organism" able to prove the superiority of the socialist system in the peaceful competition with Western capitalism. They had concluded that the Stalinist "detachment of the national economy" from the rest of the world economy had been extraordinarily harmful to the USSR, and that it even contradicted the "objective law of development of the socialist economy." CMEA members hence needed to work for a maximal level in the division of labor among themselves to build up an internationally co-dependent, modern, and complex socialist economy that could rival the rapid economic modernization of the capitalist world. This required the creation of supranational bodies, like a "unitary planning organization," joint financial institutions to stimulate economy and trade, and shared investments in cross-border infrastructure projects. Peaceful competition with capitalism in the long term would lead to the peaceful reintegration of the supposedly superior Socialist Camp into the world economy, but only under the condition of the prior end to Western economic warfare, or so the Soviet leaders hoped.[31]

The extraordinary sixteenth meeting in June 1962 once more confirmed the principles of division of labor and plan coordination, while it also created the Executive Committee, a permanent supervisory and planning body. Even if it was not explicitly called a supranational institution, it subsequently assumed *de facto* supranational functions similar to, but less extensive than, the Commission of the EEC. The sixteenth meeting also decided to open the CMEA to non-European member applicants, like Outer Mongolia. The Asian country replaced Albania, which had refused to attend meetings since late 1961 because of its ideological conflict with the USSR.[32]

In December 1962, the newly constituted Executive Committee decided to launch the transfer ruble and create the International Bank of Economic Cooperation (IBEC) as of January 1, 1964. The new monetary unit was designed to automatize multilateral clearing of trade payments within the CMEA and third parties, provide low-interest credit to member states, finance multilateral infrastructure projects, and ultimately stimulate deeper integration. It was yet another accounting tool – not a freely circulating currency – although it was pegged to a gold standard to guarantee stability beyond the CMEA. The IBEC was the bank in charge of managing the transfer ruble, associated national accounts, hard currency assets, and the provision of short-term payment credits. It was permitted to obtain hard currency loans in the capitalist world and transform them into transfer rubles on the basis of the gold standard, given that Western currencies were still pegged to gold within the Bretton Woods system of 1944. The bank would thereby provide credit to CMEA member states for trade with the capitalist world. One sympathetic Western observer optimistically viewed the IBEC as the nucleus for a future "Socialist International Monetary Fund."[33]

The sometimes heavy-handed Soviet attempts at integration naturally met with resistance from some CMEA member states, particularly Romania. Khrushchev might have correctly understood that the world economy was in a "transitional period" toward greater international division of labor, and that, in this situation, it made no sense for any country to produce "everything ... from a pin to a spaceship." But the socialist internationalist in him did not reckon with the staying power of national Stalinism in Eastern Europe and with the determination of individual countries to carve out room to maneuver. Rural Romania particularly resented his plans for socialist division of labor within the CMEA, which aimed at turning the Balkan country into a mere "vegetable garden." But dissatisfaction went even deeper. In the context of the evolving Sino–Soviet split, Bucharest first mediated between the two squabbling communist giants, and then blocked the accession of fellow CMEA member Outer Mongolia to the Warsaw Pact in June and July 1963. It feared that Moscow was trying to drag socialist Eastern Europe into its conflict with Beijing. Anyway, as early as mid July 1962, Romania had called the Soviet push for a "unitary" CMEA plan for all member economies an attack on the "sovereignty of the socialist state." The country's Communist Party announced that Romania would "not agree to delegate tasks and ... responsibilities ... to another organ," particularly one that would be "supranational." At the eighteenth meeting in late July 1963, just after it had blocked Outer Mongolian membership in WAPA, Romania managed to extract from the other CMEA members the reconfirmation of the original principle of 1949 – never enforced by Stalin, though – that decisions needed to "respect the sovereignty and the national interests" of each member. Romania had *de facto* gained a right to veto further integration, similar to the one that Charles de Gaulle's France would obtain in the Luxembourg Compromise in 1966. Stalin's empire was striking back.[34]

In the face of Romania's national Stalinism, the three CMEA countries most committed to integration – the USSR, East Germany, and Czechoslovakia – pondered far-reaching domestic reorganizations to get ready for the global economy. The reforms started in 1963 in an unexpected place – the GDR. After the closure of the Berlin borders in August 1961, Ulbricht quickly abandoned his national Stalinist policies and experimented with economic liberalization at home. His *New Economic System of Planning and Management* aimed at reducing central planning, emphasizing profitability, and creating incentives for enterprises to increase production by allowing greater flexibility in setting wages, bonuses, and prices. Ultimately, the quantity and quality of East German products was supposed to reach a level sufficient to satisfy domestic demand and fulfill international standards. The so-called Kosygin reforms, which the USSR launched in September 1965, adopted some of the East German ideas. Starting with criticism of Khrushchev's reforms – particularly his failure to catch up with the West – Aleksei N. Kosygin, the chairman of the Council of Ministers, pushed for the recentralization of overall planning. At the same time, he was willing to permit greater independence to individual enterprises, the use of scientific econometrics as a planning tool, the application of the profitability principle, and the introduction of real prices. In parallel, Czechoslovakia too introduced economic reforms, which turned out to be the most radical of the three. The country's visions included the limitation of central planning to a small number of basic economic parameters, the elimination of plan targets, greater freedom for enterprises to set investment rates, wages and prices, the softening of the state's foreign trade monopoly, and calls to use loans from the capitalist world to modernize the economy.[35]

But the emerging conservative factions in the Soviet and East German communist parties – headed by Leonid I. Brezhnev and Erich Honecker, respectively – fought Kosygin's and Ulbricht's reform ideas as a supposed sell-out to capitalism. The sudden introduction of political reforms in Czechoslovakia in the wake of the country's economic reforms triggered the Soviet-led WAPA intervention in August 1968. What Soviet propaganda publicly called the restoration of socialism in a fraternal country was, in reality, an attempt to stop the further disintegration of the Socialist Camp. But Romania remained sensitive about the so-called Brezhnev Doctrine of late 1968, which postulated limited sovereignty of all WAPA/CMEA members and arrogated the right to the USSR to intervene wherever it believed socialism in a fraternal country was in danger. The intervention in Czechoslovakia thus had primarily a stifling impact on future economic reform. Moreover, given the mixed success of Ulbricht's and Kosygin's economic ideas, domestic reform in East Germany and the Soviet Union petered out by the early 1970s.[36]

While the GDR, the USSR, and Czechoslovakia were toying with domestic reform, the CMEA continued to focus on greater internal integration. In 1964, membership countries submitted data about their future Five-Year Plans for institution-wide coordination for the first time. The following year, the CMEA addressed the problem of insufficient oil deliveries by agreeing to a diameter extension of the two-year-old *Druzhba* pipeline. However, Moscow warned, the USSR could not satisfy the annually increasing demands of the energy-hungry Eastern European economies beyond 1970 due to production limits and shipment bottlenecks. Only changes in energy consumption and supply patterns could fix the problem. After Poland had complained that economic integration among CMEA countries lagged far behind even "poorly developed capitalist countries," the organization decided in mid 1966 that integration could occur at different speeds, with a faster northern group including Hungary, and a slower southern group comprising Romania and Bulgaria. Immediately after the WAPA intervention on August 20–21, 1968, Czechoslovakia submitted a memo that proposed the adoption of some of its own domestic economic reform ideas, including the breakup of rigid trade mechanisms and the opening to world markets. Its plans also comprised the introduction of full convertibility to all CMEA national currencies, the transformation of the transfer ruble into a genuine instrument of payment, and the "creation of a financial market within the framework of CMEA." Many of the ambitious ideas, however, never saw the light of day – mostly because of the military intervention in Czechoslovakia but also because of their ideologically problematic nature. In the end, the intervention weakened the general ability of the CMEA to reform itself further. In any case, as early as 1967 East German representatives had bemoaned the fact that the CMEA was mainly a talking shop that either faced Romanian obstructionism or generally failed to implement its own decisions. This condition was, of course, primarily the result of individual members pursuing national goals above all, as Kosygin had realized shortly after Khrushchev's fall: "Nowadays, you cannot order around another country as it happened ... during Stalin's times ... Comrade Khrushchev has done many stupid things, but he was a wise man, and he proved his wisdom in the question of consensus and cooperation within the CMEA."[37]

Decline, 1968–79

Starting in the late 1960s, external shocks rattled and then paralyzed the CMEA. In this period, the organization witnessed the impact of the merger of the three European communities on January 1, 1967, the abolition of the remaining internal tariffs within the arising European Communities (EC) before the end of 1969, the launching of a common foreign trade policy on January 1, 1970, and negotiations with four membership candidates in 1970–71. On January 1, 1973, when the EC welcomed three new members, it also assumed the exclusive right to negotiate trade deals in lieu of its members. By that time, the internal and external foreign trade of the EC was four times larger than that of its Eastern European counterpart. Since the CMEA was formally an international organization without supranational treaty-making power, it increasingly struggled to come to terms with the rising supranational powerhouse in the western half of the continent. The situation developed into such an internally contested issue – and even a perceived external threat – that WAPA directed the CMEA to formulate a coherent policy toward the EC in January 1972.[38]

As early as 1967–68, the CMEA had grown concerned that EC policies could discriminate against its interests. Hungary and Czechoslovakia had proposed unsuccessfully in 1968 – even after the WAPA intervention – to adopt the market-driven process of EC integration. With the successful end of EC membership negotiations in 1971, Hungary warned that the enlarged community – "one of the most dynamic regions in world trade" – and its associated partners in the developing world encompassed half of international trade. It alerted the other socialist states that the lack of formal association between the EC and CMEA would let existing economic relations across the Iron Curtain "enter into a state of decay." Throughout 1972, the CMEA pondered the establishment of formal relations, but, as we will see below, the USSR prioritized institution-wide reform of the socialist system over a radical rethinking. In the spring,

Moscow instead offered CMEA recognition to the EC, as long as the community renounced its exclusive right to negotiate trade deals in lieu of its members. The USSR obviously sought to win the peaceful competition by emasculating the other side first. Faced with the unacceptable Soviet demand, which principally aimed at the destruction of the supranational integration process in Western Europe, the EC responded by putting talks on ice. Eventually, in 1974, CMEA members provided their organization with the limited supranational right to negotiate with the EC. However, the disparate economic developments on either side of the Iron Curtain provided the EC with few incentives to offer compromises. In the late 1970s, CMEA members repeatedly complained to each other that the EC was using the CMEA's lack of supranational character as an excuse to uphold discriminatory trading practices. Indeed, the EC picked and chose bilateral agreements with individual socialist countries in select economic branches as it pleased, while it did not allow the CMEA to apply the same practice to community members. Soviet-style socialist integration had reached a dead end in peaceful competition with Western European capitalism.[39]

Still, the WAPA intervention in Czechoslovakia in August 1968 had caused the CMEA to undertake yet another internal reassessment. Hungary and, oddly enough, Czechoslovakia continued to push for greater reform, including internal and global integration without ideological blinders, while Romania, Bulgaria, Poland, and East Germany were reluctant on nationalist and ideological grounds. The USSR believed that for an organization working on the principle of unanimity it was necessary to seek compromises from all sides. Still, Moscow rejected all proposals to introduce convertibility to all CMEA currencies on the grounds of economic security. It feared that the CMEA would turn into another United States, which at that time was suffering from a negative trading balance due to a lack of competitive products, and consequently hemorrhaged gold to members of the EC. However, the Soviet leaders also understood that even relatively developed CMEA members like Czechoslovakia, which pushed for reform, were unable to compete with "the dynamics of the most developed capitalist countries, e.g. with the European Economic Community," and that this was not "a temporary, but a long-term problem that has its roots in the 1950s." Hence, the USSR believed, the only solution was pushing for even deeper CMEA integration, greater division of labor, and more stimulation of production. At the same time, Moscow emphasized, the socialist countries needed to move away from rigid multi-year trade agreements, which reduced flexibility, and instead involve individual enterprises more closely in foreign trade. The extraordinary twenty-third meeting in April 1969 thus decided to launch a new *Complex Program* that was supposed to establish cross-border coordination between corresponding economic branches, remove parallelism in production even further, increase standardization, and create an International Investment Bank (IIB) to finance CMEA-wide infrastructure projects with capitalist credits.[40]

Negotiating the details of the Complex Program did not terminate previous debates on reform. Instead, preliminary EC talks in June 1969 about introducing a common currency once more triggered arguments within the CMEA over adopting convertibility and introducing free pricing, and even sparked an inconclusive discussion about launching a collective currency. In mid 1970, when the IIB was officially established, Romania decided to stay away for the first year because it considered the bank's right to make decisions according to the majority principle an infraction of its sovereignty. After two years of discussion, the twenty-fifth meeting in mid 1971 approved the Complex Program of "socialist integration." Romania subsequently used the reservations, which it had stated beforehand, to try to opt out from several parts. Under Nicolae Ceaușescu's leadership, the country attempted to position itself as a Yugoslav-style mediator in a wide range of Cold War conflicts. Like no other CMEA member, it aspired to economic integration in the global economy for its national modernization project. It was the first socialist state to join the IMF in late 1972. In the wake of this defection, the CMEA banned the other members from following the Romanian example. Hungary, which had been considering membership since 1968, was hung out to dry.[41]

The emphasis on further integration provided the basis for deeper co-operation in the field of energy. By the late 1960s, it had become clear that the USSR would not be able to provide the increasing amounts of oil that the Eastern European CMEA members demanded on an annual basis. Thus, in the early 1970s, Moscow started to review, and occasionally reject, justifications for delivery increases. Bottlenecks occurred due to limited supply capacities, which forced the USSR to buy oil from Iraq for shipment to CMEA partners and then to absorb the sudden price increases on the world market during the 1973–74 oil shock. In mid 1973, the USSR, Poland, East Germany, Czechoslovakia, Hungary, and Bulgaria decided to collaborate in building the *Soyuz* gas pipeline, which originated in the Orenburg gas fields in the southern Urals. The need to buy specialized pipes, technical equipment, and construction machinery in the capitalist world required the IIB to assume massive Western commercial bank credits. After interest rates on the world's financial markets skyrocketed for unrelated reasons in the late 1970s, the bank almost collapsed in the early 1980s. Moreover, at the opening of the pipeline on January 1, 1979, it was obvious that the Orenburg gas fields would run empty within twelve years. Hence, *Soyuz* needed an additional pipeline link to Siberian gas fields much further northeast. But gas was not the only solution to the energy problems. By 1976, the same group of CMEA countries and Yugoslavia had decided to establish an integrated high-voltage electricity grid to address the continued energy shortages. In its initial stage, it was supposed to be fed by existing nuclear power plants in the western USSR (for example, in Chernobyl) until similar nuclear reactors had been finished in other CMEA countries. The project was far from being complete when the CMEA collapsed in 1991.[42]

Although the Complex Program included provisions for pricing reform, the CMEA never managed to resolve this thorny problem. The USSR had brought up the issue as early as 1958 but consistently faced foot dragging from the Eastern European partners. Discussions resumed once more in November 1973 over Soviet frustrations that it had to buy Iraqi oil at prices higher than those it received for delivery to the CMEA partners. The following year, Moscow demanded an adjustment of all internal CMEA trading prices to generally rising world market levels, since the USSR was no longer capable of affording "colossal losses" that primarily benefited the other CMEA members. When negotiations started in 1975, the Soviet empire in Eastern Europe struck back by demanding "world market" prices for the semi-finished and finished goods which it sold to the USSR. Price discussions continued during the remaining fifteen years of the CMEA, with the Soviet Union subsidizing – though at a steadily declining rate – a range of raw materials until the very end. The long duration of these debates primarily stemmed from the Eastern European unwillingness to give up preferential terms of trade, and, even more, in their default inclination not to rock the boat. Memories of the consequences of the Soviet New Course in the mid 1950s and of the WAPA intervention in Czechoslovakia in 1968 made CMEA members less diposed to embark on reform. The only exceptions were Hungary and Poland, which continued with some economic experiments in the 1970s.[43]

But the development most damaging to the CMEA was the hard currency debt crisis that unfolded in the 1970s. Over the whole decade, the liabilities of the USSR and the six Eastern European member states collectively ballooned from 6.5 to 65.4 billion US dollars. Three of the four countries that generated most of the internal CMEA trade – Poland, the GDR, and the Soviet Union – also produced most of CMEA debt in the capitalist world – almost 70 percent. But it was financially weak Bulgaria that needed to be bailed out by the USSR as early as 1977, when it was no longer able to service its financial obligations to the non-socialist world. At the same time, Poland's economy slid into troubled waters, eventually bringing the CMEA to the breaking point in the early 1980s, as Chapter 22 shows.[44]

CMEA discussions to assume hard currency debt for modernization purposes had started by July 1968, if not before. The USSR itself had received long-term credits from Western European commercial banks as early as 1964. CMEA members originally envisioned a coordinated approach to the capitalist world for hard currency credits when they approved the idea of the Complex Program in 1969. While the IIB assumed the financial liabilities for the *Soyuz* pipeline, individual CMEA countries eventually sought credits for their national development projects or civilian consumption on their own and without coordination. As early as August 1973, Kosygin alerted the East German government about its ballooning debt in the capitalist world and the country's struggle to get the balance of trade back to equilibrium.[45] Three years later, he warned all CMEA members that hard currency credits were splitting the organization because they increased individual dependencies on the capitalist world. Yet the Soviet inability to deliver enough energy resources as well as increasing economic problems in the USSR itself – such as poor harvests – forced Eastern European CMEA members to turn to the world market – and to additional hard currency credits – to fix shortages.[46]

In 1977, Hungarian economists concluded that the essential institutions of the CMEA – the trade and financial mechanisms – did not function at all. Budapest instead proposed to Moscow to switch bilateral trade to convertible currencies to reflect world market practices. The two eventually decided to proceed surreptitiously in order to avoid actively "undermining CMEA." But by then, the organization was already in the process of slow dissolution, as Kosygin had noted the previous year. The incorporation of each CMEA member into the capitalist world through international financial markets was proceeding at a faster rate than the concurrent organization-wide integration. In June 1978, a Soviet review of the situation in Europe, Africa, and Asia reached a sobering conclusion: "The winds of the Cold War are blowing from many sides." Thus, it was important for the CMEA to "prove to the world that we can solve the task which we have jointly formulated" in 1971. But Kosygin poured cold water on this very expectation the following year. The CMEA lagged behind in implementing the Complex Program, had failed to catch up with the West, struggled to increase labor productivity, and had created monopoly markets for its enterprises that disincentivized product modernization and the achievement of international standards. As a result, the low quantity and quality of machines produced in the CMEA forced member countries to buy technology in the capitalist world, which undermined the existing CMEA attempts at standardization and threatened the jointly established base of technical knowledge. An East German analysis soon thereafter warned that the Soviet raw material and energy supply system so crucial to the inner workings of the CMEA was in the process of breaking down, with potentially negative ripple effects on individual economies and overall cohesion.[47]

Conclusion

The CMEA was a defective project from the very beginning. In a narrow sense, the organization was a reaction of the Marshall Plan and Western European integration, and designed to safeguard the revolutionary reconstruction of Eastern Europe from hostile Western interference. Yet Soviet domination since the end of World War II had prepared the ground for the introduction of the Stalinist economic model in each Eastern European country. In the immediate post-war period, Moscow decided to opt out of the Bretton Woods system and the Marshall Plan because it feared Western economic domination. After mid 1947, the Soviet-installed Eastern European regimes had to disengage from the global economy on Stalin's imperial edicts. The half-baked structures that he subsequently put in place in Eastern Europe from 1947 to 1949 predetermined the basic economic development path of that semi-continent for the rest of the Cold War.

The CMEA was never bigger than the sum of its parts. Its individual members were hardly compatible for integration, mostly because they enjoyed different levels of economic development while they had no shared history of substantial economic interaction. For ideological or nationalist reasons, they often pursued individual development strategies that increased this incompatibility even more. Some opposed Soviet-imposed reform as a danger to their national independence, but others considered it half-hearted and even an obstacle in their quest to keep up with the rapidly developing economy in the non-socialist world. Ultimately, however, the USSR was incapable of jettisoning its own ideological constraints and embarking on fundamental reform before the late 1980s, as described in Chapter 23.

The CMEA also lacked a deeper purpose beyond protecting the socialist system against outside interference. It did not possess the glue of Western European peacebuilding, which the long history of national enmities had stimulated, the Soviet threat had motivated, and American support had buoyed while the United States stayed outside the self-guided integration process. Instead, the USSR as the dominant member managed and subsidized the CMEA, despite the oft-repeated mantra of unanimity and the recurrent discussions on price reform. The lopsided nature of national economic sizes and natural resource distribution undermined the development of equality and cooperation among its members. Romania might have initiated the creation of the CMEA in late 1948, but since the early 1960s it influenced developments mostly by trying to block them. The GDR sought integration primarily because it wanted to detach itself from its capitalist sibling. In comparison, Poland, Czechoslovakia, and Hungary repeatedly proposed reforms that aimed at transcending the socialist character of the CMEA and, consequently, at integration into the global economy. As a result, Moscow was a target of ever increasing demands for subsidies and, at the same time, of diametrically opposed ideas about future action. The organization suffered from a paralysis caused by opposing forces. Stalin's empire was striking back from different directions. The USSR was well aware of the fundamental problems of the CMEA. Maybe Stalin himself had not liked it from the moment it was born. But even his reformist successors could not detach themselves from the ideological baggage of world revolutionary struggle against the capitalist system.

Unlike the EC, the CMEA had developed into a failure by the 1970s. It had been unable to overcome its birth defects, never managed to turn its membership economies into competitive world market participants, and eventually turned out to be unreformable. Its internal glue – annually increasing, subsidized Soviet energy and raw material deliveries – was becoming brittle just as its members were starting to integrate into the global economy, mainly via mounting external debt in the 1970s. To cut a long story short, the CMEA's very existence was its greatest obstacle to success.

Part VI

European Détente

Introduction to Chapters 17 to 19

European détente in the 1960s and 1970s comprised several parallel but related attempts to lessen the impact of the continent's division. After two decades of hostility, West Germany tried to engage with East Germany in order to reduce the human toll of division and to entangle its communist sibling economically (Chapter 17). During the Conference on Security and Cooperation in Europe (CSCE), the Soviet-led Socialist Camp hoped to get legal recognition for its contested post-World War II borders, while the *Nine* of the European Communities (EC) and Europe's neutrals tried to improve the civil, political, and human rights situation in the communist half of the continent (Chapter 18). At the same time, the Vatican attempted to engage with the Socialist Camp in order to restore the pastoral life of the Catholic Church behind the Iron Curtain (Chapter 19).

The triangular relationship among the two Germanys and Poland – or, alternatively, between one capitalist and two communist states – forms the unifying theme of Part VI. The relationship encompassed two enmities until the turn of the 1960s/1970s: a historical enmity between the two Germanys and Poland as the result of World War II, and an ideological enmity between East and West Germany as a result of the Cold War. The territorial changes, which all three had experienced at the end of 1945, posed *one* shared problem: the three had re-emerged from World War II with a new set of borders and, in Germany's case, in divided fashion. Thus, all three underwent a lengthy period of post-war state formation that displayed similarities with other territorially reconstituted or dismembered states, which we have encountered earlier in this book: China, Vietnam, India/Pakistan, and Israel/Palestine (Chapters 5–7, 10). The resolution of the parallel and interconnected conflicts between the two Germanys and Poland shaped European politics in the early 1970s. German–German rapprochement addressed the question of how the country's division affected the meaning of Germany as a nation. The CSCE focused on issues of a pan-European security structure and the future possibility of peaceful territorial changes. The Vatican's engagement with the Socialist Camp aimed at breaking open Soviet-controlled Eastern Europe.

As Chapter 17 reveals, the Big Three agreed on Germany's territorial reduction and division toward the end of World War II. At the Yalta and Potsdam Conferences in early and mid 1945, the United States and the United Kingdom had agreed to Soviet demands for the territorial westward relocation of Poland. As compensation for the eastern third of its territory lost to the USSR, Poland received the German territories of southern East Prussia, Pomerania, and Silesia, with the Oder and Neisse rivers forming its new western border. The German port-city of Stettin (Szczecin) on the western bank switched sides as well. The USSR itself annexed northern East Prussia. At the same conferences, the Big Three also decided to divide the remainder of Germany into occupation zones – a decision that predetermined the country's divided fate until 1990. At their birth in 1949, both the Federal Republic of Germany (FRG; West Germany) and the German Democratic Republic (GDR; East Germany) were firmly convinced that the country's division would be temporary until reunification under their respective leadership. But the Korean War cemented the division, driving both into opposite Cold War alliances – NATO and WAPA – by 1955. Afterward, West Germany tried to stymie East Germany's attempt at seeking separate statehood, though the East German closure of the borders in the divided capital Berlin in 1961 only deepened the estrangement. Only the election of Social Democratic Chancellor Willy Brandt in 1969 brought rapprochement, in which West Germany acknowledged the reality of the two German states but denied the emergence of a separate German nation in the GDR. Although the recognition of 1972–73 had been a long-term goal of the GDR, it brought the danger of being embraced by the FRG, and with that the possibility of future reunification.

The Conference on Security and Cooperation in Europe (CSCE) emerged at the confluence of two developments (Chapter 18). Since the early 1950s, the USSR and Poland had demanded an internationally sanctioned security arrangement against the rise of a rearmed West Germany in the form of the legal recognition of their post-World War II borders. The emerging Western European institutions of integration, in comparison, aimed at overcoming the legacy of the war through the guarantee of human rights for individual citizens throughout all of Europe. The conflict between the communist insistence on the supremacy of the territorial state and the Western emphasis on individual citizens' rights came to a denouement at the CSCE in 1972–75. The Socialist Camp did not receive a legal or even permanent guarantee of its borders but had to concede on the issue of human rights. Yet the impact of human rights on the European Socialist Camp, which Western European governments had expected for the period afterward, did not happen immediately. Poland would ultimately receive a guarantee for its post-war borders only after the end of the Cold War in 1989/91. The Final Act of the CSCE neither prevented the suppression of human rights in the Socialist Camp until the 1980s nor saved the GDR from collapse and absorption into the FRG by 1990 (Chapters 22 and 23).

As Chapter 19 shows, the Vatican was one of the seminal Cold Warriors, rejecting communism as early as the 1840s. It had hoped for the "containment" of Soviet-style expansionism into Europe as early as World War II, i.e. even before the United States adopted that term into its official Cold War vocabulary in 1946–47. However, the Vatican realized by the late 1950s that ideological rigidity damaged its own interest – ensuring the functionality of churches behind the Iron Curtain – which is why it decided to engage with the communist world. But its major success in the European regional Cold War – the restoration of the Polish Church to independence – had to wait until détente in German–German and European affairs emerged in the early 1970s.

The trajectories of Chapters 17–19 dramatically intersect on one distinct date – June 3, 1972. On this day, the four powers administering the occupation of Germany – the USSR, the United States, the United Kingdom, and France – signed the agreement on the final status of Berlin, which thereby removed the country's divided capital as a source of future Cold War crises. Having fulfilled a West German demand, this event led the FRG to exchange within hours the ratification documents of the Moscow and Warsaw Treaties, in which it normalized relations with the USSR and Poland and expressed respect for their post-war borders. The West German act in turn prompted the USSR to agree to the start of the CSCE negotiations in Helsinki in November 1972 and to task the GDR to negotiate the Basic Treaty with the FRG that normalized German–German relations. Finally, the West German–Polish exchange of the ratification documents of the Warsaw Treaty on June 3 allowed the Catholic Church in Poland to create new dioceses in the formerly German territories. The West German *de facto* recognition of the post-1945 Polish borders thus destroyed the nationalist quasi-alliance between the communist regime and the Catholic Church on the country's post-war borders, enabling Poland's clergy to play an independent role in the anti-communist opposition by the late 1970s and throughout the 1980s. Thus, the European regional Cold War experienced significant structural change in the first half of the 1970s. The normalization of relations across the Iron Curtain reduced Cold War tensions but simultaneously created the basis for further structural change by the 1980s when the Socialist Camp's declining economic health (Chapter 16) intersected with developments in European détente to produce the conditions under which the regional Cold War in Europe would end (Chapter 22).

17   Germany

Germany's division occurred as a result of its defeat in World War II, Allied occupation, and the unfolding of the early global Cold War. Internal conflict did *not* cause national dismemberment, unlike in China in 1948/49 or Vietnam in 1954. On the contrary, Germany's geographical location at the center of Europe doomed the country to its split fate from the late 1940s to 1990. The whole continent, Germany at its center, and the country's capital Berlin ultimately underwent the interrelated and concentric division into a liberal democratic, capitalist half and an authoritarian, socialist half for the whole period of the global Cold War.

At first glance, the Western and Soviet military presence until the end of the Cold War suggests that the two halves of divided Germany were mere pawns of their respective masters in Washington and Moscow. However, the leaders of both Germanys displayed remarkable talents in carving out wiggle room. Their experiences in the failed German democratic experiment of the 1920s and in the subsequent National Socialist nightmare under Adolf Hitler between 1933 and 1945 underpinned their voluntary participation in the Allied division of the country. However, in the larger western half, elected politicians quickly established a well-respected democracy with the help of the Western Allies. In the smaller eastern part, a Soviet-installed communist party dictatorship dealt with tight constraints set by its hegemon but eventually learned to force the hand of its master in Moscow.

Initially, both Germanys saw the country's division as temporary while aspiring to unite the nation under their respective leadership. But whereas the western half was able to produce internal and external legitimacy, the eastern half failed to do so and thus concluded that it needed to pursue separate statehood in order to gain some form of authority. Its attempts in the 1960s to exploit unrelated conflicts in the Middle East, South Asia, and Southeast Asia for the purpose of obtaining official recognition merely testified to its generally instrumental approach to the world outside the Socialist Camp. However, it was West Germany's pragmatic policy in the 1960s, designed to lessen gradually the human costs of the nation's division, that ultimately enabled East Germany to obtain recognition in the early 1970s.

Germany's destiny from 1945 to 1989 had structural effects on the European regional Cold War. Its *de facto* division in the immediate post-war period influenced the fate of the whole continent. Without the German division, the military and economic integration of Western Europe probably would not have happened. But West Germany's attempt to lessen the division through political and economic engagement with East Germany eventually enabled Europe to overcome some of the aspects of the continent's structural division. Ultimately, the collapse of East Germany in 1989, as described in Chapter 23, and the subsequent German reunification provided the impetus for continent-wide European integration afterward. Thus, throughout the Cold War, developments in Germany shaped developments in all of Europe.

Dividing Germany

After defeat in World War II, Germany lost territory and was divided into four Allied occupation zones. Silesia, Pomerania, Stettin (Szczecin), and the southern half of East Prussia went to Poland as compensation for the Soviet annexation of the eastern Polish territories, while the northern half of East Prussia became a part of the USSR itself. Germany's remaining territory, within today's borders, was carved up into four occupation zones controlled by the victorious Allies – the Soviet Union, the United Kingdom, the United States, and France – with the country's capital, situated in the Soviet occupation zone, divvied up into analogous occupation sectors as well. During the war, the Big Three had failed to agree on post-war plans for Germany. As early as 1943, the USSR had begun to prepare the export of its own system. For that purpose, it primed a group of German communists-in-exile in Moscow for transfer to occupied Berlin at the end of the war. Although the Soviet Union, the United States, and the United Kingdom had agreed on the principle of quadruple division before the end of the war, they failed to come up with concrete occupation policies. Washington and London had understood early on that the permanent dismemberment of Germany would break up a highly integrated national economy into dysfunctional parts. Moscow and Washington also had always kept the option for the country's unity open during the war, even if both also had simultaneously entertained the idea of permanent fragmentation.[1]

At the Potsdam Conference in mid 1945, the Big Three agreed to the four *D*s – denazification, demilitarization, decentralization, and democratization. Mainly for the practical reason of administering occupied

Map 10. Germany in 1945

Germany, the Big Three decided to divide the country into four occupation zones – one for each of them and one for France. The three still
intended to keep Germany together as one economic unit. Nonetheless,
Germany quickly suffered from a deep economic crisis after the war. The

restrictions on interzonal economic activities, which the four Allies jointly imposed, contributed much more to the post-war dislocation than the preceding war-related destruction of the country's industrial capabilities. Moreover, all four occupation powers engaged in the dismantlement of targeted assets in their respective zones, although the USSR did so to a much greater extent than the three Western Allies. In due course, the unfolding global Cold War solidified Germany's division. Once the United States realized that a unified and self-sufficient Germany was no longer a prospect, it decided to create an economically viable rump-Germany. On January 1, 1947, Washington and London merged their zones into the Bizone, followed by the creation of political structures there. When Paris joined in on June 1, 1948, the resulting Trizone foreshadowed the territorial emergence of what would become West Germany.[2]

The Cold War division of Germany's integrated economy had different consequences in each zone. Although the Anglo–American Allies had heavily bombed West German industrial assets during World War II, they considered the surviving economic capabilities increasingly crucial to the integration of Western Europe in the unfolding Cold War. Hence, they introduced monetary reforms in the Bizone/Trizone to improve macro-economic planning and speed up recovery. In comparison, the Soviet zone in general suffered less war-related destruction but experienced a greater amount of industrial and infrastructure removal by the occupation power. Since this zone was anyway more dependent on economic links to the other three zones than vice versa, Germany's economic division and Soviet removals had a much greater impact there, despite conditions being better to start with in mid 1945. Once Iosif V. Stalin had decided not to allow his Eastern European empire to participate in the Marshall Plan, the Soviet zone in Germany underwent a far-reaching economic reorientation toward the USSR and the emerging Council for Mutual Economic Assistance (CMEA) in the late 1940s.[3]

As the economic reforms in the Bizone/Trizone removed Soviet influence and the United States imposed the embargo list of the international Coordinating Committee (CoCom) in early 1948, Stalin needed to react. Through the blockade of Berlin from June 24, 1948, to May 12, 1949, he tried to eliminate the Western Allied presence in the three Western occupation sectors of the capital at the heart of the Soviet zone. The Anglo–American–French *Airlift* – an air bridge to bring supplies to over 2 million West Berliners and Western troops by plane – undercut Stalin's plans, while it endeared West Berliners and West Germans permanently to the three Western Allies. Moreover, Stalin's blockade convinced the Anglo–American–French Allies to sign the North Atlantic Treaty on

April 4, 1949, and to establish the Federal Republic of Germany (FRG) seven weeks later. Although the Soviet dictator eventually terminated the Berlin Blockade on May 12, he was unable to prevent the institutional division of Germany. Still, the foundation of the German Democratic Republic (GDR) on October 7, 1949, was not a reaction to the establishment of the FRG in May 1949. It had actually been decided by the USSR as early as October 1948. Similar to Stalin's hesitant support for the CMEA, however, Moscow had not been keen on creating a socialist East German state. One historian even called the GDR "Stalin's unwanted child." Nonetheless, in a photograph from the dictator's seventieth birthday celebration on December 21, 1949, East Germany's party boss Walter Ulbricht and China's Chairman Mao Zedong appear on either side of Stalin. The two newest additions to the socialist world from Europe and East Asia, respectively, flanked the center of world revolution in Moscow.[4]

The unplanned yet foreordained division of Germany created hostile twin states. Each was headed by a strong-willed and independent personality – the Christian Democrat Konrad Adenauer and the communist party head Walter Ulbricht. Both Germanys perceived the division as temporary while claiming to represent the whole country. In a symbolic act, the FRG chose the provincial city of Bonn as the "seat of government." The strict avoidance of the term "capital" for almost a quarter of a century was supposed to serve as a constant reminder that this arrangement was only a *Provisorium* – a provisional solution. Even if national unity was a central vision from the very beginning, Adenauer still wanted *first* to anchor the new state in the Free World *before* seeking unification on the basis of a firmly secured liberal democratic order. In comparison, East Germany expected national unification to occur under the leadership of socialism much earlier. The day after the birth of the GDR on October 7, 1949, Prime Minister Otto Grotewohl wrote in his diary: "This *Provisorium* will last no longer than one year."[5]

The outbreak of the Korean War in June 1950 deepened Germany's division once more. Fearful of the military might of the Socialist Camp, Adenauer understood the need for arming the FRG given the country's central geographical location in a divided Europe. In October 1950, the chancellor welcomed a French proposal to arm the new country within a multinational military institution – the European Defense Community (EDC). On March 10, 1952, Stalin tried to derail the negotiations on the EDC by offering talks on a peace treaty and the formation of a united German government – but failed. Anyhow, since the late 1940s, the GDR had established, on Soviet orders, paramilitary organizations – deceptively called the *Kasernierte Volkspolizei* (Garrisoned People's Police) – as a nucleus for a future army.[6]

Even in economic affairs, the two German states developed in different directions. Buttressed by the Marshall Plan, the FRG embarked on the establishment of a socially responsible market economy, which quickly led to the fondly remembered *Wirtschaftswunder* (economic miracle) in the early 1950s. As Adenauer stressed in his first declaration to the Allied High Commissioners on September 21, 1949, economic success was crucial to the inner stability of the FRG and, by extension, all of Europe. Indeed, by February 1952, the Western Allies granted greater – though still limited – sovereignty to the FRG in the context of negotiations on the EDC. In comparison, the GDR quickly adopted the Soviet-style planned economy, implementing a Two-Year Plan for 1949–50 and its first Five-Year Plan for 1951–55. At Ulbricht's urging, in July 1952 Stalin agreed to the proposal to launch socialist reconstruction with the purpose of creating a socialist model country, which was supposed to attract popular West German awe and thereby open the path to reunification. Yet the nationalization of industrial assets, the collectivization of agriculture, the increase in work norms, the militarization of many aspects of life, campaigns against the churches, and stricter border controls caused much popular dissatisfaction.[7]

Within less than a year, a countrywide workers' uprising threatened Ulbricht's high-flying dreams of creating a socialist paradise. Stalin's death in early March 1953 had quickly led to the first steps of de-Stalinization in the USSR itself. The East German leaders reacted with confusion while their new Soviet masters grew concerned about the deterioration of the political and economic situation in the GDR. The post-Stalinist leadership ordered Ulbricht and Grotewohl to appear in Moscow in early June to justify their mistaken policy of "accelerated construction of socialism" which had led to an "unsatisfactory political and economic situation" in the GDR. Particularly in view of the "Germany Question," the post-Stalinist Soviet leaders decided – despite their unrelated internal power struggle – to demand the general slowdown of socialist construction in the GDR and even the reversal of some excesses. The ensuing public announcement of policy corrections itself did not trigger labor unrest in the GDR. It was only the refusal of the East German regime to take back increased labor norms that actually sparked a strike of construction workers in East Berlin on June 16, 1953. Within twenty-four hours, workers in virtually all of East Germany's cities joined the strike. On the morning of June 17, the East German leadership fled to safety in the Soviet Army headquarters on the eastern outskirts of Berlin as the Kremlin ordered a massive military crackdown. Within days, Soviet troops suppressed the uprising and restored the Ulbricht regime to power.[8]

Paradoxically, Ulbricht emerged from his near-downfall in a strengthened position. The East German regime swiftly adopted the theory of a fascist and counter-revolutionary plot organized by Adenauer and other foreign agents. Ulbricht also exploited the unrelated arrest of Lavrentii Beria on June 26 by his fellow Soviet leaders, who feared that he had arrogated too much power to himself. After they expediently blamed Beria for the uprising in Germany, Ulbricht exploited this indictment to eliminate those in the East German party leadership who had dared to criticize his dictatorial style of rule. In the end, the Soviet leaders did not find any alternative to the unpopular Ulbricht. For the following decade, he faced neither internal challenges nor much opposition from Moscow to his radical economic policies and plans for Germany's complete territorial division in 1961.[9]

With Adenauer and Ulbricht firmly in power by the mid 1950s, the two Germanys approached the question of membership in the emerging military alliance system of the Cold War. The failure of the EDC to pass ratification in the French parliament in August 1954 marked the point of no return. In the absence of any other option, the NATO allies decided on October 23 in Paris to provide West Germany with almost all sovereign powers – including the permission to establish its own army – and membership in the alliance. The Western Allies retained only rights and obligations with regard to West Berlin (which was legally not a part of the FRG), and with regard to Germany as a whole in questions such as reunification and the final peace treaty. Despite massive domestic opposition to rearmament, the West German parliament ratified the Paris Treaty in the spring of 1955, with the FRG acquiring almost complete sovereignty on May 5 and joining NATO the following day.

The Soviet Union was not at all pleased with this rapid and unexpected development. At a conference in late November 1954, Moscow and its vassals from the Eastern European capitals denounced the one-month-old Paris Treaty and publicly discussed the foundation of a counter-NATO and the official armament of the GDR. In a desperate attempt to prevent the ratification of the Paris Treaty in West Germany, Moscow even offered free elections for all of Germany under international supervision. On May 15, a little more than a week after West Germany's entry into NATO, the socialist states signed the treaty that established the Warsaw Pact Organization (WAPA). The new alliance did not provide the USSR with any additional rights or privileges that Moscow had not previously enjoyed as a result of its military occupation of Eastern Europe and East Germany since World War II. Its establishment pursued the primary goal of creating leverage in the hoped-for negotiations with the West on the parallel dissolution of both alliances. The GDR itself saw the pact primarily as reassurance against the alleged West German militarism and as a propaganda instrument for peaceful reunification.[10]

The Geneva Summit in mid 1955, the first meeting of the Allied heads of state in ten years, failed both to dissolve the antagonistic pact systems and to resolve the Germany Question. As a consequence, the USSR was forced to transform WAPA from a hollow shell into a genuine organization and to provide the GDR with partial sovereignty. On September 20, 1955, Moscow and East Berlin signed a treaty that terminated all reparation payments and reduced the costs for the Soviet occupation. At the same time, the two also agreed that East German units could guard the country's borders, including those around West Berlin. After the establishment of the *Bundeswehr* (West Germany's Federal Defense Force) in late 1955, the formal transformation of the *Kasernierte Volkspolizei* into the *Volksarmee* (People's Army) followed.[11]

Two Germanys, Four Germany Policies

The unfulfilled dreams of unification on either side had produced, by the mid 1950s, one pair of Germany policies each in the FRG and the GDR. Adenauer's governing Christian Democrats pursued a policy of integration with the Free World *before* unification, while the opposition Social Democrats took up a position of equidistance to both the USSR and the United States. The East German communist party dictatorship, in comparison, did not have to deal with opposition parties – even if it still faced a lot of informal grassroots resistance – and thus entertained two contradictory policies by itself: unity under socialism and the Two-State solution.

Adenauer's orientation toward the West was rooted in his long-time fear of the USSR, his commitment to Christian values, and his devotion to overcoming Germany's historical conflict with France. In order to acquire sovereignty and international respect, Adenauer also believed it was not enough for the FRG to develop into a successful and internationally trusted democracy. On the contrary, Germany had to address the country's recent National Socialist past. The chancellor himself considered it a "moral obligation" to restitute property to Jewish victims and Holocaust survivors, and to pay *Wiedergutmachung* (restitution) to the newly founded state of Israel. In 1952, the FRG and Israel agreed on the payment of 3.5 billion German marks, mostly in goods and services, over ten years. Paradoxically, however, Adenauer did not push for the prosecution of those Germans who were responsible for the persecution and murder of Jews during the Holocaust.[12]

With near complete sovereignty acquired in May 1955, Adenauer had to address the issue of how to deal with the GDR – an entity he considered illegitimate. During his visit to Moscow on September 8–14, 1955, he successfully negotiated the return of the remaining German prisoners of war from the USSR but also requested – and received – full Soviet recognition. In its wake, Moscow granted East Berlin a measure of sovereignty equivalent to what Bonn had received with the Paris Treaty a year before. However, the Soviet recognition of both Germanys had set a dangerous precedent. Adenauer did not want to endanger the chances of future reunification by permitting international recognition of the GDR, or even double recognition by third parties. Thus, on September 22, he publicly announced what would become the Hallstein Doctrine. Named after a state secretary in the Foreign Office, the policy denied any state other than the Soviet Union the privilege of double recognition. Countries that had recognized West Germany would see their diplomatic relations cut as soon as they recognized East Germany. When Yugoslavia did so in October 1957, the FRG acted accordingly.[13]

The opposition Social Democrats agreed neither with Adenauer's orientation toward the West nor with his economically liberal policies. But the party's leader, Kurt Schumacher, also loathed Ulbricht's comrades, whom he called "red-lacquered Nazis," and similarly rejected their plans to introduce Soviet-style communism. Yet Schumacher's abrasive rhetorical style did not attract the majority – or even the plurality – of voters in the first federal election in August 1949. His anti-Western positions and difficult personality convinced Adenauer to shun a unity government with the Social Democrats and instead to seek a small coalition with the Free Democrats (Liberals) and a miniscule conservative party. On September 20, 1949, the West German parliament elected him first federal chancellor with the tiniest of all possible margins – by one vote ... his own. In opposition, the Social Democrats retained Schumacher's class-conscious positions and foreign policy of equidistance between the USSR and the United States beyond his death in 1952, but, at least, they supported Adenauer's hardline policy toward the GDR. It was only in 1959 that a younger generation – among them Willy Brandt, the future federal chancellor – turned the class-based party into a mass political movement. The Godesberg Program abandoned Marxist positions and, simultaneously, committed the Social Democrats to the country's integration with the West.[14]

Closely guided by their Soviet masters, the East German communists pursued a policy of national unity under socialism even before the birth of the GDR. Following the uprising in the GDR in June 1953, the Soviet Union once more offered negotiations on a peace treaty and the formation of a unified national government, albeit under communist leadership. The failure of the Geneva Summit to solve the Germany Question two years later convinced the USSR that the "conditions for Germany's unification are not yet ripe enough." Subsequently, East German appeals for national unity moved onto the level of calling for a confederation between the two states. At the same time, the East German communists tried to implement a *Westpolitik* through rapprochement with the opposition Social Democrats in the FRG – in the hope of grooming good relations with a future party-in-government, but ultimately in order to obtain recognition for the GDR.[15]

After the failure of the Geneva Summit, Soviet leader Nikita S. Khrushchev raised the Two-State Theory for the first time. It quickly became the dominant East German policy with regard to the Germany Question. In reaction to the Hallstein Doctrine, the GDR seized the initiative to establish trade relations with countries in the capitalist West and the decolonizing Afro–Asian world. By 1958, Khrushchev promised additional economic assistance to the GDR because East Germany was fighting at the first frontline of the Cold War: "If necessary, [the Soviet Union] will tighten its belt to help the GDR."[16]

The rise of the Two-State Theory went hand in hand with a rhetorical sharpening of ideological conflict. East Germany's foundational, anti-fascist myth claimed that the GDR was the nation's better half, which supposedly had broken with the terrible National Socialist past. Thus, East Berlin felt *no moral obligation* to participate in *Wiedergutmachung*, even if Israel hoped to obtain from the GDR a treaty similar to the one with the FRG. East Germany maintained that it had done everything to eradicate fascism and that it had helped *all* victims living within its borders – communists and Jews alike. In reality, the GDR hoped for recognition from Arab states, which had protested against Adenauer's agreement to pay 3.5 billion German marks to Israel. After the Suez Crisis in late 1956, East Germany even claimed that West German *Wiedergutmachung* had financed the Israeli aggression against Egypt.[17]

In that vein, the GDR instrumentalized its concocted anti-fascist tradition to accuse the FRG of allowing former Nazis to work in high-level positions. This did not hinder East Germany from recruiting members of past National Socialist organizations widely, though covertly, since early 1947 to build up its own governmental and military institutions as well. After the uprising in June 1953, the ruling communist party, however, suddenly realized that the percentage share of former Nazis among its own ranks was much higher than among those whom the state security organs had arrested for participating in the supposedly fascist counter-revolution. Still, the ideological construction of the supposedly unbroken fascist continuity from National Socialist Germany to the FRG served the GDR for a whole range of purposes. For example, during Ho Chi Minh's visit in 1957, it enabled East Germany to equate Adenauer's West Germany with Ngo Dinh Diem's South Vietnam as the greatest threat to world peace.[18]

Berlin, Refugees, and Economics

On the morning of August 13, 1961, Berliners woke up to a new reality. Overnight, the *Volksarmee* and East German border guard units had blocked the perimeter of West Berlin. The hastily erected barbed wire barricades ripped apart a city that until then had functioned as one urban unit. Over the following twenty-eight years, the improvised barriers around West Berlin and similar installations at the German–German border gave way to ever more sophisticated death strips that encompassed concrete walls, ditches, mine fields, and sharpshooting border guards. Until 1989, over 40,000 East Germans still managed to overcome these obstacles, roughly 60,000 were convicted for trying to flee, and more than 500 died in escape attempts.[19]

In late 1961, East German representatives told foreign politicians that the closure of the borders in Berlin had prevented an impending military intervention by fascist West Germany and thereby helped preserve the chance of peaceful unification. Official propaganda vilified the "imperialist and revanchist" Adenauer and his "rightist" sidekick Brandt – the Social Democratic mayor of West Berlin who had fled National Socialism in 1933 into Norwegian exile – for aggression against the peace-loving GDR. West Berliners, West Germans, and Westerners were shocked by the harsh measures that cut the last physical bond between the two Germanys. But the Western Allies quickly communicated to the USSR that they would not intervene as long as their occupation rights in West Berlin remained untouched.[20]

Ulbricht's decision to imprison East Germany's population was actually prompted by his failure to create a socialist model state that could compete with the capitalist *Wirtschaftswunder*. The increasing gap between the economic performances of the two Germanys, as Ulbricht bluntly wrote to Khrushchev in January 1961, was primarily responsible for the large number of GDR citizens leaving for the FRG. Between October 1949 and August 1961, over 2.7 million East Germans committed the crime of *Republikflucht* (absconding from the Republic), leading to a drop of 8.5 percent in the population of the GDR. Initially, the East German communist party had been content with letting go people whom it considered enemies of the socialist order. As the 1950s progressed, however, well-trained professionals left in frustration over the political and economic situation. Starting in 1952, the GDR tried to make emigrating progressively more difficult through the introduction of legal measures and physical controls at the German–German border, but Berlin remained an open escape hatch.[21]

Throughout the 1950s, Berlin had been an unresolved territorial Cold War problem. Hence, in his Berlin Ultimatum of November 1958, Khrushchev claimed that the establishment of the FRG and its accession to NATO had rendered the Potsdam agreements of 1945 moot. The Soviet leader demanded negotiations within six months of the end of the Western Allied status in West Berlin and on the conversion of that semi-metropolis into a demilitarized "free city" *on* the territory of the GDR. Otherwise, the USSR would unilaterally hand Allied rights over to East Germany. While Khrushchev saw West Berlin primarily as a tool to acquire respect from the United States, Ulbricht aimed at the removal of the capitalist outpost from within the socialist GDR. When Khrushchev acquired what he considered American respect during his official visit to the United States in September 1959, he withdrew the ultimatum. Frustrated at being denied the prize that had seemed so close at hand, Ulbricht gradually upped the ante by escalating the crisis around Berlin through words and deeds. For a long time, however, Khrushchev rejected the idea of closing the borders. In view of the increasing number of refugees leaving the GDR through West Berlin, however, he reinstated the 1958 ultimatum at the confrontational Vienna Summit with US President John F. Kennedy in June 1961. After he had finally realized that the Western Allies would not budge on their rights in West Berlin, he decided to give Ulbricht the green light on July 20, 1961 – less than a month before the actual event.[22]

Ulbricht understood that closing the borders in Berlin would increase his country's economic problems for some time. But as early as December 1960, Ulbricht had told Khrushchev that he desired to make the GDR "independent from the capitalist world." The closure of the Berlin borders in August 1961 would thus complete the reorientation of the country toward the USSR and the CMEA, which had begun in 1947. In that vein, Ulbricht tried to enlist economic support from both on March 1, and obtain political backing from WAPA on August 3–5.[23]

The closure of the Berlin borders received a wide range of assessments at the time. The *Einbetonierung* (encasement with concrete) left many East Germans in despair, anger, and bitterness, but the efficacy of the Stasi (Ministerium für Staatssicherheit; Ministry for State Security) prevented another uprising until 1989. West Berliners and West Germans called the closure of the borders a "declaration of bankruptcy" and the walled-in GDR Ulbricht's "concentration camp." The Western Allies saw it mostly as a defensive measure designed to shore up a failing socialist state.[24] Khrushchev, in comparison, was "pleased" that "East Germany ... had asserted its sovereign rights." Still, he admitted in November 1961 to a West German diplomat that the "wall is an ugly thing." His successor, Leonid I. Brezhnev, went further in the early 1970s by faulting Ulbricht for building a "Chinese wall" that was an obstacle to peace. The East German leader himself considered the imprisonment of his citizens the "second birth" of the GDR because it ensured a stable population base on which to create a socialist paradise on German soil.[25]

After the closure of the borders, Ulbricht hoped to move quickly toward the unperturbed construction of socialism in the GDR. As predicted, East Germany faced economic problems, but East Berlin firmly believed that the GDR "as the most western country of the Socialist Camp shoulders the task of demonstrating the superiority of the socialist societal order over the second strongest capitalist state." Since Germany's physical division also put a greater psychological distance between the two hostile twins, it lessened the need to construct an ideologically pure socialist system. By November 1961, Ulbricht had formulated his new ideas on socialist construction; East Germany's economy would no longer run according to political commands but according to economic calculations. For some years after 1963, when his GDR experimented with reform, the country experienced economic growth – but never at the rate of the FRG. The shortage of qualified labor, the self-delusion of using the USSR as a cheap raw material supplier and receptive market for expensive GDR products, and Ulbricht's vicious criticism of supposedly inept party cadres doomed the project to failure. Already in 1962, Moscow rejected East Berlin's request for additional economic aid: "If the German comrades believe that they could be the display case for socialism, they should fill it with goods through their own effort." But the situation was even worse: an internal report two years later revealed that the GDR had started to consume its own structural substance to survive economically.[26]

Struggling against and Living with Each Other

Ten days after the closure of the borders in Berlin, Ulbricht raised the idea of concluding a peace treaty. Stalin had brought up this idea as early as his note in March 1952, but Khrushchev had shelved the issue with the withdrawal of his Berlin Ultimatum in 1959. In August 1961, the Soviet leader clearly had not been willing to touch Western Allied rights in West Berlin, but subsequently convinced himself that the closure of the borders "was as though a peace treaty had been signed." In February 1962, however, he bluntly told his vassal from East Berlin to focus on more pressing issues: "The main thing is not the peace treaty but the consolidation of the economic situation ... What is it that makes a peace treaty attractive to us? Nothing." Since he considered the Berlin problem patched up for good, Khrushchev told UK Prime Minister Harold Wilson two years later, he was more interested in lowering the fever of the global Cold War than in aggravating the "inflamed wound" once more. Eventually, he relented to Ulbricht's constant pestering by granting a bilateral friendship treaty in mid 1964. The East German leader firmly believed that he needed such an ostentatious agreement because it would solidify the status of the GDR as a sovereign state in the eyes of the FRG.[27]

After August 13, 1961, the GDR tried to raise political support in the Afro–Asian world by portraying the closure of the borders as a measure of peace. Seemingly uninformed about the situation in Berlin, India's Jawaharlal Nehru initially fell for the propaganda about West German militarism and publicly approved East Germany's decision to close the borders. Ghana's Kwame Nkrumah even promised to work for a peace treaty. But Egypt's Gamal Abdel Nasser refused to receive the East German emissary dispatched to see him. The German division reminded him of Palestine's sorrowful "dissolution" into a Jewish and Arab part. In view of the impending first Non-Aligned Conference in Belgrade in early September 1961, the GDR tried in vain to influence delegations there. Consequently, in March 1962, the GDR decided to launch an aid offensive in the Afro–Arab world designed to achieve recognition, though it lacked the means to match FRG resources. Two years later, once the Non-Aligned had decided to convene a second conference in October 1964 in Cairo, East Germany once more tried to sway participants.[28]

The East German attempts after August 1961 to obtain UN membership fared similarly poorly. Since neither Germany was a member, accession to the international organization would have meant full recognition. Pouring cold water on these extravagant dreams, the Soviet comrades proposed a gradual approach whereby the GDR obtained observer status first before working toward double membership later. Still, around the first anniversary of the closure of the borders in Berlin, the GDR requested that the USSR influence UN General Secretary U Thant to allow both Germanys to accede on the basis of equality. Spurred by the FRG, the three Western Allies – all permanent members of the Security Council – intervened with U Thant, stating that "only the West German Government had the right to speak in the name of the German people."[29]

Twice in the mid 1960s, the GDR seemed to be close to a diplomatic breakthrough. After Chinese Premier Zhou Enlai had boasted to an East

German delegation in early November of 1964 that the recent Chinese A-bomb test had finally broken the ability of US imperialism to blackmail the rest of the world, the GDR hoped that, through mutual cooperation, both countries would obtain UN membership quickly. Little did East Berlin know that Beijing would soon publicly denounce the international organization as reactionary. Concurrent developments in the Middle East were more auspicious, however. When the news broke in October of 1964 that the FRG had shipped American weapons to Israel, Nasser retaliated in mid December by inviting Ulbricht to Cairo. The East German leader arrived in Egypt in late February of 1965 to gun salutes, the East German anthem, and the raising of his country's flag. For the FRG, a nightmare had become reality. Bonn retaliated by sending, for the first time, an ambassador to Tel Aviv. In reprisal, ten Arab states cut relations with the FRG before mid 1965, displaying their new-found unity. But the GDR could not build on the momentum of this triumph. Conservative Arab countries like Saudi Arabia had no wish to recognize a communist Germany, and radical ones like Egypt or Algeria were too dependent on West German development aid to afford doing so.[30]

In comparison, West Germany and West Berlin saw the sudden closure of the borders in 1961 primarily as a human disaster. It tore apart hundreds of thousands of extended families without any prospect of meeting each other in person again or even calling each other on the phone. In this situation, Grotewohl's November 1961 proposal to normalize relations sounded like a bad joke. But Bonn was eventually willing to deal with the devil in order to reduce the human suffering. In December 1962, the two governments agreed that the FRG would pay for the release and emigration of thousands of GDR citizens who had been arrested on political grounds. Until 1989, Bonn paid in total 3.436 billion German marks to free almost 34,000 political prisoners. In late 1963, the two hostile twins also agreed to allow West Berliners to visit their relatives in the eastern half of the divided city during the Christmas holidays. The following September, East Germany permitted retirees – i.e. people whose labor it no longer needed – to visit West Berlin and West Germany, and agreed to private visits to East Berlin.[31]

In response to East Germany's attempts to raise its profile in the Afro–Asian and Non-Aligned world after August 1961, West Germany established trade representations in Poland, Hungary, and Romania in 1963 to mark its presence there. However, the FRG explicitly did not establish embassies, since it did not want to undermine its own Hallstein Doctrine. When Bonn also offered the establishment of cultural ties to socialist states in Eastern Europe in 1964, East Berlin briefly toyed with the idea of developing an "offensive" counter-Hallstein doctrine.[32]

West Germany's relations with the USSR, in comparison, entered into a cul-de-sac. In June 1964, Bonn complained to Moscow that the recently signed Soviet–East German friendship treaty undermined the development of a mutually beneficial relationship. Khrushchev officially responded that, with August 1961, the Germany Question had developed from an international issue into an exclusively German problem, to be solved primarily by "both German states." Still, he must have sensed that the GDR was an obstacle. During a visit to the FRG in late July 1964, his son-in-law, Aleksei Adzhubei, tried to calm down West German concerns with the remark that "Ulbricht will not live much longer." But the East German leader refused to die for another nine years, while Adzhubei's father-in-law found himself overthrown within less than three months. East Berlin was convinced that Khrushchev's fall was partially the result of his recent policy toward Bonn. Still, this was of little consolation. After the Arab–West German fallout in 1965, Bonn focused on further improving its relations with the other socialist states in Eastern Europe.[33]

In this context, France was for the FRG a source of both support and irritation. Adenauer had sought reconciliation with the Western neighbor from the beginning of his chancellorship. With Charles de Gaulle's ascent to power in 1958, he found a like-minded partner in terms of political convictions. In December 1961, the chancellor asked the French president to mediate in the Berlin Question between Bonn and Moscow, but de Gaulle refused "to negotiate" with the USSR because doing so meant that "one has already made a concession." Despite disagreements, the two countries signed a friendship treaty on January 22, 1963, that committed both sides to "consultations" on "all important questions of foreign policy." Even if the West German parliament ratified the agreement, Adenauer's own party took issue with the chancellor's increasingly single-handed style of decision-making in the wake of de Gaulle's unilateral no to British membership in the European Communities. The party eventually persuaded him to step down in September 1963 – at the advanced age of eighty-seven. Ludwig Erhard, the architect of the *Wirtschaftswunder*, succeeded him, but turned out to be a hapless leader.[34]

To Bonn's great frustration, Paris did not honor the promise to consult on all important foreign political issues. Just as Adenauer was retiring, de Gaulle ordered the start of secret negotiations on the establishment of diplomatic relations with Mao's China. The announcement of the break-through agreement on January 27, 1964, fell almost on the first anniversary of the signing of the Franco–German Treaty. Paris felt compelled to reassure an apprehensive Bonn that Beijing's recognition would not set a precedent for establishing relations with East Berlin. Consequently, during his seminal visit to Moscow in June 1966, de Gaulle bluntly told his Soviet hosts that the GDR was "an artificial construct."[35]

Ostpolitik

The collapse of the three-year-old Christian Democratic–Free Democratic coalition government in November of 1966 led to the establishment of the first grand coalition between Christian Democrats and Social Democrats in West German history. Georg Kiesinger was elected third federal chancellor, and Willy Brandt, the long-time mayor of West Berlin, assumed the position of foreign minister. Even if the coalition continued to reject the recognition of the GDR, it signaled willingness to enter into a limited German–German dialogue. In view of the difficult situation in Berlin, the Social Democrats had proposed, since the early 1960s, the concept of *Wandel durch Annäherung* (change through rapprochement) and developed the *Politik der kleinen Schritte* (policy of small steps). Anyway, the new government quickly set about abolishing the Hallstein Doctrine *de facto* when it established diplomatic relations with Romania on January 31, 1967, without requesting a prior severance of relations with the GDR.[36]

In a panic at the prospect of becoming isolated among the fraternal socialist countries, the GDR adopted a slate of counter-policies. It managed to convince WAPA to adopt the so-called Ulbricht Doctrine, which permitted recognition of the FRG only after West German recognition of East Germany. Then, the GDR tried to put a greater distance between itself and the FRG by creating a separate citizenship and dropping the clause in the 1949 constitution that pronounced the indivisibility of the German nation. Finally, it reactivated its assertive policy to obtain diplomatic recognition. This included the ostentatious display of pro-Arab and anti-Israeli positions during and after the June War in 1967. Yet the Arab states, which had not yet restored their relations with the FRG, hesitated to respond for another two years. On April 30, 1969, Iraq eventually broke ranks by recognizing the GDR in exchange for economic aid. In an unrelated development ten days later, Cambodia tried to emphasize its Non-Aligned status by recognizing the GDR – eighteen months after it had done so with the FRG. With Soviet help and East German offers of money, Sudan, Egypt, Syria, and the People's Republic of Yemen established relations with the GDR in mid 1969.[37]

In the federal elections in late September 1969, the Christian Democrats gained a plurality of votes, but the combined seats of the Social Democrats and the Free Democrats gave them a tiny majority in parliament. Brandt was elected the fourth – and first non-Christian

Democratic – chancellor in the history of the FRG. The new government was quick to acknowledge in public the reality of "two German states." Brandt also swiftly signaled to the USSR that his government would officially abandon the Hallstein Doctrine. And he rapidly signed the Nuclear Non-Proliferation Treaty (NPT) of 1968, which the Christian Democrats had refused to do. In view of Brandt's positions on the Hallstein Doctrine and the NPT, the Soviet Union had anyway preferred him over the Christian Democrat Kiesinger even before the elections.[38]

Via a backchannel, the new West German government soon started to negotiate with the USSR on a non-aggression treaty, which Moscow had sought for over a decade. The military clashes at the border with the People's Republic of China (PRC) in March 1969 had increased the Soviet eagerness to solve one of the long-term problems at the western end of its empire. On August 12, 1970, the FRG and the USSR signed the Moscow Treaty, which called for the normalization of relations in Europe and respect for – though not legal recognition of – the territorial status quo. Brandt replied to domestic critics that he had "not given anything away that had not already been gambled away" twenty-five years before.[39] On the contrary, he had obtained Brezhnev's implicit backing for his *Ostpolitik* toward Poland and the GDR. Moscow sold the treaty, which it had negotiated without East German input, to East Berlin as a chance to get recognition from Bonn. But Brandt faced an uphill struggle to get it accepted in the German parliament. Even the USSR understood that the opposition Christian Democrats fundamentally rejected a treaty that went against their long-time positions. Thus, Brandt made ratification of the Moscow Treaty dependent on progress in the ongoing quadrilateral Allied negotiations on the final status of West Berlin in order to gain domestic leverage.[40] But Soviet leaders replied by imposing the precondition that the West German ratification of the Moscow Treaty needed to precede the opening of the Conference on Cooperation and Security in Europe, as covered in the following chapter.

Given that the Soviet Union and National Socialist Germany had divided up Poland in August 1939, Brandt understood that approaching Moscow without simultaneously negotiating with Warsaw would create mistrust. Brandt's reconciliation with Poland was as important as Adenauer's reconciliation with France. Poland, in turn, realized that its fate was dependent on the solution of the Germany Question, and that Bonn had to go through Moscow on this issue. On December 7, 1970, the Polish and West German governments signed the Warsaw Treaty, which, similar to the Moscow Treaty, included a non-aggression clause and West German respect for – though not legal recognition of – the existing (East) German–Polish border at the Oder–Neisse Line. Brandt acquired much good will in Poland during a scheduled short visit to the Memorial of the Warsaw Ghetto Uprising. In an unexpected gesture, the man who had himself fled the National Socialists in 1933 fell on his knees, silently asking for absolution for the crimes committed in Germany's name during occupation in 1939–44.[41]

The successes in the first year of Brandt's chancellorship would not have been possible without the backing of West Germany's most important ally – the United States. Even before he was formally elected chancellor by parliament, Brandt flew to Washington to coordinate his initiatives with President Richard M. Nixon. The US leader himself had called for negotiations in his inaugural address ten months before. But Henry Kissinger, his national security adviser, feared that Brandt was simply rehashing Schumacher's old policy of German unification through equidistance between the USSR and the United States. Yet the new chancellor stood to benefit from the publicly stated Soviet willingness to improve relations with the West, which had arisen against the background of Sino–Soviet border clashes earlier in the year. In response, the Western Allies had called on the USSR to improve the situation in Berlin. Finally, on March 26, 1970, the talks on the final status of Berlin between the four World War II Allies started.[42]

The GDR eyed Brandt's *Ostpolitik* with suspicion from the very beginning. Responding to his insistence that there was only *one German nation* despite the existence of *two German states*, it redefined itself as a "socialist German nation." Bonn took the lead in early 1970 by offering informal talks, but rejected a counterproposal to meet in East Berlin because it would have provided the GDR with a symbolic victory. The encounter between Willy Brandt and his counterpart Willi Stoph in the East German city of Erfurt on March 19 marked the first high-level talks between the two German states. For weeks, the East German population had eagerly anticipated the West German visit. On the 19th, thousands managed to break through police cordons to gather in front of Brandt's hotel in the center of Erfurt. There, they started to call on the chancellor to appear in a window. Deeply moved by this unexpected expression of *Zusammengehörigkeit* (belonging together) and yet simultaneously concerned that the situation might escalate, he briefly appeared in a hotel window, silently gesturing with his hands to the jubilant crowd below to remain calm. From behind the curtains of his room, Brandt then watched how the East German security organs cleared the square.[43]

The talks in Erfurt and subsequent negotiations in the West German provincial city of Kassel in May did not lead to any agreement. Stoph demanded full diplomatic recognition but Brandt was only willing to offer gradual steps to lessen the severity of the nation's division. Still, the GDR saw the fact that talks, even if inconclusive, had occurred at all as a victory of its peace policy. At least, the two governments managed to sign a postal agreement between the Erfurt and Kassel meetings. But in August, the Soviet Union warned East Germany: "There is, can, or shall be no process of rapprochement between the GDR and the FRG ... Brandt has different goals for the GDR than we have." The USSR emphasized that East Berlin needed to wait and see if Bonn would ever ratify the recently signed Moscow Treaty.[44]

But by then Ulbricht had decided that he wanted German–German rapprochement anyway. He took up Brandt's idea of stepwise rapprochement in the fields of traffic, trade, travel, and human contacts – for two reasons. First, he was eager to use the momentum to convince other non-socialist states to follow Brandt's example and negotiate with the GDR. But his orthodox rivals in the Politburo around his chosen successor, Erich Honecker, did not believe that the time was yet ripe for rapprochement because of its inherent dangers to the fragile stability and brittle internal legitimacy of the GDR. Opening toward the non-socialist world, they feared, would undo much of what closure of the borders in 1961 had achieved. Second, Ulbricht did not want to miss a window of opportunity that might be closing soon; the long-time East German leader feared that the Brandt government would not stay in power for long.[45]

The unexpected leadership changes in the GDR in May 1971, however, raised renewed questions about the long-term prospects of Brandt's *Ostpolitik*. In July 1970, the USSR had interceded in East Berlin to reverse Ulbricht's decision to sack his chosen successor-turned-rival Honecker. Thus, Honecker had become Brezhnev's man against the 77-year-old Ulbricht, who had run East Germany for a quarter of a century. In late July, less than three weeks before the conclusion of the Moscow Treaty, Honecker covertly visited the convalescent Brezhnev in a Moscow hospital to discuss the situation in East Berlin. The Soviet leader was "disquieted" with both Ulbricht's desire to pursue an accelerated rapprochement with West Germany and his increasingly autocratic rule. But Brezhnev still requested that Honecker try to work it out with Ulbricht, emphasizing that "it will be impossible for him [Ulbricht] to rule past us. We have troops [stationed] with you." A week after the Moscow Treaty, Brezhnev was even blunter to Honecker when it came to the need to follow Moscow's orders: "Without the Soviet Union, the GDR does not exist."[46]

In early 1971, Honecker – together with other Politburo members – wrote an alarmist letter to Brezhnev, in which he portrayed Ulbricht as a treasonous megalomaniac and demanded that the Soviet comrades convince the old leader to retire as soon as possible. After Soviet pressure,

Ulbricht asked Brezhnev to be allowed to retire by early May. Two weeks later, Honecker promised the Soviet leader that he would coordinate foreign and economic policy more closely. Brezhnev then raised what he considered more urgent business. He was convinced that the current weakness of the Brandt government – the tiny majority of his coalition was shrinking as a result of defections – was a problem that required defining "a tactical line in such a way that we [are able to] promote the ratification of the [Moscow and Warsaw] treaties." Following both Soviet instructions and his own inclinations, Honecker then went on to jettison Ulbricht's economic reform, instituting policies that focused on social welfare which, as it turned out over the course of the 1970s, were financed by ever increasing loans from the USSR and the non-socialist world, including West Germany.[47]

On September 3, 1971, after eighteen months of negotiations, the Soviet Union and the three Western Allies approved the text of the so-called Quadripartite Agreement on Berlin, but declared they would not sign until after the West German parliament had ratified the Moscow and Warsaw Treaties. In the agreement, the four World War II Allies guaranteed each other's occupation rights in the city while the Soviet Union warranted free unhindered Western access to West Berlin. This opened the avenue toward German–German negotiations on finding solutions to the many problems from which the divided city suffered. In a first step of confidence-building measures, the two Germanys had reconnected the phone lines between the two halves of Berlin beforehand, in January 1971. In the three months after the finalization of the text of the Quadripartite Agreement, the FRG and the GDR signed agreements on postal services, on transit through East German territory between West Germany and West Berlin, and on private travel and human contacts.[48]

Yet, at the same time, East Berlin reinvigorated its policy of trying to raise its international standing in response to Bonn's request from third countries to hold off double recognition until after the end of all German–German negotiations. The GDR in particular attempted to exploit the evolving East Pakistan Crisis in late 1971 by seeking close relations with the emerging Bangladeshi government. Immediately after the conclusion of the three German–German agreements and *during* the short Indo-Pakistani war in late 1971, East German diplomats in vain beleaguered India's Prime Minister Indira Gandhi with requests to recognize the GDR.[49]

But within just one year, on December 21, 1972, Bonn and East Berlin signed the *Grundlagenvertrag* (Basic Treaty). On September 18 the following year, the FRG and the GDR acceded to the United Nations as full members. The Basic Treaty normalized relations between the two states, assured each other's territorial sovereignty and autonomy in domestic and foreign affairs, ruled out the claim that one of them could represent the other or all of Germany, and established near-full diplomatic relations. Bonn insisted that the two Germanys would not exchange embassies but only "permanent representations" in order to underscore that the mutual relationship was one *between two states* but *not between two nations*.[50]

But before the Basic Treaty could be signed, two obstacles needed to be overcome – a recalcitrant GDR and the opposition Christian Democrats in the FRG. Honecker, who had exploited Ulbricht's recent promotion of supposedly lenient policies toward West Germany to overthrow his political father, resisted changing his own negative positions on rapprochement once he had gotten into power. Following the signing of the Quadripartite Agreement in September 1971, however, Moscow made it clear to East Berlin what was at stake: "Of course there is a codependency between the Quadripartite Agreement and the [future] 'German' agreement in the sense that they only work as one unit." A Soviet diplomat complained to East German representatives in late 1971 that he "unfortunately ... has the impression that not all GDR comrades understand this issue correctly." German–German rapprochement would lead to East German recognition on a global scale, he emphasized.[51]

At the same time, the opposition Christian Democrats in Bonn had openly told the Soviet leaders that they would vote against the ratification of the Moscow and Warsaw Treaties. In view of a scheduled no-confidence vote in the hung Federal German parliament on April 27, 1972, the GDR, under Soviet pressure, made concessions regarding German–German travel issues with the purpose of supporting Brandt politically. To everyone's surprise, the no-confidence vote went in Brandt's favor by two votes. The Stasi had bought at least one opposition member in the West German parliament to help Brandt survive. In its wake, the FRG ratified the Moscow and Warsaw Treaties by May 19. However, the FRG exchanged the ratification documents with the USSR and Poland, respectively, on June 3 only *after* the four occupation powers had signed the Quadripartite Agreement on Berlin earlier in the day.[52]

With the Moscow and Warsaw Treaties in force by June 3, the way to the Conference on Security and Cooperation in Europe opened, and the Soviet Union gave the GDR the go ahead to negotiate the *Grundlagenvertrag* with the FRG. It even pushed East Berlin hard to accelerate German–German rapprochement because its relations with Beijing remained poor. Following his re-election triumph in November 1972, Brandt had reached the pinnacle of his power. The *Grundlagenvertrag* was signed within five weeks and ratified within another six months. In June 1973, Brandt was the first German head of government to visit Israel, where Prime Minister Golda Meir asked him – a German after all – to mediate in the Israeli–Arab conflict. And by late 1973, Brandt signed a treaty in Prague that normalized relations with Czechoslovakia.[53]

But German–German rapprochement did not continue beyond 1973. Honecker did not want it to develop further. On the one hand, he had achieved all he wanted with the *Grundlagenvertrag*. The man who had personally overseen the closure of the Berlin borders in 1961 had always aimed at turning the GDR into an internationally recognized socialist German nation. On the other hand, Honecker simply did not share Ulbricht's preference for rapprochement, though he had to pursue it under Soviet pressure. He essentially saw further rapprochement as a threat to the GDR. Over the course of the 1970s, the number of Stasi agents doubled, largely for the purpose of controlling the re-emerging contacts between visiting West Germans and their East German relatives. Yet, at the same time, East Berlin's debt in the non-socialist world, especially in the FRG, increased to such a degree that the specter of economic dependency appeared on the horizon.[54]

Moreover, at the time of Brandt's *Ostpolitik*, the German–German competition moved from politics and economics into other fields as well. In the late 1960s, East Berlin decided to focus on the development of competitive sports in order to outcompete West Germany, which was awarded with hosting the Summer Olympic Games in September 1972 in Munich. Although the GDR succeeded, its athletes paid a steep price. The fixation on sport as a marker of socialist greatness led to the establishment of a sophisticated doping scheme that ruined the health of thousands of East German athletes. Furthermore, the GDR supported antigovernmental left-wing terrorists in the western half of the nation by providing weapons and training, and by offering sanctuary for those who wanted to quit or just needed respite from living underground over extended periods of time.[55]

Likewise, East Germany's staunchly pro-Arab and stridently anti-Israeli positions produced inconsistent and ethically questionable policies. Since the June War in 1967, the Stasi had built up close contacts with radical leftist movements in the Arab world, and since 1970 it had even helped to establish connections between Palestinian groups and West German leftist terrorists. The GDR thereby turned out to be an unwitting bedfellow with anti-Semitic Neo-Nazi groups in the FRG, which provided logistical support to the Palestinian attack on the Israeli Olympic team in Munich that killed eleven Jewish athletes, five terrorists, and one West German policeman. East Berlin was not involved in the actual planning of the attack, and also seemed not to have known anything about its preparations, but it was still embarrassed. Also, the GDR continued to reject any *Wiedergutmachung* to Israel. Since it had in total paid more reparations for World War II than the FRG, it argued, it was under no obligation to pay anything at all to Israel.[56]

Equally disturbing were the continued and intensive Stasi efforts to subvert the FRG, including the planting of spies at the highest levels of government, in spite of the explicit language about mutual respect for sovereignty in the *Grundlagenvertrag*. The discovery of the mole Günther Guillaume, who worked as a personal adviser to the chancellor, forced Willy Brandt to resign in May 1974.[57] The GDR thereby betrayed the man who had received the Nobel Peace Prize in 1971 for his *Ostpolitik* and who had helped East Germany to obtain international recognition.

Conclusion

The two Germanys that emerged in the wake of World War II could not have been more different. The Western Allies had created the FRG, but it soon developed into a stable and affluent liberal democracy. Successive governments enjoyed democratic legitimacy bolstered by recurrent free elections. Its leaders demonstrated an understanding of the crimes committed by Hitler's National Socialism in Germany's name. Adenauer sought integration with the West and reconciliation with France, and Brandt pursued rapprochement with the USSR and socialist East European countries. The Holocaust spurred both chancellors to make a commitment to Israel.

The GDR was a creation of the USSR, although probably an unsought one. Unlike its capitalist and supposedly imperialist twin in the West, the East German regime needed the presence of Soviet troops to keep itself in power. Neither Adenauer nor de Gaulle believed that the GDR was an expression of the collective will of its citizens – even Brezhnev bluntly told Honecker in 1970 that East Germany was a Soviet creation entirely dependent on Moscow. Despite recurring "elections," ordinary East Germans scornfully called the mandatory and rigged polling process *Zettelfalten* – the mechanical folding of the ballot before dropping it into the ballot box in public.[58] The GDR leaders did not succeed in producing legitimacy, or even a level of economic wellbeing similar to the FRG, despite their repeated claims that they were ruling in the name of the people and socio-economic justice. Their empty anti-fascist propaganda served as a tool to evade responsibility for National Socialist crimes while they cynically sought to obtain international recognition by supporting the Arab side in the Middle Eastern conflict.

German double statehood within internationally recognized borders and eventually within the United Nations emerged in parallel but unrelated developments of state and nation formation by several states in Asia, the Middle East, and Europe. In October 1971, a month after the four occupation powers of Germany had settled on the final text of the Quadripartite Agreement on Berlin that opened the way to the *Grundlagenvertrag*, the UN General Assembly decided to admit the PRC in lieu of the ROC. Shortly thereafter, as the USSR and the GDR struggled for the West German ratification of the Moscow and Warsaw Treaties, India broke up Pakistan and recognized Bangladesh. In its aftermath, India decided to go nuclear to become a great power while Pakistan tried to reinvent itself as an Islamic country within the larger Middle East. A month after the two Germanys signed the *Grundlagenvertrag* in late December 1972, the Paris Accords ended the American involvement in the Vietnam War, opening up the path for the DRV to pursue Vietnamese reunification and even Indochinese hegemony. Within a month of German–German accession to the United Nations in mid September 1973, Egypt went to war against Israel to force the world, particularly the United States, to address the issue of Egyptian sovereignty over the Sinai and tackle Palestinian nationhood. As the two Germanys concluded a quarter-century-long process of state formation by the early 1970s, Poland experienced a similar international recognition of its post-World War II borders and ultimate assumption of territorial control, as the following two chapters reveal.

18 The Conference on Security and Cooperation in Europe

European governments on either side of the Iron Curtain drew different lessons from World War II. On the eastern side, the Soviet-led Socialist Camp primarily pursued security and international recognition for its refashioned borders, given the multiple German invasions between 1938 and 1941. Thus, from 1954 to 1969, the Socialist Camp repeatedly sought to jumpstart a pan-European conference to obtain Western, especially West German, recognition of its disputed post-war borders in Eastern Europe. On the other side, Western European democracies made commitments to political pluralism and human rights in the post-war period against the background of authoritarianism and atrocities committed during the war. Participatory politics and individual rights were supposed to serve as models for the reform of authoritarian states on both sides of the Iron Curtain. These two incompatible but parallel pursuits, which aimed at preventing another European catastrophe and bolstering peace, intersected in 1973–75 at the Conference on Security and Cooperation in Europe (CSCE) in Geneva. Thus the CSCE turned into the principal arena in the struggle between socialist conceptions of the primacy of the state and liberal conceptions of rights of the individual citizen.

This struggle arose particularly in the space stretching from the USSR across Poland and Czechoslovakia to East and West Germany. Since the 1950s, the four socialist states had sought recognition from the Federal Republic of Germany (FRG) for their refashioned borders, and hoped to prevent its rearmament within NATO in the wake of the Korean War. West Germany refused to acknowledge the post-war borders in Eastern Europe, not because it pursued the recovery of lost territory, but because it wanted to keep a trump card up its sleeve to achieve reunification with the German Democratic Republic (GDR). The Helsinki Final Act of August 1, 1975, reconciled these seemingly incompatible goals in a political, but not legally binding, deal that traded the *de facto* respect of borders for human contacts and freedom of movement and ideas across the Iron Curtain.

438

The impact of the Helsinki deal on Europe only unfolded over time, however. The Soviet Union and East Germany continued to use repressive force to limit individual rights as if they had never signed the Final Act. The opposition in Czechoslovakia was small, elite-driven, committed to socialist ideas of societal organization, and thus unable to attract a wider audience. Only the Polish people, who had experienced political ferment since 1968, were able to benefit from the international attention that the CSCE had drawn to the human rights situation in Eastern Europe. However, the real impact of the Western European human rights agenda occurred in the second half of the 1980s and after the end of the Cold War, as the final two chapters show.

The Socialist Pursuit of Security

World War II ended several age-old territorial disputes in Europe, but simultaneously created new ones. German-annexed Alsace-Lorraine returned to France for good in 1945. A year later, Austria agreed for South Tyrol and the Trentino to stay permanently with Italy, which in turn granted the German-speaking populations minority rights. The disputed Trieste region was *de facto* divided, although Italy and Yugoslavia needed three decades to sign a final legal agreement. In comparison, Eastern Europe at the end of World War II experienced significant territorial changes that would occupy the continent's politics for decades to come. During the war, the Soviet Union had annexed the three Baltic countries Estonia, Latvia, and Lithuania. At the Tehran Conference in 1943, British Prime Minister Winston Churchill and Soviet leader Iosif V. Stalin agreed that Romania would lose Bessarabia and Poland give up its eastern third to the Soviet Union. At the Yalta and Potsdam Conferences in 1945, the Big Three agreed that Poland would be compensated with the German territories of southern East Prussia, Pomerania, and Silesia. The Oder and Neisse rivers were to form Poland's new western border, although left-bank Stettin (Szczecin) would become Polish as well. The Soviet Union itself annexed northern East Prussia and Trans-Carpathian Ruthenia, the most eastern part of Czechoslovakia.[1]

Unsurprisingly, the USSR and Poland were sensitive about their new borders. The United States never recognized the Soviet annexation of the Baltic States. Similarly, at their creation in 1949, *both* German states refused to give up legal claim to the lost eastern territories. East German leader Walter Ulbricht eventually recognized the existing border with Poland at the Oder–Neisse Line and the loss of Stettin on June 6, 1950, but the bilateral relationship remained strained for years. Soon thereafter, on June 23, the GDR also renounced claims to the Sudetenland in Czechoslovakia, which Adolf Hitler had gained in the infamous Munich agreement in 1938. While the FRG had never endorsed the territorial claims raised by the Sudeten German refugees, Article 23 of the *Grundgesetz* (Basic Law) of 1949 explicitly stressed that the West German constitution applied to Germany within the borders of 1937, i.e. the Federal Republic of Germany, the German Democratic Republic, and the eastern territories lost to Poland and the USSR. The article was primarily designed as a tool to keep the issue politically alive as leverage for future reunification, but still created much irritation in Warsaw and Moscow for decades. In June 1950, Chancellor Konrad Adenauer's government officially protested against East Berlin's supposed betrayal of German territory, but soon thereafter he privately admitted that the eastern territories were gone for good.[2]

In November 1953, less than half a year after the end of the Korean War, Poland appealed to several Western European countries to cooperate against the remilitarization of the supposedly "neo-fascist" and "imperialist" West Germany within the supranational structures of the European Defense Community (EDC). Warsaw's plea targeted NATO countries that had been fellow victims of German aggression in World War II – France, Belgium, the Netherlands, Denmark, and Norway. At the Berlin Conference in early 1954, the Big Three and France were unable to come to an agreement on the divided nation. The USSR instead proposed a pan-European collective security accord in exchange for the dissolution of NATO and American withdrawal from the continent. The three Western Allies rejected the Soviet scheme as a "poor joke," particularly since it included the idea of elevating the People's Republic of China (PRC) to co-observer in European affairs and downgrading the United States to the same level. The United States did not want to recognize communist China at all, nor see Beijing assume raised status in world affairs at Washington's expense. At least, the four World War II Allies saved the gathering from complete failure by agreeing to convene a conference on ending the Korean and Indochina conflicts in the summer of 1954 in Geneva.[3]

In the wake of the Berlin Conference, Poland approached France, which had grown uneasy about the EDC for unrelated reasons, with an appeal to support the Soviet proposal for a pan-European collective security agreement that would contain supposed West German militarism and force Adenauer to recognize the Oder–Neisse Line. In August – between the Geneva Conference and the impending vote in the French National Assembly on the EDC treaty – the Soviet Union again called for a security conference "with the participation of the United States and ...

the People's Republic of China." The successful collaboration of pro-Soviet Communists and Gaullists in the National Assembly against ratification on August 30 only amounted to a Pyrrhic victory for the Socialist Camp. On the basis of the quickly cobbled-together Paris Treaty of October 23, NATO countries granted West Germany a greater scope of sovereignty and permission to enter the alliance.[4]

The prospect of an armed West Germany, albeit under NATO control, rattled the USSR and socialist Eastern Europe even more. The Kremlin floated the idea of a mutual and "immediate withdrawal of occupation troops from the territory of East and West Germany." A conference on peace and security held in Moscow from November 29 to December 2 gathered the Soviet Union, Eastern European socialist states, and China to discuss countermeasures. Poland demanded fraternal support to guarantee its security and borders. Czechoslovakia proposed the creation of a unified military command and the armament of the GDR, although East Germany had armed itself clandestinely for years. None of these late maneuvers, however, could prevent West Germany from gaining membership in NATO on May 6, 1955. Within less than ten days, the USSR imposed the Warsaw Pact treaty (WAPA) on the Eastern European socialist states. Yet Moscow did not succeed in using the new alliance as a bargaining chip to get rid of NATO. At the Geneva Summit in July 1955, the western powers also rejected once more a Soviet proposal to create a system of pan-European collective security.[5]

Moscow returned to the general idea of a pan-European security system yet again in early 1958 when it called for a four-power summit to discuss a nuclear test moratorium and the increase of trade across the Iron Curtain. The proposal merged earlier ideas of a pan-European security system with more recent Soviet concerns over negative effects on trade following the formation of the European Economic Community (EEC) in 1957. In September 1959, Soviet leader Nikita S. Khrushchev and US President Dwight D. Eisenhower agreed on a four-power summit in Paris to discuss Berlin and Germany. But three crises in as many years – the U-2 incident that wrecked the Paris Summit in May of 1960, the Berlin Crisis in August of 1961, and the Cuban Missile Crisis in October of 1962 – sidetracked Soviet attempts to establish a pan-European collective security system.[6]

The West German hesitation to sign the Limited Test Ban Treaty (LTBT) of 1963 and concurrent NATO discussions about nuclear sharing within the Multi-Lateral Force (MLF) provided Poland and the Soviet Union with a renewed impetus to call for a pan-European security system. As early as 1957, Warsaw had grown concerned about possible West German access to nuclear weapons. Thus, a plan by Polish Foreign

Minister Adam Rapacki called for a nuclear-free zone in Europe. The proposal failed within a year because of NATO's lack of interest, and also because of East German complaints that it did not explicitly call for the international recognition of the GDR. In October 1963, two months after the Soviet–American–British signing of the LTBT in Moscow, the Polish leader Władysław Gomułka accused Khrushchev of failing to include the prohibition of the MLF in the treaty. Gomułka warned that West German access to nuclear weapons through the MLF would provide the FRG with pre-eminence over the GDR, and even enable it to conduct "nuclear blackmail" against WAPA member countries. Instead, the Polish leader demanded, the USSR should work on dividing NATO, particularly since France and Great Britain were also concerned about the MLF, and on strengthening the unity of the Socialist Camp by making compromises in the ideological conflict with Beijing. The Soviet leader eventually proposed to the new US president, Lyndon B. Johnson, that "an international agreement (or treaty) be concluded for the renunciation by the states of the use of force for the settlement of territorial disputes and boundary questions." A year later, at the United Nations, Rapacki once more criticized the MLF while proposing to convene a pan-European security conference. At East Germany's request, the Warsaw Pact met in early 1965 in the Polish capital to unveil a draft nuclear non-proliferation treaty (NPT), demand the end of the MLF (which would die within a short period of time anyway), call for a non-aggression treaty between WAPA and NATO, and propose once more a conference for pan-European security.[7]

A West German political initiative in March 1966 carried the potential of breaking the East–West deadlock. Responding to Soviet propaganda on the supposed militarist character of the FRG, Chancellor Georg Kiesinger publicly renounced his country's territorial claims, repudiated the use of military force to solve Europe's problems, and called for the gradual reduction of nuclear weapons on the continent. While the vast majority of German parliamentarians, NATO members, and even WAPA states reacted positively, Poland criticized the lack of an explicit recognition of the Oder–Neisse Line. The USSR subsequently tried to exploit what it labeled the West German peace note at a two-week WAPA conference in Bucharest in June, but the gathering struggled to find common positions. The majority – with Romania being the dissenter – wanted to elevate the solution to the Germany Question – i.e. West Germany's renunciation of nuclear weapons, recognition of the Oder–Neisse border, and the international double recognition of both German states – to a key issue at a future pan-European security conference. Despite its own internal division, the Soviet-led WAPA ultimately hoped to split Western unity by calling for a pan-European security conference of capitalist, neutral, and socialist states to discuss the recognition of post-war borders, the solution of the Germany Question, the disbanding of both military alliances, the increase of mutual trade, and scientific and cultural cooperation. The signatories of the long-winded Bucharest appeal explicitly excluded the United States from the invitation because "of its aggressive war against the Vietnamese."[8] But Moscow's position was inconsistent. While it was happy to present the Indochina conflict as an obstacle to American participation in pan-European security matters, at the same time it was willing to drop Vietnam in bilateral negotiations with Washington on nuclear non-proliferation. Both the June War in the Middle East a year later and the WAPA intervention in Czechoslovakia in 1968 undermined Soviet calls for a pan-European security conference, jeopardized Polish bids to obtain respect for the Oder–Neisse Line, and undermined East German hopes to get international recognition.

By mid March 1969, the Socialist Camp found itself in a desperate situation. The CMEA worried that the European Communities (EC) – in the wake of the merger treaty of 1967 and in view of the launch of its common foreign policy in 1970 – would implement discriminatory trade policies. And the lethal military clash at the Sino–Soviet border on March 2, 1969, turned the Sino–Soviet Split into a major security concern for Moscow. At short notice, Soviet party leader Leonid I. Brezhnev called a WAPA meeting in Budapest to discuss pan-European security. In two days of preparatory talks, he demanded a public expression of pact solidarity against China, which Romania managed to prevent. When the official meeting convened on March 17, the Soviet leader was still occupied with the Chinese security threat at the expense of any discussion of European affairs. The gathering did, however, issue a short statement – the Budapest Appeal – that called for a pan-European security conference to discuss borders, Germany, and continent-wide cooperation, but did not include *any* preconditions on agenda and participation. Afterward, Moscow informed East Berlin that it sought to convene a pan-European conference before the end of the year in Paris, Helsinki, Stockholm, or Warsaw. But despite the tame wording of the Budapest Appeal, Soviet goals still remained the same – a guarantee of post-war borders, recognition of both Germanys, containment of West German "neo-Nazism" and "revanchism," the end of the arms race, the dissolution of NATO, and the exclusion of the United States from Europe.[9]

The West European Pursuit of Human Rights

Drafted in response to the brutalities of World War II, the UN Declaration of December 10, 1948, turned out to be the seminal statement on human rights in the twentieth century. The Covenant of the League of Nations of 1919 had not contained any references to human rights. But during the interwar period, lawyers, educators, and diplomats in France and the United States pushed for the international codification of human rights. The American government insisted on a human rights declaration at the founding conference of the United Nations in San Francisco in 1945. Yet, in subsequent negotiations, the Big Three opposed the establishment of an enforcement mechanism. The United Kingdom wanted to shield itself against attacks on its Empire. The USSR objected to interference with its sovereignty. And the United States feared international criticism over racial discrimination at home. Thus, the UN Declaration did not play a meaningful role in its first two decades. The global Cold War undermined its potential to develop into a normative force, and decolonization movements, even if they used the rhetoric of human rights, focused mainly on the liberation of nations rather than individuals.[10]

In early May 1948, just before the UN General Assembly put the finishing touches on the declaration, the Congress of Europe established the Council of Europe. Within a year, the council took cues from the United Nations by launching discussions on a European Convention on Human Rights. On November 4, 1950, the council members – all Western European democracies – signed the convention. The horrors of World War II, the anti-communist instincts of Christian democrats and conservatives who had both campaigned for the council's establishment, and the explicit commitments to democracy in the Brussels Pact of 1948 and the North Atlantic Treaty of 1949 jointly drove the effort to enshrine human rights. The United Kingdom was the first country to ratify in March 1951, and the convention went into force in September 1953 with the ratification by its tenth signatory, Luxembourg.[11]

Unlike its UN model, the European Convention acquired an enforcement mechanism within a decade. At the beginning, the European Commission for Human Rights could only hear cases raised by member countries but merely assist in reaching friendly settlements. After July 1955, it was also allowed to hear petitions by individuals residing in member countries. With the ratification of an additional accord in September 1958 by eight countries, the European Court of Human Rights (ECHR) was established early the following year. Its decisions were binding to those countries that had submitted to its jurisdiction. After 1961, even individuals could file petitions. In subsequent years, the court quickly established itself as the primary tool of enforcement for a rapidly growing body of European human rights law.[12]

The court's establishment was not uncontroversial, particularly among two countries that had tried to shape European integration since the 1940s. Although British public opinion had been calling for an international human rights regime since World War II, the United Kingdom signed the convention only on the condition that it would not apply automatically to the Empire. London also did not accede to the European Court of Human Rights until 1966 out of fear that the court might supersede British civil rights, and then it only did so under permissible conditions (opt-outs). Similarly, France signed the convention, but neither ratified it until 1974 nor joined the court until 1981. This looked paradoxical for a country that had hosted the ECHR in Strasbourg since its inception in 1959. However, during the 1950s, France feared that the convention would interfere with its direct rule in Algeria. After 1962, President Charles de Gaulle loathed the idea of transferring French sovereignty to any international body – be it the European Economic Community or the ECHR.[13]

Just as the European Court of Human Rights emerged as a supranational actor in human rights politics in the early 1960s, non-governmental actors started to play an increasing role in sensitizing public opinion. NGOs had been crucial in the interwar period in creating the intellectual groundwork for the UN Declaration in 1948, but they had little influence on the state-driven European human rights approach afterward or on public opinion at large. The British-based NGO Amnesty International almost singlehandedly changed this situation after its foundation on December 10, 1961, the thirteenth anniversary of the UN Declaration. Tired of the Cold War propaganda battles, it tried to transcend them by focusing on political prisoners everywhere in the world. From the very beginning, Amnesty International emphasized its political neutrality while focusing on cases on both sides of the Iron Curtain, in the Afro–Asian world, and in South America. Mainly staffed by volunteers, the organization established chapters in several Western European countries in a short space of time. By 1964 and 1965, it obtained consultative status at the United Nations and the Council of Europe, respectively. Amnesty International lobbied the council to evict Greece after the military coup in 1967. By December 1969, Athens withdrew voluntarily to avoid the humiliation of imminent expulsion. The successful pursuit of this case helped Amnesty International to establish itself in the United States. There, civil rights activists had struggled against racial discrimination since the 1950s and had protested against US human rights abuses in the country's foreign policy – particularly in Vietnam – but had not focused on human rights abuses by other governments.[14] By the late 1960s, Amnesty International had clearly surpassed the UN Declaration in political effectiveness across the globe.

Preparing for a Pan-European Security Conference, 1969–72

The western reaction to the Budapest Appeal of March 1969 was muted but positive. On April 10–11, NATO decided to engage in "effective détente" but under the caveat of maintaining the alliance's military strength. Anyway, since early 1967, West Germany's Christian Democratic–Social Democratic coalition government had tried to engage in a limited dialogue across the Iron Curtain. This included a message to the USSR about West Germany's willingness to improve bilateral relations in the realms of trade, culture, and science and technology, to discuss borders and relations with East Germany, and to negotiate on conventional and nuclear disarmament. Late in 1967, NATO decided to pursue an active policy of seeking the relaxation of East–West tensions, though mostly in the field of conventional arms reduction. In January 1969, incoming US President Richard M. Nixon announced at his inauguration that his country was ready to enter into an "era of negotiation." However, his United States preferred to discuss security questions in a bilateral fashion – between the two exalted superpowers – rather than joining a multinational conference that involved mini-countries like Liechtenstein, Monaco, or San Marino. On May 7, neutral Finland offered to host a pan-European security conference after receiving a Soviet request. But since the Nordic country did not want to act merely as a "mailman" for the Warsaw Pact, it decided on its own to include both Germanys, the United States, and Canada in the invitation, and to insist on thorough preparations.[15]

Over the period from May to October 1969, WAPA and NATO tried to negotiate the terms for the conference. The Soviet Union was not happy with the Western insistence on American and Canadian participation, but eventually relented on the condition that both Germanys attend as equal partners. Even if Moscow thereby helped East Berlin to obtain *de facto* international recognition, it opposed making formal recognition or the solution of the Berlin Question into inflexible preconditions. On the contrary, the USSR advocated the quick convention of the pan-European conference with an agenda that was uncontroversial and likely to obtain speedy agreement. Moscow primarily wanted to focus on borders, the renunciation of the use of military force, and collaboration in trade, culture, and science and technology. By early fall 1969, the Soviet leaders sought to solve all open questions in Europe mainly because – on the other side of the USSR, in Asia – US involvement in Vietnam continued without abatement and Sino–Soviet relations remained tense.[16]

The West German elections in late September 1969 generated fresh opportunities for the USSR. The new chancellor, the Social Democrat Willy Brandt, swiftly signaled to the Soviet Union that he would seek rapprochement with East Germany and be open to participation in a pan-European security conference. However, Brandt first needed to earn trust from the White House and the Kremlin. President Nixon quickly came to see *Ostpolitik* as a trial balloon for superpower détente. But the Warsaw Pact was internally divided, despite Brandt's announcement of ratification of the one-year-old NPT. At a meeting in Moscow in early December, most of the East European members did not believe that *Ostpolitik* marked a break with the supposedly revanchist, militarist, and imperialist policies of Brandt's predecessors. Brezhnev, however, called for a cautious engagement. While Poland and East Germany essentially pursued narrow goals – i.e. the recognition of their borders by West Germany – the Soviet Union sought to establish greater influence in Europe by instituting good relations with West Germany at the expense of NATO cohesion. Ultimately, Moscow also needed détente in Europe for its economic modernization policies in the CMEA.[17]

Almost parallel to the WAPA meeting, the *Six* members of the EC met in The Hague to make several decisions that would be crucial for the community's future joint foreign policy. In the wake of de Gaulle's resignation the previous April, they had agreed to start membership negotiations with the United Kingdom, Ireland, Denmark, and Norway. Given the debate on Greece's expulsion from the Council of Europe, the *Six* emphasized the community's commitment to democracy and human rights. Eventually, they charged the Belgian diplomat Étienne Davignon with drafting proposals for the creation of a common foreign policy mechanism, designed to let the *Six* speak with one voice. Brandt explained the motivation for the new initiative with a somber reflection on the continent's contemporaneous international standing: "Europe as such is absent."[18]

But it was a NATO meeting, also in December 1969, that made the start of preparatory talks for the pan-European security conference dependent on progress in solving the Germany and Berlin Questions. This put dual pressure on the USSR to respond quickly to Brandt's *Ostpolitik* and to agree to resolve the Berlin issue in talks among the four occupation powers. As described in the previous chapter, West Germany signed a treaty with the Soviet Union in Moscow in August 1970 on the normalization of relations, the renunciation of force, and respect for post-World War II borders, followed by a similar treaty with Poland in Warsaw four months later. By September 1971, the four wartime Allies approved the final text of the Quadripartite Agreement on Berlin that guaranteed

Western access rights while requiring the two Germanys to find solutions to the myriad of problems that the division of the city and country had caused since 1945.

During the two years of negotiations following Brandt's election, Moscow managed German–German rapprochement on the eastern side of the Iron Curtain, as we saw in the previous chapter. Throughout 1970 and early 1971, the Soviet leaders constrained the East German party head Walter Ulbricht from acting on his own initiatives. After his forced resignation, they had to drag along his reticent hardline successor Erich Honecker, who feared that a West German embrace would smother his country. Furthermore, the USSR made the West German ratification of the Moscow and Warsaw Treaties – both hotly contested in the almost evenly split West German parliament – a precondition for the pan-European conference. Only after approval of the final text of the Quadripartite Agreement on Berlin in September did Moscow grow optimistic that a pan-European security conference would convene within a year, but still made signing the agreement dependent on the prior West German ratification of the Moscow and Warsaw Treaties. A British journalist compared the prospect of a future pan-European conference to a sparkling chandelier fastened to the ceiling by the unsecured link of imminent West German ratification: "If this link snaps, the chandelier of provisional détente ... will collapse on the statesmen below."[19]

As the Socialist Camp in Europe got ready for the pan-European security conference over the period 1969–72, NATO and the EC still needed to formulate their positions and demands. Following Brandt's election in September 1969, the Western alliance not only adopted his demand for linking the conference to a prior solution of the Germany and Berlin Questions, but also espoused the Franco–German idea of pressing for greater movement of individuals, ideas, and information across the Iron Curtain. Bonn and Paris had raised this proposal in the hope that its implementation would reunite divided families and spread ideas of liberal democracy and capitalism in the socialist world. Yet, between 1970 and 1971, disagreements within NATO over strategy mounted. Since Washington had only a limited interest in the multinational conference, it belligerently pursued its demands for freer movement across the Iron Curtain simply for the purpose of putting the USSR on the defensive in the global Cold War. In comparison, West Germany pursued a more realistic but limited agenda. Ultimately, the NATO partners managed to work out their differences. In December 1971, the alliance proposed negotiations at the pan-European security conference on four major issues: security; freer movement of people, information and ideas, plus cultural relations;

cooperation in trade, technology, and science; and improvement of the human environment.[20]

The prospect of the pan-European security conference worked as a catalyst for the emergence of European Political Cooperation (EPC) within the EC. On the basis of the Davignon report of October 1970, the EC implemented EPC as a voluntary mechanism to coordinate the foreign policies of the *Six*. Before the end of the year, the four membership candidates – the United Kingdom, Ireland, Denmark, and Norway – acceded as well. Although EPC initially focused on the Middle East, by May 1971, it also started to develop positions on the future pan-European security conference. But only after the NATO proposals of late 1971 did the EC begin to think more systematically about concrete foreign policy goals. As a community of democracies, it was able to bypass the non-democratic members of NATO – Greece, Turkey, and Portugal – which for obvious reasons were skeptical about including human rights in the pan-European security conference. Over the course of 1972, a series of referenda confirmed membership of the United Kingdom, Ireland, and Denmark – but not of Norway. By January 1, 1973, the *Nine* decided to demand that the USSR and the socialist states in Europe accept the norms of the European Convention on Human Rights, which they all had signed in 1950. This step logically followed an earlier decision to deny EC membership to authoritarian Western European countries – Spain, Portugal, Greece, and Turkey – unless they returned to democratic forms of government.[21]

As the likelihood of a pan-European conference increased in early 1972, the Soviet leadership grew concerned about the possibility of Chinese participation. Moscow itself had proposed making Beijing a counterweight to Washington in a pan-European security system in early 1954. In the fall of 1971, PRC propaganda used China's membership in the anti-German World War II alliance as an argument to demand formal involvement in European affairs. Beijing was particularly concerned about the implications of a pan-European settlement for its own security. The possibility that the USSR would use the conference to resolve security questions at its western borders and then turn against the PRC in the Far East led "the Chinese to be obviously afraid of détente in Europe." After its surprise accession to the United Nations in late October 1971, communist China was also the only permanent member of the Security Council not invited to the future pan-European security conference. According to an East German analysis, the PRC hence focused on establishing relations with the EC for an alliance against the USSR and other socialist countries in Europe.[22]

In the spring of 1972, the stars of the pan-European security conference finally aligned. On April 23, French voters agreed to grant EC membership to the United Kingdom, Ireland, Denmark and Norway (though Norwegian voters would nix it five months later in a separate referendum). After Brandt unexpectedly survived the no-confidence vote four days later, the West German parliament ratified the Moscow and Warsaw Treaties on May 19 but withheld the exchange of the ratification documents until after the USSR signed the Quadripartite Agreement on Berlin on June 3. At the Soviet–American Moscow Summit on May 22–30, Nixon and Brezhnev signed the SALT I and ABM treaties, agreements on collaboration in outer space and on trade, and a political statement calling for superpower collaboration to avoid nuclear war and for the use of peaceful means to solve regional crises. As Soviet Foreign Minister Andrei A. Gromyko told East German leaders in early June, all these agreements had opened the road to a pan-European security conference. The USSR, he claimed, had worked for the Soviet–American summit for three years. Because Soviet leaders wanted to achieve substantial agreements during Nixon's visit to Moscow – and not just "drink tea" as at a Chinese-style "protocollary meeting" – they were determined not to allow the concurrent escalation of the Vietnam War to wreck the summit. In fact, Moscow wanted a complete reset of relations with Washington after a quarter century of non-existent commercial and cultural ties. Brezhnev was convinced that the summit had committed Nixon to world peace, although the American president had made it clear that nothing would happen in terms of any pan-European security conference before the US presidential election on November 7. The two sides at least agreed to preparatory talks for a conference – soon to be dubbed the Conference on Security and Cooperation in Europe (CSCE) – to open in Helsinki by November 22. Moscow even believed that the summit had convinced Washington to adopt more constructive policies toward Vietnam and the Middle East. Little did Brezhnev know that Egypt would expel Soviet military advisers within six weeks in order to improve relations with the United States.[23]

At a meeting with the Eastern European communist party heads on July 21, Brezhnev bemoaned Egypt's decision to expel Soviet personnel because it would lead to a shift of the superpower balance in the Middle East. But this development was only a small black cloud in an otherwise sunny sky, he seemed to believe. The Soviet leader saw the CSCE as the crowning achievement of his country's 25-year-long "peace" policy in Europe. The sacrifice of 20 million Soviet lives in World War II had not been for naught. The West German ratification of the Moscow and Warsaw Treaties and the conclusion of the numerous Soviet–American treaties in May as well as the signing of the Quadripartite Agreement on Berlin and the exchange of the ratification documents of the Moscow and Warsaw treaties on June 3 had all together laid the basis for lasting peace in Europe. This meant that the Soviet-led Socialist Camp in Europe finally had the chance to focus on economic development and, in the process, outperform world capitalism peacefully. Hence, Brezhnev told his fellow party leaders from Eastern Europe that it was high time to determine joint negotiation positions for the preparatory talks in Finland, i.e. to aim for the legal recognition of Europe's post-World War II borders, the increase of trade, the establishment of cultural ties, and cooperation in science and technology. At the same time, the camp needed to oppose Western ideas of freedom of movement for people, ideas, and information as an attack on socialist sovereignty. Finally, the camp had to coordinate policies to prevent the EC from keeping its common market closed.[24]

On October 19–21, the EC took the basic decision to transform itself into the European Union in the long term, marking a further step toward deeper political and economic unity – a month before the start of the preparatory talks for the CSCE. On November 7, Nixon won a landslide victory. Eight days later, the Warsaw Pact decided to pursue policies to prevent "human rights" from becoming an issue at the CSCE since this could block the success of the whole conference.[25] And on November 19, Brandt was triumphantly re-elected, giving him the mandate to sign the *Grundlagenvertrag* (Basic Treaty) with East Germany that led to mutual recognition of the two states and opened up UN membership by 1973. All was ready for the East–West negotiations to start in Helsinki on November 22, 1972.

The Conference on Security and Cooperation in Europe, 1972–75

The start of the preparatory talks in Helsinki marked a new chapter in European diplomacy. For the first time since World War II, virtually all European states as well as the United States and Canada convened to discuss the continent's affairs. It was also the first meeting between NATO members, WAPA states, and neutrals in Europe, and the first multilateral conference attended by both Germanys. Nonetheless, the negotiations on procedures in the fall of 1972 quickly descended into an East–West tug-of-war because both sides had realized that the outcome of the preparatory talks would predetermine the results of the actual conference. Under the threat of an early deadlock, the neutrals Austria and Switzerland suggested suspending the talks for some weeks until mid January 1973.[26]

The main line of conflict was between the EC and the Soviet-led Socialist Camp on the issue of human rights. After the official accession of the United Kingdom, Ireland, and Denmark to the community on January 1, 1973, the *Nine* decided that the conference should aim for real agreements and not just empty declarations, and that agreements on security, economic issues, and human rights needed to balance each other. In the first days of the resumed preparatory talks in mid January, EC members submitted – in a demonstration of unity – coordinated proposals on a multitude of issues, taking WAPA members and even neutrals by surprise. In order to prevent another deadlock, Switzerland took up earlier Dutch and Austrian ideas of grouping the different proposals into four baskets: (I) security and borders; (II) cooperation in trade, science, technology, and the environment; (III) human contacts, exchange of information, and culture; and (IV) questions about the institutionalization of the conference.[27]

Put on the defensive, Brezhnev could not walk away from a conference for which the USSR had called since 1954. He himself also hoped that a success would earn him the Nobel Peace Prize. On March 1, using East Germany as a channel, the USSR made a focused counterproposal on borders, sovereignty, and peaceful settlement of conflicts. The goal was to reach a quick but limited result in Helsinki that would symbolically conclude World War II in Europe and thereby terminate US involvement on the continent. Ultimately, Moscow tried to aim for complete success in Basket I, to eliminate the discriminatory trading practices of the capitalist West (CoCom) and the EC (common market) through agreements in Basket II, to block human rights issues in Basket III, and to cement its own influence in Europe through the creation of a permanent security organization in Basket IV. The EC *Nine* and four neutrals – Switzerland, Austria, Sweden, and Finland – quickly rejected the Soviet proposal since it did not cover any aspect of human rights.[28]

At first, the United States was not interested in the preparatory talks in Helsinki, which in turn allowed the EC *Nine* to seize the moment. In the year after his re-election in November 1972, Nixon was absorbed with the end of the Indochina conflict, the unfolding crisis in the Middle East, the developing Watergate Scandal, and then the unraveling of the Paris Accords on Vietnam. The White House even concurred with the Kremlin on the need for quick results in Helsinki – but for different reasons. During his visit to Moscow in May 1972, Nixon had agreed to the multinational preparatory talks for the CSCE on the condition that bilateral conventional arms reduction talks would follow soon thereafter. Thus, an exasperated United States scolded the *Nine* for their obstinacy in Helsinki in the spring of 1973, and even requested to let the USSR have what it wanted.[29]

Yet the recommendations on the organization, agenda, and procedure of the subsequent Conference on Security and Cooperation in Europe, which the preparatory talks adopted in early July 1973, were a victory for the EC. Above all, they included the idea of the four baskets proposed by Switzerland. While Basket III on "Co-operation in Humanitarian and Other Fields" did not explicitly name human rights, Basket I on "Questions Relating to Security in Europe" nonetheless listed "respect for human rights and fundamental freedoms, including the freedom of thought, conscience, religion or belief." Although the EC had originally pushed for the explicit inclusion of a list of clearly defined human rights in Basket III, it had realized that this would only lead to endless philosophical discussions between East and West about the nature of human rights. The *Nine* instead concluded that replacing such explicit references in Basket III with a reduced number of key political demands – freedom of movement and information, and cooperation in culture and education – would ensure not only a successful conclusion of the conference but probably also achieve the desired political effects in the Socialist Camp afterward. Furthermore, the USSR had failed to obtain an agreement on the creation of a permanent pan-European security organization, which it had hoped to dominate. Instead, the final recommendations envisioned, on a proposal by Non-Aligned Yugoslavia, periodical follow-up conferences for "all European States, the United States and Canada." But Moscow did not give up on pursuing its agenda, if necessary outside the multilateral forum. After the end of the Helsinki preparatory talks, it sent out feelers to the *Nine* about direct trade talks between the EC and CMEA, but received a clear rejection. Because the final recommendations made Basket III a sore point for Moscow, the Soviet Union also tried to send a signal of discouragement to the EC through the arrest of several dissidents in August before the opening of the CSCE in Geneva.[30]

In the wake of the conclusion of the preparatory talks in Helsinki, the European socialist countries faced a barrage of Chinese criticism. PRC propaganda called the Soviet insistence on sovereignty and non-interference fraudulent given past Soviet interventions in the domestic affairs of other socialist states, particularly in Czechoslovakia in 1968. Beijing considered détente in Europe completely "illusory." Communist China warned Western European countries not to fall for Soviet tricks because the USSR, or so it claimed, continued to pursue expansionist and hegemonic goals throughout the world. Beijing feared peace in Europe because it would allow Moscow to transfer troops to East Asia.[31]

The CSCE formally opened in Geneva on September 18, 1973. Its consensus-based decision-making process was primarily responsible for the long duration of twenty-two months, until July 21, 1975. But this procedure also ensured that agreements would reflect negotiated compromises among all thirty-five participants. Negotiations on Basket II went relatively well. Despite previous Soviet concerns about commercial discrimination by the West, Moscow did not take the lead on this topic. Ultimately, the multilateral conference was not well suited to resolving conflicts that were an inherent characteristic of the East–West split between planned socialist economies and liberal capitalism.[32]

The EC, which by 1975 would appear as the major winner of the conference, had to fight several uphill battles to reach its goals with regard to Baskets I and III. Within a month of the beginning of the CSCE, the *Nine* faced an Arab oil embargo in the context of the war between Egypt, Syria, and Israel. The Middle East had been the seminal focus of EPC in early 1971. But by the turn of 1973/74, the region posed a severe test to EC unity, particularly since the United Kingdom displayed little solidarity with other community members. Also, while the *Nine* and NATO usually presented a façade of unity at the negotiation table, behind-the-scenes disagreements between Western Europeans and North Americans often taxed transatlantic relations. At least, the Western European neutrals often sided with the *Nine*.[33]

The major line of conflict still occurred between the EC and the Soviet-led Socialist Camp, which mostly acted as a unified and coordinated group, with the exception of Romania. With regard to Basket I, the USSR demanded a firm guarantee of the inviolability of all borders and, simultaneously, an implicit approval of the validity of the Brezhnev Doctrine in Eastern Europe. In comparison, the EC wanted to have greater flexibility on peaceful border changes, which was a West German demand designed to keep the chances of reunification alive, and declare interventions under the Brezhnev Doctrine illegitimate. With regard to Basket III, the Soviet Union tried to limit the scope of agreements and water down the language, but ultimately did not want to risk the failure of the whole conference over this issue. In comparison, the EC used foot dragging to extract concessions with regard to this basket, which explains the overall length of negotiations. Moscow realized that the *Nine* cooperated closely against both the Socialist Camp and the United States, concluding – erroneously – that this was a sign of weakened NATO cohesion. Fearful that the negotiations would never end, the USSR was ready in late 1974 to make concessions and even recommit itself to the UN Declaration of Human Rights of 1948, but unwilling to accept the stricter norms of the European Convention of 1950. Still, as late as February 1975, Brezhnev "attempted to belittle Basket 3" in talks with UK Prime Minister Harold Wilson.[34]

The initial nonchalant American attitude toward the CSCE had been a source of great frustration among the *Nine*, but increasing public pressure in the United States forced the White House to change its stance on Basket III over the course of 1974. After the USSR had expelled the famous dissident Aleksandr Solzhenitsyn in February, US public opinion shifted toward criticism of the immorality of superpower détente. The Watergate Scandal led to Nixon's resignation and Gerald Ford's accession to the presidency in August. In December, Congress passed the Jackson–Vanick Amendment, linking trade with the socialist world to emigration and human rights issues. By the turn of the year, the American-led NATO and the EC *Nine* finally closed ranks over human rights. During the final months of negotiations, this unified position extracted major concessions from the USSR on Basket III. WAPA accepted almost all Western proposals on this issue just to obtain a successful end to the conference.[35]

On August 1, 1975, thirty-five heads of states signed the Final Act in Helsinki. Basket I enshrined the "inviolability" of borders and "human rights," whereas Basket III covered what human rights were supposed to mean in the new Europe without mentioning them by name – human contacts, free flow of information, and cooperation in the fields of culture and education. Some observers considered the Final Act a "peace" treaty for Europe, but it was neither a legally binding contract nor did it end World War II formally. Because it was a document of non-binding political declarations, it encompassed a wide range of topics that exceeded previous European peace agreements – like the Vienna and Paris treaties of 1814–15 and 1919, respectively – in ambition and scope.[36]

The Soviet Union considered the Final Act the basis for a durable *de facto* peace in Europe. Brezhnev himself saw it as a triumph of his statesmanship. In the months after August 1, 1975, the USSR worked out strategies for the implementation of the Final Act. Moscow hoped to pursue the implementation of Basket I in an offensive fashion while planning to execute Basket III in an incomplete manner at best. This attitude was not completely unreasonable. In late 1974, during the CSCE negotiations, Ford's secretary of state, Henry Kissinger, had promised that the United States would not insist on the strict implementation of Basket III. In comparison, the Polish government was primarily content with the *de facto* international recognition of the Oder–Neisse Line, but also with the economic agreements in Basket II that would help the country to attract foreign investment and knowhow, or so it hoped. Unsurprisingly, Warsaw also saw Basket III as a potential problem, particularly since it allowed emigration from an economy that suffered from acute labor shortages. Yet, on the whole, communist Poland considered the conference a success. Czechoslovakia was mostly content to be once more recognized internationally as a respectable state, after the Soviet-led WAPA intervention in 1968.[37]

East Germany praised the international recognition of the post-World War II territorial status quo, not only because it provided the GDR with a seemingly secure title to territory but also because the conference had supposedly turned out to be a failure of US and West German imperialism to keep territorial issues unresolved for future revanchist goals. However, the GDR was unhappy that the Final Act included the principle, demanded by West Germany, that borders could be changed by peaceful means. Oddly enough, East Germany was convinced that the agreements in Basket I were legally binding. Ultimately, the GDR was content to celebrate the CSCE as a defeat of the "world-hegemonic foreign policy of Beijing's leaders," who had opposed the conference all along.[38]

The assessment of the CSCE on the Western side was mixed. The *Nine* were naturally pleased that they had forced the Socialist Camp to make concessions on Basket III. West Germany was satisfied that European borders were not completely incontestable; German reunification could still occur. But the United States was more critical. While President Ford personally believed that the achievements outweighed the disadvantages, American public opinion had turned against the conference during the last year of negotiations because it seemed to betray the interests of Eastern European people. Shortly before the signing of the Final Act, a conservative critic even carped: "World War II will soon be coming to its official end. The Russians won." Before Ford traveled to Helsinki to sign the Final Act, he publicly promised that the United States would never recognize the Soviet occupation of the Baltic countries. Given the changing public climate in the United States, Ford afterward distanced himself from superpower détente. In the end, from 1969 to 1975, American views on the CSCE had undergone a curious development: from disregard to embrace to critical reassessment. The views of the communist Chinese government oddly aligned with American public opinion. A *People's Daily* editorial "derided" the CSCE because it had installed "the Soviet Union in the role of God."[39]

A Critical Assessment of the CSCE Impact on East Europe

Despite the varied assessments by contemporary observers and scholars today, the results of the CSCE negotiations were *not* a quid-pro-quo deal of Western recognition of Soviet, Polish and East German borders and Eastern acceptance of human rights. The Final Act also did not cement the status quo. It did *not* legally recognize any borderlines nor disallow any peaceful territorial changes in the future. In any case, West Germany – the one country, from which the USSR and Poland had wanted legal recognition of the borderlines for two decades – had expressed respect for them *before* the start of negotiations, though with the proviso that a final legal recognition was dependent on a future German peace treaty. Also, the exchange of ratification documents for the Moscow and Warsaw Treaties on June 3, 1972, had been the *precondition* for the Soviet Union to agree to the start of the preparatory talks in Helsinki.[40]

Human rights did not have an immediate influence on the rise of civil societies in the Socialist Camp, as scholars have often claimed. To be sure, the EC and NATO had made human rights into an issue of Western identity in 1973–75, but during the tedious negotiations they also reduced their demands to a few key aspects. Thus, without belittling the influence of the Final Act in Europe in the second half of the 1980s and after, a nuanced assessment of its immediate impact in the late 1970s produces a more realistic picture. In general, Europe by the end of 1975 was divided into a democratic western and an authoritarian eastern half. During and immediately after the CSCE, the remaining Western European authoritarian regimes returned to constitutional government: Turkey in October 1973 after two years of military rule, Portugal in April 1974 after three decades of corporatist authoritarianism, Greece the following August after seven years of military dictatorship, and Spain after Francisco Franco's death in November 1975. The only exception was Cyprus, where the Turkish–Greek conflict over the island in 1974 led to its division. In comparison, all countries on the eastern side of the Iron Curtain remained communist party dictatorships into the late 1980s. Thus, when the signatories of the Final Act met in periodic follow-up conferences – in Non-Aligned Yugoslavia (1977–78), in democratized and unaligned Spain (1980–83), and in neutral Austria (1986–89) – the West could occupy the moral high ground in terms of human rights. Moreover, President Jimmy Carter repudiated what he considered the moral hollowness of the détente pursued by his two Republican predecessors. His commitments to human rights stemmed both from personal convictions and from a changed discourse in the public arena. During his presidency from 1977 to 1981, American activists and philanthropists established several human rights organizations to help monitor the implementation of the Helsinki agreements.[41]

In August 1975, the countries of the Socialist Camp published the Final Act at full length in their national newspapers. Thus, their citizens could read the actual document, and not only the ideologically distorted interpretation offered by party-controlled news media. Yet dissident movements remained small throughout the communist world for the following decade – though with the notable exception of Poland. Opposition movements in the Soviet Union reached back to the period after Khrushchev's Secret Speech in early 1956, and were mostly based on protest along political, religious, or national lines. By the mid 1960s, human rights activism emerged for the first time; the intervention in Czechoslovakia in 1968 provided the nascent human rights movement with additional momentum. Soviet authorities, however, were adept at suppressing dissidence. The arrest of several activists in August 1972, mentioned above, weakened and demoralized human rights campaigners. The relative calm among dissidents during the negotiations in Helsinki and Geneva might have lulled the Soviet regime into a sense of security. The award of the Nobel Peace Prize to Andrei D. Sakharov – the Soviet H-bomb designer-turned-human rights activist – in late 1975 dashed Brezhnev's dreams of getting that honor while it breathed new life into the movement. Dissidents demanded clarifications about the government's implementation of Basket III while establishing a countrywide network of Helsinki Watch Groups to observe and report human rights abuses. Initially, Soviet authorities appeared on the defensive while trying to launch a quixotic external propaganda campaign about human rights abuses in the West. Around the time of the first CSCE follow-up meeting in Belgrade, however, governmental suppression increased, leading to the arrest and internal exile of almost all human rights activists by the early 1980s.[42]

In comparison, the situation in East Germany was more complex. Over two decades, the GDR had developed its own discourse on human rights that amalgamated the issue with Marxism–Leninism into a theory of socialist human rights. Since organizations outside the state, like the docile Lutheran (Protestant) Church, espoused this discourse, no independent human rights movement developed in the country before the 1980s. Moreover, because the government's security apparatus was growing in the wake of the separate German–German agreements from the early 1970s – mainly with the goal of supervising and discouraging family visits – the conditions for independent activism in response to the Helsinki Final Act quickly deteriorated. While the regime had decided to deem the agreements in Basket I legally binding, paradoxically it considered the accords in Basket III merely advisory. In any case, the state security apparatus had warned the East German leaders since 1974 about the implications of Basket III, and in mid 1975 had prepared policies to prevent citizens from exploiting the Final Act to their advantage. East German citizens used the Helsinki agreements primarily as a last resort to bolster their often-denied applications for emigration to the western half of the country. Official requests to relocate permanently to the FRG jumped by 40 percent in the fall of 1975. Similar to Ulbricht's view that West German interference had created the economic crisis that forced the closure of the borders in Berlin in 1961, Honecker's regime saw foreign agitation, not widespread dissatisfaction with life in his walled-in GDR, as the primary reason for the spike in applications. The regime reacted with repression, harassment, and intimidation; by the late 1970s, the number of official requests to emigrate had dropped back to previous levels.[43]

In Czechoslovakia, the questions raised by Basket III faced a specific political environment. The Soviet-led WAPA intervention in August 1968 had elicited a careful economic and political stabilization of the country that occurred over a multi-year period. Dubbed "normalization," the process primarily aimed at political demobilization, first in the form of the removal of the reformist leadership until the spring of 1969 (around the time of the Budapest Appeal), then as a purge of over 20 percent of the party membership, and finally as repression of individual citizens for supposedly illegal political activities. The relatively small ranks of the political dissenters in Czechoslovakia included former party members, artists, philosophers, and journalists, who – inspired by the evolving Eurocommunism in Italy and France – aimed primarily at the reform of socialism. The signing of the Helsinki Final Act led to a flurry of activities, which triggered another round of repression in 1976, and then the establishment of Charter 77 on January 1. While the 242 signatories used the UN Declaration and the Helsinki Final Act as points of reference, they did not see themselves as an oppositional organization but rather as a partner for the government to resolve individual cases of human rights violations. But the regime quickly declared Charter 77 a counter-revolutionary movement under influence of foreign powers, and then harassed, intimidated, and persecuted signatories and other dissenters ahead of the CSCE follow-up conference in Belgrade. In the end, the influence of Charter 77 was larger abroad than at home, mainly because the number of people involved always remained small and comprised mostly well-educated urbanites.[44]

If the impact of the Helsinki Final Act on the formation of civil societies in the Soviet Union, East Germany, and Czechoslovakia was mostly inconsequential in the second half of the 1970s, the situation in Poland was different. Student unrest in March 1968 and the crushing of the Prague Spring – with the participation of Polish troops – in August had created a political ferment that reached even into the ranks of the communist party. In subsequent years, critical citizens and activists, often with support from the lower ranks of the Catholic Church, turned away from the long-held hope that Soviet-style socialism was capable of reform. The bloody suppression of labor unrest in Gdańsk and Szczecin (Stettin) in late 1970 terminated the rule of Władysław Gomułka, who had returned to power during the Polish October in 1956 on a wave of popular support. His successor, Edward Gierek, was a pragmatic manager able to address some of the economic troubles in the first years of his leadership, but proved powerless to resolve the fundamental problems of the country. Still, Poland in the early 1970s enjoyed a period of relative cultural and intellectual freedom, and its human rights situation was better than that in the Soviet Union, East Germany, or Czechoslovakia.[45]

Toward the end of the CSCE negotiations, Poland's communist government understood that it needed to make concessions domestically in the realm of Basket III to reap the international economic benefits it hoped to get from Basket II. Still, in the fall of 1975, it tried to change the constitution with amendments that seemed to contradict the Helsinki Final Act, which ignited opposition among activists. Labor strikes in the Warsaw region in mid 1976 triggered the establishment of the Workers' Defense Committee (KOR). Unlike Charter 77 in Czechoslovakia, KOR brought together intellectuals *and* workers, though mostly in Warsaw, and positioned itself explicitly as an oppositional organization. Its relationship to the Movement for the Defense of Human and Civic Rights (ROPCiO), which was established in March 1977 to force the Polish government to implement Basket III, was difficult from the beginning, however. The regime initially reacted with the suppression of KOR, but in 1977 released those arrested in view of the CSCE follow-up conference in Belgrade. By mid year, the government even recognized KOR implicitly when it invited representatives to official talks. The stinging Western, particularly American, criticism of the human rights conditions in the Socialist Camp at the CSCE follow-up conference in Belgrade convinced Gierek to tread more carefully with regard to the opposition. Furthermore, with the election of Polish Cardinal Karol Wojtyła as Pope John Paul II in October 1978, the Polish opposition obtained an ally on the global stage. In March 1979, the pontiff called for the respect of human rights in his first Encyclical *Redemptor hominis*. In early 1980, following the Soviet model, Polish activists established a Helsinki Committee, designed to provide independent information on the human rights situation in Poland to the CSCE follow-up conference in Madrid. In the wake of nationwide strikes against the economic situation the following summer, the first independent labor union in the Socialist Camp – Solidarność – was established by striking workers in the port city of Gdańsk. Although it was not the product of KOR, it benefited enormously from the successes and experiences of the Workers' Defense Committee. Its fast nationwide growth made it into the first national

Polish civil society organization. In the wake of its foundation, the country headed toward a crisis that would entirely change the regional Cold War in Europe, as we will see in Chapters 22 and 23.[46]

Conclusion

The CSCE created self-perceived and real winners in the final one and a half decades of the European regional Cold War. In 1975, the Socialist Camp believed that it had gotten real peace and stability for the development of its socialist societies in return for supposedly irrelevant concessions on human rights. But the CSCE did not fix the camp's economic problems, nor did it address the decline of socialist influence in the world, as described in earlier chapters. Likewise, the Western European human rights agenda also did not have an immediate impact on all of Eastern Europe. Where it did have an impact – in Poland – this would make a difference only by the turn of the decade. Ultimately, the crisis of the Soviet-led Socialist Camp in the early 1980s triggered the reforms in the USSR in the second half of that decade, when human rights would finally play a major role in the collapse of communist party dictatorships.

Despite all the compromises and public criticism of the Final Act, the West emerged as the long-term winner from the CSCE process. Basket III provided Western Europeans and North Americans with an elevated moral position, from which they could scrutinize the human rights record in the Socialist Camp. With democratization in Spain, Portugal, Greece, and Turkey by the mid 1970s, *all* Western CSCE members – including the Vatican, to which we turn now – were governed by elected rulers. More importantly, the CSCE was a formative experience for the EC *Six/ Nine* on the road to greater union. Finally, the conference helped to bridge the conflicts within the Western world that had emerged in the 1960s, as described in an earlier chapter. In the long-term, the CSCE was both a moral victory for the West and a norm-setting achievement for all of Europe.

19   The Vatican

"And how many divisions does the pope have?," Iosif V. Stalin once quipped during World War II.[1] Many, as it turned out, though they were not armed soldiers but defenders of the faith. Of all the large religions in Europe, the Catholic Church enjoyed the unique advantage of being a transnational organization. While popes had always been elected autocrats at the helm of a spiritual institution, they also headed a state recognized under international law since 1929. During the Cold War, Catholics numbered in the hundreds of millions in Europe and beyond. Even under the atheistic rule of communism, the Catholic Church – particularly in Poland – retained a huge following. Despite individual differences, churches in Eastern European countries – except Poland – generally fared poorly after 1945 because of systematic suppression or long-term secularization processes, most notably in Czechoslovakia and East Germany.

According to conventional wisdom, Pope John Paul II (reign 1978–2005) played a major role in the collapse of communism. Without doubt, the Polish pontiff assumed a significant political role, particularly in his home country, but such hagiographic great-man-history obscures the prior structural changes that made his rise possible in the first place. Understanding the role of Catholicism in the Cold War requires focusing on developments since the nineteenth century and the reforms under Popes John XXIII (1958–63) and Paul VI (1963–78). Already before the mid 1940s, the Holy See had been committed to anti-communism. Since communism in the Soviet Union and Eastern Europe had greater staying power than the Vatican expected in the period after World Wars I and II, respectively, John Paul II's two predecessors needed to make political compromises in order to save the church as a functioning institution capable of serving the spiritual needs of its members. These compromises first saved and then strengthened the Catholic Church, particularly in Poland.

The Foundations of Vatican Foreign Policy

In the century leading up to 1945, the Holy See underwent sweeping institutional and political changes. In the 1860s, Italy's national unification had deprived the Vatican of its extensive land holdings in the country, except for a walled city of less than half a square kilometer around St. Peter's Basilica in Rome. Until 1929, the status of the Holy See under international law remained in limbo. In these six decades, successive popes refused to leave the walled city to avoid recognizing the secular power of the Kingdom of Italy (1861–1946). Pope Pius IX (1846–78) even excommunicated King Victor Emmanuel II for ruling a secular state, and prohibited Catholics from entering its employ.[2]

The Vatican's rejection of secularism obviously included the refutation of communism, particularly against the background of its long-standing fears of radical political demands since the French Revolution of 1789. As early as 1846, two years before Karl Marx published his famous *Communist Manifesto*, Pius IX dismissed emerging communist ideas as an "unspeakable doctrine" and a "filthy medley of errors." Pope Leo XIII (1878–1903) spurned communism – together with capitalism, to be clear – in his encyclical *Rerum Novarum* (On New Things) of 1891. Pius XI (1922–39) rejected Vladimir I. Lenin's Bolshevik regime after the Battle of Warsaw in August of 1920 between Soviet troops carrying the revolution westward and the newly reconstructed Polish state – a clash he had witnessed himself as apostolic nuncio (ambassador) to Poland. Through mediation by third parties, however, the Vatican offered humanitarian aid to Soviet Russia in an attempt to protect the Catholic Church there – with mixed success until 1927, when contacts broke down. Against the background of the anti-religious persecutions during the High Stalinist period, Pius XI issued the encyclical *Divini Redemptoris* (Of the Divine Redeemer) in March 1937. It specifically addressed the threat of "Bolshevistic and atheistic Communism ... [to] the very foundations of Christian civilization," peaking in the "absolute condemnation of the impudent falsehoods of Communism."[3]

During the interwar period, this kind of anti-communism prompted the Holy See to draw near to right-wing and Catholic-authoritarian governments in Europe. The Lateran Treaty with fascist Italy created the tiny Vatican City state under international law in 1929. Beforehand, the Holy See had already concluded concordats – agreements defining the relationship of the Catholic Church with the secular state – with a series of countries that comprised sizeable Catholic communities, like Poland and Latvia in 1925, Lithuania and Romania in 1927, and Czechoslovakia and Portugal in 1928. In 1933, the Holy See even signed a concordat with

National Socialist Germany. The anti-communism of Adolf Hitler's revisionist state trumped the Vatican's concerns over its anti-democratic and even pagan features. A year later, a concordat with Catholic-authoritarian Austria followed. In 1938, the Vatican opened negotiations with Francisco Franco, Spain's right-wing dictator, whose troops were in the process of defeating the leftist Republic in the Spanish Civil War (1936–39).[4]

Yet the emphasis on anti-communism did not mean a papal *carte blanche* for the policies of European right-wing states. As the 1930s progressed, Vatican relations with Germany worsened over the maltreatment of the Catholic Church there. Pius XI's secret encyclical *Mit brennender Sorge* (With Burning Concern) of March 1937 was published in German – not in the customary Latin – for secret distribution in Hitler's *Reich*. Just a week before the publication of his anti-communist *Divini Redemptoris*, the pontiff thereby condemned National Socialism, denouncing the concept of race as un-Christian and calling Hitler a "deluded prophet." Concerned about the persecution of Jews, the pontiff intended to issue another encyclical, *Humani Generis Unitas* (On the Unity of Humankind), which explicitly denounced racism, particularly against Jews in Germany and Italy. But his untimely death in early 1939 terminated the project prematurely. Pius XII (1939–58), who was even more anti-communist than his predecessor, decided to pursue a policy of outward non-involvement in international affairs. This included dropping public criticism of Germany's racial policies, its military aggression against Catholic Poland, and the Holocaust in favor of secret but futile policies of peace and the improvement of the situation of Catholics under Nazi German rule. At least, the pontiff refused to endorse Germany's attack on the Soviet Union as an anti-Bolshevik crusade, but he also abstained from approving the alliance of the Big Three against Nazi Germany.[5]

The Vatican's participation in the ideological conflicts during the first half of the twentieth century did not leave Catholics outside Rome untouched. In *Rerum Novarum*, Pope Leo XIII had pointed to the "revolutionary changes" that industrialization and modernity had brought to humanity. Rejecting both communism and unfettered capitalism, he called for a third way that would protect workers and "their dignity as human beings." Committed to social justice, the pontiff, in parallel with the emerging Christian democratic parties, called on Catholic clerics and lay people to shape the rise of this new world, particularly by addressing the Social Question beyond the narrow confines of communism, nationalism, or capitalism. Responding both to the thinking of the medieval philosopher Thomas Aquinas favored by Leo XIII and to wider debates on human rights that emerged in the interwar period, Catholic thinkers developed a rich – though internally not cohesive – body of *personalist* thought that focused on restoring personal dignity to every human being. Among them, the French convert-philosopher Jacques Maritain particularly influenced Pius XI. He would also become an important human rights philosopher after World War II, having a major influence on the drafting of the UN Declaration of Human Rights of 1948. Some of the French activists, the *prêtres ouvriers* (worker priests), ended up collaborating closely with socialist and communist parties in the 1940s, until they were condemned by Pius XII in 1954. But probably the most important Catholic *personalist* thinker in the first half of the Cold War was the young Karol Wojtyła, the future Pope John Paul II.[6]

Pius XII, 1945–58: The Early Cold War

Consequently, the Cold War between the atheistic Soviet Union and the anti-Bolshevik Vatican was ideologically foreordained. Between 1943 and 1949, the communist suppression of the Catholic Church in Eastern Europe proceeded in clearly discernible steps, though at a different pace in each country. Two years before the end of World War II, Stalin rehabilitated the Russian Orthodox Church in order to tap into its authority as the USSR was about to reoccupy its western border lands. After his troops had arrived in Ukraine and in territories that would become Soviet after the war – Eastern Poland, Trans-Carpathian Ruthenia, and Bessarabia – Stalin and the Russian Orthodox Church collaborated in forcing the Uniate Church – Orthodox in rite but loyal to the pope – to cut relations with the Vatican in March 1946 and to integrate with the Moscow Patriarchate. The Soviet leader thereby removed foreign, i.e. papal, influence from the western territories, while the Orthodox Church eliminated a rival.[7]

The fate of the Catholic Church in Eastern Europe itself varied from country to country, depending on the nature and duration of the Soviet occupation. Yugoslavia and Czechoslovakia, for example, were only briefly occupied by Soviet troops toward the end of World War II. In Yugoslav Croatia, hundreds of Catholic clerics fell victim to persecution, lynchings, and summary executions. Despite his wartime protests against the discrimination of Serbs and Jews, Zagreb's Archbishop Aloijzije Stepinac had cooperated with the right-wing quisling regime of Ante Pavelić from 1941 to 1945. Thus, he was a highly symbolic target for retribution in Josip Broz Tito's socialist Yugoslavia. In the fall of 1946, Stepinac was sentenced to sixteen years of hard labor, but released five years later into rural house arrest where he died in 1960. In Slovakia, the

Catholic priest Josef Tiso, who had run the German vassal state from late 1939 to April 1945 and collaborated in the persecution of Jews and communists, was put on trial, sentenced to death, and hanged in April 1947. Even the anti-communist Vatican did not defend his transgressions, nor did it dispute that he deserved to be put on trial. But unlike Tito's government in Yugoslavia, the leftist coalition government of Czechoslovakia had tried, since the end of World War II, to reach out to the Catholic Church in an effort of national reconciliation between anti-communist Catholics and anti-Catholic communists. In May 1946, the Vatican and Czechoslovakia re-established diplomatic relations, which had been cut as a result of German wartime occupation. Also, in November 1946, Pius XII chose Josef Beran, a nationalist enemy of the German occupation, who had spent three years in a concentration camp, as new Archbishop of Prague and Primate of Czechoslovakia – to the applause of even the communist minister of the interior.[8]

The advent of communist rule in Soviet-occupied Eastern European countries did not lead automatically to immediate or systematic repression. But as the Soviet occupiers and their national communist minions progressively tried to nationalize all spheres of life along ideological lines, the church in each country felt the impact of these policies as hard as any other non-communist organization. Poland and Hungary serve as particularly good examples of different post-war experiences. Stalin trod carefully with regard to socialization in Poland to prevent the worsening of relations with the Western Allies and the alienation of large segments of the population. Such caution was paramount since the share of Catholics in the country's population had increased from 65 to over 90 percent as a result of the Jewish Holocaust, the territorial changes that moved Poland westward in 1945, the outbound migration of Orthodox/Uniate believers, and the forced expulsion of Lutheran (Protestant) Germans. Furthermore, its role in the resistance and underground life during German occupation had turned the church into a national rallying point. Still, the communist-dominated government abrogated the twenty-year-old concordat in September 1945 in the hope of negotiating a new one with a smaller degree of papal influence.[9] In comparison, the Soviet occupation forces in Hungary seized much of the church's vast land holdings in a countrywide land reform in spring 1945 to benefit tenant peasants. Having lost their source of income, the clergy instead became state employed. The relatively free national elections at the end of the year produced a victory for the rural Smallholders' Party, which formed a coalition government with the Socialist Democrats and Communists to proclaim the Hungarian Republic in early 1946. However, by the spring, the Communist Party and its backers in the Soviet occupation forces launched a political campaign against the church that resulted in the dissolution of Catholic organizations and schools by 1947.[10]

The Vatican's reaction to communist domination of Eastern Europe displayed great continuity with wartime positions and was colored by its long-standing anti-communism. Undeniably, Pius XII was one of the seminal Cold Warriors. As Soviet armies started to rout German troops in the wake of the Battle of Stalingrad at the turn of 1942/43, the pontiff grew anxious about the prospect of future Soviet hegemony over parts or even all of Europe. He hoped for close collaboration with the Anglo–American powers against the USSR as early as March 1943 to keep the Bolshevik enemy contained. In and after 1945, the pope emerged as a champion of the United Nations (though he was critical of the Soviet veto in the Security Council) and as a strident supporter of the Marshall Plan, Western European integration, the creation of NATO, and the Christian Democrats in the hotly contested Italian national elections against the Communists in the spring of 1948. The collaboration between Stalin and the Orthodox Church in the takeover of the Uniate Church toward the end of the war further increased the Vatican's mistrust. Moreover, after the end of the war, Pius XII displayed little sympathy for Holocaust survivors. He opposed the Zionist project in Palestine, largely because he rejected Jewish control over the Holy Sites in Jerusalem, and hence pursued an unrealistic policy of internationalization even after the Arab–Israeli war in 1947–48.[11]

Despite his long-standing concerns over the Soviet domination of Eastern Europe, Pius XII provided surprisingly little leadership to the Catholic Church there. Since he was convinced that Stalin would re-enact the rapid Bolshevization of post-World War I Russia in post-World War II Eastern Europe, he fatalistically believed that nothing was left for him to do. Hence, he did not attempt to reach out to Stalin to save the Uniate Church in Ukraine or to alleviate the anticipated persecution of the Catholic Church in Poland. Although in mid 1945 Pius XII called on the Polish Church not to fall for the false promises of Bolshevism, he gave the country's ecclesiastical hierarchy a free pass to run church affairs, particularly in view of the needs for pastoral care, as it saw fit under the unfolding circumstances. This, however, opened up opportunities for Polish Catholics to collaborate with the communist-dominated government. In August 1945, Cardinal August Hlond in effect sided with the communist-dominated Polish government when he appointed auxiliary bishops in previously German territories, thereby de facto incorporating Szczecin (Stettin) and the new Polish territories east of the Oder–Neisse Line into the Polish Church. The Vatican, in comparison, continued to consider them under German episcopal jurisdiction, as Pius XII confirmed in a letter to German bishops in 1948. The pope's abdication of political leadership in Poland also opened up opportunities for lay Catholics to work with – and, as they hoped, domesticate – the Soviet-installed regime, particularly after its leader, Władysław Gomułka, had reached out to non-fascists for the sake of gaining legitimacy in Polish society. The Polish leader hoped that by moderating Soviet-style communism he would be able to bridge the gap between communists and Catholic activists, who were deeply steeped in the long-standing debates of social reform initiated by Pope Leo XIII in the 1890s and developed by *personalist* thinkers afterward. However, the continued harassment, persecution, and even execution of Polish underground fighters and political opponents by the regime complicated cooperation.[12]

In Hungary, papal decisions in 1945 predetermined the long-term conflict between church and Communist Party. In early September, Pius XII appointed the stridently anti-communist Bishop József Mindszenty Primate of Hungary. He was a controversial figure even among the country's clergy. To his credit, he had opposed the racial policies and persecution of Jews by Hungary's own wartime right-wing government and then under German occupation, for which he was sent to prison. But as an ardent monarchist, he opposed the creation of the republic, which many Catholic Hungarians endorsed, in early 1946. Mindszenty considered himself to be the rightful head of the Hungarian nation in the absence of a reigning king. In the end, his double rejection of communism and republicanism played into the hands of those political forces in Hungary – the Communist Party and the Soviet occupation – that wanted to restrict the influence of the church on society anyway.[13]

The sharpening of the European Cold War in 1947 – in the wake of the Greek Civil War, the Truman Doctrine, the Marshall Plan, and the foundation of Cominform – had major consequences for the Catholic Church in Eastern Europe. The communist regimes in Romania and Bulgaria, where Catholic minorities lived, had resisted Soviet pressure to break off relations with the Vatican after 1944, but Bucharest abrogated the 1929 concordat in mid 1948 and Sofia followed by breaking diplomatic relations in early 1949. Despite the Soviet expulsion of Yugoslavia from the Socialist Camp in mid 1948, no rapprochement between Tito's socialist state and the Vatican occurred; harassment and persecution continued as before. In the wake of the pro-Soviet coup in Prague in February 1948, the new Czechoslovak government increased political pressure. As a reaction to its attempts at co-opting lower clerics, Archbishop Beran prohibited them from participating in political life. A year later, in mid 1949, Pius XII declared a communist-sponsored Catholic Party in Czechoslovakia schismatic, and excommunicated its leaders. In Hungary, the communists succeeded in rigging the political system and the national elections of 1947 in their favor, and then quickly started to persecute the church. Shortly after Christmas 1948, Mindszenty was arrested, put on trial for his anti-republicanism and sentenced to life in prison in early 1949. In 1953, at least, he was released into rural house arrest. In general, the harassment and persecution of the top hierarchies of the church in various Eastern European countries after mid 1947 was accompanied by a similar treatment of the lower clergy, the confiscation of property, the closure of churches and monasteries, and the harassment of practising believers.[14]

The sole exception was Poland. Throughout the late 1940s, the communist government sought negotiations with the Vatican on a new concordat, but the lack of mutual formal recognition prevented any progress. Moreover, papal resistance to the integration of the former German territories united Hlond and Gomułka in a nationalist quasi-alliance. After the cardinal had passed away in October 1948, Pius XII installed the politically moderate and relatively young Bishop Stefan Wyszyński as new primate, though his independence still irked the communist government. At least, by the spring of 1950, state and church reached an informal agreement, under which the government tolerated religious instruction in schools, the existence of the Catholic University in Lublin, pilgrimages, pastoral care, and independent monastic life in return for the ecclesiastical promise to abstain from politics. But the communist government continued to call the shots. In September 1953, for example, Wyszyński, who had just been appointed cardinal, was confined to prison and then house arrest for three years.[15]

Predictably, Pius XII reacted to the anti-Catholic offensive since mid 1947 – and particularly to Mindszenty's conviction and Beran's arrest – with an anti-communist campaign of his own, which reached its first highpoint during the Italian national elections in the spring of 1948. On July 1 the following year, the Vatican's Holy Office issued a decree announcing that communist party members and promoters of communist ideas would be excommunicated. The decree was primarily aimed at Western Europe, most notably Italy and France, where communist parties had enjoyed widespread electoral support, and not necessarily at those Eastern European Catholics who were involved in government-sponsored organizations or otherwise collaborated with communist regimes. The pontiff specifically emphasized that socialists were exempt from the decree. In the wake of its publication, Pius XII put additional emphasis on social policy in an attempt to draw communist sympathizers to his side. Still, Eastern European governments reacted to the decree with yet another round of repression; Prague's Archbishop Beran, for example, was quickly sentenced to life in prison. But Pius XII rarely used the threatened measure of excommunication; on the contrary, he even swallowed the 1950 *modus vivendi* in Poland. The reality was that the Vatican had lost virtually all of its influence in Eastern Europe. At Christmas 1951, the pontiff therefore called the suffering Catholic communities on the other side of the Iron Curtain the "Church of Silence," and he even compared their fate to the Holocaust.[16]

As the Cold War division between the Vatican and socialist Eastern Europe hardened, the pope faced new problems in East Asia in the wake of the establishment of the People's Republic of China on October 1, 1949. The new regime's campaign against the Catholic Church exploited two strategic advantages. First, the close historical bond between Western imperialism and the Christian mission provided credibility to the communist propaganda claim that Catholicism itself was imperialist. Jesuit and Franciscan missionaries had brought Catholicism to China in the sixteenth century. In 1724, however, Emperor Yongzheng expelled all missionaries and ordered churches to be closed. Since Catholic communities in China had always been relatively independent from the Vatican, this trait would become even more pronounced during their underground existence after 1724. Second, the Vatican's heavy-handed policy toward the relatively independent Chinese church in the aftermath of the Opium War (1839–42) had alienated a substantial number of Chinese believers. Catholic missionaries, who went to China in the following century, tried to impose church doctrine rigidly on existing Catholic communities, staffed newly established ecclesiastical hierarchies with Europeans, and tried to suppress independent traditions as potentially schismatic. Thus, after 1949, it was easy for the new communist regime to play on the internal conflicts of the Chinese Catholic Church, banishing or imprisoning foreign church leaders and missionaries while enticing lower-ranking Chinese clerics to work with the new regime in the establishment of an allegedly anti-imperialist Chinese Catholic Church outside papal reach. In 1955, the PRC sentenced thousands of supposedly disloyal Chinese Catholics to long prison terms. In October 1958, the PRC installed three new bishops regardless of Vatican resistance.[17]

Just as the PRC managed to contain papal influence in China, the Vatican faced yet another Catholic crisis in Asia – this time in Vietnam. The emergence of a Vietnamese Catholic Church had also been the consequence of Western imperialist presence. But the Vatican's interwar campaign to establish a national church, which was designed to shift popular loyalties from missionary enterprises to the pope and promoted a large number of trained locals in the ecclesiastical hierarchy, achieved much greater success there than in China. In any case, some of the most important Vietnamese anti-colonial and nationalist leaders in the first half of the twentieth century were Catholics. Furthermore, many believers joined the resistance against Vichy France and the Japanese occupation during World War II, and by 1945 even the revolution. Three weeks after Ho Chi Minh's declaration of Vietnamese independence on September 2, Vietnamese bishops wrote a circular letter to Pius XII, US President Harry S. Truman, and the British Prime Minister Clement Attlee in support of that very national aspiration. Yet, over the course of the First Indochina War from 1946 to 1954, Catholics got stuck between the rock of French colonial reconquest, the hard place of papal anti-communism, and the boulder of Vietnamese communism. Because the Geneva Accords of 1954 divided Vietnam into a communist and a non-communist half at the seventeenth parallel, hundreds of thousands of often well-educated Catholics left the Democratic Republic of Vietnam in the north for the southern half of the country. There, they became leaders and staunch supporters of the anti-communist southern Republic of Vietnam under President Ngo Dinh Diem, a northern Catholic, long-term nationalist, and *personalist* devotee himself. But the dream of national unification under their leadership faltered due to Vatican pressure to integrate Catholic refugees, their institutions, and their separate political agendas into the reorganized southern ecclesiastical hierarchy in 1960.[18]

These Asian developments fell within the period of de-Stalinization in the Socialist Camp in Europe and the simultaneous political stand-still at the Vatican under the increasingly infirm Pius XII. For the years of fitful de-Stalinization between the dictator's death in March 1953 and Nikita S. Khrushchev's Secret Speech in February 1956, the record of communist–Catholic relations is mixed. While the Polish government cracked down on the church in 1953, the Soviet government allowed the consecration of two Catholic bishops in Lithuania during the famous visit of the Catholic Konrad Adenauer to Moscow in September 1955. Also, in December later that year, Soviet leaders received the Austro–Luxembourgian theologian Marcel Reding, who had written on the parallels between the philosophical ideas of Thomas Aquinas and Karl Marx. Although Pius XII refused a Soviet offer for a concordat in the wake of Khrushchev's famous Secret Speech in February of 1956, he still toned down his anti-communist rhetoric because he had concluded that the dangers of nuclear war could only be overcome by an East–West dialogue. But the major problem was the clearly discernible physical and mental decline of Pius XII, which manifested itself in frequent religious apparitions and his increasing fixation on the afterlife.[19]

The year 1956 nevertheless turned out to be crucial for the Catholic Church in two Eastern European countries. Khrushchev's Secret Speech triggered political developments in Poland and Hungary that led to the famous double crisis in the fall of 1956. On October 19–21, the Soviet leadership accepted the return of Gomułka, who had been sacked for his criticism of Yugoslavia's expulsion from the Socialist Camp in 1948, to the helm of the Polish party. The restored leader quickly reviewed relations with the church, and even ordered Bishop Wyszyński's release before the end of the month. At the same time, the Hungarian Revolution began with mass demonstrations on October 23. The new government in Budapest under the rehabilitated prime minister, Imre Nagy, also swiftly released Mindszenty from rural house arrest. On November 1, both gave back-to-back radio announcements about Hungary's neutral and independent future in the aftermath of the initial Soviet failure to suppress the revolution. But on November 3, the second Soviet military intervention, which would eventually crush the revolution within a short time, began. The following day, Nagy sought refuge in the Yugoslav embassy, but was arrested on the 22nd when he left the diplomatic mission after receiving false promises of free passage. He was executed after a secret trial in mid 1958. Also on November 4, 1956, Mindszenty fled to the American embassy, where he would stay for almost fifteen years.[20]

The diverging outcomes of the Polish October and the Hungarian Revolution had a long-term impact on the development of the church in each country. On December 7, in an attempt to defuse popular passions, the Polish government signed a new agreement that reconfirmed the six-year-old *modus vivendi* and even received tacit papal endorsement. In its wake, the church in Poland re-emerged as a functioning institution in terms of self-governance (including the right to appoint bishops and priests), pastoral care, ecclesiastical life, publishing, and education. Maybe because Wyszyński carefully tried to circumnavigate the whims of communist politics in the following two decades, the church gradually transformed itself into a major political force by the late 1970s, as we will see below.[21] In Hungary, in comparison, the Soviet-installed government under János Kádár tried to impose complete control over what it considered a counter-revolutionary institution. The regime was particularly interested in sending Mindszenty into exile, but eventually had to settle for his continued stay in the US embassy. The government's attempts to entice priests to work with the communist state triggered some of the few papal excommunications.[22]

By the late 1950s, both the Socialist Camp and the Vatican surveyed a mixed picture of state–church relations. Following the double crisis in

Warsaw and Budapest, Eastern European socialist states started to collaborate with each other in dealing with Catholicism. A conference of Soviet and Eastern European national government offices in charge of church affairs decided in early September 1957 on regular exchanges of information and coordination of anti-religious policies. The gathering particularly praised the recent Hungarian suppression of the Catholic Church while it criticized "the temporary retreat" in Poland. When Pius XII died on October 9, 1958, the Vatican desperately needed to review his intransigent policies toward the communist world. In most socialist countries other than Poland, the Catholic Church was unable to function properly or, in the absence of a sufficient number of active priests, to fulfill the basic needs of pastoral care.[23]

John XXIII, 1958–63: The Opening

The new pope was the 77-year-old, worldly and gregarious John XXIII, whose papacy would be shaped by three interlinked concerns. From the very beginning, he emphasized the need for the *aggiornamento* (modernization) of the church, particularly in terms of reconciliation with the world around it. Soon, he also advocated the church's *aperturismo* (opening), which meant, literally, that the pope should travel outside Vatican City (he himself soon went on pilgrimages to Loreto and Assisi), and, figuratively, that the Vatican needed to seek active engagement with the world. Finally, in the tradition of Leo XIII, the new pontiff demanded social justice, above all for the emerging Third World. Responding to Marxist–Leninist criticism, he insisted on the close links between global equality and world peace. In terms of improving relations with the outside world, John XXIII was a fitting choice. From 1925 to 1944, he had served as apostolic nuncio to Bulgaria, Greece, and Turkey, where he had obtained an intimate understanding of Orthodoxy. While stationed in Istanbul during World War II, he had saved Jews from the Holocaust and maintained informal contacts with Soviet diplomats.[24] After his election in October 1958, Moscow publicly expressed the hope that the new pope would collaborate on world peace. But in confidential discussions with other socialist countries, the USSR continued to disparage the Vatican as a reactionary and imperialist force, and even suggested pursuing a policy of driving a wedge between the new pontiff and the Catholic Church in the Socialist Camp.[25]

John XXIII surprised the church bureaucracy and the world at large when he called, in early 1959, for an Ecumenical Council to seek unity among the Christian churches. His goal was to overcome the divisions of the Cold War and to engage with the Socialist Camp for the sake of all

Christians living under communism. This required, as the pope recognized, the willingness of both Catholics and communists to revise ingrained political views about each other. In the long-term, however, coexistence could hold the seeds for reform and change of the Socialist Camp.[26] But the resistance of the Lutheran, Anglican, and Soviet-controlled Russian Orthodox churches to attend a gathering under papal direction ensured that the focus of the future Council shifted toward internal reform of the Catholic Church. Still, John XXIII created the Secretariat for the Promotion of Unity among Christians in mid 1960 to reduce mutual mistrust through channels separate from the preparations for the Council.[27] At the same time, the USSR started to regard the Russian Orthodox Church as a political tool against the global activism of John XXIII. The Kremlin pondered whether or not the Russian Church should unite all Orthodox churches under its leadership and dispatch a delegation, representing all of them, to the future Council.[28]

As the Vatican prepared for what would become the Second Vatican Council, it got caught up in the Berlin Crisis of August 12–13, 1961. The Catholic Church in East Germany had suffered from a range of problems since 1945. It was a minority religious community in a population that was mostly Lutheran or even secular. The territorial changes that divided Germany and transformed Poland in 1945 left diocesan borders out of sync with the new political realities. Many Catholics in East Germany lived in dioceses administered by a bishop with a see in West Germany, while bishops in the German Democratic Republic (GDR) oversaw dioceses that criss-crossed the Oder–Neisse Line. The Bishop of Berlin, for example, had his see in the western half of the city, while his diocese theoretically included East Berlin, parts of East Germany, and Polish Pomerania. The onset of the Cold War, the West German policy of clinging to the lost eastern territories as a trump card for national unification, and the Vatican's doctrine of aligning diocesan boundaries with political borders only after the conclusion of international treaties all conspired against the resolution of this thorny problem. In 1958, East Germany denied entry to Berlin's Bishop Julius Döpfner. The auxiliary bishop Alfred Bengsch, who resided in East Berlin, eventually took up pastoral care for Catholics in East Germany. For some years afterward, the Vatican considered moving the bishop's see to East Berlin, which, however, would have required Döpfner's prior reassignment. In early summer 1961, Döpfner was eventually transferred to the recently vacated see in Munich. But East Germany closed the city's open borders less than a week before Bengsch was installed as Bishop of Berlin on August 18, 1961. In the aftermath of this major rupture in German post-World War II history, the new bishop found a *modus vivendi* with the communist regime. In exchange for his abstinence from politics, the government allowed Bengsch to pursue pastoral care in the walled-in GDR, to maintain contacts with his flock in West Berlin, and to keep links to the Vatican in Rome. But with the closure of the borders in Berlin, East Germany had created a *fait accompli* that turned the official readjustment of diocesan borders in Germany and Poland into a major political issue.[29]

A fortnight after the Berlin Crisis, Khrushchev's announcement that he would break the three-year-old nuclear test moratorium triggered protests not only from the West and the Non-Aligned Movement but also from the pope. In early September, John XXIII called on the United States and the USSR to remove the threat of nuclear war that was hanging over the world. Two months later, just after the politically motivated test of the militarily useless *Tsar Bomba*, the pontiff castigated the Soviet Union for the ongoing series of nuclear explosions. Faced with worldwide criticism about the ongoing tests, Khrushchev sent a congratulatory telegram to the pope on his eightieth birthday on November 25. The first message from a high-ranking Soviet leader to a pontiff since 1917 came as a surprise, leading John XXIII to comment drily: "Better than a slap in the face, isn't it?" Soviet testing ended in November but in the spring Khrushchev still decided to send nuclear missiles to Cuba covertly.[30]

In view of the impending opening of the first session of the Second Vatican Council on October 11, 1962, the Soviet Union and the socialist states tried to align their standpoints. At a meeting in Budapest in late April, the heads of various national government offices in charge of church affairs assessed what they considered the ideological threat emanating from the Council. The general consensus was that the papal repositioning of the Vatican as a third force in between capitalism and communism was a fig leaf for the continued anti-communist thrust of a church vying for global domination. The pontiff's attempt to seek unity among the world's Christians was merely a vehicle to "penetrate peacefully" the Socialist Camp. The calls for peaceful coexistence thus were not serious either, since the Vatican allegedly preferred martyrs like Mindszenty over moderates like Wyszyński. Still, the gathered communist officials criticized the behavior of Wyszyński and other Catholic Church representatives from the Socialist Camp for their unwillingness to speak out against the anti-communist tendencies in Rome. The Czechoslovak representative even suggested organizing a parallel Christian peace conference under the auspices of the United Nations in Prague to counter the anti-communism of the impending Council.[31]

But in the end Moscow did not want to be completely frozen out, given that the Lutheran and Anglican churches had decided to dispatch a small number of observers to the Council. In the summer of 1962, the Soviet Union secretly sought negotiations with the Vatican on the dispatch of Russian Orthodox delegates. This move allowed Khrushchev to appear conciliatory, while the timing of the initiative ensured that the Soviet-controlled Russian Church would exclusively represent all of Orthodoxy. The trick worked. Five days before the opening of the Council, the Vatican issued an invitation to the Moscow Patriarchate. The arrival of two Russian representatives naturally irritated the other Orthodox churches, which had been loyal to an earlier joint Orthodox decision not to send anybody.[32]

As the first session of the Second Vatican Council met on October 11 to begin eight weeks of discussions about church reform, the world was unwittingly moving toward one of the most dangerous Cold War confrontations – the Cuban Missile Crisis of October 22–28. John XXIII and the American newspaper publisher Norman Cousins played an important role, first, in defusing the crisis and, then, in reducing Soviet–American mistrust. Urged on by the Vatican, Cousins used his extensive contacts with American, Catholic, and Soviet scientists to act as a private diplomat between US President John F. Kennedy, the pontiff, and the Soviet leader. As a first result of this informal diplomacy, on October 24 John XXIII appealed in an "anguished cry of Peace" to both the USSR and the United States to step away from the brink and "negotiate" with each other. In December, Cousins successively met with Kennedy in Washington, John XXIII in the Vatican, and Khrushchev in Moscow to discuss nuclear disarmament and religious affairs in the USSR. The Soviet leader confessed to the American publisher that "the Pope's appeal was a real ray of light" during the darkest hours of the Cuban Missile Crisis, and how much the threat of nuclear war, which he had provoked, had been a cathartic passage for him to seek nuclear arms limitation. But he was reluctant to talk about religion in his country, or even to agree to the release of the imprisoned and aging Archbishop Josyf Slipij of the absorbed Ukrainian Uniate Church, which John XXIII expected as a sign of Soviet good will.[33]

Still, the papal foray into global diplomacy scored some successes in the first half of 1963. In February, Khrushchev released Slipij from prison, allowing him to relocate to Rome in retirement. On March 7, the pontiff received Khrushchev's son-in-law, Aleksei Adzhubei, in a mutual sign of good will, but the talks did not lead to political rapprochement. Five weeks later, on April 11, John XXIII released his long-expected encyclical *Pacem in Terris* (On Peace on Earth), in which he called for nuclear disarmament, social justice in the world, and "the cooperation of Catholics with men who may not be Christians but who nevertheless are reasonable men." The following day, Khrushchev received Cousins in Gagra at the Black Sea. US President Kennedy had asked the private diplomat to meet the Soviet leader in the hope of breaking the deadlock in the negotiations over a nuclear test ban treaty. The American publisher brought a papal present from Rome with him – the Russian translation of the one-day-old encyclical. Yet his talks with Khrushchev did not result in any success. Ultimately, the Soviet–American deadlock broke only in early June, when the PRC started a massive propaganda campaign against the USSR and when the United States accepted the idea of an inspection-free test ban treaty. By mid July, the Soviet–American–British negotia-tions on the Limited Test Ban Treaty started in Moscow, ending in an agreement within a fortnight.[34]

But John XXIII was unable to harvest the fruits of his international diplomacy. His health had been steadily deteriorating since the fall of 1962. He died of inoperable stomach cancer on June 3. Two days later, the United Nations Disarmament Conference in Geneva praised the pontiff for his leadership and inspiration in seeking world peace. Yet it was his attempt at opening up the communist world that would become his long-term legacy. The pope's under secretary of state, Agostino Casaroli, once characterized John XXIII's policy toward the Socialist Camp as an attempt to replace futile confrontation with a policy of small steps that was designed to "plant the seedlings of freedom in the monolith, so that they can grow over time."[35]

Paul VI, 1963–78: Détente

On June 21, 1963, the College of Cardinals elected John XXIII's preferred successor. The 65-year-old diplomat Paul VI quickly recon-vened the second session of the second Council in the fall in order to continue his predecessor's policy of *aggiornamento*. Eventually, his visits to five continents during his fifteen-year reign made him an international media star. As a sign of peace, "the Pilgrim Pope" made the first ever papal visit to the Holy Land in early 1964. He carefully balanced the visit to Jordan and Israel with the reality of a divided Jerusalem, the need to support Palestinian Christian refugees, and the necessity of placating anti-Israeli Arab states. But he also used the opportunity to meet the Ecumenical Patriarch of Constantinople (the Orthodox counterpart to the pope) and other Orthodox leaders, the first pontiff to do so after the split of the church in 1054. His visit to Jerusalem opened the path for non-Russian Orthodox representatives to attend the third session later in the year. The fourth session concluded the Council at the end of 1965, bringing several Christian churches together in a joint ecumenical service in which the 900-year-old papal condemnation of the Orthodox Church was formally repealed. With regard to internal matters, the Council approved various measures of modernization in liturgy, constitutional matters, and scriptural analysis. In a triumph for the Eastern European bishops, who had received permission from their communist governments to participate in the meetings in Rome, the Council pronounced that religious freedom was a fundamental human right everywhere in the world.[36]

Although Paul VI reconfirmed the Vatican's historical enmity toward the "putrid and lethal illness" of communism, he generally continued John XXIII's policy of trying to find a *modus vivendi* with the Socialist Camp for the sake of pastoral life there. His first encyclical *Ecclesiam Suam* (His Church) of August 1964 called for "dialogue" with other Christians and with "unbelievers." At the Council, liberal Western bishops defeated attempts by Spanish anti-communist prelates and exile bishops from China, Czechoslovakia, Yugoslavia, and Ukraine to adopt a strong anti-communist declaration. Paul VI was determined to continue John XXIII's policy of small steps toward the Socialist Camp, similar to *Ostpolitik*, which the opposition Social Democrats in West Germany were developing in parallel at that very time. Many years later, Casaroli recalled that the ensuing diplomatic dealings with the Socialist Camp became his "martyrdom of patience." But West German media called him the "Holy 007" for his ability to navigate the pitfalls of the communist world. In the wake of *Ecclesiam Suam*, Paul VI created the Secretariat for Non-Believers in April 1965. Headed by Vienna's left-leaning Archbishop Franz König, it aimed at analyzing atheism academically, at seeking dialogue for the sake of world peace, and at engaging with the Socialist Camp in parallel to Casaroli's diplomatic efforts. The members of that camp, however, grew concerned about the new pope. Recurrent conferences of the state church offices from 1964 to 1967 compared Paul VI more with the anti-communist Pius XII than with the conciliatory John XXIII. Although the gathered officials unswervingly reassured each other that the Vatican was on the losing side of history, they still acknowledged the increased moral standing of the Holy See in international affairs, which required greater coordinated engagement in order to benefit from it instrumentally. In the end, however, they were worried about Vatican attempts both to discredit atheism intellectually and to undercut socialist-sponsored Catholic conferences and movements through skillful academic debate.[37]

Paul VI's policy of small steps achieved some successes while it suffered several stinging defeats. In mid 1964, four years after Zagreb's Archbishop Stepinac's death in involuntary rural exile, the Yugoslav ambassador to Italy started a two-year negotiation marathon with Casaroli on mutual recognition. Tito wanted to defuse nationalist tensions between Catholic Croats and Orthodox Serbs through an agreement that tolerated the Catholic Church. In turn, the Vatican agreed to contain the nationalist tendencies among the Croatian clergy. The establishment of full diplomatic relations followed in August 1970.[38] Soviet diplomats, in comparison, had tried to launch informal contacts with the Vatican as early as the 1950s. After his election, Paul VI pondered meeting Khrushchev, but the Soviet leader soon fell from power. In April 1966, Foreign Minister Andrei A. Gromyko visited the pope, addressing Paul VI strictly as the leader of the Catholic Church but not as the head of the internationally recognized Vatican state. While the pontiff expressed his hopes for an improvement of the church's condition in the USSR, the Soviet visitor used the opportunity to promote his government's proposals for an anti-American security conference in Europe. During an audience with the high-ranking Soviet official Nikolai V. Podgorny in early 1967, the pontiff made future consultations about world peace dependent on improvements of religious life in the USSR. Still, Paul VI announced on New Year's Day 1971 that the Vatican would accede to the Nuclear Non-Proliferation Treaty of 1968 as a sign of its commitment to world peace. Casaroli traveled to Moscow eight weeks later to sign the pact, but the "martyr of patience" again insisted on wide-ranging negotiations on human rights and greater religious freedom in the Soviet Union.[39]

The situation in Czechoslovakia was more complicated. Economic reforms had started in the first half of the 1960s. Eventually they would trigger the Prague Spring and then lead to the Soviet-led Warsaw Pact intervention in 1968. For twenty months after Paul VI's election in mid 1963, Casaroli had negotiated with the communist government in Prague for the release of clerics and bishops, including Beran, who was freed in February 1965 for retirement in Rome. Still, only a few bishops were allowed to participate in the concurrent Council. Negotiations in late spring 1967 on the thorny issue of selecting candidates for vacant episcopal sees collapsed despite the Vatican's willingness to compromise. During the Prague Spring, both popular pressure and the government's own ideological reform policies – designed to realize a socialism with a human face – prompted a significant reduction of state interference in church affairs, the dissolution of the twenty-year-old state-sponsored Catholic Party, the release of the last imprisoned bishops and clerics, and the re-establishment of Catholic orders, charities, and publication venues. But the Vatican did not trust the sudden reform efforts before the Soviet-led intervention in August ended the possibility of rapprochement anyway. Paul VI bemoaned the fact that the suppression of the Prague Spring had "darkened" the atmosphere in Europe, but expressed his hope that "courage and realism" would unify the whole continent and ultimately bring lasting peace. Archbishop König called for continued dialogue with the "non-believers" in Czechoslovakia, even if it "won't be very easy." After the removal of the leaders of the reform government in early 1969, the repression of society at large, including the church, went into full force. Many episcopal sees fell vacant again. The resulting ecclesiastical inability to consecrate priests threatened the health of pastoral life in the whole country. In early 1973, after short negotiations, the Vatican agreed to a *modus vivendi* in which the Czechoslovak regime claimed the right to select candidates for an episcopal see while the Vatican was allowed to test their religious qualifications but not question their political loyalties. In reality, only a few bishops were enthroned before the end of the Cold War.[40]

In comparison, Poland's Church enjoyed the most favorable conditions in the Socialist Camp. In the 1960s, it counted seventy bishops and a large number of priests who maintained pastoral life. It also comprised a vibrant monastic life and ran a functioning Catholic University. Sixty-one Polish bishops participated in at least one of the four sessions of the Council. But government harassment had not stopped. In 1959, Gomułka had started to distrust the church, believing that it was fighting the communist order over the soul of Poland's population. For his part, Cardinal Wyszyński had spent much effort and many years preparing for 1966 – the millennial anniversary of the Christianization of Poland – which had triggered a widespread popular re-engagement with the church and even convinced him to invite Paul VI to come to Poland on that occasion.[41]

But the main obstacle continued to be the conflict over what Poland claimed as its western lands and what West Germany called the lost eastern territories. In his famous "Hedwig Sermon" in October 1960, Berlin's Bishop Döpfner had emphasized the common Polish–German history of these territories, bemoaned the crimes committed in Germany's name during World War II, and called for dialogue, reconciliation, and peace. At the first session of the Council in 1962, Polish and German bishops agreed to seek reconciliation but failed to follow up in the remaining three sessions. Delegates from the Polish Catholic Church and representatives of the West German Lutheran Church, some of whom were refugees from the disputed territories, drew up a program of reconciliation over the summer of 1965. One of the leading figures in this effort, the bilingual Auxiliary Bishop of Wrocław (Breslau) Bolesław Kominek, publicly acknowledged the German heritage of Szczecin

(Stettin) and the territories east of the Oder–Neisse Line in August 1965. Toward the end of the Council, on November 18, 1965, Poland's bishops sent a letter, drafted by Kominek, to their West German colleagues. Fashioned as an invitation to attend the millennium celebrations the following year, it claimed the Oder–Neisse Line as Poland's western border while it offered and asked for mutual forgiveness for past injustices. The West German episcopal reply accepted the offer of dialogue, but failed to make any reference to the Oder–Neisse Line, which deeply disappointed the Polish bishops. Enraged by the politically delicate contents of the letter exchange, the Polish government reacted with an anti-church campaign, accusing Wyszyński of sidestepping governmental authority, prohibiting him from leaving the country for three years, disrupting the planned events for the millennium celebrations throughout 1966, and even blocking the planned visit by Paul VI.[42]

The fallout of 1966 was just the prelude to a larger rupture in 1968. The anti-Zionist campaign by the government against Jewish student protesters in the wake of the June War in the Middle East in 1967, the suppression of student unrest over the cancellation of a theater performance of a play by Poland's nineteenth-century national poet Adam Mickiewicz in early 1968, and the Polish participation in the Soviet-led intervention in neighboring Czechoslovakia all disturbed many Poles, even members of the ruling party. Burnt by the events of 1966, however, the Polish Bishops Conference reacted cautiously. But the dismal realization that the reformist ideas of 1956 had vanished for good started to permeate society at large. The *personalist* dream, so vibrant in the late 1940s and early 1950s, that progressive Catholics could tame Soviet-style communism had become a faint memory. The question of cooperating with the oppressive communist state in the hope of establishing a socialism with a human face turned into a moral dilemma for many. The Polish Party realized that lower-ranking priests increasingly sympathized with a groundswell of fundamental popular opposition.[43]

The malaise in Polish society occurred at the time of West Germany's *Ostpolitik*, which Willy Brandt had promoted as Social Democratic foreign minister in the grand coalition since 1966 and as chancellor since 1969. Its rise occurred in the wake of Paul VI's 1966 musings on adjusting the borders of the dioceses that crisscrossed the Oder–Neisse Line. But since the coalition government feared that hasty steps would undermine West Germany's position vis-à-vis the Socialist Camp, the pontiff agreed to a compromise that only formally confirmed the Polish practice, customary since 1945, of appointing auxiliary bishops. After Brandt's election, the Polish bishops pushed for a quick resolution of this matter since they feared that the new chancellor's attempts to seek rapprochement with the USSR would create disadvantages for Poland – in an echo of Hitler's pact with Stalin three decades earlier. In mid July 1970, Brandt traveled to the Vatican to meet Paul VI, who promised support for *Ostpolitik* and agreed to adjust the diocesan borders only *after* the conclusion of the German–Polish treaty that concurrently was under negotiation. Brandt's trip to Warsaw in early December was symbolic beyond just the signing of the treaty that recognized the Oder–Neisse Line. The chancellor himself asked for forgiveness by falling to his knees at the Memorial of the Warsaw Ghetto Uprising. The visit ended twenty-five years of West German–Polish bitterness, but at the same time also pre-dated Gomułka's removal from office following the unrelated suppression of workers' strikes shortly thereafter.[44]

The new government under Edward Gierek hoped to regain public trust through economic reforms and rapprochement with the Catholic Church. But Brandt still needed to convince a hostile West German public and a split parliament. The Vatican ordered masses to be held in the spring of 1972 for the chancellor's survival of the scheduled no-confidence vote in the West German parliament. It was not divine intervention that saved him, however, but the East German State Security buying off at least one member of parliament before the decisive vote on April 27. The Polish–West German exchange of the ratification documents for the Warsaw Treaty on June 3, 1972, not only opened the path toward the Conference on Security and Cooperation in Europe, but also allowed Paul VI to create new episcopates formally and appoint full bishops in Poland's western territories within three weeks. Thus, June 3 fulfilled the shared long-standing dreams of the Polish government and the church, while it *simultaneously* terminated the nationalist quasi-alliance they had formed since 1945. A clash between the communist regime and the Catholic Church was in the offing. While the politically cautious church hierarchy tended to work more closely with the Gierek regime, lower-ranking clergy openly engaged with the groundswell of opposition. In West Germany, bishops and opposition Conservatives, who were still smarting over the failed no-confidence vote, protested against the adjustment of diocesan borders in Poland. But much of it was just political theater. Similarly, the events in June 1972 also augured the future readjustment of diocesan borders in East Germany, and with that a deeper division of Germany. Indeed, within one year, Paul VI appointed auxiliary bishops in the GDR despite the resistance of West German bishops. As East Germany and the Vatican established contacts in the following years, they moved toward an agreement on the readjustment of diocesan borders, but Paul VI's death on August 6, 1978, scuttled the signing of the semi-finished settlement.[45]

In parallel to the developments in Poland, the Vatican and Hungary established a *modus vivendi*. The two sides had already entered into a partial agreement in 1964, but Cardinal József Mindszenty, who had been living in the American embassy since November 1956, remained a major stumbling block. As early as April 1963, the Vatican had maintained that "Mindszenty was, in a very real sense, living and thinking thirty years in the past." Casaroli signaled to the Hungarian regime that it wanted Mindszenty to go into retirement in Rome so that the national church could return to functionality. But the stubborn cardinal primate, who had barely been able to maintain contact with his suffering church, repeatedly refused to budge, threatening instead to walk out of the embassy into the arms of the secret police in order to suffer a martyr's fate, similar to Nagy's. The deadlock lasted for the first eight years of Paul VI's reign, despite repeated visits from König and Casaroli to soften up the aging and increasingly frail Mindszenty. Though both the Vatican and Hungary wanted a resolution, they were not willing to lose face either. As the Mindszenty case progressively threatened pastoral life in Hungary, it also damaged the government's image worldwide, just at the moment when it was emerging as one of the few communist regimes in Eastern Europe still committed to a low level of economic reform in the wake of the suppression of the Prague Spring in neighboring Czechoslovakia. Ultimately, a political deal between Hungary, the Vatican, and the United States cut the Gordian knot. In exchange for a Vatican guarantee that he could remain primate and for a formal governmental pardon, the 79-year-old Mindszenty agreed in September 1971 to leave for Rome. In turn, the Hungarian state consented to restore church life, release imprisoned bishops and clerics, and allow the appointment of new (though government-sanctioned) bishops. But harassment persisted at a low level until the end of the Cold War. In his Roman exile, Mindszenty also continued his anti-communist crusade, which quickly alienated the pope, until his death in early 1975.[46]

As an advocate for world peace, Paul VI also looked beyond Europe toward Vietnam. Newly elected, he criticized the South Vietnamese government under the *personalist* Catholic Ngo Dinh Diem for its treatment of the Buddhist majority. A year after Diem's overthrow and assassination by his own generals in early November 1963, Paul VI demoted his brother, the Archbishop of Hué, to a minor position in Rome. In May 1966, the US government even sought the pontiff's good offices in the Vietnam conflict. At the turn of the year, the Vatican collaborated with the Communist Party of Italy in a peace mission to Hanoi, followed by one of its own under the leadership of the head of the West German Catholic aid organization Caritas. When the pontiff received Podgorny in late January 1967, he demanded from both superpowers an end to their military and political involvement in Vietnam for the sake of peace. But neither Washington nor Hanoi were willing to heed the pope's subsequent pleas to end the fighting in favor of negotiations. The premeditated killings of Catholic priests and missionaries by communist forces during the month-long occupation of Hué during the Tet Offensive in February 1968 shocked the Vatican. In its aftermath, the pontiff offered the Vatican as a site for the American–North Vietnamese peace talks, but lost out to Charles de Gaulle's Paris. From 1969 to 1972, Paul VI focused on working with the United States in a futile attempt to free American prisoners-of-war in North Vietnam and on ensuring that the peace negotiations in the French capital addressed the fate of the Catholic minority in the south. Yet, after the Paris Agreements of January 1973, the pontiff's interest refocused on Europe again.[47]

By 1972–73, papal foreign policy toward the European Socialist Camp had achieved all that was possible. Communist Poland and Non-Aligned Yugoslavia had agreed to accommodate working churches, Hungary and Czechoslovakia supervised semi-functional churches, and the USSR and the GDR continued to harass a minority church. As early as the beginning of 1972, the Vatican detected a hardening of socialist positions that made further progress seem difficult to achieve. Indeed, the representatives of the socialist church offices, who had resumed their periodical meetings in 1970, exuded increasing confidence that the Socialist Camp had solved the problem of the anti-communist Catholic Church – either through restrictive agreements, outright repression, political manipulation, or driving a wedge between the ecclesiastical hierarchy and the common believers. Until 1978, the year of Paul VI's death, the Catholic Church declined as the predominant topic in their discussions in favor of more general deliberations about how to exploit all religions to the benefit of the Socialist Camp.[48]

Yet the Vatican had still one arrow left in its quiver – participation in the Conference on Security and Cooperation in Europe. In the wake of the Budapest Appeal of March 1969, the Warsaw Pact had even asked the pope to mediate in favor of a pan-European security conference. The Vatican announced in July 1973 that it would join the CSCE negotiations – the first time since 1815 that it participated in an international conference of states. Casaroli deemed involvement a suitable tool to firm up those concessions that the Vatican had received in bilateral talks from individual socialist states, and more generally a key Vatican contribution to world peace. Thus, the CSCE enabled the Holy See to intensify the diplomatic dialogue with socialist states in the hope of improving the situation of the church there. It also offered the opportunity to influence the phrasing of the articles on human contacts, free flow of information, and cooperation in the fields of culture and education in Basket III.[49]

Still, with his pontificate nearing its end in August 1978, Paul VI received growing criticism for his policy toward the Socialist Camp, particularly as détente faltered at the global level. Some of the criticism came from expected quarters, like Mindszenty, the church hierarchy in West Germany, or the exiled Ukrainian Uniate bishops. But even König admitted by 1977 that the Socialist Camp was playing a "false game" with the Catholic Church. As early as February 1971, a frustrated Paul VI had been thinking about retiring within a year at the age of seventy-five, in accordance with the retirement rules that the Second Council had adopted for cardinals. Given the recent opening of the church toward the world, which he had helped along, the pontiff hoped that the next College of Cardinals would break with the century-old custom of electing an Italian pope. In the end, he stayed six years beyond his retirement age, during which he too grew critical of the limited success of his *Ostpolitik*.[50]

Conclusion

At his inauguration as Pope John Paul II on October 22, 1978, the Polish Cardinal Karol Wojtyła quoted Jesus Christ's call on the faithful not to worry about the enemy: "Be not afraid!"[51] The Polish pope was no accident of history but the product of three decades of struggle by his country's church against Soviet-style communism. He had been ordained in 1946 during the communist effort to grasp domination over Polish society, installed as bishop in 1958 in the brief period of Gomułka's reforms following the Polish October, enthroned as Archbishop of Cracow in 1964 during the Second Council, and appointed cardinal in 1967 in the wake of the ruined millennium celebrations. In 1960, he had published a widely read *personalist* exploration of love and responsibility. Wojtyła had been one of the most junior and simultaneously most articulate Eastern European participants in the Council, where he spoke passionately about human freedom. As cardinal, he increasingly disagreed with the policies of compromise, which his senior colleague, the cautious Wyszyński, and the other Polish bishops pursued. He joined lower-ranking clergy in their quest to engage with the groundswell of opposition in the wake of 1968. Over the course of the 1970s, Wojtyła challenged the communist regime in his triple role as priest, philosopher, and ambassador of the Polish Church during his many travels around the world. Once elected pope, he issued his first encyclical, *Redemptor hominis* (Redeemer of Man), within five months of his inauguration. In it, he repeatedly returned to the central *personalist* theme of "human dignity," while he called for the implementation of the UN Declaration of Human Rights of 1948. Without doubt, the new pope inspired the independent labor union Solidarność, which attracted many of those who had been raised in the *personalist* debates of the interwar and post-war periods. The Socialist Camp quickly learned to fear him. In June 1979, John Paul II returned – for the first time as pontiff – to Poland, where he celebrated an open-air mass in Cracow in front of one million people. A senior party official reportedly lamented that the Polish pope was undoing all that the Polish communists had built up since 1945. Soviet leader Leonid I. Brezhnev had warned Gierek in advance about allowing John Paul II to come to Poland unless he wanted to invite trouble. He even reminded the Polish leader how Gomułka had canceled Paul VI's visit in 1966 without protest from the Polish church or believers.[52]

Papal anti-communism pre-dated even the Bolshevik Revolution. The Vatican's response to Soviet domination of Eastern Europe underwent three distinct phases: fatalistic resistance under Pius XII, engagement under John XXIII and Paul VI to strengthen the church, and contestation under John Paul II. The Vatican seemed to have always been a step ahead of larger developments in the global Cold War. Pius XII was a Cold Warrior even before the Americans, John XXIII pursued *Ostpolitik* ahead of West Germany's Willy Brandt, and Paul VI realized that engagement had run its course before superpower détente faltered. Throughout the period of evolving relations with the Socialist Camp, the Vatican affected structural change in Eastern Europe, most notably in Poland. Although John Paul II criticized the concessions made during the three decades before his election, they had helped to restore the functionality of the church in Poland and, by extension, its clergy's capability to engage in anti-communist opposition in the 1970s. Moreover, it was precisely these concessions that made the Polish pope possible in the first place. Although the church in other communist states fared less well than in Poland, the election of John Paul II was the contagious apple of spiritual freedom that helped to infect the barrel of Soviet-style communism.

Part VII

The End of the Regional Cold Wars

Introduction to Chapters 20 to 22

The previous fifteen chapters have explored the structural changes that Asia, the Middle East, and Europe had undergone during the decades leading up to the late 1970s. In Asia, reunified Vietnam replaced the rising China as a revolutionary power, while India transformed its internationalism into a national quest for great power status. In the Middle East, the Arab–Israeli conflict went through four major wars. Israel emerged as an unacknowledged regional power, Egypt ensnared the global Cold War in the region but realized the futility of allying closely with the Soviet Union, and the Palestinians managed to put their struggle for nationhood on the international agenda despite repeated military and political defeats. Asian–African Internationalism, Non-Alignment, and pan-Islamism all formulated alternatives to the Cold War bloc system. One collapsed in the 1960s, the second moved toward the Socialist Camp, and the third, though internally not unified, formulated visions for the Middle East to transcend the Cold War. In Europe, power shifted from the United Kingdom to the continent, most notably to France and the European Communities (EC). The economic experiences on either side of the Iron Curtain diverged greatly, with the EC a success story and the Council for Mutual Economic Assistance (CMEA) a failure. European détente – between the two Germanys, the two halves of the continent, and between the Vatican and the Socialist Camp – arose in the 1960s and 1970s with the goal of decreasing the toll of the continent's division and reconciling different visions of a joint future.

The structures underlying the ends of the regional Cold Wars in Asia, the Middle East, and Europe emerged in parallel over the short period from the late 1970s to the early 1980s. But what do we use as benchmarks to assert such structural endpoints? Since the nature of the regional Cold Wars in Asia, the Middle East, and Europe had differed from each other for decades, we need to use different criteria, or combinations thereof, to define structural endpoints of the regional Cold Wars. First, the collapse of long-standing partnerships or established blocs is a good indicator to denote the beginning of the post-Cold War period. The collapse of unity among communist-led national liberation movements in East Asia in 1978–79, the Soviet abandonment of the Brezhnev Doctrine in 1981, and the economic collapse of the Socialist Camp in Europe during the concurrent Polish Crisis are fitting criteria. Second, the relatively swift transformation of enduring Cold War antagonisms into political and economic partnerships likewise represents the erosion of Cold War blocs. Here, we can think of Sino–American recognition on January 1, 1979, the Sino–American–Southeast Asian cooperation to contain hegemonic Vietnam in the same year, or the *de facto* economic integration of several Eastern European socialist states into the global economy. Finally, the emergence of phenomena that transcended the Cold War as an ordering principle of international relations also point to the dawn of a new age. The rise of Islamist movements to political influence and the establishment of the Islamic Republic of Iran in the late 1970s come to mind as examples.

How did these changes come about? For the most part, regional developments from the previous three decades merged into producing the structural ending of the regional Cold Wars. However, these changes occurred simultaneously but largely independently of each other. Still, three distinct events connected changes in Asia, the Middle East, and Europe – the Islamic Revolution in Iran in 1979, the start of the Afghanistan War late the same year, and the beginning of the Iraq–Iran War in the fall 1980. They particularly bound together developments in the Middle East and Asia in multiple ways, but they also had an impact, though less decisive, on Europe. Unlike the 1960s and early 1970s, as discussed in previous parts of this book, events in Asia hardly had an influence on changes in Europe in the late 1970s and early 1980s. Developments in all the three regions, however, benefited from the overall decline of Soviet power that started in the late 1970s. The USSR might have been able to achieve short-term successes with its alliance with hegemonic Vietnam, with its intervention in Afghanistan, or with its subversion of Non-Alignment in alliance with Cuba, but all of them quickly turned out to be major losses that weakened Soviet military, economic, and reputational power.

Part VII starts with Chapter 20 on the Middle East, where events occurred that influenced Asia and Europe. The region experienced two separate but intertwined events – Israeli–Egyptian rapprochement and the rise of Islamism. From 1977 to 1979, Israel's Prime Minister Menachem Begin and Egypt's President Anwar Sadat negotiated a bilateral peace, which, however, led neither to a region-wide peace nor to the creation of a Palestinian Arab state in the West Bank, as Sadat had hoped. On the contrary, Egypt was expelled from the Arab League – the organization which it had established in World War II and dominated for a long time – as a punishment for breaking Arab ranks. Just when Begin and Sadat signed the bilateral peace agreement in March 1979, the Iranian Revolution unfolded. Its Islamist leader, Ayatollah Khomeini, envisioned the creation of a Shia Persian-led new world system outside the existing Cold War structures and in competition with Sunni-Arab Islam. In an attempt to seize leadership in the Arab world in the wake of Egypt's expulsion from the League, Iraq launched war against Iran. The conflict pitted a secular Arab state that was supported by conservative Arab regimes against a Persian theocracy that received political and material assistance from other secular Arab states and even Israel. By late 1979, Sunni Islamists challenged Saudi royal hegemony over the Holy Cities of Mecca and Medina. Soon thereafter, the Soviet intervention in Afghanistan, which was motivated by Cold War considerations, further heated up the Iranian–Saudi competition for leadership in the Muslim world. Finally, the Israeli intervention in the Lebanese civil war in 1982 triggered the growth of Iranian influence on the side of Shia Muslims and pitted the Palestine Liberation Organization against its Syrian backers. An American–European military mission to oversee the Palestinian retreat to Tunisia withdrew after several lethal Islamist suicide bombings in 1983. By the mid 1980s, the Middle East had essentially exited the structures of the global Cold War, but the superpowers mostly failed to see it.

Chapter 21 on Asia explores the rapid realignment of regional forces in the late 1970s and early 1980s. The Sino–Vietnamese split over bilateral problems and Vietnamese designs on Cambodia preceded Sino–American recognition. Together, they signified the collapse of long-standing alignments that had defined the regional Cold War in Asia. The roles of India and the Non-Aligned Movement in the period are more complex. In 1977–79, the first Indian government led by a party other than Congress tried to reverse long-standing policies by reducing tensions with Pakistan, the People's Republic of China, and the United States, while distancing itself from the Soviet-supported Vietnamese intervention in Cambodia. The reelection of Congress leader Indira Gandhi to power in early 1980 led India to a temporary return to old positions, including the defense of the Soviet and Vietnamese interventions in Afghanistan and Cambodia, respectively. But by 1982, once she had realized that her one-sided policy hurt her country, she tried to reorient India into a position of equidistance between the superpowers, just as India had gained control over the Non-Aligned Movement for the first time. The deep involvement of the USSR in the wars in Indochina, Afghanistan, and the Middle East at the turn of the decade, as well as the Soviet attempt to infiltrate the Non-Aligned

Movement with the help of Cuba had damaged Moscow's standing in all three areas, particularly since the main participants in all three wars were members of the Non-Aligned Movement. In the early 1980s, the USSR was tied to losing Cold War causes in Indochina, South Asia, and the Middle East.

Chapter 22 on Europe focuses on how the two halves of the divided continent overcame their parallel economic crises of the 1970s. Ballooning Eastern European debt to the non-socialist world, the Polish Crisis in 1980–81, and the economic impact of the Afghanistan War and the Iraq–Iran War permanently undermined Soviet hegemony in Eastern Europe. By late 1981, the USSR had neither the economic means nor the military stomach to maintain its influence by brute force. As a consequence, Hungary, Poland, and East Germany turned to the Western world for credit and economic advice, which in turn accelerated the erosion of Soviet dominance. At the same time, Western countries underwent a conservative transformation that helped to overcome the economic crises of the late 1970s in the aftermath of the American abolition of the Bretton Woods system and the two Middle East oil shocks. In the 1980s, they emerged strengthened in economic terms and unified against the final Soviet attempt to seek supremacy in all of Europe through the stationing of intermediate-range nuclear missiles in Eastern Europe. The regional structures for the end of the global Cold War were in place.

20   The Middle East

The Cold War did not cause any of the conflicts in the Middle East before 1979. All had their roots in the collapse of the Ottoman Empire, Western colonialism, and the Arab–Israeli antagonism. The Soviet–American clash had imposed itself on the Middle East, particularly in the decade from 1964. It merely exacerbated existing conflicts, helped to shape the region until the early years of Anwar Sadat's presidency, and was then expelled by Egypt and Saudi Arabia. If the regional conflicts in the Middle East before 1979 had no Cold War roots, it is thus impossible to define the end of the regional Cold War in the context of their resolution. Indeed, the regional Cold War ended – with the exception of Afghanistan – with the emergence of actors that *transcended* the super-power antagonism as an ordering principle in the region. Egypt initiated peace negotiations with Israel without any outside involvement – and even against the plans of the superpowers – in 1977, just as an Israeli government ideologically committed to the idea of Greater Israel had come to power. That new government pursued a peace policy toward the Arab states in order to establish its grandiose ethno-nationalist plans in all of Palestine. In Egypt, Saudi Arabia, and Lebanon, Islamist parties and movements that rejected Western liberalism and Soviet communism rose to prominence by the late 1970s, though Iran was the only country where an Islamist government arose. Caught in their Cold War thinking, the superpowers, and some of their regional allies like Saudi Arabia, reacted in a Cold War fashion that only reinforced the rise of political Islam – be it in Egypt, Afghanistan, or Lebanon.

The Middle East in the Mid 1970s

Middle Eastern politics in the mid 1970s displayed a high degree of volatility. Sadat had expelled Soviet military advisers in 1972 and launched the October War against Israel a year later, in the hope of forcing the United States to engage with the Egyptian–Israeli conflict. He spent much of the following three years trying to convince Arab players of the idea of a negotiated peace. With the American-mediated second Sinai Agreement in September 1975, Egypt renounced the use of military force to solve the Arab–Israeli conflict. Sadat understood that the repudiation of a three-decade-old joint Arab position was politically sensitive. He thus publicly stressed his concerns for the fate of the Palestinians, though he simultaneously emphasized that they were primarily responsible for their own future.[1] As Sadat sought an arrangement with Israel, he continued to pursue domestic rapprochement with Islamists, even if they rejected peace with Zionism. At the global level, Egypt persisted in pursuing the strategic shift from the USSR toward the United States. Although Cairo was aware that not much would happen in Washington during the presidential election year of 1976, it still cancelled its five-year-old friendship treaty with Moscow early in the year. The People's Republic of China (PRC) reacted with "gloating." Within five weeks, Beijing replaced Moscow as supplier and maintainer of Soviet-designed weapons. In June 1976, Sadat traveled to Tehran to repair relations with his predecessor Gamal Abdel Nasser's long-term enemy, the Shah of Iran.[2]

Since 1965, King Faisal had made Saudi Arabia into the leading anti-communist and pan-Islamist country in the Arab world. He had supported Sadat in turning Egypt from the USSR toward the United States in the early 1970s, just as Saudi Arabia promoted its own conservative version of Islam in the wider Muslim world on the basis of its increasing oil wealth. The kingdom also facilitated the incorporation of rump-Pakistan into the Middle East after the bi-territorial South Asian country had collapsed at the turn of 1971/72. King Khalid and Crown Prince Fahd continued these policies after Faisal's assassination in March 1975. In mid year, Khalid visited Cairo for talks with Sadat, which resulted in additional credits to Egypt's ailing economy. Since Saudi Arabia aimed at keeping all communist – Soviet or Chinese – influence out of Egypt, it requested that the Anglo–American powers become exclusive military suppliers to the country at the Suez Canal. With the Shah's Iran, Saudi Arabia continued its policy of good relations in terms of Islamic solidarity and unity in support of the Palestinian issue.[3]

Neither Syria nor Iraq shared the pro-American policies of Egypt and Saudi Arabia in the mid 1970s. Damascus rejected the second Sinai Agreement of 1975 as treason to the Arab cause, claiming to be the new leader of the Arab world instead. Since Egypt's decision to renounce force meant that Israel was able to turn its military might against its other Arab neighbors, Hafez al-Assad's Syria pinned its hopes on an alliance with the USSR as an instrument of his pan-Arab aspirations. Its Baathist sibling, Iraq, rejected the second Sinai Agreement even more strongly, calling for

Israel's "liquidation." But Iraq neither bordered on Israel nor had territory occupied by it. Deriding Damascus as weak in the face of Zionism mainly allowed Baghdad to claim leadership in the Arab world. Nevertheless, Iraq feared that, after the recent US defeat in Indochina, "American imperialism" would turn its focus on the Middle East and create tensions in the Gulf region and the Levant.[4]

Furthermore, in 1975, Lebanon descended into a fifteen-year-long civil war. The country had faced a precarious balance between its denominational groups – Shia, Sunni, Druze, and Christian – since its emergence in the 1920s. The arrival of Palestinian refugees after 1947 and members of the Palestine Liberation Organization in 1971 further undermined stability while creating a *de facto* PLO state in southern Lebanon. In late May 1976, a year after the outbreak of sectarian fighting, Syria intervened. Assad feared that the leftist Druze and their Palestinian allies were trying to take over the country and start a radical, leftist political experiment that would provoke Israel into intervention and aggression against Syria. He further worried that the collapse of Lebanon's multi-denominational political institutions would lead to the creation of a Christian statelet in southern Lebanon under Israeli protection. In the spring of 1976, the situation in Lebanon looked eerily similar to the one in Jordan six years earlier. Assad thus intervened on the side of the Christians to keep them in a unified Lebanon while using the opportunity to discipline Druze leftists and their Palestinian allies. The gruesome battles with the PLO damaged Syria's standing in the Arab world, and exasperated Syria's superpower ally, the USSR, which feared that Assad's imperialist actions in Lebanon would ultimately "break his neck."[5]

In comparison, Yasser Arafat's PLO experienced a roller coaster ride in international relations in the mid 1970s. Arab unity had allowed the PLO to obtain non-state observer status at the United Nations in November 1974. But by early 1975, the PLO could only rely on Syria as a firm Arab promoter of a continued hardline policy toward Israel. Just as Vietnamese communists emerged victorious in late April 1975, however, Arafat grew pessimistic about the Palestinian future, given Arab disunity. At least, the PLO was able to score some diplomatic victories outside the Arab world. The PRC promised military support in July, and the Non-Aligned Movement welcomed the organization, alongside unified Vietnam, as a member the following month.[6]

In September, Arafat quickly rejected the second Sinai Agreement. "Peace will never be an American peace, ... but a Palestinian peace," he claimed. Behind the scenes, however, he hinted that the PLO was willing to recognize Israel at a time of its own choosing and after sufficient concessions. Yet, within half a year, the PLO was fighting its patron Syria in southern Lebanon, a development it considered "a tragedy for the struggle against imperialism." To make matters worse in this situation, the old factional struggles within the PLO broke out again. For some Maoist PLO members, the crisis of the national struggle and parallel reform in China after Mao Zedong's death triggered a decade-long process of rethinking, which eventually ended with membership in the Islamic Jihad Movement in Palestine.[7]

The superpowers followed their own, mutually exclusive, policies in the Middle East. The American engagement with the Arab–Israeli conflict in late 1973 – which Egypt had forced – provided the United States with elevated standing in the region, though Washington lacked concrete plans beyond the military disentanglement on the Sinai. In comparison, the USSR suffered from structural disadvantages after it had cut diplomatic relations with Israel in 1967 and lost Egypt in the early 1970s. In their place, Moscow built up closer relations with Damascus and Baghdad. After the October War in 1973, the Soviet Union also tried to improve relations with Tehran in the hope of binding that pro-American Middle Eastern country into the joint foreign policies of the Socialist Camp.[8] In May 1975, the USSR argued that the recent end of conflict in Vietnam could serve as a model for the Middle East. Moscow thus surprised its radical Arab friends when it demanded nothing less than their recognition of Israel at a future Geneva conference in exchange for Israeli withdrawal from all territories occupied in 1967 and for an Israeli agreement to a Palestinian state in the West Bank. But the American-mediated second Sinai Agreement destroyed any chance in September for a comprehensive solution at Geneva. By early 1976, the USSR and some of its Eastern European allies reduced trade and military relations with Egypt to punish the Arab country for its supposedly divisive policy toward the Arab world and its alleged refusal to pay off debt to the Socialist Camp. But this merely played into the Egyptian decision to abrogate the five-year-old Friendship Treaty in March. After losing Egypt, the Syrian intervention in Lebanon in late May further undermined the Soviet position in the Middle East.[9]

Egypt, Israel, and Palestine

On November 19, 1977, Sadat traveled to Jerusalem for talks with Israeli Prime Minister Menachem Begin. His surprise trip occurred at the confluence of several developments. The Egyptian leader had grown frustrated with the policies of the new US president, Jimmy Carter, whose call for a comprehensive solution at a future conference in

Geneva threatened to invite Soviet influence back into the Middle East and thereby prolong the stalemate that the Soviet–American Cold War had fortified since the mid 1960s. Sadat had convinced himself years earlier that the USSR was merely interested in preserving its presence in the Middle East but not in addressing the region's basic problems that were unrelated to the Cold War. The Egyptian leader was also convinced that the complexity of the Arab–Israeli conflict would condemn any international conference about a comprehensive solution to failure from the outset. Finally, since late 1973, he had managed to convince the majority of Arab states of the need to reach a deal with Israel. Following its intervention in Lebanon in 1976, even Syria was willing to moderate its position.[10]

The momentous events of Sadat's visit occurred on November 20. The Egyptian president started the day with a highly symbolic prayer in Al-Aqsa Mosque, where Jordan's King Abdullah had been assassinated for his collaboration with Israel in 1951 and where no Arab leader had publicly prayed since the June War in 1967. In a speech before the Knesset, he announced that he had come to offer peace but "not ... a separate agreement," because "in the absence of a just solution to the Palestinian problem, never will there be ... durable and just peace." Sadat called for withdrawal from all territories occupied in 1967, a Palestinian state in parts of former Mandatory Palestine, the mutual renunciation of force, and the end of the state of belligerency. Begin failed to respond to Sadat's vision in kind; he was merely willing to offer a separate deal on the Sinai.[11]

Sadat's visit took place after years of diplomatic maneuvering. In 1972, Nicolae Ceaușescu's Romania had tried to jumpstart Egyptian–Israeli talks. Three years later, the Egyptian leader himself had offered direct negotiations through Nahum Goldmann, the founder of the World Jewish Congress. During Ceaușescu's visit to Cairo on May 11–13, 1977, Sadat raised the idea of direct Arab peace talks with Israel. His optimism did not waver a week later when the Israeli elections produced, for the first time since the foundation of Israel, a plurality for a right-wing party led by Menachem Begin. Cairo was convinced that the election results reflected nothing but domestic concerns over corruption under the Labor Party.[12] In late August, Begin used the Romanian channel to signal his interest in peace to Sadat, which led to secret ministerial talks hosted by Moroccan King Hassan II. On November 9, Sadat publicly announced his willingness to travel to Israel. He was firmly convinced that Arab states would fall into line. Surprised by the offer, Begin invited Sadat in a letter transmitted through American diplomatic channels within a week. Sadat's decision to go to Jerusalem, however, did not meet with support from several of his ministers, who resigned to avoid accompanying him to Israel.[13]

Begin, however, was not interested in a comprehensive peace, nor in a Palestinian state. Since adolescence in interwar Poland, he had been a follower of the Zionist right-winger Ze'ev (Vladimir) Jabotinsky, who had broken with David Ben-Gurion's leftist Zionism in the early 1920s. For all his adult life, Begin had advocated the taking of all of *Eretz Israel* – the biblical Palestine that supposedly included Mandatory Palestine and territories in Syria and Transjordan – by military force, and thus had always supported an uncompromising policy toward the Palestinians. He had strongly opposed the UN partition plan of 1947 because it did not award all of Mandatory Palestine to Israel. After 1949, Begin had been a Knesset member for a series of right-wing opposition parties. On June 20, 1977, he assumed the office of prime minister at the helm of a right-wing coalition government that included his Likud, the National Religious Party that promoted settlement in the West Bank, and a miniscule ultra-religious party. But he offered the foreign ministry to Labor Party member Moshe Dayan, the architect of the military campaigns in 1956 and 1967, who wanted to polish his image as a peace maker after the fiasco of 1973.[14]

On his first day as prime minister, Begin publicly laid out the basics of his policies. They included the offer to negotiate with Egypt, Jordan, and Syria, but also an explicit reference to Jabotinsky as his inspiration. In September, Minister for Agriculture Ariel Sharon announced a plan to settle 2 million Israelis in the West Bank in the following two decades. Between 1967 and 1977, 40,000 Jews had moved to East Jerusalem and only 11,000 to the West Bank. By 1990, an additional 160,000 settlers would live in the Arab half of the city and in the occupied territory – in the midst of Palestinian towns of religious importance to Judaism, in agricultural settlements in the Jordan Valley, and in strategic hilltop settlements designed to project Jewish domination over Palestinian townships below.[15] Ultimately, Begin was willing to renounce Israel's holdings in the Sinai in exchange for Israel's settler colonial project in the West Bank. He thereby fashioned himself the second creator of Israel – a country that was much larger than the one which the original founder and his late nemesis, the leftist Ben-Gurion, had achieved. At the end of August, just before Sharon sketched the new settlement policy, Begin used his visit to Romania to reach out to Egypt. During Sadat's visit to Jerusalem, Israel's first right-wing prime minister recon-firmed his willingness to talk with all neighboring Arab states, but simultaneously insisted that Jews "took no foreign land" in Palestine but merely had "returned to our homeland."[16]

Under these circumstances, Sadat's gamble to get a comprehensive Arab peace with Israel by making a dramatic gesture could not succeed. Despite several rounds of diplomatic talks and even high-level meetings in late 1977 and the first half of 1978, the two sides could not agree on the Palestinian issue. Initially, President Carter was irritated by Sadat's and Begin's side-stepping of the American–Soviet-championed Geneva conference, but he eventually invited both to Camp David in September 1978 to break the deadlock. The Camp David framework agreements and the subsequent peace treaty of March 26, 1979, envisioned the end of Israeli–Egyptian belligerence, complete Israeli withdrawal from the Sinai, mutual diplomatic recognition, and free Israeli passage through the Suez Canal and the Straits of Tiran. They also included an agreement to a five-year transition period during which Israeli–Egyptian negotiations on withdrawal from the West Bank and Gaza and the establishment of a Palestinian state were supposed to occur.[17]

Begin thereby had bought five years of time to unfold his settlement policies toward East Jerusalem and the West Bank. In exchange for parliamentary endorsement of the peace treaty in March 1979, he promised Sharon he would allow the increase of settlement activities, designed to create "facts" on the ground before any agreement with Egypt about the Palestinian question was in reach. Indeed, Begin achieved much of what Theodor Herzl had dreamed in 1895 – virtually unrestricted Jewish settlement in all of Palestine. But Begin's Israel did not envision removing Palestinians or compensating them in the process. Instead, an increasingly tighter network of settlements was supposed to quarantine them, carve up their settlement patterns, and thereby undermine the chance to establish their own state.[18]

In comparison, Sadat received merely a separate peace that was territorially beneficial to Egypt. In the negotiation process, he had allowed Begin to pick and choose, which is what Nasser had feared Israel aimed at doing all along twenty years earlier. Moreover, both Nasser in early 1955 and Sadat in late 1970 had understood that any Egyptian politician who recognized Israel was gambling with his life. Upon hearing the news that the Egyptian president and the Israeli prime minister would jointly receive the Nobel Peace Prize in late 1978 for the Camp David Accords, President Carter noted in his diary: "Sadat deserved it; Begin did not."[19]

Arab Unity against Egypt

Sadat's hope that his trip to Jerusalem would trigger a positive Arab response was not fulfilled either. Syria, Iraq, Libya, Algeria, South

Yemen, and the PLO had all expected a solution at an international conference in Geneva – and they had received support from the USSR on that matter. A summit conference of self-declared progressive Arab states in Tripoli/Libya in early December 1977 was supposed to find unity in support of a Geneva conference, but Libya and Iraq demanded military action, and Baghdad's delegation even left early in protest. The compromise communiqué called for a diplomatic and economic boycott against Egypt and for its expulsion from the Arab League.[20] Sadat responded by cutting diplomatic relations with all five countries. Within a few days, he also closed the consulates and cultural centers of the USSR, Poland, Czechoslovakia, and East Germany in retaliation over Soviet support for the Tripoli meeting. Unsurprisingly, Jordan's King Hussein grew concerned about Arab disunity, but calmed down when he received Sadat's promise not to sign a separate agreement with Israel. Saudi Arabia feared that "fanatics" would "destroy" Sadat before long.[21]

Sadat's visit to Jerusalem threw Palestinians into a "hopeless situation," as Arafat told Yugoslavia's President Josip Broz Tito in December 1977. Most PLO cadres understood that Egyptian recognition of Israel had become inevitable, but they still hoped it would happen under the conditions of a prior Israeli acknowledgment of Palestinian rights. Ultimately, Arafat was unable to keep the radicals in the PLO under control. On February 18, a splinter group assassinated Yusuf al-Sibai, a close friend of Sadat and editor of the Egyptian daily *al-Ahram*, at a conference of the Afro–Asian People's Solidarity Organization in Cyprus, took hostages among the diplomats, and commandeered a civilian airliner.[22] As Arafat toured through the Soviet Union and East Germany to denounce Sadat's capitulationism, an amphibious PLO commando unit attacked Israel, killing thirty-six Israelis on March 11, 1978. Designed to undermine the Egyptian–Israeli talks, the operation provoked Begin into ordering an incursion into southern Lebanon to remove PLO military infrastructure there. The Israeli operation caused 700 civilian deaths and forced 225,000 to flee their homes. Ultimately, it also led to the creation of the United Nations Interim Force in Lebanon (UNIFIL), tasked with separating the PLO and Israel in southern Lebanon. In addition to the ensuing military weakness of the PLO, infighting and mutual assassinations among the various Palestinian factions increased.[23]

By the same token, Sadat's trip to Jerusalem damaged the status of the Palestinian superpower ally, the USSR, in the Middle East. Foreign Minister Andrei A. Gromyko publicly faulted Egypt and the United States for having wrecked the Geneva conference. Yet the sudden turn of events was only one of many symptoms of a larger decline in Soviet

Cold War policy, as an internal review of the world situation had revealed in June 1978. Domestic conflict in Ethiopia, which had recently turned toward the USSR after a coup, sapped Soviet diplomatic, military, and economic strength. The Baath Party in Iraq persecuted and executed communists. Afghanistan was sliding into internal chaos while its small communist party remained internally split. In East Asia, the PRC intervened in the domestic politics of reunified Vietnam and was in the process of dominating Cambodia, or so Moscow feared. In the North Atlantic world, détente with the West was collapsing. In short, the Soviet leaders recognized that they were facing a range of "complicated" problems along the entire periphery of their country.[24]

The Camp David Accords in September 1978 and the peace treaty the following March helped to unify the Arab world – against Egypt. The negative reactions of the self-declared progressive Arab players to the Camp David Accords were predictable. Syria saw itself forced to seek reconciliation with hardline Iraq in late October, and even agreed to joint action against "the imperialist–Zionist alliance" and "the treacherous Egyptian–Zionist agreements." The PLO protested against Egypt taking it upon itself to negotiate with Israel in the name of the Palestinians.[25] But disappointment also reigned on the side of the Arab moderates. Jordan's king was "absolutely shattered" by the Camp David Accords. Sadat had personally reassured Hussein during the negotiations at Camp David that Egypt would not pursue a bilateral agreement. In reality, however, Egypt had simply arrogated to itself the right to negotiate on a Palestinian state in the West Bank, a territory that was still formally Jordanian. Saudi Arabia was skeptical that Israel would ever concede on the West Bank, and was exasperated that Egypt had given up the third holiest city in Islam to the Jews. Arab League states met in early November in Baghdad to consult on further actions ... and reached a consensus. In the absence of Egypt, the radicals and moderates agreed not to hold any further league meetings in Cairo until Egypt had "returned to the fold," and to establish a common fund to support the economic and military needs of the PLO, the West Bank, Jordan, Syria, and Lebanon. Should Egypt sign a peace treaty with Israel, the Arab League would expel the organization's founding father and move its headquarters from Cairo to Tunis. Iraq and Syria were pleased to have forced the hand of the conservative and pro-American Saudi Arabia. Cairo was deeply disappointed by Riyadh's defection.[26]

Despite the Arab League's unified stand, Egypt signed the treaty with Israel on March 26, 1979. At the United Nations, the following day, Jordan accused Israel of undermining any chance of a comprehensive peace treaty by concurrently increasing its settlement activities. Saudi

Arabia, while admiring Carter's determination, was skeptical that the American president could ever get Israel to concede on the Palestinian issue. Indeed, once Carter left office in early 1981, his conservative successor Ronald Reagan was uncommitted to forcing Israel into any concession for almost two years. On March 27–31, 1979, the Arab League met in Baghdad, where it decided to expel Egypt, to move its headquarters to Tunis, and to commit all its members to cutting diplomatic relations with Cairo.[27]

As Egypt lost the friendship of other Arab countries, Sadat also earned the enmity of the Muslim Brothers and other Islamists. Starting as early as 1974, Islamist splinter groups had challenged the authority of the Egyptian state in a series of armed attacks on governmental institutions. After Sadat's return from Jerusalem, the Muslim Brotherhood condemned him for his rapprochement with Israel, in particular, and his pro-Western stances, liberal domestic policies, and failures in the economic sphere, in general. At the international level, the ninth and tenth Islamic Summits of the Saudi-led Organization of the Islamic Conference in April of 1978 and May of 1979, respectively, criticized Egypt for its policy toward Israel. Islamist activities in Egypt increased in 1980 and 1981 against the background of general unrest over the ailing economy and widespread frustration over Egypt's faltering Palestine talks with Israel. By September 1981, Sadat accused the Muslim Brothers, Islamists, and other opposition parties of conspiring against him. On October 2, his government launched a major political crackdown. During the military parade commemorating the anniversary of the start of the October War of 1973 four days later, soldiers with links to Islamist groups sprayed the main stand with bullets, killing nine people, including Sadat. The radical Islamists did not assassinate the Egyptian leader merely for making peace with Israel, but because he, as a self-professed devout Muslim, had failed to introduce an Islamic state in Egypt, and instead had collaborated with infidels – imperialists, Christian crusaders, communists, and Zionists.[28]

The Iranian Revolution

As the Arab world split from Egypt over Israel, Iran descended into revolution. Despite increasing popular dissatisfaction, few Iranians would have forecast in the spring of 1978 the radical transformations that would occur in their country within only one year. But over the course of twelve months, Iranians of virtually all political convictions overcame their long-standing fear of the Shah's brutal repression apparatus, joined demonstrations and strikes, and forced the hated monarch into exile in Egypt on January 16, 1979. On February 1, the Ayatollah

(Islamic scholar) Ruhollah Khomeini returned from France, where he had lived for four months after Iranian pressure had forced him out of his long-time exile in Iraq. After another ten days of clashes, the armed forces loyal to the departed Shah ended the fighting for what had clearly become a lost cause. Unwelcome in many countries, the Shah moved from Egypt to Morocco and then to Mexico. On October 22, 1979, President Carter allowed him to enter the United States temporarily for cancer treatment. After a short stay in Panama, the Shah received political asylum from Sadat in March 1980 for the last four months of his life. The Egyptian leader thereby wanted to express his gratitude for Iranian support during the October War in 1973, but only played into the hands of Egyptian Islamists, who started to see him as Egypt's Shah.[29]

Khomeini seemed an unlikely figure to lead the revolution in Iran. But his opposition to the Shah since the early 1960s and a hare-brained slander campaign by the monarch's regime in 1978 transformed him into a figure of integration for Iranians even beyond Islamist circles. In turn, this provided him with enormous charismatic power to implement an Islamist revolution that only a minority of Iranians endorsed. Within less than a fortnight of Khomeini's return to Iran, the provisional government installed by the Shah made way for a provisional revolutionary government headed by the moderate Islamist Mehdi Bazargan. Despite his charismatic power, Khomeini understood that assuming full control would take time, which is why he let a coalition government between Islamists and secularists run the country for a while. Simultaneously, he increased his appeal by focusing on socio-economic reform that benefited the impoverished masses. The non-Islamist coalition partners realized far too late that Khomeini was working for the implementation of the Islamist agenda he had developed during the 1970s in Iraqi exile. His Islamic Iran was supposed to look like a democracy but in reality it was supervised by a parallel structure of religious institutions from backstage, not unlike the Soviet system, in which the communist party controlled the government from behind the scenes. Once the new Islamic constitution was written in October, zealots among Khomeini's followers exploited Carter's decision to let the Shah enter the United States temporarily for medical treatment and occupied the US embassy on November 4. In its wake, Bazargan's coalition government collapsed.[30]

Before his return to Iran in February 1979, Khomeini had publicly announced that the new Iran would be non-aligned and abstain from interfering in the affairs of other countries. In reality, Khomeini rejected the international system of states on principle. In his conception of the world, states were the products of man's limited imagination; all of humankind was supposed to live as one under the rule of God, as revealed in the Quran. Khomeini not only aimed at establishing an Islamic order throughout the world, but also believed that his Iran was divinely mandated to do so. This meant not only that he rejected making tactical alliances with either of the two superpowers – or even playing them against each other – but also that he rebuffed the international system that they were leading. All of these ideas found their way into the constitution of the Islamic Republic of October 1979. Its adoption in an engineered referendum on December 2–3, four weeks after the fall of Bazargan's coalition government, allowed Khomeini to implement the Islamization of Iran in the following years. Once the new internal order was established, the Iranian *ulama* and sympathetic religious scholars from the Arab world – mostly Shia but also some Sunni – decided during a March 1982 conference to launch coordinated policies to carry the Islamic Revolution into all of the Middle East and eventually the whole world. In many respects, the ambitious and utopian nature of Khomeini's challenge to the existing world order – including his rejection of states as its constituent parts – had striking similarities to Lenin's challenge to the bourgeois-imperialist world order after the Bolshevik Revolution in 1917.[31]

In the meantime, Khomeini's Iran implemented revolutionary foreign policies whenever opportunities arose. The radicalized students who seized the US embassy on November 4 acted on their own, with no plan to stay there for more than a few days. Within hours they obtained Khomeini's endorsement. Initially, he exploited the militancy of the radicalized students not only for the purpose of undermining Bazargan's coalition government but also for the goal of parading the impotence of the "Great Satan," the United States, before the world's eyes. The seizure of fifty-two US citizens, who were released only in early 1981 after 444 days of captivity, was a political windfall for Khomeini, as was the botched US military rescue attempt in April of 1980.[32] Members of the same group that occupied the US embassy also tried to occupy the British mission on the evening of November 5, 1979, but Khomeini's office ordered them to retreat within hours. After the Soviet intervention in Afghanistan in late December (see below), Afghani protesters and their radicalized Iranian student supporters stormed the Soviet embassy on January 1 and were able to replace the Soviet flag with the green flag of the Islamic Republic before Iranian security forces expelled them. In August 1980, however, Khomeini for the first time also called the USSR "a Satanic superpower" given its concurrent attempts to suppress Islam in Afghanistan.[33]

American and Soviet views of Iran's revolution were tainted by their respective Cold War perceptions. The Carter administration had remained loyal to the anti-communist Shah until the end. Afterward, the United States continued to see Iran within the context of the containment of the USSR. At least, an internal national security assessment from the period between Khomeini's return on February 1 and the conclusion of the Egyptian–Israeli Peace Treaty on March 26 called for greater attention to "Islamic fundamentalism." Washington understood that political Islam was *both* anti-American and anti-Soviet. But the report still raised concerns about the possibility of the USSR using unrest in the region to make further inroads, given the communist coup in Afghanistan in April 1978 (see below) and the participation of the Tudeh (Communist) Party in the anti-Shah revolution in Iran more recently. After mid year, the United States tried to establish relations with Bazargan's coalition government. But the perception of an impending Iranian rapprochement with the United States and Carter's decision to allow the Shah medical treatment motivated students to seize the US embassy in the first place, which in turn drove Washington and Tehran into deeper hostility toward each other.[34]

In comparison, the Soviet Union initially welcomed the overthrow of the Shah and saw a revolutionary opportunity in Khomeini's return. The USSR was convinced that Iran's endorsement of Non-Alignment and the inclusion of the Tudeh Party in the revolution would lead to an anti-imperialist and possibly pro-Soviet stance. By June 1979, however, Moscow had grown disappointed with Tehran's increasing "anti-Sovietism" and Khomeini's refusal to see the USSR as a "natural ally." Soviet party leaders also misread the imposition of Islamist rule after December 1979 as the implementation of progressive reforms.[35] Only by September 1980 did Moscow register Tehran's hostility, which had increased after the Soviet intervention in Afghanistan. To a certain degree, the USSR had fallen for the overly optimistic but ideologically slanted reports from the Tudeh Party. Although Iran's communist party had suffered from political suppression as early as mid 1979, it continued to support Khomeini's supposedly progressive policies for several years. In 1983, Tudeh Party members were arrested *en masse*, the party was declared illegal, and ten of its leaders were executed within a year.[36]

In the Arab Middle East, the Iranian Revolution received an unsurprisingly hostile reception, even though Khomeini's takeover happened at a time when the Arab League was united against its founding father Egypt. Anti-Zionism, dissatisfaction with Sadat, and the dream of liberating Jerusalem could all have served as elements of cohesion between Khomeini's Iran and the Arab League. But the Sunni Arab regimes at the Gulf all had significant Shia minority populations, with Bahrain even being Shia-majority, and thus primarily feared a spillover of the revolution from Shia Iran. The Saudi monarchy in particular was nervous after it had sought reconciliation with the Shah's regime in 1977. Despite its disappointment with the US-brokered Israeli–Egypt peace treaty and its adoption of Iraq's hardline position within the Arab League on this issue, Saudi Arabia still saw the Iranian Revolution as the greatest danger to stability in the Middle East. As early as mid 1979, anti-communist Riyadh hence sought close economic and military cooperation with Washington; the Soviet intervention in Afghanistan in December additionally strengthened this burgeoning strategic partnership.[37] Arab fears of the Iranian threat were not groundless. Khomeini's Iran boycotted the Saudi-led Organization of the Islamic Conference in early 1980 simply by ignoring it completely. Instead, the Arab-language programs of Radio Tehran tried to stoke Shia unrest in Saudi Arabia. Moreover, the rise of the Islamic Republic attracted thousands of disaffected Shia youth from the Gulf countries, Iraq, Syria, and Lebanon, who received training in asymmetrical warfare, guerilla fighting, and suicide missions to create instability abroad and thereby further the Islamic Revolution there. Throughout the 1980s, Iranian pilgrims were involved in incidents in Mecca that were designed to discredit the Saudi monarchy as the guardian of the two holiest Muslim sites.[38]

The PLO, however, saw a political opportunity in the rise of the Islamic Republic at the very moment when Egypt and Israel were about to sign the peace treaty. In January 1979, Arafat had contacted Khomeini in Paris in a move to mobilize additional opposition to the peace treaty. On February 17, the Palestinian leader arrived unannounced in Tehran at the head of a large delegation. Arafat hoped to receive military support after Egypt had left the anti-Israeli front. Within two days, Khomeini handed over the former Israeli consulate as embassy building to the PLO. The Islamic Republic also stopped oil shipments to Israel and cut relations with Egypt. However, ideological differences between the Palestinian nationalist and the Islamist leader soon emerged. Unlike Arafat, Khomeini wanted to transform the Arab struggle against Zionism and for Palestinian nationhood into one by all Muslims against the worldwide enemies of Islam. When Arafat offered mediation between Tehran and Washington after the embassy seizure, Khomeini's support for the PLO quickly waned.[39]

Then, on September 22, 1980, Iraq attacked Islamic Iran. Its new supreme leader, Saddam Hussein, had come to power in July 1979 after purging the Baath Party. The secular country of 17–20 million Arabs marshalled numerous reasons for launching a war against the Islamist neighbor of 55–60 million mainly non-Arabs. Saddam's Iraq wanted to reverse a five-year-old Algerian-brokered agreement with Iran that had divided the oil-rich Shatt el-Arab at the Persian Gulf. The seeming popularity of the Islamic regime in Tehran also was an existential threat to the unpopular Baathist regime in Baghdad, particularly given that Iraq's large Shia minority had hosted Khomeini during his long exile. Finally, the disintegration of the Shah's army after the Islamic Revolution seemed to offer the opportunity for well-armed Iraq to incorporate Iran's Arab provinces while posing as the protector of the Arab world against Persian ascendency in the wake of Egypt's expulsion from the Arab League. Saddam falsely hoped that his military attack would quickly undermine Khomeini's regime and lead to an easy victory. On the contrary, the war became a rallying cry for Iranians to close ranks behind the Islamic Republic. The eight-year-long, bloody conflict saw ups and downs in the military fortunes of both sides. Until the spring of 1982, it went in Iraq's favor, but in the following two years, Iran was on the offensive, with 1985 seeing an entrenchment, and the final two years witnessing Iranian battlefield domination once more. As the war turned in his favor in 1982, Khomeini demanded total Iraqi surrender, in accordance with the recent decision to export the Islamic Revolution in a systematic fashion. In a peculiar community of interests, both superpowers steadily supported Iraq with military supplies. But at different points in time, they also offered to sell weapons to Iran, either to put pressure on Iraq or for unrelated reasons. In the end, however, neither wanted Khomeini's revolution to be victorious.[40]

Iraq's attack on Iran was not only a military blunder but also shattered the recently established Arab unity against Egypt. Oddly, conservative Arab states lined up behind leftist Iraq for anti-Iranian reasons while the PLO abandoned Iran in the expectation of a quick Iraqi victory. But the radical regimes in Damascus, Tripoli, and Algiers sided with the Islamic regime in Tehran. Particularly Syria's Assad rejected Saddam Hussein's claim to Arab leadership. As an Alawite, he shared Shia Iran's anti-Sunni reflexes, agreed with its strident anti-Zionism, and considered the Iraqi initiation of war an American-inspired scheme to smother the flame of anti-imperialism and non-alignment in Iran. Sadat's Egypt quickly declared neutrality in the conflict between its Arab rival and its Islamist enemy. This turned out to be a wise choice in the long-term, even if Sadat himself did not harvest the fruits of his decision. In need of a strong military ally against Khomeini's Iran, conservative and even radical members of the Arab League alike sought rapprochement with the banished founding father, and eventually welcomed Egypt back into the fold in 1987.[41]

Saudi Arabia

Across the Persian Gulf, Saudi Arabia did not experience an Islamist revolution in 1979, but still faced an Islamist revolutionary challenge to its own pan-Islamist project. Under King Faisal's leadership before 1975, Saudi Arabia had risen to prominence in the Arab world on the basis of its policy of triple containment of Nasserite Egypt, Soviet communism, and Israel. Following the Suez Crisis in 1956, Riyadh had been willing to associate with Washington without entering into a formal alliance. Thus, in the early 1970s, Faisal supported Sadat's turn away from the USSR for anti-communist reasons, and agreed with his rapprochement with the United States for the purpose of overcoming the long-standing Arab–Israeli paralysis. But after the October War, the monarch also started to buy up shares of American oil companies operating in the kingdom to reduce the country's political and economic dependency on the United States.[42]

Despite the rapid modernization of Saudi Arabia in the 1960s and 1970s, the Saudi monarchy was able to maintain good relations with large sections of the Wahhabist *ulama*, whose support had been crucial for internal peace and the maintenance of dynastic rule for two centuries. In exchange for the right to enforce the conservative lifestyles of the king's subjects, the *ulama* acquiesced to its own economic decline as oil proceeds paid to the monarchy gradually exceeded income to the religious establishment from pilgrims to Mecca and Medina. Still, Saudi Arabia could not insulate itself from the rise of Islamist politics. On the one hand, Faisal himself had supported oppositional Islamists abroad – in Egypt and Pakistan, for example – since the early 1960s. On the other hand, the clash of religious conservatism and rapid modernization had created a homegrown Islamist scene, particularly among ultra-conservative lower-class theology students at the Islamic University in Medina. These students rejected the kingdom's relationship with the United States while charging the royal family with corruption, apostasy, and associating with infidels.[43]

On the morning of November 20, 1979 – the first day of the year 1400 in the Islamic calendar – a radical Islamist group seized the Grand Mosque in Mecca, the holiest place of Islam, with thousands of pilgrims in it. The group was funded, armed, and supported by a Saudi network of businessmen, military officials, and even members of the *ulama*. Its leader claimed to be the *Mahdi*, the prophesied messiah who would rid the world of all evil before the Day of Judgement. The Islamist seizure of the center of Islam, which had been so crucial to the legitimacy of the Saudi kingdom since the mid 1920s, and the claim to have the religious right to judge the royal family, the *ummah*, and even the world of infidels beyond was a direct challenge to the ruling monarchy. Moreover, the news of the seizure paralleled unrest among the marginalized Shia minority populations in eastern Saudi cities. Even more embarrassing to the monarchy was the inability of its own security forces to retake the mosque from the hundreds of heavily armed radicals. Eventually, the Saudi royal house, which was supposed to guard the holiest sites of Islam against infidels, resorted to the help of French special forces to break the Islamist occupation of the Grand Mosque. After a hastily arranged cursory conversion to Islam, they succeeded in doing so on December 4.[44]

After defeating the radical occupiers of the mosque, the Saudi monarchy quickly grabbed the offensive in rewriting the narrative of the Islamist challenge to its rule. The extensive damage to the building was hurriedly and secretly repaired. Saudi Arabia downplayed the number of casualties among the pilgrims, its security forces, and the radicals. Observers estimated the toll to stand at over one thousand. In a show of force and political determination, sympathizers were rounded up and imprisoned. Sixty-three captured radicals were publicly beheaded in eight different Saudi cities in early 1980 as a deterrent. In order to co-opt potential future radicals, the monarchy and the *ulama* enforced ultra-conservative lifestyles, which particularly affected women. But the radical challenge in Mecca echoed in the wider Muslim world. A fortnight into the Iranian occupation of the US embassy in Tehran, Khomeini exploited the incident in Mecca for propaganda about supposed American and Israeli schemes against Islam. The radical occupiers of the Grand Mosque inspired both Egyptian Islamists, who would assassinate Sadat in 1981, and Saudi sympathizers, many of whom would soon decide to go to Afghanistan to defend their co-religionists against the invading Soviet infidels.[45]

Afghanistan

Afghanistan had been sliding into internal disorder long before the communist coup in April 1978 and the Soviet intervention twenty months later. King Zahir's perfunctory attempt to introduce parliamentary rule had triggered a bloodless takeover by the monarch's cousin Daud and then the establishment of a republic in 1973. Led by local army units, the coup by the small communist party on April 27, 1978, was the first successful one in a series of competing attempts by the army and the small, home-grown Islamist movement. On April 30, a revolutionary council announced the creation of the Democratic Republic of Afghanistan, headed by President Nur Muhammad Taraki. However, the success of the coup came as a surprise to most observers. The Afghan communists had not established a party until 1965. Within two years, it had split into two rival factions, one led by the party's General Secretary Taraki, and the other by his deputy Babrak Karmal. After the coup in 1978, Taraki managed to outmaneuver Karmal, who went into exile abroad. Karmal's followers joined him there, or were imprisoned or even executed. Alone in power, Taraki's faction not only fell into internal conflict between the president himself and his new deputy, Hafizullah Amin, but also misread the supposedly revolutionary atmosphere in the country. By early 1979, all but four of the twenty-eight provinces had experienced rebellions.[46]

The USSR greeted the Afghan Revolution as a "fortunate" development – the first socialist revolution at the Soviet border since the Chinese Revolution in 1949, and the first ever in the larger Middle East. But Soviet leaders understood that the communist party was small, internally divided, and confronted with the difficult task of attracting the "Islamic-clerical chieftains" of the "tribes." As early as June 1978, however, Moscow placed the Afghan Revolution into the arch of other problematic developments in the larger Middle East. The Soviet leaders worried about the continued persecution of communists in Iraq, the fraternal infighting within the PLO, and the rising civil war in Ethiopia, which might lead to the breakaway of an Egyptian-dominated Eritrea. In Afghanistan itself, or so Soviet leaders believed, counter-revolutionary infiltration by the Muslim Brotherhood, the Pakistani government, the CIA, and Afghan "reactionary forces" threatened peace and stability. Despite all these warning signs, the USSR agreed to the Afghan request to sign a twenty-year friendship and cooperation treaty, which included economic, military, and organizational support, in December 1978.[47]

As Soviet advisers and their families entered Afghanistan, they were not immune to the insurgency. During an uprising in the provincial capital Herat in mid March 1979, several Soviet citizens were killed. In its aftermath, the Afghan government called for a Soviet military intervention but received a rebuff. Moscow feared that this would threaten détente with Washington, expected that Iran, Pakistan, the PRC, and the United States would oppose the intervention, and understood that its troops would fight against the majority of the Afghan people. Yet, at the same time, the Soviet leaders were afraid that a lack of action might lead to a loss of Afghanistan to the United States in the global Cold War. Moreover, the USSR was unnerved by the excitement which the Islamist revolution in Iran and the resistance against Afghan communism created in its own Muslim regions in the Trans-Caucasus and Central Asia.[48]

By mid September, the situation in Afghanistan deteriorated once more. Taraki tried to move against his deputy-turned-rival Amin to pre-empt a coup, but ended up imprisoned and then dead within less than a month. The clearly perceptible anti-Sovietism of Khomeini's revolution, the US dispatch of a naval force to the Persian Gulf in response to the events in Iran, and the fear that "Amin ... [would] walk the path of union with imperialism, as Sadat in Egypt had done," led the Soviet leaders to rethink their stance on Afghanistan. In the absence of the skeptical but ailing Soviet Premier Aleksei N. Kosygin, KGB Chairman Yuri V. Andropov, Defense Minister Dmitri F. Ustinov, and Foreign Minister Andrei A. Gromyko convinced the sick Leonid I. Brezhnev on December 12 – the day of the NATO double-track decision – to agree to a military intervention that aimed at saving the Afghan Revolution by replacing Amin with the exiled Karmal.[49]

Convinced that the operation would last only a few months – similar to the one in Czechoslovakia in 1968 – the USSR blundered into its own eight-year quagmire – as the United States had done in 1965 in Vietnam. Soviet special forces landed at Kabul airport on December 22–23, attacked Amin's residence on the 27th, and executed him the following day. By January, the Soviet Union still believed that it would be able to withdraw its troops, which had grown to 75,000 in the meantime, within a few weeks. But after another month, the Soviet army had taken over the fight against insurgents, who were hiding among the civilian population, from the disintegrating Afghan army. Andropov understood that the USSR had passed a point of no return with the intervention; backing out after two months would have been a sign of weakness in the global Cold War. By May, CPSU Central Committee member Boris N. Ponomarev admitted to Eastern European party representatives that Afghanistan had created many obstacles to the hoped-for Soviet-led transformation of global "anti-socialism" into global "anti-imperialism."[50]

Throughout 1979, the US government had been occupied with Israeli–Egyptian negotiations and the Iranian Revolution. Still, the Afghan drama injected itself into US policy-making on February 14, when a communist splinter group kidnapped US Ambassador Adolph Dubs. The American diplomat was killed the following day in a firefight with Afghan and Soviet forces sent to free him. Within a week, Washington cut its development aid to Kabul, and after another month, the United States warned the USSR not to intervene in Afghanistan. In the spring, American newspapers observed the similarities between the contemporaneous Afghanistan and the Vietnam of the early 1960s. Moscow faced the same dilemma that Washington had encountered: whether or not to engage in a hostile country in support of an unpopular government. In July, Carter approved a covert program of medical aid and propaganda support for the insurgency. Despite intelligence that the USSR was preparing an intervention, the United States was caught off guard in late December 1979 when it actually happened.[51]

In a letter to Brezhnev on December 28, Carter called the Soviet intervention in a "previously non-aligned country" a "threat to the peace," and compared it to the past Soviet interventions in Hungary and Czechoslovakia. The US government reacted by imposing political and economic sanctions – the withdrawal of the second Strategic Arms Limitation Treaty (SALT II) from consideration in Congress, the cancellation of grain supplies, and a boycott of the Olympic Games in Moscow in the summer of 1980. On January 23, Carter announced in Congress that the United States would repel any outside intervention in the Persian Gulf area, which his administration believed was the focus of Soviet strategy in the wake of instability caused by the Afghan communist and the Iranian Islamist revolutions. Along the lines of this threat perception, the American president approved the delivery of US-made rifles to Afghan insurgents. American diplomats even asked Egypt to provide Soviet-produced arms, which US military planes flew to Pakistan for onward supply to Afghanistan.[52]

It was at this juncture that the combined networks of new Islamic solidarity and old Cold War partnerships between Pakistan, Saudi Arabia, and the United States sprang into action. In need of redefining Pakistan's national identity and in an attempt to buy off the Islamist opposition, Prime Minister Zulfikar Ali Bhutto had rewarmed Pakistani concepts of pan-Islamism from the 1940s, and then even adopted Islamist policies at home after 1971. He had also supported Afghan Islamists opposing Daud's regime in Kabul, while he had relied on Saudi Arabia to act as a patron for Pakistan's inclusion in the wider Middle East. Eventually, Bhutto was overthrown in July 1977 by an unlikely alliance ranging from secular leftists to Islamists. But his successor, General Muhammad Zia-ul-Haq, continued Pakistan's Islamization at a greater pace, and even received the support of the aging Abul Ala Maududi, who had opposed the creation of Pakistan three decades earlier. After the Afghan coup in April 1978, Pakistan provided military supplies to some of the anti-communist insurgents, served as their organizational rear base, and was the recipient of an increasing stream of refugees. Taraki's overthrow in September 1979 convinced the Pakistani foreign ministry of the imminence of a Soviet military intervention. Early the following year, Zia saw Soviet actions in Afghanistan in a similar light to Soviet collusion with India in the dismemberment of Pakistan in 1971 – as a Soviet imperialist attempt to undermine, divide, and dominate countries at the superpower's periphery.[53]

As the Afghan Revolution unfolded, Pakistan's and Saudi Arabia's relations with the United States greatly improved. The Afghan crisis helped to overcome the chill between Islamabad and Washington that had emerged over Pakistan's nuclear bomb project. Similarly, the Iranian Revolution and the seizure of the Grand Mosque in Mecca had triggered the deepening of the long-standing anti-communist partnership between Saudi Arabia and the United States, as described above. At the turn of 1979/80, Saudi Arabia placed the Soviet intervention in Afghanistan in the context of the "chaos" in Iran. But the Pakistani–Saudi–American alignment of interests was one only among *governments*, each of which perceived external Cold War threats and, in the Pakistani and Saudi cases, were under intense Islamist, and even anti-American, *popular* pressure at home. On November 21, 1979, for example, Pakistani Islamist students burned down the US embassy in Islamabad after rumors had spread that the United States and Israel were behind the seizure of the Grand Mosque in Mecca, which home-grown Saudi Islamists had occupied the previous day.[54]

The Afghan insurgents who rose up in 1979 against the Soviet intervention were not an internally cohesive force. Resistance in the initial period occurred in an uncoordinated manner and in successive spasms at different locations. Much of the resistance was led by members of the *ulama*, which traditionally had been independent from the government. Apart from disagreements with the Shia minority, the Sunni majority itself was also internally divided. Foreign Islamists who called for *jihad* against the infidel invaders and their Afghani allies were rare in Afghanistan itself at the time of the Soviet intervention, although homegrown Islamists had received targeted Pakistani support since Bhutto had come to power in the early 1970s. Many of them had studied in Pakistan and Egypt in the 1950s and the 1960s, where they had come under the influence of the writings of Maududi and Sayyid Qutb, respectively. *Jihadi* influence greatly increased only in March 1980, when seven exiled groups formed a shaky alliance in Pakistan. The radical Islamists among them aimed at the creation of an Islamic state in Afghanistan. Others primarily worked for the liberation of their homeland from infidel occupation. Still, the geographical and political closeness of these *mujahideen* (holy warriors) to the Pakistani government allowed them to benefit from the flow of external aid. Only over the full course of the eight-year conflict, however, did the radical Islamists become the spokesmen of the resistance, crowding out local and moderate Afghan groups.[55]

From January 1980 on, Pakistan controlled the influx of external military aid from the United States, Egypt, China, the United Kingdom, France, and Israel. The purpose was to manage resistance activities while keeping aid clandestine to avoid providing the USSR with a pretext to expand military activities beyond Afghanistan. American military aid increased sharply after Ronald Reagan's ascent to the US presidency in early 1981. That the United States worked together indirectly with anti-American Islamists seemed not to have weighed much on the minds of US decision-makers, as long as the two sides collaborated in resisting the same enemy – the Russian infidels in Islamist eyes, the Soviet communists in the American view. But the external military support for the chosen radical groups had long-term effects on Afghanistan and the world. Unlike the second Vietnam War that lasted from 1964 to 1975 and ended with a central government in firm control of the whole country, the equally long Afghan War caused the complete destruction of Afghanistan's state, society, and infrastructure. Furthermore, the long and brutal war was a breeding and training ground for hardline Islamists, 25,000 of whom were foreign fighters who would carry their war experience into the world after Soviet withdrawal in 1989. In the end, Egypt and Saudi Arabia provided not only military and financial aid to these groups, but also exported their own domestic Islamists, who rejected the secular Egyptian state – led by Sadat and his successor Hosni Mubarak – and the supposedly apostate Saudi monarchy, respectively.[56]

With the Soviet intervention in Afghanistan at the turn of 1979/80, Khomeini's Iran encountered a complex problem at its eastern border. The intervention occurred just at the time when the Islamization of Iran began. Afghan Shia were split among themselves and about the communist government. Tehran faced the elementary dilemma of whether to over-throw the communist regime in Kabul in an informal alignment with the Great Satan in Washington, or to pursue an independent policy against the other Satan in Moscow. Only by late 1981 did Iran formulate a coherent policy that aimed at excluding both superpowers from the whole "Islamic world." It demanded the creation of a Pakistani–Iranian peacekeeping force that would replace the Soviet occupation in Afghanistan and establish a state along the lines of the Islamic Republic of Iran. The existence of a bilateral force from neighboring Muslim countries was also supposed to remove the pretext for the United States to maintain a naval presence in the Gulf. Unsurprisingly, the USSR rejected the replacement of its client regime in Afghanistan with a "reactionary" Iranian puppet state. The implementation of the Iranian proposal would have doubled not only the number of Islamist countries at its southern border but also their appeal to Muslims in the Soviet Union. Pakistan similarly saw "no merit in the proposals," but still believed that any form of Iranian involvement would increase pressure on the USSR.[57]

Lebanon

While the Iranian Islamic Revolution and the Afghanistan War unfolded, Israel, the PLO, and Iran came to blows in Lebanon. As mentioned above, the arrival of the PLO in 1971 had undermined the precarious political stability between Sunni, Shia, Druze, and Christians in the

Lebanese population. After the civil war had started in 1975, the PLO used southern Lebanon as a staging ground for attacks on Israel. One of these attacks had provoked the Israeli intervention in March 1978, which in turn had led to the creation of UNIFIL. The following four years witnessed a period of relative stability in that part of the country but not in the rest, where intra-communal conflict – with Syria maintaining the balance among them – laid waste to the cities and the infrastructure of the country.[58]

Continued conflict in Lebanon opened up political opportunities for Begin to accelerate the implementation of his policy of *Eretz Israel* by sending Jewish settlers to East Jerusalem and the West Bank. This, however, triggered the resignation of Foreign Minister Moshe Dayan and Defense Minister Ezer Weizman, his internal critics, in October 1979 and May 1980, respectively. But developments in international relations still helped Begin to further his agenda. The election of Ronald Reagan in early November 1980 brought to power a president who was not only staunchly anti-communist but also steadfastly pro-Israeli. Yet the outbreak of the Iraq–Iran War six weeks earlier, on September 22, had posed a major security problem; a victory by either of the two equally anti-Israeli sides seemed not to be beneficial to the country's security. To keep the balance in the war, Israel clandestinely supported Khomeini's Islamic Iran in an effort to weaken Saddam's Iraq. In that vein, on October 14, 1980 – three weeks after the start of the Iraq–Iran War – the Israeli government began the planning for an air strike against the Iraqi nuclear bomb project. The attack on the Osirak nuclear reactor near Baghdad on June 7, 1981, was a military success. The daring military operation secured Begin's re-election three weeks later. Ariel Sharon, the architect of Jewish settlement policies in the West Bank, was subsequently elevated to defense minister in the new government.[59] Unsurprisingly in this situation, a Saudi proposal in August to jumpstart the Arab–Israeli peace process, which contained a withdrawal-for-recognition principle, met with immediate Israeli rejection. In any case, the plan collapsed at the Arab League meeting in Fez in late November because of the negative attitude of Syria, which collaborated closely with the non-member Iran on this issue. Three weeks later, Israel responded by annexing the Golan Heights in violation of the 1974 withdrawal agreement and the 1977 Camp David Accords. In the wake of Sadat's assassination in October of 1981, Begin also had started to dismantle the cosmetic Palestinian self-government, which he had allowed to emerge in the West Bank after late 1977.[60]

On June 6, 1982, Israel invaded Lebanon, easily overrunning the small number of UNIFIL peacekeeping troops in the south of the country. The pretext for the Israeli intervention was an assassination attempt on the

Israeli ambassador in London by a PLO splinter group. The war, however, was Sharon's brainchild. Planned since the summer of 1981, it had been scheduled to take place in the period after April 25, 1982, when the last Israeli troops had left the Sinai in line with the 1978/79 agreements. The war in Lebanon was supposed to destroy the PLO as a military threat and political organization, which in turn would have simplified the integration of the West Bank into Israel politically. The ensuing refugee stream to Jordan was supposed to make that kingdom into a Palestinian state, which would have further lessened international pressure to allow the creation of such an entity in the West Bank and East Jerusalem. In the process of the intervention, Begin's government also wanted to expel Syrian forces from Lebanon and impose a subservient, Christian-dominated government.[61]

Even if the Israel Defense Forces (IDF) succeeded in occupying the southern third of Lebanon and parts of Beirut, the war did not bring the expected results. The only tangible success was the US-brokered evacuation of the PLO from Lebanon to Tunisia in August 1982. What even Begin himself called a "war of choice" also triggered criticism within the IDF and the Israeli population at large, particularly with regard to the war's aggressive nature, the Israeli aerial bombing of Beirut, and the indiscriminate attacks by allied Christian militias on two Palestinian refugee camps in Beirut that cost several hundreds of civilian lives. In the end, Israel did not get a pliant client state in Lebanon. While it succeeded in having the Christian Bachir Gemayel elected as president on August 23 in a poll that was marred by Israeli interference, the new Lebanese leader was assassinated by pro-Syrian forces within three weeks. His brother Amine stepped in, but he had little legitimacy and was pro-Syrian anyway.[62]

Peace between Israel and Lebanon was not on the horizon, even though Israel's intervention had spurred Reagan on September 1, 1982, to propose both a "far-reaching peace effort" in the Middle East and the dispatch of American troops to oversee PLO withdrawal. At least, the American president finally confirmed his adherence to the Camp David Accords, particularly with regard to the Israeli withdrawal from many of the territories occupied since 1967, a "freeze" on Jewish settlement activities, the creation of a Palestinian entity in the West Bank and Gaza, and Arab recognition of Israel. After Bachir Gemayel's assassination and the ensuing resumption of fighting in Lebanon, France and Italy joined the United States to form the Multinational Force (MNF) to pursue the peace effort in Lebanon itself. Seeing his dreams in the West Bank threatened by Reagan's proposal, Begin rejected the US peace effort. But in the short run, Israel still benefited from American pressure on Lebanon, which resulted in the imposition of a *de facto* bilateral peace agreement on May 17, 1983.[63] But pro-Syrian, Shia, Druze, and Palestinian groups resisted the agreement because they saw its contents as a national humiliation and even rejected the Christian-led government that had signed it. By early 1984, Amine Gemayel was forced to renounce the agreement and resign; a multi-religious national reconciliation government officially abrogated it in March. Begin thereby had not only failed to obtain a lasting, Egyptian-style peace but also alienated the Lebanese people in the process. Even worse, Israel's intervention had strengthened Syria's position in Lebanon and convinced Moscow to make additional military and political commitments to Damascus and the PLO in the summer of 1982. Having chosen to go to war, Begin and Sharon faced the consequences of their hubris. The prime minister retired in August 1983 out of guilt over the unnecessary loss of Jewish life – but with no remorse over the 30,000 Arab deaths in Lebanon. Half a year before, the defense minister had been forced to resign over his role in the allied Christian-inflicted massacres of Palestinian civilians in Beirut's refugee camps. Ultimately, Israel's blunder strengthened the Lebanese Shia and Iran's influence. As the PLO pulled out in August 1982, Shia militias occupied its positions in southern Lebanon.[64]

Islamist Shia activism in Lebanon dated back to the early 1960s. While in exile in Iraq, Khomeini and his associates had helped to build up militias in Lebanon. In 1979, Lebanese Shia activists quickly established relations with revolutionary Iran. For Khomeini, the Israeli intervention in June 1982 was yet another proof of the moral and political bankruptcy of Arab governments and the PLO. Only Islamic ideology and the desire for martyrdom would be able to defeat American and Zionist imperialism, or so he believed. Within a week of the war's start, he sent the Revolutionary Guards to Lebanon – in line with the decision in March to export the Iranian Revolution – where they provided military support and political indoctrination to the local Shia population. Khomeini's Iran also opposed the dispatch of the American–French–Italian MNF as another infidel invasion of Muslim lands. Within weeks of the Israeli intervention, the Iranian ambassador in Syria initiated the foundation of Hizbullah (Party of God) in Lebanon, which permitted only Shia Islamists to join as members. Although the party's aim was to remake the dysfunctional, multi-confessional Lebanese state into a Shia Islamic one, its initial priority was a divinely mandated *jihad* against Zionism, support for the Palestinian cause, and the liberation of Jerusalem. In this context, Hizbullah saw the six Arab–Israeli wars (1948, 1956, 1967, 1973, 1978, and 1982) as closely tied to Western, particularly American, support for Zionism. Hizbullah's revolutionary, anti-imperialist discourse and its military activities appealed to some Lebanese (Shia) communists, who compared the party's activities in southern Lebanon to the Vietnamese guerilla experience a decade earlier in South Vietnam. Echoing Khomeini's call for martyrdom, the first Islamist suicide bombing attack occurred on November 11, 1982, against the IDF in Tyre.[65]

In 1983, more suicide attacks followed. On April 28, the truck bombing of the US embassy compound in Beirut killed 63 persons, including 17 American embassy personnel. A double truck bombing on October 23 killed 241 US marines and 58 French paratroopers. Within ten days, yet another truck bombing, once more in Tyre, killed 30 Israeli soldiers and 29 Lebanese and Palestinian prisoners. Hizbullah publicly called the attacks on the American embassy and the US marines a "punishment," but the United States subsequently was unable to establish a firm link between the suicide attackers and the Islamist party. After the October bombing, the Reagan administration was adamant that the United States "was not going to cut and run" but rather would continue national reconciliation in Lebanon. However, within two months, it dawned on the American president that the world was faced with a "fundamentally new phenomenon," though he was firmly convinced that "the problem of terrorism will not disappear if we run from it." In reality, however, the MNF pulled out by February and March of 1984, and the Reagan administration gave up on its own peace effort just at the moment when Lebanon abrogated the US-brokered deal with Israel.[66]

Conclusion

By the early 1980s, the Cold War ceased to be the critical structure that shaped the regional system in the Middle East – despite the Soviet intervention in Afghanistan in 1979. The Iraqi attack on Iran in 1980 was about leadership in the Arab world. The Israeli intervention in Lebanon two years later stemmed from the extravagant political aims of the Begin government. Iran's claims to export its revolution heralded a "new phenomenon" in international relations. Khomeini's ambitions were as grandiose as Lenin's six decades before – to transform the world according to his own ideological visions. The dichotomous superpower division of the world crumbled in the Middle East because Khomeinism and other strains of political Islam simply rejected it. Iran's foreign policy revealed this better than any other example: in Afghanistan, the Islamist country indirectly fought with the United States against the USSR, in Lebanon it struggled together with Soviet-allied Syria against the United States and Israel, and in the war against Iraq it battled against and occasionally fought alongside the superpowers.

The late 1970s thus witnessed a series of events that undermined the Cold War as an ordering principle in the region. Begin initiated what he considered the second birth of Israel by opposing Ben-Gurion's vision of Zionism. His aggressive pursuit of an *Eretz Israel* enabled him to make peace with Egypt while implementing a colonial policy that aimed at transforming all of Mandatory Palestine into Israel. Begin thereby turned the wheel of time back to the colonial and pre-Cold War period. His botched intervention in Lebanon at least checkmated Israel's appetite for more external adventures. The Egyptian–Israeli rapprochement transcended the long-standing superpower policy of finding a global solution to Middle Eastern problems by means of an international conference. On the Arab side, it accelerated the transformation of the anti-imperialist roots of political Islam into Islamist movements that rejected the Cold War. Some, such as the Egyptian Muslim Brothers, the Saudi radicals, and Afghan members of the *ulama* aimed at cleansing the *ummah* from infidel – Western and communist alike – influence at the national level. Others like Khomeini, the radical Afghani Islamists, the foreign fighters whom they attracted, and members of Hizbullah had a world revolutionary Islamist agenda. In essence, the international policies of the Islamists did not end the regional Cold War by resolving conflicts in the Middle East, but by transcending the international system which the global Cold War had fortified there. Starting from these kinds of political objectives, it was not difficult for Islamists – mostly Sunni, however – to arrive at the *jihadi* visions of the 1990s, which embraced attacking the outside world of the infidels on their turf – be it in the United States, post-Soviet Russia, or Europe – with the goal of affecting profound change in the Muslim world.[67] The superpowers were not completely blind to the rise of Islamism, but still perceived it in the context of the Cold War. In the spring of 1979, both Washington and Moscow noticed the threat of political Islam – mostly in its Iranian version – to their strategic interests. But their reactions were still shaped by age-old Cold War thinking. Instead of engaging with the rising post-Cold War world, they decided to contain it in Cold War fashion.

21 Asia

Three major factors defined the regional Cold War in Asia: the historical concord between the communist-led national liberation movements of China and Indochina since the 1920s, the antagonism between the United States and East Asian communist countries during the Cold War, and the Indian definition of non-alignment as an alternative to Cold War bloc formation. The late 1970s and early 1980s witnessed fundamental changes with respect to all three. While the concord had been under duress since the mid 1960s, three communist countries eventually went to war against each other in Indochina in 1978–79. The antagonism with the United States had been softened by Sino–American rapprochement in 1971–72 and the US military withdrawal from Indochina in 1973. But it was the emergence of anti-Vietnamese collaboration between the People's Republic of China (PRC), the United States, and the Association of Southeast Asian Nations (ASEAN) in 1978–79 that symbolized the transition from US containment of communism to a cross-ideological policy of restraining a rising regional hegemon – Vietnam. Finally, Non-Alignment experienced its political nadir in 1980. Associated with Hanoi and Moscow since the first half of the 1970s, Delhi emerged isolated in the world after it failed to censure the DRV for occupying Non-Aligned Cambodia in late 1978 and the Soviet Union for overrunning Non-Aligned Afghanistan a year later. Even worse, after India had managed to bring Pakistan and Islamic Iran into the Non-Aligned Movement in 1979, it quickly found itself at loggerheads with its Muslim neighbor, while it faced an embarrassing war between the founding Non-Aligned member Iraq and new member Iran in 1980. Early in the decade, Non-Alignment lost its credibility as an actor in the Cold War and its *raison d'être* as a force for peace.

Asia in the Mid 1970s

After the American opening toward China and the US withdrawal from Indochina, the Cold War in Asia remained fluid, similar to its counterpart in the Middle East. The PRC had undergone an economic resurgence since 1971 in parallel with the rebuilding of government and party structures. But these reforms did not put an end to Cultural Revolution strife within the Chinese leadership; the radical Gang of Four around Mao's wife Jiang Qing tried to block changes for years. It was not inconceivable that the radicals would try to seize power in September 1976 – after Zhou Enlai's and Mao Zedong's successive deaths within eight months. But Zhou's successor, Hua Guofeng, quickly had the Gang of Four arrested, terminated ideological radicalism among the top leaders, and secured the path toward economic transformation. The reform's eventual standard bearer, Deng Xiaoping, had questioned ideology as a means for economic development since mid 1959. By March 1975, he had even announced that the "socialist camp no longer exists, and that the concept of the two camps is not compatible with today's reality."[1]

The lack of development in Sino–American relations after US President Richard M. Nixon's seminal visit in 1972 was a major disappointment for the PRC, particularly since Sino–Soviet relations remained tense. At least, the PRC was pleased that the American "wolf has been thrown out" of Indochina by 1973, though it simultaneously understood that only this wolf was able to contain the Soviet "tiger." Thus, China was ready to accept the continued presence of US naval bases in the Philippines in the Western Pacific and on Diego Garcia in the Indian Ocean. Against this background, the Chinese leaders had developed, since the spring of 1973, what would become the Three-World theory, according to which the superpowers formed the First World, all of Europe, Canada, and Japan represented the Second World, and the underdeveloped rest came together as the Third World. With the goal of forming a global "'anti-hegemonist' united front" against the domineering superpowers, Beijing focused on the European Communities, which it misunderstood as a rising third military bloc.[2] But its long-term goal to lead the Third World ran into problems because of the deterioration of its relationship with Hanoi over the 1970s.

In comparison, 1975 was the year of triumph for the DRV. After three decades of struggle, it had unified Vietnam and established its political hegemony over Laos. But several blemishes diminished this double accomplishment. The Cambodian communist movement, which the DRV had helped to establish in the 1950s, emerged as an antagonist after its defeat of Lon Nol's pro-American government in the spring of 1975. At the same time, Hanoi reversed its temporary suspension of its world revolutionary agenda after American withdrawal in early 1973. Even before the final military push to unify the country at the turn of 1974/75, Vietnam's General Secretary Le Duan yet again dreamt about fulfilling "our international duty in South East Asia," i.e. about expelling US imperialism from and extending socialist hegemony over all of Indochina, Thailand, and eventually the whole of Southeast Asia. But Vietnam's relations with its long-term Chinese ally had been deteriorating over military and political strategy as early as the second half of the 1960s. In 1971, Hanoi had concluded that Beijing was marching "against the world revolutionary process" when the PRC pursued rapprochement with US imperialism.[3]

As Sino–Vietnamese relations deteriorated, the un-demarcated state of the bilateral borders led to low-level armed conflict as early as 1973. Hence, Hanoi was seeking closer relations with Beijing's main antagonists – Moscow and Delhi. It had anyway pursued a strategic partnership with the USSR since the start of the Cultural Revolution in the PRC in the mid 1960s. In Delhi, Hanoi found a partner that could help the DRV establish itself in the Afro–Asian world. India had recognized communist Vietnam in early 1972 in an attempt to detach it from the PRC and in the context of the simultaneous East Pakistan Crisis and Sino–American rapprochement. The South Asian country had also been instrumental in admitting the Provisional Revolutionary Government – the communist pseudo-government that the DRV had established in the southern part of the country – at the Non-Aligned Foreign Ministers Conference in Georgetown, Guyana, in August 1972. Three years later, a follow-up conference in Lima, Peru, even accepted unified Vietnam, the socialist associate of the USSR, as a member in its midst.[4]

India, in comparison, suffered from a range of domestic and foreign problems in the mid 1970s. Economically, the South Asian country had experienced several years of crisis, made worse by the OAPEC oil embargo in 1973–74. Its prime minister, Indira Gandhi, had faced accusations of election fraud since the national polls in the spring of 1971. On June 12, 1975, the High Court in Allahabad convicted her of a minor breach of the electoral law, which raised the likelihood of her political downfall. On the 25th, she declared a State of Emergency – the third since the Sino–Indian War in October 1962. In a circular letter to foreign statesmen, Gandhi claimed that the state of emergency served both to overcome the divisive domestic political climate and to implement necessary economic reforms which the opposition had blocked.[5]

In international affairs, the situation was not better. The nuclear test in May 1974 and the third State of Emergency thirteen months later both isolated India. After being broken up by its giant neighbor in 1971, Pakistan gladly seized on the nuclear test to paint India as a danger to world peace. Relations with Bangladesh soured in 1975, a year after Delhi had successfully prodded the two Muslim neighbors to establish formal relations. Further afield, a rapport with the PRC remained difficult to achieve, although Yugoslav mediation accomplished an agreement to exchange ambassadors in late 1975, after a hiatus of thirteen years.[6] But even after Mao's death, Gandhi entertained little hope of a resolution of the long-standing bilateral conflict. To increase India's room to maneuver, she had tried to improve relations with ASEAN in 1975. However, her country's firm support of the DRV – and a parallel Chinese political opening toward the association designed to exploit anti-Vietnamese feelings in Southeast Asia – ensured that Gandhi's initiative failed. Above all, her country's relations with the United States remained unfriendly because of the Sino–American rapprochement, the US naval presence on Diego Garcia, and Washington's criticism of Delhi's nuclear program.[7]

The only silver lining was the continued good relationships with the USSR (despite Soviet misgivings about the Indian nuclear test), anti-imperialist Vietnam, and the Non-Aligned Movement. Surprisingly, the nuclear test did not do much to undermine India's standing within the Non-Aligned Movement, although the country decided to keep a low profile at the Lima Foreign Ministers Conference in 1975 to evade anticipated criticism. But a year later, at the fifth tri-annual Non-Aligned Conference in Colombo, India cooperated closely with Yugoslavia and the host Sri Lanka (formerly Ceylon) to contain the radical communist members – like Cuba – even if it could not prevent the Caribbean island from being selected as host for the sixth tri-annual conference in September 1979.[8]

Toward the Cambodian Crisis, 1977–78

In the late 1970s, a series of unrelated events triggered developments that would lead to the Vietnamese military invasion of Cambodia in December 1978 and the Chinese punitive war against Vietnam two months later. In the wake of formal reunification of the two Vietnams in mid 1976, the newly established Socialist Republic of Vietnam (SRV) had introduced economic reforms in the southern half of the country. This included the socialization of private businesses, which often happened to belong to members of the Hoa, the Chinese ethnic minority, whom the new government anyway suspected of being counter-revolutionary. On top of economic persecution came political pressure to renounce Chinese citizenship, which altogether triggered the collapse of Sino–Vietnamese relations by mid 1978. Similar to Maoist claims about Soviet revisionism fifteen years earlier, the SRV publicly accused the PRC of turning from a socialist friend into a "reactionary" enemy. Hanoi even announced a "Cold War" between the two erstwhile communist allies. At the same time, relations between Vietnam and Cambodia, led by Khmer Rouge leader Pol Pot, worsened over territorial disputes, the treatment of the Vietnamese minority there, and Phnom Penh's anxieties over Hanoi's domination of Laotian politics. More importantly, the SRV had not given up its world revolutionary goals. After obtaining Non-Aligned membership in 1975, it dreamt of turning the movement – in cooperation with Cuba and other "avant-gardist countries" – into an instrument for fighting US imperialism on a global scale. Responding to an ASEAN offer to develop relations in 1977, Hanoi officially announced the pursuit of a policy of peaceful coexistence but clandestinely remained committed to the support of "revolution in Southeast Asia."[9]

The deterioration of Sino–Vietnamese relations paralleled, and to a certain degree even triggered, the Sino–American establishment of full diplomatic relations by January 1, 1979. During most of 1977, however, Beijing's post-Cultural Revolution leadership focused on stabilizing the government and the economy. On December 17, eventually, Deng called on all Asian countries "to solve their disagreements in mutual consultations and without the interference of the superpowers." A month later, China and Japan initiated negotiations on a peace treaty that was supposed to conclude World War II in East Asia and end their ancillary Cold War antagonism. It benefited from Japan's determination to follow a more independent and assertive policy since Sino–American rapprochement and US withdrawal from Vietnam earlier in the decade. The treaty was signed on August 12, 1978. The previous May, Deng had even emphasized to foreign diplomats that the arrest of the Gang of Four had "reopened the path to *sihua*" (Four Modernizations), which Mao's ideological radicalism had repeatedly stymied for a quarter of a century. By December, the third plenum of the Eleventh Central Committee officially approved the modernization program, thus marking the beginning of China's rise to this day. But Deng's launch of *sihua* required closer relations with the world's technologically most developed country – the United States. Alas, throughout most of 1977 the new US president, Jimmy Carter, focused on the Middle East. However, Soviet and Cuban military support for Ethiopia in its conflict with Somalia over Ogaden eventually alarmed the United States. In order to counter the perceived Soviet foray into the Horn of Africa and possibly the Middle East, the Carter administration decided in the spring of 1978 to play the China card. Against the background of the collapsing Sino–Vietnamese relationship, Washington and Beijing negotiated normalization in the three months leading up to mid December 1978.[10]

Sino–American normalization talks caught Hanoi on the wrong foot, just as the SRV visibly prepared for a war against Cambodia that aimed at achieving hegemony over all of Indochina. Normalization not only divulged that Hanoi's long-term policy of seeking rapprochement with Washington had been a pipe dream all along but it also deepened the Vietnamese exasperation over the discord with Beijing and China's ensuing support for Cambodia. To mask Vietnam's aggressive policy toward Cambodia and its revolutionary goals in Southeast Asia, Prime Minister Pham Van Dong visited the five ASEAN member countries in September and the first half of October. During his travels, he repeatedly reconfirmed Vietnam's commitment to peaceful coexistence while publicly renouncing Vietnamese plans of creating an Indochinese confederation. Prudent, his hosts remained skeptical about the sincerity of the Vietnamese peace offensive. Indeed, after his return home, Pham told the East German ambassador that his country would not honor any of its promises but instead continue to support revolutions in Southeast Asia.[11] Beijing, in turn, grew concerned about Vietnamese regional plans, which it considered "not an isolated development but a part of the Soviet strategic plans to prepare for a final war." Fearing Vietnamese duplicity, Deng followed in Pham's footsteps in the first half of November, though he could not dispel some of the historical mistrust about China's hegemonic goals. Still, in Thailand, he accused Vietnam of being the "Cuba of the Orient" that executed the policy of the Soviet "hegemonists" throughout all of Southeast Asia. As Deng toured ASEAN, Le Duan and Pham visited Moscow to sign a Treaty of Defense and Friendship on November 3. Even if this agreement turned the *supposedly Non-Aligned* SRV into a *formal Soviet Cold War ally*, it did not commit the USSR to military action in Indochina in the event of war. Its implicit goal was to deter the PRC in view of the impending war in Cambodia, which in turn drove Beijing further into Washington's arms. In order to get American diplomatic recognition quickly, Deng made far-reaching concessions on Taiwan to the Carter administration in late 1978.[12]

India's foreign policy in 1977–78 evolved against the background of these realignments in East Asia. In March of 1977, Indians went to the polls despite the two-year third State of Emergency. To the surprise of most observers, Indira Gandhi's Congress lost against the Janata (People's) Party, which had been founded just two months earlier and included former Congress ministers and members. Not only did Congress thereby squander its thirty-year control of the central government, but Gandhi herself failed even to keep her own seat in parliament. Janata's lack of political cohesion, its chronic internal squabbles, and its domestic policy failures quickly undermined popular respect for the new government, however. Its attempts to humiliate Gandhi through legal prosecution, including her short arrest in October 1977, further damaged its reputation while they helped to restore her popularity. In external affairs, however, Janata was more successful in its attempts at breaking with her foreign policy priorities. Within a short time, new foreign minister, Atal Bihari Vajpayee, announced that India would create equidistance from the superpowers by improving relations with the United States and maintaining its traditional friendship with the USSR. The country would return to being non-aligned in word and deed, develop its links to Southeast Asia even-handedly, and improve relations with all of its neighbors.[13]

But good will alone was not sufficient to refashion the complex web of foreign relations that the previous three decades had woven. President Carter's visit to India in early 1978 and the resumption of US aid after a seven-year suspension heralded the possibility of a new start following a decade of acrimonious relations. The main bone of contention, however, remained India's refusal to join the Nuclear Non-Proliferation Treaty of 1968, even if the new government called the 1974 test a mistake. India's negative stance was based on principle, not on fears about Chinese and future Pakistani nuclear capabilities. As long as other states continued to test nuclear devices and refused to disarm, Delhi would not sign. Out of fear that India under Janata might "do an Egypt" and turn to the United States, the USSR quickly dispatched Foreign Minister Andrei A. Gromyko in late April of 1977, only weeks after the elections. Delhi reassured Moscow it would observe the letter of the 1971 treaty but insisted that the relationship had to be mutually beneficial. In order to prove equidistance ahead of Carter's impending visit to India, new Prime Minister Morarji Desai and Vajpayee visited Moscow in October 1977.[14]

With Cuba scheduled to host the sixth tri-annual Non-Aligned Conference in September 1979, India focused on the preparatory meetings during the preceding eighteen months. Several Non-Aligned members had expressed concerns about pro-Soviet Cuba trying to weaken the movement's non-aligned nature. Yugoslavia also hoped to enlist India for a mediation attempt in the brewing conflict between the member states Vietnam and Cambodia. To make matters worse, the communist coup in Non-Aligned Afghanistan on April 27, 1978, forced the hurried relocation of a scheduled foreign ministers meeting from Kabul to . . . Havana, of all places! At the meeting in the Cuban capital, delegations from India, Yugoslavia, and Sri Lanka cooperated closely to block the host's attempts to present the Socialist Camp as the movement's natural ally. A second Foreign Ministers Conference in Belgrade in late July allowed Yugoslavia to push for a demonstration of unity and prevent another Cuban attempt to impose its anti-imperialist, i.e. anti-American, agenda. Havana failed mainly because of the resistance by moderate participants and African countries that faced Cuban military interventions on their continent. Arab member states at least managed to agree on the text of a declaration in support of Palestinian rights, despite their internal controversies following Egypt's President Anwar Sadat's surprise visit to Jerusalem in November 1977.[15]

Similarly, the new Indian government tried to undo Indira Gandhi's pro-Vietnamese tendencies in the country's policy toward ASEAN, but faced difficulties given popular Indian opinion, which held Vietnam's thirty-year anti-imperialist struggle in high esteem. Also, the Vietnamese government had invited Indian companies to invest and help reconstruct the recently unified country without attaching political conditions. Moreover, the Janata government underestimated the scope of Vietnamese hegemonic aims; it was not concerned at all about the breakdown of Sino–Vietnamese relations, the Vietnamese–Soviet alliance, or even the possibility of Vietnamese expansionism.[16]

With regard to South Asia, Janata-ruled India tried to improve relations as well. In late 1977, it settled a long-standing dispute with Bangladesh over the use of Ganges waters. The circumstance that Janata was not associated with the thirty-year-long hostility toward Pakistan also worked in favor of the new government. In a gesture of good will, India decided not to react to Pakistan's propaganda campaign on Kashmir in May 1977 – a political response unthinkable in previous years. Delhi also welcomed London's proposal a year later to readmit Pakistan to the Commonwealth after the Muslim country had left the organization in protest over UK recognition of Bangladesh. Beyond Pakistan, however, long-time Non-Aligned member Afghanistan gave the Janata government a headache, particularly after the coup in April 1978. India worked closely with the Shah's Iran to maintain contacts with the new regime in the hope that this would help limit Soviet influence. But it also realized that Pakistan was gravely concerned about the developing crisis in Afghanistan, though it believed its own "steadying" influence there would defang the problem.[17]

The trickiest issue, however, was how to reduce the two-decade-long Sino–Indian hostility. Initially, the Janata government did not expect any betterment, though it acknowledged that post-Maoist China was "prudent." In the fall of 1977, Delhi grew concerned over renewed Sino–American rapprochement and the possible threat to India that could emanate from US arms deliveries to the PRC. Even after Deng's call on all Asian nations to improve relations through mutual consultations, India's Prime Minister Desai remained certain that China would continue "to take advantage of India." Nonetheless, in January 1978, Indian companies invited a Chinese trade delegation, which came to India on the first visit of higher-ranking Chinese officials since the early 1960s.[18] In response, Deng expressed his hope for an improvement of Sino–Indian relations during his visit to Nepal in early February 1978. Within a fortnight of the conclusion of the Sino–Japanese peace treaty on August 12, Beijing and Delhi agreed on a visit of India's foreign minister. But Vajpayee remained skeptical about the success of his future "exploratory" trip. His sudden hospitalization just before his scheduled departure in early November necessitated the visit's postponement to mid February – a fateful development, as future events would reveal.[19]

The Third Indochina War, 1978–79

On December 25, 1978, Vietnam started its full-scale invasion of Cambodia. Pol Pot's ragtag army had little chance against the well-armed and battle-hardened Vietnamese troops. His brutal misrule since 1975 had killed millions and weakened the country economically and militarily. On January 8, the SRV established the People's Republic of Kampuchea in Phnom Penh – a Vietnamese-controlled government that would remain in power until 1991. In reaction to the outbreak of war, the Politburo of the Chinese Communist Party (CCP) approved a punitive strike against Vietnam in late December. Deng believed that the PRC needed to take the lead in the global struggle against Soviet expansionism, discourage further Vietnamese aggression, and thereby also create a safe international environment for *sihua*. Some months later, he placed the decision to wage war against the SRV into an even larger context: The USSR was using Cuba and Vietnam to "run wild" in Africa, the Middle East, and Asia while the world was standing idly by.[20] In early 1979, Deng secretly visited Thailand with the plan of setting up a Sino–ASEAN quasi-alliance. Vice-Foreign Minister Han Nianlong negotiated an agreement in Bangkok to ship weapons to Pol Pot's insurgency through Thai territory. In comparison, the Carter administration, which at that time was preoccupied with the Egyptian–Israeli peace process, primarily wanted to use diplomatic means "to urge Hanoi to act with great caution on the Thai–Cambodian border." Bangkok itself was deeply concerned about the possibility of being drawn into the war, particularly since it believed that ASEAN had failed to take a hard stand. Thus Thailand was willingly cooperating with the PRC against a hegemonic Vietnam.[21]

When Deng arrived in Washington on January 28 for the first high-level communist Chinese visit to the White House, he was obsessed with Indochina. After the end of the formal talks the following day, he announced that his country had no choice but to combat strategic expansionism by the USSR and its regional Vietnamese sidekick. Deng recounted his visit to ASEAN in November, lamenting that his hosts there had realized only recently how Pham Van Dong had deceived them all along. The Chinese leader compared his country's impending military action against Vietnam with the punitive war against India in 1962, emphasizing that "if we do not punish them, their violent actions will continue on a greater scale." In any case, the PRC planned only "a limited action," similar to the one seventeen years before in the Himalayas: "Our troops will quickly withdraw." Deng warned that only appropriate steps against Hanoi would send a strong message to Moscow, but ultimately a global "united front" that included "the United States, Japan, Western Europe, and the Third World" would be necessary. President Carter counseled against a "punitive strike" on Vietnam because any "token action" would not be effective. After Deng's departure, the United States planned political and military support for Thailand in order to protect it from the fallout of the impending Chinese strike.[22]

On February 17, Chinese troops invaded northern Vietnam, but withdrew on March 5 with a declaration of mission accomplished. Unlike in the Himalayas almost two decades before, the foray turned out to be a military disappointment. Vietnamese troops had put up fierce resistance and caused high Chinese casualties. All the same, Deng stressed after the war that if "the Vietnamese continue to make trouble they [the Chinese] in turn reserved the right to continue to teach them a lesson."[23] Hanoi, in comparison, concluded that it had actually taught the lesson to Beijing. But even for Vietnam, the war turned out to be costly. The Chinese invasion displaced 800,000 people and caused major damage in five provinces. The continued Chinese military threat afterward forced the SRV to reallocate military and economic resources from many other provinces and even from Cambodia. Still, for the DRV, the attack was once more proof of the reactionary nature of the PRC. In a mirror image of Chinese views, Hanoi believed that Beijing was pursuing a policy of "expansionism and great power chauvinism" which was "directed against socialism … and peace and stability in Southeast Asia and the world." Ultimately, however, the SRV gave up pursuing its revolutionary dreams in Southeast Asia in subsequent years. China's botched punitive strike and its quasi-containment alliance with ASEAN had the desired deterrent effect.[24]

In the wake of the establishment of full Sino–American diplomatic relations on January 1, 1979, the Kremlin engaged in mirror imaging as well. Moscow believed that Beijing was joining Washington and NATO in an attempt to encircle the Soviet Union. But the USSR was also convinced that its enemies were on the losing side of history: the quick

Vietnamese victory in Cambodia and Khomeini's revolution in Iran supposedly had damaged American global plans. Still, the Soviet leaders emphasized the necessity of preventing India from joining the new bloc, particularly in view of the recent improvement of relations between Delhi and Moscow. Nonetheless, the Chinese attack on Vietnam had caused a "loss of face" because it had revealed the ineffectiveness of Soviet deterrent capabilities in Asia. Two days into the war, Soviet party leader Leonid I. Brezhnev informed Carter that "the Soviet Union cannot remain a non-participant." Moscow even ordered troop movements at China's northern border to intimidate Beijing. During Pham Van Dong's visit in late February, the USSR promised to accelerate contractually agreed military supplies and to deliver additional quantities of food and oil.[25]

For the Janata government in Delhi, the Chinese punitive war against Vietnam turned into an embarrassment. India had criticized its Vietnamese friend for the intervention in Cambodia, and thus was not willing to heed Hanoi's request to recognize the newly installed regime in Phnom Penh. Some segments in the Indian public even believed that Sino–American normalization provided a "propitious" setting for Vajpayee's delayed visit to Beijing on February 11–19. But at his departure from Delhi airport, demonstrators help up placards with slogans like "Don't forget 1962" and "Bring back the occupied territory."[26] During the visit itself, both countries agreed to exclude the territorial disputes and instead to focus on the improvement of relations in all other spheres. When the PRC attacked Vietnam on February 17 while Vajpayee was still in Beijing, news agencies quickly pointed out the similarities to 1962. To add insult to injury, within ten days Deng publicly compared the recent war with the events almost seventeen years earlier, making the situation even worse by claiming that "Vietnam is stronger than India." Humiliated by Chinese actions in Vietnam, Prime Minister Desai had ordered Vajpayee back home one day before the official end of the visit. While Indian public opinion quickly turned against the PRC, Vajpayee continued to be convinced of the trip's success – until Deng's public statement a week later. Even if Desai considered the Vietnamese attack on Cambodia "wrong," he could not refrain from publicly gloating that "the Vietnamese would defeat the Chinese." Why Beijing chose to attack *during* Vajpayee's visit and thereby humiliate India publicly is still a mystery. China may have exploited the visit of Vietnamese top leaders to Cambodia on February 16–19 to surprise a temporarily rudderless SRV.[27] If this was the case, then Deng had sacrificed strategic rapprochement with India for tactical gains in Indochina.

The Sino–Indian crisis occurred just before a long-scheduled visit by Soviet Premier Kosygin to Delhi on March 9. The Indian tilt back to the

USSR in the wake of Vajpayee's spoilt China visit must have reassured
Soviet leaders that their South Asian friend indeed would not "do an
Egypt." Desai emphasized that he would not endanger the close bilateral
relationship through a rushed rapprochement with either the PRC or the
United States. Both sides agreed on increased military and economic
cooperation. But they still failed to see eye to eye on recognition of the
new Cambodian government. After Kosygin's departure, Vajpayee publicly reconfirmed India's commitment to friendship with the USSR by
declaring that Deng's recent public "references to the 1962 attack on
India ... had dealt a blow to the process of normalization."[28]

The ongoing Cambodian crisis and its brewing Afghanistan counterpart
drove the PRC further away from the USSR. In early April 1979, Beijing
officially informed Moscow of its decision not to seek negotiations on the
renewal of the thirty-year Friendship and Alliance Treaty of 1950. Since
Beijing had come to consider the communist coup of April 1978 in Kabul
a Soviet "strategic" move, it unsurprisingly reacted sharply to the Soviet
intervention in Afghanistan in late 1979. A PRC spokesman called on the
world to stop appeasing the USSR: "One should not feed the Tiger until it
is big and dangerous."[29] Foreign Minister Huang Hua claimed shortly
thereafter that Vietnam and Afghanistan were merely staging grounds for
the Soviet Union to grasp control over the international shipping routes in
the Strait of Malacca and the Indian Ocean, while Sino–ASEAN containment at least had prevented Vietnam from "advancing into Thailand and
the rest of Southeast Asia." Ultimately, China's renewed attempt to
improve relations with Delhi in early 1980 failed because of Indira
Gandhi's return to power. Given the grave Chinese concerns about
a Soviet encirclement, Deng pronounced on April 11, 1980, that Sino–
Soviet normalization would only be possible through Moscow's removal of
"three obstacles" – its troop massing at the Chinese border, its military
presence in Afghanistan, and its support for the Vietnamese "federation
policy" in Indochina.[30]

The Non-Aligned Crucible, 1979–81

For the Non-Aligned Movement, the turn of the decade proved fateful. The
double crises in Cambodia and Afghanistan in 1978–79 preceded another
crisis within a year – the Iraq–Iran War that started in September of 1980.
Apart from Indian and Yugoslav criticism, the movement had not shown
much concern about the attack by one of its Indochinese members against
another one in late 1978. An extraordinary conference in Maputo,
Mozambique, which occurred in parallel to Deng's visit to the United
States, only focused on apartheid in South Africa. In late February, after

the Chinese punitive strike against Vietnam, the ambassador of Cuba – the host of the impending sixth Non-Aligned Conference – told British officials that his country "could not accept there was a parallel between the Chinese invasion of Vietnam and the Vietnamese involvement in Kampuchea." In an exercise of rhetorical acrobatics, he claimed that one was an unjustified punitive strike, while the full-scale invasion of a whole country was a justified fraternal intervention in support of an uprising. Soon thereafter, Havana publicly offered the dispatch of troops to Indochina in support of Hanoi's anti-Chinese struggle. The Non-Aligned Movement obviously lacked any political cohesion or direction, as an Indian diplomat bemoaned. Some members, like India, were "post-imperialist," while others remained staunchly "anti-imperialist."[31] Some, like anti-imperialist Cuba, simply aligned with Vietnamese imperialism.

As Indochina receded into the background over the late spring of 1979, the parallel collapse of Cold War alignments in the Middle East and South Asia shook the movement. Before his return to Tehran from Paris on February 1, 1979, Ayatollah Ruhollah Khomeini had announced that revolutionary Iran would pursue a non-aligned foreign policy. On the 6th, the Iranian foreign ministry announced the country's impending withdrawal from CENTO – from the Western anti-Soviet alliance in the Middle East that had emerged in the wake of Iraq's withdrawal from the Baghdad Pact two decades earlier. In early March, Pakistan sent diplomats to Islamic Iran to prepare the coordinated withdrawal, eventually scheduled for the 13th. Pakistan had been dissatisfied with CENTO for a long time, or so its ambassador to London explained, and thus the time had come to pursue an independent policy. On March 15, the last remaining Middle Eastern member, Turkey, pulled out of the collapsing alliance too. As a long-standing critic of Western alliance formation, India welcomed Pakistan's and Islamic Iran's subsequent applications for Non-Aligned membership. The movement admitted the two Muslim countries shortly before its sixth conference in Cuba. In late September, CENTO was officially disbanded – just three months before the Soviet invasion of Afghanistan, which it was supposed to deter.[32]

In view of the sixth Non-Aligned Conference in Cuba in early September, the moderate member states grew worried about the host's ideological radicalism. In April, a Yugoslav delegation to Havana managed to obtain a Cuban promise not to "re-orientate the movement" toward the Socialist Camp. A subsequent Indian delegation reminded the Cuban leader Fidel Castro about the "concept of Non-Alignment as independence of all blocs." High-level Yugoslav–Indian talks in early May focused on how to overcome disagreements among the Non-Aligned. They particularly dealt with bilateral conflicts like the one in Southeast Asia, or the

Arab demand to expel Egypt because of its recent peace treaty with Israel. A preparatory conference in Colombo rejected the Arab demand, though it issued a call on all members "not to extend recognition" to the Egyptian–Israeli peace treaty. But in the summer, the ideological conflicts between Cuba, on the one hand, and Yugoslavia and India, on the other, broke out again. The prospect of discord in Havana convinced the 87-year-old Josip Broz Tito to travel early to Cuba in order to use his personal influence as the last living founding father of Non-Alignment. Just before he sat down with Castro for talks on August 30, the Janata government in India collapsed and national elections were called for early January 1980.[33]

Representatives from more than half of the world's countries attended the opening of the sixth Non-Aligned Conference on September 3. The Cuban hosts used a heavy hand to manipulate official proceedings, to control access to the conference, to deny participation of official delegates, and to present draft documents with radical positions. Yugoslavia and India were able to soften some but not all of the anti-imperialist, anti-American, and anti-Chinese rhetoric. Cuba was "reasonably pleased" with the conference's outcome as it had managed to outmaneuver the moderates on many issues. But Belgrade accused Moscow of subterfuge because many of the Cuban drafts contained word-for-word passages from documents which the Soviets had presented to the Yugoslavs in unrelated bilateral meetings weeks before. Obviously, the "Cubans and Russians had worked together." "Disappointed and disillusioned," founding member Burma (today's Myanmar) withdrew from the movement altogether.[34]

This internal disarray explained why the Non-Aligned Movement was unable to deal effectively with a series of crises that unfolded in 1979–80. Its response to the Soviet intervention in Non-Aligned Afghanistan was muted at best. Yugoslav diplomats tried to mobilize the Non-Aligned ambassadors at the United Nations, but they were keenly aware that Tito's terminal illness had created an "undeniable vacuum." In the end, the Non-Aligned preferred to support UN diplomatic efforts in lieu of directly helping a founding member state in distress. At least, Soviet aggression in Afghanistan had emasculated Moscow's close Non-Aligned friend Havana.[35] However, within a fortnight of Soviet troops entering Kabul, Indira Gandhi triumphed in the Indian elections, which initiated a return to the country's foreign policies of the mid 1970s. Even before being sworn in as new prime minister in January 14, she announced her willingness to recognize the Vietnamese-installed government in Cambodia. To visiting British Foreign Secretary Lord Carrington, Gandhi admitted that Moscow ought to withdraw its troops from Afghanistan – although she did not know how to achieve this – but felt they were no threat to Pakistan. Nonetheless, she excused the Soviet intervention with the argument that the USSR was "obsessed by China" and felt "encircled" by Sino–American normalization. By the same token, the new prime minister emphasized, the "Indians too felt encircled. Pakistan was on one side, and the Chinese were on the other." Paradoxically, Beijing was at that very time reaching out to Delhi because of its own fears of Soviet encirclement, as mentioned above, but without success. To Australian representatives, Gandhi railed against Western double standards; the Soviet occupation in Afghanistan had attracted loud condemnation while the Chinese attack in Vietnam the previous year had met only with a muted response. But she herself failed to remember Vietnam's prior invasion of Cambodia. Ultimately, however, Gandhi feared a return of the Cold War to South Asia. Western weapons delivered to Pakistan in response to the Afghanistan crisis primarily posed a threat to India, or so she claimed, but would not help contain the USSR.[36]

Tito's death on May 5, 1980, hurled the Non-Aligned Movement into even greater disarray. At his funeral in Belgrade, Gandhi discussed with Hua Guofeng the improvement of relations, but Cambodia and Afghanistan remained intractable obstacles. Similarly, Yugoslavia and India could not resolve their "sharp differences" over "the interpretation of foreign interventions" in Southeast and South Asia. With Tito gone, the danger of a split within the Non-Aligned Movement arose. In the hope that internal discord would abate with time, the movement decided to postpone the impending foreign ministers meeting to spring 1981.[37] But on July 9, Delhi recognized the Hanoi-installed government in Phnom Penh, which elicited sharp criticism from Belgrade and Beijing. By then, Gandhi's return to pro-Vietnamese policies had already managed to alienate ASEAN. Unsurprisingly, India found itself isolated in South and Southeast Asia, given its accommodation of Vietnamese hegemony and its apologetic views on Soviet intervention in Afghanistan.[38] Within only a few short months, Gandhi had gambled away much of the good will that the Desai government had built up between 1977 and 1979.

The Iraqi attack on Iran on September 22, 1980, complicated Non-Aligned relations once more. After Vietnam's invasion of Cambodia in 1978, once again two Non-Aligned member states went to war against each other. Beijing saw the attack as more proof of Soviet expansionism in West Asia, at the time when Moscow and Hanoi continued to refuse to withdraw from Afghanistan and Cambodia, respectively. But as Indian President Neelam Sanjiva Reddy realized during his visit to the USSR in early October, the Kremlin was literally losing its senses. Brezhnev was "not capable of sustaining even a social dialogue," Kosygin "incapacitated," and Gromyko "visibly deteriorated." But Gandhi still did not reconsider her pro-Soviet inclinations, blaming instead Pakistan and China for the mess in Afghanistan. In late 1980, Yugoslavia spearheaded a mediation effort to end the war between Iraq and Iran – to no avail. Nonetheless, Belgrade insisted that Baghdad should act as the host of the seventh Non-Aligned Conference in September 1982, as decided in Havana in 1979. By April 1981, however, India found it "embarrassing to attend the next Non-Aligned Summit in Baghdad if the Iran/Iraq war was still in progress." Iran's opposition to the conference site ultimately forced the cancellation of the summit in Baghdad and its postponement to Delhi in the spring of 1983.[39] To cut a long story short, throughout 1980–81, the Non-Aligned Movement staged a self-harming theater of the absurd.

Attempts at Relaxation, 1982

After a year of standstill throughout 1981, Asian politics experienced renewed movement the following year. In Tashkent on March 24, 1982, Brezhnev expressed his country's desire to end two decades of Sino–Soviet hostilities and improve economic and political relations. The announcement was an attempt to play the China card against the United States at a time when the USSR suffered from the collapse of détente and faced multiple self-inflicted injuries in the Global South, including the Middle East. Some days later, against the background of a massive economic crisis, the Vietnamese party held its fifth congress. In its wake, war hero Vo Nguyen Giap openly talked about the failings in domestic politics and about the problems that the idea of the "Greater Vietnamese Empire" in Laos and Cambodia had caused. Chinese diplomatic observers concluded that the rhetorical attacks on the PRC during the congress were merely a façade to conceal "self-criticism." Vietnam's commitment to Laos and Cambodia, the PRC believed, had drained resources to such a degree that the SRV could not use them for internal development. Economic support from the USSR and the European Socialist Camp had helped to "solve some tasks" but the current political line would still prevent Vietnam from fixing the "enormous problems" that the country faced. At least, in July, the SRV offered the PRC the resumption of bilateral talks after a hiatus of three years.[40]

Responding to Brezhnev's Tashkent speech, Beijing quickly indicated that Moscow needed to let deeds follow words, particularly with regard to the three obstacles. In mid April, Deng asked visiting Romanian leader Nicolae Ceauşescu to convey to Brezhnev the Chinese demand for the USSR "to start with one or two" of the obstacles, otherwise the PRC would not negotiate at all. But the aging Soviet leader for his part was not willing to make any concessions on Soviet global "revolutionary theory." The PRC was equally suspicious of the Vietnamese request to resume talks, mainly because of Vietnam's unappealing propaganda rhetoric. Beijing's hesitant attitude in turn reconfirmed Hanoi's deep mistrust. In view of the twelfth CCP congress in early September of 1982, Deng decided to continue to insist on the "three obstacles" but agreed to a Soviet offer to resume bilateral border negotiations in October. At the congress itself, General Secretary Hu Yaobang rejected the promotion of revolution abroad as "absolutely impermissible," and thanked the world for its help in the recent economic development of the PRC.[41] Moscow picked up on these encouraging signals, but continued to blame Beijing's "three obstacles" for the lack of any improvement of relations. Unsurprisingly, the Chinese side remained pessimistic that Soviet policy would change at all. Prime Minister Zhao Ziyang emphasized to his British colleague Margaret Thatcher that even Brezhnev's looming death would not affect anything, despite the problems that the USSR faced at home and particularly abroad – in Indochina, Afghanistan, and Poland. High-level talks during Brezhnev's funeral in Moscow in mid November did not resolve any of the issues, either.[42]

As Sino–Soviet–Vietnamese relations experienced minute changes, Gandhi's India restored its international status and equidistance between the superpowers. The official decision in mid 1982 to reschedule the seventh tri-annual conference from Baghdad to Delhi for the spring of 1983 bestowed on India *de facto* leadership of the Non-Aligned Movement – for the first time since its inception in 1961. At this juncture, Gandhi's government also grew concerned with the overall "rapid deterioration of East–West relations" at the global level.[43] Her visit to the United States in mid summer of 1982 helped to "lay some groundwork for elevating ... US Indian relations from the disrepair." Despite initial apprehensions about the visit, both sides were pleasantly surprised by how successfully it turned out. Gandhi liked Ronald Reagan's amicability, openness, and "honesty," as she confessed to British officials during her stopover in London on the way home. Still, the two "agreed ... on almost no issue of policy." Six weeks later, she visited Moscow in a public show of equidistance. She returned content that the trip's specific goal of "reaffirm-[ing] ... the bilateral relationship ... while distancing India from the Soviet Union on major international issues" had been accomplished. In contrast to the energetic and engaging Reagan, however, Brezhnev appeared to her in "bad shape" and unable "to sustain a lengthy conversation."[44]

Conclusion

The transformation of the Asian Cold War in the late 1970s created the structural preconditions in that region for the end of the global Cold War in the second half of the 1980s. Deng was convinced as early as 1975 that the global Cold War made no sense as an ordering principle for East Asia any longer, and thus worked for international collaboration after the arrest of the Gang of Four in 1976. Some aspects of the structural changes in 1979–80 are self-evident: the collapse of communism as a unifying program for national liberation, the end of the Sino–American antagonism, and the conversion of US policy of containing communism into Chinese–American–ASEAN cooperation against Vietnamese aspirations. Unlike in the Middle East, where Islamic Iran tried to transcend the regional Cold War, East and Southeast Asia experienced the resolution of some of the conflicts that had defined the regional Cold War there. While Khomeini's Iran embarked on a revolution to remake the international system of states in the image of his Islam, post-Maoist China repudiated its own world revolutionary policies by joining this system while smothering – successfully – Vietnam's world revolutionary ambitions.

In comparison, the structural changes which India and Non-Alignment underwent during the same time period are less obvious on first glance. The interlude of the Janata government in between Indira Gandhi's two premierships appears, in retrospect, a trial period for new approaches to old Indian foreign policy problems. Although Gandhi rejected much of Desai's outlook at the beginning of her second premiership, she resurrected some of its aspects, like achieving equidistance from both superpowers, by 1982. Under Indian leadership, the Non-Aligned Movement tried to embrace once more its founding principle in international relations, attempting to re-establish its former influence through closer cooperation at the United Nations.[45] In the end, the rattling years of 1979–80 and structural changes in the international system in Asia and the Middle East – including a pair of wars among two Non-Aligned members each – left Non-Alignment weakened. Accepting communist and pro-Soviet countries had exposed the movement to the danger of Moscow's subversion, as the Havana conference in 1979 revealed. Pro-Soviet forces from within and outside undermined Non-Alignment as an alternative vision to the Cold War. Ultimately, however, the lack of internal cohesion was also due to the sheer size of membership – the vast majority of the world's countries. The movement's political decline created the conditions under which Asia helped end the global Cold War in the remainder of the 1980s, as Chapter 23 shows.

The structural changes of international relations in Asia in 1979–80, as far-reaching as they turned out to be, were not yet sufficient to bring about the immediate end of the global Cold War. The old guard in the Soviet leadership was committed to revolutionary regimes in Vietnam and Afghanistan until its death, and thereby continued to fan many of the conflicts on the continent. The end of the global Cold War primarily required a strategic rethinking in Moscow which would only come in March 1985 with Mikhail S. Gorbachev's ascent to power.

Over the course of three decades after World War II, significant structural changes had occurred in the regional Cold War of divided Europe. Starting in the late 1940s, Western Europe had sought unity through the Council of Europe and the emerging European Communities while the Soviet Union tried to enforce political conformity and economic integration in the continent's eastern half. The 1960s had witnessed the peak of Europe's division with the closure of the borders in Berlin and the Soviet-led Warsaw Pact (WAPA) intervention in Czechoslovakia. But during that decade, West Germany and the Vatican pursued policies of engaging with the Socialist Camp in Eastern Europe in the hope of reducing the human toll of the continent's division. With the Conference on Security and Cooperation in Europe (CSCE), the Soviet-led Socialist Camp sought territorial security whereas Western Europe aimed at instilling basic political and civic rights there. At the same time, Europe's socialist states were increasing their dependency on the world economy, mostly via debt.

In the late 1970s and early 1980s, Soviet economic, military, and political authority in Eastern Europe eroded with remarkable swiftness. Incapable of supporting its empire with subsidized energy and raw material supplies by 1980–81, the USSR thrust aside, in the face of the Afghanistan War and the Polish Crisis, its self-arrogated right to intervene with military force to restore the socialist order in Eastern Europe. Hence, in late 1981, Hungary, Poland, and East Germany sought even greater economic integration with the West in order to overcome domestic problems. Poignantly, this happened in a period of a long-drawn-out economic crisis in the Western world in the wake of the American abrogation of the Bretton Woods system in 1971 and the Middle Eastern oil shocks in 1973–74 and 1979–80. But just as socialist economic integration eroded in the first half of the 1980s, Western Europe and the United States underwent reforms that ultimately helped them return to economic health. By mid decade, the structures for the end of the regional Cold War in Europe had been put in place.

Europe by the late 1970s

Both halves of divided Europe faced economic hardship in the late 1970s, though at different levels of intensity. The continent's western half suffered from a long-drawn out economic downturn. President Richard M. Nixon's *de facto* obliteration of the Bretton Woods system in 1971 had triggered painful readjustments within the Western European currency exchange regime, which lasted for several years. Moreover, the jump in oil price during and after the Middle East Crisis of 1973 triggered an energy crisis, followed by high unemployment, ballooning budget deficits, rising inflation, and elevated interest rates in Western Europe and North America. Western European left-wing terrorism, which several Eastern European secret services supported financially and logistically, created an atmosphere of public angst, particularly in West Germany, France, and Italy.[1]

Yet, despite this malaise, the European Communities (EC) did not fall apart. With the May 1974 elections of Helmut Schmidt and Valéry Giscard d'Estaing as chancellor and president, respectively, the sputtering Franco–German engine of European integration received an urgently needed upgrade. The Euroskeptic attitude of the British government and public – despite the positive referendum of 1975 – further helped to bring Germany and France closer to each other. Schmidt in particular wanted to deepen Western European integration in order to turn the EC into a partner equal to the United States. In 1978, the community agreed to launch the European Monetary System by January 1 the following year. Under the new arrangement the exchange rates of member state currencies were fixed (or pegged) to each other, but fluctuations within a certain bandwidth were allowed, in the hope of calming and stabilizing the common market. The Western European replacement for the old Bretton Woods currency system was born.[2]

At the same time, discord between the United States and its European NATO members over Western Europe's security had increased following the emergence of the Soviet–American nuclear duopoly in the late 1960s. The two superpowers had almost single-handedly imposed the Nuclear Non-Proliferation Treaty on the Eighteen-Nation Committee on Disarmament at the United Nations in 1968, negotiated on strategic nuclear arms limitation for years without the inclusion of any other party, and signed the Strategic Arms Limitation Treaty (SALT) in 1972 on a bilateral basis. In early 1977, the incoming US president, Jimmy Carter, committed himself to turning the tentative Vladivostok agreements of 1974 between his predecessor Gerald Ford and Soviet leader Leonid I. Brezhnev into a firm bilateral nuclear arms limitation treaty replacing the interim agreements of SALT. The superpower commitment to reaching SALT II was sufficiently firm to survive Sino–American rapprochement, the Soviet–Vietnamese alliance, and the Indochina wars at the turn of 1978/79. In June 1979, Moscow and Washington finally signed SALT II. However, European NATO members had increasingly feared that the US commitment to nuclear arms limitation problems exclusively at the strategic level and only within the framework of the Soviet–American nuclear duopoly undermined their security. This was particularly disconcerting given that the USSR had enjoyed conventional military superiority in Europe since World War II and had stationed large numbers of medium-range nuclear rockets – the mobile SS-20 missiles – in its western territories and Eastern Europe since the mid 1970s. Dispirited by Carter's indifference to European security interests, Chancellor Schmidt publicly insisted on the resumption of conventional disarmament talks and the inclusion of the SS-20 missiles in the ongoing SALT II negotiations in 1977. Only after the signing of SALT II did Carter agree to address European concerns. The NATO double-track decision of December 12, 1979, demanded that the USSR negotiate on the withdrawal of the SS-20 missiles but also included a warning that in case of failure to reach an agreement the alliance would station similar Pershing II missiles and Tomahawk cruise missiles by late 1983 to redress the balance of nuclear deterrence in Europe.[3]

In comparison to the Western European countries, the Socialist Camp in Eastern Europe experienced a rapidly deepening economic crisis in the second half of the 1970s. The Council for Mutual Economic Assistance (CMEA) had turned out to be incapable of basic reform in the wake of the Soviet-led WAPA intervention in Czechoslovakia in 1968. The implementation of the Complex Program of socialist integration of 1971 quickly fell behind schedule, while the economic gap between the CMEA and the EC – even if the community at that time faced its own economic problems – grew year by year. The inability of the USSR to increase fossil fuel deliveries, either because of the lack of shipment capabilities or due to delays in the exploration of new oil and gas fields in Siberia, arrested the further development of the energy-hungry, Soviet-style economies of Eastern Europe. In the early 1970s, the USSR was forced to buy oil in Iraq to fulfill its supply obligations to CMEA partners, sustaining financial losses in the process.[4]

Yet the largest problem was the mounting debt of CMEA states to the non-socialist world. Member countries had hoped to modernize their economies with Western commercial bank credits and repay debt through the ensuing production and export increases, but they ended up misspending much of the hard currency windfall. Over the period from 1970 to 1979, the collective debt of CMEA members increased tenfold to 65.4 billion US dollars. The financial liabilities were distributed asymmetrically across the CMEA; the USSR (21.6 billion US dollars) and Poland (18.5 billion US dollars) alone assumed over 61 percent of the total. Still, the other five Eastern European members held individual debt between 3.9 and 6.9 billion US dollars. Even at this comparatively low level, Bulgaria defaulted on its liabilities to the non-socialist world in 1977 and needed to be bailed out by the Soviet Union in an effort to preserve the international creditworthiness of the whole Socialist Camp in Europe. To add insult to injury, rising interest rates in the non-socialist world by the late 1970s made refinancing debt increasingly difficult. By 1978, Soviet economic specialists understood that the capitalist world economy, even if it was concurrently suffering from hardships, was increasing its influence in the Socialist Camp and the Global South.[5]

While the USSR led a Socialist Camp in economic decline, it continued to seek hegemony in Europe. It had sought supremacy since 1954 through repeated demands for American withdrawal from the continent. In 1975, its leaders had come to believe that the Final Act of the CSCE had achieved something akin to that goal. The concurrent deployment of the SS-20 missiles served, in *defensive* terms, as a counterbalance to American military bases stationed at the periphery of the USSR since the 1950s, but also, in *offensive* terms, as an attempt to achieve final predominance in Europe given that NATO had no comparable system available. In late November 1978, Brezhnev told a gathering of CMEA leaders that he was convinced that Soviet nuclear policies had forced US President Carter to agree to negotiations on SALT II. He marveled that the SS-20 missiles managed to occupy a "grey zone" in between the ongoing SALT II negotiations on strategic nuclear weapons, on the one side, and talks on conventional disarmament, on the other. The mobile rockets, he forecast, would become the trump card in negotiations on the final withdrawal of American troops from Western Europe. But this all meant that the Socialist Camp needed to focus on improving its external peace propaganda and, particularly, mobilize Western European public opinion to split NATO. Unsurprisingly, given this mindset, Soviet leaders concluded a year later that the NATO double-track decision was an "aggressive" but desperate move by the supposedly doomed Western alliance. In turn, they even considered demanding the inclusion of British and French nuclear forces in future negotiations – which *de facto* aimed at the denuclearization of the United Kingdom and of France, which had withdrawn from the military structures of NATO in 1966.[6]

Afghanistan and Iran, 1979–80

On December 25, 1979, within less than two weeks of the NATO double-track decision, the USSR invaded Afghanistan. The intervention would quickly become entangled with the six-month-old SALT II agreement. The decision to intervene had been made on short notice against the background of the quickly deteriorating situation in Afghanistan. In the months before, Moscow had increasingly placed the failing Afghan communist revolution into the context of the concurrent decline of Soviet influence in several Middle Eastern countries, the danger of Islamist influence in Muslim Soviet Central Asia, and eventually also of the NATO double-track decision.[7]

For Washington, the Soviet intervention in Afghanistan killed what remained of détente. President Carter reacted by withdrawing the SALT II agreement from consideration in the Senate, where it had encountered opposition over its verification clauses anyway. Within weeks, he also approved the delivery of light arms to anti-communist insurgents in Afghanistan and convinced Egypt's President Anwar Sadat to supply Soviet-made weapons. Over the course of 1980, the United States and its European NATO allies started to pressure commercial banks to reduce credit to both the USSR and socialist states supportive of the Soviet military presence in Afghanistan. Yet most of the other measures – particularly in the spheres of trade and the politics of symbolism – were less effective. In January, Carter imposed an embargo on grain – i.e. on the commodity that formed the mainstay of Soviet–American trade – with the purpose of undermining the Soviet economy. But the embargo mostly damaged grain farmers at home – and in Canada and Australia which joined it – while the country's competitors in the international grain market, most notably Argentina, benefited. The boycott of the Summer Olympic Games in Moscow similarly was more a symbolic show of force than an effective tool to get Soviet troops out of Afghanistan. The International Olympic Committee met in February 1980 in the American town of Lake Placid, where the Winter Olympic Games happened to occur, to discuss a US proposal to cancel or reschedule the summer games, but ultimately refused to allow what it considered the politicization of the Olympic Movement. At least, the United States got its revenge in the Cold War-like Olympic ice hockey final, where an assorted team of US college students unexpectedly defeated the *crème de la crème* of Soviet players. But Washington could not even convince most of its own Cold War allies to boycott the games in Moscow. Only two NATO allies – Canada and West Germany – joined the United States, along with another sixty-three countries from Latin America, Africa, the Middle East, and Asia (including China).[8]

Moscow was still able to exploit the Summer Olympic Games for its peace propaganda, convinced that the American reaction to Afghanistan was just a US imperialist storm in the teacup of Cold War propaganda. Nonetheless, the Soviet leaders understood that they had received "a negative echo" to the intervention in Afghanistan from more than just the United States. Foreign Minister Andrei A. Gromyko admitted to East German visitors in late February that the international situation had worsened. Yet he simultaneously saw divisions emerging between Carter's hardline United States and moderate NATO members, however, which in due course would open up political opportunities in Europe. The mounting international pressure in early 1980 still had some impact on Soviet nerves. The Kremlin sent the renowned dissident and Nobel Peace Prize winner Andrei D.Sakharov into internal exile in Gorki in late January after he had publicly supported international sanctions against the USSR because of the intervention in Afghanistan. But at the Central Committee plenum in June, a month before the opening of the Olympic Games, Brezhnev was certain that the Soviet Union continued to be leading the world's peace camp while the imperialist United States had irresponsibly thrown away détente by refusing to ratify SALT II and by imposing economic and "sports" sanctions.[9]

The Afghan drama and its Olympic sideshow occurred in parallel to the Islamic Revolution in Iran and the Iraq–Iran War. Within a year of the 1979 revolution, both superpowers found themselves targets of Khomeini's ideological wrath. Young radicals occupied the American embassy in October 1979 for 444 days, following up with a short occupation of the Soviet mission on New Year's Day of 1980 in response to the Soviet intervention in Afghanistan. The economic impact of the revolution in 1979 and the Iraq–Iran War a year later was significant for both the Western world and the Socialist Camp. Over the course of 1973, the oil price had already tripled to a level where it would remain for the rest of the decade, but doubled once more from June 1979 to early 1980 though it gradually fell to the pre-crisis level by mid decade. The second oil shock hit Western European countries particularly hard since they could no longer resort to another round of deficit spending to soften the crisis. The increase in inflation and debt in the six years leading up to 1979 had limited many of the Keynesian options of government intervention. In tune with the partial NATO boycott of the Moscow Summer Games in 1980, European alliance members showed once again only limited solidarity with the United States with regard to sanctions against the Islamic Republic of Iran. Many Western European governments had concluded that Carter's policies toward the larger Middle East throughout 1980 were erratic if not amateurish.[10]

The impact of the Iranian Revolution and the Iraq–Iran War on the CMEA was vastly different and even more foreboding in character. The lopsided character of fossil energy supplies, structural deficiencies in shipping networks, the onset of the decline of Soviet oil production at the turn of the decade, and the energy-hungry nature of Soviet-style economies all came to bite the Socialist Camp. Before the Shah's regime fell in early 1979, the USSR had contracted Iranian gas deliveries to the Caucasus in order to free up gas supplies from Siberia to Eastern Europe. But the sudden Islamic Revolution threatened Soviet investments in Iranian gas infrastructure.[11] To make matters worse, the Iraq–Iran War of 1980 reduced oil deliveries from Baghdad and cut all gas deliveries from Tehran. This sudden drop in energy supplies from the Middle East hit the Socialist Camp at the very time when the Polish Crisis unfolded, which required the emergency sale of Soviet oil on the world market to support Poland financially at the expense of energy deliveries to CMEA partners in Europe.

The Polish Crisis, 1980–81

Poland's predicaments in the years of 1980–81 played a *fundamental* role in the structural transformation of the regional Cold War in Europe. Both the decades-long struggle of the Polish people against the communist regime and the Final Act of the CSCE in 1975 had triggered the emergence of a civil society in a Soviet-style communist country for the first time. Unlike in the German Democratic Republic (GDR) in 1953, Hungary in 1956, Czechoslovakia in 1968, or even Afghanistan in 1979, the Soviet inability to maintain its hegemony in Poland through economic assistance or even by brute military force in 1980–81 marked an important milestone in the global decline of the USSR. The collapse of the Polish economy further damaged the fragile CMEA. By the fall of 1981, Hungary, Poland, and East Germany decided to seek rapprochement with the capitalist world economy.

The Polish Crisis was a chronicle of a death foretold. The technocrat Edward Gierek, who had succeeded the disgraced Władysław Gomułka as Polish leader in late 1970, proved unable to solve the structural problems of the economy and overcome the mounting political disaffection among the Polish people, although the West German ratification of the Warsaw Treaty in 1972 had brought a short-lived feeling of success. The Final Act of the CSCE in 1975 had a particular impact on Poland since it provided the politically restless population with yet another weapon in the struggle against the regime. The election of a Polish pope – John Paul II – in 1978 and his triumphal visit to Poland the following year further revealed the deep chasm between regime and people. To make matters worse for Gierek's government, his country had accumulated the largest – and utterly unsustainable – per capita debt in the non-socialist world among all CMEA member states over the course of the 1970s, without showing anything of significance created by the hard currency windfall.

The troubles in Poland erupted just when the Soviet leaders feted themselves as promoters of world peace during the Summer Olympic Games in Moscow in the second half of July of 1980. In a bizarre sideshow, Polish communist diplomats had to calm the nerves of their Soviet colleagues over a politically inflated incident at the games. The Polish athlete Władysław Kozakiewicz not only managed to eclipse his Soviet rival Konstantin Volkov by winning gold in the pole vault competition, but also made an obscene gesture – the *bras d'honneur* – to the booing Soviet crowd immediately after his decisive leap. Made in frustration over the unsportsmanlike behavior of the home crowd during the whole competition, the gesture delighted Polish spectators in the stadium and, as legend has it, many Eastern Europeans in front of their TV sets. Polish diplomats solved the diplomatic crisis by claiming that Kozakiewicz suffered from incontrollable muscle spasms, but they were powerless when it came to explaining the rapidly unfolding economic crisis in their home country.[12]

The Polish Crisis broke out on July 1 when yet another increase in consumer goods prices triggered a wave of strikes afflicting one factory after another. Once workers at the Lenin Shipyards in Gdańsk stopped work on August 14, strike action across the nation became more coordinated. Within days, Solidarność arose as an independent labor union, with the Gdańsk shipyard electrician Lech Wałęsa as leader. By August 30, the government agreed to legalization because Gierek was unwilling to use the kind of lethal military force against striking workers that had disgraced his predecessor Władysław Gomułka in late 1970. The August 30 agreements helped to reduce much of the strike activity but also meant that, for the first time, a Soviet-style communist government had recognized an independent union movement. Stanisław Kania, who succeeded the heart-attack stricken Gierek five weeks later, quickly came to believe that the events of the previous months posed "a danger to socialism" in Poland and even other socialist countries. The Polish comrades understood clearly that the deficient economic policies of the previous decade were at the heart of the problem, but hastened to reassure WAPA partners that they would prevent a situation similar to the one in Czechoslovakia in 1968 from developing. Still, by mid September, the Polish party was convinced that "counter-revolutionary" elements of the Workers' Defense Committee (KOR), which had been established in 1976 in the wake of the Helsinki Final Act, controlled Solidarność. But a month later, Kania acknowledged the continued "crisis of trust" within society, and warned about the ballooning debt of 26 billion US dollars and the possibility of the country's economic collapse. In early November, he decided to retain martial law as an option of last resort.[13]

Soviet reactions to the crisis, which unfolded so unexpectedly during and after the Olympic Games, appeared to be calm. But by late August, the Politburo of the Communist Party of the Soviet Union (CPSU) approved the planning of a military intervention. Two months later, Brezhnev advocated the imposition of martial law, while Gromyko asserted that Soviet sacrifices in World War II would not allow the USSR to "lose Poland" to "a counter-revolution." But Yuri V. Andropov was skeptical about the use of military force so soon after Afghanistan, as he told an assistant: "The quota of interventions abroad has been exhausted." Nevertheless, East German leader Erich Honecker reminded the Polish comrades in late November that "bloodshed" was the only correct lesson learned from the counter-revolutions in Berlin in 1953, in Hungary in 1956, and in Czechoslovakia in 1968. Some days later, he requested that Brezhnev call a WAPA meeting "to work out collective measures" to prevent "the death of socialist Poland." By early December, WAPA worked on plans for a 1968-style intervention.[14]

The Polish pope, John Paul II, followed the developments in his native country from the Vatican. Without doubt, Solidarność had emerged from the long-time struggle of Polish society, which he had personally supported as a priest, bishop, and cardinal. The pontiff decided to intervene in early September by inviting Wałęsa to Rome. On the basis of intelligence coming from the Vatican, the East German secret service concluded – correctly – that the pope planned to use his personal influence in Poland to create a "united Christian Europe." In mid December, just as the WAPA planned its intervention, John Paul II reminded Brezhnev in a personal letter that Poland had been "the first victim of an aggression" in 1939 – by Hitler's Germany and Stalin's Soviet Union – and was also "one of the signatories of the Helsinki Final Act," which included "the principle of non-intervention in internal affairs." Brezhnev's reaction to the letter is unknown, but the statesman-like reception of Wałęsa by John Paul II in mid January 1981 could not have endeared the pontiff to the Soviet leader. To this day, it is not entirely clear whether or not the Soviet leadership ordered the assassination attempt on the pontiff on May 13, 1981, even though there are credible connections between the hired gun and the Bulgarian secret service. The event came as a shock to many Poles, as did Stefan Wyszyński's death from stomach cancer a fortnight later. The Polish regime hoped that his successor – Józef Glemp – would continue on the path of political realism, which he actually did. But Soviet church specialists did not share such optimism in 1981. They believed that the convalescent John Paul II would continue to transform the church into a major political force in Poland. Ultimately, they feared, the Polish pope aimed at the "liberalization" of his home country and at the injection of his influence into what they freely admitted was an emerging ideological vacuum in the Socialist Camp.[15]

The Polish party reacted to the ongoing domestic crisis by appointing General Wojciech Jaruzelski prime minister in February 1981. At the beginning, the USSR was ready to trust the Kania–Jaruzelski duumvirate to suppress the Solidarność-led counter-revolution, particularly since the two were working on plans for martial law. But by mid May, the Soviet leaders pondered replacing the duo, and even met with East Germany's Erich Honecker and Czechoslovakia's Gustáv Husák to vet more pliable candidates in the Polish party. Despite encouragement from Moscow, hardliners in Warsaw failed to overthrow Kania and Jaruzelski at a Central Committee meeting in June.[16] The two came under pressure again in early September 1981 when Solidarność held its first congress. The independent labor union not only announced its ultimate goal of taking over the government but also issued an appeal to all workers in socialist Eastern Europe and the USSR to follow the Polish example. An irate Brezhnev called the appeal an attempt to "stir up sedition." On the phone, he accused Kania of being "in a grip of illusion" about Poland's domestic situation, calling Solidarność a fascist, terrorist, and anti-Soviet organization. Although the Polish party soon declared Solidarność in violation of the year-old agreements, it again put off the decision to impose martial law. Yet, on the day of Brezhnev's acrimonious telephone conversation with Kania, John Paul II happened to release his new encyclical *Laborem Exercens* (Through Work). Referring to Pope Leo XIII's *Rerum Novarum* from 1891 and his own *Redemptor Hominis* from 1979, it emphasized the right of all workers to form independent labor unions.[17]

The Soviet-induced replacement of Kania with Jaruzelski as party leader on October 18 set the Polish Crisis on the road to final confrontation. The following day, Brezhnev demanded "decisive actions . . . against the counter-revolution" during a congratulatory phone conversation. But within ten days, the CPSU leaders became convinced that Jaruzelski too was unwilling to change Kania's weak course, while they rejected the general's concurrent request for the dispatch of Soviet troops. After November had passed without any solution, the new Polish party leader asked WAPA for military support in early December, but the alliance's supreme commander, Dmitri F. Ustinov, merely promised moral and political assistance. On December 10, Andropov told the CPSU Politburo that the USSR would not use military force in Poland, even if this meant that the Eastern European country might fall under the "authority of Solidarity." The CPSU was primarily responsible for protecting the Soviet Union, he insisted. In a desperate phone call on the 12th, Jaruzelski once more asked for a military intervention, but Politburo member Mikhail A. Suslov retorted that Soviet troops would be used only to protect Poland from *external* enemies. In the afternoon, Jaruzelski ordered the implementation of martial law as of December 13. Although he had asked multiple times for a Soviet military intervention to avoid imposing martial law, Jaruzelski later claimed that he had imposed martial law primarily to pre-empt an impending external intervention. Under martial law, the Polish government arrested Solidarność leaders, bloodily suppressed labor strikes, and purged unreliable cadres. Pope John Paul II sent a personal letter to General Jaruzelski with a request to stop the bloodshed; Poles should defend the nation but not have the blood of their compatriots dripping from their hands. Jaruzelski understood that martial law was just one victory in a larger struggle to regain the "trust" of the population.[18] But how could he ever believe that martial law was the proper way to regain that trust? Despite the formal end of martial law in July 1983, the rupture between the communist regime and the Polish people was final.

The Soviet refusal to intervene in Poland was surprising, given the previous use of military force in the GDR, Hungary, and Czechoslovakia to suppress supposed counter-revolutions. In spite of extended WAPA exercises in Poland in the spring of 1981, designed to intimidate Kania and Jaruzelski, the same Soviet leaders who had decided on intervention in Afghanistan two years earlier did not have the stomach for another military intervention. But all three previous cases in Europe shared one basic characteristic: they happened to be at the geographical frontline in the European Cold War. Poland was only a second-line country in the military defense of the Socialist Camp. On December 10, 1981, when Andropov was pondering the possibility of a Solidarność government, his minimal demands were a guarantee of Soviet prerogatives in the country and security for the lines of communication to the frontline state East Germany. Yet, there was a range of other reasons that convinced the Soviet leaders not to use military force. First of all, they had no alternative to Jaruzelski, unlike in Hungary in 1956, when they could use János Kádár to replace Imre Nagy. Second, the USSR and the Socialist Camp suffered from economic problems, described further below, which questioned Soviet capabilities to help restore Poland to stability after intervention. The Soviet interventions in the GDR and Hungary in the 1950s had saddled the USSR with the task of providing substantial economic aid, which in turn had repercussions for the development of the Soviet economy itself. Third, as Politburo member Boris N. Ponomarev had explained to Eastern European visitors in early November, the costs of the concurrent political and economic reconstruction of Afghanistan were mounting. The Soviet leaders recalled that, a year before, NATO had accused the

USSR of violating international law in Afghanistan, insisted on the stipula-
tions of non-interference from the Helsinki Final Act, and warned of
serious economic consequences "if the Soviet Union were again to violate
the basic rights of any state to territorial integrity and independence."
Andropov explicitly warned the Politburo on December 10, 1981, that
Western sanctions in the aftermath of a Soviet intervention in Poland "will
be very difficult for us."[19] Interestingly, the Final Act of the CSCE seemed
not to have weighed heavily on Soviet minds. Still, with the refusal to
intervene in Poland in 1981, the Brezhnev Doctrine – the self-arrogated
right of the USSR to intervene in other socialist states to restore the
socialist order there – had died.

The Dissolution of the Soviet Economic Empire, 1981–84

The Polish Crisis unfolded just as the USSR faced a serious economic
malaise that questioned its capability to maintain hegemony in all of its
Eastern European empire. For decades before, the lopsided nature of
energy and raw material deliveries within the CMEA had provided the
USSR with leverage over the Eastern European members but had also
required the continued flow of supplies below world market prices to
maintain political loyalty and economic stability. By the mid 1970s,
however, the CMEA had entered into a crisis of purpose; increasing
unilateral nationalist demands, mounting ideological disagreements,
and fundamental differences over economic reform had paralyzed the
integration process. Moreover, by the turn of the decade, overall Soviet
oil production went into decline. In early November of 1980, just as oil
supplies from Iraq shrank and gas deliveries from Iran vanished, the
USSR demanded that its Eastern European allies agree to reductions in
energy supplies so that more Soviet oil could be sold on the world market
to raise hard currency in fraternal support for Poland. Ultimately,
Poland's economic collapse after mid 1980 had major ripple effects
through the CMEA. The country's anthracite (black coal) production
was crucial to the heavy industries in East Germany and the USSR.
Contractual deliveries to the GDR had started to fall behind schedule as
early as 1976, but collapsed completely in the fall of 1980, wreaking havoc
on East Germany's planned economy. Fraternal solidarity within the
Socialist Camp, which had been evoked for decades on all kinds of
occasions, suddenly evaporated. In early 1981, East Berlin resorted to
economic warfare against Warsaw, announcing cuts to its goods deliveries
to struggling Poland proportional to Polish failures to supply anthracite.[20]

But the situation took a turn for the worse in the summer of 1981 when
one Eastern European leader after another visited Brezhnev for the

annual Crimea meetings. Apart from the decline in oil production, the USSR endured its fourth consecutive harvest failure. Brezhnev demanded that Honecker and Husák agree to a 20 percent cut in oil deliveries so that the USSR could sell more of its oil on the world market to buy grain for itself and to raise funds for Poland. After complaining that such cuts "undermined the fundamental pillars of the existence of the German Democratic Republic," Honecker negotiated a 10 percent cut, but his country in return needed to deliver over 400,000 tons of potatoes as emergency food aid to the starving Soviet Union. By November, Czechoslovakia, Hungary, and Bulgaria had also agreed to similar cuts in oil supplies. Only the Polish comrades received promises of additional economic aid during their Crimea meeting in mid August 1981 – on top of strident advice to crack down on the counter-revolutionary Solidarność once and for all.[21]

The Soviet inability to sustain the empire economically convinced several of the indebted Eastern European socialist states to look to the West for a solution. The only exceptions were Bulgaria and Czechoslovakia, which had both managed to achieve positive trade balances with the non-socialist world by 1980 through a variety of measures, such as austerity, export increases, and import cuts. Nicolae Ceauşescu's Romania, which suffered from high debt and, particularly, the collapse of Iranian oil supplies in 1980, tried to escape the debt trap with a combination of rescheduling negotiations and severe austerity, which impoverished the country within one decade.[22]

On November 4, 1981, Hungary applied for membership in the International Monetary Fund (IMF) to get access to credit at preferential interest rates in order to refinance its debt held by private Western banks. Budapest had considered this step since the 1960s but had been prevented from taking it when the CMEA explicitly prohibited membership in the IMF in 1973 in an attempt to stop further disintegration after Romania's accession. But by the fall of 1981, Soviet control over the Eastern European empire had slipped to such a degree that Hungary neither consulted with nor even informed the USSR of its decision to apply. The fast acquisition of membership by the spring of 1982 helped Hungary to avoid international insolvency just in time, but also convinced the country to accelerate economic reforms that included regulatory and ministerial reforms, the legalization of private businesses, and the opening toward the global economy.[23]

In comparison, Poland only started to consider IMF membership in early 1981 when it faced talks with more than four hundred commercial banks from fifteen Western countries on the rescheduling of its exploding debt. By August, an agreement was reached to defer the interest payment for 95 percent of all Polish liabilities – totaling five billion US dollars – by four years. In a media statement after its application to the IMF on November 10, Poland announced that membership would reverse its Soviet-enforced exit from the institution in 1950 and thus "re-establish connections that had been cut by the crisis of the Cold War." Yet Jaruzelski must have known that the WAPA intervention, for which he concurrently hoped, or the imposition of martial law, which he still tried to avoid, would damage the application. Indeed, by the turn of 1981/82, the United States and its NATO allies imposed economic sanctions on Poland. Martial law delayed Poland's entry into the International Monetary Fund by four years until 1986.[24]

Given the competition with its capitalist sibling, the GDR faced a unique dilemma. Romanian-style austerity was not an option for political reasons since it would have amounted to a *de facto* declaration of bankruptcy of the socialist experiment on German soil. Joining the IMF was not possible either for ideological reasons because it would have meant submission to the financial system of the supposedly doomed capitalist world. Yet, turning to the German sibling, even if it was capitalist, was possible *as long as* it was depicted as the continuation of détente in Europe. During the annual Crimea meeting in August 1980, Brezhnev had complained to Honecker about East Germany's increasing debt dependency on West Germany and warned of the country's resulting "disintegration from the USSR." In the Crimea meeting a year later, mentioned above, Brezhnev was still concerned about GDR debt but also obsessed with cutting Soviet oil supplies. Given the massive drop in Polish anthracite supplies in 1980 and the 10 percent reduction of Soviet oil deliveries the following year, the East German regime decided in the fall of 1981 on strict budgetary controls and on "flexible [attitudes] toward the Western countries." During a bilateral meeting in the GDR on December 11 – two days before Jaruzelski imposed martial law in neighboring Poland – Honecker proposed to the visiting Chancellor Schmidt far-reaching bilateral economic integration even if this would contravene East German membership in the CMEA, as he freely admitted. Although the chancellor did not agree to the idea, because he was more interested in improving human contacts, the East German regime afterward convinced itself that the meeting had opened up new opportunities.[25] But since GDR debt continued to balloon, the country's Foreign Trade Bank issued an internal warning by early 1982 that the country, like Poland, would soon be incapable of servicing its debt. An attempt via a well-connected German banker in Switzerland to get an economic framework agreement with West Germany in exchange for concessions in human affairs faltered over the summer when Schmidt's coalition government was sliding into collapse. The Christian Democratic successor government under Helmut Kohl, however, was at war with itself over policy toward East Germany, which meant that the GDR received a windfall loan of one billion German marks (400 million US dollars) in mid 1983 at virtually no political cost. In a tasteless joke, Honecker boasted that the GDR had gotten the loan like "the Virgin had become with child."[26]

The crisis in Poland further undermined the shaky financial health of the CMEA. When Warsaw announced in the late summer of 1980 that it could no longer service its massive debt of 25 billion US dollars in the non-socialist world, it was obvious that it would soon fail to do so with regard to its one billion US dollar debt to the CMEA's International Investment Bank (IIB). By the turn of the year 1980/81, when Poland finally faltered, the IIB was forced to assume hard currency debt in the non-socialist world at high-rate interest to maintain its own liquidity and, by extension, its international creditworthiness. Despite this looming bank crisis, the socialist states, which collectively owned the IIB, still narcissistically followed their own national economic interest by refusing to repay their US dollar debt at an earlier date in order to help keep the bank afloat. As all IIB members, including recalcitrant Poland, played a game of chicken with the CMEA bank, they just postponed the inevitable year by year. By October 1984, finally, they were forced to cut a deal that was much worse for the CMEA than the agreement that the Western banks had negotiated in the summer of 1981. It encompassed the rescheduling of Poland's complete CMEA debt for ten years without any interest payments. In the end, the deal kept a massive bad Polish loan on the books, depriving the IIB of the possibility of financing further economic integration projects within the CMEA.[27]

Moscow understood that its empire in Eastern Europe was slipping. At the annual Crimea meeting in August 1982, Brezhnev openly discussed with Honecker the Soviet need for purchases of grain and food from the non-socialist world, which, given the negative attitude of NATO, was "expensive and politically undesirable." The increasing technological and financial dependency of all CMEA countries on the non-socialist world, Brezhnev continued, had reached a "worrying character." At the same time, supply delays and the low quality of goods produced in CMEA countries further undermined the viability of the economic organization. During a Politburo meeting shortly after Brezhnev's death in November 1982, the CPSU discussed the urgent need to find strategic solutions to the economic development problems in the USSR and the CMEA. While remaining critical, the Soviet comrades at least took note of the nascent success of the Hungarian economic reforms, including the exploitation of private initiative. Yet Brezhnev's successor Andropov seemed to see the economic problems plaguing the USSR and the CMEA purely in terms of Western economic and ideological warfare, counselling Honecker in March 1983 to keep up political vigilance in order to defeat international capitalism in the long term.[28] But Andropov's commitment to ideological purity did not reverse the economic disintegration of the CMEA. Domestic pressures forced the USSR in 1983 to become inflexible in the pricing of Soviet energy and raw materials while simultaneously demanding greater flexibility from Eastern European CMEA members in terms of quantity and variety of goods to be delivered. The economic downward slide and disintegration of the CMEA continued after Andropov's death in February 1984. His successor, Konstantin U. Chernenko, warned Honecker in June that West Germany, with its strategy of embracing the GDR economically, intended to "liquidate" socialism on German soil and to "expand power into the east." But Honecker only poured salt into the open wound. The combination of the Polish Crisis and Soviet failures to provide sufficient quantities of energy and raw materials had forced the GDR to seek economic rapprochement with the FRG.[29]

The Conservative Turn in the West, 1979–83

Similar to the Polish role in the transformation of the Socialist Camp, the parallel rise of conservative leaders – the two ideologues Margaret Thatcher and Ronald Reagan, the pragmatic Socialist François Mitterrand, and the Christian Democrat Helmut Kohl – brought long-term changes to the Western world. All four faced comparable problems at home – an economic and political malaise that seemed to question the continuation of decades-long policies of Keynesian deficit spending. And they shared a strident anti-communism in foreign relations.

Margaret Thatcher was elected prime minister of the United Kingdom in early May of 1979, just before the beginning of the second oil shock that would lead to a doubling of prices within less than a year. Soon nicknamed the Iron Lady, she was convinced that the United Kingdom needed a complete economic reconstruction because socialist, bureaucratic, and interventionist policies since 1945 had ruined the country. Her first goal was to tackle high inflation through a combination of sharp increases in interest rates, budget cuts, and a shift of taxation from income to consumption. However, her policies did not stop the decline of the British economy but instead quickly produced high unemployment. The Falklands War in 1982 reversed her sagging popularity, and the drop in global oil prices and decline in inflation shortly thereafter brought some success to her economic policies. In 1984–85, she was determined to break the power of the labor unions, which she saw as the greatest obstacle to necessary reform, and then to sell off nationalized industries and infrastructure to raise government revenue. While the British economy grew in the second half of the 1980s in aggregate terms, Thatcher did not achieve her goal of reducing the government's share in the economy. Savings from cuts in public expenditure were devoured by unemployment benefits for an increasing number of workers who had lost their jobs in inefficient factories, which Thatcher's free market ideology-driven policies allowed to go bankrupt.[30]

Thatcher's relationship with Europe was more complex than her Tory successors in Great Britain nowadays claim. Shortly after her election and half a year before the NATO double-track decision, she agreed with Schmidt on the military and psychological need to counterbalance the Soviet deployment of SS-20 intermediate range nuclear missiles. She was also not a fervent Euroskeptic; on the contrary, as the new Conservative leader in 1975, she had been a pro-campaigner in the referendum against the Euroskeptic Labour government under Harold Wilson. Yet, when she became prime minister four years later, the ongoing economic malaise in the United Kingdom had gradually eroded public support for EC membership. In the first direct elections to the European Parliament in June 1979 – a month after her triumph – only a third of the eligible voters participated in the United Kingdom while two-thirds did so in the rest of the EC. Despite recommendations by her advisers to stay out of the European Monetary System, Thatcher was unwilling to shut the door on negotiations completely. Most importantly, however, she tried as early as 1980 to change the way member states contributed to the community budget because the allocation formula put the United Kingdom at a disadvantage. Based on the rate of the internal consumption tax and the overall size of external customs revenue, it required London to pay a higher-than-average contribution, while the budget's focus on the Common Agricultural Policy primarily benefited farmers in France.[31]

With the promise to "Make America Great Again" after a decade of economic decline and political unease, Ronald Reagan won the presidential election in November 1980, twenty months after Thatcher's victory. His success marked the rejection of the country's post-war liberal consensus, which had been based on Keynesian policies by a fiscally interventionist federal government. The economy had started to suffer in the late 1960s as a result of the Vietnam War and the declining competitiveness of American products on the international market, and then buckled in the wake of the first oil shock in 1973–74. Increasing unemployment, high inflation, and economic contraction provided conservative politicians and academic free market advocates with the opportunity to attack Keynesianism. The retreat from Vietnam in 1973 and the Watergate Scandal, which forced Nixon to resign a year later, added political discontent to economic discomfort. In 1976, Americans voted for the Democrat Jimmy Carter because, as an outsider to Washington, he was untainted by scandal and seemed to promise a new beginning. A technocrat without much charismatic appeal, he not only failed to solve the country's economic problems but was also prone to political gaffes. In foreign policy, he did not depart much from his predecessors Nixon and Ford – continuing rapprochement with China, seeking SALT II in the context of the Soviet–American nuclear duopoly, and emphasizing human rights in the wake of the Helsinki Final Act – but suffered from conflict among his top advisers. Ultimately, the humiliating hostage-taking of American diplomats in the Islamic Republic of Iran in late 1979 and the botched American military rescue attempt the following spring undermined Carter's appeal to voters in a presidential election year.[32]

A charismatic former Hollywood actor and California governor, Reagan won the presidency on his second attempt. He had started his political career in the campaign for the arch-conservative Barry Goldwater in 1964. Twelve years later, he lost the Republican primaries against the sitting President Ford by only a slim margin. Following Goldwater's crushing defeat by Lyndon B. Johnson, Reagan had led the conservative revival by opposing the liberal social engineering policies of the 1960s and the Keynesianism that underpinned the economic policies from John F. Kennedy to Jimmy Carter. Like Thatcher, he embraced the rise of conservative economic thought that included free market capitalism, tax cuts to jumpstart private investment, and a reduction of state intervention in the form of spending cuts, deregulation, and the shrinking of the welfare state. He also had some clear ideas about foreign policy long before he assumed office. Convinced that the USSR was a "temporary aberration" and vulnerable in the sphere of ideas, he envisioned a restoration of a US Cold War foreign policy to political and military strength. Given these viewpoints, Reagan considered US participation in the recently ended Vietnam War honorable, which at the time was a controversial minority view.[33]

On the day of his inauguration, January 20, 1981, Reagan benefited from the concurrent release of the American hostages by the Islamic Republic of Iran, which had been negotiated by outgoing President Carter. Like Thatcher, the new president quickly tackled inflation, but his free market policies, unlike hers, showed quick success by the second half of 1982 when an unbroken seven-year expansion of the economy started. On the flipside, however, recovery caused huge budget deficits and let socio-economic inequality rise dramatically. In foreign policy, Reagan acted equally quickly. Shortly after inauguration, he declared détente dead. The new president was convinced that his predecessors Nixon, Ford, and Carter had allowed the USSR to consolidate its positions in Europe and advance its interests in Asia and Africa. His foreign policy returned to earlier containment ideas – such as resistance to Soviet expansion everywhere – but also included offers of genuine negotiations to resolve disagreements peacefully. However, this was only possible, he believed, after increasing the military budget and implementing assertive Cold War policies to force the hand of the USSR. But as an evangelical, he also abhorred the possibility of nuclear war since it posed a severe threat to God's creation. Consequently, he disliked the nuclear duopoly, which the USSR and the United States had formed since the late 1960s and cemented in two sets of nuclear arms limitation treaties in the 1970s, because it had not led to nuclear *disarmament*. The new president was determined to break the duopoly either through immediate negotiations on disarmament or through unilateral nuclear armament intended to force the Soviet Union to the negotiation table. Hence, Reagan quickly endorsed the NATO double-track decision of December 1979. By March 1983, he proposed the Strategic Defense Initiative – an ambitious space-based defense system designed to lower the chances of a Soviet nuclear first strike.[34]

In terms of containment at the Soviet periphery, Reagan continued Carter's anti-Soviet policy of standing firm on non-intervention in Poland and supporting Islamist insurgents in Afghanistan. His pressure policies against the USSR also extended, much more than Carter's, to the sphere of rhetoric and propaganda, as his two "evil empire" speeches before the British parliament and a gathering of Florida evangelicals in June 1982 and March 1983, respectively, testify. Yet his disproportionate focus on strident anti-communism created new dangers and made him blind to issues that arose outside the Cold War paradigm. His assertive military stance toward the other superpower caused a nuclear crisis during the NATO Able Archer maneuvers in November of 1983, which, however, was far less serious than the Cuban Missile Crisis in 1962. He was incapable of seeing the concurrent rise of the post-Cold War world in the Middle East. When armed Lebanese groups, probably linked to the Shia Islamist Hizbullah, bombed the American embassy and the headquarters of the US Marines in Beirut in 1983, he ordered withdrawal early the following year. In order to free American hostages held in Beirut by Islamist groups connected to Tehran, Reagan even agreed to sell weapons to the Islamic Republic of Iran, currently at war with Iraq, and to use the proceeds to fund illegally the bloody struggle of anti-communist guerrillas against the supposed Soviet takeover of Nicaragua.[35]

In May 1981, six months after the conservative Reagan was voted into office, the Socialist François Mitterrand won the French presidency. His election was primarily a vote against the conservative Valéry Giscard d'Estaing, who paid for the economic downturn that spanned his entire seven-year presidency following the first oil shock of 1973–74. While the election of a Socialist president looked, at least at first glance, like an odd event given the conservative turns in the United Kingdom and the United States, it reflected major long-term shifts in the French political system. On the one hand, Catholicism and class had lost their defining political role since the end of World War II. France's economy and society had undergone massive transformations even under the conservative Charles de Gaulle, who had himself often pushed for change. On the other hand, Mitterrand was the only electable candidate on the left. He and his party had become co-dependent in the long march back to power after the humiliating defeat in the national election of June 1968. Mitterrand needed the party's organizational prowess, while the party needed his political appeal to regain power in order to implement the envisioned socialist reconstruction of the country.[36]

Mitterrand's slim victory was not a mandate for radical reform. But his quick decision to call for snap elections for the National Assembly in June secured a clear majority of seats for his Socialist Party. His invitation to the Communist Party to join him in government initially worried Thatcher and Reagan, especially since the small far-left party had parted ways with the Italian Eurocommunists by the late 1970s and realigned with the USSR. From afar, it thus appeared that France sought a "rupture with capitalism" while pursuing its own "road to Socialism." But Mitterrand primarily wanted social and political peace in France in the face of high unemployment and inflation. He aimed, as he told American officials, at binding the hard-line communists into the government so that he could discredit their radical political platform in the long term with the adoption of policies that contradicted their convictions. To mollify Western worries, he quickly committed France to the anti-Soviet NATO double-track decision of late 1979, even though his country had left the military structures of the alliance in 1966. Still, during the first year of his presidency, Mitterrand enacted the radical polices of the joint Socialist–Communist program of 1972, which had been formulated at a time of economic health and international détente. Antithetical to what Thatcher and Reagan were pursuing at the time, this included the nationalization of banks and industries, the increase of minimum wages and pensions, cuts to working hours, tax hikes for the rich, and the increase of public sector jobs to fight unemployment.[37]

By mid 1982, Mitterrand undertook his famous U-turn. The policies of his first year had not helped to revive the economy, which had been flagging since the mid 1970s. Hovering at 10 to 14 percent, inflation caused the French franc to depreciate in international markets at a similar rate, despite the limits that the European Monetary System allowed currencies to swing. While Mitterrand would never subscribe to the newly reigning Anglo–American free market ideology, he still used a "dose of Thatcherism" in June 1982. Abandoning Keynesianism, the French president enacted austerity with cuts to public spending as well as the imposition of price and wage freezes to bring inflation down to concurrent West German or American rates of 5 and 7 percent, respectively. The results of his new policies were similar to those in Thatcher's United Kingdom; until the mid 1980s, unemployment rose from 7 to 11 percent. In 1983, Mitterrand even decided to fight inflation by pegging the franc to the resilient West German mark, a step that forestalled further devaluations and forced France to seek another round of European integration to reap economic benefits. Although the French public generally agreed with the radical measures Mitterrand had implemented, the unified left still lost the municipal elections in 1983. Soon, however, the president ended the coalition with the communists, who had greatly suffered at the ballot box due to their association with the austerity policies. Despite massive labor protests throughout 1984, Mitterrand continued his policies of economic reconstruction by forcing state-owned companies to forego government subsidies and to balance books through job cuts, and by allowing inefficient industries to go bankrupt. At least, after the mid 1980s, inflation came down, but unemployment remained stubbornly high.[38]

West Germany's turn toward conservatism in October 1982 unfolded in a fashion different again from Thatcher's United Kingdom, Reagan's United States, and Mitterrand's France. The country had suffered from high unemployment and economic stagnation in the wake of Nixon's abolition of the Bretton Woods agreement in 1971 as well as the first oil shock in 1973–74. However, the legal mandate of price stability forced the Federal Bank to tighten money supply early on, which resulted in a comparatively low inflation rate. In the federal elections of October 1980, the Social Democratic Party under the moderate Chancellor Schmidt and its Free Democratic (Liberal) coalition partner enlarged their combined majority of seats against the center-right coalition headed by the Bavarian Franz-Josef Strauss. But Schmidt's coalition started to fray within a year over disagreements about domestic and foreign policy. The Free Democratic Party stressed the need to address continued economic difficulties and to reform the welfare state, which faced problems of long-term sustainability as a result of population aging. In foreign policy, however, conflict did not emerge *between* the coalition partners but rather *within* the Social Democratic Party. The party's rank-and-file was deeply engaged in the country's influential peace and environmental movement. Fears that Germany would become the main battlefield in a future nuclear war led many party members to turn against the NATO double-track decision. But the father of that decision, Chancellor Schmidt, continued to stick to his guns against his own party – in a strange alliance with the increasingly restless Free Democratic coalition partner and the Christian Democratic opposition.[39]

Schmidt's government fell as the result of a no-confidence vote on October 1, 1982, after the Free Democratic Party had abandoned the Social Democrats and joined Helmut Kohl's coalition of the Christian Democratic Union and its Bavarian sister party, the Christian Social Union. The new three-party coalition government promised a "conservative turn-around" in economic and foreign policy. Like Reagan, the new chancellor spoke about the need for a moral regeneration in domestic politics. He sought close Franco–German cooperation with the Socialist Mitterrand in the spirit of Konrad Adenauer's rapprochement with Charles de Gaulle in the late 1950s and early 1960s. Like the French president, he too quickly pursued a clear popular mandate, which he received in a snap election in March 1983.[40]

But Kohl's conservative turnaround paled in comparison to what Thatcher, Reagan, and even Mitterrand were undertaking. Unemployment remained high throughout the 1980s, while the announced cuts to the welfare state were minimal. Kohl's government mainly benefited from the American recovery, which took off just as he became chancellor, and the resulting rebound of the world economy, all of which allowed him to avoid radical reform at home. In foreign policy, he embraced continuity in terms of Schmidt's commitment to the NATO double-track decision and close collaboration with France for the sake of further EC integration. At least, he could overcome the famously difficult relationship between his predecessor and Carter by establishing a close working relationship with Reagan. But in domestic affairs, personal gaffes and party slush fund scandals weakened the new chancellor for many years. Even in relations with East Germany, his government missed the chance of lessening the nation's division. His struggle with Strauss about control over German–German relations first led to the abrogation of Schmidt's attempts to get political concessions from the GDR in exchange for economic assistance, and then allowed the Bavarian right-winger to seize the initiative and provide Honecker with a one-billion mark (400 million US dollar) loan without any political strings attached, as mentioned above.[41]

The NATO Double-Track Decision Implemented, 1983

The collapse of economic hegemony in the Socialist Camp in 1980–81 did not convince the Soviet leaders to question their policy of trying to split Western public opinion in order to scuttle the NATO double-track decision. On the contrary, the emerging conflict between Schmidt and the majority of the Social Democratic Party, which they noticed by mid 1981, encouraged them to stick to the policy. In an interview in late October – a month before martial law was imposed in Poland – Brezhnev once more offered talks on the parallel reduction of SS-20 missiles and similar NATO systems including those of Great Britain and France. Given his own visions of complete nuclear disarmament, Reagan replied on November 18 in his first foreign policy speech as president with a proposal to withdraw *all* American and Soviet intermediate range nuclear missiles from Europe: "With Soviet agreement, we could together substantially reduce the dread threat of nuclear war which hangs over the people of Europe. This, like the first footstep on the Moon, would be a giant step for mankind." But within days, Brezhnev rejected Reagan's zero-proposal as an attempt to "disarm" the USSR. The Kremlin was still betting on its ability to split Western public opinion.[42]

In the spring of 1982, eventually, the Soviet leaders started to worry that time was running out. Yet even Kohl's rise in October of 1982 and his victory in the snap election half a year later failed to convince the Kremlin to change tack. On the contrary, the "decisive phase" to influence Western public opinion supposedly began in the spring of 1983, though it too would prove futile. In September, the desperate WAPA members decided to launch a final coordinated propaganda campaign against the supposed NATO plan to nuclearize Europe while again promoting a zero-solution proposal that included British and French nuclear weapons. But nothing helped to rescue the flawed campaign of thwarting the implementation of the four-year-old NATO double-track decision. By 1983, Western unity was based on the public endorsement for the stationing of Pershing II intermediate nuclear rockets in an attempt to counterbalance the SS-20 missiles. On November 22, the West German parliament formally agreed to their deployment; the following day, the first Pershing II arrived on German soil.[43]

Although the USSR had failed in its campaign since early 1954 to establish its hegemony over all of Europe at the expense of the United States, the aging men in the Kremlin stuck to their course. After Andropov's death in early 1984, Chernenko hoped that Reagan would lose his bid for re-election against the Democratic challenger Walter Mondale, whom the Soviet leaders considered gullible. The president's landslide victory in November 1984 once more revealed Soviet miscalculations. At the same time, Soviet influence in Eastern Europe continued to collapse. Kohl and Honecker had agreed in early October of 1983 to pursue a bilateral "partnership of reason" despite the deployment of the Pershing II missiles the following month. While détente was dead on the global plane, it flourished at the lower level in Europe. By April 1984, Strauss promised yet another one-billion mark loan to help stabilize East Germany. All Chernenko could do was warn Honecker about West German plans for economic embracement and geographic expansion, but, as mentioned above, the East German party head responded by reminding the economically impotent Soviet leader of the lack of energy and raw material support.[44]

Conclusion

The mid 1980s marked the crossroads in the economic development of divided Europe. The CMEA suffered from a lack of will to continue integration while some of its core members deepened their financial and economic links to the non-socialist world. Despite repeated discussions of various ideas, no new economic initiative was launched except in the field of extending the gas pipeline network to replace declining Soviet oil supplies. By 1988, when the USSR was undergoing its own economic and political reforms under the new Soviet leader Mikhail S. Gorbachev, it eventually demanded the introduction of free market principles to save the CMEA.[45] Around that time, the conservative turn in the West showed results in terms of aggregate economic growth, though at the cost of increased budget deficits and sustained high unemployment. More important, however, was the renewed round of Western European integration that started in 1984. With the admission of three military dictatorships-turned-democracies – Greece in 1982, and Spain and Portugal two years later – the EC had grown to a dozen members. At Franco–German prodding, the *Twelve* cut a deal on British contributions – the so-called rebate – at the Fontainebleau Summit in June 1984, which in turn unblocked revisions to the Rome Treaties that allowed further economic integration beyond just the abolition of customs. In February 1986, the *Twelve* signed the Single European Act, which aimed at harmonizing commercial standards and at establishing the four freedoms – free movement of goods, persons, services, and capital – within six years. Even though Thatcher had agreed to the Single European Act because of its emphasis on the old British obsession with free trade, she subsequently became a critic of the EC as the only possible version of a united Europe. Her disapproval primarily aimed at the community's long-term goal of seeking the dissolution of national sovereignty, but it definitely did not envision overcoming the continent's forty-year Cold War division.[46]

By the mid 1980s, the structures for the end of the regional Cold War in Europe had been put in place. The initiative had come from Eastern European countries, particularly Hungary, Poland, and East Germany. Even after 1968, Budapest had continued to advocate economic reform and the opening toward the non-socialist world, but had been stymied by the CMEA. Once Soviet military and economic hegemony crumbled in the fall of 1981, Hungary joined the IMF within less than half a year, avoided external default, and continued with its economic reforms and its own integration into the global economy. Poland followed closely, driven by its external default and its massive domestic problems. At virtually the same time, the GDR decided to seek economic rapprochement with the FRG. However, there were also obstacles to all of these overtures. The USSR tried to prevent the economic disintegration of its Eastern European empire while it continued to pursue hegemony over Western Europe. Ultimately, it failed in both endeavors. Equally noteworthy were the different Western responses to the Eastern European overtures. Despite Poland's application to the IMF, the imposition of martial law resulted in NATO sanctions that delayed membership and, consequently, greater economic integration with the non-socialist world. During the transition from Schmidt to Kohl, West Germany was hesitant to embark on economic integration with East Germany in tandem with political concessions. Instead, the FRG provided funds to stabilize the economy, and thereby the dictatorship, in the GDR for some more years without demanding anything in return. In general, in the second half of the 1980s, Western Europeans were more interested in their own integration process than in integration with an opening socialist Eastern Europe. The final collapse of the regional Cold War in Europe required the emergence of a new generation of Soviet reformist leaders – like Mikhail S. Gorbachev – which accelerated this process, as described in the next chapter.

The seemingly sudden end of the Cold War in 1989 has surprised parti-cipants, observers at the time, and scholars to this day. It destroyed near-unshakable assumptions about the long-lasting division of Europe, Germany, and Berlin. As a result, the air was filled with awe and excite-ment – but also with concerns that the new situation would not hold. Too many Cold War crises – in 1948–49, 1953, 1956, 1961, 1968, 1979, and 1980–81 – had prematurely ended spells of hope. Yet the notion that the global Cold War ended in 1989 is *primarily* a Eurocentric interpretation. The year had little meaning in Asia or the Middle East, apart from the Vietnamese withdrawal from Cambodia and the Soviet pull-out from Afghanistan. As the previous chapters reveal, the superpower conflict had mostly lost its meaning as an ordering paradigm in both world regions a decade before. Even in Europe, the Cold War of the early 1980s looked vastly different from that of the late 1940s. The continent's division had become less rigid, and most of Eastern Europe was in an economic downward spiral and rife with popular disaffection.

As Chapters 5 to 22 reveal, by the early 1980s, over three decades of structural change in Asia, the Middle East, and Europe had put in place the conditions under which the superpower conflict could actually have ended earlier. At the beginning of the Cold War, three great powers had run the world – the United Kingdom, the USSR, and the United States. The collapse of their World War II alliance divided Asia, the Middle East, and Europe, though in regionally different ways. East and Southeast Asia were divided into communist states on the mainland and pro-American countries along the continent's shoreline, while India tried to keep the Cold War out of South Asia. The Middle East was split between members of the British-led Baghdad Pact/CENTO and Non-Aligned countries, and between Soviet-supported Arab states and American-backed Israel. Europe was broken up along the Iron Curtain into a communist East and a non-communist West, with Non-Aligned Yugoslavia and the neutrals Austria, Switzerland, and Sweden in between. By the early 1980s, the United Kingdom had long ceased to be a great power, the colonial empires had unraveled, and the appeal of socialism had declined. The division in East Asia now ran *among* communist countries, with different non-communist states supporting either side. In the Middle East, new conflicts emerged along sectarian lines and between Arab states and Iran. Europe witnessed the collapse of communist cohesion and the partial economic integration of Eastern Europe into the global economy.

But if the regional structures for the end of the global Cold War were in place in the first half of the 1980s, *why, then, did the superpower conflict take so long to end?* The answer is remarkably simple: both superpowers were Cold Warriors almost until the very end. America-centric interpretations to the contrary the final years of the Cold War did not resemble a boxing match that Ronald Reagan's United States won with a knockout punch. They actually looked more like an endurance race, in which Mikhail S. Gorbachev's Soviet Union simply ran out of steam. There is no doubt that the American president was a committed Cold Warrior. He said so before the 1980 election, and he acted accordingly in his eight years in office from 1981 to 1989. Under him, the United States turned into a resurgent military and economic power. Moreover, Reagan extended the Cold War geographically into Africa and Latin America – most notably Nicaragua – as well as into outer space with his Strategic Defense Initiative (SDI). His rhetoric denounced communism and championed unfettered free-market capitalism. In his intellectual world, the USSR was an evil empire and Gorbachev could tear down the Berlin Wall simply at the snap of his fingers.[1] But all things considered, his uncompromising style and confrontational policies did not drive the Soviet Union to surrender. To be fair, Reagan was at least committed to nuclear disarmament from his first year in office, i.e. he was dedicated to dismantling those weapons that had made the United States and the USSR into superpowers in their own class by the 1960s.

Gorbachev was a Cold Warrior as well. Since his teenage years, he had been a dedicated Marxist–Leninist, though he had rejected Stalinism shortly before the death of the Great Dictator. When he became general secretary in 1985, he displayed the same anti-Americanism that his predecessors had embraced. His *New Thinking* in economic and foreign policy was about ensuring that a reinvigorated Soviet Union would stay in the superpower race against the imperialist–capitalist United States. But the new approach never amounted to a coherent set of policies, as Gorbachev admitted early on. It evolved over time through trial and error, and encompassed contradictory elements toward the end of the decade. For example, Gorbachev retreated from economic reform at home in the late 1980s while he continued to shed revolutionary liabilities abroad – in Cuba, Vietnam, Afghanistan, and Eastern Europe. Only by 1988 did

Gorbachev start to question his belief in Marxism–Leninism.[2] When communism collapsed in Eastern Europe in 1989, because the USSR was politically, economically, and militarily no longer capable of supporting its empire, the sudden political changes there triggered similar developments within the Soviet Union in the following two years. Thus, the focus of this chapter is not on Reagan's fictitious victory in the Cold War, but on Gorbachev's failed attempts to maintain the superpower status of the USSR.

Gorbachev's Rise

Gorbachev's election as general secretary of the Communist Party of the Soviet Union (CPSU) in mid March of 1985 marked the advent of a younger generation of Soviet leaders, whose formative years had not occurred during the Stalin period but during Nikita S. Khrushchev's Thaw. According to conventional wisdom, his three predecessors, Leonid I. Brezhnev (died in November 1982), Yuri V. Andropov (died in February 1984), and Konstantin U. Chernenko (died in March 1985), were mentally beyond their prime, physically ailing, and ideologically inflexible representatives of the old guard. Of course, Andropov had advocated the interventions in Hungary in 1956, in Czechoslovakia in 1968, and in Afghanistan in 1979, but flinched in 1981 when it came to Poland. During his fifteen-month tenure as general secretary, he believed that the Soviet problems were not structural but rather the result of a lack of ideological commitment and low work discipline. In comparison, his successor Chernenko sought rapprochement with the People's Republic of China (PRC) in late 1984. Shortly before his death, he decided to improve relations with the United States by redispatching a delegation to the nuclear disarmament talks after his predecessor had withdrawn it in response to the implementation of the NATO double-track decision over a year earlier.[3]

Gorbachev was not only substantially younger than his two immediate predecessors at the time of ascent to power, but also better educated. Although he came from a humble background in rural southern Russia, he managed to enroll in the country's premier university in Moscow in 1950. There he became life-long friends with a Czechoslovak student – Zdeněk Mlynář – who would become a reformer during the Prague Spring in 1968 and then one of the signers of Czechoslovakia's Charter 77 a decade later. During their initial years at the university, the two became doubters of Stalinism but not of Marxism–Leninism. In their final two years at university, they witnessed the start of Khrushchev's Thaw. For over two decades after graduation in 1955, Gorbachev made his career in agricultural affairs in southern Russia, where he earned a reputation as a hard-working and incorruptible technocrat. By 1978, he returned to Moscow as a member of the Central Committee and then even of the Politburo. He shared several characteristics with his political patron Andropov – a southern Russian background, the belief in Marxism–Leninism, work discipline, and displeasure at the corruption even at the highest level during Brezhnev's later years. At the turn of 1983/84 Gorbachev *de facto* ran the USSR during Andropov's final illness, as he did again the following summer during Chernenko's temporary absence for health reasons. Interested in reducing Cold War tensions with the United States, he met Prime Minister Margaret Thatcher, Ronald Reagan's fellow conservative in Europe, in December 1984 to send a signal to the other superpower. Indeed, when the Iron Lady traveled to Washington soon thereafter, she impressed her positive evaluation of the Soviet deputy leader on the American president.[4]

At the point of his election, Gorbachev had no set of fully developed ideas to reform Soviet communism. He understood that the USSR had fallen behind the West in the fields of technology, economics, and living standards, though not in the realms of space exploration and arms development. Nonetheless, in a speech to the leaders of the Warsaw Pact member states three days after Chernenko's death, Gorbachev regurgitated the old mantras, stressing the "continuity of the political line," calling for greater economic integration of the Socialist Camp, and warning about the assertiveness of the United States and NATO. Soon thereafter, he came up with his own slogan – *uskorenye* (acceleration) – which revived Khrushchev's policies of additional investment in heavy industry and Andropov's ideas of increased work discipline. But Gorbachev also understood that the implementation of new policies required getting rid of the members of the old guard, like long-time foreign minister Andrei A. Gromyko, who were poised to slow down changes to a system that had been established during their entire political life.[5]

Reforming the Soviet Union

The explosion of the nuclear power plant in Chernobyl on April 26, 1986, which massively contaminated the adjacent city of Pripyat – and, even to a lesser degree, parts of Europe – played a central role in Gorbachev's opening of Soviet politics and society. The lack of a functioning civil defense system, the paralysis of decision-making in Moscow, and the government's customary tendency to keep the public at home and abroad in the dark about the gravity of the situation all revealed that the seven-decade-old secretive communist political system was poorly equipped for the modern world. It convinced Gorbachev to push *glasnost* (openness) for the rest of the year, making frequent public statements about the many crises in all aspects of Soviet life. In the summer of 1987, he even wrote a book to explain his "revolutionary" visions about perfecting Marxist–Leninist socialism.[6]

In parallel to the promotion of *glasnost*, Gorbachev abandoned Andropov's emphasis on work discipline in favor of political liberalization, although competitive elections would not follow until 1989. In the fall of 1986, censorship was abolished, long-banned novels were allowed to be published, and newspapers started to print increasingly critical assessments of contemporaneous problems and the Stalin period. Gorbachev preferred a complete condemnation of the dictator – thereby going much further than Khrushchev in February 1956 – but older Politburo members, whose careers had started under Iosif V. Stalin, opposed radical steps. After Gorbachev had convinced the Politburo that the modernization of Soviet society would not allow the continued criminalization of dissidents, 140 political prisoners – among them Andrei D. Sakharov – were released from prison or allowed to return from internal exile at the turn of the year 1986/87. But the new Soviet leader still needed to overcome skeptics from far and wide. Predictably, cadres feared for their privileges, and citizens – even if they yearned for the improvement of their difficult material situation – disliked the uncertainties that change might bring.[7]

The most important reform, however, was *perestroika* – the reconstruction or remodeling of the Soviet economy – which started in earnest in 1987, just after the US and Western European economies had re-emerged from the malaise of the previous decade. Despite the repeated growth forecasts of successive Five-Year Plans since the 1960s, the economy stagnated two decades later; some Soviet specialists even believed it was contracting. In the 1970s, the export of oil and raw materials to the non-socialist world had financed the purchase of technology, consumer products, grain, and food there. But these imports declined when Soviet oil production and world market prices successively fell in the first half of the 1980s. The technocrats and specialists, whom Gorbachev had promoted, understood many of the underlying economic problems but often shied away from radical economic reforms that could possibly produce a revolutionary situation like that in Poland in 1980. As late as September 1988, Gorbachev compared his visions with Lenin's New Economic Policy of the 1920s when ideological retreat "had saved Russia."[8]

But where did *perestroika* come from? Gorbachev abhorred the unfettered free market capitalism championed by Thatcher and Reagan. Similarly, François Mitterrand's reformed French system and the West

German social market economy were not points of reference, nor were the reforms in Hungary. Even though a Soviet spokesman explained in April 1987 that the sole difference between *perestroika* and the Prague Spring was "nineteen years," Czechoslovak economic reforms before 1968 did not have a significant influence on Gorbachev's policies either. At least, some of Gorbachev's economic reforms resembled Aleksei N. Kosygin's technocratic ideas of the 1960s.[9] In effect, since the early 1980s Soviet economic specialists had looked toward the PRC, which was reaping the benefits of the economic reforms officially adopted by Deng Xiaoping in late 1978. They understood that China's economic reform had started in the countryside with rural policies similar to Lenin's New Economic Policy. But the Chinese leaders were even more radical. They had dismissed Marxist–Leninist economic theory and had decollectivized agriculture, introducing market mechanisms instead. Given his own involvement in Soviet agriculture from the 1950s to the 1970s, Gorbachev had recognized the pressing need for rural reform, which is why he quickly went about reshaping the relevant Soviet ministerial bureaucracy to break old thinking and command structures in 1985. But the introduction of Chinese-style economic reforms still met with resistance from cadres at all levels while it suffered from structural problems. The PRC had been able to tap into the underused economic potential of the vast majority of the Chinese people, whom the internal passport system had forced to live in the countryside since the 1950s. The USSR, in comparison, lacked this kind of labor reserve, because the country had undergone swift urbanization since the 1930s while its demographic growth had declined. Ultimately, however, Gorbachev's reforms were well-intentioned but half-hearted trial-and-error policies. The man himself was a consensus builder, and thus his policy decisions were compromises among different factions of reformers and between reformers and conservatives within the party apparatus.[10]

Gorbachev's reforms triggered opposition on both flanks of the party. He was the target of criticism from some of the reformers, who had received his backing in 1985 but increasingly disagreed with the slow pace of change. One of the most vociferous critics was Boris N. Yeltsin, the populist party boss of the industrial city of Sverdlovsk (today's Yekaterinburg) to the east of the Ural Mountains. Appointed by Gorbachev as Moscow city party boss in late 1985, Yeltsin quickly sacked the vast majority of the corrupt higher city administration. Within two years, he openly attacked Gorbachev in the Politburo over personal grievances and political differences. The general secretary reacted by demoting him to a ministerial bureaucracy in late 1987. On the other side of the political spectrum, conservative forces rejected changes to the Soviet system. While Gorbachev had been able to pension off many of the old guard in the leadership, their followers still populated all ranks of the party. Many believed that his reforms would endanger what they considered Soviet achievements – social justice, affordable food and housing, or guaranteed employment. Some agreed with Gorbachev's criticism of Stalin but still believed in Lenin's world revolutionary dreams. Others were unreconstructed Stalinists, who believed Gorbachev was selling the USSR out to the imperialist–capitalist enemy. On March 13, 1988, just as he left Moscow on a five-day trip to Yugoslavia, an orchestrated conservative attack started with the publication of an alleged letter-to-the-editor written by a Leningrad university professor, Nina Andreyeva, in the newspaper *Sovetskaya Rossiya*. Gorbachev was able to parry this particular attack in the Politburo. But he had been put on notice about the possibility of future surprise attacks and possibly even coup attempts, and thus felt under pressure to make more concessions to the conservatives.[11]

Reorganizing Eastern Europe

Reforming the Soviet Union went hand in hand with reorganizing relations with the Socialist Camp in Eastern Europe, given that by the 1970s and the early 1980s the USSR had reached its economic and military limits in maintaining its empire there. Because Eastern European socialist countries had accumulated much debt to the non-socialist world, their integration into the global economy was proceeding throughout the 1980s. Until 1988, Gorbachev did not intend to give up Soviet influence in Eastern Europe voluntarily, although in the fall of 1981 Andropov had accepted the possibility that a non-communist government might arise in Poland, as did some of Gorbachev's aides in the spring of 1985. In mid 1986, Gorbachev himself recognized that a Polish departure from the Socialist Camp was a possible scenario that might precipitate East Germany's exit and even the collapse of Soviet hegemonic positions in all of Eastern Europe. Like Khrushchev after Stalin's death, Gorbachev hoped that Eastern European governments would introduce political and economic reforms by themselves. He himself was not willing to impose a New Course that could backfire, as it had in the mid 1950s after Stalin's death. But his goal remained the same as Khrushchev's three decades before – to reform the Soviet clones, which Stalin had imposed, and thereby guarantee their long-term survival.[12]

In a repetition of the 1950s, the socialist regimes in Eastern Europe resisted Gorbachev's advice to reform – with the exception of Hungary. The Uprising in East Germany in 1953, the Hungarian Revolution in 1956, the Prague Spring in 1968, and the Polish Crisis in 1980–81 had taught most of them to value stability over experiments. It did not help that Gorbachev failed to get along with many of their leaders, except Poland's Wojciech Jaruzelski. All of them were almost a generation older and dogmatic in outlook. In addition to their fear of the destabilizing nature of reform, East Germany's Erich Honecker, for example, even believed that his country's supposedly perfect socialist system needed no reform at all. The continued Soviet economic demise provided a perfect pretext to deride Gorbachev's reforms. Romania's Nicolae Ceaușescu wondered about the new phenomenon of breadlines in Moscow, as if there were none in Bucharest at all. Bulgaria's Todor Zhivkov warned that Gorbachev's reforms would lead to the kind of instability that Khrushchev's de-Stalinization had created in Hungary in 1956; he would be proven right. But the combination of Gorbachev's mid 1986 rejection of the "methods used in relation to Czechoslovakia (in 1968) and Hungary (in 1956)" and his irritation at the Eastern European scorn for his reforms played important roles in his decision to abstain from intervention in 1989, as described below.[13]

Gorbachev experienced a similar disappointment with his reform attempts in the Council for Mutual Economic Assistance (CMEA). In 1985, he hoped to use the modernized organization to improve the economic situation in the USSR and Eastern Europe, despite the thirty-year history of failed attempts to shake it up. He believed that a great but unused economic potential existed in the Socialist Camp while capitalism was on its final downward path, as the crisis in the West since the early 1970s seemed to prove. Poignantly, he still called on CMEA members to learn from the West, which was concurrently using the scientific-technological revolution, particularly in microelectronics, to try to gain strategic advantages in the Cold War. If the CMEA adopted this method, he concluded, the Socialist Camp would beat the capitalist world at its own game by 2000. In early 1986, for example, Gorbachev was convinced that the USSR, the German Democratic Republic (GDR), and Czechoslovakia were capable of building up a powerful microelectronic industry within a few years as an engine for modernization to take on the United States, Western Europe, and Japan in that field. The decline of Soviet oil exports and falling world market prices, however, required substituting the purchase of the relevant technology in the West with greater socialist development efforts, as Gorbachev told Honecker in April. While gambling on the use of high technology, the Soviet leader simultaneously advocated trimming the CMEA down by getting rid of all the non-functional "junk" projects that had accumulated since the 1970s. Within two years, however, his own high-technology plans had become junk too, when it turned out that East Germany, which had promoted itself as the technological leader, was merely capable of producing microchips that were 100 times more expensive than similar products in the West and a decade behind the global standard.[14]

Soviet and Western experts alike noted the negative impact of declining Soviet economic potency on the Socialist Camp. Hence, in late 1986, Moscow's planners declared both the existing model of goods exchange within the CMEA and the Soviet delivery of subsidized oil and raw materials "outdated." A year later, West German economists noted that the debt levels of the USSR and all Eastern European CMEA member states – except Romania – were rising again. In late 1987, Hungary flatly stated what had been obvious since the 1970s: the CMEA was "a brake to the development of the socialist community" and should be replaced with "goods–money relationships" – market relations, in non-communist speak. Within a short time, the tide turned from attempting to reform the CMEA toward adopting the economic system of the non-socialist world. In July 1988, the organization officially decided to institute market relations in trade among its members. A month before, it had even achieved a two-decade-old goal – official relations with the European Communities (EC). A year later, Hungary, Poland, and the USSR pushed for allowing commercial contracts between enterprises in different member countries. Ultimately, the rapprochement with the EC also opened up the opportunity for Gorbachev to use his good contacts with Mitterrand to get CoCom restrictions lifted. But this development raised the fundamental question as to what the Soviet Union would do if CMEA members decided to withdraw from the decrepit Eastern European organization and join the thriving Western European alternative.[15]

As Gorbachev was rethinking his county's relationship with the Socialist Camp, he also reconsidered Soviet attitudes toward the Vatican, headed by the formidable Polish pope. In 1985, Soviet church officials still clung to old perceptions of a fundamentally reactionary Vatican that the Socialist Camp should simply exploit instrumentally to influence public opinion in Europe in favor of Soviet peace initiatives and disarmament proposals. In early 1987, Soviet diplomats countered the pontiff's desire to visit Catholic Lithuania for the country's 600th anniversary of the adoption of Christianity with the demand of a prior visit by Gorbachev to the Vatican. Early in 1988, the pontiff made his participation in the millennial celebration of Christianity in Russia dependent on prior Soviet admission of accountability for the forced absorption of the Ukrainian Uniate Church into the Russian Orthodox Church in 1946. Soviet media replied with a campaign accusing John Paul II of having used his third trip to Poland in mid 1987 for anti-Russian and anti-Soviet propaganda. As in Lithuania in 1987, it was only a Vatican delegation that participated in the celebrations in Moscow in June 1988. At least, Secretary of State Agostino Casaroli met

with Gorbachev in the first official encounter between a Vatican representative and a general secretary of the CPSU. While the Soviet host spoke
about peace and disarmament in Europe, the visitor handed over a papal
memorandum about the lack of religious freedom in the USSR. Whether
or not Vatican pressure had any impact on Gorbachev's rethinking of
religious policies is unclear. Within half a year, however, the Soviet government accepted a proposal on religious freedom that the Vatican had submitted to the Conference on Security and Cooperation in Europe (CSCE)
follow-up meeting in Vienna in 1987. Even if Soviet authorities would not
relegalize the Uniate Church until 1990, they still allowed its followers in
1989 to celebrate large open-air masses and memorialize its victims of
Stalinism, despite protests by the Moscow Patriarchate.[16]

Shedding Liabilities

In foreign policy toward the world at large, Gorbachev quickly tackled
a series of financially and politically expensive problems that the USSR
had amassed since the 1960s. Again, Gorbachev did not plan on ending
the global competition that had been running between the Soviet Union/
the Socialist Camp and the imperialist–capitalist world since 1917. He
was primarily interested in reducing Cold War commitments to reap
a "peace dividend" that would enable the USSR to implement economic
reform successfully and then reappear as the triumphant winner over the
doomed imperialist–capitalist world system. His speeches and conversations with socialist leaders in his first years in power consistently reveal
this thinking, as do his actual policies.[17]

Most importantly, Gorbachev needed to rethink aid commitments to
Third World countries like Cuba and Vietnam, which received one-half
and one-sixth, respectively, of all Soviet foreign aid in 1985. Over
the second half of the decade, total Soviet aid fell by a mere 10 percent,
with Cuba bearing most of the reduction. From the beginning, Gorbachev
and his advisers had been critical of Fidel Castro's revolutionary dogma-
tism, which resembled the worldviews of most of the Eastern European
leaders. During a long-delayed visit to the Caribbean island in April 1989,
Gorbachev eventually convinced Castro to engage in economic reform and
terminate expensive revolutionary projects in Latin America and sub-
Saharan Africa.[18] The revolutionary "outpost" on the other side of the
globe – the Socialist Republic of Vietnam (SRV) – was similarly doctrinaire
when Gorbachev came to power. The 79-year-old Le Duan displayed his
unchanged ideological worldviews during his last visit to Moscow in mid
1985. Swapping cause for effect, he claimed that the counter-revolutionary
alliance between China, Thailand, and the United States was responsible

for his country's miserable economic performance, high defense spending, and the need to maintain hundreds of thousands of Vietnamese troops in Laos and Cambodia. And he still promoted his world revolutionary dreams by fantasizing about the strengthening of revolutionary movements in ASEAN countries. Yet, even before 1985, the USSR had grown frustrated at Vietnam's wasteful use of the annual one billion US dollars of Soviet aid. Nevertheless, Gorbachev initially increased assistance to appease Vietnamese concerns over his attempts to seek rapprochement with China, as described below. In late 1986, less than half a year after Le Duan's death, the Vietnamese Party sensibly decided to reverse his emphasis on world revolution, to adopt Gorbachev's idea of New Thinking in foreign and domestic affairs, to prepare for withdrawal from Cambodia within three years, and to introduce market mechanisms in the economy. Soon thereafter, Gorbachev decided to end "revolutionary solidarity" and instead base bilateral relations on internationally "accepted principles" of aid. Soviet economic pressure and political advice pushed the new Vietnamese leadership to seek rapprochement with the PRC and ASEAN. But by 1989, the level of Soviet aid to Vietnam had merely fallen back to where it had been in 1985.[19]

Although the USSR provided Afghanistan with a paltry 2.25 percent of its foreign economic aid in 1985, Moscow had still made an expensive commitment in terms of human lives and military materiel since the late 1970s. Early on, Gorbachev intended to end the Soviet military involvement in Afghanistan; even conservative Politburo members and generals had understood that the war was lost. But how to achieve a face-saving withdrawal? Like Fidel Castro in Cuba and Le Duan in Vietnam, the Afghan leader Babrak Karmal was a doctrinaire revolutionary who headed a country in economic disarray. At a meeting in October 1985, Gorbachev told the flummoxed Karmal that "you will need to learn to defend your revolution by yourself" by the following summer. To that end, he proposed turning toward Islam as state ideology and introducing markets to revive the economy. Four months later, the general secretary even publicly called the Soviet involvement in Afghanistan a "bleeding wound." In the end, the USSR aimed at implementing policies that would enable the Afghan regime to survive for some time after withdrawal so that the Soviet military departure would not look like a defeat in the global Cold War. This required shoring up support for the regime through the de-emphasis of its communist character, attempts to seek national reconciliation, and replacing the inflexible Karmal with Mohammed Najibullah, who seemed to be a capable pragmatist with good connections to Pashtun tribes.[20]

Moscow's plans to pull out of Afghanistan did not go unnoticed in Tehran, where half a decade of grueling warfare with Iraq at the western border had temporarily dampened some of the Islamic revolutionary fervor. In October 1986, Ruhollah Khomeini hinted at his willingness to collaborate with the USSR in seeking peace in Afghanistan. The offer included accepting a pro-Soviet government after withdrawal, as long as it was anti-imperialist and kept influence from Sunni Saudi Arabia and the Great American Satan at bay. Islamic Iran also hoped that Soviet withdrawal would remove the pretext for the United States to station troops in the whole region. With regard to Iraq, the Islamic country informed the USSR that conservative Sunni Arabs and the imperialist Americans supported the war effort. Oddly enough, in spite of this anti-American rhetoric, Iran at that very time collaborated with the United States and Israel in a deal that included the delivery of US arms for the war against Iraq in exchange for Iranian cash – used by the American government to fund anti-communist guerrillas in Nicaragua illegally – and the release of American hostages held by Hizbullah in Lebanon. The Soviet Union agreed in principle to the Iranian view that the never-ending Afghanistan War, which it had started, and the Iraq–Iran conflict, which it had not caused, had provided the United States with the pretext to increase its military presence in the region. Thus, in early 1987, Moscow decided to reduce its contacts with Baghdad and improve relations with Tehran in the hope of receiving support for its policies in Afghanistan. But no anti-American collaboration with Islamic Iran ever materialized.[21]

Instead, Gorbachev decided to seek a stable coalition government in Afghanistan that would prevent the outbreak of a civil war after Soviet withdrawal. By 1987, however, Najibullah's national reconciliation attempts had failed while the economic situation in the country continued to deteriorate. Attempts at the beginning of 1988 to win Pakistani political support for a Najibullah-led coalition government also went nowhere, as did a similar diplomatic appeal to the United States shortly thereafter. In February, Gorbachev publicly announced withdrawal within thirteen months – no matter what. He was aware that this would not resolve any of the problems in Afghanistan, despite a bilateral aid agreement that was supposed to run "until the year 2000." The last Soviet troops left a year later – under fire from American weapons handled by Islamist rebels with ideological ties to Saudi Arabia. Moscow understood that its "departure will be regarded as a major political and military defeat." Nine years of the military conflict had cost hundreds of thousands of Afghan lives and 14,000 Soviet lives, and caused enduring damage to the social fabric, the political system, and the economic structure of the country to this day.[22]

Furthermore, Moscow's close association with a small number of radical Arab regimes and its lack of diplomatic relations with Israel for almost two decades hampered Soviet policies in the Middle East. At the beginning, Gorbachev continued to follow the twenty-year policy of seeking a comprehensive solution to the Middle East problems through an international conference, as if the Israeli–Egyptian peace in 1979 had never occurred. Accordingly, the Soviet leadership disparaged the Palestinian leader Yasser Arafat as insufficiently revolutionary because of his willingness to make concessions to Egypt, Jordan, and the United States in order to get a Palestinian state in the West Bank and Gaza. Only after Arafat's death, or so Moscow believed, would the pacification of the Middle East really start on the basis of a strict implementation of all UN resolutions since 1947. Given this attitude, the USSR was willing to re-establish diplomatic relations with Israel, but only on condition of a prior multilateral peace treaty in the Middle East, as Gorbachev emphasized in November 1985. Yet, by the following spring, he was searching for new policies that could help "unblock" the logjam in the Middle East.[23]

When Arafat's Palestine Liberation Organization and Assad's Syria independently of each other approached the USSR late in April 1986 with a request for support for the relaunching of an international Middle East conference, Gorbachev believed his chance to solve the Arab–Israeli conflict had come. He reassured both that the Soviet Union would re-establish diplomatic relations with Israel only after its withdrawal from the territories occupied in 1967, i.e. Gaza, the West Bank, and East Jerusalem. But the outbreak of the first *Intifada* in the Palestinian territories in December 1987 undermined the chances of such a conference, though Moscow was still determined to pursue "an active approach" to the solution of the Middle East conflict. Gorbachev thus met with the previously scorned Arafat in Moscow in April 1988 to coordinate policies. Two months later, the Soviet Union even re-engaged with Israel – despite the lack of diplomatic relations – in high-level talks at the United Nations. In the end, diplomatic relations were re-established in October 1991, just before the opening of the multilateral Madrid Conference that was supposed – but failed – to disentangle the legacies of 1967. Gorbachev had not gotten withdrawal prior to establishing diplomatic relations. Anyway, by the fall of 1991, the USSR was in the process of fading away.[24]

Rearranging Global Affairs

All in all, Gorbachev's policies toward China, India, and Europe displayed most visibly his original insistence on ideologically predetermined, anti-American positions. His attempt to establish a Sino–Indian–Soviet triangle against the United States once more pursued the old aim of winning the global Cold War. In Europe, he stuck for some years to the three-decade-old policy of trying to split NATO and force the American military presence out of Europe.

Unsurprisingly, Moscow was obsessed with its hostile former ally Beijing. The two had fallen out over ideology in the 1960s, Vietnam in the 1970s, and Afghanistan in the 1980s. Even before Gorbachev's ascent to power, the Kremlin had understood that the USSR bore co-responsibility for the split. A visit to Beijing by China specialist Ivan Arkhipov in December 1984 led to agreements on economic cooperation and even netted China's repudiation of its two-decade-long denial that the USSR was a "socialist country." But the Soviet side still took issue with Deng Xiaoping's "three obstacles" to improved relations – Soviet military concentrations at the Chinese border, Soviet support for Vietnam's policies in Indochina, and Soviet troops in Afghanistan. By April 1985, the Chinese leader acknowledged that removing all three obstacles at once would be difficult; he even hinted that he would consider Soviet pressure on Vietnam to withdraw from Cambodia an encouraging signal. Yet Gorbachev rejected the three obstacles as unreasonable preconditions, while he was upset with what he believed was a Chinese policy of weakening the CMEA by driving a wedge between the USSR and Eastern Europe.[25]

When Gorbachev received Li Peng, a member of the Chinese Politburo, in late 1985, he expressed his belief in a renewed Cold War partnership: "The Soviet leadership is convinced that the USSR and the PRC are on the same side in the historical struggle between the two world systems, and will not allow the plans of imperialism to succeed." But his implicit claim that support for Vietnam and troop concentrations in Siberia and Afghanistan only served to deter American imperialism did not convince Li. In the New Year, Beijing agreed to Moscow's proposal for a summit meeting in principle, but only on condition of a prior Vietnamese withdrawal from Cambodia. In December 1988, Moscow eventually obtained Beijing's green light for the summit. But by then, the USSR and the SRV were in the final stages of their respective withdrawals from Afghanistan and Cambodia, and bilateral negotiations over Soviet troop withdrawal from the Chinese border were progressing. Gorbachev had bowed to all of Deng's three conditions, while the PRC had proven that it was unwilling to become a pawn in Soviet great power policies. Thus, in February 1989, Gorbachev signaled to incoming US president, George H. W. Bush, that the two superpowers "will have to proceed from the premise that China will be neither yours nor ours." When Gorbachev visited Beijing in May, the two former allies agreed that Sino–Soviet rapprochement did not mean "a return to the 1950s" and that it was "in no way directed against third parties."[26]

Gorbachev approached relations with India in 1985 with a similar Cold War mindset. The South Asian country and the USSR had established close relations in the first five years of Indira Gandhi's premiership two decades earlier. In the wake of her assassination in 1984, Gorbachev was interested in reaffirming the friendship with her successor-son Rajiv Gandhi to prevent the Non-Aligned country from drifting toward the West. Like Deng Xiaoping in the late 1970s, the new Indian leader had concluded that closer economic cooperation with the West could help his country to develop. During Rajiv Gandhi's visit to Moscow in May 1985, Gorbachev was delighted to hear that the Indian guest opposed US military support for Pakistan in the context of the Afghanistan War, the continued American naval presence in the Persian Gulf and the Indian Ocean, and the implementation of the NATO double-track decision. Gandhi's desire to improve relations with China also seemed to fit Soviet plans for rapprochement with the PRC. Gorbachev thus raised the idea of creating an Asian collective security system, which Kosygin had originally proposed in the wake of the Sino–Soviet border clashes of March 1969 with the goal of isolating China. One and a half decades later, however, the Soviet leader was thinking about including the PRC in a triangular relationship against the United States. But like his grandfather Jawaharlal Nehru, the young Indian prime minister did not like superpower influence in South Asia. Thus, when Gorbachev went on a return visit to Delhi in late 1986, he was more attuned to Indian sensibilities. The two sides signed a declaration calling for the denuclearization of the world, which Gorbachev hoped would help convince Ronald Reagan to agree to nuclear disarmament (see below). Moscow sold the Delhi Summit to the Eastern European allies as a "strategic" success for the struggle against "American neoglobalism." Yet the envisioned Sino–Indian–Soviet strategic cooperation against the United States still did not materialize. After his second visit to India in November 1988, Gorbachev regretted that his plan to use the triangle "India–China–USSR" to counterbalance the triangle "US–EC–Japan" had flopped.[27]

In 1985, the Soviet leader also perceived his country's policies toward Western Europe through a comparable anti-American lens. As late as February 1987, he hoped "to force the United States out of Europe" – a policy that the USSR had pursued since 1954. In response to Reagan's SDI – the ambitious space-based defense system against a Soviet nuclear first strike – Gorbachev proposed, on a visit to France in October 1985, an alternative European security system – eventually nicknamed the "Common European Home" – that called for nuclear and conventional disarmament on the continent. What looked great on the surface, however, had a disguised strategic purpose. As before, the ultimate Soviet goal still was to split NATO by driving a wedge between the Western Europeans and the United States.[28] In the same vein, Gorbachev envisioned detaching the Federal Republic of Germany (FRG) from its American superpower ally by claiming that the historical obligation for peace on the continent could only be fulfilled through close cooperation within the "triangle of the USSR, the GDR, and the FRG." The plan collapsed in October 1986 when Chancellor Helmut Kohl compared Gorbachev to the Nazi propagandist Joseph Goebbels in an undeniably grave diplomatic *faux pas*. But Kohl's histrionics also divulged West Germany's continued distrust of Soviet intentions and, as a consequence, undercut Gorbachev's strategic schemes for a future Europe without the United States. Both sides tried to repair the damage in the following year, but the personal relationship between Gorbachev and Kohl remained frozen until 1988.[29]

The Lone Success: Nuclear Disarmament

Gorbachev achieved his greatest success in the sphere of his most antagonistic relationship – with Reagan. But it was only a *limited* accomplishment in the field of nuclear disarmament, not the great victory of winning the global Cold War. Reagan had offered talks on nuclear disarmament on an annual basis since his first year in office. In late 1981, he had even proposed a zero solution for Soviet and American intermediate range nuclear missiles in Europe, but the USSR failed to reply except with peace propaganda designed to split NATO over the 1979 double-track decision. Just after Reagan's second inauguration in early 1985, the dying Chernenko had redispatched a Soviet delegation to the Geneva nuclear disarmament talks after a hiatus of over a year. At Chernenko's funeral, Vice-President Bush invited Gorbachev to Washington in order to reset US–Soviet relations. But the new general secretary did not trust the president, particularly since Reagan asked him in a personal letter to stop speaking in "two languages" – spouting peace rhetoric for public consumption on the one hand while making inflexible demands in bilateral negotiations on the other.[30]

By and large, Gorbachev was sandwiched between the ongoing stationing of SS-20 missiles and the perceived threat emanating from the SDI. His foreign policy adviser Anatoly S. Chernyaev understood that the deployment of the SS-20s in the western Soviet Union and Eastern Europe since the mid 1970s was "as stupid as Khrushchev's missiles in Cuba in 1962." Even the conservative Gromyko admitted that it was a "gross mistake." But Gorbachev was concerned that the SDI was not only an outer-space platform for offensive nuclear weapons but also one of many examples of a general scientific-technological breakthrough for the United States. In terms of military security, he feared that the SDI would provide the United States with a first strike capability that could "destroy the Warsaw Pact in depth." At a pact meeting in April of 1985, he admitted that the USSR was also working on such weapons systems, but, unlike the United States, the Soviet Union supposedly was abiding by the Anti-Ballistic Missile (ABM) Treaty of 1972 and did not intend to change the strategic balance of deterrence. At least, by July Gorbachev announced a moratorium on nuclear testing as a gesture of good will.[31]

As Reagan's invitation turned into an agreement to meet at a summit in Geneva on November 19–20, 1985, Gorbachev continued to cling to Brezhnev's rigid positions. Any agreement on the pullout of SS-20s would require the concurrent withdrawal of similar US missiles – stationed on the basis of the NATO double-track decision of 1979 – as well as the dismantling of the unrelated British and French nuclear arsenals. The demand fit into Gorbachev's pursuit of the "Common European Home" with its concealed goal of achieving Soviet supremacy in Europe at the expense of the United States. Given this approach, he considered the official talks in Geneva – including the famous unscheduled personal meeting with Reagan – a failure, largely because the president was unwilling to forego the SDI. Even though by the fall of 1985 the general secretary had understood that the SDI would not become operational until several decades into the future, he still insisted in Geneva that the American initiative was an offensive system.[32] On January 15, 1986, however, Gorbachev went public with a package offer to regain the upper hand. He proposed the complete destruction of all Soviet and American strategic nuclear weapons and of all intermediate range nuclear missiles in Europe by 2000 – under the condition of the cancellation of the SDI and the inclusion of British and French (and even Chinese) nuclear weapons. Soviet diplomats admitted to Warsaw Pact members shortly thereafter that the offer was politically impossible to implement and primarily about mobilizing world opinion, particularly in Western Europe, against the United States. But Gorbachev also feared that a renewed nuclear arms race would deprive the USSR of the peace dividend that he needed for his reforms at home.[33]

The Chernobyl disaster in late April 1986 worked as an important catalyst on Gorbachev's rethinking about international affairs as well. In the months before, he had already rejected Stalin's two-camp approach and even started to reconceptualize the world as an interdependent system. But the massive radioactive contamination of Pripyat near the burst Chernobyl reactor taught Gorbachev the same lesson that Georgii M. Malenkov and Dwight D. Eisenhower had learned in the 1950s and Khrushchev during the Cuban Missile Crisis in 1962: fallout from nuclear war would destroy the ecological basis for human civilization worldwide. The general secretary thus decided to pursue new efforts to end the nuclear arms race. Stopping nuclear tests on a global scale would be a good first step, he believed, which is why he extended the year-old test moratorium for another twelve months.[34]

In September, Gorbachev proposed a second summit to Reagan, mainly because he wanted to give the Soviet–American dialogue a "serious impulse." He was unwilling to wait for another two years until a new president emerged, who "could hardly be worse than Reagan." Gorbachev thus was ready "to give something to Reagan in order to sway him," otherwise the American leader would not forego the SDI. At the Reykjavik Summit on October 11–12, 1986, the US president quickly agreed in principle to the Soviet proposal of a 50 percent reduction of strategic nuclear weapons. The general secretary even offered the elimination of all Soviet and American intermediate nuclear missiles in Europe *without* including British and French nuclear forces. But the two sides could not reach an understanding on the SDI, which the Soviet leader continued to consider an offensive platform.[35] After the failure of the summit, Gorbachev returned to Moscow convinced that the United States still aimed at restoring the kind of strategic superiority that it had enjoyed before both superpowers had reached strategic parity in the 1960s. But he was determined to continue with the struggle for nuclear disarmament in order to benefit economic development at home and the "world revolutionary process" abroad. He used his visit to India a month later to enlist Rajiv Gandhi for a global campaign to denuclearize the world, as mentioned above. But soon thereafter he cancelled the nuclear moratorium of mid 1985 because the United States continued with testing.[36]

Ultimately, the momentum from Reykjavik was not lost, even if the USSR roundly rejected an American proposal in early 1987 to "untie" the package deal, which Gorbachev had offered in Iceland. A month later, however, he himself proposed exactly that, after he had grown concerned about NATO plans to develop a separate European SDI. In February, Gorbachev called for negotiations on intermediate nuclear missiles – now called intermediate nuclear forces (INF) – without the inclusion of British and French nuclear forces, as he had done in Reykjavik. Two months later, he even agreed to use Reagan's zero proposal from 1981 as a negotiation basis.[37] Over the summer, he still tried to use the INF negotiations to push Reagan to delay the SDI by ten years, hoping that this would provide sufficient time to conclude disarmament agreements on strategic nuclear weapons that would render the SDI unnecessary. The INF Treaty that Gorbachev and Reagan signed at the Washington Summit on December 8, 1987, committed both sides to destroying an entire class of nuclear weapon delivery systems – missiles with a range between 50 and 5,500 km – within three years.[38] It was the first ever nuclear arms *reduction* agreement between the two superpowers. At the end of the day, NATO had obtained more from Gorbachev in 1987 than it had expected to receive from Brezhnev back in 1979.

The USSR hoped to use the INF Treaty as stimulus for further nuclear disarmament talks, particularly with regard to Gorbachev's Reykjavik proposal of a 50 percent cut in strategic nuclear weapons. But Moscow understood that 1988 was a US presidential election year, during which little progress would be possible. Still, Gorbachev wanted to create a good atmosphere for negotiations with Reagan's successor, even if the Moscow Summit in late spring predictably did not bring tangible results. At a meeting of the Warsaw Pact (WAPA) in July, Gorbachev stated that he was relieved that "Reagan's presidency, which was not easy for us, was finally coming to an end." On the whole, the general secretary was more hopeful about relations with Western Europe. The concurrent deeper integration of the EC and its recent agreement with the CMEA, Gorbachev claimed, had "opened the possibility to develop stable and partnership-like relations between the two parts of Europe." Rejecting the anti-American ideas in his own proposal for the "Common European Home," the general secretary finally accepted that "the Europe of today is an indispensable part of an integrated world and linked by thousands of threads to the other continents. This is a reality."[39] However, the end of Europe's division would happen faster than – and definitely in a manner different from – what Gorbachev probably expected in 1988.

The Transformations of Poland and Hungary, 1988–89

Geographically, the Cold War's reach had shrunk to encompass no more than Europe by 1988. Gorbachev had failed to bind China and India into an anti-American triangle. Vietnam was withdrawing from Cambodia, as was the USSR from Afghanistan. In the Middle East, Gorbachev was giving up Brezhnev's rigid positions as well. And the general secretary had failed to reform the decrepit CMEA. Thus, by 1988, Europe was slated to become the the final arena of the superpower clash, which is why the collapse of communism in Eastern Europe the following year has come to signify – inaccurately – the end of the global Cold War.

Gorbachev and his advisers understood as early as 1987 that the situation in repressive Poland and reform Hungary was becoming politically and economically unstable. During his visit to Yugoslavia in March 1988 – just as the Nina Andreyeva affair exploded at home – he publicly announced that the Soviet Union would respect "the independence of parties and socialist countries to define, for themselves, the path of their own development." But this path could lead to external default, as Gorbachev's adviser Georgii Shakhnazarov warned in October with an eye on the hard currency debt levels of Poland, Hungary, East Germany, and Bulgaria. Shakhnazarov even raised the question of why the USSR had stationed so many troops in Eastern Europe since 1945 in the first place. Soon thereafter, the general secretary decided to support peaceful transformations in Eastern Europe actively, while ruling out military intervention in case of political and economic collapse. At the United Nations in December, Gorbachev publicly denounced the right of interfering in other countries, and then even announced troop withdrawals from Eastern Europe within two years.[40]

By 1988, it was clear that the communist regime in Poland had lost much of its legitimacy, with Solidarność emerging as a self-organized counter-society. Through the mediation of the Catholic Church, Jaruzelski had tried to sound out the union movement, but recurrent price increases triggered ever-intensifying labor strikes throughout 1987 and the first half of the following year. The Polish leader told Honecker in June of 1988 that the situation in his country resembled the late 1970s, including the continued debt problem toward the non-socialist world, but promised that he would not "retreat in the question of relegalizing Solidarność."[41] Still, through the church, Jaruzelski's government reached out to the banned union in late August in the hope of ending the strikes, but Lech Wałęsa demanded legalization in return. In November, the Polish party agreed with Cardinal Jósef Glemp on the formation of a three-way coalition government that included the communists, forces allied with them, and members of the independent union. Soon thereafter, however, Jaruzelski's government decided to abandon the deal and instead resolve the economic and political problems through administrative and repressive measures. The prohibition of private businesses and the renewed increase of prices at the end of 1989, however, set off an inflationary spiral that led to the *de facto* replacement of the Polish złoty with the US dollar and the West German mark as a means of daily payment. With his leadership weakened even more, in January 1989 Jaruzelski decided to engage with the still illegal Solidarność and agree to the previously floated idea of a roundtable.[42]

The two-month-long roundtable negotiations, which began in early February, ended with an agreement to allow the legalization of Solidarność and to hold snap elections on June 4, 1989. The government hoped that the compromise of permitting competitive races for only 35 percent of the seats in the Sejm (lower house) but for all seats in the Senate would guarantee communist preponderance in the new parliament. In a meeting with Jaruzelski in April, Gorbachev wholeheartedly supported the scheduled elections, particularly since he himself had just become chairman of the Supreme Soviet (a position renamed president of the Soviet Union within a year) in the first competitive elections in the USSR on March 26. Jaruzelski considered the roundtable agreements the "worst compromise" possible, but he was firmly convinced that he would be able "to control the situation" after June 4. To the surprise of all, Solidarność won all competitive races except one, ensuring a legislative stalemate given that the results provided it with a *de facto* veto in parliament. While Jaruzelski did not face any resistance to his election as president, he ran into determined opposition when he tried to install a communist prime minister despite the election results. On August 21, he eventually appointed Tadeusz Mazowiecki, a long-time dissident and Solidarność adviser, as the first non-communist prime minister since World War II. In a phone call the following day, Gorbachev counseled Jaruzelski against imposing martial law, while also ruling out a Soviet intervention.[43]

The concurrent changes in Hungary were equally peaceful and by no means less far-reaching. By the spring of 1988, the ruling Hungarian Socialist Workers' Party faced the question of whether or not to replace its increasingly senile leader, the 76-year-old János Kádár. Gorbachev helped by gently urging the symbol of the suppression of the Hungarian Revolution of 1956 to step down. Like Jaruzelski, the new general secretary, Károly Grósz, did not intend to open up the political system to non-communist participants but to save single party rule through token reforms. Yet the continued parallel collapse of party legitimacy and the country's economy, accompanied by the rise of a reform wing within the party, undermined Grósz's shaky authority. By late 1988, almost two dozen independent (but still illegal) parties had appeared. In early February 1989, the Hungarian government decided in principle to bring down the Iron Curtain along the border with Austria, which consisted mostly of a rusting barbed wire fence anyway, in the near future. Since Hungarians had anyway the right of visa-free travel to Austria, the fence had only served to prevent a handful of Romanians and East Germans from escaping to the West. In late March, Gorbachev welcomed the decision to remove the Iron Curtain and even the introduction of a multi-party system in Hungary, which he himself had not yet been ready to introduce in the USSR for the impending elections (see below). Following the Polish example, the Socialist Party and the opposition in Hungary discussed political reforms at a roundtable over the course of three months starting on June 13. Three days into the talks, Imre Nagy – the leader of the 1956 revolution, who had been secretly executed in 1958 – was symbolically reinterred at a public funeral attended by 250,000 people. By September, however, some of the opposition parties refused to sign the roundtable agreements on constitutional changes and demanded a referendum on the role of the ruling Socialist Party in government and society. As Hungarians prepared for the referendum in November, the refounding of the party as a reformed social democratic organization almost failed in early October, when over 90 percent of the 725,000 members refused to join. In the spring elections of 1990, six different parties gathered almost all seats in parliament; the reformed Socialists only obtained a little over 10 percent.[44]

Gorbachev had followed the events in Poland and Hungary closely throughout 1989. In March, he had supported Hungary's one-month-old decision to remove the Iron Curtain, and in August he counseled Jaruzelski against imposing martial law. On October 25, 1989, during Gorbachev's visit to Finland, his speaker announced that "the Brezhnev Doctrine is dead." Instead, the Soviet Union had adopted the "Sinatra Doctrine," pointing out that Poland and Hungary had acted according to the American singer's famous song "I did it my way," without any Soviet interference.[45]

Four Revolutions, 1989

By early 1989, the remaining four communist regimes in Eastern Europe – East Germany, Czechoslovakia, Romania, and Bulgaria – were still headed by doctrinaire leaders unable or unwilling to accept the social and economic malaise in their countries. The collapse of the communist regime in the German Democratic Republic in the fall of 1989 played a particularly crucial role in the final demise of communism in Eastern Europe. Not only did it provide a trigger, or at least the context, for the quick changes in the other three countries, but its collapse was also critical to the European Cold War, given the country's central role in the ideological competition between Soviet-style communism and liberal capitalism at the heart of the continent.

Throughout the 1980s, the rise of a diverse opposition milieu in the GDR had paralleled the accelerating economic decline of the country. Initially, the Final Act of the CSCE of 1975 had only a short-lived impact on East Germany. Still, the Europe-wide focus on human rights and religious freedom had buoyed dissidents since the late 1970s, although they only made infrequent reference to the Final Act or to Poland's Solidarność. At least, in the 1980s, the politically docile but geographically omnipresent Lutheran (Protestant) Church finally emerged as an institution that provided moral encouragement and physical space for civil rights and environmental activists, although the Stasi (Ministry for State Security) was effective in penetrating and disrupting their activities. Nonetheless, by 1987 the security organs noted increasing political unrest, partially influenced by Gorbachev's *perestroika*. But Honecker remained resistant to any reform of his supposedly perfect socialist system, even if internal assessments in late 1987 warned of state bankruptcy within a decade should no changes in economic policy occur. Eventually, the communal elections in May 1989 undermined what little was left of the regime's credibility. For the first time, citizens in great numbers refused to vote or spoiled ballots while activists in many parts of the country insisted on their legal right to observe the voting and subsequent counting process. When the regime announced the customary results of absurdly high victories for party-endorsed candidates, most people knew for certain that the election results were rigged.[46]

By then, Gorbachev had already decided to establish closer relations with the FRG at the expense of the reform-adverse GDR, despite Kohl's imprudent Goebbels comparison of late 1986. However, this did not mean that he was willing to endorse changes to the status quo that had existed in Europe since 1945, as he told a West German representative in early 1988. The FRG needed to accept the "realities" of a divided Germany and Berlin, as decided by the victorious World War II Allies at the Yalta and Potsdam Conferences in 1945, and the treaties that former Chancellor Willy Brandt had signed in the early 1970s. During a visit to West Germany in early June 1989 – one month after the rigged East German elections – Gorbachev agreed with Kohl that nothing should be done from the outside to destabilize the GDR, although the chancellor was convinced that Honecker was unwittingly doing exactly this by himself. Gorbachev publicly reconfirmed in early July 1989 during a visit to France that, despite all the transformations in Eastern Europe and the USSR, German reunification would never happen.[47]

Developments on the ground drove high politics in the second half of 1989. On June 27, Hungary finally implemented its February decision to remove the Iron Curtain. The event happened just before the start of summer vacations in the GDR. East German tourists in Hungary quickly tried to escape across the now unfortified border, though Hungarian border patrols often turned them back. By mid August, tens of thousands waited in Hungary in often squalid conditions for another opportunity. On September 10, the Hungarian government decided unilaterally to allow East German citizens to exit to any third country. As they left through Austria for West Germany, other East Germans used the visa-free travel to Czechoslovakia to enter the West German embassy grounds in Prague. By September 30, the East German regime agreed to allow 4,700 citizens occupying the embassy and its garden to leave for West Germany as well.[48]

As tens of thousands were turning their back on East Germany, the Lutheran Nikolai Church in Leipzig resumed its customary Monday peace prayers in early September after the two-month-long hiatus of the summer break. Now, however, participants staged spontaneous demonstrations after the prayers – demanding not so much the right to emigrate but fundamental reform in the GDR. Within six weeks, the Monday demonstrations grew from one thousand to over one hundred thousand. Predictably, the doctrinaire Honecker regime toyed with the idea of using force. In June, it had publicly supported the military suppression of the "counter-revolution" in Beijing, where students had openly demonstrated against the regime in the wake of Gorbachev's visit. Unlike Honecker, Gorbachev was appalled by the reappearance of ideological rigidity in the PRC a month after Sino–Soviet normalization.[49] In late September, Honecker's sidekick Egon Krenz flew to Beijing to reaffirm socialist "solidarity" against the "ideological infiltration" from the imperialist–capitalist world. But the aging East German despot had lost touch with reality. In early October, he personally amended a newspaper editorial that disparaged East German citizens, who had fled, as amoral scum for whom no tear was worth being shed. The Politburo even decided to confiscate their left-behind property. By now, Moscow realized that Honecker was politically untenable. Fortunately, lower-level cadres of his own regime decided not to follow through with his plans to apply the Chinese solution in Leipzig on October 9, which would have caused massive bloodshed among 70,000 demonstrators.[50]

Two days earlier, on October 7, Honecker had received representatives from the socialist world in East Berlin to celebrate the fortieth anniversary of the GDR in the Palace of the Republic in East Berlin. While he gave a speech in honor of the socialist paradise on German soil, Stasi agents beat up and arrested demonstrators shouting "Gorbi, Gorbi" two blocks down the road in front of Western news cameras. Gorbachev attended the festivities without much enthusiasm, but also without the intention of interfering in the domestic developments of East Germany. At least, he cryptically warned his host with the often-cited words: "Life punishes those who come too late." The next morning, Gorbachev returned to Moscow convinced that Honecker was a "dumbass."[51]

The days of Honecker and East Germany alike were numbered. After the Politburo forced him to resign ten days later, the Central Committee made Krenz his successor on October 18. In view of their first meeting in Moscow two weeks later, Krenz and Gorbachev tried to assess the political and economic crisis in the GDR. Both were shocked when they realized the unsustainable debt of 26.5 billion US dollars to the non-socialist world and the associated danger of external default. East German financial experts and the Stasi had warned throughout October that political unrest and economic decline formed a vicious cycle that could trigger the loss of international creditworthiness, and that the opening of the borders would only lead to further instability and possibly complete economic collapse. On November 1, Krenz and Gorbachev agreed to seek help in West Germany to solve East Germany's financial and economic problems in the absence of available Soviet economic resources, but ruled out reunification and shirked discussing the opening of the walled borders. Like his predecessor Honecker in the early 1980s, Krenz did not want to turn to the International Monetary Fund (IMF) for ideological reasons. Still, a mere two days later, Gorbachev and his advisers speculated whether Krenz and the GDR would survive at all, and even pondered the possibility of opening the borders.[52]

On November 9, Krenz and his Politburo decided to allow visa-free travel for GDR citizens to the non-socialist world in principle. But at the subsequent media conference, the speaker of the Politburo fumbled the announcement, proclaiming instead the opening of the borders with immediate effect. The Berlin Wall fell within hours in an unplanned but peaceful manner when East German citizens arrived in increasing numbers at the hitherto closed border crossings. Moscow was taken by surprise, with Gorbachev only hearing about the momentous event the next morning. His adviser Chernyaev confided that day to his diary "*that a whole epoch in history ... has ended. ... here is the end of Yalta, the finale of Stalin's legacy.*" Gorbachev himself did not yet see it that way. On the 13th, he reminded Kohl of the post-war realities – "the factual existence of two German states." But the opening of the wall put the GDR back to July 1961, before the country had closed the borders around West Berlin to stem the refugee flow that had destabilized the country's economy for years. After November 9, the number of mostly younger and well-educated GDR citizens who left for the West jumped dramatically. In total, almost 350,000 left in all of 1989 – a ninefold increase from 1988 – and another 240,000 in 1990, amounting to a net loss of almost 4 percent of the country's population.[53] This, and the saturation of the GDR with

Western consumer goods in the wake of November 9, pushed the East German economy over the brink, which in turn provided an important impetus for reunification on October 3, 1990.

The night when the Berlin Wall fell was the moment of political high noon in Bulgaria. Todor Zhivkov had run the country since 1954, posed as the eternal reformer (though without ever succeeding), and accumulated 11 billion US dollars of debt to the non-socialist world by 1989. He had always been effective at splitting any opposition and buying off dissidents. Zhivkov at all times had followed Moscow's line, particularly in 1956 and 1968, to avoid conflict with the Soviet hegemon, but was flabbergasted by Gorbachev's *glasnost* and *perestroika*. Since the 1300th anniversary of the foundation of Bulgaria in 1981, Zhivkov had used nationalism to divert public attention from the mounting economic problems. In 1984–85, he launched a campaign to *slavicize* the Turkish names of Muslim citizens, who made up approximately 10 percent of Bulgaria's population. After four years of low-level conflict, Muslim unrest exploded in March 1989. Within two months, Zhivkov expelled the supposed leaders – all Bulgarian citizens – to Turkey. In response to international criticism, he accused Turkey of Greater Ottoman designs and demanded the neighboring country take in 900,000 Bulgarian citizens of Muslim faith. Within weeks, 300,000 fled state repression. According to Soviet assessments, the sudden departure of 3 percent of the country's population paralyzed the fragile Bulgarian economy immediately. By the summer of 1989, Politburo members in Sofia started to conspire. Like Honecker, the long-time Bulgarian leader failed to realize that his own comrades were abandoning him. Public demonstrations in the context of the CSCE-inspired Environmental Forum in Sofia in late October convinced the plotters to move. By November 4, they had received political backing from the Soviet embassy. News of the momentous events in Berlin on November 9 most likely provided the final impetus to sack Zhivkov in a nocturnal palace coup. However, the attempt of the party to save its rule by sacrificing the despised long-time leader did not work out. Gorbachev urged the new leader, Petar Mladenov, on December 6, to introduce *glasnost* and *perestroika*. After transforming itself into a socialist political organization, the former Communist Party won a plurality in the elections of June 1990 but decided to let the Union of Democratic Forces, established on December 7, 1989, head the first non-communist government since 1944.[54]

In Czechoslovakia, the communist regime was successful in maintaining power until November 1989 as well. Normalization after 1968 had driven most citizens into political apathy, while the regime was able to provide consumer goods at an acceptable level of quality and in sufficient quantity. Still, debt to the non-socialist world was approaching 7 billion US dollars in 1989/90. At any rate, the opposition was weak and barely visible before

1988. The CSCE-inspired Charter 77, which was mostly based in Prague, always remained a tiny movement of dissident intellectuals better known outside the country. The first organized mass resistance occurred in 1988 with a signature campaign by Slovak Catholics in the wake of the pontiff's third visit to Poland and the 600th anniversary celebrations in Lithuania in 1987, and in parallel with the officially sanctioned millennial celebration of the Russian Orthodox Church in Gorbachev's Soviet Union. But police had no problem in breaking up small public demonstrations in Prague in mid August 1988 in commemoration of the twentieth anniversary of the Soviet-led Warsaw Pact intervention and on October 28 on the seventieth anniversary of the foundation of the Czechoslovak state. But the year's end witnessed the rise of informal political networks that took cues from the political changes in Poland and Hungary. Still, in mid August and late October 1989, security forces again broke up demonstrations commemorating 1968 and 1918. Poignantly, the citizens of Prague did not take much note of the drama of thousands of East Germans crowding the West German embassy in September. Only when the police used force against demonstrating students on November 17 – on the fiftieth anniversary of the murder of a Czech student by German occupation troops during World War II – did the dams of popular restraint break. Within two days, tens of thousands demonstrated against the regime, with the security forces suddenly afraid to interfere. The hardline and reform-adverse regime finally recognized that the game was up. Within two weeks, its long-time leaders resigned, Charter 77 transformed itself into the party-like Civil Forum, the analogous Public against Violence emerged in Slovakia, a two-hour general strike occurred on November 27, a roundtable met for two days, and a coalition government of non-communists, including former leaders of the Prague Spring, and communists formed. The revolution in Czechoslovakia – a compromise deal – turned out to be a quick and relatively civil affair. On December 4, at a Warsaw Pact meeting, the USSR called the intervention of 1968 a mistake.[55]

The Romanian Revolution was an equally short, but still bloody affair. In power since 1965, Nicolae Ceaușescu firmly believed in Stalin's economic policies of seeking a self-sufficient national economy. This was one of the reasons for his opposition to the integration of the CMEA and the division of labor within it since the 1960s. In the following decade, he maintained close connections with the Shah's Iran, which netted him cheap oil imports that substituted for the declining production from exhausted Romanian oil fields – until the Islamic Revolution in 1979. Romania had joined the IMF in 1972 and received Western commercial credits, which by 1982 meant that, despite austerity policies, the country was forced to reschedule its debt, as Poland had done the year before.

Recalling his earlier ideas of economic independence, Ceaușescu ordered the repayment of all foreign debt within a decade. By 1989, that goal was almost reached, but at the cost of mass impoverishment of the citizenry. Yet this did not prevent him from wasting money on megalomaniacal projects or a lavish personal life style. Predictably, he opposed Gorbachev's reforms. In late August 1989, he demanded an emergency meeting of the Warsaw Pact to decide on a military intervention in Poland against the new Solidarność-led government, which he saw as a threat to socialism in all of Eastern Europe – but Gorbachev refused. Oddly, this request came from the very man who had made his career in 1968 by denouncing the intervention in Czechoslovakia, and who had criticized the Soviet intervention in Afghanistan a decade later. As Ceaușescu's senility and detachment from reality became obvious in the fall of 1989, high-ranking party cadres conspired to ditch him in order to keep the party in power, as had happened in Bulgaria. Sensing danger, Ceaușescu tried to improve relations with Gorbachev at the WAPA meeting on December 4. To his request for a bilateral summit in the second week of the New Year, the Soviet leader sarcastically responded: "You shall still be alive on January 9."[56]

On December 15, the Romanian revolution started in the provincial city of Timișoara. Despite the lethal suppression of the mass demonstrations by the armed forces, the revolution spread to Bucharest within days. A week later, Ceaușescu tried to mollify a rowdy crowd with an impromptu speech on the balcony of the Central Committee building – the very spot from where he had publicly denounced the intervention in Czechoslovakia over two decades earlier. But the people on the square below shouted him down and then broke into the building. Ceaușescu and his wife managed to flee by helicopter from the rooftop, but ended up in the hands of army units within hours. The same evening, the party appointed Ion Iliescu, who would run the country until 1996, as successor. On December 25, on Christmas Day, a kangaroo court sentenced the Ceaușescus to death, with the verdict carried out immediately. Obviously, the armed forces wanted to discourage Ceaușescu's supporters from continuing the struggle. His violent death shocked the Chinese leaders, not only because they had considered him a close ally for many years but also since this drove the point home that they had probably escaped a similar fate during the student demonstrations in Beijing six months earlier.[57]

By early December, Gorbachev was willing to declare the formal end of the Cold War. On December 1, he met John Paul II in the Vatican during the first official visit by the highest Soviet leader. In the hour of triumph, the Polish pope emphasized that Europe was coming together from the "Urals to the Atlantic," in an echo of Charles de Gaulle's *Europe of*

Fatherlands, though with a religious tilt. Gorbachev acknowledged the pontiff's historical role in overcoming the continent's division, while he announced the formal end of seventy years of Soviet hostility toward the Vatican and promised that the USSR would permit the Uniate Church in Ukraine to register as an independent institution. The next day, Gorbachev flew to Malta to meet US President Bush for a two-day summit. After reviewing global affairs, the leaders of the two superpowers agreed to declare the Cold War over, reset bilateral relations, restart nuclear disarmament talks, and not interfere in developments in Germany, even if Gorbachev was unhappy with how Kohl had started to push reunification in previous weeks.[58]

The End of the Soviet Union, 1991

The disintegration of the USSR started with the elections on March 26, 1989, which Gorbachev had hoped would break the party's control over the state and shift actual power to elected bodies. As before, this reform was half-hearted, since many candidates were officially approved and seats were reserved for the party and organizations affiliated with it. The new Congress of People's Deputies replaced the rubberstamp Supreme Soviet in May 1989. Initially, the newly elected parliament fulfilled Gorbachev's hopes for an arena of free debate, but soon it turned into a place of political intrigue and infighting. The elections had also brought in anti-communist delegates, particularly from the Baltic republics, and enemies of Gorbachev – above all Yeltsin. Within fourteen months, Yeltsin was elected chairman of the Supreme Soviet of the Russian Federation – the largest of the fifteen republics of the USSR – and by June 1991 even president of the renamed Russian Republic. Gorbachev, as president of the Soviet Union, faced in Yeltsin an increasingly powerful rival in the parallel system at the republic level.[59]

The rapid changes in Eastern Europe in 1988–89 naturally produced feedback effects in the USSR itself. Particularly the emergence of the Polish roundtable talks inspired Baltic independence movements in early 1989. In February, all three elevated their national languages to official status alongside Russian. In the Soviet elections in March, virtually all party-supported candidates in the three republics failed to be elected. But conservative forces in Moscow tried to stem the tide of nationalism in the Soviet republics. In April 1989, they tried to suppress demonstrations in the Georgian capital Tbilisi with lethal force. Even if Gorbachev had probably not approved this, it still contradicted his rejection of using force in Eastern Europe. Once a Solidarność-led government was in power in Poland by late summer, it supported the Baltic States passively as a model and actively with political assistance, although Gorbachev tried to prevent the Eastern European revolutions from spilling over into the USSR through public statements and political pressure. In early January of 1990, Soviet security forces quelled unrest in Baku, the capital of Azerbaijan, at the cost of over one hundred civilian lives. With Polish support, Lithuania, Estonia, and Latvia declared independence between March and May. Yeltsin's Russia followed in mid June, and Armenia and Georgia in August and November, respectively. Thus, Gorbachev scheduled a union-wide referendum on the preservation of a reformed USSR for the spring of 1991. As early as the end of 1989, he had understood that the centralized Soviet Union needed to change into a genuine federation otherwise it would perish. Over three-fourths of the votes cast in the referendum were in favor of the proposed federalization of the USSR, but six of the fifteen republics – Moldavia plus all six independent republics except Russia – refused to participate. A new proposal, renegotiated between the central government and the other nine republics – was scheduled to be signed at an official ceremony on August 20, 1991.[60]

In global affairs, the decline of Soviet standing was even more pronounced. Gorbachev's adviser Chernyaev bemoaned in early 1990 that "Eastern Europe falls away from us completely and uncontrollably ... And it is more and more obvious that the Common European Home will be built without us, without the USSR." Indeed, Moscow was losing its increasingly dull instruments of control over Eastern Europe. Poignantly, the documents of a Warsaw Pact meeting in late October 1989 read as if nothing had happened in Poland, Hungary, or in East Germany in the previous weeks. But by March of 1990, the military organization finally understood that it was out of tune with the times. In June, it still decided to reform itself in view of the "democratic revolutions" in Eastern Europe, but by February of 1991, it simply dissolved itself. The CMEA vanished in a similar way. Unlike WAPA, the organization in late October of 1989 realized that "the transformations in individual CMEA member states" were so far-reaching that they did not yet allow for the formulation of new common policies. In November, it envisioned adopting the lessons and practices of the EC and the G-7 (the group of the world's seven largest economies). The organization lumbered aimlessly on for another one and a half years. Three months after WAPA, it too decided to dissolve itself. The only success Gorbachev's Soviet Union could celebrate in international relations was the signing of the first Strategic Arms Reduction Treaty (START) on July 30–31, 1991, which reduced American and Soviet strategic nuclear weapons by 25 and 35 percent, respectively, after nine years of negotiations. It was a far cry from Gorbachev's proposal in 1986 to cut 50 percent, but it opened the way to the 1993 START II agreement with cuts of two-thirds to each side's arsenals. Even then, both countries still played in a league of their own in terms of sheer numbers of nuclear weapons, but the quantitative advantage, which they had enjoyed since the 1960s, was shrinking. The superpower rivalry was ending in its most distinct sphere as well.[61]

On August 19, 1991, while Gorbachev was on vacation at the Black Sea, a group of generals, ministers, secret service members, and party leaders staged a coup in Moscow to prevent the signing of the new union treaty the following day. A farcical shadow of the Bolshevik Revolution seventy-four years prior, the putsch was poorly organized, did not offer any plans for the future, and unraveled quickly. Its leaders were convinced that the majority of the citizenry would back their attempt to turn the wheels of time back to a mythical version of a better and more harmonious Soviet Union. Yeltsin, president of Russia, rallied Muscovites against the coup while placing Soviet ministries and the central bank under Russian control by decree. When Gorbachev returned to Moscow on August 22 after the end of the putsch, he arrived in a different country. The president of a gravely weakened USSR, he resigned as general secretary on August 24. Five days later, the Congress of People's Deputies even ordered the dissolution of the CPSU. Lenin's party was gone! With the tables turned, Yeltsin publicly humiliated Gorbachev time and again in the congress for the remainder of the year. With more and more republics declaring independence, Yeltsin and the leaders of Ukraine and Belarus decided to dissolve the Soviet Union by December 8, 1991.[62] Left without any option, on December 25 Gorbachev announced on television both his resignation as president and the dissolution of the USSR. Lenin's challenge to the world had come to an end too!

Conclusion

By 1988 at the latest, Gorbachev realized that the Soviet Union was in losing positions in virtually every field of policy. Almost all of its closest allies were ideologically dogmatic and economically broken regimes – Vietnam, Afghanistan, the Eastern European socialist states, and Cuba. Gorbachev himself had failed to enlist China and India in an anti-American triangle, or to split NATO on the SS-20. Since 1967, the USSR had miscalculated in the Middle East. The CMEA had turned out to be unreformable. The ideologically predetermined collapse of the imperialist–capitalist world had not happened either. On the contrary, the West had overcome the economic crises of the 1970s and early 1980s. At least, Gorbachev had gotten an agreement on nuclear disarmament in late 1987, but at the price of giving up all Soviet preconditions. Even economic reform at home did not bring the desired effects. At the end of 1991, the greatest revolutionary experiment of the twentieth century simply vanished into thin air.

Gorbachev did not intend to dissolve the USSR, but his reform attempts still finished off the long-standing Bolshevik challenge to the world. John Paul II once called the last Soviet leader "a providential man" incapable of understanding his role in the unfolding of the divine scheme.[63] To come back to Richard Wagner's *Ring*, with which I started this book, Gorbachev looks to me more like Siegfried – a free-willed but unsuspecting agent. In the cycle's third opera, the hero learns from the birds about Brünnhilde, asleep since his own conception and waiting to be kissed awake by him. As he storms off in search of her, he encounters his disguised grandfather Wotan, who uses the divine spear as a barrier to block his progress. Annoyed, Siegfried cuts the spear in two with a stroke of his mighty sword. Obsessed with winning Brünnhilde, he leaves his shaken grandfather behind, without realizing that he had just smashed the old order. The spear's shaft had held engraved the contract by which the Gods had ruled the world.

24　Legacies of the Cold War

Most scholars and commentators agree that the Cold War is over, even if some suggest that one between Russia and the United States might arise anew. Yet great powers have often clashed in history, and will do so in the future. Without a doubt, the Cold War was a great power conflict, but what set it apart from other great power clashes was its ideological dimension. Communism, which fired up the global Cold War, has disappeared as a credible ideological force in international relations. Although there are still communist parties in power today – in China, North Korea, Vietnam, and Cuba – they are communist (Leninist, to be precise) in name and organization only. Soviet-style communism (or Marxism–Leninism, as it was called back then), including the numerous variations which it had spawned during the twentieth century, has been relegated to the proverbial trash heap of history, to which its adherents had wanted to dispatch capitalism and liberal democracy after 1917.

What are the legacies of the Cold War in Asia, the Middle East, and Europe? Some of them are easily discernible, while others are less apparent. At this point, we need to remind ourselves that there are two kinds of legacies. One category includes direct legacies of the Cold War, i.e. policies, structures, organizations, etc., which the ideological conflict had created. The other category comprises legacies that had roots mainly elsewhere but were shaped by the Cold War. Also, some legacies have global relevance, while others carry only regional significance.

The decline and eventual collapse of the USSR heralded a general fading of the left – communist and non-communist – on a global scale. The Communist Party of the Soviet Union (CPSU) was outlawed in August 1991, only days after the harebrained coup attempt by members of the old guard. Its successor in Russia has developed into an ideologically confused and ultimately irrelevant opposition party. In other former Soviet republics, communist parties either disappeared, made common cause with nationalists, or their communist party elites established autocratic rule. Only in East Asia did several communist parties manage to remain in power, although they jettisoned ideological substance.[1] In the

Middle East, most communist parties faced repression during the Cold War. Occasionally, though rarely, they managed to become members of coalition governments for short periods of time, such as in Iraq from 1958 to 1963. Where communists survived the Cold War as individuals or parties, they had the opportunity to join Islamist parties to continue the struggle against outside influence.[2] In former Eastern Europe, communist parties either vanished into political irrelevance if they refused to reform, or pragmatically reinvented themselves as social democratic outfits to stay in power. On the continent's western side, both pro-Soviet communists and Eurocommunists evaporated almost completely.[3]

After the end of the Cold War, non-communist leftist parties in Europe – i.e. the social democrats – also lost support at the ballot box if they did not reinvent themselves by moving toward the political center, as happened in Germany and the United Kingdom in the 1990s, for example. But social democracy suffered from unrelated long-term problems; it had achieved many of its traditional goals by the late twentieth century. Even if some Western European countries trimmed the welfare state in the 1990s and in the early 2000s, mass poverty was a rare phenomenon for two decades after the Cold War. The successive global financial crisis and the European debt crisis in 2007–9, which were both unrelated to the Cold War, have recently helped to increase the appeal of new leftist, but not communist, parties and protest movements in southern Europe.[4]

The decline of the left, both communist and non-communist, throughout most of the world after the end of the Cold War created a unipolar moment in two respects. First, even if the United States did not win the Cold War, it still benefited from the collapse of the USSR by becoming the only remaining superpower. Second, the parallel collapse of the Soviet alternative and the rise of neo-liberalism – the ideology of free markets, trade liberalization, deregulation, and the small state – in the United States and in some Western European countries since the 1970s made neo-liberalism appear as the victor in the global Cold War. However, the resilience of the Free World throughout most of the Cold War had not been the result of the full embrace of such ideological tenets as early as the mid 1940s. On the contrary, it was based on a variety of different but compatible sets of interventionist socio-economic policies, ranging from New Deal Keynesianism in the United States to the socially responsible market economy (*soziale Marktwirtschaft*) in West Germany and state guidance of the economy (*dirigisme*) in France. For a quarter century after 1945, the Bretton Woods agreements had bound these variations of the same capitalist theme together. Only US President Richard M. Nixon's decision to end rigid currency exchange rates and to abolish gold pegging in 1971, and the economic crises in the wake of the subsequent oil shocks, foreshadowed the rise of neo-liberalism, which now pretends to be the winner of the global Cold War.[5]

The decline and collapse of Soviet-style communism in the second half of the 1980s, however, paralleled democratization in South Korea and the Philippines, triggered democratization in Eastern Europe in 1989/90, and created the context for democratization in Indonesia, sub-Saharan Africa, and Latin America in the 1990s. The allure of undemocratic rule – on the left or the right – vanished quickly, but only temporarily. Democratization has been neither persistent nor well founded in several parts of the world. Political and economic instability have frequently opened the door to populist policies or even internal military interventions. By 2020, the world has been sliding back on democratization for many years.[6]

The world's post-Cold War record on human rights is equally mixed. Certainly, the number of human rights organizations and activists has dramatically increased in the last three decades. Yet there is a Cold War legacy in prioritizing some human rights over others, if we use the almost universally ratified 1948 UN Declaration as a benchmark. Political and civic rights still take precedence over socio-economic rights, which are all listed side by side in the seven-decade-old declaration. But international human rights debates since the 1960s had focused on violations of specific human rights – mostly political and civic rights – in the Socialist Camp, particularly. Also, NGOs like Amnesty International found it easier to focus on egregious individual human rights violations, like torture or the denial of civic rights, than on less visible structural injustices, like poverty. And Basket III of the Conference on Security and Cooperation in Europe (CSCE) turned an even smaller subset of political and civic rights into an important norm-setting yardstick in the East–West debates in the late 1970s and throughout the 1980s. But this all meant that other elements of the 1948 UN Declaration slipped away from the discourse, even if the United Nations endorsed an International Covenant on Economic, Social, and Cultural Rights in 1976, one year after the Final Act was signed at the end of the conference in Helsinki. The collapse of the Socialist Camp, which had championed socio-economic human rights since the 1940s, further lessened the likelihood of them reappearing at the top of the agenda of international human rights debates.[7]

The end of the global Cold War delegitimized not only autocratic systems across the world but also some of the third-way options that had emerged during the East–West confrontation. For example, Non-Alignment, after it barely survived the early 1980s and re-emerged mid-decade under Indian leadership, was still incapable of reviving its international influence from the 1960s, despite its attempts to struggle against post-Cold War globalization, particularly in the form of trade liberalization. After 1989, it strenuously tried to redefine itself as more than just the voice of the ill-treated Global South, which had other and more effective avenues, such as G-77 and UNESCO, to raise its concerns. Anyway, its last two summits, in Mahmoud Ahmadinejad's Islamic Iran in 2012 and in Nicolás Maduro's Bolivarian Venezuela in 2016, further removed the little polish that had remained.[8]

Even one of the lasting legacies of the Cold War, nuclear disarmament, is a mixed bag of success. The Strategic Arms Reduction Treaties (START) of 1991, 1993, and of 2010 greatly reduced the number of nuclear warheads of the United States and Russia (the legal successor of the defunct USSR). As a part of the 1993 agreement, Belarus, Kazakhstan, and Ukraine handed over those nuclear weapons that had ended up on their respective territories, to Russia. France and the United Kingdom have also reduced their stockpiles of warheads by a little less than 50 percent since the end of the Cold War, but China and Israel increased them, though only moderately, to a relatively low level. On the whole, the United States and Russia still play in their own league of nuclear powers, controlling many thousands of warheads, while others possess only a few hundred or even less. Even if these arms reduction agreements greatly reduced both the number of weapons and the likelihood of global nuclear war, they did not completely stop proliferation. India and Pakistan conducted nuclear tests in 1998 in a competition for mutual deterrence and regional status, but also in a continuation of Cold War policies. North Korea and Islamic Iran have pursued nuclear weapons for decades to obtain respect from and possibly equal status with the remaining American superpower, but in the process they have threatened to undermine non-proliferation efforts since the 1960s. Fears over the insufficient security of nuclear sites in some countries, most notably in Pakistan, or the likelihood of commercial sale of technological components by North Korea have raised apprehensions that fissile material might fall into the hand of rogue states, criminal organizations, or extremist groups to be used for terror attacks with radiological devices in asymmetrical warfare.[9] The vestiges of the Cold War nuclear arms race will continue to haunt humanity for a long time to come.

Cold War conflicts in continental East and Southeast Asia reached back to the interwar ideological clash between the Soviet-founded Comintern, French–British–Japanese imperialism, and Western democratic liberalism and capitalism. In the post-World War II period, domestic struggles over nation building in Korea, China, and Indochina quickly turned into clashes of decolonization, Cold War conflicts, or both. The global conflict between the USSR and the United States cemented the division of China and Korea to this day, and of Vietnam for several decades until 1975. Leninist parties with roots in the interwar period survived the end of the Cold War and are still in power in all three. But the People's Republic of China (PRC) and the Socialist Republic of Vietnam (SRV) both gave up their world revolutionary goals in the 1970s and 1980s, respectively, while embracing Western capitalism (and, increasingly, neo-liberalism) without political liberalization. In comparison, after 1953 the Democratic People's Republic of Korea (North Korea) developed into a dynastical system that merged older political traditions, or their more recent reinventions, with Leninist styles of party and government organization.[10]

During most of the Cold War, liberal democracy was in a difficult position in East and Southeast Asia, and still is today. The long nature of the ideological conflict produced strong communist parties, on the one hand, and a number of authoritarian anti-communist regimes, on the other. Without doubt, Japan, by far, has the longest continuous democratic tradition in the region, even if its political system comprises paternalistic characteristics that produced predominant rule by one elected party for several decades during the Cold War. In comparison, both South Korea and the Philippines experienced long periods of dictatorial rule in the second half of the Cold War. Yet, by the late 1980s, the two countries and the Republic of China (ROC) returned to or introduced, respectively, democratic rule, even if the Philippines has slid back lately. Asia's one great success of post-Cold War democratization is Indonesia, which since the late 1990s has experienced several cycles of vibrant electoral contests and peaceful power transitions. In comparison, Malaysia, Singapore, and Cambodia have developed electoral-authoritarian hybrid systems. In Thailand, the undemocratic legacies of the Cold War are still present, as the country regularly oscillates between military dictatorship and democracy.[11]

The abandonment of authoritarian economic development models, both communist and non-communist, in the PRC, the ROC, South Korea, and the SRV in the waning Cold War has produced economic prosperity on a previously unknown scale in the region. While the four have experienced a long-time economic rise since at least the 1980s – even if they suffered from the global crises in the late 1990s and the late 2000s – the Cold War's long-time economic champion, Japan, has been afflicted by a relative economic standstill for three decades. The end of the Cold War also had positive economic effects on Southeast Asia in general, even if direct foreign investment and an emphasis on export-oriented production has not led to greater democratization except in Indonesia, nor helped to insulate the region from international economic downturns.[12]

The situation in South Asia is similarly mixed. Since its third State of Emergency in 1975–77, India has enjoyed democratic rule and recurrent peaceful power transitions for over forty years. Economically, the country has tried for almost three decades to shed its Nehruvian socialist economic system, which has hampered the development of the country, but reform is slow, patchy, and hotly contested in the federally organized and regionally diverse country.[13] Although formally a democracy for seventy years, Sri Lanka had suffered from a civil war unrelated to the Cold War for a quarter of a century after 1983. Myanmar, Bangladesh, and Pakistan continue to vacillate between military rule and democracy. Domestic conflicts, military rule, and ethnic and sectarian strife, all of which have roots in the Cold War period, have dampened economic development in all of India's neighboring countries.[14]

Except for the Afghanistan War in 1979–89, no conflict in the larger Middle East stemmed from the interwar ideological clash or the post-World War II Soviet–American global struggle. But the East–West conflict exacerbated many of the pre-existing conflicts that had their roots in the collapsing Ottoman Empire, British and French colonialism, and the Zionist project in Mandatory Palestine. After the end of the Cold War, the wave of democratization in other parts of the world did not really touch the Middle East, with Israel and Turkey continuing to be the only (semi-) democratic systems. At least, the decline of the global Cold War and the armistice in the Iraq–Iran War in 1988 created an atmosphere that enabled the Arab League, under Saudi leadership, to mediate in Lebanon's civil war. In its wake, the Levantine country returned to democratic rule after fifteen years of devastating domestic turmoil.[15]

The Cold War, however, left three major legacies in the Middle East – political Islam, the unresolved Palestine Question, and American influence. Pan-Islamism emerged as a reaction to Western imperial intervention, the search for identity after the Turkish abrogation of the Caliphate in 1924, and the conflict with secularism at home and on the global plane. Two major strands of political Islam survived into the post-Cold War world. Islamic Iran promotes the Shia version, mainly in the Gulf region and in Lebanon, while Saudi Arabia advances the Sunni version, though radicalized Sunni groups have been contesting its leadership. The Soviet-caused Afghanistan War had brought together Sunni Islamists regardless of Saudi support; after its end, some radicalized fighters joined civil wars in southern Russia and in Bosnia-Herzegovina, where they supposedly fought for fellow Muslims, in the 1990s. Others returned to their home countries in the Middle East to establish underground organizations designed to cleanse the Muslim world of infidel influence and apostate – be they secular or moderately Islamic – rulers. One of these groups – al-Qaida – organized and executed the terrorist attacks with hijacked planes in the United States that cost almost 3,000 civilian lives on September 11, 2001.[16]

The conference in Madrid in the fall of 1991 tried to take advantage of the end of the superpower conflict and restart the Arab–Israeli peace process, which had been stalled for almost a decade. Within three years, Jordan, as the second Arab country after Egypt in 1979, signed a peace treaty with Israel after almost a quarter of a century of intermittent negotiations. But the Palestine issue remained open. Israel refused to negotiate with PLO representatives in Madrid, though Palestinian representatives at the conference worked closely with the PLO. Eventually, with mediation by US President Bill Clinton, Israeli Prime Minister Yitzhak Rabin and PLO Chairman Yasser Arafat agreed in 1993 on a framework for the resolution of the Israeli–Palestinian conflict, for which the two received the Nobel Peace Prize the following year. Rabin's assassination by an Israeli right-wing student two years later derailed the process, however. The Israeli elections in mid 1996 produced a narrow victory for Benjamin Netanyahu of Likud, who ran on a platform of rescinding the four-year-old moratorium on settlements in the West Bank. After September 11, 2001, Israel exploited the so-called American War on Terror to squash Palestinian resistance in the West Bank and Gaza, to continue with its settlement policy, and to ignore an explicit Arab peace initiative in 2002 that offered peace-for-land while dropping the demand of Palestinians to return to their pre-1948 homes.[17]

Finally, the unparalleled American post-Cold War influence in the Middle East emerged as a result of the Soviet loss of influence since the early 1970s and Russia's *de facto* retreat from the region after the collapse of the USSR. The Madrid Conference briefly helped restore some prestige to Moscow after it had embarked on a lost cause in Afghanistan and pursued unconstructive policies in Lebanon, Syria, and Palestine throughout most of the 1980s. But one of its former clients and weapons customers, Saddam Hussein's Iraq, had misjudged post-Cold War developments in international affairs by attacking Kuwait in August 1990. Before starting the war, Saddam had feared that his regime would suffer a fate like that of the Eastern European socialist states in 1989, and after his country's occupation of Kuwait, he hoped that he could split the USSR and the United States along old Cold War conflict lines. Both his futile attempts to get support from the Soviet Union, which ultimately sided with the United States, and the American military intervention tipped the balance of outside influence in the Middle East further in favor of Washington.[18] Yet the United States damaged its long-term influence in the region with its interventions in Afghanistan and Iraq. In the wake of the terror attacks in September 2001, the United States planned to overthrow the Islamist Taliban regime and root out al-Qaida bases in Afghanistan. Two years later, it occupied Iraq on trumped-up charges of Iraq's production of weapons of mass destruction and Saddam's links to al-Qaida. Neither war led to peaceful reconstruction in either country but to the strengthening and geographical spread of al-Qaida and similar radical groups throughout the Muslim world and even beyond. This included the Islamic State of Iraq and Syria (ISIS), established in 2014, that claimed to recreate the Caliphate, abolished by the secular Turkish Republic in 1924, and to lead the *ummah*. But its extreme brutality failed to generate much approval among Muslims worldwide.[19]

Many of the current international structures and organizations in Europe are a direct legacy of the Cold War – NATO, the Council of Europe, the European Union, and the Organization for Security and Cooperation in Europe (OSCE). Even if three of the four had strong anti-Soviet objectives, they survived into the post-Cold War world for structural reasons. The sudden collapse of communism in Eastern Europe in 1989 and of the USSR in 1991 both created a window of opportunity for Eastern European countries and for West Germany to seek parallel integration processes in which the existing structures and organizations served as indispensable vehicles.

Particularly Estonia, Latvia, Lithuania, Poland, Czechoslovakia, and Hungary used the rapid shifts in political and military power in 1989–91 to escape control and influence of the dying USSR. After over four decades of domination, they sought both protection by integrating into the military structures of NATO and support for economic development from the European Communities/European Union. Because the Council of Europe since 1948 and the EC since 1993 have made democratic institutions, the rule of law, and respect for human rights preconditions of membership, this in turn incentivized continued democratization in the formerly socialist states of Eastern Europe. The transformation of the CSCE into the OSCE by the mid 1990s created a larger framework for democratization and human rights that included the United States, Canada, and the successor states of the USSR after 1991.[20]

Initially, the collapse of communism in Eastern Europe and the fall of the Berlin Wall in 1989 opened up a range of possible futures of a unified Europe and a unified Germany within it. At the European level, this included Mikhail S. Gorbachev's Common European Home (which would have left out the United States), the creation of a completely new order on the basis of the CSCE/OSCE, or the extension of NATO and the EC (which would have left the USSR out). At the German level, two options were conceivable at the end of 1989 – a federation between East and West Germany, or reunification on the basis of the West German constitution. Yet East Germany's economic collapse in early 1990 and elections in March – the first free elections since 1946 – pushed developments toward speedy economic and then political reunification under West German leadership. This, however, required the prior negotiation and conclusion of a peace treaty with all four World War II Allies, which eventually was signed on November 14, 1990. Nevertheless, Chancellor Helmut Kohl understood that reunifying Germany would only be possible within a greater unified Europe that would help pin down the enlarged Germany and thereby diminish fears of future German revanchism. Thus, Eastern European security needs and German national interests aligned with extending NATO and the EEC/EU at the expense of the USSR/Russia and to the benefit of the United States.[21]

Similar to the global decline of leftist parties, the end of the Cold War also led to the relative weakening of Christian democracy in Europe. Christian democrats since the late nineteenth century had tried to define a third option between the revolutionary left and unfettered capitalism by emphasizing traditional Christian values and addressing the emerging Social Question in a progressive manner. They had been crucial in establishing the Council of Europe and the European Coal and Steel Community/the European Economic Community in the 1940s and 1950s, respectively. In several Western European countries, particularly in West Germany and Italy, Christian democrats had led post-war economic and political reconstruction. Yet, by the 1980s, they were not immune to the rise of Anglo–American free-market capitalism and social conservatism. With Helmut Kohl's "conservative turn" in 1982, the socially progressive tradition was increasingly pushed aside. The further political demise of Christian democracy in Europe occurred in the 1990s when parties in several countries – in Western Europe and formerly socialist Eastern Europe – started to embrace traditional conservative or neo-liberal ideas, or even both. In Italy, the Democrazia Cristiana imploded in the early 1990s, together with Italy's Socialist Party, when judicial investigations uncovered long-standing systematic party corruption and links to organized crime at the highest level.[22]

Similarly, the Vatican did not reap the long-term benefits from its engagement with the Socialist Camp during the Cold War. Like the Christian democrats, various popes since Leo XIII had sought a third option between communism and capitalism. John Paul II saw his policies since 1978 as an attempt to re-Christianize Eastern Europe, which Soviet officials had clearly understood in the early 1980s. But the pontiff had mistaken the political appeal of the Catholic Church in Poland for a popular embrace of its religious and missionary agenda. As the Cold

War ended, Eastern European socialist states adopted reforms along neo-liberal lines, which the Holy See abhorred.[23]

Finally, a long-term consequence of the Cold War in Europe is the resurgence of ethno-nationalism and national conservative movements and parties. The catastrophe of World War II and the Cold War enemy – the USSR – had brought Western Europeans together in an alliance to overcome the threat of identity politics and to generate collective strength. Yet identity politics sprang back to life at the end of the Cold War. The rise of ethno-nationalism started in the early 1990s with the collapse of Yugoslavia, followed by the emergence of national conservative parties in Hungary, Poland, and the Czech Republic, and the ascent of right-wing parties in Austria, Italy, France, the Netherlands, Germany, Denmark, Sweden, the United Kingdom, and other Western European countries. Furthermore, the economic problems since the global financial crises and the European debt crisis in 2007–9 as well as the refugee crisis in 2015 – which was mostly caused by ISIS in the Middle East – have increasingly seduced politicians in various European countries to blame the European Union for problems that had essentially been caused by national politics. This rhetorical buck-passing emerged not only in crisis-ridden countries like Greece or Italy, but also in the United Kingdom, where it probably helped to swing the Brexit referendum in 2016. While the European Union in its current state deserves constructive criticism, its populist enemies cynically exploit anti-EU rhetoric for short-term political gain while forgetting that the Western European integration process has guaranteed peace and prosperity since 1945. Given the European national enmities and recurrent large-scale war in the preceding 150 years, this is an achievement that should not be easily gambled away.[24]

Conclusion

As the centennial commemorations for World War I and the Paris Peace Conference of 1919 have come to an end, historians will likely turn their attention to the long-term effects of the first global war of the twentieth century. The four-year-long conflict had caused the collapse of the Russian, German, and Ottoman Empires, but at the same time initiated new imperialist endeavors by Great Britain, France, Japan, and Italy. The interwar period witnessed economic upheaval at a global level and the stirrings of decolonization in the Afro–Asian world, both of which were related to World War I. By the late 1930s, the world was at war again, followed by the Cold War a decade later.

The post-World War I period witnessed the greatest geographical extent of imperialist rule throughout the world since the American Revolution and the independence of Latin America over a century before. Great Britain and France benefited from the collapse of the Ottoman Empire by extending their control into the Levant. Japan's imperialist desires focused on the Asian mainland from Siberia to China. And Italy eyed Ethiopia, the last independent African country. Yet, just as global imperialism experienced its last peak, Great Britain was forced to agree to gradual devolution of power in South Asia. Against the background of this imperialist world system, the Bolshevik challenge arose from the ruins of the Russian Empire. Vladimir I. Lenin's Soviet Russia/ USSR entertained the ambition of replacing it with a new global communist order by stoking anti-imperialist revolutions in colonial possessions and anti-capitalist revolutions in the developed world. Partially as a reaction to the Bolshevik challenge, the United States proposed the transformation of the international system, which until World War I had favored conflict resolution by war, into one of peaceful conflict resolution within the League of Nations. Yet many of Woodrow Wilson's reformist ideas concentrated on reordering Europe and not abolishing imperialism in the world. His successor in World War II, Franklin D. Roosevelt, eventually understood that continued imperialist rule was a potential source of a future global conflict. After World War I, pan-Europeanists also

605

pondered how to reorganize the continent – not because they were Wilsonians, but because they wanted to overcome Europe's historical conflicts. Ultimately, they aimed at restoring Europe to its former position of influence in the world and at strengthening it against the Soviet threat. Finally, the collapse of the Ottoman Empire in 1918 and the abrogation of the Caliphate six years later sparked an identity crisis in the Muslim world that gave rise to pan-Arabism in the Levant and to pan-Islamism in South Asia and Egypt.

During World War II, the Big Three established an imperialist–communist–capitalist alliance to defeat right-wing and militarist regimes in Europe and Asia. Hence, by 1945, the United Kingdom was the world's undisputed imperialist power. It ruled over a large empire that stretched from Africa to the Middle East, the Persian Gulf, South and Southeast Asia, and included Australia, New Zealand, and Canada through the Commonwealth. But London understood that its formal empire was under threat, though it hoped to transform its worldwide domains into a reformed and enlarged Commonwealth and the Arab League under its global leadership. Yet the United Kingdom lost not only its formal empire over the course of the 1940s, 1950s, and 1960s but also much of its informal influence throughout the world, particularly after the Suez Crisis in late 1956. It was able to extend its great power status once more for a decade on the basis of its small nuclear weapons program. But the Suez Crisis and the subsequent but unrelated signing of the Rome Treaties on Western European integration raised questions about Britain's long-term future as a great power. Although London had been a supporter of some form of European integration during and immediately after World War II, it withdrew from engaging with the continent by the late 1940s due to its perception of itself as a great power and its commitment to Commonwealth and Empire. By the early 1960s, the United Kingdom eventually understood that participation in the Western European integration process was the only avenue to preserve some of its global standing.

As a result of World War II, the Soviet Union obtained for the first time a sphere of influence. It had sought international authority through the Comintern since 1919, but had abandoned promoting world revolution actively before the end of the 1920s. The USSR emerged rather fortuitously on the winning side of World War II after Iosif V. Stalin had made common cause in 1939 with Adolf Hitler's Germany against the Western democracies. The German attack on the Soviet Union in 1941 opened the way to join what eventually would become the alliance of the Big Three. As a result, Stalin ended up in military control of Eastern Europe from the Baltics to Bulgaria. While the USSR claimed this sphere of influence for security reasons, it simultaneously looked at Eastern Europe as a place of communist revolution for export further west. In a similarly auspicious manner, Stalin ended up with Asian allies who voluntarily joined his Socialist Camp – the People's Republic of China (PRC) and communist Vietnam – in 1949/50. But until his death in 1953, Stalin showed little interest in the Middle East and South Asia – with the exception of Turkey and Iran in the immediate post-war period. He generally abstained from exploiting the problems which the British Empire faced in Palestine and India in 1947, and he even sided with the United Kingdom and the United States in recognizing Israel against Arab opposition. Only after his death did his successor, Nikita S. Khrushchev, attempt to increase influence outside Europe and East Asia, most notably in Egypt during the Suez Crisis. Locked into a nuclear competition with the United States, the Soviet Union caught up in terms of missiles and warheads by the 1960s, turning the great power arrangement of the Big Three from the World War II period into a nuclear superpower duopoly.

By 1945, the United States was the militarily and economically dominant power in the world. Its land forces had fought in all major theaters of World War II, and its navy patrolled all of the world's seas. Unlike the near-bankrupt United Kingdom and the partially destroyed Soviet Union, the United States had benefited from the war-induced economic boom to overcome the last vestiges of the Great Depression. During the war, Roosevelt had promoted upgraded versions of Wilsonian ideas to ensure worldwide peace. He had revamped the League of Nations to become the United Nations, and created the International Monetary Fund and the World Bank to guarantee financial stability and provide resources to rebuild the world. Still, immediately after the war, the United States was hesitant to follow the United Kingdom and the Soviet Union in establishing its own zone of influence, with the exception of Japan. By late 1946, Washington eventually started to take the initiative in Germany by proposing to London the creation of the Bizone. The following spring, responding to the British military withdrawal from Greece, President Harry S. Truman committed American military resources to that Balkan country and to Turkey to contain the expected Soviet expansionism. The Marshall Plan for Europe and a similar economic reconstruction policy for Japan helped to shore up the American zone of influence among the re-emerged and reconstructed democracies in Western Europe and in East Asia. But until 1950, the United States was hesitant in supporting anti-communist causes in Indochina or the Middle East. In the case of China, it even decided to scale down its commitment. Only the foundation of the PRC, the signing of the Sino–Soviet alliance, and the Korean War triggered a major overhaul of American policy, with defensive and economic commitments to virtually all countries at the periphery of the

Socialist Camp. Washington completed its network of containment alliances by the mid 1950s, despite de-Stalinization in Moscow after the Great Dictator's death. Throughout the 1950s and the 1960s, the United States continued to enjoy a preponderance of economic and military power. But while the United Kingdom was declining as a great power, the USSR reached parity, at least in the nuclear arms race, in the second half of the 1960s.

Despite their elevated position in 1945, each of the Big Three quickly realized that their *political, economic, and military power had surprisingly tight limits*. Heavy-handed interventions generally did not solve problems. On the contrary, they either failed outright or produced costly long-term commitments. The United Kingdom learned this lesson in Palestine after World War II and at Suez in 1956. The Soviet Union assumed staggering long-term commitments when it asserted ultimate control in Eastern Europe at the turn of 1947/48. Its military occupation and politico-economic domination of the semi-continent created much resistance, either through foot-dragging by the Soviet-imposed elites there, or through outright mass defiance that required military interventions as in East Germany in 1953, Hungary in 1956, Czechoslovakia in 1968, and Afghanistan in 1979. By the early 1980s, Moscow could no longer afford to intervene in a similar manner in Poland since its political and economic resources were depleted. The United States had a similar experience in Vietnam, where, however, it did not occupy a country but tried to prop up an unpopular regime against outside subversion.

The Great Powers were more successful when they were able *to nudge pre-existing regional developments* in their favor. London opportunistically seized on the emerging Arab League in 1943–45 to acquire a zone of influence that was strategically crucial to the future of the British Empire. Moscow benefited from similar developments in China and Vietnam in 1949–50. And starting in 1947, the United States took advantage of a nascent European integration project that had been in the making for a quarter of a century. Still, opportunities did not always translate into long-term partnerships. British imperialist reflexes in 1956 destroyed influence in the Arab world. The People's Republic of China fell out with the Soviet Union, while communist Vietnam first remained distant, then sought closeness for anti-Chinese reasons, and eventually quit the partnership. Even the American political commitment to the Western European integration process waned, though the two sides never really fell out. In 1977–79, the United States could once more benefit from the Egyptian–Israeli peace initiative, which arose to the complete surprise of the superpowers and regional actors alike.

Particularly in the Middle East, the great powers experienced *major difficulties in shaping regional developments*. Instead of using force, the great powers in the early 1950s decided to impose an arms embargo on themselves in an attempt to defuse the tensions in the Arab–Israeli conflict that pre-dated the Cold War. While American economic and political pressure compelled Great Britain, France, and Israel out of Egypt at the turn of 1956/57, Washington still failed to reap any benefits among Arab states. Poignantly, Moscow obtained an undeserved political boost from the crisis, which it, however, was unable to transform into long-term influence either. Similarly, neither the United States nor the Soviet Union were able to affect significantly the advent, the course, and the aftermath of the June War in 1967 and the October War in 1973. Initiatives for regional peace mainly came from Egypt in the 1970s. Early in the decade, the United States was still unprepared for major structural changes in the Middle East, but later it at least served as a midwife to a flawed Egyptian–Israeli bilateral peace.

In Asia and Europe, the great powers encountered problems similar to those in the Middle East, though to a lesser degree. The United Kingdom could not influence developments in South Asia since the 1930s and in Greece before 1947. The United States and the Soviet Union repeatedly experienced the limits of their influence in Asia; for instance, China turned out to be a major headache for both. Washington faced resistance to necessary reforms in South Korea and South Vietnam, while Moscow was confronted with a recalcitrant communist Vietnam and an obstinate Eastern Europe. Even the United States encountered challenges in Western Europe, from Charles de Gaulle's France in the 1960s and Helmut Schmidt's West Germany in the 1970s.

In the end, Great Britain and the Soviet Union failed as great powers since they were unable to maintain their status in view of resistance from below, though London experienced this in the 1950s, several decades before Moscow. Both suffered from expansive commitments that had turned sour or from problems that required resources beyond their means. But how about the United States? Even Washington did not always succeed where it made commitments – in Korea, Vietnam, Pakistan, and even France. Yet it benefited from two distinct characteristics of its worldwide influence – its general flexibility in dealing with difficult allies and obstinate partners, and the collapse of the Soviet Union by the late 1980s. The United States did not win the global Cold War; it just outlived its great power rivals. Structural transformations had ended the regional Cold Wars long before.

Three different types of conflicts and developments occurred in the regional Cold Wars in Asia, the Middle East, and Europe. Many of the conflicts and developments in the *first* category had their roots entirely outside the Bolshevik challenge of 1917 and the Cold War after 1945, such as India's decolonization, Asian–African Internationalism, pan-Arabism, pan-Islamism, and the Arab–Israeli antagonism. Until the late 1980s, they interacted loosely with the global conflict. India tried to keep the Cold War out of South Asia. Arab actors and Israel attempted to instrumentalize the global conflict for their own ends without ever providing any outside power with real influence. Some forms of pan-Islamism even rejected engaging with the Soviet–American ideological conflict in principle. *Second*, a small number of developments in the regional Cold Wars stemmed directly from the Bolshevik challenge since 1917. The Chinese and Vietnamese revolutions were kick started by the Comintern but developed their own dynamics outside of Soviet control by World War II. Both the anti-Soviet characteristics of Western European integration and the Vatican's foreign policy were reactions to the Bolshevik threat in the 1920s and carried over into the Cold War period. Only the *third* group comprised developments and conflicts that were clearly tied to the Cold War after 1945. The nuclear arms race amounted to the most obvious expression of the Soviet–American competition. The German division, the creation of the Council for Mutual Economic Assistance, and the Conference on Security and Cooperation in Europe all were creations of or reactions to the global Cold War. Non-Alignment rejected the Cold War, but still got entangled with it by the 1960s. But all *three* forms of regional conflict and development contributed to structural changes of the global Cold War.

Of course, the middle powers and smaller countries in Asia, the Middle East, and Europe enjoyed *different levels of agency*. The degree of their individual tie to the global Cold War mattered to their actual capacity to exert influence abroad, but so did their specific political, military, and economic power, and even moral, charismatic, and organizational capacity. The PRC, communist Vietnam, India, the Middle Eastern countries, and France all enjoyed high levels of independence from the great powers, though other regional powers frequently limited their agency. Both Vietnam and India suffered from Chinese pressure, and the Arab countries and Israel impeded each other. At the mid level of agency in the Cold War stood most of the European countries, though members in the Socialist Camp faced greater constraints than those in the western half of the continent. But even East Germany and Poland over time obtained surprisingly far-reaching leeway to defy the wishes of the Soviet superpower. Finally, at the lower end of agency we find agents with little power, like the Palestinians, some of the pan-Islamists, or the Vatican.

Middle powers and smaller countries *individually* and *collectively* exerted a major impact on the structural development of the Cold War across the three regions. The PRC voluntarily joined the Socialist Camp in the late 1940s, and then gladly defected from it in the early 1960s. The first event influenced Indochina, India, and even the Middle East and Europe, while the second development affected North Vietnamese war policies and compelled the Soviet Union to shore up a rump-Socialist Camp in 1968, rendering Eastern Europe unreformable in the process. The Suez Crisis, the June War, and the October War all had an impact on Europe – on the United Kingdom after 1956, on German–German relations after 1967, and on the European Communities after 1973. West Germany's *Ostpolitik* in the 1960s and 1970s shaped politics in Eastern Europe, opened the door to the Conference on Security and Cooperation in Europe, and had an influence on the Catholic Church and popular resistance in Poland.

The agency of middle powers and smaller countries *gradually increased over the course of the Cold War* during four major periods. From 1945 to 1957, the unfolding Cold War put the structures of the post-World War II system in place. The Socialist Camp in Europe and East Asia emerged, while the Anglo–American great powers increasingly worked together to establish a ring of containment alliances, including NATO, the Baghdad Pact/CENTO, SEATO, and the East Asian system of parallel alliances. But the emerging bloc system was unstable from the very beginning; Yugoslavia left the Socialist Camp in 1948 and France set out on an independent path in 1954. Non-aligned India grew frustrated by the globalization of the Cold War in the wake of the Korean War, and thus agreed to the Indonesian plea to call for an Asian–African Conference in April of 1955 to counter bloc formation. The Anglo–American push for an anti-Soviet alliance system in the Middle East divided the Arab League temporarily and helped to foment the Suez Crisis in 1956.

In the following dozen years until 1969, the Soviet Union and the United States formed a nuclear superpower duopoly. Yet the pre-eminent position of the two superpowers in the international system did not translate into increased power at the lower levels. The Socialist Camp unraveled with the defection of the PRC, Albania, and Romania. Simultaneously, communist Vietnam rose as a major actor, which neither communist China nor the Soviet Union was able to control. The Arab League set out on an independent path in parallel to the decline of the United Kingdom as a great power after Suez. After engaging in a Cold War of its own, the league was able to restore a semblance of unity by 1964, which, however, put it on the path to the June War of 1967. Neither the two superpowers nor the United Nations could prevent that war or solve its aftermath. Gaullist France undermined unity within NATO throughout the 1960s. The Vatican and West Germany started to develop and test-run *Ostpolitik* – i.e. the policy of long-term subversion of Eastern Europe and the Soviet Union – independently from American Cold War policies. At the same time, the Western European NATO allies were among the strongest critics of US containment policies in Indochina.

Throughout the 1970s, the two superpowers sought détente by renegotiating the terms of their global engagement, i.e. by limiting their nuclear arms race and agreeing to compete peacefully in all other spheres of conflict. But the decade experienced massive structural change at all levels below. Communist China sought rapprochement with the United States after its border clashes with the Soviet Union. Washington reacted to the Chinese entreaty with the parallel policies of putting pressure on Moscow and demanding help from Beijing to end the Indochina conflict. Still, communist Vietnam won the three-decade-long war by 1975. While the PRC decreased the emphasis on ideology in foreign policy by the early 1970s – and even questioned the usefulness of the Cold War paradigm in general – unified communist Vietnam replaced China as the world revolutionary leader in Asia. By mid decade, India claimed great power status equal to all five United Nations Security Council members with a demonstration of its nuclear capabilities, which it had developed as a consequence of its rivalry with China and despite Soviet–American détente. In the Middle East, the Arab League reached the greatest measure of unity in 1973 as Egypt tried to push the Cold War out of the Arab world, and then attempted to solve the Arab–Israeli conflict bilaterally. Wedded to their bilateral détente, neither superpower understood the long-term consequences of this momentous development. In parallel, pan-Islamism rose to political influence over the course of the whole decade. While some Middle Eastern governments – Saudi Arabia, Pakistan, and Egypt – used pan-Islamism as a basis for strategic regional cooperation that was mostly unrelated to the superpower conflict, opposition movements in Egypt and Iran envisioned it as a means to transcend the regional Cold War once and for all. In Europe, West Germany's *Ostpolitik* celebrated its first successes in the early 1970s, convincing the United States to use it as a trial balloon for superpower détente. But while the relaxation of superpower relations aimed at a redefinition of their bilateral competition, *Ostpolitik* worked to embrace and subvert Eastern Europe. Likewise, Western European countries imposed a human rights discourse on the Conference on Security and Cooperation in Europe in the first half of the 1970s in the face of parallel superpower opposition.

The end of superpower détente in the late 1970s led to what some historians have called the Second Cold War in the 1980s. Yet, at the beginning of this very period, all three regional Cold Wars ended in structural terms. In the wider Middle East, pan-Islamist movements emerged as dominant political forces, either as opposition in Egypt or in power in Iran. Although the Soviet intervention in Afghanistan was a Cold War conflict, it was motivated by the rise of pan-Islamism, while it in turn stimulated the further rise of pan-Islamism. In Asia, China agreed to end its antagonism with the United States and even cooperated with the anti-communist Association of Southeast Asian Nations in thwarting Vietnamese hegemonic aspirations. Thus, Vietnam quickly gave up its world revolutionary ambitions. The old anti-imperialist networks of fraternal communist movements, which dated to the 1920s, had collapsed. In Europe, despite the end of superpower détente, relations across the Iron Curtain deepened. The economic collapse of the Socialist Camp and its integration into the world economy via debt forced Eastern European countries to transcend the Cold War constraints, which Stalin's Soviet Union had put in place three decades before. Eventually, the last Soviet leader, Mikhail S. Gorbachev, realized by 1988 that the game was up, and grudgingly admitted Soviet defeat in the global Cold War within a year. Structural changes at all lower levels of the international system had helped him to get there. By doing so, these changes assisted the United States in outliving its last great power rival.

Notes

Introduction

1. In defining structure in international relations, I follow Colin Wight, *Agents, structures and international relations: politics as ontology* (Cambridge University Press, 2006), pp. 121–76. Accordingly, structure is a pattern of relatively stable – though not unchangeable – behavior among actors, displays "law-like regularities," includes "collective rules and resources," contains a system of relationships, and comprises "relations of difference that constitute and define properties" of the actors.
2. For a summary introduction to agency in international relations, see Wight, *Agents, structures and international relations*, pp. 177–225.
3. See, for example, William Appleman Williams, *The tragedy of American diplomacy* (Ivan R. Dee, 1959). Walter LaFeber, *America, Russia, and the Cold War, 1945–1966* (Wiley, 1967). Herbert Feis, *From trust to terror* (W. W. Norton, 1970). John Lewis Gaddis, *Strategies of containment* (Oxford University Press, 1982). Michael F. Hopkins, "Continuing debate and new approaches in Cold War history," *The Historical Journal*, 50/4 (2007), pp. 913–34.
4. Bradley R. Simpson, *Economists with guns* (Stanford University Press, 2008). Robert J. McMahon, *The Cold War on the periphery* (Columbia University Press, 1996). Piero Gleijeses, *Conflicting missions* (University of North Carolina Press, 2002). Gilbert M. Joseph, and Daniela Spenser, eds., *In from the Cold* (Duke University Press, 2007).
5. Allen Hunter, ed., *Rethinking the Cold War* (Temple University Press, 1998). Matthew Connelly, "Taking off the Cold War lens," *American Historical Review*, 105/3 (2000), pp. 739–69. Efraim Karsh, "Cold War, Post-Cold War: does it make a difference for the Middle East?," *Review of International Studies*, 23/3 (1997), pp. 271–91. Hope M. Harrison, *Driving the Soviets up the wall* (Princeton University Press, 2003).
6. Chen Jian, *Mao's China and the Cold War* (University of North Carolina Press, 2001). Zhai Qiang, *China and the Vietnam Wars, 1950–1975* (University of North Carolina Press, 2000). Pierre Asselin, *Hanoi's road to the Vietnam War, 1954–1965* (University of California Press, 2013). Lien-Hang T. Nguyen, *Hanoi's war* (University of North Carolina Press, 2012). Srinath Raghavan, *War and peace in modern India* (Permanent Black, 2010). Paul T. Chamberlin, *The global offensive* (Oxford University Press, 2012). Jesse Ferris, *Nasser's gamble*

(Princeton University Press, 2013). Matthew J. Connelly, *A diplomatic revolution* (Oxford University Press, 2002). Jeffrey J. Byrne, *Mecca of revolution* (Oxford University Press, 2012). William G. Gray, *Germany's Cold War* (University of North California Press, 2003). Mary E. Sarotte, *Dealing with the devil: East Germany, Détente, and Ostpolitik, 1969–1973* (University of North Carolina Press, 2001).

7. O. Arne Westad, *The global Cold War* (Cambridge University Press, 2005). Even many of the contributors to the three-volume *Cambridge history of the Cold War* are wedded to the bipolar interpretation: Melvyn P. Leffler and O. Arne Westad, eds., *The Cambridge history of the Cold War*, 3 volumes (Cambridge University Press, 2010).

8. Jessica C. E. Gienow-Hecht, ed., *Decentering America* (Berghahn Books, 2007). Jadwiga E. Pieper Mooney and Fabio Lanza, eds., *De-centering Cold War history* (Routledge, 2012). Meghana Nayak and Eric Selbin, *Decentering international relations* (Zed Books, 2010). Ingo Peters and Wiebke Wemheuer-Vogelaar, eds., *Globalizing international relations* (Palgrave Macmillan, 2016).

9. Fraser J. Harbutt, *The Cold War era* (Blackwell, 2002). John Lewis Gaddis, *The Cold War: a new history* (Penguin Press, 2005). Melvyn P. Leffler, *For the soul of mankind* (Hill and Wang, 2007). John Lamberton Harper, *The Cold War* (Oxford University Press, 2011). Carole Fink, *Cold War* (Westview Press, 2014).

10. Edward G. Miller and Tuong Vu, "The Vietnam War as a Vietnamese War: agency and society in the study of the Second Indochina War," *Journal of Vietnamese Studies*, 4/3 (2009), pp. 1–16. Andrew Preston, "Rethinking the Vietnam War: orthodoxy and revisionism," *International Politics Reviews*, 1/1 (2013), pp. 37–48.

11. Andrew J. Rotter, "Saidism without Said," *American Historical Review*, 105/4 (2000), pp. 1205–17. Nathan J. Citino, "Between global and regional narratives," *International Journal of Middle East Studies*, 43/2 (2011), pp. 313–16.

12. Only a few books have a distinct regional or comparative approach to Europe in the Cold War; see David Reynolds, ed., *The origins of the Cold War in Europe* (Yale University Press, 1994). Wilfried Loth, ed., *Europe, Cold War and coexistence, 1953–1965* (Frank Cass, 2004).

13. For integrated histories, see Peter Bender, *Episode oder Epoche?* (Deutscher Taschenbuchverlag, 1996). Peter Bender, *Deutschlands Wiederkehr* (Klett-Cotta, 2007). Peter Graf Kielmansegg, *Das geteilte Land* (Pantheon, 2007).

14. For separate histories, see Manfred Görtemaker, *Geschichte der Bundesrepublik Deutschland* (Fischer Taschenbuch, 1999). Edgar Wolfrum, *Die geglückte Demokratie* (Klett-Cotta, 2006). Eckart Conze, *Die Suche nach Sicherheit* (Siedler Verlag, 2009). Klaus Schroeder, *Der SED Staat* (Carl Hanser, 1998). Andreas Malycha and Peter Jochen Winters, *Die SED* (Munich: C. H. Beck, 2009). For the argument of East Germany as an aberration, see Werner Abelshauser, *Deutsche Wirtschaftsgeschichte* (Bundeszentrale für politische Bildung, 2011).

15. Paul T. Chamberlin, *The Cold War's killing fields* (Harper, 2018).

16. For the Cold War in Africa and Latin America, see Westad, *The global Cold War*.

17. George Orwell, "You and the atomic bomb," *Tribune*, October 19, 1945, http://
orwell.ru/library/articles/ABomb/english/e_abomb, accessed on September 10,
2019.

18. Larry Wolff, *Inventing Eastern Europe* (Stanford University Press, 1994), pp.
1–16. Timothy Garton Ash, "The puzzle of Central Europe," *New York
Review of Books*, 46/5 (1999), p. 18.

1   From High Imperialism to Cold War Division

1. P. J. Cain and A. G. Hopkins, *British imperialism: 1688–2000*, 2nd ed.
(Pearson Education, 2002), pp. 411–63. Lawrence James, *The rise and the
fall of the British Empire* (St. Martin's Griffin, 1994), p. 353. Nicholas Owen,
The British Left and India (Oxford University Press, 2007), pp. 235–98.

2. Cain and Hopkins, *British imperialism*, pp. 543–64. Lawrence, *Rise and fall*,
pp. 412–27.

3. Lawrence, *Rise and fall*, pp. 386–411. Susan Pederson, "Getting out of Iraq –
in 1932," *American Historical Review*, 115/4 (2010), pp. 975–1000.

4. Vladimir I. Lenin, "The crisis has matured," September 29, 1917, *Collected
works*, vol. 26 (Progress Publishers, 1964), pp. 74–84. Iosif V. Stalin, "Two
camps," February 22, 1919, *Works*, vol. 4 (Foreign Languages Publishing
House, 1953), pp. 240–44 (first quote). Donald I. Buzinkai, "The Bolsheviks,
the League of Nations and the Paris Peace Conference, 1919," *Soviet Studies*, 19/
2 (1967), pp. 259–60 (second quote). Vladimir I. Lenin, "Report of the
Commission on the National and the Colonial Questions," July 26, 1920,
Collected works, vol. 31, pp. 240–45. Christopher Read, *Lenin* (Routledge,
2005), pp. 116–26. Margaret MacMillan, *Paris 1919* (Random House, 2001),
pp. 78–81. Vladimir I. Lenin, "Speech delivered at a meeting in the People's
House, Petrograd," March 13, 1919, *Collected works*, vol. 29, p. 53.

5. Jon Jacobson, *When the Soviet Union entered world politics* (University of California
Press, 1994), pp. 11–26. Erik van Ree, *The political thought of Joseph Stalin*
(RoutledgeCurzon, 2003), pp. 84–95. R. Craig Nation, *Black earth, red star*
(Cornell University Press, 1992), pp. 74–112. Jonathan Haslam, "The
Comintern and the origins of the Popular Front 1934–1935," *The Historical
Journal*, 22/3 (1992), pp. 673–91. Daniel Kowalsky, *Stalin and the Spanish Civil
War* (Columbia University Press, 2001). Bert Hoppe, *In Stalins Gefolgschaft*
(Oldenbourg Wissenschaftsverlag, 2007). Edward H. Carr, *Twilight of the
Comintern, 1930–1935* (Pantheon Books, 1982). Tareq Y. Ismael, *The communist
movement in the Arab world* (Routledge, 2005), pp. 8–20. Michael M. Sheng,
Battling Western imperialism (Princeton University Press, 2008).

6. Jonathan Haslam, *The Soviet Union and the threat from the East, 1933–41*
(University of Pittsburgh Press, 1992). Gerhard L. Weinberg, *Germany, Hitler
and World War II* (Cambridge University Press, 1995), pp. 153–67.
Geoffrey Roberts, *Stalin's wars* (Yale University Press, 2006), pp. 30–60,
63–64, 245–46. Arkadi I. Vaksberg, *Hôtel Lux* (Fayard, 1993).

7. Thomas J. Knock, *To end all wars* (Oxford University Press, 1992). Gordon
N. Levin, *Woodrow Wilson and world politics* (Oxford University Press, 1968).
Betty Miller Unterberger, "The United States and national self-determination,"
Presidential Studies Quarterly, 26/4 (1996), pp. 926–41.

8. Niels Aage Thorsen, *The political thought of Woodrow Wilson, 1875–1910* (Princeton University Press, 2014), pp. 165–66. John Milton Cooper, "American sphinx," John Milton Cooper and Thomas J. Knock, eds., *Jefferson, Lincoln, and Wilson* (University of Virginia Press, 2010), pp. 145–62. Erez Manela, *The Wilsonian moment* (Oxford University Press, 2007), pp. 19–34. Erez Manela, "Imagining Woodrow Wilson in Asia," *American Historical Review*, 111/5 (2006), pp. 1327–51. Sophie Quinn-Judge, *Ho Chi Minh* (University of California Press, 2002), pp. 11–42.

9. Stephen A. Schuker, *The end of French predominance in Europe* (University of North Carolina Press, 1976), pp. 9–10. Robert H. Ferrell, *Woodrow Wilson and World War I, 1917–1921* (Harper & Row, 1985), pp. 156–77. Warren I. Cohen, *Empire without tears* (Temple University Press, 1987), pp. 45–55. Frank Costigliola, *Awkward dominion* (Cornell University Press, 1984), pp. 111–27. Charles P. Kindleberger, *The world in depression, 1929–1939* (University of California Press, 1973), pp. 108–231. Robert Dallek, *Franklin D. Roosevelt and American foreign policy, 1932–1945* (Oxford University Press, 1979), pp. 101–43.

10. Dallek, *Roosevelt*, pp. 144–68, 434–39, 503–19. "Joint statement by President Roosevelt and Prime Minister Churchill, August 14, 1914," United States, Department of State, *Foreign relations of the United States [FRUS]*, 1941, vol. I (US Government Printing Office, 1958), pp. 367–69. Fred E. Pollock and Warren F. Kimball, "'In search of monsters to destroy'," Warren F. Kimball, *The juggler* (Princeton University Press, 1991), pp. 127–58. "Memorandum of conversation, by Adviser of Caribbean Affairs (Taussig)," March 15, 1945, *FRUS*, 1945, I, p. 124 (quote). "Memorandum of conversations, by the Secretary of States," March 27, 1943, *FRUS*, 1943, III, p. 37.

11. Warren F. Kimball, "The sheriffs," David B. Woolner, Warren F. Kimball, and David Reynolds, eds., *FDR's world* (Palgrave Macmillan, 2008), pp. 91–121. Eric Rauchway, *The money makers* (Basic Books, 2015). Benn Steil, *The battle of Bretton Woods* (Princeton University Press, 2013), pp. 125–249. Dallek, *Roosevelt*, pp. 505–7.

12. Cain and Hopkins, *British Imperialism*, pp. 627–32.

13. John Morton Blum, *V was for victory* (Harcourt Brace Jovanovich, 1976), pp. 90–92. Wm. Roger Louis, *Imperialism at bay* (Oxford University Press, 1978).

14. Vladislav M. Zubok, *A failed empire* (University of North Carolina Press, 2007), pp. 17–49. Ralph B. Levering, Vladimir O. Pechatnov, Verena Botzenhart-Viehe, and C. Earl Edmondson, *Debating the origins of the Cold War* (Rowman & Littlefield, 2002), pp. 90–100. Tsuyoshi Hasegawa, *Racing the enemy* (Belknap Press, 2005), pp. 186, 252–89. Robert Dallek, *The lost peace* (Harper, 2010), pp. 100–2. John Lewis Gaddis, *Strategies of containment*, 2nd and rev. ed. (Oxford University Press, 2005), p. 15. van Ree, *Political thought*, p. 237. Harold James and Marzenna James, "The origins of the Cold War," *The Historical Journal*, 37/3 (1994), pp. 615–22. Harold James, *International monetary cooperation since Bretton Woods* (Oxford University Press, 1996), pp. 60–71. McGeorge Bundy, *Danger and survival* (Random House, 1988), p. 81. David Holloway, *Stalin and the bomb* (Yale University Press, 1994), p. 129.

15. Zubok, *Failed empire*, pp. 65–69. Stephen Denis Kertesz, *Last European peace conference, Paris, 1946* (Hunyadi M. Mk, 1992), pp. 22–43. Various documents: *FRUS*, 1946, III and IV.

16. "The Chargé in the Soviet Union (Kennan) to the Secretary of State," February 22, 1946, *FRUS*, 1946, VI, pp. 696–709. Melvyn P. Leffler, *A preponderance of power* (Stanford University Press, 1992), pp. 100–40, 157–64, 253–58. Gaddis, *Strategies*, pp. 24–52. George F. Kennan, *Memoirs, 1925–1950* (Little, Brown, 1967), p. 368. Manfred Görtemaker, *Geschichte der Bundesrepublik Deutschland* (Fischer Taschenbuch, 1999), pp. 37–38. Michael Schaller, *American occupation of Japan* (Oxford University Press, 1987), pp. 110–40.

17. Kennan, *Memoirs, 1925–1950*, pp. 313–24. Nicklaus Thomas-Symonds, *Attlee* (I. B. Tauris, 2010), p. 152. Wm. Roger Louis, *The British Empire in the Middle East, 1945–1951* (Clarendon Press, 1984), pp. 82–102. Leffler, *Preponderance*, pp. 142–46.

18. Zubok, *Failed empire*, pp. 73–78. William I. Hitchcock, *France restored* (University of North Carolina Press, 1998), pp. 99–116.

19. Holloway, *Stalin*, pp. 196–223. Sheng, *Battling*, pp. 15–56. O. Arne Westad, *Cold War and revolution* (Columbia University Press, 1993). Leffler, *Preponderance*, pp. 291–93. Chen Jian, *Mao's China and the Cold War* (University of North Carolina Press, 2001), pp. 38–48. Lorenz M. Lüthi, *The Sino-Soviet split* (Princeton University Press, 2008), pp. 31–33.

20. Leffler, *Preponderance*, pp. 323–40. John Lewis Gaddis, *George F. Kennan* (Penguin Press, 2011), pp. 365–70. "A report to the president pursuant to the president's directive of January 31, 1950 [NSC-68]," April 7, 1950, *FRUS*, 1950, IX, pp. 235–92. Alonzo L. Hamby, *Man of the people* (Oxford University Press, 1995), pp. 527–29.

21. Lüthi, *Sino-Soviet split*, pp. 32–33. Chen, *Mao's China*, p. 54.

22. William Stueck, *Rethinking the Korean War* (Princeton University Press, 2002), pp. 11–38, 87–88. Bruce Cumings, *Korea's place in the sun*, upd. ed. (W. W. Norton, 2005), pp. 183–260. Sergei N. Goncharov, John W. Lewis, and Xue Litai, *Uncertain partners* (Stanford University Press, 1993), pp. 136–48.

23. Gaddis, *Strategies*, pp. 106–12. Goncharov, *Uncertain Partners*, p. 161. Chen Jian, *China's road to the Korean War* (Columbia University Press, 1994), pp. 125–213. "UN gives go-ahead with 47–5 vote," *Globe and Mail*, October 9, 1950, p. 1.

24. Gaddis, *Strategies*, pp. 106–62. Lawrence S. Kaplan, *NATO divided, NATO united* (Praeger, 2004), pp. 9–11. Hitchcock, *France*, pp. 133–47.

25. Steven Hugh Lee, *Outposts of empire* (McGill-Queen's University Press, 1995), pp. 80–83. Schaller, *American occupation*, pp. 292–94. Victor D. Cha, "Powerplay," *International Security*, 34/3 (2010), pp. 158–96 (quote). Mark Atwood Lawrence, *Assuming the burden* (University of California Press, 2005).

26. For a British assessment of the pact, see "Arab League Collective Security Pact," January 15, 1952, National Archives of the United Kingdom [NAUK], FO 371/97862, pp. 1–3. Aran Sanjian, "The formulation of the Baghdad Pact," *Middle Eastern Studies*, 33/2 (1997), pp. 226–66.

27. Kathryn C. Statler, *Replacing France* (University of Kentucky Press, 2007), pp. 78–95. Roger Dingman, "John Foster Dulles and the creation of the South-East Asia Treaty Organization in 1954," *International History Review*, 11/3 (1989), pp. 457–77.

28. William Taubman, *Khrushchev* (W. W. Norton, 2003), pp. 241–44. Lorenz M. Lüthi, "A window of opportunities in Europe," Lorenz M. Lüthi, ed., *The regional Cold Wars in Europe, East Asia, and the Middle East* (Woodrow Wilson Center Press / Stanford University Press, 2015), p. 46. Ilya V. Gaiduk, *Confronting Vietnam* (Stanford University Press, 2003), pp. 28–53. Zhai Qiang, *China and the Vietnam Wars, 1950–1975* (University of North Carolina Press, 2000), pp. 49–63. Li Lianqing, *Dawai jiaojia Zhou Enlai*, vol. 2 (Tian ditushu youxian gongsi, 1994), pp. 348–52. Svetozar Rajak, *Yugoslavia and the Soviet Union in the early Cold War* (Routledge, 2011), pp. 66–126. Vojtech Mastny, "The Soviet Union's partnership with India," *Journal of Cold War Studies*, 12/3 (2010), p. 53.

29. "Indonesian proposal for an Afro-Asian Conference," September 24, 1954, Jawaharlal Nehru, *Selected Works*, 2nd series [*JNSW*2], vol. 26 (Nehru Memorial Museum and Library, 2000), pp. 429–30. "My Dear Chief Minister," November 15, 1954, *JNSW*2, vol. 27, p. 549. "Memo No. 940/53," May 5, 1953, National Archives of Australia [NAA], Series A1838, 181/2/1 Part 3, p. 1. "No. 24. Saving," February 1, 1954, NAUK, FO 371/108349, p. 1.

30. Hitchcock, *France*, pp. 169–202.

31. Vojtech Mastny and Malcolm Byrne, eds., *A cardboard castle?* (Central European University Press, 2005), pp. 2–4. Lüthi, "Window," pp. 49–50.

32. Eckart Conze, *Die Suche nach Sicherheit* (Siedler Verlag, 2009), pp. 89–93. Lüthi, "Window," pp. 57–60.

33. Michael Ottolenghi, "Harry Truman's recognition of Israel," *The Historical Journal*, 47/4 (2004), pp. 963–88. Jerome Slater, "The superpowers and an Arab–Israeli political settlement," *Political Science Quarterly*, 105/4 (1990–91), pp. 562–63. Shlomo Slonim, "The 1948 American embargo on arms to Palestine," *Political Science Quarterly*, 94/3 (1979), pp. 495–514. Zubok, *Failed empire*, p. 109.

34. "Conversation with Gamal Abdel Nasser," *JNSW*2, vol. 28, pp. 216–17. Muhammad H. Haykal, *The sphinx and the commissar* (Harper & Row, 1978), pp. 57–59.

35. Avi Shlaim, "The protocol of Sèvres, 1956," *International Affairs*, 73/3 (1997), pp. 509–30. "W. No. 304 Top Secret," July 31, 1956, NAUK, FO 371/119078, p. 24 (quote).

36. Diane B. Kunz, *The economic diplomacy of the Suez Crisis* (University of North Carolina Press, 1991), pp. 116–52. Lüthi, "Window," pp. 59–60.

37. Salim Yaqub, *Containing Arab nationalism* (University of North Carolina Press, 2004). Harry N. Howard, "The regional pacts and the Eisenhower Doctrine," *Annals of the American Academy of Political and Social Science*, 401/1 (1972), pp. 85–94. Various documents: Politisches Archiv des Auswärtigen Amtes, Bestand: Ministerium für Auswärtige Angelegenheiten [PAAA-MfAA], A 12559; National Archives of India [NAI], External Affairs, 8 (108) Eur.E/58.

2   The United Kingdom and the Arab League

1. Correlli Barnett, *The lost victory* (Macmillan, 1995), pp. 42 (quote), 46–53. Leonard Beaton, "Imperial defence without the Empire," *International Journal*, 23/4 (1968), pp. 531–33. Anne Deighton, "Britain and the Cold War, 1945–1955," Melvyn P. Leffler and O. Arne Westad, eds., *The Cambridge history of the Cold War*, vol. 1, *Origins* (Cambridge University Press, 2010), pp. 112–32.

2. Aiyaz Husain, *Mapping the end of empire* (Harvard University Press, 2014), pp. 179–86. Barnett, *Lost victory*, p. 56. W. David McIntyre, *Commonwealth of Nations* (University of Minnesota Press, 1971), pp. 181–93, 343–54.

3. Elisabeth Åsbrink, *1947: Als die Gegenwart began* (btb, 2017), p. 40. A. G. Hopkins, "Rethinking decolonization," *Past & Present*, 200 (2008), pp. 211–47. Nicholas J. White, "The business and the politics of decolonization," *Economic History Review*, 53/3 (2000), pp. 544–64.

4. Donald Quataert, *The Ottoman Empire, 1700–1922* (Cambridge University Press, 2005), pp. 21–59, 68–72. Suraiya Faroqhi, *The Ottoman Empire and the world around it* (I. B. Tauris, 2004), pp. 75–77. Marian Kent, ed., *The Great Powers and the end of the Ottoman Empire* (Frank Cass, 1996).

5. Mustafa Aksakal, *The Ottoman road to war in 1914* (Cambridge University Press, 2008), pp. 57–118, 188–94. Eugene L. Rogan, *The fall of the Ottomans* (Basic Books, 2015). Helmut Mejcher, *The struggle for a new Middle East in the 20th century* (Lit Verlag, 2007), pp. 1–32. David Fromkin, *A peace to end all peace* (Henry Holt, 1989), pp. 173–99, 383–454.

6. Steven A. Cook, *The struggle for Egypt* (Oxford University Press, 2012), pp. 20–25. Donald M. Reid, "Nationalizing the Pharaonic past," James Jankowski and Israel Gershoni, eds., *Rethinking nationalism in the Arab Middle East* (Columbia University Press, 1997), pp. 127–49. Reeva S. Simon, "The imposition of nationalism on a non-nation state," Jankowski and Gershoni, *Rethinking nationalism*, pp. 87–104. James L. Gelvin, "The other Arab nationalism," Jankowski and Gershoni, *Rethinking nationalism*, pp. 231–48. Beshara Doumani, *Rediscovering Palestine* (University of California Press, 1995). Muhammad Y. Muslih, *The origins of Palestinian nationalism* (Columbia University Press, 1988). C. Ernest Dawn, "The formation of pan-Arab ideology in the interwar years," *International Journal of Middle East Studies*, 20/1 (1988), pp. 67–91. Reeva S. Simon, "The Hashemite 'conspiracy'," *International Journal of Middle East Studies*, 5/3 (1974), pp. 314–27.

7. Rogan, *Fall*, pp. 355–95. Bülent Gökay, *A clash of empires* (Tauris Academic Studies, 1997). Joshua Teitelbaum, *The rise and fall of the Hashemite Kingdom of Arabia* (New York University Press, 2001), pp. 243–48. David Holden and Richard Johns, *The house of Saud* (Holt, Rinehart and Winston, 1981), pp. 78–86.

8. "No. 556," November 3, 1932, British Library [BL], IOR/L/PS/12/2110, p. 541a (quote). Basheer M. Nafi, "King Faysal, the British and the project for a pan-Arab congress, 1931–33," *Islamic Studies*, 37/4 (1998), pp. 479–503.

9. Nir Arielli, *Fascist Italy and the Middle East, 1933–40* (Palgrave Macmillan, 2013), pp. 41–75. Laila Morsy, "The military clauses of the Anglo-Egyptian

Treaty of Friendship and Alliance, 1936," *International Journal of Middle East Studies*, 16/1 (1984), pp. 67–97.

10. Various documents: BL, IOR/L/PS/12/2110. Mehmet Akif Kumral, *Rethinking Turkey–Iraq relations* (Palgrave Macmillan, 2016), pp. 54–69.

11. David K. Fieldhouse, *Western imperialism in the Middle East, 1914–1958* (Oxford University Press, 2006), pp. 165–71, 269–73, 322–23. Various documents: Anita L. P. Burdett, ed., *The Arab League*, vol. 1 (Archive Editions, 1995), pp. 339–414.

12. "Material for a history of the Arab Union, 1939–1945," no date, National Archives of the United Kingdom [NAUK], FO 371/45241, pp. 1–11. David Motadel, *Islam and Nazi Germany's War* (Harvard University Press, 2014), pp. 73–132. "Parliamentary Question," October 16, 1940, NAUK, FO 371/24548, p. 48 (quote). James Barr, *A line in the sand* (Simon & Schuster, 2011), pp. 201–32. Various documents: NAUK, FO 371/23195 and 24548.

13. F. Eshraghi, "Anglo-Soviet occupation of Iran in August 1941," *Middle Eastern Studies*, 20/1 (1984), pp. 27–52. Mustafa Sitki Bilgin and Steven Morewood, "Turkey's reliance on Britain," *Middle Eastern Studies*, 40/2 (2004), p. 28. Majid Khadduri, "The Arab League as a regional arrangement," *American Journal of International Law*, 40/4 (1946), pp. 760–61. Various documents: BL, IOR/L/PS/12/2110 and NAUK, FO 371/31337.

14. "Arab unity must come from Arabs," *Palestine Post*, February 25, 1943, p. 1 (quote). John Keegan, "Churchill's strategy," Robert Blake and Wm. Roger Louis, eds., *Churchill* (Oxford University Press, 1996), pp. 327–52. Julian Lewis, *Changing direction* (Frank Cass, 2003), pp. 31–54. Meir Zamir, "The 'missing dimension'," *Middle Eastern Studies*, 46/6 (2010), pp. 791–814.

15. Yehoshua Porath, *In search of Arab unity, 1930–1945* (Frank Cass, 1986), pp. 257–77. Various documents: NAUK, CO 732/87/8–732/87/11, FO 141/866, FO 371/34961–34963, 39987–39989. Ahmed M. Gomaa, *The foundation of the League of Arab States* (Longman, 1977), pp. 91–97.

16. "E 6477/41/65," October 7, 1944, NAUK, CO 732/88/11, pp. 1–4 (quote). Various documents: NAUK, FO 371/39991, FO 371/45235, and FO 816/44. "N.E. through Counsellor," [October 12, 1944], NAUK, FO 624/35, p. 1. "Dear Charles," February 8, 1945, NAUK, FO 371/45236, pp. 11–12a.

17. "No. 539," April 23, 1945, NAUK, FO 371/45238, pp. 102–4. Various documents: NAUK, PREM 4/77/1a, and Meir Zamir, ed., *The Secret Anglo-French War in the Middle East* (Routledge, 2015), pp. 224–31. Khadduri, "Arab League," p. 771. "From Palestine (Field Marshal Viscount Gort)," February 27, 1945, NAUK, PREM 4/77/1a, p. 1 (quotes).

18. Various documents: NAUK, FO 371/45237, CO 732/88/12, FO 921/3262. "Memorandum," March 20, 1945, NAUK, FO 371/45238, pp. 14–14a. "No. 263," February 13, 1945, NAUK, FO 371/45236, p. 81 (quote).

19. "President Quwatli's report to this Cabinet ministers on his agreement with Kings Faruq and Ibn Sa'ud," February 20, 1945, Zamir, *Secret Anglo-French War*, pp. 229–31. Barr, *Line in the sand*, pp. 297–311. Bruce Maddy-Weitzman, *The crystallization of the Arab state system 1945–1954* (Syracuse University Press, 1993), p. 31. "No. 500," March 2, 1945, NAUK, FO 921/323, pp. 1–2.

20. J. A. Hail, *Britain's foreign policy in Egypt and Sudan, 1947–1956* (Ithaca Press, 1996), pp. 15–121. Cook, *Struggle*, pp. 35–38.

21. Martin Thomas, "France accused," *Contemporary European History*, 10/1 (2001), pp. 91–121. Matthew J. Connelly, *A diplomatic revolution* (Oxford University Press, 2002).
22. Various documents: NAUK, FO 371/45240 and FO371/45396. Gershon Meron, "Economic repercussions of Arab policy toward Israel," *Journal of Educational Sociology*, 27/8 (1954), p. 353. Donald L. Losman, "The Arab boycott of Israel," *International Journal of Middle East Studies*, 3/2 (1972), p. 99. Various documents: Burdett, *Arab League*, vol. 5, pp. 257–329, 684–707.
23. Walid Khalidi, "The Arab perspective," Wm. Roger Louis and Robert W. Stookey, eds., *The end of the Palestine Mandate* (London: I. B. Tauris, 1986), pp. 104–14. Various documents: NAUK, FO 371/52313–52314. Douglas Little, "Pipeline politics," *Business History Review*, 64/2 (1990), pp. 255–85.
24. Khalidi, "Arab perspective," p. 113. Avi Shlaim, *Collusion across the Jordan* (Clarendon Press, 1988), pp. 78–84.
25. Khalidi, "The Arab perspective," 118–21. Muhammad F. Jamali, *Inside the Arab nationalist struggle* (I. B. Tauris, 2012), pp. 108–13. "Arabs call Palestine report source of Third World War," *New York Times* [*NYT*], September 9, 1947, p. 1. Various documents: NAUK, FO 371/61529–61530. Laila Parsons, *The commander* (Hill and Wang, 2016), pp. 195–240. Joshua Landis, "Syria and the Palestine War," Eugene L. Rogan and Avi Shlaim, eds., *The war for Palestine*, 2nd ed. (Cambridge University Press, 2007), pp. 191–93.
26. Rashid Khalidi, "The Palestinians and 1948," and Fawaz A. Gerges, "Egypt and the 1948 War," Rogan and Shlaim, *War for Palestine*, pp. 12–36, 79–103. Avraham Sela, "Transjordan, Israel and the 1948 war," *Middle Eastern Studies*, 28/4 (1992), pp. 623–88.
27. Shlomo Slonim, "The 1948 American Embargo on Arms to Palestine," *Political Science Quarterly*, 94/3 (1979), pp. 495–514. "No. 74A," February 24, 1948, NAUK, CO 537/3984, p. 1. Jamali, *Inside*, pp. 117–19. "Israel scores Egypt on Suez ship grabs," May 29, 1948, *NYT*, p. 4. Uri Bialer, *Oil and the Arab–Israeli conflict, 1948–63* (Macmillan, 1999), p. 128. Neil Caplan, *The Lausanne Conference, 1949* (The Mosche Dayan Center for Middle Eastern and African Studies, 1993).
28. Shlomo Slonim, "Origins of the 1950 tripartite declaration on the Middle East," *Middle Eastern Studies*, 23/2 (1987), pp. 135–49. Guy Laron, *Origins of the Suez Crisis* (Woodrow Wilson Center Press/ Johns Hopkins University Press, 2013), pp. 24–29. "No. 1125," October 25, 1949, NAUK, FO 371/75076, pp. 28–30. "Q. No. 15 Saving," July 6, 1950, NAUK, FO 371/81933, pp. 1–2.
29. Michael Doran, *Pan-Arabism before Nasser* (Oxford University Press, 1999), pp. 80–84. Various documents: Burdett, *Arab League*, vol. 5, pp. 61–100.
30. Ilan Pappé, *Britain and the Arab–Israeli conflict, 1948–51* (Macmillan, 1988), pp. 89–96. Maddy-Weitzman, *Crystallization*, pp. 105–25. Shlaim, *Collusion*, pp. 522–33.
31. Various documents: NAUK, FO 371/81931, and 82707, 81933, and FO 1018/71. Philip Robins, *A history of Jordan* (Cambridge University Press, 2004), p. 73. Ronen Yitzhak, "The assassination of King Abdallah," *Diplomacy & Statecraft*, 21/1 (2010), pp. 68–86.

32. Fayez A. Sayegh, "Neutralism in the United Arab Republic," Fayez A. Sayegh, ed., *The dynamics of neutralism in the Arab world* (Chandler, 1964), pp. 173–74. "Egypt may close canal to Korea help," *Jerusalem Post*, July 2, 1950, p. 1. "Arab League rent by stand on Korea," *NYT*, July 11, 1950, p. 17. Elie Podeh, *The quest for hegemony in the Arab world* (E. J. Brill, 1995), p. 39.

33. Various documents: NAUK, FO 371/81934. "Arab delegations: neutrality as a bargaining counter," *Times of India*, September 14, 1950, p. 6.

34. "The League of Arab States," February 2, 1951, NAUK, FO 371/91205, pp. 89–92. "Arab League asks defense bid talks," *NYT*, October 31, 1951, p. 12. "Dear Archie," February 28, 1952, NAUK, FO 371/97862, 1. Podeh, *Quest*, pp. 54–55. "Jordan to sign Arab security pact," January 21, 1952, NAUK, FO 371/97862, 1. "No. 34," August 28, 1952, NAUK, FO 371/97863, 1–2. Only Yemen and Lebanon had not ratified by August 1952. Various documents: NAUK, FO 371/97863.

35. Podeh, *Quest*, pp. 59–63. "Memo No. 600/53," March 3, 1953, NAA, Series A1838, 163/11/148, pp. 1–2. "10613/1/53," April 13, 1953, NAUK, FO 371/104195, p. 1. "Memo No. 940/53," May 5, 1953, NAA, Series A1838, 181/2/1 Part 3, p. 1. "No. 202," August 29, 1953, NAUK, FO 371/104196, p. 1 (first quote). "Cairo projecting neutralist role," *NYT*, December 28, 1953, p. 3 (second quote).

36. Podeh, *Quest*, pp. 64–76. "No. 139 Saving," May 31, 1954, NAUK, FO 371/108349, pp. 1–2 (quote). Various documents: NAUK, FO 371/115489–115492.

37. Zach Levey, "Israel's quest for a security guarantee from the United States, 1954–1956," *British Journal of Middle Eastern Studies*, 22/1–2 (1995), pp. 49–51. Various documents: NAUK, FO 371/115495–115499. "Memo No. 200," March 24, 1955, NAA, Series A1838, 3002/1 Part 3, p. 1. "Conversation with Gamal Abdel Nasser," April 14, 1955, Jawaharlal Nehru, *Selected Works*, 2nd series [*JNSW*2], vol. 28 (Nehru Memorial Museum and Library, 2001), p. 217. "Memorandum of conversation by the Ambassador of Egypt D. S. Solod with Prime Minister of Egypt G. Nasser," May 21, 1955, V. V. Naumkin, ed., *Blizhnevostochnyi konflikt*, vol. 1 (Mezhdunarodnyi Fond Demokratiya, 2003), pp. 276–77.

38. "No. 218," August 17, 1955, NAUK, PREM 11/943, pp. 1–2. Various documents: NAUK, FO 371/115525. "Fm Embassy Cairo May 20/56 Secret," Library and Archives Canada [LAC], RG25, box 8152, pp. 1–2. "Memorandum of a conversation, Department of State, Washington," July 19, 1956, United States, Department of State, *Foreign relations of the United States* [*FRUS*], 1955–57, XV (US Government Printing Office, 1989), pp. 867–73. "Speech by President Nasser at Alexandria on July 26 [1956]," NAUK, FO 371/119088, pp. 1–16 (quotes).

39. Shlaim, "The protocol," pp. 514–15. Howard J. Dooley, "Great Britain's 'last battle' in the Middle East," *International History Review*, 11/3 (1989), pp. 486–517.

40. Various documents: NAUK, FO 371/119080, 119088, 119090, 119092, 119106, 119160. Shlaim, "Protocol," p. 509.

41. "Secretary of State," July 30, 1956, NAUK, FO 371/119088, p. 1 (first to third quote). "My Dear Harold," August 13, 1956, NAUK, FO 371/120754, pp. 1–2 (fourth quote). "No. 836," September 22, 1956, NAUK, FO 371/119141, p. 1 (fifth quote).Various documents: NAUK, FO 371/119121 and FO 371/118951. "No. 2260," September 21, 1956, NAUK, FO 371/119141, p. 1 (sixth quote).

42. Kunz, *The economic diplomacy of the Suez Crisis* (University of North Carolina Press, 1991), pp. 116–52. "No. 419," November 16, 1956, NAUK, FO 371/121800, p. 1 (first quote).

43. "Note on a conversation with Foreign Minister Shepilov," July 31, 1956, Politisches Archiv des Auswärtigen Amtes, Bestand: Ministerium für Auswärtige Angelegenheiten [PAAA-MfAA], A 17207, pp. 16–17. "No. 1196," August 30, 1956, LAC, RG25, box 6108, p. 1 (first quote). "No. 433," August 8, 1956, NAUK, FO 371/119094, pp. 1–2 (second quote). "Protocol no. 49, session October 31, 1956," Aleksandr A. Fursenko, ed., *Prezidium TsK KPSS 1954-1964*, vol. 1 (ROSSPEN, 2003), p. 191.

44. The Bulganin letters to the British and French governments, dated November 5, were published in *Pravda* on November 6, 1956, pp. 1–2. Muhammad H. Haykal, *Cutting the lion's tail* (André Deutsch, 1986), pp. 191–92.

45. Various documents: NAUK, FO 371/120772. "No. 479," November 21, 1956, LAC, RG25, box 5835, p. 1 (first and second quotes). "No. 510," December 13, 1956, LAC, RG25, box 4069, pp. 1–2. "No. 1103," December 20, 1956, NAUK, PREM 11/1793, p. 1 (third and fourth quotes).

46. Fieldhouse, *Western imperialism*, pp. 241–42. "No. 419," November 16, 1956, NAUK, FO 371/121800, p. 1. Salim Yaqub, *Containing Arab nationalism* (University of North Carolina, 2004), pp. 57–267.

47. Malcolm H. Kerr, *The Arab cold war* (Oxford University Press, 1971). Various documents: NAUK, FO 371/128047 and 157396, and LAC, RG25, box 4069.

48. "Soviet loan to assist Aswan Dam," *Globe and Mail*, December 27, 1958, p. 1. Various documents: LAC, RG 25, 7812.

49. David W. Lesch, "Gamal Abd al-Nasser and an example of diplomatic acumen," *Middle Eastern Studies*, 31/2 (1995), pp. 362–74. "Liberation start seen by Nasser," February 24, 1958, *New York Herald Tribune*, in LAC, RG25, box 6142, p. 1. "Fm Ldn Mar 7/1958 Secret Cdn eyes only," LAC, RG25, box 6142, p. 1. "United Arab States," March 14, 1958, LAC, RG25, box 6142, p. 1. Podeh, *Quest*, pp. 237–40.

50. Tawfiq Y. Hasou, *The struggle for the Arab world* (KPI, 1985), pp. 89–104. Various documents: NAUK, FO 371/132658, 133154, and 150869 (quote). Avshalom H. Rubin, "Abd al-Karim Qasim and the Kurds of Iraq," *Middle Eastern Studies*, 43/3 (2007), pp. 357–58.

51. Abraham Ben-Zvi, *Decade of transition* (Columbia University Press, 1998). Various documents: PAAA-MfAA, A 224, A 12559, A 12775. Cook, *Struggle*, p. 76. Ferris, *Nasser's gamble*. Various documents: NAUK, FO 371/163978.

52. Elie Podeh, "To unite or not to unite," *Middle Eastern Studies*, 39/1 (2003), pp. 150–85. "UAR–Soviet relations," June 13, 1963, NAA, Series A1838,

69/1/4/31 Part 1, pp. 253–52. "Note," [September 1964], Stiftung Archiv der Parteien und Massenorganisationen der DDR im Bundesarchiv [SAPMO-BArch], DY 30/IV A 2/20/894, pp. 1–9.

53. Various documents: Waijiaobu Dang'anguan [WJBDAG], 107–00523-03, 107–01027-04 to 107–01027-08.
54. Various documents: NAUK, FO 371/175556–371/175558; LAC, RG25, box 8897.
55. Various documents: NAUK, FO 371/175559; LAC, RG25, box 8885.

3   The Soviet Union and the Socialist Camp

1. John Lewis Gaddis, *Strategies of containment*, 2nd and rev. ed. (Oxford University Press, 2005), p. 384. Milovan Djilas, *Conversations with Stalin* (Harcourt, Brace & World, 1962), p. 114 (quote).
2. See, for example, Karl Marx and Friedrich Engels, *Critique of the Gotha Programme* (Electric Book, 2001).
3. Leszek Kolakowski, *Main currents of Marxism*, vol. 3 (Oxford University Press, 1978), pp. 1–182, 494–552.
4. Tim Rees and Andrew Thorpe, eds., *International communism and the Communist International, 1919–43* (Manchester University Press, 1998).
5. Arkadi I. Vaksberg, *Hôtel Lux* (Fayard, 1993). Mario Frank, *Walter Ulbricht* (Siedler Verlag, 2011), pp. 143–88. Mark Kramer, "Stalin, Soviet policy, and the consolidation of a communist bloc," Vladimir Tismaneanu, ed., *Stalin revisited* (Central European University Press, 2009), pp. 51–81.
6. Andreas Malycha and Peter Jochen Winters, *Die SED* (C. H. Beck, 2009), pp. 26–37. Kevin McDermott, *Communist Czechoslovakia, 1945–1989* (Palgrave, 2015), pp. 36–39. Marie-Janine Calic, *Geschichte Jugoslawiens im 20. Jahrhundert* (C. H. Beck, 2010), pp. 171–76. Miranda Vickers, *The Albanians* (I. B. Tauris, 1995), pp. 156–61.
7. Anne Applebaum, *Iron curtain* (Doubleday, 2012), pp. 192–222. Melvyn P. Leffler, "The beginning and the end," Olav Njølstad, ed., *The last decade of the Cold War* (Frank Cass, 2004), p. 28. Vladimir Tismaneanu, *Stalinism for all seasons* (University of California Press, 2003), p. 92.
8. Scott D. Parrish and Mikhail M. Narinsky, "New evidence on the Soviet rejection of the Marshall Plan, 1947," Cold War International History Project [CWIHP], Working Paper 9 (2011). Benn Steil, *The Marshall Plan* (Simon & Schuster, 2018), pp. 117–45.
9. "Session VI, September 25, 1947," Giuliano Procacci, ed., *The Cominform* (Fondazione Giangiacomo Feltrinelli, 1994), pp. 217–51.
10. Tismaneanu, *Stalinism*, p. 93. McDermott, *Communist Czechoslovakia*, pp. 54–57. Applebaum, *Iron Curtain*, pp. 221–22. Malycha and Winters, *SED*, pp. 60–92.
11. Grant Adibekov, "How the first conference of the Cominform came about," Procacci, *The Cominform*, p. 6. Agosti Aldo, *Palmiro Togliatti* (I. B. Tauris, 2008), pp. 189–99. Stéphane Courtois and Marc Lazar, *Histoire du Parti communiste français*, 2nd ed. (Presses universitaires de France, 1995), pp. 257–84.

12. Ivo Banac, *With Stalin against Tito* (Cornell University Press, 1988), pp. 3–44. Leonid Gibianskii, "The beginning of the Soviet-Yugoslav conflict and the Cominform," and Silvio Pons, "The twilight of the Cominform," and "On the situation in the Communist Party of Yugoslavia," [June 23, 1948], Procacci, *The Cominform*, pp. 465–503, 611–21 (quote). Calic, *Geschichte Jugoslawiens*, pp. 189–91. Various documents: United States, Department of State, *Foreign relations of the United States [FRUS]*, 1951, IV/2 (US Government Printing Office, 1985), pp. 1677–1863.

13. Niu Jun, *From Yan'an to the world* (EastBridge, 2005), pp. 322–23 (first and second quotes). Shi Zhe, "Mao Zedong fangSu de ririyeye," Zhonggong zhongyang wenxian yanjiushi, ed., *Bujin de simian* (Zhongyang wenxian chubanshe, 1991), p. 79. Vickers, *Albanians*, pp. 173–75. Zhai Qiang, *China and the Vietnam Wars, 1950–1975* (University of North Carolina Press, 2000), pp. 10–18.

14. Julia Strauss, "Morality, coercion and state building by campaign in the early PRC," *China Quarterly*, 188 (2006), pp. 891–912. Li Hua-yu, "Instilling Stalinism in Chinese party members," Thomas P. Bernstein and Hua-yu Li, eds., *China learns from the Soviet Union, 1949–Present* (Lexington Books, 2010), pp. 107–30. Balázs Szalontai, *Kim Il Sung in the Khrushchev era* (Woodrow Wilson Center Press / Stanford University Press, 2005), pp. 25–34.

15. Applebaum, *Iron Curtain*, p. 250. Andrzej Paczkowski, *The spring will be ours* (Pennsylvania State University Press, 2003), pp. 211–42. McDermott, *Communist Czechoslovakia*, pp. 58–90. László Borhi, *Hungary in the Cold War, 1945–1956* (Central European University Press, 2004), pp. 197–225. Tismaneanu, *Stalinism*, pp. 107–35. R. J. Crampton, *Bulgaria* (Oxford University Press, 2007), pp. 327–43. Vickers, *Albanians*, pp. 173–80. Quote from André Steiner, *Von Plan zu Plan* (Aufbau Taschenbuch, 2007), pp. 81–87.

16. Ilya Ehrenburg, *The thaw* (H. Regnery Co., 1955). Andrei Artizov, ed., *Reabilitatsia* (Mezhdunarodnyi fond 'Demokratiya,' 2000), pp. 8–15.

17. Christian F. Ostermann, ed., "This is not a Politburo, but a madhouse," *Cold War International History Project [CWIHP] Bulletin*, 10 (1998), pp. 61–66. Ilko-Sascha Kowalczuk, *17. Juni 1953* (Bundeszentrale für politische Bildung, 2013). "Situation report, 18 June 1953," Christian F. Ostermann, ed., *Uprising in East Germany, 1953* (Central European University Press, 2001), pp. 208–9. Borhi, *Hungary*, pp. 239–321. Enver Hoxha, *The artful Albanian* (Chatto & Windus, 1986), pp. 157–61. Vickers, *Albanians*, pp. 179–80. Tismaneanu, *Stalinism*, p. 139. Crampton, *Bulgaria*, pp. 343–45. Paczkowski, *Spring*, pp. 262–64. McDermott, *Communist Czechoslovakia*, pp. 92–94.

18. Lorenz M. Lüthi, "A window of opportunities in Europe," Lorenz M. Lüthi, ed., *The regional Cold Wars in Europe, East Asia, and the Middle East* (Woodrow Wilson Center Press / Stanford University Press, 2015), p. 49. Svetozar Rajak, *Yugoslavia and the Soviet Union in the early Cold War* (Routledge, 2011), pp. 66–126.

19. Artizov, *Reabilitatsia*, pp. 317–48. Lüthi, "Window," pp. 53–54.

20. Paweł Machcewicz, *Rebellious satellite* (Woodrow Wilson Center Press/ Stanford University Press, 2009). Lorenz M. Lüthi, *The Sino-Soviet split* (Princeton University Press, 2008), pp. 54–57.

21. Victor Sebestyen, *Twelve days* (Pantheon Books, 2006), pp. 79–272.

22. Lüthi, *Sino-Soviet split*, pp. 49–53.

23. Wu Lengxi, *Shinian lunzhan, 1956–1966* (Zhongyang wenxian, 1999), p. 68 (quote, italics added). Lüthi, *Sino-Soviet split*, pp. 69–72.

24. Lüthi, *Sino-Soviet split*, pp. 76, 81–90, 116–23, 158–60, 186–87, 195–201. Bo Yibo, *Ruogan zhongda juece yu shijian de huigu*, vol. 1 (Zhonggong zhongyang dangxiao, 1991), p. 704. Mao Zedong, "Talk at Beidaihe conference (draft transcript)," August 21, 1958, Afternoon, Roderick MacFarquhar, Timothy Cheek, and Eugene Wu, eds., *The secret speeches of Chairman Mao* (Harvard University Press, 1989), p. 421.

25. Wu, *Shinian*, 241–65. Lüthi, *Sino-Soviet split*, pp. 164–90. "Report," July 16, 1960, Rossiiskii Gosudarstvennyi Arkhiv Noveishei Istorii [RGANI], fond 2, opis 1, delo 484, pp. 69–87a (quote).

26. Steiner, *Plan*, pp. 93–138. Damian von Melis, *Republikflucht* (Oldenbourg Verlag, 2006), pp. 73–120. "Dear Comrade Nikita Sergeyevich," January 18, 1961, Stiftung Archiv der Parteien und Massenorganisationen der DDR im Bundesarchiv [SAPMO-BArch], DY 30/3508, pp. 59–73. Hope M. Harrison, *Driving the Soviets up the wall* (Princeton University Press, 2003), pp. 161–66.

27. Harrison, *Driving*, pp. 81–93, 163. Gerhard Wettig, *Chruschtschows Berlin-Krise 1958 bis 1963* (Oldenbourg Verlag, 2006), pp. 31–45, 71–73. Liu Xiao, *Chushi Sulian banian* (Dangshi ziliao chubanshe, 1998), pp. 88–91. Wu, *Shinian*, pp. 220–27.

28. Harrison, *Driving*, pp. 139–92.

29. Wettig, *Chruschtschows Berlin-Krise*, pp. 84–87, 148–56.

30. "The speech of Comrade Khrushchev," [August 4, 1961], in Bernd Bonwetsch and Alexei Filitow, eds., "Chruschtschow und der Mauerbau," *Vierteljahreshefte für Zeitgeschichte*, 48/1 (2000), pp. 191 (quotes). Norbert Podewin, *Walter Ulbricht* (Dietz, 1995), p. 359.

31. Bonwetsch, "Chruschtschow," pp. 164–65. Vickers, *Albanians*, pp. 180–84. Lüthi, *Sino-Soviet split*, pp. 170–74, 201–3.

32. Lüthi, *Sino-Soviet split*.

33. Tismaneanu, *Stalinism*, pp. 136–67. Dennis Deletant, "Introduction," Dennis Deletant and Mihail E. Ionescu, eds., *Romania and the Warsaw Pact, 1955–1989* (Politeia-SNSPA, 2004), pp. 15–19. Lüthi, *Sino-Soviet split*, pp. 167–74, 236–44, 26–70. Raymond L. Garthoff, "When and why Romania distanced itself from the Warsaw Pact," *Cold War International History Project [CWIHP] Bulletin*, 5 (1995), p. 111.

34. Chen Jian, *Mao's China and the Cold War* (University of North Carolina Press, 2001), pp. 53–61. Lüthi, *Sino-Soviet split*, pp. 313–39. "Excerpts from a note on the two talks with Comrade Hoang Muoi, chargé d'affaires of the DRV, on February 16 and 17, 1967," March 9, 1967, SAPMO-BArch, NY 4182/1271, pp. 23–26.

35. "CPSU Plenum, April 9–10, 1968," RGANI fond 2, opis 3, delo 100, pp. 4–47. Frank, *Walter Ulbricht*, pp. 378–89.

36. "The CPCz CC action program, April 1968 (excerpts)," Jaromír Navrátil, ed., *The Prague Spring, 1968* (Central European University Press, 1998), pp. 92–95.

37. A. M. Aleksandrov-Agentov, *Ot Kollontai do Gorbacheva* (Mezhdunarodnye otnosheniya, 1994), pp. 147–49. "Cable to Moscow from Soviet Ambassador to Warsaw Averki Aristov regarding Władysław Gomułka's views on the situation in Czechoslovakia, April 16, 1968," and "Minutes of the Secret Speech meeting of the 'Five' in Moscow, May 8, 1968 (excerpts)," Navrátil, *Prague Spring*, pp. 103, 137 (first quote). "On the situation in the CSSR," July 28, 1968, SAPMO-BArch, DY 30/3619, p. 140 (second and third quotes). Matthew J. Ouimet, *The rise and the fall of the Brezhnev Doctrine in Soviet foreign policy* (University of North Carolina Press, 2003), pp. 66–69.

38. Stefan Wolle, *Aufbruch nach Utopia* (Bundeszentrale für politische Bildung, 2011), pp. 381–90. Paulina Bren, "Weekend getaways," David Crowley and Susan E. Reid, eds., *Socialist spaces* (Berg, 2002), pp. 123–40.

39. Manfred Hildermeier, *Geschichte der Sowjetunion, 1917–1991* (C. H. Beck, 1998), pp. 877–99. Lorenz M. Lüthi, "Drifting apart," Jeronim Perović, ed., *Cold War energy* (Macmillan, 2017), pp. 383–89.

40. "Note," August 27, 1968, Arhiv Jugoslavije [AJ], KPR I-3-a/97–22, pp. 1–43. "Romanian position on CSSR," [mid July 1968], Politisches Archiv des Auswärtigen Amtes, Bestand: Ministerium für Auswärtige Angelegenheiten [PAAA-MfAA], C 1030/72, pp. 47–48. Mihai Retegan, *In the shadow of the Prague Spring* (Center for Romanian Studies, 2000), pp. 187–95. Calic, *Geschichte Jugoslawiens*, p. 236. Thomas Kunze, *Nicolae Ceaușescu*, 3rd, upd. ed. (Ch. Links Verlag, 2009), pp. 176–83, 211–19, 264–358. Lorenz M. Lüthi, "Non-Alignment, 1961–1974," Sandra Bott, Jussi M. Hanhimäki, Janick Schaufelbuehl, and Marco Wyss, eds., *Neutrality and neutralism in the global Cold War* (Routledge, 2016), p. 98.

41. "Speech by the Prime Minister Zhou Enlai at the reception by the ambassador of Vietnam on the occasion of the national holiday of the DRV," September 2, 1968, Schweizerisches Bundesarchiv [SBA], E 2200.174 Peking, Akzession 1985/195, box 11, pp. 1–7 (first quote). Lorenz M. Lüthi, "Restoring chaos to history," *China Quarterly*, 210 (2012), pp. 382–84, 388–91, 392–97. "Note for file no. 76/68," April 29, 1968, PAAA-MfAA, G-A 321, p. 123. "Fm HKong Sep 20/ 68 confd," Library and Archives Canada [LAC], RG25, box 8893, pp. 1–3.

42. "Togliatti's revolutionary testament," *Boston Globe*, September 20, 1964, A3. Alexander Höbel, *Il PCI di Luigi Longo (1964–1969)* (Edizioni Scientifiche Italiane, 2010), pp. 209–29, 525–26. "On the talks," July 26, 1968, SAPMO-BArch, DY 30/3619, pp. 128–30. "Western Reds bar action now," *The Sun*, August 2, 1968, pp. A1, A6. "Obituaries: Maurice Thorez dies," *Boston Globe*, July 13, 1964, p. 21. "Reds in France assert autonomy of world parties," *New York Times*, October 15, 1964, pp. 1, 6. David S. Bell and

Byron Criddle, *The French Communist Party in the Fifth Republic* (Clarendon Press, 1994), pp. 88–93. Gino G. Raymond, *The French Communist Party during the Fifth Republic* (Palgrave Macmillan, 2005), pp. 151, 192–203. "Conference of Communist Parties," June 26, 1969, SBA, E 2300–01, Akzession 1977/28, box 5, pp. 1–5. Robert Gualteri, "Il PCI, la DC e il 'vincolo esterno'," Robert Gualteri, ed., *Il PCI nell'Italia Repubblicana 1943–1991* (Carocci editore, 2001), pp. 73–88.

43. Silvio Pons, "The rise and fall of Eurocommunism," Melvyn P. Leffler and O. Arne Westad, eds., *The Cambridge history of the Cold War*, vol. 3 (Cambridge University Press, 2010), pp. 45–50. "French, Italian communists reject interference," *Boston Globe*, November 18, 1975, p. 14. "Report on the Berlin Conference of the Communist and Workers Parties of Europe (June 29 and 30, 1976)," no date, SAPMO-BArch, DY 30/IV 2/2.035/35, pp. 14–24.

4   The United States and the Free World

1. "A Supreme Hour," *New York Herald Tribune*, May 22, 1940, p. 26. "Nazi world revolution is Hitler's objective," *New York Times* [*NYT*], May 12, 1940, p. 73 (first quote). "Text of President Roosevelt's message to Congress on defense requirements and plans," *Chicago Daily Tribune*, January 7, 1941, p. 8 (second quote). "Creed for the Free World," *Globe and Mail*, Nov 17, 1942, p. 1 (third quote). "Russia will be world puzzle," *Times Pictorial*, June 2, 1945, p. 4.

2. See various chapters in David Reynolds, ed., *The origins of the Cold War in Europe* (Yale University Press, 1994). John O. Iatrides and Nicholas X. Rizopoulos, "The international dimension of the Greek Civil War," *World Policy Journal*, 17/1 (2000), pp. 87–96.

3. See various chapters in Reynolds, *Origins*. Emmanuel Cartier, "The Liberation and the institutional question in France," Andrew Knapp, ed., *The uncertain foundation* (Palgrave Macmillan, 2007), pp. 23–40. John O. Iatrides, "Greece at the crossroads, 1944–1950," John O. Iatrides and Linda Wrigley, eds., *Greece at the crossroads* (Pennsylvania State University Press, 1995), pp. 1–30.

4. James Edward Miller, *The United States and the making of modern Greece* (University of North Carolina Press, 2009), pp. 136–56. James Maxwell Anderson, *The history of Portugal* (Greenwood Press, 2000), pp. 146–72. William I. Hitchcock, *France restored* (University of North Carolina Press, 1998), pp. 203–9.

5. Charles L. Robertson, *When Roosevelt planned to govern France* (University of Massachusetts Press, 2011). Natalia Naoumova, "Moscow, the Parti Communiste Français, and France's political recovery," Knapp, *Uncertain foundation*, pp. 176–78. The reasons for the departure of communist members from the unity governments of Luxembourg and Belgium were disagreements over railroad administration and coal prices, respectively; see "Govt of Luxembourg," *South China Morning Post*, March 3, 1947, p. 6. "Government quits today in Belgium," *NYT*, March 12, 1947, p. 10.

6. Geir Lundestad, "'Empire by invitation' in the American century," *Diplomatic History*, 23/2 (1999), pp. 189–217. Warren F. Kimball, *The juggler* (Princeton University Press, 1991), pp. 83–105.

7. Various documents: United States, Department of State, *Foreign relations of the United States* [*FRUS*], 1943, *Conferences of Washington and Quebec* (US Government Printing Office, 1970), pp. 788–829 (first quote from p. 814). "Moscow Declaration text," *Austin Statesman*, November 1, 1943, p. 9 (second quote). Robert Dallek, *Franklin D. Roosevelt and American foreign policy, 1932–1945* (Oxford University Press, 1979), pp. 371–75, 472–75. Michael Schaller, *American occupation of Japan* (Oxford University Press, 1987), pp. 24–25.

8. Indro Montanelli and Mario Cervi, *L'Italia della Guerra Civile, 8 settembre 1940 – 9 maggio 1946* (Rizzoli, 1983), pp. 160–63.

9. Dallek, *Roosevelt*, pp. 415–16. Montanelli, *Italia della Guerra Civile*, pp. 264–82. Indro Montanelli and Mario Cervi, *L'Italia della Repubblica, 2 giugno 1946 – 18 aprile 1948* (Rizzoli, 1985), pp. 11–23, 83–90. Aurelio Lepre, *Storia della prima Repubblica* (Il Mulino, 1993), pp. 87–89.

10. Edgar Wolfrum, *Die geglückte Demokratie* (Klett-Cotta, 2006), pp. 23–27. Werner Abelshauser, *Deutsche Wirtschaftsgeschichte* (Bundeszentrale für politische Bildung, 2011), pp. 82–87. Andrew J. Williams, "'Reconstruction' before the Marshall Plan," *Review of International Studies*, 31/3 (2005), pp. 548–56. Nicolaus Mills, *Winning the peace* (John Wiley & Sons, 2008), pp. 24–25. Manfred Görtemaker, *Geschichte der Bundesrepublik Deutschland* (Fischer Taschenbuch, 1999), pp. 37–38.

11. Schaller, *American occupation*, p. 27. Tsuyoshi Hasegawa, *Racing the enemy* (Belknap Press, 2005), pp. 195–201, 252–89. Harry S. Truman, *Memoirs*, vol. 1, *Year of decisions* (Doubleday, 1955), p. 432. William J. Sebald, *With MacArthur in Japan* (W. W. Norton, 1965), pp. 45–46, and footnote.

12. John W. Dower, *Embracing defeat* (W. W. Norton, 1999), pp. 73–84. Schaller, *American occupation*, pp. 27–48. Various documents: *FRUS*, 1947 VI, pp. 186–89, 205.

13. Konosuke Odaka, "The evolution of social policy in Japan," *World Bank Papers*, 2002, p. 2. Schaller, *American occupation*, pp. 85–97. George F. Kennan, *Memoirs*, vol. 1, *1925–1950* (Little, Brown, 1967), p. 382.

14. "The Ambassador in France (Caffery) to the Secretary of States," October 7, 1947, *FRUS*, 1947, III, pp. 764–65. "Report by the National Security Council, NSC 1/1, November 14, 1947," *FRUS*, 1948, III, pp. 724–26 (quotes). Trevor Barnes, "The secret Cold War (Part I)," *The Historical Journal*, 24/2 (1981), pp. 408–10. Lepre, *Storia*, pp. 100–14.

15. Kennan, *Memoirs*, vol. 1, p. 368. Ronald L. McGlothlen, *Controlling the waves* (W. W. Norton, 1993), pp. 30–40. Indro Montanelli and Mario Cervi, *L'Italia del Miracolo, 14 Iuglio 1948 – 19 agosto 1954* (Rizzoli, 1987). Abelshauser, *Deutsche Wirtschaftsgeschichte*, pp. 173–98. Aaron Forsberg, *America and the Japanese miracle* (University of North Carolina Press, 2000).

16. Douglas J. Macdonald, *Adventures in chaos* (Harvard University Press, 1992).

17. Bruce Cumings, *The origins of the Korean War*, vol. 1 (Princeton University Press, 1981), pp. 101–264. Young Ick Lew, *The making of the first Korean president*

(University of Hawai'i Press, 2013), pp. 64–280. Gregg Brazinsky, *Nation building in South Korea* (University of North Carolina Press, 2007), p.24.

18. Brazinsky, *Nation building*, pp. 13–40.
19. Denny Roy, *Taiwan* (Cornell University Press, 2003), pp. 105–37.
20. Mark Atwood Lawrence, *Assuming the burden* (University of California Press, 2005).
21. Kathryn C. Statler, *Replacing France* (University of Kentucky Press, 2007), pp. 60–70. Fredrik Logevall, *Embers of war* (Random House, 2012), pp. 476–594. Jessica M. Chapman, *Cauldron of resistance* (Cornell University Press, 2013). Edward G. Miller, *Misalliance* (Harvard University Press, 2013).
22. Bradley R. Simpson, *Economists with guns* (Stanford University Press, 2008). David P. Chandler, *The tragedy of Cambodian history* (Yale University Press, 1991), pp. 192–215. Various chapters in Mark J. Gasiorowski and Malcolm Byrne, eds., *Mohammad Mosaddeq and the 1953 coup in Iran* (Syracuse University Press, 2004). Christopher de Bellaigue, *Patriot of Persia* (Bodley Head, 2012), pp. 217–39. Kuross A. Samii, *Involvement by invitation* (Pennsylvania State University Press, 1987) (quote).
23. Logevall, *Embers*, pp. 549–613. Hitchcock, *France*, pp. 147–68, 190–202.
24. Diane B. Kunz, *Butter and guns* (The Free Press, 1997), pp. 84–87. Keith Kyle, *Suez* (I. B. Tauris, 2003), pp. 581–85. Jean Guisnel and Bruno Tertrais, *Le Président et la Bombe* (Odile Jacob, 2016), pp. 24–25. Maurice Vaïsse, "Post-Suez France," Wm. Roger Louis and Roger Owen, eds., *Suez 1956* (Clarendon Press, 1989), pp. 335–36.
25. William I. Hitchcock, *The struggle for Europe* (Doubleday, 2003), p. 189.
26. Sebastian Ryen, *Atlantis lost* (Amsterdam University Press, 2010), pp. 25–305. Maurice Vaïsse, *La Grandeur* (Fayard, 1998), pp. 111–61, 381–86.
27. Guisnel, *Président*, pp. 29–42, 60–63, 295.
28. Thomas Gomart, *Double détente* (Presses de la Sorbonne, 2003), pp. 221–398.
29. Eckart Conze, *Die gaullistische Herausforderung* (Oldenbourg Verlag, 1995), pp. 72–87, 112–20, 211–21, 238–94. Ronald J. Granieri, "More than a geriatric romance," Carine Germond and Henning Türk, eds., *A history of Franco-German relations in Europe* (Palgrave Macmillan, 2008), pp. 192–97.
30. Vaïsse, *Grandeur*, pp. 60–79. Jeffrey J. Byrne, "'Je ne vous ai pas compris'," Christian Nuenlist, Anna Locher, and Garret Martin, eds., *Globalizing de Gaulle* (Lexington Books, 2010), pp. 227–34. Frederick Cooper, *Citizenship between empire and nation* (Princeton University Press, 2014), pp. 279–430. Jean Lacouture, *De Gaulle: the ruler, 1945–1970* (W. W. Norton, 1992), pp. 315–30.
31. Lorenz M. Lüthi, "Rearranging international relations?," *Journal of Cold War Studies*, 16/1 (2014), pp. 111–45.
32. Lüthi, "Rearranging," pp. 131–32, 138. Eugenie M. Blang, *Allies at odds* (Rowman & Littlefield, 2010), pp. 75–152. Yuko Torikata, "The U.S. escalation in Vietnam and de Gaulle's secret search for peace, 1964–1966," Nuenlist *et al.*, *Globalizing de Gaulle*, pp. 155–80.
33. Walter LaFeber, *The clash* (W. W. Norton, 1997), pp. 314–24.
34. Mark H. Lytle, *America's uncivil wars* (Oxford University Press, 2006), pp. 1–265.

35. Norbert Frei, *1968* (Deutscher Taschenbuchverlag, 2008), pp. 79–130. Stefan Wolle, *Der Traum der Revolte* (Ch. Links Verlag, 2008); *Aufbruch nach Utopia* (Bundeszentrale für politische Bildung, 2011), pp. 332–34.
36. "Protests halted Paris talks bring student gains," *Christian Science Monitor*, May 10, 1968, p. 2. Ingrid Gilcher-Holtey, "France," Martin Klimke and Joachim Sharloth, eds., *1968 in Europe* (Palgrave Macmillan, 2008), pp. 111–24. Hitchcock, *Struggle*, pp. 250–51.
37. Frei, *1968*, pp. 153–208. Paulina Bren, "1968 East and West," Padraic Kenney and Gerhard-Rainer Horn, eds., *Transnational moments of change* (Rowman & Littlefield, 2004), pp. 124–26.
38. Gael-Georges Moullec, *Pour une Europe de l'Atlantique à l'Oural* (Les Éditions de Paris, 2016), pp. 78–94. Guisnel, *Président*, pp. 27–29. Görtemaker, *Geschichte*, pp. 489–90. "Objectives – France," February 13, 1969, Richard Nixon Presidential Library [RMN], NSC, box 442, pp. 1–4. For the talks, see RMN, NSC, Box 1023. Lacouture, *De Gaulle*, pp. 571–97.
39. Lytle, *America's uncivil wars*, pp. 269–374. Peter N. Carroll, *It seemed like nothing happened* (Rutgers University Press, 1982), pp. 185–206.
40. Geir Lundestad, *The United States and Western Europe since 1945* (Oxford University Press, 2003), pp. 156–61. Pierre Journod, "La France, cinquième partie aux négociations?," Pierre Journod and Cécile Menétrey-Monchau, eds., *Vietnam, 1968–1976* (PIE Peter Lang, 2011), pp. 198–203.
41. Serge Bernstein and Jean-Pierre Rioux, *The Pompidou years, 1969–1974* (Cambridge University Press, 2000), p. 16. Eric Roussel, *Georges Pompidou, 1911–1974*, new ed. (J. C. Lattès, 1994), pp. 333–67. Claudia Hiepel, *Willy Brandt und Georges Pompidou* (Oldenbourg Verlag, 2012), pp. 38–44. Kenneth O. Morgan, *The people's peace* (Oxford University Press, 1990), pp. 338–39. Helga Haftendorn, "German *Ostpolitik* in a multilateral setting," Helga Haftendorn, Georges-Henri Soutou, Stephen F. Szabo, and Samuel F. Wells, eds., *The strategic triangle* (Woodrow Wilson Center Press/Johns Hopkins University Press, 2006), pp. 212–22.
42. Francis J. Gavin, *Gold, dollars, and power* (University of North Carolina Press, 2004), pp. 166–96. Robert Leeson, *Ideology and the international economy* (Palgrave Macmillan, 2003), pp. 63–88, 167–180. Ronald I. McKinnon, *The unloved dollar standard* (Oxford University Press, 2012), pp. 50–55.
43. Henning Türk, "The oil crisis of 1973 as a challenge to multilateral energy cooperation among western industrialized countries," *Historical Social Research*, 39/4, (2014), pp. 209–30. Roy Licklider, "The power of oil," *International Studies Quarterly*, 32/2 (1988), pp. 205–26.

Part II   Asia. Introduction to Chapters 5 to 7

1. Pierre Grosser, *L'histoire du monde se fait en Asie* (Odile Jacob, 2017), pp. 127–30.

5   China

1. Edward L. Dreyer, *China at war, 1901–1949* (Longman, 1995), pp. 329–49. Mao Zedong, "The Chinese people have stood up!," September 21, 1949,

and "Long live the great unity of the Chinese people," September 30, 1949, *Selected Works*, vol. 5, pp. 15–21.

2. Jonathan D. Spence, *The Chan's great continent* (W. W. Norton, 1998); *The search for modern China*, 2nd ed. (W. W. Norton, 1999), pp. 139–313.

3. Marie-Claire Bergère, *Sun Yat-sen* (Stanford University Press, 1998), pp. 289, 298–99. Hans van de Ven, *From friend to comrade* (University of California Press, 1991), pp. 99–146. Jay Taylor, *The Generalissimo* (Belknap Press, 2009), pp. 41–55. Pierre Grosser, *L'histoire du monde se fait en Asie* (Odile Jacob, 2017), pp. 127–30. Jonathan Fenby, *Chiang Kai Shek* (Carroll & Graf, 2004), pp. 114–62. John W. Garver, "The origins of the 2nd united front," *China Quarterly*, 113 (1988), pp. 29–59. Shum Kui-Kwong, *The Chinese Communists' road to power* (Oxford University Press, 1988), pp. 184–91.

4. Noriko Kawamura, "Wilsonian idealism and Japanese claims at the Paris Peace Conference," *Pacific Historical Review*, 66/4 (1997), pp. 503–26. Sören Urbansky, *Kolonialer Wettstreit* (Campus Verlag, 2008), pp. 144–71. K. C. Chan, "The abrogation of British extraterritoriality in China 1942–43," *Modern Asian Studies*, 11/2 (1977), pp. 257–91. Brian Hook and Miguel Santos Neves, "The role of Hong Kong and Macau in China's relations with Europe," *China Quarterly*, 169 (2002), p. 109.

5. Chen Hao, "Negotiating for alliance at war," unpublished MA thesis, McGill University, 2015. Robert Dallek, *Franklin D. Roosevelt and American foreign policy, 1932–1945* (Oxford University Press, 1979), pp. 389–90. O. Arne Westad, *Cold War and revolution* (Columbia University Press, 1993); *Decisive encounters* (Stanford University Press, 2003).

6. Michael Y. L. Luk, *The origins of Chinese Bolshevism* (Oxford University Press, 1990), pp. 35–60. Tony Saich, ed., *The Rise to power of the Chinese Communist Party* (M. E. Sharpe, 1996), pp. 277–330. Lloyd E. Eastman, *The Nationalist era in China, 1927–1949* (Cambridge University Press, 1991), pp. 53–114. Steven M. Goldstein, "The Chinese revolution and the colonial areas," *China Quarterly*, 75 (1978), pp. 594–622. Mao Zedong, "On the international united front against fascism," June 23, 1941, *Selected Works*, vol. 3, p. 29 (first quote). Mao Zedong, "The present situation and our tasks," December 25, 1947, *Selected Works*, vol. 4, p. 158 (second and third quotes). Dreyer, *China*, pp. 329–49.

7. Chen Jian, *Mao's China and the Cold War* (University of North Carolina Press, 2001), pp. 21–23, 40. Mao Zedong, "On the people's democratic dictatorship," June 30, 1949, *Selected Works*, vol. 4, pp. 415–16 (all quotes). Iosif V. Stalin, "Two camps," February 22, 1919, *Works*, vol. 4 (Foreign Languages Publishing House, 1953), pp. 240–44. Chen Jian, *China's road to the Korean War* (Columbia University Press, 1994), p. 19.

8. Mao Zedong, "Telegram of August 16 [1945]," *Selected Works*, vol. 4, p. 36. Zhonggong zhongyang wenxian yanjiushi, ed., *Zhou Enlai nianpu, 1949–1976*, vol. 1 [*ZELNP1*] (Zhongyang wenxian chubanshe, 1997), p. 11. Samuel S. Kim, "The People's Republic of China in the United Nations," *World Politics*, 26/3 (1974), p. 304. "Nationalist China stays in," January 14, 1950, *Daily Boston Globe*, p. 1.

9. Chen Jian, *China's road*, p. 93. Lorenz M. Lüthi, *The Sino-Soviet split* (Princeton University Press, 2008), pp. 31–34.
10. UN Security Council, "Resolution 82 (1950) of 25 June 1950," S/RES/82 (1950), www.refworld.org/docid/3b00f15960.html, accessed May 19, 2015. UN Security Council, "Resolution 83 (1950) of 27 June 1950," S/RES/83 (1950), www.refworld.org/docid/3b00f20a2c.html, accessed May 19, 2015. Chen, *Mao's China*, p. 55. Chen, *China's road*, pp. 111–13, 130–89. Zhai Qiang, *China and the Vietnam Wars, 1950–1975* (University of North Carolina Press, 2000), p. 26.
11. Chen Jian, "China and the first Indo-China War, 1950–54," *China Quarterly*, 133 (1993), pp. 89–90. "Chinese troops in heavy attack on U.N. units," November 4, 1950, *Irish Times*, p. 1. "U.N. body invites Red China to discuss troops in Korea," November 9, 1950, *New York Times* [*NYT*], p. 1. Wu Xiuquan, *Eight years in the Ministry of Foreign Affairs (January 1950 – October 1958)* (New World Press, 1985), pp. 44–83. Chen, *China's road*, pp. 116–17.
12. Zhou Enlai, "Five Principles of Peaceful Coexistence," December 31, 1953, *Selected Works* (Foreign Languages Press, 1989), vol. 2, p. 128. New China News Agency, "Agreement between India and China on trade and intercourse between Tibet region of China and India," April 29, 1954, Harold C. Hinton, ed., *The People's Republic of China, 1949–1979*, vol. 1 (Scholarly Resources, 1980), pp. 165–66. The principles are: 1. Mutual respect for each other's territorial integrity and sovereignty, 2. Mutual non-aggression, 3. Mutual non-interference in each other's internal affairs, 4. Equality and cooperation for mutual benefit, 5. Peaceful co-existence. *Panchsheel*, however, is an Indian term used by Nehru, first coined by Sukarno in 1945 denoting the unrelated five principles of the Indonesian Republic.
13. Li Lianqing, *Dawai jiaojia Zhou Enlai*, vol. 2 (Tian Ditushu Company, 1994), pp. 34–501. Ilya V. Gaiduk, *Confronting Vietnam* (Stanford University Press, 2003), pp. 28–53. Chen, *Mao's China*, pp. 138–44. Zhai, *China*, pp. 49–63. "No. 75," May 15, 1954, Library and Archives Canada [LAC], RG25, box 3262, pp. 1–2. J. Y. Ra, "The politics of conference," *Journal of Contemporary History*, 34/3 (1999), pp. 399–416. "Geneva Conference (1954) Documentation," [July 23, 1954], Virtual Vietnam Archive [VVA], 2410404001. "Editorial note," and "Memorandum of conversation, by the Special Adviser to the United States Delegation (Heath)," June 19, 1954, United States, Department of State, *Foreign relations of the United States* [*FRUS*], 1952–54, XVI (US Government Printing Office, 1981), pp. 1503 (first quote), 1198 (second quote).
14. Zhonggong zhongyang wenxian yanjiushi, ed. *Zhou Enlai zhuan*, vol. 2 (Zhonggong zhongyang wenxian chubanshe, 1998), pp. 1534–36. Zhou Enlai, "Turning China into powerful, modern, socialist, industrialized country," September 23, 1954, *Selected Works*, vol. 2, p. 142. Lüthi, *Sino-Soviet split*, pp. 43–44, 73–74, 81–90.
15. "Chou proposes Pan-Asia security bloc," *Christian Science Monitor* [*CSM*], July 21, 1954, p. 14. "No. 362," August 27, 1954, LAC, RG 25, box 8146, pp. 1–2. "No. 222," May 24, 1954, LAC, RG 25, box 8146, pp. 1–2.

16. "Report on foreign affairs," August 11, 1954, Labour History Archive and Study Centre, People's History Museum, Labour Party Int'l Dept, box "Delegation to Moscow & China 1954, Morgan Philips," pp. 1–9. "Telegram: Instructions on the military news on the Taiwan Question," July 24, 1954, Jiangsu Sheng Dang'anguan [JSSDAG], 3011, zhang 144, no page numbers. Thomas E. Stolper, *China, Taiwan, and the offshore Islands* (M. E. Sharpe, 1985), p. 39. Mao Zedong, "Application of the Five Principles of Peaceful Coexistence should be extended to state relations among all countries," October 1954, *On diplomacy* (Foreign Languages Press, 1998), pp. 127–28. "Telegram: CC instructions on the guiding principles of the liberation of Taiwan," September 25, 1954, JSSDAG, 3011, zhang 144, no page numbers. "13 U.S. Flyers Sentenced by Red China," *Chicago Daily Tribune*, November 24, 1954, p. 1.

17. "Indonesian proposal for an Afro-Asian conference," September 24, 1954, Jawaharlal Nehru, *Selected Works*, 2nd series [*JNSW2*], vol. 26 (Nehru Memorial Museum and Library, 2002), pp. 429–34. "A great event in history," October 15, 1954, and "Foreign policies of America and China," Minutes of talks with Chou En-lai, October 20, 1954, *JNSW2*, vol. 27, pp. 3–6, 16–18. "U.N. vote, 47 to 5, condemns Peiping for jailing fliers," *NYT*, December 11, 1954, p. 1. "Cable to V. K. Krishna Menon," December 9, 1954, *JNSW2*, vol. 27, pp. 213–15 (quote). ZELNP1, p. 431. Various documents: Kungliga biblioteket [KB], MS L 179:80.

18. "Note for file," no date, PAAA-MfAA, A 6399, p. 3 (first quote). Mao Zedong, "On the correct handling of contradictions among the People," February 27, 1957, *Selected works*, vol. 5, p. 417. Mao Zedong, "Talks at a Conference of Secretaries of Provincial, Municipal, and Autonomous Region Party Committees: the talk of January 27 [1957]," *Selected works*, vol. 5, p. 363 (second quote). "Mr. Prime Minister," January 15, 1955, National Archives of Australia [NAA], Series A1838, 3002/1 Part 3, p. 1. Mao Zedong, "The Chinese people cannot be cowed by the atom bomb," January 28, 1955, *Selected works*, vol. 5, p. 153 (third quote).

19. Dangdai Zhongguo congshu bianjibu, ed., *Dangdai Zhongguo he gongye* (Zhongguo shehui kexue chubanshe, 1987), pp. 13–18. Sergei N. Goncharov, John W. Lewis, and Xue Litai, *China builds the bomb* (Stanford University Press, 1988), pp. 22–27, 35–46. Mao Zedong, "Talk with the American correspondent Anna Louise Strong," August 6, 1946, *On diplomacy*, p. 46 (quote). Song Renqiong, *Huiyilu* (Jiefangjun chubanshe, 1994), p. 337.

20. John K. Cooley, "China and the Palestinians," *Journal of Palestine Studies*, 1/2 (1972), pp. 22–23. Nigel Disney, "China and the Middle East," *Middle East Research and Information Project [MERIP] Report*, 63 (1977), p. 4. Chen Laiyuan, "Zhong yi jianjiao weihe tuole sishi duo nian," *Bainianchao*, 2007/11, p. 71. ZELNP1, pp. 459–65. Li, *Dawai jiaojia*, vol. 3, pp. 255–70. "Outwards cable 121," April 16, 1955, NAA, Series A11604, 604/2/2 Part 2, pp. 1–2. Steve Tsang, "Target Zhou Enlai," *China Quarterly*, 139 (1994), pp. 766–82.

21. Li, *Dawai jiaojia*, vol. 3, pp. 234–384. "Peiping accuses U.S. in air crash," *NYT*, April 13, 1955, p. 3. "Supplementary remarks," no date, Zhou, *Selected Works*, vol. 2, pp. 162–65 (quote). For a summary of the closed meetings, see "[Letter]

23," April 28, 1955, Jawaharlal Nehru, *Letters to Chief Ministers, 1947–1964*, vol. 4 (Oxford University Press, 1988), pp. 166–69. "Report on Asian–African Conference – Bandung," no date, NAA, Series A1838, 3002/1 Part 8, pp. 76–75. Zhou Enlai, "China wishes to enter into talks with the United States over the Taiwan Question," April 23, 1955, Zhou Enlai, *Zhou Enlai waijiao wenxuan* (Zhongyang wenxian chubanshe, 2000), p. 130. *ZELNP1*, pp. 474–75. Xia Yafeng, *Negotiating with the enemy* (Indiana University Press, 2006), pp. 81–89. "U.S. hails fliers release as talks with Peking begin," *CSM*, August 1, 1955, p. 1. On Indian mediation, various documents: KB, MS L 179:82.

22. The Pakistani government even believed that Zhou had surrendered to pro-US Western positions on all issues, see: "The Pakistani ambassador (Khaliquzzaman)," no date, NAA, Series A1838, 3002/1 Part 6, p. 1. Hashim S. H. Behbehani, *China's foreign policy in the Arab world, 1955–75* (Kegan Paul International, 1981), p. 4. "The report," [May 13, 1955], PAAA-MfAA, A 6662, pp. 40–68 (quote).

23. Chapters 2 and 3 in Lüthi, *Sino-Soviet split*.

24. Lüthi, *Sino-Soviet split*, pp. 104, 119.

25. Xinhua News Agency, *China's foreign relations* (Foreign Languages Press, 1989), p. 317. John Calabrese, "From flyswatters to silkworms," *Asian Survey*, 30/9, (1990), pp. 864–65. "45 to 9 Vote by UN demands rights of Tibetans be respected," *Globe and Mail*, October 21, 1959, p. 1. Roderick MacFarquhar, *The origins of the Cultural Revolution*, vol. 3 (Columbia University Press, 1997), p. 300. Wu Lengxi. *Shinian lunzhan, 1956–1966* (Zhongyang wenxian chubanshe, 1999), pp. 205–27. Lüthi, *Sino-Soviet split*, pp. 137–38, 149.

26. Lüthi, *Sino-Soviet split*, pp. 158–91. "Khrushchev to the SED CC," July 18, 1960, Stiftung Archiv der Parteien und Massenorganisationen der DDR im Bundesarchiv [SAPMO-BArch], DY 30/3605, pp. 21–27.

27. Lüthi, *Sino-Soviet split*, pp. 196–99. Dangdai Zhongguo congshu bianjibu, *Dangdai Zhongguo duiwai maoyi*, vol. 2 (Zhongguo shehui kexue chubanshe, 1992), pp. 371–88. Xiao Donglian, *Qiusuo Zhongguo*, vol. 2 (Hongqi chubanshe, 1999), p. 919. Lorenz M. Lüthi, "Chinese foreign policy, 1960–79," Tsuyoshi Hasegawa, ed., *The Cold War in East Asia, 1945–1991* (Stanford University Press, 2011), p. 157. Zhonggong zhongyang wenxian yanjiushi, *Zhou Enlai zhuan*, vol. 2, pp. 1534–36.

28. Eric Hyer, *The pragmatic dragon* (University of British Columbia Press, 2015). Lorenz M. Lüthi, "Rearranging international relations?," *Journal of Cold War Studies*, 16/1 (2014), pp. 111–45.

29. Lüthi, *Sino-Soviet split*, pp. 220–28. "No title," September 1963, JSSDAG, 3124, zhang 177, pp. 1–25 (quote). MacFarquhar, *Origins*, vol. 3, p. 312. "The record of the talk of Zhou Enlai receiving the Egyptian Ambassador in China Iman," 21 April 1963, Waijiaobu Dang'anguan [WJBDAG], 107–01004-01, pp. 7–12. Lüthi, "Chinese foreign policy," p. 165. Mao Zedong, "Two intermediate zones (1963/9, 1964/1 and 7)," *Mao Zedong wenji*, vol. 8 (Renmin chubanshe, 1999), pp. 343–44.

30. "Statement of the Chinese Government," July 31, 1963, *Survey of China Mainland Press*, 3032, pp. 30–33. Liu Xiyao, *Panfeng yu chuan wu* (Wuhan

daxue chubanshe, 2000), p. 111. Various documents: WJBDAG, 106–00778-02, 106–00778-03, 107–00597-01, 107–00835-03, 113–00395-10, 113–00396-07, and 113–00396-09 (quote). "Memorandum," [November 1964], PAAA-MfAA, A 17424, pp. 3–6.

31. "Indonesia quitting U.N.," *Boston Globe*, January 2, 1965, p. 1. "China will not enter UN," February 13, 1965, PAAA-MfAA, C 588/77, pp. 166–67. "Premier Chou En-lai's Statement of 24 January 1965," January 28, 1965, United Nations Archive [UNA], S-0884–0010-05, pp. 1–3. "No. 916," April 30, 1965, National Archives of the United Kingdom [NAUK], FO 371/180378, pp. 1.

32. "The matter of the talks of the Algerian ambassador in Syria talking about the Second Afro-Asian Conference," March 21, 1965, WJBDAG, 107–00636-04, pp. 43–46. "Resubmitting the circumstances of the talks of Ambassador Hui with head of Political Department of the Egyptian foreign ministry," March 27, 1965, WJBDAG, 107–00636-04, pp. 55–58. "Chou, in Tanzania, calls U.S. a bully," *NYT*, June 6, 1965, p. 1. "Political Report no. 42," December 16, 1965, Schweizerisches Bundesarchiv [SBA], E 2300, Akzession 1000/716, box 361, pp. 1–4. Lorenz M. Lüthi and Chen Jian, "China's turn to the world," Lorenz M. Lüthi, ed., *The regional Cold Wars in Europe, East Asia, and the Middle East* (Woodrow Wilson Center Press/ Stanford University Press, 2015), pp. 152–53. "Indonesia resumes her seat in U.N.," *NYT*, September 29, 1966, p. 6.

33. Shi Yanchun, "Zhou Enlai yu Zhongdong," *Dangshi zongheng*, 2006/1, p. 8. Zhai, *China*, pp. 82–83, 130–52. Lorenz M. Lüthi, "Reading and warning the likely enemy," *The International History Review*, 35/4 (2013), pp. 807–16.

34. M. N. Sladkovskii, O. B. Rakhmanin, G. V. Astafev, V. N. Glunin, V. A. Krivtsov, M. L. Titarenko, and K. K. Shirinya, eds., *Ocherki kommunisticheskoi partii Kitaya, 1921–1969* (SSSR AN, Institut Dalnego Vostoka, 1971), p. 405. Lüthi, "Chinese foreign policy," pp. 158–59. Lüthi, *Sino-Soviet split*, pp. 285–99. Ma Jisen, *The cultural revolution in the foreign ministry of China* (The Chinese University Press, 2004), pp. 73–77.

35. "Memo about Mao Zedong on foreign propaganda," July 12, 1968, JSSDAG, 3072 Provincial People's Committee General Office, 3124, zhang 305, pp. 1–3. Mao Zedong, "We do not want to impose propaganda abroad," [May 16, 1968], *Mao Zedong wenji*, vol. 8, pp. 430–31 (quote).

36. Chen, *Mao's China*, p. 243. Li Jie, "Changes in China's domestic situation in the 1960s and Sino-U.S. relations," Robert S. Ross and Jiang Changbin, eds., *Re-examining the Cold War* (Harvard University Press, 2001), pp. 310–11. Zhonggong zhongyang wenxian yanjiushi, ed., *Mao Zedong zhuan*, vol. 2 (Zhongyang wenxian chubanshe, 2003), pp. 1530–37.

37. "Speech by the Prime Minister Zhou Enlai at the banquet in honor of the Albanian party and government delegation," September 29, 1968, SBA, E 2200.174 Peking, Akzession 1985/195, box 11, pp. 1–7. Richard M. Nixon, "Asia after Viet Nam," *Foreign Affairs*, 46/1 (1967), pp. 111–25. Mao Zedong, "We agree with Vietnam's policy to both fight and negotiate (November 17, 1968)," *On diplomacy*, pp. 441–43. Zhonggong zhongyang wenxian yanjiushi, ed., *Mao Zedong nianpu, 1949–1976*, vol. 3

[*MZDNP3*] (Zhongyang wenxian chubanshe, 2013), pp. 216–18. Chen, *Mao's China*, p. 238. Lorenz M. Lüthi, "Restoring chaos to history," *China Quarterly*, 210 (2012), pp. 382–83.

38. Lüthi, "Restoring chaos," pp. 385–86.

39. Lüthi, "Restoring chaos," pp. 391–96.

40. Lüthi, "Chinese foreign policy," pp. 162–65. Yang Kuisong and Xia Yafeng, "Vacillating between revolution and détente," *Diplomatic History*, 34/2 (2010), pp. 401–2. Ma, *Cultural Revolution*, p. 321. Lüthi and Chen, "China's turn to the world," p. 159.

41. Chen, *Mao's China*, pp. 262–69. Chris Tudda, *A Cold War turning point* (Louisiana State University Press, 2012), pp. 120–43. Li Jiasong, ed., *Zhonghua renmin gongheguo waijiao dashiji*, vol. 3 (Shijie zhishi chubanshe, 2002), p. 210 (first quote). "Talking points of conversation with Chou En-lai," September 5, 1972, UNA, S-0987-0002-10, p. 4. *MZDNP3*, pp. 412–13 (second quote).

42. Chen, *Mao's China*, pp. 269–76. Tudda, *Cold War turning point*, pp. 169–81. "Why did our country accede to Nixon's request for a visit?," December 1971, King C. Chen, ed., *China and the three Worlds* (M. E. Sharpe, 1979), pp. 133–42. "Joint statement following discussions with leaders of the People's Republic of China," February 27, 1972, *FRUS*, 1969–1976, XVII, pp. 812–16.

43. "Memorandum from John H. Holdridge," November 22, 1971, *FRUS*, 1969–1975, V, pp. 888–95. Kim, "The People's Republic of China in the United Nations," pp. 306–30. "Chou-Goto interview (1) and (2)," November 5 and 9, 1972, PAAA-MfAA, C 587/77, p. 105. Andrew J. Nathan, "Human rights in Chinese foreign policy," *China Quarterly*, 139 (1994), p. 622.

44. "Meeting with Premier Chou," August 14, 1972, UNA, S-0904-0010-09, p. 2 (first quote). Various documents in *FRUS*, 1969–1967, XVIII, pp. 126, 210–23, 859 (second quote). Kuisong, "Vacillating," pp. 410–12.

45. Chen, *China and the Three Worlds*, p. 39. Mao Zedong, "On the question of the differentiation of the Three Worlds," February 22, 1974, *On diplomacy*, p. 454. Lüthi, "Chinese foreign policy," p. 167. Kuisong, "Vacillating," pp. 408–22.

46. Gregg Brazinsky, "Between ideology and strategy," Robert A. Wampler, ed., *Trilateralism and beyond* (Kent State University Press, 2012), pp. 163–71. Gregg Brazinsky, "Korea's Great Divergence," Hasegawa, *The Cold War in East Asia*, pp. 242–46. Wang Taiping, *Zhonghua renmin gongheguo waijiaoshi*, vol. 3, *1970–1978* (Shijie zhishi chubanshe, 1999), pp. 18, 41–43.

47. Lüthi, "Chinese foreign policy," pp. 158–67. Brazinsky, "Korea's Great Divergence," pp. 255–61.

48. Keith Foster, "China's coup of October 1976," *Modern China*, 18/3 (1992), pp. 263–303. Zhou Enlai, "Marching towards the splendid goal of the Four Modernizations," January 13, 1975, *Selected works*, vol. 2, p. 504 (quote). Zhonggong zhongyang wenxian yanjiushi, ed., *Deng Xiaoping nianpu (1975–1997)*, vol. 1 (Zhongyang wenxian chubanshe, 2004), p. 307. Ezra Vogel, *Deng Xiaoping and the transformation of China* (Belknap Press, 2011), pp. 217–48.

6   Vietnam

1. William J. Duiker, *The communist road to power in Vietnam*, 2nd ed. (Westview Press, 1996), p. 1. Christopher E. Goscha, *Historical dictionary of the Indochina war (1945–1954)* (University of Hawai'i Press, 2012), pp. 260–61, 375, 471–72, 491. Dennis Ducanson, "'Limited sovereignty' in Indochina," *The World Today*, 34/7 (1978), p. 262. Christopher E. Goscha, *Going Indochinese* (NIAS, 2012).
2. Thomas R. Metcalf, *Ideologies of the Raj* (Cambridge University Press, 1994), pp. 66–112. Goscha, *Going Indochinese*.
3. "Comintern directive 27 Oct. 1929 on formation of the ICP," Virtual Vietnam Archive [VVA], 2410210006, pp. 1–6 (quote). Christopher E. Goscha, *Thailand and the Southeast Asian networks of the Vietnamese revolution, 1885–1954* (Curzon Press, 1999), pp. 76–96. William J. Duiker, *Ho Chi Minh* (Hyperion, 2000), pp. 162–67, 195–97. Sophie Quinn-Judge, *Ho Chi Minh* (University of California Press, 2002), pp. 177–83, 191–246.
4. Mao Zedong, "On new democracy," January 1940, *Selected works*, vol. 2 (Foreign Languages Press, 1965), pp. 339–84. Duiker, *Communist road*, pp. 70–73, 277–82. Arthur J. Dommen, *The Indochinese experience of the French and the Americans* (Indiana University Press, 2001), pp. 47–75.
5. "De Gaulle forces will fight Japan," *The Sun*, August 30, 1944, p. 2. Kiyoko Kurusu Nitz, "Japanese military policy towards French Indochina during the Second World War," *Journal of Southeast Asian Studies*, 14/2 (1983), pp. 333–47. Vu Ngu Chieu, "The other side of the 1945 Vietnamese Revolution," *Journal of Asian Studies*, 45/2 (1986)," pp. 295–96. Ralph B. Smith, *Communist Indochina* (Routledge, 2009), p. 85. Dommen, *Indochinese experience*, pp. 85–89.
6. "Instructions of the Standing Bureau of the Central Committee of the Indochinese Communist Party Issued on March 12, 1945," [Vietnam, Democratic Republic], *Breaking our chains* (Foreign Languages Publishing House, 1960), pp. 7–17 (quotes). Goscha, *Thailand*, pp. 127–29. Luu Van Loi, *50 years of Vietnamese diplomacy, 1945–1995*, vol. 1 (The Gioi Publishers, 2002), p. 7.
7. Various documents: [Vietnam,] *Breaking our chains*, pp. 63–74 (quotes). Dommen, *Indochinese experience*, p. 101.
8. Dommen, *Indochinese experience*, pp. 107–10, 113–16. David G. Marr, *Vietnam 1945* (University of California Press, 1995), pp. 357, 382–472. Fredrik Logevall, *Embers of war* (Random House, 2012), pp. 96–97. "Address to the entire nation by the provisional government," August 27, 1945, [Vietnam,] *Breaking our chains*, pp. 94–97 (quote).
9. Duiker, *Ho*, pp. 326, 337–40. Charles de Gaulle, *War memoirs*, vol. 3, *Salvation, 1944–1946* (Simon and Schuster, 1960), p. 221 (first quote). "My Dear Admiral," September 16, 1945, Archives du Ministère des Affaires Étrangères [AMAE], 174QO/9, pp. 1–3 (second quote). John Springhall, "'Kicking out the Vietminh'," *Journal of Contemporary History*, 40/1 (2005), pp. 118–30.

10. Duiker, *Communist road,* 119–22. Dommen, *Indochinese experience,* pp. 145–46. Smith, *Communist Indochina,* pp. 87–88. Christopher E. Goscha, "Courting diplomatic disaster?," *Journal of Vietnamese Studies,* 1/1–2 (2006), pp. 60–62. François Guillemot, "A coeur de la fracture viêtnamienne," Christopher E. Goscha, and Benoît De Tréglodé, eds., *Naissance d'un État* (Les Indes Savantes, 2004), pp. 175–85.

11. Duiker, *Ho,* pp. 369–98. Christopher E. Goscha, *Viêtnam* (Armand Colin, 2011), p. 19. Logevall, *Embers,* pp. 161–71, 208–9. Duiker, *Communist road,* p. 141. Christopher E. Goscha, "Une guerre pour l'Indochine?," *Guerres mondiales et conflits contemporains,* 211 (2003), pp. 30–41. Goscha, *Thailand,* pp. 181–265.

12. Duiker, *Ho,* pp. 415–6. Mark Atwood Lawrence, *Assuming the burden* (University of California Press, 2005), pp. 179–232.

13. Lawrence, *Assuming,* pp. 259–75. Goscha, *Thailand,* pp. 314–39.

14. Zhai Qiang, *China and the Vietnam Wars, 1950–1975* (University of North Carolina Press, 2000), pp. 26–33. "Answers to the press on U.S. intervention in Indochina," July 25, 1950, VVA, 2410502014, p. 95 (quote).

15. Dommen, *Indochinese experience,* p. 205. Pierre Asselin, "Le Duan, the American War, and the confrontation of an independent Vietnamese state," *Journal of American-East Asian Relations,* 10/1–2 (2001), pp. 3–4. Duiker, *Ho,* p. 437–41. Various documents: National Archives of Australia [NAA], Series A1838, 3020/2/1/1 Part 1 (first and second quotes). Third quote from Duiker, *Communist road,* p. 150 (italics added). Christopher E. Goscha, "Vietnam and the world outside," *South East Asia Research,* 12/2 (2004), pp. 149–51. Goscha, *Historical dictionary,* p. 81, 257. David P. Chandler, "Revising the past in Democratic Kampuchea," *Pacific Affairs,* 56/2 (1983), pp. 289–90.

16. Duiker, *Communist road,* pp. 156–60. Goscha, *Viêtnam,* pp. 434–49.

17. Logevall, *Embers,* pp. 358, 381–94. "France open to truce in Indo-China," *Washington Post,* August 9, 1953, p. B3 (quote). Duiker, *Ho,* p. 451. Duiker, *Communist road,* pp. 166–67.

18. Various documents: United States, Department of State, *Foreign relations of the United States [FRUS],* 1952–54, VII (US Government Printing Office, 1984), pp. 601–1207. Duiker, *Communist road,* pp. 169–71. Logevall, *Embers,* pp. 563, 575.

19. Various documents: *FRUS,* 1952–1954, XVI, pp. 734–36, 753–55, 909, 1540–42, 1548–49. Zhai, *China,* pp. 53–59. Pierre Asselin, "The Democratic Republic of Vietnam and the 1954 Geneva Conference," *Cold War History,* 11/2 (2011), pp. 176–83. Li Lianqing, *Dawai jiaojia Zhou Enlai,* vol. 2 (Tian ditushu youxian gongsi, 1994), pp. 348–52.

20. Various documents: *FRUS* 1952–54, XVII, pp. 399–899, 1503 (first quote), 1505–42. "Text of Manila Treaty," *Manchester Guardian,* September 9, 1954, p. 7 (second quote).

21. Zhai, *China,* p. 62. Dommen, *Indochinese experience,* pp. 261–69. Charles Keith, *Catholic Vietnam* (University of California Press, 2012), pp. 242–48. Pierre Asselin, *Hanoi's road to the Vietnam War, 1954–1965* (University of California Press, 2013), pp. 18–19.

22. "To Edwina Mountbatten," November 2, 1954, Jawaharlal Nehru, *Selected Works*, 2nd series [*JNSW2*], vol. 27 (Nehru Memorial Museum and Library, 2002), p. 70 (quote). Logevall, *Embers*, p. 619. Duiker, *Ho*, p. 470–81. Asselin, *Hanoi's road*, p. 24. Florence Yvon, "The construction of socialism in North Vietnam," *South East Asia Research*, 16/1 (2008), pp. 47–50.

23. "Viet Minh policy document on post-Geneva strategy, probably issued by the Central Committee of the Lao Dong Party to the eastern interzone of Nambo," November 1954, VVA, 4080125001, pp. 1–12 (quote). Edward G. Miller, *Misalliance* (Harvard University Press, 2013), pp. 19–53, 85–157. Duiker, *Communist road*, pp. 184–86. Asselin, *Hanoi's road*, pp. 28–32.

24. Asselin, *Hanoi's road*, pp. 41–43. Duiker, *Communist road*, pp. 184–87. "Talks with Pham Van Dong," April 9, 1955, *JNSW2*, vol. 28, pp. 188–90. "No. 250," April 14, 1955, Library and Archives Canada [LAC], RG25, box 7720, p. 2. "Laos and Cambodia," May 12, 1955, NAA, Series A11604, 604/2/2 Part 2, pp. 1–2. "Report," no date, Politisches Archiv des Auswärtigen Amtes, Bestand: Ministerium für Auswärtige Angelegenheiten [PAAA-MfAA], A 8465, pp. 25–44. Ben Kiernan, "Origins of Khmer communism," *Southeast Asian Affairs*, 1981, pp. 174–77. Goscha, "Vietnam and the world outside," pp. 161–75.

25. Asselin, *Hanoi's road*, pp. 36–41. Duiker, *Ho*, pp. 499–500. "South Vietnam's revolutionary line," VVA, 2320102006, pp. 1–33 (quotes).

26. Asselin, *Hanoi's Road*, pp. 51–69, 87–89. Duiker, *Communist road*, p. 199, 207–9.

27. Zhai, *China*, pp. 95–96, 109. Duiker, *Communist road*, p. 221.

28. Lien-Hang T. Nguyen, *Hanoi's war* (University of North Carolina Press, 2012), pp. 49–70. Duiker, *Communist road*, pp. 215–24. Asselin, *Hanoi's road*, pp. 107–12.

29. Miller, *Misalliance*, pp. 214–318. Asselin, *Hanoi's road*, pp. 162–73. "Resolution: ninth conference of Central [Committee] 12/1963," VVA, 2120302009, p. 9 (quote).

30. Asselin, *Hanoi's road*, pp. 177–78. Fredrik Logevall, *Choosing war* (University of California Press, 1999).

31. Duiker, *Communist road*, pp. 260–70. Nguyen, *Hanoi's war*, pp. 75–77. Dommen, *Indochinese Experience*, pp. 611–16. "Note for file," March 23, 1965, PAAA-MfAA, G-A 340, pp. 1–4. Lorenz M. Lüthi, *The Sino-Soviet split* (Princeton University Press, 2008), pp. 273–339. Zhai, *China*, pp. 136, 157–75.

32. Asselin, *Hanoi's road*, pp. 190–96. "Reception for the General Director of MID PRP comr. E. Michalowski," January 15, 1966, Arkhiv Vneshnei Politiki Rossiiskoi Federatsii [AVPRF], fond 0100, opis 59, delo 5, papka 525, p. 2 (first quote). "Note for file," June 2, 1966, PAAA-MfAA, G-A 321, p. 9 (second quote). "From: Anh Sau," no date, National Archives of the United Kingdom [NAUK], FCO 15/757, pp. 7–8 (third quote). "The situation in Vietnam after the start of the U.S. aggression," August 25, 1966, Stiftung Archiv der Parteien und Massenorganisationen der DDR im Bundesarchiv [SAPMO-BArch], NY 4182/1270, pp. 133–36.

33. "Information on the economic situation in the DRV," July 11, 1967, PAAA-MfAA, G-A 319, pp. 88–92. "Letter by Kohrt," May 23, 1967, SAPMO-BArch, DY 30/3382, pp. 128–34. "Note for file Nr. 77/67," May 12, 1967,

PAAA-MfAA, G-A 319, pp. 83–87. "Note," March 6, 1967, PAAA-MfAA, G-A 358, pp. 19–20.

34. Nguyen, *Hanoi's war*, pp. 77–109. "Note for file," February 1, 1967, PAAA-MfAA, G-A 329, p. 24 (quote). "Brief assessment," November 21, 1968, PAAA-MfAA, G-A 357, pp. 150–51. "Excerpts from a letter," [December 1967?], SAPMO-BArch, NY 4182/1271, pp. 104–6. "Dear Comrade Hegen," December 11, 1967, PAAA-MfAA, G-A 358, pp. 51–52.

35. Nguyen, *Hanoi's war*, pp. 113–24. Mark Bowden, *Hue 1968* (Atlantic Monthly Press, 2017), pp. 495–96. Thomas L. Ahern, *The CIA and rural pacification in South Vietnam* (Center for the Study of Intelligence, 2001), pp. 307–38. "Number 178," May 22, 1968, LAC, RG25, box 8893, p. 2 (first quote). "Report by Vasil Dimitrov," March 30, 1968, Arkhiv na Ministerstvoto na Vnshnite Raboti [AMVnR], opis 24, a.e. 876, pp. 68–75. "The Truong Chinh Report," [early May 1968], LAC, RG25, box 8893, p. 3 (second quote).

36. Sean Fear, "The ambiguous legacy of Ngo Dinh Diem in South Vietnam's Second Republic (1967–1975), *Journal of Vietnamese Studies*, 11/1 (2016), pp. 30–34. "Transcript of the President's Address on the Vietnam War and His Political Plans," *New York Times* [*NYT*], April 1, 1968, p. 26. "Text of Hanoi's message agreeing to talks", April 4, 1968, *Boston Globe*, p. 9. "Protocol," [April 4–10, 1968], PAAA-MfAA, C 1081/73, pp. 27–28 (quote). "Report by Vasil Dimitrov," [April 1968], AMVnR, opis 24, a.e. 876, p. 66.

37. "Dear Comrades," June 12, 1968, PAAA-MfAA, G-A 416, pp. 62–63. "Transcript of a telegram from our Ambassador in Hanoi, comrade Bergold," [June 1968], SAPMO-BArch, NY 4182/1271, p. 142. "Number 463," October 23, 1968, LAC, RG25, box 8893, pp. 1–2.

38. Various documents: O. Arne Westad, Chen Jian, Stein Tønnesson, Nguyen Vu Tung, and James G. Hershberg, eds., "77 conversations," Cold War International History Project, Working Paper 22 (1998), pp. 121–37. "Note for file no. 23/69," March 11, 1969, PAAA-MfAA, G-A 357, pp. 31–32. Chen Jian, *Mao's China and the Cold War* (University of North Carolina Press, 2001), p. 243. "Fm HKong Sep 20/68 confd," LAC, RG25, box 8893, pp. 1–3. Mao Zedong, "We agree with Vietnam's policy to both fight and negotiate (November 17, 1968)," *On diplomacy* (Foreign Languages Press, 1998), pp. 441–43. "Note for file," January 15, 1969, PAAA-MfAA, C 1365/74, pp. 1–4.

39. "Fm Saign Dec 14/68 confd no/no standard," LAC, RG25, box 8893, pp. 1–2. "Dear comrade Fischer," April 10, 1969, PAAA-MfAA, G-A 357, pp. 33–39. Nguyen, *Hanoi's war*, pp. 129, 155–56.

40. Various documents: *FRUS*, 1969–1976, VI, pp. 50 (first quote), 195–96 (second quote), 267–72. "Report by Vladislav Videnov," December 25, 1968, AMVnR, opis 20p, a.e. 124, pp. 80, 82 (third and fourth quotes). "Report on the first official talk," May 10, 1969, SAPMO-BArch, DY 30/IV 2/2.035/27, pp. 14–21.

41. Nguyen, *Hanoi's war*, p. 140. "Fm Mosco Nov 27/69," LAC, RG25, box 8893, pp. 1–4.

42. Ben Kiernan, *How Pol Pot came to power*, 2nd ed. (Yale University Press, 2004), pp. 249–96. "Political report no. 3/1970," March 25, 1970, Schweizerisches Bundesarchiv [SBA], E 2300–01, Akzession 1977/28, box 15, pp. 1–6. "[No

title]," March 22, 1970, NAA, Series A1838, 3006/3/6 Part 5, p. 67. "Proposals of Samdech Norodom Sihanouk and the National United Front of Cambodia," November 30, 1971, VVA, 2320703003, pp. 13–14. "Fm Saign Apr 25/70 Cdn eyes only," LAC, RG25, box 8893, pp. 1–5 (first quote). "Joint declaration," no date, PAAA-MfAA, C 5449, pp. 4–16 (second quote). "Telno 461," June 16, 1970, NAUK, FCO 15/1180, pp. 1–4.

43. Nguyen, *Hanoi's war*, pp. 196–97. "Memorandum of the President's Assistant for National Security Affairs (Kissinger) to President Nixon," July 20, 1970, *FRUS*, 1969–1976, VI, pp. 1134–35 (quote). Jeffrey Kimball, *Nixon's Vietnam War* (University of Kansas Press, 1998), p. 241. Lorenz M. Lüthi, "Beyond betrayal," *Journal of Cold War Studies*, 11/1 (2009), p. 63.

44. "Transcript of telephone conversation," April 27, 1971, *FRUS*, 1969–1976, vol. XVII, p. 306. "Political report no. 10," August 4, 1971, SBA, E 2300–01, Akzession 1977/29, box 7, p. 3 (quote). Lüthi, "Beyond betrayal," pp. 67–68, 70, 79, 81.

45. "Note," February 8, 1972, PAAA-MfAA, C 222/76, p. 172. "Dear Comrade Minister," April 26, 1972, PAAA-MfAA, G-A 358, p. 59 (first and second quote). "Report by Vladislav Videnov," June 22, 1972, AMVnR, opis 23p, a. e. 33, p. 20 (third and fourth quotes). Lüthi, "Beyond betrayal," pp. 92–97.

46. "An interview in Hanoi," September 28, 1972, NAUK, FCO 15/1675, p. 1 (first and second quotes). "Fm Saigon 090330Z," October 9, 1972, NAUK, FCO 15/1675, p. 1. Lüthi, "Beyond betrayal," pp. 97–105. "Zhou Enlai and Le Duc Tho, Beijing, 5:30 pm, 3 January 1973," Westad, "77 Conversations," p. 186 (third and fourth quotes). "Stenographic transcript," March 16, 1973, PAAA-MfAA, C 218/78, p. 173.

47. "Note," February 5, 1973, PAAA-MfAA, C 927/76, pp. 64–65 (quote). "Stenographic transcript," March 16, 1973, PAAA-MfAA, C 218/78, p. 186. "Information," February 26, 1973, Der Bundesbeauftragte für die Unterlagen des Staatssicherheitsdienstes der ehemaligen Deutschen Demokratischen Republik [BStU], MfS HVA 91, p. 61. "Information on some aspects of the domestic and foreign policy of the DRV and the political situation in Cambodia," January 22, 1974, BStU, MfS HVA 104, p. 236. "Dear Comrade Minister," December 8, 1973, PAAA-MfAA, G-A 348, p. 155. Merle L. Pribbenow, "North Vietnam's final offensive," *Parameters* 29 (1999–2000), pp. 58–71. "Information on some development tendencies in the DRV," January 24, 1975, BStU, MfS HVA 114, pp. 289–90 (third quote). Fear, "Ambiguous legacy," pp. 46–54.

48. "Information on statements of leading cadres of the DRV on a visit of Le Duan to the GDR and on the cooperation of the DRV and the RSV," November 23, 1975, BStU, MfS HVA 118, pp. 51–52. "Information," March 27, 1974, SAPMO-BArch, DY 30/IV 2/2.033/75, p. 9 (quote). Dommen, *Indochinese experience*, pp. 942–51.

49. "Despatch No. 3/75," May 9, 1975, NAA, Series A4231, 1975/South Asia, pp. 1–8. "Report," May 30, 1975, SAPMO-BArch, DY 30/IV 2/2.033/76, p. 131 (first and second quotes). "Note," February 17, 1972, PAAA-MfAA, C 222/76, pp. 177–96. "Number PR-16," February 22, 1972, LAC, RG25, box 10850, pp. 1–2. "Samdech Norodom Sihanouk enjoys Tet with Vietnam

people," February 18, 1972, VVA, 2430403046, pp. 1–2. Zhai, *China*, p. 208. Dommen, *Indochinese experience*, pp. 929–32.

50. "Information on the situation in the DRV leadership and the military-political situation in Cambodia," May 18, 1973, BStU, MfS HVA 95, pp. 291. Kiernan, *Pol Pot*, pp. 412–14. Various documents: NAA, Series A1838, 3006/3/6 Part 9, pp. 68–67, 30–29. "Information," December 1, 1975, PAAA-MfAA, C 6675, p. 1. "Note," June 15, 1976, PAAA-MfAA, C 5397, pp. 9–11.

51. "Political Report no. 11," May 24, 1972, SBA, E 2300–01, Akzession 1977/ 29, box 17, p. 3 (first and second quotes). "Note," February 8, 1972, PAAA-MfAA, C 222/76, p. 173 (third quote). Lüthi, "Beyond betrayal," pp. 93, 105. Zhai, *China*, pp. 208–15. "New aspects in the policy of the People's Republic of China toward the countries of Indochina," December 12, 1975, PAAA-MfAA, C 216/78, pp. 1–8. "Information No. [??]/1978," October 11, 1978, SAPMO-BArch, DY 30/J IV 2/2J/8140, p. 10.

52. "Truong Chinh addresses third congress of Viet-Nam Fatherland Front," December 17, 1971, VVA, 2322509031, pp. 43–46. "Note," December 23, 1974, SAPMO-BArch, DY 30/IV B 2/20/169, pp. 11–12 (first and second quotes). "Stenographic report," [December 2, 1977], SAPMO-BArch, DY 30/11496, pp. 1–2. Note," January 23, 1978, PAAA-MfAA, C 5459, p. 47 (third to fifth quotes). Amitav Acharya, "The Association of Southeast Asian Nations," *Pacific Affairs*, 64/2 (1991), pp. 159–78.

53. "Transcript of President Eisenhower's press conference," *NYT*, April 8, 1954, p. 18.

54. Lorenz M. Lüthi, "Reading and warning the likely enemy," *International History Review*, 35/4 (2013), pp. 807–16.

7   India

1. P. J. Cain and A. G. Hopkins, *British Imperialism: 1688–2000*, 2nd ed. (Pearson Education, 2002), pp. 543–64. Lawrence James, *The rise and the fall of the British Empire* (St. Martin's Griffin, 1994), pp. 412–27. Nicklaus Thomas-Symonds, *Attlee* (I. B. Tauris, 2010), p. 152.

2. "Despatch no. 59," September 8, 1950, National Archives of Australia [NAA], Series A4231, 1950/New Delhi, p. 1 (fourth quote).

3. Burton Stein, *A history of India*, 2nd ed. (Blackwell, 1998), pp. 68–73, 159.

4. Jawaharlal Nehru, *The discovery of India* (The John Day Company, 1946), pp. 49–61. "The limits of self-determination," August 2, 1945, Jawaharlal Nehru, *Selected works*, 1st series [*JNSW*1], vol. 14 (Nehru Memorial Museum and Library, 1981), p. 440 (quotes).

5. Ramachandra Guha, *India after Gandhi* (Picador, 2012), pp. 3–24. Prem Shankar Jha, *Kashmir, 1947* (Oxford University Press, 1996).

6. "The army as the defender of freedom," December 9, 1948, Jawaharlal Nehru, *Selected works*, 2nd series [*JNSW*2], vol. 8 (Nehru Memorial Museum and Library, 1989), p. 4 (quote). John Lall, *Aksaichin and the Sino-Indian conflict* (Allied Publishers, 1989), pp. 217–30.

7. Srinath Raghavan, *War and peace in modern India* (Permanent Black, 2010), pp. 229–40. M. L. Bose, *History of Arunachal Pradesh* (Concept Publishing

Co., 1997). "To John Matthai," *JNSW*2, vol. 13, p. 260 (first quote). "Importance of the North East Frontier," *JNSW*2, vol. 12, p. 431 (second quote). "My dear Chief Minister," November 17, 1950, Jawaharlal Nehru, *Letters to chief ministers, 1947–1964*, vol. 2 (Oxford University Press, 1986), pp. 267–68 (third and fourth quotes). Sarvepalli Gopal, *Jawaharlal Nehru*, vol. 2 (Jonathan Cape, 1979), p. 177. "Indo-Chinese border," *Times of India* [*ToI*], February 22, 1951, p. 1.

  8. Various documents: *JNSW*2, vol. 15/1, p. 429, 438 (first quote). "My dear Premier," December 1, 1949, *JNSW*2, vol. 14-I, p. 367 (second quote). "My dear Chief Minister," August 2, 1952, *JNSW*2, vol. 19, p. 694 (third and fourth quotes).

  9. Various documents: *JNSW*1, vol. 14, pp. 439–42 (first quote). "India's foreign policy," March 8, 1948, *JNSW*2, vol. 5, p. 496. "Report on his trip abroad," November 6, 1948, *JNSW*2, vol. 8, p. 298 (second quote).

 10. Andrew B. Kennedy, *The international ambitions of Mao and Nehru* (Cambridge University Press, 2011), pp. 159, 206. "Disarmament," December 12, 1946, *JNSW*2, vol. 2, p. 469 (first quote). "The policy of Free India," August 7, 1947, *JNSW*2, vol. 3, p. 37 (second quote). "Keeping to the path of Mahatma Gandhi," April 26, 1948, *JNSW*2, vol. 6, pp. 15–16 (third quote). Raghavan, *War*, p. 307. "Changes in Asia," April 7, 1954, *JNSW*2, vol. 25, p. 396.

 11. "My dear Chief Minister," July 2, 1950, *JNSW*2, 14/2, p. 479 (first quote). "My dear Chief Minister," April 4, 1954, *JNSW*2, 25, p. 550 (second quote). "India and the International Situation," May 15, 1954, *JNSW*2, 25, p. 400 (third quote; italics added). "Cable to N. Raghavan," April 16, 1954, *JNSW*2, 25, pp. 467–68. "Proposals on Indo-China," April 24, 1954, *JNSW*2, 25, pp. 439–44. "I.6048," May 24, 1954, NAA, Series A1838, 3012/11/147, pp. 78–77.

 12. Various documents: *JNSW*2, vol. 20, pp. 561–62; vol. 22, pp. 464, 501, 511, 556; vol. 24, pp. 554, 659–60. "I.4474," April 20, 1954, NAA, Series A1838, 3012/11/147, p. 71. "From the High Commissioner for Canada, New Delhi, India," May 8, 1954, Library and Archives Canada [LAC], RG25, box 8230, p. 1. "India warns Soviet on red spread in Asia," *Washington Post*, June 3, 1954, p. 6. Li Lianqing, *Dawai jiaojia Zhou Enlai*, vol. 2 (Tian ditushu youxian gongsi, 1994), pp. 348–52. Ramesh Thakur, *Peacekeeping in Vietnam* (University of Alberta Press, 1984), p. 58.

 13. "Message to Ali Sastroamidjojo," July 22, 1954, *JNSW*2, vol. 26, pp. 359–60 (first quote). "A great event in history," October 15, 1954, *JNSW*2, vol. 27, p. 5 (second quote). "My dear Chief Minister," January 27, 1953, *Letters*, vol. 3, p. 237 (third and fourth quotes). "Notes on Asian–African Conference – Djakarta," no date, NAA, Series A1838, 3002/1 PART 8, p. 102 (fifth quote). "Despatch no. 6," February 20, 1956, NAA, Series A4231, 1956/ New Delhi, pp. 1–2 (sixth and seventh quotes).

 14. "My dear Chief Minister," June 16, 1952, *Letters*, vol. 3, pp. 20–21. "Restrictions on Indian Representatives in Tibet," September 2, 1953, *JNSW*2, vol. 23, p. 487. "Cable to KM. Panikkar," June 16, 1952,

JNSW2, vol. 18, pp. 474–75. "India foreign policy and Mr. Nehru," August 16, 1952, NAA, Series A1838, 169/11/87 Part 2, p. 66 (quotes).

15. "My dear Chief Minister," March 1, 1950, *JNSW2*, vol. 14-I, p. 410 (quote). Anton Harder, "Not at the cost of China," Cold War International History Project [CWIHP], Working Paper 76 (2015).

16. Nehru's long reflection about 1952 in "My dear Chief Minister," July 1, 1954, *Letters*, vol. 3, pp. 580–86. "My dear Premier," December 1, 1949, *JNSW2*, vol. 14-I, p. 367 (first quote). "Prime Minister Secretariat," June 18, 1954, Nehru Memorial Museum and Library [NMML], Subimal Dutt Papers, Subject Files, file no. 6, pp. 4–7. "My dear Chief Minister," August 1, 1953, *JNSW2*, vol. 23, p. 581. The five principles are: 1. mutual respect for each other's territorial integrity and sovereignty, 2. mutual non-aggression, 3. mutual non-interference in each other's internal affairs, 4. equality and mutual benefit, and 5. peaceful co-existence. "India and the international situation," May 15, 1954, *JNSW2*, vol. 25, p. 398. "Prime Minister Secretariat," June 18, 1954, NMML, Subimal Dutt Papers, Subject Files, file no. 6, p. 4 (second and third quotes). "I.7279," June 24, 1954, NAA, Series A1838, 3004/13/3 Part 9, p. 1.

17. "Future negotiations with China," May 12, 1954, *JNSW2*, vol. 25, pp. 469–70. "Conversation with Chou En-lai IV," June 26, 1954, *JNSW2*, vol. 26, p. 393. "Implications of China visit," November 14, 1954, *JNSW2*, vol. 27, p. 83. "Indonesian proposal for an Afro-Asian Conference," September 24, 1954, *JNSW2*, vol. 26, pp. 429–34. "A great event in history," October 15, 1954, *JNSW2*, vol. 27, pp. 3–6. "Talks with the American ambassador," May 5, 1955, *JNSW2*, vol. 28, p. 283 (first quote). "The Pakistani ambassador (Khaliquzzaman)," no date, NAA, Series A1838, 3002/1 Part 6, p. 1 (second and third quotes). "Chou and Nehru open India talks," *New York Times* [*NYT*], November 29, 1956, p. 1. "Joint efforts for peace," *ToI*, November 30, 1956, p. 9. "Stronger Afro-Asian ties to defend peace," *ToI*, December 1, 1956, p. 1. "Talks with Chou En-lai I," December 31, 1956, and January 1, 1957, and "Talks with Zhou Enlai II," January 1, 1957, *JNSW2*, vol. 36, pp. 600–1, 614 (fourth quote).

18. "Prime Minister's Secretariat," June 15, 1958, NMML, Subimal Dutt Papers, Subject Files, file no. 32, p. 48. Raghavan, *War*, p. 245. "To Chou En-lai," December 14, 1958, *JNSW2*, vol. 45, pp. 702–6. Zhou Enlai, "Letter to Nehru," January 23, 1959, Harold C. Hinton, ed., *The People's Republic of China, 1949–1979*, vol. 2 (Scholarly Resources, 1980), pp. 807–8.

19. Liu Xuecheng, *The Sino-Indian border dispute and Sino-Indian relations* (University Press of America, 1994), p. 26. "My dear Chief Minister," October 1, 1959, *Letters*, vol. 5, pp. 285, 288 (quotes).

20. Zhonggong zhongyang wenxian yanjiushi, ed., *Zhou Enlai nianpu, 1949–1976*, vol. 2 (Zhongyang wenxian chubanshe, 1997), pp. 302–3. Nehru–Zhou conversations: NMML, P. N. Haksar Papers, I and II Installments, Subject Files, files nos. 24–26. "Premier Chou En-lai's press conference held on April 25, 1960," no date, NMML, P. N. Haksar Papers, I and II Installments, Subject Files, file no. 25, pp. 59–79. K. Natwar Singh,

My China diary, 1956–88 (Rupa & Co., 2009), p. 110. "Chou 'hard rock,' Nehru declares," *NYT*, April 27, 1960, p. 5 (quote).

21. Various documents: *JNSW*2, vol. 22, p. 68; vol. 26, p. 63; vol. 27, pp. 3–11, 47–50; vol. 30, pp. 85, 116–17; vol. 31, pp. 30–31, 36; vol. 40, pp. 57–58. Raghavan, *War*, pp. 262–63. Jagat S. Mehta, *Negotiating for India* (Manohar, 2006), pp. 79–80. "Hindi-Chini bye-bye," June 18, 1967, *TofI*, p. 1 (quote).

22. Mehta, *Negotiating*, pp. 86–106. Raghavan, *War*, pp. 271–98. Gopal, *Jawaharlal Nehru*, vol. 3, pp. 138–44, 204–21. Steven A. Hoffmann, *India and the China crisis* (University of California Press, 1990), pp. 75–114. "I.14793," June 7, 1962, NAA, Series A1838, 169/10/1 Part 6, p. 61 (quote).

23. Lorenz M. Lüthi, *The Sino-Soviet split* (Princeton University Press, 2008), pp. 220–22. Zhonggong zhongyang wenxian yanjiushi, ed., *Mao Zedong nianpu, 1949–1976*, vol. 5 [*MZDNP*5] (Zhongyang wenxian chubanshe, 2013), pp. 113, 117, 138, 148, 162, 164–65.

24. *MZDNP*5, p. 165 (first quote). Raghavan, *War*, pp. 304–8. "Letter," October 24, 1962, Der Bundesbeauftragte für die Unterlagen des Staatssicherheitsdienstes der ehemaligen Deutschen Demokratischen Republik [BStU], MfS – HA XX 17469, pp. 27–29. "Chinese proposal for cease-fire in border struggle with India," November 21, 1962, *NYT*, p. 2 (second and third quotes). "Fm Jakarta Jan 12/63 confd," LAC, RG25, box 5201, p. 1 (fourth quote). "Fm Delhi Aug 20/63 confd," LAC, RG25, box 5284, p. 1 (fifth quote).

25. "Bombay PTI in English to Tokyo 1800 22 Oct 62 B," LAC, RG25, box 5201, p. 1 (first quote). See chapters by Imtiaz Omar, Payal Banerjee, and Subho Basu in Amit R. Das Gupta and Lorenz M. Lüthi, eds., *The Sino-Indian War of 1962* (Routledge, 2017). "My dear Chief Minister," October 21, 1962, *Letters*, vol. 5, pp. 535–36. "Record of conversation with R. K. Nehru," November 14, 1962, NAA, Series A1838, 169/10/1 Part 6, p. 1 (second quote). "Sino-Indian conflict," November 26, 1962, LAC, RG25, box 5201, p. 1 (third quote). Paul M. McGarr, *The Cold War in South Asia* (Cambridge University Press, 2013), pp. 149–82. "Note for file," December 17, 1962, Politisches Archiv des Auswärtigen Amtes, Bestand: Ministerium für Auswärtige Angelegenheiten [PAAA-MfAA], A 13919, pp. 117–18. "Memorandum for the Minister," November 19, 1962, LAC, RG25, box 5201, p. 1 (fourth quote).

26. "Record of conversation with Sir Arthur Tange and Mr. S. S. Khera, secretary of the Cabinet, India," April 26, 1963, NAA, Series A1838, 169/10/1 Part 6, p. 1. "O. 8718," April 30, 1963, NAA, Series A1838, 169/7/1 Part 9, p. 1. See chapters by Paul M. McGarr and Jovan Čavoški in Das Gupta and Lüthi, *Sino-Indian War*.

27. "I.17488," September 23, 1959, NAA, Series A1838, 189/7/1 Part 3, pp. 298–97. "I.11168," May 18, 1960, NAA, Series A1838, 169/11/148 Part 10, pp. 224–23. "I.11168," May 18, 1960, NAA, Series A1838, 169/11/148 Part 10, pp. 224–23. "I.1831," January 18, 1960, NAA, Series A1838, 189/7/1 Part 3, p. 314 (first quote). "I.13298," June 10, 1960, NAA, Series A1838, 189/7/1 Part 4, pp. 4–3. "FBIS 52," May 3, 1962, LAC, RG25, box 8152, p. 1. "My dear Chief Minister," July 10, 1962, *Letters*, vol. 5, p. 508 (second quote).

28. Various documents: NAA, Series A1838, 169/11/148 Part 13.
29. Christopher Tang, "Trust exercises," unpublished MA thesis, McGill University, 2010, p. 17. "My dear Chief Minister," May 21, 1963, *Letters*, vol. 5, pp. 592–602. "I.18473," July 10, 1963, NAA, Series A1838, 189/7/1 Part 5, pp. 24–23. "Talk with Mr. T. T. Krishnamachari," August 23, 1963, NAA, Series A1838, 169/11/52 Part 7, pp. 156–52 (first quote). "I.16116," June 18, 1963, NAA, Series A1838, 169/11/148 Part 14, p. 89 (second quote).
30. "Note," February 20, 1964, PAAA-MfAA, A 14013, pp. 141–43. "Memo no. 283," March 18, 1963, NAA, Series A1838, 169/10/1 Part 6, p. 1. "I.17610," May 27, 1964, NAA, Series A1838, 169/10/10/1 Part 7, p. 224. "Brief assessment," June 24, 1964, PAAA-MfAA, C 640/70, p. 104 (quote).
31. "Prime Minister Shastri presents five-point peace programme," October 8, 1964, NAA, Series A1838, 169/11/87 Part 26, p. 125 (first quote). "Memorandum no. 1965," October 20, 1964, NAA, Series A1838, 169/11/87 Part 26, pp. 153–52. "Record of conversation," May 29, 1965, NAA, Series A1838, 169/11/87 Part 27, p. 60 (second quote). Kennedy, "India's nuclear odyssey," pp. 128. George Perkovich, *India's nuclear bomb*, upd. ed. (University of California Press, 1999), pp. 66–83.
32. "Domestic political report," January 9, 1965, PAAA-MfAA, A 14028, pp. 1–3 (quote). "Talk with Mr. T. T. Krishnamachari," January 28, 1965, NAA, Series A1838, 169/10/1 Part 8, p. 3. "The matter of the talks of the Algerian ambassador in Syria talking about the Second Afro-Asian Conference," March 21, 1965, Waijiaobu Dang'anguan [WJBDAG], 107–00636-04, pp. 43–46. "India's delegation to the second Afro-Asian Conference to be held in Algiers from June 24, 1965," National Archives of India, New Delhi [NAI], External Affairs, 122 (51)-GA, 1965, pp. 31–35. Satya B. Jain, *India's foreign policy and non-alignment* (Anamika Publishers, 2000), p. 146.
33. Jain, *India's foreign policy*, pp. 146–47. Various documents: NAA, Series A1838, 169/11/148 Parts 20 and 21, and 3107/40/147 Part 24. Mehta, *Negotiating*, pp. 106–8. Christopher Tang, "Beyond India," CWIHP, Working Paper 64 (2012), p. 12.
34. Various documents: SBA, E 2300, Akzession 1000/716, box 303. Jain, *India's foreign policy*, pp. 156–65. "I.44873," October 4, 1965, NAA, Series A1838, 169/11/148 Part 22, pp. 319–14. "[No title]," no date, NMML, T. N. Kaul Papers, I to III Installment, Subject Files, file no. 15, pp. 63–68.
35. Jain, *India's foreign policy*, p. 154. Various documents: LAC, RG25, box 8913. "Prime Minister's Secretariat," February 9, 1966, NMML, T. N. Kaul Papers, I to III Installment, Subject Files, file no. 18, pp. 1–5.
36. Gandhi Jee Roy, *The non-aligned diplomacy of Mrs. Indira Gandhi* (Janaki Prakashan, 1983), p. 9. Guha, *India after Gandhi*, pp. 402, 409–10, 421–44. "I.23335," May 12, 1966, NAA, Series A1838, 3107/40/147 Part 25, p. 97 (first quote). "Memo no. 106," January 16, 1970, NAA, Series A1838, 720/5/7 Part 2, pp. 1–2 (second quote). Andrew B. Kennedy, "India's nuclear odyssey," *International Security*, 36/2 (2011), p. 133.
37. "Minutes of the meeting of the secretaries, joint secretaries, and directors held on 20th May, 1967," NMML, M. C. Chagla Papers, I Installment, Subject Files, file no. 91, p. 192 (first quote). "Instructions to India's representative to U.N. on non-proliferation treaty," April 20, 1968, NMML,

P. N. Haksar Papers, I and II Installments, Subject Files, file no. 35, p. 6 (second quote). Michael J. Sullivan, "Re-orientation of Indian arms control policy, 1969–1972," *Asian Survey*, 13/7 (1973), p. 696. "Record of conversation with Mr. Lalit Sen," August 14, 1968, NAA, Series A1838, 3107/40/ 147 Part 27, p. 17 (third quote).

38. "Talk with Chief of Army Staff," no date, NAA, Series A1838, 3107/40/147 Part 22, p. 114 (first quote). Ramesh Thakur, "India's Vietnam policy, 1946–1979," *Asian Survey*, 19/10 (1979), p. 965. "Record of conversation," May 14, 1965, NAA, Series A1838, 3107/40/147 Part 22, p. 190 (second quote). "Information," October 25, 1968, PAAA-MfAA, C 1739/76, p. 251 (third quote). "Indian views on Vietnam (draft)," no date, NAA, Series A1838, 169/10/10/10 Part 1, p. 94 (fourth to sixth quotes). "Information," September 25, 1969, PAAA-MfAA, C 1739/76, p. 9. Various documents: NAA, Series A1838, 3006/3/6 Part 5.

39. "Memo no. 122," February 6, 1968, NAA, Series A1838, 169/11/52 Part 9, p. 95. Kennedy, "India's nuclear odyssey," p. 135. "Political letter no. 5," August 27, 1968, SBA, E 2300–01, Akzession 1973/156, box 27, p. 1 (quote). "Memo no. 630," April 9, 1969, NAA, Series A1838, 169/11/52 Part 9, pp. 176–74. "Telex (coded) from: London, no. 1229 from June 16, 1969," Politisches Archiv des Auswärtigen Amtes [PAAA], B41, Sowjetunion Referat IIA4, vol. 95, pp. 29–30. "Fm Isbad Jun 24/69 no/no std," LAC, RG25, box 8913, pp. 1–2. "Telex (coded) from New Delhi no. 472," June 18, 1969, PAAA, B37, Süd- und Ostasien, Australien, Neuseeland und Ozeanien, 1950–1972, vol. 441, pp. 1–3.

40. Iftikhar H. Malik, *The history of Pakistan* (Greenwood Press, 2008), pp. 129–57. Srinath Raghavan, *1971* (Harvard University Press, 2013), pp. 14–53.

41. "Extract from record of conversation," June 20, 1963, NAA, Series A1838, 169/11/148 Part 14, p. 101 (quotes). Raghavan, *1971*, pp. 54–183.

42. "I.73177," July 18, 1971, NAA, Series A1838, 169/10/1 Part 18, p. 169 (first quote). "Political report no. 25," July 19, 1971, SBA, E 2300–01, Akzession 1977/29, box 6, p. 2 (second quote). Kennedy, "India's nuclear odyssey," pp. 135–36. "I.83249," August 13, 1971, NAA, Series A1838, 169/10/1 Part 19, pp. 41–36. "Fm Isbad 858 Aug 13/71," LAC, RG25, box 8914, p. 2 (third quote).

43. "Fm Delhi 4271 Nov 11/71," LAC, RG25, box 8915, p. 1 (first and second quotes). "Secret 03 Nov 71," LAC, RG25, box 8915, p. 2. "Fm Pekin 1134 Nov 10/11," LAC, RG25, box 8923, p. 1. "Political report no. 40," November 2, 1971, SBA, E 2300–01, Akzession 1977/29, box 6, pp. 1–4 (third quote). Raghavan, *1971*, pp. 231–34. "I.124433," December 7, 1971, NAA, Series A1838, 3107/40/148 Part 11, pp. 117–15. "I.129412," December 21, 1971, NAA, Series A1838, 169/10/1 Part 20, pp. 1–4. "India and South East Asia," December 14, 1971, NAA, Series A1838, 169/10/1 Part 20, pp. 1–2 (fourth quote). "Information," February 7, 1972, PAAA-MfAA, C 93/78, pp. 1–2.

44. "China, Russ veto U.N. truce bid," *Chicago Tribune*, December 6, 1971, p. 1. "I.124301," December 7, 1971, NAA, Series A1838, 3107/40/148 Part 11, pp.

102–1. "Final report," no date, LAC, RG25, box 8915, pp. 1–3. "Aide mem-oire," December 14, 1971, LAC, RG25, box 8915, pp. 1–7 (quote).

45. "Information," January 14, 1972, PAAA-MfAA, C 1739/76, pp. 124–26. "President Nixon's visit to Peking," no date, NAI, External Affairs, WII/104/18/72, pp. 286–87 (quote). "Indira ushers in Meghalaya & Arunachal Pradesh," January 21, 1972, *TofI*, p. 1. V. Venkata Rao, "Reorganization of North East India," *Indian Journal of Political Science*, 33/2 (1972), pp. 123–44. Sanjib Baruah, "Minority policy in the North-East," *Economic and Political Weekly*, 24/37 (1989), pp. 2087–88. Bose, *History*, pp. 239–47.

46. Perkovich, *India's nuclear bomb*, pp. 169–72. "O.ND6399," February 2, 1976, NAA, Series A1838, 169/10/1 Part 31, p. 33 (quote).

47. "Fm Delhi 170740Z," July 17, 1974, NAUK, FO 37/1472, p. 1 (first quote). "Nuclear club keeps growing," *Christian Science Monitor*, June 21, 1974, p. 2. "Despatch no. 8/74," December 31, 1974, NAA, Series A4231, 1974/South Asia, p. 1. "Nuclear guarantee by U.N. sought," June 26, 1974, *TofI*, p. 1 (second quote).

48. Perkovich, *India's nuclear bomb*, p. 175. Nayantara Saghal, *Indira Gandhi* (Penguin Books India, 2012), pp. 98–110. The second state of emergency had been called during the East Pakistan Crisis. Guha, *India after Gandhi*, pp. 488–95, 522–25. "Mrs. Gandhi is arrested on 2 charges," October 4, 1977, *Globe and Mail*, p. 1.

8   Arab–Israeli Relations, 1948–64

1. Shlomo Ben-Ami, *Scars of war, wounds of peace* (Oxford University Press, 2006), pp. 88–89. James L. Gelvin, *The Israel–Palestine conflict* (Cambridge University Press, 2005), pp. 14–50, 56. Gudrun Krämer, *Geschichte Palästinas* (Bundeszentrale für politische Bildung, 2015), pp. 125–39.

2. Howard M. Sachar, *A history of Israel*, 2nd, rev., upd. ed. (Alfred A. Knopf, 1996), pp. 39–41. "Zionist Congress in Basel," *New York Times* [*NYT*], August 31, 1897, p. 7 (first quote). "Basel Program," August 1897, www.jewishvirtuallibrary.org/first-zionist-congress-and-basel-program-1897, accessed on June 19, 2017 (second quote). Theodor Herzl, *Tagebücher*, vol. 1 (Jüdischer Verlag, 1922), pp. 98–99 (third and fourth quotes).

3. Krämer, *Geschichte*, pp. 165–79, 200–9. Neil Caplan, *Futile diplomacy*, vol. 1 (Frank Cass, 1983), pp. 34–54. Neil Caplan, *The Israel–Palestine conflict* (Wiley-Blackwell, 2010), pp. 8–9.

4. Krämer, *Geschichte*, pp. 142–45, 158–64, 221–71. Beshara Doumani, *Rediscovering Palestine* (University of California Press, 1995).Gelvin, *Israel–Palestine conflict*, pp. 92–102. Caplan, *Israel–Palestine conflict*, pp. 12–27, 80–89. "No. 556," November 3, 1932, British Library [BL], IOR/L/PS/12/2110, p. 541a (quote).

5. Sachar, *History of Israel*, pp. 189, 199–201. Krämer, *Geschichte*, pp. 314–23. Caplan, *Futile diplomacy*, vol. 2, 58–84. Caplan, *Israel–Palestine conflict*, p. 88. Rashid Khalidi, "The Palestinians and 1948," Eugene L. Rogan and Avi Shlaim, eds., *The war for Palestine*, 2nd ed. (Cambridge University Press, 2007), pp. 25–28.

6. Avi Shlaim, *The iron wall* (W. W. Norton, 2000), pp. 22–24. "Your Excellency," April 30, 1943, National Archives of the United Kingdom [NAUK], FO 141/866, p. 1 (first quote). "E 6477/41/65," October 7, 1944, NAUK, CO 732/88/11, pp. 1–4 (second quote). "Memorandum of conversation," February 14, 1945, United States, Department of State, *Foreign relations of the United States [FRUS]*, 1945, VIII (US Government Printing Office, 1969), p. 2 (third and fourth quotes). For Covenant and Annex: "No. 539," April 12, 1945, BL, IOR/L/PS/12/2110, pp. 67–69. "My dear Dixon," June 11, 1945, NAUK, FO 371/45417, p. 44 (fifth quote).

7. Margarete Myers Feinstein, *Holocaust survivors in postwar Germany, 1945–1957* (Cambridge University Press, 2014), pp. 11–63. Hans-Peter Föhrding and Heinz Verfrüth, *Als die Juden nach Deutschland flohen* (Kiepenheuer & Witsch, 2017), p. 19. Avinom J. Patt, *Finding home and homeland* (Wayne State University Press, 2009).

8. Krämer, *Geschichte*, pp. 355–56. Ritchie Ovendale, "The Palestine policy of the British Labour government 1945-1946," *International Affairs*, 55/3 (1979), pp. 410–17. "Truman opposes British White Paper on Palestine state," *Daily Boston Globe*, August 17, 1945, p. 13. "President Truman to Prime Minister Churchill," July 24, 1945, *FRUS* 1945, II, p. 1402. Various documents: *FRUS*, 1945, VIII, pp. 721–58. "No. 2541," December 5, 1945, NAUK, FO 371/45396, pp. 39–40 (quotes).

9. Krämer, *Geschichte*, pp. 357–58. Shlaim, *Iron wall*, p. 25. Wm. Roger Louis, *The British Empire in the Middle East, 1945–1951* (Clarendon Press, 1984), pp. 474–87. Rami Ginat, "Soviet policy towards the Arab world, 1945-48," *Middle Eastern Studies*, 32/4 (1996), pp. 328–30.

10. Sachar, *History of Israel*, pp. 284–85. "Arabs call Palestine report source of Third World War," *NYT*, September 9, 1947, p. 1 (first quote). "No. 740," October 11, 1947, NAUK, FO 371/61530, pp. 49–50. "Immediate steps for military action decreed by League at Cairo session," *Washington Post [WaPo]*, December 9, 1947, p. 1. Eitan Barak, "On the power of tacit understandings," *Middle East Journal*, 58/3 (2004), p. 445. "My dear Burrows," February 17, 1948, NAUK, FO 371/68381, pp. 1–2 (second quote). "No. 74A," February 24, 1948, NAUK, FO 371/68381, pp. 1–2. Krämer, *Geschichte*, p. 367.

11. Avi Shlaim, "Britain and the Arab-Israeli war of 1948," *Journal of Palestine Studies*, 16/4 (1987), p. 52. Krämer, *Geschichte*, pp. 362–75. Yezid Sayigh, *Armed struggle and the search for state* (Oxford University Press, 1997), pp. 37, 39–41. Benny Morris, "Revisiting the Palestinian exodus of 1948," Rogan and Shlaim, *War for Palestine*, p. 38. "UNGA Resolution 194," December 11, 1948, Caplan, *Futile diplomacy*, vol. 3, pp. 284–86 (quote).

12. Caplan, *Israel–Palestine conflict*, pp. 111–12. "Arab League bars direct peace talk," *NYT*, August 11, 1948, p. 10. "No. 883," November 13, 1948, NAUK, FO 371/68382, pp. 1–2.

13. Shabtai Teveth, *Ben-Gurion and the Palestinian Arabs* (Oxford University Press, 1985). Morris, "Revisiting," pp. 40–56. Khalidi, "Palestinians and 1948," pp. 15–16. David Tal, *War in Palestine 1948* (Routledge, 2003), pp. 3–4, 161, 471. Walid Khalidi, "The Arab perspective," Wm. Roger Louis

and Robert W. Stookey, eds., *The end of the Palestine Mandate* (I. B. Tauris, 1986), pp. 104–20.

14. Caplan, *Futile diplomacy*, vol. 3, pp. 37–53. Neil Caplan, *The Lausanne Conference, 1949* (The Mosche Dayan Center for Middle Eastern and African Studies, 1993). Sayigh, *Armed struggle*, p. 37.

15. "Israel wins a seat in U.N. by 37-12 vote," *NYT*, May 12, 1949, p. 1. Donald L. Losman, "The Arab boycott of Israel," *International Journal of Middle East Studies*, 3/2 (1972), p. 100. "Arabs accept defense plan," *The Sun*, October 30, 1949, p. 13. "Arab countries bar direct Israel talks," *NYT*, November 1, 1949, p. 18. Avi Shlaim, *The politics of partition* (Oxford University Press, 1990), pp. 355–98. "No. 37 Saving," April 3, 1950, NAUK, FO 371/81931, p. 2 (quote). Eitan Barak, "Between reality and secrecy," *Middle East Journal*, 61/4 (2007), pp. 659–60.

16. Caplan, *Israel–Palestine conflict*, pp. 137–40. Uri Bialer and Moshe Tlamim, "Top hat, tuxedo and cannons," *Israel Studies*, 7/1 (2002), pp. 37–41. Efraim Karsh, "Israel," Yezid Sayigh and Avi Shlaim, eds., *The Cold War and the Middle East* (Clarendon Press, 1997), pp. 159–60. Avi Shlaim, "Israel between east and west, 1948-56," *International Journal of Middle East Studies*, 36/4 (2004), p. 657–73. "No. 411," September 9, 1950, NAUK, FO 371/81934, pp. 1–2.

17. Caplan, *Futile diplomacy*, vol. 3, pp. 127–256.

18. Bialer, "Top hat," pp. 4–5, 8. "Despatch no. S-505," July 18, 1952, Library and Archives Canada [LAC], RG25, box 8431, p. 1. "Memo no. 1468/52," December 17, 1952, National Archives of Australia [NAA], Series A1838, 175/11/20 Part 1, p. 1 (first and second quotes). "Memorandum of conversation, by Theodore R. Frye of the Office of Near Eastern Affairs," September 10, 1953, *FRUS*, 1952-54, IX, p. 1304 (third quote). Barak, "Power," p. 445.

19. Shlaim, *Iron wall*, pp. 95–123.

20. Uri Bialer, *Oil and the Arab–Israeli conflict, 1948–1963* (Macmillan, 1999), pp. 57, 86–92, 115–93. "No. 612," September 22, 1951, NAUK, FO 371/91318, p. 1. Various documents: NAUK, POWE 33/2106.

21. Howard A. Patten, *Israel and the Cold War* (I. B. Tauris, 2013), pp. 7, 20. Mansour Farhang, "The Iran–Israel connection," *Arab Studies Quarterly*, 11/1 (1989), pp. 86–87. "No. 189," February 29, 1955, NAUK, FO 371/115510, pp. 3–4 (first quote). R. K. Srivastava, "India–Israel relations," *Indian Journal of Political Science*, 31/3 (1970), pp. 241–55. Frank N. Trager, "Burma's foreign policy, 1948-56," *Journal of Asian Studies*, 16/1 (1956), pp. 93–99. "Short report on the second session," [December 29, 1954], National Archives of India [NAI], External Affairs, 1 (44)-AAC, 1955, p. 32 (second quote). Pei Jianzhang, *Zhonghua renmin gongheguo waijiaoshi*, vol. 1 (Shijie zhishi chubanshe, 1994), pp. 289–90. John K. Cooley, "China and the Palestinians," *Journal of Palestine Studies*, 1/2 (1972), pp. 21–23.

22. Howard M. Sachar, *Israel and Europe* (Alfred A. Knopf, 1999), pp. 32–52. Various documents: NAUK, FO 371/100009.

23. Neil Caplan, *Futile diplomacy*, vol. 4, p. 25. Peter L. Hahn, *The United States, Great Britain, and Egypt, 1945–1956* (University of North Carolina Press,

1991), pp. 155–79. Various documents: *FRUS*, 1952-54, IX, pp. 1528–36. "Aide Memoire," September 17, 1954, NAUK, FO 371/111074, pp. 1–7. "No. 202," October 25, 1954, NAUK, FO 371/111076, p. 2 (first and second quotes). "No. 228," December 15, 1954, NAUK, FO 371/108349, p. 1 (third quote). "No. 24," January 12, 1955, LAC, RG25, box 7719, p. 1 (fourth and fifth quotes). Steven A. Cook, *The struggle for Egypt* (Oxford University Press, 2012), pp. 32–36, 60. "Palestine settlement," [March? 1955], NAUK, FO 371/115867, pp. 1–2. For more documentation: NAUK, FO 371/115864-115867, and *FRUS*, 1955-57, XIV, pp. 1–107. Caplan, *Futile diplomacy*, vol. 4, pp. 67–95.

24. "Pact of mutual co-operation between His Majesty the King of Iraq and the President of the Republic of Turkey," February 24, 1955, NAUK, FO 371/115493, 1–13. Shlaim, *Iron wall*, pp. 123–29. "Despatch no. 1/55," March 6, 1956, NAA, Series A4231, 1956/Cairo, p. 3 (quote). Various documents: *FRUS*, 1955-57, XIV, pp. 90–133, 151–53. "No. 487," April 6, 1955, NAUK, FO 371/115867, pp. 1–2.

25. "Radio news service," April 22, 1955, NAA, Series A1838, 3002/1 Part 5, p. 1. "Memo no. 199/55," April 28, 1955, NAA, Series A1838, 3002/1 Part 6, pp. 1–2 (first quote). "No. 640," May 19, 1955, NAUK, FO 371/115869, p. 1 (second quote). "Memorandum of conversation by the Ambassador of Egypt D. S. Solod with Prime Minister of Egypt G. Nasser," May 21, 1955, V. V. Naumkin, ed., *Blizhnevostochnyi konflikt*, vol. 1 (Mezhdunarodnyi Fond Demokratiya, 2003), pp. 276–77. "I.7077," June 2, 1955, NAA, Series A1838, 163/11/24 Part 2, p. 1 (third and fourth quotes). Zach Levey, "Israel's quest for a security guarantee from the United States, 1954–1956," *British Journal of Middle Eastern Studies*, 22/1-2 (1995), p. 44. Shlaim, *Iron wall*, pp. 135–37.

26. "Sir I. Kirkpatrick," July 8, 1955, NAUK, FO 371/115871, p. 1. Hahn, *United States*, p. 191. "Proposals by Secretary of State Dulles for a settlement in the Arab–Israel Zone," August 26, 1955, Caplan, *Futile diplomacy*, vol. 4, pp. 304–7. Various documents: *FRUS*, 1955-57, XIV, pp. 304–68, 451–53, 457–61, and NAUK, FO 371/115875-115878.

27. "Record of conversation by the Soviet ambassador in Egypt D. S. Solod with the head of cabinet of the prime minister of Egypt A. Sabri," August 30, 1955, Naumkin, *Blizhnevostochnyi konflikt*, vol. 1, p. 318. Caplan, *Futile diplomacy*, vol. 4, pp. 152–61. "Record of conversation by the Soviet ambassador in Egypt D. S. Solod with prime minister of Egypt G. Nasser," September 29, 1955, Naumkin, *Blizhnevostochnyi konflikt*, vol. 1, p. 342. Various documents: NAUK, FO 371/115521. Levey, "Israel's quest," pp. 57–60.

28. "Flare-up of Arab–Israeli war feared near," *Boston Globe*, October 12, 1955, p. 20. "Memo no. 511/55," November 7, 1955, NAA, Series A1838, 175/11/20 Part 3, p. 1. Shlaim, *Iron wall*, pp. 144–46. "No. 1615," November 3, 1955, NAUK, FO 371/115908, p. 9. "Report on the Arab oil Experts committee," [November 1955], NAUK, POWE 33/2106, 1–3.

29. "Memorandum of a conversation, Geneva, November 9, 1955," *FRUS*, 1955-57, XIV, pp. 720–23. "Anthony Eden's Guildhall (Mansion House)

Speech," November 9, 1955, Caplan, *Futile diplomacy*, vol. 4, pp. 309–11. Caplan, *Futile diplomacy*, vol. 4, pp. 178–83, 220–42. "Memorandum of conversation," November 11, 1955, LAC, RG25, box 4422, pp. 1–5.

30. "Memo no. 154," March 1, 1956, NAA, Series A1838, 175/11/20 Part 4, p. 1. "No. 516," March 15, 1956, NAUK, FO 371/121773, pp. 1–2. "Selwyn Lloyd – Nasser talks, March 2, 1956," no date, NAA, Series A1838, 175/11/20 Part 5, p. 1 (first quote). Hahn, *United States*, pp. 200–3. Various documents: Kungliga biblioteket [KB], MS L 179:70, 179:109, 179:110. "I.6491," May 9, 1956, NAA, Series A1838, 175/11/20 Part 6, p. 1. "No. 379," May 18, 1956, NAUK, FO 371/121740, p. 1 (second quote).

31. Various documents: LAC, RG25, box 8152. Pei, *Zhonghua*, vol. 1, pp. 279, 293. "Recognition of China by Egypt," May 25, 1956, NAA, Series A1838, 163/11/87, p. 1. "Memo no. 294," May 29, 1956, NAA, Series A1838, 163/11/52 Part 2, p. 1 (quote). Various documents: *FRUS*, 1955-57, XV, pp. 645–874.

32. David Tal, "Israel's road to the 1956 War," *International Journal of Middle East Studies*, 28/1 (1996), pp. 74–75. Shlaim, *Iron wall*, pp. 160–62. Various documents: LAC, RG25, boxes 6108 and 6109.

33. As the British government told the U.N. Secretary General after the crisis: "Memorandum," [date made illegible], KB, MS L 179:111, "Middle East/Suez Story – Nr. 17 12-24 Oct. 56," p. 1 (quote). Avi Shlaim, "The protocol of Sèvres, 1956," *International Affairs*, 73/3 (1997), pp. 509–30. S. Ilan Troen, "The protocol of Sèvres," *Israel Studies*, 1/2 (1996), pp. 122–39.

34. Shlaim, *Iron wall*, pp. 178–85. Shabtai Teveth, *Moshe Dayan* (Weidenfeld and Nicolson, 1972), p. 267. Cook, *Struggle*, p. 69.

35. Diane B. Kunz, *The economic diplomacy of the Suez Crisis* (University of North Carolina Press, 1991), pp. 116–53. "Israel captures port, wins victory in week," *Daily Boston Globe*, November 5, 1956, p. 13. "Fm Tel Aviv Nov 9/56 secret," LAC, RG25, box 5835, pp. 1–2. "Israel to demand Cairo peace vow," *NYT*, November 3, 1956, p. 6. "British, French are out of Suez," *NYT*, December 23, 1956, p. 1.

36. "Peace left up to U.S. and Soviets," *Los Angeles Times* [*LAT*], November 2, 1956, p. 26. "No. 830," November 26, 1956, NAUK, FO 371/121803, p. 1 (quotes). Barak, "Power," p. 446. Barak, "Between reality and secrecy," p. 664. "Oil route alternative to Suez Canal, Tiran, Gaza, Palestine settlement," December 11, 1956, NAA, Series A1838, 175/11/20 Part 8, pp. 1–2. Bialer, *Oil*, p. 224.

37. "Memorandum," January 5, 1957, *KB*, MS L 179:113, "Middle East/Suez Story – Nr. 26 5 Jan. 57," p. 5. "Fm Candel NY Jan 8/57 confd," LAC, RG 25, box 8431, pp. 1–6. "Notes on meeting with President Nasser – in Cairo," January 19, 1957, NAUK, PREM 11/1918, p. 1. Barak, "Power," pp. 446–47. Barak, "Between reality and secrecy," pp. 665–66. "Israel's right to self-defence," *Manchester Guardian*, March 1, 1957, p. 1 (quote).

38. See several documents: KB, MS L 179:114-116, 130. Barak, "Between reality and secrecy," p. 668. Barak, "Power," p. 448–55

39. "Extracts," April 2, 1957, LAC, RG 25, box 8431, pp. 1–6. "Meeting of the Secretary-General," [March 21, 1957], KB, MS L 179:130, "Middle East/

Suez Story 21-26 March 57," p. 1 (quote). Barak, "Between reality and secrecy," pp. 670–73. "Letter dated 24 April 1957," April 24, 1957, KB, MS L 179:130, "Middle East – Fawzi, Mahmoud – 37 letters/messages to D. H., 1956-61," pp. 1–5. "Israel pipes first oil to Beersheba," *WaPo*, April 25, 1957, p. A7.

40. "Fm Cairo Jun 17/57 confd," NAA, Series A1838, 163/11/20, p. 1.
41. Avner Cohen, *Israel and the bomb* (Columbia University Press, 1998), pp. 52–75. Shlaim, *Iron wall*, p. 188.
42. Abraham Ben-Zvi, *Decade of transition* (Columbia University Press, 1998). Warren Bass, *Support any friend* (Oxford University Press, 2003), pp. 64–143. Zach Levey, "The United States' *Skyhawk* sale to Israel, 1966," *Diplomatic History*, 28/2 (2004), pp. 255–76.
43. Shlaim, *Iron wall*, p. 193. Patten, *Israel*, pp. 36–58, 81–97, 116–40. Zach Levey, "Israel's strategy in Africa, 1961-67," *International Journal of Middle East Studies*, 36/1 (2004), pp. 71–87.
44. Various documents: LAC, RG25, boxes 8863, 8885 and 8897. Moshe Shemesh, "Prelude to the Six-Day War," *Israel Studies*, 9/3 (2004), pp. 1–45.
45. Various documents: LAC, RG25, box 8885, and NAA, Series A1838, 69/1/4/31 Part 1.
46. Various documents: LAC, RG25, box 8897.
47. "On some aspects of the visit by comrade Khrushchev to Egypt," April 6, 1964, Politisches Archiv des Auswärtigen Amtes, Bestand: Ministerium für Auswärtige Angelegenheiten [PAAA-MfAA], A 224, pp. 195–201. Various documents: NAA, Series A1838, 69/1/4/31 Part 1.
48. "No. 750," September 13, 1964, NAUK, FO 371/175559, p. 2 (first quote). "No. 10 Saving," September 18, 1964, NAUK, FO 371/175559, p. 1 (second and third quotes).

9   Arab–Israeli Relations, 1964–75

1. Guy Laron, *The Six-Day War* (Yale University Press, 2017), pp. 23–32. Various documents: Politisches Archiv des Auswärtigen Amtes, Bestand: Ministerium für Auswärtige Angelegenheiten [PAAA-MfAA], A 13627, and Waijiaobu Dang'anguan [WJBDAG], 107–01061-05 and 107–01061-18.
2. Patrick Seale, *Asad* (University of California Press, 1988), pp. 104–5. "Arab unit plans aid for Vietcong," *New York Times* [*NYT*], June 10, 1966, p 3. Laron, *Six-Day War*, pp. 39–43. Nigel J. Ashton, *King Hussein of Jordan* (Yale University Press, 2008), pp. 107–11.
3. Steven A. Cook, *The struggle for Egypt* (Oxford University Press, 2012), pp. 77–78. "Fm Cairo Oct 24/64 confd," Library and Archives Canada [LAC], RG25, box 8885, p. 1 (quote). Various documents: WJBDAG, 107–00566-01, 107–01030-03, and 203–00652-02.
4. "The Under Secretary of State for External Affairs, Ottawa," July 12, 1965, LAC, RG25, box 8885, p. 4 (quote). "Telegram no. 234/65," April 20, 1965, PAAA-MfAA, G-A 408, p. 100. "Report on the talks of Nasser in Moscow,"

September 28, 1965, Stiftung Archiv der Parteien und Massenorganisationen der DDR im Bundesarchiv [SAPMO-BArch], DY 30/J IV 2/2J/1512, pp. 1–7. Lorenz M. Lüthi, "The Non-Aligned Movement and the Cold War, 1961–1973," *Journal of Cold War Studies*, 18/4 (2016), p. 126. "Soviet said to offer Cairo atom defense," *NYT*, February 4, 1966, pp. 1, 12.

5. "Fm Cairo Nov 20/65 confd," LAC, RG25, box 8885, p. 1 (quote). Various documents: LAC, RG25, box 8885. Cook, *Struggle*, p. 90.

6. Cook, *Struggle*, pp. 71, 107, 112, 121. "Islamic summit conference," March 16, 1966, National Archives of Australia [NAA], Series A1838, 181/2/3/11 Part 1, pp. 26–25. "Nasser says U.S. and Britain back his rightist foes," February 23, 1966, *NYT*, p. 1. Various documents: LAC, RG25, box 8897.

7. "Information on the speech by President Nasser on the Day of Unity on February 22, 1967," PAAA-MfAA, C 953, pp. 60–62. "Political report no. 14," March 9, [1967], Schweizerisches Bundesarchiv [SBA], E 2300–01, 1973/156, box 16, p. 1. "Telno 261," April 12, 1967, National Archives of the United Kingdom [NAUK], PREM 13/2208, p. 1. "Guidance no. 116," May 23, 1967, NAUK, PREM 13/1618, pp. 1–3. "Excerpts of a speech by President Nasser on the occasion of May 1st, 1967," no date, PAAA-MfAA, C 896, pp. 64–67 (quotes). "Saudi Arabia during and after the Arab–Israeli War," August 18, 1967, NAUK, FCO 8/760, p. 1.

8. Laron, *Six-Day War*, pp. 48–54, 78–85. Various documents: United Nations Archive [UNA], S-0861–0003-09, S-0862–0001-03, S-0861–0005-04. "Note," May 31, 1967, PAAA-MfAA, C 1156/70, pp. 99–100 (first quote). Various documents: UNA, S-0865–0001-01 (second quote). "Note for the file," July 11, 1968, UNA, S-0865–0001-04, p. 1 (third and fourth quotes).

9. "Telno 417," May 23, 1967, NAUK, PREM 13/1617, p. 1 (first quote). "Dear Murray," May 23, 1967, NAUK, FCO 8/760, p. 1 (second and third quotes). Laron, *Six-Day War*, pp. 243–44. Various documents: NAUK, PREM 13/1617 and 13/1618.

10. Laron, *Six-Day War*, pp. 106–8. "Fm TAviv Feb10/66 confd," LAC, RG25, box 8897, p. 1 (quote). "Memo no. 207," February 15, 1966, NAA, Series A1838, 175/11/20 Part 14, pp. 32–31. "Fm Cairo Jun 13/66 confd," LAC, RG 25, 8863, pp. 1–3. "Record of conversation," October 5, 1966, NAA, Series A1838, 175/11/20 Part 14, pp. 58–57.

11. Laron, *Six-Day War*, pp. 140–48, 201–7, 254–55. William B. Quandt, *Peace process*, 3rd ed. (Brookings Institution Press, 2005), p. 37–38.

12. Benny Morris, *Righteous victims* (Alfred A. Knopf, 1999), p. 306. Laron, *Six-Day War*, pp. 264–302. Avi Shlaim, *The iron wall* (W. W. Norton, 2000), p. 238.

13. First quote from Said K. Aburish, *Nasser* (St. Martin's Press, 2004), p. 260. Michael B. Oren, *Six days of war* (Ballantine Books, 2003), pp. 170–304. Richard B. Parker, *The politics of miscalculation in the Middle East* (Indiana University Press, 1993), pp. 52–98. Hisham Sharabi, "Prelude to war," Ibrahim Abu Lughod, ed., *The Arab–Israeli confrontation of June 1967* (Northwestern University Press, 1970), p. 63 (second quote).

14. "My dear Azim," June 19, 1967, Nehru Memorial Museum and Library [NMML], Apa B. Pant, Subject Files, no. 16-I, p. 27 (first quote). "Trip to the United Arab Republic," June 17, 1967, Arhiv Jugoslavije [AJ], KPR I-2/35–3, pp. 18–20 (second quote). "United Arab Republic, Ministry of Foreign Affairs," June 6, 1967, LAC, RG25, box 8885, pp. 1–2. Abdel Magid Farid, *Nasser* (Ithaca Press, 1994), p. 1. Cook, *Struggle*, pp. 91–92, 100. Various documents: PAAA-MfAA, G-A 412 (third quote). "Information no. 254/VI," June 28, 1967, SAPMO-BArch, DY 30/J IV 2/ 2J/1999, pp. 1–2 (fourth and fifth quotes). "Note," [July 5, 1967], PAAA-MfAA, C 327, p. 32 (sixth quote).
15. Avi Shlaim, *Lion of Jordan* (Alfred A. Knopf, 2008), pp. 255–57. "A brutal price for our stupidity," *Spiegel*, February 3, 1969, p. 110 (first quote). Various documents: NAUK, PREM 13/1622. "Outgoing telegram 009614," July 18, 1967, Lyndon Baines Johnson Presidential Library [LBJ], NSF 1963–1969, Files of the Special Committee of the NSC, box 12, p. 1 (first quote).
16. David W. Lesch, "Syria," Wm. Roger Louis and Avi Shlaim, eds., *The 1967 Arab–Israeli War* (Cambridge University Press, 2012), pp. 86–91. Various documents: SAPMO-BArch, DY 30/J IV 2/2J/1968 and DY 30/IV A 2/ 20/872.
17. "Telno. unnumbered," June 9, 1967, NAUK, PREM 13/1620, pp. 1–2 (first quote). Various documents: NAUK, PREM 13/1622 (second and third quotes). "Copy of telegram no. 264/67 of 6/20/67 by Comrade Lösch, Algiers," no date, PAAA-MfAA, G-A 412, p. 240 (fourth and fifth quotes). M. S. Daoudi and M. S. Dajani, "The 1967 oil embargo revisited," *Journal of Palestine Studies*, 13/2 (1984), pp. 68–72. "Information no. 191/VI," June 21, 1967, SAPMO-BArch, DY 30/J IV 2/2J/1979, p. 1. "Dear Michael," July 1, 1967, NAUK, FCO 8/760, p. 1.
18. "Telegram of the Minister of Foreign Affairs of the USSR, A. A. Gromyko, to the Ambassador of the USSR in the UAR," May 24, 1967, V. V. Naumkin, ed., *Blizhnevostochnyi konflikt*, vol. 2 (Mezhdunarodnyi Fond Demokratiya, 2003), p. 566 (first quote). Yaacov Roi, "Soviet policy towards the Six Day War," Yaacov Roi and Boris Mozorov, eds., *The Soviet Union and the June 1967 Six Day War* (Woodrow Wilson Center Press / Stanford University Press, 2008), p. 16. "Note on the consultations," [June 9, 1967], AJ, KPR I-2/33, 1–29a (second and third quotes). "Telegram by Kormes to Markowski and Fischer," June 29, 1967, SAPMO-BArch, DY 30/IV A 2/20/360, pp. 1–2. Various documents: Farid, *Nasser*, pp. 1–17. Muhammad H. Haykal, *The Cairo documents* (Doubleday, 1973), p. 312. "Political report no. 11," July 17, 1967, SBA, E 2300–01, 1973/156, box 18, p. 4 (fourth quote).
19. "Telegram number 1936," June 5, 1967, NAUK, PREM 13/1620, pp. 1–3 (first quote). Charles D. Smith, "The United States and the 1967 war," Louis and Shlaim, *The 1967 Arab–Israeli war*, pp. 166, 170–84. "Text of Johnson speech on Mideast situation," *The Sun*, June 20, 1967, p. A8 (second to fifth quote). Howard M. Sachar, *Israel and Europe* (New York: Alfred A. Knopf, 1999), pp. 174–93, 214–16. "Record of a discussion," June 19, 1967,

NAUK, PREM 13/1622, p. 4 (sixth and seventh quotes). "Information no. 219/VI," June 26, 1967, SAPMO-BArch, DY 30/J IV 2/2J/1982, p. 2.

20. "Statement by the Prime Minister, Mr. Levi Eshkol in the Knesset, 12 June 1967," LAC, RG 25, 8863, p. 13 (first and second quotes). "Telno. 1001," June 13, 1967, NAUK, PREM 13/1621, pp. 1–2. Gershon Gorenberg, *The accidental empire* (Times Books, 2006), pp. 39–41, 46. Avi Raz, "The generous peace offer that was never offered," *Diplomatic History*, 37/1 (2013), pp. 85–108. "Telno. 670," June 21, 1967, NAUK, PREM 13/1622, p. 1. "Incoming telegram 011223," June 13, 1967, LBJ, NSF 1963–1969, files of the Special Committee of the NSC, box 4, pp. 1–3.

21. Various documents: LBJ, NSF 1963–1969, Country file, box 195 and files of the Special Committee of the NSC, boxes 7 and 12.

22. Various documents: NAUK, FCO 17/7; PAAA-MfAA, C 896; SAPMO-BArch, DY 30/IV A 2/20/889; Farid, *Nasser*, pp. 21–49 (quotes); NMML, Apa B. Pant, Subject files, no. 16-I. Daoudi, "1967," pp. 75–76.

23. Various documents: NAUK, FCO 17/301; Farid, *Nasser*, pp. 51–67; AJ, KPR I-2/35; and NAUK, FCO 17/36 (quote).

24. "Note," September 18, 1967, SAPMO-BArch, DY 30/3666, p. 76 (quotes). Shlaim, *Iron wall*, p. 259. Ashton, *King Hussein*, pp. 121–29. Jesse Ferris, *Nasser's gamble* (Princeton University Press, 2013), p. 291.

25. Shlaim, *Iron wall*, p. 259. Various documents: LAC, RG25, box 8898 (first and second quotes). "Information no. 68/X," October 10, 1967, SAPMO-BArch, DY 30/IV A2/20/875, pp. 259–62. "Faster than the thought," *Spiegel*, October 30, 1967, pp. 148–50. "Egyptian leader believed to feel U.S. holds key to solution in Mideast," *NYT*, September 18, 1967, p. 1 (third quote). "Excerpt," September 19, 1967, PAAA-MfAA, C 996/71, p. 194.

26. "Telegram number 3356," October 25, 1967, NAUK, PREM 13/1623, p. 2. Quandt, *Peace process*, p. 47.

27. "Resolution on the Mideast," *NYT*, November 23, 1967, p. 5 (first quote). James L. Gelvin, *The Israel–Palestine conflict* (Cambridge University Press, 2005), pp. 176–79. "Dear Mr. President," December 9, 1967, LBJ, NSF 1963–1969, Head of State correspondence file, box 55, p. 1 (second quote).

28. "Statement by the Secretary-General," November 22, 1967, UNA, S-0861–0003-09, p. 1. "A suggested alternative course of action," September 10, 1969, UNA, S-0865–0001-09, p. 1 (first and second quotes). Various documents: UNA, S-0353–0002-11, S-0862–0001-05, and S-0865–0001-09. Shlaim, *Iron wall*, pp. 260–61. Shlaim, *Lion*, pp. 281–314. "Supreme Executive Committee, 12 November 1968," Farid, *Nasser*, pp. 99–103 (third quote).

29. Shlaim, *Iron wall*, pp. 264–89. Craig Daigle, *The limits of détente* (Yale University Press, 2012), pp. 37–38. Morris, *Righteous victims*, p. 355.

30. Various documents: Richard Nixon Presidential Library [RMN], NSC, Numeric files, box 1023 (first quote). "Views to be conveyed to Ambassador Jarring," UNA, S-0865–0001-05, pp. 1–2 (second and third quotes). Lorenz M. Lüthi, "Restoring chaos to history," *China Quarterly*, 210 (2012), p. 384. "Note for file," March 27, 1969, PAAA-MfAA, C 996/71, p. 2.

31. Laura M. James, "Military/political means/ends," Nigel J. Ashton, ed., *The Cold War in the Middle East* (Routledge, 2007), pp. 97–98. "Israel has gambled away its victory," *Spiegel*, March 10, 1969, p. 110 (first quote). Various documents: NAUK, PREM 13/2609 (second quote). "Meeting of the council of ministers, 16 February 1969," Farid, *Nasser*, p. 135 (third quote). "Information," no date, SAPMO-BArch, NY 4182/1338, p. 65 (fourth quote).

32. Various documents: UNA, S-0865–0001-05; LAC, RG25, box 8899; RMN, NSC, Country files, box 634; SAPMO-BArch, NY 4182/1338. Dima P. Adamsky, "How American and Israeli intelligence failed to estimate the Soviet intervention in the war of attrition," Ashton, *Cold War in the Middle East*, pp. 113–14.

33. Various documents: LAC, RG25, box 8899; Farid, *Nasser*, pp. 146–52; UNA, S-0865–0001-09. Quandt, *Peace process*, p. 66. Shlaim, *Iron wall*, p. 290.

34. Quandt, *Peace process*, pp. 75–83. Daigle, *Limits*, pp. 48–51.

35. "Conversation," December 19, 1969, SAPMO-BArch, DY 30/IV A 2/20/889, p. 2. Various documents: Farid, *Nasser*, pp. 154–62 (quote), and NAUK, FCO 17/1151. Shlaim, *Iron wall*, pp. 291–94. Daigle, *Limits*, pp. 83–113.

36. Quandt, *Peace process*, pp. 72–73. "Appeal from President Gamal Abd El Nasser," [May 1, 1970], PAAA-MfAA, C 1293/76, pp. 52–54 (quote). Daigle, *Limits*, pp. 113–14, 136–43. "On the visit," July 24, 1970, SAPMO-BArch, NY 4182/1338, pp. 140–42. "Nasser's meeting with the Higher Executive Committee," 20 July 1970, Farid, *Nasser*, pp. 186–91. Various documents: RMN, NSC, Country files, box 636 and HAK Office files, box 129; LAC, RG 25, 8900.

37. Quandt, *Peace process*, pp. 90, 98–108. Various documents: PAAA-MfAA, C 7662. Farid, *Nasser*, 205–13. Joel Gordon, *Nasser* (Oneworld Publications, 2006), pp. 114–15. "Fm TAviv Sep 29/70 no/no standard," LAC, RG 25, 8900, p. 1 (quote).

38. Cook, *Struggle*, pp. 119–27. "Note on a conversation," [December 19, 1970], AJ, KPR I-3-a/121–51, pp. 8–10. "Cairo 2798," December 24, 1970, RMN, NSC, Country files, box 636, pp. 1–2 (first quote). "Excerpts from the interview with President Sadat of Egypt," *NYT*, December 28, 1970, p. 15 (second quote). "The Saudi/Egyptian honeymoon," October 6, 1971, NAUK, FCO 8/1739, pp. 1–8 (third quote). "Fm Cairo 064 Feb4/71," LAC, RG 25, 8900, pp. 1–3.

39. "Report," no date [January 1971], SAPMO-BArch, DY 30/IV A 2/20/884, pp. 2–4. Shlaim, *Iron wall*, p. 302. "Statement by the Prime Minister of Israel Mrs. Golda Meir in the Knesset on 9 February 1971," no date, UNA, S-0884–0010-13, pp. 1–10. Various documents: RMN, NSC, HAK Office files, box 129 (first quote). "Fm Tel Aviv 251400Z," March 25, 1971, NAUK, PREM 15/540, p. 1 (second quote). "Fm Cairo 164 Apr6/71," LAC, RG 25, 8901, pp. 1–2. Various documents: RMN, NSC, HAK Office files, box 129.

40. Various documents: RMN, NSC, Country files, box 636 (quote). "Record of a meeting," January 5, 1971, NAUK, PREM 15/532, p. 3. "Telegram from the Section in Egypt to the Department of State," May 9, 1971, United

States, Department of State, *Foreign relations of the United States* [*FRUS*], 1969–1974, XXIII (US Government Printing Office, 2016), p. 851.

41. Various documents: PAAA-MfAA, C 1113/75 and C 1304/76. "Fm Mosco 1259 May11/71," LAC, RG25, box 8928, p. 1 (first quote). "Information," June 2, 1971, Der Bundesbeauftragte für die Unterlagen des Staatssicherheitsdienstes der ehemaligen Deutschen Demokratischen Republik [BStU], MfS HVA 182, pp. 88–91 (second quote). "Fm TAviv 322 Jun 03/71," LAC, RG25, box 8928, pp. 1–2.

42. "Aide memoire for the conversation with the Ambassador of the UAR, Saad Afre," September 1, 1971, AJ, KPR I-3-a/121-55, p. 2. "Fm Rabat 152230Z," September 15, 1971, NAUK, PREM 15/1091, p. 1 (first quote). "[Information from the CPSU]," October 25, 1971, SAPMO-BArch, DY 30/13911, p. 3 (second quote). Saad Shazly, *The crossing of the Suez* (American Mideast Research, 1980), p. 113. "Fm Cairo 544 Nov22/71," LAC, RG 25, 8901, p. 1 (third quote). "Egyptian involvement in Soviet arms supplies to India in 1971," April 15, 1976, NAUK, FCO 37/1723, p. 1.

43. "Strictly confidential," February 9, 1972, SAPMO-BArch, DY 30/13911, pp. 1–3. Various documents: AJ, KPR I-3-a/121-58. "Note for file," May 4, 1972, PAAA-MfAA, C 578/77, p. 123. Various documents: RMN, NSC, Country files, box 638. "[Information from the CPSU]," May 16, 1972, SAPMO-BArch, DY 30/13911, pp. 1–4. Thomas Kunze, *Nicolae Ceauşescu*, 3rd, upd. ed. (Ch. Links Verlag, 2009), p. 218. Daigle, *Limits*, pp. 213–27.

44. "Saudi Prince Sultan's involvement," no date, RMN, NSC, Country files, box 638, p. 1. Quandt, *Peace process*, pp. 95–96. Yoram Meital, "The October War and Egypt's multiple crossings," Asaf Siniver, ed., *The October 1973 War* (Hurst & Company, 2013), p. 51. Various documents: SAPMO-BArch, DY 30/13911; PAAA-MfAA, C 174/75; RMN, NSC, Country files, box 638.

45. Quandt, *Peace process*, p. 86. "Secret Cairo 2153," August 2, 1972, RMN, NSC, Country files, box 638, pp. 1–2. "Fm Cairo 250910Z," August 25, 1972, NAUK, PREM 15/1483, pp. 2–3 (quote). Various documents: SAPMO-BArch, DY 30/IV B 2/20/431; and NAUK, FCO 17/1647. Shazly, *Crossing*, pp. 171–83.

46. Various documents: NAUK, FCO 17/1379 and FCO 93/195 (quote). Seale, *Asad*, p. 197. Shazly, *Crossing*, p. 205.

47. "Fm Cairo 091200Z May," May 9, 1973, NAUK, PREM 15/1764, p. 1 (first and second quotes). "Memorandum for the President," March 6, 1973, RMN, NSC, Country files, box 638, p. 2 (third and fourth quotes). Shlaim, *Lion*, pp. 364–65.

48. "Information," March 16, 1973, BStU, MfS HVA 91, pp. 28–31. Shazly, *Crossing*, pp. 197–98. Avraham Sela, *The decline of the Arab–Israeli conflict* (State University of New York Press, 1998), p. 143. Various documents: NAUK, PREM 15/1483. Daniel Yergin, *The prize* (Free Press, 2008), pp. 545–69, 579. Sheikh Rustum Ali, *Saudi Arabia and oil diplomacy* (Praeger, 1976), pp. 107–8. "Sadat vows action and says Arabs will aid him with 'oil weapon'," May 2, 1973, NAUK, PREM 15/1764, p. 1. "Oil issues to be raised at OAPEC session: Kuwait, Sept. 4," *South China Morning Post*, September 5, 1973, p. 24 (quote).

49. "Foreign policy," February 21, 1973, PAAA-MfAA, C 329/75, p. 89. "Algiers: the Non-Aligned Conference," September 26, 1973, NAUK, FCO 93/9, p. 7–9. Zach Levey, "Israel's exit from Africa, 1973," *British Journal of Middle Eastern Studies*, 35/2 (2008), pp. 205–26.

50. "Telegram no. 184," May 18, 1973, SBA, E 2300–01, 1977/30, box 4, pp. 1–2. Uri Bar-Joseph, "Last chance to avoid war," *Journal of Contemporary History*, 41/3 (2006), pp. 545–56. Boaz Vanetik and Zaki Shalom, "The White House Middle East policy in 1973 as a catalyst for the outbreak of the Yom Kippur War," *Israel Studies*, 16/1 (2011), pp. 53–78. Various documents: NAUK, PREM 15/1484; RMN, NSC, Country files, box 638; and PAAA-MfAA, C 4255.

51. Uri Bar-Joseph, *The watchman fell asleep* (State University of New York Press, 2005). Shlomo Ben-Ami, *Scars of war, wounds of peace* (Oxford University Press, 2006), p. 144. Shlaim, *Iron wall*, p. 319.

52. Various chapters in Siniver, *October 1973 War*, pp. 59–61, 75, 177. Victor Israelyan, *Inside the Kremlin during the Yom Kippur War* (Pennsylvania State University Press, 1995), pp. 56–61. Quandt, *Peace process*, pp. 106–20. Ali, *Saudi Arabia*, p. 109. Cook, *Struggle*, p. 135.

53. Various documents: RMN, NSC, HAK Office files, box 132 and NSC, Country files, box 638; and NAUK, PREM 15/1765. Israelyan, *Inside the Kremlin*, pp. 103–49. "Secret/Sensitive," October 16, 1973, RMN, NSC files, HAK Office files, box 132, p. 1 (quote). Quandt, *Peace process*, pp. 118–20.

54. Daigle, *Limits*, pp. 332–37. "7 Arab states end US oil embargo," *Boston Globe*, March 19, 1974, pp. 1, 14. "Suez Canal reopens today after 8 years," *Boston Globe*, June 5, 1975, pp. 1, 15.

55. Daigle, *Limits*, p. 338. Gorenberg, *Accidental empire*, pp. 258–59. Shlaim, *Iron wall*, p. 323.

56. Kenneth W. Stein, *Heroic diplomacy* (Routledge, 1999), pp. 117–86. Quandt, *Peace process*, pp. 154–56.

10   The Palestinians

1. Yezid Sayigh, *Armed struggle and the search for state* (Oxford University Press, 1997), pp. 37, 39–41. Edward H. Buehrig, *UN and the Palestinian refugees* (Indiana University Press, 1972), p. 41.

2. "Memorandum," June 29, 1945, National Archives of the United Kingdom [NAUK], FO 371/45239, pp. 93–94.

3. Rashid Khalidi, *The iron cage* (OneWorld Publications, 2007), pp. 31–90, 108–24. Bayan Nuweihid al-Hout, "The Palestinian political elite during the mandate period," *Journal of Palestine Studies*, 9/1 (1979), pp. 85–111. Benny Morris, *The birth of the Palestinian refugee problem revisited* (Cambridge University Press, 2004), pp. 12–13, 28–29. Zvi Elpeleg, *The Grand Mufti* (Frank Cass, 1993), pp. 63–73. Klaus Gensicke, *Der Mufti von Jerusalem und die Nationalsozialisten* (Wissenschaftliche Buchgesellschaft, 2001).

4. Morris, *Birth*, pp. 65–139, 163–265, 309–34, 342–95. Nafez Nazzal, *The Palestinian exodus from Galilee, 1948* (Institute for Palestine Studies, 1978), pp. 102–11. Sayigh, *Armed struggle*, p. 37. Walid Khalidi, ed., *All that remains* (Institute for Palestine Studies, 1992). Don Peretz, "Problems of Arab refugee compensation," *Middle East Journal*, 8/4

(1954), pp. 403–16. Ilan Pappé, *A history of modern Palestine*, 2nd ed. (Cambridge University Press, 2006), p. 138.

5. Sayigh, *Armed struggle*, pp. 39–41. Pappé, *History*, pp. 142. Buehrig, *UN and the Palestinian refugees.*

6. Ilan Pappé, *Britain and the Arab–Israeli Conflict, 1948–51* (Macmillan, 1988), pp. 89–96. Avi Shlaim, "The rise and the fall of the all-Palestine government in Gaza," *Journal of Palestine Studies*, 20/1 (1990), pp. 37–53. Elpeleg, *Grand Mufti*, pp. 124–38. "New rebuff to Mufti," *New York Times* [*NYT*], March 19, 1952, p. 2. "Ex-Mufti ordered to leave Cairo," *Jerusalem Post*, January 17, 1955, p. 1.

7. Sayigh, *Armed struggle*, pp. 59–60. Various documents: NAUK, FO 371/115866–115867. Neil Caplan, *The Lausanne Conference, 1949* (The Moshe Dayan Center for Middle Eastern and African Studies, 1993), p. 20. "Mr. Shuckburgh's conversations with Egyptian ministers," December 20, 1954, National Archives of Australia [NAA], Series A1838, 163/7/1 Part 1, p. 1.

8. Sayigh, *Armed struggle*, pp. 60–65.

9. Sayigh, *Armed struggle*, p. 96. Philip Mattar, ed., *Encyclopedia of the modern Middle East and North Africa* (Thomson Gale, 2004), pp. 2061–62. Taysir Jbara, *Palestinian leader Hajj Amin Al-Husayni* (Kingston Press, 1985), p. 191. Various documents: NAUK, FO 371/ 97863 and 104196.

10. Elpeleg, *Grand Mufti*, pp. 131–32. Ahmad al-Shuqayri, *Min al-qimma ila al-hazima ma' al-muluk wa al-ru'asa'* (Dar al-awda, 1971), pp. 264–65. Various documents: NAUK, FO 371/127152. Ahmad al-Shuqayri, *Arba'un 'aaman fi al-haya al-'arabiyya wa al-duawaliyya* (Dar al-nahar, 1969), pp. 745, 784–85, 840–55.

11. Laurie Brand, "Nasir's Egypt and the reemergence of the Palestinian national movement," *Journal of Palestine Studies*, 17/2 (1988), pp. 29–41. Sayigh, *Armed struggle*, pp. 75–92. Abdel Razzaq Takriti, *Monsoon revolution* (Oxford University Press, 2013), pp. 50–52. James L. Gelvin, *The Israel–Palestine conflict* (Cambridge University Press, 2005), pp. 199–202. Said K. Aburish, *Arafat*, upd. ed. (Bloomsbury, 2004), pp. 52–56. Xiao Sike, "Zhonggong dangshi shang de 'bange renwu'," *Dangde jianshe* 2006/4, pp. 25–26.

12. Moshe Shemesh, "The founding of the PLO 1964," *Middle Eastern Studies*, 20/4 (1984), pp. 107–17. Various documents: NAUK, FO 371/150869. Sayigh, *Armed struggle*, p. 96. Elpeleg, *Grand Mufti*, pp. 138–45. Aburish, *Arafat*, pp. 55–57.

13. "No. 46," January 18, 1964, NAUK, FO 371/175556, pp. 1–2 (quotes). Sayigh, *Armed struggle*, pp. 96–97, 122. Shemesh, "Founding," pp. 126–35. Various documents: NAUK, FO 371/175556, 175558, and 175562.

14. Sayigh, *Armed struggle*, p. 99. Shemesh, "Founding," pp. 122–29. "National Covenant of the Palestine Liberation Organisation, First Arab Palestine Congress," Jerusalem, May 28, 1964, Mahdi abdul Hadi, *Documents on Palestine*, vol. 2 (Palestinian Academic Society for the Study of International Affairs, no year), pp. 230–31 (quote). Various documents: NAUK, FO 371/175560, 175562 and 175563.

15. Shemesh, "Founding," p. 131. Abu Iyad, and Eric Rouleau, *My home, my land* (Times Books, 1981), p. 41–49. Aburish, *Arafat*, pp. 8–9. Janet Wallach

and John Wallach, *Arafat*, rev., upd. ed. (Birch Lane, 1997), pp. 123–24. Moshe Shemesh, "The Fida'iyyun organization's contribution to the descent to the Six-Day War," *Israel Studies*, 11/1 (2006), pp. 24–26.

16. "The record of the second talk of Premier Zhou Enlai with President Nasser," December 17, 1963, Waijiaobu Dang'anguan [WJBDAG], 107–01027-06, pp. 32–33 (first quote). Several documents in WJBDAG, 107–01065-01, 107–01065-06. Al-Shuqayri, *Min al-qimma*, pp. 132, 266, 302–7, 323–24. John K. Cooley, "China and the Palestinians," *Journal of Palestine Studies*, 1/2 (1972), p. 21. Shi Yanchun, "Zhou Enlai yu Zhongdong," *Dangshi zongheng*, 2006/1, p. 8. Sayigh, *Armed struggle*, p. 141. "Information," November 23, 1965, Stiftung Archiv der Parteien und Massenorganisationen der DDR im Bundesarchiv [SAPMO-BArch], DY 30/IV A 2/20/833, p. 8 (second quote).

17. "Note on a talk with Mister Bassam Atary," July 21, 1966, SAPMO-BArch, DY 30/IV A 2/20/859, pp. 1–5. "Shukairy speaks at rally," *NYT*, November 28, 1966, p. 17. Cooley, "China," p. 27. Huang Hua, *Memoirs* (Foreign Languages Press, 2008), p. 199–200. Nigel Disney, "China and the Middle East," *Middle East Research and Information Project [MERIP] Report*, 63 (1977), p. 8. "Statement of Ahmed Shuqayri," June 1, 1967, Arhiv Jugoslavije [AJ], KPR I-5-c/85, p. 1 (first quote). "News conference," June 1, 1967, Fuad A. Jabber, ed., *International documents on Palestine 1967* (Institute for Palestine Studies, 1970), p. 571 (second quote).

18. Paul T. Chamberlin, *The global offensive* (Oxford University Press, 2012), p. 18. Gershon Gorenberg, *The accidental empire* (Times Books, 2006), pp. 42–46. Avi Raz, *The bride and the dowry* (Yale University Press, 2012), pp. 104–13.

19. "Telno. 601," June 14, 1967, NAUK, PREM 13/1621, p. 1 (first quote). Raz, *Bride*, pp. 3, 38–43. "Incoming telegram 011223," June 13, 1967, Lyndon Baines Johnson Presidential Library [LBJ], National Security File 1963–1969, Files of the Special Committee of the NSC, box 4, p. 1 (second to fourth quote). "Memorandum for Mr. Rostow," June 26, 1967, LBJ, National Security File 1963–1969, Files of the Special Committee of the NSC, box 12, pp. 1–2.

20. Raz, *Bride*, pp. 57–65, 122–25. Gorenberg, *Accidental Empire*, pp. 84, 99–120. "Fm TAviv Jul 24/67 confd Cdn eyes only," Library and Archives Canada [LAC], RG25, box 8897, pp. 1–2. "Fm TAviv Aug 2/67 confd," LAC, RG 25, 8863, pp. 1–2. Buehrig, *UN and the Palestinian refugees*, p. 41.

21. Raz, *Bride*, p. 25. Sayigh, *Armed struggle*, pp. 169–70. "Brief information," February 28, 1968, SAPMO-BArch, DY 30/IV A 2/20/859, pp. 1–5. "Political report no. 11," July 17, 1967, SBA, E 2300–01, Akzession 1973/156, box 18, pp. 5–6. "Copy of a telegram no. 291/67," no date, Politisches Archiv des Auswärtigen Amtes, Bestand: Ministerium für Auswärtige Angelegenheiten [PAAA-MfAA], G-A 412, p. 199. Cooley, "China," pp. 21, 28. Hashim S. H. Behbehani, *China's foreign policy in the Arab world, 1955–75* (Kegan Paul International, 1981), p. 62. Zhonggong zhongyang wenxian yanjiushi, ed., *Zhou Enlai nianpu, 1949–1976*, vol. 3 [ZELNP3] (Zhongyang wenxian chubanshe, 1997) p. 256.

22. Sayigh, *Armed struggle*, pp. 155–64, 196–96. Aburish, *Arafat*, pp. 70–71. Wallach, *Arafat*, pp. 135–41. Helena Cobban, *The Palestinian Liberation Organisation* (Cambridge University Press, 1984), pp. 36–37.
23. Cobban, *Palestinian Liberation Organisation*, pp. 41–42. Iyad, *Home*, pp. 58–59. Chamberlin, *Global offensive*, pp. 44–49. Sayigh, *Armed struggle*, pp. 179–81. Aburish, *Arafat*, pp. 88–89. Wallach, *Arafat*, pp. 147–50.
24. "Individual information on the visit of UAR President Nasser," June 27, 1968, Der Bundesbeauftragte für die Unterlagen des Staatssicherheitsdienstes der ehemaligen Deutschen Demokratischen Republik [BStU], MfS HVA 131, pp. 121–23. Aburish, *Arafat*, p. 89. "Moscow tries to ease tensions in Mideast," *Christian Science Monitor* [*CSM*], August 21, 1968, p. 15. "Political report no. 18," August 28, 1968, SBA, E 2300–01, Akzession 1973/156, box 24, pp. 1–3. Chamberlin, *Global offensive*, p. 61. "Fm Beirut Jan23/69 confd no/no standard," LAC, RG25, box 8899, pp. 1–3. "Soviets deny arms to Arab guerrillas," *CSM*, January 25, 1969, p. 1 (quote).
25. Aburish, *Arafat*, p. 90. Cobban, *Palestinian Liberation Organisation*, p. 218. Chamberlin, *Global offensive*, pp. 61–62. John Calabrese, "From flyswatters to silkworms," *Asian Survey*, 30/9, (1990), p. 866. Gulshan Dhanani, "PLO," *Social Scientist*, 10/9 (1982), pp. 54–55. *ZELNP3*, p. 288.
26. Chamberlin, *Global offensive*, p. 71. Bassam Abu Sharif, *Arafat and the dream of Palestine* (Palgrave Macmillan, 2009), pp. 3–4. Sayigh, *Armed struggle*, p. 230. "Note," [April 1968], PAAA-MfAA, C 636/73, p. 43a. Aburish, *Arafat*, p. 96.
27. Chamberlin, *Global offensive*, pp. 26–27, 62–64. "No. 455," September 12, 1969, LAC, RG25, box 8899, p. 1. Behbehani, *China's foreign policy*, pp. 68, 76. "Note," March 19, 1970, PAAA-MfAA, C 641/73, pp. 23–24. Iyad, *Home*, pp. 67–70.
28. Sayigh, *Armed struggle*, pp. 243–53. Avi Shlaim, *Lion of Jordan* (Alfred A. Knopf, 2008), pp. 315–24. Aburish, *Arafat*, pp. 107–8. Iyad, *Home*, p. 73.
29. "Statement of the Palestinian commando organizations," August 9, 1970, Walid Khadduri, ed., *International documents on Palestine, 1970* (Institute for Palestine Studies, 1973), pp. 887–88. "Memorandum for Mr. Henry A. Kissinger," July 31, 1970, Richard Nixon Presidential Library [RMN], NSC, Country files, box 636, pp. 1–3. "Commandos' chief sees Iraqi leaders," *NYT*, August 18, 1970, p. 2 (first and second quotes). Third and fourth quotes from Chamberlin, *Global offensive*, p. 111.
30. "Marxist leader of commandos," *NYT*, June 13, 1970, p. 12. George Habash, *Les révolutionnaires ne meurent jamais* (Fayard, 2008), pp. 92–96, 103. Shlaim, *Lion*, p. 327–28. Sharif, *Arafat*, pp. 26–30. Aburish, *Arafat*, pp. 109–10.
31. Sayigh, *Armed struggle*, pp. 263–67. Said K. Aburish, *Nasser* (St. Martin's Press, 2004), pp. 310–11. Various documents: PAAA-MfAA, C 7662.
32. Lillian Craig Harris, "China's relations with the PLO," *Journal of Palestine Studies*, 7/1 (1977), p. 138. Cooley, "China," p. 30. "Text of Mao's statement urging world revolution against U.S.," *NYT*, May 21, 1970, p. 6. "Political report no. 2," March 4, 1971, SBA, E 2300–01, Akzession 1977/29, box 7, pp. 1–8. Behbehani, *China's foreign policy*, pp. 98–101.

33. "Translation from 'Le Monde' of November 12, 1970, page 14," no date, PAAA-MfAA, C 7662, pp. 84–90. Chamberlin, *Global offensive*, pp. 136–37. Sayigh, *Armed struggle*, pp. 274–79. Shlaim, *Lion*, pp. 346–60.

34. Sayigh, *Armed struggle*, pp. 39, 296–317. David Hirst, *Beware of small states* (Nation Books, 2010), pp. 86–98. Cobban, *Palestinian Liberation Organisation*, p. 64. Chamberlin, *Global offensive*, pp. 73–75. "Stenographic transcript," November 11, 1971, PAAA-MfAA, C 7678, p. 147.

35. Iyad, *Home*, p. 95, 105–8. Sayigh, *Armed struggle*, pp. 307–11. Chamberlin, *Global offensive*, pp. 161–67. "Mister President of the German Democratic Republic," September 17, 1972, PAAA-MfAA, C 7667, pp. 48–51.

36. *ZELNP3*, pp. 456, 486. "Political report no. 32," September 20, 1972, SBA, E 2300–01, Akzession 1977/29, box 17, p. 2 (quote). "Political report no. 30," October 12, 1972, SBA, E 2300–01, Akzession 1977/29, box 13, pp. 1–4.

37. Sayigh, *Armed struggle*, p. 312. "Information on the visit of the PLO delegation in the GDR," March 28, 1973, PAAA-MfAA, C 7678, pp. 43–47 (quote). Chamberlin, *Global offensive*, pp. 175–78.

38. Sayigh, *Armed struggle*, pp. 330–39. Cobban, *Palestinian Liberation Organisation*, pp. 58–59. "Political report no. 22," June 17, 1974, SBA, E 2300–01, Akzession 1977/30, box 13, pp. 1–6. Chamberlin, *Global offensive*, pp. 235–39. "Militants quit Palestine group," *NYT*, September 27, 1974, p. 5. "Brief information no. 32/74," October 24, 1974, PAAA-MfAA, C 7670, p. 90 (quote).

39. Aburish, *Arafat*, pp. 134–35. Chamberlin, *Global offensive*, pp. 225–44. Various documents: RMN, NSC files, HAK Office files, box 139. Victor Israelyan, *Inside the Kremlin during the Yom Kippur War* (Pennsylvania State University Press, 1995), pp. 214, 218. "Brezhnev, Tito focus on Mideast," *NYT*, November 16, 1973, p. 7. "Fm Beirut 270845Z," [November 27, 1973], LAC, RG25, box 8679, pp. 1–2 (quote). "[No title]," August 15, 1974, SAPMO-BArch, DY 30/13970, pp. 1–5. Behbehani, *China's foreign policy*, pp. 116–33.

40. "Arabs seek a Palestine debate at U.N." *NYT*, September 14, 1974, p. 3. "Palestinians win right to appear in U.N. assembly," *NYT*, October 15, 1974, p. 1. "Transcripts of addresses to the U.N. assembly by Arafat and Israeli delegate," *NYT*, November 14, 1974, pp. 22–23 (quotes). Chamberlin, *Global offensive*, pp. 247, 250.

41. See the website, including personal testimonies, at: learnpalestine .politics.ox.ac.uk/learn/part/3, accessed on September 29, 2018.

42. "Statements by Y. Arafat on the situation in the Near East," April 17, 1975, PAAA-MfAA, C 7663, pp. 167–68. "Despatch no. 6/75," October 3, 1975, NAA, Series A4231, 1975/Africa & The Middle East, pp. 5–10 (quote). Sayigh, *Armed struggle*, pp. 358–67. Hirst, *Beware*, pp. 99–102.

11   Asian–African Internationalism

1. Seng Tan and Amitav Acharya, eds., *Bandung revisited* (National University of Singapore Press, 2008). G. H. Jansen, *Afro-Asia and non-alignment* (Faber, 1966), p. 182 (quote). Robert Vitalis, "The midnight ride of Kwame

Nkrumah and other fables of Bandung (Ban-doong)," *Humanity*, 4/2 (2013), p. 266.

2. Vijay Prashad, *The darker nations* (New Press, 2008), pp. 16–30.
3. Michele L. Louro, *Comrades against imperialism* (Cambridge University Press, 2018). Vineet Thakur, "An Asian drama," *International History Review* (online), February 2018, pp. 4–7. Various chapters in Sven Saaler and J. Victor Koschmann, eds., *Pan-Asianism in modern Japanese history* (Routledge, 2007).
4. Jansen, *Afro-Asia*, pp. 41–42 (first quote). Thakur, "Asian drama," p. 5. Various documents: *Selected works of Jawaharlal Nehru*, first series [*JNSW*1], vol. 14 (Orient Longman, 1981), pp. 439, 455–460 (second and third quotes).
5. Various documents: *JNSW*1, vol. 14, pp. 470–473 (first, third and fourth quotes). "Asian Countries' Conference," *New York Times* [*NYT*], May 29, 1946, p. 7 (second quote). Jansen, *Afro-Asia*, p. 43.
6. "Inter-Asian relations," August 22 [16?], 1946, *JNSW*1, vol. 15, pp. 560–66.
7. Asian Relations Organization, *Asian Relations, being report of the proceedings and documentation of the first Asian Relations conference, New Delhi, March–April, 1947* (Asian Relations Organization, 1948), pp. 4–5.
8. "Invitation to inter-Asian relations conference," September 7, 1946, *JNSW*2, vol. 1, pp. 482–83. *Asian Relations*, pp. 8, 263–69. "Soviet looms large at Pan Asiatic parley," *Christian Science Monitor* [*CSM*], March 28, 1947, p. 6.
9. "Strife rakes Delhi as Asia talks open," *Washington Post*, March 24, 1947, p. 2. "Troops enforce curfew to end riots in Delhi," *Globe and Mail*, March 24, 1947, p. 12.
10. "A united Asia for world peace," March 23, 1947, *JNSW*2, vol. 2, pp. 503–9 (quote). *Asian Relations*, pp. 255–57, 311–14.
11. "Arab League agreement on Palestine," March 23, 1947, *Observer*, p. 5. "Fireworks at Delhi talks," *Palestine Post*, March 25, 1947, p. 1. "Breeze in Asian conference," *Times of India* [*ToI*], March 26, 1947, p. 7.
12. "Asiatic ties forged at New Delhi parley," *CSM*, June 13, 1947, p. 6. "Permanent group set up to aid darker peoples," *Afro-American*, April 19, 1947, p. 5. Jansen, *Afro-Asia*, pp. 71–73.
13. "Departmental despatch 52/48," July 9, 1948, National Archives of Australia [NAA], Series A4231, 1948/New Delhi, p. 3. "Asian aid to Indonesia," December 31, 1948, *Palestine Post*, p. 1 (first quote). "Proposal for ministerial conference of Asian countries at New Delhi," December 31, 1948, *JNSW*2, vol. 9, p. 152–53. "My dear Premier," January 17, 1949, Jawaharlal Nehru, *Letters to Chief Ministers, 1947–1964*, vol. 2 (Oxford University Press, 1986), p. 261 (second quote). "India and the world," November 12, 1948, *JNSW*2, vol. 8, p. 318 (third quote).
14. "Basic principles," September 12, 1948, *JNSW*2, vol. 2, p. 611 (first and second quotes). "India's foreign policy," March 8, 1948, *JNSW*2, vol. 5, p. 499 (third quote). "I.1133," January 20, 1949, NAA, Series A1838, 169/11/106A Part 1, p. 1.
15. India, Ministry of Information and Broadcasting, Publications Division, ed., *The Conference on Indonesia, January 20–23, 1949* (United Press, 1949), p. 13.

"Memorandum for the Minister," January 26, 1949, NAA, Series A1838, 383/1/2/5, pp. 1–2. "O.865," January 20, 1949, NAA, Series A1838, 383/1/2/5, pp. 1–2.

16. Various documents: NAA, Series A1838, 383/1/2/5. *Conference on Indonesia*, pp. 14, 33–37, 66–71 (text of resolution). "The voice of the East," *Daily Boston Globe*, August 14, 1947, p. 14. "Palestine partition approved by U. N.," *TofI*, December 1, 1947, p. 8.

17. Various documents: NAA, Series A1838, 169/11/6 Part 1.

18. "Indonesia admitted to United Nations," September 30, 1950, *TofI*, p. 6. "Notes on private conversation with Ambassador Mohammed Mir Khan," no date [April 1954], NAA, Series A1838, 3002/1 Part 5, p. 1. "13-nation red bid hits snags," December 7, 1950, *The Sun*, p. 1 (quote). "U.N. to get Arab–Asian truce plan," *Los Angeles Times* [*LAT*], December 12, 1950, p. 6.

19. "U.N. opens China talks tomorrow," *Daily Boston Globe*, November 15, 1950, pp. 1, 10. "U.S., Red China trade charges in U.N. Council," *Chicago Daily Tribune*, November 29, 1950, p. 1.

20. Wu Xiuquan, *Eight years in the Ministry of Foreign Affairs (January 1950 – October 1958)* (New World Press, 1985), pp. 58–70. "13-nation red bid hits snags," *The Sun*, December 7, 1950, pp. 1, 9. "India's envoy sees Peiping's U.N. aide," *NYT*, December 8, 1950, p. 8. "I.20806," December 19, 1950, NAA, Series A1838, 169/7/1 Part 1, p. 1.

21. "Arab–Asiatic bloc studies India's plan," *The Sun*, December 11, 1950, p. 1. "U.N. picks 3-man team to seek Korea cease-fire," *Daily Boston Globe*, December 15, 1950, pp. 1, 14 (first quote). "Peace in Korea," *CSM*, June 7, 1951, p. 13 (second quote). "Red Chinese reject U.N.'s peace scheme," *The Sun*, December 23, 1950, p. 2 (third quote).

22. "12 to push peace accord," *NYT*, January 4, 1951, p. 4. "Arab-Asian leaders meet in Cairo today," *The Sun*, January 20, 1951, p. 2. "Asian-Arab bloc seeks way to 'clarify' Peiping proposal," *NYT*, January 25, 1951, p. 3 (quote). "U.S. rejects Arab–Asian peace plan," *Hartford Courant*, January 28, 1951, p. 1. "Arab–Asian truce move rejected at night session," *Washington Post*, January 31, 1951, p. 1.

23. "Africans, Arabs, Asians demand Tunisia hearing," *Chicago Daily Tribune*, January 31, 1952, p. 9. "France urged to quit U.N.," *TofI*, November 1, 1952, p. 1. "French shun U.N. in Tunisia debate," *NYT*, December 5, 1952, p. 1. "Arabs, Asians seek support on Morocco," *Jerusalem Post*, December 15, 1952, p. 1. "Tunis accord urged in U.N.," *The Sun*, December 9, 1952, p. 1. "U.N. urges France and Tunisia to negotiate," *LAT*, December 18, 1952, p. 10.

24. "Asian–Arab bloc meets," *NYT*, December 24, 1952, p. 4 (first quote). "Arab–Asian setbacks," *CSM*, December 19, 1952, p. 22. "Arab committee meets," *Hartford Courant*, December 21, 1952, p. A16. "13 nations warn France," *Chicago Daily Tribune*, December 25, 1952, p. 20 (second and third quotes).

25. "Cairo rally sponsored," *NYT*, August 27, 1953, p. 5. "Big Three solid, against U.N. action on Morocco," *LAT*, August 28, 1953, p. 8.

26. "Afro-Asian group in U.N.," October 12, 1953, *JNSW2*, vol. 24, pp. 553–54 (first to fourth quote). "Egypt's bid for Arab–Asian chiefs' talks," *TofI*,

February 1, 1954, p. 1 (fifth quote). "Arab–Asian Conference," March 25, 1954, Library and Archives Canada [LAC], RG25, box 8146, pp. 1–2 (sixth quote).

27. "Indonesian proposal for an Afro-Asian conference," April 6, 1954, and "India and the international situation," May 15, 1954, *JNSW2*, vol. 25, pp. 503, 398 (quote).

28. "Ministers gather in Colombo," *Globe and Mail*, April 28, 1954, p. 32. "Six point proposal on Indo-China," *JNSW2*, vol. 25, pp. 423–26. "Pakistan newsletter," *TofI*, April 27, 1954, p. 6. "Ceylon to stress red period to Asia," *NYT*, April 25, 1954, p. 2. "Development of S.-E. Asia," *TofI*, April 27, 1954, p. 1. "Permanent body to deal with Asian affairs," *TofI*, April 17, 1954, p. 11. Cindy Ewing, "The Colombo Powers," *Cold War History*, 18/2 (2018), pp. 1–19.

29. "Text of South Asian Prime Ministers' communiqué," *NYT*, May 2, 1954, p. 2 (first quote). "Vain Pak bid to raise Kashmir issue at Premiers' talks," *TofI*, April 29, 1954, p. 1. "Asia ministers reach deadlock on Indo-China," *Globe and Mail*, April 30, 1954, p. 10. "Asia chiefs split in liberty perils," *NYT*, April 30, 1954, p. 3. "Five Asians will extend conference," *Hartford Courant*, May 1, 1954, p. 6D. "Talks show India doesn't rule Asia," *NYT*, May 3, 1954, p. 8 (second and third quotes).

30. Jansen, *Afro-Asia*, p. 170. Ewing, "Colombo Powers," pp. 12–14. "To Ali Sastroamidjojo," August 18, 1954, *JNSW2*, vol. 26, pp. 424–28 (quote). Various documents: NAA, Series A1838, 3002/1 Part 1, and *JNSW2*, vol. 26, pp. 318–32, 429–34.

31. "I.14900," December 30, 1954, NAA, Series A1838, 851/19/11, p. 62 (quote). Various documents: *JNSW2*, vol. 27, pp. 107–12; NAA, Series A11604, 604/2/2 Part 2 and Series A1838, 3002/1 Part 2. "Joint communiqué," no date, National Archives of India [NAI], External Affairs, 1 (44)-AAC, 1955, pp. 54–59. Apart from the five Colombo Powers, the invited nations were: Afghanistan, Cambodia, the PRC, the Central African Federation, Egypt, Ethiopia, the Gold Coast (Ghana), Iran, Iraq, Japan, Jordan, Laos, Lebanon, Liberia, Libya, Nepal, the Philippines, Saudi Arabia, Sudan, Syria, Thailand, Turkey, the DRV, the SVN, and Yemen.

32. "I.58," January 3, 1955, *NAA*, Series A1838, 851/19/11, p. 63. "Note," no date, Arhiv Jugoslavije [AJ], KPR I-2/4–1, p. 1 (first quote). "Memo. no. 30/ 54," January 10, 1955, NAA, Series A1838, 3002/1 Part 2, p. 2 (second and third quotes). "Despatch no. 4," April 6, 1955, NAA, Series A1838, 3002/1 Part 4, p. 1 (fourth and fifth quotes). "Memo. no. 31/55," January 14, 1955, NAA, Series A1838, 3002/1 Part 2, p. 1 (sixth and seventh quotes).

33. Jansen, *Afro-Asia*, pp. 188–89. Various documents: NAA, Series A11604, 604/2/2 Part 2 and Series A1838, 3002/1 Part 8. Ewing, "Colombo Powers," pp. 14–15.

34. "Talks with Pham Van Dong," April 9, 1955, *JNSW2*, vol. 28, pp. 188–90. "Outwards cable 121," April 16, 1955, NAA, Series A11604, 604/2/2 Part 2, p. 1 (quote). "Conversation with Gamal Abdel Nasser," April 14, 1955, *JNSW2*, vol. 28, pp. 216–17. Muhammad H. Haykal [Heikal], *The sphinx and the commissar* (Harper & Row, 1978), pp. 57–59.

35. "Memo no. 439," May 9, 1955, NAA, Series A1838, 3002/1 Part 6, pp. 1–2. "Some impressions of the Bandung conference," no date, NAA, Series A1838, 3002/1 Part 7, pp. 198–90 (quote).
36. "Bandung," no date, NAA, Series A11604, 604/2/2 PART 2, p. 5 (first to third quote). "Some impressions of the Bandung Conference," no date, NAA, Series A1838, 3002/1 Part 7, pp. 193–92 (fourth quote).
37. "Nehru's temper flares at talks," April 19, 1955, *NYT*, p. 3. Various documents: NAA, Series A1838, 3002/1 Parts 5 and 8. "Some impressions of the Bandung conference," no date, NAA, Series A1838, 3002/1 Part 7, pp. 198–97 (first and second quotes). "Bandung meeting asked to assail red colonialism," *NYT*, April 22, 1955, p. 1. "Notes on Asian–African conference – Djakarta," no date, and "Report on Asian–African conference – Bandung," no date, NAA, Series A1838, 3002/1 Part 8, pp. 107 (third quote) and 81 (fourth quote).
38. "Rebuffs to Reds and Nehru bring Bandung discord," *NYT*, April 19, 1955, p. 1. Various documents: NAA, Series A1838, 3002/1 Part 8. For talks: "[Letter] 23," April 28, 1955, Nehru, *Letters*, vol. 4, pp. 167–68. "Mr. Nehru," no date, NAA, Series A1838, 3002/1 Part 6, p. 1. "Report on Asian–African Conference – Bandung," no date, NAA, Series A1838, 3002/1 Part 8, pp. 76–75 (first quote). "Neighbor nations get Red's pledge," *NYT*, April 24, 1955, p. 6. "Record of talk given by Dr. Charles Malik," April 28, 1955, NAA, Series A1838, 851/19/11, p. 141 (second quote).
39. "Some impressions of the Bandung Conference," no date, NAA, Series A1838, 3002/1 Part 7, p. 196. "The Asian–African Conference," no date, NAA, Series A1838, 3002/1 Part 5, p. 2 (quote). Mohamed Abdel Khalek Hassouna, *The first Asian–African Conference held at Bandung, Indonesia (April 18–24, 1955)* (Misr Imprimerie, 1955), pp. 25–26. Ahmad al-Shuqayri, *Min al-qimma ila al-hazima ma' al-muluk wa al-ru'asa'* (Dar al-awda, 1971), p. 265.
40. "Arab states map Bandung tactics," *NYT*, April 18, 1955, p. 2. "Radio News Service," April 22, 1955, NAA, Series A1838, 3002/1 Part 5, p. 1. Al-Shuqayri, *Min al-qimma*, p. 265. "Bandung meeting asked to assail red colonialism," *NYT*, April 22, 1955, pp. 1, 2.
41. "Pacts cause war," *Irish Times*, April 23, 1955, NAA, Series A1838, 3002/1 Part 6, p. 1. "The Asian–African Conference," no date, NAA, Series A1838, 3002/1 Part 5, p. 3. "From the speech by Nehru," no date, Politisches Archiv des Auswärtigen Amtes, Bestand: Ministerium für Auswärtige Angelegenheiten [PAAA-MfAA], A 6662, p. 92. "Report on Asian–African Conference – Bandung," no date, NAA, Series A1838, 3002/1 Part 8, p. 77 (first quote). "Some impressions of the Bandung Conference," no date, NAA, Series A1838, 3002/1 Part 7, pp. 195–94 (second quote).
42. "Bandung Conference communiqué," April 24, 1955, NAA, Series A1838, 3002/1 Part 5, pp. 1–7 (quote).
43. "Nasir proposes second Asian-African conference in Cairo," April 23, 1955, NAA, Series A1838, 3002/1 Part 5, p. 1. Jansen, *Afro-Asia*, p. 221. Mao Yufeng, "When Zhou Enlai met Gamal Abdel Nasser," Antonia Finnane and Derek McDougall, eds., *Bandung 1955* (Monash University Press, 2010), p. 98.

44. Jansen, *Afro-Asia*, p. 74. "Reds beaten by one vote at Bandoeng," *The Herald*, April 26, 1955, NAA, Series A1838, 3002/1 Part 5, p. 1."Notes of a conversation with General Raza," May 3, 1955, NAA, Series A11604, 604/2/2 Part 2, p. 1 (first quote). "The Pakistani Ambassador (Khaliquzzaman)," no date, NAA, Series A1838, 3002/1 Part 6, p. 1 (second and third quotes).

45. "Conversation on 9th May, 1954 with Mr. Max Maramis," no date, NAA, Series A4231, 1954/Djakarta, p. 1 (first quote). "I.14553," November 4, 1956, NAA, Series A1838, 169/7/1 Part 6, p. 1. "I.15444," November 12, 1956, NAA, Series A1838, 189/11/20 Part 1, p. 1 (second quote). "Memo no. 1045," June 30, 1964, NAA, Series A1838, 169/11/106 Part 3, pp. 1–2.

46. "Mr. Nehru," no date, NAA, Series A1838, 3002/1 Part 6, p. 1. "Despatch no. 11/55," May 30, 1955, NAA, Series A1838, TS654/8/10/5, p. 1 (first quote). "Memo no. 488," May 4, 1955, NAA, Series A1838, 3002/1 Part 6, pp. 1–2 (second and third quotes). "Telegram no. 9," May 2, 1955, NAA, Series A1838, 3002/1 Part 5, pp. 1–2 (fourth quote).

47. "A commonwealth of Afro-Asian countries," March 9, 1957, *JNSW*2, vol. 37, p. 555. "Memo no. 853," October 24, 1962, NAA, Series A1838, 169/7/1 Part 9, p. 1.

48. "Nkrumah and Nasser rivalry is friendly," *Philadelphia Tribune*, July 22, 1958, p. 1. Vitalis, "Midnight ride," p. 275. "Nkrumah calls for unity to bring freedom to Africa," *Irish Times*, December 9, 1958, p. 1.

49. Various documents: NAA, Series A1838, 3002/1 Part 4 and 69/1/4/31 Part 1. "Two conferences," *Jerusalem Post*, December 15, 1958, p. 4 (quote).

50. "Conference of Bandung," January 8, 1960, Schweizerisches Bundesarchiv [SBA], E 2300, Akzession 1000/716, box 302, pp. 1–2. "Fm Jakarta Jan12/63 confd," LAC, RG25, box 5201, p. 1. Zhonggong zhongyang wenxian yanjiushi, ed., *Zhou Enlai nianpu, 1949–1976*, vol. 2 (Zhongyang wenxian chubanshe, 1997, pp. 550–51, 603, 612, 6161, 620, 757–59 (second quote). "Fm Colombo Oct17/63 conf," LAC, RG25, box 8885, p. 1 (first quote). "Conc.: 2nd Afro-Asian conference in Algiers," January 3, 1965, PAAA-MfAA, A 13344, pp. 1–5. "Report on the talks of Nasser in Moscow," September 28, 1965, Stiftung Archiv der Parteien und Massenorganisationen der DDR im Bundesarchiv [SAPMO-BArch], DY 30/J IV 2/2J/1512, pp. 1–7. "Chou, in Tanzania, calls U.S. a bully," *NYT*, June 6, 1965, p. 1. "Africa–Asia talk off indefinitely," *NYT*, November 2, 1965, p. 6.

51. Robert S. Walters, "International organizations and political communication," *International Organization*, 25/4 (1971), pp. 818–35.

52. "The glory of Islam," no date, NAA, Series A1838, 3002/1 Part 7, p. 1. Various documents: National Archives of the United Kingdom [NAUK], FO 371/180378 and 185517, and FCO 8/1201.

12   Non-Alignment

1. "Enclosure," August 15, 1956, Jawaharlal Nehru, Jawaharlal Nehru, *Letters to Chief Ministers, 1947–1964*, vol. 4 (Oxford University Press, 1988), p. 416 (quote). "Joint communiqué," [July 18, 1956], Arhiv Jugoslavije [AJ], KPR I-4-a/6, pp. 7–8.

2. Lorenz M. Lüthi, "Non-Alignment, 1946–1965," *Humanity*, 7/2 (2016), pp. 201–23.
3. "No departure from past pledges," May 2, 1949, *JNSW2*, vol. 11, p. 300 (first quote). "Free India's foreign policy," March 15, 1946, *JNSW1*, vol. 15, p. 525 (second quote). "Basic principles," September 12, 1948, *JNSW2*, vol. 7, p. 612 (third quote). "Salient features of India's foreign policy," March 16, 1950, *JNSW2*, vol. 14-I, p. 475 (fourth quote). "To James Loeb Jr.," October 25, 1951, *JNSW2*, vol. 16-II, p. 599 (fifth and sixth quotes). "My dear Chief Minister," January 27, 1953, *JNSW2*, vol. 21, p. 581. "My dear Chief Minister," December 22, 1962, Nehru, *Letters*, vol. 5, p. 564 (seventh quote).
4. "Tito to shut his door on Greek fight," *Chicago Daily Tribune*, July 11, 1949, p. 1. "Tito signs agreement with U.S.," *Washington Post* [*WaPo*], November 15, 1951, p. 2. "Editorial note," United States, Department of State, *Foreign relations of the United States* [*FRUS*], 1951, IV (U.S. Government Printing Office, 1985), pp. 1862–63. "The Ambassador in Yugoslavia (Allen) to the Department of State," January 8, 1953, *FRUS*, 1952–54, VIII, p. 1334 (quotes). Svetozar Rajak, *Yugoslavia and the Soviet Union in the early Cold War* (Routledge, 2011), pp. 38–44, 88, 91. "Tito denies he'll join Nehru's neutral bloc," *WaPo*, October 4, 1954, p. 13.
5. Various documents: AJ, KPR I-2/4–1, pp. 1–3. "Text of the Nehru–Tito joint statement," *New York Times* [*NYT*], December 24, 1954, p. 2 (quotes). "My dear Chief Minister," December 24, 1954, *JNSW2*, vol. 27, p. 558.
6. Elie Podeh, "The drift towards neutrality," *Middle Eastern Studies*, 32/1 (2006), pp. 159–78. "Memo no. 600/53," March 3, 1953, National Archives of Australia [NAA], Series A1838, 163/11/148, pp. 1–2. "Memo no. 940/53," May 5, 1953, NAA, Series A1838, 181/2/1 Part 3, p. 1 (first and second quotes). "My dear Chief Minister," July 2, 1953, *JNSW2*, vol. 23, p. 571 (third quote). "Memo no. 60," January 12, 1954, NAA, Series A1838, 163/7/1 Part 1, pp. 1–2 (fourth quote). "Memo no. 511," April 20, 1954, NAA, Series A1838, 163/7/1 Part 1, p. 1 (fifth quote). "Conversation," February 5, 1955, AJ, KPR I-2/4–3, pp. 1–21. "Egyptian premier backs Nehru View," *NYT*, February 17, 1955, p. 2. "My dear Chief Minister," February 23, 1955, *JNSW2*, vol. 28, p. 567 (sixth quote).
7. "Nehru and Nasser score alliances," *NYT*, July 13, 1955, p. 8 (first quote). "To Ali Yavar Jung," September 8, 1954, *JNSW2*, vol. 26, p. 525. Jovan Čavoški, "Constructing Nasser's neutralism," Lorenz M. Lüthi, ed., *The regional Cold Wars in Europe, East Asia, and the Middle East* (Woodrow Wilson Center Press / Stanford University Press, 2015), pp. 88–107. "Note," [January 5, 1956], AJ, KPR I-2/5–2, p. 2 (second quote).
8. "Enclosure," August 15, 1956, Nehru, *Letters*, vol. 4, p. 416. "Despatch no. 10/56," July 26, 1956, NAA, Series A4231, 1956/Cairo, pp. 1–2 (first quote). "Joint communiqué," [July 18, 1956], AJ, KPR I-4-a/6, pp. 7–8 (second and third quotes). "Enclosure," August 15, 1956, Nehru, *Letters*, vol. 4, p. 416 (fourth quote).
9. Several documents: *JNSW2*, vol. 34, 318–20, and LAC, RG25, boxes 6107–6109.

10. "Mister Minister," May 31, 1957, Schweizerisches Bundesarchiv [SBA], E 2300, Akzession 1000/716, box 301, pp. 1–2. "Nasir proposes second Asian-African conference in Cairo," April 23, 1955, NAA, Series A1838, 3002/1 Part 5, p. 1. "Note on Interview," June 9, 1958, Nehru Memorial Museum and Library [NMML], Subimal Dutt Papers, Subject Files, file no. 32, pp. 3–5.

11. "Note on interview," June 11, 1958, NMML, Subimal Dutt Papers, Subject Files, file no. 32, p. 9 (first quote). In the original, Yugoslavia is underlined, not in italics. "Message to Djuanda Kartawidjaja," July 23, 1958, *JNSW2*, vol. 43, p. 491. "Memo no. 3," January 4, 1959, NAA, Series A1838, 3016/11/147 Part 1, p. 213 (second and third quotes).

12. "Nasser calls for summit talks by leaders of neutralist bloc," *NYT*, May 18, 1959, p. 3. "Conference of the 'big four' and the 'non-aligned' countries," May 25, 1959, SBA, E 2300, Akzession 1000/716, box 302, pp. 1–2. "Tito sees neutrals in jeopardy," *Hartford Courant*, November 23, 1959, p. 13B. "CCB no. 16338," December 12, 1959, National Archives of India [NAI], External Affairs, 21-A (2)-WANA, 1960, p. 1.

13. "My dear Dutt," January 7, 1960, NAI, External Affairs, 21-A (2)-WANA, 1960, p. 7. "Conference of Bandung," January 8, 1960, SBA, E 2300, Akzession 1000/716, box 302, p. 1 (first quote). "Official visit by Nasser to India (March 29 to April 9)," April 5, 1960, SBA, E 2300, Akzession 1000/716, box 302, p. 1 (second and third quotes).

14. "Note," [June 14, 1960], AJ, KPR I-3-a/121–15, pp. 1–15. "Bigger say in UN urged for uncommitted nations," *Christian Science Monitor* [*CSM*], June 21, 1960, p. 6 (quotes).

15. "Neutrals come into their own at U.N. General Assembly," *WaPo*, September 21, 1960, p. A6.

16. "Tito as mediator," October 6, 1960, *NYT*, p. 17. No Indian and Yugoslav documents on the proceedings in New York have surfaced, with the exception of Tito's 25-page report on mostly unrelated issues: "Report," October 13, 1960, AJ, KPR I-2/12, pp. 1–25; I am grateful to Jovan Čavoški and Lyubodrag Dimić for this document. "Neutralist bloc forming at U.N.," *NYT*, September 24, 1960, p. 1. "Tito host to neutralist chiefs in private 'summit' session," *WaPo*, September 30, 1960, p. A13 (first quote). "Nasser and Tito weigh mediation," *NYT*, September 25, 1960, p. 1. "Neutralists assert their power at U.N.," *NYT*, October 2, 1960, p. E4. "Neutrals woo Asia–Africa bloc," *NYT*, October 5, 1960, p. 1. Lorenz M. Lüthi, *The Sino-Soviet split* (Princeton University Press, 2008), p. 185. "Tito thinks neutrals failed at mediation," *Globe and Mail*, October 5, 1960, p. 3 (second quote). "My dear Chief Minister," October 23, 1960, Nehru, *Letters*, vol. 5, p. 413 (third quote).

17. Dragan Bogetič and Lyubormir Dimić, *Beogradska Konferenziya nesvrstanikh zemela 1–6, Septembra 1961* (Zavod za Uzbenike, 2013), pp. 95–108. "Report," no date, AJ, KPR I-2/13, pp. 1–40. "On the summit meeting," May 18, 1961, Politisches Archiv des Auswärtigen Amtes, Bestand: Ministerium für Auswärtige Angelegenheiten [PAAA-MfAA], A 12618, pp. 97–99. The letter is in "To remind," no date, AJ, KPR I-4-a/1, 1, pp. 1–2

(quote). The countries invited were Afghanistan, the "Maghreb," Brazil, Burma, Cambodia, Ceylon, Cuba, Egypt, Ethiopia, Ghana, Guinea, India, Indonesia, Iraq, Mali, Mexico, Nepal, Saudi Arabia, Somalia, Sudan, Yemen, Venezuela, and Yugoslavia.

18. "Summit conference of non-aligned nations," *Times of India* [*TofI*], May 6, 1961, p. 1. "On the planned conference of the so-called non-aligned countries," May 15, 1961, PAAA-MfAA, A 5298, p. 54. "My dear Chief Minister," June 27, 1961, Nehru, *Letters*, vol. 5, p. 449 (first quote). "Neutrals revise plans for talks," *NYT*, May 14, 1961, p. 7 (second quote). "Final report," June 12, 1961, AJ, KPR I-4-a/1, pp. 9–10 (third and fourth quotes).

19. The participating countries were Afghanistan, Algeria, Burma, Cambodia, Ceylon, the Congo (Léopoldville), Cuba, Cyprus, Egypt, Ethiopia, Ghana, Guinea, India, Indonesia, Iraq, Lebanon, Mali, Morocco, Nepal, Saudi Arabia, Somalia, Sudan, Tunisia, Yemen, and Yugoslavia. "Khrushchev asserts his aim is to shock allies into a parley," *NYT*, September 2, 1961, p. 1. Test mentioned: "Moscow agrees to resume talks on atom test ban," *NYT*, November 22, 1961, p. 1.

20. "Neutrals at Belgrade talk angered by Kremlin move," *NYT*, September 1, 1961, p. 1. For all speeches: [Yugoslavia,] *The Conference of Heads of State or Government of Non-Aligned Countries, Belgrade, September 1–6, 1961* (Publicističko-Izdavački Zavod Jugoslavija, 1961), pp. 25–152. "Memo no. 1280," August 30, 1961, NAA, Series A1838, 169/7/1 Part 9, p. 1 (first quote). "Nehru among the neutrals," *CSM*, September 6, 1961, p. 14. "Belgrade conference appeal," no date, John F. Kennedy Presidential Library [JFK], online archive: www.jfklibrary.org/Asset-Viewer/Archives/JFKPO F-104–004.aspx (accessed on July 8, 2014), no page numbers (second quote). "Declaration," September 6, 1961, AJ, KPR I-4-a/2, pp. 1–14 (third quote).

21. "Your Excellency," no date, AJ, KPR I-4-a/2, pp. 1–2. "Joint message," September 27, 1961, AJ, KPR I-4-a/2, pp. 1–33 (first quote). "Your excellency," September 5, 1961, JFK, online archive: www.jfklibrary.org/Asset-Viewer/Archives/JFKPOF-104–004.aspx (July 8, 2014), no page numbers (second quote). "Memorandum of conversation," September 12, 1961, *FRUS*, 1961–63, V, pp. 288–91.

22. "U.N. asks return to test-ban talk," *NYT*, November 9, 1961, p. 11. "Asians, Africans pass plea to limit a-bombs," *Los Angeles Times*, November 15, 1961, p. A13. "Nehru agrees his neutral camp is too soft on Soviet a-tests," *Boston Globe*, November 13, 1961, p. 8. "Tito seeking support for stand on U.S.," *The Sun*, November 19, 1961, p. 2. "Protocol," [November 19, 1961], AJ, KPR I-2/14, pp. 1–17. "Secret and guard," November 21, 1961, National Archives of the United Kingdom [NAUK], FO 371/161228, p. 6 (quotes).

23. "Moscow agrees to resume talks on atom test ban," *NYT*, November 22, 1961, p. 1. "Test ban parley in Geneva ended," *NYT*, January 30, 1962, p. 1. "U.S.–Soviet accord on U.N. arms unit wins full backing," *NYT*, December 14, 1961, p. 1. "Moscow proposes 18-nation Geneva talks," *CSM*, February 12, 1962, p. 1 (first quote). "JFK orders Air Nuclear Tests," *Newsday*, March 3, 1962, p. 1 (second quote). "Allies back atom tests; neutrals voice regrets," *Hartford Courant*, March 4, 1962, p. 7A (third quote).

24. "17-Nation arms cut talks open today," *Jerusalem Post*, March 14, 1962, p. 1. "Arms talks open as Gromyko says 'no' to inspection," *NYT*, March 15, 1962, p. 1. "Neutral camp is active at Geneva," *TofI*, March 19, 1962, p. 7. "Neutrals add pressure for ban on a-tests," *WaPo*, March 21, 1962, p. A14. "The crucial Soviet equation," *Observer*, March 25, 1962, p. 11 (quote). Lorenz M. Lüthi, "Non-Alignment, 1961–1974," Sandra Bott, Jussi M. Hanhimäki, Janick Schaufelbuehl, and Marco Wyss, eds., *Neutrality and neutralism in the global Cold War* (Routledge, 2016), p. 93. "Neutral nations disappointed," *Guardian*, April 26, 1962, p. 1. "U.S. defends new a-tests to neutrals," *Chicago Daily Tribune*, May 4, 1962, p. 9.

25. Aleksandr A. Fursenko and Timothy Naftali, *One hell of a gamble* (Norton, 1997), pp. 177–97. Lüthi, *Sino-Soviet split*, pp. 251–52. "Disillusionment of neutral powers over disarmament," *Irish Times*, August 27, 1962, p. 9.

26. Lüthi, *Sino-Soviet split*, pp. 246–72. "Atom test ban hailed as big step to peace," *Chicago Tribune*, July 28, 1963, p. N4.

27. "Main points," no date, Library and Archives Canada [LAC], RG25, box 5201, p. 1 (quote). Various documents: LAC, RG25, box 5201, 6083–40, part 9.1 and 9.2.

28. "Colombo: fear of China is haunting," *NYT*, December 17, 1962, p. 11. Various documents: LAC, RG25, box 5201.

29. "The record of the talk of Zhou Enlai receiving the Egyptian ambassador in China, Iman," April 21, 1963, Waijiaobu Dang'anguan [WJBDAG], 107–01004-01, pp. 7–12. "I. 12211," May 6, 1963, NAA, Series A1838, 169/7/1 Part 9, pp. 1–2. "Information," February 6, 1963, PAAA-MfAA, C 1738/76, pp. 22–33.

30. "The circumstance of the talk of Fekki with Ambassador Chen," September 9, 1963, WJBDAG, 107–00523-03, pp. 24–25. "No. 706," November 30, 1962, LAC, RG25, box 5201, p. 1. "Outline of the report of the visit to 14 countries," May 27, 1964, WJBDAG, 203–00495-01, pp. 1–26. "Great and good friend," February 16, 1964, AJ, KPR I-4-a/4, pp. 1–3. "Copy of letter dated March 7, 1964, from Dr. Subandrio," no date, NAI, External Affairs, 118 (78)/WII/64, pp. 1–4. "Statements by Nehru on foreign policy before the Lok Sabha on April 13, 1964," April 17, 1964, Bundesarchiv Koblenz [BA Koblenz], B 136/3045, p. 5 (quote). "Chinese govt. bid to prevent meeting: summit conference of non-aligned states," *TofI*, May 17, 1961, p. 7.

31. "List," no date, PAAA-MfAA, A 17984, pp. 109–11. "Declaration," no date, AJ, KPR I-4-a/6, pp. 17–31. "Declaration of Cairo second non-aligned conference on non-dissemination of nuclear weapons, issued at Cairo, October 11, 1964," Lyndon Baines Johnson Presidential Library [LBJ], National Security File 1963–1969, Committee on Nuclear Proliferation, box 5, p. 1 (quote).

32. "Prime Minister Shastri presents five-point peace programme," October 8, 1964, NAA, Series A1838, 169/11/87 Part 26, p. 125 (quote). Zhonggong zhongyang wenxian yanjiushi, ed., *Zhou Enlai nianpu, 1949–1976*, vol. 2 (Zhongyang wenxian chubanshe, 1997), pp. 675–76. "[UAR President Nasser's telegram to Premier Zhou Enlai]," October 20, 1964, WJBDAG,

107–00575-09, pp. 197–98. "Memorandum no. 1965," October 20, 1964, NAA, Series A1838, 169/11/87 Part 26, pp. 153–52.

33. "Note," [September 1, 1965], AJ, KPR I-3-a/121–36, pp. 1–49. "The Under Secretary of State for External Affairs, Ottawa," September 13, 1965, LAC, RG25, box 8885, pp. 1–4. "[No title]," no date, NMML, T. N. Kaul Papers, I to III Installment, Subject Files, file no. 15, pp. 63–68.

34. Various documents: AJ, KPR I-5-b/117–5. "Political letter no. 11," May 12, 1966, and "Political report no. 11," November 10, 1966, SBA, E 2300–01, Akzession 1973/156, box 6, pp. 1–4 (quote). "Note for file," November 1, 1966, PAAA-MfAA, C 637/70, pp. 37–41. For the transcripts of talks and communiqué: AJ, KPR I-4-a/6. "Additional information," November 29, 1966, PAAA-MfAA, C 637/70, pp. 12–17.

35. Various reports: AJ, KPR I-5-c/85. "The reaction," no date, PAAA-MfAA, C 453, p. 10. "Note," [July 11–12, 1967], AJ, KPR I-2/34, pp. 1–59. "Information," [September 4–6, 1967], Stiftung Archiv der Parteien und Massenorganisationen der DDR im Bundesarchiv [SAPMO-BArch], DY 30/ J IV 2/2A/1247, pp. 56–63. "Second day of consultations: Wednesday, December 20, 1967," PAAA-MfAA, C 899, pp. 25–68.

36. "Incoming telegram 7533," June 8, 1967, LBJ, National Security File 1963–1969, Files of the Special Committee of the NSC, box 7, p. 1. "Note," no date, AJ, KPR I-5-b/39–7, pp. 1–2. "Break in grain aid looms," NYT, June 16, 1967, p. 13. "My dear Azim," June 19, 1967, and "No. CAI/ 413/A/67," June 22, 1967, NMML, Apa B. Pant, Subject Files, file no. 16, part I, pp. 26–31 (quote) and 59. "Information," no date, PAAA-MfAA, G-A 413, pp. 131–37. "No. CAI/599/A/67," September 21, 1967, NMML, Apa B. Pant, Subject Files, file no.16, part I, p. 269.

37. "Note," April 4, 1968, PAAA-MfAA, C 1575/72, p. 10. Mentioned: "Note on a conversation with the Soviet ambassador, Comrade Abrassimov," February 28, 1968, SAPMO-BArch, DY 30/3634, p. 91.

38. "Yugoslavia bolstering defense against a Soviet intervention," NYT, August 27, 1968, p. 6. "delhi, broj 740," August 21, 1968, AJ, KPR I-5-b/39–8, pp. 1–3 (quotes). "Dear Comrade Minister," September 16, 1968, PAAA-MfAA, C 1194/71, p. 2. "Political report no. 18," August 28, 1968, SBA, E 2300–01, Akzession 1973/156, box 24, pp. 1–3.

39. "Conversation with Mr. Pekic," July 3, 1969, NAUK, FCO 28/867, p. 1. "Note," October 24, 1968, PAAA-MfAA, C 1575/72, pp. 1–2. "Memorandum," no date, NAUK, FCO 28/868, p. 1. "Foreign policy," no date, PAAA-MfAA, C 341/75, pp. 19–20. "Non-Alignment consultative meeting in Belgrade," July 25, 1969, NAUK, FCO 28/868, pp. 1–2 (quote). "Nonaligned bloc ends 4-day talks," NYT, July 12, 1969, p. 5.

40. Peter Willetts, The Non-Aligned Movement (F. Pinter, 1978), pp. 36–43.

41. Lorenz M. Lüthi, "The Non-Aligned Movement and the Cold War, 1961–1973," Journal of Cold War Studies, 18/4 (2016), pp. 42–48. "On the preparations," April 27, 1970, PAAA-MfAA, C 522/72, pp. 60–61. "Report," September 14, 1970, AJ, KPR I-4-a/9, pp. 1–2.

42. "Fm Georgetown 11/1240Z," August 11, 1972, NAUK, FCO 15/1503, pp. 1–2. "Resolution on Indochina," no date, NAUK, FCO 15/1503, pp. 1–3.

43. "Information," no date, AJ, KPR I-2/53, pp. 1–25. "[No title]," November 28, 1973, SAPMO-BArch, DY 30/13951, p. 21.

44. "I.124445," December 7, 1971, NAA, Series A1838, 3107/40/148 Part 11, pp. 114–13. Srinath Raghavan, *War and peace in modern India* (Permanent Black, 2010), p. 242. "The U.N. vote on India," *Chicago Tribune*, December 9, 1971, p. 28. "India losing world sympathy," *CSM*, December 9, 1971, p. 1. "After India's war," *Jerusalem Post*, January 21, 1972, p. A5.

45. "Despatch no. 4/74," July 29, 1974, NAA, Series A4231, 1974/South Asia, pp. 1–8. "Nuclear club keeps growing," *CSM*, June 21, 1974, p. 2.

46. "The Colombo summit of non-aligned states (August 9 – 19th, 1976)," no date, NAUK, FCO 58/980, p. 1. "Non-aligned bloc adds 4 members," *NYT*, August 27, 1975, p. 9. "Position," May 22, 1976, PAAA-MfAA, C 5445, pp. 8–12. "Preparations for the non-aligned Summit," [March? 1976], NAUK, FCO 58/978, p. 1. "Dear Michael," September 23, 1975, NAUK, FCO 58/ 855/1, p. 1. "P.R. no. 8," May 10, 1976, SBA, E 2300–01, Akzession 1988/91, box 5, pp. 1–6. "Dear Peter," May 20, 1976, NAUK, FCO 58/978, p. 1 (quote). "On the position of Egypt," August 26, 1976, PAAA-MfAA, C 6518, pp. 7–13. "Fm Clmo Yhgr0547 Aug11/76," NAUK, FCO 58/980, pp. 1–2.

47. Various documents: NAUK, FCO 58/982. "Cuba and the non-aligned conference," September 27, 1976, NAUK, FCO 58/983, pp. 1–6. "Note for file," August 30, 1976, PAAA-MfAA, C 5445, pp. 1–7.

48. "The fourth non-Aligned summit conference at Algiers," September 19, 1973, NAUK, FCO 93/7, p. 2.

13   Pan-Islamism

1. "Mr. Jinnah meets Nokrashy Pasha," *Times of India* [*ToI*], December 18, 1946, 1. For photo, see www.siasat.pk/forum/showthread.php?221389-Quaid-e-Aazam-Muhammad-Ali-Jinnah-ra-Treasure-of-Pictures-in-TIME -Line, accessed on September 14, 2017. The website misidentifies the Egyptian prime minister as Ibrahim Abdel Hadi Pasha. "After the creation of Pakistan," June 26, 1947, *Le Progrès Egyptien*, Anita L. P. Burdett, ed., *Islamic movements in the Arab World, 1913–1966*, vol. 3 (Archive Editions, 1998), p. 499.

2. Cemil Aydin, *The idea of the Muslim world* (Harvard University Press, 2017), pp. 14–132.

3. M. Naeem Qureshi, *Pan-Islam in British Indian politics* (Brill, 1999), pp. 1, 88–173, 363–413. Ayesha Jalal, *The sole spokesman* (Cambridge University Press, 1985), pp. 7–71. Sikandar Hayat, *The charismatic leader*, 2nd ed. (Oxford University Press, 2014), pp. 63–110. Stephen P. Cohen, *The idea of Pakistan* (Brookings Institution Press, 2004), p. 29.

4. Faisal Devji, *Muslim Zion* (Harvard University Press, 2013), p. 17. "No discussion of politics," *ToI*, December 27, 1946, p. 8. "Mr. Jinnah leaving for India today," *ToI*, December 20, 1946, p. 1.

5. "No. 139," May 17, 1950, Library and Archives Canada [LAC], RG25, box 6137, pp. 1–2. Devji, *Muslim Zion*, pp. 3–5 (quote). Beverley Milton-Edwards, *Islamic fundamentalism since 1945* (Routledge, 2005), p. 40. Mohammed Ayoob, *The many faces of political Islam* (University of

Michigan Press, 2008), pp. 65–66. Richard Bonney, *Jihad* (Palgrave Macmillan, 2004), pp. 205–8. Vernie Liebl, "The Caliphate," *Middle Eastern Studies*, 45/3 (2009), p. 376.

6. Cohen, *Idea of Pakistan*, pp. 45–51. Tariq Ali, *The duel* (Scribner, 2008), p. 32.

7. Devji, *Muslim Zion*, pp. 47, 84, 135, 189. "Jinnah assures support to Indonesia," [July 26, 1947], Mahomed Ali Jinnah, *Selected speeches and statements of the Quaid-i-Azam Mohammad Ali Jinnah (1911–34 and 1947–48)* (Research Society of Pakistan, University of the Punjab, 1973), pp. 425–26. "Pakistan joins opponents of Palestine split," *Chicago Daily Tribune*, October 8, 1947, p. 11. "Pakistan will not be in Arab League," *Palestine Post*, June 22, 1947, p. 1.

8. Firoz Khan Nun [Noon], *From memory* (Feroz, 1966), pp. 219–20. "Pakistan leader asks all Moslems to unite," *Hartford Courant*, August 7, 1948, p. 12. "Pakistan gives up Islamic union," *Palestine Post*, December 5, 1948, p. 4.

9. Nehemia Levtzion, *International Islamic solidarity and its limitations* (Magnes Press, 1979), p. 12. "Islamistan in Middle East," *TofI*, July 4, 1949, p. 9 (first quote). Various documents: Burdett, *Islamic Movements*, vol. 4, pp. 9, 32. "Islamistan and Arab League," *TofI*, December 10, 1949, p. 9. Jacob M. Landau, *The politics of pan-Islam* (Clarendon Press, 1993), pp. 269–70. "The glory of Islam," no date, National Archives of Australia [NAA], Series A1838, 3002/1 Part 7, p. 1 (second quote).

10. "Mr. Liaquat Ali tells congress of Pakistan's aims," *Manchester Guardian*, May 5, 1950, p. 10 (quote). "Islamistan," *TofI*, December 10, 1949, p. 6.

11. S. S. Pirzada "Pakistan and the OIC," *Pakistan Horizon*, 40/2 (1987), pp. 22–24. "Memorandum for the Secretary," November 28, 1949, NAA, Series A1838, 181/2/3/1, p. 1 (quote). Levtzion, *International Islamic solidarity*, pp. 12–13. "World Moslem parley ends," *New York Times* [*NYT*], February 21, 1951, p. 2. Agha [Aga] Khan III, *Address of H.R.H. Prince Aga Khan at the session of Motamer-e-Alam-e-Islami on Friday the 9th February 1951 at Karachi* (Motamer-e-Alam-e-Islami, 1951?). "Medina-Pakistan railway plan," *Manchester Guardian*, February 12, 1951, p. 8. Muḥammad Reza Kazmi, *Liaquat Ali Khan* (Oxford University Press, 2003), p. 303.

12. "Political report no. 7," March 21, 1952, Schweizerisches Bundesarchiv [SBA], E 2300, Akzession 1000/716, box 178, pp. 1–2. "Proposed Islamic conference at Karachi," May 14, 1952, NAA, Series A1838, 189/7/1 Part 1, p. 1 (quote).

13. "Pakistan avoids joining any Blocs," April 15, 1950, *NYT*, p. 6. "Pakistan clings to middle of international highway," *Christian Science Monitor* [*CSM*], September 21, 1950, p. 14. Shahid M. Amin, *Pakistan's foreign policy* (Oxford University Press, 2000), pp. 42–43. "Memo no. 600/53," March 3, 1953, NAA, Series A1838, 163/11/148, pp. 1–2 (quote).

14. "Memo no. 322," March 5, 1954, NAA, Series A1838, 189/7/1 Part 1, p. 1 (quote). "Egypt snubs Pakistan," April 12, 1954, *TofI*, p. 1. "Political report no. 1," January 8, 1954, SBA, E 2300, Akzession 1000/716, 178, p. 1. Amin, *Pakistan's Foreign Policy*, pp. 39–73.

15. Huseyn Shaheed Suhrawardy, *Memoirs of Huseyn Shaheed Suhrawardy* (University Press, 1987), p. 56 (quotes). "From Office of the High Commissioner for Canada, Karachi," November 7, 1956, LAC, RG25, box 6137, p. 2. Various documents: NAA, Series A1838, 189/11/20 Part 1. "Pakistan turns against Nasser," *NYT*, December 20, 1956, p. 3. "No. 14444," November 21, 1956, Burdett, *Islamic movements*, vol. 4, pp. 341–42.

16. Levtzion, *International Islamic solidarity*, p. 9. Steven A. Cook, *The struggle for Egypt* (Oxford University Press, 2012), pp. 27–30. Reinhard Schulze, *Islamischer Internationalismus im 20. Jahrhundert* (Brill, 1990), p. 105. Richard P. Mitchell, *The society of the Muslim Brothers* (Oxford University Press, 1969), pp. 7–19. "The Moslem Brotherhood," *Palestine Post*, December 18, 1946, p. 5.

17. "Threaten revolt unless Egypt calls off talks with Britain," *Globe and Mail*, August 30, 1946, p. 2. Mitchell, *Society*, pp. 49–58. "Aim to oust Jews pledged by sheikh," *NYT*, August 2, 1948, p. 4 (quote).

18. Various documents: Burdett, *Islamic movements*, vol. 3, pp. 548–49, 577–78. Cook, *Struggle*, pp. 35–36. Mitchell, *Society*, pp. 58–84.

19. "No. 492," September 16, 1949, Burdett, *Islamic movements*, vol. 4, pp. 10–11. "Foreign relations," no date, NAA, Series A1838, 181/2/1 Part 2, p. 1. "Ministerial despatch no. 11/52," March 7, 1952, NAA, Series A1838, 189/11/20 Part 1, pp. 2–3.

20. Kirk J. Beattie, *Egypt during the Sadat years* (Palgrave, 2000), p. 3. Cook, *Struggle*, pp. 46–54. "Political report no. 24," August 19, 1952, SBA, E 2300, Akzession 1000/716, box 172, p. 4.

21. Schulze, *Islamischer Internationalismus*, pp. 113–15. "No. 58," January 14, 1954, Burdett, *Islamic movements*, vol. 4, p. 196. "Political report no. 26," September 19, 1953, SBA, E 2300, Akzession 1000/716, box 173, pp. 1–6.

22. Various documents: NAA, Series A1838, 163/7/1 Part 1, and Burdett, *Islamic movements*, vol. 4, pp. 201–16. "Moslem urges 'holy war' on British in Suez," *CSM*, March 27, 1954, p. 7.

23. "Ministerial despatch no. 8/54," February 24, 1954, NAA, Series A1838, 181/2/1 Part 4, pp. 1–4. "Political report no. 16," April 29, 1954, SBA, E 2300, Akzession 1000/716, box 178, pp. 4–5. "Memo no. 631," May 19, 1954, NAA, Series A1838, 189/7/1 Part 1, pp. 1–2.

24. "Unified command for Egypt & Saudi Arabia," *TofI*, June 13, 1954, p. 10. Various documents: NAA, Series A1838, 181/2/1 Part 4. "Political report no. 17," August 18, 1954, SBA, E 2300, Akzession 1000/716, box 173, pp. 1–5. Schulze, *Islamischer Internationalismus*, pp. 117–19. "Bid to make Cairo Islamic centre," *Jerusalem Post*, September 3, 1954, p. 5.

25. Mitchell, *Society*, pp. 137–50. "Nasser censures Moslem fanatics," *NYT*, August 22, 1954, p. 30. "A thorn in Nasser's side," *CSM*, September 16, 1954, p. 4. "Regime to write sermons in Egypt," *NYT*, September 14, 1954, p. 6.

26. Cook, *Struggle*, pp. 60–61, 82–84. Mitchell, *Society*, pp. 150–62. "Egypt defies Arab world," *Manchester Guardian*, December 8, 1954, p. 7. Gamal Abdel Nasser, "The Egyptian revolution," *Foreign Affairs*, 33/2 (1955), p. 209 (quote).

27. "Dear Department," April 21, 1955, Burdett, *Islamic movements*, vol. 4, pp. 331–33.
28. Levtzion, *International Islamic solidarity*, p. 15. "Pakistan adheres to Turco-Iraqi Treaty," *Jerusalem Post*, July 3, 1955, p. 4. "Political letter," April 26, 1956, SBA, E 2300, Akzession 1000/716, box 174, pp. 1–4. "Nasser joins talks of two Arab rulers in anti-British plan," April 21, 1956, *NYT*, p. 1.
29. Levtzion, *International Islamic solidarity*, pp. 16–17. Malcolm H. Kerr, *The Arab cold war* (Oxford University Press, 1971). "Nasser's Islamic Campaign," *Jerusalem Post*, January 24, 1961, p. 4. Ali E. Hilal Dessouki, "The limits of instrumentalism," Adeed Dawisha, ed., *Islam in foreign policy* (Cambridge University Press, 1983), pp. 87–88.
30. Adnan A. Musallam, *From secularism to Jihad* (Prager, 2005), pp. 137–65. Cook, *Struggle*, pp. 90. "Saudi Prince killed while leading plot against Faisal," *NYT*, September 27, 1965, p. A2. Various documents: National Archives of the United Kingdom [NAUK], FO 371/190186 and 190187.
31. Stephan Conermann, *Mustafa Mahmud (geb. 1921) und der modifizierte islamische Diskurs im modern Ägypten* (Klaus Schwarz Verlag, 1996), pp. 110–13, 130–35. Fouad Ajami, *The Arab predicament*, upd. ed. (Cambridge University Press, 1993), pp. 64–65. Cook, *Struggle*, pp. 101–7. Fawaz A. Gerges, *The far enemy* (Cambridge University Press, 2005), pp. 4–7.
32. Cook, *Struggle*, pp. 115–16. Musallam, *From Secularism*, pp. 182–98. Gabriel R. Warburg, "Islam and politics in Egypt," *Middle Eastern Studies*, 18/2 (1982), p. 147. Malek Abisaab, "The so-called Arab Spring, Islamism and the dilemma of the Arab left, 1970–2012," *R/evolutions: Global Trends & Regional Issues*, 4/1 (2016), pp. 41–42.
33. Nadav Safran, *Saudi Arabia* (Belknap Press, 1985), pp. 9–27. "The Caliphate," [December 1954], NAUK, FO 371/110840, p. [18].
34. Rachel Bronson, *Thicker than oil* (Oxford University Press, 2006), pp. 17–24, 34–35.
35. Various documents: NAA, Series A1838, 181/2/1 Part 4. Safran, *Saudi Arabia*, pp. 103–10. "Fm Cairo Jan 19/57 secret," LAC, RG25, box 6141, pp. 1–2. Salim Yaqub, *Containing Arab nationalism* (University of North Carolina Press, 2004), pp. 87–145.
36. "Political letter," April 12, 1958, SBA, E 2300, Akzession 1000/716, box 174, pp. 1–5. Ellinor Schöne, *Islamische Solidarität* (Klaus Schwarz Verlag, 1997), pp. 23–26. Schulze, *Islamischer Internationalismus*, p. 160. Bronson, *Thicker than oil*, pp. 75–76, 141–42, 181–212. Levtzion, *International Islamic solidarity*, p. 18. Landau, *Politics*, pp. 283–87.
37. Bronson, *Thicker than oil*, pp. 84–92. "Ex-king Saud given refuge by Nasser," *Globe and Mail*, December 19, 1966, p. 9. "No. 57," January 26, 1964, NAUK, FO 371/175556, pp. 1–2. "Dear Derek," March 17, 1965, NAUK, FO 371/180378, various page numbers. "Islamic congress attacks communism," no date, NAA, Series A1838, 181/2/3 Part 1, p. 183. Levtzion, *International Islamic solidarity*, p. 19.
38. "Shah and Faisal in accord," *NYT*, December 14, 1965, p. 14. "Feisal Is rallying Moslem conservatives," *Washington Post* [*WaPo*], December 16, 1965, p. F4. "Hussein opposes 'Islamic Pact'," *Jerusalem Post*, January 30, 1966, p. 1. "Feisal indicates he is going ahead with Islamic bid," no date,

NAA, Series A1838, 181/2/3 Part 1, pp. 190–89. "Feisal plea to 'doubters' on summit," *Jerusalem Post*, March 29, 1966, p. 5.

39. "UAR disappointed by Pak stand," *TofI*, April 22, 1966, p. 9. "Pakistan to get loan," *WaPo*, April 20, 1966, p. C1. "Turkey refuses to take part," *TofI*, November 7, 1966, p. 8. "Faisal seeks African support," *Irish Times*, September 14, 1966, p. 7. "Cairo opens own Islamic congress," *Jerusalem Post*, October 2, 1966, p. 2. "Islamic pact plan seen withering," *Los Angeles Times [LAT]*, March 5, 1967, p. J4.

40. "Pak move for Islamic summit," *TofI*, August 15, 1967, p. 1. "No. CAI/565/A/67," September 3, 1967, Nehru Memorial Museum and Library [NMML], Apa B. Pant, Subject Files, file no. 16, part I, p. 196. "Saudi-Persian coolness a bonus for Nasser," *Guardian*, February 5, 1968, p. 17. "Islamic diplomacy and the 'jihad'," October 21, 1968, NAUK, FCO 8/1201, pp. 1–6. Schulze, *Islamischer Internationalismus*, p. 271.

41. "Nasser and Faisal call for holy war," *Observer*, August 24, 1969, p. 1. "Arab states delay call for summit," *WaPo*, August 26, 1969, p. A1.

42. Schöne, *Islamische Solidarität*, p. 36–45. "Moslem summit on Jerusalem opens," *WaPo*, September 23, 1969, p. A18. "Moslem leaders approve condemnation of Israel," *Globe and Mail*, September 24, 1969, p. 8. "A struggle between Nasser and Faisal over Islamic summit is reported," *NYT*, September 17, 1969, p. 13. "Syria, Iraq boycott Islamic parley," *Jerusalem Post*, September 23, 1969, p. 1.

43. "The Feisal/Nasser meeting and the Rabat Summit," January 13, 1970, NAUK, FCO 17/1151, pp. 1–3. "Conference of Islamic foreign ministers," March 31, 1970, NAA, Series A1838, 181/2/3/11 Part 1, pp. 35–34. Johannes Grundmann, *Islamische Internationalisten* (Reichert Verlag, 2005), pp. 80. "King Faisal seeks Islamic leadership," *CSM*, March 25, 1970, p. 12. "Arabs split as Islamic meet ends," *Jerusalem Post*, March 27, 1970, p. 3.

44. Levtzion, *International Islamic solidarity*, p. 24. Naif Bin Hethlain, *Saudi Arabia and the US since 1962* (Saqi Books, 2010), pp. 84–86. "Despatch no. 1/1972," January 17, 1972, NAA, Series A4231, 1972/Africa & The Middle East, pp. 15–24. "King Feisal dubs Bangla events anti-Islamic," *TofI*, March 1, 1972, p. 9. "Islam meeting ok's fund to fight Israel," *LAT*, March 5, 1972, p. A7. "Secret Cairo 1495," May 21, 1973, Richard Nixon Presidential Library [RMN], NSC files, box 638, Country files: Middle East, pp. 1–4. Bronson, *Thicker than oil*, pp. 116–18.

45. Naveed Ahmad, "Pakistan-Saudi relations," *Pakistan Horizon*, 35/4 (1982), pp. 52–53, 61. Schöne, *Islamische Solidarität*, p. 54, 94–117. Dennis Kux, *The United States and Pakistan, 1947–2000* (Woodrow Wilson Center Press / Johns Hopkins University Press, 2001), pp. 204–45. Tariq, *Duel*, pp. 44–49, 97–133. "I.129412," December 21, 1971, NAA, Series A1838, 169/10/1 Part 20, pp. 1–4. Mehrunnisa Ali, "The second Islamic summit conference, 1974," *Pakistan Horizon*, 27/1 (1974), pp. 29–49.

46. Joseph A. Kechichian, *Faysal* (University Press of Florida, 2008), p. 121. Grundmann, *Islamische Internationalisten*, pp. 84–90.

47. Amin Saikal, *The rise and fall of the Shah* (Princeton University Press, 2009), pp. 71–131.

48. Charles Kurzman, *The unthinkable revolution in Iran* (Harvard University Press, 2004), pp. 12–32. Qureshi, *Pan-Islam*, p. 1. Nikki R. Keddie, "The roots of the Ulama's power in modern Iran," *Studia Islamica*, 29 (1969), p. 51. Hamid Dabashi, *Theology of discontent* (Routledge, 2015), pp. 39–101. Mohsen M. Milani, *The making of Iran's Islamic revolution*, 2nd ed. (Westview, 1994), pp. 47–52.

49. Ervand Abrahamian, *Khomeinism* (University of California Press, 1993), pp. 20–26, 47–50. Hamid Mavani, "Ayatullah Khomeini's concept of governance (*wilayat al-faqih*) and the classical Shi'i doctrine of Imamate," *Middle Eastern Studies*, 47/5 (2001), pp. 807–8. Mansoor Moaddel, *Islamic modernism, nationalism, and fundamentalism* (University of Chicago Press, 2005), pp. 251–63. Bonney, *Jihad*, p. 247.

50. Ayoob, *Many faces*, p. 63. R. K. Ramazani, "Khumayni's Islam and Iran's foreign policy," Dawisha, *Islam in foreign policy*, pp. 9–32. H. E. Chehabi, *Iranian politics and religious modernism* (I. B. Tauris, 1990), p. 215. Dabashi, *Theology*, pp. 409–84.

14   Nuclear Weapons

1. For a discussion on status, see T. V. Paul, Deborah Welch Larson, and William C. Wohlforth, eds., *Status in world politics* (Cambridge University Press, 2014).

2. Campbell Craig and Sergey Radchenko, *The atomic bomb and the origins of the Cold War* (Yale University Press, 2008), pp. 4–33, 62–89. David Holloway, *Stalin and the bomb* (Yale University Press, 1994), p. 129. Quote from Robert H. Ferrell, ed., *Off the record* (Harper & Row, 1980), p. 53 (quotes). Tsuyoshi Hasegawa, *Racing the enemy* (Belknap Press, 2005), pp. 136–40. Robert L. Messer, *The end of an alliance* (University of North Carolina Press, 1982), p. 86.

3. Holloway, *Stalin*, pp. 72–133. Hasegawa, *Racing the enemy*, pp. 154–251. Vladislav M. Zubok, "Stalin and the nuclear age," John Lewis Gaddis, Philip H. Gordon, Ernest R. May, and Jonathan Rosenberg, eds., *Cold War statesmen confront the bomb* (Oxford University Press, 1999), pp. 39–61. Craig, *Atomic bomb*, pp. 97–98.

4. Craig, *Atomic bomb*, pp. 15–18. Samuel R. Williamson and Steven L. Rearden, *The origins of U.S. nuclear strategy, 1945–1953* (St. Martin's Press, 1993), pp. 35–44. Shane J. Maddock, *Nuclear apartheid* (University of North Carolina Press, 2010), pp. 40–68. David W. Kearn, "The Baruch Plan and the quest for atomic disarmament," *Diplomacy and Statecraft*, 21/1 (2010), pp. 41–67.

5. Charles R. Loeber, *Building the bombs*, 2nd ed. (Sandia National Laboratories, 2005), p. 83. Holloway, *Stalin*, pp. 196–220. John Lewis Gaddis, *The Cold War* (Penguin Press, 2005), pp. 61–63. McGeorge Bundy, *Danger and survival* (Random House, 1988), pp. 201–14. Robert S. Norris and Hans M. Kristensen, "Global nuclear weapons inventories, 1945–2010," *Bulletin of the Atomic Scientists*, 66/4 (2010), p. 81. David S. McDonough, "Nuclear superiority or mutually assured deterrence," *International Journal*,

60/3 (2005), p. 814. Christoph Bluth, *Soviet strategic arms policy before SALT* (Cambridge University Press, 1992), pp. 174–98.

6. Craig, *Atomic bomb*, pp. 7–15. Quote from Jonathan Clarke, "Repeating British mistakes," *National Interest*, 39 (spring 1995), pp. 72–73. Matthew Jones, *The official history of the UK strategic nuclear deterrent*, vol. 1 (Routledge, 2017), pp. 1–43, 365–83.

7. John Baylis, *Ambiguity and deterrence* (Clarendon Press, 1995), pp. 35–205, 262. Jonathan Rosenberg, "Before the bomb and after," Gaddis *et al.*, *Cold War statesmen*, pp. 183–92. Jones, *Official history*, vol. 1, pp. 25–43, 365–93, and vol. 2, pp. 399–400.

8. "Talk with the American correspondent Anna Louise Strong," August 1946, Mao Zedong, *Selected works*, vol. 4 (Foreign Languages Press, 1961), p. 100 (first quote). "[Speech held in Moscow, November 18, 1957]," Mao Zedong, *Jianguo yilai Mao Zedong wengao*, vol. 6 (Zhongyang wenxian chubanshe, 1992), p. 636 (second quote). Zhang Shu Guang, "Between 'paper' and 'real tigers'," Gaddis *et al.*, *Cold War statesmen*, pp. 199–201. Lorenz M. Lüthi, *The Sino-Soviet split* (Princeton University Press, 2008), pp. 74, 137, 148. "Memorandum," [November 1964], Politisches Archiv des Auswärtigen Amtes, Bestand: Ministerium für Auswärtige Angelegenheiten [PAAA-MfAA], A 17424, pp. 3–6. Sergei N. Goncharov, John W. Lewis, and Litai Xue, *China builds the bomb* (Stanford University Press, 1988), pp. 190–218.

9. Avner Cohen, *Israel and the bomb* (Columbia University Press, 1998), pp. 1–21, 42–43, 52–55, 195–291. Zaki Shalom, *Israel's nuclear option* (Sussex Academic Press, 2005), pp. 1–8. Michael Karpin, *The bomb in the basement* (Simon & Schuster, 2006), pp. 57–95, 168–77. Norris, "Global nuclear weapons inventories," p. 81.

10. Bertrand Goldschmidt, *The atomic complex* (American Nuclear Society, 1982), pp. 136–37. Lawrence Scheinman, *Atomic energy policy in France under the Fourth Republic* (Princeton University Press, 1965), pp. 111–201. Jean Guisnel and Bruno Tertrais, *Le Président et la Bombe* (Odile Jacob, 2016), pp. 29–31 (quote). Beatrice Heuser, *NATO, Britain, France and the FRG* (Palgrave Macmillan, 1997), pp. 101–5.

11. Jones, *Official History*, vol. 1, pp. 393–401. Guisnel, *Président*, pp. 42–46.

12. Annette Messemer, "Konrad Adenauer," Gaddis *et al.*, *Cold War statesmen*, pp. 236–59. Oliver Bange, "NATO as a frame work for nuclear nonproliferation," *International Journal*, 64/2 (2009), pp. 364–69. Dieter Mahncke, *Nukleare Mitwirkung* (Walter de Gruyter, 1972).

13. Gaddis, *Cold War*, pp. 66–68. Michael D. Gordin, *Red cloud at dawn* (Farrar, Straus and Giroux, 2009), pp. 91–104. Benjamin P. Greene, *Eisenhower, science advice, and the nuclear test-ban debate, 1945–1963* (Stanford University Press, 2007), pp. 62–86. "Memorandum of discussion at the 415th Meeting of the National Security Council," July 30, 1959, United States, Department of State, *Foreign relations of the United States* [FRUS], 1958–60, III (U.S. Government Printing Office, 1996), p. 288 (quote). Charles R. Morris, *Iron destinies, lost opportunities* (Harper & Row, 1988), pp. 109–12. Lüthi, *Sino-Soviet split*, p. 95.

14. Vladislav M. Zubok, "The nuclear education of Nikita Khrushchev," Gaddis *et al.*, *Cold War statesmen*, pp. 143–49. Norris, "Global nuclear weapons inventories," p. 81. Bluth, *Soviet strategic arms policy*, pp. 174–98. Sergei Khrushchev, *Nikita Khrushchev* (Pennsylvania State University Press, 2000), pp. 279–83, 313–17. Philip Nash, *The other missiles of October* (University of North Carolina Press, 1997), pp. 45–75. Morris, *Iron destinies*, pp. 120–31. Matthias Uhl, *Krieg um Berlin?* (Oldenbourg Verlag, 2008), pp. 201–7.
15. Lawrence S. Wittner, *The struggle against the bomb*, vol. 1 (Stanford University Press, 1993), pp. 20–168. Andrei Sakharov, *Memoirs* (Vintage Books, 1992), pp. 197–209. Ira Chernus, *Eisenhower's atoms for peace* (Texas A&M University Press, 2002). Maddock, *Nuclear apartheid*, pp. 81–114. Wittner, *Struggle*, vol. 2, pp. 1–183.
16. Zubok, "Nuclear education," pp. 162–63. Stephen Twigge, "Disarmament and non-proliferation," Matthew Grant, *The British way in cold warfare* (Continuum, 2009), pp. 40–42. Lüthi, *Sino-Soviet split*, pp. 93–115.
17. Greene, *Eisenhower*, pp 165–232. Francis J. Gavin, *Nuclear statecraft* (Cornell University Press, 2012), pp. 66–70. J. P. G. Freeman, *Britain's nuclear arms control policy in the context of Anglo-American relations, 1957–68* (St. Martin's Press, 1986), pp. 79–83, 91–102. Khrushchev, *Nikita Khrushchev*, pp. 365–77.
18. Piero Gleijeses, "Ships in the night," *Journal of Latin American Studies*, 27/1 (1995), pp. 1–42. William Taubman, *Khrushchev* (W. W. Norton, 2003), pp. 490–96. Viktor Adamsky and Yuri Smirnov, "Moscow's biggest bomb," *Cold War International History Project [CWIHP] Bulletin*, 4 (1994), pp. 19–21 (quote). Sakharov, *Memoirs*, pp. 188–232. "Information," August 28, 1961, Stiftung Archiv der Parteien und Massenorganisationen der DDR im Bundesarchiv [SAPMO-BArch], DY 30/3497, pp. 202–5. "Joint Message," September 27, 1961, Arhiv Jugoslavije [AJ], KPR I-4-a/2, pp. 1–33. Maddock, *Nuclear apartheid*, p. 171.
19. Lüthi, *Sino-Soviet split*, pp. 249–52. Khrushchev, *Nikita Khrushchev*, pp. 468–82. Aleksandr A. Fursenko and Timothy Naftali, *One hell of a gamble* (Norton, 1997), pp. 170–72 (quote).
20. Don Munton and David A. Welch, *The Cuban Missile Crisis*, 2nd edition (Oxford University Press, 2012), pp. 63–93. Bluth, *Soviet strategic arms policy*, pp. 184–92. Norris, "Global nuclear weapons inventories," p. 81. Norman Cousins, *The improbable triumvirate* (W. W. Norton, 1972), pp. 45–46 (quote; italics added).
21. Albert Legault and Michel Fortmann, *A diplomacy of hope* (McGill-Queen's University Press, 1992), pp. 172, 197.
22. Lüthi, *Sino-Soviet split*, pp. 254–69. Lorenz M. Lüthi, "Rearranging international relations?," *Journal of Cold War Studies*, 16/1 (2014), pp. 111–45.
23. Lüthi, *Sino-Soviet split*, pp. 265–68.
24. Matthias Küntzel, *Bonn and the bomb* (Pluto Press, 1995), pp. 32–26. Susanna Schrafstetter, *Die dritte Atommacht* (Oldenbourg Verlag, 1999), pp. 107–19. Douglas Selvage, "The Warsaw Pact and nuclear nonproliferation, 1963–1965," Cold War International History Project [CWIHP],

Working Paper 32 (2001), pp. 3–17. Freeman, *Britain's nuclear arms control policy*, pp. 190–92.

25. Cohen, *Israel*, pp. 101–136, 153–75. Various documents: Lyndon Baines Johnson Presidential Library [LBJ], National Security File 1963–1969, Files of Robert W. Komer, boxes 30 and 53, and National Security File 1963–1969, Subject File, boxes 8, 9, and 34. Shalom, *Israel's nuclear option*, pp. 69–152.

26. Lorenz M. Lüthi, "The Non-Aligned Movement and the Cold War, 1961–1973," *Journal of Cold War Studies*, 18/4 (2016), pp. 125–26. "Memorandum no. 1965," October 20, 1964, National Archives of Australia [NAA], Series A1838, 169/11/87 Part 26, pp. 153–52. "Changes in Asia," April 7, 1954, Jawaharlal Nehru, *Selected works*, 2nd series [*JNSW2*], vol. 25 (Nehru Memorial Museum and Library, 1999), p. 396. Raj Chengappa, *Weapons of peace* (HarperCollins, 2000), pp. 85–87. "Record of conversation with R. K. Nehru, Secretary-General, Minister of External Affairs," November 14, 1962, NAA, Series A1838, 169/10/1 Part 6, pp. 1–4. "Record of conversation," May 29, 1965, NAA, Series A1838, 169/11/87 Part 27, p. 60 (second quote).

27. Hal Brands, "Rethinking nonproliferation," *Journal of Cold War Studies*, 8/2 (2006), pp. 83–113. Maddock, *Nuclear apartheid*, pp. 237–68. "Information no. 102/IX," September 16, 1965, PAAA-MfAA, A 4270, pp. 60–63. "Visit of the prime minister to the Soviet Union," February 21–24, 1966, National Archives of the United Kingdom [NAUK], PREM 13/1216, pp. 11–12 (quotes).

28. "Record of conversation," July 18, 1966, NAUK, PREM 13/1218, pp. 21–23. Maddock, *Nuclear apartheid*, pp. 269–70. Hal Brands, "Progress unseen," *Diplomatic History*, 30/2 (2006), p. 279. Dimitris Bourantonis, "The negotiation of the non-proliferation treaty, 1965–1968," *International History Review*, 19/2 (1997), pp. 347–54. Gavin, *Nuclear statecraft*, pp. 97–100. "Instructions to India's Representative to U.N. on Non-Proliferation Treaty," April 20, 1968, Nehru Memorial Museum and Library [NMML], P. N. Haksar Papers, I and II Installments, Subject Files, file no. 35, p. 6 (quote).

29. Jonathan Hunt, "The birth of an international community," Robert Hutchings and Jeremi Suri, eds., *Foreign policy breakthroughs* (Oxford University Press, 2015), pp. 89–94. See also various contributions in Jozef Goldblat, ed., *Non-proliferation* (SIPRI, 1985). Maddock, *Nuclear apartheid*, pp. 282–83.

30. Bluth, *Soviet strategic arms policy*, pp. 174–98. Vladislav M. Zubok, *A failed empire* (University of North Carolina Press, 2007), p. 205. Lawrence Freedman, *The evolution of nuclear strategy*, 3rd ed. (Palgrave Macmillan, 2003), pp. 232–57.

31. Niklas H. Rossbach, *Heath, Nixon and the rebirth of the special relationship* (Palgrave Macmillan, 2009), pp. 84–121. Helen Parr, "'The nuclear myth'," *International History Review*, 35/3 (2013), pp. 534–55. Kristan Stoddart, *The sword and the shield* (Palgrave Macmillan, 2014), pp. 11–42.

32. Raymond L. Garthoff, *Détente and confrontation*, rev. ed. (Brookings Institution, 1994), pp. 77–87, 100–6. Richard M. Nixon, "Asia after Viet Nam," *Foreign Affairs*, 46/1 (1967), pp. 122–23 (quotes). "Chinese threat

obsesses table-pounding Brezhnev," *Washington Post*, March 19, 1969, p. A1. Lorenz M. Lüthi, "Restoring chaos to history," *China Quarterly*, 210 (2012), pp. 390–91.

33. Chen Jian, *Mao's China and the Cold War* (University of North Carolina Press, 2001), pp. 258–73. Zubok, *Failed empire*, p. 216. Various documents in William Burr, ed., *Negotiating U.S.–Chinese rapprochement*, National Security Archive Electronic Briefing Book no. 70, nsarchive2.gwu.edu/NS AEBB/NSAEBB70/, accessed on February 3, 2018.

34. Garthoff, *Détente*, pp. 326–38. Morris, *Iron destinies*, 295–98. Lorenz M. Lüthi, "Beyond betrayal," *Journal of Cold War Studies*, 11/1 (2009), pp. 89–92. "Statements," June 6, 1971, SAPMO-BArch, DY 30/ IV 2/2.035/55, pp. 42–46.

35. Feroz Hassan Khan, *Eating grass* (Stanford University Press, 2012), pp. 43–88, 109. "The brown bomb," *Guardian*, March 11, 1965, p. 10 (quote).

36. Chengappa, *Weapons of peace*, pp. 116–18. "Sino-American detente," no date, National Archives of India [NAI], External Affairs, WII/104/18/72, p. 266 (quotes).

37. K. Subramanyam, "'Indian nuclear policy, 1964–98," Jasjit Singh, ed, *Nuclear India* (Institute for Defense Studies and Analyses, 1998), p. 30. "India's response to the nuclear explosion," June 7, 1974, NAUK, FCO 37/1469, p. 4 (first quote). "Fm Delhi 170740Z," July 17, 1974, NAUK, FCO 37/1471, p. 1 (second quote). "Nuclear guarantee by U.N. sought," *Times of India*, June 26, 1974, p. 1.

38. Chengappa, *Weapons of peace*, pp. 232–34, 278–80, 428–33. Hasan-Askari Rizvi, "Pakistan's nuclear testing," *Asian Survey*, 41/6 (2001), pp. 943–45. J. Michael Martinez, "The Carter administration and the evolution of American nuclear nonproliferation policy, 1977–1981," *Journal of Policy History*, 14/3 (2002), pp. 261–92. Malcolm M. Craig, *America, Britain and Pakistan's nuclear weapons programme, 1974–1980* (Palgrave Macmillan, 2017).

39. Garthoff, *Détente*, pp. 360–812.

40. "Information," February 7, 1978, PAAA-MfAA, C 6549, pp. 36–37. "Information," June 9, 1978, SAPMO-BArch, DY 30/IV 2/2.035/56, pp. 192–93 (quotes). "Information," [January 25–26, 1979], SAPMO-BArch, DY 30/2378, pp. 51–52. "Note," February 9, 1979, PAAA-MfAA, C 3655, pp. 5–8.

41. Garthoff, *Détente*, p. 814. Bange, "NATO," pp. 273–74. Helmut Schmidt, "The 1977 Alastair Buchan Memorial Lecture," October 28, 1977, *Survival*, 20/1 (1978), pp. 3–5. Gerhard Wettig, "Die Sowjetunion in der Auseinandersetzung über den NATO-Doppelbeschluss 1979–1983," *Vierteljahrshefte für Zeitgeschichte*, 2/2009, pp. 217–20. Klaus Wiegrefe, *Das Zerwürfnis* (Propyläen Verlag, 2005), pp. 252–77. Manfred Görtemaker, *Geschichte der Bundesrepublik Deutschland* (Fischer Taschenbuch, 1999), p. 591.

42. John Lewis Gaddis, *The long peace* (Oxford University Press, 1987), pp. 215–45.

15   Western European Integration

1. "Kennedy bars quiz on Cuba," *Washington Post*, April 22, 1961, p. A7.

2. Guido Thiemeyer, *Europäische Integration* (Böhlau Verlag, 2010), pp. 41–45. Martin Horn, *Britain, France, and the financing of the first World War* (McGill-Queen's University Press, 2002), pp. 7–27.
3. Frederick Stirton Weaver, *The United States and the global economy* (Rowman & Littlefield, 2011), p. 10. V. I. Zolotarev, "Main stages of development of USSR foreign trade, 1917–1967," *Soviet and Eastern European Foreign Trade*, 4/2 (1968), pp. 4–5. Charles P. Kindleberger, *The world in depression, 1929–1939* (University of California Press, 1973), pp. 34–42, 199–231. John Gillingham, *Coal, steel, and the rebirth of Europe, 1945–1955* (Cambridge University Press, 1991), p. 13. Derek Howard Aldcroft, *The European economy, 1914–2000*, 4th ed. (Routledge, 2001), pp. 45–46, 61–69.
4. Dietmar Rothermund, *The global impact of the Great Depression, 1929–1939* (Routledge, 1996), pp. 74–135.
5. Barry J. Eichengreen, *The European economy since 1945* (Princeton University Press, 2007), pp. 54–58. Oscar Sanchez-Sibony, *Red globalization* (Cambridge University Press, 2014), p. 64.
6. G. John Ikenberry, "A world economy restored," *International Organization*, 46/1 (1992), pp. 289–321.
7. Richard N. Coudenhove-Kalergi, *Pan-Europa* (Pan-Europa-Verlag, 1923). D. K. M. K., "The United States of Europe," *The World Today*, 3/4 (1947), pp. 156–57.
8. Richard N. Coudenhove-Kalergi, *Europe Seeks Unity* (New York University Press, 1948), pp. 15–16. Stephen A. Schuker, *The end of French predominance in Europe* (University of North Carolina Press, 1976), pp. 232–382. "Paris and Berlin open trade parley," *New York Times* [*NYT*], October 2, 1924, p. 6 (first quote). Gillingham, *Coal*, p. 5. "M. Herriot on German armament," *Manchester Guardian*, January 29, 1925, p. 10 (second quote). Thiemeyer, *Europäische Integration*, p. 40.
9. Gillingham, *Coal*, pp. 18–28. "French Premier espouses compulsory arbitration," *NYT*, September 6, 1929, p. 1. Aristide Briand, *Memorandum sur l'organisation d'un régime d'union fédérale européenne* ([Ministère des Affaires étrangères], 1930), pp. 1–16 (quotes). D. K. M. K., "United States of Europe," pp. 158–60. Jean-Luc Chabot, *Aux origines intellectuelles de l'Union européenne* (Presses universitaires de Grenoble, 2005), pp. 192–217.
10. "The report," *Manchester Guardian*, June 27, 1930, p. 15 (first quote). Coudenhove-Kalergi, *Europe*, p. 17. "The United States of Europe," *Saturday Evening Post*, February 15, 1930, pp. 25, 48, 51 (second quote). Martin Gilbert, *Winston S. Churchill*, vol. 5 (Houghton Mifflin Company, 1977), p. 408. "Churchill sees U.S. of Europe," *Daily Boston Globe*, March 11, 1932, p. 12.
11. "Why not 'The United States of Europe'?," *Saturday Evening Post*, May 9, 1938, reprinted in *Finest Hour*, 130 (2006), pp. 45–47. "Spiritual values linked with peace aims by Halifax," *Christian Science Monitor*, November 8, 1939, p. 6 (first and second quotes). Martin Dedman, *The origins and development of the European Union 1945–2008*, 2nd ed. (Routledge, 2010), pp. 16–18. Avi Shlaim, "Prelude to downfall," *Journal of Contemporary History*, 9/3 (1974), pp. 27–63. Benjamin Grob-Fitzgibbon, *Continental drift*

(Cambridge University Press, 2016), pp. 18–26. Frederick L. Schuman, "The Council of Europe," *American Political Science Review*, 45/3 (1951), p. 725. "Text of Prime Minister Churchill's speech," *NYT*, March 22, 1943, p. 4 (third and fourth quotes).

12. "United States of Europe," *Manchester Guardian*, November 17, 1945, p. 5. "Text of Churchill talk to Dutch parliament," *Globe and Mail*, May 10, 1946, p. 10. "Text of Churchill's Zurich address," *NYT*, September 20, 1946, p. 2 (first quote). "Text of Churchill's address at Westminster College in Missouri," *Daily Boston Globe*, March 6, 1946, p. 2 (second quote). Grob-Fitzgibbon, *Continental drift*, pp. 34–59. D. K. M. K., "United States of Europe," p. 168. Jonathan Clarke, "Repeating British mistakes," *National Interest*, 39 (Spring 1995), p. 71. "Text of Churchill's speech advocating formation of United Europe," *NYT*, May 15, 1947, p. 16 (third quote).

13. D. K. M. K., "United States of Europe," p. 162. "Benelux Pact ratified," *NYT*, October 30, 1947, p. 11.

14. Frederick F. Ritsch, "Origins of the Council of Europe," *Il Politico*, 35/1 (1970), p. 71. Richard N. Coudenhove-Kalergi, *Crusade for Pan-Europe* (G. P. Putnam's Sons, 1943), pp. 219–24. "Pan Europe body meets," *NYT*, April 11, 1947, p. 14 (quote).

15. John Baylis, "Britain, the Brussels Pact and the continental commitment," *International Affairs*, 60/4 (1984), pp. 618–27. Cees Wiebes and Bert Zeeman, "Benelux," David Reynolds, ed., *The origins of the Cold War in Europe* (Yale University Press, 1994), pp. 179–80. Lawrence S. Kaplan, *NATO 1948* (Rowman & Littlefield, 2007), pp. 105–228. Quote from Joseph Nye, *The paradox of American power* (Oxford University Press, 2002), p. 33.

16. Geir Lundestad, "Empire by invitation?," *Journal of Peace Research*, 23/3 (1986), p. 269. Aldcroft, *European economy*, p. 113. Weaver, *United States*, pp. 18–22. "Federated Europe urged in Congress," *NYT*, March 22, 1947, p. 1 (first quote). "Text of Churchill's speech advocating formation of United Europe," *NYT*, May 15, 1947, p. 16 (second quote). Melvyn P. Leffler, *A preponderance of power* (Stanford University Press, 1992), pp. 173–74, 184–86. "The address of Secretary Marshall at Harvard," *NYT*, June 6, 1947, p. 2 (third and fourth quotes). Benn Steil, *The Marshall Plan* (Simon & Schuster, 2018), pp. 85–115.

17. The sixteen were Austria, Belgium, Denmark, France, Greece, Iceland, Ireland, Italy, Luxembourg, the Netherlands, Norway, Portugal, Sweden, Switzerland, Turkey, and the United Kingdom. Steil, *Marshall Plan*, pp. 147–217. William I. Hitchcock, *France restored* (University of North Carolina Press, 1998), pp. 87–98. Stephen George, *An awkward partner* (Oxford University Press, 1990), pp. 17–18. Walter Lipgens, *A history of European integration, 1945–1947* (Clarendon Press, 1982), pp. 548–71. Dedman, *Origins*, pp. 39.

18. Lipgens, *History of European integration*, pp. 523–35. Thiemeyer, *Europäische Integration*, pp. 47–48. Eichengreen, *European economy since 1945*, pp. 79–85. Alan S. Milward, *The reconstruction of Western Europe, 1945–51* (Taylor & Francis, 1984), pp. 230–57.

19. Dedman, *Origins*, pp. 16–19. Lipgens, *History of European integration*, pp. 107–53, 283–457, 571–614, 623–28, 659–64. Gerhard Brunn, *Die*

Europäische Einigung von 1945 bis heute, 4th, rev. ed. (Reclam, 2017), pp. 51–63. Ritsch, "Origins," pp. 77–79, 87. "Pride in being 'a European'," *Manchester Guardian*, May 10, 1948, p. 6 (quotes).

20. Frederick F. Ritsch, "Origins of the Council of Europe," *Il Politico*, 35/2 (1970), p. 205–27. Grob-Fitzgibbon, *Continental drift*, pp. 99–110. Dedman, *Origins*, p. 24.

21. "Statute of the Council of Europe," May 5, 1949: www.coe.int/en/web/con ventions/full-list/-/conventions/rms/0900001680306052, accessed on November 19, 2017 (quotes; italics added). Grob-Fitzgibbon, *Continental drift*, p. 110. Dedman, *Origins*, p. 25.

22. Peter Pulzer, "Nationalism and internationalism in European Christian Democracy," Michael Gehler and Wolfram Kaiser, eds., *Christian Democracy in Europe since 1945*, vol. 2 (Routledge, 2004), pp. 8–20. Wolfram Kaiser, *Christian democracy and the origins of European Union* (Cambridge University Press, 2007), pp. 163–65. Giuseppe Audisio, and Alberto Chiara, *Les fondateurs de l'Europe unie selon le projet de Jean Monnet* (Salvator, 2004), pp. 20–31, 35–40, 111–15, 152–99. Hans-Peter Schwarz, *Adenauer*, vol. 1 (Deutsche Verlags-Anstalt, 1986), pp. 225–29. Milward, *Reconstruction*, pp. 279–324.

23. Desmond Dinan, *Europe recast*, 2nd ed. (Lynne Rienner, 2014), p. 43. Gillingham, *Coal*, pp. 173–74. Gilbert Trausch, "Der Schuman-Plan zwischen Mythos und Realität," *Historische Zeitschrift*, 21 (1995), p. 119. Ulrich Lappenküper, "Der Schuman-Plan," *Vierteljahreshefte für Zeitgeschichte*, 42/3 (1994), p. 411. Konrad Adenauer, *Erinnerungen*, vol. 1 (Deutsche Verlags-Anstalt, 1965), pp. 311–16. Ennio Di Nolfo, "Das Problem der europäischen Einigung als ein Aspekt der italienischen Außenpolitik 1945–1954," *Vierteljahreshefte für Zeitgeschichte*, 28/2 (1980), pp. 166–67. Adrian F. Manning, "Die Niederlande und Europa von 1945 bis zum Beginn der fünfziger Jahre," *Vierteljahreshefte für Zeitgeschichte*, 29/1 (1981), pp. 11–14. "Technicians start arguing over Europe's steel pool," *NYT*, May 28, 1950, p. 95.

24. Trausch, "Schuman-Plan," pp. 121–28. Lappenküper, " Schuman-Plan," pp. 418–38. Dedman, *Origins*, pp. 55–56. John W. Young, "Churchill's 'No' to Europe," *The Historical Journal*, 28/4 (1985), pp. 924–26. Grob-Fitzgibbon, *Continental drift*, pp. 129–52. Quote from Clarke, "Repeating British mistakes," p. 72. Sebastian Rosato, *Europe united* (Cornell University Press, 2011), p. 94.

25. Geir Lundestad, *The United States and Western Europe since 1945* (Oxford University Press, 2003), pp. 80–81. Hitchcock, *France restored*, pp. 152–202. Lawrence S. Kaplan, *NATO divided, NATO united* (Praeger, 2004), p. 18. Rosato, *Europe united*, pp. 142–51. Philippe Buton, "La CED, l'Affaire Dreyfus de la Quatrième République?," *Vingtième Siècle*, 84 (2004/4), pp. 43–59. Grob-Fitzgibbon, *Continental drift*, pp. 195–203.

26. H.-J. Braun, *The German economy in the twentieth century* (Routledge, 2003), pp. 144–75. Vera Zamagni, *The economic history of Italy, 1860–1990* (Clarendon Press, 1993), pp. 321–46. J. L. van Zanden, *The economic history of the Netherlands, 1914–1995* (Routledge, 1998), pp. 120–54. Manning, "Niederlande und Europa," pp. 11–14. André Mommen, *The Belgian*

economy in the twentieth century (Routledge, 1994), pp. 104–26. François Caron, *An economic history of modern France* (Columbia University Press, 1979), pp. 182–96, 242–363. Dedman, *Origins*, p. 37. Wolfram Kaiser, *Using Europe, abusing the Europeans* (St. Martin's Press, 1996), pp. 4–5. Brunn, *Europäische Einigung*, pp. 44–48.

27. Rosato, *Europe united*, p. 168 (quote). Lundestad, *United States*, pp. 84–87. Brunn, *Europäische Einigung*, pp. 100–28.

28. Rosato, *Europe united*, pp. 169, 210–14. Andrew Moravcsik, *The choice for Europe* (Cornell University Press, 1998), pp. 126–35. Kaiser, *Using Europe*, pp. 30–50, 88–107. Rolf Steininger, "Grossbritannien und de Gaulle," *Vierteljahreshefte für Zeitgeschichte*, 44/1 (1996), pp. 88–89 (quote). Clarke, "Repeating British mistakes," p. 72. Grob-Fitzgibbon, *Continental drift*, pp. 219–45. Eichengreen, *European economy since 1945*, p. 177.

29. Paul M. Pitman, "The French crisis and the dissolution of the European Payments Union, 1956–1958," and Richard T. Griffiths, "'An act of creative leadership'," Richard T. Griffiths, ed., *Explorations in OEEC history* (OECD Publishing, 2009), pp. 219–25, 235–50.

30. Buton, "La CED," pp. 44–46. J. B. Duroselle, "General de Gaulle's Europe and Jean Monnet's Europe," *The World Today*, 22/1 (1966), pp. 4–7. Mathieu Segers, "De Gaulle's race to the bottom," *Contemporary European History*, 19/2 (2010), pp. 119–23. Meir Zamir, ed., *The secret Anglo-French War in the Middle East* (Routledge, 2015), p. 134. Grob-Fitzgibbon, *Continental drift*, pp. 235–37. Brunn, *Europäische Einigung*, pp. 133–57. Gregor Schöllgen, *Die Aussenpolitik der Bundesrepublik Deutschland* (C. H. Beck, 2004), pp. 67–69.

31. George W. Ball, *The past has another pattern* (W. W. Norton, 1982), p. 209 (quotes). Ferdinand Leikam, "A strategy that failed," Morten Rasmussen and Ann-Christina L. Knudsen, eds., *The road to a United Europe* (PIE Peter Lang, 2009), pp. 106–17. Grob-Fitzgibbon, *Continental drift*, pp. 249–300. N. Piers Ludlow, *Dealing with Britain* (Cambridge University Press, 1997), pp. 63–64. Dinan, *Europe recast*, pp. 102–4.

32. Steininger, "Grossbritannien," pp. 94–95. Philip Robert Bajon, "The empty chair crisis of 1965–1966," Rasmussen and Knudsen, *The road to a United Europe*, pp. 205–21. Brunn, *Europäische Einigung*, pp. 144–48. N. Piers Ludlow, *The European Community and the crises of the 1960s* (Routledge, 2006), pp. 45–48, 71–118, 126. Eichengreen, *European economy since 1945*, p. 186.

33. Ludlow, *European Community*, pp. 137–40. Brunn, *Europäische Einigung*, p. 157. John W. Young, *Britain and the world in the twentieth century* (Arnold, 1997), p. 190. Wilfried Loth, *Europas Einigung* (Campus Verlag, 2014), pp. 163–69.

34. John R. Oneal and Mark A. Elrod, "NATO burden sharing and the forces of change," *International Studies Quarterly*, 33/4 (1989), pp. 436–37. Francis J. Gavin, *Gold, dollars, and power* (University of North Carolina Press, 2004), pp. 166–96. Eichengreen, *European economy since 1945*, pp. 242–51. Robert Leeson, *Ideology and the international economy* (Palgrave Macmillan, 2003), pp. 63–88, 167–180. Werner Abelshauser, *Deutsche Wirtschaftsgeschichte* (Bundeszentrale für politische Bildung, 2011), pp. 392–96.

35. Young, *Britain*, pp. 191–94. Grob-Fitzgibbon, *Continental drift*, pp. 334–66. Andrew D. Devenney, "Joining Europe," *Journal of British Studies*, 49/1 (2010), p. 101. Gene G. Gage, "Denmark's road to the European Communities," *Scandinavian Studies*, 46/4 (1974), p. 348. Tor Bjørklund, "Old and new patterns," *Acta Sociologica*, 40/2 (1997), p. 140. "The French 'Yes' on the larger EEC," *The Sun*, April 25, 1972, p. A16.

36. Young, *Britain*, p. 194. Götz von Groll, "The Nine at the Conference on Security and Cooperation in Europe," David Allen, Reinhard Rummel, and Wolfgang Wessels, eds., *European political cooperation* (Butterworth Scientific, 1982), p. 60. Mauro Elli, "The UK role in the European Community," Michele Affinito, Guia Migani, and Christian Wenkel, eds., *The two Europes* (PIE Peter Lang, 2009), pp. 303–5. Grob-Fitzgibbon, *Continental drift*, pp. 367–99. George, *Awkward partner*, pp. 50–96.

37. Jonathan Story, "The Franco-German alliance within the Community," *The World Today*, 36/6 (1980), pp. 209–17. John Pinder, "Economic and monetary union," *Publius*, 26/4 (1996), p. 130. Moravcsik, *Choice*, pp. 238–302. Eichengreen, *European economy since 1945*, pp. 187–94, 282–90.

38. Dedman, *Origins*, p. 84.

39. Brunn, *Europäische Einigung*, pp. 129–31. Dinan, *Europe recast*, pp. 163, 175–76, 258.

16   The Council for Mutual Economic Assistance

1. Iosif V. Stalin, *Economic Problems of Socialism in the U.S.S.R.* (Foreign Languages Press, 1972), p. 30.

2. Marie Lavigne, *International political economy and socialism* (Cambridge University Press, 1991), p. 7.

3. For the opposite argument of Soviet integration into the world economy, see Oscar Sanchez-Sibony, *Red globalization* (Cambridge University Press, 2014).

4. Alec Nove, *An economic history of the U.S.S.R.*, 2nd ed. (Penguin Books, 1989), pp. 39–64. Vincent Barnett, *The revolutionary Russian economy, 1890–1940* (Routledge, 2004), pp. 56–65. V. I. Zolotarev, "Main stages of development of USSR foreign trade, 1917–1967," *Soviet and Eastern European Foreign Trade*, 4/2 (1968), pp. 4–7.

5. Zolotarev, "Main stages," pp. 8–12. Sanchez-Sibony, *Red globalization*, pp. 29, 34. Nove, *Economic history*, pp. 73–83. Barnett, *Revolutionary Russian economy*, pp. 68–69. Peter Krüger, "Das doppelte Dilemma," *German Studies Review*, 22/2 (1999), pp. 247–67.

6. "Once more on the social-democratic deviation in our party," December 7, 1926, Iosif V. Stalin, *Works*, vol. 9 (Foreign Languages Publishing House, 1954), pp. 21–37 (quotes). Nove, *Economic history*, pp. 83–149.

7. Sanchez-Sibony, *Red globalization*, pp. 47–55. Nove, *Economic history*, pp. 146–259. Barnett, *Revolutionary Russian economy*, pp. 100–4. Lee Kendall Metcalf, *The Council of Mutual Economic Assistance* (Columbia University Press, 1997), pp. 31–37. Ralf Ahrens, *Gegenseitige Wirtschaftshilfe?* (Böhlau Verlag, 2000), p. 33. Michael R. Dohan, "The economic origins of Soviet autarky 1927/28–1934," *Slavic Review*, 35/4 (1976), pp. 603–35. "Notes from the meeting between Comrade Stalin and economists concerning questions

in political economy, 29 January 1941," Ethan Pollock, ed., "Conversations with Stalin on questions of political economy," Cold War International History Project [CWIHP], Working Paper 33 (2001), p. 19 (second quote).

8. Sanchez-Sibony, *Red globalization*, pp. 60–67. Nove, *Economic history*, pp. 260–79. Harold James, *International monetary cooperation since Bretton Woods* (Oxford University Press, 1996), pp. 60–71. Vladimir O. Pechatnov, "The Soviet Union and the Bretton Woods Conference," G. Scott-Smith and J. S. Rofe, eds., *Global perspectives on the Bretton Woods Conference and the post-war world order* (Palgrave Macmillan, 2017), pp. 103–4.

9. Mark Pittaway, *Eastern Europe 1939–2000* (Arnold, 2004), pp. 17–33. Thomas W. Simons, *Eastern Europe in the postwar world* (St. Martin's Press, 1991), pp. 38–43. E. A. Radice, "The collapse of German hegemony and its economic consequences," Michael C. Kaser and E. A. Radice, eds., *The economic history of Eastern Europe 1919–1975*, vol. 2 (Clarendon Press, 1986), pp. 495–519. Adam Zwass and Michel Vale, "Monetary cooperation between East & West," *Soviet and Eastern European Foreign Trade*, 10/3–4 (1974/1975), p. 49. Kazimierz Grzybowski, "Foreign trade policy of the Soviet bloc," *Polish Review*, 1/2–3 (1956), pp. 99–100.

10. Mark Kramer, "Stalin, Soviet policy, and the consolidation of a communist bloc in Eastern Europe, 1944–53," Valdimir Tismaneanu, ed., *Stalinism revisited* (Central European University Press, 2009), pp. 59–81. Simons, *Eastern Europe*, pp. 47–79. Pittaway, *Eastern Europe*, pp. 35–61. Ben Fowkes, *Eastern Europe, 1945–1969* (Longman, 2000), pp. 22–31. Z. A. B. Zeman, *Pursued by a bear* (Chatto & Windus, 1989), pp. 170–95. Eduard Mark, "Revolution by degrees," CWIHP, Working Paper 31 (2001). Gerhard Wettig, "Die sowjetische Wirtschaftspolitik in der SBZ/ DDR 1945–1954," Walter M. Iber and Peter Ruggenthaler, eds., *Stalins Wirtschaftspolitik an der sowjetischen Peripherie* (StudienVerlag, 2011), pp. 73–75. W. Brus, "Postwar reconstruction and socio-economic transformation," Kaser and Radice, *Economic history*, vol. 2, pp. 596–608.

11. R. Nötel, "International finance and monetary reforms," Kaser and Radice, *Economic history*, vol. 2, pp. 536–51. Brus, "Postwar reconstruction," pp. 608–21. Vladislav M. Zubok, *A failed empire* (University of North Carolina Press, 2007), pp. 69–93. Peter Heumos, "Die Konferenzen der sozialistischen Parteien Zentral- und Osteuropas in Prag und Budapest 1946 und 1947," *Jahrbücher für Geschichte Osteuropas*, 31/2 (1983), pp. 244–84. Grzybowski, "Foreign trade policy," pp. 100, 105.

12. André Mommen, *Stalin's economist* (Routledge, 2011), pp. 157–58. Nötel, "International finance," pp. 572–76. Wettig, "Sowjetische Wirtschaftspolitik," p. 78. Bogdan Musial, "Sowjetische Demontagen und Beschlagnahmungen in Polen und in den ehemaligen deutschen Ostgebieten," Iber and Ruggenthaler, *Stalins Wirtschaftspolitik*, pp. 45–71. United States, Department of State, *Treaties of peace with Italy, Bulgaria, Hungary, Roumania, and Finland* (US Government Printing Office, 1947), pp. 10 (Hungarian Treaty), 28 (Romanian Treaty). Italy and Finland paid 100 and 300 million US dollars, respectively, of reparations to the Soviet Union. Derek Howard Aldcroft, *The European economy, 1914–2000*,

4th ed. (Routledge, 2001), pp. 113, 184. Nötel, "International finance," pp. 576–79.

13. Geoffrey Roberts, "Moscow and the Marshall Plan," *Europe-Asia Studies*, 46/8 (1994), pp. 1371–86. Scott D. Parrish and Mikhail M. Narinsky, "New evidence on the Soviet rejection of the Marshall Plan, 1947," CWIHP, Working Paper 9 (2011). Benn Steil, *The Marshall Plan* (Simon & Schuster, 2018), pp. 117–45. Wettig, "Sowjetische Wirtschaftspolitik," pp. 87–91. Mommen, *Stalin's economist*, pp. 162–64. Sanchez-Sibony, *Red globalization*, pp. 67–69. Wolfgang Mueller, "Die UdSSR und die europäische Integration," Michael Gehler, ed., *Vom gemeinsamen Markt zur europäischen Unionsbildung* (Böhlau Verlag, 2009), pp. 620–21. Xenia J. Eudin, "Moscow's views of American imperialism," *Russian Review*, 13/4 (1954), pp. 280–84. First quote from Richard B. Day, *Cold War capitalism* (M. E. Sharpe, 1995), p. 49. Valerie Bunce, "The empire strikes back," *International Organization*, 39/1 (1985), pp. 1–46 (second quote).

14. Mommen, *Stalin's economist*, p. 164. Roberts, "Moscow," p. 1378.

15. Nötel, "International finance," p. 579. Grzybowski, "Foreign trade policy," p. 107. Various documents on East German monetary reform: L. N. Dobrokhotov, *Denezhnaya reforma v SSSR 1947 goda* (ROSSPEN, 2010), pp. 683–744. "Poland withdraws from World Bank," *Los Angeles Times*, March 16, 1950, p. 32 (quote). "World Bank, Fund expels the Czechs," *New York Times* [*NYT*], January 6, 1955, p. 37.

16. Zeman, *Pursued by a bear*, p. 223. Michael Mastanduno, *Economic containment* (Cornell University Press, 1992), pp. 64–106. A. Köves, "The impact of Western trade restrictions on East–West trade after World War II," *Acta Oeconomica*, 19/1 (1977), pp. 69–73. Metcalf, *Council*, pp. 21–28.

17. Quotes from Elena Dragomir, "The formation of the Soviet bloc's Council for Mutual Economic Assistance," *Journal of Cold War Studies*, 14/1 (2012), pp. 34–47. Leonid Gibianskii, "Die Gründung des Rates für gegenseitige Wirtschaftshilfe," Iber and Ruggenthaler, *Stalins Wirtschaftspolitik*, pp. 24–40. Arie Bloed, *The external relations of the Council for Mutual Economic Assistance* (Martinus Nijhoff Publishers, 1988), p. 6. Various documents: *Bundesarchiv* [*BArch*], DC 20/22080–22082.

18. For good statistics in absolute terms, see P. W., "East-West Trade," *The World Today*, 10/1 (1954), pp. 19–31. Pavel Szobi, "Die Tschechoslowakei im RGW," Iber and Ruggenthaler, *Stalins Wirtschaftspolitik*, pp. 102–9. Oleg Hoeffding, "Recent trends in Soviet foreign trade," *Annals of the American Academy of Political and Social Science*, 303 (1956), p. 76.

19. W. Brus, "1950 to 1953," Kaser and Radice, *Economic history*, vol. 3, pp. 12–24. Stephen Kotkin, *Magnetic mountain* (University of California Press, 1997). Katherine Lebow, *Unfinished utopia* (Cornell University Press, 2013). Ruth May, "Planned city Stalinstadt," *Planning Perspectives*, 18/1 (2010), pp. 47–78. Mark Pittaway, "Creating and domesticating Hungary's socialist industrial landscape," *Historical Archaeology*, 39/3 (2005), pp. 75–93. "Protocol no. 2/1," [April 27–29, 1949], BArch, DC 20/22080, p. 3. The names of the steel cities in the GDR and Hungary were de-Stalinized in 1961

into the current names. Nicolas Spulber, *The economics of communist Eastern Europe* (Greenwood Press, 1957), p. 416. Metcalf, *Council*, p. 53.

20. Brus, "1950," pp. 7–11. Fowkes, *Eastern Europe*, pp. 41–44.
21. Ahrens, *Gegenseitige Wirtschaftshilfe*, pp. 35–85. Lavigne, *International political economy*, pp. 9–25, 241–43.
22. Margarita M. Balmaceda, "Der Weg in die Abhängigkeit," *Osteuropa*, 54/9–10 (2004), p. 163. Randall W. Stone, *Satellites and commissars* (Princeton University Press, 1996), pp. 5–9.
23. Stalin, *Economic problems*, pp. 30–31 (first and second quotes). This is also how the CMEA saw itself in retrospect a decade later: "Information," [October 1963], BArch, DN 1/12422, p. 3. Austin Jersild, "The Soviet state as imperial scavenger," *American Historical Review*, 116/1 (2011), pp. 109–32 (third quote). Austin Jersild, *The Sino-Soviet alliance* (University of North Carolina Press, 2014), pp. 58–81.
24. Jana Wüstenhagen, *Blick durch den Vorhang* (Nomos Verlag, 2001), pp. 34–39, 107–41. Stalin, *Economic problems*, pp. 35–37 (quotes).
25. Geoffrey Roberts, "A chance for peace?," CWIHP, Working Paper 57 (2008). Matthew Evangelista, "'Why keep such an army?'," CWIHP, Working Paper 19 (1997). Metcalf, *Council*, p. 56. Sanchez-Sibony, *Red globalization*, pp. 91–124. See the chapters by Niklas Jensen-Eriksen, Robert Cantoni, and Vyacheslav Nekrasov in Jeronim Perović, ed., *Cold War energy* (Palgrave Macmillan, 2017), pp. 105–99. [Communist Party of the Soviet Union], *Programme of the Communist Party of the Soviet Union* (Foreign Languages, 1961).
26. Quote from "Khrushchev under fire," *NYT*, October 18, 1964, p. 32. Day, *Cold War capitalism*, pp. 87–88. Yakov Feygin, "Reforming the Cold War state," unpublished PhD thesis, University of Pennsylvania, 2017, pp. 37–154. Day, *Cold War capitalism*, pp. 93–130. Philip Hanson, *The rise and fall of the Soviet economy* (Pearson, 2003), pp. 70–97.
27. "Speech by Comrade Mikoyan," March 26, 1954, BArch, DC 20/22083, pp. 1–8 (first to third quote). "Protocol no. 1/5," [June 24–25, 1954], BArch, DC 20/22084, pp. 1–14 (fourth and fifth quotes). "Protocol no. 1/6," [December 7–11, 1955], BArch, DC 20/22085, pp. 11–20 (sixth quote). Michael C. Kaser, *Comecon* (Oxford University Press, 1967), p. 69.
28. Kaser, *Comecon*, pp. 77–79, 169–70. Lorenz M. Lüthi, *The Sino-Soviet split* (Princeton University Press, 2008), pp. 110–11. Various documents: Arkhiv Vneshnei Politiki Rossiiskoi Federatsii [AVPRF], fond 0100, opis 49, delo 37, papka 414. Metcalf, *Council*, pp. 55–71. "Information," June 27, 1957, Stiftung Archiv der Parteien und Massenorganisationen der DDR im Bundesarchiv [SAPMO-BArch], DY 30/3404, p. 33 (quote).
29. "Calculation of quotas for membership countries," [1963?], BArch, DN 6/1443, p. 1. David D. Finley, "A political perspective of economic relations in the communist camp," *Western Political Quarterly*, 17/2 (1964), p. 305. Various documents: BArch, DC 20/22084–22089. Falk Flade, *Energy infrastructures in the Eastern Bloc* (Otto Harrassowitz, 2017), pp. 75–88. Lorenz M. Lüthi, "Drifting apart," Perović, *Cold War energy*, p. 374. "Protocol no. 1/11," [May 13–16, 1959], BArch, DC 20/22090, pp. 28–32. Flade, *Energy infrastructures*, pp. 59–72. Kaser, *Comecon*, pp. 80–81.

30. As Ulbricht told Khrushchev in December 1960: "I. The Moscow meeting," [December 19–20, 1960], Politisches Archiv des Auswärtigen Amtes, Bestand: Ministerium für Auswärtige Angelegenheiten [PAAA-MfAA], A 15489, p. 42. "Speech," [March 1, 1961], SAPMO-BArch, DY 30/3405, pp. 1–8. "Speech," [August 3, 1961], PAAA-MfAA, G-A 476, pp. 31–36. "Proposal," September 9, 1961, SAPMO-BArch, DY 30/J IV 2/2A/851, pp. 30–41. Ahrens, *Gegenseitige Wirtschaftshilfe*, pp. 124–25.

31. "Protocol," December 15, 1961, BArch, DE 1/61248, pp. 4–12. Mueller, "UdSSR," pp. 828–43. "The position of the Soviet Union regarding some CMEA problems," July 22, 1963, SAPMO-BArch, DY 30/IV A 2/20/158, pp. 1–12 (quotes). Harry G. Shaffer, "Comecon integration," *Soviet and Eastern European Foreign Trade*, 9/3 (1973), p. 5.

32. "Protocol," [June 1962], BArch, DE 1/61367, pp. 1–18. "Communiqué," [June 1962], SAPMO-BArch, DY 30/3406, p. 2. Lüthi, *Sino-Soviet split*, pp. 171–74, 201–5. "Protocol," December 15, 1961, BArch, DE 1/61248, pp. 3–4.

33. "[No title]," [July 17, 1962], SAPMO-BArch, DY 30/3417, pp. 1–7. "The significance of the CMEA decision to create a system of multilateral clearance and to establish an international bank of the socialist states," [December 16–20, 1962], BArch, DN 1/11206, pp. 1–9. "The international bank," [1964?], BArch, DN 1/11206, pp. 1–12. Zdzisław Osiecki and Michel Vale, "The international banks of the COMECON countries," *Soviet and Eastern European Foreign Trade*, 12/1 (1976), pp. 13–15. Leslie Szeplaki, "A socialist 'International Monetary Fund'," *Journal of Economic Issues*, 5/4 (1971), pp. 29–30 (quote).

34. "Notes," February 21, 1963, SAPMO-BArch, DY 30/3420, p. 2 (first and second quotes). Third quote from Bloed, *External relations*, pp. 9, 29. Lüthi, *Sino-Soviet split*, p. 269. "Statement," [July 17, 1962], SAPMO-BArch, DY 30/3417, pp. 11–12 (fourth to seventh quote). Metcalf, *Council*, p. 50. "Protocol," [July 25–26, 1963], SAPMO-BArch, DY 30/3408, p. 74 (eighth quote).

35. Ahrens, *Gegenseitige Wirtschaftshilfe*, pp. 133–90. Feygin, "Reforming," pp. 155–20. W. Brus, "1966 to 1975," Kaser and Radice, *Economic history*, vol. 3, pp. 207–16. Henry Wilcox Schaefer, *Comecon and the politics of integration* (Praeger, 1972), pp. 10–12.

36. Stone, *Satellites*, pp. 39–41. Feygin, "Reforming," pp. 203–59. Ahrens, *Gegenseitige Wirtschaftshilfe*, pp. 191–213.

37. Richard F. Staar, *Communist regimes in Eastern Europe*, 5th ed. (Hoover Institution Press, 1988), p. 302. Lüthi, "Drifting apart," pp. 374–75. "Information," January 26, 1965, SAPMO-BArch, DY 30/3428, pp. 1–3. "Conc.: Preparations of the 20th session of the Executive Committee of CMEA," November 22, 1965, BArch, DN 1/11209, p. 1 (first quote). "Information," June 14, 1966, SAPMO-BArch, DY 30/3434, pp. 6–9. "Proposals," [August 22, 1968], BArch, DE 1/54661, pp. 1–20 (second quote). "Coordination," February 15, 1967, BArch, DE 1/54661, pp. 1–2. "Note," December 2, 1964, SAPMO-BArch, DY 30/3466, p. 206 (third quote).

38. Metcalf, *Council*, p. 91. Wüstenhagen, *Blick*, pp. 176–82. Kazimierz Grzybowski, "The Council for Mutual Economic Assistance and the European Community," *American Journal of International Law*, 84/1 (1990), p. 287. Suvi Kansikas, *Socialist countries face the European Community* (PIE Peter Lang, 2014), p. 102.

39. Various documents: SAPMO-BArch, DY 3023/807. "Position paper," November 12, 1968, SAPMO-BArch, DY 30/3294, pp. 337–56. "Dear Comrade Deputy," October 12, 1971, BArch, DC 20/12410, pp. 4–5 (quotes). Various documents: SAPMO-BArch, DY 30/3460, 3461, and 13859. Wolfgang Mueller, "Recognition in return for détente?," *Journal of Cold War Studies*, 13/4 (2011), pp. 94–95. Kansikas, *Socialist countries*, pp. 134–70. Various documents: SAPMO-BArch, DY 30/IV 2/2.036/68 and 69. Lavigne, *International political economy*, pp. 81–82.

40. Schaefer, *Comecon*, pp. 15–35. "Information," [January 21–23, 1969], SAPMO-BArch, DY 30/3412, pp. 42–50. The Hungarian and Czechoslovak proposals: "Program," November 21, 1968, PAAA-MfAA, C 273/76, pp. 1–55. "Nyers Rezső," [January 23, 1969], PAAA-MfAA, G-A 449, pp. 135–55. Various documents: SAPMO-BArch, DY 3023/784, pp. 156–280 (quotes on p. 261). "Protocol," [April 23, 1969], SAPMO-BArch, DY 30/3415, pp. 1–19a.

41. Various documents: SAPMO-BArch, DY 3023/696, 782 and 783, and DC 20/4499, BArch, DE 1/54661 and DN 1/27981. Metcalf, *Council*, pp. 108–9. "Information," [July 27–29, 1971], BArch, DC 20/I/3/873, pp. 4–12 (quote). "Dear Comrade Secretary," June 18, 1975, SAPMO-BArch, DC 20/16860, pp. 174–205. For the reservations, see "Information," June 28, 1971, SAPMO-BArch, DY 30/3458, pp. 2–8. For a good overview of Romanian goals in international affairs in 1971, see "Memorandum of conversation," August 31, 1971, United States, Department of State, *Foreign relations of the United States* [*FRUS*], 1969–76, XXIX (US Government Printing Office, 2007), pp. 506–11. "Romania joins IMF, first in Soviet bloc," *Washington Post*, December 7, 1972, p. El. For decision to ban membership: "30. Argumentation," January 17, 1983, Der Bundesbeauftragte für die Unterlagen des Staatssicherheitsdienstes der ehemaligen Deutschen Demokratischen Republik [BStU], MfS HA XVIII, 16068, p. 11. For Hungary's interests since 1968: "Memorandum for Dr. Kissinger," February 8, 1971, Richard Nixon Presidential Library [RMN], NSC, Country files, box 693, Hungary, vol. I, pp. 1–2.

42. Lüthi, "Drifting apart," pp. 375–89. Flade, *Energy infrastructures*, pp. 106–74.

43. "Estimates," May 7, 1958, BArch, NY 4090/470, pp. 7–17. "Note," [November 1973], SAPMO-BArch, DC 20/16863, pp. 52–56. "Transcript," August 7, 1974, SAPMO-BArch, DY 30/IV 2/2.036/58, pp. 85–94 (first quote). "Tentative report," April 21, 1975, SAPMO-BArch, DY 30/IV 2/2.036/60, pp. 86–94 (second quote). Ahrens, *Gegenseitige Wirtschaftshilfe*, pp. 302–40. Stone, *Satellites*, pp. 94–102. Brus, "1966," pp. 160–85.

44. Krzystof Czerkawski and Don Hank, "The indebtedness of socialist countries to the West," *Eastern European Economics*, 21/1 (1982), pp. 77–90. "Information," August 15, 1977, SAPMO-BArch, DY 30/IV 2/2.036/65, pp. 124–30. Lüthi, "Drifting apart," pp. 383–89.

45. "Report," July 3, 1968, BArch, DN 1/20061, pp. 4–5. Metcalf, *Council*, pp. 90–91. "Protocol," [April 23, 1969], SAPMO-BArch, DY 30/3415, pp. 14–15. "Transcript," August 20, 1973, BArch, DC 20/4415, pp. 97–98.
46. "Statements," [July 8, 1976], SAPMO-BArch, DC 20/16861, pp. 106–7. "Transcript," December 13, 1976, BArch, DC 20/5149, pp. 12–31.
47. "Information," May 30, 1977, SAPMO-BArch, DY 30/IV 2/2.036/64, pp. 327–28 (first quote). "Statements," [July 8, 1976], SAPMO-BArch, DC 20/16861, p. 108. "Information," June 9, 1978, SAPMO-BArch, DY 30/IV 2/2.035/56, 180–241 (second and third quotes from pp. 193 and 239). "Speech," [June 26–28, 1979], BArch, DC 20/5135, 33–57. "Information," September 1979, BArch, DC 20/4324, pp. 20–42.

17   Germany

1. Gerhard Wettig, *Bereitschaft zur Einheit in Freiheit?* (Olzog, 1999), pp. 36–39, 57–68. Werner Abelshauser, *Deutsche Wirtschaftsgeschichte* (Bundeszentrale für politische Bildung, 2011), pp. 59–87.
2. Edgar Wolfrum, *Die geglückte Demokratie* (Klett-Cotta, 2006), p. 26. Abelshauser, *Wirtschaftsgeschichte*, pp. 64–82. Manfred Görtemaker, *Geschichte der Bundesrepublik Deutschland* (Fischer Taschenbuch, 1999), pp. 37–38.
3. Abelshauser, *Wirtschaftsgeschichte*, pp. 112–29, 404–11. André Steiner, *Von Plan zu Plan* (Aufbau Taschenbuch, 2007), pp. 21–37. Hermann Wentker, *Aussenpolitik in engen Grenzen* (Oldenbourg Verlag, 2007), pp. 63–67.
4. Wettig, *Bereitschaft*, pp. 140–52. Wolfrum, *Die geglückte Demokratie*, pp. 38–39. Görtemaker, *Geschichte*, pp. 43–65. Klaus Schroeder, *Der SED Staat* (Carl Hanser, 1998), p. 75. Wilfried Loth, *Stalin's unwanted child* (Macmillan, 1998). Chen Jian, *Mao's China and the Cold War* (University of North Carolina Press, 2001), p. 53.
5. Wolfrum, *Die geglückte Demokratie*, pp. 43, 51. For first and second quotes from the Basic Law, see www.documentarchiv.de/brd/1949/grundgesetz.html, accessed on August 24, 2015. Andreas Salz, *Bonn–Berlin* (Monsenstein und Vannerdat, 2006), pp. 28–43. Eckart Conze, *Die Suche nach Sicherheit* (Siedler Verlag, 2009), pp. 45–89. Third quote from Stefan Wolle, *Der Grosse Plan* (Bundeszentrale für politische Bildung, 2013), pp. 53, 95 (italics added).
6. Gregor Schöllgen, *Die Aussenpolitik der Bundesrepublik Deutschland* (C. H. Beck, 2004), pp. 26–27. Wettig, *Bereitschaft*, pp. 205–34.
7. Abelshauser, *Wirtschaftsgeschichte*, pp. 87–213. "Declaration," September 21, 1949, Institut für Zeitgeschichte [Institute for Contemporary Research], ed., *Akten zur Auswärtigen Politik der Bundesrepublik Deutschland, 1949/50* (R. Oldenbourg Verlag, 1997), pp. 3–4. Adolf M. Birke, *Nation ohne Haus*, upd. ed. (Siedler, 1994), pp. 296–305. Wolle, *Grosse Plan*, pp. 116–19, 237–41. Steiner, *Plan*, pp. 81–87. Gary Bruce, *Resistance with the People* (Rowman & Littlefield, 2003), pp. 159–217.
8. Wolle, *Grosse Plan*, pp. 246–63. Ilko-Sascha Kowalczuk, *17. Juni 1953* (Bundeszentrale für politische Bildung, 2013), pp. 22–25, 34–105. "[No title]," no date, Stiftung Archiv der Parteien und Massenorganisationen der DDR im Bundesarchiv [SAPMO-BArch], DY 30/J IV 2/2A/3196, 1–8 (quotes).

9. Wolle, *Grosse Plan*, pp. 271–303. Andreas Malycha and Peter Jochen Winters, *Die SED* (C. H. Beck, 2009), p. 120. Wentker, *Aussenpolitik*, pp. 126–27.

10. "Armament demands in Moscow: Grotewohl for a regular army," *Der Tag*, December 1, 1954, Bundesarchiv [BArch], DC 20/18555, p. 152. Schroeder, *SED Staat*, p. 90. Vojtech Mastny and Malcolm Byrne, eds., *A cardboard castle?* (Central European University Press, 2005), pp. 2–3. "Stenographic transcript," June 1–2, 1955, SAPMO-BArch, DY 30/IV 2/1/147, pp. 1–46.

11. Mastny and Byrne, *Cardboard castle?*, p. 5. Various documents: BArch, NY 4090/471, pp. 198–201. Torsten Diedrich, "Die DDR zwischen den Blöcken," Torsten Diedrich, Winfried Heinemann, and Christian F. Ostermann, eds., *Der Warschauer Pakt* (Ch. Links, 2009), pp. 69–72.

12. "Interview given by the Federal Chancellor to Herr Ernst Friedländer on 12th November 1952," National Archives of the United Kingdom [NAUK], FO 371/97857, p. 1 (quote). Konrad Adenauer, *Erinnerungen*, vol. 2, 4th ed. (Deutsche Verlags-Anstalt, 1966), pp. 132–62. Jeffrey Herf, *Divided memory* (Harvard University Press, 1997), pp. 267–323.

13. Werner Kilian, *Die Hallstein Doktrin* (Duncker & Humblot, 2001), pp. 14–30. William Glenn Gray, *Germany's Cold War* (University of North California Press, 2003), pp. 30–86.

14. Quote from Manfred Uschner, *Die Ostpolitik der SPD* (Dietz, 1991), pp. 33–53. Peter Graf Kielmansegg, *Das geteilte Land* (Pantheon Verlag, 2007), p. 135. Adenauer, *Erinnerungen*, vol. 2, pp. 223–31. Görtemaker, *Geschichte*, pp. 375–77.

15. Kielmansegg, *Das geteilte Land*, pp. 75–79. Wentker, *Aussenpolitik*, pp. 81, 141–44. "Copy," August 1, 1955, BArch, NY 4090/463, 151 (quote). Heike Amos, *Die Westpolitik der SED 1948/49–1961* (Akademie Verlag, 1999), pp. 188–335.

16. Schroeder, *SED Staat*, p. 132. "Decision of the collegium from April 25, 1956," no date, BArch, DC 20/591, pp. 2–11. Wentker, *Aussenpolitik*, p. 123 (quote).

17. "German–Israeli Agreement," September 10, 1952, NAUK, FO 371/100009, pp. 1–2. "Aide memoire," November 29, 1955, BArch, DC 20/16943, pp. 11–13. Wentker, *Aussenpolitik*, pp. 109–18. "Note," March 4, 1957, SAPMO-BArch, DY 30/J IV 2/2J/335, pp. 1–4.

18. Wolfgang Buschfort, "Wie die SED und MfS in Westdeutschland 'Faschisten' suchten und bei sich selbst 'übersahen'," Manfred Agethen , Eckhard Jesse, and Ehrhart Neubert, eds., *Der missbrauchte Antifaschismus* (Herder, 2002), pp. 237–47. "Draft communiqué," [August 1957], SAPMO-BArch, NY 4090/488, pp. 65–68.

19. Gerhard Sätler, "Die Sperranlagen," Klaus-Dietmar Henke, ed., *Die Mauer* (Deutscher Taschenbuchverlag, 2011), pp. 152–62. Jürgen Ritte and Peter H. Lapp, *Die Grenze* (Ch. Links, 2001), p. 167.

20. "Report," December 15, 1961, SAPMO-BArch, DY 30/IV 2/20/373, p. 239. "Declaration," August 31, 1961, BArch, DC 20/I/3/346, pp. 5–9 (quotes). Gerhard Wettig, *Chruschtschows Berlin-Krise 1958 bis 1963* (Oldenbourg Verlag, 2006), pp. 191–213.

21. "Dear comrade Nikita Sergeyevich," January 18, 1961, www.chronik-der-mauer.de, accessed on June 23, 2011. Damian von Melis, *Republikflucht* (Oldenbourg Verlag, 2006), pp. 38–72, 255.

22. *Wettig, Chruschtschows Berlin-Krise*, pp. 129–72. Hope M. Harrison, *Driving the Soviets up the wall* (Princeton University Press, 2003).
23. Steiner, *Plan*, p. 141. "The Moscow meeting," [December 19–20, 1960], Politisches Archiv des Auswärtigen Amtes, Bestand: Ministerium für Auswärtige Angelegenheiten [PAAA-MfAA], A 15489, p. 42 (quote).
24. Heinrich Potthoff, *Im Schatten der Mauer* (Propyläen Verlag, 1999), pp. 22–24. Quotes from in Helge Heidemeyer, "Antifaschistischer Schutzwall oder Bankrotterklärung des Ulbricht-Regimes?," Udo Wengst and Hermann Wentker, eds., *Das doppelte Deutschland* (Ch. Links, 2008), pp. 87–109. Christof Münger, *Kennedy, die Berliner Mauer und die Kubakrise* (Ferdinand Schöningh, 2003), pp. 102–10.
25. Sergei Khrushchev, ed., *Memoirs of Nikita Khrushchev*, vol. 3 (Pennsylvania State University Press, 2007), p. 311 (first and second quotes). "Report of the ambassador of the Federal Republic of Germany in Moscow, Kroll," November 9, 1961, Germany, Bundesministerium des Innern, ed., *Dokumente zur Deutschlandpolitik*, ser. 4, vol. 7, part 2 (Oldenbourg Verlag, 1976), p. 925 (third and fifth quotes). Vladislav M. Zubok, *A failed empire* (University of North Carolina Press, 2007), p. 203. Norbert Podewin, *Walter Ulbricht* (Dietz, 1995), p. 359.
26. Various documents: SAPMO-BArch, DY 30/J IV 2/2A/851. "Theses," [September 1961], PAAA-MfAA, A 1149, p. 41 (first quote). Podewin, *Ulbricht*, pp. 360–79. Steiner, *Plan*, pp. 164–71. Ralf Ahrens, *Gegenseitige Wirtschaftshilfe?* (Böhlau Verlag, 2000), p. 124 (second quote). Jeffrey Kopstein, *The politics of economic decline in East Germany, 1945–1989* (University of North Carolina Press, 1997), pp. 45–56. "Report," August 21, 1964, BArch, DE 1/54913, pp. 1–25.
27. "Report," [August 23, 1961], SAPMO-BArch, DY 30/J IV 2/2J/759, pp. 1–4. Khrushchev, *Memoirs of Nikita Khrushchev*, vol. 3, p. 311 (first quote). "Note," [February], 1962, PAAA-MfAA, G-A 476, pp. 88 (second quote). "Summary of Khrushchev's references to Berlin in a conversation with Harold Wilson in Moscow on June 2nd," [June 1964], Labour History Archive and Study Centre, People's History Museum [LHASC-PHM], Labour Party Int'l Dept, box "International Dept, LP/ID/USSR/20 – USSR/38, USSR: Correspondence + Memos," p. 1 (third quote). Wentker, *Aussenpolitik*, pp. 211–33. "Dear comrade Khrushchev," May 6, 1964, SAPMO-BArch, DY 30/3513, p. 62.
28. "Dear comrade Vosseler," August 4, 1961, PAAA-MfAA, A 5295, pp. 128–32. "Note on a talk with Prime Minister Nehru on August 18, 4 to 5 p.m.," PAAA-MfAA, A 13911, pp. 101–4. "Assessment," September 7, 1961, PAAA-MfAA, A 14336, pp. 82–84. "Excerpt from information I/16.8.61," PAAA-MfAA, A 12617, pp. 373–74 (quote). "On the Conference of Non-Aligned Nations in Belgrade, September 1–5, 1961," September 23, 1961, SAPMO-BArch, NY 4182/1236, pp. 40–49. "Session of the State Council on March 29, 1962," PAAA-MfAA, A 14819, 2–9. "Dear Comrade Stainer," November 5, 1964, PAAA-MfAA, A 17441, pp. 236–38.
29. "Information," November 20, 1961, PAAA-MfAA, A 1149, pp. 1–16. "Note for file," February 6, 1962, PAAA-MfAA, G-A 478, pp. 39–44. "Dear

comrade Winzer," August 9, 1962, PAAA-MfAA, A 1149, pp. 18–19. "[No title]," December 13, 1963, PAAA-MfAA, A 1149, pp. 25–26 (quote).

30. Zhonggong zhongyang wenxian yanjiushi, ed., *Zhou Enlai nianpu, 1949–1976* [*ZELNP*], vol. 2 (Zhongyang wenxian chubanshe, 1997), p. 672. "On the relations to the People's Republic of China 1965," December 14, 1964, PAAA-MfAA, C 6565, pp. 193–95. "Dear comrades," December 18, 1964, BArch, DC 20/10170, pp. 1–2. Gray, *Germany's Cold War*, p. 181. "Information," June 23, 1965, SAPMO-BArch, DY 30/IV A 2/20/230, pp. 1–3.

31. Potthoff, *Schatten*, pp. 21–33. Schroeder, *SED Staat*, pp. 151–53.

32. Christian Hacke, *Die Aussenpolitik der Bundesrepublik Deutschland*, upd. ed. (Ullstein Taschenbuch, 2003), p. 111. "References," May 23, 1964, PAAA-MfAA, G-A 428, pp. 62–63.

33. "[No title]," June 19, 1964, SAPMO-BArch, DY 30/3513, pp. 160–68. "Reply letter of comrade N. S. Khrushchev on the letter by Federal Chancellor L. Erhard," July 29, 1964, SAPMO-BArch, DY 30/3513, pp. 176–83. "Material on some aspects of Adzhubei's trip to West Germany and on remarks by Kroll," November 3, 1964, SAPMO-BArch, DY 30/3497, pp. 262–70. "Information," October 27, 1964, SAPMO-BArch, DY 30/3497, pp. 259–61.

34. Jean Lacouture, *De Gaulle* (Norton, 1992), pp. 215–16. Adenauer, *Erinnerungen*, vol. 3, pp. 119–32 (first quote). Second and third quotes from treaty: web.archive.org/web/20001020051830/www.dhm.de/lemo/html/dokumente/ DieZuspitzungDesKaltenKrieges_vertragElyseeVertrag/index.html, accessed on August 27, 2015. Görtemaker, *Geschichte*, pp. 389–437.

35. "Note," July 26, 1966, SAPMO-BArch, DY 30/3517, p. 60.

36. Potthoff, *Schatten*, p. 57. Uschner, *Ostpolitik*, pp. 57–73. Schroeder, *SED Staat*, p. 156.

37. "Statement," February 7, 1967, SAPMO-BArch, DY 30/3396, pp. 226–30. Wentker, *Aussenpolitik*, pp. 243, 272–73. "Comrades Ulbricht, Stoph, Honecker, Axen," May 2, 1969, PAAA-MfAA, G-A 419, pp. 1–8. Gray, *Germany's Cold War*, pp. 210–12. "Dear comrades," May 27, 1969, BArch, DC 20/13066, pp. 30–39.

38. Potthoff, *Schatten*, pp. 73–74. "From the Statement of Government by the Federal Chancellor, Brandt, before the German Federal Parliament," October 28, 1969, Willy Brandt, *Berliner Ausgabe*, vol. 6 (Dietz, 2005), p. 237 (quote). "Note," June 16, 1969, PAAA-MfAA, C 975/71, p. 13.

39. "Proposals of the Soviet government," January 8, 1958, BArch, NY 4090/ 474, pp. 83–97. Peter Merseburger, *Willy Brandt, 1913–1992* (Deutscher Taschenbuchverlag, 2004), pp. 608–9. Quote from Frank Fischer, "Einleitung", Brandt, *Berliner Ausgabe*, vol. 6, pp. 47–52.

40. "Note," August 27, 1970, PAAA-MfAA, C 57/73, pp. 70–73. "Information," [October 1970], BArch, DY 30/J IV 2/2J/3150, pp. 1–8. "Information," December 24, 1970, PAAA-MfAA, G-A 453, pp. 157–58.

41. Katarzyna Stokłosa, *Polen und die deutsche Ostpolitik 1945–1990* (Vandenhoeck & Ruprecht, 2011), pp. 219–20. Fischer, "Einleitung," p. 56. Merseburger, *Willy Brandt*, pp. 612–15.

42. "Inaugural Address," January 20, 1969, www.presidency.ucsb.edu/ws/ ?pid=1941, accessed on August 30, 2015. Schöllgen, *Aussenpolitik*, pp.

110–13. Anatoly F. Dobrynin, *In confidence* (Times Books, 1995), pp. 201–2. Schroeder, *SED Staat*, p. 160.

43. Quoted from Schroeder, *SED Staat*, p. 206. Fischer, "Einleitung," pp. 52–53. Jan Schönfelder and Rainer Erices, *Willy Brandt in Erfurt* (Ch. Links, 2010), pp. 202–8.

44. Podewin, *Ulbricht*, p. 416. "The position," no date, PAAA-MfAA, C 74/74, p. 86. Schroeder, *SED Staat*, p. 160. "On the talks [with] Comr. L. I. Brezhnev," August 20, 1970, SAPMO-BArch, DY 30/3295, p. 40 (quote). "Note," [August 21, 1970], SAPMO-BArch, DY 30/3295, p. 44.

45. Monika Kaiser, *Machtwechsel von Ulbricht to Honecker* (Akademie Verlag, 1997), p. 385. Podewin, *Ulbricht*, pp. 419–20. Schroeder, *SED Staat*, pp. 206–8.

46. Kaiser, *Machtwechsel*, pp. 372–75. "[No title]," July 28, 1970, SAPMO-BArch, DY 30/3295, pp. 27–35 (quotes). "On the talks [with] Comr. L. I. Brezhnev," August 20, 1970, SAPMO-BArch, DY 30/3295, pp. 38–42.

47. "Dear comrades," January 21, 1971, SAPMO-BArch, DY 30/3295, pp. 141–47. "Dear Comrade Leonid Ilyich Brezhnev," April 27, 1971, SAPMO-BArch, DY 30/3295, p. 153. "Information," no date, SAPMO-BArch, DY 30/11466, pp. 1–42 (quote). Steiner, *Plan*, pp. 187–209.

48. Schöllgen, *Aussenpolitik*, pp. 113–16. Schroeder, *SED Staat*, p. 200.

49. Various documents: PAAA-MfAA, C 1044/77, C 1046/71, C 1052/77, C 1739/76, C 1752/76, C 1756/76, C 1762/76. "Flash telegram," December 23, 1971, SAPMO-BArch, DY 30/IV B 2/20/432, p. 6.

50. Görtemaker, *Geschichte*, pp. 560–61. Mary E. Sarotte, *Dealing with the Devil* (University of North Carolina Press, 2001), pp. 140–44.

51. Schroeder, *SED Staat*, pp. 201–2. "Report," October 21, 1971, PAAA-MfAA, C785/75, p. 4. "Note," December 17, 1971, PAAA-MfAA, C 1204/73, pp. 3–4.

52. "Political report no. 19," December 20, 1971, Schweizerisches Bundesarchiv [SBA], E 2300-01, Akzession 1977/29, box 2, pp. 1–3. Wentker, *Aussenpolitik*, pp. 337–38. Markus Wolf, *Spionagechef im geheimen Krieg* (List, 1997), pp. 260–62. "Big 4 sign agreement to end Berlin role as source of tension," *Los Angeles Times*, June 4, 1972, p. 1.

53. "Stenogram," July 31, 1972, SAPMO-BArch, DY 30/J IV 2/2A/1617, pp. 46–169. "Wie Willy Brandt die Friedenskarte verspielte," *Die Welt*, June 9, 2013, www.welt.de/print/wams/politik/article116950837/Wie-Willy-Brandt -die-Friedenskarte-verspielte.html, accessed on August 30, 2015. "Information," December 14, 1973, BArch, DY 30/J IV 2/2J/5074, pp. 1–7.

54. Sarotte, *Dealing*, p. 169. Jens Gieseke, *Der Mielke-Konzern*, enl. ed. (Deutsche Verlags-Anstalt, 2006), pp. 72, 86–89. "Problems and consequences," November 6, 1973, SAPMO-BArch, DY 30/25761, pp. 449–56.

55. "The further systematic promotion of high-performance sport," [April 8, 1969], SAPMO-BArch, DY 30/J IV 2/2A/1365, pp. 85–112. Thomas Raithel, "Das Sparwasser Tor," Wengst, *Das doppelte Deutschland*, p. 271. Giselher Spitzer, *Doping in der DDR*, fourth, enl. ed. (Sportverlag Strauss, 2013). Willi Winkler, *Die Geschichte der RAF* (rororo, 2007).

56. John C. Schmeidel, *Stasi* (Routledge, 2008), pp. 144–55. Peter Onnertz, *München Olympia 1972 und die Stasi* (Agon Sportverlag, 2014), pp. 99–100. "Position paper," no date, BArch, DC 20/11784, pp. 69–76.

57. Hubertus Knabe, *Die unterwanderte Republik* (Propyläen Verlag, 1999). Eckard Michels, *Guillaume, der Spion* (Berlin: Ch. Links, 2013).
58. Hans Michael Kloth, *Vom 'Zettelfalten' zum freien Wählen* (Ch. Links, 2000), pp. 101–8.

18   The Conference on Security and Cooperation in Europe

1. R. Gerald Hughes, "Unfinished business from Potsdam," *International History Review*, 27/2 (2005), p. 263. R. C. Raack, "Stalin fixes the Oder–Neisse Line," *Journal of Contemporary History*, 25/4 (1990), p. 474. David Wolff, "Stalin's postwar border-making tactics," *Cahiers du Monde russe*, 52/2–3 (2011), p. 278.
2. Hughes, "Unfinished business," pp. 263–68. Sheldon R. Anderson, *A Cold War in the Soviet bloc* (Westview Press, 2001), pp. 52–65. "East Germans sign pact giving Poles Oder–Neisse area," *New York Times* [*NYT*], June 8, 1950, p. 1. "East Germans sign Sudetenland pact renouncing claims," *NYT*, June 24, 1950, p. 1.
3. "Dear Mr. Minister President," November 21, 1953, Bundesarchiv [BArch], DC 20/15236, pp. 2–10 (first and second quote). Various documents: United States, Department of State, *Foreign relations of the United States* [*FRUS*], 1952–54, VII/1 (US Government Printing Office, 1986), pp. 1018–1167 (third quote on p. 1023).
4. "Statement," [spring 1954], BArch, DC 20/15235, pp. 2–6. "[No title]," no date, BArch, DC 20/6890, pp. 2–3 (quote).
5. "No. 36/3eo-GE," no date, BArch, DC 20/15396, p. 5 (quote). Various documents: BArch, DC 20/6891 and DC 20/18555. Vojtech Mastny and Malcolm Byrne, eds., *A cardboard castle?* (Central European University Press, 2005), pp. 3–5, 77–79. Various documents: *FRUS*, 1955–57, V, pp. 368–424, 503–19.
6. "Proposals of the Soviet Government," January 8, 1958, BArch, NY 4090/474, pp. 83–97.
7. Anderson, *Cold War*, pp. 204–11. "Letter of W. Gomułka to N. Khrushchev," October 8, 1963, Andrzej Paczkowski, ed., *Tajne dokumenty Biura Politycznego* (Aneks, 1998), pp. 170–78 (first quote). "My dear Mr. President," December 31, 1963, John F. Kennedy Presidential Library [JFK], National Security Files, Robert W. Kromer, box 446, p. 14 (second quote). "Mr. Rapacki urges talks before MLF decision," *Guardian*, December 15, 1964, p. 1. Wanda Jarząbek, "Hope and reality," Cold War International History Project [CWIHP], Working Paper 56 (2008), p. 6. "Memory protocol," January 26, 1965, Politisches Archiv des Auswärtigen Amtes, Bestand: Ministerium für Auswärtige Angelegenheiten [PAAA-MfAA], G-A 541, pp. 64–74. Douglas Selvage, "The Warsaw Pact and nuclear nonproliferation, 1963–1965," CWIHP, Working Paper 32 (2001), pp. 1–17.
8. Rainer A. Blasius, "Erwin Wickert und die Friedensnote der Bundesregierung vom 25. März 1966," *Vierteljahreshefte für Zeitgeschichte*, 43/3 (1995), pp. 539–53. "Ambassador Emmel, in Warsaw, to Foreign Office," March 26,

1966, Institut für Zeitgeschichte, ed., *Akten zur Auswärtigen Politik der Bundesrepublik Deutschland, 1966* (R. Oldenbourg Verlag, 1997), pp. 402–3. Various documents: PAAA-MfAA, G-A 545. "Public declaration on security of Europe," July 8, 1966, Parallel History Project on Cooperative Security [PHP], www.php.isn.ethz.ch/lory1.ethz.ch/collections/colltopic7644.html?lng=en&id=17953&navinfo=14465, accessed on February 25, 2018 (quote).

9. Lorenz M. Lüthi, "Restoring chaos to history," *China Quarterly*, 210 (2012), p. 384. "Public appeal for a European security conference," March 17, 1969, PHP, www.php.isn.ethz.ch/lory1.ethz.ch/collections/colltopic032c.html?lng=en&id=18022&navinfo=14465, accessed on February 25, 2018. "Note," March 24, 1969, Stiftung Archiv der Parteien und Massenorganisationen der DDR im Bundesarchiv [SAPMO-BArch], DY 30/3524, pp. 79–81 (quote).

10. Charles R. Beitz, *The idea of human rights* (Oxford University Press, 2009), pp. 13–18. Samuel Moyn, *The last utopia* (Harvard University Press, 2010), pp. 2, 68–119.

11. J. G. Merills, and A. H. Robertson, *Human rights in Europe*, 4th ed. (Juris Publishing, 2001), pp. 1–13. Moyn, *Last Utopia*, pp. 77–79. Ralph Beddard, *Human rights in Europe*, 2nd ed. (Sweet & Maxwell, 1980), p. 29.

12. A. H. Robertson, "The European Court of Human Rights," *American Journal of Comparative Law*, 9/1 (1960), pp. 11–14. J. E. S. Fawcett, "The European Commission of Human Rights at work," *The World Today*, 28/5 (1972), p. 210. Thomas Buergenthal, "The evolving international human rights system," *American Journal of International Law*, 100/4 (2006), p. 792.

13. William K. Coblentz and Robert S. Warshaw, "European Convention for the Protection of Human Rights and Fundamental Freedoms," *California Law Review*, 44/1 (1956), p. 103. Mikael Rask Madsen, "From Cold War instrument to supreme European court," *Law & Social Inquiry*, 32/1 (2007), pp. 145–46. F. E. Dowrick, "Juristic activity in the Council of Europe," *International and Comparative Law Quarterly*, 23/3 (1974), pp. 621, 627.

14. Moyn, *Last Utopia*, pp. 122–33. Tom Buchanan, "'The truth will set you free'," *Journal of Contemporary History*, 37/4 (2002), pp. 575–97. Linda Rabben, "Amnesty International," *Agni*, 54 (2001), pp. 8–28. Sarah B. Snyder, "Exporting Amnesty International to the United States," *Human Rights Quarterly*, 34/3 (2012), pp. 779–99. Barbara Keys, "Anti-torture politics," Akira Iriye, Petra Goedde, and William I. Hitchcock, eds., *The human rights revolution: an international history* (Oxford University Press, 2012), pp. 210–21.

15. "NATO to explore outlook on talks with Soviet bloc," *NYT*, April 12, 1969, pp. 1, 14 (first quote). "[No title]," June 16, 1967, SAPMO-BArch, DY 30/3520, pp. 48–50. Thomas Fischer, *Neutral power in the CSCE* (Nomos, 2009), pp. 93–94. "Nixon: 'We enter era of negotiation'," January 21, 1969, *Guardian*, p. 2 (second quote). Michael C. Morgan, "North America, Atlanticism, and the making of the Helsinki Final Act," Andreas Wenger, Vojtech Mastny, and Christian Nuenlist, eds., *Origins of the European security system* (Routledge, 2008), pp. 27–30. Christian Nuenlist, "Expanding the East–West dialog beyond the bloc division," Wenger *et al.*, *Origins*, pp. 202–4 (third quote).

16. Various documents: SAPMO-BArch, DY 30/3398, 3399, 3524; and PAAA-MfAA, C 833/75.

17. "[Information]," October 15, 1969, SAPMO-BArch, DY 30/3500, pp. 299–300. Gregor Schöllgen, *Die Aussenpolitik der Bundesrepublik Deutschland* (C. H. Beck, 2004), pp. 110–13. Various documents: PAAA-MfAA, G-A 557. Douglas Selvage, "The Warsaw Pact and the European Security Conference, 1964–69," Wenger *et al.*, *Origins*, pp. 94–96.

18. Angela Romano, *From détente in Europe to European détente* (PIE Peter Lang, 2009), p. 78. Daniel C. Thomas, *The Helsinki effect* (Princeton University Press, 1993), pp. 39–42. Simon J. Nuttall, *European Political Co-operation* (Oxford University Press, 1992), p. 49 (quote).

19. "The 24th CPSU congress on the struggle of the USSR for the implementation of European security," May 18, 1971, PAAA-MfAA, C 69/74, p. 26. "Note," October 14, 1971, PAAA-MfAA, G-A 444, pp. 30–34. "Comrades," May 1972, Der Bundesbeauftragte für die Unterlagen des Staatssicherheitsdienstes der ehemaligen Deutschen Demokratischen Republik [BStU], MfS HA I, 16197, pp. 2–17. British journalist quoted in Michael C. Morgan, *The Final Act* (Princeton University Press, 2018), p. 225.

20. Michael C. Morgan and Daniel Sargent, "Helsinki, 1975," Kristina Spohr and David Reynolds, eds., *Transcending the Cold War* (Oxford University Press, 2016), p. 99. Petri Hakkarainen, *A state of peace in Europe* (Berghahn Books, 2011), pp. 109–36. Thomas, *Helsinki effect*, p. 47.

21. Daniel Möckli, "The EC Nine, the CSCE, and the changing pattern of European security," Wenger *et al.*, *Origins*, pp. 148–49. Thomas, *Helsinki effect*, pp. 42–44, 50–51.

22. "Note," January 17, 1972, PAAA-MfAA, G-A 17, p. 5. "On the West Europe policy of the Mao group," September 29, 1971, SAPMO-BArch, DY 30/IV A 2/20/220, pp. 4–5. "Note," February 11, 1970, PAAA-MfAA, C 1362/74, p. 145 (quote). "Study," December 15, 1971, PAAA-MfAA, C 599/77, p. 181.

23. Mary E. Sarotte, *Dealing with the Devil* (University of North Carolina Press, 2001), pp. 136–37. "Statements," June 6, 1971, SAPMO-BArch, DY 30/IV 2/2.035/55, pp. 40–52.

24. "Stenogram," July 31, 1972, SAPMO-BArch, DY 30/J IV 2/2A/1617, pp. 51–84.

25. Götz von Groll, "The Nine at the Conference on Security and Cooperation in Europe," David Allen, Reinhard Rummel, and Wolfgang Wessels, eds., *European political cooperation* (Butterworth Scientific, 1982), p. 60. "Report," November 16, 1972, PAAA-MfAA, G-A 435, p. 74 (quote).

26. Thomas, *Helsinki effect*, p. 100. Philip Rosin, *Die Schweiz im KSZE-Prozeß 1972–1983* (Oldenbourg Verlag, 2014), pp. 68–71.

27. Romano, *From détente*, pp. 135–39. Möckli, "EC Nine," pp. 151–57. Fischer, *Neutral power*, pp. 173–75.

28. Marie-Pierre Rey, "The USSR and the Helsinki process, 1969–75," Wenger *et al.*, *Origins*, p. 68. Thomas, *Helsinki effect*, p. 59. "Report," [May? 1973], PAAA-MfAA, G-A 21, pp. 1–8.

29. John J. Maresca, *To Helsinki* (Duke University Press, 1987), pp. 31–37. Michael C. Morgan, "The United States and the making of the Helsinki Final Act," Fredrik Logevall and Andrew Preston, eds., *Nixon in the world* (Oxford University Press, 2008), p. 170. Möckli, "EC Nine," p. 151.

30. Rosin, *Schweiz im KSZE-Prozeß*, pp. 79–83. "Final recommendation of the Helsinki consultations," Helsinki 1973, www.osce.org/mc/40213, accessed on April 1, 2018 (quotes). Fischer, *Neutral power*, p. 181. "Dear comrades," July 19, 1973, SAPMO-BArch, DY 30/13862, p. 1. Morgan, *Final Act*, pp. 299–305. Thomas, *Helsinki effect*, p. 65. Douglas Selvage and Walter Süß, *Staatssicherheit und KSZE-Prozess* (Vandenhoeck & Ruprecht, 2019), pp. 60–63.

31. "On the reaction of the PR China to the Helsinki Conference," July 20, 1973, PAAA-MfAA, C 582/77, pp. 34–36 (quote). "Record of conversation," [June 7, 1973], National Archives of the United Kingdom [NAUK], FCO 21/1106, pp. 1–8. "Political report no. 20," July 10, 1973, Schweizerisches Bundesarchiv [SBA], E 2300–01, Akzession 1977/30, box 7, pp. 1–4.

32. Maresca, *To Helsinki*, pp. 175–80. Morgan, *Final Act*, pp. 313–58.

33. Thomas, *Helsinki effect*, p. 70.

34. Thomas, *Helsinki effect*, pp. 68–77, 81–85. Maresca, *To Helsinki*, pp. 110–16. Morgan, "Helsinki, 1975," pp. 102–3. "Speech," [April 17, 1974], PAAA-MfAA, G-A 567, p. 40. "Fm Moscow 171630Z," February 17, 1975, NAUK, FCO 37/1714, p. 4 (quote).

35. Morgan, "North America," pp. 32–33. Maresca, *To Helsinki*, pp. 119–60. Selvage, *Staatssicherheit*, pp. 64–68.

36. "Helsinki Final Act," August 1, 1975, www.osce.org/helsinki-final-act, accessed on April 4, 2018. Duccio Basosi, "Helsinki and Rambouillet," Wenger *et al.*, *Origins*, p. 222. Thomas, *Helsinki effect*, p. 86. Morgan, "Helsinki, 1975," p. 96.

37. Morgan, "Helsinki, 1975," pp. 86–87. Vladislav M. Zubok, *A failed empire* (University of North Carolina Press, 2007), pp. 237–38. "On the approach of the USSR," no date, PAAA-MfAA, G-A 22, pp. 64–69. Sarah B. Snyder, *Human rights activism and the end of the Cold War* (Cambridge University Press, 2011), p. 31. Jarząbek, "Hope and reality," pp. 43–45. Thomas, *Helsinki effect*, p. 95.

38. Various documents: SAPMO-BArch, DY 30/J IV 2/2A/1901, pp. 14–18 and DY 30/J IV 2/2A/1917, pp. 87–88, 91–102 (quote), 132–33.

39. Thomas, *Helsinki effect*, pp. 85–87. "Conversation of Federal Minister Genscher with the British Foreign Minister Callaghan in Hamburg," July 24, 1975, *Akten, 1975*, p. 219. Morgan, "Helsinki 1975," pp. 111–14. "Ending World War II: essay," *NYT*, April 14, 1975, p. 31 (first quote). "Dear John," August 13, 1975, NAUK, FCO 21/1379, p. 1 (second and third quotes).

40. Morgan, *Final Act*, pp. 29, 291–97.

41. Morgan, *Final Act*, p. 274. Aryeh Neier, *The international human rights movement* (Princeton University Press, 2013), pp. 204–13. Tony Judt, *Postwar* (Penguin Press, 2005), pp. 508–23. William I. Hitchcock, *The struggle for Europe* (Doubleday, 2003), pp. 169–88. Snyder, *Human rights*, pp. 81–114.

42. Rosin, *Schweiz im KSZE-Prozeß*, p. 126. Ann Komaromi, "Samizdat and Soviet dissident publics," *Slavic Review*, 71/1 (2012), pp. 79–88. Svetlana Savranskaya, "Human rights movement in the USSR after the signing of the Helsinki Final Act, and the reaction of Soviet authorities," Leopoldo Nuti, ed., *The crisis of détente in Europe* (Routledge, 2010), pp. 30–35. Snyder, *Human rights*, pp. 53–80.
43. Ned Richardson-Little, "Dictatorship and dissent," Jan Eckel and Samuel Moyn, eds., *The breakthrough* (University of Pennsylvania Press, 2013), pp. 49–67. Selvage, *Staatssicherheit*, pp. 132–35, 172–76. Anja Hanisch, "Trügerische Sicherheit," Helmut Altrichter and Hermann Wentker, eds., *Der KSZE-Prozess* (Oldenbourg Verlag, 2011), pp. 75–86. Oliver Bange, "Onto the slippery slope," *Journal of Cold War Studies*, 18/3 (2016), p. 85.
44. Jonathan Bolton, *Worlds of dissent* (Harvard University Press, 2014). Thomas, *Helsinki effect*, pp. 174–83, 212–15.
45. David Ost, *Solidarity and the politics of anti-politics* (Temple University Press, 1990), pp. 49–53. Jarząbek, "Hope and reality," pp. 45–55.
46. Ost, *Solidarity*, pp. 55–74. Michael H. Bernhard, *The origins of democratization in Poland* (Columbia University Press, 1993), pp. 76–208. Thomas, *Helsinki effect*, pp. 173–74.

19   The Vatican

1. Quote from Piotr H. Kosicki, *Catholics on the barricades* (Yale University Press, 2018), p. 1.
2. David I. Kertzer, *The Pope and Mussolini* (Random House, 2014), pp. 98–100.
3. "Qui Pluribus," 1846, www.papalencyclicals.net/pius09/p9quiplu.htm, accessed on April 15, 2018 (first quote). "Rerum Novarum," 1891, w2.vatican.va/content/leo-xiii/en/encyclicals/documents/hf_l-xiii_en c_15051891_rerum-novarum.html, accessed on April 15, 2018. Hansjakob Stehle, *Geheimdiplomatie im Vatikan* (Benziger Verlag, 1993), pp. 15–150, 168–185. "Divini Redemptoris," 1937, w2.vatican.va/con tent/pius-xi/en/encyclicals/documents/hf_p-xi_enc_19370319_divini-redemptoris.html, accessed on April 14, 2018 (second and third quotes). Giuliana Chamedes, "The Vatican, Nazi-Fascism, and the making of transnational anti-communism in the 1930s," *Journal of Contemporary History*, 51/2 (2016), pp. 261–90.
4. Stehle, *Geheimdiplomatie*, pp. 151–57. Frank J. Coppa, *Politics and the papacy in the modern world* (Praeger, 2008), pp. 8, 102. For the 1941 convention and the 1953 concordat, see www.concordatwatch.eu/showsite.php?org_id=845, accessed on April 14, 2018.
5. Kertzer, *Pope*, pp. 255–369. Georges Passelecq and Bernard Suchecky, *The hidden encyclical of Pius XI* (Harcourt, Brace, 1997). Robert A. Ventresca, *Soldier of Christ* (Harvard University Press, 2013), pp. 129–218. "Mit bren-nender Sorge," 1937, w2.vatican.va/content/pius-xi/de/encyclicals/documents/hf_p-xi_enc_14031937_mit-brennender-sorge.html, accessed

on April 15, 2018 (quotes). Peter C. Kent, *The lonely Cold War of Pope Pius XII* (McGill-Queen's University Press, 2002), p. 75. Hubert Wolf, *Pope and Devil* (Belknap Press, 2010), pp. 252–71.

6. "Rerum Novarum," 1891, w2.vatican.va/content/leo-xiii/en/encyclicals/documents/hf_l-xiii_enc_15051891_rerum-novarum.html, accessed on April 15, 2018 (quotes). Kosicki, *Catholics*. Charles Suaud and Nathalie Viet-Depaule, *Prêtres et ouvriers*, 2nd ed. (Éditions Karthala, 2004). Samuel Moyn, "Personalism, community, and the origins of human rights," Stefan-Ludwig Hoffmann, ed., *Human rights in the twentieth century* (Cambridge University Press, 2010), pp. 85–106. Karol Wojtyła, *Love and responsibility* (Ignatius Press, 1981). Originally published in Polish in 1960.

7. Steven M. Miner, *Stalin's holy war* (University of North Carolina Press, 2003). Kent, *Lonely Cold War*, pp. 69–73.

8. Owen Chadwick, *The Christian church in the Cold War* (Penguin Books, 1992), pp. 60–67. Kent, *Lonely Cold War*, pp. 129–31, 162–76. Stehle, *Geheimdiplomatie*, p. 256.

9. Stehle, *Geheimdiplomatie*, pp. 218–20. Kent, *Lonely Cold War*, pp. 120–25.

10. Chadwick, *Christian church*, pp. 67–68. Kent, *Lonely Cold War*, pp. 115–17. Csaba Szabó, "Die katholische Kirche Ungarns bis zum Prozeß gegen Jósef Kardinal Mindszenty," Hartmut Lehmann and Jens Holger Schjørring, eds., *Im Räderwerk des real existierenden Sozialismus* (Wallstein Verlag, 2003), pp. 50–58.

11. Stehle, *Geheimdiplomatie*, pp. 224–27. Coppa, *Politics*, pp. 136–54.

12. Stehle, *Geheimdiplomatie*, pp. 233–38. Kosicki, *Catholics*, pp. 96–100, 110.

13. Kent, *Lonely Cold War*, pp. 112–20.

14. Kent, *Lonely Cold War*, pp. 108–20, 214–36. "Rumania ends papal tie," *New York Times* [*NYT*], July 18, 1948, p. 17. "Bulgaria bans all papal missions," *NYT*, February 24, 1949, p. 3. Szabó, "Katholische Kirche Ungarns," pp. 58–62. Gabriel Adriány, *Geschichte der Kirche Osteuropas im 20. Jahrhundert* (Ferdinand Schöningh, 1992), pp. 71–72, 87–88, 104–5, 132–34, 148–49, 158–59.

15. Michael Fleming, *Communism, nationalism and ethnicity in Poland, 1944–50* (Routledge, 2010), pp. 102–8. Kent, *Lonely Cold War*, pp. 230–31. Stehle, *Geheimdiplomatie*, pp. 260–61. Piotr H. Kosicki, ed., *Vatican II behind the Iron Curtain* (Catholic University of America Press, 2016), p. 14. Piotr H. Kosicki, "The Catholic Church and the Cold War," Artemy M. Kalinovsky and Craig Daigle, eds., *The Routledge handbook of the Cold War* (Routledge, 2014), p. 262.

16. "Papal decree against communism," July 14, 1949, *NYT*, p. 14. Roland Cerny-Werner, *Vatikanische Ostpolitik und die DDR* (V&R unipress, 2011), pp. 52–53. Kent, *Lonely Cold War*, pp. 237–51. "Socialism as such not banned," July 23, 1949, *NYT*, p. 3.

17. David E. Mungello, *The Catholic invasion of China* (Rowman & Littlefield, 2015), pp. 15–69, 109–16. Anthony E. Clark, "Sealing fate and changing course," and Amanda C. R. Clark, "Adjustment and advocacy: Charles McCarthy, SJ, and China's Jesuit mission in transition," Anthony E. Clark, ed., *China's Christianity* (Brill, 2017), pp. 121–40, 199–218.

Jonathan Luxmoore and Jolanta Babiuch, *The Vatican and the red flag* (Geoffrey Chapman, 1999), p. 155. Gerald Chan, "Sino-Vatican diplomatic relations," *China Quarterly*, 120 (1989), p. 818.

18. Charles Keith, *Catholic Vietnam* (University of California Press, 2012). Edward G. Miller, *Misalliance* (Harvard University Press, 2013), pp. 54–123. Phi-Vân Nguyen, "Fighting the First Indochina War again?," *SOJOURN: Journal of Social Issues in Southeast Asia*, 31/ 1 (2016), pp. 207–46.

19. Luxmoore and Babiuch, *Vatican*, p. 77. Stehle, *Geheimdiplomatie*, pp. 272–78. Coppa, *Politics*, p. 156. Ventresca, *Soldier*, pp. 286–97.

20. Stehle, *Geheimdiplomatie*, pp. 274–83. János M. Rainer, *Imre Nagy* (Ferdinand Schöningh, 2002), pp. 158–75.

21. Adriány, *Geschichte*, pp. 72–73. Andrzej Micewski, *Cardinal Wyszyński* (Harcourt Brace Jovanovich, 1984), pp. 160–423. Various documents: Bundesarchiv [BArch], DO 4/395, 498, 500, 833, 2383.

22. "Transmission of information material on the Hungarian People's Republic," May 14, 1957, BArch, DO 4/2382, p. 1. "Reds favor exile for Mindszenty," *NYT*, April 15, 1957, p. 7. John Pollard, *The Papacy in the age of totalitarianism, 1914–1958* (Oxford University Press, 2014), p. 371.

23. "Report," September 10, 1957, BArch, DO 4/2382, pp. 1–4 (quote). Rudolf Lill, "Zur Vatikanischen Ostpolitik unter Johannes XXIII. und Paul VI.," Karl-Joseph Hummel, ed., *Vatikanische Ostpolitik unter Johannes XXIII. und Paul VI. 1958–1978* (Ferdinand Schöningh, 1999), p. 20.

24. Luxmoore and Babiuch, *Vatican*, p. 112. Coppa, *Politics*, pp. 157–65. Chadwick, *Christian church*, pp. 115. Stehle, *Geheimdiplomatie*, p. 217.

25. "Soviet bid to Vatican," *NYT*, October 20, 1958, p. 6. "Report," January 6, 1959, BArch, DO 4/2384, pp. 7–9.

26. Stehle, *Geheimdiplomatie*, p. 285. Coppa, *Politics*, pp. 164–66.

27. Roberto de Mattei, *Das Zweite Vatikanische Konzil* (Sarto Verlag, 2012), pp. 177–80.

28. A. Roccucci, "Russian observers at Vatican II," Alberto Melloni, ed., *Vatican II in Moscow, 1959–1965* (Library of the Faculty of Theology, 1997), pp. 53–59.

29. Bernd Schäfer, *Staat und katholische Kirche in der DDR* (Böhlau Verlag, 1999), pp. 57–64, 160–70. Josef Pilvousek, "Vatikanische Ostpolitik," Hummel, *Vatikanische Ostpolitik*, pp. 113–18. Various documents: BArch, DO 4/115, 116, 464, 824, 836.

30. "Pope bids chiefs end war threat," *NYT*, September 11, 1961, p. 1. "World's threats deplored by Pope," *NYT*, November 5, 1961, p. 1."Vatican prints texts," *NYT*, December 17, 1961, p. 19. Stehle, *Geheimdiplomatie*, p. 283 (quote).

31. Various documents: BArch, DO 4/498 and 1154.

32. Stehle, *Geheimdiplomatie*, pp. 286–87. Roccucci, "Russian observers," pp. 60–69. "Russian church assailed for sending 2 to Rome," *NYT*, October 13, 1962, p. 4.

33. Mattei, *Das Zweite Vatikanische Konzil*, pp. 222–319. "[Public appeal of John XXIII]," [October 1962], University of California at Los Angeles Library [UCLA], Norman Cousins Papers, Box 1221, pp. 1–5 (first

quote). Various documents: John F. Kennedy Presidential Library [JFK], Personal Papers of Arthur Schlesinger Jr., box WH-23. Norman Cousins, *The improbable triumvirate* (W. W. Norton, 1972), pp. 17–57 (second quote).

34. Stehle, *Geheimdiplomatie*, pp. 228–32, 290–91. Various documents: JFK, National Security Files, box 191. "Pacem in Terris," April 11, 1963, w2 .vatican.va/content/john-xxiii/en/encyclicals/documents/hf_j-xxiii_en c_11041963_pacem.html, accessed on May 5, 2018 (quote). Various documents: *UCLA Library*, Norman Cousins Papers, box 1221. Cousins, *Improbable Triumvirate*, pp. 79–110. Lorenz M. Lüthi, *The Sino-Soviet split* (Princeton University Press, 2008), pp. 256–59.

35. "Department of State memorandum," December 11, 1962, JFK, National Security Files, box 191, pp. 1–2. "East and West laud Pope at arms talks," *NYT*, June 6, 1963, p. 3. Quote from Stehle, *Geheimdiplomatie*, p. 10.

36. Jörg Ernesti, *Paul VI* (Herder Verlag, 2012), pp. 67–126, 188–202. Kosicki, *Vatican II*, pp. 16–20. Chadwick, *Christian church*, pp. 120–21.

37. "Clear statement of Vatican against communism," *Deutsche Zeitung*, September 9, 1963, BArch, DO 4/107, unnumbered (first quote). "Ecclesiam Suam," August 6, 1964, w2.vatican.va/content/paul-vi/en/ency clicals/documents/hf_p-vi_enc_06081964_ecclesiam.html, accessed on May 11, 2018 (second and third quotes). Chadwick, *Christian church*, pp. 121–22. Luxmoore and Babiuch, *Vatican*, p. 156. Agostino Casaroli, *Il martirio della pazienza* (Einaudi, 2000) (fourth quote). "Casaroli: Holy 007," *Spiegel*, November 7, 1966, BArch, DO 4/5469, unnumbered (fifth quote). Erhard Mayerhofer, *Kirche im Dialog* (PIE Peter Lang, 1999), pp. 45–74. Various documents: BArch, DO 4/497, 506, and 1155.

38. Stehle, *Geheimdiplomatie*, pp. 305–8. Ivo Banac, "Vatican II and Yugoslavia," Kosicki, *Vatican II*, pp. 78–98.

39. Cerny-Werner, *Vatikanische Ostpolitik*, pp. 59–69. "Gromyko sees pope," *NYT*, April 28, 1966, p. 1. "Vatican to sign pact for nuclear curb," *NYT*, January 2, 1971, p. 21. "To the Federal Ministry for External Affairs," March 10, 1971, Österreichisches Staatsarchiv [ÖStA], AdR/01, BMfaA, Sektion II-pol, box 1821, pp. 1–3.

40. James Ramon Felak, "Vatican II and Czechoslovakia," Kosicki, *Vatican II*, p. 100–10. Casaroli, *Martirio*, pp. 128–67. Stehle, *Geheimdiplomatie*, pp. 315–20. "Pope urges Europe to unite for peace," *NYT*, September 3, 1968, p. 17 (first and second quotes). "Cardinal Konig urges a 'dialogue' with nonbelievers, including communists," *NYT*, September 22, 1968, p. 2 (third and fourth quotes).

41. Stehle, *Geheimdiplomatie*, pp. 321–23. Piotr H. Kosicki, "Vatican II and Poland," Kosicki, *Vatican II*, p. 129. Leonid Luks, "Die Politik von Staat und Kirche in Polen (1956–1978)," Hummel, *Vatikanische Ostpolitik*, p. 143. Luxmoore, *Vatican*, p. 146. "Wyszynski received by pope," *NYT*, May 21, 1965, p. 8.

42. "In the Spirit of Saint Hedwig," October 16, 1960, Julius Kardinal Döpfner, *Wort aus Berlin* (Morus-Verlag, 1961), pp. 98–104. Basil Kerski, Thomas Kycia, and Robert Żurek, eds., *Wir vergeben und bitten um*

Vergebung (fibre, 2006), pp. 18–27, 211–28 (texts of letters). Piotr H. Kosicki, "Caritas across the iron curtain?," *East European Politics and Societies*, 23/2 (2009), pp. 213–43.

43. Luxmoore, *Vatican*, p. 140–45. Kosicki, *Catholics*, pp. 114–302. Adam Michnik, *The church and the left* (University of Chicago Press, 1993), pp. 97–215. Andrzej Paczkowski, *The spring will be ours* (Pennsylvania State University Press, 2003), pp. 325–50.

44. Rudolf Morsey, "Die Haltung der Bundesregierung," Hummel, *Vatikanische Ostpolitik*, pp. 43–64. Kerski, *Wir vergeben*, pp. 46–49. "Conversation of Chancellor Brandt with Pope Paul VI in the Vatican," July 13, 1970, Institut für Zeitgeschichte, ed., *Akten zur Auswärtigen Politik der Bundesrepublik Deutschland, 1949/50* (Oldenbourg Verlag, 2001), pp. 1297–1300.

45. Various chapters in Hummel, *Vatikanische Ostpolitik*, pp. 28–29, 75–78, 101–3. Paczkowski, *Spring*, pp. 353–60, 388–89. "Masses for the Coalition," *Zeit*, November 24, 1972, BArch, DO 4/227, p. 1. Cerny-Werner, *Vatikanische Ostpolitik*, pp. 124–314.

46. "Memorandum of conversation," April 25, 1963, JFK, National Security Files, box 191, p. 11a (quote). "Part I," December 12, 1964, BArch, DO 4/505, pp. 8–9. Hubert Feichtlbauer, *Franz König* (Holzhausen Verlag, 2003), pp. 125–28. Casaroli, *Martirio*, pp. 77–109. Stehle, *Geheimdiplomatie*, pp. 297–305. Various documents: Richard Nixon Presidential Library [RMN], NSC, Country files, box 693.

47. "Vatican asserts fight is political," *NYT*, August 23, 1963, p. 2. "Diem's brother loses rule over Archdiocese of Hue," *NYT*, November 12, 1964, p. 12. Alberto Melloni, "La politica internazionale della Santa Sede negli anni sessanta," Alberto Melloni, ed., *Il filo sottile* (Il Mulino, 2006), pp. 29–31. Ernesti, *Paul VI*, p. 186. Various documents: Archiv des Deutschen Caritasverbandes, AB 11; and Lyndon Baines Johnson Presidential Library [LBJ], National Security File 1963–1969, Country file, box 231. "Recent losses by Catholics in Vietnam termed serious," *NYT*, March 13, 1968, p. 20. "Pontiff discloses he offered Vatican as a site for talks," *NYT*, May 6, 1968, p. 15. Various documents: RMN, NSC, Country files Europe, box 732. Luxmoore and Babiuch, *Vatican*, p. 170.

48. "To the Federal Ministry for External Affairs," January 26, 1972, ÖStA, AdR/01, BMfaA, Sektion II-pol, box 1959, p. 1. Various documents: BArch, DO 4/496, 502, 503, 1156–1158, 4740, and 4758.

49. Giovanni Barberini, *L'Ostpolitik della Santa Sede* (Il Mulino, 2007), pp. 325–78. Marco Lavopa, "Mgr Agostino Casaroli, un habile 'tisseur de dialogues européens' (1963–1975)," *Revue de l'histoire des religions*, 231/1 (2014), pp. 104–15.

50. "Dialogue to get power," *Frankfurter Allgemeine*, October 26, 1977, BArch, DO 4/5329, p. 1 (quote). Several newspaper clippings: BArch, DO 4/227, 3759, 3764, 3765, 5329, and 5559. "Pope Paul wants to resign, Austrian Cardinal says," *NYT*, February 12, 1971, p. 2. "A break in Ostpolitik," January 29, 1976, BArch, DO 4/5051, p. 1.

51. Luke 12:4. Stehle, *Geheimdiplomatie*, p. 10.

52. Wojtyła, *Love and Responsibility*. Kosicki, "Vatican II," p. 186. Carl Bernstein and Marco Politi, *His Holiness* (Doubleday, 1996), pp. 101–47, 191. "Redemptor hominis," March 4, 1979, w2.vatican.va/content/john-paul-ii/en/encyclicals/documents/hf_jp-ii_enc_04031979_redemptor-hominis.html, accessed on May 14, 2018. "[Soviet assessment]," December 5, 1978, Der Bundesbeauftragte für die Unterlagen des Staatssicherheitsdienstes der ehemaligen Deutschen Demokratischen Republik [BStU], MfS XX/4, 233, pp. 178–79. "Protocolary note," [October 1979], BArch, DO 4/501, pp. 280–85. "Pope ends his trip to Poland," *NYT*, June 11, 1979, p. A1. Matthew J. Ouimet, *The rise and the fall of the Brezhnev Doctrine in Soviet foreign policy* (University of North Carolina Press, 2003), pp. 113–22.

20   The Middle East

1. "Despatch no. 3/74," December 2, 1974, National Archives of Australia [NAA], Series A4231, 1974/Africa & The Middle East, pp. 60–68. Various documents: Politisches Archiv des Auswärtigen Amtes, Bestand: Ministerium für Auswärtige Angelegenheiten [PAAA-MfAA], C 1439/78. "Political report no. 5," March 3, 1976, Schweizerisches Bundesarchiv [SBA], E 2300–01, Akzession 1988/91, box 3, pp. 1–3. Adel Safty, "Sadat's negotiations with the United States and Israel," *American Journal of Economics and Sociology*, 50/3 (1991), p. 288. Various documents: Anwar Sadat, *The public diary of President Sadat* (E. J. Brill, 1979), pp. 627, 810–11, 927, 1020, 1114.
2. "Note of a meeting," [February 27, 1976], National Archives of the United Kingdom [NAUK], PREM 16/840, p. 3. "Dear John," March 23, 1976, NAUK, FCO 21/1499, p. 1 (quote). "O.CA2920," April 27, 1976, NAA, Series A1838, 169/11/52 Part 19, pp. 115–14. "Dear Michael," June 23, 1976, NAUK, PREM 16/1370, pp. 1–3.
3. "Summary of conversation," May 13, 1975, NAUK, PREM 16/2227, pp. 1–6. "Information," July 22, 1975, PAAA-MfAA, C 1439/78, pp. 72–75. "Record of conversation," November 23, 1975, NAUK, PREM 16/1444, pp. 2–3. "Shah of Iran ends Saudi Arabian visit," *The Sun*, April 30, 1975, p. A5.
4. "Information," October 22, 1975, Stiftung Archiv der Parteien und Massenorganisationen der DDR im Bundesarchiv [SAPMO-BArch], DY 30/13982, pp. 27–30. "Brief information no 60/75," November 9, 1975, PAAA-MfAA, C 1015/77, pp. 3–4. "Brief information no. 35/75," June 29, 1975, PAAA-MfAA, C 1017/77, pp. 1–5. "Information," October 19, 1975, PAAA-MfAA, C 1277/78, pp. 1–6 (first quote). "Report," [December 1975], SAPMO-BArch, DY 30/J IV 2/2A/1940, pp. 25–27. Patrick Seale, *Asad of Syria* (University of California Press, 1988), p. 262. "Information," April 24, 1975, SAPMO-BArch, DY 30/13943, pp. 27–30 (second quote).
5. Dilip Hiro, *Lebanon* (St. Martin's Press, 1993), pp. 31–51. David Hirst, *Beware of small states* (Nation Books, 2010), pp. 99–147. Seale, *Asad*, pp. 276–88. "Consultation," [June 1976], Bundesarchiv [BArch], DY 30/J IV 2/2J/7243, pp. 3–4 (quote).

6. "Information," January 15, 1975, PAAA-MfAA, C 7673, pp. 116–20. "Statements by Y. Arafat," April 17, 1975, PAAA-MfAA, C 7663, pp. 167–68. "Brief information," July 31, 1975, PAAA-MfAA, C 7674, pp. 8–9. "Non-aligned bloc adds 4 members," *New York Times* [*NYT*], August 27, 1975, p. 9.
7. "Despatch no. 6/75," October 3, 1975, NAA, Series A4231, 1975/Africa & The Middle East, p. 5 (quote). "Information for the Politburo," December 5, 1975, SAPMO-BArch, DY 30/J IV 2/2J/7010, p. 3. "Note on a talk in the Fatah office in Cairo," August 4, 1976, PAAA-MfAA, C 1432/78, p. 184 (quote). "Information no. 1/77," January 6, 1977, PAAA-MfAA, C 7670, pp. 68–75. Manfred Sing, "Brothers in arms," *Die Welt des Islams*, 51/1 (2011), pp. 1–44.
8. William B. Quandt, *Peace process*, 3rd ed. (Brookings Institution Press, 2005), pp. 155–73. Craig Daigle, "A crescent of crisis," Lorenz M. Lüthi, ed., *The regional Cold Wars in Europe, East Asia, and the Middle East* (Woodrow Wilson Center Press / Stanford University Press, 2015), p. 255. "On the work visit of the Shah to the USSR November 18–20, 1974," November 26, 1974, SAPMO-BArch, DY 30/13940, pp. 1–5.
9. "Near East: the hour of Soviet diplomacy," *Spiegel*, May 12, 1975, pp. 88–89. "Dear Comrade Dr. Willerding," May 27, 1975, PAAA-MfAA, C 853/77, pp. 4–8. "Information," October 22, 1975, SAPMO-BArch, DY 30/13982, pp. 27–30. "Report," January 19, 1976, BArch, DC 20/13068, pp. 60–64. "O. CA2799," March 15, 1976, NAA, Series A1838, 169/11/52 Part 19, pp. 86–85. "Political report no. 12," July 21, 1976, SBA, E 2300–01, Akzession 1988/91, box 3, pp. 1–3.
10. Quandt, *Peace process*, pp. 177–85. Seale, *Asad*, pp. 290–98.
11. Steven A. Cook, *The struggle for Egypt* (Oxford University Press, 2012), p. 145. "Sadat Addresses the Knesset in Jerusalem," November 20, 1977, Harry Hurwitz and Yisrael Medad, eds., *Peace in the making* (Gefen, 2015), pp. 16–28 (quotes). Information from Egypt and Israel, as relayed from the United States to the United Kingdom: "Fm Washington 252320Z," November 25, 1977, NAUK, PREM 16/1372, p. 1.
12. "Rabin insists Israel had no objection to talks," *Jewish Advocate*, November 18, 1976, p. 1. Various documents: PAAA-MfAA, C 7468 and C 7468. "Fm Cairo 240925Z May," May 24, 1977, NAUK, PREM 16/1727, pp. 1–2.
13. Avi Shlaim, *The iron wall* (W. W. Norton, 2000), pp. 357–59. Various documents: NAUK, PREM 16/1372. "Begin's Official Invitation," November 15, 1977, Hurwitz, *Peace*, pp. 12–13. Boutros Boutros-Ghali, *Egypt's road to Jerusalem* (Random House, 1997), p. 16.
14. Daniel Gordis, *Menachem Begin* (Schocken, 2014), pp. 10–140. Seth Anziska, *Preventing Palestine* (Princeton University Press, 2018), pp. 49–53, 97–111. Nur Masalha, *Imperial Israel and the Palestinians* (Pluto Press, 2000), pp. 55–74. Ilan Peleg, *Begin's foreign policy, 1977–1983* (Greenwood Press, 1987), pp. 1–43. Mordechai Bar-On, *Moshe Dayan* (Yale University Press, 2012), pp. 193–95.
15. Anziska, *Preventing Palestine*, pp. 53–79. Several documents: Meron Medzini, ed., *Israel's foreign relations*, vol. 4 (Ministry of Foreign Affairs, 1981), pp. 1–5. Masalha, *Imperial Israel*, p. 74. Idith Zertal and

Akiva Eldar, *Lords of the land* (Nation Books, 2009), pp. 58–61. Gershon Gorenberg, *The accidental empire* (Times Books, 2006), p. 358. James L. Gelvin, *The Israel–Palestine conflict* (Cambridge University Press, 2005), pp. 189–94.

16. Shlomo Ben-Ami, *Scars of war, wounds of peace* (Oxford University Press, 2006), pp. 161–62. Shlaim, *Iron wall*, p. 361. "Begin addresses the Knesset after Sadat," November 20, 1977, Hurwitz, *Peace*, pp. 28–36 (quotes).

17. Ben-Ami, *Scars of war*, pp. 158–72. Anziska, *Preventing Palestine*, pp. 17–36. Quandt, *Peace process*, pp. 191–237. Various documents: United States, Department of State, *Foreign relations of the United States* [*FRUS*], 1977–80, IX (U.S. Government Printing Office, 2014), pp. 1–800. The texts of the agreement and the treaty: Medzini, *Israel's foreign relations*, vol. 5, pp. 514–24, 696–720. Lawrence Wright, *Thirteen days in September* (Vintage Books, 2014).

18. "Fm Tel Aviv 281030Z Mar," March 28, 1979, NAUK, PREM 16/2170, pp. 1–3 (quote). Ben-Ami, *Scars of war*, pp. 174–77. Zertal, *Lords*, pp. 58–61. Anziska, *Preventing Palestine*, pp. 136–61.

19. Jimmy Carter, *White House Diary* (Farrar, Straus & Giroux, 2010), p. 256.

20. Seale, *Asad*, pp. 304–5. "[No title]," December 8, 1977, SAPMO-BArch, DY 30/IV 2/2.033/122, pp. 79–80. "Telegram vvs 550/77," December 6, 1977, BArch, DC 20/12792, pp. 27–28.

21. "Egypt cuts ties with Syria, 4 other countries," December 5, 1977, *Los Angeles Times* [*LAT*], p. A1. "Egypt orders Soviet and allies to close all culture offices," *NYT*, December 8, 1977, p. 57. Various documents: NAUK, PREM 16/1372. "Sadat plays his last card," *Spiegel*, December 12, 1977, p. 119. "Fm Jedda 280700Z," November 28, 1977, NAUK, PREM 16/1372, pp. 1–3 (quotes). Various documents: NAUK, PREM 16/1753 and 16/1758.

22. "Conversation," December 25, 1977, Arhiv Jugoslavije [AJ], KPR I-5-b/91-2, p. 1 (quote). "Current problems of the policy of the PLO," November 28, 1977, PAAA-MfAA, C 7663, p. 182. Ben-Ami, *Scars of war*, p. 164. "Diary of events," February 28, 1978, NAUK, FCO 9/2730, pp. 1–9.

23. "Information," March 20, 1978, SAPMO-BArch, DY 30/13970, pp. 1–5. "Information," March 16, 1978, BArch, DY 30/J IV 2/2J/7946, pp. 1–11. Yezid Sayigh, *Armed struggle and the search for state* (Oxford University Press, 1997), pp. 426–27. Avi Shlaim, *Lion of Jordan* (Alfred A. Knopf, 2008), p. 420. "Information no. 54/78," June 13, 1978, SAPMO-BArch, DY 30/J IV 2/2J/8024, p. 4. "Information," July 24, 1978, PAAA-MfAA, C 7670, pp. 21–24.

24. "Gromyko attacks Cairo plan," *NYT*, November 30, 1977, p. 6. "Information," June 12, 1978, SAPMO-BArch, DY 30/IV B 2/20/153, pp. 1–38 (quote).

25. Various documents: NAUK, PREM 16/2169 (quotes). "Comrade Erich Honecker," September 25, 1978, SAPMO-BArch, DY 30/2499, p. 7.

26. Various documents: NAUK, PREM 16/1759 (quotes) and PREM 16/2169. Shlaim, *Lion*, pp. 405–6. Seale, *Asad*, p. 313.

27. Various documents: NAUK, PREM 16/2170. Quandt, *Peace process*, pp. 335–39. Anziska, *Preventing Palestine*, pp. 162–93. "Fm Baghdad 011022Z Apr," April 1, 1979, NAUK, PREM 16/2170, pp. 1–3.

28. Ali E. Hilal Dessouki, "The limits of instrumentalism," Adeed Dawisha, ed., *Islam in foreign policy* (Cambridge University Press, 1983), p. 92. Saad Eddin Ibrahim, "An Islamic alternative in Egypt," *Arab Studies Quarterly*, 4/1–2 (1982), pp. 77–93. Nehemia Levtzion, *International Islamic solidarity and its limitations* (Magnes Press, Hebrew University, 1979), pp. 55–56, 67. Cook, *Struggle*, pp. 152–56. Richard Bonney, *Jihad: from Quran to bin Laden* (Palgrave Macmillan, 2004), pp. 286–92.

29. Charles Kurzman, *The unthinkable revolution in Iran* (Harvard University Press, 2004). Mohsen M. Milani, *The making of Iran's Islamic revolution*, 2nd ed. (Westview Press, 1994), pp. 105–33. Sandra Mackey, *The Iranians* (Penguin, 1996), pp. 271–94. "Telegram Nr 255 of 25 Mar 80," NAUK, FCO 93/2377, pp. 1–2. Robin Wright, *Sacred rage*, upd. ed. (Touchstone, 2001), pp. 176–77.

30. Mackey, *Iranians*, pp. 274–93. David W. Lesch, *1979* (Westview Press, 2001), p. 33. Milani, *Making of Iran's Islamic revolution*, pp. 143–54, 162–67.

31. "Khomeini demands review of Iran's foreign deals," *NYT*, January 22, 1979, p. A11. R. K. Ramazani, "Khumayni's Islam and Iran's foreign policy," Dawisha, *Islam in foreign policy*, pp. 16–18. Milani, *Making of Iran's Islamic revolution*, pp. 156–58. Mackey, *Iranians*, pp. 296–99. Wright, *Sacred rage*, pp. 31–36.

32. David Farber, *Taken hostage* (Princeton University Press, 2005), pp. 126–90. David Patrick Houghton, *US foreign policy and the Iran hostage Crisis* (Cambridge University Press, 2001), pp. 50–74.

33. Various documents: NAUK, FCO 8/3378. "Moscow's embassy stormed in Tehran," *Washington Post* [*WaPo*], January 2, 1980, p. A1. Quote from "Khomeini seeks overthrow in Egypt, Iraq," *Hartford Courant*, August 10, 1980, p. 26A.

34. Christian Emery, *US foreign policy and the Iranian Revolution* (Palgrave Macmillan, 2013), pp. 29–70. "NSC Weekly Report #87," February 2, 1979, Jimmy Carter Presidential Library [JC], Zbigniew Brzezinski Collection, Subject File, box 42, pp. 1–5 (quote). Farber, *Taken hostage*, pp. 119–28. Milani, *Making of Iran's Islamic revolution*, pp. 164–67.

35. "[No title]," February 5, 1979, SAPMO-BArch, DY 30/13940, pp. 1–2. Various documents: NAUK, FCO 8/3371. "vvs 113/79," June 5, 1979, SAPMO-BArch, DY 30/IV B 2/20/369, pp. 60–61 (quotes). "On the situation in Iran," February 4, 1980, SAPMO-BArch, DY 30/IV B 2/20/370, [pp. 1–5].

36. "Information on Iran," September 16, 1980, SAPMO-BArch, DY 30/IV B 2/20/370, [pp. 1–5]. "Foreign policy information summary no. 30/79," July 23, 1979, Der Bundesbeauftragte für die Unterlagen des Staatssicherheitsdienstes der ehemaligen Deutschen Demokratischen Republik [BStU], MfS HVA 82, pp. 120–21. Various documents: SAPMO-BArch, DY 30/IV 2/2.035/142. "Information for the Politburo," May 26, 1981, SAPMO-BArch, DY 30/11537, pp. 1–17. Milani, *Making of Iran's Islamic revolution*, pp. 192–93. "Members of Tudeh party executed," February 28, 1984, BStU, MfS HA II/6 1762, p. 3.

37. Lesch, *1979*, pp. 59–60. Nadav Safran, *Saudi Arabia* (Belknap Press, 1985), pp. 270–73. Naif Bin Hethlain, *Saudi Arabia and the US since 1962* (Saqi

Books, 2010), pp. 117–23. Rachel Bronson, *Thicker than oil* (Oxford University Press, 2006), pp. 149–50.

38. "Fm Jedda 190915Z Jan 81," NAUK, PREM 19/530, p. 1. Bronson, *Thicker than oil*, pp. 146–47. Wright, *Sacred rage*, pp. 33–36, 42–45, 178–80. Mackey, *Iranians*, pp. 310, 312.

39. "Information on some aspects of the situation in the Near East," February 6, 1979, BStU, MfS HVA 75, p. 156. Chris P. Ioannides, "The PLO and the Islamic Revolution in Iran," August Richard Norton and Martin H. Greenberg, eds., *The international relations of the Palestine Liberation Organization* (Southern Illinois University Press, 1989), pp. 74–86.

40. Lesch, *1979*, p. 70. Milani, *Making of Iran's Islamic revolution*, pp. 205–13. Ramazani, "Khumayni's Islam," pp. 14, 23–24. Charles Tripp, *A history of Iraq*, 3rd ed. (Cambridge University Press, 2007), pp. 212–25. Mackey, *Iranians*, pp. 320–21. Yevgeny Primakov, *Russia and the Arabs* (Basic Books, 2009), pp. 309–12.

41. Ioannides, "PLO," pp. 87–88. "Report," [November 1980], SAPMO-BArch, DY 30/IV B 2/20/381, pp. 88–107. "Information," August 10, 1987, SAPMO-BArch, DY 30/13943, pp. 59–63. Marius Deeb, *Syria, Iran, and Hezbollah* (Hoover Institution Press, 2013), pp. 1–2. "Fm Cairo 060910Z Oct 80," NAUK, PREM 19/813, pp. 1–2. "Arab leaders blast Iran, open door to renewed Egypt ties," *LAT*, November 11, 1987, p. 2.

42. Bin Hethlain, *Saudi Arabia*, pp. 33–116.

43. Alexei Vassiliev, *The history of Saudi Arabia* (Saqi Books, 1998), pp. 439–41. Wright, *Sacred rage*, pp. 152–53. Pascal Ménoret, "Fighting for the Holy Mosque," C. Christine Fair and Sumit Ganguly, eds., *Treading on hallowed ground* (Oxford University Press, 2008), pp. 118–24. Thomas Hegghammer and Stéphane Lacroix, "Rejectionist Islamism in Saudi Arabia," *International Journal of Middle East Studies*, 39/1 (2007), `pp. 103–22.

44. Wright, *Sacred rage*, pp. 146–50. Yaroslav Trofimov, *The siege of Mecca* (Doubleday, 2007), pp. 19–219. Ron E. Hassner, *War on sacred grounds* (Cornell University Press, 2009), p. 146–49. Ménoret, "Fighting," pp. 124–30

45. Wright, *Sacred rage*, p. 155. Trofimov, *Siege*, pp. 108, 220–59. Vassiliev, *History*, p. 397. Hassner, *War*, pp. 150–51.

46. Gilles Dorronsoro, *Revolution unending* (Columbia University Press, 2005), pp. 70–86. Martin Evans, *Afghanistan* (Perenniel, 2002), pp. 176–205. Larry P. Goodson, *Afghanistan's endless war* (University of Washington Press, 2001), p. 56.

47. "Information on the current situation," May 16, 1978, SAPMO-BArch, DY 30/IV B 2/20/229, pp. 1–6 (first to third quote). "Information," June 12, 1978, SAPMO-BArch, DY 30/IV B 2/20/153, pp. 6–21 (fourth quote). "Information," December 18, 1978, SAPMO-BArch, DY 30/13909, pp. 1–4.

48. Artemy M. Kalinovsky, *A long goodbye* (Harvard University Press, 2011), p. 19. Matthew J. Ouimet, *The rise and the fall of the Brezhnev Doctrine in Soviet foreign policy* (University of North Carolina Press, 2003), pp. 89–92. As the Soviet leaders told Indian Prime Minister Vajpayee in May 1979: "From C. L. Mallaby," July 16, 1979, NAUK, FCO 8/3372, pp. 1–3.

49. Ewans, *Afghanistan*, pp. 199–200. As the Soviets told the East Germans: "Information material," February 26, 1980, SAPMO-BArch, DY 30/13674, p. 88 (quote). "Strictly confidential," December 28, 1979, SAPMO-BArch, DY 30/13909, pp. 1–3. Kalinovsky, *Long goodbye*, pp. 20–21. Ouimet, *Rise and fall*, pp. 93–94. Anatoly F. Dobrynin, *In confidence* (Times Books, 1995), pp. 442–44.

50. Kalinovsky, *Long goodbye*, pp. 21–24. John K. Cooley, *Unholy wars* (Pluto Press, 1999), p. 10. Dorronsoro, *Revolution unending*, p. 92. Dobrynin, *In confidence*, pp. 445–46. Kalinovsky, *Long goodbye*, p. 27. Markus Wolf, *Spionagechef im geheimen Krieg* (List, 1997), p. 326. Ouimet, *Rise and fall*, pp. 94–95. "Dear comrades," [May 15, 1980], SAPMO-BArch, DY 30/11870, p. 10 (quotes).

51. Dorronsoro, *Revolution unending*, p. 87. "A problem of empire" *Christian Science Monitor*, August 9, 1979, p. 23. See, for example, "Afghanistan: Moscow's Vietnam," *WaPo*, May 10, 1979, p. A33. Cooley, *Unholy wars*, p. 10. Burton I. Kaufman and Scott Kaufman, *The presidency of James Earl Carter*, 2nd rev. ed. (University of Kansas Press, 2006), p. 196.

52. "Dear President Brezhnev," December 28, 1979, JC, Zbigniew Brzezinski Collection, Geographic File, box 18, pp. 1–3 (quote). Zbigniew Brzezinski, *Power and principle* (Farrar, Straus & Giroux, 1983), pp. 430–37. Cooley, *Unholy wars*, pp. 10, 22.

53. Ḥusain Ḥaqqani, *Pakistan* (Brookings Institution Press, 2005), pp. 96–140. Iftikhar H. Malik, *The history of Pakistan* (Greenwood Press, 2008), pp. 167–70. Ewans, *Afghanistan*, p. 207. "Fm Islamabad 200850Z Sep 79," NAUK, FCO 37/2130, p. 1. "Summary record," January 15, 1980, NAUK, FCO 37/2316, pp. 1–5.

54. Dennis Kux, *The United States and Pakistan, 1947–2000* (Woodrow Wilson Center Press / Johns Hopkins University Press, 2001), pp. 178–245. "Fm Jedda 020830Z Jan," January 2[, 1980], NAUK, PREM 19/1126, pp. 1–2 (quote).

55. Dorronsoro, *Revolution unending*, pp. 48–60, 93–29, 137–72. M. Hassan Kakar, *Afghanistan* (University of California Press, 1995), pp. 81–92. Ewans, *Afghanistan*, pp. 213–17.

56. Cooley, *Unholy wars*, pp. 10–47. Kux, *Disenchanted Allies*, pp. 246–53. William Maley, *The Afghanistan wars* (Palgrave Macmillan, 2002), p. 80. Beverley Milton-Edwards, *Islamic fundamentalism since 1945* (Routledge, 2005), p. 76. Bin Hethlain, *Saudi Arabia*, pp. 137–49.

57. Kakar, *Afghanistan*, pp. 94–95. "Foreign political information overview," June 1, 1981, BStU, HVA 12, pp. 261–62. Various documents: NAUK, FCO 37/2406 (first and second quotes). "Partial record," December 14, 1981, NAUK, FCO 37/2399, pp. 2–3 (third quote).

58. Charles Winslow, *Lebanon* (Routledge, 1996), pp. 221–30.

59. Ben-Ami, *Scars of war*, p. 175. Shlaim, *Iron wall*, pp. 382–91. Shlaim, *Lion*, p. 419. Donald Neff, "The U.S., Iraq, Israel, and Iran," *Journal of Palestine Studies*, 20/4 (1991), pp. 29–30. Various documents: NAUK, PREM 19/531.

60. Ioannides, "PLO," p. 90. "Israel says nothing is new in peace ideas by Saudis," *Globe and Mail*, August 10, 1981, p. A8. Helena Cobban, *The*

Palestinian Liberation Organisation (Cambridge University Press, 1984), pp. 112–16. Various documents: NAUK, PREM 19/1126. Shlaim, *Iron wall*, pp. 393–95. Peleg, *Begin's foreign policy*, p. 97.

61. Javier Pérez de Cuéllar, *Pilgrimage for peace* (St. Martin's Press, 1997), pp. 36–37. Shlaim, *Iron wall*, pp. 396–403, 422 (quote). Peleg, *Begin's foreign policy*, pp. 151–55. Hiro, *Lebanon*, pp. 81–110. Hirst, *Beware of small states*, pp. 116–47.

62. Cobban, *Palestinian Liberation Organization*, pp. 123–24. Peleg, *Begin's foreign policy*, pp. 156–65. Shlaim, *Iron wall*, pp. 398–416.

63. "Text of President Reagan's speech on the Mideast," *Boston Globe*, September 2, 1982, p. 1 (quotes). Naomi Joy Weinberger, "Peacekeeping options in Lebanon," *Middle East Journal*, 37/3 (1983), pp. 356–63. Shlaim, *Iron wall*, p. 415. "Agreement between the Government of the State of Israel and the Government of the Republic of Lebanon," Medzini, *Israel's foreign relations*, vol. 8, pp. 402–14. Ben-Ami, *Scars of war*, pp. 181–82.

64. Hirst, *Beware of small states*, pp. 148–73. Peleg, *Begin's foreign policy*, p. 171. Various documents: SAPMO-BArch, DY 30/13982. "Fm Amman 301735Z Jun 82," NAUK, PREM 19/1087, pp. 1–3. Shlaim, *Iron wall*, p. 419. Bonney, *Jihad*, p. 295. Jacob Høigilt, "Islamism, pluralism and the Palestine question," *British Journal of Middle Eastern Studies*, 34/2 (2007), p. 129.

65. Ioannides, "PLO," pp. 91–92. Naim Qassem, *Hizbullah* (Saqi Books, 2005), pp. 13–17, 66–67, 89, 151–85. Milton-Edwards, *Islamic fundamentalism*, pp. 86–87. Mackey, *Iranians*, pp. 313–15. Bonney, *Jihad*, pp. 295–98. Rula Jurdi Abisaab and Malek Abisaab, *The Shi'ites of Lebanon* (Syracuse University Press, 2014), pp. 159–61. Amal Saad-Ghorayeb, *Hizbullah* (Pluto Press, 2002), pp. 35–95.

66. First quote from Bonney, *Jihad*, pp. 298. Wright, *Sacred rage*, pp. 72–73. Saad-Ghorayeb, *Hizbullah*, pp. 100–2. "Fm Washington 260001Z," October 25, 1983, NAUK, PREM 19/1075, p. 1 (second quote). "Fm Washington 282252Z," December 28, 1983, NAUK, PREM 19/1077, p. 1 (third and fourth quotes). Lesch, *1979*, p. 66.

67. Fawaz A. Gerges, *The far enemy* (Cambridge University Press, 2005).

21   Asia

1. Zhang Shu Guang, *Economic Cold War* (Stanford University Press, 2001), p. 256. Andrew G. Walder, *China under Mao* (Harvard University Press, 2015), pp. 293–95. Li Zhisui and Anne F. Thurston, *The private life of Chairman Mao* (Random House, 1994), pp. 629–38. Ezra Vogel, *Deng Xiaoping and the transformation of China* (Belknap Press, 2011), pp. 41–45. Zhonggong zhongyang wenxian yanjiushi, ed., *Deng Xiaoping nianpu (1975–1997)* [*DXPNP*], vol. 1 (Zhongyang wenxian chubanshe, 2004), p. 22 (quote).

2. Yang Kuisong and Xia Yafeng, "Vacillating between revolution and détente," *Diplomatic History*, 34/2 (2010), p. 410. "Record of conversation," July 9, 1975, National Archives of Australia [NAA], Series A1838, 3107/40/5 Part 6, pp. 252–51 (first quote). "Ambassador Pauls, Beijing, to the Foreign Office," June 19, 1975, Institut für Zeitgeschichte, ed., *Akten zur Auswärtigen Politik der Bundesrepublik Deutschland, 1975* (R. Oldenbourg Verlag, 2006),

pp. 807–8 (second quote). Various documents: King C. Chen, ed., *China and the three Worlds* (M. E. Sharpe, 1979), pp. 85–98, 143–73, 183–93, 303–13. "Wider options in China's foreign policy," November 1978, National Archives of the United Kingdom [NAUK], FCO 21/1612, p. 1 (third quote). Various documents: NAUK, FCO 21/1097, 1098, 1101, and 1106.

3. "Note," December 23, 1974, Stiftung Archiv der Parteien und Massenorganisationen der DDR im Bundesarchiv [SAPMO-BArch], DY 30/IV B 2/20/169, p. 12 (first quote). Zhang Xiaoming, *Deng Xiaoping's long war* (University of North Carolina Press, 2015), pp. 24–29. "Information," no date, Arkhiv na Ministerstvoto na Vnshnite Raboti [AMVnR], opis 22p, a.e. 33, p. 220 (second quote).

4. Zhai Qiang, *China and the Vietnam Wars, 1950–1975* (University of North Carolina Press, 2000), pp. 208–15. "Note on a talk of the Secretary of Comecon, N. V. Faddeyev, with the Extraordinary and Plenipotentiary Ambassador of the DRV in Moscow, Vo Thuc Dong, on April 3, 1973," April 5, 1973, SAPMO-BArch, DY 30/J IV 2/2J/4662, pp. 1–6. Various documents: NAUK, FCO 15/1503. "Non-aligned bloc adds 4 members," *New York Times* [*NYT*], August 27, 1975, p. 9.

5. Paul F. Power, "The energy crisis and Indian development," *Asian Survey*, 15/4 (1975), pp. 328–45. Ramachandra Guha, *India after Gandhi* (Picador, 2012), pp. 488–95. The second had occurred in 1971 during the East Pakistan Crisis. "Your Excellency," July 11, 1975, SAPMO-BArch, DY 30/2448, pp. 24–30.

6. "My dear Lucy," July 16, 1975, NAUK, FCO 37/1600, pp. 1–3. "Excellency," May 24, 1974, NAUK, PREM 16/1182, pp. 1–4. Stephen Oren, "After the Bangladesh coups," *The World Today*, 32/1 (1976), pp. 18–24. "Dear Prime Minister," April 26, 1974, NAA, Series A1838, 169/10/1 Part 27, pp. 188–87. "Information," November 3, 1975, Politisches Archiv des Auswärtigen Amtes, Bestand: Ministerium für Auswärtige Angelegenheiten [PAAA-MfAA], C 902/78, pp. 25–28.

7. Various documents: NAUK, FCO/1600, 1608, 1723, and 1729. "Record of conversation," July 9, 1975, NAA, Series A1838, 3107/40/5 Part 6, pp. 253–50.

8. "Soviet relations with India," June 8, 1976, NAA, Series A1838, 169/11/52 Part 19, pp. 153–47. "Commonwealth heads of government meeting Kingston, Jamaica," [May 1975], NAUK, FCO 37/1600, p. 2. "Dear Michael," September 23, 1975, NAUK, FCO 58/855/1, p. 1. Various documents: NAUK, FCO 58/982 and 983.

9. "Note," April 11, 1977, PAAA-MfAA, C 5396, pp. 5–6. "Information no.[?], 1978," October 11, 1978, SAPMO-BArch, DY 30/J IV 2/2J/8140, p. 10. "Information no. 61, 1978," July 4, 1978, SAPMO-BArch, DY 30/J IV2/2J/8051, p. 2 (first and second quotes). Lorenz M. Lüthi, "Strategic shifts in East Asia," Lorenz M. Lüthi, ed., *The regional Cold Wars in Europe, East Asia, and the Middle East* (Woodrow Wilson Center Press / Stanford University Press, 2015), pp. 224–26. "Position," May 22, 1976, PAAA-MfAA, C 5445, pp. 8–9 (third quote). "Note," January 23, 1978, PAAA-MfAA, C 5459, p. 47 (fourth quote).

10. First quote from "On the policy," June 1, 1978, PAAA-MfAA, C 6576, p. 2. Lorenz M. Lüthi, "Chinese foreign policy, 1960–79," Tsuyoshi Hasegawa, ed., *The Cold War in East Asia, 1945–1991* (Stanford University Press, 2011), p. 168. *DXPNP*1, p. 307 (second quote). Dangdai Zhongguo congshu bianjibu, ed., *Dangdai Zhongguo de jingji tizhi gaige* (Dangdai Zhongguo chubanshe, 1984), pp. 160–66. Gong Li, *Deng Xiaoping yu Meiguo* (Zhonggong dangshi chubanshe, 2004), p. 206. Lüthi, "Strategic shifts," pp. 232–33.

11. Cécile Menétrey-Monchau, *American–Vietnamese relations in the wake of the war* (McFarland, 2006), pp. 177–202. Lüthi, "Strategic shifts," pp. 225–26. "Assessment," October 23, 1978, PAAA-MfAA, C 5459, pp. 49–51. "Political report no. 6," September 26, 1978, Schweizerisches Bundesarchiv [SBA], E 2300–01, Akzession 1988/91, box 21, p. 2. "Statements," November 6, 1978, PAAA-MfAA, C 5487, p. 19.

12. "Notes on a meeting held in the Secretary-General's office on Thursday, 28 September 1978, at 10.30 am," United Nations Archive [UNA], S-0904–0010-07, p. 1 (first quote). Lüthi, "Strategic shifts," p. 231. "Teng tells the Thais Moscow–Hanoi treaty perils world's peace," *NYT*, November 9, 1978, p. A9 (second and third quotes). "On the results of the official friendship visit," November 14, 1978, SAPMO-BArch, DY 30/13994, pp. 1–4. Enrico Fardella, "The Sino-American normalization," *Diplomatic History* 33/4 (2009), pp. 566–70.

13. Guha, *India after Gandhi*, pp. 522–42. "O.ND11148," July 1, 1977, NAA, Series A1838, 169/10/1 Part 34, pp. 203–2.

14. Ramesh Thakur, "India's Vietnam policy, 1946–1979," *Asian Survey*, 19/10 (1979), pp. 969–70. Various documents: NAUK, FCO 37/1942, 1963, 1968, 1969, 2095, 2096, 2097, and PREM 16/1691; SAPMO-BArch, DY 30/13941. "Fm Delhi 020600Z," May 2, 1977, NAUK, FCO 37/1946, pp. 1–2 (quote).

15. Various documents: NAUK, FCO 58/1307. "Information," May 10, 1978, PAAA-MfAA, C 6359, pp. 30–32. "The Belgrade conference of the Non-Aligned foreign ministers," August 2, 1978, NAUK, FCO 58/1310, pp. 1–15.

16. "Record of discussion," October 3, 1977, NAUK, FCO 37/1950, pp. 1–2. "Record of conversation with Mr. E. Gonsalves," August 23, 1978, NAA, Series A1838, 169/10/1 Part 36, pp. 208–7.

17. Guha, *India after Gandhi*, p. 528. "Record of conversation with Mr. E. Gonsalves," August 23, 1978, NAA, Series A1838, 169/10/1 Part 36, p. 209. "Second session," May 17, 1977, NAUK, FCO 37/1943, [p. 5]. "Record of conversation," June 6, 1978, NAUK, FCO 37/2097, pp. 2–3. "Record of a meeting," June 6, 1978, NAUK, FCO 37/2093, p. 1 (quote).

18. "Information," May 9, 1977, SAPMO-BArch, DY 30/13941, pp. 40–43. "Second session," May 17, 1977, NAUK, FCO 37/1943, [p. 1] (first quote). "Record of discussion," October 3, 1977, NAUK, FCO 37/1950, p. 2. "Note of a conversation," January 7, 1978, NAUK, PREM 16/1692, p. 1 (second quote). "P.R. no. 6," February 23, 1978, SBA, E 2300–01, Akzession 1988/

91, box 23, pp. 1–3. "Chinese team to visit India," *South China Morning Post* [*SCMP*], February 2, 1978, p. 26.

19. "Teng for closer ties with India," *Times of India* [*TofI*], February 5, 1978, p. 1. *DXPNP*1, p. 265. "Vajpayee makes it official," *SCMP*, August 22, 1978, p. 5. "Record of conversation with Mr. E. Gonsalves," August 23, 1978, NAA, Series A1838, 169/10/1 Part 36, p. 208 (quote). "Information," October 2, 1978, SAPMO-BArch, DY 30/13941, p. 61. "P.R. no. 21," November 2, 1978, SBA, E 2300–01, Akzession 1988/91, box 23, pp. 1–2.

20. Nayan Chandra, *Brother enemy* (Collier Books, 1986), pp. 341–47. Zhang Zhen, *Zhang Zhen huiyilu*, vol. 2 (Jiefangjun chubanshe, 2003), pp. 165–66. Zhang, *Deng Xiaoping's long war*, pp. 54–55. "Record of a meeting," March 21, 1979, NAUK, FCO 21/1705, p. 1 (quote).

21. Christopher E. Goscha, "Vietnam, the Third Indochina war and the meltdown of Asian internationalism," O. Arne Westad and Sophie Quinn-Judge, eds., *The Third Indochina war* (Routledge, 2006), p. 179. Mentioned: "Memorandum of conversation," February 1, 1979, Jimmy Carter Presidential Library [JC], NSA, 26 Staff Material Far East, box 66, p. 2. "Memorandum from Brzezinski for the Secretary of State," January 12, 1979, JC, NSA, 26 Staff Material Far East, box 66, p. 1 (quote). "Fm Bangkok 101040Z," January 10, 1979, NAUK, PREM 16/2292, p. 1.

22. "Memorandum of conversation," January 29, 1979, United States, Department of State, *Foreign relations of the United States* [*FRUS*], 1977–80, XIII (US Government Printing Office, 2013), pp. 767–69 (first and second quotes). Gong Li, "1979nian ZhongYue bianjing chongtu de MeiZhongSu sanjiao guanxi," *Guoji Guancha*, 2004 (3), pp. 66–72 (third and fourth quotes). "Oral presentation by President Carter to Chinese Vice Premier Deng Xiaoping," January 30, 1979, *FRUS*, 1977–80, XIII, p. 770 (fifth and sixth quotes). Lüthi, "Strategic shifts," p. 235.

23. Gong Li, "1979nian," p. 70. Grant Evans and Kelvin Rowley, *Red brotherhood at war*, rev. ed. (Verso, 1990), p. 115–19. "Record of a meeting," March 21, 1979, NAUK, FCO 21/1705, p. 1 (quote).

24. Sergey Radchenko, *Unwanted visionaries* (Oxford University Press, 2014), p. 127. "Impact of Chinese aggression on SR Vietnam," June 26, 1979, Der Bundesbeauftragte für die Unterlagen des Staatssicherheitsdienstes der ehemaligen Deutschen Demokratischen Republik [BStU], MfS ZAIG 14070, pp. 95–96. "Telegram vvs 33/79," March 1, 1979, Bundesarchiv (BArch), DC 20/12792, p. 87 (quotes). Lüthi, "Strategic shifts," p. 236.

25. "Information," no date, SAPMO-BArch, DY 30/IV B 2/20/154, pp. 1–24. According to the Soviet ambassador to India: "Fm Delhi 261050Z Feb 79," NAUK, FCO 37/2159, p. 1 (first quote). "L. Brezhnev to Jimmy Carter," February 18, 1979, JC, Zbigniew Brzezinski Collection, Geographic File, box 10, p. 2 (second quote). Radchenko, *Unwanted visionaries*, p. 128. "Information," March 13, 1979, SAPMO-BArch, DY 30/13994, pp. 1–6.

26. "O.ND18861," February 2, 1979, NAA, Series A1838, 3016/11/147 Part 2, pp. 221–20. "Opening dialogue with China," *TofI*, February 7, 1979, p. 8 (first quote). "India's foreign minister leaves on visit to Peking," *NYT*, February 12, 1979, p. A3 (second and third quotes).

27. *DXPNP*1, p. 489. Jagat S. Mehta, "Diplomatic amnesia on successful bipartisanship," *India International Centre Quarterly*, 30/1 (2003), p. 164. "Attack on Vietnamese compared to the drive against India in 1962," *NYT*, February 18, 1979, p. 10. "Teng says war to last another week or more," *Boston Globe*, February 27, 1979, p. 1 (first quote). "Indian's visit to China cut off in protest," *NYT*, February 19, 1978, p. A10. "Fm Delhi 211515Z Feb," NAUK, PREM 16/2292, p. 1. "Fm Delhi 280550Z Feb," NAUK, FCO 21/1703, p. 1 (second and third quote). Masashi Nishihara, "The Sino-Vietnamese war of 1979," *Southeast Asian Affairs*, 1980, p. 72.
28. "Information," April 3, 1979, SAPMO-BArch, DY 30/13941, pp. 69–74 (first quote). "India," March 19, 1979, NAA, Series A1838, 3016/11/147 Part 2, pp. 233–30 (second quote).
29. Dangdai Zhongguo congshu bianjibu, ed., *Dangdai Zhongguo waijiao* (Zhongguo shehui kexue chubanshe, 1988), p. 245. "Fm Peking 120730Z Jun 81," NAUK, PREM 19/387, p. 1 (first quote). "Don't feed the tiger until it is big," *Spiegel*, February 18, 1980, p. 152 (second quote). Gong Li, *Deng Xiaoping*, p. 287.
30. "Record of a conversation," October 1, 1980, NAUK, FCO 21/1816, [p. 5]. "Record of a conversation," October 2, 1980, NAUK, FCO 21/1816, p. 2 (first quote). "Fm Peking 300822Z Jan 80," NAUK, FCO 37/2319, pp. 1–3. *DXPNP*1, pp. 612, 619 (second and third quotes).
31. Various documents: NAUK, FCO 51/1572 and 1573. "From FCO 201845Z Feb 79," NAUK, FCO 58/1573, pp. 1–2 (first quote). Nishihara, "The Sino-Vietnamese War," p. 74. "Session III," March 3, 1979, NAUK, FCO 37/2164, p. 2 (second and third quotes).
32. "Khomeini demands review of Iran's foreign deals," *NYT*, January 22, 1979, p. A11. "Iran says it will abandon military pact," *Los Angeles Times*, February 7, 1979, p. B1. "Pakistan quits CENTO in the wake of Iran," *Jerusalem Post*, March 13, 1979, p. 4. "Turkish withdrawal finishes CENTO," *Guardian*, March 16, 1979, p. 6. "Record of conversation," March 22, 1979, NAUK, FCO 58/1574, pp. 1–4. "Vajpayee hails Pindi bid to join neutrals," *TofI*, June 9, 1979, p. 9. "Pakistan admitted to non-aligned bloc," September 1, 1979, *TofI*, p. 1. "CENTO group is dissolved," *The Sun*, September 27, 1979, p. A7.
33. "Fm Havana 041600Z," May 4, 1979, NAUK, FCO 28/3923, p. 1 (first quote). "Non-Aligned matters," May 4, 1979, NAUK, FCO 58/1575, p. 1 (second quote). "Dear Howard," May 16, 1979, NAUK, FCO 58/1576, pp. 1–3. "Non-Aligned Movement (NAM): essential facts," June 22, 1979, NAUK, FCO 58/1577, p. 2 (third quote). For Tito's trip: NAUK, FCO 58/1579. "Fm Belgrade 190835Z Jul 79," NAUK, FCO 28/3923, p. 1. Mentioned: "Fm Belgrade 010930Z Aug 79," NAUK, FCO 58/1582, pp. 1–2. "India: into the dust," *Spiegel*, August 27, 1979, p. 134.
34. "The sixth Non-Aligned conference at Havana," no date, NAUK, FCO 58/1584, pp. 7–14. "From Havana 131900Z Sep," NAUK, FCO 28/3877, p. 1 (first quote). "Non-Aligned summit," October 3, 1979, NAUK, FCO 58/1585, p. 1 (second quote). "Fm UKmis New York 031635Z Oct 79," NAUK, FCO 58/1584, p. 1 (third quote).

35. "Yugoslavia external," February 26, 1980, NAUK, FCO 28/4243, p. 1 (quote). "Afghanistan and the Non-Aligned Movement," January 8, 1980, NAUK, FCO 28/4243, p. 1. "Setbacks in the Non-Aligned Movement," August 1980, NAUK, FCO 58/1952, pp. 1–4.

36. Guha, *India after Gandhi*, pp. 546–48. "O.ND22222," January 8, 1980, NAA, Series A1838, 3016/11/147 Part 2, pp. 263–61. "Summary record," January 16, 1980, NAUK, FCO 37/2316, pp. 1–5 (quotes). "Fm Delhi 1230z 29 Jan," NAUK, FCO 37/2311, p. 2. "Visit of FM Offergeld with Ms. Gandhi," January 30, 1980, Politisches Archiv des Auswärtigen Amtes [PAAA], AV Neues Amt, vol. 9553, pp. 1–4.

37. Various documents: SBA, E 2010–02 (A), Akzession 1991/19, box 13. "Dear Charles," June 18, 1980, NAUK, FCO 37/2311, p. 1 (quotes). Various documents: NAUK, FCO 58/1951–1952.

38. "Fm Peking 090835z Jul 80," NAUK, FCO 21/1806, p. 1. "Dear Charles," July 16, 1980, NAUK, FCO 37/2311, pp. 1–2. "Visit of Indian Secretary for External Affairs," May 9, 1980, NAUK, FCO 15/2591, pp. 1–2. "My dear Graham," August 12, 1980, NAUK, FCO 37/2311, pp. 1–4.

39. Various documents: NAUK, FCO 21/1816. As the Indian government told the American ambassador in Delhi: "Telegram from AmEmbassy to SecState," October 16, 1980, JC, Zbigniew Brzezinski Collection, Subject File, box 42, p. 1 (first to third quote). "Note of a conversation," December 4, 1980, NAUK, FCO 37/2311, p. 1. Various documents: NAUK, FCO 58/1952. "Record of a conversation," April 16, 1981, NAUK, PREM 19/487, p. 2 (fourth quote). "Non-Aligned summit a - $6 billion war victim," *SCMP*, September 6, 1982, p. 32.

40. "Essential facts," no date, NAUK, FCO 21/2051, p. 1. Radchenko, *Unwanted visionaries*, pp. 23–24. "Information on the assessment of the internal and external developments of the SRV," March 30, 1982, BStU, MfS ZAIG 14071, pp. 75–77. "Note," no date, BStU, MfS – Abt. X 341, p. 63 (first quote). "Information on Chinese reactions to the 5th Party Congress of the CPV," May 6, 1982, BStU, MfS ZAIG 14071, p. 72 (all other quotes). "Fm Hanoi 2107201Z Jul 82," NAUK, FCO 21/2073, p. 1.

41. Radchenko, *Unwanted visionaries*, pp. 24–25. *DXPNP2*, p. 815. "Transcript of the meeting of comrade Erich Honecker with Comrade Leonid I. Brezhnev on the Crimea on August 11, 1982," SAPMO-BArch, DY 30/11854, p. 33 (first quote). "Fm Hanoi 2107201z Jul 82," NAUK, FCO 21/2073, p. 1. "Hanoi teletter 283," August 27, 1982, NAUK, FCO 21/2073, pp. 1–4. *DXPNP2*, p. 835 (second quote). "Hu Yaobang's report to the 12th Party Congress," Xinhua, Beijing, September 7, 1982, Foreign Broadcast Information Service, 1:174 (September 8, 1982), p. K4 (third quote).

42. "Talk of the Ambassador of the USSR with the Chinese Ambassador in the GDR on September 21st," September 25, 1982, SAPMO-BArch, DY 30/13932, pp. 5–6 (quote). *DXPNP2*, p. 851. "Note of a meeting," September 22, 1982, NAUK, PREM 19/962, pp. 1–12. Various documents: NAUK, FCO 21/2053.

43. "Dear George," April 2, 1982, NAUK, FCO 37/2797, p. 1.

44. "Fm Washington 032330z Aug 82," NAUK, FCO 37/2789, p. 1 (first quote). Various documents: NAUK, FCO 37/2790 (second and third quotes). "Mrs Gandhi's visit to the Soviet Union," October 6, 1982, NAUK, FCO 37/2787, p. 1 (fourth quote). "Brezhnev's health," October 8, 1972, NAUK, FCO 37/2787, p. 1 (fifth and sixth quotes).
45. A. K. Damodaran, "Non-aligned movement and its future," Atish Sinha and Madhup Mohta, eds., *Indian foreign policy* (Academic Foundation, 2007), p. 133.

22   Europe

1. Tony Judt, *Postwar* (Penguin Press, 2005), pp. 453–77. Derek Howard Aldcroft, *The European economy, 1914–2000*, 4th ed. (Routledge, 2001), pp. 188–210.
2. Andrew Moravcsik, *The choice for Europe* (Cornell University Press, 1998), pp. 238–302. Matthias Schulz, "The reluctant European," Matthias Schulz and Thomas A. Schwarz, eds., *The strained alliance* (Cambridge University Press, 2010), pp. 292–305. Barry J. Eichengreen, *The European economy since 1945* (Princeton University Press, 2007), pp. 242–86.
3. Helga Haftendorn, *Deutsche Aussenpolitik zwischen Selbstbeschränkungen und Selbstbehauptung 1945–2000* (Deutsche Verlags-Anstalt, 2001), pp. 92–114. Geir Lundestad, *The United States and Western Europe since 1945* (Oxford University Press, 2003), pp. 201–7.
4. Lorenz M. Lüthi, "Drifting apart," Jeronim Perović, ed., *Cold War energy* (Macmillan, 2017), pp. 374–78.
5. Krzystof Czerkawski and Don Hank, "The indebtedness of Socialist countries to the West," *Eastern European Economics*, 21/1 (1982), pp. 77–90. Lüthi, "Drifting apart," p. 378. "Information," February 5, 1979, Der Bundesbeauftragte für die Unterlagen des Staatssicherheitsdienstes der ehemaligen Deutschen Demokratischen Republik [BStU], MfS HA XVIII 12478, pp. 12–15. "Speech," [late February 1978], Stiftung Archiv der Parteien und Massenorganisationen der DDR im Bundesarchiv [SAPMO-BArch], DY 30/11862, pp. 95–101.
6. Gerhard Wettig, "Die Sowjetunion in der Auseinandersetzung über den NATO-Doppelbeschluss 1979–1983," *Vierteljahreshefte für Zeitgeschichte*, 2/2009, pp. 217–20. A. M. Aleksandrov-Agentov, *Ot Kollontai do Gorbacheva* (Mezhdunarodnye otnosheniya, 1994), p. 269. "Stenographic transcript," [November 22–23], Bundesarchiv [BArch], DC 20/5200, pp. 4–25 (first quote). "Argumentation materials of the CC of the CPSU," [December 1979], SAPMO-BArch, DY 30/13904, 89–103 (second quote).
7. Vladislav M. Zubok, *A failed empire* (University of North Carolina Press, 2007), p. 263.
8. "Report," November 2, 1981, BStU, MfS AIM 15827/89, vol. 4, p. 6. Kim Richard Nossal, "Knowing when to fold," *International Journal*, 44/3 (1989), pp. 703–5. Various documents: *International Olympic Committee*, JO-1980s-Boyco. Nicholas Evan Sarantakes, *Dropping the torch* (Cambridge University Press, 2011), pp. 1–243.

9. "Note on a meeting of the heads of the missions of the SSG, on 1/17/1980," January 19, 1980, SAPMO-BArch, DY 30/IV B 2/20/229, pp. 1–2. "Information," February 20, 1980, SAPMO-BArch, DY 30/J IV 2/2A/ 2305, pp. 42–44. "On Sakharov," January 26, 1980, SAPMO-BArch, DY 30/14021, pp. 71–75. "CPSU plenum, June 23, 1980," Rossiiskii Gosudarstvennyi Arkhiv Noveishei Istorii [RGANI], fond 2, opis 3, delo 528, p. 14 (quote).

10. Historical oil prices: https://tradingeconomics.com/commodity/crude-oil, accessed on June 16, 2018. Aldcroft, *European economy*, pp. 215–18. Joe Renouard and D. Nathan Vigil, "The quest for leadership in a time of peace," Schulz, *Strained Alliance*, pp. 324–27.

11. Various documents: National Archives of the United Kingdom [NAUK], FCO 8/3371.

12. "Their moments will last forever," *Los Angeles Times*, July 21, 1992, pp. WA8–WA9.

13. Various documents: Andrzej Paczkowski and Malcolm Byrne, eds., *From Solidarity to martial law* (Central European University Press, 2007), pp. xxxiii, 66–80. Andrzej Paczkowski, "Playground of superpowers, Poland 1980–89," Olav Njølstad, ed., *The last decade of the Cold War* (Frank Cass, 2004), p. 312. "Note," September 12, 1980, SAPMO-BArch, DY 30/IV 2/ 2.035/44, pp. 2–37 (first quote). "Telegram vvs b 7/3 – 70/80," September 17, 1980, and "Telegram vvs b 7/3 – 77/80," October 17, 1980, BArch, DC 20/13014, pp. 164–65, 181–82 (second and third quotes).

14. Matthew J. Ouimet, *The rise and the fall of the Brezhnev Doctrine in Soviet foreign policy* (University of North Carolina Press, 2003), pp. 136–37. "Transcript of CPSU CC Politburo meeting," October 29, 1980, Paczkowski and Byrne, *From Solidarity*, pp. 124–25 (first and second quotes). Zubok, *Failed empire*, p. 267 (third quote). "Note," November 21, 1980, SAPMO-BArch, DY 30/IV 2/2.035/44, p. 192 (fourth quote). "Dear Comrade Leonid Ilyich," November 26, 1980, SAPMO-BArch, DY 30/ 13973, p. 26 (fifth and sixth quotes). Various documents: Paczkowski and Byrne, *From Solidarity*, pp. 139–61.

15. Hansjakob Stehle, *Geheimdiplomatie im Vatikan* (Benziger Verlag, 1993), p. 355. "Telegram vvs b 7/3 – 67/80," September 9, 1980, BArch, DC 20/ 13014, pp. 159–60. "Information on the opinions of clerical representatives of the Vatican," October 17, 1980, BStU, MfS ZAIG/3062, p. 1–2 (first quote). Letter printed in George Weigel, *Witness to hope* (Cliff Street Books, 2001), pp. 422–25 (second to fourth quote). "CPSU CC instructions to the Soviet ambassador concerning Lech Wałęsa Visit to Italy," January 14, 1981, Paczkowski and Byrne, *From Solidarity*, pp. 176–78. *Tribunale di Roma, L'attentato al Papa* (Kaos Edizioni, 2002), pp. 227–61. Ouimet, *Rise*, pp. 120–22. "Wyszynski dies," *New York Times* [NYT], May 28, 1981, p. A1. "Information," June 26, 1981, BArch, DO 4/501, pp. 212–19. "On some tendencies in the policy of the Vatican with regard to the socialist states," July 27, 1981, BStU, MfS XX/4, 414, pp. 128–31 (fifth quote).

16. Various documents: SAPMO-BArch, DY 30/13973 and 30/IV 2/2.035/48. Vojtech Mastny, "The Soviet non-invasion of Poland in 1980/81 and the end

of the Cold War," Cold War International History Project [CWIHP], Working Paper 23, p. 22. Paczkowski., "Playground," p. 313.

17. "Information," September 16, 1981, SAPMO-BArch, DY 30/IV 2/2.035/48, pp. 69–70. "Transcript of CPSU CC Politburo meeting," September 10, 1981, and "Information on the Brezhnev–Kania telephone conversation," September 15, 1981, Paczkowski and Byrne, *From Solidarity*, pp. 348–49 (first quote), pp. 360–61 (second quote). "Laborem Exercens," September 15, 1981, w2.vatican.va/content/john-paul-ii/en/encyclicals/docu ments/hf_jp-ii_enc_14091981_laborem-exercens.html, accessed on June 19, 2018.

18. Paczkowski, "Playground," p. 313. Various documents: Paczkowski and Byrne, *From Solidarity*, pp. xlv, 392 (first quote), 397, 423, 450 (second quote). Mark Kramer, "Jaruzelski, the Soviet Union, and the imposition of martial law in Poland," *Cold War International History Project [CWIHP] Bulletin*, 11 (1998), p. 6. Wojciech Jaruzelski, *Hinter den Türen der Macht* (Militzke, 1996), pp. 432–45. "Telegram vvs b 7/3 – t – 137/81," December 16, 1981, and "Telegram vvs b 7/3 – t – 146/81," December 30, 1981, BArch, DC 20/13014, pp. 69–71, 86 (third quote). Papal letter reprinted in Stehle, *Geheimdiplomatie*, p. 359.

19. Mastny, "Soviet non-invasion," pp. 18–22. Ouimet, *Rise*, pp. 180–86. "Transcript of CPSU CC Politburo meeting," December 10, 1981, Paczkowski and Byrne, *From Solidarity*, p. 450. Paczkowski, "Playground," p. 313. André Steiner, *Von Plan zu Plan* (Aufbau Taschenbuch, 2007), p. 90. "Stenographic account of the CPSU CC plenum," [11/5/1958], RGANI, fond 2, opis 1, delo 332. "Speech," [November 3–4, 1981], SAPMO-BArch, DY 30/ 11871, pp. 38–39. "Final communiqué," December 11–12, 1980, www.nato.int /docu/comm/49–95/c801211a.htm, accessed on June 20, 2018 (first quote). "Transcript of CPSU CC Politburo meeting," December 10, 1981, Paczkowski and Byrne, *From Solidarity*, p. 450 (second quote).

20. "Information," November 10, 1980, SAPMO-BArch, DY 30/IV 2/2.036/76, pp. 131–32. "Information," December 5, 1981, BStU, MfS HA XVIII 2815, pp. 23–25. Lüthi, "Drifting apart," pp. 381–83.

21. Lüthi, "Drifting apart," pp. 381–82. "Transcript," August 3, 1981, SAPMO-BArch, DY 30/11853, pp. 2–4. "Note," September 30, 1981, SAPMO-BArch, DY 30/IV 2/2.036/79, pp. 119–20. "Dear Leonid Ilyich," September 4, 1981, SAPMO-BArch, DY 30/J IV 2/2/1909, pp. 11–13 (quote). "Dear Comrade Leonid Ilyich," October 2, 1981, SAPMO-BArch, DY 30/14018, pp. 141–43. "Final information," October 26, 1981, SAPMO-BArch, DY 30/250, p. 1. "[No title]," November 19, 1981, SAPMO-BArch, DY 30/14018, p. 148. "Information on Brezhnev meeting with Kania and Jaruzelski on August 14, 1981," Paczkowski and Byrne, *From Solidarity*, pp. 342–47.

22. Laura D'Andrea Tyson, "The debt crisis and adjustment responses in Eastern Europe," *International Organization*, 40/2 (1986), p. 261. Thomas Kunze, *Nicolae Ceaușescu*, 3rd, upd. ed. (Ch. Links Verlag, 2009), pp. 303–5.

23. "Assessment," November 16, 1981, BStU, MfS AIM 15827/89, Band 5, pp. 11–18. "[No title]," November 20, 1981, BStU, MfS HA XVIII, 16067, pp. 51–53. Ellen Comisso and Paul Marer, "The economics and politics of reform in Hungary," *International Organization*, 40/2 (1986), pp. 430–54.
24. "Dear Comrade Stoph," July 30, 1981, BArch, DC 20/5136, pp. 163–64. "Poles agree to debt plan," *NYT*, August 21, 1981, p. D8. "ADN-information," November 13, 1981, SAPMO-BArch, DY 30/IV 2/2.036/80, pp. 84–85 (quote). Paczkowski and Byrne, *From Solidarity*, pp. xlvi–xlvii. "Hungary joins IMF, but Poland must wait," *NYT*, May 6, 1982, p. D16. "Poland gains admission to the International Monetary Fund," *NYT*, June 1, 1986, p. 13.
25. "Information," August 25, 1980, BStU, MfS HA XVIII, 18843, p. 21 (first quote). "Transcript," August 3, 1981, SAPMO-BArch, DY 30/11853, pp. 1–60. "[No title]," December 12, 1981, SAPMO-BArch, DY 30/25759, pp. 47–48 (second quote). "Memory Protocol," [December 11, 1981], SAPMO-BArch, DY 30/2408, p. 13. "On the assessment (draft)," December 30, 1981, SAPMO-BArch, DY 30/IV 2/2.035/86, pp. 12–22.
26. "Information," January 16, 1982, BStU, MfS-HA XVIII 13329, pp. 9–11. Lorenz M. Lüthi, "How Udo wanted to save the world in 'Erich's lamp shop'," *Contemporary European History*, 24/1 (2015), pp. 98–99. Quote from Margit Roth, *Innerdeutsche Bestandsaufnahme der Bundesrepublik 1969–1989* (Springer Fachmedien, 2013), p. 461.
27. Lüthi, "Drifting apart," p. 384–85.
28. "Transcript," August 11, 1982, SAPMO-BArch, DY 30/11854, pp. 4–7 (quote). "Dear comrade Honecker," December 8, 1982, BArch, DY 30/11357, pp. 96–97. "Transcript," [March 5, 1983], SAPMO-BArch, DY 30/J IV 2/2A/2560, pp. 38.
29. "Dear comrade Honecker," September 14, 1983, BArch, DY 30/11357, pp. 129–30. "Transcript," June 15, 1984, SAPMO-BArch, DY 30/IV 2/2.035/58, pp. 55–62 (quotes).
30. Benjamin Grob-Fitzgibbon, *Continental drift* (Cambridge University Press, 2016), pp. 400–22, 426. William I. Hitchcock, *The struggle for Europe* (Doubleday, 2003), pp. 315–32. Eichengreen, *European economy*, pp. 277–82. Judt, *Postwar*, pp. 539–47.
31. Various documents: Institut für Zeitgeschichte, ed., *Akten zur Auswärtigen Politik der Bundesrepublik Deutschland, 1979* (R. Oldenbourg, 2010), pp. 598–99, 614–16, 648–49. Grob-Fitzgibbon, *Continental Drift*, pp. 400–22.
32. Robert M. Collins, *Transforming America* (Columbia University Press, 2007), pp. 7–27. John Ehrman, *The eighties* (Yale University Press, 2005), pp. 23–45. John Lewis Gaddis, *Strategies of containment*, 2nd and rev. ed. (Oxford University Press, 2005), pp. 343–49.
33. Collins, *Transforming America*, pp. 29–91. Ehrman, *The eighties*, pp. 2–22, 49–89. Gaddis, *Strategies*, pp. 349–62. Chester J. Pach, "Sticking to his guns," W. Elliot Brownlee and Hugh Davis Graham, eds., *The Reagan presidency* (University Press of Kansas, 2003), p. 86 (quote).
34. Collins, *Transforming America*, pp. 193–218. Gaddis, *Strategies*, pp. 353–62.

35. "Message from President Reagan to Soviet General Secretary Brezhnev," [April 1981], United States, Department of State, *Foreign relations of the United States [FRUS]*, 1981–88, III (US Government Printing Office, 2016), pp. 101–2. Pach, "Sticking," pp. 104–7. Nate Jones, *Able Archer 83* (The New Press, 2016). "Text of Reagan's address to parliament on promoting democracy," *NYT*, June 9, 1982, p. A16. "Excerpts from President's speech to National Association of Evangelicals," *NYT*, March 9, 1983, p. A18. Lou Cannon, *President Reagan* (Public Affairs, 2000), pp. 339–401.

36. George Ross, "The limits of political economy," Anthony Daley, ed., *The Mitterrand era policy alternatives and political mobilization in France* (New York University Press, 1996), p. 35. Judt, *Postwar*, pp. 548–51. Serge Bernstein, "The crisis of the left and the renaissance of the Republican model, 1981–1995," Mairi Maclean, ed., *The Mitterrand years* (Macmillan, 1998), pp. 53–54.

37. Judt, *Postwar*, pp. 552–54. Ronald Tiersky, *François Mitterrand* (Rowman & Littlefield, 2003), 125–51. Wayne Northcutt, *Mitterrand* (Holmes & Meier, 1992), pp. 84–115. Ross, "Limits," pp. 36–37. Joseph P. Morray, *Grand disillusion* (Praeger, 1997), pp. 101, 109 (quotes). Bernstein, "Crisis," p. 55.

38. Judt, *Postwar*, p. 553 (quote). Morray, *Grand Disillusion*, pp. 107–10. Northcutt, *Mitterrand*, pp. 116–70. Ross, "Limits," pp. 37–38.

39. Manfred Görtemaker, *Geschichte der Bundesrepublik Deutschland* (Fischer Taschenbuch, 1999), pp. 699–704. Edgar Wolfrum, *Die geglückte Demokratie* (Klett-Cotta, 2006), pp. 354–56.

40. Heinrich August Winkler, *Germany* (Oxford, 2007), pp. 357–72. Görtemaker, *Geschichte*, pp. 687–90.

41. Edgar Wolfrum, *Die geglückte Demokratie*, pp. 356–64. Görtemaker, *Geschichte*, pp. 704–9. Lüthi, "How Udo wanted to save the world," pp. 98–99.

42. "Moscow flash vvs 13/81," June 12, 1981, SAPMO-BArch, DY 30/IV 2/ 2.035/65, pp. 82–84. "Try to see it from our point . . . ," *Spiegel*, November 2, 1981, pp. 46–47, 52. "Excerpts from President's address," *Boston Globe*, November 19, 1981, p. 1 (first quote). "Brezhnev rejects Reagan missile plan," *Washington Post*, November 24, 1981, p. A1 (second quote). "Letter to the communist and worker parties in the non-socialist countries," March 8, 1982, SAPMO-BArch, DY 30/14005, pp. 69–81.

43. "Dear Comrades," May 27, 1982, SAPMO-BArch, DY 30/IV 2/2.035/65, pp. 126–33. "[No title]," September 12, 1983, SAPMO-BArch, DY 30/J IV 2/2A/2594, pp. 45–49 (quote). "Report," [September 1983], SAPMO-BArch, DY 30/11877, pp. 235–47. "Moscow negotiations in September 1983," [September 1983], SAPMO-BArch, DY 30/27125, pp. 103–27. Lüthi, "How Udo wanted to save the world," p. 93.

44. Lüthi, "How Udo wanted to save the world," pp. 93, 99. Letter exchange of October 5 and 24, 1983: SAPMO-BArch, DY 30/2398, pp. 44–54 (quote). "Transcript," June 15, 1984, SAPMO-BArch, DY 30/IV 2/ 2.035/58, pp. 55–62.

45. Various documents: BArch, DC 20/5161, 5162, 5164, 5330, 5352, 22119–22123, and SAPMO-BArch, DY 30/2358 and DY 30/IV 2/2.039/ 291. Lüthi, "Drifting apart," pp. 388–89.

46. Moravcsik, *Choice*, pp. 314–78. Grob-Fitzgibbon, *Continental drift*, pp. 429–44.

23   The End of the Superpower Cold War

1. O. Arne Westad, "Reagan's anti-revolutionary offensive in the Third World," Olav Njølstad, ed., *The last decade of the Cold War* (Frank Cass, 2004), pp. 201–19. "Mr. Gorbachev, open this gate, tear down this wall," *Los Angeles Times*, June 12, 1987, p. 1.

2. "Politburo," January 23, 1986, Anatoly S. Chernyaev, ed., *V Politbyuro TsK KPSS* (Alpina, 2006), pp. 28–29. Anatoly S. Chernyaev, *Sovmestnyi iskhod* (ROSSPEN, 2010), p. 776.

3. Vladislav M. Zubok, *A failed empire* (University of North Carolina Press, 2007), pp. 208, 259–70. Gerd Ruge, *Michail Gorbatschow* (S. Fischer Verlag, 1990), pp. 180–81. "Dear comrade Honecker," December 8, 1982, Bundesarchiv [BArch], DY 30/11357, pp. 96–104. "More information," January 9, 1985, Stiftung Archiv der Parteien und Massenorganisationen der DDR im Bundesarchiv [SAPMO-BArch], DY 30/11608, pp. 1–4. Eduard Shevardnadze, *Als der Eiserne Vorhang zerriss* (Peter W. Metzler Verlag, 2007), p. 56.

4. Ruge, *Gorbatschow*, pp. 16–23, 68–70, 118–21, 142–45, 178–84. William Taubman, *Gorbachev* (W.W. Norton, 2017), pp. 53–58, 119–57, 180–82, 196–201. Mária Huber, *Moskau, 11. März 1985* (Deutscher Taschenbuchverlag, 2002), pp. 14–15, 33. Archie Brown, *The Gorbachev factor* (Oxford University Press, 1996), pp. 47–52, 62–77.

5. Ruge, *Gorbatschow*, pp. 190–91. Taubman, *Gorbachev*, pp. 219–40. "Note," March 14, 1985, SAPMO-BArch, DY 30/J IV 2/2A/2739, pp. 25–30 (quote). Zubok, *Failed empire*, p. 279. Brown, *Gorbachev factor*, pp. 97–117.

6. Taubman, *Gorbachev*, pp. 240–51. György Dalos, *Gorbatschow* (C. H. Beck, 2012), pp. 86–93. "Note," [October 2, 1986], SAPMO-BArch, DY 30/J IV 2/2A/2937, p. 37. Mikhail Gorbachev, *Perestroika* (Harper & Row, 1987).

7. Huber, *Moskau*, pp. 98–104. Brown, *Gorbachev factor*, pp. 155–68. Dalos, *Gorbatschow*, pp. 136–49.

8. Huber, *Moskau*, pp. 80–81 (first quote). Various documents: Politisches Archiv des Auswärtigen Amtes, Bestand: Ministerium für Auswärtige Angelegenheiten [PAAA-MfAA], G-A 592, G-A 597, G-A 598; and Daniel Küchenmeister, ed., *Honecker-Gorbachev* (Dietz, 1993), pp. 57, 83, 95–96, 127, 131–32, 157, 205 (second quote).

9. Brown, *Gorbachev factor*, pp. 130–54. Chris Miller, *The struggle to save the Soviet economy* (University of North Carolina Press, 2016), pp. 17–23. Huber, *Moskau*, p. 84. Brown, *Gorbachev factor*, p. 155. "Gorbachev alludes to Czech invasion," *New York Times* [*NYT*], April 12, 1987, p. 12 (quote). Stephen G. Brooks and William C. Wohlforth, "Economic constraints and the turn towards superpower cooperation in the 1980s," Njølstad, *Last decade*, pp. 73–81. "Transcript," September 29, 1988, Küchenmeister, *Honecker-Gorbachev*, pp. 205 (quote). Brown, *Gorbachev factor*, pp. 130–31. Huber, *Moskau*, pp. 57, 66–97. Ruge, *Gorbatschow*, p. 245.

10. Miller, *Struggle*, pp. 31–54, 119–40. "Report," [April 1982], SAPMO-BArch, DY 30/J IV 2/2A/2469, pp. 107–25. Lorenz M. Lüthi, "China's Wirtschaftswunder," Bernd Greiner, Tim B. Müller, and Klaas Voß, eds. *Erbe des Kalten Krieges* (Hamburger Editionen, 2013), pp. 453–62. Taubman, *Gorbachev*, pp. 310–14. Ruge, *Gorbatschow*, pp. 245–79. Huber, *Moskau*, pp. 95–97.

11. Ruge, *Gorbatschow*, pp. 245–313. Taubman, *Gorbachev*, pp. 322–75. Dalos, *Gorbatschow*, pp. 170–80.

12. "Politburo meeting of July 11, 1986," Chernyaev, *V Politbyuro*, p. 69. Brooks, "Economic constraints," pp. 81–84. Taubman, *Gorbachev*, pp. 378–83.

13. Dalos, *Gorbatschow*, pp. 197–218. Constantine Pleshakov, "In a blind spot," Lorenz M. Lüthi, ed., *The regional Cold Wars in Europe, East Asia, and the Middle East* (Woodrow Wilson Center Press / Stanford University Press, 2015), pp. 305–6. "Politburo meeting of July 3, 1986" and "Politburo meeting of January 29, 1987," Chernyaev, *V Politbyuro*, pp. 61 (quote), 141. Taubman, *Gorbachev*, pp. 383–86.

14. "Speech by the Secretary General of the CC of the CPSU, comrade Gorbachev," [May 5, 1985], SAPMO-BArch, DY 30/J IV 2/2A/2759, pp. 132–36. "Information," [February 27, 1986], SAPMO-BArch, DY 30/IV 2/2.035/58, pp. 143–45. "Information," [April 20–22, 1986], BArch, DY 30/2382, pp. 18–22. "Politburo meeting of September 29, 1986," Chernyaev, *V Politbyuro*, p. 81. André Steiner, *Von Plan zu Plan* (Aufbau Taschenbuch, 2007), pp. 237–39.

15. "Report on the 42nd Session of CMEA (Bucharest November 3–5, 1986)," BArch, DC 20/5161, pp. 7–8 (first quote). "East trade," November 10, 1987, Der Bundesbeauftragte für die Unterlagen des Staatssicherheitsdienstes der ehemaligen Deutschen Demokratischen Republik [BStU], MfS AG BKK, 1342, pp. 17–19. "Report," [October 13–14, 1987], BArch, DC 20/5352, p. 146 (second and third quotes). Various documents: SAPMO-BArch, DY 30/IV 2/2.039/291. "Politburo meeting of December 1988" and "Politburo meeting of January 24, 1989," Chernyaev, *V Politbyuro*, pp. 425–36.

16. "On the proposal," June 3, 1985, SAPMO-BArch, DY 30/11885, p. 4. "Report," [January 27, 1986], BArch, DO 4/1320, pp. 1–2. "Falin," February 26, 1987, BArch, DO 4/3765, p. 1. Hansjakob Stehle, *Geheimdiplomatie im Vatikan* (Benziger Verlag, 1993), pp. 366–74. "Conversation of M. S. Gorbachev with A. Casaroli," July 7, 1988, BArch, DO 4/3765, p. 1.

17. Huber, *Moskau*, pp. 80–81 (quote). Various documents: PAAA-MfAA, G-A 592, G-A 597, G-A 598. Küchenmeister, *Honecker–Gorbachev*, pp. 83, 95–96, 127, 131–32, 157, 205.

18. Svetlana Savranskaya, "Gorbachev and the Third World," Artemy Kalinovsky and Sergey Radchenko, eds., *The end of the Cold War and the Third World* (Routledge, 2011), p. 34–42. W. Donald Bowles, "Perestroika and its implications for Soviet foreign aid," Marie Lavigne, ed., *The Soviet Union and Eastern Europe in the global economy* (Cambridge University Press, 1992), p. 69.

19. "Information," July 19, 1985, SAPMO-BArch, DY 30/13994, pp. 1–5 (first quote). Various documents: SAPMO-BArch, DY 30/13848. "Information on the recent problems with regard to the 6th Party Congress of the CPV (12/15–18/1986)," December 11, 1986, BStU, MfS ZAIG 8290, pp. 1–3. "Politburo meeting of March 26, 1987," Chernyaev, *V Politbyuro*, p. 161 (second quote). Balázs Szalontai, "From battlefield into marketplace," Kalinovsky and Radchenko, *End of the Cold War*, pp. 158–63. Bowles, "Perestroika," p. 69. Tuong Vu, *Vietnam's communist revolution* (Cambridge University Press, 2017), pp. 245–58.

20. Bowles, "Perestroika," p. 69. Chernyaev, *Sovmestnyi iskhod*, p. 650 (first quote). Artemy M. Kalinovsky, *A long goodbye* (Harvard University Press, 2011), pp. 80–93 (second quote).

21. "Note," [October 13–15, 1986], BArch, DC 20/5337, pp. 196–98. Lou Cannon, *President Reagan* (Public Affairs, 2000), pp. 339–401. "Information," January 21, 1987, SAPMO-BArch, DY 30/12383, pp. 42–45.

22. "Information," January 15, 1987, SAPMO-BArch, DY 30/IV 2/2.035/72, pp. 45–47. Kalinovsky, *Long goodbye*, pp. 100–8, 122–46. Taubman, *Gorbachev*, pp. 376–78. "Dear Comrade Erich Honecker," May 12, 1988, SAPMO-BArch, DY 30/J IV 2/2A/3121, pp. 24–27 (first quote). "Politburo meeting of January 24, 1989," Chernyaev, *V. Politbyuro*, p. 434 (second quote).

23. Various documents: SAPMO-BArch, DY 30/13790. "[No title]," November 19, 1985, SAPMO-BArch, DY 30/13945, p. 52. Savranskaya, "Gorbachev," p. 28 (quote).

24. "Note," June 12, 1987, SAPMO-BArch, DY 30/13792, pp. 25–29. "[No title]," May 4, 1987, SAPMO-BArch, DY 30/13982, pp. 123–28. "Information," June 11, 1987, SAPMO-BArch, DY 30/12383, pp. 61–67. "Continued information," March 11, 1988, SAPMO-BArch, DY 30/12383, p. 102 (quote). "[No title]," April 20, 1988, SAPMO-BArch, DY 30/13970, pp. 1–6. "Information," June 21, 1988, SAPMO-BArch, DY 30/13945, pp. 54–57. "Mideast talks to start Oct. 30," *Houston Chronicle*, October 18, 1991, p. 1.

25. Sergey Radchenko, "Gorbachev in Europe and Asia," Lüthi, *Regional Cold Wars*, pp. 275–76. "More information," January 9, 1985, SAPMO-BArch, DY 30/11608, pp. 1–4 (quotes). Zhonggong zhongyang wenxian yanjiushi, ed., *Deng Xiaoping nianpu (1975–1997)* [*DXPNP*], vol. 1 (Zhongyang wenxian chubanshe, 2004), p. 1041. "Information," August 1, 1985, Küchenmeister, *Honecker–Gorbachev*, pp. 51–55.

26. "[No title]," December 30, 1983, SAPMO-BArch, DY 30/13932, pp. 1–8 (first quote). "[No title]," February 7, 1986, SAPMO-BArch, DY 30/13933, pp. 1–3. "Information," February 13, 1989, SAPMO-BArch, DY 30/13933, pp. 1–9. "Politburo meeting of February 16, 1989," Chernyaev, *V Politbyuro*, pp. 451–52 (second quote). "Visit of Mikhail Gorbachev to China," May 30, 1989, SAPMO-BArch, DY 30/13933, p. 2 (third and fourth quotes).

27. Various documents: SAPMO-BArch, DY 30/13941, pp. 124–140 (first and second quotes), pp. 148–51. Radchenko, "Gorbachev," pp. 279–80. "Politburo meeting of November 24, 1988," Chernyaev, *V Politbyuro*, p. 421 (third and fourth quotes).

28. First quote from Taubman, *Gorbachev*, p. 387. "Initial assessment of the visit of Comrade M. Gorbachev to France," [October 1985], SAPMO-BArch, DY 30/11608, pp. 1–5. "On some recent aspects of the policy of the USSR towards the imperialist states," June 18, 1986, SAPMO-BArch, DY 30/12386, p. 82. "Additional information," November 20, 1985, SAPMO-BArch, DY 30/12381, pp. 66–69.

29. "Note on a conversation," [October 1986], Küchenmeister, *Honecker–Gorbachev*, pp. 113–14 (quote). Various documents: SAPMO-BArch, DY 30/2383. Hannes Adomeit, *Imperial overstretch* (Nomos Verlag, 1998), pp. 259–71.

30. Melvyn P. Leffler, *For the soul of mankind* (Hill and Wang, 2007), pp. 338–65. Shevardnadze, *Als der Eiserne Vorhang zerriss*, p. 56. Chernyaev, *Sovmestnyi iskhod*, p. 624 (quote).

31. Chernyaev, *Sovmestnyi iskhod*, p. 621 (first quote). "Politburo meeting of October 8, 1986," Chernyaev, *V Politbyuro*, p. 86 (second quote). "Dear comrades," [April 1985], PAAA-MfAA, G-A 592, pp. 41–45 (third quote). "[No title]," July 29, 1985, SAPMO-BArch, DY 30/13905, pp. 171–72.

32. "Speech of Comrade M. S. Gorbachev," [October 22–23, 1985], BArch, DC 20/5163, pp. 147–64 (quote). "Transcript," November 21, 1985, SAPMO-BArch, DY 30/J IV 2/2A/2825, pp. 21–26. Raymond L. Garthoff, *The great transition* (Brookings Institution Press, 1994), pp. 234–48.

33. "[No title]," January 15, 1986, SAPMO-BArch, DY 30/13906, pp. 1–5. "Report," [January 29, 1986], SAPMO-BArch, DY 30/11889, pp. 3–5. "Information," April 20–22, 1986, SAPMO-BArch, DY 30/2382, p. 28.

34. Zubok, *Failed empire*, pp. 285–89. "Dear Comrade Erich Honecker," June 2, 1986, SAPMO-BArch, DY 30/13906, pp. 42–48.

35. "Comrade E. Honecker," September 29, 1986, SAPMO-BArch, DY 30/IV 2/2.035/63, p. 76 (first quote). "Note," [October 2, 1986], SAPMO-BArch, DY 30/J IV 2/2A/2937, pp. 29–32 (second quote). "Politburo meeting of October 4, 1986," Chernyaev, *V Politbyuro*, p. 83 (third quote). Garthoff, *Great transition*, pp. 285–91.

36. Zubok, *Failed empire*, pp. 290–94. "Telegram," [October 14–15, 1986], PAAA-MfAA, G-A 603, p. 69. "Transcript," [November 10–11, 1986], SAPMO-BArch, DY 30/2358, p. 89 (quote). "[No title]," December 15, 1986, SAPMO-BArch, DY 30/13906, pp. 112–15.

37. "Speech," [January 23, 1987], SAPMO-BArch, DY 30/11892, pp. 52–54 (quote). "[No title]," February 17, 1987, SAPMO-BArch, DY 30/13906, pp. 127–28. Garthoff, *Great transition*, p. 305. Zubok, *Failed empire*, p. 300.

38. "Information," June 9, 1987, SAPMO-BArch, DY 30/12384, pp. 37–44. Garthoff, *Great transition*, p. 326.

39. "Main directions of policy of the USSR," February 15, 1988, SAPMO-BArch, DY 30/12384, pp. 56–70. Garthoff, *Great transition*, pp. 338–68. "Speech," [July 15–16, 1988], PAAA-MfAA, G-A 600, pp. 32–38 (quote).

40. Taubman, *Gorbachev*, p. 378. Quote from Mark Kramer, "Gorbachev and the demise of East European communism," Silvio Pons and Federico Romero, eds., *Reinterpreting the end of the Cold War* (Frank Cass, 2005), pp. 181, 184. "For the Politburo meeting on October 6, 1988,"

Georgii Shakhnazarov, *Tsena svobody* (Rossiska, 1993), p. 368. "Speech at the United Nations Organization," December 7, 1988, Mikhail Gorbachev, *Sobranie sochinenii*, vol. 13 (Ves Mir, 2009), pp. 18–37.

41. Tony Judt, *Postwar* (Penguin Press, 2005), p. 606. Włodzimierz Borodziej, *Geschichte Polens im 20. Jahrhundert* (C. H. Beck, 2010), p. 378. "Transcript," June 24, 1988, SAPMO-BArch, DY 30/IV 2/2.039/284, 117–19 (quote).

42. Kramer, "Gorbachev," pp. 187–88. Borodziej, *Geschichte*, pp. 378–80. Andrzej Paczkowski, *The spring will be ours* (Pennsylvania State University Press, 2003), pp. 491–92. "Information," November 11, 1988, SAPMO-BArch, DY 30/IV 2/2.039/284, p. 127.

43. Paczkowski, *Spring will be ours*, pp. 498–509. Borodziej, *Geschichte*, pp. 381–92. Mikhail Gorbachev, *Erinnerungen* (Siedler Verlag, 1995), p. 870. "Report," October 18, 1988, SAPMO-BArch, DY 30/I V 2/2.035/47, p. 162 (quote). Kramer, "Gorbachev," pp. 189–90. "Gorbachev to Mieczysław Rakowski," August 22, 1989, Stefan Karner, Mark Kramer, Peter Ruggenthaler, Manfred Wilke, Viktor Iščenko, Olga Pavlenko, Efim Pivovar, Michail Prozumenščikov, Natalja Tomilina, and Alexander Tschubarjan, eds., *Der Kreml und die "Wende" 1989* (Studienverlag, 2014), pp. 434–36.

44. Dalos, *Gorbatschow*, pp. 204–7. Gorbachev, *Erinnerungen*, pp. 855–60. Paul Lendvai, *Hungary between democracy and authoritarianism* (Columbia University Press, 2012), pp. 1–28. "Hungary wants to open its border to Austria," March 3, 1989, Karner *et al.*, *Kreml*, p. 303. "ct 202/89 [Information on Gorbachev's visit to Hungary]," [March 1989], SAPMO-BArch, DY 30/IV 2/2.039/294, pp. 274–76. Zubok, *Failed empire*, pp. 321–22. Various chapters in András Bozóki, ed., *The roundtable talks of 1989* (Central European University Press, 2002).

45. "Gorbachev, in Finland, disavows any right of regional intervention," *NYT*, October 26, 1989, p. A1.

46. Ilko-Sascha Kowalczuk, *Endspiel* (C. H. Beck, 2009), pp. 91, 243–91. Ehrhardt Neubert, *Geschichte der Opposition in der DDR 1949–1989*, 2nd ed. (Ch. Links, 1998), pp. 248–770, 810–15. "Information," December 18, 1987, BStU, MfS AG BKK, 1342, p. 16.

47. Zubok, *Failed empire*, p. 324. "Conversation of Gorbachev with the Premier of Baden-Württemberg Späth," February 9, 1988, Aleksandr Galkin and Anatoly Chernyaev, eds., *Mikhail Gorbachev i germanskii vopros* (Ves Mir, 2006), p. 81 (quote). "Conversation of Chancellor Kohl with Secretary General Gorbachev," June 12, 1989, Hanns Jürgen Küsters and Daniel Hofmann, eds., *Deutsche Einheit* (Oldenbourg Wissenschaftsverlag, 1998), p. 283. Various documents: SAPMO-BArch, 30/IV V 2/2.035/60. "Gorbachev says change will sweep bloc," *NYT*, July 6, 1989, p. A1.

48. Kowalczuk, *Endspiel*, pp. 337–54. "Hungary allows thousands of East Germans to flee to West," *Washington Post*, September 11, 1989, A1.

49. Kowalczuk, *Endspiel*, pp. 360–77. "Situation in the People's Republic of China," no date, BArch, DC 20/4302, pp. 1–3 (quote). Various documents: Karner *et al.*, *Kreml*, pp. 361–63, 377–80, 384–87.

50. "Report," no date, SAPMO-BArch, DY 30/J IV 2/2A/3247, pp. 59–67 (quotes). "Self-excluded from the socialist society," *Neues Deutschland*,

October 2, 1989, p. 2. "Proposal to the Politburo," October 6, 1989, SAPMO-BArch, DY 30/J IV 2/2A/3245, pp. 7–8. Zubok, *Failed empire*, p. 325. Walter Süss, *Staatssicherheit am Ende* (Ch. Links, 1999), pp. 301–14.

51. Kowalczuk, *Endspiel*, pp. 386–401. Zubok, *Failed empire*, p. 325. "Stenographic transcript," [October 7, 1989], SAPMO-BArch, DY 30/IV 2/2.035/60, p. 225 (second quote). "October 11, 1989," Galkin and Chernyaev, *Mikhail Gorbachev*, p. 215 (third quote).

52. Ulrich Völklein, *Honecker* (Aufbau Verlag, 2003), pp. 368–70. "Suggestions," no date, SAPMO-BArch, DY 30/IV 2/2.039/329, p. 21. "The GDR is dangerously highly indebted in capitalist countries," October 31, 1989, Karner et al., *Kreml*, pp. 493–97. Various documents: BStU, MfS-HA XVIII 3314 and 16883. "Conversation of M. S. Gorbachev with E. Krenz," November 1, 1989, Galkin and Chernyaev, *Mikhail Gorbachev*, pp. 232–45. Chernyaev, ed., *V Politbyuro*, p. 524.

53. Kowalczuk, *Endspiel*, pp. 453–69. Karner et al., *Kreml*, pp. 505. Chernyaev, *Sovmestnyi iskhod*, pp. 816–17 (first quote; italics added). "Oral Message," November 13, 1989, SAPMO-BArch, DY 30/IV 2/2.039/319, p. 15 (second quote). For statistics, see appendix in Hans Hermann Hertle, Konrad H. Jarausch, and Christoph Kleßmann, eds., *Mauerbau und Mauerfall* (Ch. Links, 2002), pp. 310–14.

54. György Dalos, *Der Vorhang geht auf* (C. H. Beck, 2009), pp. 144–71. Gale Stokes, *The walls came tumbling down* (Oxford University Press, 1993), pp. 49–52, 141–48. Various documents: Karner et al., *Kreml*, pp. 426–29, 523–26.

55. Stokes, *Walls*, pp. 148–57. Dalos, *Vorhang*, pp. 172–204. Judt, *Postwar*, pp. 616–22. Various documents: Karner et al., *Kreml*, pp. 363–69, 488–90.

56. Thomas Kunze, *Nicolae Ceaușescu*, 3rd, upd. ed. (Ch. Links Verlag, 2009), pp. 302–405. Șerban Săndulescu, *Decembrie '89* (Omega, 1996), p. 292 (quote).

57. Kunze, *Ceaușescu*, pp. 302–405. Vladimir Tismaneanu, *Stalinism for all seasons* (University of California Press, 2003), pp. 187–235. Various documents: Karner et al., *Kreml*, pp. 437–41, 620. Liu Xiaoyuan and Vojtech Mastny, eds., *China and Eastern Europe, 1960s-1980s* (Center for Security Studies, ETH Zürich, 2004), p. 204.

58. George Weigel, *Witness to hope* (Cliff Street Books, 2001), pp. 600–5 (quote). Stehle, *Geheimdiplomatie*, pp. 368–74. Chernyaev, *Sovmestnyi iskhod*, pp. 817–28. "Transcript of the Bush–Gorbachev news conference in Malta," *NYT*, December 4, 1989, pp. A12–A13.

59. Brown, *Gorbachev factor*, pp. 186–221. Taubman, *Gorbachev*, pp. 428–33, 513–38. Dalos, *Gorbatschow*, pp. 236–40.

60. Mark Kramer, "The collapse of East European communism and repercussions with the Soviet Union," *Journal of Cold War Studies*, 5/4 (2003), pp. 206–14. Taubman, *Gorbachev*, pp. 435–37. Dalos, *Gorbatschow*, pp. 224–26, 240–50. Manfred Hildermeier, *Geschichte der Sowjetunion, 1917–1991* (C. H. Beck, 1998), pp. 1050–52.

61. Chernyaev, *Sovmestnyi iskhod*, p. 838 (first quote). Various documents: PAAA-MfAA, G-A 612 and 613. "Report," June 8, 1990, BArch, DC20/I/

3/3000, pp. 66–71 (second quote). "Information," October 28, 1989, BArch, DC 20/19336, p. 95. "To take into account the integration experiences of the EEC," November 23, 1989, Karner *et al.*, *Kreml*, pp. 531–35. Garthoff, *Great transition*, pp. 461–67.

62. Zubok, *Failed empire*, pp. 331–35. Dalos, *Gorbatschow*, pp. 262–73. Taubman, *Gorbachev*, pp. 620–50.

63. Quote from Weigel, *Witness to hope*, pp. 604–5.

24 Legacies of the Cold War

1. Luke March, "For victory?," *Europe-Asia Studies*, 53/2 (2001), pp. 263–90. Michael McFaul, "Political transitions," *Harvard International Review*, 28/1 (2007), pp. 40–45. Graeme J. Gill, *Democracy and post-communism* (Routledge, 2002). Tuong Vu, "The making and unmaking of the Communist Party and single-party system of Vietnam," and Yongnian Zheng, "The institutionalization of the Communist Party and the party system in China," Allen Hicken and Erik Martinez Kuhonta, eds., *Party system institutionalization in Asia* (Cambridge University Press, 2014), 136–60, 162–88. Kee Kwang-seo, "The historical origins and formation of the monolithic political system in North Korea," Jongwoo Han, Lee Ju-cheol, Jung Tae-hern, Chin Hee-gwan, Kee Kwang-seo, Kim Gwang-oon, Kim Keun-sik, Kim Yeon-chul, Lee Gee-dong, and Lee Jong-seok, eds., *Understanding North Korea* (Lexington Books, 2013), pp. 13–35.

2. Sandra Halperin, "The post-Cold War political topography of the Middle East: prospects for democracy," *Third World Quarterly*, 26/7, pp. 1135–56. Rula Jurdi Abisaab and Malek Abisaab, *The Shi'ites of Lebanon* (Syracuse University Press, 2014), pp. 160–61.

3. Anna M. Grzymala-Busse, *Redeeming the communist past* (Cambridge University Press, 2002). Silvio Pons, "Western communists, Mikhail Gorbachev and the 1989 revolutions," *Contemporary European History*, 18/3 (2009), pp. 349–62.

4. John Callaghan, Nina Fishman, Ben Jackson, and Martin McIvor, eds., *In search of Social Democracy* (Manchester University Press, 2009). John Milios, "Does Social Democracy hold up half the sky?," Ingo Schmidt, ed., *The three worlds of Social Democracy* (Pluto Press, 2016), pp. 127–45. Lorenzo Mosca and Valeria Calderoni, "A year of social movements in Italy," *Italian Politics*, 28 (2012), pp. 267–85.

5. Hal Brands, *Making the unipolar moment* (Cornell University Press, 2016). Susanne Soederberg, Georg Menz, and Philip G. Cerny, eds., *Internalizing globalization* (Palgrave Macmillan, 2005).

6. Lorenz M. Lüthi, "The global meaning of 1989," Stanisław Latek, ed., *From totalitarianism to democracy* (Polish Academy of Arts and Sciences, 2011), pp. 269–83. Gabrielle Lynch and Gordon Crawford, "Democratization in Africa 1990–2010," *Democratization*, 18/2 (2001), pp. 273–310. Ignacio Walker, *Democracy in Latin America* (University of Notre Dame Press, 2013).

7. Mark Goodale, ed., *Human rights at the crossroads* (Oxford University Press, 2013). Makau Mutua, *Human rights* (University of Pennsylvania Press, 2002).

8. Surander Singh, "NAM in the contemporary world order," *Indian Journal of Political Science*, 70/4 (2009), pp. 1213–26. "Nonalignment misconceived," *New Indian Express*, April 2, 2012. "End of the road for the Non-Aligned Movement," *Epoch Times*, October 7, 2016, p. A15.

9. Robert S. Norris and Hans M. Kristensen, "Global nuclear weapons inventories, 1945–2010," *Bulletin of the Atomic Scientists*, 66/4 (2010), p. 82. Raymond L. Garthoff, *The great transition* (Brookings Institution Press, 1994), pp. 778–79. Sumit Ganguly and Devin T. Hagerty, *Fearful symmetry* (University of Washington Press, 2015). Wade L. Huntley, "Rebels without a cause," *International Affairs*, 82/4 (2006), pp. 723–42. Deepti Choubey, "From sprint to marathon," *Arms Control Today*, 44/4 (2014), pp. 16–23.

10. Balázs Szalontai, *Kim Il Sung in the Khrushchev era* (Woodrow Wilson Center Press / Stanford University Press, 2005). Bruce Cumings, *North Korea* (New Press, 2003).

11. Alisa Gaunder, *Japanese politics and government* (Routledge, 2017), pp. 46–60. David C. Kang, *Crony capitalism* (Cambridge University Press, 2002). Charles Chi-hsiang Chang and Hung-Mao Tien, eds., *Taiwan's electoral politics and democratic transition* (M. E. Sharpe, 1996). Richard Javad Heydarian, *The rise of Duterte* (Palgrave Macmillan, 2018). Edward Aspinall, "The surprising democratic behemoth," *Journal of Asian Studies*, 74/4 (2015), pp. 889–902. Meredith L. Weiss, "Of inequality and irritation," *Democratization*, 21/5 (2014), pp. 867–87. Aries A. Arugay and Aim Sinpeng, "Varieties of authoritarianism and the limits of democracy in Southeast Asia," Alice D. Ba and Mark Beeson, eds., *Contemporary Southeast Asia*, 3rd ed. (Palgrave, 2018), pp. 91–110.

12. Ivan Tselichtchev and Philippe Debroux, *Asia's turning point* (Wiley, 2012). Gaunder, *Japanese politics*, pp. 83–94. Greg Felker, "The political economy of Southeast Asia," Ba and Beeson, *Contemporary Southeast Asia*, pp. 70–90.

13. Bipan Chandra, Mridula Mukherjee, and Aditya Mukherhee, *India since independence*, rev. and upd. (Penguin Books India, 2008), pp. 331–90, 475–93.

14. Veena Kukreja and Mahendra Prasad Singh, eds., *Democracy, development and discontent in South Asia* (Sage Publications, 2008). Bhumitra Chakma, ed., *South Asia in transition* (Palgrave Macmillan, 2014).

15. Dilip Hiro, *Lebanon* (St. Martin's Press, 1993), pp. 161–84. David Hirst, *Beware of small states* (Nation Books, 2010), pp. 206–42.

16. Murad Batal al-Shishani, "From Chechen mafia to the Islamic Emirate of the Caucasus," and Jana Arsovska, "Bosnia-Herzegovina," Svante Cornell and Michael Jonsson, eds., *Conflict, crime, and the state in postcommunist Eurasia* (University of Pennsylvania Press, 2014), pp. 82–102, 151–76. Fawaz A. Gerges, *The far enemy* (Cambridge University Press, 2005).

17. Seth Anziska, *Preventing Palestine* (Princeton University Press, 2018), pp. 267–87. Abdul Salam Majali, Jawad A. Anani, and Munther J. Haddadin, *Peacemaking* (Ithaca Press, 2006). Elie Podeh, "Israel and the Arab peace initiative, 2002–2014," *Middle East Journal*, 68/4 (2014), pp. 584–603.

18. F. Gregory Gause, "Iraq's decisions to go to war, 1980 and 1990," *Middle East Journal*, 56/1 (2002), pp. 53–61.

19. Robert K. Brigham, "The lessons and legacies of the war in Iraq," and Aaron B. O'Connell, "The lessons and legacies of the war in Afghanistan," Beth Bailey and Richard H. Immerman, eds., *Understanding the U.S. wars in Iraq and Afghanistan* (New York University Press, 2015), pp. 286–332. Abdel Bari Atwan, *After Bin Laden* (Saqi Books, 2012). Joel Rayburn, *Iraq after America* (Hoover Institution Press, Stanford University Press, 2014). Mohammad-Mahmoud Ould Mohamedou, *A theory of ISIS* (Pluto Press, 2018).

20. Geoffrey Pridham, *Designing democracy* (Palgrave Macmillan, 2005). Wojciech Sadurski, Adam W. Czarnota and Martin. Krygier, eds., *Spreading democracy and the rule of law?* (Springer, 2006). Piotr Dutkiewicz and Robert J. Jackson, eds., *NATO looks east* (Praeger, 1998). Janie Leatherman, *From Cold War to democratic peace* (Syracuse University Press, 2003).

21. Mary E. Sarotte, *1989* (Princeton University Press, 2009).

22. Beata Kosowska-Gąstoł, "A truly 'European' Christian Democracy?," Piotr H. Kosicki and Sławomir Łukasiewicz, eds., *Christian Democracy across the Iron Curtain* (Palgrave Macmillan, 2017), pp. 127–44. James L. Newell, *Parties and democracy in Italy* (Routledge, 2000).

23. Jonathan Luxmoore and Jolanta Babiuch, *The Vatican and the red flag* (Geoffrey Chapman, 1999), pp. 302–22.

24. Robert M. Hayden, *From Yugoslavia to the western Balkans* (Brill, 2013). Michael Zantovsky, "Continental drift," *World Affairs*, 178/2 (2015), pp. 74–81. Turkuler Isiksel, "Square peg, round hole," Benjamin Martill and Uta Staiger, eds., *Brexit and beyond* (UCL Press, 2018), pp. 239–50.

Index

Abdullah (king of Jordan), 55, 56, 57
Adenauer, Konrad
  armament policies of, 417
  economic policies of, 418
  foreign policies of, 103, 369, 417, 420–21
  nuclear weapons strategy of, 341
  retirement of, 428
Adzhubei, Aleksei, 428, 476
Afghanistan
  and India, 527
  Soviet intervention in, 491, 509–13, 548
    and China, 531
    end of, 573–74
    Islamist opposition against, 513–14
    and Non-Aligned Movement, 533
    and United States/NATO, 541–43
  US intervention in, 601
Africa
  and Israel, 209, 235
  representation in Asian–African
    Movement from, 283, 286
Aga Khan III, 312
agency of middle and smaller powers, 4, 5,
  610–11
al-Alami, Musa, 51
Albania, communist regime in, 71
  independence from Soviet Union, 75, 77,
    82–83
Ale-Ahmad, Jalal, 327
Algeria, independence of, 53, 104
All-Indian Muslim League, 309
Amin, Hafizullah, 510
Amnesty International, 445
Andropov, Yuri V., 546, 547, 548, 552, 565
Anti-Ballistic Missile (ABM) Treaty
  (1972), 353
anti-communism
  at Bandung Conference, 279, 281
  of Free World alliance, 90–91
  of India, 168
  of Pakistan, 173
  of Reagan, 556

  of Saudi Arabia, 49, 494
  of Vatican, 462, 463–64, 467, 469
anti-imperialism/anti-colonialism, 186
  of Arab League, 52–54
  of PLO, 256
  of Soviet Union, 605
  of United States, 19, 21
anti-Westernism, of Khomeini, 327
anti-Zionism
  in British Mandatory Palestine, 191
  in Ottoman Palestine, 190
Arab League, 8, 611
  anti-imperialism of, 52–54
  and Arab–Israeli conflict, 54–57, 62, 193,
    194, 210, 240, 242, 243,
    245–46, 254
    Israeli Independence war
      (1948–1949), 196, 198
    June War defeat, 224–25
    Palestinian issue, 241, 256
    rejection of Camp David Accords, 501
    rejection of UN partition plan for
      Palestine, 195
    Suez Crisis, 61
  and Cold War, 58, 66
  creation of, 42, 45, 50–52, 66, 308
  Egyptian membership
    expulsion, 490, 500, 502
    readmission, 507
  internal divisions, 43, 63–66, 210
  and Iranian Islamic Revolution, 505
  and Korean War, 58–59
  leadership of, 311
    by Egypt, 50, 53, 63, 64, 314
  Pakistan seeking membership of, 311
  Saudi criticism of, 320
  UK influence in, 39–40, 42–43, 67
Arab Liberation Army, 195
Arab nationalism, 17, 49
  British support for, 46, 50
Arab states / Arab world
  and Arab–Israeli conflict